Frommer's

S0-BCQ-985

Denmark

6th Edition

by Darwin Porter & Danforth Prince

Here's what the critics say about Frommer's:

"Amazingly easy to use. Very portable, very complete."
—BOOKLIST

"Detailed, accurate, and easy-to-read information
for all price ranges."
—GLAMOUR MAGAZINE

"Hotel information is close to encyclopedic."
—DES MOINES SUNDAY REGISTER

"Frommer's Guides have a way of giving you a real feel
for a place."
—KNIGHT RIDDER NEWSPAPERS

WILEY
Wiley Publishing, Inc.

Published by:

WILEY PUBLISHING, INC.

111 River St.
Hoboken, NJ 07030-5774

ISBN: 978-0-470-43212-9

Editor: William Travis, with Kathleen Warnock
Production Editor: Lindsay Conner
Cartographer: Elizabeth Puhl
Photo Editor: Richard Fox
Production by Wiley Indianapolis Composition Services

Front cover photo: Helsingør, Frederiksborg
Back cover photo: some of the 50 million bricks that make up Legoland, in Billund, Ribe.

For information on our other products and services or to obtain technical support, please contact our Customer Care Department within the U.S. at 877/762-2974, outside the U.S. at 317/572-3993 or fax 317/572-4002.

Wiley also publishes its books in a variety of electronic formats. Some content that appears in print may not be available in electronic formats.

Manufactured in the United States of America

5 4 3 2 1

CONTENTS

WHAT'S NEW IN DENMARK   1

1 THE BEST OF DENMARK   4

1 The Best Danish Experiences 4

2 The Best Hotels 5

3 The Best Restaurants 6

4 The Best Buys 6

5 The Most Scenic Towns & Villages 7

6 The Best Active Vacations 8

7 The Best Castles & Palaces. 9

8 The Best Offbeat Experiences 9

2 DENMARK IN DEPTH   11

1 Denmark Today .... .11

2 Looking Back at Denmark .... .13

   Dateline. 13

3 Denmark's Art & Architecture .... .24

4 Denmark in Books, Films & Music .... .26

5 Eating & Drinking in Denmark. ... .27

3 PLANNING YOUR TRIP TO DENMARK   29

1 Visitor Information .... .29

2 Entry Requirements & Customs ...29

3 When to Go. .... .30

   Denmark Calendar of Events. 30

4 Getting There & Getting Around. .... .32

5 Money & Costs. .... .38

   What Things Cost in Copenhagen 39

6 Health .... .40

7 Safety. .... .42

8 Specialized Travel Resources ..... .42

9 Sustainable Tourism. .... .45

   It's Easy Being Green 46

   Frommers.com: The Complete Travel Resource 47

10 Special-Interest Tours. .... .48

   Heritage—The Search for Roots. ... .49

11 The Active Vacation Planner. ..... .50

12 Staying Connected. .... .51

   Online Traveler's Toolbox. 52

13 Tips on Accommodations .... .53

4 SUGGESTED ITINERARIES FOR DENMARK · 56

1 The Regions in Brief 56
2 Denmark in 1 Week 58
3 Denmark in 2 Weeks 61
4 The Islands of Denmark in 1 Week 64
5 Denmark for Families in 1 Week ..66

5 SETTLING INTO COPENHAGEN · 69

1 Orientation 70
 Neighborhoods in Brief..............71
2 Getting Around 73
 Copenhagen........................75
3 Where to Stay.....................77
 Family-Friendly Accommodations....................90
4 Where to Dine 95
 Family-Friendly Restaurants........104
 Quick Bites in Copenhagen 108

6 EXPLORING COPENHAGEN · 120

1 Seeing the Sights 121
 Frommer's Favorite Copenhagen Experiences 125
 Danish Design 126
 Special & Free Events 141
 Walking Tour 1: The Old City 143
 Walking Tour 2: Kongens Nytorv to Langelinie.......................144
2 Shopping 150
3 Copenhagen After Dark.........155
 Nighttime Experiences for Free (Well, Almost)......................158
4 Side Trips from Copenhagen 163

7 NORTH ZEALAND · 170

1 Hillerød 172
2 Fredensborg 177
3 Helsingør: In Search of Hamlet ... 180
4 Hornbæk.........................186
5 Gilleleje 189
6 Tisvildeleje 193
7 Roskilde 195
 Czarina's Remains Returned to Russia...........................198

8 SOUTH ZEALAND & MØN · 206

1 Køge 206
 Zealand's Link to the Continent 215
2 Ringsted 215
3 Slagelse.........................219
4 Næstved 223
5 Møn 228

9 BORNHOLM 237

1 Rønne 239

2 Nexø 247

3 Svaneke 251

4 Gudhjem 253

5 Christiansø 256

6 Allinge & Sandvig 257

10 FUNEN 260

1 Nyborg: Gateway to Funen...... 260

2 Odense: Birthplace of Hans Christian Andersen 265

3 Svendborg 279

4 Faaborg 287

5 Ærø 292

11 SOUTH JUTLAND 301

1 Kolding 301

2 Haderslev 307

3 Tønder 311

4 Rømø 317

5 Ribe 321

6 Fanø 330

12 CENTRAL JUTLAND 336

1 Vejle 336

2 Jelling 341

Discovering a Viking Past 342

3 Billund & Legoland 343

4 Ringkøbing 345

Windsurfing on Ringkøbing Fjord 349

5 Ry 350

6 Silkeborg........................ 354

7 Århus 360

8 Ebeltoft 375

13 NORTH JUTLAND 379

1 Mariager 379

2 Aalborg 384

3 Frederikshavn................... 396

4 Skagen 402

APPENDIX: FAST FACTS, TOLL-FREE NUMBERS & WEBSITES 408

1 Fast Facts: Denmark............. 408

2 Toll-Free Numbers & Websites... 412

INDEX 416

General Index................... 416

Accommodations Index......... 427

Restaurants Index............... 429

LIST OF MAPS

Denmark. 57

Denmark in 1 Week. 59

Denmark in 2 Weeks. 63

The Islands of Denmark
in 1 Week. 65

Denmark for Families
in 1 Week. 67

Copenhagen Accommodations . . . 78

Copenhagen Dining 96

Copenhagen Attractions. 122

Walking Tour 1: The Old City 145

Walking Tour 2: Kongens
Nytorv to Langelinie 147

Copenhagen & Environs 165

North Zealand 171

Helsingør 181

Roskilde 197

South Zealand 207

Møn 229

Bornholm. 241

Funen 261

Odense 267

Svendborg. 281

South Jutland 303

Rømø. 319

Ribe 323

Central Jutland. 337

Århus. 361

North Jutland 381

Aalborg. 383

Frederikshavn. 397

ABOUT THE AUTHORS

As a team of veteran travel writers, **Darwin Porter** and **Danforth Prince** have produced numerous titles for Frommer's which have included Italy, France, the Caribbean, Spain, England, Scotland, and Germany. A film critic, columnist, and broadcaster, Porter is also a Hollywood biographer. Recent releases by Darwin include *Merv Griffin: A Life in the Closet*, documenting the private life of the richest and most notorious man in television, and *Paul Newman, The Man Behind the Baby Blues*. Prince was formerly employed by the Paris bureau of the *New York Times* and is today the president of Blood Moon Productions and other media-related firms.

AN INVITATION TO THE READER

In researching this book, we discovered many wonderful places—hotels, restaurants, shops, and more. We're sure you'll find others. Please tell us about them, so we can share the information with your fellow travelers in upcoming editions. If you were disappointed with a recommendation, we'd love to know that, too. Please write to:

Frommer's Denmark, 6th Edition
Wiley Publishing, Inc. • 111 River St. • Hoboken, NJ 07030-5774

AN ADDITIONAL NOTE

Please be advised that travel information is subject to change at any time—and this is especially true of prices. We therefore suggest that you write or call ahead for confirmation when making your travel plans. The authors, editors, and publisher cannot be held responsible for the experiences of readers while traveling. Your safety is important to us, however, so we encourage you to stay alert and be aware of your surroundings. Keep a close eye on cameras, purses, and wallets, all favorite targets of thieves and pickpockets.

FROMMER'S STAR RATINGS, ICONS & ABBREVIATIONS

Every hotel, restaurant, and attraction listing in this guide has been ranked for quality, value, service, amenities, and special features using a **star-rating system.** In country, state, and regional guides, we also rate towns and regions to help you narrow down your choices and budget your time accordingly. Hotels and restaurants are rated on a scale of zero (recommended) to three stars (exceptional). Attractions, shopping, nightlife, towns, and regions are rated according to the following scale: zero stars (recommended), one star (highly recommended), two stars (very highly recommended), and three stars (must-see).

In addition to the star-rating system, we also use **six feature icons** that point you to the great deals, in-the-know advice, and unique experiences that separate travelers from tourists. Throughout the book, look for:

(Finds	Special finds—those places only insiders know about
(Fun Facts	Fun facts—details that make travelers more informed and their trips more fun
(Moments	Special moments—those experiences that memories are made of
(Overrated	Places or experiences not worth your time or money
(Tips	Insider tips—great ways to save time and money
(Value	Great values—where to get the best deals

The following **abbreviations** are used for credit cards:

AE	American Express	**DISC**	Discover	**V**	Visa
DC	Diners Club	**MC**	MasterCard		

FROMMERS.COM

Now that you have this guidebook to help you plan a great trip, visit our website at **www. frommers.com** for additional travel information on more than 4,000 destinations. We update features regularly to give you instant access to the most current trip-planning information available. At Frommers.com, you'll find scoops on the best airfares, lodging rates, and car rental bargains. You can even book your travel online through our reliable travel booking partners. Other popular features include:

- Online updates of our most popular guidebooks
- Vacation sweepstakes and contest giveaways
- Newsletters highlighting the hottest travel trends
- Podcasts, interactive maps, and up-to-the-minute events listings
- Opinionated blog entries by Arthur Frommer himself
- Online travel message boards with featured travel discussions

What's New in Denmark

Many of the old towns and villages remain relatively the same year after year, but we've noted some updates and changes below. Of course, in cosmopolitan Copenhagen, the pulse always beats faster, so there's lots to report. Here are some of the newest developments in various categories.

COPENHAGEN Accommodations Massive renovations have returned **Le Meridien Palace Hotel,** at Rådhuspladsen 57 (*℃* **800/543-4300** or 33-14-40-50), to its former glory. Long a celebrity favorite, it completed restoration work in January 2009, when it was granted a five-star rating by the government. Our favorite wing is called "The Night Wing," inspired by the mystical hues of the night; each accommodation here is individually designed.

Sharing the Rådhuspladsen with the above-recommended Palace is the elegant hotel **The Square,** Rådhuspladsen 14 (*℃* **33-38-12-00**), a modern property overlooking the Town Hall. Minimalist lines characterize this exquisitely designed hotel, where bedrooms open onto panoramic views of Copenhagen. The furnishings are tastefully and stylishly modern, and there are imaginative Danish design touches throughout, including Arne Jacobsen's famous circular chair, "The Egg."

AXEL Hotel Guldsmeden, Helgolandsgade 11 (*℃* **33-31-32-66**), is the latest member of the Guldsmeden family chain to open in Copenhagen in the Vesterbro district near the Central Station behind the Tivoli Gardens. Bedrooms are attractively decorated in a Balinese style, with original paintings, Persian carpets, and wooden floors; some of the most luxurious and elegant accommodations—also the most expensive—are penthouse suites.

Scandinavia's only floating hotel, **CPH Living,** has opened at 570 Langebrogade Kaj (*℃* **30-41-02-11**), with 12 rooms furnished with the best of Scandinavian design, each room definitely nautical, with steel and hardwood deck materials used throughout. This is elegant houseboat living, a novelty and a marvelous change of pace for those wishing to experience the pulsating harbor life of Copenhagen. All rooms are equipped with floor-to-ceiling windows.

Restaurants In the increasingly trendy district of Vesterbro, **Kiin Kiin,** at Guldbergsgade 21 (*℃* **35-35-75-55**), reigns as Copenhagen's finest Thai dining room, serving only a fixed-price menu nightly that is sublime but very expensive. For those who can afford it, it's worth it. This bastion of modern Thai cooking feeds you one delectable dish after another, with some surprise ingredients in certain cases, including fresh orchids for you to eat. Try such delights as red coconut curry with litchi nuts and fresh shellfish.

Also in the Vesterbro district, a Danish and Asian restaurant, **Karriere,** is now serving delectable food at Flaesketorvet 57–67 (*℃* **33-21-55-09**). The skilled chefs feature set menus of 2 to 10 courses, the latter a treat for gourmets and gourmands. The kitchen makes great use of organic produce, and the restaurant is owned by a famous

Danish artist, Jeppe Hein, who naturally decorates his dining room in the meat-packing district of Copenhagen with paintings, not just his own, but those of other international artists.

In another emerging district, Langebro, you can dine on seafood as well as both Danish and Mediterranean specialties at **VIVA,** Langebrok Kaj 570 (✆ **27-25-05-05**). The dining room is on a remodeled barge opening onto a view of the Royal Library. In summer, guests prefer to dine on the sun deck, where the music from a DJ fills the night. The chefs provide an elegant ambience for a quality cuisine. An evening menu is based on tapas, allowing you to enjoy several different taste sensations.

In the Copenhagen Admiral Hotel, **Salt,** Toldbodgade 24–28 (✆ **33-74-14-44**), is the creation of British designer Sir Terence Conran. Enjoying a waterside setting, it serves a superb international cuisine. The chefs use some of the most high-quality and market-fresh ingredients, which are reflected in their constantly changing fixed-price menus.

Geranium, Kronprinsessegade 13 (✆ **33-11-13-04**), near the Nørreport Station, is a bastion of gourmet food and the home base for two of the most brilliant and talented chefs in Copenhagen, Rasmus Kofoed and Soren Ledet. In 2008, they were awarded "Restaurant of the Year" accolades by several Danish gourmet societies. An inventiveness and precision with regional products characterize their sublime cuisine.

In the Radisson SAS Royal Hotel, **Albert K,** Hammerichsgade 1 (✆ **38-15-65-00**), is one of the most successful fusions of Danish raw materials with the culinary techniques of the new Italian kitchen. A great emphasis on freshness characterizes the kitchen, and you can order every item from North Sea cod and oysters to just-caught lobster. The restaurant is panoramic, lying on the 20th floor of this elegant hotel.

Shopping There are more and more showcases of Danish design opening in Copenhagen, including **The House,** Nyhavn 11 (✆ **32-95-00-24**), which is a virtual museum of Danish designers, both the golden oldies and the most futuristic of today. There's everything here from Arne Jacobsen's celebrated Swan Chair to the most avant-garde designs of artisans today.

After Dark Hailed as the best bar in Copenhagen, **Ruby,** Nybrogade 10 (✆ **33-93-12-03**), turns out the most original cocktails in the city. The demimonde flock to its door, which looks like the entrance to a private home. The bar was created from a restored warehouse from the 18th century.

AALBORG One of the most exclusive and finest seafood restaurants in Jutland, **Rosdahls,** at Strandvejen 6 (✆ **98-12-05-80**), is housed today in an old converted sugar warehouse along the banks of the Limfjord River. The fresh fish is purchased each day by the chefs at a nearby auction. In spite of its rustic setting, this is one of the most elegant restaurants in the area, with a kitchen that is a fusion of the best of Danish flavors with Mediterranean recipes.

In hotel dining, the best news is coming from the opening of a first-rate Danish restaurant, **Kong Richard,** in the Radisson SAS Hotel at Ved Stranden 14–16 (✆ **98-12-39-99**). The skilled chefs produce five- and six-course menus that are changed nightly, featuring some of the best of Danish regional produce, such as fresh game dishes in the autumn.

ÅRHUS Accommodations A small boutique hotel, **Villa Provence,** Fredens Torv 12 (✆ **86-18-24-00**), opens onto a tranquil square in the city. This designer hotel evokes an inn in the south of France. Each room is individually designed and furnished in a typical Provençal style. In the rear is a cobblestone courtyard graced with tall lime trees. Wrought-iron beds sit on wide-planked oak floors.

Restaurants Thorsten Schmidt reigns today as the most inventive chef on Jutland at his **Malling & Schmidt,** Jægergårdsgade 81 (© **86-17-70-88**), specializing in Scandinavian cuisine. All of his raw ingredients come from the Nordic countries, ranging from rapeseed oil to dehydrated pumpkin to pickled cloudberries and seaweed. He attempts to create a taste sensation with every dish, and his combinations of flavors shock some first-timers; yet the result is almost always harmonious.

To break from the Nordic kitchen, **Forlaens & Baglaens** has opened at Jægergårdsgade 23 (© **86-76-00-70**), serving the best and most authentic tapas in Jutland. In the center of town, the chefs nightly prepare a fine array of varied tapas—meat, vegetable, or seafood. You can also order one of the tastiest fixed-price menus in Århus.

HELSINGØR It's only appropriate that a **Hotel Hamlet,** Bramstrasse 5 (© **49-21-05-91**), would exist in this town made famous by the Shakespeare play. The hotel has been around for some time but was getting a bit battered until a major renovation made it one of the most acceptable and affordable choices in town. Located near the harbor, it is also a good choice for those arriving by ferryboat from Sweden and seeking a desirable address for the night.

NAESTVED In the largest town of South Zealand, lying 80km (50 miles) southwest of Copenhagen, sits **Mogenstrup Kro,** at Praestø Landevej 25 (© **55-76-11-30**), which has been putting up wayfarers for 200 years. It was certainly beginning to show its age until 2008, when it underwent a much-needed renovation, with a spa added to keep up with the demands of modern travelers. Slated for reopening in 2009, it will make one of the best centers for exploring South Zealand. Danish country cooking will still be a feature of the inn.

RIBE In a city long known for its storks, **Danhostel Ribe** has opened at Ribehallen, Skt. Peders Gade 16 (© **75-42-06-20**), with 152 beds. Rooms with private bathroom can also be rented, and many standard bedrooms can also be booked by families—up to five guests. This brick-built hostel is one of the finest in Denmark, and there is a cafeteria on-site, as well as a kitchen set aside for the use of guests.

SVENDBORG On the Hans Christian Andersen island of Funen, **Hotel Ærø,** Brogade 1, Ærøfaergen (© **62-21-07-60**), is the oldest hotel in this port city. After a major restoration, it is now an acceptable and affordable choice for overnighting. Even if you don't stay here, consider it for dinner. Locals claim it serves the most authentic Danish cuisine in Svendborg.

The Best of Denmark

Denmark presents visitors with everything from a world-class city in Copenhagen to historic castles, wind-swept offshore islands, quaint villages, and more. To help you decide how best to spend your time in Denmark, we compiled a list of our favorite experiences and discoveries. In the following pages, you'll find the kind of candid advice we'd give our close friends.

1 THE BEST DANISH EXPERIENCES

- **A Day (and Night) at Tivoli Gardens:** These 150-year-old pleasure gardens are almost worth the trip to Copenhagen by themselves. They offer a little bit of everything: open-air dancing, restaurants, theaters, concert halls, an amusement park . . . and, oh yes, gardens. From the first bloom of spring until the autumn leaves start to fall (*note:* Tivoli's closed in the winter), they're devoted to lighthearted fun. The gardens are worth a visit anytime but are especially pleasant at twilight, when the lights begin to glint among the trees. See p. 156.

- **A Week down on the Farm:** The best way to see the heart of Denmark and meet the Danes is to spend a week on one of their farms. Nearly 400 farms all over the country take in paying guests. Stick a pin anywhere on a map of Denmark away from the cities and seacoast, and you'll find a thatched and timbered farm, or perhaps a more modern homestead. Almost any place makes a good base from which to explore the rest of the country on day trips. You join the host family and other guests for meals. You can learn about the farm and help with the chores if you like. Activities range from bonfires and folk dancing to riding lessons or horse-and-buggy rides. Although there's no official agency to arrange such holidays, many visitors

seeking this kind of accommodation surf the Internet for farms that advertise their willingness to receive guests. Another way to hook up is to decide what part of Denmark you'd like to visit, then contact the tourist office for a list of farms willing to accept paying guests.

- **On the Trail of the Vikings:** Renowned for centuries of fantastic exploits, the Vikings explored Greenland to the north, North America to the west, and the Caspian Sea to the south and east from roughly A.D. 750 to 1050. Their legacy lives on in Denmark. Relive the age of Vikings at the **Nationalmuseet** in Copenhagen, which displays burial grounds of the Viking period, along with the largest and richest hoards of treasure, including relics from the "Silver Age." Even Viking costumes are exhibited. See p. 133. At Roskilde, explore the **Viking Ship Museum,** containing five vessels found in a fjord nearby, the largest of which was built in Ireland around 1060 and manned by 60 to 100 warriors. See p. 199. If you're in Ribe, check out the **Museum of the Viking Age,** where a multimedia room, "Odin's Eye," introduces the visitor to the world of the Vikings through a vivid sound and vision experience. See p. 324. And, at Jelling, see two **enormous mounds** (the largest in Denmark), one of which was the burial ground of King Gorm. See "Jelling," in chapter 12.

- **In the Footsteps of H. C. Andersen:** To some visitors, this storyteller is the symbol of Denmark itself. The fairy tale lives on in Odense, on the island of Funen, where Andersen was born the son of a shoemaker in 1805. His childhood home, a small half-timbered house on Munkemøllestræde, where he lived from 1807 to 1817, has been turned into a museum. You can also visit **H. C. Andersen's Hus,** where much of his memorabilia is stored (including his walking stick and top hat), and take a few moments to listen to his tales on tape. But mostly you can wander the cobblestone streets that he knew, marveling at the life of this man and his works, which, in the words of his obituary, struck "chords that reverberated in every human heart"—as they still do today. See "Odense: Birthplace of Hans Christian Andersen," in chapter 10.

- **Cycling Around Ærø:** Regardless of how busy our schedule, we always like to devote at least one sunny day to what we view as the greatest cycling trip in Denmark: a slow, scenic ride around the island of Ærø, lying off the coast of Funen. Relatively flat, its countryside dotted with windmills, the island evokes the fields of Holland, but is unique unto itself. Country roads will take you across fertile fields and into villages of cobbled streets and half-timbered houses. This is small-town Denmark at its best. Yes, you'll even pass a whistling postman in red jacket and gold-and-black cap looking like an extra in one of those Technicolor MGM movies from the '40s. See p. 294.

2 THE BEST HOTELS

- **Phoenix Copenhagen** (Copenhagen; ℂ 33-95-95-00; www.phoenix copenhagen.com): The Danish Communist Party used to have its headquarters here, but the "Reds" of the Cold War era wouldn't recognize this pocket of posh today. It reeks of capitalistic excess and splendor, from its dazzling public rooms with French antiques to its rooms with Louis XVI styling. See p. 81.

- **Hotel d'Angleterre** (Copenhagen; ℂ 33-12-00-95; www.remmen.dk): Some critics rate this as the finest hotel in Denmark. As it drifted toward mediocrity a few years back, a massive investment was made to save it. Now the hotel is better than ever—housing a swimming pool and a nightclub. Behind its Georgian facade, much of the ambience is in the traditional English mode. Service is perhaps the finest in Copenhagen. See p. 77.

- **Falsled Kro** (Falsled; ℂ 62-68-11-11; www.falsledkro.dk): Not only is this Funen Island's finest accommodation, but it's the quintessential Danish inn, with origins going back to the 1400s. This Relais & Châteaux property is now a stellar inn, with elegant furnishings as well as a top-quality restaurant, rivaling the best in Copenhagen. See p. 289.

- **Hotel Hesselet** (Nyborg; ℂ 65-31-30-29; www.hesselet.dk): This stylish modern hotel on Funen Island occupies a woodland setting in a beech forest. The spacious rooms are artfully decorated, often with traditional furnishings. A library, Oriental carpets, and an open fireplace add graceful touches to the public areas. Many Copenhagen residents come here for a retreat, patronizing the hotel's gourmet restaurant at night. See p. 263.

- **Hotel Dagmar** (Ribe; $\mathcal{C}$ 75-42-00-33; www.hoteldagmar.dk): Jutland's most glamorous hotel was converted from a private home in 1850, although the building itself dates back to 1581. This half-timbered hotel encapsulates the charm of the 16th century, with such adornments as carved chairs, sloping wooden floors, and stained-glass windows. Many bedrooms are furnished with antique canopy beds. A fine restaurant, serving both Danish and international dishes, completes the picture. See p. 326.

3 THE BEST RESTAURANTS

- **Era Ora** (Copenhagen; $\mathcal{C}$ 32-54-06-93): This is the best Italian restaurant in Denmark. This 20-year-old restaurant is the domain of two Tuscan-born partners who have delighted some of the most discerning palates in Copenhagen. Denmark's superb array of fresh seafood, among other produce, is given a decidedly Mediterranean twist at this citadel of refined cuisine. See p. 95.
- **Godt** (Copenhagen; $\mathcal{C}$ 33-15-21-22): Even the Queen of Denmark dines at this superb restaurant, celebrated for its international cuisine. The best and freshest produce and various ingredients at the market are fashioned into the most pleasing and quintessential dishes. See p. 98.
- **The Paul** (Copenhagen; $\mathcal{C}$ 33-75-07-75): Winning a coveted Michelin star, this is the best restaurant among the deluxe dining rooms of the Tivoli Gardens. Drawing gourmet diners with its carefully crafted international menu, it offers an inspired cuisine in these

pleasure gardens. There is a daring and innovation here found in no other Tivoli restaurant. See p. 118.
- **Marie Louise** (Odense; $\mathcal{C}$ 66-17-92-95): Glittering with crystal and silver, this dining room on a pedestrian street is one of the finest on the island of Funen. In an antique house, this Danish/Franco alliance offers a cuisine that's the epitome of taste, preparation, and service. Seafood and fish are the favored dishes. See p. 276.
- **Falsled Kro** (Falsled; $\mathcal{C}$ 62-68-11-11): Even if you don't stay at the hotel, consider stopping for a meal. A favorite among well-heeled Europeans, this restaurant produces a stellar French-inspired cuisine and uses seasonal produce from its own gardens. The succulent salmon is smoked in one of the outbuildings, and the owners breed quail locally. Such care and attention to detail make this one of Denmark's top restaurants. See p. 291.

4 THE BEST BUYS

- **Danish Design:** It's worth making a shopping trip to Denmark for this. The simple but elegant style that became fashionable in the 1950s has made a comeback. Danish modern chairs, glassware, and even buildings have returned. Collectors celebrate "old masters," such as Arne Jacobsen, Hans Wegner, and Poul Kjærholm, whose designs from the 1940s and 1950s are sold in antiques stores. Wegner, noted for his sculptured teak chairs, for example, is now viewed as the grand old man of Danish design. Younger designers have followed in the old masters' footsteps, producing carefully crafted items for the home—everything from chairs, desks, and furnishings to table settings and silverware. For the best display of Danish design today, walk along the pedestrian-only Strøget, the major shopping street in Copenhagen. The best single showcase for modern Danish design may be **Illums Bolighus,** Amagertorv 10 (© **33-14-19-41**). See p. 154.

- **Crystal & Porcelain:** Holmegaard crystal and Royal Copenhagen porcelain are household names, known for their beauty and craftsmanship. These items cost less in Denmark than in the United States, although signed art glass is costly everywhere. To avoid high prices, you can shop for seconds, which are discounted by 20% to 50% (some-

times the imperfection can be detected only by an expert). The best center for these collectors' items in Copenhagen is **Royal Copenhagen Porcelain,** Amagertorv 6 (© **33-13-71-81**). See p. 154.

- **Silver:** Danish designers have made a name for themselves in this field. Even with taxes and shipping charges, you can still save about 50% when purchasing silver in Denmark as compared with in the United States. If you're willing to consider "used" silver, you can get some remarkable discounts. The big name in international silver—and you can buy it at the source—is **Georg Jensen,** Amagertorv 6, Copenhagen (© **33-11-40-80**). See p. 155.

5 THE MOST SCENIC TOWNS & VILLAGES

- **Dragør:** At the doorstep of Copenhagen, this old seafaring town once flourished as a bustling herring port on the Baltic. Time, however, has passed it by, and for that we can be grateful, because it looks much as it used to, with half-timbered ocher and pink 18th-century cottages topped with thatch or red-tile roofs. The entire village is under the protection of the National Trust of Denmark. A 35-minute ride from the Danish capital will take you back 2 centuries. See "Side Trips from Copenhagen," in chapter 6.

- **Ærøskøbing:** This little village on the country's most charming island (Ærø) is storybook Denmark. A 13th-century market town, Ærøskøbing is a Lilliputian souvenir of the past, complete with gingerbread houses. You expect Hansel and Gretel to arrive at any moment. See "Ærø," in chapter 10.

- **Odense:** The birthplace of Hans Christian Andersen is Denmark's third-largest city, and still has a medieval core. You can walk its cobblestone streets and admire its half-timbered houses. Other than its associations with the writer,

Odense is a worthwhile destination in its own right, filled with attractions (including **St. Canute's Cathedral**). On the outskirts, you can explore the 1554 Renaissance castle, Egeskov, as well as a 10th-century Viking ship at Ladby. See "Odense: Birthplace of Hans Christian Andersen," in chapter 10.

- **Ribe:** On the Jutland peninsula (the European mainland), this is the best-preserved medieval town in Denmark, and is known for its narrow cobblestone lanes and crooked, half-timbered houses. An important trading center during the Viking era, today it's known as the town where the endangered stork—the subject of European myth and legend—nests every April. The National Trust protects the medieval center. From April to mid-September a night watchman circles Ribe, spinning tales of the town's legendary days and singing traditional songs. See "Ribe," in chapter 11.

- **Ebeltoft:** On Jutland, this well-preserved town of half-timbered buildings is the capital of the Mols hill country. It's a town of sloping row houses, crooked streets, and local handicraft shops. The town hall looks as if it had been erected for kindergarten children;

in Ebeltoft you can also visit the 1860 frigate *Jylland*, the oldest man-of-war in Denmark. See "Ebeltoft," in chapter 12.

6 THE BEST ACTIVE VACATIONS

- **Fishing:** For centuries, much of Denmark relied on the sea and whatever the country's fishermen could pull out of it for its diet. Since then, no *smørrebrød* (open-faced sandwich) buffet has been complete without a selection of shrimp, herring, and salmon. The preparations of plaice, cod, eel, perch, and trout are culinary art forms. The seas off Funen, especially within the Great Belt, have yielded countless tons of seafood, and that tradition has encouraged anglers and sports enthusiasts to test their luck in the rich waters of the Baltic. Many outfitters can introduce you to the mysteries of fresh- and saltwater fishing.

- **Biking:** A nation of bikers, Denmark has organized the roads to suit the national sport. A network of bike routes and paths is protected from heavy traffic, and much of the terrain is flat. Bicycling vacations are available as inclusive tours that cover bike rental, ferry tickets, and accommodations en route. Some deluxe tours transport your luggage from one hotel to the next. For more information, contact the **Danish Cycling Federation,** Rømersgade 7, DK-1362 Copenhagen (© **33-32-31-21;** www.dcf.dk).

- **Camping:** With about 550 officially sanctioned campgrounds, Denmark has one of the highest numbers, per capita, of campgrounds of any nation in the world, and living in a tent or a pop-up trailer in the great outdoors is something of a national obsession. There are

plenty of campsites near the city limits of Copenhagen, and many more are located around the country in areas of scenic or historic interest, some near the sea. The official website and address of the **Danish Camping Federation** is www.campingraadet.dk. Either via their website, or by calling or writing them at Campingrådet, Mosedalsvej 15, DK-2500 Valby (© **39-27-88-44**), you can request that the staff send you information about the nation's campsites. Other sources of information about camping are available at www.visitdenmark.com (the official website of the Danish Tourist Board), or an equivalent site, **www.dk-camp.dk**, which lists more than 300 campsites that are privately owned. You can obtain a free *DK Camping Danmark* catalog at all DK-CAMP camping grounds, tourist offices, and many service stations.

- **Golf:** There are about 130 golf courses scattered across the flat, sandy, and sometimes windy landscapes of Denmark, many of them landscaped around the sand dunes, ponds, forests, and rocky outcroppings for which the country is well-known. Most clubs welcome visitors, although in some cases you might be asked to present a membership card from your club at home. Local tourism offices are usually well versed in steering golfers to worthwhile courses, but for some insight into what's available, visit **www.golfonline.dk**.

7 THE BEST CASTLES & PALACES

- **Christiansborg Palace** (Copenhagen): The queen receives official guests here in the Royal Reception Chamber, where you must don slippers to protect the floors. The complex also holds the Parliament House and the Supreme Court. From 1441 until the fire of 1795, this was the official residence of Denmark's monarchy. You can tour the richly decorated rooms, including the Throne Room and banqueting hall. Below, you can see the well-preserved ruins of the 1167 castle of Bishop Absalon, founder of Copenhagen. See p. 132.

- **Rosenborg Castle** (Copenhagen): Built by Christian IV in the 17th century, this red-brick Renaissance castle remained a royal residence until the early 19th century, when the building was converted into a museum. It still houses the crown jewels, and its collection of costumes and royal memorabilia is unequaled in Denmark. See p. 130.

- **Kronborg Slot** (Helsingør): Shakespeare never saw this castle, and Hamlet (if he existed at all) lived centuries before it was built. But Shakespeare did set his immortal play here. Intriguing secret passages fill its cannon-studded bastions, and it often serves as the backdrop for modern

productions of *Hamlet*. The brooding statue of Holger Danske sleeps in the dungeon, but according to legend, this Viking chief will rise again to defend Denmark if the country is endangered. See p. 182.

- **Frederiksborg Castle** (Hillerød): Known as the Danish Versailles, this moated *slot* (castle) is the most elaborate in Scandinavia. It was built in the Dutch Renaissance style of red brick with a copper roof, and its oldest parts date from 1560. Much of the castle was constructed under the direction of the "master builder," Christian IV, from 1600 to 1620. Fire ravaged the castle in 1859, and the structure had to be completely restored. It is now a national history museum. See p. 173.

- **Egeskov Castle** (Kværndrup): On the island of Funen, this 1554 Renaissance "water castle" is set amid splendid gardens. The most romantic example of Denmark's fortified manors, the castle was built in the middle of a moat, surrounded by a park. The best-preserved Renaissance castle of its type in Europe, it has many attractions on its grounds, including airplane and vintage-automobile museums. See p. 270.

8 THE BEST OFFBEAT EXPERIENCES

- **Journeying Back to the 1960s:** If you're nostalgic for the counterculture of the 1960s, it lives on in Christiania, a Copenhagen community located at the corner of Prinsessegade and Badsmandsstræde, on Christianshavn. Founded in 1972, this anarchists' commune occupies former army barracks; its current residents preach a gospel of drugs and peace. Christiania's residents have even organized their own government and passed laws, for example, to

legalize drugs. They're not complete anarchists, however, as they venture into the city at least once a month to pick up their social welfare checks. Today you can wander about their community, which is complete with a theater, cafes, grocery stores, and even a local radio station. See chapter 5.

- **Exploring Erotica:** Denmark was the first country to "liberate" pornography, in 1968, and today there's a museum in Copenhagen devoted to the subject. In the **Erotica Museum** (at Købmager-gade 24; © **33-12-03-11**), you can learn about the sex lives of such famous figures as Nietzsche, Freud, and even Duke Ellington. Founded by a photographer of nudes, the museum has exhibits ranging from the tame to the tempestuous—starting from Etruscan drawings and progressing to the further reaches of the erotic and sexual. See p. 133.

- **Calling on Artists and Craftspeople:** West Jutland has many open workshops where you can see craftspeople in action; you can meet the potter, the glass blower, the painter, the textile designer, and even the candlestick maker. Local tourist offices can tell you which studios are open to receive guests in such centers as Ærø, Tønder, and Ribe.

Denmark in Depth

The Danes may live in a small country, but they usually extend an enthusiastic welcome to visitors. The British novelist Evelyn Waugh called the Danes "the most exhilarating people of Europe." Few Danes would dispute this, and neither would we. Made up mostly of islands, Denmark is a heavily industrialized nation, known for its manufactured products as well as its arts and crafts. However, it also boasts a quarter of a million farmers.

1 DENMARK TODAY

Denmark has been called a bridge because it links northern Europe with the Scandinavian Peninsula. In 2000, that became literal, as the Øresund Bridge opened across the sound, connecting the island of Zealand, on which Copenhagen sits, with southern Sweden, at the city of Malmö, for the first time in history.

The smallest of the Scandinavian countries (about half the size of Maine), it has a total land mass of about 41,400 sq. km (16,000 sq. miles), most of which is on the peninsula of Jutland, which borders Germany. The major islands are Zealand, Funen, and Bornholm. Denmark has adequate space for its population of 5.5 million people, but its population density is much greater than that of the other Scandinavian countries. About 1.4 million Danes live in the capital city, Copenhagen, on the island of Zealand.

About 98% of all native-born Danes belong to the Danish Lutheran Church, the state church, although church attendance is actually low. The second-largest group is Catholics (30,000), and there are about 6,500 Jews.

Only 4.5% of the population is made up of immigrants, including refugees identified as Palestinians, Somalis, Bangladeshis, Kurds, and Iraqis, among others. Some immigrants, such as the Vietnamese,

seem to fit smoothly into Danish life. Among some members of the Muslim and Arab communities, there have been cultural conflicts—as blaring world headlines about those Danish cartoons revealed.

Technically, Denmark is a parliamentary democracy and constitutional monarchy. Its territories include the Faroe Islands (an autonomous area under the Danish Crown) and Greenland (which was granted regional autonomy in 1985). The sovereign is Queen Margrethe II, who ascended the throne in 1972; her husband is a Frenchman, Prince Henrik. Margrethe is the first woman sovereign in Denmark in 6 centuries. Real power is vested in the unicameral parliament (the *Folketing*), which citizens older than 23 elect every 4 years. The royal family's primary function is ceremonial.

Although it has been a NATO member since 1949, Denmark does not permit nuclear weapons to be deployed on its soil. Denmark became the first NATO country to grant women the right to serve in frontline units. It's also an active member of the European Union (but not part of the Eurozone, having voted in Sept 2000 to retain the Danish kroner), and enjoys harmonious relations with its Scandinavian neighbors and other European countries.

Fun Facts   **Did You Know?**

- Denmark is a nation of nearly 500 islands.
- The reigning queen, Margrethe II, designs postage stamps, as well as opera and ballet sets.
- Second only to the Bible, the writings of Hans Christian (H. C.) Andersen are the most widely translated literary works in the world.
- Some historians argue that the fairy-tale writer Andersen wasn't the son of a poor cobbler but the child of the 19th-century Danish king Christian VIII.
- Denmark has the highest proportion of female clerics per capita.
- The country has a celebration honoring America's Fourth of July.
- Chilly Denmark used to grow grapes for winemaking in the Middle Ages.
- Danes pay the highest taxes on earth.

Denmark boasts one of the world's highest standards of living plus a comprehensive social welfare system, which is funded through extremely high taxes. Danes enjoy 7^1/$_2$-hour workdays, cradle-to-grave security, state-funded hospitals and schools, and a month-long vacation every year. During their vacations, Danes tend to travel extensively. By and large the Danes are extremely well educated; they have pioneered the establishment of adult education centers (for those ages 18–35), a movement that has spread to other countries of Europe.

No country in the European Union has less poverty or a fairer distribution of wealth than Denmark. Both the poor and the rich get richer, and in most cases young people have little trouble finding employment.

Although a progressive, modern, and liberal state (it was one of the first countries to recognize same-sex marriages), Denmark has its share of problems. Drug use among young people is a growing concern, and the young are increasingly rejecting the institution of marriage, with common-law relationships becoming the norm. Also, the divorce rate is rising.

The "melancholy Dane" aspect of their character (if there is one) is reflected in a relatively high suicide rate. Otherwise, their general health is excellent—a Danish girl born today has a life expectancy of 78 years; a Danish boy, 72 years.

Culturally, Denmark is an avid producer and consumer of art and culture. Some 12,000 books a year are published in Denmark. There are 42 newspapers, and the theater and film industries are thriving in spite of cutbacks in government funding.

Denmark in the late '90s built bridges to the world. On June 14, 1998, Queen Margrethe II cut a ribbon before driving across the Great Belt Bridge, a span that links the island of Zealand (on which Copenhagen sits) with the island of Funen. Because Funen is linked by bridge to Jutland (part of mainland Europe), and with Malmö across the Øresund Sound, Copenhageners can now drive to Germany or Sweden without having to rely on ferries.

Composed of a flat and sandy peninsula and a cluster of islands, Denmark is tiny. But despite its small size, its strategic position at the mouth of the Baltic has made Denmark one of the most coveted terrains in the world. Consequently, Denmark's struggles to secure its sovereignty and independence from the larger, stronger military forces that surround it on every side have repeatedly shaped Danish history. And although modern Danes are somewhat embarrassed when confronted with their country's militaristic past, Denmark used to be known as a fiercely aggressive nation, jockeying for territory, prestige, and strategic advantage with other empire-building nations such as England, Austria, and the precursors of modern-day Germany.

PREHISTORIC DENMARK & THE ROMANS

The mystery that surrounds early Denmark stems from the fact that the Romans and their legions never managed to transform it into a colony. Consequently, while former Roman provinces like France and Germany were depicted by numerous historians, including Julius Caesar himself, little was ever recorded about ancient Denmark. There is evidence of early trade.

Amber found only in the Baltic has been identified within Egyptian jewelry, and some historians cite Danish trade with the Eastern Mediterranean, in which the Danes exchanged fur and slaves for bronze utensils and gold jewelry.

Concentrations of bones from various grave sites, and stone implements that archaeologists estimate at 80,000 years old, have been unearthed in regions of Jutland, but despite those discoveries, Denmark has never produced the wealth of archaeological finds that are commonplace, say, in Greece, Italy, or Egypt. Part of the reason might stem from the great ice sheets that made much of Denmark uninhabitable for thousands of years.

Later, as the ice sheets receded northward, hunter-gatherers eked out a modest living. Their communal grave sites and the stone dolmens that mark their entrances show proficiency at erecting stone lintels and markers.

Ironically, the high acid and iron content within Denmark's peat bogs has had the macabre effect of preserving the bodies of at least 160 unfortunates, all of whom died violently, in some cases many thousands of years ago, and all of whom appear to have been unceremoniously dumped into bogs. Among the most famous of

DATELINE

- **810** The reign of the first recorded Danish king, Godfred, ends.
- **811** The southern boundary of the Danish kingdom is established at the banks of the Eider River, where it remains for almost a thousand years.
- **800–950** Vikings emerge to plunder the monasteries and settlements of England, France, and Russia.

- **940–985** Harald Bluetooth brings Christianity to Denmark.
- **1013–43** The crowns of Denmark and England are united.
- **1104** The foundation is laid for a Danish national church that is distinctly different from that within German lands to the south.
- **1397** The Union of Kalmar, under the leadership of Queen Margrethe, unites

Denmark, Norway, and Sweden. Meanwhile, high percentages of Danes are allowed to work their own farmland, forming the basis of Denmark's eventual strength as an agrarian nation.

- **1471** Sweden abandons the union; Denmark and Norway remain united under Christian I (1426–81).

continues

these is the well-preserved, 2,400-year-old body of the Tollund Man, who was probably strangled to death, and whose body was discovered in the 1950s in a Jutland peat bog. His body revealed some clues about what life was like in prehistoric Denmark: A wool cap covered his head, stubble on his chin and cheeks indicated that the fashion at the time involved shaving, and the remains in his stomach showed that his last meal consisted mostly of barley.

As for literary references, other than a few cryptic comments that appear within such early English sagas as *Beowulf,* and the cryptic descriptions by the medieval Scandinavian historian Saxo Grammaticus of a long line of (otherwise undocumented) early medieval Danish warlords, there isn't a lot of documentation about post-Roman Denmark. Historians conclude that Denmark was a land of frequent migrations, frequent annihilations of one tribal unit by another, and continual changeovers of the racial texture of the peninsula as one tribe of people was either annihilated or ousted by others.

VIKINGS TERRORIZE EUROPE

Denmark developed a reputation for violence as the Vikings ravaged regions of central and southern Europe.

So, ironically, the country with one of the most peaceful reputations in Europe today was originally a hell-raising land that, along with such other Viking areas as Norway and Sweden, was associated with terror for the rest of Europe. Lustfully pagan and undeterred by the belief that Christian churches and monasteries were sanctified, they exacted rich plunder from whatever monastery or convent they happened to judge as weak enough to be attractive.

Their longboats were especially feared: Measuring about 18m (60 ft.) from the dragon-shaped prow to stern, longboats were powered by 30 oars and a sail. They were still light enough, however, that their crews could drag them across land, thereby "hopping" from rivers to lakes, across sandbars, and across isthmuses that would otherwise have been unnavigable. It's no small wonder that the Danes would eventually become proficient as both mariners and traders.

Through rape and intermarriage, the Vikings mingled bloodlines with future English, French, Germans, and Russians. Despite the mayhem they unleashed on conquered lands, Vikings brought with them regimented rituals; for example, unlike most European peoples at the time, they bathed every Sunday, regardless of temperature or weather.

- **1530** Lutheran preachers bring the Reformation to Denmark.
- **1536** After a siege of Copenhagen, most of the lands and assets owned by the Catholic Church are seized by the Danish crown.
- **1577–1648** The long reign of Christian IV brings prosperity but ends in a losing war with Sweden.
- **1675–79** The Skane War is fought, and Denmark loses large territories to Sweden, including the "château country" of southern Sweden.
- **1801–07** England, in a black chapter of its foreign policy, bombards Copenhagen and confiscates the ships of Denmark's navy as a means of ensuring that the Danes don't cooperate with Napoleon.
- **1813** The national treasury of Denmark, faced with punitive clauses in the treaty at the end of the Napoleonic Wars, goes bankrupt.
- **1810–30** The creation of works by Søren Kierkegaard and Hans Christian Andersen defines this period as the golden age of Danish Literature.
- **1849** Simultaneous with revolutions that break out across Europe, liberal reforms are activated in the form of a new Danish constitution.

The most distinct threat to Danish territoriality came from Charlemagne, whose Frankish empire covered what is today France and Germany. If Charlemagne hadn't focused most of his territorial ambitions on richer, more fertile lands in central Europe and Spain, it's likely that what's known today as Denmark would have become a vassal state of the Franks. As it was, the Franks only took a slight imperial interest in Jutland. Godfred, the first recorded Danish king, died in 810 after spending most of his reign battling the Franks.

Godfred's successor, Hemming, signed a treaty with the Franks marking the Eider River, an east-west stream that flanks southern Jutland, as the southern boundary of his sovereignty. That boundary functioned more or less as the Danish border until 1864.

Two famous kings emerged from Denmark during the 10th century, Gorm the Old (883–940) and his son, Harald Bluetooth (935–85). Their reigns resulted in the unification of Denmark with power centralized at Jelling in Jutland. Harald, through the hard work of a core of Christian missionaries trained in Frankish territories to the south (especially in Hamburg), also introduced Christianity, which eventually became the country's predominant religion. As part of his attempt to obliterate Denmark's pagan past, he transformed his father's tomb, which honored a roster of pagan gods and spirits, into a site of Christian worship.

Harald eventually extended Danish influence as far as neighboring Norway. The links he established between Denmark and Norway weren't severed, at least politically, until the 1800s. Harald's son, Sweyn I, succeeded in conquering England in 1013, more than 50 years before the Norman invasion in 1066. The Normans, ironically, were also of Danish origin, through invasions several centuries before.

Under Sweyn's son, Canute II (994–1035), England, Denmark, and part of Sweden came under the rule of one crown. After Canute's death, however, the Danish kingdom was reduced to only Denmark. Canute's nephew, Sweyn II, ruled the Danish kingdom, and, upon his death, his five sons governed Denmark successfully. In 1104, the foundation was laid for a Danish national church that was distinct from the ecclesiastical administration in Hamburg.

THE BALTIC: A DANISH "LAKE"

The few remaining links between Denmark and the Frankish Holy Roman Empire were severed under Archbishop Eskil (1100–82) and King Valdemar I (1131–82). During a celebration at

---

- **1866** Denmark loses Schleswig-Holstein to Prussia.
- **1890s** Many liberal reforms in education and health insurance act as precursors of the liberal social policies of Denmark in the 20th century.
- **1914** Denmark struggles to maintain neutrality in World War I.
- **1915** A new constitution gives Denmark universal suffrage.

- **1916** Denmark sells some of the Virgin Islands to the U.S. for $25 million.
- **1926–40** Economic depression causes great suffering in Denmark
- **1940–45** Denmark is invaded and occupied by Nazi Germany.
- **1949** Over some protests, Denmark joins NATO.
- **1953** A new constitution provides for a single-chamber parliament.

- **1972** Denmark joins the European Economic Community; Margrethe, daughter of Frederik IX, becomes queen of Denmark.
- **1982** Poul Schluter becomes the first Conservative prime minister since 1894.
- **1989** Denmark leads the world in certain social policies: the first NATO country to allow women in front-line military units and the first

continues

Ringsted in 1190, the Danish church and state were united, partly because of the influence of Archbishop Absalon (1128–1201), a soldier and statesman who is honored today as the patron saint of Copenhagen. Inspired by monarchical ideas, Absalon became a fierce and militaristic guardian of Danish independence. The hostilities became a religious confrontation, pitting the Christian Danes against the pagans to the south, as well as a territorial conflict. Absalon's most dramatic disfigurement of a pagan god occurred on the now-German island of Rügen around 1147, when he chopped *Svantevit,* the four-headed wooden figure, into little pieces and distributed them as firewood among his nominally Christian soldiers.

In 1169, Denmark began what would evolve into a long series of conquests that increased its sphere of influence within city-states along the Baltic, including the ports of Estonia (which was conquered by the Danes in 1219), Latvia, eastern Germany, Poland, Sweden, and Russia. Part of Denmark's military and mercantile success derived from the general weakness of the German states to the south; part of it was because of a population explosion within Denmark, which increased the pressure for colonization.

Valdemar II (1170–1241) strengthened Denmark's control over the Baltic and came close to transforming it into a Danish lake. Grateful for their help, he ennobled many of his illegitimate sons and empowered many of his military cohorts with aristocratic titles and rewarded them with land.

The result was a weakening of the monarchy in favor of an increasingly voracious group of nobles, whose private agendas conflicted with those of the king. Valdemar's son, Eric IV (1216–50), also known as Eric Ploughpenny, argued with church bishops and with his brothers over royal prerogatives, and was assassinated by his younger brother, Duke Abel of Schleswig, who proclaimed himself king of Denmark in 1250.

Civil wars ensued, and three of the four successive kings were killed in battle. Eric VI (1274–1319) also waged wars with Norway and Sweden, which led to Denmark's debilitation and the mortgaging of large parcels of the kingdom to pay for unsuccessful military campaigns.

Between 1332 and 1340, Denmark had no king and was ruled by an uneasy coalition of nobles. Valdemar IV Atterdag (1320–75) retained his grip on the Danish throne only by signing the peace treaty of Stralsund in 1370 with the towns of the Hanseatic League (a federation of free towns in northern Germany and adjoining countries formed around 1241 for economic advancement and mutual protection). Its enactment did a lot to improve the fortunes of the city-states of the Hanseatic

country to recognize same-sex marriages.

- **1992** Denmark votes against the Maastricht Treaty, which establishes the framework for the European Economic Union.
- **1993** Denmark votes to support the Maastricht Treaty, and then presides over the European Union for the first half of the year.

- **1996** Copenhagen is designated the "Cultural Capital of Europe"; the "Copenhagen '96" festival attracts artists and performers from all over the world, with more than 25,000 performances staged.
- **1998** By a narrow margin, Denmark votes to enlarge its ties with the European Union.

- **2000** Danes vote not to join the Eurozone; Øresund Bridge links the island of Zealand with Sweden.
- **2004** Crown Prince Frederik takes a bride, HRH Crown Princess Mary.
- **2005–06** Muhammad cartoons published in Denmark set off worldwide protests in the Muslim world.
- **2006** Prince Joachim divorces Asian bride.

League, as it granted them enviable commercial privileges. The resulting prosperity of the Hanseatic League led to architectural enhancements, whose effects were visible all around the Baltic.

A UNITED SCANDINAVIA

Valdemar IV died in 1375, leaving Denmark without a male heir. Finally, Olaf (1375–87), the infant son of Valdemar's daughter Margrethe, through her marriage with King Haakon VI Magnusson (1339–80) of Norway, came to the throne. (Through a complicated chain of bloodlines, the infant Olaf was the nominal heir to all of Norway, Denmark, and Sweden.)

During Olaf's infancy, Margrethe ruled the country as regent. When her husband, Haakon, and 12-year-old Olaf both died, she was acknowledged as queen of Norway and Denmark. A patroness of the arts and a savvy administrator of the national treasury, she was eventually granted wide political leeway in Sweden.

Although the three nations had already been combined under the stewardship of Margrethe, they were merged into a united Scandinavia in 1397 as The Union of Kalmar. One of the largest political unions since the collapse of the Roman Empire, it extended from Iceland and the fledging communities in Greenland as far east as the western coast of Finland. It included the entire Danish archipelago as well as the Faroe, Shetland, and Orkney islands.

Acknowledging her advanced age and the need for a male figurehead at the reigns of power, Margrethe arranged for her nephew, Eric of Pomerania (1382–1459), to be crowned king of all three countries as Eric VII. Margrethe, however, firmly committed to the superiority of Denmark within the trio, continued to rule behind the scenes until her death in 1412. (A contemporary historian said of Margrethe's comportment at public events, "All the nobility of Denmark were seized by fear of the wisdom and strength of this lady.") Despite later attempts to expand

the Scandinavian union to northeastern Germany, the concept of a united Scandinavia was never as far-reaching or powerful as it was under Margrethe. There were many 19th- and 20th-century visionaries who hoped in vain for the eventual unification of "the three separate nations of the Scandinavian north."

Margrethe's designated heir, Eric VII, was childless. He was dethroned in 1439 and replaced by his nephew Christopher of Bavaria. His reign lasted only about 9 years, after which Sweden pressed for autonomy. It elected Karl Knutson (Charles VIII) as its Stockholm-based king in 1471. Denmark and the relatively weak Norway shared King Christian I (1426–81). Although Christian I lost control of Sweden, he did gain sovereignty over Schleswig and Holstein, ancient territories to the south of modern-day Denmark. But it was a troubled and culturally ambiguous acquisition that would vex the patience of both Denmark and the German states for centuries, as its citizens waffled in their allegiances.

Throughout the rest of the 15th century, the Danish church accumulated great wealth, and the merchant class profited from increases in agricultural production. By around 1500, about 12,000 Danes were estimated to own their own farms; about 18,000 Danes operated farms on land leased by the Danish king, and some 30,000 Danes maintained lease lands belonging to either Danish nobles or the increasingly wealthy (tax-exempt) Catholic Church. Denmark became an exporter of foodstuffs, especially beef and grain, and livestock, especially horses.

The early 15th century marked a fundamental change in the definition of nobility. Prior to that, any Dane could become a noble by contributing a fully equipped private army, invariably composed of feudal-style serfs and vassals, to the king's war efforts. In exchange for this, he would be granted an exemption from all taxes generated by his estates. After around 1400, however, only nobles who could prove at least three generations of aristocratic lineage could define themselves as noble, with all the attendant privileges that such a title implied. With no new blood coming into the pool of Danish aristocrats, the number of noble families decreased from 264 to 140 between 1450 and 1650. Shakespeare borrowed the names of two of those families, the Rosencrantz and the Guildenstern, for his drama about the mythical Danish prince, Hamlet.

The 16th century also saw changes in Danish religious practice as critiques of Catholicism began to gain currency across Europe. One of Denmark's most devoted Reformation-era theologians was Paul Helgesen, a staunch opponent of the corruption of Denmark's church. He was appointed to a position of academic prominence within the University of Copenhagen in 1519 and was a particularly vocal critic of the idea of buying salvation through the sale of indulgences. Ironically, Martin Luther's break with the Catholic Church in 1521, from a base in nearby Germany, transformed the reputation of Paul Helgesen into something of an archconservative defender of Danish Catholicism.

THE 16TH CENTURY

Christian II (1481–1559) ascended the throne in 1513. Sympathetic to the common man during his regency over the throne of Norway, he was mistrusted by conservative nobles. Their distrust was exacerbated by his commitment to seeking financial and military advice from commoners. He went so far as to turn over control of the kingdom's finances to his mistress's mother, Sigbrit Villoms, the frugal and canny widow of a Dutch burgher. A former alchemist, who claimed to have a telepathic hold over the king, she contributed to a reign alternating between bouts of genius and bouts of blood-soaked madness. Despite the massacre of more than 600 Danish and Swedish nobles in

the "bloodbath of Stockholm" in 1520 and other violent atrocities, many Renaissance-style reforms were activated under Christian II's reign, without which Denmark might have erupted into full-fledged revolution.

Christian II recaptured Sweden in 1520 but was defeated by the Swedish warrior-king Gustavus Vasa a year later. Christian was deposed in 1522, whereupon he fled to the Netherlands. In the spring of 1532, he returned to Denmark, where he was incarcerated until his death, first in Sønderborg Castle and then in Kalundborg castle.

His successor, Frederik I (1471–1533), signed a charter granting the nobility many privileges. Under his regime, the Franciscans, an order of Roman Catholic monks, were expelled from their conspicuously wealthy houses of worship, and Lutheran ministers were granted the freedom to roam throughout Denmark preaching. Upon Frederik's death, the Reformation took earnest hold within Denmark. Conflicts between Lutherans and Catholics erupted in a civil war, with Catholic power centered in Copenhagen and with Lutherans mainly based on the islands of Funen and Jutland. The war ended in 1536 with the surrender of Copenhagen. In the process, vast Catholic-owned estates were forfeited to the Danish crown.

The Danish Lutheran Church was founded in 1536 during the reign of Christian III (1534–59). Before the end of the 1570s, Protestantism was firmly entrenched within Denmark. A Danish church organized in accordance with German Lutheran models ousted virtually every trace of Catholicism. Disciples of Martin Luther were brought in to organize the new Reformed Church of Denmark, which soon took on patriotic and nationalistic overtones, as hymn books, liturgies, and sermons were eventually conducted exclusively in vernacular Danish. As for the monarchy, its finances were vastly improved at the end of the Reformation thanks to its confiscation of the vast wealth formerly controlled by the Catholic Church.

WARS WITH SWEDEN

Much of the 17th century in Denmark was consumed with an ongoing series of wars with its archenemy, Sweden. Despite that, the reign of the Danish king Christian IV (1577–1648) was one of relative prosperity. The Danes worked hard, investing time and money in the development of their "overseas territory," Norway. That territory's capital, Christiania (now known as Oslo), was named after their king.

Sweden was understandably concerned about Denmark's control of the entrance to the Baltic, the sea on which Sweden and many members of the Hanseatic League depended. Denmark, thanks to its control of the narrow straits near Copenhagen, its ownership of such Baltic islands as Ösel and Gotland, and, in the Atlantic, its control of Iceland and the Faroe Islands, could be accused of being far more imperial than its size and present-day pacifism would imply.

Denmark continued to meddle in German and English politics throughout the 1600s, notably in the Thirty Years' War, which ripped apart the principalities of Germany.

Tensions between Denmark and Sweden also intensified during this period and were exacerbated by Sweden's emperor Charles V, who argued that Sweden held the right of succession to the Danish throne.

Sweden invaded Jutland and quickly defeated the Danes. Military scholars attribute the victory to Sweden's reliance on well-trained Swedish peasants who filled the ranks of the Swedish army. The Danes, in contrast, relied on paid, and less committed, mercenaries. By the Treaty of Christianople, Denmark was forced to cede to Sweden many of its former possessions, including scattered communities in Norway and the Baltic island of Gotland. Simultaneous with the loss of its territories in southern Sweden was the completion of two of Denmark's most-photographed castles: Frederiksborg, in Hillerød, and Rosenborg, in Copenhagen, both finished under the regime of Christian IV.

Danish king Frederik III (1609–70) tried to regain the lost territories when Sweden went to war with Poland, but Charles X defeated him. Frederik ended up giving Sweden additional territory, including the island of Bornholm. Charles X attacked Denmark in an attempt to take control of the whole country, but this time Denmark won, regaining its lost territories. Sweden ended the war after the death of Charles X in 1660.

The Skane War (1675–79) was an ill-advised military campaign started by the Danish king Christian V (1646–99). Its outcome included Denmark's loss of Skane, a valuable territory in southern Sweden, which, because of its architectural appeal, is known today as Sweden's "château country." After the signing of the peace treaty that ended the war, Denmark managed to retain its claim on the island of Bornholm and on cities in northern Norway, such as Trondheim.

Frederik IV (1671–1730), Christian V's successor, resumed the war with Sweden in 1699. Named the Great Northern War, it raged, more or less inconclusively, from 1699 to 1730. Southern Sweden was not recovered, but part of Schleswig-Holstein (northern Germany) was ceded to Denmark by the German states.

During the 18th century, Denmark achieved many democratic reforms. Thanks to its navy and its seasoned core of merchant vessels, it also gained control of a group of islands in the West Indies (now the U.S. Virgin Islands) as well as the barren, snowy expanse of Greenland. Agriculture and trade prospered, and Copenhagen developed into a quietly prosperous but formidable guardian of the western entrance of the Baltic Sea.

THE 19TH CENTURY & THE NAPOLEONIC WARS

At the start of the Napoleonic wars, with France squarely opposed to most of the other nations of Europe, Denmark was engaged in a booming business of selling grain to both England and France. Despite the sweeping changes in the map of Europe engendered by Napoleon's military campaigns, Denmark strongly defended its right to remain neutral, and, as such, worked hard to ensure free passage of ships from other neutral nations within the Baltic.

This refusal to take sides, combined with the rich contracts that Danish merchants were able to acquire transporting supplies between hostile parties, infuriated England—the sworn enemy of Napoleon's France. In 1801, fearing that Denmark's formidable navy might be persuaded to cooperate with the French, England destroyed part of the Danish fleet in a battle at sea.

In 1807, as the threat of Napoleon's conquest of Europe became more and more of a reality, in one of the most arrogant acts of coercion in 19th-century history, England ordered the Danes to transfer their navy to British rule within 8 days or be bombarded. When the Danes refused, English warships opened fire on Copenhagen and destroyed the city's cathedral, its university, and hundreds of homes. England's treatment of Denmark forced the youthful king Frederik VI (1808–39) to ally Denmark with France and the policies of Napoleon. Later, after all of Napoleon's European allies abandoned him, Denmark remained loyal.

This led to a series of humiliating disasters for Denmark, especially when Napoleon was roundly defeated by an alliance of European countries in 1814. Because of England's embargoes on Denmark and the

destruction of many Danish ships, Denmark lost control over its overseas colony of Norway, and its trade came to an almost complete standstill after the loss of its navy.

At a treaty that was signed at Kiel the same year, Denmark was forced to yield Norway to Sweden and Heligoland to England. The only remaining gems in Denmark's once-mighty empire included Greenland, Iceland, and the Faroe Islands.

Without a navy and crippled by huge debts and a loss of much of its prestige, Denmark sank into poverty. In 1813, the national treasury went bankrupt. Several years later, especially between 1818 and 1824, the price of grain virtually collapsed, which culminated in many farm failures and a massive exodus from Denmark to the New World. The country's precarious financial and military position also put a virtual end to any hope of liberal reforms.

Following the Napoleonic wars, the rulers Frederik VI and his successor, Christian VIII, formed very conservative governments. In 1848, as revolts and revolutions broke out across Europe, the Danes demanded a more liberal constitution. Representatives elected under a new constitution that was signed on June 5, 1849, tempered the absolute rule of the Danish monarchs.

The liberal reforms inaugurated in 1849 eventually applied to a smaller, more compact nation. In 1850, after a 2-year revolution, Schleswig-Holstein seceded from Denmark and allied itself with its German-speaking neighbor to the south, Prussia. After several years of indecisive referendums, military interventions, and the politicking of such European nations as Austria, Schleswig-Holstein was ceded to Prussia in 1866 under the Treaty of Prague.

On July 28, 1866, a new constitution was adopted, but it was more conservative than the earlier one (1849), and granted more power to those who paid the highest taxes—in other words, the landowners.

Throughout the rest of the 19th century, Denmark's conservatives struggled against reform-minded liberals. Conservatives pledged to build up trade incentives and military fortifications around Copenhagen. In the event of war, liberals argued, most of the Danish countryside would be sacrificed to the invaders, and only Copenhagen would be defended.

Members of the left favored social reforms, a downsizing of the Danish army, and an official allegiance to political neutrality. Despite opposition, a process of liberalization continued apace with the changes wrought by the Industrial Revolution. In 1891, a system of old-age pensions was introduced; in 1892 came an early form of health insurance; and in 1899, funds were allocated for the acquisition of farmland by individuals who qualified for assistance from the Danish government.

WORLD WAR I & ECONOMIC CHAOS

When World War I broke out, Denmark found itself on a razor's edge and struggled to remain neutral, but its position astride the shipping lanes favored by both England and Germany made this especially perilous. On August 14, 1914, Germany laid mines in the sea channels of southern Denmark and then strongly implied that Denmark would be well advised to lay other mines in the channels leading toward Copenhagen. Fearing that if they didn't comply, Germany would lay the mines anyway and then commandeer parcels of Danish soil for installation of German naval bases, Denmark began laying mines.

Danish king Christian X had the unfortunate task of phoning his cousin, the king of England, about the situation. England agreed not to interpret Denmark's action as a direct act of hostility. Consequently,

all the waters around Denmark were peppered with high-powered explosives, a situation that had a disastrous effect on Danish trade and the Danish treasury. Later, German U-boats sank at least 30% of Denmark's merchant fleet.

Eventually, through cooperation and joint commitments with Sweden and Norway, Denmark managed to retain its fragile hold on wartime neutrality, but at a high price in terms of unemployment, higher taxes, and endless neuroses and self-doubts.

Partly in reaction to the traumas of their untenable situation, the Danes signed a new constitution on June 5, 1915, establishing a two-chamber parliament and granting equal voting rights to men and women. In 1916, a law was passed that compelled industries to insure their workers against accidents. Also in 1916, a financially strapped Denmark concluded a treaty with the United States, selling the Danish West Indies (later known as the U.S. Virgin Islands) for $25 million.

In 1919, a land reform act resulted in the breakup of many large estates, with lands passing into the hands of greater numbers of farmers.

Because Germany was defeated in World War I, many people felt that all of Schleswig should be returned to Denmark and that the details should be hammered out during the Versailles Conference. But in an act that was later interpreted as remarkably callous, Denmark, because of its official neutrality during World War I, was not invited to the conference, despite the extreme losses its navy and merchant marine had suffered. Under pressure, the conventioneers eventually agreed to return North Schleswig, but not South Schleswig or Holstein, to Denmark.

A new treaty was drawn up between Iceland and Denmark in 1918. Although they functioned as separate, sovereign states, the two countries were united under one king, with Iceland under Denmark's protection. Danish ships were appointed as the official inspectors of Icelandic fisheries, and plans were laid for Iceland's eventual independence.

Denmark participated in the creation of the League of Nations and joined it in 1920. A crisis arose when Norway claimed jurisdiction over the territory of Greenland. However, in April 1933, the Permanent Court of International Justice granted Denmark sovereignty over Greenland, nullifying Norway's claim.

Although the Great Depression didn't begin in the United States until October 1929, Denmark was plunged into high levels of unemployment (30%) as early as 1926. Poor harvests and a 1926 tariff imposed on Danish grain by Germany, one of Denmark's largest trading partners, contributed to Denmark's fiscal woes. By 1932, a fiscal collapse of the Danish government seemed imminent. Fueled by the uncertainty, Danish branches of both the Fascist and the Nazi parties were established by the mid-1930s, although they remained relatively small. Part of their lack of success derived from the Danish government's policy of forbidding the civilian use of any kind of uniform in public, with the exception of the Boy Scouts. As a result, no mass demonstrations in the style of what the Germans later developed into the Third Reich ever took place on Danish soil.

THE COMING OF HITLER & NAZI OCCUPATION

In May of 1939, Hitler asked Denmark to sign a non-aggression pact. Denmark accepted it; Norway and Sweden did not, and as such, any semblance of a united Scandinavian front collapsed. The pact specified that Denmark and Germany would not go to war with each other for 10 years, and that Denmark would not give aid or assistance to any nation with which Germany was at war. When war broke out in 1939, Denmark declared its

neutrality. Denmark's ties with Iceland were severed, and the United States and Great Britain occupied Greenland and the Faroe Islands, respectively.

Despite the nonaggression pact, Nazi forces invaded and occupied Denmark in 1940. In 1943, Hitler sent General Hermann von Hanneken to impose martial law on Denmark and commandeered two Danish destroyers. Danish resistance continued against the German occupying forces, often in the form of sabotage of German-controlled industries and military installations. In many cases, Danish sailors scuttled their own ships to prevent them from falling under Nazi control. Danish Jews and homosexuals were arrested and sent to concentration camps beginning in 1942, but most, aided by the brave Danish people, were able to escape to Sweden. Danish civil servants tended to remain at their posts, as a means of ensuring an orderly administration of the country during terrible times.

In September 1944, many members of the Danish police, suspected (often correctly) of helping the Danish resistance, were imprisoned. The same year, a general strike among the Danes crippled Copenhagen, until the Germans accepted an uneasy compromise, and the Nazi troops became less visible in the capital.

On March 21, 1945, the Gestapo's headquarters (in what had been the Danish headquarters for Shell Oil) were demolished during an Allied air raid, sending most of the Gestapo's archives up in flames, much to the regret of later historians. Later, the Gestapo's Danish strongholds in Odense and Århus were also bombarded.

Beginning in February 1945, as the defeat of Germany appeared imminent, thousands of refugees from Germany poured across the border, seeking safety in Denmark. When Germany surrendered in 1945, British troops occupied most of Denmark. The island of Bornholm, however, was occupied by Soviet troops, who bombed parts of the island in a successful effort to dislodge the occupying Nazi forces. After the war, Denmark joined the United Nations.

POSTWAR DENMARK

After 1945, the Liberal Party, under Knud Kristensen, assumed control of Denmark. In 1947, Kristensen resigned. The Social Democratic Party, who governed under Frederik IX, then governed the country. The economy remained sluggish until 1948.

In 1949, Denmark joined NATO. In 1953, the Scandinavian Council was formed, composed of Denmark, Norway, Sweden, and Iceland; the council lasted until 1961. Also in 1953, Denmark adopted a new constitution, providing for a single-chamber parliament.

In 1972, Denmark became the sole Nordic member of the EEC. That same year, Queen Margrethe, born in 1940 (the year of the Nazi invasion), became queen of Denmark upon the death of her father, Frederik IX.

In 1982, Denmark seemed to abandon its long-cherished liberalism when it elected Poul Schluter, its first conservative prime minister since 1894. However, by 1989 Denmark was leading the world in the development of a liberal social agenda. It became the first NATO country to allow women to join frontline military units. Later, it became the first country to recognize marriages between partners of the same sex.

The early 1990s were dominated by Denmark's continuing debate over its role (or lack thereof) in the European Union. In 1992, Denmark rejected the Maastricht Treaty, which had established a framework for the European Economic Union. However, in a 1993 referendum Denmark reversed its position (by a close vote), voting to support the Maastricht Treaty and its own limited involvement in it. Denmark

presided over the European Union for the first part of that year.

In 1993, Denmark also observed the 50th anniversary of the virtual overnight rescue of 8,000 of its Jewish citizens, who were smuggled out of the country in 1943 into neutral Sweden. That same year the Tivoli Gardens celebrated its 150th year, and *The Little Mermaid* statue, inspired by the famous character from H. C. Andersen's fairy tales, turned 80.

In 1996, Copenhagen was named the "Cultural Capital of Europe." Following in the footsteps of other European cities (including Athens, Florence, Paris, and Madrid), Copenhagen celebrated with a year of festivities. A massive campaign of restorations and new construction revitalized the city.

In May 1998, Denmark held a referendum on extending its ties and connections with the European Union. Danes, Greenlanders, and Faroese voted for enlargement of their position within the EU. The margin was extremely narrow, indicating how divided Danes remain on this important issue.

Denmark had a royal wedding on May 14, 2004. His royal highness, Crown Prince Frederik, married Mary Elizabeth Donaldson. She is now HRH Crown Princess of Denmark. The wedding took place in the Copenhagen Cathedral. Copenhagen is now her address, but the Crown Princess of Denmark was born in the Australian state of Tasmania, the daughter of two educators.

When the Danish newspaper *Jyllands-Posten,* in autumn of 2005, published 12 editorial cartoons, it set off worldwide violence and protests in the Muslim world. Most of the cartoons depicted the Islamic prophet Muhammad, which is against Islamic law. Danish Prime Minister Anders Fogh Rasmussen called the controversy "Denmark's worst international crisis since World War II." Massive protests from Morocco to Indonesia led to violence. The protest also led to a boycott of Danish products in the Muslim world. Danish flags and effigies of the prime minister were burned.

Another royal marriage in 2006 became a tabloid feeding frenzy. Prince Joachim and Princess Alexandra announced their divorce, the first in Europe's oldest monarchy in nearly 160 years. The couple has two sons, and Joachim is the second in line to the throne after his older brother Frederik.

The couple met in Hong Kong when he was working for a Danish shipping company. Alexandra became the first person of Asian heritage to marry into a sitting royal family in Europe.

No reason was given for the divorce, but tabloids and paparazzi have dubbed Joachim "the party prince," a man known for his wild visits to nightclubs, where he drank heavily and flirted with beautiful women.

3 DENMARK'S ART & ARCHITECTURE

EARLY & VIKING ART

The first masterpiece discovered in Denmark was *The Sun Chariot* from the 14th century B.C. Found on the island of Zealand, it is a horse-drawn wagon with the image of a solar disk. It's made of bronze and laminated gold, revealing the high level of craftsmanship possible in Denmark at this time.

In the Viking Age (800–1100), Danish Vikings were influenced by the countries they conquered, especially Anglo-Saxon art styles. This fusion led to the creation of ferocious dragons and griffins, beasts with gaping jaws, and birds of prey. Christianity came in 826 and would have a great influence on art and architecture for centuries to come.

THE COMING OF ROMANESQUE

The Romanesque period (1000–1250) overlapped the Viking period. In this era, wooden ecclesiastical buildings were the dominant theme, especially with the early churches made of wooden beams. In church architecture, wood eventually gave way to travertine, as evoked by the Church of Our Lady (c. 1110) in Roskilde.

Granite came into use later, and sections of the original Viborg Cathedral still remain to exemplify this style. In time, sandstone replaced granite. When supplies ran out, the Danes introduced brick, following examples set by the Lombards and Germans.

The oldest known ecclesiastical Danish paintings date from around 1100. Frescoes were used to decorate churches, such as those found in a rural church at Jelling.

THE GOTHIC ERA

The building of the great cathedrals of Denmark occurred in the Gothic period, roughly from 1250 to 1536. The French Gothic style prevailed in the reconstruction of St. Canute's, the cathedral of Odense, in 1250. Except for this cathedral, the French Gothic style did not catch on in Denmark.

The German influence prevailed in sculpture in Denmark during the medieval era. A masterpiece, the tomb of Queen Margaret (1423), in Roskilde Cathedral, was actually the work of a German, Johannes Junge, who was active in the early years of the 15th century.

Fresco paintings dominated in the small village churches, and they were fairly simple pastoral scenes—somewhat like a flat tapestry design.

Later in the 14th century, French Gothic painting, as practiced in Lübeck, Germany, came to Denmark, inspiring such works as the Chapel of the Three Kings (1450) in Roskilde Cathedral.

THE RENAISSANCE ARRIVES

With the collapse of the Catholic Church, Protestantism was introduced in 1536. This marked a period of great artistic decline in Denmark, and much previous art was destroyed.

From the mid-1500s to the mid-1800s, the greatest architectural achievements were not reflected in cathedrals, but in castles, private villas, and royal palaces. For the most part, Flemish architects were imported to carry out the work. They constructed the original Kronborg Castle at Helsingør. Tourists today refer to it as "Hamlet's Castle."

During the reign of Christian IV (1577–1648), the reliance on foreign architects continued. However, he did employ several Danish architects in his attempt to turn Copenhagen into a modern city. They included Jorgen Friborg, who rebuilt Frederiksborg Castle, and the Steenwinkel brothers, who designed the original Stock Exchange in Copenhagen in 1619. Borrowing features derived from the architecture of The Netherlands, the brothers dominated building trends in Denmark in the latter half of the 1600s.

In sculpture, foreign artists dominated the medium, introducing French Baroque painting into Denmark. Painting during the Renaissance consisted mainly of court artists imported from Amsterdam.

THE NEOCLASSICAL ERA

In the reign of Frederick IV (1671–1730), Italian architecture heavily influenced Danish building, although French baroque and German Rococo were also dominant features.

A Dane, Nikolai Eigtved (1701–54), designed the palace at Roskilde (1733). He also drew up plans for the Amalienborg in Copenhagen, and was heavily influenced by his studies of architecture in Italy.

By the late 1700s, the Neoclassical style was firmly established in both architecture and sculpture in Denmark. Out of the many artists working at the time, the giant of Danish sculpture emerged, Bertel Thorvaldsen (1768–1844). His work evoked that of Antonio Canova in Italy, and there is a museum today in Copenhagen devoted to Thorvaldsen's sculpture.

Another major sculptor emerged in Kai Nielsen (1882–1924), who was influenced by August Rodin. Painting was somewhat lackluster during this era as various schools came and went, including the Skagen School, which was organized in North Jutland in 1880.

THE MODERN PERIOD

Modern Danish architecture was born "between the wars." Such innovations occurred as housing projects for working people. Apartment houses were designed for city dwellers. Scale, materials, and color were of paramount importance to Danish architects. Interiors were made bright to fight against the bleakness of the Danish winter, and low and comfortable proportions were maintained.

From an array of architects at the time, Arne Jacobsen emerged as the leader of the pack. Since the 1930s, he produced Denmark's most original buildings, including terraced houses and several town halls.

Danish sculptors continued to follow contemporary international trends. Drawing the most attention was the Cobra group formed in 1948, its name based on the cities of Copenhagen, Brussels, and Amsterdam. The most outstanding Cobra artist from Denmark was Anger Jorn, born in 1914. His style was influenced by the more famous Edvard Munch of Norway.

In the closing years of the 20th century, Danish architecture increasingly was oriented toward Neo-Modernism. Both building forms and room layouts can be either severe and calm or highly dynamic, as evoked by Terminal 3 at Copenhagen's Airport. The most dramatic postmillennium structure in Denmark is the new Opera House in Copenhagen, dating from 2004.

4 DENMARK IN BOOKS, FILMS & MUSIC

BOOKS

HISTORY & PHILOSOPHY *A Kierke-gaard Anthology,* edited by Robert Bretall (Princeton University Press), explores the work of the Copenhagen-born philosopher who developed an almost-pathological sense of involvement in theology. A representative selection of some of his more significant works is included.

Copenhagen, A Historical Guide, by Torben Ejlersen (published by Høst & Søn in Denmark, and available at most bookstores there), an 88-page guide, takes you on a brief tour of the city that began as a ferry landing and became one of the most important capitals of Europe.

Of Danish Ways, written by two Danish-Americans, Ingeborg S. MacHiffic and Margaret A. Nielsen (Harper & Row, 1984), is a delightful account of this land and its people. It has a little bit of everything: history, social consciousness, customs, food, handicrafts, art, music, and theater.

BIOGRAPHY & LITERATURE *Andersen's Fairy Tales,* by H. C. Andersen (New American Library), and *The Complete Hans Christian Andersen Fairy Tales* (Crown) are anthologies that include all of his most important works, such as *The Little Mermaid, The Tinderbox,* and *The Princess and the Pea.*

Danish Literature: A Short Critical Guide, by Paul Borum (Nordic Books), is a well-written review that explores Danish literature from the Middle Ages to the 1970s.

Out of Africa (Modern Library), *Letters from Africa* (University of Chicago Press), and *Seven Gothic Tales* (Random House) are all by Karen Blixen (who wrote under the name Isak Dinesen), one of the major authors of the 20th century, who gained renewed fame with the release of the 1985 movie *Out of Africa,* with Meryl Streep

and Robert Redford. *Isak Dinesen,* by Judith Thurman (St. Martin's Press), chronicles Blixen's amazing life from an unhappy childhood in Denmark to marriage to Baron Blixen to immigration to Kenya to her passionate love affair with Denys Finch Hatton.

FILMS

Basically controlled by the state through the Danish Film Institute, founded in 1972, Danish cinema still enjoys international renown. Most movies coming out of Denmark today deal with social realism, in both comedy and drama, as well as films for children and a series of documentaries, which have received many awards at international film festivals.

In spite of this acclaim, the Golden Age of Danish cinema was before 1914. Denmark was one of the major European centers of film production, giving the world such stars as Asta Nielson and Valdemar Psilander. The coming of World War I and the rapidly growing American film industry sent the Danish film industry into decline.

Denmark gave the world one truly great director in the 1920s, Carl Dreyer, who was born in 1889. His greatest films include *Blades of Leaves from Satan's Book* in 1920 and *The Parson's Widow* in 1921. His masterpiece, *La Passion de Jeanne d'Arc,* shot in France and released in 1928, was filmed almost entirely in close-ups. The lyric power of that film had been rarely achieved in cinema.

In the postmillennium Per Fly achieved international acclaim with a trio of movies—*The Bench* in 2000, *Inheritance* in 2003, and *Manslaughter* in 2005. These films depicted three distinct social classes in Denmark. Suzanne Bier's *After the Wedding* (2006) was nominated for an Oscar as Best Foreign Language Film.

Lars von Trier is a bit of an oddity in the history of Danish cinema. He became known in the 1990s when he was nominated for numerous awards for such films as *Europa, Breaking the Waves, The Idiots,* and *Dancer in the Dark.* He shocked the film world when his company, Zentropa, became the world's first mainstream film company to produce hard-core porn, including the notorious *Constance* in 1998 and much later *All About Anna* in 2005. These films were made for a primarily female audience, and became wildly successful across the continent.

In a non-porno film, Nicole Kidman starred in von Trier's *Dogville* in 2003. This was a provocative stylistic experiment filmed on a black sound stage. Von Trier has not been successful in his latest films, leading one critic to note that "the film party of the '90s has ended for him."

MUSIC

Lurs, long bronze trumpets, dating from the Bronze Age, have been excavated in Denmark. They are the oldest musical relics found on the continent. With the coming of Christianity in the 9th century, church music was the dominant note.

Beginning with the Reformation in the 16th century, the royal court became the center of music. Under the reign of Christian IV (1577–1648), some of the greatest musicians in Europe visited the Danish court.

Dietrich Buxtehude (1637–1707) composed organ and instrumental music and became a major musical influence in North Europe.

Danish music came into its own during the middle of the 1800s, as such great

composers arose as Niels Wilhelm Gade (1817–90). His works included symphonies, a violin concerto, piano and organ compositions, and operas.

Denmark's greatest composer came along in the works of Carl August Nielsen (1865–1931), who developed a unique polytonal and contrapuntal musical form. Some of his most famous operas include *Saul og David* in 1903 and *Maskerade* in 1906.

In the countryside, Danish folk music prevailed. It was most often dominated by a fiddle player and an accordion duo. Unlike most Nordic countries, Denmark still uses the guitar prominently in its folk music.

Today rock and pop bands rule the night in the underground cellars of big cities in Denmark, including Copenhagen and Århus. Formerly known as Disneyland After Dark, rockers D-A-D have found many international fans with such recordings as "Sleeping My Day Away." Currently, the major bands in Denmark are garage rockers such as The Raveonettes.

Enjoying the most popularity is the band Nephew, which mixes both Danish and English lyrics. Their lead singer, Simon Kvamm, is quite charismatic and is one of the biggest rock stars in Denmark.

You can often see the biggest names in music displaying their talents at the annual Roskilde Festival.

In pop music, the group Aqua is the most celebrated in Denmark, enjoying such worldwide hits as "Turn Back Time," "Doctor Jones," and "Barbie Girl."

5 EATING & DRINKING IN DENMARK

Danish food is the best in Scandinavia—in fact, it's among the best in Europe.

Breakfast is usually big and hearty, just right for a day of sightseeing. It usually consists of homemade breads, Danish

cheeses, and often a boiled egg or salami. In most establishments you can order bacon and eggs, two items that are well stocked here. However, you may prefer a simple continental breakfast of Danish *wienerbrød* (pastry) and coffee. The "Danish" is moist, airy, and rich.

The favorite dish at midday is the ubiquitous *smørrebrød* (open-faced sandwiches)—a national institution. Literally, this means "bread and butter," but the Danes stack this sandwich as if it were the Leaning Tower of Pisa—and then throw in a slice of curled cucumber and bits of parsley, or perhaps sliced peaches or a mushroom for added color.

Two of these sandwiches can make a more-than-filling lunch. They're everywhere—from the grandest dining rooms to the lowliest pushcart. Many restaurants offer a wide selection; guests look over a checklist and then mark the ones they want. Some are made with sliced pork (perhaps a prune on top), roast beef with béarnaise sauce and crispy fried bits of onion, or liver paste adorned with an olive or cucumber slice and gelatin made with strong beef stock.

Smørrebrød is often served as an hors d'oeuvre. The most popular, most tempting, and usually most expensive of these delicacies is prepared with tiny Danish shrimp, on which a lemon slice and caviar often perch, perhaps even with fresh dill. The "ugly duckling" of the *smørrebrød* family is anything with a cold sunny-side-up egg on top of it.

For dinner, the Danes tend to keep farmers' hours: 6:30pm is common, although restaurants remain open much later. Many main-course dishes are familiar to North Americans, but they're prepared with a distinct flourish in Denmark—for example, *lever med løg* (liver and fried onion), *bøf* (beef, in a thousand different ways), *lammesteg* (roast lamb), or that old reliable staple, *flæskesteg med rødkål* (roast pork with red cabbage).

Danish chefs are really noted for their fresh fish dishes. The tiny Danish shrimp, *rejer,* are splendid; herring and kippers are also greeted with much enthusiasm. Top-notch fish dishes include *rodspætte* (plaice), *laks* (salmon), *makrel* (mackerel), and *kogt torsk* (boiled cod).

Danish cheese may be consumed at any meal and then eaten again on a late-night *smørrebrød* at Tivoli. Danish bleu is already familiar to most people. For something softer and milder, try havarti.

Danish specialties that are worth sampling include *frikadeller,* the Danish meatballs (prepared in various ways); a Danish omelet with a rasher of bacon covered with chopped chives and served in a skillet; and Danish hamburger patties topped with fried onions and coated with a rich brown gravy.

Two great desserts are Danish apple Charlotte, best when decorated with whipped cream, dried bread crumbs, and chopped almonds; and *rødgrød med fløde*—basically a jellied fruit-studded juice, served with thick cream.

As for drinks, Carlsberg and Tuborg beer are Denmark's national beverages. A bottle of Pilsner costs about half the price of a stronger export beer with the fancy label. Value-conscious Danes rely on the low-priced *fadøl* (draft beer); visitors on a modest budget might want to do the same.

You may gravitate more toward *akvavit* (schnapps), which comes from the city of Aalborg, in northern Jutland. The Danes, who usually drink it at mealtime, follow it with a beer chaser. Made from a distilling process using potatoes, it should be served only icy cold.

For those with a daintier taste, the world-famous Danish liqueur, Cherry Herring, is a delightful drink; made from cherries, as the name implies, it can be consumed anytime, except with meals.

Planning Your Trip to Denmark

In the following pages, we've compiled all of the practical information you'll need to plan your trip in advance—airline information, what things cost, a calendar of events, and more.

1 VISITOR INFORMATION

TOURIST OFFICES

In the **United States,** contact the **Scandinavian Tourist Board,** 655 Third Ave., 18th Floor, New York, NY 10017 (© **212/885-9700;** www.goscandinavia.com), for maps, sightseeing information, ferry schedules, or whatever other travel information you need. You can also try the **Danish Tourist Board,** 655 Third Ave., 18th Floor, New York, NY 10017 (© **212/885-9700;** www.visitdenmark.com).

In the **United Kingdom,** contact the **Danish Tourist Board,** 55 Sloane St., London SW1X 9SY (© **020/7259-5959**).

WEBSITES

To begin your exploration of Denmark, visit the **Scandinavian Tourist Board** (www.goscandinavia.com), the **Danish Tourist Board** (www.visitdenmark.com), and **Wonderful Copenhagen** (www.visitcopenhagen.dk), all of which offer extensive links to other organizations, accommodations, attractions, and other information. Get information on Danish culture, tour suggestions, and events at **CultureNet Denmark** (© 45/33-74-51-00; www.kulturarv.dk).

MAPS The best map for touring Denmark is part of the series published by Michelin. It's for sale at all major bookstores in Copenhagen, including the most centrally located one, **Boghallen,** Rådhuspladsen 37 (© **33-47-25-60**), in the Town Hall Square.

2 ENTRY REQUIREMENTS & CUSTOMS

ENTRY REQUIREMENTS

U.S., Canadian, U.K., Irish, Australian, and New Zealand citizens with a **valid passport** don't need a visa to enter Denmark if they don't expect to stay more than 90 days and don't expect to work there. If after entering Denmark you want to stay more than 90 days, you can apply for a permit for an extra 90 days at your home country's consulate, which as a rule is granted immediately. If your passport is lost or stolen, head to your consulate as soon as possible for a replacement.

CUSTOMS
What You Can Bring into Denmark

Foreign visitors can bring along most items for personal use duty-free, including fishing tackle, a pair of skis, two tennis rackets, a baby carriage, two hand cameras with 10 rolls of film, and 400 cigarettes or a quantity of cigars or pipe tobacco not exceeding 500 grams (1.1 lb.). There are strict limits on importing alcoholic beverages. However, for alcohol bought tax-paid, limits are much more liberal than in other countries of the European Union.

What You Can Take Home from Denmark

U.S. CITIZENS: or specifics on what you can bring back and the corresponding fees, download the invaluable free pamphlet *Know Before You Go* online at **www.cbp.gov**. (Click on "Travel," and then click on "Know Before You Go! Online Brochure.") Or contact the **U.S. Customs & Border Protection (CBP),** 1300 Pennsylvania Ave. NW, Washington, DC 20229 (© **877/287-8667**), and request the pamphlet.

CANADIAN CITIZENS: For a clear summary of Canadian rules, write for the booklet *I Declare,* issued by the **Canada**

Border Services Agency (© **800/461-9999** in Canada, or 204/983-3500; www.cbsa-asfc.gc.ca).

U.K. CITIZENS: For information, contact **HM Revenue & Customs** at © **02920/501-261** (from outside the U.K., 020/8929-0152), or consult their website at www.hmrc.gov.uk.

AUSTRALIAN CITIZENS: A helpful brochure available from Australian consulates or Customs offices is *Know Before You Go.* For more information, call the **Australian Customs Service** at © **1300/363-263,** or log on to www.customs.gov.au.

NEW ZEALAND CITIZENS: Most questions are answered in a free pamphlet available at New Zealand consulates and Customs offices: *New Zealand Customs Guide for Travellers, Notice no. 4.* For more information, contact **New Zealand Customs,** The Customhouse, 17–21 Whitmore St., Box 2218, Wellington (© **04/473-6099** or 0800/428-786; www.customs.govt.nz).

3 WHEN TO GO

CLIMATE

Denmark's climate is mild for a Scandinavian country—New England farmers experience harsher winters. Summer temperatures average between 61°F and 77°F (16°C–25°C). Winter temperatures seldom go below 30°F (–1°C), thanks to the warming waters of the Gulf Stream. From the weather perspective, mid-April to November is a good time to visit.

Denmark's Average Daytime Temperatures

	Jan	Feb	Mar	Apr	May	June	July	Aug	Sept	Oct	Nov	Dec
°F	32	32	35	44	53	60	64	63	57	49	42	37
°C	0	0	2	7	12	16	18	17	14	9	6	3

DENMARK CALENDAR OF EVENTS

Exact dates below apply for 2009. Should you be using this guide in 2010, check with local tourist boards for exact dates.

MAY

Carnival in Copenhagen. A great city-wide event. There's also a children's carnival. For information, call © **35-38-85-04;** www.karneval.dk. Mid-May.

Ballet and Opera Festival ★★★ (Copenhagen). Classical and modern dance and two operatic masterpieces are presented at the Old Stage of the Royal Theater in Copenhagen. For tickets, contact the Royal Theater, Box 2185, DK-1017 Copenhagen (℃ 33-69-69-69-33; www.kglteater.dk). Mid-May to June.

Aalborg Carnival ★ This is one of the country's great spring events. The streets fill with people in colorful costumes. Thousands take part in the celebration, which honors the victory of spring over winter. For information, call ℃ 98-13-72-11; www.karnevaliaalborg.dk. Late May.

JUNE

Viking Festival ★★★(Frederikssund, 8 miles southwest of Hillerød). For 2 weeks every summer, "bearded Vikings" present old Nordic sagas in an open-air setting. After each performance, a traditional Viking meal is served. Call ℃ 47-31-06-85 or visit www.vikingespil.dk for more information. Late June to early July.

Midsummer's Night (countrywide). This age-old event is celebrated throughout Denmark. It is the longest day of the year. Festivities throughout the nation begin at around 10pm with bonfires and celebrations along the myriad coasts. June 21.

JULY

Roskilde Festival ★ Europe's biggest rock festival has been going strong for 30 years, now bringing about 90,000 revelers each year to the central Zealand town. Besides major rock concerts, which often draw big names, scheduled activities include theater and film presentations. For more information, call ℃ 46-36-66-13; www.roskilde-festival.dk. Early July.

Copenhagen Jazz Festival. International jazz musicians play in the streets, squares, and theaters. Pick up a copy of *Copenhagen This Week* to find the venues. For information, call ℃ 33-93-20-13; www.jazzfestival.dk. Early July.

July 4th (Rebild). Rebild National Park, near Aalborg, is one of the few places outside the United States to honor American Independence Day. For more information, contact the Aalborg Tourist Bureau, Østerågade 8, DK-9000 Aalborg (℃ 99-31-75-00; www.visitaalborg.com). July 4th.

Funen Festival. This annual musical extravaganza draws big, international headliners. The festival's music is often hard-core rock, but gentler, classical melodies are presented as well. It takes place in the city of Odense, on the island of Funen. For more information, call the Odense tourist bureau (℃ 66-12-75-20; www.visitodense.com). Early July.

AUGUST

Fire Festival Regatta (Silkeborg). Denmark's oldest and biggest festival features nightly cruises on the lakes, with thousands of candles illuminating the shores. The fireworks display on the last night is the largest and most spectacular in northern Europe. Popular Danish artists provide entertainment at a large, fun fair. For more information, contact the Turistbureau, Godthåbsuej 4, DK-8600 Silkeborg (℃ 86-85-31-55; www.ildregatta.dk). Mid-August.

Fall Ballet Festival ★★★(Copenhagen). The internationally acclaimed Royal Danish Ballet returns home to perform at the Old Stage of the Royal Theater just before the tourist season ends. For tickets, contact the Royal Theater, Box 2185, DK-1017 Copenhagen (℃ 33-69-69-69; www.kglteater.dk). Mid-August to September.

Århus Festival Week ★ A wide range of cultural activities, including opera, jazz, classical and folk music, ballet, and theater, is presented. It's the largest cultural festival in Scandinavia. Sporting activities and street parties abound as well. For more information, contact ℃ 87-30-83-00 or go to www.aarhusfestival.dk. Late August to early September.

4 GETTING THERE & GETTING AROUND

GETTING TO DENMARK
By Plane

Flying in winter—Scandinavia's off season—is cheapest; summer is the most expensive. Spring and fall are in between. In any season, midweek fares (Mon–Thurs) are the lowest.

FROM NORTH AMERICA SAS (Scandinavian Airlines Systems; © 800/221-2350 in the U.S., or 0870/6072-7727 in the U.K.; www.flysas.com) has more nonstop flights to Scandinavia from more North American cities than any other airline, and it has more flights to and from Denmark and within Scandinavia than any other airline in the world. From Seattle and Chicago, SAS offers nonstop flights to Copenhagen daily in midsummer and almost every day in winter; from Newark, New Jersey, there are daily flights year-round to Copenhagen. SAS's agreement with United Airlines, the "Star Alliance," connects the gateway cities of Seattle, Chicago, New York, and Washington, D.C., to other U.S. cities (such as Dallas/Fort Worth, Denver, Houston, Los Angeles, Minneapolis/St. Paul, and San Francisco).

Nonstop flights to Copenhagen from the greater New York area take about $7^{1}/_{2}$ hours; from Chicago, around $8^{1}/_{2}$ hours; from Seattle, $9^{1}/_{2}$ hours.

FROM THE U.K. British Airways (© 800/AIRWAYS [247-9297], or 0870/850-9850 in the U.K.; www.british airways.com) offers convenient connections through Heathrow and Gatwick to Copenhagen. The price structure (and discounted prices on hotel packages) sometimes makes a stopover in Britain less expensive than you might have thought. SAS offers five daily nonstop flights to Copenhagen from Heathrow ($1^{3}/_{4}$ hr.), two daily nonstops from Glasgow (2 hr.), and three daily nonstops from Manchester (2 hr., 20 min.). Other European airlines

with connections through their home countries to Copenhagen include **Iceland-air** (© 800/223-5500 in the U.S., or 0870/787-4020 in the U.K.; www.iceland air.com); **KLM** (© 800/225-2525 in the U.S., or 0870/507-4074 in the U.K.; www.klm.com); and **Lufthansa** (© 800/645-3880 in the U.S., or 0870/8377-747 in the U.K.; www.lufthansa.com). Be aware, however, that unless you make all your flight arrangements in North America before you go, you might find some of these flights prohibitively expensive.

Flying for Less: Tips for Getting the Best Airfare

Passengers sharing the same airplane cabin rarely pay the same fare. Travelers who need to purchase tickets at the last minute, change their itinerary at a moment's notice, or fly one-way often get stuck paying the premium rate. Here are some ways to keep your airfare costs down:

- Passengers who can book their ticket **far in advance,** who can **stay over Saturday night,** or who **fly midweek** or **at less-trafficked hours** may pay a fraction of the full fare. If your schedule is flexible, say so, and ask if you can secure a cheaper fare by changing your flight plans.
- You can also save on airfares by keeping an eye on local newspapers for **promotional specials** or **fare wars,** when airlines lower prices on their most popular routes. You rarely see fare wars offered for peak travel times, but if you can travel in the off months, you may snag a bargain.
- Search **the Internet** for cheap fares.
- Join **frequent-flier clubs.** Accrue enough miles, and you'll be rewarded with free flights and elite status. It's free, and you'll get the best choice of seats, faster response to phone inquiries, and

prompter service if your luggage is stolen, your flight is canceled or delayed, or you want to change your seat. You don't need to fly to build frequent-flier miles—**frequent-flier credit cards** can provide thousands of miles for doing your everyday shopping.

By Car

You can easily drive to Denmark from Germany. Many people drive to Jutland from Hamburg, Bremerhaven, and Lübeck. A bridge links Jutland and the central island of Funen. In 1998, a bridge opened that goes across the Great Belt from Funen to the island of Zealand, site of the city of Copenhagen. The bridge lies near Nyborg, Denmark. Once in West Zealand, you'll still have to drive east across the island to Copenhagen.

Car-ferry service to Denmark from the United Kingdom generally leaves passengers at Esbjerg, where they must cross from Jutland to Copenhagen. From Germany, it's possible to take a car ferry from Travemünde, northeast of Lübeck, which will deposit you at Gedser, Denmark. From here, connect with the E55, an express highway north to Copenhagen.

By Train

If you're in Europe, it's easy to get to Denmark by train. Copenhagen is the main rail hub between Scandinavia and the rest of Europe. For example, the London–Copenhagen train—through Ostende, Belgium, or Hook, Holland—leaves four times daily and takes 22 hours. About 10 daily express trains run from Hamburg to Copenhagen ($5^{1}/_{2}$ hr.). There are also intercity trains on the Merkur route from Karlsruhe, Germany, to Cologne to Hamburg to Copenhagen. The Berlin–Ostbahnhof–Copenhagen train ($8^{1}/_{2}$ hr.) connects with Eastern European trains. Two daily express trains make this run.

Thousands of trains run from Britain to the Continent, and at least some of them go directly across or under the Channel, through France or Belgium and Germany into Denmark. For example, a train leaves London's Victoria Station daily at 9am and arrives in Copenhagen the next day at 8:25am. Another train leaves London's Victoria Station at 8:45pm and arrives in Copenhagen the next day at 8:20pm. Both go through Dover–Ostende, or with a connection at Brussels. Once you're in Copenhagen, you can make rail connections to Norway, Finland, and Sweden. Because of the time and distances involved, many passengers rent a couchette (sleeping berth), which costs around £20 ($38) per person. Designed like padded benches stacked bunk-style, they're usually clustered six to a compartment.

If you plan to travel extensively on European and/or British railroads, it would be worthwhile for you to get a copy of the latest edition of the *Thomas Cook European Timetable of Railroads*. It's available online at **www.thomascooktimetables. com.**

Rail Passes for North American Travelers

EURAILPASS The Eurailpass permits unlimited first-class rail travel in any country in western Europe except the British Isles (good in Ireland). Passes are available for purchase online (**www.eurail.com**) and at various offices/agents around the world. Travel agents and railway agents in such cities as New York, Montreal, and Los Angeles sell Eurailpasses. You can purchase them at the North American offices of CIT Travel Service, the French National Railroads, the German Federal Railroads, and the Swiss Federal Railways.

It is strongly recommended that you purchase passes before you leave home as not all passes are available in Europe; also, passes purchased in Europe will cost about 20% more. Numerous options are available for travel in France.

The **Eurail Global Pass** allows you unlimited travel in 20 Eurail-affiliated countries. You can travel on any of the days within the validity period, which is available for 15 days, 21 days, 1 month, 2 months, 3 months, and some other possibilities as well. Prices for first-class adult travel are US$745 for 15 days; US$965 for 21 days; US$1,199 for 1 month; US$1,695 for 2 months; and US$2,089 for 3 months. Children 4 to 11 pay half fare; those 3 and under travel for free.

A **Eurail Global Pass Saver,** also valid for first-class travel in 20 countries, offers a special deal for two or more people traveling together. This pass costs US$629 for 15 days; US$819 for 21 days; US$1,019 for 1 month; US$1,439 for 2 months; and US$1,785 for 3 months.

A **Eurail Global Youth Pass** for those 12 to 25 allows second-class travel in 18 countries. This pass costs US$485 for 15 days; US$625 for 21 days; US$779 for 1 month; US$1,099 for 2 months; and US$1,359 for 3 months.

The **Eurail Select Pass** offers unlimited travel on the national rail networks of any three, four, or five bordering countries out of the 22 Eurail nations linked by train or ship. Two or more passengers can travel together for big discounts, getting 5, 6, 8, 10, or 15 days of rail travel within any 2-month period on the national rail networks of any three, four, or five adjoining Eurail countries linked by train or ship. A sample fare: For 5 days in 2 months you pay US$469 for three countries. **Eurail Select Pass Youth,** for travelers 25 and under, allows second-class travel within the same guidelines as Eurail Select Pass, with fees starting at US$305. **Eurail Select Pass Saver** offers discounts for two or more people traveling together, first-class travel within the same guidelines as Eurail Select Pass, with fees starting at US$399.

WHERE TO BUY RAIL PASSES Travel agents in all towns and railway agents in major North American cities sell all these tickets, but the biggest supplier is **Rail Europe** (℡ **877/272-RAIL** [272-7245];

www.raileurope.com), which can also give you informational brochures.

Many different rail passes are available in the United Kingdom for travel in Britain and continental Europe. Stop in at the **International Rail Centre,** Victoria Station, London SW1V 1JY (℡ **0870/5848-848** in the U.K.). Some of the most popular passes, including Inter-Rail and Euro Youth, are offered only to travelers 25 and under; these allow unlimited second-class travel through most European countries.

SCANRAIL PASS If your visit to Europe will be primarily in Scandinavia, the Scanrail pass may be better and cheaper than the Eurailpass. This pass allows its owner a designated number of days of free rail travel within a larger time block. (Presumably, this allows for days devoted to sightseeing scattered among days of rail transfers between cities or sites of interest.) You can choose a total of any 5 days of unlimited rail travel during a 15-day period, 10 days of rail travel within a 1-month period, or 1 month of unlimited rail travel. The pass, which is valid on all lines of the state railways of Denmark, Finland, Norway, and Sweden, offers discounts or free travel on some (but not all) of the region's ferry lines as well. The pass can be purchased only in North America. It's available from any office of **RailEurope** (℡ **800/848-7245**) or **ScanAm World Tours,** 108 N. Main St., Cranbury, NJ 08512 (℡ **800/545-2204;** www.scandinaviantravel.com).

Depending on whether you choose first- or second-class rail transport, 5 days out of 10 days costs $249 to $329, 8 days out of 2 months costs $180 to $360, 10 days out of 22 days costs $359 to $489, and 21 consecutive days of unlimited travel costs $469 to $629. Seniors get an 11% discount, and students receive a 30% discount.

EURAIL DENMARK PASS For those who plan to travel only in Denmark, a series of cost-cutting passes are offered. The major one is the **Eurail Denmark**

Pass, offering both first- and second-class unlimited travel on Denmark's national rail network. For travel any 3 or 7 days within a 1-month period, the 3-day pass costs $98 to $149 for adults (first and second class), or $50 to $75 for children ages 4 to 11. The 7-day pass goes for $149 to $230 for adults or $75 to $116 for children.

Two or more passengers traveling together can take advantage of the **Eurail Denmark Saverpass,** offering unlimited travel in first and second class. On this deal, you get 3 days of travel in 1 month for $85 to $126 for adults or $44 to $64 for children 4 to 11. For 7 days in 1 month, the cost ranges from $126 to $197 for adults or $64 to $99 for children.

A better deal for passengers 25 and under is the **Eurail Denmark Youthpass,** costing $76 for 3 days in 1 month, or $113 for 7 days.

Rail Passes for British Travelers

If you plan to do a lot of exploring, you may prefer one of the three rail passes designed for unlimited train travel within a designated region during a predetermined number of days. These passes are sold in Britain and several other European countries.

An **InterRail Pass** is available to passengers of any nationality, with some restrictions—they must be under age 26 and able to prove residency in a European or North African country (Morocco, Algeria, and Tunisia) for at least 6 months before buying the pass. It allows unlimited travel through Europe, except Albania and the republics of the former Soviet Union. Prices are complicated and vary depending on the countries you want to include. For pricing purposes, Europe is divided into eight zones; the cost depends on the number of zones you include. For ages 25 and under, the most expensive option (£399) allows 1 month of unlimited travel in all

eight zones and is known to the staff as a "global." The least expensive option (£159) allows 5 days of travel within 10 days.

Passengers age 26 and older can buy an **InterRail 26-Plus Pass.** The cost varies from £359 to £489 for 16 days to £599 to £809 for 1 month. Passengers must meet the same residency requirements that apply to the InterRail Pass (described above).

For information on buying individual rail tickets or any of the just-mentioned passes, contact **National Rail Inquiries,** Victoria Station, London (© 08705/848-848). Tickets and passes also are available at any of the larger railway stations, as well as selected travel agencies throughout Britain and the rest of Europe.

By Ship & Ferry

It's easy to travel by water from several ports to Denmark. Liners carrying cars and passengers operate from England, Germany, Poland, Norway, and Sweden. Check with your travel agent about these cruises.

FROM BRITAIN DFDS Seaways (© 0871/522-9955; www.dfdsseaways.com) runs vessels year-round between Harwich, England, and Esbjerg in West Jutland. The crossing takes 16 to 20 hours. The same line also sails from Newcastle upon Tyne to Esbjerg, but only in the summer, as part of a 22-hour passage. Overnight cabins and space for cars are available on both routes.

FROM NORWAY & SWEDEN Norwegian Coastal Voyage Inc. (© 866/257-6071 or 212/319-1390 in the U.S.; www.hurtigruten.com) operates vessels from Oslo to Hirtshals in North Jutland.

Stena Line runs popular sea links from Oslo to Frederikshavn, North Jutland (11¹⁄₂ hr.), and from Gothenburg, Sweden, to Frederikshavn (3 hr.). For information, schedules, and fares, contact **Stena Line UK, Ltd.** (© 08705/70-70-70; www.stenaline.co.uk). For 24-hour updates on sailing, call © 08705/755-755.

GETTING AROUND DENMARK

By Plane

The best way to get around Denmark is by private car on the excellent road network. In lieu of that, nearly all major towns, and certainly most Danish cities, are serviced by trains, except certain offshore islands, which can be reached only by ferryboat. If you're traveling extensively in Europe, special European passes are also available.

SAS'S "VISIT SCANDINAVIA" FARE The vast distances encourage air travel between Norway's far-flung points. One of the most worthwhile promotions is SAS's **Visit Scandinavia Pass.** Available only to travelers who fly SAS across the Atlantic, it includes up to six coupons, each of which is valid for any SAS flight within or between Denmark, Norway, and Sweden. Each coupon costs $60, $80, and $100, depending on the route. The pass is especially valuable if you plan to travel to the far northern frontiers of Sweden or Norway; in that case, the savings over the price of a regular economy-class ticket can be substantial. For information on buying the pass, call **SAS** (✆ **800/221-2350;** www.flysas.com).

WITHIN DENMARK For those in a hurry, **SAS** (✆ **32-32-00-00** in Denmark) operates daily service between Copenhagen and points on Jutland's mainland. From Copenhagen, it takes about 40 minutes to fly to Aalborg, 35 minutes to Århus, and 30 minutes to Odense.

Fares to other Danish cities are sometimes included in a transatlantic ticket at no extra charge, as long as the additional cities are specified when the ticket is written.

By Train

Flat, low-lying Denmark, with its hundreds of bridges and absence of mountains, has a large network of railway lines that connect virtually every hamlet with the largest city, Copenhagen. For **information, schedules, and fares** anywhere in Denmark, call ✆ **70-13-14-15.** Waiting times for a live person on this telephone line range from long to very long. Alternatively, you can check the Danish National Railways website, **www.dsb.dk,** for schedules and prices, and to reserve seats.

A word you're likely to see and hear frequently is *Lyntog* ("Express Trains"), which are the fastest trains presently operational in Denmark. Be warned in advance that the most crowded times on Danish trains are Fridays, Sundays, and national holidays, so plan your reservations accordingly.

On any train in Denmark, children between the ages of 4 and 15 are charged half-price if they're accompanied by an adult, and up to two children 3 and under can travel free with an adult on any train in Denmark. Seniors 65 or older receive a discount of 20% for travel on Fridays, Sundays, and holidays, and a discount of 45% every other day of the week. No identification is needed when you buy your ticket, but the conductor who checks your ticket might ask for proof of age.

The Danish government offers dozens of discounts on the country's rail networks—depending on the type of traveler, days or hours traveled, and destination. Because discounts change often, it's best to ask for a discount based on your age and the number of days (or hours) you intend to travel.

By Bus

By far, the best way to visit rural Denmark is by car, but if you want or need to travel by bus, be aware that you'll probably get your bus at the railway station. (In much of Scandinavia, buses take passengers to destinations not served by the train; therefore, the bus route often originates at the railway station.) The arrival of trains and departure of buses are usually closely timed.

For seniors 65 and over, round-trip bus tickets are sometimes offered at one-way prices (excluding Sat, Sun, and peak travel periods around Christmas and Easter).

Most discounts are granted only to seniors who are traveling beyond the city limits of their point of origin.

By Car

RENTALS Avis, Budget, and Hertz offer well-serviced, well-maintained fleets of cars. You may have to reserve and pay for your rental car in advance (usually 2 weeks, but occasionally as little as 48 hr.) to get the lowest rates. Unfortunately, if your trip is canceled or your arrival date changes, you might have to fill out a lot of forms for a refund. All three companies may charge slightly higher rates to clients who reserve less than 48 hours in advance and pay at pickup. The highest rates are charged to walk-in customers who arrange their rentals after they arrive in Denmark. **If at all possible, you should reserve a car before you leave North America.**

The Danish government imposes a whopping **25% tax on all car rentals.** Agencies that encourage prepaid rates almost never collect this tax in advance—instead, it's imposed as part of a separate transaction when you pick up the car. Furthermore, any car retrieved at a Danish airport is subject to a one-time supplemental tax of DKK255 ($43/£26), so you might prefer to pick up your car at a downtown location. Membership in certain travel clubs or organizations (such as AAA or AARP) might qualify you for a modest discount.

Avis (© **800/331-1212** in the U.S. and Canada; www.avis.com) maintains four offices in Copenhagen: two at the arrivals hall of the airport, one at Landgreven 10 (© **70-24-77-64**), and another at Kampmannsgade 1 (© **70-24-77-07**).

Budget (© **800/527-0700** in the U.S.; © **800/472-3325** in Canada; www.budget.com) has two rental locations in Copenhagen. The larger branch is at the Copenhagen airport (© **35-53-39-00**), and the other office is at Vesterfarimagsgade 7 (© **33-55-70-00**).

Hertz (© **800/654-3001** in the U.S. and Canada; www.hertz.com) has two offices in Copenhagen, one at the airport (© **33-17-90-20**) and the other at Ved Vesterport 3 (© **33-17-90-20**).

Also consider using a small company. **Kemwel** (© **800/678-0678** in the U.S.; www.kemwel.com) is the North American representative for two Denmark-based car companies, Van Wijk and Hertz. It may be able to offer attractive rental prices to North Americans who pay in full at least 10 days before their departure. Seniors and members of AAA get a 5% discount.

DRIVING RULES A valid driver's license from your home country is required. If you are in your own car, you need a certificate of registration and national plates. This is especially important for the people of Britain, who often drive to Denmark. Each rental agency should provide you with a triangular hazard warning sign. It's Danish law that you have this signal. Seat belts are required in both the front and the rear of the vehicle, and you must drive with low beams on at all times, even in the bright sunlight. Talking on a cellphone while driving is illegal. Be on the lookout for bicycle riders, who have the right of way if they are heading straight and an auto is making a turn.

GASOLINE (PETROL) Stations are plentiful throughout the land, and prices—subject to almost daily fluctuations—are extremely high. Most stations take credit cards and are self-service. In general, stations open daily at 6 or 7 in the morning, usually shutting down at 9pm (later in more congested areas).

5 MONEY & COSTS

CURRENCY

Although Denmark is a member of the European Union, the Danes rejected the euro as their form of currency. They continue to use the **krone** (crown), which breaks down into 100 **øre**. The plural is **kroner.** The international monetary designation for the Danish kroner is "DKK." (The Swedish currency is the kronor, but note the different spelling.)

At this writing, in the wake of some of the most unpredicted economic swings since before World War II, $1 US = 5.85 kroner, or 1 DKK = 17¢; £1 = 10 DKK, or 1 DKK = 10p; and one Danish krone = 13 europence, or 1€ = DKK7.5.

It's a good idea to exchange at least some money—just enough to cover airport incidentals and transportation to your hotel—before you leave home (though don't expect the exchange rate to be ideal) so that you can avoid lines at airport ATMs. You can exchange money at your local American Express or Thomas Cook office or at your bank. American Express also dispenses traveler's checks and foreign currency via www.americanexpress.com or © **800/807-6233,** but they'll charge a $15 order fee and additional shipping costs. American Express cardholders should dial © **800/221-7282;** this number accepts collect calls, offers service in several foreign languages, and exempts Amex gold and platinum cardholders from the 1% fee.

ATMS

PLUS, Cirrus, and other networks connecting automated teller machines (ATMs)

operate throughout Denmark. The easiest and best way to get cash away from home is from an ATM. The **Cirrus** (© **800/424-7787;** www.mastercard.com) and **PLUS** (© **800/843-7587;** www.visa.com) networks span the globe; look at the back of your bank card to see which network you're on, and then call or check online for ATM locations at your destination. Be sure you know your personal identification number (PIN) before you leave home, and be sure to find out your daily withdrawal limit before you depart. Also keep in mind that many banks impose a fee every time a card is used at a different bank's ATM, and that fee can be higher for international transactions (up to $5 or more) than for domestic ones. On top of this, the bank from which you withdraw cash may charge its own fee. To compare banks' ATM fees within the U.S., use www.bankrate.com. For international withdrawal fees, ask your bank.

You can also get cash advances on your credit card at an ATM. Keep in mind that credit card companies try to protect themselves from theft by limiting the funds someone can withdraw outside their home country, so call your credit card company before you leave home. And keep in mind that you'll pay interest from the moment of your withdrawal, even if you pay your monthly bills on time.

Important note: Make sure that the PINs on your bank cards and credit cards will work in Austria. You'll need a **four-digit code** (six digits won't work); if you have a six-digit code, you'll have to go into

---

Bank Fees for Charge Cards
For all restaurants in Denmark, there is an assessed bank fee from 3% to 7% on charge cards if the card is not a Danish card.

What Things Cost in Copenhagen	DKK	US$	UK£
Train from the airport to the City Center	180.00	3.10	1.80
Subway from the Central Station to the outlying suburbs	15.00	2.55	1.50
Double room at the Hotel d'Angleterre (very expensive)	3,060.00	520.00	306.00
Double room, with bathroom, at the Kong Arthur (moderate)	1,320.00	224.00	132.00
Double room, without private bathroom, at the City Hotel Nebo (inexpensive)	850.00	145.00	85.00
Lunch for one at the Café Victor (moderate)	185.00	31.00	19.00
Lunch for one at CH14 (inexpensive)	110.00	19.00	11.00
Dinner for one, without wine, at Godt (very expensive)	480.00	82.00	48.00
Dinner for one, without wine, at Søren K (moderate)	365.00	62.00	37.00
Pint of beer (draft pilsner or lager)	55.00	9.35	5.50
Cup of coffee in a cafe or bar	35.00	5.95	3.50
Coca-Cola in a cafe or bar	30.00	5.10	3.00
Admission to Tivoli Gardens	85.00	15.00	8.50
Movie ticket	75.00–90.00	13.00–15.00	7.50–9.00
Ticket to the Royal Theater	80.00–720.00	14.00–122.00	72.00

your bank and get a new PIN for your trip. If you're unsure about this, contact Cirrus or PLUS (see above). Be sure to check the daily withdrawal limit at the same time.

TRAVELER'S CHECKS

You can buy traveler's checks at most banks. They are offered in denominations of $20, $50, $100, $500, and sometimes $1,000. Generally, you'll pay a service charge ranging from 1% to 4%.

The most popular traveler's checks are offered by **American Express** (© 800/528-4800 or 800/221-7282 for card holders; this number accepts collect calls, offers service in several foreign languages, and exempts Amex gold and platinum cardholders from the 1% fee); **Visa** (© 800/732-1322; AAA members can obtain Visa checks for a $9.95 fee [for checks up to

$1,500] at most AAA offices or by calling © 866/339-3378); and **MasterCard** (© 800/223-9920).

American Express, Thomas Cook, Visa, and **MasterCard** offer **foreign currency traveler's checks,** which are useful if you're traveling to one country, or to the Euro zone; they're accepted at locations where dollar checks may not be.

If you carry traveler's checks, keep a record of their serial numbers separate from your checks in the event that they are stolen or lost. You'll get a refund faster if you know the numbers.

CREDIT CARDS

Credit cards are a safe way to carry money. They also provide a convenient record of all your expenses, and they generally offer relatively good exchange rates. You can also withdraw cash advances from your credit cards at banks or ATMs, provided you know your PIN. If you've forgotten yours, or didn't even know you had one, call the number on the back of your credit card and ask the bank to send it to you. It usually takes 5 to 7 business days, though some banks will provide the number over the phone if you tell them your mother's maiden name or some other personal information. Keep in mind that when you use your credit card abroad, most banks assess a 2% fee above the 1% fee charged by Visa, MasterCard, or American Express for currency conversion on credit charges. But credit cards still may be the smart way to go when you factor in things like exorbitant ATM fees and higher traveler's check exchange rates (and service fees).

For tips and telephone numbers to call if your wallet is stolen or lost, see "Lost & Found" in the "Fast Facts" section of the Appendix.

In Denmark, the most commonly accepted credit cards are MasterCard and Visa. Of secondary importance are American Express and Diners Club.

CURRENCY EXCHANGE

Banks offer the best rates for performing currency exchanges. Most hotels will exchange money but usually at an unfavorable rate.

Many hotels in Denmark simply do not accept a dollar- or pound-denominated personal check; those that do will certainly charge for making the conversion. In some cases, a hotel may accept countersigned traveler's checks or a credit or charge card.

If you're making a deposit on a hotel reservation, it's cheaper and easier to pay with a check drawn from a Norwegian bank. This can be arranged by a large commercial bank or by a specialist such as **Ruesch International,** 700 11th St. NW, Fourth Floor, Washington, DC 20001 (© **800/424-2923** or 202/408-1200; www.ruesch.com), which performs a wide variety of conversion-related tasks, usually for about $15 per transaction.

If you need a check payable in Danish currency, call Ruesch's toll-free number, describe what you need, and write down the transaction number. Mail your dollar-denominated personal check (payable to Ruesch International) to the Washington, D.C., office. When it's received, the company will mail you a check denominated in the requested currency for the specified amount, minus the $3 charge. The company can also help you with wire transfers, as well as converting VAT (value-added tax) refund checks. Information is mailed upon request.

In England, contact **Ruesch International Ltd.,** Lower Cookham Road, Maidenhead Berkshire SL6 8XY (© **0845/880-0400**).

---

6 HEALTH

STAYING HEALTHY

Denmark is viewed as a "safe" destination, although problems, of course, can and do occur anywhere. You don't need to get shots, most foodstuff is safe, and the water in cities and towns is potable. If you're concerned, order bottled water. It is easy to get a prescription filled in towns and cities, and nearly all places throughout Denmark contain hospitals with English-speaking doctors and well-trained medical staffs.

Denmark is part of the civilized world. In fact, it's one of the most advanced countries on the planet.

Availability of Healthcare

If a medical emergency arises, your hotel staff can usually put you in touch with a

Avoiding "Economy-Class Syndrome"

Deep vein thrombosis, or as it's known in the world of flying, "economy-class syndrome," is a blood clot that develops in a deep vein. It's a potentially deadly condition that can be caused by sitting in cramped conditions, such as an airplane cabin, for too long. During a flight (especially a long-haul flight), get up, walk around, and stretch your legs every 60 to 90 minutes to keep your blood flowing. Other preventive measures include frequent flexing of the legs while sitting, drinking lots of water, and avoiding alcohol and sleeping pills. If you have a history of deep vein thrombosis, heart disease, or another condition that puts you at high risk, some experts recommend wearing compression stockings or taking anticoagulants when you fly; always ask your physician about the best course for you. Symptoms of deep vein thrombosis include leg pain or swelling, or even shortness of breath.

reliable doctor. If not, contact the American embassy or a consulate; each one maintains a list of English-speaking doctors. Medical and hospital services aren't free, so be sure that you have appropriate insurance coverage before you travel.

Contact the **International Association for Medical Assistance to Travelers** (IAMAT; *©* **716/754-4883** or, in Canada, 416/652-0137; www.iamat.org) for tips on travel and health concerns in the countries you're visiting, and for lists of local, English-speaking doctors. The United States **Centers for Disease Control and Prevention** (*©* **800/311-3435** or 404/498-1515; www.cdc.gov) provides up-to-date information on health hazards by region or country and offers tips on food safety. **Travel Health Online** (www.tripprep.com), sponsored by a consortium of travel medicine practitioners, may also offer helpful advice on traveling abroad. You can find listings of reliable medical clinics overseas at the **International Society of Travel Medicine** (www.istm.org).

WHAT TO DO IF YOU GET SICK AWAY FROM HOME

For travel abroad, you may have to pay all medical costs upfront and be reimbursed later. Medicare and Medicaid do not provide coverage for medical costs outside the U.S. Before leaving home, find out what medical services your health insurance covers. To protect yourself, consider buying medical travel insurance (see the appendix, "Fast Facts: Denmark," p. 408).

Very few health insurance plans pay for medical evacuation back to the U.S. (which can cost US$10,000 and up). A number of companies offer medical evacuation services anywhere in the world. If you're ever hospitalized more than 150 miles from home, **MedjetAssist** (*©* **800/527-7478;** www.medjetassistance.com) will pick you up and fly you to the hospital of your choice virtually anywhere in the world in a medically equipped and staffed aircraft 24 hours day, 7 days a week. Annual memberships are US$225 individual, US$350 family; you can also purchase short-term memberships.

U.K. nationals will need a **European Health Insurance Card (EHIC)** (*©* **0845/606-2030;** www.ehic.org.uk) to receive free or reduced-cost health benefits during a visit to a European Economic Area (EEA) country (European Union countries plus Iceland, Liechtenstein, and Norway) or Switzerland. The European Health Insurance Card replaces the E111 form, which is no longer valid. For advice, ask at your local post office or see **www.dh.gov.uk/travellers.**

We list **hospital** and **emergency numbers** in the Appendix, under "Fast Facts: Denmark," p. 408.

If you suffer from a chronic illness, consult your doctor before your departure. Pack **prescription medications** in your carry-on luggage, and carry them in their original containers, with pharmacy labels—otherwise, they won't make it through airport security. Carry the generic name of prescription medicines, in case a local pharmacist is unfamiliar with the brand name.

---

7 SAFETY

STAYING SAFE

Denmark has a relatively low crime rate with rare, but increasing, instances of violent crime. Most crimes involve the theft of personal property from cars or residences or in public areas. Pickpockets and purse snatchers often work in pairs or groups, with one distracting the victim while another grabs valuables. Often they operate in or near the major rail stations in Copenhagen. Hotel breakfast rooms and lobbies attract professional, well-dressed thieves who blend in with guests and target purses and briefcases left unguarded by unsuspecting tourists and business travelers. Valuables should not be left unguarded in parked vehicles.

The loss or theft abroad of a U.S. passport should be reported immediately to the local police and the nearest U.S. Embassy or Consulate. If you are the victim of a crime while overseas, in addition to reporting to local police, contact the nearest U.S. Embassy or Consulate for assistance. The Embassy/Consulate staff can, for example, assist you in finding appropriate medical care and contacting family members or friends, and explain how funds can be transferred. Although the investigation and prosecution of the crime is solely the responsibility of local authorities, consular officers can help you to understand the local criminal justice process and to find an attorney if needed.

U.S. citizens may refer to the Department of State's pamphlet *A Safe Trip Abroad* for ways to promote a trouble-free journey. The pamphlet is available by mail from the **Superintendent of Documents, U.S. Government Printing Office,** Washington, DC 20402; via the Internet at **www.gpoaccess.gov;** or via the Bureau of Consular Affairs home page at http:// travel.state.gov.

---

8 SPECIALIZED TRAVEL RESOURCES

TRAVELERS WITH DISABILITIES

Most disabilities shouldn't stop anyone from traveling. There are more options and resources out there than ever before.

In general, Denmark's trains, airlines, ferries, department stores, and malls are accessible. For information about wheelchair access, ferry and air travel, parking, and other matters, contact the **Danish Tourist Board** (see "Visitor Information," earlier in this chapter).

Useful information for people with disabilities is provided by *De Samvirkende Invalideorganisationer* (**Danish Disability Council,** abbreviated in Denmark as DSI), Bredgade 25, 1260 Copenhagen, Denmark (℃ **33-11-10-44;** www.dch.dk). Established in 1934, it organizes 29 smaller organizations, each involved with issues of concern to physically challenged people, into one coherent grouping that represents the estimated 300,000 persons with disabilities living in Denmark today.

Many travel agencies offer customized tours and itineraries for travelers with disabilities. **Flying Wheels Travel** (*©* 507/451-5005; www.flyingwheelstravel.com) offers escorted tours and cruises that emphasize sports and private tours in mini-vans with lifts. **Access-Able Travel Source** (www.access-able.com) offers extensive access information and advice for traveling around the world with disabilities. **Accessible Journeys** (*©* 800/846-4537 or 610/521-0339; www.disabilitytravel.com) caters specifically to slow walkers and wheelchair travelers and their families and friends.

Organizations that offer assistance to travelers with disabilities include **Moss-Rehab** (*©* 800/CALL-MOSS [225-5667]; www.mossresourcenet.org), which provides a library of accessible-travel resources online; **SATH** (**Society for Accessible Travel and Hospitality;** *©* 212/447-7284; www.sath.org; annual membership fees: $45 adults, $30 seniors and students), which offers a wealth of travel resources for all types of disabilities and informed recommendations on destinations, access guides, travel agents, tour operators, vehicle rentals, and companion services; and the **American Foundation for the Blind** (**AFB;** *©* 800/232-5463; www.afb.org), a referral resource for travelers who are blind or visually impaired that includes information on traveling with Seeing Eye dogs.

For more information specifically targeted to travelers with disabilities, check out the quarterly magazine *Emerging Horizons* (www.emerginghorizons.com) and *Open World Magazine,* published by SATH.

FOR BRITISH TRAVELERS

The **Royal Association for Disability and Rehabilitation (RADAR),** Unit 12, City Forum, 250 City Rd., London EC1V 8AF (*©* 020/7250-3222; www.radar.org.uk),

publishes three holiday "fact packs." The first provides general information, including tips for planning and booking a holiday, obtaining insurance, and handling finances; the second outlines transportation available when going abroad and equipment for rent; and the third deals with specialized accommodations. Another good resource is **Holiday Care Service,** Seventh Floor, Sunley House, 4 Bedford Park, Croydon, Surrey CR0 2AP (*©* 0845/124-9971; www.holidaycare.org.uk), a national charity advising on accessible accommodations for seniors and persons with disabilities. Annual membership is £37 ($63).

GAY & LESBIAN TRAVELERS

In general, Denmark is one of the most gay-friendly countries in Europe and was one of the first to embrace same-sex marriages. Antidiscrimination laws have been in effect since 1987. Most Danes are exceptionally friendly and tolerant of lifestyles of either sexual preference. Obviously, an urban center such as Copenhagen will have a more openly gay life than rural areas. In many ways, the Erotic Museum in Copenhagen illustrates the city's attitudes toward sex—both heterosexual and homosexual. The history of both forms of sexual pleasure is presented in an unprejudiced manner.

The **Danish National Association for Gays and Lesbians** (Landsforeningen for Bøsser og Lesbiske, abbreviated as LBL) maintains its headquarters at Teglgaardstræde 13, 1007 Copenhagen (*©* 33-13-19-48; www.lbl.dk), with branches in at least four of the larger cities of Denmark. You might find it hard to reach a live person on their telephone line (their hours of operation are limited), but they maintain one of the most informative and user-friendly websites of any gay organization in Europe, complete with maps on how to reach the gay and lesbian venues they describe on their site.

The **International Gay and Lesbian Travel Association** (IGLTA; © 954/630-1637; www.iglta.org) is the trade association for the gay and lesbian travel industry, and offers an online directory of gay- and lesbian-friendly travel businesses and tour operators.

Many agencies offer tours and travel itineraries specifically for gay and lesbian travelers. **Above and Beyond Tours** (© 800/397-2681; www.abovebeyondtours.com) can arrange independent travel in Scandinavia. San Francisco–based **Now, Voyager** (© 800/255-6951; www.nowvoyager.com) offers worldwide trips and cruises. And **Olivia** (© 800/631-6277; www.olivia.com) offers lesbian cruises and resort vacations.

Gay.com Travel (© 415/834-6500; www.gay.com/travel or www.outandabout.com) is an excellent online successor to the popular *Out & About* print magazine. It provides regularly updated information about gay-owned, gay-oriented, and gay-friendly lodging, dining, sightseeing, nightlife, and shopping establishments in every important destination worldwide.

The Canadian website **GayTraveler** (www.gaytraveler.ca) offers ideas and advice for gay travel all over the world.

The following travel guides are available at many bookstores, or you can order them from any online bookseller: *Spartacus International Gay Guide* (Bruno Gmünder Verlag; www.spartacusworld.com/gayguide) and *Odysseus: The International Gay Travel Planner, 17th Edition*; and the *Damron* guides (www.damron.com), with separate, annual books for gay men and lesbians.

For more gay and lesbian travel resources, visit **Frommers.com**.

SENIOR TRAVEL

Mention the fact that you're a senior when you first make your travel reservations. All major airlines and many Norwegian hotels offer discounts for seniors. In Denmark people over age 67 are entitled to 50% off the price of first- and second-class train tickets. Ask for the discount at the ticket office.

Members of **AARP**, 601 E St. NW, Washington, DC 20049 (© 888/687-2277; www.aarp.org), get discounts on hotels, airfares, and car rentals. AARP offers members a wide range of benefits, including *AARP: The Magazine* and a monthly newsletter. Anyone over 50 can join.

Many reliable agencies and organizations target the 50-plus market. **Elderhostel** (© 800/454-5768; www.elderhostel.org) arranges worldwide study programs for those ages 55 and over.

INTRAV (© 800/680-2858; www.tourvacationstogo.com) is a high-end tour operator that caters to the mature, discerning traveler, not specifically seniors, with trips around the world that include guided safaris, polar expeditions, private jet adventures, small boat cruises down jungle rivers, and trips to the Norwegian fjords.

Recommended publications offering travel resources and discounts for seniors include the quarterly magazine *Travel 50 & Beyond* (www.travel50andbeyond.com) and the bestselling paperback *Unbelievably Good Deals and Great Adventures That You Absolutely Can't Get Unless You're Over 50* (McGraw-Hill), by Joann Rattner Heilman.

Frommers.com offers more information and resources on travel for seniors.

FAMILY TRAVEL

The family vacation is a rite of passage for many households, one that in a split second can devolve into a *National Lampoon* farce. But as any veteran family vacationer will assure you, a family trip can be among the most pleasurable and rewarding times of your life.

Most Danish hoteliers let children 12 and under stay in a room with their parents free; others do not. Sometimes this requires a little negotiation at the reception desk.

Danes like kids but don't offer a lot of special amenities for them. For example, a kiddies' menu in a restaurant is a rarity. You can, however, order a half portion, and most waiters will oblige.

At attractions, even if it isn't specifically posted, inquire if a kids' discount is available. European Community citizens 17 and under are admitted free to all state-run museums.

To locate those accommodations, restaurants, and attractions that are particularly kid-friendly, refer to the "Kids" icon throughout this guide.

Recommended family travel Internet sites include **Family Travel Forum** (www.familytravelforum.com), a comprehensive site that offers customized trip planning; **Family Travel Network** (www.familytravel network.com), an award-winning site that offers travel features, deals, and tips; **Traveling Internationally with Your Kids** (www.travelwithyourkids.com), a comprehensive site offering sound advice for long-distance and international travel with children; and **Family Travel Files** (www.thefamilytravel files.com), which offers an online magazine and a directory of off-the-beaten-path tours and tour operators for families.

SINGLE TRAVELERS

Single travelers are often hit with a "single supplement" to the base price of accommodations. To avoid it, you can agree to room with other single travelers on the trip, or before you go you can find a compatible roommate from one of the many roommate-locator agencies.

Travel Buddies Singles Travel Club (℅ 800/998-9099; www.travelbuddies worldwide.com), based in Canada, runs intimate, single-friendly group trips and will match you with a roommate free of charge. **TravelChums** (℅ 212/787-2621; www.travelchums.com) is an Internet-only travel-companion matching service with elements of an online personals-type site, hosted by the respected New York–based Shaw Guides travel service.

Many reputable tour companies offer singles-only trips. **Singles Travel International** (℅ 877/765-6874; www.singlestravelintl. com) offers singles-only trips to such places as Scandinavia. **Backroads** (℅ 800/462-2848; www.backroads.com) offers more than 160 active-travel trips to 30 destinations worldwide, including Denmark.

For more information, check out Eleanor Berman's latest edition of *Traveling Solo: Advice and Ideas for More Than 250 Great Vacations* (Globe Pequot), a guide with advice on traveling alone, whether on your own or on a group tour.

9 SUSTAINABLE TOURISM

Sustainable tourism is conscientious travel. It means being careful with the environments you explore, and respecting the communities you visit. Two overlapping components of sustainable travel are **ecotourism** and **ethical tourism.** The **International Ecotourism Society** (TIES) defines ecotourism as responsible travel to natural areas that conserves the environment and improves the well-being of local people. TIES suggests that ecotourists follow these principles:

- Minimize environmental impact.
- Build environmental and cultural awareness and respect.
- Provide positive experiences for both visitors and hosts.
- Provide direct financial benefits for conservation and for local people.
- Raise sensitivity to host countries' political, environmental, and social climates.
- Support international human rights and labor agreements.

It's Easy Being Green

Here are a few simple ways you can help conserve fuel and energy when you travel:

- Each time you take a flight or drive a car, greenhouse gases release into the atmosphere. You can help neutralize this danger to the planet through "carbon offsetting," paying someone to invest your money in programs that reduce your greenhouse gas emissions by the same amount you've added. Before buying carbon offset credits, just make sure that you're using a reputable company, one with a proven program that invests in renewable energy. Reliable carbon offset companies include **Carbonfund** (www.carbonfund.org), **TerraPass** (www.terrapass.org), and **Carbon Neutral** (www.carbonneutral.org).

- Whenever possible, choose nonstop flights; they generally require less fuel than indirect flights that stop and take off again. Try to fly during the day—some scientists estimate that nighttime flights are twice as harmful to the environment. And pack light, as each 15 pounds of luggage on a 5,000-mile flight adds up to 50 pounds of carbon dioxide emitted.

- Where you stay during your travels can have a major environmental impact. To determine the green credentials of a property, ask about trash disposal and recycling, water conservation, and energy use; also question if sustainable materials were used in the construction of the property. The website **www.greenhotels.com** recommends green-rated member hotels around the world that fulfill the company's stringent environmental requirements. Also consult **www.environmentallyfriendlyhotels.com** for more green accommodation ratings.

- At hotels, request that your sheets and towels not be changed daily. (Many hotels already have programs like this in place.) Turn off the lights and air-conditioner (or heater) when you leave your room.

- Use public transport where possible; trains, buses, and even taxis are more energy-efficient forms of transport than driving. Even better is to walk or cycle; you'll produce zero emissions and stay fit and healthy on your travels.

- If renting a car is necessary, ask the rental agent for a hybrid, or rent the most fuel-efficient car available. You'll use less gas and save money at the tank.

- Eat at locally owned and operated restaurants that use produce grown in the area. This contributes to the local economy and cuts down on greenhouse gas emissions by supporting restaurants where the food is not flown or trucked in across long distances.

Frommers.com: The Complete Travel Resource

It should go without saying, but we highly recommend **Frommers.com,** voted Best Travel Site by *PC Magazine*. We think you'll find our expert advice and tips; independent reviews of hotels, restaurants, attractions, and preferred shopping and nightlife venues; vacation giveaways; and online booking tool indispensable before, during, and after your travels. We publish the complete contents of more than 128 travel guides in our **Destinations** section covering nearly 3,600 places worldwide to help you plan your trip. Each weekday, we publish original articles reporting on **Deals and News** via our free **Frommers.com Newsletter** to help you save time and money and travel smarter. We're betting you'll find our new **Events** listings (http://events.frommers.com) an invaluable resource; it's an up-to-the-minute roster of what's happening in cities everywhere—including concerts, festivals, lectures, and more. We've also added weekly **podcasts, interactive maps,** and hundreds of new images across the site. Check out our **Travel Talk** area featuring **Message Boards** where you can join in conversations with thousands of fellow Frommer's travelers and post your trip report once you return.

You can find some eco-friendly travel tips and statistics, as well as touring companies and associations—listed by destination under "Travel Choice"—at the **TIES** website, **www.ecotourism.org**. Also check out **Ecotravel.com,** which lets you search for sustainable touring companies in several categories (water-based, land-based, spiritually oriented, and so on).

While much of the focus of ecotourism is about reducing impacts on the natural environment, ethical tourism concentrates on ways to preserve and enhance local economies and communities, regardless of location. You can embrace ethical tourism by staying at a locally owned hotel or shopping at a store that employs local workers and sells locally produced goods.

Responsible Travel (www.responsibletravel.com) is a great source of sustainable travel ideas; the site is run by a spokesperson for ethical tourism in the travel industry. **Sustainable Travel International** (www.sustainabletravelinternational.org) promotes ethical tourism practices, and

manages an extensive directory of sustainable properties and tour operators around the world.

In the U.K., **Tourism Concern** (www.tourismconcern.org.uk) works to reduce social and environmental problems connected to tourism. The **Association of Independent Tour Operators** (AITO; www.aito.co.uk) is a group of specialist operators leading the field in making holidays sustainable.

Volunteer travel has become popular among those who want to venture beyond the standard group-tour experience to learn languages, interact with locals, and make a positive difference while on vacation. Volunteer travel usually doesn't require special skills—just a willingness to work hard—and programs vary in length from a few days to a number of weeks. Some programs provide free housing and food, but many require volunteers to pay for travel expenses, which can add up quickly.

For general info on volunteer travel, visit **www.volunteerabroad.org** and **www.idealist.org**.

Before you commit to a volunteer program, it's important to make sure any money you're giving is truly going back to the local community, and that the work you'll be doing will be a good fit for you. **Volunteer International** (www.volunteer international.org) has a helpful list of questions to ask to determine the intentions and the nature of a volunteer program.

10 SPECIAL-INTEREST TOURS

BUS TOURS

ScanAm World Tours (© 800/545-2204; www.scanamtours.com) offers a tour through the "Heart of Fairy Tale Denmark." You can choose a 5-day, 4-night trip through Hans Christian Andersen country, including a visit to Odense (his birthplace) and an excursion to Legoland. Tours begin at $620 per person.

SELF-DRIVE TOURS

Several companies offer self-drive tours, which usually include accommodations, rental cars, and customized itineraries. **Scantours Inc.** (© 800/545-2204; www.scantours.net) features the 5-day "Taste of Danish Castles & Manor Houses" tour, which is available year-round. Prices begin at $785 per person. The company also sponsors a tour of Danish inns. The 4-day self-drive tour includes accommodations, breakfast, car rental, and an itinerary. The typical price for an inn is $182 per night in a double room, and the trip builds from there.

BICYCLE TOURS

An excellent way to explore the flat, rolling Danish countryside is on a bicycle. Numerous organizations (including Scantours Inc. and ScanAm Tours) sponsor bike tours through various regions of the country. You can choose one that covers the castles, beaches, and fjords of northern Denmark; the southern Funen islands; the beaches and marshland of western Jutland; or the lake country in eastern Jutland. **Blue Marble Travel** (© 800/BLUE-8689

[258-3868] or 215/923-3788; www.blue marble.org) offers 7-day excursions to Hans Christian Andersen country and several small islands in the Baltic for $1,508 per person. **Dansk Cyklist Forbund,** Rømersgade 7, DK-1362 Copenhagen (© 33-32-31-21; www.dcf.dk), can provide the latest information on cycling tours in Denmark.

ADVENTURE TRAVEL OPERATORS

In North America

Crossing Latitudes, 420 W. Koch St., Bozeman, MT 59715 (© 800/572-8747 or fax 406/585-5356; www.crossing latitudes.com), offers sea kayaking and backpacking expeditions throughout the region; and **Blue Marble Travel,** 211 South St., Philadelphia, PA 19147 (© 215/923-3788; www.bluemarble.org), features reasonably priced biking and hiking trips in Denmark and Norway.

In the U.K.

The oldest travel agency in Britain, **Cox & Kings,** Gordon House 10, Greencoat Place, London SW1P 1PH (© 020/7873-5000; www.coxandkings.co.uk), was established in 1758. Today the company specializes in unusual, if pricey, holidays. Its offerings in Scandinavia include cruises through the spectacular fjords and waterways, bus and rail tours through sites of historic and aesthetic interest, and visits to the region's best-known handicraft centers, Viking burial sites, and historic churches. The company's staff is noted for its focus on tours of ecological and environmental interest.

Heritage—The Search for Roots

More than 12 million North Americans have Scandinavian roots, many in Denmark. To help you trace your ancestry, Danish consulates can furnish fact sheets. Many original Danish records are available on microfilm from **The Family History Library,** 35 N. West Temple, Salt Lake City, UT 84150 (© **801/240-2331).**

Established in 1992, the **Danish Immigrant Museum,** Elk Horn, Iowa (© **712/764-7001;** www.dkmuseum.org), is devoted to telling the story of migration to the United States.

In Denmark itself, the major archives concerning immigration are held at **Det Danske Udvandrerarkiv** (Danes' Worldwide Archives), Arkivstræde 1, P.O. Box 1731, DK-9100 Aalborg (© **99-31-42-20;** fax 98-10-22-48; www.emiarch.dk).

To cycle through the splendors of Scandinavia, you can join Britain's oldest and largest association of bicycle riders, the **Cyclists' Touring Club** (CTC Parklands, Railton Road, Guildford, Surrey GU2 9JX; www.ctc.org.uk). Founded in 1878, it charges £12 to £35 ($23 to $60) a year for membership, which includes information, maps, and a subscription to a newsletter packed with practical information and morale boosters, plus recommended cycling routes through virtually every country in Europe. The organization's information bank on scenic routes through Scandinavia is especially comprehensive. Membership can be arranged over the phone with a credit card (such as MasterCard, Visa, Access, or Barclaycard).

LEARNING VACATIONS

Danish Cultural Institute (Det Danske Kultur Institutu), Farvergade 27L, DK-1463 Copenhagen (© **33-13-54-48;** fax 33-15-10-91; www.dankultur.dk), offers summer seminars in English, including a course in Danish culture. Credit programs are available, but many courses are geared toward professional groups from abroad. An especially interesting course for those with some knowledge of

Danish is "Danmark, Danskerne, Dansk," which includes language instruction.

An international series of programs for persons over 50 who are interested in combining travel and learning is offered by **Interhostel,** developed by the University of New Hampshire. Each program lasts 2 weeks, is led by a university faculty or staff member, and is arranged in conjunction with a host college, university, or cultural institution. Participants may stay longer if they want. Interhostel offers programs consisting of cultural and intellectual activities, with field trips to museums and other centers of interest. For information, contact the University of New Hampshire, Division of Continuing Education, 6 Garrison Ave., Durham, NH 03824 (© **800/313-5327** or 603/862-2015; www.learn.unh.edu).

Another good source of information about courses in Denmark is the **American Institute for Foreign Study (AIFS),** River Plaza, 9 W. Broad St., Stamford, CT 06902 (© **866/906-2437;** www.aifs.org). This organization can set up transportation and arrange for summer courses, with bed and board included.

The largest organization dealing with higher education in Europe is the **Institute**

of International Education (IIE), 809 United Nations Plaza, New York, NY 10017 (© **212/883-8200;** www.iie.org). A few of its booklets are free, but for $47, plus $6 for postage, you can buy the more definitive *Vacation Study Abroad.* The Information Center in New York is open to the public Tuesday through Thursday from 11am to 4pm. The institute is closed on major holidays.

One well-recommended clearinghouse for academic programs throughout the world is the **National Registration Center for Study Abroad (NRCSA),** 823 N. 2nd St., P.O. Box 1393, Milwaukee, WI 53203 (© **414/278-0631;** www.nrcsa.com). The organization maintains language study programs throughout Europe.

11 THE ACTIVE VACATION PLANNER

BEACHES

With some 8,000km (5,000 miles) of coastline, Denmark has many long strips of sandy beaches. In many cases, dunes protect the beaches from sea winds. Most of these beaches are relatively unspoiled, and the Danes like to keep them that way (any polluted beaches are clearly marked). Many Danes like to go nude at the beach. Nudist beaches aren't clearly identified; often you'll see bathers with and without clothing using the same beach. The best beach resorts are those on the north coast of Zealand and the southern tip of the island of Bornholm. Beaches on the east coast of Jutland are also good, often attracting Germans from the south. Funen also has a number of good beaches, especially in the south.

BIKING

A nation of bikers, the Danes have organized their roads to suit this national sport. Bikers can pedal along a network of biking routes and paths protected from heavy traffic. The Danish landscape is made for this type of vacation. Most tourist offices publish biking-tour suggestions for their own district; it's a great way to see the sights and get in shape at the same time. The **Dansk Cyklist Forbund** (Danish Cycling Federation), Rømersgade 5, DK-1362 Copenhagen (© **33-32-31-21;** www.dcf.dk), publishes excellent guides covering the whole country. They can also provide information about a number of prepackaged biking vacations that are available.

FISHING

Because no place in Denmark is more than 56km (35 miles) from the sea, fishing is a major pastime. Denmark also has well-stocked rivers and lakes, including fjord waters around the Limfjord. Anglers between the ages of 18 and 67 must obtain a fishing permit from the Danish Directorate of Fisheries for DKK30 ($5.10/£3) for 1 day, DKK90 ($15/£9) for 1 week; these are available at any post office. Jutland is known for its good trout fishing; salmon is also available, but it is found more readily in Norway. Anglers who fish from the beach can catch eel, mackerel, turbot, sea trout, plaice, and flounder. For more information about fishing in Denmark, contact **Sportsfiskerforbund,** Worsåesgade 1, DK-7100 Vejle (© **75-82-06-99;** www.sportsfiskeren.dk).

GOLF

Denmark's undulating landscape is ideal for the construction of golf courses. Prospective golfers should bring with them a valid golf club membership card from home. For information on the best courses near where you're staying, contact local tourist offices.

HANG GLIDING & PARAGLIDING

Although Denmark is a relatively flat country, good possibilities for paragliding do exist. **The Danish Union of Windgliders** provides information about suitable locations. As a rule, the union has arranged with local landowners that a slope or some other suitable place may be used. Since equipment cannot be rented in Denmark, clients must bring their own. More information is available from **Dansk Drageflyver Union** (© **46-14-15-01;** www.dansk drageflyverunion.dk).

SAILING

Denmark has about 600 harbors, both large and small, including the island of Bornholm. Those who like to sail have many opportunities to do so, especially in the open waters of the Baltic or in the more sheltered waters of the South Funen Sea between Lolland/Falster and Zealand. The Limfjord in North Jutland is also ideal for sailing. Many sailing boats are available for rent, as are cruisers. For information, contact the tourist offices.

WALKING

About 20 pamphlets describing walks of short or long duration in Danish forests are printed in English and are available from local tourist offices.

---

12 STAYING CONNECTED

TELEPHONES

The country code for Denmark is **45.** For international calls, dial **00,** then the country code, the area code, and the number. Try to avoid calling from your hotel. The surcharges are often outrageous.

Dial **118** to find out a number in Denmark, or **113** for international assistance. If you need operator assistance for international calls, dial **115.** Virtually all international operators speak English.

Coin-operated phones are being phased out. Visitors can purchase a telephone card at most kiosks, groceries, and post offices in Denmark. If you face a coin-operated phone, know that these take 1-, 2-, 5-, 10-, or 20-kroner coins.

CELLPHONES

The three letters that define much of the world's wireless capabilities are GSM (Global System for Mobiles), a big, seamless network that makes for easy cross-border cellphone use throughout dozens of countries worldwide. In general, reception is good.

For many, **renting** a phone is a good idea. (Even World Phone owners will have to rent new phones if they're traveling to non-GSM regions.) While you can rent a phone from any number of overseas sites, including kiosks at airports and at car-rental agencies, we suggest renting the phone before you leave home. North Americans can rent one before leaving home from **InTouch USA** (© **800/872-7626** or 703/222-7161; www.intouch global.com) or **RoadPost** (© **888/290-1616** or 905/272-5665; www.roadpost. com). InTouch will also, for free, advise you on whether your existing phone will work overseas.

Buying a phone can be economically attractive, as many nations have cheap prepaid phone systems. Once you arrive at your destination, stop by a local cellphone shop and get the cheapest package; you'll probably pay less than US$100 for a phone and a starter calling card. Local calls may be as low as 10¢ per minute, and in many countries incoming calls are free.

Online Traveler's Toolbox

Veteran travelers usually carry some essential items to make their trips easier. Following is a selection of handy online tools to bookmark and use.

- **Airplane Food** (www.airlinemeals.net)
- **Airplane Seating** (www.seatguru.com and www.airlinequality.com)
- **Foreign Languages for Travelers** (www.travlang.com)
- **Maps** (www.mapquest.com)
- **Time and Date** (www.timeanddate.com)
- **Travel Warnings** (http://travel.state.gov, www.fco.gov.uk/travel, www.voyage.gc.ca, or www.dfat.gov.au/consular/advice)
- **Universal Currency Converter** (www.xe.com/ucc)
- **Visa ATM Locator** (www.visa.com); **MasterCard ATM Locator** (www.mastercard.com)
- **Weather** (www.intellicast.com and www.weather.com)

INTERNET & E-MAIL
With Your Own Computer

More and more hotels, cafes, and retailers are signing on as Wi-Fi (wireless fidelity) "hot spots." Mac owners have their own networking technology: Apple AirPort. **T-Mobile Hotspot** (www.t-mobile.com/hotspot or www.t-mobile.co.uk) serves up wireless connections at coffee shops nationwide. **Boingo** (www.boingo.com) and **Wayport** (www.wayport.com) have set up networks in airports and high-class hotel lobbies. IPass providers (see below) also give you access to a few hundred wireless hotel lobby setups. To locate other hot spots that provide **free wireless networks,** go to **www.jiwire.com**.

For dial-up access, most business-class hotels offer Wi-Fi for laptop modems. In addition, major Internet service providers (ISPs) have **local access numbers** around the world, allowing you to go online by placing a local call. The **iPass** network also has dial-up numbers around the world. You'll have to sign up with an iPass provider, who will then tell you how to set up your computer for your destination(s). For a list of iPass providers, go to www.ipass.com and click on "Individuals Buy Now." One solid provider is **i2roam** (© **866/811-6209** or 920/233-5863; www.i2roam.com).

Wherever you go, bring a **connection kit** of the right power and phone adapters, a spare phone cord, and a spare Ethernet network cable—or find out whether your hotel supplies them to guests.

Without Your Computer

To find cybercafes check **www.cybercaptive.com** and **www.cybercafe.com**. Cybercafes are found in all large cities, especially Copenhagen and Århus. But they do not tend to cluster in any particular neighborhoods because of competition.

Aside from formal cybercafes, most **youth hostels** and **public libraries** have Internet access. Avoid **hotel business centers** unless you're willing to pay exorbitant rates.

Most major airports now have **Internet kiosks** scattered throughout their gates. These give you basic Web access for a per-minute fee that's usually higher than cybercafe prices.

There are other alternatives, but most visitors to Denmark check into a hotel. Accommodations range from the most basic, perhaps lacking private bathrooms, to the most deluxe. Outside of Copenhagen, you are likely to encounter first class in the top category instead of luxe accommodations. The one thing you'll not find is a truly cheap hotel. Even the most inexpensive hotels might be considered a bit pricey in some parts of the world. To compensate, many hotels, especially chain members, offer discounted rates on weekends, when hotels lose their most reliable client—the commercial traveler.

Our accommodation listings include service charges and taxes so you won't be shocked when the time comes to pay the bill and a lot of extras are added on, as is the situation in many European countries.

Denmark classifies its hotels by stars ranging from one (the most basic) to five (deluxe). A hotel without a restaurant is called Hotel *Garni*. One-star hotel rooms have a hand basin with hot and cold running water and at least one communal bathroom per 10 rooms; two-star hotels have at least 30% of the units with private bathrooms; three-star hotels offer rooms with their own private bathroom (such hotels also have an elevator if there are more than two floors). Moving up, four-star hotels offer round-the-clock reception, an a la carte restaurant, room service, minibars, laundry service, and a bar. The best hotels in Denmark are five-stars, with luxuriously appointed rooms, often indoor pools, professionally staffed fitness centers, air-conditioning, safes in the rooms, and round-the-clock room service, among other luxuries.

If you have not booked a room prior to your arrival in Copenhagen, you may call personally at **Wonderful Copenhagen Tourist Information** at Bernstorffsgade 1,

opposite the Central Station next to Tivoli. A handling fee of $9 is charged. There is also a booking desk, charging the same handling fee, at the **Copenhagen Airport Arrival Hall.**

Advance booking online is possible through **Wonderful Copenhagen Tourist Information & Booking Center,** Gammel Kongevej 1, DK 1610 Copenhagen (© **70-22-24-42**; www.visitcopenhagen. dk). Outside Copenhagen, bookings can be made online at www.visitdenmark. com, through local tourist offices, or directly with the hotel.

ALTERNATIVE ACCOMMODATIONS

If you'd like to avoid a stay in a hotel, consider these other options:

Bed & Breakfast

Dansk Bed & Breakfast publishes a catalog of guesthouses throughout Denmark that receive visitors for overnight stays, fortifying them the next morning with a hearty Danish breakfast. A typical B&B might be an 18th-century farmhouse built of granite and half-timbering. Contact **Dansk Bed & Breakfast,** at Sankt Peders Stræde 41, DK-1453 Copenhagen (© **39-61-04-05**; www.bedandbreakfast.dk).

The densest concentration of B&Bs is found on the Hans Christian Andersen island of Funen. There is a separate organization handling these bookings: **Nyborg Tourist Office,** Torvey 9, DK-5800 Nyborg (© **65-31-02-80**; www.bed-breakfast-fyn. dk). A typical overnight price for a double room in a B&B is DKK170 ($29/£17).

Castles & Manor Houses

Denmark is riddled with old manor houses and even a few small castles that receive paying guests all year. In our view, this type of lodging is the most exciting way to stay in Denmark, because of the grandeur of the buildings. You get to feel like a king (or queen), or at least a prince or princess for the night. Some of the establishments in this category are more like country homes than castles or manors. By taking in boarders, many of the owners of these privately owned estates are preserving Denmark's cultural heritage. For more information, contact **Danish Castles & Manor Houses,** Sankt Leonis Stræde 1A, DK-8800 Viborg (© **86-60-38-44;** www. slotte-herregaarde.dk).

Danish Inns

Nearly 100 atmospheric, old-world accommodations spread across the country have formed an association, offering rooms in *kros* (inns) that often date back hundreds of years. The bedrooms, however, are mostly renovated in the modern style. You get atmosphere and comfort, and most often good, solid food, both regional dishes and in many cases French specialties as well. For this type of accommodation, book through **Danska Kroer og Hoteller,** Vejlevej 16, DK- 8700 Horsens (© **75-64-87-00;** www.krohotel.dk).

Farm Holidays

Some 110 farms all over Denmark receive paying guests. To get close to the heart of the country and to meet the Danes, there is no better way than spending a week on one of these farms. In addition to an atmospheric stay, you can enjoy good country cooking with fresh vegetables, newly laid eggs, and rich butter. You stay on a farm as the guest of the family, joining members and other guests for meals. Often lodgings are in a small apartment on the grounds or even a cottage near the main building. In many cases you do your own housekeeping. Prices average around $35 per person, including a full Danish breakfast. You can book with the farm directly or else go through **Landsforeningen for Landboturisme,** Lerbakken 7,

DK-8410 Rønde (© **87-37-39-00;** www. bondegaardsferie.dk).

Holiday Homes

Yes, it's possible to rent your own house—most often a seaside cottage—throughout Denmark. The house may be a snug retreat for two or spacious enough to accommodate 10 to 12 guests. Some of these holiday homes are within a 30-minute drive of Copenhagen. They are available all year, and prices begin at around $600 per week, the rates depending on the season, size, and location. Naturally, seaside holiday homes are the most sought after and most expensive in July and August. Many of the best homes are found on the west coast of Jutland, often with an indoor swimming pool and sauna. To book one of these homes, contact one of the following organizations: **Dansommer** (© **86-17-61-22;** www.dansommer.com); **Novasol AS** (© **73-75-66-11;** www. novasol.com); and **Sol og Strand** (© **99-44-44-44;** www.sologstrand.com).

Home Stays

Friendship Force, 34 Peachtree St. NW, Suite 900, Atlanta, GA 30303 (© **404/522-9490;** www.thefriendshipforce.org), is a nonprofit organization that encourages friendship among people worldwide. Dozens of branch offices throughout North America arrange visits, usually once a year. Because of group bookings, the airfare to the host country is usually less than the cost of individual APEX tickets. Each participant spends 2 weeks in the host country, the first as a guest in the home of a family and the second traveling in the host country.

Servas, 1125 16th St., Suite 201, Arcata, CA 95521 (© **707/825-1714;** www.us servas.org), is an international nonprofit, nongovernmental, interfaith network of travelers and hosts whose goal is to help promote world peace, goodwill, and understanding. Servas hosts offer travelers hospitality for 2 days. Travelers pay an $85 annual fee and a $25 list deposit after filling out an application and being approved by an interviewer (interviewers are located across the U.S.). They then receive Servas directories listing the names and addresses of Servas hosts.

Home Exchanges

One of the most exciting breakthroughs in modern tourism is the home exchange. Sometimes the family automobile is even included. Of course, you must be comfortable with the idea of having strangers in your home, and you must be content to spend your vacation in one place. One potential problem, though, is that you may not get a home in the area you request.

Intervac USA, 30 Corte San Fernando, Tiburon, CA 94920 (© **800/756-HOME** [756-4663]; www.intervacus.com), is part of the largest worldwide exchange network. It contains more than 10,000 homes in more than 36 countries. Members contact each other directly. The cost is $85 plus postage, which includes the purchase of three of the company's catalogs, plus the inclusion of your own listing in whichever catalog you select. If you want to publish a photograph of your home, there is an additional charge of $15. Fees begin at $90, going up to $150.

The Invented City (© **415/846-7588;** www.invented-city.com) publishes home-exchange listings three times a year. For the $50 membership fee, you can list your home with your own written descriptive summary.

Home Link, 2937 NW 9 St., Fort Lauderdale, FL 33311 (© **800/638-3841** or 954/566-2687; www.homelink.org), will send you five directories a year for $130.

Chain Hotels & Discounts

The most prevalent chain hotel in Denmark is **Best Western** (© **800/937-8376;** www.bestwestern.com). It offers a Best Western Advance Card that allows you to take advantage of special "summer low" or "winter special" promotion rates, and grants such privileges as allowing one child under the age of 12 to stay free in a room shared with parents.

Suggested Itineraries for Denmark

Vacations are getting shorter, and a "lean and mean" schedule is called for if you want to experience the best of Denmark in a relatively small amount of time.

Fortunately, the country is small and enjoys a good road system or else an efficient network of ferryboats to take you to its off-shore islands in all weather conditions.

1 THE REGIONS IN BRIEF

ZEALAND

Home to Denmark's capital, **Copenhagen,** the island of Zealand draws more visitors than any other region. The largest island in Denmark, Zealand is also the wealthiest and most densely populated. Other cities include **Roskilde,** about 30km (19 miles) west of Copenhagen, which is home to a landmark cathedral (burial place of many kings) and a collection of Viking vessels discovered in a fjord. In the medieval town of **Køge,** witches were burned in the Middle Ages. One of the most popular attractions on the island is **Helsingør** ("Elsinore" in English), about 40km (25 miles) north of Copenhagen, where visitors flock to see "Hamlet's castle." Off the southeast corner of the island lies the island of **Møn,** home to Møns Klint, an expanse of white cliffs that rises sharply out of the Baltic.

JUTLAND

The peninsula of Jutland links the mostly island nation of Denmark with Germany. It is the only part of Denmark on the European continent. Jutland has miles of coastline, with some of northern Europe's finest sandy beaches. Giant dunes and moors abound on the west coast, whereas the interior has rolling pastures and beech forests. Jutland's more interesting towns and villages include **Jelling,** heralded as the birthplace of Denmark and the ancient seat of the Danish kings; here you can see an extensive collection of Viking artifacts excavated from ancient burial mounds. The Viking port of **Ribe** is the oldest town in Denmark. It's known throughout the world as the preferred nesting ground for numerous endangered storks. The resort of **Fanø,** with its giant dunes, heather-covered moors, and forests, is an excellent place to bird-watch or view Denmark's varied wildlife. The university city of **Århus** is Jutland's capital and second only to Copenhagen in size. **Aalborg,** founded by Vikings more than 1,000 years ago, is a thriving commercial center in northern Jutland. It lies close to Rebild National Park and the Rold Forest.

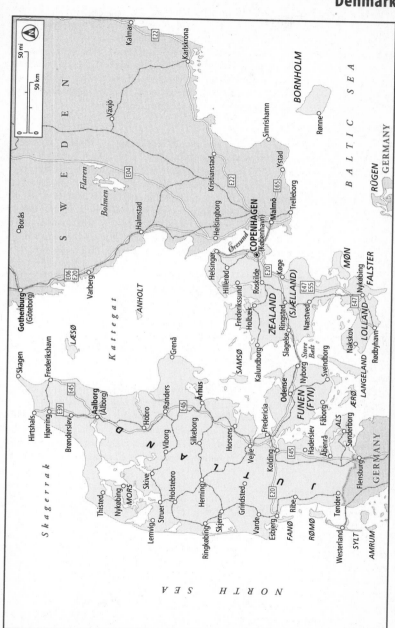

FUNEN

With an area of 2,980 sq. km (1,150 sq. miles), Funen is Denmark's second-largest island. Called the "garden of Denmark," Funen is known to the world as the birthplace of Hans Christian Andersen. Orchards, stately manors, and castles dot its rolling countryside. **Odense,** Andersen's birthplace, is a mecca for fairy-tale writers and fans from around the world. Nearby stands Egeskov Castle, resting on oak columns in the middle of a small lake. It's Europe's best-preserved Renaissance castle. Funen has a number of bustling ports, including **Nyborg** in the east and **Svendborg** at the southern end of the island. **Ærøskøbing** is a medieval market town that's a showplace of Scandinavian heritage.

BORNHOLM

In the Baltic Sea, southeast of Zealand and close to Sweden, lies the island of Bornholm. Prehistoric monuments and runic stones pepper the countryside, and numerous fishing villages dot the shoreline. On the northern coast, near **Hammerhus,** the Bornholm Animal and Nature Park is home to many native species as well as some that have been introduced from other parts of Scandinavia. Some of Europe's largest castle ruins dot this region of the island. The town of **Rønne** is the site of Denmark's oldest regional theater; it stages numerous concerts and shows year-round. The island of **Christiansø,** off the coast of Bornholm, was the site of Denmark's penal colony. Criminals sentenced to life imprisonment were deported to the island, where they spent their lives in slavery.

2 DENMARK IN 1 WEEK

Use the following itinerary to make the most out of a week in Denmark, but feel free to drop a place or two to save a day to relax. One week provides just enough time to take in the major attractions of **Zealand** (an island dominated by Copenhagen) and the neighboring island of **Funen,** centering on the birthplace of Hans Christian Andersen at Odense.

On the first day, you can see **Louisiana,** the most acclaimed modern art museum outside of Copenhagen, and also the so-called "Hamlet's Castle" at **Helsingør.** The following day you can head for **Roskilde** to see both its famous cathedral and its **Viking Ship Museum.** After a 2-night stopover, you can motor south to the yachting port of **Svendborg,** your launch pad for the island of **Ærø** for a 2-night visit. This tiny island is the most enchanting in all of the Scandinavian countries—and almost no one disputes that.

Day ❶: Louisiana Museum ★★★ & Helsingør ★

On **Day 1** of our driving tour, after wrapping up your visit to Copenhagen and renting a car, head north in the morning to the town of Humlebæk, 30km (19 miles) north of Copenhagen, for a morning visit to the **Louisiana Museum of Modern Art** (p. 167), which opens at 10am. This is one of the greatest art museums of Scandinavia,

and you'll want to give it at least an hour or two.

From Copenhagen, follow coastal road 152, known as Strandvej. Depending on traffic, the scenic drive takes some 45 minutes. After a visit, continue north from Humlebæk into Helsingør, a distance of 14km (8²/₃ miles), following the same Strandvej route. Once in Helsingør, you can check into a hotel for the night, but if you don't want to change hotels so often,

DAY 1: LOUISIANA MUSEUM & HELSINGØR

  1 Copenhagen
  2 Humlebæk
  3 Helsingør

DAY 2: THE CATHEDRAL CITY OF ROSKILDE

  4 Roskilde
  5 Hillerød

DAYS 3 & 4: ODENSE & H.C. ANDERSEN

  6 Odense

DAY 5: SVENDBORG, FAVORITE PORT FOR YACHTIES

  7 Svendborg

DAYS 6 & 7: ÆRØ, DENMARK'S MOST BEAUTIFUL ISLAND

  8 Ærø

you can use Copenhagen as your base and return there for the night.

There are many attractions in Helsingør, but the one magnet for most visitors is **Kronborg Slot** (p. 182), fabled as "Hamlet's Castle," even though Shakespeare presumably never visited it and Hamlet may never have existed. Allow at least an hour for an afternoon visit here after lunch in Helsingør.

Day ➋: The Cathedral City of Roskilde ★★

On the morning of **Day 2,** leave Helsingør (or Copenhagen if you spent the night there) for a drive west to **Roskilde.** The distance is 30km (19 miles) west of Copenhagen, but a distance of 72km (45 miles) southwest of Helsingør. From Copenhagen, head west on the E21 express highway; from Helsingør follow Route 6 southwest.

If you're on Route 6 from Helsingør, you can stop off for a morning visit to **Hillerød,** a distance of 25km (16 miles) southwest of Helsingør, or a jaunt of 35km (22 miles) north of Copenhagen. This town possesses one of the great treasures of Denmark and is well worth a detour regardless of where you spent the night. Hillerød is the home of **Frederiksborg Castle** (p. 173), which has been called "the Danish Versailles." Surrounded by a moat, it is the most beautiful royal residence in Denmark and the setting for the Museum of National History, with one of Denmark's greatest collections of historical paintings. Allow at least 1 1/2 hours for a visit.

From Hillerød, continue along Route 6 southwest into **Roskilde,** where you can check into a hotel for the night. In the afternoon, visit the **Roskilde Domkirke** (p. 196) and try to take a 90-minute boat tour of the **Roskilde Fjord** (p. 201). If you can't schedule a visit to the fjord, then call on the **Lejre Research Center** (p. 200), which, in spite of its dull name, is actually a reconstructed Iron Age village.

Days ❸ & ❹: Odense ★★ & H. C. Andersen

On the morning of **Day 3,** leave Zealand altogether and drive west to the neighboring island of Funen, whose capital is **Odense,** lying 134km (83 miles) to the west of Roskilde. From Roskilde, take Route 14 southwest to the express highway E20, continuing west to the port of Korsør, where you cross the Great Belt Bridge into Funen, entering the island through its gateway city of Nyborg. Once on land in Funen, continue west along E20 until you see the cutoff arteries leading north into the center of Odense. Once here, book into a hotel for a 2-night stay.

After lunch you can take in some of the major sights of the city, including the **H. C. Andersen's Childhood Home** (p. 269). If it's summer, you might even hook up with

a 2-hour walking tour, taking in all the highlights. Check with the tourist office.

On the morning of **Day 4,** visit **Funen Village** (p. 269), an open-air regional museum depicting life in Denmark in the 1700s and 1800s. In a busy afternoon you can visit both **Egeskov Castle** (p. 270), one of the grandest in Denmark, and **Ladbyskibet** (p. 271), 19km (12 miles) northeast of Odense, to see the ruins of a 10th-century Viking ship.

Day ❺: Svendborg ★: Favorite Port for Yachties

On the morning of **Day 5,** check out of your hotel in Odense and drive 43km (27 miles) south to the port city of **Svendborg,** following Route 9. Once in Svendborg, check into a hotel for the night and set out to see the rather minor sights in town, including **Anne Hvides Gård** (p. 280), **Skt. Jorgens Kirke** (p. 280), and **Skt. Nicolai Kirke** (p. 280). After lunch, you can explore nearby islands, each linked to Svendborg by bridge. These include the horseshoe-shaped **Thurø** (p. 285), called "The Garden of Denmark," and **Tåsinge** (p. 285), where you can visit several attractions such as the church tower at **Bregninge Kirkebakke** (p. 286) for its panoramic views. After a call on the 17th-century **Valdemars Slot** (p. 286), you can spend the rest of the afternoon just exploring at random. Because the island is so small, it's almost impossible to get lost. Return to Svendborg for the night.

Days ❻ & ❼: Ærø ★★: Denmark's Most Beautiful Island

On the morning of **Day 6,** leave Svendborg by driving to the port, where you can board a car ferry heading for the island of **Ærø,** lying 29km (18 miles) across the water south of Svendborg. Check into a hotel in the little picture-postcard capital of **Ærøskøbing** for 2 nights, and set out to explore the island.

Begin first on foot by walking the cobblestone streets of this most enchanting of Danish villages, saving the driving tour of the island for the following day. The main attraction of the town is Ærøskøbing itself, although there are specific sights of minor interest, including the **Ærø Museum** (p. 296) and an 18th-century church, **Ærøskøbing Kirke** (p. 295). Dine in an old *kro* (inn), and later walk down by the water to watch the yachts and other boats bobbing in the harbor at night.

On the morning of **Day 7,** while still based in Ærøskøbing, set out on a leisurely motor tour of the island, stopping at random to enjoy anything that fascinates you. We'd head east to the "second city" on

Marstal, really just a modest port town. After a 2-hour visit here, you can take the southern road all the way to the little port of **Søby** in the northwest. From Søby, you can drive southeast back to Ærøskøbing for the night.

The following morning, you can take the ferryboat back to Svendborg, where you can drive north once again toward Odense, and link with the E20 to carry you east across the Great Belt Bridge to Zealand and back to Copenhagen. Here you can make air or rail connections to your next destination.

3 DENMARK IN 2 WEEKS

After having driven through the highlights of the islands of Zealand and Funen, we tackle the largest landmass of Denmark, the peninsula of **Jutland** linking Denmark with the continent of Europe—Germany in this case. In just 1 week you can skim the highlights of this history-rich part of Denmark.

Our tour continues in the marshlands of South Jutland in the area's capital, **Tønder,** and proceeds north to **Ribe,** which, for most visitors, is the sightseeing highlight of the entire peninsula. This is followed by a trip to **Fanø,** the most beautiful island off the coast of Jutland.

We'll follow that with a trip to **Silkeborg** to call on the Tollund Man (who is 2,400 years old). Both of the two leading cities of Jutland, **Århus** and **Aalborg,** can be visited before we head for the northernmost point of Jutland, the artists' colony and summer resort of **Skagen.**

Day ❽: Tønder ★: Capital of the Marshlands

Our tour begins in South Jutland in one of Denmark's oldest towns, **Tønder,** lying on the banks of the River Vidå in the center of the southern marshlands, a section of Denmark that once belonged to Germany. Tønder lies at a distance of 277km (172 miles) southwest of Copenhagen. To arrive in Jutland, you can use the port of Kolding as your gateway. Driving distance from Copenhagen to Kolding is 208km (129 miles). You can cross the bridge from Funen in the east, then follow Route 161 into Kolding. The final trip from Kolding to Tønder is a distance of 85km (53 miles). From Kolding take Route 25 southwest to

the junction with Route 11, which will carry you to the turnoff for Tønder, reached along Route 419 heading west.

Once in Tønder, check into a hotel for the night and set out to explore the area, whose highlight will be the little village of **Møgeltønder,** lying 4km (2¹/₂ miles) west from Tønder via Route 419.

This charming old-world village is one of the highlights of South Jutland (our coverage begins on p. 315). Back in Tønder, you can wander up and down its old town, taking in its quaintness. Specific visits aren't necessary as it form its appeal, although you might drop into the 16th-century church of **Kristkirken** (p. 312).

Day ❾: Ribe ★★: Nesting Place for Storks

On the morning of **Day 9,** leave Tønder and head north for 47km (29 miles) to **Ribe,** which, like Tønder itself, is one of Denmark's oldest towns. From Tønder, follow Route 11 north all the way. You should arrive in Ribe in time to see all its highlights in 1 day, after checking into a hotel for the night.

Spend 2 or 3 hours exploring its **Gamle Stan** (Old Town), centered on the Torvet, the town's ancient market square. Our full coverage of the sightseeing highlights of Ribe begins on p. 321. Its chief attractions include **Ribe Domkirke,** site of Denmark's earliest wooden church, and the **Ribe VikingeCenter,** 2km (1¼ miles) south of the center, a re-creation of Ribe in the early Middle Ages.

Day ❿: Fanø ★★: Beautiful Island in the North Sea

On the morning of **Day 10,** leave Ribe and drive to the island of **Fanø,** 47km (29 miles) northwest of Ribe. From Ribe, head north on Route 11 to Route 24, which you follow northwest into the city of Esbjerg, where you can board a car ferry to Fanø. Once on the island, check into a hotel for the night, then set out to explore. Our coverage of the attractions of Fanø begins on p. 330. But most motorists will want to skip any of the man-made attractions and devote the rest of the day to exploring this most beautiful of North Sea islands itself. If the weather's fair, try to get in some beach time.

Day ⓫: Silkeborg & the Oldest Man in the World

On the morning of **Day 11,** leave Fanø and return by car ferry to the port of Esbjerg. Head northeast to the city of **Silkeborg,** a distance of 139km (86 miles). From Esbjerg follow Route 12 north. Near the town of Varde it becomes Route 11, which you follow all the way to the junction of Route 15, which takes you due east into Silkeborg.

Once here, check into a hotel for the night. Call first at the **Silkeborg Museum** (p. 356), where you can see the 2,400-year-old "Tollund Man," who was discovered in an amazing state of preservation in a peat bog in 1950. Other attractions include the **Silkeborg Kunstmuseum** (p. 355), one of the finest provincial art museums in Scandinavia, and **AQUA Ferskvands Akvarium** (p. 355), North Europe's largest freshwater aquarium.

Day ⓬ Århus ★★★: "World's Smallest City"

On the morning of **Day 12,** leave Silkeborg and drive 43km (27 miles) to the west, following Route 15. Once at **Århus,** check into a hotel for the night and set about to spend 1 busy day. Because Århus is hard to cover in just 1 day, as it's so much larger than the previous destinations, we suggest you take a 2-hour tour, leaving in summer at 10am and covering all the major highlights. After lunch you can spend another 2 hours wandering **Den Gamle By** (p. 364), an open-air museum of historic buildings. If time remains, pay a visit to the **Århus Kunstmuseum** (p. 363) and the **Århus Domkirke** (p. 363), the cathedral honoring St. Clemens.

Day ⓭ Aalborg ★: Capital of North Jutland

On the morning of **Day 13,** leave Århus heading for **Aalborg,** the largest city in Jutland, a distance of 112km (70 miles) north of Århus. From Århus take the express highway, E45, north into Aalborg, where you can check into a hotel for the night. For the best overview, head for the lookout tower, **Aalborg Tårnet** (p. 385), for a panoramic view of this vast (in Denmark's terms) city. The **Aalborg Zoologiske Have** (p. 386) is usually a must on many a visitor's itinerary, as are stopovers at **Jens Bangs Stenhus** (p. 387) and **Nordjyllands Kunstmuseet** (p. 387), the best museum of modern art in North Jutland. Cap your day with an evening visit to the

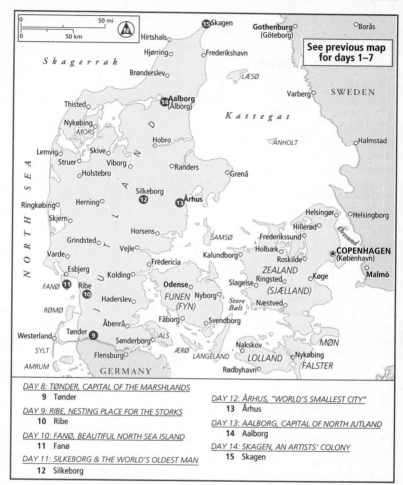

DAY 8: TØNDER, CAPITAL OF THE MARSHLANDS
   9 Tønder

DAY 9: RIBE, NESTING PLACE FOR THE STORKS
   10 Ribe

DAY 10: FANØ, BEAUTIFUL NORTH SEA ISLAND
   11 Fanø

DAY 11: SILKEBORG & THE WORLD'S OLDEST MAN
   12 Silkeborg

DAY 12: ÅRHUS, "WORLD'S SMALLEST CITY"
   13 Århus

DAY 13: AALBORG, CAPITAL OF NORTH JUTLAND
   14 Aalborg

DAY 14: SKAGEN, AN ARTISTS' COLONY
   15 Skagen

major amusement park in the north of Jutland, **Tivoliland** (p. 388). Okay, so it's not as great as Copenhagen's Tivoli Gardens (but, what is?).

Day ⑭ Skagen ★★: An Artists' Colony

On the morning of **Day 14,** leave Aalborg and drive northeast for about 100km (60 miles) to **Skagen,** at the tip of Jutland, where you can check into a hotel for your final night. While enjoying the bracing air of the North Sea, you can set about to explore **Skagen Havn** (p. 403), the colorful harbor, followed by visits to **Den Tilsandede Kirke** (p. 403), an old church mostly buried in the sand dunes. You'll definitely want to visit the **Skagens Museum** (p. 405), the best showcase for the Skagen School of painting that was launched here between the 1870s and the

1900s. If you've finished in time, you can also drive 50km (31 miles) to Hirtshals, a neighboring town, to see the spectacular **Nordsømuseet** (p. 404), an aquarium of North Sea marine life. From Aalborg, you can drive back to Copenhagen, or else return your car in Aalborg if you made arrangements in advance. You can also take a plane or train ride back to the Danish capital for transportation links to the rest of the world.

4 THE ISLANDS OF DENMARK IN 1 WEEK

We've already visited the two major islands of Denmark, both Funen and Zealand, even the peninsula of Jutland. The two tours above have covered all the highlights of the island, even the offshore islands of **Fanø** and **Ærø.** There are many other offshore islands, some of little interest to visitors. But Denmark has some major vacation islands not documented, notably **Bornholm, Møn,** and **Rømø.** We'll visit all of them in this nutshell tour. Except for the longer passage to Bornholm, all of these islands can be quickly reached by causeway or car ferries.

Days ❶ & ❷: Bornholm ★★: Pearl of the Baltic

On the morning of **Day 1,** assuming you've wrapped up your visit to Copenhagen, you can sail over to the island of Bornholm in the Baltic. This is where Copenhageners themselves go for their vacations. From Copenhagen, you can take a 7-hour car ferry to **Bornholm,** where you can check into a hotel for 2 nights, as you will have spent most of Day 1 getting to the island.

On the morning of **Day 2,** you can set out to explore most of the island, which can be easily accomplished in 1 day. Highlights of a visit to the island include the capital of **Rønne,** where you can visit **Ericksson's Gård** (p. 241), a well-preserved 19th-century farmhouse. Other major stopovers include **Svaneke** (p. 251) and **Gudhjem** (p. 253). Pick up a map from the tourist office and plot a day tour to see how much ground you can cover. Complete coverage of Bornholm's highlights is found in chapter 9.

Day ❸: Møn ★★ & its Chalk Cliffs

On the morning of **Day 3,** return to Copenhagen by the 7-hour car ferry. Once in the capital, head south to **Møn,** an island lying off the eastern coast of Zealand, a drive of 130km (81 miles) south of Copenhagen. From Copenhagen, follow the express highway E20 south (it becomes the E47/E55). At the junction with Route 59, follow it east, crossing the Dronning Alexandrines Bridge, which will take you into **Stege,** the capital of Møn. You can overnight here.

Because you won't have time until the following day, you can save the sights of Møn until the morning of Day 4.

Days ❹ & ❺: Ærø ★★★: The Most Beautiful Island

Plan an early-morning visit to **Møns Klint** (p. 234), the famous chalk cliffs on Møn. After a drive around the scenic highlights of the island (our coverage begins on p. 228), you can cross the bridge back onto the island of Zealand. From here you can drive to our next destination, **Ærø,** an island off the southern coast of Funen.

From Stege, drive west along Route 59 to the express highway, E47/E65. Follow it north to E20, cutting west toward the port of Korsør. Once here you can drive across the Great Belt Bridge. In Funen continue along the E20 to the junction of Route 9 going south to **Svendborg.** At Svendborg,

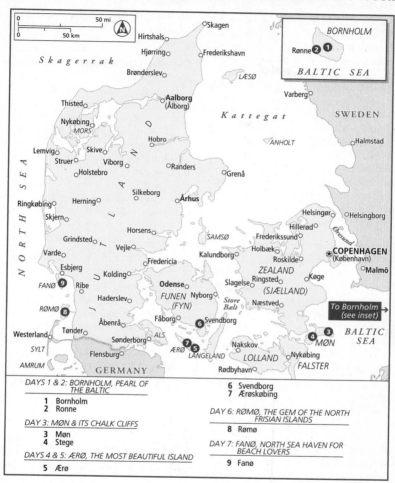

DAYS 1 & 2: BORNHOLM, PEARL OF
THE BALTIC

   1 Bornholm
   2 Ronne

DAY 3: MØN & ITS CHALK CLIFFS

   3 Møn
   4 Stege

DAYS 4 & 5: ÆRØ, THE MOST BEAUTIFUL ISLAND

   5 Ærø

   6 Svendborg
   7 Ærøskøbing

DAY 6: RØMØ, THE GEM OF THE NORTH
FRISIAN ISLANDS

   8 Rømø

DAY 7: FANØ, NORTH SEA HAVEN FOR
BEACH LOVERS

   9 Fanø

you'll be at a point 146km (91 miles) west of Copenhagen. Because the distances are so short, you can hop across the country, going from island to island easily in just 1 day.

From Svendborg take a car ferry to the island of **Ærø,** where you can book into a hotel for 2 nights. You'll need the second night here because you will have spent a good part of 1 day reaching **Ærø** itself.

The best bet for a hotel stay is in the little capital of **Ærøskøbing,** which can easily be explored on foot in the late afternoon of your arrival on the island.

On the morning of **Day 5,** while still based in Ærøskøbing, follow the suggestion for Day 7, as outlined earlier in this chapter, in "Denmark in 1 Week."

Day ❻: Rømø ★: The Gem of North Frisian Islands

On the morning of **Day 6,** leave Ærø, taking the car ferry back to the port of Svendborg. Follow Route 9 north to the junction with express highway E20, heading west to the peninsula of Jutland. Stay on E20 all the way to the city of Esbjerg, on the west coast of Jutland, where you take Route 11 continuing south, cutting west across the causeway leading to the island of **Rømø.** The stone causeway from the mainland is a 10km (6¼-mile) drive. Once at Rømø, you will have come a total distance of 288km (179 miles) southwest from Copenhagen.

Check into a hotel on Rømø and set out for a wild romp on the beach, if the weather's warm and sunny. Like most offshore islands of Denmark, the man-made attractions here hardly compete with the beauty of the island itself. The best sandy beaches are found on the west side of the island.

Day ❼: Fanø ★★: North Sea Haven for Beach Lovers

On the morning of **Day 7,** leave Fanø and cross back over the causeway to the mainland of Jutland. Once here, return to Route 11 heading north toward Ribe. Bypass Ribe, taking Route 24 to the port of Esbjerg. From Esbjerg, a car ferry transports motorists to **Fanø,** where you can check into a hotel for your final night. For more details, see Day 10 for Fanø under "Denmark in 2 Weeks," above.

---

5 DENMARK FOR FAMILIES IN 1 WEEK

Denmark offers many attractions that kids enjoy, none more notable than the Tivoli Gardens in Copenhagen. Perhaps your main concern with having children along is pacing yourself with museum time. Our suggestion is to explore **Copenhagen** for 2 days with family in tow, then spend Day 3 visiting "Hamlet's Castle" in the north. Then head over to the island of Funen, centering at its capital, **Odense,** birthplace of Hans Christian Andersen, whose work is known to children around the world because of his massive number of foreign translations. Finally, we go to Jutland, which is Denmark's mainland link to the continent (via Germany). Here we visit its two major attractions, **Århus** and **Aalborg,** both containing Tivoli-like amusement parks of their own, plus numerous other attractions.

Days ❶ & ❷: Arrival in Copenhagen ★★★

Before renting a car to explore the countryside, you can take in the glories of Copenhagen itself, the most kid-friendly of all Scandinavia capitals. After your arrival and after you've checked into a hotel for 2 nights, take one of the bus and boat tours to orient yourself. See "Organized Tours" (p. 148). Follow this up with a guided tour of **Amalienborg Palace** (p. 124), where Queen Margrethe II lives with her royal family. After lunch, descend on the **Tivoli Gardens** (p. 156), where you and your kids can wander for hours and also eat dinner.

On the morning of **Day 2,** pay a call on **Den Lille Havfrue** (*The Little Mermaid;* p. 128), the most photographed statue in Scandinavia. After that, explore **Ny Carlsberg Glyptotek** (p. 121), one of the greatest art museums in Europe. If your child is older, he or she will find much art to fascinate here, perhaps a prehistoric sculpture of a hippopotamus. In the afternoon, visit **Frilandsmuseet** (p. 139), an open-air museum and reconstructed village that evokes life in the 19th century, lying at Lyngby on the fringe of Copenhagen.

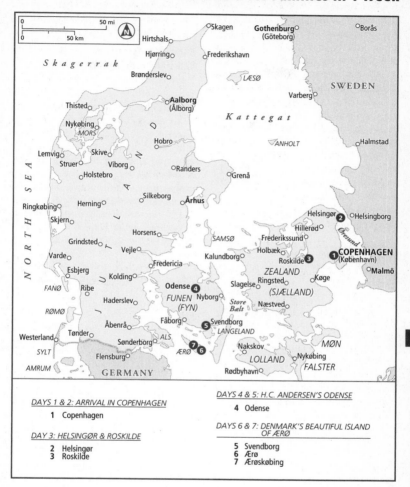

DAYS 1 & 2: ARRIVAL IN COPENHAGEN
  1 Copenhagen

DAY 3: HELSINGØR & ROSKILDE
  2 Helsingør
  3 Roskilde

DAYS 4 & 5: H.C. ANDERSEN'S ODENSE
  4 Odense

DAYS 6 & 7: DENMARK'S BEAUTIFUL ISLAND OF ÆRØ
  5 Svendborg
  6 Ærø
  7 Ærøskøbing

When you return to Copenhagen, you can do as many families do and pay a final visit to **Tivoli Gardens,** or else you can visit another amusement park, **Bakken** (p. 140), on the northern fringe of the city. If you like merry-go-rounds and roller coasters, Bakken is even more fun for some families than the more carefully manicured Tivoli.

Day ❸: Helsingør ★ & Roskilde ★★
On the morning of **Day 3,** check out of your hotel and drive 40km (25 miles) north of Copenhagen, taking the E4 express highway. Once at Helsingør, you can pay a morning visit to the Dutch-Renaissance–style **Kronborg Castle,** legendary home of Shakespeare's fictional Hamlet. Kids may think that Walt Disney created this dank, spooky place, which is surrounded by a deep moat.

After a 1-hour visit, you can head for our final destination of the day, the cathedral city of **Roskilde,** lying 72km (45 miles) southwest. It's reached by following Route 6 all the way. Check into a hotel in Roskilde for the day and set about to explore this ancient city. Call first at the **Roskilde Domkirke** (p. 196). Kids delight in seeing the 16th-century clock where a tiny sculpted St. George on horseback marks the hour by charging a dragon. Afterward, drive 20km (12 miles) north of Roskilde to see the **Viking Ship Museum** (p. 199), displaying the remains of five wrecked Viking-era ships. Return to Roskilde for the night.

Days ❹ & ❺: H. C. Andersen's Odense ★★

On the morning of **Day 4,** drive west from Roskilde for 134km (83 miles) until you reach Odense. To do so, you have to cross the Great Belt Bridge into Nyborg, lying west on the Funen side. From Nyborg, E20 will carry you to Odense, where you can check into a hotel for 2 nights. In Odense, follow the same family-friendly itinerary as outlined in Days 3 and 4 under "Denmark in 1 Week" (earlier in this chapter).

Days ❻ & ❼: Denmark's Beautiful Island of Ærø ★★★

Leave Odense on the morning of **Day 6,** driving south to Svendborg, a distance of 43km (27 miles), following Route 9. Once at Svendborg, take a car ferry over to the island of Ærø, a distance of 29km (18 miles) from Svendborg. Once here, check into a hotel in the tiny island's capital, **Ærøskøbing,** for 2 nights and set about to explore this Lilliputian town, with a driving tour of the island to follow on Day 7.

Use the same family-friendly itinerary as outlined under **Days 6 and 7,** under "Denmark in 1 Week" (earlier in this chapter).

After a visit to Ærø, you can easily return to Copenhagen the following day, using a bridge and a ferryboat. Copenhagen lies 176km (109 miles) to the east of Ærø.

Settling into Copenhagen

Like Mighty Mouse, Denmark may be small but it packs a powerful punch. Its capital, Copenhagen, seems to be the seat of everything Danish—artistic, financial, and political.

But Copenhagen still remains the "fun" capital of Scandinavia—and also the most affordable—and the Danes continue to practice their own *joie de vivre*. There is an enthusiasm for life here that always sweeps us up in its spell.

The city continues to change. Middle Eastern restaurants now compete with old-fashioned eateries serving food that Grandmother Denmark used to cook. Internet cafes have become the rendezvous point of choice for young Danes instead of the traditional sudsy taverns beloved by their parents. The city isn't as safe as it used to be: Crime and drugs are on the rise. In other words, welcome to the modern world.

But some things never change. Many Copenhageners still bike to work along the city's canals. We still join the locals who follow their noses to the cafes where the smell of freshly baked bread lures us in for a morning Danish and a cup of freshly brewed coffee. Along the way, we still pass that little old shopkeeper out soaping down his glass windows.

Copenhagen, the capital of Denmark, got its name from the word *køben-havn,* which means "merchants' harbor." It grew in size and importance because of its position on the Øresund (the Sound), the body of water between Denmark and Sweden, guarding the strategic passage of all maritime traffic heading into or out of the Baltic.

From its humble beginnings, Copenhagen has become the largest city in Scandinavia, home to 1.8 million people, the seat of one of the oldest kingdoms in the world.

Over the centuries, Copenhagen has suffered more than its share of invasions and disasters. In the 17th century, the Swedes repeatedly besieged it, and in the 18th century, it endured the plague and two devastating fires. The British attacked twice during the Napoleonic wars in the early 1800s. In 1940, the Nazis invaded Denmark and held onto Copenhagen until 1945, when the British army moved in again, this time as liberators.

Copenhagen is a city with much charm, as reflected in its canals, narrow streets, and old houses. Its most famous resident was Hans Christian Andersen, whose memory lives on. Another of Copenhagen's world-renowned inhabitants was Søren Kierkegaard, who used to take long morning strolls in the city, planning his next addition to the collection of essays that eventually earned him the title "father of existentialism."

In 2000, the Øresund Bridge was officially opened, physically linking Sweden and Denmark for the first time. Today there's a 15km (9$\frac{1}{3}$-mile) car and train link between Zealand (the eastern part of Denmark, the island on which Copenhagen sits) and Skane (the southern part of Sweden). If you'd like to link a visit with Copenhagen to Malmö, Copenhagen's fast-growing counterpart across the border in Sweden, or perhaps visit some of the châteaus of southern Sweden, just drive across the bridge.

Copenhagen still retains some of the characteristics of a village. If you ignore the suburbs, you can cover most of the central belt on foot. It's almost as if the city were designed for strolling, as reflected by its Strøget, the longest and oldest pedestrians-only street in Europe.

1 ORIENTATION

GETTING THERE

BY PLANE   You arrive at **Kastrup Airport** (© 32-31-32-31; www.cph.dk), 12km (7¹/₂ miles) from the center of Copenhagen. Air-rail trains link the airport with the Central Railway Station in the center of Copenhagen. The ride takes 13 minutes, and costs DKK27 ($4.60/£2.70). Located right under the airport's Arrivals and Departures halls, the Air Rail Terminal is a short escalator ride from the gates. You can also take an SAS bus to the city terminal; the fare is DKK26 ($4.40/£2.60). A taxi to the city center costs DKK180 to DKK220 ($31–$37/£18–£22).

BY TRAIN   Trains arrive at the **HovedBanegården** (Central Railway Station; © 70-13-14-15 for rail information), in the center of Copenhagen, near Tivoli Gardens and the Rådhuspladsen. The station operates a luggage-checking service, but room bookings are available only at the tourist office (see "Visitor Information," below).

From the Central Railway Station, you can connect with the **S-tog**, a local train; trains depart from platforms in the terminal itself. The information desk is near tracks 5 and 6.

BY BUS   Buses from Zealand and elsewhere pull into the Central Railway Station. For bus information, call © 36-13-14-15 daily 7am to 9:30pm.

BY CAR   If you're driving from Germany, a car ferry will take you from Travemünde to Gedser in southern Denmark. From Gedser, get on E55 north, an express highway that will deliver you to the southern outskirts of Copenhagen. If you're coming from Sweden via the Øresund Bridge, it will deposit you on the city's eastern outskirts, close to Kastrup airport. From here, it's a short drive into the center.

VISITOR INFORMATION

The **Copenhagen Tourist Information Center,** Vesterbrogade 4A (© 70-22-24-42; www.visitcopenhagen.dk), adjacent to the main entrance of Tivoli, dispenses information. It's open in July and August, Monday to Saturday 9am to 8pm; May and June, Monday to Saturday 9am to 6pm; September to April, Monday to Friday 9am to 4pm, Saturday 9am to 2pm.

CITY LAYOUT

MAIN ARTERIES & STREETS   The heart of Old Copenhagen is a warren of pedestrian streets, bounded by Nørreport Station to the north, Rådhuspladsen (Town Hall Square) to the west, and Kongens Nytorv, a busy square that's positioned at the top of the Nyhavn Canal, to the east. **Strøget,** the longest continuous pedestrian-only route in Europe, goes east from Town Hall Square to Kongens Nytorv, and is made up of five interconnected streets: Frederiksberggade, Nygade, Vimmelskaftet, Amagertorv, and Østergade. Strøget is lined with shops, bars, restaurants, pizza parlors, and, in summer, sidewalk cafes. **Pistolstræde** contains a maze of galleries, restaurants, and boutiques, housed in restored 18th-century buildings.

Fiolstræde (Violet St.), a dignified street with antiques shops and bookshops, cuts through the university (Latin Quarter). If you turn into Rosengaarden, at the top of Fiolstræde, you'll come to **Kultorvet** (Coal Square), just before you reach Nørreport Station. Here you join the third main pedestrian street, **Købmagergade** (Butcher St.), which winds around and finally meets Strøget at Amagertorv.

At the end of Strøget, you approach **Kongens Nytorv** (King's Square). This is the site of the Royal Theater and Magasin, the largest department store in Copenhagen. This will put you at the beginning of **Nyhavn,** the former seamen's quarter that has been gentrified into an upmarket area of expensive restaurants, apartments, cafes, and boutiques.

The government of Denmark has been centered, for the past 800 years, on the small and very central downtown island of **Slotsholmen,** which is connected to the center by eight different bridges. The island's most immediately visible attraction is the imperial-looking granite mass of Christiansborg Castle, home of the Danish parliament, the prime minister's offices, the country's Supreme Court, and several museums.

The center of Copenhagen is **Rådhuspladsen** (Town Hall Square). From here it's a short walk to the Tivoli Gardens, the major attraction of Copenhagen; the Central Railway Station; and the Bus Station terminus. **Vesterbrogade,** a wide, densely trafficked boulevard, passes by Tivoli en route to the Central Railway Station. **H. C. Andersens Boulevard,** a major avenue named after Denmark's most famous writer, runs beside the Rådhuspladsen and Tivoli Gardens.

FINDING AN ADDRESS All even numbers are on one side of the street, all odd numbers on the other. Buildings are listed in numerical order. A, B, or C is often inserted after the street number.

NEIGHBORHOODS IN BRIEF

For a map of Copenhagen, see p. 78.

Tivoli Gardens Steeped in nostalgia, these amusement gardens were built in 1843 on the site of former fortifications in the heart of Copenhagen, on the south side of Rådhuspladsen. Some 160,000 flowers and 110,000 electric lights set the tone, and a collection of restaurants, dance halls, theaters, beer gardens, and lakes attracts many thousands of visitors every year.

Strøget This pedestrian-only urban walkway stretches between Rådhuspladsen and Kongens Nytorv, two of the city's most visible and busiest plazas. En route along its trajectory are two spectacular, although smaller, squares, Gammeltorv and Nytorv, "old" and "new" squares, which seem to blossom during the warm-weather months with outdoor seating—extensions of the many restaurants that line its edges. The word "Strøget" usually doesn't appear on maps. Instead, Strøget encompasses five interconnected streets: Frederiksberggade, Nygade, Villelskaftet, Amagertorv, and Østergade.

Nyhavn/Kongens Nytorv Nyhavn ("New Harbor") was originally conceived in the 1670s by the Danish king as a shelter from the storms of the North and Baltic Sea, and as a means of hauling building supplies into central Copenhagen. Nyhavn today is the site of a denser concentration of restaurants than any other neighborhood in Copenhagen. Moored beside its granite embankments, you'll see old or even antique fishing boats, some of which remain in place to preserve the sense of old-fashioned nostalgia. For many generations, Nyhavn was the haunt of sailors looking for tattoos, cheap drinks, and other diversions. Nowadays it's one of the most obviously gentrified sections of the city, with outdoor terraces that are mobbed during warm-weather months with chattering, sometimes hard-drinking Danes on holiday. At the top, or western terminus, of the Nyhavn canal is the five-sided Kongens Nytorv (King's New Market), site of the deluxe Hotel d'Angleterre and the Royal Theater.

Indre By This is the Old Town, the heart of Copenhagen. Once filled with monasteries, it's a maze of streets, alleyways, and squares. The neighborhood around Gammeltorv and Nørregade, sometimes called "The Latin Quarter," contains many buildings linked with the university. The **Vor Frue Kirke** (cathedral of Copenhagen) is here, as is the **Rundetårn** (Round Tower).

Slotsholmen This island, site of Christiansborg Palace, was where Bishop Absalon built Copenhagen's first fortress in 1167. Today it's the seat of the Danish parliament and home of Thorvaldsen's Museum. Bridges link Slotsholmen to Indre By. You can also visit the Royal Library (site of a recent hypermodern new wing described as the "Black Diamond"), the Theater Museum, and the Royal Stables. The 17th-century Børsen (stock exchange) is also here.

Christianshavn Set on the opposite side of Copenhagen's harbor from the rest of the city, this was the "new town" ordered by master builder King Christian IV in the early 1500s. The town was originally constructed in the Dutch Renaissance style to house workers in the shipbuilding industry. Visitors come today mainly to see the Danish Film Museum, on Store Søndervoldstræde, and **Vors Frelsers Kirke,** on the corner of Prinsessegade and Skt. Annægade. Sightseers can climb the spire of the old

church for a panoramic view. Within the Christianshavn district is the offbeat community of **Christiania.** In 1971, many young and homeless people moved in, without the city's permission, proclaiming Christiania a "free city" (that is, partially exempt from the rules and regulations of the Danish government) within the orbit of Greater Copenhagen. It has been a freewheeling and controversial place ever since.

Once filled with barracks for soldiers, Christiania is within walking distance of Vor Frelsers Kirke at Christianshavn. You can enter the area on Prinsessegade. The craft shops and restaurants here are fairly cheap because the residents refuse to pay Denmark's crippling 25% sales tax.

Vesterbro Once a hotbed slum loaded with junkies and prostitutes, Vesterbro would be comparable to the East Village or Williamsburg in New York City. Its main street, **Istedgade,** runs west from the Central Railway Station. Don't come here for monuments or museums, but for hip cafes, bars, music, and ethnic restaurants. No longer a slum, Vesterbro's sense of newfound hipness centers on the cafes and bars around the Halmtorvet, Vesterbro's main square. Expect gentrification but also cultural diversity such as Turkish-Kurdish gift shops, food markets loaded with fruits you might not immediately recognize, barbers from Istanbul, and, from time to time, a sex shop like those that proliferated here during the '70s and '80s.

Nørrebro Adjacent to Vesterbro (see above), Nørrebro takes the immigrant overflow, and is also rich in artisan shops and ethnic restaurants, especially Turkish and Pakistani. This area has been a blue-collar neighborhood since the middle of the 19th century. The original Danish settlers have long since departed, replaced by immigrants who are not always greeted with a friendly reception in Copenhagen. The area also abounds with trend-conscious artists, students, and musicians, who can't afford the high rents elsewhere. Numerous secondhand clothing stores—especially around Sankt Hans Torv—give Nørrebro the flavor of a Middle Eastern bazaar. Antiques shops (believe us, many of the furnishings and objets d'art aren't authentic) also fill the area. Most of these "antiques" stores lie along Ravnsborgade. The district is also home to a historic cemetery, Assistens Kirkegård, burial ground of both Hans Christian Andersen and Søren Kierkegaard, just to the west of Nørrebrogade. If you're looking for the densest concentrations of the nightlife that the district has become famous for, head for either **Sankt Hans Torv** or **Blågårdsgade.**

Frederiksberg Heading west of the inner city along Vesterbrogade, you will reach the residential and business district of Frederiksberg. It grew up around **Frederiksberg Palace,** constructed in the Italianate style, with an ocher facade. A park, Frederiksberg Have, surrounds the palace. To the west of the palace is the **Zoologisk Have,** one of the largest zoos in Europe.

Dragør Dragør is a fishing village south of the city that dates from the 16th century. Along with Tivoli, this seems to be everybody's favorite leisure spot. It's especially recommended for its aura of an 18th-century Danish village, if you only have time to see the Copenhagen area. Walk its cobblestone streets and enjoy its 65 old red-roofed houses, designated as national landmarks.

2 GETTING AROUND

Copenhagen is a walker's paradise, neat and compact. Many of the major sightseeing attractions are close to one another.

BY PUBLIC TRANSPORTATION

A joint zone fare system includes Copenhagen Transport buses; State Railway, Metro, and S-tog trains in Copenhagen and North Zealand; and some private railway routes within a 40km (25-mile) radius of the capital, enabling you to transfer from train to bus and vice versa with the same ticket.

BASIC FARES A *grundbillet* (basic ticket) for buses and trains costs DKK15 ($2.60/£1.50). Up to two children, age 11 and under, ride for half fare when accompanied by an adult. For DKK90 ($15/£9), you can purchase a ticket allowing 24-hour bus and train travel through nearly half of Zealand; it's half-price for children 7 to 11, and free for children 6 and under.

DISCOUNT PASSES The **Copenhagen Card** (www.copenhagencard.dk) entitles you to free and unlimited travel by bus and rail throughout the metropolitan area (including North Zealand), 25% to 50% discounts on crossings to and from Sweden, and free admission to many sights and museums. The card is available for 1 or 3 days and costs DKK199 ($34/£20) and DKK429 ($73/£43), respectively. Up to two children under the age of 10 are allowed to go free with each adult card. Otherwise, children ages 10 to 15 pay DKK129 ($22/£13) and DKK299 ($51/£30) for 1 or 3 days. Buy the card at tourist offices, at the airport, at train stations, and at most hotels. For more information, contact the Copenhagen Tourist Information Center (see the previous section, "Orientation") or click on **www.cphcard.com.**

For information about low-cost train, ferry, and plane trips, go to **Wasteels,** Skoubogade 6 (© **33-14-46-33**), in Copenhagen. It's open Monday to Friday 9am to 5pm and Saturday 10am to 3pm.

Eurailpasses (which must be purchased in the U.S.) and **Nordturist Pass** tickets (which can be purchased at any train station in Scandinavia) can be used on local trains in Copenhagen. (For a more complete discussion of the cost/use of these passes, see p. 33.)

BY BUS Copenhagen's well-maintained buses are the least expensive method of getting around, and most buses leave from Rådhuspladsen in the heart of the city. A basic ticket allows 1 hour of travel and unlimited transfers within the zone where you started your trip. For information, call © **36-13-14-15.**

BY METRO In 2002, Copenhagen launched its first Metro line, taking passengers from east to west across the city or vice versa. Operating 24 hours, the Metro links the western and eastern sections of Copenhagen to the center. Eventually, when completed, the Metro will run all the way to the airport. Nørreport is the transfer station to the **S-tog** system, the commuter rail link to the suburbs. Metro trains run every 2 minutes during rush hours and every 15 minutes at night. Fares are integrated into the existing zonal systems (see "Basic Fares," above).

BY S-TOG The S-tog connects the heart of Copenhagen, most notably the Central Station, with the city's suburbs. Use of the tickets is the same as on buses (see "Basic Fares," above). You can transfer from a bus line to an S-tog train on the same ticket. Eurailpass holders generally ride free. For more information, call © **70-13-14-15.**

BY CAR

Because of the widespread availability of traffic-free walkways in Copenhagen, and its many parks, gardens, and canalside promenades, the Danish capital is well suited to pedestrian promenades. It's best to park your car in any of the dozens of city parking lots, then retrieve it when you're ready to explore the suburbs or countryside. Many parking lots are open 24 hours, but a few close between 1 and 7am; some close on Saturday afternoon and on Sunday, when traffic is generally lighter. The cost ranges from DKK9 to DKK26 ($1.60–$4.40/90p–£2.60) per hour. Two centrally located parking lots are **Industriens Hus,** H. C. Andersens Blvd. 18 (© **33-91-21-75**), open Monday to Friday 7am to midnight, Saturday 9am to 1am, Sunday 9am to midnight; and **Park City,** Israels Plads (© **70-22-92-20**), open daily from 6am to midnight for entry. (You can exit from this facility any time, 24 hr. a day.) For more information about parking in Copenhagen, call © **47-70-80-80-90** or go online to www.parking.dk.

BY TAXI

Watch for the FRI (free) sign or green light to hail a taxi, and be sure the taxis are metered. **Taxa 4x35** (© **35-35-35-35**) operates the largest fleet of cabs. Tips are included in the meter price: DKK19 to DKK32 ($3.30–$5.50/£1.90–£3.20) at the drop of the flag and DKK12 ($2.10/£1.20) per kilometer (about ²/₃ mile) thereafter, Monday to Friday 7am to 4pm. From 6pm to 6am, and all day Saturday and Sunday, the cost is DKK15 ($2.60/£1.50) per kilometer. Many drivers speak English.

BY BICYCLE

To reduce pollution from cars (among other reasons), many Copenhageners ride bicycles. In her younger days, even the queen of Denmark could be seen cycling around just like her subjects. You can rent a bike at **Københavns Cyklebors,** Gothersgade 157 (© **33-14-07-17**). Depending on the bike, daily rates range from DKK60 to DKK150 ($10–$26/£6–£15), with deposits from DKK200 to DKK300 ($34–$51/£20–£30). Hours are Monday to Friday 8:30am to 5:30pm and Saturday 10am to 1:30pm.

⟨Fast Facts⟩ Copenhagen

American Express Amex is represented throughout Denmark by **Nyman & Schultz,** Nørregade 7A (© **33-13-11-81;** bus: 34 or 35), with a branch in Terminal 3 of the Copenhagen Airport. Fulfilling all the functions of American Express, except for foreign exchange services, the main office is open Monday to Thursday 8:30am to 4:30pm, and Friday 8:30am to 4pm. The airport office remains open until 8:30pm Monday to Friday. On weekends, and overnight on weekdays, a recorded message, in English, will deliver the phone number of a 24-hour Amex service in Stockholm. This is useful for anyone who has lost a card or traveler's checks.

Bookstores One of the best and most centrally located is **Politikens Boghallen,** Rådhuspladsen 37 (© **33-47-25-60;** www.boghallen.dk; bus: 2, 8, or 30), offering more English titles than its competitors. Hours are Monday to Friday 10am to 7pm, and Saturday 10am to 4pm.

Business Hours Most **banks** are open Monday to Friday 10am to 4pm (to 6pm Thurs). **Stores** are generally open Monday to Thursday 9am to 6pm, Friday 9am to 7 or 8pm, and Saturday 9am to 2pm; most are closed Sunday. **Offices** are open Monday to Friday 9 or 10am to 4 or 5pm.

Currency Exchange Banks give better rates than currency kiosks. The main branch of Den Danske Bank (The Danish Bank), Holmens Kanal, 2–12 (© **33-44-00-00**), is open Monday to Friday from 10am to 4pm (to 5:30pm Thurs). When banks are closed, you can exchange money at **Forex** (© **33-11-29-05**) in the Central Railway Station, daily 8am to 10pm, or at the **Change Group,** Østergade 61 (© **33-93-04-55;** bus: 9 or 10), daily 8:30am to 8:15pm.

Dentists During regular business hours, ask your hotel to call the nearest English-speaking dentist. For emergencies, go to **Tandlægevagten,** Oslo Plads 14 (© **35-38-02-51;** bus: 6 or 9), near Østerport Station and the U.S. Embassy. It's open Monday to Friday 8am to 9:30pm and Saturday, Sunday, and holidays 10am to noon. Be prepared to pay in cash.

Doctors To reach a doctor, dial © **38-11-40-00** 24 hours a day (www.copenhagen doctors.dk). The doctor's fee is payable in cash and visits cost DKK1,400 ($238/£140) per visit from Monday to Friday 8am to 4pm and DKK1,800 ($306/£180) all other times. The doctor will arrive within 45 minutes and provide most medication. Language is hardly a problem in Denmark, where virtually all doctors speak English.

Emergencies Dial © **112** to report a fire or to call the police or an ambulance. State your phone number and address. Emergency calls from public telephones are free (no coins needed).

Hospitals   In cases of illness or accident, even foreigners are entitled to free medical treatment in Denmark. One of the most centrally located hospitals is **Rigshospitalet,** Blegdamsvej 9 (© **35-45-35-45;** bus: 10).

Internet Access   To check your e-mail or to send messages, go to **Copenhagen Hovedbibliotek,** Krystalgade 15 (© **33-73-60-60;** bus: 5, 14, or 16), open Monday to Friday 10am to 7pm, Saturday 10am to 2pm.

Lost Property   The Lost and Found Property office at Slotsherrensvej 113, 2720 Vanløse (© **38-74-88-22;** bus: 12 or 22), is open Monday, Wednesday, and Friday 9am to 2pm, Tuesday and Thursday 9am to 5:30pm.

Luggage Storage & Lockers   Luggage can be stored in lockers at Central Railway Station. Lockers are accessible Monday to Saturday 5:30am to 1am and Sunday 6am to 1am. The cost is DKK30 to DKK40 ($5.10–$6.80/£3–£4) for 24 hours, depending on the size of your luggage.

Newspapers   Foreign newspapers, particularly the *International Herald Tribune* and *USA Today,* are available at the Central Railway Station in front of the Palladium movie theater on Vesterbrogade, at many newspaper kiosks on Strøget, and at the newsstands of big hotels. Foreign fashion and lifestyle magazines are also widely sold.

Pharmacies   An *apotek* (pharmacy) open 24 hours a day is **Steno Apotek,** Vesterbrogade 6C (© **33-14-82-66;** bus: 6), lying opposite the Central Railway Station.

Police   In an emergency, dial © **112.** For other matters, go to the police station at Halmtorvet 20 (© **33-25-14-48**).

Post Office   For information about the Copenhagen post office, phone © **80-20-70-30.** The main post office, where your *poste restante* (general delivery) letters can be picked up, is located at Tietgensgade 37, DK-1704 København (© **80-20-70-30;** bus: 10 or 46). It's open Monday to Friday 11am to 6pm and Saturday 10am to 1pm. The post office at the Central Railway Station is open Monday to Friday 8am to 9pm, Saturday 9am to 4pm, and Sunday 10am to 4pm.

Safety   Compared with other European capital cities, Copenhagen is relatively safe. However, since the early 1990s, with the increase of homelessness and unemployment, crime has risen. Guard your wallet, purse, and other valuables as you would when traveling in any big city.

Taxes   Throughout Denmark you'll come across MOMS on your bills, a government-imposed value-added tax of 25%. It's included in hotel and restaurant bills, service charges, entrance fees, and repair of foreign-registered cars. No refunds are given on these items. For more information, see "Shopping," in chapter 6.

Toilets   Public toilets are at Rådhuspladsen (Town Hall Square), at the Central Railway Station, and at all terminals. Look for the signs TOILETTER, WC, DAMER (women), or HERRER (men). There is no charge.

Transit Information   Day or night, phone © **70-13-14-15** for bus, Metro, and S-tog information.

High season in Denmark is May to September, which pretty much coincides with the schedule at Tivoli Gardens. Once Tivoli closes for the winter, lots of rooms become available. Make sure to ask about winter discounts, and ask if breakfast is included (usually it isn't).

Nearly all doubles come with a private bathroom. Find out, though, whether this means a shower or a tub. At moderate and inexpensive hotels, you can save money by requesting a room without a bathroom. Keep in mind that in most moderate and nearly all of the inexpensive hotels, bathrooms are cramped, and there's never enough room to spread out all of your stuff. Many were added to older buildings that weren't designed for bathrooms. Also, get used to towels that are much thinner than you might like—not the thick, fluffy types always demanded by Frank Sinatra when he checked into a hotel anywhere in the world.

Several moderately priced hotels in Copenhagen are known as **mission hotels;** they were originally founded by a temperance society, but now about half of them are fully licensed to serve alcohol. They tend to cater to middle-class families.

RESERVATIONS SERVICE At Bernstorffsgade 1, across from the Tivoli's main entrance, the Tourist Information Center maintains a useful hotel-booking service, **Værelsænvisningen** (*C* **70-22-24-42**). In person, the charge, whether you book into a private home, a hostel, or a luxury hotel, is DKK100 ($17/£10) per person. This fee is waived when booking by telephone or Internet. You'll also be given a city map and bus directions. This particular office doesn't accept advance reservations; it can arrange private accommodations if the hotels in your price range are already full. The office is open April 19 to September 30, daily 9am to 9pm, and October to April 18, Monday to Friday 9am to 5pm and Saturday 9am to 2pm.

In the same building is another service—the **Hotel Booking Service** (*C* **70-22-24-42;** www.hotel.denmark.com)—that will reserve hotel rooms in advance.

NEAR KONGENS NYTORV & NYHAVN

Once the home of sailor bars and tattoo parlors, Nyhavn is now a chic, up-and-coming section of Copenhagen. The central canal, filled with 19th-century boats and the 18th-century facades of the buildings around it, contributes to the area's evocative ambience.

Very Expensive

Hotel d'Angleterre ★★★ **Kids** With 250 years of history, the d'Angleterre is one of the oldest deluxe bastions in the world, although it's kept abreast of the times with modern comforts. The seven-story property at the top of Nyhavn is a member of the Leading Hotels of the World. It was built as a private club for English merchants before its transformation into a hotel in 1805. Hans Christian Andersen was among the first celebrity guests. The midsize-to-spacious bedrooms are beautifully furnished in a medley of styles. We prefer the Empire and Louis XVI rooms, though you may opt for the conservatively modern. Each high-ceilinged bedroom comes with a private marble bathroom. The deluxe rooms are in front; those facing the courtyard are smaller but more tranquil.

Kongens Nytorv 34, DK-1050 København. *C* **33-12-00-95.** Fax 33-12-11-18. www.remmen.dk. 123 units. DKK3,060–DKK4,300 ($520–$731/£306–£430) double; from DKK5,530 ($940/£553) suite. AE, DC, MC, V. Parking DKK400 ($68/£40). Bus: 1, 6, or 9. **Amenities:** Restaurant; bar; indoor heated pool; fitness center;

Absalon Hotel og
  Absalon Annex **23**
Ascot Hotel **10**
Avenue Hotel **1**
AXEL Hotel
  Guldsmeden **21**
Bertram Hotel
  Guldsmeden **13**
Carlton Hotel
  Gudlsmeden **12**
City Hotel Nebo **20**
Clarion Collection
  Hotel Neptun **40**
Clarion Collection
  Mayfair **16**
Comfort Hotel
  Esplanaden **43**
Copenhagen Admiral
  Hotel **42**
Copenhagen Crown **14**
Copenhagen Island
  Hotel **28**
Copenhagen Plaza **19**
Copenhagen Strand **37**
CPH Living **30**
Danhostel Copenhagen
  City **31**
DGI-byen's Hotel **26**
First Hotel Vesterbro **15**
Front Hotel
  Copenhagen **41**
Grand Hotel **17**
Hotel Alexandra **9**
Hotel Ansgar **25**
Hotel d'Angleterre **34**
Hotel Fox **5**
Hotel Jørgensen **4**
Hotel Opera **35**
Hotel Selandia **22**
Hotel Skt. Petri **33**
Hotel 27 **32**
Ibsens Hotel **3**
Kong Arthur **2**
Kong Frederik **6**
Maritime **36**
Marriott Copenhagen **27**
Phoenix Copenhagen **39**
Radisson SAS Royal **18**

Radisson SAS
  Scandinavian Hotel **29**
Saga Hotel **24**
Scandic Copenhagen **11**
Scandic Palace Hotel **7**
71 Nyhavn **38**
The Square **8**

(i) Information
✉ Post office
--ⓢ-- S-Tog (S-Train)
----Ⓜ---- Metro
═══ Pedestrians-
      only streets

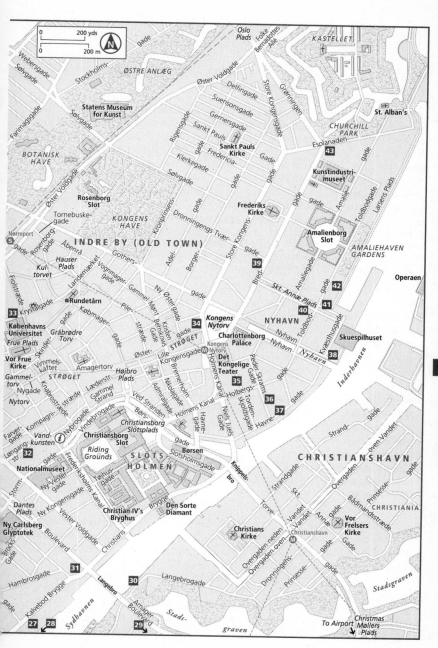

spa; sauna; room service; babysitting; laundry service; dry cleaning; nonsmoking rooms. *In room:* A/C, TV, Wi-Fi, minibar, hair dryer, safe.

Expensive

Clarion Collection Hotel Neptun ★

The dream of this place never quite came true. Founded in 1854, the hotel was meant to be the gathering place for the bohemian and literati set. These days, commercial clients, a scattering of tourists, and even tour groups dominate the client list, but the main lounge still evokes an upper-crust living room in an English country house, with its traditional furnishings and even a chess table. Many of the bedrooms open onto two covered interior courtyards, adding a little glamour to the joint. Ask for one of the bedrooms that open onto a courtyard, as they are the brightest during the day and the most tranquil in the evening. Bedrooms are tastefully furnished in a modern style, and most of them are either small or midsize. Another feature of the hotel is an outdoor terrace on the sixth floor where you can order drinks in the summer. Some bright young chefs operate the hotel's restaurant, lying next door. **The Gendarmen** offers a seasonally adjusted menu that respects traditional Danish recipes but prepares many of them with a lighter touch.

Skt. Annæ Plads 18–20, DK-1250 København. © **877/424-6423** or 33-96-20-00. Fax 33-96-20-66. www.clarionhotel.com. 133 units. DKK2,295–DKK2,595 ($390–$441/£230–£260) double; DKK2,700 ($459/£270) suite. Rates include breakfast. AE, DC, MC, V. Parking DKK270 ($46/£27). Bus: 1, 6, 9, or 19. **Amenities:** Restaurant; bar; room service; babysitting; laundry service; dry cleaning; nonsmoking rooms. *In room:* A/C, TV, dataport (in some), Wi-Fi, minibar, hair dryer, safe.

Front Hotel Copenhagen ★

From the outside, this boxy-looking building might remind you of the rash of angular modern construction that blossomed throughout Central Europe during the Cold War. On the inside, however, it's one of the hottest and most appealing hotels in town, enjoying a connection with the nearby Hotel d'Angleterre, and a location close to the very central Nyhavn Canal. Throughout, the decor is minimalist and somewhat self-consciously linked to the Spartan-looking heyday of Denmark's modern design movement. In fact, it's so minimalist that some parts of it, including the lobby area, might remind you of a college dormitory. Bedrooms benefit from very large windows, high-quality Danish modern furniture, lots of sunlight, and panoramic views, and are accessible via the hotel's only really visible drawback—small, awkwardly configured elevators that are simply too cramped for the amount of use they get. Bedrooms contain furniture, some of it upholstered with black leather, that evoke the best in post-millennium design.

Skt. Annæ Plads 21, P.O. Box 9076, DK-1022 København. © **33-13-34-00.** Fax 33-11-77-07. www.front.dk. 31 units. DKK1,700–DKK4,980 ($289–$847/£170–£498) double. AE, DC, MC, V. Metro: Kongens Nytorv. **Amenities:** Restaurant; bar; health club and exercise area; laundry service; dry cleaning. *In room:* A/C, TV, Wi-Fi, minibar.

Hotel Skt. Petri ★★★

For the world's fashionistas and interior designers, this is a mandatory stopover. Since the 1930s, the site of this hotel was the much-loved department store Dalle Valle. Today, in a reincarnation, it's become one of the grandest hotels in Copenhagen. Modern Danish design, as interpreted by interior designer Per Arnoldi, is showcased here. Rooms are individually done in a minimalist yet elegant style, with bright, cheerful colors and such touches as Mondrian-inspired headboards. Opt for a double with terrace on the fifth or sixth floors. The ceilings in most rooms are a bit low, but the lobby rises three floors, embracing an atrium garden. Musicians, artists, and designers are among those we've seen in the fashionable **Bar Rouge** or in **Brasserie Bleu.**

Krystalgade 22, DK-1172 København. ℂ **33-45-91-00.** Fax 33-45-91-10. www.hotelsktpetri.com. 268 units. DKK1,695 ($288/£170) double; from DKK3,095 ($526/£310) suite. AE, DC, MC, V. Parking DKK195 ($33/£20). S-tog: Nørreport. **Amenities:** Restaurant; bar; fitness room; room service; laundry service; dry cleaning; nonsmoking rooms; rooms for those w/limited mobility. *In room:* A/C, TV, Wi-Fi, minibar, hair dryer, safe.

Phoenix Copenhagen ★★

Though it falls a bit short of its goal, this government-rated four-star hotel poses a serious challenge to the discreet grandeur of the d'Angleterre. It saw the light of day in the 1680s, when it was constructed to accommodate the aristocratic courtiers of Amalienborg Palace, visible from the rear of the hotel. In 1847, the guesthouse was torn down and rebuilt as a luxury Victorian-style hotel, attracting the English nobility. Tons of white and colored marble were imported to create a modern version of the Louis XVI style. Beautiful wool carpeting and chandeliers add glamour to the standard guest rooms, but many are a bit too small for our tastes. If you're willing to pay more, opt for one of the business-class rooms or perhaps a suite. You'll catch us hanging out with Danish publishers in the English-style pub, **Murdock's Books & Ale,** with its mahogany and brass.

Bredgade 37, DK-1260 København. ℂ **33-95-95-00.** Fax 33-33-98-33. www.phoenixcopenhagen.com. 213 units. DKK995–DKK2,825 ($169–$480/£100–£283) double; DKK2,165–DKK7,525 ($368–$1,279/£217–£753) suite. AE, DC, MC, V. Parking DKK225 ($38/£23). Bus: 1, 6, 9, or 10. **Amenities:** Restaurant; bar; car rental; room service; babysitting; laundry service; dry cleaning; nonsmoking rooms. *In room:* A/C, TV, Wi-Fi, minibar, hair dryer, iron, trouser press (in some), safe.

71 Nyhavn ★★

Few people dream of sleeping in a warehouse, until they check in here. Back in 1804, this building on the corner between the harbor and Nyhavn Canal housed everything from bales of cotton from America to live chickens from the Danish countryside. Today the massively restored redbrick structure, converted into a hotel in 1971, is one of the most successful examples of recycling in the Danish capital. The smell of spices from the Far East has long faded, but the architects wisely kept the Pomeranian fir beams for atmosphere. That the building is standing at all today is something of a miracle because an 1807 British bombardment destroyed most of the surrounding structures. We like to wake up in the morning here, pulling back the draperies for a view of the old ships anchored at Nyhavn. If there's a downside, it's the smallness of most of the bedrooms, though each comes with a tiled bathroom with a tub/shower combo. However, with crisscrossing timbers, soft leather furniture, and dark wood accents, the rooms are pretty cozy.

Nyhavn 71, DK-1051 København. ℂ **33-43-62-00.** Fax 33-43-62-01. www.71nyhavnhotel.com. 150 units. DKK1,195–DKK2,050 ($203–$349/£120–£205) double; DKK2,295–DKK3,825 ($390–$650/£230–£383) suite. Rates include breakfast (weekends only). AE, DC, MC, V. Free parking. S-tog: Kongensnytorv. **Amenities:** Restaurant; bar; car rental; room service; babysitting; laundry service; dry cleaning; nonsmoking rooms. *In room:* A/C, TV, Wi-Fi, minibar, hair dryer, iron, trouser press, safe.

Moderate

Comfort Hotel Esplanaden

This hotel is a bit dull, but it's comfortable and moderately priced—reason enough to recommend it. It occupies a much-upgraded mid–19th-century building, with a pair of long-suffering caryatids—human figures supposedly bearing the weight of the building's facade—flanking the front entrance. Inside, you'll find a functionally modern interior with very few antique touches, a roster of much-used but well-maintained bedrooms, and a simple decor that's efficient and aggressively unpretentious. Don't expect frills or very many grace notes, as everything is fast-paced with frequent turnover. But the location is on the stylish Bredgade (albeit at its less stylish end), close to the museum of the Danish Resistance and the northern end of Copenhagen's harborfront.

Bredgate 78, DK-1260 København. © 33-48-10-00. Fax 33-48-10-66. www.choicehotels.dk. 117 units. DKK1,271–DKK1,695 ($216–$288/£127–£170) double; DKK1,551–DKK1,825 ($264–$310/£155–£183) suite. AE, DC, MC, V. **Amenities:** Restaurant; bar; free Internet use in lobby; room service. *In room:* TV, Wi-Fi, minibar.

Copenhagen Admiral Hotel   In 1787, the building housing this hotel put bread on the table of many Copenhageners. The former grain warehouse was turned into a hotel in 1988, and in terms of its physical plant, it is the most serious rival of 71 Nyhavn, which has a slight edge. Its location is 2 blocks from the Nyhavn Canal, where sailors of yore went for tattoos and prostitutes. Today many rooms with French balconies open onto harbor views. But thousands of tourists have replaced those sailors of yesterday. Huge timber ceiling beams and roof supports evoke the warehouse; otherwise, the hotel is completely modern, carrying a four-star rating from the government. No two of the midsize rooms here are identical, but each comes with rustic wooden beams and tasteful Danish furniture from classic designers. All the furniture is custom-made of solid teak. The split-level sixth-floor suites—actually studios—are the best accommodations, with large sitting areas and upgraded furnishing. On-site is the **SALT Restaurant & Bar** (p. 101).

Toldbodgade 24–28, DK-1253 København. © 33-74-14-14. Fax 33-74-14-16. www.admiralhotel.dk. 366 units. DKK1,660–DKK1,715 ($282–$292/£166–£172) double; DKK1,755–DKK2,720 ($298–$462/£176–£272) suite. AE, MC, V. Free parking. Bus: 1, 9, 10, 28, or 41. **Amenities:** Restaurant; bar; nightclub; sauna; room service; laundry service; dry cleaning; nonsmoking rooms; solarium. *In room:* TV, Wi-Fi, minibar, hair dryer.

Copenhagen Strand ★ (Value)   This hotel is rated only three stars by the government, but, frankly, we think that only its lack of a restaurant keeps it from four-star status. In 2002, two 18th-century brick-and-timber warehouses were recycled into this hotel only a 5-minute walk from Nyhavn. Because of its harborfront location, the snug lobby has a maritime theme with pictures of ships on the walls and chic brown leather sofas. Many of the old-fashioned architectural details of the building have been retained, and there is a certain nautical gloss here, with varnished wood, brass hardware, and marine artifacts. We like to drop in at the bar in the lobby, where the reception staff works double time mixing drinks and pulling pints.

The medium-size rooms are cozy but predictably less richly decorated than the lobby. For the most part, they are small, cozy, and both tastefully and comfortably furnished with Danish modern. The best accommodations, if you can afford them, are 16 double executive rooms, plus junior suites and deluxe suites, each of which open onto a panoramic view of the harbor.

Havnegade 37, DK-1058 København K. © 33-48-99-00. Fax 33-48-99-01. www.copenhagenstrand.dk. 174 units. Mon–Thurs DKK1,670–DKK2,360 ($284–$401/£167–£236) double, DKK2,875–DKK3,290 ($489–$559/£288–£329) suite; Fri–Sun DKK1,330–DKK1,875 ($226–$319/£133–£188) double, DKK2,085–DKK3,115 ($354–$530/£209–£312) suite. Rates include buffet breakfast. AE, DC, MC, V. Parking DKK225 ($38/£23). Tram: 1 or 6. **Amenities:** Breakfast room; bar; car rental; business center; room service; babysitting; laundry service; dry cleaning; nonsmoking rooms. *In room:* TV, Wi-Fi, minibar, hair dryer, iron, trouser press.

Hotel Opera ★ (Finds)   Discreet, traditional, and inviting, this five-story member of a well-respected Danish chain lies on a tranquil, old-fashioned street just behind what used to be the opera house. All those opera stars who used to stay here now lodge elsewhere and perform at the new opera house. Despite the change in the opera's venue, this hotel retains its original name, along with an elegant wood-paneled lobby that evokes a sense of Britannic charm. In the lobby, directly in front of you as you enter, is an exact copy of the most famous statue in Denmark, *The Little Mermaid*. According to the staff, it was cast as one of three identical statues, one of which is the famous version sitting on the rocks near the entrance to the city's harbor. The midsize bedrooms are conservatively and traditionally furnished and comfortable—appropriate refuges from the madding crowds at the nearby Nyhavn. Only breakfast is served within this hotel, but there are many good restaurants nearby.

Tordenskjoldsgade 15, DK-1055 København. (C) **33-47-83-00.** Fax 33-47-83-01. www.operahotel copenhagen.com. 92 units. Mon–Thurs DKK1,625–DKK2,125 ($276–$361/£163–£213) double, DKK3,035–DKK3,225 ($516–$548/£304–£323) suite; Fri–Sun DKK1,315–DKK1,875 ($224–$319/£132–£188) double, DKK2,475–DKK2,595 ($421–$441/£248–£260) suite. AE, DC, MC, V. **Amenities:** Bar; laundry service; dry cleaning. *In room:* TV, Wi-Fi, minibar, beverage maker, hair dryer.

Maritime   This hotel on a tranquil street near the waterfront has some expensive neighbors, such as the d'Angleterre, but it keeps its prices more affordable. For its location alone, near Nyhavn Canal, it's a recommendable choice. We used to be put off by a certain rigid staff attitude, but, on our last visit, we found the staff far more helpful and cooperative. The hotel has benefited from some refurbishing and updating, while keeping to its maritime theme. Even though the building itself is a century old—maybe older—all the well-furnished, midsize bedrooms are up-to-date and both comfortably and tastefully furnished.

Peder Skrams Gade 19, DK-1054 København. (C) **33-13-48-82.** Fax 33-15-03-45. www.hotel-maritime.dk. 64 units. DKK925–DKK1,700 ($157–$289/£93–£170) double; DKK1,350–DKK2,200 ($230–$374/£135–£220) triple. Rates include breakfast. AE, DC, DISC, MC, V. Bus: 1, 6, or 9. **Amenities:** Restaurant; bar; lounge; laundry service; dry cleaning; nonsmoking rooms. *In room:* TV, Wi-Fi, hair dryer.

NEAR RÅDHUSPLADSEN & TIVOLI GARDENS

Some of the most expensive hotels in Copenhagen are here. In the heart of the city, around Rådhuspladsen (Town Hall Square), Tivoli Gardens, and the Central Railway Station, you'll be near all public transportation and many attractions.

Expensive

Alexandra ★ Kids   Some of its overnight guests have called this long-time favorite the most authentic Danish hotel in Copenhagen. It may be a bit threadbare in places, but much of its furniture is by such Danish modern masters as Arne Jacobsen and Ole Wanscher, with lighting by Paul Henningsen. Its managers refer to it as a "designer and concept hotel." Bedrooms are comfortable and well maintained, done in a striking Danish design. The staff will add an extra bed for families traveling together. The on-site restaurant serves a French-inspired cuisine with many Scandinavian flavors. Because of its extensive collection of wines, the restaurant might be called a wine brasserie.

H. C. Andersens Blvd. 8, DK-1553 København. (C) **33-74-44-44.** Fax 33-74-44-88. www.hotel-alexandra. dk. 61 units. DKK1,425–DKK2,125 ($242–$361/£143–£213) double. Extra bed DKK375 ($64/£38). Rates include breakfast. AE, DC, MC, V. Parking: DKK120 ($20/£12). Bus: 1, 2, 5, 6, 8, or 10. **Amenities:** Restaurant; bar; Wi-Fi in lobby; room service; laundry service; dry cleaning. *In room:* TV, hair dryer, trouser press.

Bertram Hotel Guldsmeden ★   This is the more elegant twin of the also-recommended Carlton Hotel Guldsmeden. Both lie within about 274m (899 ft.) of one another, on a wide and busy boulevard that runs into the rear of Copenhagen's Central Railway station, within about a 10-minute walk. Rising six stories, the hotel originated in 2006, after a 19th-century town house was restored, with special emphasis on the landscaping within the building's central courtyard. Rooms overlook the courtyard, the noisy Vesterbrogade, or the quieter neighborhood in back. Furniture in the bedrooms was imported from Indonesia, including four-poster beds and the heavy, artfully simple lines in natural wood, which go well with the concepts of Danish modern design and the bright pastel colors in which the rooms are painted.

Vesterbrogade 107, 1620 København V. ℂ 33-25-04-05. Fax 33-25-04-02. www.hotelguldsmeden.dk. 47 units. DKK1,795–DKK1,995 ($305–$339/£180–£200) double; DKK2,245–DKK2,495 ($382–$424/£225–£250) suite. Rates include breakfast buffet. AE, DC, MC, V. Parking DKK95 ($16/£9.50). Bus: 6A. **Amenities:** Restaurant; bar; limited room service; babysitting; laundry service; dry cleaning; nonsmoking rooms. *In room:* TV, Wi-Fi, minibar, hair dryer, safe.

Copenhagen Plaza ★★   If we told you that the likes of Keith Richards and Tina Turner have checked in, would that be a plus or a minus—perhaps a plus for Turner, a minus for the poor, beaten-up Richards. The hotel is still going strong, but actually it is past its heyday. Commissioned by King Frederik VIII in 1913, it once hosted its share of big-name celebrities to Copenhagen, even royalty. Today queens and kings stay elsewhere, although rock stars find it suits them just fine, especially its location opposite the Tivoli Gardens and close to the Central Railway Station.

Still imbued with a turn-of-the-20th-century atmosphere, it has been successfully overhauled for first-class comfort, with items such as antique furnishings, without losing its ambience. As befits the age and era of this hotel, guest rooms come in various sizes and configurations, many evoking an English country house. Antiques, double-glazed windows, and views of the cityscape make this a winning choice. For a kind of Paris garret atmosphere, book one of the top-floor rooms with dormered windows, among the coziest in Copenhagen, especially if you're a romantic duo on an off-the-record weekend.

Bernstorffsgade 4, DK-1577 København. ℂ 800/221-4542 in the U.S., or 33-14-92-62. Fax 33-93-93-62. www.profilhotels.se. 93 units. DKK2,150 ($366/£215) double; DKK6,695 ($1,138/£670) suite. 1 child stays free in parent's room. AE, DC, MC, V. Parking DKK235 ($40/£24). Bus: 1 or 6. **Amenities:** Restaurant; bar; fitness center; car rental; room service; babysitting; laundry service; dry cleaning; nonsmoking rooms. *In room:* A/C, TV, Wi-Fi, minibar, hair dryer, safe.

First Hotel Vesterbro ★★   Just a 5-minute walk from the Tivoli Gardens, this luxury hotel is the third largest in Denmark. Of course, big doesn't always mean best, but in this case Vesterbro is a standout. Rooms are midsize to spacious and as modern as tomorrow. In the so-called "Lady Rooms," we were impressed with the robes laid out, the makeup mirror, the beauty products from Clarins, the dress hangers, even an assortment of women's magazines. The sun-flooded lobby sets the high sense of style and fashion, with windows going from floor to ceiling. The furnishings are like a showcase of Danish design with much use of blond wood. We loved the style, comfort, and taste of the bedrooms, with their pastel-colored walls that brighten a dull gray day in Copenhagen, along with the Spanish cherrywood furniture and the modern lithographs. Our favorite spot here is the atrium garden, lined in brick, and a suntrap on a fair day. The hotel lies just a short walk to the Central Railway Station. Guests can use a fitness center nearby for free.

Vesterbrogade 23–29, DK-1620 København. ℂ 33-78-80-00. Fax 33-78-80-80. www.firsthotels.com. 403 units. DKK1,295–DKK1,695 ($220–$288/£130–£170) double. AE, DC, MC, V. Parking DKK200 ($34/£20). **Amenities:** Restaurant; bar; room service; laundry service; dry cleaning; nonsmoking rooms; rooms for those w/limited mobility. *In room:* A/C, TV, Wi-Fi, minibar, hair dryer, iron, trouser press, safe.

Grand Hotel ★   This 1880 landmark hotel near the Central Railway Station was growing a bit stale, but a major postmillennium overhaul has given it a new lease on life.

It should be around for at least another 100 years if it keeps having those periodic face-lifts. The charm of the old structure, where celebrities—the "Who's Who of Yesterday"—used to stay, was preserved and respected. But all the midsize-to-spacious bedrooms were tastefully and comfortably updated with modern amenities installed. Singles opening onto the courtyard are more tranquil but don't have views, and the corner rooms are the best and most expensive because they have been the most recently renovated and are larger. The **Frascati Bar** overflows in summer onto a sidewalk cafe, and the **Restaurant Frascati** serves freshly prepared Italian specialties.

Vesterbrogade 9A, DK-1620 København. (C) **33-27-69-00.** Fax 33-27-69-01. www.grandhotel copenhagen.com. 161 units. DKK1,195–DKK1,755 ($203–$298/£120–£176) double; DKK2,455–DKK2,775 ($417–$472/£246–£278) suite. Rates include buffet breakfast. AE, DC, MC, V. Bus: 1, 6, 16, 27, 28, or 29. **Amenities:** Restaurant; bar; car rental; business center; room service; laundry service; dry cleaning; non-smoking rooms. *In room:* A/C, TV, Wi-Fi, minibar, hair dryer, trouser press.

Kong Frederik ★★ Finds

There are two "Kongs" among the hotels of Copenhagen, both Kong Frederik and Kong Arthur. Of the two, we think Frederik is "King Kong." The smallest of the ultrachic hotels in Copenhagen, Kong Frederik has the feeling of an unpretentious but elegant private club thanks to discreet service, dark paneling, and a labyrinth of antiques-filled lounges. Many guests, and we agree, feel that it's much cozier than the Hotel d'Angleterre. Originally built around 1850 as two separate hotels, and then combined around a central courtyard about 1990, it has always appealed to glamorous showbiz types. The midsize rooms are conservatively decorated in a wide array of styles, with striped fabrics, overstuffed chairs, and antique prints.

Vester Voldgade 25, DK-1552 København. (C) 33-12-59-02. Fax 33-93-59-01. www.remmen.dk. 110 units. DKK1,730–DKK2,210 ($294–$376/£173–£221) double; DKK3,890–DKK5,450 ($661–$927/£389–£545) suite. AE, DC, MC, V. Parking DKK175 ($30/£18). Bus: 1, 6, or 28. **Amenities:** Restaurant; bar; fitness center; spa; room service; laundry service; dry cleaning; nonsmoking rooms. *In room:* TV, Wi-Fi, minibar, hair dryer, safe.

Radisson SAS Royal ★★★ Kids

There are two Radisson SAS hotels in Copenhagen, but we infinitely prefer this one because of its pedigree, although its competitor, the Radisson SAS Scandinavia, attracts those with more modern tastes. The Royal, Copenhagen's first skyscraper, in the city center near Tivoli and Town Hall Square, is famous within the orbit of the Danish design world because of the role of Arne Jacobsen, one of the patriarchs of Danish design. Between 1958 and 1960, he designed not only the hotel but also most of the furnishings within it. Today the building is classified as a historic monument that retains most, if not all, of Arne Jacobsen's original mandates. Rooms are beautifully furnished and well maintained, with light maple furnishings and the world-famous Jacobsen lamps. The most requested chamber is no. 606, which is kept just as it was in 1960, except for paint and repairs. All the Jacobsen furnishings in this room are original, including the radiators. Several of the units open onto views over the Tivoli Gardens and the rooftops of Copenhagen. At the Business Club, on the top floors, guests can take advantage of a lounge and speedier check-ins.

Hammerichsgade 1, DK-1611 København. (C) **800/333-3333** in the U.S., or 33-42-60-00. Fax 33-42-63-00. www.radissonsas.com. 260 units. DKK1,595–DKK1,995 ($271–$339/£160–£200) standard double; DKK1,895–DKK2,395 ($322–$407/£190–£240) executive double; DKK2,395–DKK9,000 ($407–$1,530/£240–£900) suite. AE, DC, MC, V. Parking DKK240 ($41/£24). Bus: 14 or 16. **Amenities:** Restaurant; bar; fitness room; sauna; kids' playroom; room service; massage; babysitting; laundry service; dry cleaning; nonsmoking rooms; solarium. *In room:* A/C, TV, Wi-Fi, minibar, coffeemaker, hair dryer, iron, safe.

Radisson SAS Scandinavia Hotel ★★ Talk about keeping up with the times: This hotel seems in constant renovation, and we find it looking better than the day it opened in 1975. Our hearts still belong to the Radisson SAS Royal, however. But for a sleek, modern, skyscraper look, this hotel, a 15-minute walk east of Tivoli, reigns supreme. The hotel's most winning feature is that it is run in a rather personal way, filled with an enthusiastic, professional staff who will ease your adjustment into the Danish capital. First-class, midsize rooms are attractive and comfortable, with many luxuries including beautifully kept bathrooms. Greater comfort is found on the top floors at the Business Club, where guests also have such complimentary amenities as free cable and Internet connections.

Amager Blvd. 70, DK-2300 København. ⓒ 800/333-3333 in the U.S., or 33-96-50-00. Fax 33-96-55-00. www.radissonsas.com. 542 units. Mon–Thurs DKK1,700–DKK2,095 ($289–$356/£170–£210) double, DKK2,295–DKK3,595 ($390–$611/£230–£360) suite; Fri–Sun DKK1,195–DKK1,600 ($203–$272/£120–£160) double, suites same as above. Rates in suites include breakfast. 1 child stays free in parent's room. AE, DC, MC, V. Parking DKK160 ($27/£16). Bus: 15. **Amenities:** 4 restaurants; 2 bars; indoor heated pool; squash court; fitness center; sauna; boutiques; room service; massage; babysitting; laundry service; dry cleaning; nonsmoking rooms; rooms for those w/limited mobility; casino; solarium. *In room:* TV, Wi-Fi, coffeemaker, iron.

Scandic Copenhagen ★★ The Radisson SAS Scandinavia does it better and more dramatically, but this 18-story steel-and-glass member of a chain is serious competition. Built near the Tivoli Gardens in 1972, and much renovated and improved since then, it rises over the city's lakes near the Tycho Brahe Planetarium. In winter, businesspeople fill up the hotel, where the concierge staff can arrange for typists, translators, and other services. In summer, most of the clients are here for the sights and attractions. As in all hotels in these high-rises, the higher up you go, the more panoramic the view, of course. The so-called "cozy" economy singles are just too tiny. The "superior rooms" are among the best of the modern hotel rooms in Copenhagen, and the top-floor "superior plus" units approach a luxury standard. Opening onto panoramic views, the suites are spacious and luxurious.

Vester Søgade 6 (Box 337), DK-1601 København. ⓒ 33-14-35-35. Fax 33-32-12-23. www.scandichotels. com. 486 units. DKK1,450–DKK3,890 ($247–$661/£145–£389) double; DKK2,150–DKK16,700 ($366–$2,839/£215–£1,670) suite. Rates include continental breakfast. AE, DC, MC, V. Parking DKK140 ($24/£14). Bus: 1 or 14. **Amenities:** 3 restaurants; bar; exercise room; sauna; concierge; room service; massage; laundry service; dry cleaning; nonsmoking rooms; rooms for those w/limited mobility. *In room:* A/C, TV, Wi-Fi, minibar, hair dryer, iron, trouser press.

Scandic Palace Hotel ★★ Opened in 1910 and declared a historic landmark in 1985, the Palace Hotel has been a respite for countless camera-shy celebrities. Renovations completed in January 2009 brought this hotel to the status of a government-rated five-star accommodation. The transformation includes "The Night Wing," with all new interiors, carpets, draperies, and plumbing. The decor in this wing is individually designed, and, as its name suggests, inspired by the "mystical hues of night." The other contemporary-looking rooms are attractively furnished in an updated version of the Danish modern style—elegant and comfortable. The best rooms are on the top floor, away from street noise. If you're assigned a room on floors two or three, you are still in luck—they have high ceilings and tasteful furnishings and appointments. Notice the soaring tower associated with this hotel—it rivals that of Town Hall, which lies almost immediately next door.

Rådhuspladsen 57, DK-1550 København. ⓒ 800/543-4300 in the U.S., or 33-14-40-50. Fax 33-14-52-79. www.scandichotels.com. 162 units. DKK1,385–DKK1,585 ($235–$269/£139–£159) double; DKK2,695

($458/£270) suite. 20% discount may be available on weekends and in midwinter, depending on occupancy. AE, DC, MC, V. Parking DKK300 ($51/£30). Bus: 2, 30, 32, 33, 34, or 35. **Amenities:** Restaurant; bar; room service; massage; babysitting; laundry service; dry cleaning; nonsmoking rooms. *In room:* TV, Wi-Fi, minibar, beverage maker, hair dryer, trouser press, safe.

The Square ★★   In the bull's-eye center of Copenhagen, the elegant Square, a completely modern property, overlooks Town Hall Square. Tight, minimalist lines characterize this exquisitely designed hotel, which lies close to the Strøget shopping street, the Tivoli, and the Central Railway Station. Most bedrooms open onto a spectacular view of the city, and are filled with stylish modern furnishings in a simple, tasteful format. The reception room is integrated with the lobby bar, which contains specially designed furnishings punctuated by Arne Jacobsen's famous circular chair, "The Egg." The breakfast room lies on the sixth floor, opening onto the rooftops of the city.

Rådhuspladsen 14, DK-1550, København. ℂ 33-38-12-00. Fax 33-38-12-01. www.thesquare copenhagen.com. 267 units. DKK1,195–DKK1,590 ($203–$270/£120–£159) double; DKK1,690–DKK2,265 ($287–$385/£169–£227) suite. AE, DC, MC, V. Parking DKK200 ($34/£20). Bus: 1, 6, or 8. **Amenities:** Breakfast restaurant; car rental; room service; laundry service; dry cleaning; nonsmoking rooms. *In room:* A/C, TV, Wi-Fi, minibar, hair dryer, iron, trouser press, safe.

Moderate

Ascot Hotel ★ (Value)   The word "ascot," because of its British associations, usually suggests elegance—but not so here. This is one of the best small hotels in Copenhagen, despite the perception that it's in need of some sprucing up. On a side street about a 2-minute walk from Town Hall Square, the inn of personality and charm was built in 1902 (on 492 wooden pilings rescued from a medieval fortification that had previously stood on the site). In 1994, the hotel annexed an adjacent building designed in the 19th century as a bathhouse; its black-marble columns and interior bas-reliefs are historically notable. Martin Nyrop, who designed the landmark Town Hall, also was the architect for the bathhouse. The furniture is rather standard, but the finest units open onto the street. Nevertheless, the units in the rear get better air circulation and more light.

Studiestræde 61, DK-1554 København. ℂ 33-12-60-00. Fax 33-14-60-40. www.ascot-hotel.dk. 120 units. DKK1,790–DKK1,890 ($304–$321/£179–£189) double; DKK2,290 ($389/£229) suite. Rates include buffet breakfast. Winter discounts available. AE, DC, MC, V. Parking DKK125 ($21/£13). Bus: 14 or 16. **Amenities:** Restaurant; bar; fitness center; room service; laundry service; dry cleaning; nonsmoking rooms. *In room:* TV, Wi-Fi, hair dryer.

Carlton Hotel Guldsmeden ★ (Finds)   Housed in a much-renovated 19th-century townhouse in the heart of the rapidly gentrifying Vesterbro neighborhood, within a 15-minute walk west from Tivoli and the Central Railway Station, this is a government-rated three-star hotel offering good value and occasional doses of genuine charm. The structure might be old, but the bedrooms are contemporary-looking and up-to-date, ranging from small to midsize. Each is handsomely decorated in a vaguely French-Colonial style, with high ceilings, wood paneling, and four-poster beds imported from Indonesia. The best rooms contain such luxuries as fireplaces, balconies with summer furniture, and claw-foot bathtubs instead of showers. The place is made more homelike and inviting by the original art decorating the walls and a judicious use of elegant teak furnishings, along with carpets from Pakistan and pottery from Mexico. Its sister hotel, Bertram's Hotel Guldsmeden, is more charming and a bit more plush, and, unlike the Carlton, contains its own restaurant.

Vesterbrogade 66, DK-1620 København. ℂ 33-22-15-00. Fax 33-22-15-55. www.hotelguldsmeden.dk. 64 units. DKK1,595–DKK1,795 ($271–$305/£160–£180) double; DKK2,395 ($407/£240) junior suite. Rates include buffet breakfast. AE, DC, MC, V. Parking DKK130 ($22/£13). Bus: 6A. **Amenities:** Breakfast room; bar; bike rentals; room service; laundry service; nonsmoking rooms. *In room:* TV, Wi-Fi, minibar, hair dryer, safe.

DGI-byen's Hotel ★ (Kids) (Finds)   There's no hotel like this one in all Copenhagen. Right behind the Central Railway Station and convenient to most public transportation, this government-rated three-star hotel attracts sports lovers to its precincts, which contain a bowling alley, a gigantic swim center, a spa, a "climbing wall," a shooting range, and, oh yes, a hotel. (The "DGI" within its name translates as "Danish Gymnastics Association.") This is a dynamic, flexible so-called multicenter attracting schoolchildren, sports clubs, company executives, and regular visitors. Bedrooms, midsize to large, reflect the presuppositions and tenets of Danish modern design. Interiors are simple yet tasteful and comfortable with dark wood furnishings and blond wood floors. Swimming is free to hotel guests within the public indoor pool, located a short distance from the hotel, but access to the spa costs extra. The on-site **restaurant,** serving good and reasonably priced food, was created from an old cattle market that stood here in 1870.

Tietgensgade 65, DK-1704 København. © **33-29-80-50.** Fax 33-29-80-59. www.dgi-byen.dk. 104 units. DKK1,595 ($271/£160) double. AE, DC, MC, V. Parking DKK140 ($24/£14). **Amenities:** Restaurant; bar; lounge; 5 indoor heated pools; sports center; spa; Jacuzzi; sauna; babysitting; laundry service; dry cleaning; nonsmoking rooms; rooms for those w/limited mobility; solarium. *In room:* TV, Wi-Fi, hair dryer.

Hotel Fox ★ (Kids)   In 2005, one of Copenhagen's most unusual and trend-conscious hotels opened within the premises of what until then had been a staid and predictable staple (the Park Hotel) on the Copenhagen hotel scene. The owners solicited the talents of 21 separate designers from throughout Europe, each of whom submitted plans for new interior decors that reflected their individual whims and priorities. The result is a small-scale hotel that really appreciates the concept of "design" and which, in the opinion of some detractors, has carried it to levels that are almost overwhelming. Its white-painted facade carries renditions of street graffiti that might be almost too artful or too "carefully rehearsed." Each room is a highly idiosyncratic work of art, ranging from tongue-in-cheek enclaves of camp to rigorously streamlined case studies for postindustrial minimalism. Unless you've already requested a particular theme in advance, a computer at the reception desk will show you the visuals of where you're about to sleep. Choices, among many others, include a room dominated by a theme related to boxing, a unit filled with taurine (bull-inspired) souvenirs, an accommodation with syrupy reminders of Heidi, and one devoted to an all-American theme that features extra-wide beds for fullbacks and their Brunhilds.

Jarmers Plads 3, DK-1551 København. © **33-13-30-00.** Fax 33-14-30-33. www.hotelfox.dk. 61 units. Doubles DKK970–DKK1,390 ($165–$236/£97–£139). AE, DC, MC, V. Parking DKK175 ($30/£18) nearby, DKK16 ($2.70/£1.60) per hour on street. Bus: 14 or 16. **Amenities:** Restaurant; bar; laundry service; dry cleaning. *In room:* TV, Wi-Fi, hair dryer, safe.

Hotel 27 ★   This is the most recent incarnation of a large and highly visible hotel that lies within a short walk from Tivoli. It's a large, six-story hotel that opened in 2006. Rooms feature Danish modern design in color schemes of white, black, and soft reds, each with a modestly sized but serviceable bathroom trimmed in slabs of polished stone. Hotel 27 is a well-managed, up-to-date member of Copenhagen's middle-bracket hotel scene.

Løngangstræde 27, DK-1468 København. © **70-27-56-27.** Fax 70-27-96-27. www.hotel27.dk. 203 units. DKK1,095–DKK1,895 ($186–$322/£110–£190) double. Rates include buffet breakfast. AE, DC, MC, V. Bus: 1, 5, or 6. **Amenities:** Bar; laundry service; dry cleaning; nonsmoking rooms. *In room:* TV, Wi-Fi, hair dryer.

Kong Arthur ★ (Kids) Most guests checking in here think this hotel was named after England's legendary King Arthur. Actually, the Arthur in its name comes from Arthur Frommer, one of the early owners of this hotel and the founding father of the Frommer guides. Right by the Copenhagen lakes and close to Rosenborg Palace, Kong Arthur is a government-rated four-star hotel lying a 15-minute walk from the Tivoli Gardens. Charm, high-quality comfort, and a welcoming atmosphere greet you today, but back in 1882, things were a bit more rawboned here. The building was once a home for Danish orphans leading a Dickensian existence. We like to go down to breakfast because it's served in a large greenhouselike room that's flooded with light on sunny days. Bedrooms range from midsize to spacious, and each is tastefully and comfortably furnished with carpets and spacious.

Nørre Søgade 11, DK-1370 København. ✆ **33-11-12-12.** Fax 33-32-61-30. www.kongarthur.dk. 155 units. DKK1,320–DKK1,530 ($224–$260/£132–£153) double; DKK2,100–DKK3,500 ($357–$595/£210–£350) suite. AE, DC, MC, V. Free parking. Bus: 5, 7, or 16. **Amenities:** Restaurant; bar; sauna; car rental; room service; massage; babysitting; laundry service; dry cleaning; nonsmoking rooms. *In room:* TV, Wi-Fi, minibar, hair dryer, trouser press, safe.

Inexpensive

City Hotel Nebo (Value) The neighborhood that surrounds this hotel, alas, is still the heart of Copenhagen's "red light" district, but families have been checking in and out of the hotel for generations, finding it perfectly adequate in spite of the surreal quality of a seedy neighborhood that is slowly but inexorably becoming more respectable. In the vicinity of the train station, the hotel opened back in the 1930s as an alcohol-free mission hotel. Its owners are still a Christian foundation whose philosophy is that "everyone should be able to afford an accommodation in Copenhagen." Backpackers often rent the "low economy" rooms, sharing the adequate hallway facilities. For more money, you can rent small but tastefully decorated doubles, or even some family rooms sleeping up to four guests.

Istedgade 6, DK-1650 København. ✆ **33-21-12-17.** Fax 33-23-47-74. www.nebo.dk. 128 units, 88 w/ bathroom. DKK650–DKK699 ($111–$119/£65–£70) double w/shared bathroom, DKK850–DKK899 ($145–$153/£85–£90) double w/private bathroom; DKK750–DKK1,200 ($128–$204/£75–£120) family room for 3, DKK990–DKK1,300 ($168–$221/£99–£130) family room for 4. Extra bed DKK150 ($26/£15) extra. Rates include buffet breakfast. AE, DC, MC, V. Parking DKK50 ($8.50/£5). Bus: 1, 6, 16, 28, or 41. **Amenities:** Breakfast room; lounge. *In room:* TV.

Copenhagen Crown (Value) In business for more than a century, this welcoming hotel lies only a short walk from the Tivoli Gardens and the main train station. You enter through a tranquil, beautiful courtyard, evoking Copenhagen of long ago. The traffic-clogged Vesterbrogade is a short distance away, but you feel that this is a well-maintained, safe, and quiet haven once you enter. The midsize bedrooms are classically and tastefully decorated, some of them opening onto Vesterbrogade, the rest onto the courtyard. The most attractive feature of this hotel is its rooftop **restaurant,** where a varied Scandinavian breakfast buffet is served overlooking the rooftops of the city.

Vesterbrogade 41, DK-1620 København. ✆ **33-21-21-66.** Fax 33-21-00-66. www.profilhotels.dk. 80 units. DKK1,050 ($179/£105) double. Rates include breakfast. AE, DC, MC, V. Bus: 6. **Amenities:** Restaurant; bar; laundry service; dry cleaning; nonsmoking rooms. *In room:* TV, Wi-Fi, minibar, hair dryer.

ON HELGOLANDSGADE & COLBJØRNSENSGADE

In the 1970s, this area behind the Railway station became one of the major pornography districts of Europe, but subsequent hotel renovations, much-publicized civic efforts, and

(Kids) **Family-Friendly Accommodations**

DGI-byen's Hotel (p. 88). For many kids, staying here is like being in a deluxe playground, with a multicenter designed especially for children, plus five indoor heated swimming pools. If your kid is athletic, this hotel has more sporting facilities than any other in Denmark.

Hotel d'Angleterre (p. 77). This elegant hotel contains a swimming pool and in-house video; both help keep children entertained. The hotel provides an appropriate setting for the Danish equivalent of Eloise's adventures at New York's old Plaza Hotel.

Hotel Fox (p. 88). Each room has its own decor, with some that appeal directly to children, including the whimsical if surreal room devoted to Heidi and a few of the pastures in Switzerland's high Alps.

Ibsens Hotel (p. 92). This hotel caters to families on a budget, as many of its triple rooms are large enough to house mom, dad, and one or two kids. There are no other special features for kids, however.

Kong Arthur (p. 89). Once a home for Danish orphans, this is a safe haven in a residential section near tree-lined Peblinge Lake.

the gradual decline of the porno shops have led to a continuing gentrification. Today, with the original 19th-century facades mostly still intact and often gracefully restored, the district is safer than you might think and offers some of the best hotel values in Copenhagen.

Expensive

AXEL Hotel Guldsmeden ★★   This luxurious choice is the latest member of the Guldsmeden family, lying as it does in the Vesterbro district, behind the Tivoli and the Central Railway Station. Seemingly, it has everything, including a spa, private penthouse suites, an organic restaurant, teak four-poster beds, and small balconies, plus the latest technology. Bedrooms blend a traditional Balinese style with original paintings, Persian rugs on wooden floors, and attractively designed and most comfortable bedrooms. Your choice is of standard doubles, junior suites, and penthouse suites. Organic products are used in the spa, and special features include energizing salt, sugar, and coffee scrubs. Each suite has its own private rooftop terrace.

Helgolandsgade 11, DK-1653 København. ℭ **33-31-32-66.** Fax 33-31-69-70. www.hotelguldsmeden. com. 129 units. DKK1,155–DKK1,255 ($196–$213/£116–£126) double; DKK1,555 ($264/£156) junior suite; DKK4,995 ($849/£500) penthouse suite. AE, DC, MC, V. Bus: 6, 10, 16, 27, or 28. **Amenities:** Restaurant; bar; spa; room service; laundry service; dry cleaning; nonsmoking rooms. *In room:* TV, Wi-Fi, minibar, hair dryer, safe.

Moderate

Clarion Collection Mayfair ★   Those Clarion Collection people, a hotel chain known for creating havens of charm and comfort, have moved in on the long-established Mayfair, 2 blocks west of the Central Railway Station to give it a new zest for life. Rated three stars by the government, the hotel isn't as well known as it should be, but has enjoyed refurbishing and redecorating, making it a choice address in Copenhagen. In some of its furnishings and decor, it evokes a well-heeled private home in England. Bedrooms come in a wide range of sizes, but each is tastefully furnished and comfortable, with full marble bathrooms. The best accommodations here have small sitting areas, so you don't feel you're living in a box. The district around the hotel is becoming increasingly trendy, with the opening of new shops, cocktail lounges, and restaurants.

Helgolandsgade 3, DK-1653 København. ✆ **877/424-6423** in the U.S., or 70-12-17-00. Fax 33-23-96-86. www.choicehotels.no. 105 units. DKK1,356 ($231/£136) double; from DKK1,795 ($305/£180) suite. AE, DC, MC, V. Bus: 6, 16, 28, 29, or 41. **Amenities:** Breakfast room; bar; lounge; bike rentals; babysitting; laundry service; dry cleaning; nonsmoking rooms. *In room:* TV, fax, dataport, Wi-Fi, minibar, hair dryer, iron, trouser press, safe.

Inexpensive

Absalon Hotel og Absalon Annex ★ (Value)

In the increasingly gentrified Vesterbro area, the Absalon traces its origins to a love story that unfolded at the nearby Railway station. Shortly after the yet-to-be father of the present owners began his first job as a porter at a neighboring hotel, he was asked to go to the station to pick up a new babysitter who had just arrived from Jutland. They fell in love, married, and bought the first of the buildings that became the hotel. Two of their children were born in Room 108. This family-run lodging, one of the best-managed hotels in the neighborhood, consists of four townhouses that were joined into one building and became a hotel in 1938. It has a spacious blue-and-white breakfast room, and an attentive staff directed by third-generation owners. The guest rooms are simple and modern, and come in various sizes ranging from cramped to spacious. We find that those on the fifth floor have the most character. These rooms get the most light and are elegantly furnished in a modified Louis XIV style or in a classical English style, with marble bathrooms with tubs. Overflow guests are housed in one of the rather functional rooms in the Absalon Annex. Bathrooms are equipped with tub/shower combinations.

Helgolandsgade 15, DK-1653 København. ✆ **33-24-22-11.** Fax 33-24-34-11. http://absalonhotel.dk. 262 units. DKK990–DKK1,290 ($168–$219/£99–£129) double; DKK1,190–DKK1,590 ($202–$270/£119–£159) triple; DKK1,590–DKK1,890 ($270–$321/£159–£189) suite. Rates include buffet breakfast. AE, DC, MC, V. Bus: 6, 10, 16, 27, or 28. **Amenities:** Breakfast room; lounge; laundry service; dry cleaning; nonsmoking rooms. *In room:* TV, Wi-Fi, beverage maker, hair dryer (in some), trouser press.

Hotel Ansgar

Just when we were about to drop this tired old workhorse from the guide, it burst into bloom again, with renovated and modernized bedrooms. Decorating magazines may not be too impressed but you get tasteful rooms that are comfortable but plain in Danish modern—no clutter here. Although its prices have risen, the hotel is still a good value and has been ever since it opened in 1885 in a five-story structure. Think of the rooms as cozy instead of small—it's better that way. Two dozen large rooms can accommodate up to six (that's a bit crowded) and are suitable for Brady Bunch–style families. The bedrooms contain well-kept bathrooms with Danish modern shower units (no great compliment). Guests arriving at Kastrup Airport can take the SAS bus to the Air Terminal at the Central Railway Station, walk through the station, and be inside the hotel in less than 4 minutes.

Colbjørnsensgade 29, DK-1652 København. ✆ **33-21-21-96.** Fax 33-21-61-91. www.ansgar-hotel.dk. 81 units. DKK750–DKK1,100 ($128–$187/£75–£110) double. Rates include buffet breakfast. Extra bed DKK200 ($34/£20). AE, DC, MC, V. Bus: 6, 10, 28, or 41. **Amenities:** Breakfast room; Internet cafe; room service; laundry service; dry cleaning; nonsmoking rooms. *In room:* TV, Wi-Fi.

Hotel Selandia Thousands upon thousands of budget-conscious visitors have been making their way from the railway station to the doors of this hotel ever since it opened in 1928. "We're not glamorous and we attract no movie gods or rock stars," a member of the staff told us, "but we do get budget-conscious visitors from abroad, plus regular clients and their families who journey to Copenhagen from the countryside of Denmark." An elevator carries visitors to all floors, one of which features superior units decorated in the style of Louis XVI (before he was beheaded, of course). Such extras in these upgraded rooms include a Bang & Olufsen TV, a minibar, and a beverage maker. In a ground-floor room, an impressive Danish buffet breakfast is laid out each morning, and hot and cold drinks are available throughout the day.

Helgolandsgade 12, DK-1653 København. ℗ **33-31-46-10.** Fax 33-31-46-09. www.hotel-selandia.dk. 87 units, 57 w/bathroom. DKK675–DKK765 ($115–$130/£68–£77) double w/shared bathroom; DKK875–DKK1,295 ($149–$220/£88–£130) double w/private bathroom. Extra bed DKK200 ($34/£20). Rates include breakfast. AE, DC, MC, V. Closed Dec 20–Jan 2. Bus: 1, 6, 10, 14, 16, 27, or 28. **Amenities:** Breakfast room; lounge. *In room:* TV, Wi-Fi, minibar (in some), fridge, beverage maker (in some), hair dryer, trouser press (in some).

Saga Hotel In 1947, two developers purchased two late-19th-century apartment buildings that had survived the Nazi occupation and set out to gut them and turn them into hotel rooms. One of the owners told the press at the time, "We predicted that many tourists would return to Denmark after the war years and many of them would need a clean, respectable, but affordable place to stay." Those long-ago words still ring true today. As trendy, boutique hotels rise up almost yearly, the Saga is rather like it was when it was created, although it has kept up with the times with improvements such as Internet access. The five-story building still has no elevator and some of its rooms are still without a private bathroom. As such, it attracts groups of international visitors in summer and Danish student and convention groups in winter. The rooms are small to midsize, each furnished in Danish modern, and most are equipped with a private bathroom with a tub/shower combination. The hotel is especially attractive to families in that it offers some very spacious units with three, four, or even five beds. A generous Scandinavian buffet breakfast is another temptation, and the hotel will also allow you to use its storage facilities at no extra charge.

Colbjørnsensgade 18–20, DK-1652 København. ℗ **33-24-49-44.** Fax 33-24-60-33. www.sagahotel.dk. 79 units, 31 w/private bathroom. DKK480–DKK750 ($82–$128/£48–£75) double w/shared bathroom; DKK600–DKK950 ($102–$162/£60–£95) double w/private bathroom. Extra bed DKK150 ($26/£15). Modest winter discounts. AE, DC, MC, V. Bus: 6, 10, 16, 28, or 41. **Amenities:** Breakfast room; lounge; nonsmoking rooms. *In room:* TV, Wi-Fi.

AT NANSENSGADE
Moderate

Ibsens Hotel ★ Kids The Brøchner-Mortensen family succeeds in combining an old-fashioned nostalgia with all the modern amenities today's traveler demands. A charming, government-rated three-star hotel in the Nansensgade area, right by the lakes, it is convenient for trips to both Rosenborg Palace and the Tivoli Gardens. In an area filled with cafes and trendy restaurants, the hotel first opened its doors in 1906, surviving wars, occupation, and changing tastes, and somehow keeping abreast of it all. The guest rooms are comfortably and tastefully furnished, each well maintained and containing private bathrooms that are a bit cramped but have tub/shower combinations. These cozy rooms open onto a beautiful courtyard. We like the way the hotel offers you a choice of decor on each floor. One floor, for example, showcases Danish modern, whereas another floor has more of a bohemian aura and is filled with antiques.

Vendersgade 23, DK-1363 København. 📞 **33-13-19-13.** Fax 33-13-19-16. www.ibsenshotel.dk. 118 units. DKK1,150–DKK1,310 ($196–$223/£115–£131) double; DKK1,920 ($326/£192) suite. Rates include buffet breakfast. AE, DC, MC, V. Bus: 5, 14, or 16. **Amenities:** 2 restaurants; bar; car rentals; babysitting; laundry service; dry cleaning; nonsmoking rooms. *In room:* TV, Wi-Fi.

Inexpensive

Hotel Jørgensen   When this hotel first opened in 1984, it became Denmark's first gay hotel, and many of its foreign guests thought it'd been named in honor of a former American GI, George, who later, after a little surgery, became famous as the transgendered Christine Jorgensen, making headlines around the world with her sex change. In a stucco-fronted building that opened in 1906 as the headquarters of a publishing house, the hotel has changed over the decades. Located on a busy boulevard in central Copenhagen, it now caters to a conventional mix of clients of all sexual persuasions. Many of its guests are backpackers drawn to its cheap lodgings in dormitory rooms segregated by genders and holding between 6 and 12 beds. Although clients over 35 are aggressively discouraged from renting any of the dormitory rooms, they're welcome within the conventional bedrooms. The hotel is reasonably well-maintained, prices are more or less affordable, and the small rooms are conventional and well organized.

Rømersgade 11, DK-1362 København. 📞 **33-13-81-86.** Fax 33-15-51-05. www.hoteljoergensen.dk. 24 units; 13 dorm rooms (150 beds). DKK750 ($128/£75) double; DKK150 ($26/£15) per person in dorm. Rates include breakfast. MC, V. Parking DKK140 ($24/£14). Bus: 14 or 16. **Amenities:** Breakfast room; lounge. *In room:* TV.

THE SOUTHERN HARBORFRONT

Much of Copenhagen is expanding westward onto the harborfront of Copenhagen. This expansion of the city includes such hot new hotels as the Marriott and the Copenhagen Island Hotel, both of which are recommended below. City planners for this new district have insisted that pedestrians be granted unrestricted access to the harborfront promenade, allowing them to stroll between *Den Lille Havfruen (The Little Mermaid)* near the northern entrance to the harbor, as far south as the Copenhagen Island Hotel and the immediately adjacent Tyske Shopping Plaza. En route, across the harbor, rise hypermodern structures of international renown, among them the new Opera House.

Expensive

Copenhagen Island Hotel ★   This wildly innovative hotel rises from a position that's adjacent to the waterfront of Copenhagen's south harbor. It all began in 1999 with the filling in of marshy lowlands, then proceeded with the dredging of a canal that now surrounds it, like a medieval moat, on three sides. The result is literally an "island" ringed with boardwalks. Once you're inside, you'll find the place either fascinating or terrifying—or perhaps a combination of both—thanks to vertigo-inducing catwalks that crisscross the soaring glass-enclosed lobby.

In contrast to the minimalism of the lobby area, bedrooms are compact, even claustrophobic, much akin to white-walled cabins within a cruise ship. Each contains some jazzy decorative touches and fancy-schmancy lighting tricks, but nothing that really masks the cramped dimensions and the sense of cookie-cutter regularity. "Executive" status will get you a balcony that juts out above the cobblestones of the harborfront promenade, but not a lot more.

Kalvebod Brygg 53, DK-1560 København. © **33-38-96-00.** Fax 33-38-96-01. www.copenhagenisland.dk. 326 units. DKK995–DKK2,365 ($169–$402/£100–£237) double; DKK3,500 ($595/£350) suite. AE, DC, MC, V. S-tog: Dybbølsbro. **Amenities:** Restaurant; bar; business center; laundry service; dry cleaning. *In room:* A/C, TV, Wi-Fi, minibar, hair dryer.

CPH Living ★ Finds This is Scandinavia's only floating hotel, lying as it does in the harbor of Copenhagen. For another more substantial waterfront hotel, see Copenhagen Island Hotel (p. 93). Furnished with the best of Scandinavian design, the hotel is definitely nautical, with steel and hardwood deck material used as recurrent themes throughout. With a dozen rooms, this is a houseboat—not just a hotel on the waterfront. Scheduled to open in 2009, the floating hotel lies 90m (299 ft.) north of Havnebadet. Bathrooms are a special feature; you can enjoy the pulsating harbor life while taking your shower. Bedrooms are midsize, and all accommodations are equipped with floor-to-ceiling windows, original artwork, heated floors, and modern bathrooms. The hotel is fully electronic. A key card is issued to you and you come and go as you please, night and day.

570 Langebrogade Kaj, DK-1411 København. © **30-41-02-11.** Fax 61-60-85-46. www.cphliving.com. 12 units. DKK1,495 ($254/£150) double; extra bed DKK395 ($67/£40). Rates include breakfast. AE, MC, V. S-tog: Dybbølsbro. **Amenities:** Sun deck; nonsmoking rooms. *In room:* TV, Wi-Fi, beverage maker.

Marriott Copenhagen ★ One of the capital's newest blockbuster hotels rises like a glassy, postmodern cube from a position a few feet from the pedestrian promenade facing Copenhagen's southern harborfront. The lobby is pleasing, plush, and upscale, with carpets, elegant upholstery, and deep sofas, providing a dramatic contrast to the Spartan angularity of such nearby competitors as the also-recommended Copenhagen Island Hotel. Most of the public areas, and half of the accommodations, open onto sweeping views of the harbor and its dramatic combination of antique and hypermodern architecture, just across the channel. The midsize bedrooms are comfortably and tastefully furnished, with sleek Danish modern styling and tiled bathrooms that are well equipped and provided with tub/shower combinations. During clement weather, tables are set out on flowering terraces beside the harbor; the rest of the year, the action moves inside into the hermetically sealed, mostly glass-lined interior.

Kalvebod Brygge 5, DK-1560 København. © **88-33-99-00.** Fax 88-33-99-99. www.marriott.com/cphdk. 401 units. DKK1,199–DKK2,999 ($204–$510/£120–£300) double; DKK2,299–DKK5,129 ($391–$872/£230–£513) suite. S-tog: Dybbølsbro. **Amenities:** Restaurant; bar; health club; business center; room service; massage; babysitting; laundry service; dry cleaning. *In-room:* A/C, TV, Wi-Fi, minibar, hair dryer, iron, safe.

Inexpensive

Danhostel Copenhagen City Value This addition to the country's roster of youth hostels opened in 2005 in a white-sided high-rise venue that's one of the most visible buildings along the harborfront, and within a 15-minute walk from Tivoli and the Central Railway Station. Rising 16 floors (highly unusual for a youth hostel), it contains room for more than 1,000 occupants at a time, making it the largest youth hostel in Europe. The hostel used to be an office building. It does a roaring business throughout the year, welcoming individual travelers of any age over 18. Each of the accommodations contains between 4 and 12 beds; a bathroom with toilet, sink, and shower; and virtually no other amenities. Don't expect luxury. Other than breakfast, no meals are served onsite, but there are many restaurants and bars nearby; and the views (which face either the old town and the Town Hall or Copenhagen's harbor and Christianshavn) are spectacular. If you don't already have a youth hostel card, the front desk at this place will sell you one. It costs DKK35 ($6/£3.50) for a one-time stay within this particular hostel, or DKK160 ($27/£16) for a card that's universally accepted and valid for a full year.

H. C. Andersens Blvd. 50, DK-1553 København. ✆ **33-18-83-32.** Fax 33-11-85-88. www.danhostel.dk/copenhagencity. 1,020 beds. DKK580–DKK1,720 ($99–$292/£58–£172) double, triple, or quad. Rental of bed linen DKK60 ($10/£6) extra. Breakfast DKK65 ($11/£6.50) extra per person. AE, DC, MC, V. Bus: 5A. **Amenities:** Breakfast room. *In room:* No phone.

FREDERIKSBERG
Expensive

Avenue Hotel ★★ Ⓚids   Cozy, inviting, and of immense appeal, the Avenue is housed in a building from 1898 that was designed by architect Emil Blichfeldt, known mostly for having designed the main entrance to the Tivoli Gardens. The site was formerly a poorhouse, lunatic asylum, and forced labor camp for "drunks, beggars, and vagabonds." Today the Avenue is filled with grace notes such as a lounge with a sandstone fireplace and comfortable sofas, a secluded courtyard patio in summer, and even a sandpit for children, with toys provided. Bedrooms have been completely restored, with the latest conveniences added. None of the rooms is the exact same size or shape, although each has a high ceiling and, in most cases, small bay windows and French doors. Many accommodations are large enough for families. The hotel is only a 5-minute ride from the Central Station.

Åboulevard 29, DK-1960 Frederiksberg. ✆ **35-37-31-11.** www.avenuehotel.dk. 68 units. DKK1,195–DKK1,495 ($203–$254/£120–£150) double, DKK1,695 ($288/£170) family unit. Rates include breakfast buffet. AE, DC, MC, V. Bus: 12, 66, or 69. **Amenities:** Room service; laundry service; dry cleaning; non-smoking rooms. *In room:* TV, Wi-Fi, fridge, minibar.

---

4 WHERE TO DINE

It's estimated that Copenhagen has more than 2,000 cafes, snack bars, and restaurants, and a higher number of Michelin-starred restaurants than any other city in Europe in 2008 (10 with at least one Michelin star), each within an area measuring 4 sq. km (about 1¹⁄₂ sq. miles) on each side. The most convenient restaurants are in Tivoli Gardens, around Rådhuspladsen (Town Hall Square), around the Central Railway Station, and in Nyhavn. Others are in the shopping district, on streets off of Strøget.

You pay for the privilege of dining in Tivoli; prices are always higher. Reservations are not usually important, but it's best to call in advance. Nearly everyone who answers the phone at restaurants speaks English.

NEAR KONGENS NYTORV & NYHAVN
Very Expensive

Era Ora ★★★ ITALIAN   A Danish friend confided that whenever his wife discovers he's been cheating on her, he always takes her for dinner here—"and all is forgiven." This reminder of the "Golden Age" is on virtually everyone's list as the very best Italian restaurant in Denmark and is one of the best restaurants in Copenhagen. Established in 1982 by Tuscan-born partners Edelvita Santos and Elvio Milleri, it offers an antique-looking dining room, with additional seating for parties of up to 12 in the wine cellar. The cuisine is based on Tuscan and Umbrian models, with sophisticated variations inspired by Denmark's superb array of fresh seafood and produce. Traditional favorites include a platter of 10 types of antipasti, arguably the best version of these Italian hors

Alberto K **10**
Atlas Bar/Restaurant
  Flyvefisken **5**
Axelborg Bodega **9**
Bøf & Ost **40**
Brasserie Le Coq Rouge **7**
Café Lumskebugten **31**
Café à Porta **49**
Café Sorgenfri **38**
Café Victor **51**
Café Zeze **21**
Cap Horn **18**
Chili **33**
Copenhagen Corner **8**
Domhus Kælderen **37**
Era Ora **16**
Formel B. **11**
Fox Kitchen and Bar **4**
Geranium **27**
Godt **22**
Husmann Vinstue **6**
Karriere **12**
Kiin Kiin **1**
Københavner Cafeen **39**
Kong Hans Kælder **46**
Krogs Fiskerestaurant **43**
L'Alsace **50**
Le Sommelier **32**
M.R. (Mads Reflund) **25**
Murdoch's Books & Ale **29**
NOMA **17**
Nørrebro Bryghus **3**
Nyhavns Færgekro **19**
Parnas **47**
Pasta Basta **42**
Peder Oxe's Restaurant/
  Vinkælder Wine Bar **41**
Pierre Andre **23**
Puk's Restaurant **34**
Pussy Galore's
  Flying Circus **2**
Restaurant /
  Café Nytorv **35**
Restaurant Els **20**
Riz Raz **36**
St. Gertruds Kloster **26**
Salt **30**
Skindbuksen **48**
Slotskælderen **45**

Søren K **15**
Sult **24**
Thorvaldsens **44**
Tivoli Gardens
  Restaurants **13**
  Café Ketchup
  Divan II
  Færgekroen
  La Crevette
  The Paul
Umami **28**
VIVA **14**

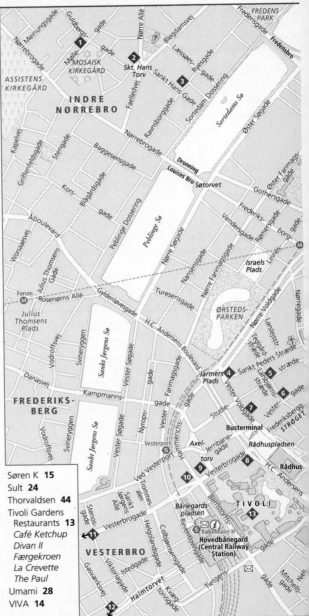

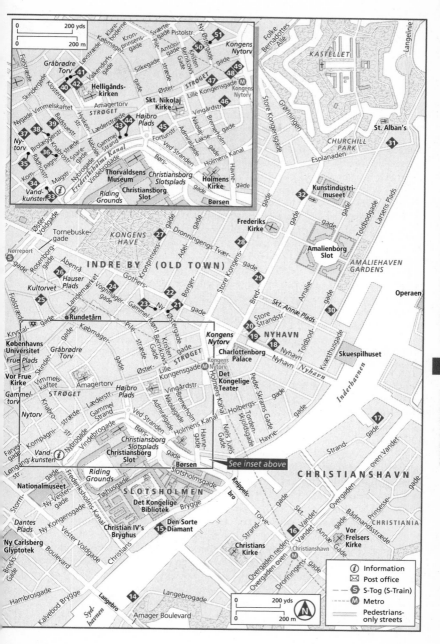

d'oeuvres in the country. The menu offers a mouthwatering array of classics combined with more imaginative dishes created by the produce of the season and the inspiration of the highly skilled chefs. Dishes have subtle flavorings and "sing" in harmony when ingredients are mixed. The chefs continue to invent and reinvent flavor combinations with a wizardry that's nothing short of staggering.

Their homemade pastas, with the town's most savory Italian sauces, are freshly made each day—and are succulent. In autumn, the rack of venison is justifiably praised by food critics, and the veal dishes are the best we've sampled in Copenhagen.

Overgaden Neden Vandet 33B. (✆ **32-54-06-93.** www.era-ora.dk. Reservations required. Fixed-price dinner menus DKK800–DKK3,800 ($136–$646/£80–£380); lunch main courses DKK325–DKK495 ($55–$84/£33–£50). AE, DC, MC, V. Mon–Sat noon–3pm and 7pm–1am. Bus: 2 or 8.

Godt ★★★ INTERNATIONAL   Its cuisine is as haute as ever, but Godt's reputation has been eclipsed by trendier and more newsworthy restaurants just as good. Nonetheless, it still remains a favorite of ours. A consistent small-scale choice that's known to everyone in the neighborhood, including the queen, this very formal restaurant offers two floors of minimalist and modern decor that never exceeds more than 20 diners at a time. Food is prepared fresh every day, based on what's best at the market. The chefs have prodigious talent and imagination, and the dishes are constantly changing. The sauces are sublime, as are the herbs and seasonings. Certain dishes appear frequently on the menu—perhaps the sautéed Norwegian redfish with a purée of celery and watercress sauce, which is an example of the chef's prowess. Using hand-picked ingredients, the chef turns out a perfectly roasted rack of hare, with fresh cranberries and roasted chanterelles. Desserts are a high-flying trip to Valhalla, especially the fresh figs marinated with black currant liqueur, wrapped in phyllo pastry, and served with a coulis of pears and a velvety chocolate mousse.

Gothersgade 38. (✆ **33-15-21-22.** www.restaurant-godt.dk. Reservations required. Fixed-price menus DKK480–DKK660 ($82–$112/£48–£66). AE, MC, V. Tues–Sat 6pm–midnight. Closed July and Dec 23–Jan 3. Bus: 6, 10, or 14.

Kong Hans Kælder ★★★ FRENCH/DANISH/ASIAN   This vaulted Gothic cellar, once owned by King Hans (1455–1513), not only lies in the oldest building in Copenhagen, but also is the site of the best restaurant. Five centuries ago, the site of the restaurant was a vineyard, a tradition still honored by the name of the street—Vingårdsstræde. Grapes were an ingredient in many of the dishes of the time. Hans Christian Andersen once lived upstairs, writing *Love in the Nicola Tower.*

Chef Thomas Rode Andersen has turned the cellar into a *Relais Gourmands* (a member of the exclusive society of gourmet restaurants), and he creates dishes whose arrangement on a platter might have been done by an inspired impressionist painter.

The chef is mainly inspired by the classic traditions of French gastronomy, though he feels free to draw upon the cuisines and raw materials of other countries. He doesn't believe in drowning a dish, and he allows its natural flavor to shine through. In autumn, fresh partridge and pigeon arrive from the fields, the same place where the mushrooms are gathered. He even smokes his own salmon on-site for 36 hours in an antique oven. Blue lobsters are yanked from a tank, and other freshly caught fish and shellfish come from harbors nearby. The menu is inventive, sublime, and full of flavor, with market-fresh ingredients decisively seasoned and appearing in combinations perhaps unknown to you.

Vingårdsstræde 6. (✆ **33-11-68-68.** www.konghans.dk. Reservations required. Main courses DKK435–DKK750 ($74–$128/£44–£75); fixed-price menu DKK1,100–DKK2,800 ($187–$476/£110–£280). AE, DC, DISC, MC, V. Mon–Sat 6pm–midnight. Closed July 20–Aug 10 and Dec 24–26. Bus: 1, 6, or 9.

MR (Mads Reflund) ★★★ MODERN CONTINENTAL   It's posh, it's trendy, and if you're a visiting celebrity, this would be a discreet address. The decor is bright and cheerful, with contrasting textures in a theme that evokes a Danish fairy tale. Not that he's ego crazed, but the owner and head chef, Mads Reflund, chose his own initials for this swank rendezvous for discerning palates. All menu items are configured as a series of set-price menus based on between three and seven courses. Expect creative, imaginative combinations of scallops, lobster, vanilla, cardamom seed, and truffles, and many more delights, each configured into novel concoctions that you might not have thought of without the superb intervention of MR himself. Everything is calm, hushed, impeccably decorated, and in all ways social and culinary, very savvy.

5 Kultorvet. ✆ **33-91-09-49.** http://en.mr-restaurant.dk. Reservations recommended. Set-price menus DKK600–DKK750 ($102–$128/£60–£75). AE, DC, MC, V. 6pm–midnight. S-tog: Nørreport.

NOMA ★★★ NORDIC   With a certain testosterone-driven enthusiasm, the chefs here celebrate the cuisine of the cold North Atlantic. In fact, the name of the restaurant is short for *nordatlantiskl mad,* or North Atlantic food. During its relatively short life, this showcase of Nordic cuisine has received greater amounts of favorable press than virtually any other restaurant in Denmark. Positioned within an antique, stone-sided warehouse in Christianshavn, it makes it an almost religious duty to import ultrafresh fish and shellfish three times a week from Greenland, Iceland, and the Faroe Islands. Chef Rene Redzepi concocts platters in which fish is poached, grilled, pickled, smoked, or salted according to old Nordic traditions, then served in ways that are sometimes more elaborately decorated, and more visually flamboyant by far, than the decor of the white, rather Spartan setting in which they are served. Come here for crayfish, lobster, halibut in a foamy wasabi-flavored cream sauce, and practically any other creature that thrives in the cold waters of Nordic Europe. You expect to see, within the simple, stripped-down decor of this place, celebrities from throughout Northern Europe, including members of the Danish royal family.

Strandgade 93. ✆ **32-96-32-97.** Reservations recommended. Main courses DKK345–DKK445 ($59–$76/£35–£45); set-price menus DKK745–DKK1,150 ($127–$196/£75–£115). AE, DC, MC, V. Mon–Fri noon–2pm and Mon–Sat 6–10pm. Bus: 2 or 8.

Pierre André ★★★ FRENCH   The fickle local media have deserted this place and moved on to other grazing fields. Pierre André is viewed as "no longer on the cutting edge." What is overlooked is that Pierre André chefs are still among the finest in Copenhagen, if you're lured by their take on a classic French cuisine. Named after the two sons of the Danish/French couple who own the place, this restaurant is painted a warm shade of terra cotta and is close to Nyhavn and the Hotel d'Angleterre. Menu items are elegant and stylish, as shown by a house specialty of carpaccio of foie gras "Emilia-Romagna," served with shaved Parmesan and truffles. Other winning starters include a salad of curried lobster with broccoli; braised filet of turbot with mushrooms, leeks, and—a surprise and a delight—mango sauce; wild venison with a bitter chocolate sauce, corn, and cranberries; and a dessert specialty of chocolate cake, wherein the innards are partially liquefied in a gooey but delectable concoction that runs onto your plate. Everything we've sampled has been a burst of flavor, ranking with the top restaurants of Paris or London. The chefs have considerable talent to create imaginative dishes packed with robust flavors, but nothing that's overpowering.

Ny Østergade 21. ✆ **33-16-17-19.** www.pierreandre.dk. Reservations required. Main courses DKK295–DKK395 ($50–$67/£30–£40); fixed-price menus DKK675–DKK850 ($115–$145/£68–£85). AE, DC, MC, V. Tues–Sat noon–2pm and 6–10pm. Closed 3 weeks July–Aug. Bus: 6, 10, or 14.

Café Lumskebugten ★ (Finds) DANISH   This spic-and-span, well-managed bastion of Danish charm has an unpretentious elegance that's admired throughout the capital. A now-legendary matriarch named Karen Marguerita Krog established it in 1854 as a tavern for sailors. As the tavern's reputation grew, aristocrats, artists, and members of the Danish royal family came to dine. Today a tastefully gentrified version of the original beef hash is still served.

Antique ship models decorate two glistening-white dining rooms, and in summer, service spills onto the tables on the outdoor terraces. The food is excellent, but be prepared for a long experience here, as the staff tends to move politely but slowly through the service rituals, sometimes making meals here more lengthy and drawn out than you might have wanted. The selection of dishes takes you back to the way Danes ate in the 1950s, and that's not meant as a put-down by us. Danes like their own version of soul food. In this case it means fried platters of herring or Danish fish cakes with mustard sauce and minced beet root. The sugar-marinated salmon with a mustard cream sauce remains one of the delights of the Danish kitchen, as does a "symphony" of fish with saffron sauce and new potatoes. You might order as a starter another classic: herb-flavored tartare of salmon.

Esplanaden 21. ℂ 33-15-60-29. www.lumskebugten.dk. Reservations recommended. Main courses DKK185–DKK275 ($31–$47/£19–£28); 5-course fixed-price dinner DKK345–DKK690 ($59–$117/£35–£69). AE, DC, MC, V. Mon–Fri 11:30am–10pm; Sat 5–10pm. Bus: 1, 6, or 9.

Le Sommelier ★ FRENCH   With a name like Sommelier, you expect some of Copenhagen's finest wine to be served here, and you're not disappointed. The good news is that many of the best selections are sold by the glass. The restaurant, which opened in 1997, offers more than 850 different bottles, and, as might be predicted, the sommelier here is one of the sharpest in the business. Chef Francis Cardenau's cuisine is inspired, especially his luncheon and dinner set menus, which are created fresh every day depending "on whatever inspiration the market provides." His cooking is characterized by virtuoso presentations such as foie gras poached in consommé with Sauternes *gelée* as a starter. Habitués find his main courses "seductive," and we agree, especially when we sample such dishes as a filet and loin of roast suckling pig with a velouté of fresh morels.

The chef never overextends himself or prepares dishes too elaborate. A savory stuffed rabbit appears frequently on the menu, or else you may want to sample the *poisson du jour*, or fish of the day. For our kroner, the chef still makes the best crème brûlée in town. Perhaps it's putting gilt on the lily, but he also serves it with marinated melon and a velvety vanilla ice cream.

Bredgade 63. ℂ 33-11-45-15. Reservation recommended. Main courses DKK195–DKK375 ($33–$64/£20–£38); fixed-price menus DKK395 ($67/£40). AE, DC, MC, V. Mon–Thurs noon–2pm and 6–10pm; Fri noon–2pm and 6–11pm; Sat 6–11pm; Sun 6–10pm. Bus: 1A, 2A, 3A, or 4A.

Restaurant Els DANISH/FRENCH   This former coffeehouse is one of the most upscale restaurants in Nyhavn, and certainly the one with the best decor. Meticulously preserved since it was installed in 1854, it's lined with murals that feature maidens in diaphanous dresses cavorting beneath trellises in a mythical garden. Dripping with Art Nouveau grace notes, they're believed to be the work of 19th-century muralist Christian Hitsch, who adorned parts of the interior of the Danish Royal Theater. Hans Christian Andersen was a regular here, and just before our arrival, novelist John Irving dropped in for lunch with a Danish journalist, discussing the European marketing for one of his novels.

Each day there's a different fixed-price menu, as well as a la carte offerings. Most dishes are well prepared, including pepper-pickled salmon served with fresh herbs and watercress; lobster soup; grilled scallops with chestnuts and a confit of tomatoes; grilled calf's liver with onion marmalade, tomatoes, and thyme; breast of chicken roasted with honey and ginger, and served with vermouth sauce; and saddle of lamb with a compote of plums and red onions. You might follow all this with black-currant sorbet with cassis. The restaurant was named, incidentally, after the nickname of the wife ("Elsa") of its founder.

Store Strandstræde 3 (off Kongens Nytorv). ✆ **33-14-13-41.** www.restaurant-els.dk. Reservations recommended. Main courses DKK185–DKK285 ($31–$48/£19–£29); sandwiches (lunch only) DKK95–DKK135 ($16–$23/£9.50–£14); fixed-price 3-course lunch DKK348 ($59/£35); fixed-price 4-course dinner DKK448 ($76/£45); fixed-price 5-course dinner DKK1,598 ($272/£160) w/wine. AE, DC, MC, V. Mon–Sat noon–3pm; daily 5:30–10pm. Closed July. Bus: 1, 6, or 10.

Salt ★★★ INTERNATIONAL   Two centuries earlier the British fleet leveled the harborfront here, but the British have returned, this time to design one of the most gorgeous waterside settings for dining in Copenhagen. The chefs take superb and market-fresh ingredients to the limits of their innate possibilities, without relying on culinary artifice. Some of their most sublime concoctions are braised oxtail with sweetbreads, blackberries, and schnapps of wild berries; braised pork shank with truffle oil and almonds; or saddle of rabbit poached in Calvados with stewed apples. Their desserts are worthy of awards, especially their chocolate layer cake with nutmeg ice cream, cloudberries from the Arctic, and burnt almonds, or their baked citrus cake with caramelized lemon ice cream, plus licorice and vanilla cream.

In the Copenhagen Admiral Hotel, Toldbodgade 24–28. ✆ **33-74-14-44.** Reservations required. Fixed-price menus: DKK285 ($48/£29) for 2 courses, DKK345 ($59/£35) for 3 courses, and DKK415 ($71/£42) for 4 courses. AE, DC, MC, V. Mon–Thurs 10am–1am; Fri 10am–2am; Sat 10:30am–2am; Sun 10:30pm–midnight. Bus: 1, 9, 10, 28, or 41.

Umami ★★ JAPANESE   One dinner at the übertrendy restaurant Nobu in Manhattan did it all for the owners of this restaurant. Returning to Copenhagen, they created their own version of a gastronomic sushi temple, luring the power players and major celebs who come to Copenhagen. The setting is beneath the high ceilings of what was originally built as a bank during the 19th century. Permeated with a sense of Japanese minimalism, within sightlines of the kind of clientele who knows precisely how fashionable this place is, you can enjoy creative cuisine that's been written about almost as a matter of course within the Danish press. Don't overlook the place as a potential lounge and club, especially on Friday and Saturday nights, when a DJ spins tunes from a spot near the bar. Drink suggestion? Try sake infused with lemongrass, or any of several kinds of hallucinogenic martini. The street level is the site of the cocktail bar; upstairs is the restaurant, and sushi is available virtually anywhere. ***Note:*** One of the most whimsical corners of the place is within the former vault, site of today's men's and ladies' toilets.

If you're not quite sure what Japanese cooking is with a French touch, try the seared foie gras with eel, Nashi pear, and seafood salad, or the sake-steamed mussels with chili and cilantro, or even the grilled scallops with Yuzu-chili. Ingredients are fresh, flavor combinations are novel, and presentation is elegant and stylish, as evoked by such dishes as Wagyu beef with three sauces or rabbit loin stuffed with shiitake mushrooms and served with pickled eggplant. Minimal cooking makes for a superb texture, as represented by the breast of guinea fowl teriyaki.

The restaurant has even claimed to have discovered five tastes to add to already accepted sour, sweet, salty, and bitter that can be distinguished by the human tongue. Chefs used *kombu*, a special type of seaweed made into crystals of amino acid glutamine and monosodium glutamate, to produce a flavor enhancer for many of their more inspired dishes.

59 Store Kongensgade. © 33-38-75-00. www.restaurantumami.dk. Reservations recommended. Main courses DKK175–DKK245 ($30–$42/£18–£25); set-price menus DKK510–DKK850 ($87–$145/£51–£85). AE, DC, MC, V. Sun–Thurs 6–10pm; Fri–Sat 6–11pm. No lunch during July. Metro: Kongens Nytorv.

Moderate

Brasserie Le Coq Rouge DANISH/FRENCH   In 2005, when one of the most elegant hotels in Copenhagen reconfigured what had been a rather staid and doddering old bar and grill, diners took notice. Today, this snappy and stylish replica of a Parisian brasserie attracts busy crowds at both lunch and dinner. The food is as good as it should be, but that is good enough for most of the savvy foodies seen ordering here. The terrine of foie gras is sublime, but we also go for the charcuterie platters, especially at lunch. The seafood platter has an assortment of some of the best fish caught off Danish waters, and the confit of duckling with lentils takes us back on a journey to southwest France. One of us more discreetly ended our meal with a divine cheese platter, our invited guest opting for pure sin—chocolate cake topped with chocolate mousse and Grand Marnier.

In the Kong Frederick Hotel, Vester Voldgade 25. © 33-12-59-02. Lunch main courses DKK98–DKK165 ($17–$28/£9.80–£17); dinner main courses DKK95–DKK205 ($16–$35/£9.50–£21); set-price 4-course menu DKK395 ($67/£40). AE, DC, MC, V. Daily 11:30am–10pm. Bus: 1, 6, or 28.

Café à Porta ★ DANISH/ENGLISH   Hans Christian Andersen used to come here for takeout, but he'd have to peddle a lot of fairy tales to be able to afford this place today. This is Copenhagen's version of a high-ceilinged, congenially battered grand cafe. Set directly on Copenhagen's most central square, close to the posh dining terrace of Hotel d'Angleterre, it's a comforting and generously proportioned lineup of rooms from the Belle Epoque, with some add-on layers of decor from the *La Dolce Vita* era of the '50s. It was established nearly 200 years ago by a Portuguese merchant, Señor à Porta, who gave it his name. Old-fashioned accents include zinc-topped bars, evoking Emile Zola's Paris, marble and wood parquet floors, and some of the most intricate ceiling decors in town. Menu items range from the straightforward and simple, such as freshly made, crisp salads, to well-stuffed sandwiches. As the day goes on, more complicated dishes appear at the tables, including grilled lobster and a tender, plate-sized Wiener schnitzel. That all these same dishes were being served at the turn of the 20th century doesn't bother the chefs at all, as they prepare old favorites such as flank steak with french fries or a tournedos Rossini like Hemingway ate at the liberation of Paris in 1944.

Kongens Nytorv 17. © 33-11-05-00. Salads and sandwiches DKK95–DKK125 ($16–$21/£9.50–£13); main courses DKK185–DKK275 ($31–$47/£19–£28); 3-course fixed-price dinner DKK495 ($84/£50). AE, DC, MC, V. Aug–June daily 8am–midnight; July daily 11am–10pm. Kitchen closed daily 4–5pm. Bus: 1, 6, 9, or 10.

Café Victor DANISH/FRENCH   Since 1981, this cafe/restaurant has been a Copenhagen tradition, and its cappuccino machine is hard at work all day long. Hip, artsy, and boasting Parisian decor and service, this is a Danish version of a bustling French bistro, replete with zinc bar tops, a staff clad in black and white, and row upon row of expensive whiskeys and cognacs lined up on the bar like religious icons on an altar. The arts-oriented crowd sits at the curved, illuminated bar or at tables, contributing to a "see and be seen" ethic that manages to be both fun and stylish at the same time—sort of a hip, Scandinavian interpretation of *La Dolce Vita*. At lunchtime, menu items include meal-size servings that focus on, among others, club sandwiches; a platter piled high with five different kinds of herring; smoked eel with scrambled eggs and chive; steamed paupiette of fish; terrine of foie gras; and filet of pork with cream sauce. At dinner, look for Victor's "Crazy" Caesar salad; mussels in white wine; seared tuna with fennel, spinach, and lime-flavored salsa; grilled rib-eye steak; and asparagus-studded risotto.

Ny Østergade 8. ✆ **33-13-36-13.** www.cafevictor.dk. Reservations recommended. Lunch platters, salads, and sandwiches DKK49–DKK185 ($8.40–$31/£4.90–£19); dinner main courses DKK125–DKK205 ($21–$35/£13–£21). AE, DC, MC, V. Mon–Wed 8am–1am; Thurs–Sat 8am–2am; Sun 11am–11pm. Bus: 1, 6, or 9.

Cap Horn ★ ORGANIC/INTERNATIONAL   This is one of the best of the restaurants along the Nyhavn waterfront, thanks to a solid and sustained concentration on high-quality food and organic ingredients. It has an outdoor terrace where, during warm weather, competition is fierce for a table. Otherwise you can retreat from the outside melee to three cozy inside dining rooms. The decor was inspired by the interior of a late-19th-century ship: polished brass, mahogany, teak, nautical accessories, a blazing fireplace that's strategically positioned to be visible from throughout most of the interior, and even a skylight removed intact from an antique fishing craft. There's yet another dining area at the top of a steep flight of steps that manages to be both minimalist and severely antique at the same time. It's rumored to shelter an angry ghost—supposedly the spirit of a local woman (Isabella) whose favorite sailor (Peter) scorned her, leading to her suicide. She's occasionally seen around midnight, shattering a plate or upsetting a vase in a fit of pique.

Salads, when configured as a lunch in their own right, can be glorious—crisp and fresh with a wide choice of dressings. Lunches also focus on some of the area's best *smørrebrød,* those open-faced sandwiches. It may seem a strange marriage, but many locals prefer the combination platter of herring and steak. "Cap burgers," made from chopped organic sirloin of beef, are a justifiably popular dish. The fare grows more elaborate at dinner, allowing you to dip into nostalgia as you order a classic Andalusian-style gazpacho, followed by a leg of venison with potatoes in a parsley-flavored butter sauce.

Nyhavn 21. ✆ **33-12-85-04.** Reservations recommended. Lunch platters DKK98–DKK198 ($17–$34/£9.80–£20); dinner main courses DKK129–DKK199 ($22–$34/£13–£20). AE, DC, MC, V. Daily 9am–5pm and 7–11pm. Bus: 1, 6, 9, or 10.

Geranium ★★★ DANISH/INTERNATIONAL   Under two brilliant chefs, Rasmus Kofoed and Soren Ledet, this bastion of gourmet food serves one of the most inventive cuisines in Denmark. In 2008, some Danish gourmet societies named Geranium "restaurant of the year." Special features include a small, cozy lounge, plus a summer terrace. There is more than the geranium theme that is great about this restaurant. The chefs are particularly concerned as to how livestock is handled on the way to their kitchen.

The moment you taste such appetizers as smoked salmon topped with a quail egg and salmon roe, you know you're in for something special. For a main course, their white-pink tenderloin of pork is both tender and juicy, served with slow-cooked marinated mushrooms and red berries. From their king crab to the lemon sole to the roe deer, dishes reflect the chefs' inventiveness and precision with regional products.

Family-Friendly Restaurants

Copenhagen Corner (p. 108)   A special children's menu features such dishes as shrimp cocktail and grilled rump steak.

Kobenhavner Cafeen (p. 111)   Sturdy and reliable, this has long been a family favorite in Copenhagen with both locals and foreigners, who dig into old-fashioned Danish fare. Kids go for the *frikadeller,* or ping-pong-size meatballs.

Restaurant/Café Nytorv (p. 105)   One of the best children's menus in town is a regular feature at this landmark cafe/restaurant on Copenhagen's most elegant square.

Kronprinsessegade 13. ℂ **33-11-13-04.** www.restaurantgeranium.dk. Reservations required. Main courses DKK238–DKK355 ($40–$60/£24–£36); fixed-price menus DKK298–DKK865 ($51–$147/£30–£87). AE, DC, MC, V. Tues–Fri noon–1:30pm; Tues–Sat 6:30–9:30pm. S-tog: Nørreport.

L'Alsace ★ CONTINENTAL   We have only one "beef" about this place. It's so intimate, you can hear personal conversations at the next table. One night Elton John told his table that religion is such an evil force in the world that it should be done away with. Queen Margrethe was overheard speaking about Queen Elizabeth II, but the Danish queen was discreet and made only flattering references. It is not known if Pope John Paul II uttered any indiscreet remarks while dining here. He spoke in such a soft whisper, he could not be overheard. Most diners come not to eavesdrop but to partake of some of the best recipes from the continental kitchen. In summer, weather permitting, meals are served in a cobblestone-studded courtyard that's directly accessible from the all-pedestrian Strøget. In an 18th-century building, an Austrian established the restaurant in 1978, and it's been a durable fixture on the Copenhagen dining scene ever since, providing a welcome change from too constant a diet of Danish food. Amid a striking collection of modern paintings, many of them by an artist named Wilhelm Fredy, you can order dishes from across the culinary divides of Europe. Many derive from Alsace, including sauerkraut studded with pork knuckles and pork sausages, and a terrine of foie gras. There are also succulent oysters from the Atlantic coast of France, plate-sized Wiener schnitzels, *tafelspitz* (Habsburg-style boiled beef with horseradish), carpaccio from Italy, bouillabaisse inspired by the traditions of Provence, savory Spain-derived tapas, Austrian-style roulades of beef, pepper steaks, roasted duck with orange sauce, Chilean sea bass with Pernod sauce, and other items that change according to the whim of the chef and the availability of ingredients.

Ny Østerg 9. ℂ **33-14-57-43.** www.alsace.dk. Reservations recommended. Lunch main courses DKK132–DKK188 ($22–$32/£13–£19); dinner main courses DKK154–DKK282 (26–$48/£15–£28); rice menus DKK362–DKK452 ($62–$77/£36–£45). AE, DC, MC, V. Mon–Sat 11:30am–midnight; first Sun of the month 11:30am–4pm. Bus: 5.

Inexpensive
Café Zeze CONTINENTAL   On some days, if you have an ambitious sightseeing agenda, only a cafe will do to get you in and out quickly. Set in a neighborhood with a dense collection of shops and offices, this hip bistro and cafe has a reputation for good

food and brisk service. You'll find a cheerful-looking setup with a high ceiling, mirrors, and a mostly yellow interior. Noise levels can get a bit high, especially late at night, when more folk seem to be drinking than eating, but overall the place can be a lot of fun. Menu items change frequently, but expect a well-prepared medley of dishes. The menu is better than some fast-food joint, and the cooks use market-fresh ingredients to create old favorites such as grilled chicken breast with fresh mushrooms or filet of lamb with shiitake mushrooms. Sometimes they even use their imaginations, dressing up a sautéed turkey breast with coconut and chili sauce or else roasted guinea fowl with fresh shrimp and braised arugula.

Ny Østergade 20. © **33-14-23-90.** Reservations recommended. Lunch main courses DKK80–DKK110 ($14–$19/£8–£11); dinner main courses DKK125–DKK189 ($21–$32/£13–£19). AE, DC, MC, V. Mon–Sat 11:30am–4:30pm and 5:30–10pm (last order). Bar and cafe Mon–Thurs 9am–midnight; Fri–Sat 9am–3am. Bus: 350 F.

Nyhavns Færgekro ★ (Finds) DANISH/FRENCH   The "Nyhavn Ferry Inn" near the harbor has a long tradition and many loyal fans, of which we include ourselves. The house is old, dating from the final years of the 18th century. Diners enjoy not only their food but also a view of the surrounding 18th-century houses and the canal from the popular summer terrace. Inside, the decor is unusual, with a spiral stairway from an antique tram and a black-and-white "checkerboard" marble floor. Lights serve as call buttons to summon the staff when you want service.

The kitchen prepares a daily homemade buffet of 10 types of herring in different styles and sauces, including fried, *rollmops* (rolled or curled herring), and smoked. Some people make a full meal of the herring. You can also order *smørrebrød*—everything from smoked eel with scrambled eggs to chicken salad with bacon. A true Dane, in the tradition of Nyhavn, orders a schnapps or akvavit at lunch. Denmark has a tradition of making spicy akvavit from the herbs and plants of the land—Saint-John's-wort from Tisvilde Hegn, sloe-leaf from the wild moors, green walnuts from the south of Funen, and many other varieties. Dinners here are relatively limited, usually configured as a fixed-price menu, with main courses including a choice of either grilled salmon or grilled entrecote—nothing particularly imaginative but perfectly adequate and well-prepared.

Nyhavn 5. © **33-15-15-88.** www.nyhavnsfaergekro.dk. Reservations required. Lunch herring buffet DKK99 ($17/£9.90); fixed-price dinner DKK239 ($41/£24). DC, MC, V. Daily 11:30am–4pm and 5–11:30pm. Closed Jan 1 and Dec 24–25. Bus: 1, 6, or 9.

Parnas DANISH   This is the best place in Copenhagen for late-night refugees to satisfy their munchies. The food may not be the best, but where else can you order a grilled steak and a beer at 3 o'clock in the morning? Opposite the city's largest department store, Magasin, this late-night refuge is decorated like a warm, rustic, old-fashioned Danish *kro* (inn). Begin with three different kinds of herring or marinated salmon, followed by fried sliced pork with parsley sauce, several different preparations of sole and salmon, or the house specialty—*Parnas Gryde,* which combines grilled sirloin with bacon, marrow, and mushrooms, with béarnaise sauce on the side. This platter has been on the menu since the restaurant opened in the 1930s. After midnight, a limited menu is available, and live music begins at 8:30pm.

Lille Kongensgade 16. © **33-11-49-10.** Reservations required. Main courses DKK128–DKK198 ($22–$34/£13–£20). AE, DC, MC, V. Mon–Thurs noon–3am; Fri–Sat noon–5am. Bus: 1 or 6.

Restaurant/Café Nytorv (Kids) DANISH   It occupies a building at the most distant end of the most elegant square in central Copenhagen, a baroque perimeter that's particularly charming on warm summer nights. Inside, you'll find a warren of cozy dining areas, each low-ceilinged, each evoking 19th-century Copenhagen, and each a bastion of uncompromising Danish nationalism in all things cultural and culinary. The place, like so many others in the area, used to shelter drunks, sailors, and prostitutes. Don't come here expecting cutting-edge cuisine or decor, as very little has changed since the early 1960s in terms of decor—and since the early 1920s in terms of cuisine. But prices are relatively affordable for this part of town; the *smørrebrød* are suitably thick; and the *Københavner platte,* a platter piled high with Danish herring, cheese, meatballs, and more, is suitably filling. If you happen to have children in tow, there's a kids' menu, and it's otherwise hard to turn down for diners of any age. Menu items include Danish pork sausage with potatoes, beef sirloin with béarnaise, *frikadeller* with potatoes, *biksemal* (Danish hash), and Madagascar-style pepper steak.

Nytorv 15. ✆ **33-11-77-06.** Reservations recommended. Sandwiches DKK49–DKK99 ($8.40–$17/£4.90–£9.90); main courses DKK109–DKK179 ($19–$30/£11–£18); children's menu DKK49 ($8.40/£4.90). AE, DC, MC, V. Mon–Fri 11am–10pm; Sat noon–9pm. Bus: 1, 6, or 10.

Skindbuksen (Moments) DANISH   Call this a local favorite. This place is more Danish than the queen, and probably a lot more fun. Although it's in an expensive neighborhood, it not only is reasonable in price but also is a down-home type of place (that is, down-home Danish style). This atmospheric landmark has long drawn beer drinkers in the neighborhood. Many locals, often old sailors, swear by its *skipperlabskovs,* the Danish version of a meat-and-potato hash that has kept many a mariner from starvation over the years. This popular dish is often sold out at noon. A good variety of *smørrebrød* is always a luncheon favorite. You can order other dishes too, including homemade soups, pâtés, fresh shrimp, and a local favorite, tender beef served with a béarnaise sauce. There is live piano music Monday to Saturday from 8pm to 12:30am.

Lille Kongensgade 4 (off Kongens Nytorv). ✆ **33-12-90-37.** www.skindbuksen.dk. Reservations recommended. Main courses DKK109–DKK189 ($19–$32/£11–£19). MC, V. Daily 11:30am–midnight (kitchen closes at 10pm). Bus: 1, 6, 15, or 26.

NEAR ØSTERBRO
Moderate

Le Saint-Jacques ★ FRENCH   Rather bizarrely, this place designed its interior to look like a small church in the heart of Østerbro. Set in a single dignified dining room, in a building that's at least a century old, this well-respected French restaurant has a talent for defining itself as an unofficial embassy of Gallic goodwill. During mild weather, you can escape from the somewhat cramped interior in favor of a table on the street outside, adding a flavor that might remind you of something in the south of France. Menu items change frequently, based on the inspiration of the chef and the availability of ingredients. A steady hand in the kitchen admirably presents dishes to diners who usually have traditional tastes. Excellent ingredients also go into this skillful cuisine, and the wide-ranging wine list includes vintages from around the world. The waiters promise you they will deliver good food, and they do, as exemplified by the North Atlantic scallops with salmon roe and leeks in a beurre blanc sauce. One couldn't hope to do better than order one of the free-range chickens with a cream-flavored morel sauce. Finally, you also can't go wrong with the filet of sole enlivened with a slight balsamic glaze.

Skt. Jacobs Pladsen 1. ✆ **35-42-77-07.** Reservations recommended. Lunch main courses DKK88–DKK147 ($15–$25/£8.80–£15); dinner main courses DKK215 ($37/£22); 3-course menu DKK335 ($57/£34); 4-course menu DKK405 ($69/£41); 5-course menu DKK485 ($82/£49). AE, DC, MC, V. Daily noon–midnight. Bus: 1A or 14.

Very Expensive

Alberto K. ★ DANISH/ITALIAN   Named for the innovative hotelier and international gourmet Alberto Kappenberger, this restaurant is the most successful in wedding Danish raw materials with the culinary techniques of the new Italian kitchen. From the homemade durum bread freshly baked that morning to the just-caught lobster, the chefs here place a great emphasis on freshness. Most fusion dishes are successful, including Danish rabbit with Umbrian truffle oil, or Danish lump fish with fresh rosemary grown in the Tuscan countryside. Pigeon and woodland mushrooms are served with polenta, pumpkin, chestnuts, and wood sorrel, or North Sea cod and oysters arrive with tiny spheres of fresh apple, each drizzled in Prosecco. The restaurant lies on the 20th floor of this previously recommended hotel.

In the Radisson SAS Royal Hotel, Hammerichsgade 1. © **38-15-65-00.** Reservations required. Fixed-price menus DKK555 ($94/£56), DKK675 ($115/£68), and DKK750 ($128/£75). AE, DC, MC, V. Mon–Sat 6–10pm. Bus: 14 or 16.

Expensive

Fox Kitchen and Bar ★ SCANDINAVIAN   This is the fashionable and trend-conscious restaurant that's associated with the also-recommended hotel—the one where each room is the often-eccentric decorative statement of an individual artist. They don't serve lunch, but every afternoon, the bar area of this restaurant is filled to capacity with the young, the restless, the bored, and, sometimes, the beautiful. Expect earth tones, wood chairs, and a judicious use of plastic mixed with fine hardwoods. Menu items are competently prepared, often with flair, and might include marinated hake with nasturtium flowers and mildly smoked rapeseed oil. Or else you might try the pan-seared filet of plaice, with celeriac, cauliflower, and two real delights: a parsley-flavored sorbet and a foamy dill sauce. Innovation combined with carefully crafted dishes is the house style, as exemplified by the anise- and chervil-marinated tenderloin of lamb with tender green

---

In Praise of the *Smørrebrød*

The favorite Danish dish at midday is the ubiquitous *smørrebrød* (open-faced sandwiches)—a national institution. Literally, this means "bread and butter," but the Danes stack this sandwich as if it were the Leaning Tower of Pisa—and then throw in a slice of curled cucumber and bits of parsley, or perhaps sliced peaches or a mushroom for added color.

Two of these sandwiches can make a more-than-filling lunch. They're everywhere—from the grandest dining rooms to the lowliest pushcart. Many restaurants offer a wide selection; guests look over a checklist and then mark the ones they want. Some are made with sliced pork (perhaps a prune on top), roast beef with béarnaise sauce and crispy fried bits of onion, or liver paste adorned with an olive or cucumber slice and gelatin made with strong beef stock.

Smørrebrød is often served as an hors d'oeuvre. The most popular, most tempting, and usually most expensive of these delicacies is prepared with tiny Danish shrimp, on which a lemon slice and caviar often perch, perhaps even with fresh dill. The "ugly duckling" of the *smørrebrød* family is anything with a cold sunny-side-up egg on top of it.

Tips **Quick Bites in Copenhagen**

Copenhagen has many hot dog stands, chicken and fish grills, and *smørrebrød* counters that serve good, fast, inexpensive meals.

Hot dog stands, especially those around Rådhuspladsen, offer *polser* (steamed or grilled hot dogs) with shredded onions on top and *pommes frites* (french fries) on the side.

The *bageri* or *konditori* (bakery), found on almost every block, sells fresh bread, rolls, and Danish pastries.

Viktualiehandler (small food shops), found throughout the city, are the closest thing to a New York deli. You can buy roast beef with free *log* (fried onions). The best buy is smoked fish. Ask for a Bornholmer, a large, boneless sardine from the Danish island of Bornholm, or for *røgost*, a popular and inexpensive smoked cheese. Yogurt fans will be delighted to know that the Danish variety is cheap and tasty. It's available in small containers—just peel off the cover and drink it right out of the cup as the Danes do. *Hytte ret* (cottage cheese) is also good and cheap.

The favorite lunch of Scandinavians, particularly Danes, is the open-faced sandwich called **smørrebrød.** The purest form is made with dark rye bread, called *rugbrød.* Most taverns and cafes offer *smørrebrød,* and many places serve it as takeout food.

You can picnic in any of the city parks in the town center. Try Kongsgarten near Kongens Nytorv; the Kastellet area near *Den Lille Havfrue;* Botanisk Have (site of the Botanical Gardens); the lakeside promenades in southeastern Copenhagen; and the old moat at Christianshavn. Remember not to litter!

---

lentils and cold yogurt. Flavors are blended beautifully in the spinach lasagna with savory goat cheese and a rich vegetable bouillon. After the dishes are tucked away, the bar area here continues on till at least midnight.

In the Hotel Fox, 3 Jarmers Plad. ☏ **33-13-30-00.** www.hotelfox.dk. Reservations recommended. Main courses DKK75–DKK129 ($13–$22/£7.50–£13); fixed-price menu DKK315 ($54/£32). AE, DC, MC, V. Daily 5–11pm. Bus: 5A, 14, or 16.

Moderate

Atlas Bar/Restaurant Flyvefisken DANISH/THAI/INTERNATIONAL This joint has always been a darling of local hipsters, and you may want to join them for a slice of Copenhagen life often not seen by the casual visitor. The cuisine at these two restaurants (prepared in the same kitchen) includes lots of vegetarian food inspired by the fare of Thailand, Mexico, and India, with a Danish overview toward tidiness and coziness. On the street level, the cramped, cozy Atlas Bar serves a busy lunchtime crowd, but slackens off a bit at night, when the wood-sheathed Flyvefisken (Flying Fish) opens for dinner upstairs. Upstairs, expect a bit more emphasis on Thai cuisine and its fiery flavors, including lemongrass, curries, and several of the hot, spicy fish soups native to Bangkok. Although the authenticity of the Thai cuisine has lost a bit of its zest in the long jump from Thailand, it's still a change of pace from typical Danish fare. Expect crowds here, especially at lunch, when the place is likely to be full.

Lars Bjørnstræde 18. ℂ **33-14-95-15**. www.atlasbar.dk. Reservations recommended. Lunch main courses DKK82–DKK128 ($14–$22/£8.20–£13); dinner main courses DKK110–DKK135 ($19–$23/£11–£14). AE, DC, MC, V. Atlas Bar Mon–Sat noon–10pm. Restaurant Flyvefisken Mon–Sat 5:30–10pm. Bus: 5 or 6A.

Copenhagen Corner (Kids) INTERNATIONAL/FRENCH This is no doubt the most convenient place for a good meal in the heart of Copenhagen. It's an especially good choice if you're going to the Tivoli Gardens nearby and don't want to pay the inflated food prices charged there. Set amid some of the heaviest pedestrian traffic in Copenhagen, this deeply entrenched landmark restaurant opens onto Rådhuspladsen, around the corner from the Tivoli Gardens. Outfitted with some of the accessories of a greenhouse-style conservatory for plants, it offers well-prepared, unpretentious meals to dozens of city residents throughout the day and evening. The menu, which offers many Danish favorites, will place you deep in the heart of Denmark, beginning with three kinds of herring or freshly peeled shrimp with dill and lemon. There's even a carpaccio of filet of deer for the most adventurous palates. The soups are excellent, such as the consommé of white asparagus flavored with chicken and fresh herbs. The fish is fresh and beautifully prepared, especially the steamed Norwegian salmon with a "lasagna" of potatoes, or the baked halibut with artichokes. Meat and poultry courses, although not always equal to the fish, are tasty and tender, especially the veal liver Provençal.

H. C. Andersens Blvd. 1A. ℂ **33-91-45-45**. www.nphotels.dk. Reservations recommended. Main courses DKK198–DKK265 ($34–$45/£20–£27). AE, DC, MC, V. Daily 11:30am–11pm. Bus: 1, 6, or 8.

Søren K ★ INTERNATIONAL/FRENCH Named after Denmark's most celebrated philosopher, this is an artfully minimalist dining room that's on the ground floor of the Black Diamond (the ultramodern, intensely angular addition to the Royal Library). It has the kind of monochromatic gray and flesh-toned decor you might find in Milan, and glassy, big-windowed views that stretch out over the nearby canal. Menu items change frequently, but the chef never cooks with butter, cream, or high-cholesterol cheese, making a meal here a low-cholesterol and savory experience. In a land known for its "butter-and-egg men," this type of cooking is heresy. Some Danes boycott it, but foreign visitors, especially those watching their waistlines, flock here for a superb meal. Your taste buds will love you if you order such dishes as a velvety foie gras, a carpaccio of veal, and a truly superb oyster soup. Attention to detail and a proud professionalism distinguish such main dishes as veal chops served with lobster sauce and a half-lobster or else roasted venison with nuts and seasonal berries with a marinade of green tomatoes, the latter providing a wonderful savory taste that we enjoy. To reach this place, you'll have to enter the library, and pass through the lobby of the new Black Diamond Wing.

On the ground floor of the Royal Library's Black Diamond Wing, Søren Kierkegaards Plads 1. ℂ **33-47-49-49**. Reservations recommended. Lunch main courses DKK75–DKK195 ($13–$33/£7.50–£20); dinner main courses DKK195–DKK345 ($33–$59/£20–£35); fixed-price 3-course dinner DKK365–DKK420 ($62–$71/£37–£42); 6-course tasting menu DKK415–DKK470 ($71–$80/£42–£47). AE, DC, MC, V. Mon–Sat 11am–10:30pm. Bus: 1, 2, 5, 8, or 9.

Sult ★ DANISH/FRENCH If you, like us, were turned on by the novel *Sult*, by Norwegian author Knut Hamsun, you might want to try out the restaurant whose moniker pays homage to the book. This fashionable, trendy eatery is inside the Danish Film Institute's center and is both a cultural and a gourmet experience. The setting is like a modern museum with wood floors, towering windows, and lofty ceilings. Chef Fredrik

Ohlsson has traveled the continent for his culinary inspiration, although he specializes in French cuisine. Using market-fresh ingredients, he often elevates his food to the sublime. Just describing the rather simple dishes does not suggest their artfulness in seasonings and natural flavors. The chef will take a grilled tuna or a filet of lamb, even oven-baked lemon sole, and make something special out of it. If you don't want to make decisions, opt for one of the fixed-price menus, which are innovative and engaging to the palate. The wine list is impressive but rather high-priced.

Vognmagergade 8B. ⓒ **33-74-34-17.** Reservations recommended. Main courses DKK155–DKK225 ($26–$38/£16–£23); fixed-price menus DKK400–DKK500 ($68–$85/£40–£50). AE, DC, MC, V. Tues–Sat noon–midnight; Sun 11am–10pm. S-tog: Nørreport.

Inexpensive

Axelborg Bodega DANISH   Since 1912, down-home cooking Danish style has been served in this cafe across from Benneweis Circus and near Scala and the Tivoli. In fair weather, you can sit out enjoying a brisk Copenhagen evening and people-watching. Most regulars here opt for the *dagens ret* (daily special), which is the equivalent of the old blue-plate special served at diners throughout America in the 1940s. Typical Danish dishes are featured on those specials, invariably *frikadeller* and the inevitable pork chops, which was the favorite dish of the Nazi occupation forces in the early '40s. A wide selection of *smørrebrød* is also available, costing DKK57 to DKK99 (9.70–$17/£5.70–£9.90) each. Although the atmosphere is somewhat impersonal, this is a local favorite; diners enjoy the recipes from grandma's attic.

Axeltorv 1. ⓒ **33-11-06-38.** Reservations recommended. Main courses DKK109–DKK199 ($19–$34/£11–£20). DC, MC, V. Restaurant daily 11am–9pm. Bar daily 11am–2am. Bus: 1 or 6.

Café Sorgenfri ⟨**Value**⟩ SANDWICHES   The English translation for this place means "without sorrows." Should you have any sorrows, you can drown them in your beer here, in a cafe sheltered in a house from 1796. The draft beer flows freely throughout the day in the cafe's antique interior, with its subdued lighting and fresh flowers. Don't come here expecting grand cuisine, or even a menu with any particular variety. This place has thrived for 150 years selling beer, schnapps, and a medley of *smørrebrød* that appeal to virtually everyone's sense of workaday thrift and frugality. With only about 50 seats, the joint is likely to be crowded around the lunch hour, with somewhat more space during the midafternoon. Everything inside reeks of old-time Denmark, from the potted shrubs that adorn the facade to the well-oiled paneling that has witnessed many generations of Copenhageners selecting and enjoying sandwiches. Between two and four of them might compose a reasonable lunch (sandwiches, not Copenhageners!), depending on your appetite. You'll find it in the all-pedestrian shopping zone, in the commercial heart of town.

Brolæggerstræde 8. ⓒ **33-11-58-80.** www.cafesorgenfri.dk. Reservations recommended for groups of 4 or more. Smørrebrød DKK49–DKK159 ($8.40–$27/£4.90–£16). AE, DC, MC, V. Daily 11am–9pm. Bus: 5 or 6.

Chili AMERICAN   Boisterous, informal, and with an American theme, this is the most recent incarnation of a once-famous 19th-century establishment known to many generations of Danes as Tokanten and our favorite hangout from long ago. Today, lacking its former bohemian atmosphere, Chili serves at least 17 versions of burgers, available in quarter- and half-pound sizes, whose descriptions read like a map of the world. Choices include Hawaii burgers (with pineapple and curry), English burgers (with bacon and fried eggs), French burgers (with mushrooms in cream sauce), Danish burgers (with fried onions), and all the Texas burgers and chili burgers you could want. Also available are well-stuffed sandwiches and grilled steak platters. Service is fast, and the ambience is unpretentious.

Vandkunsten 1. ✆ **33-91-19-18.** Main courses DKK78–DKK116 ($13–$20/£7.80–£12); burgers and sandwiches DKK55–DKK110 ($9.40–$19/£5.50–£11). No credit cards. Mon–Sat 11am–midnight; Sun 11am–11pm. Bus: 6A.

Domhus Kælderen DANISH/INTERNATIONAL   For some reason this eatery seems to attract a lot of foreign visitors, especially English hipsters. To understand some of the dialogue, you may need a translator, unless you understand "Did you see that bird kick that bloke in the huevos?" Its good food, and a location across the square from City Hall also guarantees a large number of lawyers and their clients. This is a bustling and old-fashioned emporium of Danish cuisine. The setting is a half-cellar room illuminated with high lace-draped windows that shine light down on wooden tables and 50 years of memorabilia. Menu items at lunch might include *frikadeller,* and heaping platters of herring, Danish cheeses, smoked meats and fish, salads, and a worthy assortment of *smørrebrød.* The dinner menu is more ambitious, calling for a harder effort on the part of the kitchen staff, who turn out pickled salmon and several fine cuts of beef—our favorite choices—served with either a béarnaise or pepper sauce. Also look for the catch of the day, prepared virtually any way you like. The food is typically Danish and well prepared, and you get no culinary surprises here; but then, you are rarely disappointed.

Nytorv 5. ✆ **33-14-84-55.** Reservations recommended. Lunch main courses DKK70–DKK176 ($12–$30/£7–£18); dinner main courses DKK128–DKK200 ($22–$34/£13–£20); set menus DKK265–DKK285 ($45–$48/£27–£29). AE, DC, MC, V. Daily 11am–9:30pm. Bus: 5.

Husmann Vinstue ⟨Value⟩ SANDWICHES   Would you believe that when we worked on an earlier version of this guide prior to 1980, a single woman wasn't allowed in this joint without a male escort? Now that women are allowed, one might ask why they fought to gain entrance in the first place. It's not that special, but we love it for its old-time atmosphere. It was founded back in 1888 as an all-male tavern, and the decor hasn't changed much since then in this two-fisted, bustling luncheon stopover. In spite of the somewhat seedy atmosphere, we find that the cooks make some of the most satisfying *smørrebrød* in town. The fresh raw materials and the homemade cooking are first-rate, as you devour ping-pong-size meatballs, several varieties of herring, and small cuts of tender Danish beef. Surely you will agree with us that Danish cheese is among the finest in the world.

Larsbjørnsstræde 2. ✆ **33-11-58-86.** Reservations recommended. Main courses DKK61–DKK109 ($10–$19/£6.10–£11). AE, DC, MC, V. Daily 11:30am–4pm (last order). Bus: 5.

Kobenhavner Cafeen DANISH ⟨Kids⟩   Danes go here for their comfort-food fix, and we like to join them. One of the smallest (about 45 seats) restaurants in this pedestrian-only zone, the Kobenhavner works hard to convey a sense of old-time Denmark. There's been an inn on this site since the 12th century, but the current structure dates from the 19th century. The setting is cozy, and you can enjoy authentically old-fashioned food items whose preparation adheres to methods practiced by many Danish grandmothers. Expect a roster of open-faced sandwiches at both lunch and dinner; *frikadeller;* grilled filets of plaice with butter sauce and fresh asparagus; roasted pork with braised red cabbage; and *biksemal,* a type of seafood hash that was served several times a week in many Danish homes throughout World War II. One of the most appealing items, a specialty of the house, is the *Københavner platte,* which features several preparations of herring, marinated salmon, shrimp, meatballs, fresh vegetables, and fresh-baked, roughly textured bread with butter. Be warned that Santa impersonators might be entertaining the children in the crowd during your visit, even if your visit happens to fall during the month of August.

Badstuestæde 10. ☎ **33-32-80-81**. Reservations recommended. *Smørrebrød* DKK49–DKK105 ($8.40–$18/£4.90–£11); main courses DKK95–DKK179 ($16–$30/£9.50–£18). AE, DC, MC, V. Daily 11am–midnight. Bus: 5 or 6.

Puk's Restaurant DANISH   We admire this eatery for never pretending to be more than what it is, which is a place to go for real Danish cooking. Without any particular flair, it dispenses hearty and filling meals based on market-fresh ingredients. Solid and reliable, this restaurant is housed inside the thick stone walls of a former 18th-century brewery. You can enjoy a drink or two in the atmospheric pub next door. Most serious diners head down a flight of stairs from the street into the cellar-level restaurant. Menu selections include Danish meatballs, platters of *smørrebrød* or several kinds of smoked fish, herring offered either cold and marinated or fried and served with dill and new potatoes, and tournedos of beef with a sauce made from fresh tomatoes and herbs. The cooks prepare these dishes like your mother does—assuming she's Danish.

Vandkunsten 8. ☎ **33-11-14-17**. Reservations required in summer and Dec only. Main courses DKK128–DKK168 ($22–$29/£13–£17). AE, DC, MC, V. Daily 11:30am–10pm. Bus: 1A, 2A, or 6A.

Riz Raz ★ (Value) MIDDLE EASTERN/VEGETARIAN   If you're ravenous, this is the best food deal we can find in Copenhagen. Imagine an all-you-can-eat Mediterranean buffet at a very decent price in high-priced Denmark. Bustling and unpretentious, this decidedly un-Danish hideaway offers the best all-vegetarian buffet in Copenhagen. There's additional seating outdoors during mild weather. Expect a medley of virtually every vegetable known to humankind, prepared either au naturel or as part of a marinated fantasy that might include the antipasti of Italy, the hummus of Lebanon, or an array of long-simmered casseroles inspired by the cuisine of the Moroccan highlands. There's also a selection of pastas, some of them redolent with garlic, oil, and Mediterranean spices, as well as a limited array of meat and fish dishes. Service staff is composed mostly of students from countries around the world. Beer and wine are served, which means that the staff doesn't take any hair shirt, holier-than-thou attitude as they do in so many other vegetarian restaurants.

Kompagnistræde 20 (at Knabrostræde). ☎ **33-15-05-75**. Vegetarian buffet DKK80 ($14/£8) per person; main courses DKK120–DKK190 ($20–$32/£12–£19). AE, DC, MC, V. Daily 11:30am–midnight. Bus: 5 or 6.

Slotskælderen DANISH   A star on the *smørrebrød* circuit, this landmark opened in 1797 but since 1910 has been owned by the same family. Habitués call the place "Gitte Kik," the name of the owner and granddaughter of the founder, and a woman who's often identified, along with her arch rival, Ida Davidsen, as "*smørrebrød* queen" of Copenhagen. We have long grown bored with Ida's sandwiches, and her joint is far too touristy for our tastes; so we've passed the crown of "sandwich queen" along to Gitte Kik. Everything—the Danish wood trim, the old photographs, and the gold walls—adds up to *hygge*, a coziness that has attracted such notables as the prince of Denmark, the king and queen of Sweden, and the late Victor Borge, one of the most famous entertainers to ever emerge from Denmark, and once adored by American TV audiences—and still remembered by those of a certain age. Try the marinated salmon, fresh tiny shrimp, or hot *frikadeller*. The smoked-eel and scrambled-egg sandwich is the best of its kind, although we admit that this is an acquired taste—an eel sandwich is not everybody's idea of a good time.

Fortunstræde 4. ☎ **33-11-15-37**. Reservations recommended. *Smørrebrød* DKK42–DKK78 ($7–$13/£4.20–£7.80). AE, DC, MC, V. Tues–Sat 11am–3pm. Bus: 1A, 15, or 19.

NEAR ROSENBORG SLOT
Very Expensive

St. Gertruds Kloster ★★★ **Finds** INTERNATIONAL   Surely this is how the medieval kings of Denmark must have dined, with Hamlet pondering the question in the background. It is the most romantic restaurant in Denmark, a great place to pop the question or tell your spouse you want a divorce. There's no electricity in the labyrinth of 14th-century underground vaults, and the 1,500 flickering candles, open grill, iron sconces, and rough-hewn furniture create an elegant ambience. Enjoy an aperitif in the darkly paneled library. The chefs display talent and integrity, their cuisine reflecting precision and sensitivity. Every flavor is fully focused, each dish balanced to perfection. Try the fresh, homemade foie gras with black truffles, lobster served in a turbot bouillon, venison (year-round) with green asparagus and truffle sauce, or a fish-and-shellfish terrine studded with chunks of lobster and salmon. These dishes range from being merely good to being sublime.

Hauser Plads 32. ⓒ **33-14-66-30.** Reservations required. Main courses DKK250–DKK300 ($43–$51/£25–£30); fixed-price menu DKK488–DKK528 ($83–$90/£49–£53). AE, DC, MC, V. Daily 5–11pm. Closed Dec 25–Jan 1. Bus: 4E, 7E, 14, or 16.

AT GRÅBRØDRETORV

Gråbrødretorv (Grey Friars Square), in the heart of Copenhagen's medieval core, is named after the monks who used to wander through its premises in medieval times. Now viewed as charming and hip, the area is a late-night destination that's not unlike what you'd find in the Latin Quarter of Paris. The setting is low-key, unpretentious, and representative of the brown-brick architecture that fills most of the rest of historic Copenhagen.

Moderate

Bøf & Ost DANISH/FRENCH   Even if the food weren't good, we'd like to come here on a summer evening to occupy a cafe-style table overlooking Grey Friars Square. We consider this eatery the best people-watching place in Copenhagen. This neighborhood favorite created a bit of a buzz when it first opened in a 1728 building constructed over cellars from a medieval monastery. But that buzz has long died down as fickle foodies have found newer places other than "Beef & Cheese" to pamper their stomachs. But, even though abandoned by the media in search of something new, the place still turns out food as good as it was the day it opened. The lobster soup still wins us over, and we often follow with some of the best beef tenderloin steaks in town. After all, Bøf & Ost has to live up to its namesake. The cheese in its name is justified when a platter with six different selections of the best cheese in the country arrives for you to devour with crusty and freshly baked bread.

Gråbrødretorv 13. ⓒ **33-11-99-11.** www.boef-ost.dk. Reservations required. Main courses DKK169–DKK225 ($29–$38/£17–£23); fixed-price lunch menu DKK138 ($23/£14). DC, MC, V. Mon–Sat 11:30am–10:30pm. Closed Jan 1. Bus: 5.

Peder Oxe's Restaurant/Vinkælder Wine Bar ★ DANISH   The setting alone has a certain romance, as in the Middle Ages it was the site of a monastery for gray-robed friars who couldn't own anything and were forced to beg for a living. Although fresh salad buffets now stretch from the New York islands to the Pacific coastline, the idea had never been introduced into Denmark until Peder Oxe pioneered the concept. The restaurant continues to this day to select its mesclun, arugula, escarole, watercress, iceberg, spinach, and other popular lettuce greens, and it also uses fine raw materials for its classic dishes.

The cooks serve only beef from free-range cattle, along with freshly caught fish and shellfish. Game from the Danish countryside appears on the menu in autumn, and Danish lamb, among the best in Europe, is a standard feature. Other dishes include a tantalizing lobster soup and those tiny Danish bay shrimp we like to devour. You can also drop in for lunch at any time of the day to order lighter fare, such as open-faced sandwiches or even a Danish hamburger. ("Do you want chili mayonnaise with that?")

We have found that the chefs cook the best fried herring in all of Copenhagen here, and we'll let you in on their secret. They coat filleted fish with Dijon mustard, grated fresh horseradish, and even caviar before rolling them in rye flour and pan-frying them in Danish country butter.

Gråbrødretorv 11. ℂ **33-11-00-77.** Reservations recommended. Main courses DKK119–DKK209 ($20–$36/£12–£21); fixed-price lunch menu DKK69–DKK129 ($12–$22/£6.90–£13). DC, MC, V. Daily 11:30am–midnight. Bus: 5.

Inexpensive

Murdoch's Books & Ale DANISH   Many of the patrons of this relatively inexpensive old-fashioned pub realize only belatedly that it's associated with the very upscale Phoenix Hotel, which occupies the upper floors of the same building, immediately across the Bredgade from the baroque grandeur of the rear side of Amalienborg Palace. Inside, you'll find a long and narrow room with a prominent and very accommodating mahogany bar, an entire wall of purely decorative books (they're not actually intended for reading); leather banquettes, and a menu that's devoted to the kind of platter that usually suffices as a meal in its own right. Menu items include, among others, a lunch plate loaded with three oft-changing Danish delicacies and cheese; vitello tonnato, the Italian version of thin-sliced veal with liquefied tuna; small-scale sirloin steaks with butter-fried onions and a cucumber salad; and "Murdoch's burger" with pecorino cheese, tomatoes, bacon, and fried potatoes. There's also a platter devoted exclusively to walnuts and a selection of Danish cheeses.

In the Phoenix Hotel, 37 Bredgade. ℂ **33-95-92-00.** Main courses DKK115–DKK235 ($20–$40/£12–£24). AE, DC, MC, V. Daily 6pm–1am. Bus: 1.

Pasta Basta Value ITALIAN   When the kroner in your pocket becomes the jangle of coins—not the rustle of paper—head here for a great deal on dining. This restaurant's main attraction is a table loaded with cold antipasti and salads, one of the best deals in town. With more than nine selections on the enormous buffet, it's sometimes called the "Pasta Basta Table." The restaurant itself is divided into half a dozen cozy dining rooms, each decorated in the style of ancient Pompeii, and is located on a historic cobblestone street off the main shopping boulevard, Strøget. Its fans and devotees praise it for its policy of staying open late.

Every day the chefs prepare 15 different homemade pastas. How to choose? You can, if you wish, go with our favorite—saffron-flavored fettuccine in a white-wine sauce with grilled salmon strips and a garnish of salmon caviar. Other menu choices include carpaccio served with olive oil and basil, a platter with three kinds of Danish caviar (whitefish, speckled trout, and vendace), thin-sliced salmon with a cream-based sauce of salmon roe, and Danish suckling lamb with fried spring onions and tarragon.

Valkendorfsgade 22. ℂ **33-11-21-31.** Reservations recommended. Main courses DKK98–DKK189 ($17–$32/£9.80–£19). DC, MC, V. Daily 11:30am–2am. Bus: 5.

Very Expensive

Krogs Fiskerestaurant ★★★ SEAFOOD   Orson Welles claimed that this fish restaurant was the only place north of the Riviera that knew how to make a bouillabaisse. The great actor/director and gourmet/gourmand was just one of the celebrities who has praised this seafood restaurant, one of the oldest in Copenhagen, dating from 1910. Only a short walk from Christiansborg Castle, the restaurant stands in a historic district of 19th-century houses, and its building dates from 1789 when it opened as a fish shop. The canalside plaza, where fishermen moored their boats, is now the site of the restaurant's outdoor terrace. The walls of the high-ceilinged restaurant are covered with gold-plated mirrors and paintings from the 1800s, the work of a Danish artist, Valdemar Andersen.

The chefs strike a studied balance between modernized traditional dishes and updated haute cuisine classics—all at celestial prices. With the main courses, "nouvelle" cuisine here is something served at the turn of the 20th century, including a divine plaice meunière with lemon, parsley, and brown butter. The Dover sole is even prepared at the table, and the shellfish selection, served hot or cold, is without equal in Copenhagen. This is a most engaging restaurant, especially if you're over 50—the "sweet young things" of Copenhagen dine at trendier joints. Before the waiter arrives with the bill, make sure you've taken your heart medication.

Gammel Strand 38. 🕐 **33-15-89-15.** www.krogs.dk. Reservations required. Main courses DKK385–DKK480 ($65–$82/£39–£48); fixed-price 5-course menu DKK795 ($135/£80). AE, DC, MC, V. Mon–Sat 6–11pm. Bus: 1 or 2.

Inexpensive

Thorvaldsen DANISH   For some odd reason, with seemingly no connection, this affordable eatery is named for Bertel Thorvaldsen, Denmark's greatest sculptor, who was born in Copenhagen on November 19, 1768. This restaurant is hardly a citadel of grand cuisine, but it offers some of the best tasting and least expensive *smørrebrød* in town, along with a changing daily array of old-fashioned Danish cookery. Against a backdrop of walls covered with old tapestries, you can partake of this hearty and very filling cuisine. Locals begin with various versions of herring or smoked salmon. You can go on to the typical dishes of the day, which almost invariably include fried plaice. An occasional special appears with flair and flavor, including, for example, free-range Danish roasted chicken with a saffron sauce, accompanied by a helping of risotto. For dessert, opt for the fresh fruit with vanilla ice cream. Tables are placed outside in a courtyard if the weather allows.

Gammel Strand 34. 🕐 **33-32-04-00.** Reservations recommended. Main courses DKK89–DKK259 ($15–$44/£8.90–£26). MC, V. Mon–Thurs 11am–10pm; Fri–Sat 11am–10:30pm. Bus: 1A.

IN NØRREBRO
Moderate

Nørrebro Bryghus ★ ⒻⒾⓃⒹⓈ DANISH   This is the best and most appealing restaurant in the Nørrebro district, a big-time, big-city brewery restaurant that dwarfs almost every other restaurant in the neighborhood. Occupying two floors of what was originally built in 1857 as a metal foundry, it brews between 10,000 and 20,000 liters (2,600–5,200 gallons) of beer per month, as many as 10 different kinds, all of which are dispensed in copious amounts within the restaurant. In addition, many of the dishes served here are braised, fried, or stewed in beer. And if you're interested in how the fruit of the hops is actually concocted, you can sign up for any of the free brewery tours conducted here every Monday to Thursday from 5 to 6pm (Danish-language versions) and from 6 to 7pm (English-language versions). Menu items change with the season and with whatever beer happens to have been brewed within the previous week or so. Examples include crisp-fried whitefish served with roasted and glazed fennel in Pacific Pale Ale in a coriander beurre blanc and tarragon sauce; cold tomato consommé flavored with Çeske Böhmer beer, smoked shrimps, scallops, and shellfish oil; poached filet of beef served with mangetout peas, new carrots, and haricots verts, served with sage sauce flavored with La Granja Stout; Parmesan (aged 36 months) with flower honey flavored with lemon zest and Skt. Hans Dubbel; and raspberry sorbet with Stuykman Wit beer, and sugar cookies. One of the genuinely sought-after facets of this place involves reserving the "brewmaster's table" for a specially composed seven- or eight-course meal, each course liberally soused with a different beer, with a minimum of eight diners needed for the full-fledged experience.

Ryesgade 3. (✆ **35-30-05-30.** http://noerrebrobryghus.dk. Reservations not necessary, except for brewmaster's table. Lunch platters DKK88–DKK172 ($15–$29/£8.80–£17); dinner main courses DKK219–DKK245 ($37–$42/£22–£25); fixed-price menus DKK325–DKK398 ($55–$68/£33–£40). AE, DC, MC, V. Sun–Wed 11:30am–3pm and 5:30–10pm (bar till midnight); Thurs–Sat 11:30am–3pm and 5:30–10:30pm (bar till 2am). Bus: 3A.

Pussy Galore's Flying Circus ★ INTERNATIONAL   No restaurant in Copenhagen has such an amusing name. Named after the James Bond character, this trendy eatery is in a trendy neighborhood. From inexpensive fresh salads to some of the juiciest burgers in town, it's a great place to eat, drink, and make the scene. The location is a bit away from the center, but that doesn't seem to bother one of its patrons, Prince Frederik, the playboy heir to the throne. Media types also flock here.

In summer, tables overflow onto the sidewalk. Many books that review the world's best bars, including one by "Black Bush Whiskey," list this place among the globe's best watering holes. As an attractive waiter confided to us, "Café Ketchup gets the young and beautiful; we get the younger and more beautiful." Against a 1990s minimalist decor, with Arne Jacobsen chairs, partake of great cocktails (especially those mojitos). Many regulars drop in every morning for eggs and bacon, returning in the evening for, perhaps, a wok-fried delight.

Sankt Hans Torv 30. (✆ **35-24-53-00.** Reservations not accepted. Main courses DKK95–DKK130 ($16–$22/£9.50–£13). AE, DC, MC, V. Mon–Fri 8am–2am; Sat–Sun 9am–2am. Bus: 3A.

VESTERBRO
Very Expensive
Kiin Kiin ★★ THAI   At this restaurant, the Baltic kitchen meets up with Bangkok. The result is a delight at this chic little bastion of modern Thai cookery. Many Danes stop off in the lounge to feast on such treats as roasted lotus root with lime leaves, soy-roasted cashews, or tapioca crisps with dried shrimp. Those seeking more formal dining can order one of the fixed-price menus. A typical one might feature shellfish soup; green curry with mussels and fresh seafood; crispy fried garfish with orchids (this is not a misprint); Pad Thai with tamarind and bean sprouts; fried rice with braised oxtail; and pigeon, in soy honey and ginger, with hand-rolled noodles; finished off with passion fruit, kumquats, and banana cake. One of the chef's best dishes is red coconut curry with litchi nuts and fresh shellfish.

Guldbergsgade 21. (✆ **35-35-75-55.** www.kiin.dk. Reservations required. Fixed-price menu DKK750 ($128/£75). AE, MC, V. Mon–Sat 5:30pm–midnight. Bus: 5A.

Moderate

Karriere ★ DANISH/ASIAN   Located on Flaesketorvet in Copenhagen's meat-packing district, this cafe, bar, and restaurant is in the heart of the increasingly trendy Vesterbro district. The restaurant is owned by Danish artist Jeppe Hein, who displays the art of some 30 international artists. Regular concerts and lectures are also given here, but most patrons come to eat and dine, and they can do so exceedingly well here.

The kitchen makes much use of organic produce and many of the dishes show the influence of Asia, including the steamed scallops with sesame-chili seaweed salad, or the sautéed breast of duck resting on a mound of noodles, fresh apple slices, and beetroot. Other well-recommended dishes include Jerusalem artichoke soup with truffle oil and chervil, or veal sweetbreads with pasta and Parmesan cream. An excellent cheesecake is flavored with rum-braised pineapple. The chefs feature set menus ranging from DKK180 ($31/£18) for 2 to 10 courses, or wine menus going from 4 to 8 courses. On the latter, each dish is accompanied by the appropriate wine.

Flaesketorvet 57–67. (©) **33-21-55-09.** Reservations required. Fixed-price menus DKK180–DKK825 ($31–$140/£18–£83); wine menus DKK340–DKK650 ($58–$111/£34–£65). AE, DC, MC, V. Restaurant Mon–Fri 6–10pm, Sat–Sun 10am–4pm; bar Mon–Thurs 6pm–midnight, Fri 4pm–4am, Sat 10am–4am, Sun 10am–6pm. Bus: 10.

LANGEBRO
Expensive

VIVA ★★ DANISH/MEDITERRANEAN/SEAFOOD   On a stylish ship near Langebro, this is a remodeled barge with a view over the Royal Library (called "Black Diamond"). A modern restaurant with a chic lounge, it seats 75 diners, but in summer that number can go up to 100 guests on the sun deck and wharf, when drinks and a DJ's music fill the night. A creative quality cuisine is provided in an elegant ambience. Fish and shellfish, as in any good Mediterranean kitchen, predominate on the menu, including one page devoted to shellfish. The evening menu is based on small appetizers—*tapas*—really giving you a chance to explore a lot of different tastes.

Langebro Kaj 570. (©) **27-25-05-05.** Reservations required. Main courses DKK90–DKK135 ($15–$23/£9–£14); 4-course fixed-price menu DKK345 ($59/£35), shellfish menu DKK455 ($77/£46). AE, DC, MC, V. Mon–Thurs 11:30am–3pm and 5:30–10pm; Fri–Sat 11:30am–3pm and 5:30–11:30pm; Sun 11:30am–4pm and 5:30–9pm. Bus: 1, 2, 5, 6, 8, or 9.

IN FREDERIKSBERG
Very Expensive

Formel B. ★★★ DANISH/FRENCH   On the border between the Frederiksberg and Vesterbro neighborhoods, the formal and ultrastylish restaurant is the culinary show-case of two local geniuses, Kristian Møller and Rune Jochumsen, who justifiably are having a torrid romance with the Danish press. No chefs in Copenhagen are as fanatical about serving fresh ingredients as this pair, who take the best of Danish raw materials and transform them into classical French dishes. On a daily basis, their specially picked suppliers arrive—fresh vegetables from their own farm in Lammefjorden, dairy products from Grambogård. They even have their own mushroom grower who brings them fresh cèpes and chanterelles. Their menu is seasonally adjusted and changes every 2 weeks. You might begin, for example, with a terrine of foie gras with truffles and gooseberries and follow with monkfish with lemon chutney and a lightly salted and glazed quail with fresh chanterelles, perhaps tender rack of veal with foie gras and fresh cherries. For a finish, the fresh raspberries with a licorice sorbet provides a grand finale.

Vesterbrogade 182, Frederiksberg. (🕾 **33-25-10-66.** Reservations required. Fixed-price menu DKK850 ($145/£85). AE, DC, MC, V. Mon–Sat 6–10pm. Bus: 6A.

IN TIVOLI

Food prices in the Tivoli Gardens restaurants are about 30% higher than elsewhere. To compensate for this, skip dessert and buy something less expensive (perhaps ice cream or pastry) later at one of the many stands in the park. Take bus no. 1, 6, 8, 16, 29, 30, 32, or 33 to reach the park and any of the following restaurants. *Note:* These restaurants are open only May to mid-September.

Very Expensive

The Paul ★★★ INTERNATIONAL   Winning a coveted Michelin star, the first for a restaurant in the Tivoli Gardens, this is one of the three or four most-sought-after culinary landmarks in town, lying in The Glassalen, a greenhouse-style building once used as a concert hall and designed by Poul Henningsen as a statement of Danish Pride immediately after World War II. The mastermind behind this sophisticated venue is British-born Chef Paul Cunningham, whose stated desire is to provide Tivoli revelers "with an intense gourmet experience."

The staff might not even bring table settings to your table until they (or Paul himself) engage you in a dialogue about what the kitchen can offer on any given night—a selection which will invariably be spectacular. Come here for superb food, a sense of international and very hip whimsy, and a creative and upbeat sense of fun. ("I was raped and pillaged and imported into Denmark when I married my Danish wife.") And how does Paul describe the "Gubi Chairs" that line the edges of his bar area? "Like a combination between a tongue and a toilet seat." Paul, more than any other chef in Copenhagen, brings fresh, new, and exciting ideas to his cuisine, spending his winters when the restaurant is closed "traveling, tasting, experiencing, and absorbing new inspirations." The first time we visited, we asked Paul to serve us what Bill Clinton had tasted on his visit. What arrived was hardly Bubba food but a divine free-range chicken from the island of Bornholm served with a confit of veal sweetbreads. We also tasted a perfect butter-roasted Dover sole with corn, capers, and chanterelles. The rhubarb-and-vanilla terrine for dessert brought an enchantment to the already enchanted setting of the Tivoli.

Tivoli. (🕾 **33-75-07-75.** www.thepaul.dk. Reservations recommended. Fixed-price 3-course menu w/ wine DKK850 ($145/£85). AE, DC, MC, V. Mon–Sat noon–2pm and 6–8pm. Closed Oct–Mar.

Expensive

Divan II ★★ DANISH/FRENCH   This landmark restaurant in a garden setting is one of the finest in Tivoli, and certainly one of the most expensive, though not the rival of Paul. It was established in 1843, the same year as Tivoli itself, and long ago witnessed the demise of its less-expensive associate, Divan I. Expect garden terraces that seem forever flowering, splashing fountains, and an interior decor, renovated in 2006, that was inspired by a lattice-ringed greenhouse. The service is uniformly impeccable, a fact that's appreciated by such recent clients as, among others, retired U.S. General and former Secretary of State Colin Powell. The cuisine is among the most sophisticated in Copenhagen. The credo of the chefs is to create excellent meals using the best ingredients, but without audacious inventions. Try the breast of free-range cockerel from Bornholm, which is braised in white wine and served with morels and fresh shallots. Roasted rack of

Danish veal with new peas and morels, or tournedos Rossini, are always appealing. An ongoing staple, served successfully many hundreds of times here, is the "Madame Waleska," steamed filets of sole that are elaborately presented with truffles and a lobster-studded Mornay sauce. Strawberries Romanoff finishes off the meal delightfully.

Tivoli. © **33-75-07-50.** www.divan2.dk. Reservations recommended. Main courses DKK285–DKK335 ($48–$57/£29–£34); fixed-price menus DKK535–DKK895 ($91–$152/£54–£90). AE, DC, MC, V. Daily, during opening dates of Tivoli, noon–4:30pm and 7–10:30pm. It's closed whenever Tivoli is closed.

Moderate

Café Ketchup INTERNATIONAL
Set within the direct sightline of Tivoli's biggest stage, and loaded with contented or animated drinkers during concerts, this is the most consistently popular middle-bracket restaurant in Tivoli, the grounds of which are loaded with worthy competitors. It radiates outward like the spokes of a wheel from a central Beaux Arts core, a glass-ceilinged pavilion ringed with covered terraces, a boon whenever it rains. If there's a trendy lounge-bar within Tivoli that's favored by the young, the beautiful, and the restless, this is it. Some paparazzi hang out here in summer, hoping to catch a visiting celebrity picking his (or her) nose. In fact, it might remind you of the postmodern hip of a secluded bar in such newly fashionable outlying districts as Nørrebro, but with more flowers and an enhanced sense of whimsy. There's a nearly hallucinogenic collection of cocktails offered (martinis, sours, juleps, and more). The cuisine is competent without being great. The best food items include Brittany oysters with lemon and shallot-flavored vinegar; mussels in a Pernod-flavored cream sauce with fennel and summer onions; miso-baked halibut with spinach and garlic-flavored potatoes; venison with sautéed foie gras; and pear-flavored sorbet with Danish raspberries and cream.

Tivoli. © **33-75-07-57.** www.cafeketchuptivoli.dk. Main courses DKK185–DKK395 ($31–$67/£19–£40). AE, DC, MC, V. Daily noon–4pm and 5–10pm (bar till midnight).

Færgekroen DANISH
If you like honest, straightforward fare, without a lot of trimmings, and don't like to spend "Tivoli prices," a mug of cold beer is waiting for you here. Nestled in a cluster of trees at the edge of the lake, this restaurant resembles a pink half-timbered Danish cottage. In warm weather, try to sit on the outside dining terrace. The menu offers drinks, snacks, and full meals. The latter might include an array of omelets, beef with horseradish, fried plaice with melted butter, pork chops with red cabbage, curried chicken, and fried meatballs. The food, prepared according to old recipes, is like what you might get down on a Danish farm. If you like honest, straightforward fare, without a lot of trimmings, and don't like to spend a lot of money, this might be the place for you. A pianist provides sing-along music from Tuesday to Saturday starting at 8pm. The owners of this place recently invested in their own on-site microbrewery, which produces two kinds of beer, both of which taste wonderful.

Tivoli. © **33-75-06-80.** www.faergekroen.com. Main courses DKK175–DKK189 ($30–$32/£18–£19). AE, DC, MC, V. Daily 11am–midnight (hot food until 9:45pm).

Exploring Copenhagen

There is talk of a Renaissance in Copenhagen, as Denmark moves deeper into the 21st century. Much of the city, with its copper-domed landmarks, is cutting edge. A sea of change is sweeping across Copenhagen as tired, seedy old buildings are restored—many turned into boutique hotels. At trendy restaurants, young Danes are reinventing the cuisine of their ancestors, too long dominated by the Danish pig.

Museums are becoming more user-friendly, and even the Queen is appearing on the streets in scarlet red. The culture and charm of old Copenhagen is still here, but in a word the city has become "cool."

A dynamic new life, spurred in part by the young and the changes brought by newly arriving immigrants, has made this venerable old city more vibrant than it's ever been in its history.

"You couldn't be bored here if you tried," a visiting dancer from London told us. He was referring to the around-the-clock summer fun offered in the Danish capital, everything from a free-love-and-drug commune to beer breweries, baroque palaces, and art-filled museums.

On a summer evening, there is no greater man-made attraction in all of Scandinavia than a stroll through the Tivoli pleasure gardens, which seems to have emerged intact from the days when the world was young . . . and so were we. The Danes love childhood too much to abandon it forever, no matter how old they get—so Tivoli keeps alive the magic of fairy lights and the wonder of yesteryear.

Although many visitors arrive in Copenhagen just to visit the Tivoli, there's a lot more going on here. The city is proud of its vast storehouse of antiquities and holds its own with most other capitals of Europe, although dwarfed, of course, by London, Paris, and Rome.

People come to Copenhagen for various reasons—some to absorb the city's art, others merely to have fun. Copenhagen hasn't become another Hamburg yet, but it still peddles miles of porno and sex toys, for which it became infamous in the 1970s. Several annual summer festivals take place here, and live bands—some of the best in Europe—appear in parks to keep Copenhagen rocking around the clock when the sun shines. One actor who settled into Copenhagen found it an "orgy" of boats, bikes, joggers, in-line skaters, and beer.

Shopping is another reason visitors show up here, as the city is world famous for its beautifully designed wares for the home, including porcelain by Bing & Grøndahl and Royal Copenhagen, and sterling silver by Georg Jensen, among other big names. Strøget remains one of the most fabled shopping streets of Europe.

The summer sun may not set until 11pm, but in winter expect cold, cloudy, dark, rainy weather. "We brood like Hamlet then," said a local. "But winter or summer, we're super friendly and welcoming . . . and in English too."

After years of traveling to Denmark, we heartily agree with that assessment.

1 SEEING THE SIGHTS

IN & AROUND THE TIVOLI GARDENS

Tivoli Gardens ★★★ (Moments   Created in 1843, the Tivoli Gardens gave Walt Disney an idea, and look what he did with it. The original is still here, standing in an 8-hectare (20-acre) garden in the center of Copenhagen. Its greatest admirers call it a pleasure park or flower garden, its critics suggesting that it's one giant beer garden. Michael Jackson, after appearing here, tried to buy the entire complex but was turned down, as were the Disney interests as well. The Tivoli is the virtual symbol of Denmark, and no Dane wants to see it go to foreigners.

Let's face it: The Tivoli is filled with schmaltz but somehow with its glitz, glamour, and gaiety it manages to win over hardened cynics. Children prefer it during the day, but adults tend to like it better at night, when more than 100,000 specially made soft-glow light bulbs and at least a million regular bulbs are turned on—what an electric bill.

It features thousands of flowers, a merry-go-round of tiny Viking ships, games of chance and skill (pinball arcades, slot machines, shooting galleries), and a Ferris wheel of hot-air balloons and cabin seats. The latest attraction at Tivoli, "The Demon," is the biggest roller coaster in Denmark. Passengers whiz through three loops on the thrill ride, reaching a top speed of 80kmph (50 mph). There's also a playground for children.

An Arabian-style fantasy palace, with towers and arches, houses more than two dozen expensive restaurants, from a lakeside inn to a beer garden. Take a walk around the edge of the tiny lake with its ducks, swans, and boats.

A parade of the red-uniformed Tivoli Boys Guard takes place on weekends at 5:20 and 7:20pm (also on Wed at 5pm), and their regimental band gives concerts on Saturday at 3pm on the open-air stage. The oldest building at Tivoli, the Chinese-style Pantomime Theater, with its peacock curtain, offers pantomimes in the evening.

For more on the nighttime happenings in Tivoli—fireworks, bands, orchestras, dance clubs, variety acts—see "Copenhagen After Dark," later in this chapter.

Vesterbrogade 3. ℂ **33-15-10-01.** www.tivoli.dk. Admission DKK85 ($14/£8.50) adults, DKK45 ($7.70/£4.50) children 3–11; combination ticket including admission and all rides DKK225–DKK600 ($38–$102/£23–£60) adults, DKK125 ($21/£13) children 3–11. Closed mid-Sept to mid-Apr. Bus: 1, 16, or 29.

Ny Carlsberg Glyptotek ★★★   Talk about putting sudsy beer money to good use. The Glyptotek, behind Tivoli, is one of the great art museums of Europe. Founded by the 19th-century art collector Carl Jacobsen, Mr. Carlsberg himself, the museum includes modern art and antiquities. It reopened in June of 2006 after a 3-year closing and the expenditure of 100 million DKK ($17 million/£10 million), part of which was spent for the construction of a wing that celebrates the ancient Mediterranean world.

The modern section has both French and Danish art, mainly from the 19th century. Sculpture, including works by Rodin, is on the ground floor, and works of the Impressionists and related artists, including van Gogh's *Landscape from St. Rémy* ★, are on the upper floors. Egyptian, Greek, and Roman antiquities are on the main floor; Etruscan, Greek, and Cypriot, on the lower floor. The Egyptian collection ★★ is outstanding; the most notable piece is a prehistoric rendering of a hippopotamus. Fine Greek originals (headless Apollo, Niobe's tragic children) and Roman copies of Greek bronzes (4th-c. Hercules) are also displayed, as are some of the noblest Roman busts—Pompey, Virgil, Augustus, and Trajan. The Etruscan collection ★★★—sarcophagi, a winged lion, bronzes, and pottery—is a favorite of ours and the best such collection outside Italy.

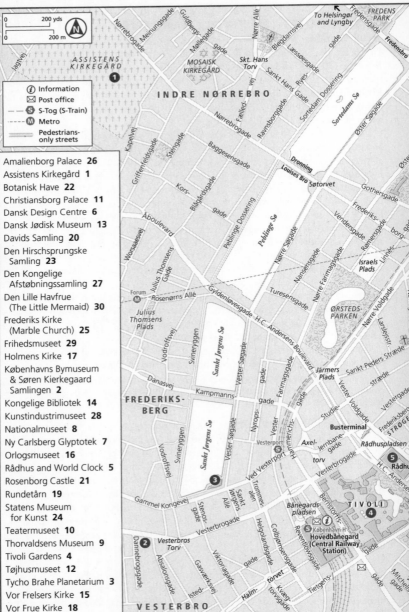

EXPLORING COPENHAGEN

6

SEEING THE SIGHTS

Amalienborg Palace **26**
Assistens Kirkegård **1**
Botanisk Have **22**
Christiansborg Palace **11**
Dansk Design Centre **6**
Dansk Jødisk Museum **13**
Davids Samling **20**
Den Hirschsprungske
  Samling **23**
Den Kongelige
  Afstøbningssamling **27**
Den Lille Havfrue
  (The Little Mermaid) **30**
Frederiks Kirke
  (Marble Church) **25**
Frihedsmuseet **29**
Holmens Kirke **17**
Københavns Bymuseum
  & Søren Kierkegaard
  Samlingen **2**
Kongelige Bibliotek **14**
Kunstindustrimuseet **28**
Nationalmuseet **8**
Ny Carlsberg Glyptotek **7**
Orlogsmuseet **16**
Rådhus and World Clock **5**
Rosenborg Castle **21**
Rundetårn **19**
Statens Museum
  for Kunst **24**
Teatermuseet **10**
Thorvaldsens Museum **9**
Tivoli Gardens **4**
Tøjhusmuseet **12**
Tycho Brahe Planetarium **3**
Vor Frelsers Kirke **15**
Vor Frue Kirke **18**

(i) Information
✉ Post office
Ⓢ S-Tog (S-Train)
Ⓜ Metro
Pedestrians-
only streets

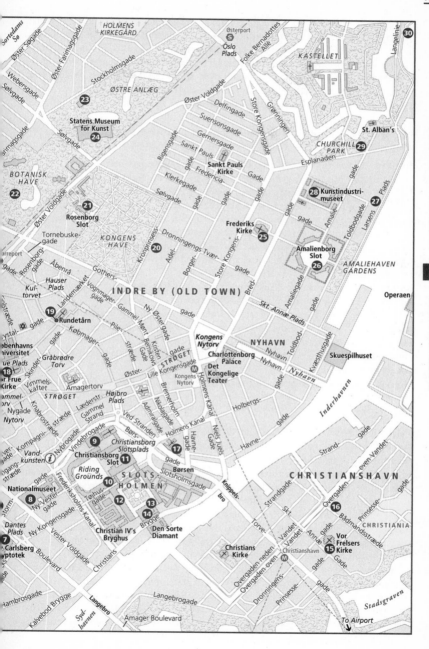

In 1996, the Ny Glyptotek added a French masters' wing. Constructed of white marble and granite, it's in the inner courtyard, which can be reached only through the Conservatory. In a climate- and light-controlled environment, you'll find an extensive collection of French masterpieces, including works by Manet, Monet, Degas, and Renoir, as well as an impressive collection of French sculpture, such as Rodin's *The Burghers of Calais*, plus 30 of his other works. The display features Cézanne's famous *Portrait of the Artist* ★★, as well as about 35 paintings ★★ by former Copenhagen resident Paul Gauguin. Consider dropping into the museum's restaurant, Café Glyptoteket, which some locals find so appealing that they come here for its sake alone, with no intention of visiting the museum.

Dantes Plads 7. ℂ **33-41-81-41**. www.glyptoteket.dk. Admission DKK50 ($8.50/£5) adults, free for children 17 and under, free for everyone Wed and Sun. Tues–Sun 10am–4pm. Bus: 1, 2, 5, 6, 8, or 10.

Rådhus (Town Hall) and World Clock We have never been able to work up much enthusiasm for this towering monument, the City Hall of Copenhagen. It was said to have been inspired by the main tower at the Piazza del Campo in Siena. The original is magnificent, the one in Copenhagen a bit dull. The architect, Martin Nyrop, wanted to create a building that would "give gaiety to everyday life and spontaneous pleasure to all." We're not so sure he succeeded, but check it out anyway. Statues of Hans Christian Andersen and Niels Bohr (the Nobel Prize–winning physicist) are worth a look. Jens Olsen's **World Clock** is open for viewing Monday to Friday 10am to 4pm and Saturday at 1pm. Frederik IX set the clock on December 15, 1955. The clockwork is so exact that it's accurate to within half a second every 300 years. Climb the tower for an impressive view, but it's not for the faint of heart—300 steps with no elevator.

To the east of the Rådhus is one of Copenhagen's most famous landmarks, the **Lurblæserne** (Lur Blower Column), topped by two Vikings blowing an ancient trumpet called a *lur*. There's a bit of artistic license taken here. The *lur* actually dates from the Bronze Age (ca. 1500 B.C.), while the Vikings lived some 1,000 years ago. But it's a fascinating sight anyway.

Rådhuspladsen. ℂ **33-66-25-82**. Admission to Rådhus DKK30 ($5.10/£3), DKK5 (85¢/50p) children 5–12, free for children 4 and under. Guided tour of Rådhus DKK30 ($5.10/£3) Mon–Sat 3pm. Guided tour of tower Oct–May Mon–Sat noon; June–Sept Mon–Fri 10am, noon, and 2pm, Sat noon. Bus: 1, 6, or 8.

AMALIENBORG PALACE & ENVIRONS

Amalienborg Palace ★★ If the beloved Dronning is in residence, a swallowtail flies from the roof of this palace. The Dronning is the queen, Margrethe II, who became the ruler of Denmark in 1953 only after the laws of succession were changed to allow a woman to ascend to the throne. The daughter of King Frederik IX and Queen Ingrid was born in 1940, during one of her country's darkest hours—the Nazi takeover of Denmark.

She studied at universities in London and the Sorbonne in Paris before becoming a member of the Women's Flying Corps and the Women's Auxiliary Air Force in England. After her marriage to a French diplomat, Henri Comte de Laborade de Monpezat, in 1967, she had two sons, Frederik, born in 1968, and Joachim, born in 1969.

She has turned out to be a hardworking, progressively modern royal who is more accessible and beloved by her subjects than her counterpart, the queen of England. Although not true monarchists and a very liberal people with a tradition of democratic equality, the Danes love their queen. A survey revealed one of the reasons. "She puffs cigars like a smokestack," claim her admirers. Come with us as we visit where she lives, and don't forget to bring along a package of cigarettes in case you run into Her Majesty.

Frommer's Favorite Copenhagen Experiences

Sitting at an Outdoor Cafe Because of Copenhagen's long gray winters, sitting at an outdoor cafe in the summer and drinking beer or eating is always a favorite pastime. The best spot is at Nyhavn (New Harbor), beginning at Kongens Nytorv, where you can enjoy ice cream while admiring the tall rigged ships with bowsprits moored in the canal.

Going to Tivoli This is the quintessential summer adventure in Copenhagen, a tradition since 1843. It's an amusement park with a difference—even the merry-go-rounds are special, using a fleet of Viking ships instead of the usual horses.

Strolling Strøget In Danish, the word *strøget* means "to stroll"—and that's exactly what all born-to-shop addicts do along this nearly 1.2km (³/₄-mile) stretch, from Rådhuspladsen to Kongens Nytorv. For a change of pace, midway along the Strøget's length, consider a detour onto the Vestergade, which runs parallel to the Strøget. It's lined with historic buildings and a roster of cozy bars.

Exploring Alternative Lifestyles Not for everybody, but worth a look, is a trip to the Free City of Christiania, on the island of Christianshavn (bus: 8 from Rådhuspladsen). Since 1971, some 1,000 squatters have illegally taken over 130 former army barracks (spread across 8 hectares/20 acres) and declared the area a free city. You can shop, dine, and talk to the natives about this community with its own doctors, clubs, stores, and even its own flag. Exercise caution here, however; there are pickpockets about.

Charting the Development of Modern Danish Design Two museums offer an overview of furniture designs that changed the look of the post–World War II universe. They include the **Danish Design Centre (www.ddc.dk)**, opened in 2001, and the older, more extensive, and more eclectic exhibits within the always-fascinating Copenhagen Museum of Decorative and Applied Art. Hungry for more? The comprehensive collections at **Louisiana,** in Humlebæk, almost always focus on some aspect of the "structural vigor" of top-notch Danish design, in permutations that are wide and broad enough to keep you absorbed and fascinated for at least a day.

These four 18th-century French-style rococo mansions—opening onto one of the most attractive squares in Europe—have been the home of the Danish royal family since 1794, when Christiansborg burned. Visitors flock to see the changing of the guard at noon when the royal family is in residence. This has been called Copenhagen's greatest photo op, but it doesn't impress us as much as the changing of the guard at London's Buckingham Palace.

The Royal Life Guard in black bearskin busbies (like the hussars) leaves Rosenborg Castle at noon and marches along Gothersgade, Nørre Voldgade, Frederiksberggade, Købmagergade, Østergade, Kongens Nytorv, Bredgade, Skt. Annæ Plads, and Amaliegade, to Amalienborg. After the event, the Guard, still accompanied by the band, returns to Rosenborg Castle via Frederiksgade, Store Kongensgade, and Gothersgade.

(Fun Facts) Danish Design

While there's been a massive postwar output of modern furniture in Norway and Sweden, and architectural innovations by such Finnish designers as Alvar Aalto, the streamlined, uncluttered look of modern Scandinavian design is most associated with Denmark. That's because innovations were made during the 1950s by such local luminaries as Hans Wegner, Poul Kjærholm, and Arne Jacobsen, who were trained as architects. Connoisseurs who appreciate their radical departures from previous styles avidly showcase their midcentury furniture and tableware designs.

The original inspiration for Danish design is believed to be the organic curves of Art Nouveau, wherein critics have defined sinuousness and an uncluttered elegance as "the curved line in love with itself." Danish modern managed to transform Art Nouveau from a decorative, nonessential adornment into an aesthetically pleasing, utilitarian stylistic approach that coincided with the industrial boom in Europe after World War II.

What makes a desirable and sought-after piece of Danish design? Some critics have referred to it as "structural vigor," others as "the visual expression of a socially just society" or "aesthetic functionalism," through simple and straightforward materials, including wood (usually oak, maple, ash, and, to a lesser degree, walnut and teak), steel, aluminum, silver, and copper. The best pieces of Danish modern stress flawless craftsmanship, a design that suits the ergonomics of the object's intended use, and subservience of form to function. Respect for the beauty of the components of a piece demands use of the finest materials. The artful simplicity of each piece is achieved only after laborious hours of lathing, polishing, mortise-and-tenoning, and fitting the components into a simple whole.

As the postwar years progressed, new industrial processes developed experimental materials (which later became mainstream): Bakelite, high-grade

---

In 1994, some of the official and private rooms in Amalienborg were opened to the public. The rooms, reconstructed to reflect the period 1863 to 1947, all belonged to members of the royal family, the Glücksborgs, who ascended the throne in 1863. The highlight is the period devoted to the long reign (1863–1906) of Christian IX (1818–1906) and Queen Louise (1817–98). The items in his study and her drawing room—gifts from their far-flung children—reflect their unofficial status as "parents-in-law to Europe." Indeed, the story of their lives has been called "the Making of a Dynasty." Both came from distant sides of the then-heirless royal family to create a "love match." The verses for their 1842 wedding song (a Danish tradition) were written by Hans Christian Andersen.

Christian and Louise gave their six children a simple (by royal standards) but internationally oriented upbringing. One daughter, Alexandra, married Edward VII of England; another, Dagmar, wed Czar Alexander III of Russia. The crown prince, later Frederik VIII, married Louise of Sweden-Norway; another son became king of Greece, and yet another declined the throne of Bulgaria. In 1905, a grandson became king of Norway.

plastics, spun aluminum, and spun steel. All these were carefully integrated into the growing canon of tenets associated with Danish modern, especially the integrity of design plus aesthetically pleasing functionalism.

Home design before World War II embodied clunky bourgeois ideals. Following the devastation of the war and its aftermath, the modern design movement emerged from the peculiar corner of the world that was Denmark, a land that during the 1950s found itself uncomfortably positioned between eastern and western Europe. Danish *joie de vivre* rose to the challenge. Within the streamlined designs, there's an implicit belief in the intelligence of the consumer as typified in the socialist idealism of the 1930s, and an implied rejection of the romantic ideals, arrogant nationalism, and imperialism that motivated some of the carnage of World War II. There's also an endearing (perhaps even quaint) sense of optimism that science and technology can alleviate many of society's problems and ills.

The style was unusual for what it was, and perhaps even more unusual for what it was not. There isn't a trace of kitsch about it—the very fact that the best examples of the style have endured for almost half a century (with few alterations or adaptations) attests to its timelessness. In contrast, the Naugahyde sofas and Eisenhower-era "moderne" accessories that swept across other parts of the world look hopelessly outdated today.

The allure of Danish modern hasn't been lost on art historians: Most visitors to Copenhagen's Museum of Decorative and Applied Art head straight for the Danish modern exhibits, featuring works that were purchased directly from the designers and artists in the 1950s. Hot objects on the auction circuit that fetch high prices today include midcentury cocktail shakers and the ergonomically balanced "egg chairs."

In the 1880s, members of the Danish royal family, numbering more than 50, got together regularly each summer at the Fredensborg Palace, north of Copenhagen. The children, now monarchs in their own right, brought Christian IX and Louise presents—works of art from the imperial workshops and from jewelers such as Fabergé—as well as souvenirs, embroideries, and handicrafts made by the grandchildren. All became treasures for the aging king and queen, and many are exhibited in the museum rooms today.

Also open to the public are the studies of Frederik VIII and Christian X. Thanks to his marriage to Louise of Sweden-Norway, the liberal-minded Frederik VIII (1843–1912), who reigned from 1906 to 1912, had considerable wealth, and he furnished Amalienborg Palace sumptuously. The king's large study, decorated in lavish neo-Renaissance style, testifies to this.

The final period room in the museum is the study of Christian X (1870–1947), the grandfather of current queen Margrethe II, who was king from 1912 to 1947. He became a symbol of national resistance during the German occupation of Denmark during

World War II. Along with the period rooms, a costume gallery and a jewelry room are open to the public. The Amalienborg Museum rooms compose one of two divisions of the Royal Danish Collections; the other is at Rosenborg Palace in Copenhagen.

Christian VIII's Palace. © **33-40-10-10.** www.rosenborgslot.dk. Admission DKK70 ($12/£7) adults, DKK45 ($7.70/£4.50) students, free for children 17 and under. May–Oct daily 10am–4pm; Nov–Apr daily 11am–4pm. Closed Mon. Bus: 1, 6, 9, or 10.

Den Lille Havfrue (The Little Mermaid) ★ Moments

The statue *everybody* wants to see in Copenhagen is the slightly smaller than life-size bronze of *Den Lille Havfrue,* inspired by Andersen's famous fairy tale *The Little Mermaid.* Edvard Eriksen sculpted the statue, unveiled in 1913. It rests on rocks right off the shoreline of the seagoing entrance to Copenhagen's harbor, close to Castellet and the Langelinie cruise piers.

In spite of its small size, the statue is as important a symbol to Copenhageners as the Statue of Liberty is to New Yorkers. Tragedy struck on January 6, 1998. An anonymous tipster called a freelance television cameraman in the middle of the night to check out the 1.2m (4-ft.) bronze Mermaid. She'd lost her head. Most of the city responded with sadness. "She is part of our heritage, like Tivoli, the Queen, and stuff like that," said local sculptor Christian Moerk.

The Mermaid had also been decapitated in 1964. The culprits at that time were never discovered, and the head was never recovered. In the early 1900s, some unknown party or parties cut off her arm. The original mold exists so it's possible to recast the bronze and weld back missing body parts. The arm was replaced.

Although not taking blame for the last attack in 1998, the Radical Feminist Faction sent flyers to newspapers to protest "the woman-hating, sexually fixated male dreams" allegedly conjured by the statue's bronze nudity. After the last decapitation, the head turned up at a TV station, delivered by a masked figure. In the spring, welders put her head back on, making the seam invisible. Today *The Little Mermaid*—head, fishy tail, and all—is back to being the most photographed nude woman in Copenhagen.

Because of all these attacks, the statue, seen by about one million visitors a year, may actually be moved out of the reach of both vandals and tourists to a safer, more secure place. City officials are considering such a proposal. At present, many visitors claim they can't see the statue because throughout the day other tourists are constantly climbing all over her to have their picture taken.

In 2006, another sculpted little mermaid was unveiled, a "genetically modified sister," lying 400m (1,312 ft.) from the original *Little Mermaid.* The new bronze is by Bjørn Nørgaard, a professor at the Royal Danish Academy of Fine Arts. Like the original, Nørgaard's mermaid also sits on a rock, but her features are twisted and her limbs exaggeratedly long and skeletal. Nørgaard created the sculpture for the Danish Pavilion at Expo 2002, the World's Fair held in Hanover, Germany.

Near *The Little Mermaid* statue is **Gefion Springvandet** (Gefion Fountain), sculpted by Anders Bundgaard. Gefion was a Scandinavian goddess who plowed Zealand away from Sweden by turning her sons into oxen.

Also in the area is **Kastellet** at Langelinie (© **33-11-22-33**), a pentagonal citadel, replete with moats, constructed by King Frederik III in the then-virtually-impregnable style of the 1660s. Some of Copenhagen's original ramparts still surround the structure. Although today the site is brightened with beds of seasonal flowers and statues honoring prominent Danes, the Citadel functioned as the capital's first line of defense from seagoing invasion until the 18th century. During the Nazi occupation of Copenhagen, the Germans made it their headquarters. Today the Danish military occupies the buildings.

You can, however, explore the beautiful grounds of Churchillparken surrounding Kastel-let. At the entrance to the park stands St. Albans, the English church of Copenhagen. You can still see the double moats built as part of Copenhagen's defense in the wake of the Swedish siege of the capital on February 10, 1659. The ruined citadel can be explored daily from 6am to sunset.

Langelinie on the harbor. Free admission. Bus: 1, 6, or 9.

Frihedsmuseet (Museum of Danish Resistance, 1940–45) ★

As World War II buffs, we always pay at least one visit here on every trip to Copenhagen. There's always some new piece of information to learn. In 1942, Hitler sent King Christian X a birthday greeting. The response was terse. In retaliation, Hitler sent Werner Best, one of the architects of the Gestapo, to rule Denmark. Hitler used Denmark mainly as a "larder" to feed his Nazi armies during the war. The Danes resisted at every turn, including spiriting away 7,000 Danish Jews to neutral Sweden before they could be deported to Germany. This museum also reveals the tools of espionage and sabotage that the Danes used to throw off the Nazi yoke in World War II. Beginning softly with peace marches in the early days of the war, the resistance movement grew from a fledgling organization into a highly polished and skilled underground that eventually electrified and excited the Allied world: "Danes Fighting Germans!" blared the headlines.

The museum highlights the workings of the outlaw press, the wireless communications equipment, and illegal films; relics of torture and concentration camps; British propaganda leaflets dropped in the country; satirical caricatures of Hitler; information about Danish Jews, and, conversely, about Danish Nazis; and material on paralyzing nationwide strikes. In all, this moment in history is graphically and dramatically preserved. An armed car, used against Danish Nazi informers and collaborators, is displayed on the grounds.

Churchillparken. ⓒ 33-13-77-14. www.frihedsmuseet.dk. Free admission. May–Sept 15 Tues–Sat 10am–4pm, Sun 10am–5pm; Sept 16–Apr Tues–Sat 11am–3pm, Sun 11am–4pm. Bus: 1, 6, or 9.

Kunstindustrimuseet (Museum of Decorative and Applied Art) ★

Admittedly, this museum of decorative and applied art is for aficionados and is not everyone's "cuppa," but for what it is, it is the finest such museum in Scandinavia. With more than 300,000 decorative objects on view, it's a lot to digest but worth at least 2 hours of your time.

The rococo building itself is one of the historic landmarks of Copenhagen, containing four wings surrounding a garden. It was part of the Royal Frederik Hospital, built from 1752 to 1757 during the reign of King Frederik V; it was here, in a hospital bed, that Søren Kierkegaard drew his last breath in 1855.

Allowed to rot and grow seedy, in the 1920s the building was taken over by the city, restored, and turned into a series of rooms, arranged in chronological order, that trace living rooms from the Middle Ages up to the 20th century.

Pride of place is given to furniture, tapestries, other textiles, pottery, porcelain, glass, and silver, and there are many exhibits focusing on the innovative role of Danish modern design—mostly furniture and fabrics—since the 1930s. There are also rare collections of Chinese and Japanese art and handicrafts. The library contains around 65,000 books and periodicals dealing with arts and crafts, architecture, costumes, advertising, photography, and industrial design. The gardens surrounding the museum are open during museum hours. In summer, theatrical performances are staged here for adults and children alike, and the museum restaurant offers alfresco cafe-style tables when the weather is fair. With its manicured grounds and beautiful old linden trees, as well as strategically placed sculptures, we find these gardens one of the most charming of the outdoor spaces of Copenhagen, an ideal place to take a break.

Bredgade 68. ℂ **33-18-56-56.** www.kunstindustrimuseet.dk. Admission to museum DKK50 ($8.50/£5) adults, free for children 17 and under. Free admission to library. Museum Tues–Fri 11am–4pm; Sat–Sun noon–4pm. Library Tues–Sat 10am–4pm. S-tog: Østerport. Bus: 1, 6, or 9.

Davids Samling ★ ⟨Finds⟩   When we first climbed the stairs to the top floor of this museum, we were astonished to discover an unheralded surprise—the Nordic world's greatest collection of art from the **World of Islam** ★★★, dating from the 7th to the 19th century and looted from such distant points as Spain or West India. An astonishing array of pottery, weaponry, glassware, silverware, texts, and textiles, among other exhibits, awaits you.

Christian Ludvig David, a lawyer in the Danish High Court with wide-ranging tastes, began this collection. He died in 1960, leaving his carefully chosen treasure-trove to the city, and since that time the museum has added to his bequests.

It's true that most visitors ignore the barrister's collection as they rush to take in the wonders of Rosenborg Slot or the Statens Museum for Kunst, both of which are nearby, but the Samling collection deserves at least 1¹/₂ hours of your time. In addition to those Islamic treasures, the museum includes floors devoted to European fine and applied art from the 18th to the 20th century. After closing for renovations, the museum is scheduled to reopen in May 2009.

David's other major bequest was his summer villa in the northern suburbs of Copenhagen at Marienborg, reserved for the Danish prime minister's use.

Kronprinsessegade 30. ℂ **33-73-49-49.** www.davidmus.dk. Free admission. Tues–Sun 1–4pm. Bus: 1, 6, 9, 10, 19, 29, 31, 42, or 43.

ROSENBORG CASTLE, THE BOTANICAL GARDENS & ENVIRONS

Rosenborg Slot (Rosenborg Castle) ★★★   With a facade that hasn't changed since 1633, the Rosenborg is the greatest and purest Renaissance structure in Denmark. It has survived fires and wars and stands to delight us today, or at least those of us who have 2 hours to spare.

Christian IV conceived of the palace in 1606 but it began with **Kongens Have** ★, the King's Garden, which still surrounds the palace today, and is one of the more delightful places in Copenhagen for a stroll. The king liked the place so much he built a summer pavilion here, which eventually led to the creation of this monumental red-brick *slot* (castle), inspired by the Dutch Renaissance style, and today one of the most beautiful and evocative monuments of Denmark.

It houses everything from narwhal-tusked and ivory coronation chairs to Frederik VII's baby shoes—all artifacts from the Danish royal family, who for many generations relegated this elegant building to the role of a storage bin for royal artifacts. Officially, its biggest draws are the dazzling **crown jewels and regalia** ★★★, in the basement Treasury, which houses a lavishly decorated coronation saddle from 1596 and other treasures. Try to see the **Knights Hall** ★ in Room 21, with its coronation seat, three silver lions, and relics from the 1700s. Room 3 was used by founding father Christian IV (lucky in love, unlucky in war), who died in this bedroom, which is decorated with Asian lacquer art and a stucco ceiling.

Øster Voldgade 4A. © **33-15-32-86.** www.rosenborgslot.dk. Admission DKK70 ($12/£7) adults, DKK45
($7.70/£4.50) students and seniors, free for children 16 and under. Palace and treasury (royal jewels) Jan–Apr Tues–Sun 11am–2pm; May and Sept–Oct daily 10am–4pm; June–Aug daily 10am–5pm; Nov–Dec 17 Tues–Sun 11am–2pm. S-tog: Nørreport. Bus: 5, 10, 14, 16, 31, 42, 43, 184, or 185.

Botanisk Have (Botanical Gardens) ★ Cactuses, orchids, and palm trees always draw us to the most splendid 10 hectares (25 acres) in all of Denmark. Planted from 1871 to 1874—and still around to thrill us to this day—these botanical gardens are on a lake that was once part of the city's defensive moat around Rosenborg Slot, which fronts the gardens. In fact, after a visit to Rosenborg, we always like to come here to wind down after devouring so many royal treasures. Greenhouses grow both tropical and subtropical plants, none finer than the **Palm House ★★**, which appears even more exotic this far north. Retreat here on a rainy day and imagine you're in the tropics. An alpine garden also contains mountain plants from all over the world.

Gothersgade 128. © **35-32-22-22.** www.botanic-garden.ku.dk. Free admission. May–Sept daily 8:30am–6pm; Oct–Apr Tues–Sun 8:30am–4pm. Closed Dec 24 and Jan 1. S-tog: Nørreport. Bus: 5A, 14, 40, 42, or 43.

Statens Museum for Kunst (Royal Museum of Fine Arts) ★★★ **Kids** We could spend an entire day here and still find some new artistic discovery. If you can't afford so much time, give it at least 2 hours, or more if you can spare it. The largest museum in Denmark houses painting and sculpture from the 13th to the present century, the collection originally acquired by the kings of Denmark.

The old museum building dates back to 1896, the creation of architect Wilhelm Dahlerup, but it has been greatly extended with modern wings. In 1750, Frederik V launched the collection by purchasing vast art from the continent, especially Flemish and Dutch paintings, but also Italian and German works. Bruegel, Rubens, Rembrandt, and Memling are just some of the artists waiting to dazzle you. Of all these works, we are drawn to a masterpiece by Andrea Mantegna, *Christ as the Suffering Redeemer* ★★★.

The so-called Danish Golden Age of painting from the 19th century forms one of the greatest treasures of the museum. Except for Edvard Munch from Norway, most of these Scandinavian artists will not be known to the general public. One of the best treats here is a mighty symbolist work, *Christ in the Kingdom of Death* ★★, by P. C. Skovgaard, representing a milestone in Danish art. Nearly all the Danish masters of the era are exhibited, including the famous Skagen and Funen painters.

Generous donations or long-term loans have beefed up the former royal collection of paintings and sculptures. In 1928, Johannes Rump donated a huge collection of early French modernists. The predictable Braque and Picasso works are here, but there is a stunning collection of **25 paintings by Henri Matisse ★★**.

The **Italian school ★★** is also a rich trove of art, with works by Filippino Lippi, Titian, and Tintoretto. The museum also contains one of the world's oldest collections of **European prints and drawings ★★★**, including contributions from Giacometti, Rembrandt, Degas, and Toulouse-Lautrec. Some of these copper prints, drawings, etchings, watercolors, and lithographic works go back to the 1400s.

Also on-site is a **Children's Museum** on the ground floor, with hands-on displays. At a workshop held daily from 2 to 4pm, kids can draw and paint and, if a budding Rodin, sculpt. If you want to take a break, head for the stylish cafe decorated by artist Viera Collaro and offering a view of the greenery of Østre Anlæg, a park, and a lake.

Sølvgade 48–50. © **33-74-84-94.** www.smk.dk. Free admission. Tues and Thurs–Sun 10am–5pm; Wed 10am–8pm. Bus: 10, 14, 26, 40, 43, 184, or 185.

Den Hirschsprungske Samling (Hirschsprung Collection) ★ The setting for the museum is romantic, as it's beautifully situated in the green parklands of Østre Anlæg on the old ramparts of Copenhagen. Never has the "dancing light and sparkling waters" of the Danish seashore and countryside been so evocatively captured as it is in this highly personal collection of art from Denmark's so-called "Golden Age" of painting (1800–50), when naturalism was not just in bloom, but flowering at its zenith.

You may not even recognize the names of any of the artists on display, but you can still have a visual treat for 1 to 1¹⁄₂ hours by wandering through, focusing on whatever captures your fancy. The collection was financed by the smoking of tobacco. Heinrich Hirschsprung (1836–1908), a tobacco manufacturer, bequeathed his treasures to the Danish state, which housed them in a neoclassical building constructed in 1911 in back of the Fine Arts Museum.

Just as long as the painters were Danish, Hirschsprung collected their art over a period of 40 years—paintings, drawings, and sculptures, including the Skagen artists, the Symbolists, and the *Fynboerne* (Natives of Funen). We feel a great intimacy was created here by the museum's wise decision to exhibit beautiful interiors featuring furniture from the homes and studios of many of the artists. Captivating us were such artists as Eckersberg, Købke, and Lundbye, and the Skagen painters P. S. Krøyer and Anna and Michael Ancher.

Stockholmsgade 20. ℂ **35-42-03-36.** www.hirschsprung.dk. Admission DKK50 ($8.50/£5) adults, free for children 17 and under, free to all Wed. Wed–Mon 11am–4pm. Bus: 6A, 14, 40, 42, or 43.

CHRISTIANSBORG PALACE & ENVIRONS

Christiansborg Slot (Christiansborg Palace) ★★★ Over the centuries Christiansborg Castle has led a rough life ever since the founding father of Copenhagen, Bishop Absalon, completed the first castle here in 1167. That one burned down—and so did the next two palaces.

Christiansborg Slot was a royal residence beginning in 1416, when Erik of Pomerania moved in. The royals lived here until fleeing to more comfortable quarters at Amalienborg Slott in 1794. Christian VI ordered that the entire castle be torn down in 1732: He didn't like Frederik IV's aesthetic tastes, finding Christiansborg "an eyesore." But his new place burned down on the night of February 26, 1794.

What is left standing today is a granite-and-copper palace from 1928. It stands on Slotsholmen, a small island in the center of Copenhagen that has been the seat of political power in Denmark for 800 years. Today it houses the Danish parliament, the Supreme Court, this prime minister's offices, and the Royal Reception Rooms. A guide will lead you through richly decorated rooms, including the Throne Room, Banqueting Hall, and the Queen's Library. Before entering, you'll be asked to put on soft overshoes to protect the floors.

Under the palace, visit the well-preserved ruins of the 1167 castle of Bishop Absalon.

You can also see **Kongelige Stalde & Kareter** ★, Christiansborg Ridebane 12 (ℂ **33-40-10-10**), the royal stables and coaches. Elegantly clad in riding breeches and jackets, riders exercise the royal horses. Vehicles include regal coaches and "fairy tale" carriages, along with a display of harnesses in use by the royal family since 1778. Free admission. The site can be visited May to October Saturday to Sunday 2 to 4pm.

Christiansborg Slotsplads. ℂ **33-92-64-92.** Guided tour of Royal Reception Rooms DKK65 ($11/£6.50) adults, DKK30 ($5.10/£3) children 4–17. Admission to castle ruins DKK40 ($6.80/£4) adults, DKK15 ($2.60/£1.50) children 4–17. Free admission to parliament. Guided tours of Reception Rooms May–Sept

daily 11am, 1pm, and 3pm; Oct–Apr Tues–Sun at 3pm. Ruins May–Sept daily 10am–4pm; Oct–Apr Tues– **133**
Sun 10am–4pm. English-language tours of parliament year-round daily 11am, 1pm, and 3pm. Bus: 1, 2, 5,
8, or 9.

Nationalmuseet (National Museum) ★★★ (Kids) The nucleus of this museum
started out as Frederik II's "Royal chamber of Curiosities" in 1650. It just grew and grew
until it's now the Nordic world's greatest repository of anthropological artifacts. There's
something here for everyone, even for kids who gravitate to the on-site Children's
Museum geared to ages 4 to 12. You never know what you'll come upon, including the
lur horn, a Bronze Age instrument that is among the oldest of its kind in Europe. It still
makes music. The world-famous *Sun Chariot* ★★★ is an elegant Bronze Age piece of
pagan art. Dating from around 1,200 B.C., the rare find was unearthed by a farmer plowing his ground in 1902.

The museum is divided into five different departments, beginning with the Prehistoric
Wing on the ground floor, with artifacts from the reindeer stalkers of the Ice Age to the
Vikings, with runic stones, helmets, and fragments of battle gear.

In the Runic Stone Hall, the **Hjortespring Boat** ★★ dates from around 300 B.C.
This "war canoe" is the oldest plank-built boat unearthed in the north of Europe. One
of the most stunning displays in this hall is the **Golden Age Room** ★★★, with its dazzling display of gold objects, some dating back to 1,000 B.C.

One of the richest sections of the museum lies upstairs in the Medieval and Renaissance departments, covering both the pre- and post-Reformation eras. Naturally exhibits
are strong in ecclesiastical art but also well represented in the decorative art accumulated
by a trio of Danish Renaissance kings, including Christian III and IV, as well as Frederik
II. A rare treasure here are Frederik II's tapestries made for the Great Hall of Kronborg
Slot.

The Peoples of the World Department is one of the oldest ethnographical collections in
the world, with artifacts ranging from Papua New Guinea to Central America. This section
also displays artifacts of the Eskimo culture that still flourishes in Greenland, which is under
the control of Denmark. The **Royal Collection of Coins and Medals** ★★ lies in one of
the loveliest rooms (no. 146) in Copenhagen, with views over Christiansborg Slot. The
salon displays various coins from antiquity. The **Collection of Antiquities** ★★★ has been
called "the British Museum in miniature." It contains everything from two fragments from

Top of the Pops in Denmark

Rock and pop bands rule the night in the underground cellars of big cities in
Denmark, including Copenhagen and Århus. Formerly known as Disneyland After
Dark, rockers D-A-D have found many international fans with such recordings as
"Sleeping My Day Away." Currently, the major bands in Denmark are garage rock-
ers such as The Raveonettes.

Enjoying the most popularity in Denmark is the Århus-based band Nephew,
which mixes both Danish and English lyrics. Their lead singer, Simon Kvamm, is
quite charismatic and is one of the biggest rock stars in Denmark.

You can often see the biggest names in music displaying their talents at the
annual Roskilde Festival.

the Parthenon, stolen by a Danish naval officer in 1687, to Holy Roman cups depicting Homeric legends.

Ny Vestergade 10. ℂ **33-13-44-11.** www.natmus.dk. Free admission. Tues–Sun 10am–5pm. Closed Dec 24–25 and Dec 31. Bus: 1, 2, 5, 6, 8, 10, or 41.

Tøjhusmuseet (Royal Arsenal Museum) ★ If in your darkest soul you have a bloody heart, and want to see the weapons that man has used to kill his fellow man over the centuries, you've come to the gruesome doorstep. Actually, the long Arsenal Hall on the ground floor is an architectural curiosity, the longest arched hall in Europe, with its cross vaults supported by 16 heavy center pillars. Displayed here is an armada of weapons, some 350 historical guns, mortars, and howitzers, with artillery equipment dating from 1500 up to the present day. The Armory Hall upstairs was once a storehouse for hand weapons, and today has 7,000 of these killers, some dating as far back as 1300. Christian IV's original arsenal building was constructed between 1589 and 1604 with the thickest walls in Copenhagen, measuring 4m (13 ft.). The most beautiful weapons—if such a word can be used in this context—are the ivory-inlaid pistols and muskets. The royal suits of armor are almost works of art unto themselves. Here is where we'll go out on a limb: This arsenal museum is the finest of its kind in the world.

Tøjhusgade 3. ℂ **33-11-60-37.** www.thm.dk. Admission DKK30 ($5.10/£3) adults, DKK20 ($3.40/£2) students and seniors, free for children 17 and under. Tues–Sun noon–4pm. Closed Jan 1, Dec 23–26, and Dec 31. Bus: 1, 2, 5, 8, and 9.

Thorvaldsens Museum ★ This is the oldest art gallery in Denmark, having opened on September 18, 1848. This museum on Slotsholmen, next door to Christiansborg, houses the greatest collection of the works of Bertel Thorvaldsen (1770–1844), the biggest name in neoclassical sculpture. Thorvaldsen's life represented the romanticism of the 18th and 19th centuries: He rose from semipoverty to the pinnacle of success in his day. He's famous for his most typical, classical, restrained works, taken from mythology: Cupid and Psyche, Adonis, Jason, Hercules, Ganymede, Mercury—all of which are displayed at the museum. His *Jason* was one of his first works and remains one of our favorites. It brought fame and success to him throughout Europe and set him off on a long career after its completion in 1803. In addition to the works of this latter-day exponent of Roman classicism, the museum also contains Thorvaldsen's personal, and quite extensive, collection—everything from the Egyptian relics of Ptolemy to the contemporary paintings he acquired during his lifetime (*Apollo Among the Thessalian Shepherds*). After many years of self-imposed exile in Italy, Thorvaldsen returned in triumph to his native Copenhagen, where he died a national figure and was buried here in the courtyard of his own personal museum.

Bertel Thorvaldsens Plads 2. ℂ **33-32-15-32.** www.thorvaldsensmuseum.dk. Admission DKK20 ($3.40/£2) adults, free for children 17 and under, free to all Wed. Tues–Sun 10am–5pm. Closed Jan 1, Dec 24–25, and Dec 31. Bus: 1A, 2, 15, 26, 29, or 650S.

IN THE OLD TOWN (INDRE BY)

Rundetårn (Round Tower) For the most **panoramic view** ★★★ of the city of Copenhagen, climb the spiral ramp (no steps) leading up to the top of this tower, which was built in 1642. The spiral walk to the top is unique in European architecture, measuring 268m (880 ft.) and winding itself seven times around the hollow core of the tower, forming the only link between the individual parts of the building complex. Obviously not wanting to walk, Peter the Great, in Denmark on a state visit, galloped up the ramp on horseback, preceded by his carriage-drawn czarina. Rundetårn is also the oldest functioning observatory in Europe, in use until 1861 by the University of Copenhagen. Now anyone can observe the night sky through the astronomical telescope in the winter months.

Købmagergade 52A. ✆ **33-73-03-73.** www.rundetaarn.dk. Admission DKK25 ($4.30/£2.50) adults, DKK5 (85¢/50p) children 5–15. Tower June–Aug Mon–Sat 10am–8pm, Sun noon–8pm; Sept–May Mon–Sat 10am–5pm, Sun noon–5pm. Observatory Oct 15–Mar 22 Tues–Wed 7–10pm; June 20–Aug 10 Sun 1–4pm. Bus: 5, 7E, 14, 16, or 42.

Vor Frue Kirke (Copenhagen Cathedral)   For such an important European capital as Copenhagen, the cathedral of the Danish capital is relatively modest. The reason that it's so lacking in art and treasures was because of a fanatical attack by Lutheran zealots during the darkest days of the Reformation. They came through here destroying precious treasures that should have been saved for future generations to appreciate.

The cathedral itself, designed by C. F. Hansen, was the third such building erected here. The original Gothic structure was destroyed by fire in 1728, and the second cathedral was damaged by British bombardments in 1807.

The church is often used for funerals of the country's greatest men and women—the funeral of Hans Christian Andersen took place here in 1875, and that of Søren Kierkegaard in 1855.

Nørregade. ✆ **33-37-65-40.** www.domkirken.dk. Free admission. Mon–Fri 8am–5pm. Bus: 5 or 6A.

MORE MUSEUMS

Arken Museum for Moderne Kunst (Arken Museum of Modern Art) ★ (Finds)
Of the major modern art museums of Copenhagen, this one is the most undiscovered because it lies in the dreary suburb of Ishøj, although just a 15-minute train ride from the center of Copenhagen. Constructed of white concrete and steel, and evoking the hull of a beached ship, the museum was built in 1996 to celebrate Copenhagen's designation as European City of Culture for that year. Architectural critics were appalled when 25-year-old Søren Robert Lund was selected to design the museum while still a student at the Royal Danish Academy of Fine Arts.

Artists who show their works here remain almost universal in their condemnation of Lund, feeling that the frame with its curious "marine architecture" competes with the picture—that is, the art exhibited inside. The museum owns some 300 works of art (not all on exhibit at once), but it supplements this trove with temporary exhibitions devoted to, say, the works of Picasso. In addition to gallery space, the museum has a concert hall, sculpture courtyards, and a restaurant.

Ishøj Strandpark, Skovvej 100. ✆ **43-54-02-22.** www.arken.dk. Admission DKK85 ($14/£8.50) adults, DKK70 ($12/£7) seniors and students, free for children 17 and under. Tues–Sun 10am–5pm; Wed until 9pm. Train: E or A to Ishøj Station, then bus 128.

Danish Design Centre ★   According to the Danes—and we're inclined to agree with them—no people on earth are as quick to embrace modern design as the people of Copenhagen. Locals rarely find almost any design "over the top." They are more likely to say, in the words of one critic, "Too much? Hell! We'll take two for the living room and one for the bedroom." Architect Henning Larsen designed the five-story center, which hides behind a smoked-glass exterior although announcing that it's a "window to the world" as far as avant-garde design is concerned. Through "golden oldie" exhibits and contemporary shows, the center focuses on Danish designers but also provides a showcase "for innovators from across the planet." This is the best place for not only looking at the work of classic designers, but seeing the "hotties" among the cream of young Danish designers as well. You can also enjoy soups, sandwiches, pastries, salads, and coffees in the on-site **Café Dansk,** which, naturally, has the most sophisticated design of any cafe in Copenhagen.

27 H. C. Andersens Blvd. (©) **33-69-33-69.** Admission DKK50 ($8.50/£5) adults, DKK25 ($4.30/£2.50) children 12–18, free for children 11 and under. Mon–Tues and Thurs–Fri 10am–5pm; Wed 10am–9pm; Sat–Sun 11am–4pm. Bus: 5A, 6A, 10, or 12.

Dansk Jødisk Museum   Daniel Libeskind, the architect who submitted the winning design for the World Trade Center Memorial in New York, also designed this museum in a wing of the Royal Library. It's been turned into the national center for Jewish art and culture, with both secular and religious exhibits ranging from films to paintings. The most dramatic exhibits focus on the rescue of Danish Jews in 1943—despite Denmark's occupation by the Nazis. Unlike many societies, Danish Jews and "Danish Danes" successfully merged into a single culture, with little tension between them.

The first minority museum ever to open in Denmark, the museum also holds interest for people who aren't Jewish. In 1906, when the Royal Library was built, it enclosed the Royal Boat House, which was ordered constructed by Christian IV in 1622. The Jewish Museum is in a wing of the Royal Library, which includes the Royal Boat House, making it "a building within a building within a building."

Proviantpassagen 6. (©) **33-11-22-18.** www.jewmus.dk. Admission DKK50 ($8.50/£5) adults, DKK25 ($4.30/£2.50) students, free for children 15 and under. June–Aug Tues–Sun 10am–5pm; Sept–May Tues–Fri 1–4pm, Sat–Sun noon–5pm. Bus: 1, 2, 5, 6, 8, or 9.

Den Kongelige Afstøbningssamling (Royal Cast Collection)   On any afternoon, you might find a lonely would-be sculptor wandering about. This museum, founded in 1895 as a branch of the Statens Museum for Kunst, seems little known. But it's such a curiosity, we had to recommend it; in fact, it contains one of the largest and oldest cast collections in the world, comprising some 2,000 plaster casts modeled from famous sculptures from the past 4,000 years of western culture. The best-known original works from antiquity and the Renaissance are scattered throughout the museums of the world, but this world of plaster unites many of them—Egyptian sphinxes, gold from Atreus's treasury, *Venus de Milo,* the Pergamon altar, and marble sculpture from the Acropolis. Most of the collection was made from 1870 to 1915 by leading European plaster workshops.

Vestindisk Pakhus, Toldbodgade 40. (©) **33-74-84-94.** www.smk.dk. Free admission. Tues and Thurs–Sun 10am–5pm; Wed 10am–8pm. Bus: 1, 6, or 9.

Kongelige Bibliotek (Royal Library) ★   It's not London's British Library, but the Danish Royal Library, dating from the 1600s, is the largest and most impressive in the Norse countries. The classical building with its high-ceilinged reading rooms is a grand and impressive place. The library owns original manuscripts by such Danish writers as H. C. Andersen and Karen Blixen (Isak Dinesen). In 1998, sorely in need of more storage space for its many historically important records, the library was expanded with the addition of a gargantuan and sharply angular granite annex, the Black Diamond, which extended the venerable antique structure out and over the waterfront traffic artery, expanding it in a dazzling (and dizzying) study in architectural contrasts.

If you have the time, don't suffer from any kind of vertigo, and aren't stopped by a security guard, consider taking the elevator to the highest floor of the echoing interior spaces of the Black Diamond. Because of locked doors and security codes on that level, you'll probably remain within the hallways, and not within any of the "Sanctum sanctorums"; but even from the catwalks and walkways of the top floor, the sense of height, the interplay of sunlight and shadows, and the perspectives from the topmost floor can be both terrifying and awe-inspiring. An irony? In keeping with the Black Diamond's role as a repository for books, its floors, as designated by the elevators inside, are labeled as Levels A, B, and C rather than the more conventional designations as 1, 2, and 3. Likened to Sydney's Opera House for its evocative and enigmatic appearance, the Black Diamond's progressive but boxy-looking design adds to the monumentality of the waterfront promenade—by the harbor between the bridges Langebro and Knippelsbro. A myriad of dazzling, reflective slabs of black granite from Zimbabwe cover the facade, and its exterior walls slant sharply at disconcerting angles. Along with space for 200,000 books, the Black Diamond features a bookshop, an upscale restaurant (Søren K, which is recommended in chapter 5, under "Where to Dine"), six reading rooms, a courtyard for exhibitions, and a 600-seat concert hall. After viewing the interiors of both the old and new sections of the library, you can wander through its formal gardens, past the fishpond and statue of philosopher Søren Kierkegaard.

Søren Kierkegaards Plads 1. ℂ **33-47-47-47.** www.kb.dk. Free admission. Mon–Fri 10am–5pm. Bus: 1, 2, 5, 6, 8, or 9.

Orlogsmuseet (Royal Naval Museum)

Do you ever lie awake at night wondering what happened to the propeller from the German U-boat that sank the *Lusitania?* Look no further: It's here at this former naval hospital in Søkvasthuset, opening onto the Christianshavn Kanal. That's not all that's here, as you can follow the history of Denmark, a maritime nation, through the exhibits of its royal navy. Although there are a lot of artifacts that won't interest you, many will. More than 300 model ships, many based on designs that date from as early as 1500, are on view, and some of them were designed and constructed by naval engineers, serving as prototypes for the construction of actual ships that ventured into the cold, dark waters of the North Sea. The models are wide ranging—some are fully "dressed," with working sails, whereas others are cross-sectional with their frames outlined. You get a vast array of other naval artifacts too, including an intriguing collection of figureheads, some of which are artworks themselves. For us, nothing is as glamorous or splendid as an ornate state barge from 1780.

Overgaden Oven Vandet 58. ℂ **33-11-60-37.** www.orlogsmuseet.dk. Admission DKK40 ($6.80/£4) adults, free for children 16 and under. Tues–Sun noon–4pm. Bus: 2, 19, or 350S.

Teatermuseet

Hans Christian Andersen was once a ballet student here, although we can't imagine how this awkward "ugly duckling" looked onstage performing *Swan Lake.* Theater buffs flock to this museum in the Old Court Theater that was constructed by King Christian VII in 1767 as the first court theater in Copenhagen. In 1842, the theater was overhauled and given its present look, but the curtain went down for the last time in 1881. It made a "comeback" as a museum in 1992, tracing the history of the Danish theater from the 18th century to modern times. The public has access to the theater boxes, the stage, and the old dressing rooms. Some of the great theatrical performances of Europe, from Italian opera to pantomime, took place on this stage, and photographs, prints, theatrical costumes, and even old stage programs tell the story, from Ludvig Holberg to the present day.

Christiansborg Ridebane 18. © **33-11-51-76.** Admission DKK30 ($5.10/£3) adults, free for children 17 and under. Tues and Thurs 11am–3pm; Wed 11am–5pm; Sat–Sun 1–4pm. Bus: 1, 2, 12, 15, 19, 26, 29, 33, or 650.

THE CHURCHES OF COPENHAGEN

For a visit to the Copenhagen Cathedral, see p. 135.

Frederikskirke (Marble Church) ★   In many ways, this landmark church is more richly decorated and impressive than Copenhagen's cathedral, Vor Frue Kirke. Instead of Frederikskirke, Danes often call this building *Marmorkirken* (Marble Church). Lying just a short walk from Amalienborg Palace, it began unsuccessfully in 1749. The original plan was to use "quarries" of expensive Norwegian marble. The treasury dried up in 1770, and work came to a halt. It wasn't resumed until late in the 19th century when an industrialist, C. F. Tietgen, put up the money for its completion. This time a cheaper Danish marble was used instead. The original design was for neoclassical revival, but in the end the church was constructed in the Roman baroque style, opening in 1894. Inspired by Michelangelo's dome for St. Peter's in Rome, the Danish church was crowned with a copper dome, measuring 46m (151 ft.) high, making it one of the largest in the world.

Frederiksgade 4. © **33-15-01-44.** Free admission. Church Mon–Thurs 10am–5pm; Fri–Sun noon–5pm. Dome June 15–Aug daily 1 and 3pm; Sept–June 14 Sat–Sun 1 and 3pm. Bus: 1, 6, or 9.

Holmens Kirke   This Lutheran church became world famous in 1967 when Queen Margrethe II married Prince Henrik here. Built in 1619, this royal chapel and naval church lies across the canal from Slotsholmen, next to the National Bank of Denmark. Although the structure was converted into a church for the Royal Navy in 1619, its nave was built in 1562 as an anchor forge. By 1641, the ever-changing church was renovated to its current, predominantly Dutch Renaissance style. The so-called "royal doorway" was brought from Roskilde Cathedral in the 19th century. Inside, the extraordinary feature of this church is its ostentatious **baroque altar** ★★ of unpainted oak, a carved pulpit by Abel Schrøder the Younger that extends right to the roof. In the burial chamber are the tombs of some of Denmark's most towering naval figures, including Admiral Niels Juel, who successfully fought off a naval attack by Swedes in 1677 in the Battle of Køge Bay. Peder Tordenskjold, who defeated Charles XII of Sweden during the Great Northern War in the early 1700s, is also entombed here.

Holmens Kanal. © **33-13-61-78.** Free admission. Mon–Fri 9am–2pm; Sat 9am–noon. Bus: 1, 2, 6, 8, 9, 10, 31, 37, or 43.

Vor Frelsers Kirken   The architect of the 1752 staircase of the "Church of Our Savior" was Laurids de Thurah. A legend still persists about him. It is said that he constructed the staircase encircling the building the wrong way. Climbing to the top, and belatedly realizing what he'd done, he jumped to his death. A good story, but it's not true. According to more reliable reports, he died poverty-stricken in his sleep in his own bed in 1759. The green-and-gold tower of this Gothic structure is a Copenhagen landmark, dominating the Christianshavn area. Inside, view the splendid baroque altar, richly adorned with a romp of cherubs and other figures. There are also a lovely font and an immense three-story organ from 1698. Four hundred vertigo-inducing steps will take you to the top, where you'll see a gilded figure of Christ standing on a globe, and a **panoramic view** ★★★ of the city. *Warning:* Those steps grow narrower as they reach the pinnacle.

Skt. Annægade 29. ☎ **32-54-68-83.** Free admission to church. Admission to tower DKK20 ($3.40/£2) adults, DKK10 ($1.70/£1) children 5–14, free for children 4 and under. Apr–Aug Mon–Sat 11am–4:30pm, Sun noon–4:30pm; Sept–Oct Mon–Sat 11am–3:30pm, Sun noon–3:30pm; Nov–Mar daily 11am–3:30pm. It is possible to visit the tower only Apr–Oct. Metro: Christianshavn.

A GLIMPSE INTO THE PAST RIGHT OUTSIDE COPENHAGEN

Frilandsmuseet (Open-Air Museum) ★★★   Your schedule may allow you to visit only Copenhagen with no time for the Danish countryside. But there is a way out of that—call it a look at "Denmark in a Nutshell." At one of the largest and oldest (1897) open-air museums in the world, you can wander into a time capsule of long ago—a sort of Danish version of the Scottish Brigadoon—and return to a town that still lives on in the 19th century, when Hans Christian Andersen was writing all those fairy tales. This reconstructed village in Lyngby, on the fringe of Copenhagen, recaptures Denmark's one-time rural character. The "museum" is nearly 36 hectares (89 acres), a 3km (1³/₄-mile) walk around the compound, and includes more than 50 re-created buildings—farmsteads, windmills, and fishermen's cottages. Exhibits include a half-timbered 18th-century farmstead from one of the tiny windswept Danish islands, a primitive longhouse from the remote Faroe Islands, thatched fishermen's huts from Jutland, tower windmills, and a potter's workshop from the mid-19th century. Folk dancers in native costume perform, and there are demonstrations of lace making and loom weaving.

Adjacent to the open-air museum stands **Brede Værk** ★, an intact industrial plant that gives a complete picture of a former factory community which closed in 1956. The Nationalmuseet moved to preserve it as a reminder of Denmark's past. Still intact are the cottages of the working-class families, even the houses of the foremen. Their former eating house has been turned into a restaurant today, and there are even an orphanage and a nursery garden. The old factory buildings house exhibitions illustrating "The Cradle of Industry." Our delight here is touring **Brede House** ★★, a neoclassical manor dating from 1795. The owner of the mill, Peter van Hemert, lived here with his family before he went bankrupt in 1805. He pictured himself a fanciful decorator, decking his halls like he was Louis XVI.

The park is about 14km (8²/₃ miles) from the Central Railway Station. There's an old-style restaurant at the entryway to the museum.

Kongevejen 100. ☎ **33-13-44-11.** www.natmus.dk. Free admission. Apr 4–Oct 22 Tues–Sun 10am–5pm. Closed Oct 23–Apr 3. S-tog: Sorgenfri (leaving every 20 min. from Central Railway Station). Bus: 184 or 194.

LITERARY LANDMARKS

Fans of **Hans Christian Andersen** may want to seek out the various addresses where he lived in Copenhagen, including Nyhavn 18, Nyhavn 20, and Nyhavn 67. He also lived for a time at Vingårdsstræde 6.

Assistens Kirkegård (Assistens Cemetery) ★   Dating from 1711, and the largest burial ground in Copenhagen, this is the liveliest cemetery we've ever encountered in Europe. Instead of a tranquil "rest in peace" kind of place, it's been turned into a public park. Families come here for picnics, and aspirant rock bands use it as an open-air venue to perform before a live, captive audience. Sunbathers don't seem to mind stripping down for a "bath" on the grave of the dear departed.

It also contains the graves of the two towering literary figures of Denmark, both Hans Christian Andersen and Søren Kierkegaard. These men were rivals in life, but in this graveyard they are at peace with one another. Many critics today believe both men were latent homosexuals. Martin Andersen Nexø, a famous novelist of his time who depicted the struggles of the working class, is also buried here, as are many other famous Danes, a sort of "Who Was Who." Even the brewer who still keeps half of Denmark drunk at night, Carlsberg patriarch Christen Jacobsen, is interred here.

Nørrebrogade/Kapelvej 4. ℂ **35-37-19-17.** Free admission. Jan–Feb 8am–5pm; Mar–Apr and Sept–Oct 8am–6pm; May–Aug 8am–8pm; Nov–Dec 8am–4pm. Bus: 5, 7E, or 16.

Københavns Bymuseet & Søren Kierkegaard Samlingen   We come here not to see the city museum exhibits so much, but to learn more about one of Denmark's most enigmatic authors, Søren Kierkegaard. A section of the museum is devoted to the "Father of Existentialism," his life illustrated by personal belongings, drawings, letters, books, and old photographs. Born in Copenhagen on May 3, 1813, he eventually died in his beloved city in October of 1855, when he collapsed on the street. He was only 42. As a hedonistic youth, he indulged himself—not in liquor, like some writers, but in the consumption of pastry. His pastry bill in 1836 was said to equal the annual wage of a typical Danish family. His most famous work was created in 1843, when he wrote his philosophical novel, *Enten/Eller (Either/Or)*. From an early age, Kierkegaard proclaimed himself a genius—and so he was.

If you hang around, you can check out some of the city museum collections. Unless you're interested in sewers and gas pipes, we'd suggest you skip the "Underground Exhibition." The section on old shop fronts evoking Copenhagen of yesterday is intriguing if you'd like to see the city the way it was.

Vesterbrogade 59. ℂ **33-21-07-72.** www.kbhbymuseum.dk. Admission DKK20 ($3.40/£2) adults, free for children 17 and under, free to all Fri. Thurs–Mon 10am–4pm; Wed 10am–9pm. Bus: 6, 16, 27, or 28.

ESPECIALLY FOR KIDS

Copenhagen is a wonderful place for children, and many so-called adult attractions—except the Erotica Museum—also appeal to kids. **Tivoli** is an obvious choice, as is the statue of *Den Lille Havfrue (The Little Mermaid)* at Langelinie. Try to see the changing of the Queen's Royal Life Guard at **Amalienborg Palace,** including the entire parade to and from the royal residence. Kids also enjoy **Frilandsmuseet,** the open-air museum. (For details on these sights, see listings earlier in this chapter.) Other attractions great for kids include the following.

Bakken Amusement Park   This is the Tivoli on a bad hair day but a lot of fun if you don't like your amusement parks too manicured. On the northern edge of Copenhagen, about 12km (7¹⁄₂ miles) from the city center, this amusement park was created 35 years before the Pilgrims landed at Plymouth Rock. It's a local favorite, featuring roller coasters, dancing, a tunnel of love, and a merry-go-round. Open-air restaurants are plentiful, as are snack bars and ice-cream booths. Some individual attractions—100 or so rides—charge a separate admission fee—proceeds support this unspoiled natural preserve. We like to visit to see the singing girls and cabaret at **Bakkens Hvile** ★★. They rival the Rockettes at New York City's Radio City Music Hall and remain the most popular revue in Denmark. There are no cars in the park—only bicycles and horse-drawn carriages are allowed.

Dyrehavevej 62, Klampenborg. ℂ **39-63-35-44.** www.bakken.dk. Free admission; 10 rides cost DKK199 ($34/£20). Summer daily noon–midnight. Closed mid-Sept to late Mar. S-tog: Klampenborg (about 20 min. from Central Railroad Station); then walk through the Deer Park or take a horse-drawn cab.

Tips **Special & Free Events**

Much of Copenhagen is a summer festival, especially at the **Tivoli Gardens** (p. 121). Although the gardens have an entrance fee, once you're inside, many of the concerts and other presentations are free. A total of 150 performances each summer are presented at the Concert Hall (which seats 1,500), or in the smaller Glassalen Hall (seats 700). Of these, more than 100 are free. Pantomime performances at the Pantomime Theater are also free. Performances on the open-air stage are free every night (closed Mon). Likewise, **Bakken Amusement Park** (p. 140), which, by most yardsticks, is the oldest amusement park in the world, offers many free events. And you don't have to pay an admission to enter—only if you patronize the various attractions.

The **birthday of Queen Margrethe,** on April 16, is a celebration with the queen and the royal family driving through the pedestrian street, Strøget, in a stagecoach escorted by hussars in full regalia. People also gather in Amalienborg Slotsplads (the square that's the focal point of the Royal Family's residence in Copenhagen), usually cheering wildly in a style that some observers claim evokes star worship at a rock concert.

The **Copenhagen Jazz Festival** (www.jazzfestival.dk) in early July is one of the greatest in the world, and many of the concerts are free. Squares, parks, and a wide range of cafes and clubs resound with the sound of jazz—in all, some 450 concerts are staged at this time. Visitors arrive for the festival from as far away as China and Australia, and over the years the festival has attracted such jazz greats as Ray Charles and Dizzy Gillespie. For more information, check out www.festival.jazz.dk.

Danmarks Akvarium (Denmark's Aquarium)   Opened in 1939, a year before the Nazi invasion of Denmark, this is not among the world-class aquariums such as the one that opened in Atlanta, Georgia. Give it a look only if you happen to be visiting the grounds of **Charlottenlund Slot** at Hellerup, a coastal suburb of Copenhagen. After walking through the grounds (the palace is not open), site of a royal residence since 1690, drop in at the aquarium. Although it was enlarged in 1974, it still features only 90 or so tanks of the usual marine "suspects"—sharks, turtles, piranhas, and fish that can survive in the North Sea as well as those from more tropical waters.

Strandvejen, in Charlottenlund Fort Park, Charlottenlund. (℃) **39-62-32-83.** www.akvarium.dk. Admission DKK90 ($15/£9) adults, DKK50 ($8.50/£5) children 3–11, free for children 2 and under. May–Aug daily 10am–6pm; Sept–Oct and Feb–Apr daily 10am–5pm; Nov–Jan daily 10am–4pm. S-tog: Charlottenlund. Bus: 14 or 166.

Experimentarium (Hands-On Science Center)★★   It is said that curators from all over the world come here to plan the science museums of the 21st century. This is the most interactive museum in the Nordic world. In the old mineral-water-bottling hall of Tuborg breweries 5km (3 miles) north of Copenhagen in Hellerup, this museum has a hands-on approach to science. Visitors use not only their hands but all five of their senses as they participate in some 300 interactive exhibitions and demonstrations divided into three themes: "Man," "Nature," and "The Interaction Between Man and Nature." Visitors hear what all the world's languages sound like, make a wind machine blow up to hurricane force, check their skin to test how much sun it can take, dance in an inverted disco, program a robot, gaze at an optical illusion, experience a human-size gyroscope, or visit a slimming machine. Families can work as a team to examine enzymes, make a camera from paper, or test perfume. Exhibitions change frequently and—from what we've seen—thrill adults almost more than the kids.

Tuborg Havnevej 7, Hellerup. ℂ **39-27-33-33**. www.experimentarium.dk. Admission DKK135 ($23/£14) adults, DKK90 ($15/£9) children 3–11, free for children 2 and under. Mon and Wed–Fri 9:30am–5pm; Tues 9:30am–9pm; Sat–Sun 11am–5pm. Closed Dec 23–25, Dec 31, and Jan 1. S-tog: Hellerup or Svanemøllen. Bus: 1, 14, or 21.

Tycho Brahe Planetarium   When E.T. makes his first real earth landing—that is, not in a film—he'll no doubt set down here first to honor the famed Danish astronomer Tycho Brahe (1546–1601). Of course, Brahe got a lot of things wrong—after all, he disagreed with Copernicus and still believed that the earth stood at the center of the universe. But he did some things right, including mapping the position of more than 1,000 fixed stars—and he did all this with the naked eye since Galileo didn't emerge with his telescope until 1610. Long before those stories about Michael Jackson's alleged faux nose surfaced, Brahe actually had a silver snout. The original fell to the ground after a duel in Rostock.

On a dome-shaped screen, IMAX films are shown, creating the marvel of the night sky, with its planets, galaxies, star clusters, and comets. If Brahe could have lived to see this enthralling film, he obviously would no longer believe the earth was the center of the universe. The permanent exhibition, "The Active Universe," doesn't quite answer all the questions of the mysteries of space, but it deals with a lot of them. Exhibitions on natural science and astronomy may leave you with a lingering feeling for space travel if the Tycho Brahe of tomorrow could only find more inhabitable planets than Mars and Jupiter.

Gammel Kongevej 10. ℂ **33-12-12-24**. www.tycho.dk. Admission DKK125 ($21/£13) adults, DKK75 ($13/£7.50) children 10–15, free for children 9 and under. Mon–Fri 10am–9pm; Sat–Sun 10:30am–9pm. Bus: 1 or 14.

Zoologisk Have (Copenhagen Zoo)   This zoo has come a long way, baby, since 1859, when it opened with stuffed birds, a seal in a bathtub, and a turtle in a bucket. Today at its location in Frederiksberg, west of the center of Copenhagen, it is home to 3,300 animals and 264 species. The zoo, in fact, is a window to the wilds of the world, with animals from the icy snowfields of Greenland to the hot, dusty savannas of Africa. You get to see everything from the musk oxen and reindeer of the far north to the hungry lions of Kenya. Expect the usual apes and elephants from a Tarzan movie, but thrill also to a close encounter with a polar bear. The world is filled with ragtag children's zoos, but the one here is exceptional. Kids can pet beasts who are "not too wild." The highlight for the kiddies is an Eiffel Tower–like structure that rises 40m (131 ft.), dating from 1905. *Warning:* The zoo is mobbed on Sundays in summer.

Roskildevej 32, Frederiksberg. ℂ **72-20-02-00**. www.zoo.dk. Admission DKK130 ($22/£13) adults, DKK70 ($12/£7) children 3–11, free for children 2 and under. Nov–Feb daily 9am–4pm; Mar Mon–Fri 9am–4pm, Sat–Sun 9am–5pm; Apr–May and Sept Mon–Fri 9am–5pm, Sat–Sun 9am–6pm; June–Aug daily 9am–6pm; Oct daily 9am–5pm. S-tog: Valby. Bus: 4A, 6A, 26, or 832.

START: Rådhuspladsen.
FINISH: Tivoli Gardens.
TIME: 1½ hours.
BEST TIMES: Any sunny day.
WORST TIMES: Rush hours (Mon–Fri 7:30–9am and 5–6:30pm).

Start in the center of Copenhagen at:

❶ Rådhuspladsen (Town Hall Square)

Pay a visit to the bronze statue of Hans Christian Andersen, the spinner of fairy tales, which stands near a boulevard bearing his name. Also on this square is a statue of two *lur* horn players that has stood here since 1914.

Bypassing the *lur* horn players, walk east along Vester Voldgade onto a narrow street on your left:

❷ Lavendelstræde

Many houses along here date from the late 18th century. At Lavendelstræde 1, Mozart's widow (Constanze) lived with her second husband, Georg Nikolaus von Nissen, a Danish diplomat, from 1812 to 1820.

The little street quickly becomes:

❸ Slutterigade

Courthouses rise on both sides of this short street, joined by elevated walkways. Built between 1805 and 1815, this was Copenhagen's fourth town hall, now the city's major law courts. The main courthouse entrance is on Nytorv.

Slutterigade will lead to:

❹ Nytorv

In this famous square, you can admire fine 19th-century houses. Philosopher Søren Kierkegaard (1813–55) lived in a house adjacent to the courthouse.

Cross Nytorv, and veer slightly west (to your left) until you reach Nygade, part of the:

❺ Strøget

At this point, this traffic-free shopping street has a different name. (It actually began at Rådhuspladsen and was called

Frederiksberggade.) The major shopping street of Scandinavia, Strøget is a stroller's and a shopper's delight, following a 1km (.6-mile) path through the heart of Copenhagen.

Nygade is one of the five streets that compose Strøget. Head northeast along this street, which becomes winding and narrow Vimmelskaftet, then turns into Amagertorv. Along Amagertorv, on your left, you'll come across the:

❻ Helligåndskirken (Church of the Holy Ghost)

Complete with an abbey, Helligåndshuset is the oldest church in Copenhagen, founded at the beginning of the 15th century. Partially destroyed in 1728, it was reconstructed in 1880 in a neoclassical style. Some of the buildings on this street date from 1616. The sales rooms of the Royal Porcelain Factory are at Amagertorv 6.

Next you'll come to Østergade, the last portion of Strøget. You'll see Illum's department store on your left. Østergade leads to the square:

❼ Kongens Nytorv

Surrounding Copenhagen's largest square, with an equestrian statue of Christian IV in the center, are many restored antique buildings. The statue is a bronze replica of a 1688 sculpture.

At Kongens Nytorv, head right until you come to Laksegade. Then go south along this street until you reach the intersection with Nikolajgade. Turn right. This street will lead to the:

❽ Nikolaj Kirke

The building dates from 1530 and was the scene of the thundering sermons of Hans Tausen, a father of the Danish Reformation.

TAKE A BREAK
A mellow spot for a pick-me-up, either a refreshing cool drink or an open-faced sandwich, **Cafeen Nikolaj,** Nikolaj Plads 12 (© **33-11-63-13**), attracts both older shoppers and young people. You can sit and linger over a cup of coffee, and no one is likely to hurry you. You can visit anytime in the afternoon, perhaps making it your luncheon stopover. The setting is within the interior of (during cold weather), or in the shadow of (during warm weather), this charming antique redbrick church.

After seeing the church, head left down Fortunstræde to your next stop, a square off Gammel Strand:

9 Højbro Plads

You'll have a good view of Christiansborg Palace and Thorvaldsens Museum on Slotsholmen. On Højbro Plads is an equestrian statue honoring Bishop Absalon, who founded Copenhagen in 1167. Several old buildings line the square.

Continue west along:

10 Gammel Strand

From this waterfront promenade—the name means "old shore"—the former edge of Copenhagen, you'll have a panoramic look across to Christiansborg Palace. A number of antique buildings line this street, and at the end you'll come upon the

Ministry of Cultural Affairs, occupying a former government pawnbroking establishment, dating from 1730.

To the right of this building, walk up:

11 Snaregade

This old-fashioned provincial street is one of the most evocative of the old city. Walk until you reach Knabrostræde. Both streets boast structures built just after the great fire of 1795. Where the streets intersect, you'll see the Church of Our Lady.

Make your way back to Snaregade, and turn right to one of Copenhagen's best-preserved streets:

12 Magstræde

Proceed along to Rådhusstræde. Just before you reach Rådhusstræde, notice the two buildings facing that street. These are the oldest structures in the city, dating from the 16th century.

Walk across Vandkunsten, a square at the end of Magstræde, then turn right down Gasegade, which doesn't go very far before you turn left along Farvergade. At this street's intersection with Vester Voldgade, you'll come to the Vartov Church. Continue west until you reach Rådhuspladsen. Across the square, you'll see the:

13 Tivoli Gardens

You'll find the entrance at Vesterbrogade 3. Attracting some 4.5 million visitors every summer, this amusement park has 25 different entertainment choices and attractions and just as many restaurants and beer gardens.

WALKING TOUR 2   **KONGENS NYTORV TO LANGELINIE**

START:	Kongens Nytorv.
FINISH:	*Den Lille Havfrue (The Little Mermaid).*
TIME:	1½ hours.
BEST TIME:	Any sunny day.
Worst Times:	Rush hours (weekdays 7:30–9am and 5–6:30pm).

Although Nyhavn, once a boisterous sailors' quarter, has quieted down, it's still a charming part of old Copenhagen, with its 1673 canal and 18th-century houses.

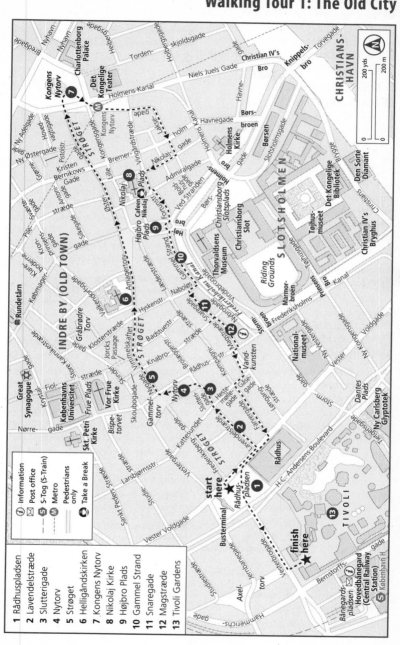

1 Rådhuspladsen
2 Lavendelstræde
3 Slutterigade
4 Nytorv
5 Strøget
6 Helligåndskirken
7 Kongens Nytorv
8 Nikolaj Kirke
9 Højbro Plads
10 Gammel Strand
11 Snaregade
12 Magstræde
13 Tivoli Gardens

(i) Information
⊠ Post office
Ⓢ S-Tog (S-Train)
Ⓜ Metro
Pedestrians only
☕ Take a Break

Begin at:

❶ Kongens Nytorv

The "King's New Market" dates from 1680. It's the home of Magasin, the biggest department store in the capital, plus an equestrian statue of Christian IV.

On the northeast side of the square is:

❷ Thott's Mansion

Completed in 1685 for a Danish naval hero and restored in 1760, it now houses the French Embassy. Between Bredgade and Store Strandstræde, a little street angling to the right near Nyhavn, is Kanneworff House, a beautifully preserved private home that dates from 1782. On the west side of the square, at no. 34, is the landmark Hotel d'Angleterre. Also here is an old anchor memorializing the Danish seamen who died in World War II.

On the southeast side of the square is:

❸ The Royal Theater

Founded in 1748, the theater presents ballet, opera, and plays. Statues of famous Danish dramatists are out front. The present theater, constructed in 1874, has a neo-Renaissance style.

With your back to the Hotel d'Angleterre, walk toward the water along:

❹ Nyhavn

Once filled with maritime businesses and seamen's bars and lodgings, Nyhavn is now "restaurant row." First, walk along its north (left) side. In the summer, cafe tables border the canal, giving it a festive atmosphere. Beautiful old homes, antiques shops, and more restaurants line the southern bank. Nyhavn was the home of Hans Christian Andersen at various times. He lived at no. 20, where he wrote his first fairy tales, in 1835, and at no. 67 from 1845 to 1864. He spent the last 2 years of his life at no. 18, where he died in 1875.

On the quieter (south) side of the canal, you can see:

❺ Charlottenborg Palace

The style of the building, now the Danish Academy of Fine Arts, is pure baroque.

The name comes from Queen Charlotte Amalie, who moved there in 1700.

Walk back to the harbor end of Nyhavn and turn left onto Kvæsthusgade, which will take you to:

❻ Skt. Annæ Plads

Before the radical transformation of Copenhagen's harborfront, ferries used to depart from piers here for other destinations in Scandinavia, including Oslo. Now, however, the harborfront, and the back of this desirable long and narrow square, is the site of one of the biggest urban transformations in the city's history. The ferryboat terminals have moved to the commercial neighborhood of Nordhavn, and the city seems to be watching what will eventually emerge from this site, just a short walk from Nyhavn and its rows of restaurants. Many consulates, two hotels, and fine old buildings open onto it.

Walk inland along the plaza and turn right onto Amaliegade, which leads under a colonnade into symmetrical majesty of the cobble-covered Amalienborg Plads, site of:

❼ Amalienborg Palace

In the square's center is a statue of Frederik V. When the queen is in residence, the changing of the guard takes place here daily at noon. The palace is the official residence of the queen and her French prince, but sections of it are open to visitors. The palace is actually composed of a quartet of nearly identical baroque mansions, each interconnected with galleries or subterranean passages, and each positioned at cardinal points of the same octagon-shaped square. The queen lives in a wing that's adjacent to the neoclassical colonnade.

Between the square and the harbor are the gardens of:

❽ Amaliehavn

Among the most beautiful in Copenhagen, these gardens were laid out by Jean Delogne, who made lavish use of Danish granite and French limestone. The bronze pillars around the fountain were the work

1 Kongens Nytorv
2 Thott's Mansion
3 Royal Theater
4 Nyhavn
5 Charlottenborg Palace
6 Skt. Annæ Plads
7 Amalienborg Palace
8 Amaliehavn
9 Frederiks Kirke
10 Medicinsk Museion
11 Frihedsmuseet
12 *The Little Mermaid*

— **S** S-Tog (S-Train)
---- **M** Metro
⬤ Take a Break

of Arnaldo Pomodoro, an Italian sculptor. From this point, look across the harbor at the most exciting and unusual recently constructed building in town, the **Danish Opera House.** With a soaring rooftop that evokes the reinforced concrete structures of Le Corbusier, and a design that evokes the outspread wings of a dove, it was created by Henning Larsen, "The House Architect of Copenhagen," with perfect acoustics and "chandeliers that might have been inspired by a show palace in Las Vegas." From your waterfront vantage, notice the way that the location of the Opera House repeats the rectilinear layout of Amalienborg Palace and the nearby Marble Church; the buildings each line up along the same lines, a brilliant combination of baroque and post-modern architecture combined into a coherent whole.

After viewing the waterfront gardens, walk away from the water, crossing Amalienborg Plads and emerging onto Frederiksgade. Continue along this street until you reach:

⑨ Frederikskirke

This church is often called the *Marmorkirken* (marble church). Construction began in 1740, but had to stop in 1770 because of the costs. The church wasn't completed until 1894—using Danish marble instead of more expensive Norwegian marble. The church was modeled on and intended to rival St. Peter's in Rome; indeed, it ended up with one of the largest church domes in Europe. Supported on a dozen towering piers, the dome has a diameter of 32m (105 ft.).

Facing the church, turn right and head north along Bredgade, passing at no. 62 the:

⑩ Medicinsk Museion (Medical History Museum)

The collection is gruesome, with fetuses, dissected heads, and the like.

TAKE A BREAK
Before you approach *Den Lille Havfrue*, consider tea and a snack at **Café Lumskebugten,** Esplanaden 21 (☎ **33-15-60-29;** see "Where to Dine," in chapter 5). Dating from 1854, and permeated with a sense of the cozy, old-fashioned Denmark of long ago, this cafe offers a cold plate served throughout the afternoon. There are five specialties: beef tartare, fish cakes with mustard sauce, marinated salmon, baked cod, and shrimp.

Bredgade ends at Esplanaden, which opens onto Churchillparken, a green belt bordering the water. Turn right and walk along Esplanaden until you come to Churchillparken and the:

⑪ Frihedsmuseet

The Danish Resistance museum commemorates the struggle against the Nazis from 1940 to 1945.

After leaving the museum, walk toward the water along Langelinie, where signs point the way to:

⑫ The Little Mermaid

Perched on rocks just off the harbor bank, *Den Lille Havfrue,* the most photographed statue in Scandinavia, dates from 1913. The bronze figure, by Edvard Eriksen, was modeled after the figure of prima ballerina Ellen Price. In time, this much-attacked and abused statue became the symbol of Copenhagen.

ORGANIZED TOURS

BUS & BOAT TOURS   The boat and bus sightseeing tours in Copenhagen range from get-acquainted jaunts to in-depth excursions. Either of the following tours can be arranged through **Copenhagen Excursions** (☎ **32-54-06-06**) or **Vikingbus** (☎ **32-66-00-00;** www.vikingbus.com). Inexpensive bus tours depart from the *lur* blowers' statue at Town Hall Square, and boat trips leave from Gammel Strand (the fish market) or Nyhavn. Visit **www.sightseeing.dk** for more information.

For orientation, hop on a bus for the 1½-hour **City Tour,** which covers scenic highlights like *The Little Mermaid,* Rosenborg Castle, and Amalienborg Palace. Tours depart from the City Hall Square daily at 9:30am, 11:30am, and 1:30pm May 15 to September 30. They cost DKK140 ($24/£14) for adults, DKK65 ($11/£6.50) for children 11 and under.

We heartily recommend the **City and Harbor Tour,** a 2½-hour trip by launch and bus that departs from Town Hall Square. The boat tours the city's main canals, passing *The Little Mermaid* and the Old Fish Market. It operates May 15 to September 30, daily at 9:30am, 11:30am, and 1:30pm. It costs DKK175 ($30/£18) for adults, DKK80 ($14/£8) for children 11 and under.

Shakespeare buffs may be interested in an afternoon excursion to the castles of North Zealand. The 7-hour tour explores the area north of Copenhagen, including Kronborg (Hamlet's castle); briefly visits Fredensborg, the queen's residence; and makes a stopover at Frederiksborg Castle and the National Historical Museum. Tours depart from Town Hall Square, running February to April and October to December Wednesday and Sunday at 9:30am; May to September Wednesday, Saturday, and Sunday at 9:30am. The cost is DKK480 ($82/£48) for adults, DKK230 ($39/£23) for children 11 and under.

GUIDED WALKS THROUGH COPENHAGEN Staff members of the Copenhagen Tourist Information Office conduct 2-hour guided walking tours of the city every Monday and Friday to Sunday at 10am, between May and September. The price is DKK80 ($14/£8) for adults, DKK25 ($4.30/£2.50) for children age 10 to 15, free for children 9 and under. For information, contact the **Copenhagen Tourist Information Center,** Vesterbrogade 4A (© **70-22-24-42;** www.visitcopenhagen.com).

A VISIT TO COPENHAGEN'S MOST FAMOUS BREWERY **Carlsberg** is the most famous beer in Denmark and the country's best-known brand internationally. Much of it is produced within an old-fashioned brewery constructed in 1847, which was enlarged in 2005 with the addition of a spanking-new microbrewery that's devoted to the production of at least four "affiliated" brews which are being marketed under the brand name of "Jacobsen." Jointly, the brewery turns out at least three million bottles of beer a day. Even Danny Kaye, in Denmark to film *Hans Christian Andersen* for Samuel Goldwyn, drank a beer here, although this gourmet later admitted, "I infinitely prefer French wine." From within the newly redesigned Visitors' Center, you can take a self-guided tour of both sides of the brewery, walking around an observation gallery whose English-language signs and flickering video screens will explain the brewing process. The factory is open for visits Tuesday to Sunday 10am to 4pm. Entrance (and access to the self-guided tours) costs DKK45 ($7.70/£4.50) per person (there's no discount for children), and each adult visitor is given a free beer at the end of the tour, with the option of buying more at the on-site pub. The entrance to the brewery is graced with a pair of sculpted elephants, each with armored regalia that includes a swastika. That doesn't mean the company was a Nazi sympathizer—Carlsberg used the symbol as part of its image long before Hitler. Take bus no. 26 from Copenhagen Central Station or from the Town Hall Square in Copenhagen to **Carlsberg Brewery,** Gamle Carlsberg Vej 11 (© **33-27-13-14**).

ACTIVE SPORTS

BICYCLING The absence of hills and the abundance of parks and wide avenues with bicycle lanes make cycling the best way to explore Copenhagen. Bike-rental shops and stands are scattered throughout the city. Two suggestions are **Københavns Cyker,** Reventlowsgade 11 (© **33-33-86-13;** bus: 6 or 10), and **Dan Wheel,** Colbjørnsensgade

3 (✆ **33-21-22-27;** bus: 28 or 41). A deposit of DKK500 ($85/£50) is required. Alternatively, **City Bike** is a great way to get around central Copenhagen. Bike racks are located throughout the city center; the service is free and you unlock your bike with a DKK25 ($4.30/£2.50) deposit. When you return the bike, your deposit is returned. The bikes are available from May to December (**www.bycyklen.dk**).

JOGGING   The many parks (known to locals as "green lungs") of Copenhagen provide endless routes for joggers. Our favorite, just west of the city center, circles Lakes Sortedams, St. Jorgens, and Peblinge. The paths that wind through the Frederiksborg gardens are also well suited for joggers.

SWIMMING   In spite of an often bone-chilling climate, swimming is a favorite Danish pastime. The **Frederiksborg Svømmehal,** Helgesvej 29 (✆ **38-14-04-04;** bus: 6 or 18), is open to the public Monday to Friday 7am to 9pm, Saturday 9am to 4pm, and Sunday 9am to 2:30pm. Tickets cost DKK35 ($6/£3.50). You can also try **Sundby Swimming Pool,** Sundbyvestervej 50 (✆ **32-58-55-68;** bus: 30 or 31); or **Kildeskovshallen,** Adolphsvej 25 (✆ **39-77-44-00;** bus: 165).

2 SHOPPING

Copenhagen is in the vanguard of shopping in Europe, and much of the action takes place on **Strøget,** the pedestrian street in the heart of the capital. Strøget begins as Frederiksberggade, north of Rådhuspladsen, and winds to Østergade, which opens onto Kongens Nytorv. The jam-packed street is lined with stores selling everything from porcelain statues of *Youthful Boldness* to open-faced sandwiches piled high with Greenland shrimp, pizza slices, all kinds of clothing, and some of the most elegant porcelain in Europe. There are also high-volume franchises of both McDonald's and Burger King.

Between stops, relax with a drink at an outdoor cafe, or just sit on a bench and people-watch.

In two nearby walking areas—**Gråbrødretorv** and **Fiolstræde**—you can browse through antiques shops and bookshops.

Bredgade, beginning at Kongens Nytorv, is the antiques district, where prices tend to be very high. **Læderstræde** is another shopping street that competes with Bredgade in antiques.

BEST BUYS   In a country famed for its designers and craftspeople, the best buys are in stainless steel, porcelain, china, glassware, toys, functionally designed furniture, textiles, and jewelry—especially silver jewelry set with semiprecious stones.

SHIPPING IT HOME & RECOVERING VAT   Denmark imposes a 25% tax on goods and services, a "value-added tax" known in Denmark as **MOMS** (pronounced "mumps," and every bit as painful). Tax-free exports are possible. Many stores will mail goods to your home so you can avoid paying the tax. If you want to take your purchases, look for shops displaying Danish tax-free shopping notices. Such shops offer tourists tax refunds for personal export. This refund applies to purchases of over DKK300 ($51/£30) for visitors from the United States and Canada—spent at the same store, but not necessarily all at once. For more information, see "Taxes" in "Fast Facts: Denmark," in the appendix. For answers to tax refund questions, call **Global Refund** (✆ **32-52-55-66**).

STORE HOURS   In general, shopping hours are 9:30 or 10am to 5:30pm Monday to Thursday, to 7 or 8pm on Friday, and to 2pm on Saturday. Most shops are closed Sunday,

except the kiosks and supermarket at the Central Railroad Station. Here you can purchase food until 10pm or midnight. The Central Railroad Station's bakery is open until
9pm, and one kiosk at Rådhuspladsen, which sells papers, film, and souvenirs, is open
24 hours.

SHOPPING A TO Z
Amber
The Amber Specialist The owners, known to customers as the "Amber Twins," will
sell you "the gold of the north." This petrified resin originated in the large coniferous
forests that covered Denmark some 35 million years ago. The forest disappeared, but the
amber lasted, and is now used to create handsome jewelry. This shop carries a large collection of stunning amber set in 14-karat gold. Frederiksberggade 28. (✆ **33-11-88-03.** Bus:
28, 29, or 41.

Art Galleries & Auction Houses
Bruun Rasmussen Established shortly after World War II, this is Denmark's leading
auction house. July is usually quiet, although the premises remain open for appraisals and
purchases. The season begins in August, with an auction of paintings and fine art. Viewing time is allowed before auctions, which are held about once a month. There are also
auctions of art, wine, coins, books, and antique weapons. Bredgade 33. (✆ **88-18-11-11.**
www.bruun-rasmussen.dk. Bus: 1, 6, 9, or 10.

Galerie Asbæk This modern-art gallery has a permanent exhibit of the best local
artists, along with changing shows by Scandinavian and foreign artists. A bookshop and
cafe serving French-inspired Danish food is on the premises. Graphics and posters are for
sale. Bredgade 20. (✆ **33-15-40-04.** www.asbaek.dk. Bus: 1, 6, 9, 10, 28, 29, or 41.

Books
Boghallen This big store at Town Hall Square carries many books in English, as well
as a wide selection of travel-related literature, including maps. It stocks books in English
on Danish themes, such as the collected works of Hans Christian Andersen. Rådhuspladsen 37. (✆ **33-47-25-60.** www.boghallen.dk. Bus: 2, 8, or 30.

Coffee & Tea
Specialkobmanden It's the best-scented store in Copenhagen, thanks to hundreds
of containers of exotic coffees, teas, and spices that would send any caffeine addict into
orbit. Scattered within this cornucopia of abundance are coffee varieties from Jamaica,
Cuba, and Kenya; teas from the slopes of Mount Kilimanjaro; olive oils from Italy and
France; and even a blend of tea named after (and presumably favored by) Princess Mary,
the (relatively) new Australia-born bride of Denmark's crown prince. Established in
1972, the shop is a favorite of local residents, who seek out the place for the new, the
unusual, and the esoteric. Hovedvagtsgade 6. (✆ **33-15-12-88.** Bus: 1, 6, or 9.

Danish Design
Bald & Bang ★ Finds Its name sounds gimmicky, but this outlet showcases what are
perhaps the most sophisticated lamps in Europe. Launched by entrepreneurs Anders
Bang and Gitte Bald, it began by selling only one item, the IQlight, a lampshade from
the heyday of disco in the '70s. Designed by Holger Strøm in 1972, the lamp had long
become passé until Bald and Bang brought it back in 2000. The lampshade is made from
linking pieces of off-white plastic that can be combined in different sizes and shapes.

Some of their latest lamp designs include the futuristic "Fuse." They also go back in Denmark's design past to rediscover golden oldies, including Louis Weisdorf's 1965 "Turbo," made from a dozen pieces of interlocking aluminum. Rømersgade 7. ℃ **33-36-07-76**. www.bald-bang.com. Bus: Any bus going to Nørreport Station.

DDC Shop ★ Finds   On the premises of the Danish Design Centre (p. 135), this store is like a small exhibition of Danish design . . . except everything is for sale. The shop showcases products that evoke some of the best craftsmanship of modern Danish designers today. The assortment of items for sale is always changing and continuously expanding, but invariably only high-quality items are offered for sale. 27 H. C. Andersens Blvd. ℃ **33-69-33-69**. www.ddc.dk. Bus: 5A, 6A, 10, or 12.

Georg Jensen Damask ★★   This store is not to be confused with the more famous Georg Jensen, the purveyor of the nation's finest silver. This George Jensen family has been turning out the nation's finest home textiles since the 15th century. Nearly all fine households in Denmark contain the firm's high-quality and well-designed table linens and towers. Some major designers are also showcased here, including geometrically patterned cloth in anthracite and white, the design of the legendary Arne Jacobsen. Ny Østergade 19. ℃ **33-12-26-00**. www.damask.dk. Bus: 1, 6, or 9.

The House ★★   Is this a shop or a museum of Danish design? Opened in 2007, this outlet set about to showcase the most iconic of Danish designers. Its selections of chairs, for example, may be the most bizarre or unique on the planet. You can purchase reproductions of not only Arne Jacobsen's celebrated Swan Chair (1958), but also Vernere Panton's Panton Chair (1960), or even Nanna Ditzel's Trinidad Chair (1993). Christian Flindt's Orchid Chair (2000) is ultrafuturistic. The shop is somewhat of a cultural center, hosting interviews with designers, even performances by singers, actors, and musicians. Nyhavn 11. ℃ **32-95-00-24**. Bus: 1, 6, or 9.

Jørgen L. Dalgaard ★ Finds   This relatively small shop has been hailed as one of Copenhagen's best-kept design secrets. Opened in 1974, it is a showcase for the decorative arts of the 20th century, and its owner is a specialist in Danish stoneware, porcelain, and glass. There is also a wide range of Danish furniture from 1920 to 1980. The big names in Swedish glass, Orrefors and Kosta Boda, are on display, but you can also see the work of lesser-known Finnish designers such as Tapio Wirkkala and Timo Sarpaneva. Bredgade 2. ℃ **33-14-09-05**. Bus: 1, 6, 9, or 10.

Klassik Moderne Møbelkunst ★   This shop specializes in furniture design from 1920 to 1975, and it also specializes in lamps and lighting by Paul Henningsen. It also offers a selection of Danish arts and crafts from "The Golden Age" of Scandinavian design, including glass, ceramics, and woodworks. The golden age refers to that period after World War II. Also on display is a wide range of Danish modern art, paintings, and sculpture going back to early Modernism. Bredgade 3. ℃ **33-33-90-60**. Bus: 1, 6, 9, or 10.

Normann Copenhagen   In the Østerbro district, this is an international design firm installed in a long-deserted old movie house. Jan and Poul are the two Normanns, one with the last name of Andersen and the other called Madsen. Locals flock here to purchase ever-changing furniture and objects in Danish design, including avant-garde ceramics. Østerbrogade 70. ℃ **35-27-05-40**. www.normann-copenhagen.com. Bus: 3.

Rosendahl ★★   It all started with a wine stopper when this company's founder, Erik Rosendahl, invented a cone-shaped object that would fit all wine bottles. It took

Denmark by storm. Today Rosendahl is one of the country's leading producers of gifts for the home, each object from clear glass to bone china based on fine craftsmanship and practical design. The company is known for its innovative accessories for the table and its professional, easy-to-use kitchen utensils. Bremerholm 1. ℂ **70-27-66-33.** www.rosendahl. dk. Bus: 1, 6, 8, 9, or 10.

Department Stores

Birger Christensen ★★ This spacious store is one of the most luxe in Copenhagen, filled with beautiful and expensive clothes, even seal and sable furs from the far north of Scandinavia. In addition to clothing from Danish designers, the store carries all the big names such as Prada and Chanel, and it clothes both men and women rather glamorously. The 20th century in fashion is a distant memory. This store's clothing is as modern as tomorrow. Østergade 38. ℂ **33-11-55-55.** www.birger-christensen.com. Bus: 1, 6, or 9.

Bruuns Bazaar ★★ Starting out small in 1995, two brothers, Teis and Bjørn Brunn, soon had fashionistas beating a path to their door. Their clothing is now seen on the catwalks of Paris and has, in fact, gone around the world. Today the Bazaar is an innovative and international design company, creating beautiful clothing for both men and women, as well as accessories. Somehow they manage to blend a classic style with cutting-edge designs. The shop also designs a trendy line for younger women and carries a collection of delicate footwear for women, in the most seductive colors. Krønprinsensgade 8 and 9. ℂ **33-32-19-99.** www.bruunsbazaar.com. Bus: 1, 6, or 9.

Illum ★ One of Denmark's top department stores, Illum is on Strøget. Take time to browse through its vast store of Danish and Scandinavian design. There are a restaurant and a special export cash desk at street level. Østergade 52. ℂ **33-14-40-02.** Bus: 1, 6, 9, or 10.

Mads Nørgaard All the big names in international labels are sold here, but Mads, lying along the Strøget, turns out some beautifully made clothing on its own label. The women's jeans look street-smart, and the menswear is fashionable and right up-to-date. The selection of elegant T-shirts—if a T-shirt can be elegant—is the best in town. Amagertorv 15. ℂ **33-32-01-19.** www.madsnorgaard.dk. Bus: 1, 6, 8, 9, or 10.

Magasin ★★ A classy department store, Magasin is the biggest in Scandinavia. It offers a complete assortment of Danish designer fashion, a large selection of glass and porcelain, and souvenirs. Goods are shipped abroad tax-free. Kongens Nytorv 13. ℂ **33-11-44-33.** www.magasin.dk. Bus: 1, 6, 9, or 10.

Munthe plus Simonsen ★ This is where the Danish supermodel Helena Christensen and even Crown Princess Mary go to shop. The walls are lined with buffalo skin to create a warm, cozy mood for the fashion on parade. Designers Naja Munthe and Karen Simonsen founded this award-winning design company in 1994, and they still select the colors, individual designs, and fabrics used in their line of women's wear. Their line also includes men's' suit jackets and tailored outerwear jackets and coats in alpaca wool. Grønnegade 10. ℂ **33-32-00-12.** www.muntheplussimonsen.dk. Bus: 1, 6, or 9.

Sneaky Fox Although these designers turn out seductive, "foxy" party dresses, the owners earned their fame for their Sneaky Fox hosiery, which has swept Denmark and spilled over into Norway, Sweden, Germany, France, and Holland. Created in 1986 in a basement location, the company grew and grew with its unique "one size fits all" concept in hosiery. Studiestræde 25A. ℂ **33-91-25-20.** www.sneakyfox.dk. Bus: 14 or 16.

Furs

Birger Christensen   This is one of Scandinavia's leading fur shops. It has its own designer line, two well-stocked floors of inventory, and furs and fashions by some of the world's leading designers, including Valentino and Oscar de la Renta. You can also purchase—cheaper than the furs—a selection of cashmere or wool-blended coats with fur lining and fur trim, and conventional (nonfur) sportswear from Chanel, Yves St-Laurent, Marc Jacobs, and Prada. This is swank shopping and very, very expensive. Østergade 38. © 33-11-55-55. www.birger-christensen.com. Bus: 1, 6, 9, 10, 19, 29, 31, 42, or 43.

Glassware, Porcelain & Crystal

Rosenthal Studio-Haus ★★★   You'll find an array of ceramic works here, especially by well-known Danish artist Bjørn Wiinblad, whose figures we find whimsical and delightful. You can also get some good buys on Orrefors crystal, including some stunning bowls. The sculptural reliefs, handmade in lead crystal, range from miniatures to giant animals in limited world editions of 199 pieces. They often depict the animals of the far north. Frederiksberggade 21. © 33-14-21-01. www.rosenthal.dk. Bus: 28, 29, or 41.

Royal Copenhagen Porcelain ★★★   Royal Copenhagen's trademark, three wavy blue lines, has come to symbolize quality. Founded in 1775, the factory was a royal possession for a century before passing into private hands in 1868. Royal Copenhagen's Christmas plates are collectors' items. The factory has turned out a new plate each year since 1908, most of the designs depicting the Danish countryside in winter. There's a huge selection of seconds on the top floor, and unless you're an expert, you probably can't tell the difference. Visitors are welcome at the **factory** at Søndre Fasanvej 5 (© **38-14-48-48**), where tours are given Monday to Friday from 9am to 3pm. (These tours, which occur at a location about 15km [9¹/₃ miles] west of Copenhagen, can be arranged, along with transportation from central Copenhagen, by contacting the Royal Copenhagen store at the phone number listed above.) Purchases cannot be made at the factory.

There are also various porcelain and silver retailers in this same location, as well as the Royal Copenhagen Antiques shop, which specializes in buying and selling antique Georg Jensen, Royal Copenhagen, Bing & Grøndahl porcelain, and Michelson Christmas spoons. In November 2006, the showrooms of this place were radically renovated into a pale blue-and-white design that include plays of both natural and artificial light, sound, and perfume. In the Royal Scandinavia retail center, Amagertorv 6 (Strøget). © **33-13-71-81**. www.royalcopenhagen.com. Bus: 1, 2, 6, 8, 28, 29, or 41 for the retail outlet; 1 or 14 for the factory.

Home Furnishings

Illums Bolighus ★★★   A center for modern Scandinavian and Danish design, this is one of Europe's finest showcases for household furnishings and accessories. It stocks furniture, lamps, rugs, textiles, bedding, glassware, kitchenware, flatware, china, jewelry, and ceramics. The store also sells women's and men's clothes and accessories, and there's even a gift shop. Amagertorv 10 (Strøget). © 33-14-19-41. www.royalshopping.com. Bus: 28, 29, or 41.

Lysberg, Hansen & Therp   This major interior-decorating center offers fabrics, carpets, and furniture. The model apartments are furnished in impeccable taste. The company manufactures its own furniture in traditional design and imports fabrics, usually from Germany or France. The gift shop has many hard-to-find creations. Bredgade 77. © 33-14-47-87. Bus: 1, 6, 9, or 10.

Paustian ★★★ Copenhagen's leading furniture showroom, in the somewhat distant industrial Nordhavn section, will ship anywhere in the world. The finest of Scandinavian design is on display, along with reproductions of the classics. There's a well-recommended adjoining restaurant. Kalkbrænderiløbskaj 2. © **39-16-65-65.** www.paustian.dk. S-tog: Nordhavn.

Jewelry

Hartmann's Selected Estate Silver & Jewelry ★ (Finds) This shop buys silver and jewelry from old estates and sells it at reduced prices. Sometimes it's possible to purchase heirloom Georg Jensen estate silver. Ulrik Hartmann, the store's owner, launched his career as a 10-year-old trading at a local flea market, but went on to greater things. The shop is near Kongens Nytorv. While in the neighborhood, you can walk for hours, exploring the auction rooms, jewelry shops, and art galleries in the vicinity. Bredgade 4. © **33-33-09-63.** Bus: 1, 6, 9, or 10.

Kære Ven One of the city's oldest diamond dealers, in business for more than 100 years, this outlet advertises itself as offering "prices from another century." That's a gross exaggeration, but you can often find bargains in antique jewelry, even old Georg Jensen silver. An array of rings, earrings, necklaces, and bracelets are sold, along with other items. A few items in the store are sold at 50% off competitive prices, but you have to shop carefully and know what you're buying. Star Kongens Gade 30. © **33-11-43-15.** www.kaereven.dk. Bus: 1, 6, 9, or 10.

Music

Axel Musik One of the best-stocked music stores in the Danish capital, Axel also has another branch in the city's main railway station. In Scala Center (ground floor), Axeltorv 2. © **33-14-05-50.** Bus: 1, 6, or 8.

Pewter & Silver

Georg Jensen ★★★ Georg Jensen is legendary for its silver. For the connoisseur, there's no better address. On display is the largest and best collection of Jensen Holloware in Europe. The store also features gold and silver jewelry in traditional and modern Danish designs. In the Royal Scandinavia retail center, Amagertorv 6 (Strøget). © **33-11-40-80.** www.georgjensen.com. Bus: 1, 6, 8, 9, or 10.

3 COPENHAGEN AFTER DARK

Danes know how to party. A good night means a late night, and on warm weekends, hundreds of rowdy revelers crowd Strøget until sunrise. Merrymaking in Copenhagen is not just for the younger crowd; jazz clubs, traditional beer houses, and wine cellars are routinely packed with people of all ages. Of course, the city has a more highbrow cultural side as well, exemplified by excellent theaters, operas, ballets, and one of the best circuses in Europe.

To find out what's happening at the time of your visit, pick up a free copy of *Copenhagen This Week* at the tourist information center. The section marked "Events Calendar" has a week-by-week roundup of the "hottest" entertainment and sightseeing events in the Danish capital.

TIVOLI GARDENS ★★★

In the center of the gardens, the large **open-air stage** books vaudeville acts (tumbling clowns, acrobats, aerialists) who give performances every Friday night at 10pm, and on an arbitrary, oft-changing schedule that varies from week to week and summer to summer. Spectators must enter through the turnstiles for seats, but there's an unobstructed view from outside if you prefer to stand. Jazz and folkloric groups also perform here during the season. Admission is free.

The 150-year-old outdoor **Pantomime Theater,** with its Chinese stage and peacock curtain, is near the Tivoli's Vesterbrogade 3 entrance and presents shows Tuesday to Thursday at 6:15 and 8:15pm; Friday at 7:30 and 9pm; Saturday at 8:15 and 9:30pm; and Sunday at 4:30 and 6:30pm. The repertoire consists of 16 different commedia dell'arte productions featuring the entertaining trio Pierrot, Columbine, and Harlequin—these are authentic pantomimes that have been performed continuously in Copenhagen since 1844. Admission is free.

The modern **Tivolis Koncertsal** (concert hall) is a great place to hear top artists and orchestras, led by equally famous conductors. Opened in 1956, the concert hall can seat 2,000, and its season—which begins in late April and lasts for more than 5 months—has been called "the most extensive music festival in the world." Performances of everything from symphony to opera are presented Monday to Saturday at 7:30pm, and sometimes at 8pm, depending on the event. Good seats are available at prices ranging from DKK275 to DKK800 ($47–$136/£28–£80) when major artists are performing—but most performances are free. You can buy tickets at the main booking office on Vesterbrogade 3 (✆ 33-15-10-10 or 45-70-15-65) or on the Web at www.billetnet.dk.

Tivoli Glassalen (✆ 33-15-10-12) is housed in a century-old octagonal gazebolike building with a glass, gilt-capped canopy. Shows are often comedic/satirical performances by Danish comedians in Danish, and these usually don't interest non-Danish audiences. A noteworthy exception to this are the annual Christmas programs, presented in November and December, in English. There are also musical reviews, with a minimum of any spoken language, presented throughout the year. Tickets range from DKK250 to DKK475 ($43–$81/£25–£48).

THE PERFORMING ARTS

For tickets to most of the musical, cultural, and sports-themed entertainment venues of Denmark, check out **Billetnet,** a local branch of Ticketmaster. You can purchase tickets through www.billetnet.dk or by calling ✆ **45/70-15-65-65.**

For **discount seats** (sometimes as much as 50% off), go in person to a ticket kiosk at the corner of Fiolstræde and Nørre Voldgade, across from the Nørreport train station. Discount tickets are sold the day of the performance and may be purchased Monday to Friday noon to 5pm and Saturday noon to 3pm.

Copenhagen Opera House ★★★   Opened by Queen Margrethe, this 1,700-seat opera house is the luxurious home of the Royal Danish Opera. The opera house is the gift of the A. P. Møller and Chastine McKinney Møller Foundation, which is headed by Mærsk McKinney-Møller, one of the wealthiest men in the country. Prior to his donation of the opera house, he had already received, directly from the Queen, Denmark's highest honor, the coveted and intensely prestigious Order of the Elephant. Designed by Danish architect Henning Larsen, the opera house uses precious stones and metals, including 105,000 sheets of gold leaf, and chandeliers which out-sparkle and outshine anything in Las Vegas. In addition to the international artists, the opera house showcases the works of such Danish composers as Carl Nielsen and Poul Ruders. You can dine at the on-site **Restauranten** before curtain time, with a three-course menu costing DKK425 ($72/£43). In addition, there is an **Opera Café**, serving sandwiches, salads, and light Danish specialties. The season runs from mid-August until the beginning of June. During that period, tours of the building are offered daily on a frequently changing schedule, which usually requires a phone call as a means of hammering out the schedule. The box office is open Monday to Saturday noon to 6pm. Ekuipagemesteruej 10. ℂ **33-69-69-33**, or box office ℂ 33-69-69-69. www.operaen.dk. Tickets standing-room space DKK85 ($14/£8.50); seats DKK250–DKK500 ($43–$85/£25–£50).

Det Kongelige Teater (Royal Theater)   Performances by the world-renowned **Royal Danish Ballet ★★★** and **Royal Danish Opera ★★★**, dating from 1748, are major winter cultural events in Copenhagen. Because the arts are state-subsidized in Denmark, ticket prices are comparatively low, and some seats may be available at the box office the day before a performance. The season runs August to June. Kongens Nytorv. ℂ **33-69-69-69**. www.kgl-teater.dk. Tickets DKK80–DKK720 ($14–$122/£8–£72); half-price for seniors 66 and over and people 25 and under. Bus: 1, 6, 9, or 10.

THE CLUB & MUSIC SCENE
Dance Clubs
Den Røde Pimpernel   Throughout most of the day, this place functions as a lively dining and drinking emporium within the heart of Tivoli, whose walls are painted a vivid shade of red in honor of its gallant 17th-century namesake, *The Scarlet Pimpernel.* Every evening after 10pm, however, its tables are moved away to create a wide-open dance floor. The youngest clients, those in their 30s, tend to appear on Thursday and Sunday; other nights, the patrons are a bit more staid, ages anywhere from 30 to a youthful 50-ish. It's open daily noon to 4am. Bernstorffsgade 3, Tivoli. ℂ **33-75-07-60.** Cover DKK70 ($12/£7); free before 10pm. Bus: 2, 8, or 30.

NASA   Its name has changed several times in the past decade, but even so, this is the most posh and prestigious of three nightclubs that occupy three respective floors of the same building. The late-night crowd of 25- to 40-year-olds includes many avid fans of whatever musical innovation has just emerged in London or Los Angeles. The decorative theme includes lots of white, lots of mirrors, and lots of artfully directed spotlights. Don't be surprised to see a room full of expensively, albeit casually, dressed Danes chattering away in a cacophony of different languages. Technically, the site is a private club, but polite and presentable newcomers can usually gain access. It's open only Friday and Saturday midnight to 6am. Gothersgade 8F, Bolthensgaard. ℂ **33-93-74-15.** Cover DKK150 ($26/£15) for nonmembers. Bus: 1, 6, or 9.

The Rock   Thanks to an armada of designers who developed it, and thanks to its self-appointed role as a "Design Disco," its interior is more artfully outfitted than any other in Copenhagen. Expect lots of postmodern gloss, references to the California rave movement, an occasional emphasis on dance music of the 1980s, a small corner outfitted like a cozy beer hall, and a clientele that seems familiar with the music and ambience of some very hip clubs in Europe and the United States. Part of its interior was based on a waiting room of a 1970s Scandinavian airport, complete with then-innovative streamlined design that's been associated with Denmark ever since. It's open Friday and Saturday 11pm till at least 5:30am. Skindergade 45. ℂ **33-91-39-13.** www.the-rock.dk. Cover DKK80 ($14/£8). Bus: 1 or 6.

Nighttime Experiences for Free (Well, Almost)

You don't have to go to clubs or attend cultural presentations to experience Copenhagen nightlife. If you want to have a good time and save money too, consider doing as the Danes do: Walk about and enjoy the city and its glittering lights for free, perhaps stopping at a lovely square to have a drink and watch the world pass by.

Copenhagen's elegant spires and tangle of cobbled one-way streets are best viewed at night, when they take on the aura of the Hans Christian Andersen era. The old buildings have been well preserved, and at night they're floodlit. The city's network of drawbridges and small bridges is also particularly charming at night.

One of the best places for a walk is **Nyhavn** (New Harbor), which, until about 25 years ago, was the haunt of sailors and some of the roughest dives in Copenhagen. Today it's gone upmarket and is the site of numerous restaurants and bars. In summer, you can sit out at one of the cafe tables watching life along the canal and throngs of people from around the world passing by—all for the price of your Carlsberg. Along the quay you can also see a fleet of old-time sailing ships. Hans Christian Andersen lived at three different addresses along Nyhavn: nos. 18, 20, and 67.

Another neighborhood that takes on special magic at night is **Christianshavn,** whose principal landmark is **Christiansborg Slot** (castle), a massive granite pile surrounded by canals on three sides. The ramparts of Christianshavn are edged with walking paths, which are lit at light. This neighborhood, which glows under the soft, forgiving light of antique street lamps, is the closest Copenhagen comes to the charm of the Left Bank in Paris. You can wander for hours through its cobbled streets and 18th-century buildings. The area also

Rust   Rust sprawls over a single floor in the Nørrebro district, where the clientele is international and high-energy. Since 1989, faithful patrons have been flocking to its restaurant, several bars, a dance floor, and a stage where live musicians perform every Thursday night beginning around 9pm. Meals are served Wednesday to Saturday 5:30pm to around midnight, and at least someone will begin to boogie on the dance floor after 9:30pm, as drinks flow. The setting is dark and shadowy, "a great place to feel up your partner—or someone else's," one of the patrons told us. There are places to sit, but none so comfortable that you'll stay in one spot for too long. No one under age 21 is admitted, but you'll see very few over age 45. Open Wednesday to Saturday 9pm to at least 5am. Guldbergsgade 8. (℃ **35-24-52-00.** www.rust.dk. Cover DKK30–DKK120 ($5.10–$20/£3–£12). Bus: 5 or 6.

Vega   Consider this brick-built circular 19th-century monument as the closest thing in town to an old hippie be-in, where you'll enter a multifaceted, multipurpose environment with an open mind and then pick the site that best suits your mood of the minute.

abounds with cafes, bars, and restaurants. Originally the section was built by King Christian IV to provide housing for workers in the shipbuilding industry, but in the past decades real estate prices here have soared.

For a more offbeat adventure—although it's not the safest place at night—you can head for the commune of **Christiania,** a few blocks to the east of Vor Frelsers Kirke. This area once housed Danish soldiers in barracks. When the soldiers moved out, the free spirits of Copenhagen moved in, occupying the little village, even though—technically speaking—they are squatters and in violation of the law. They declared the area a "free city" on September 24, 1971. Copenhagen authorities have not moved in to oust them in all this time, fearing a full-scale riot. The area is a refuge for petty criminals and drug dealers. But there has been success in the community as well, evoking the communes of the 1960s. For example, the villagers have helped hundreds of addicts kick heroin habits.

At night, adventurous visitors enter Christiania to eat at one of the neighborhood's little restaurants, many of which are surprisingly good. Prices here are the cheapest in Copenhagen, because the restaurant managers refuse to pay taxes. You can also wander through some of the shops selling handmade crafts. Because most establishments are small and personal, you can also invite yourself in, perhaps to listen to innovative music or see some cultural presentation. Currently your best bet for dining is **Spiseloppen.** Later you can visit the jazz club **Loppen,** where you'll hear some of the best jazz in the city. If you're a vegetarian, as are many members of the commune, head for the vegetarian restaurant **Morgensted.** (These two restaurants and the club don't have addresses, but they're easy to spot.)

At least two of the venues inside are devoted to live concerts that begin, according to a baffling and oft-changing schedule, any time between 8 and 11pm, depending on the inclinations of the musicians, and for which entrance usually varies from DKK100 to DKK180 ($17–$31/£10–£18). And when the concert ends, you'll still find at least three other dining and drinking emporiums inside, some with live music of their own, and each with a distinctly different ambience. On nights when there happens not to be any live music, the smaller bars and dining areas inside are likely to be rocking and rolling the night away. Most venues inside require a minimum age of 20, and except for the concerts, whose prices are noted above, entrance to each of the bars and restaurants is free. It lies in Vesterbrø, behind the railway station. Phones may or may not be answered, depending on the whim of whomever is tending house. Enghavevej 40. © **33-26-70-11** or 33-25-70-11. For concert schedules, go to www.vega.dk. Bus: 1, 6, 9, or 19.

Copenhagen's Biggest Nightclub

Cirkusbygningen Wallmans   In a former circus building near Town Hall Square, this is the best place for patrons who like a spectacular Las Vegas–style dinner show. It's a bit corny and very Scandinavian, but it enjoys great success with both visitors and locals. Some 1,000 guests can be entertained here by 22 artists on nine stages while enjoying a four-course dinner. After the show, the interior is transformed into a gigantic nightclub with dancing. Incidentally, the artists also wait on your table.

Open Wednesday to Saturday only, except in November, when it is also open on Tuesday. The bar opens at 6pm, and the restaurant serves until 6:45pm. Shows stretch out with breaks from 7 to 11:15pm, followed by dancing that goes on till around 2am, including dinner. Admission to the show is DKK575 ($98/£58) except on Friday and Saturday, when it rises to DKK695 ($118/£70). Jernbanegade 8. ✆ **33-16-37-00.** www.wallmans.com. Bus: 1, 16, or 29.

Jazz, Rock & Blues

Copenhagen JazzHouse ★ The decor is modern and uncomplicated and serves as a consciously simple foil for the music and noise. This club hosts more performances by non-Danish jazz artists than any other jazz bar in town. Shows begin relatively early, at around 8:30pm, and usually finish early, too. Around midnight on Friday and Saturday, the club is transformed from a live concert hall into a dance club (open until 5am). It's closed Mondays; otherwise, it keeps a confusing schedule that changes according to the demands of the current band. Niels Hemmingsensgade 10. ✆ **33-15-26-00.** www.jazzhouse.dk. Cover charge DKK75–DKK300 ($13–$51/£7.50–£30) when live music is performed. Bus: 10.

La Fontaine This is a dive that hasn't changed much since the 1950s, but it's the kind of dive that—if you meet the right partner, or if you really groove with the music—can be a lot of fun. Small, and cozy to the point of being cramped, it functions mostly as a bar, every Tuesday to Saturday 8pm to 6am or even 8am. Sunday hours are 9pm to 1am. Live music is performed on Friday and Saturday, when free-jazz artists play starting around 11:30pm. Kompagnistræde 11. ✆ **33-11-60-98.** www.lafontaine.dk. Cover DKK65 ($11/£6.50) Fri–Sat. Bus: 5 or 10.

Mojo Blues Bar "Our clients come here for the booze and the blues," the manager rather accurately told us. Mojo is a candlelit drinking spot that offers blues music, 90% of which is performed by Scandinavian groups. This grubby but strangely appealing joint is open daily 8pm to 5am. Løngangstræde 21C. ✆ **33-11-64-53.** www.mojo.dk. Cover DKK60 ($10/£6) Fri–Sat. Bus: 2, 8, or 30.

THE BAR SCENE

Café Zirup Set on a street that's packed with worthy competitors, this cafe and bar is loaded with people who seem fun, charming, and engaged with life and the well-being of their companions. Its name translates as "syrup." The venue is youthful and hip. Salads, sandwiches, and platters cost from DKK79 to DKK139 ($13–$24/£7.90–£14). Open Monday to Thursday 10am to midnight, Friday and Saturday 10am to 2am. Læderstræde 32. ✆ **33-13-50-60.** http://zirup.dk. Bus: 1, 6, 9, or 10.

Library Bar ★★★ Frequently visited by celebrities and royalty, the Library Bar was once rated by the late Malcolm Forbes as one of the top five bars in the world. In a setting of antique books and works of art, you can order everything from a cappuccino to a cocktail. The setting is the lobby level of the landmark Hotel Plaza, commissioned in 1913 by Frederik VIII. The bar was originally designed and built as the hotel's library; Oregon pine was used for the paneling, and hundreds of books line the walls. It's open daily from noon to midnight (till 2am on Fri and Sat). Beer costs DKK60 ($10/£6);

drinks cost from DKK75 to DKK95 ($13–$16/£7.50–£9.50). In the Hotel Plaza, Bernstorffsgade 4. ℂ **33-14-92-62.** Bus: 10, 15, or 26.

Nyhavn 17   This is the last of the honky-tonk pubs that used to make up the former sailors' quarter, and even this last bastion has seen a rapid gentrification in recent years. This cafe is a short walk from the patrician Kongens Nytorv. In summer, you can sit outside. It's open Sunday to Thursday 10am to 2am and Friday and Saturday to 3am. Beer costs DKK55 ($9.40/£5.50), and drinks start at DKK65 ($11/£6.50). Nyhavn 17. ℂ **33-12-54-19.** www.nyhavn17.dk. Bus: 1, 6, 27, or 29.

Ruby ★★★   This is arguably the best bar in Copenhagen. Danes are caught up in a cocktail boom right now, each bartender competing to see who can come up with the greatest concoction. The bartenders at Ruby are the leaders of the pack, coming up with such drinks as "Burnt Fig" (caramelized fig syrup with cognac and cream) or a "Thai'ed Up Martini" (Plymouth gin with Thai basil). Behind an unmarked door, you enter the demimonde world of Copenhagen, attracting the widest possible base of clients in all forms of dress. As a bartender told us, "We play host to all of God's children." Two rooms have been created out of a building from the 1700s, with high ceilings and gray wainscoting. Open Monday to Saturday 4pm to 2am. Nybrogade 10. ℂ **33-93-12-03.** Bus: 1A, 2, 15, 26, or 650S.

Copenhagen's Best Wine Bar

Hvids Vinstue ★★   Built in 1670, this old wine cellar is a dimly lit safe haven for an eclectic crowd, many patrons—including theatergoers, actors, and dancers—drawn from the Royal Theater across the way. In December only, a combination of red wine and cognac is served. It's open Monday to Saturday 10am to 1am; Sunday from 10am to 8pm. Beer costs DKK45 ($7.70/£4.50); wine costs DKK39 ($6.70/£3.90). Open-faced sandwiches are DKK60 to DKK85 ($10–$14/£6–£8.50), and include a free beer. Kongens Nytorv 19. ℂ **33-15-10-64.** Bus: 1, 6, 9, or 10.

GAY & LESBIAN CLUBS

Boiz Bar   Two hundred years ago, the antique and richly beamed interior of this place was used to shelter cattle. Today, in a much-sanitized format, it's a whimsically outfitted men's bar and restaurant contained within one large room with a cozy annex bar a few paces away. There are at least three separate bars/drinking areas within this establishment, a cluster of tables in the center of the larger of the two rooms, with leather upholstery and the kind of lighting that makes everyone look dramatic, especially the crowd of mostly gay men ages 20 to 50. Main courses in the restaurant cost from DKK159 to DKK229 ($27–$39/£16–£23), and a glass of beer costs DKK42 ($7.20/£4.20). Most of the time, this place functions as a flamboyant version of an old Danish *kro* (inn), but every Friday and Saturday beginning at 10pm, there's a drag show, with artists imported from London, followed by a high-energy scene on the dance floor that is active till around 5am. Hours are Sunday to Thursday 4pm to 2am, Friday and Saturday 4pm to 5am. Magstræde 12–14. ℂ **33-14-52-70.** Bus: 6A.

Centralhjornet   This is the oldest gay bar in Copenhagen, having attracted a clientele of self-styled "pederasts and queers" as far back as the early 20th century, when same-sex love was identified in terms very different from what it is today. Old-fashioned, wood-paneled, and cozy, it's absolutely mobbed with gay and, to a lesser extent, lesbian tourists during the Christmas holidays. It's open every day of the year from 2pm to midnight.

Between October and May, there's a drag show presented here every Thursday night beginning around 10pm. Kattesundet 18. ℂ **33-11-85-49.** www.centralhjornet.dk. Bus: 14 or 16.

Cosy Bar It runs a fine line between a crowd that favors leather, and what you'd expect from a working crew of men performing manual labor down by the harborfront. Popular and cruisy, it's open daily 11pm till 8am, dispensing ample amounts of schnapps and suds during the course of a working night. Studiestræde 24. ℂ **33-12-74-27.** Bus: 6 or 29.

Jailhouse Copenhagen The name of this bar reminds us of Elvis's "Jailhouse Rock." It's set amid the densest concentration of gay men's bars in town, about a block from its nearest competitor (the also-recommended Men's Bar, which attracts a similar clientele). This is the bar most quickly cited as an amicable and amenable watering hole for the leather, bear, and S&M communities—or those who merely dream about them. The name of the place influences its decor: Imagine a large, shadowy space with a prominent, beer-soaked bar, battered walls and floors, and iron bars that subdivide the space into a series of simulated jail cells. If you're in the mood for a meal, there's a restaurant upstairs, where crisp white napery contrasts with simulations of cellblocks. Food is Danish and Scandinavian, with specialties that focus on old-fashioned, tried-and-true comfort food, with some modern and somewhat experimental twists. Overall, food is a lot better than what you might have expected in jail. The bar is open from 2pm to 2am (Thurs and Fri until 5am), and entrance is free, with a beer costing DKK45 ($7.70/£4.50). The restaurant is open only Thursday to Saturday 6 to 11pm, with a fixed-price, three-course meal going for DKK285 ($48/£29). Studiestræde 12. ℂ **33-15-22-55.** www.jailhousecph.dk. Bus: 2, 8, or 30.

The Men's Bar This is the only leather bar in town, filled with a bemused collection of uniforms, leather, Levi's, and gay-icon memorabilia. Amicable and fraternal, it showcases a framed portrait, in full military uniform, of "the cutest prince in Europe," Crown Prince Frederik, happily and recently married to "that woman." Note that if it's a particularly hot day, someone might encourage you to take off your shirt, in exchange for which, if you're a newcomer, the bartender is likely to give you a free glass of schnapps. It's open daily 3pm to 2am. A beer will set you back DKK26 ($4.40/£2.60). Teglgaard-stræde 3. ℂ **33-12-73-03.** www.mensbar.dk. Bus: 2, 8, or 30.

Pan Club This nationwide organization was established in 1948 for the protection and advancement of gay and lesbian rights in headquarters in a 19th-century yellow building off the Strøget. A dance club occupies three of its floors, and a modern cafe is on the ground level. Every night is gay night, although a lot of straights come here for the music. The cafe is open Thursday 9pm to 4am; Friday and Saturday 10pm to 5am. The dance club is open Friday 10pm to 5am and Saturday 10pm to 6am. Knabrostræde 3. ℂ **33-11-19-50.** Cover DKK70 ($12/£7) for dance club. Bus: 28, 29, or 41.

XXX COPENHAGEN

The heady "boogie nights" of the '70s, when pornography aficionados flocked to Copenhagen to purchase X-rated materials, are long gone. Copenhagen is no longer the capital of sex, having long ago lost out to Hamburg and Amsterdam, but many city residents can quote the year when a landmark ruling from Denmark's supreme court made printed pornography legal (1967). Despite the fact that pornographic Copenhagen is not as cutting edge or raunchy as it was (and we're all somewhat more jaded these days), it's still possible to take a walk here on the wild side any night of the week. Two of the densest concentrations of porno and the sex industry still lie on **Istedgade** and **Helgolandsgade,** both of them near the rail terminus in the center of the city. Ironically, the sex shops peddling magazines and X-rated films stand virtually adjacent to decent and well-recommended family hotels. Mothers can often be seen hustling their sons past the window displays.

---

4 SIDE TRIPS FROM COPENHAGEN

BEACHES

Locals and visitors are flocking to a newly created beach, **Amager Beach Park ★,** which opened in 2006, lying only a 15-minute drive from the center of Copenhagen, a distance of 5km (3 miles). The beach lies on the Øresund coastline with a view of Sweden and the Øresund Bridge that now links Denmark with Sweden. You can swim, sunbathe, scuba dive, race boats, or just admire the ships on the Øresund Sound while having a cup of coffee. Off the existing Amager Beach, a completely new island was created with wide, sandy beaches and bathing jetties. Tons of sand were brought in to create the island beach, which is about 2km (1¼ mile) long and 50m (164 ft.) wide. In a newly dug lagoon are paddling beaches for children. By the time you read this, three Metro stations should be open right by the beach, which will make it easy to zip over here from Copenhagen if the sun's out. For more information, visit www.amager-strand.dk.

The beach closest to Copenhagen is **Bellevue** (S-tog: Klampenborg), but the water is not recommended for swimming. (Klampenborg, the community that's adjacent to Bellevue Beach, can provide distractions in addition to a beach: It's the site of the "White City" or "White Town," a residential community designed in the 1930s by modernist master Arne Jacobsen, and revered by Danes as a prime example of the workability of Danish architecture and design.

If you don't mind traveling farther afield, take a trip (by train or car) to the beaches of North Zealand—**Gilleleje, Hornbæk, Liseleje,** and **Tisvildeleje** (see chapter 7). Although these are family beaches, minimal bathing attire is worn.

To reach any of these beaches, take the train to Helsingør and then continue by bus. Or you can make connections by train to Hillerød and switch to a local train; check at the railroad station for details. If you drive, you may want to stay for the evening dance clubs at the little beach resort towns dotting the north coast of Zealand.

DRAGØR ★★

5km (3 miles) S of Copenhagen's Kastrup Airport

Even if you have to skip the rest of Denmark, head to this little fishing port to see what an idyllic Danish village looks like. Though we don't mean to put it down, the Frilandsmuseet (p. 139) was an artificially created site—and a grand one at that—but Dragør is the real thing. Young professionals are flocking here from Copenhagen to purchase homes. They're within an easy commute of the city, but in the old-fashioned world of Dragør that goes back to the 19th century at night (albeit with modern conveniences).

This old seafaring town on the island of Amager is filled with well-preserved half-timbered ocher and pink 18th-century cottages with steep red-tile or thatched roofs, many of which are under the protection of the National Trust.

Dragør (pronounced *Drah*-wer) was a busy port on the herring-rich Baltic Sea in the early Middle Ages, and when fishing fell off, it became a sleepy little waterfront village. After 1520, Amager Island and its villages—Dragør and Store Magleby—were inhabited by the Dutch, who brought their own customs, Low-German language, and agricultural expertise to Amager, especially their love of bulb flowers. In Copenhagen, you still see wooden-shoed Amager locals selling their hyacinths, tulips, daffodils, and lilies in the streets.

Essentials

GETTING THERE   By Bus   Take bus nos. 30, 33, or 73E from Rådhuspladsen (Town Hall Square) in Copenhagen (trip time: 35 min.).

Seeing the Sights

Amager Museum   This museum is only of passing interest and could be skipped in favor of spending more time walking the streets of Dragør. But if you do duck into it, you'll learn how strong the influence of the Dutch used to be here, ever since farmers from Holland settled Dragør in the 16th century. King Christian II ordered them to provide fresh flowers and produce for his court and so they did. The interiors of a Dutch house reveal how they decorated their homes and lived in modest comfort, and the Amager Dutch, as they were known, live again in the exhibits of their rich textiles, fine embroidery, and such artifacts as silver buckles and buttons.

Hovedgaden 4–12, Store Magleby. ✆ **32-53-02-50.** www.amagermuseet.dk. Admission DKK30 ($5.10/£3) adults, DKK15 ($2.60/£1.50) children 5–14, free for children 4 and under. May–Sept Tues–Sun noon–4pm; Oct–Mar Wed and Sun noon–4pm. Closed in Apr. Bus: 30, 33, or 350S.

Dragør Museum   As you're wandering along Dragør's harborfront, you can spend 20 minutes or so looking inside the town's oldest fisherman's cottage, dating from 1682. The exhibits are modest but reveal how the Amager Dutch lived here when they settled Dragør. Pictures and artifacts reveal that their lives were devoted to farming, goose breeding, seafaring, fishing, ship piloting, and salvaging the cargo of ships wrecked off the coast.

Havnepladsen 2–4. ✆ **32-53-41-06.** www.dragoermuseum.dk. Admission DKK20 ($3.40/£2) adults, free for children 17 and under. May–Sept Tues–Sun and holidays noon–4pm. Closed Oct–Apr. Bus: 30, 32, or 350S.

Where to Stay

Dragør Badehotel   Back in 1907 a railway line was extended from Copenhagen to this fishing hamlet, and this government-rated three-star hotel opened that same year to greet visitors. The rail line is long gone but the much-improved and modernized hotel still remains. Restoration in recent years has brought much-needed change but the old style that prevailed around the turn of the 20th century was respected. The midsize bedrooms are furnished in Nordic modern with exceedingly comfortable beds, and maintenance is top rate around here. Most of the accommodations come with a view of the sea, and the most desirable units open onto their own private balconies. Traditional Danish cuisine is served in the main restaurant or else you can dine on the open-air terraces in summer. Nonguests are welcome to enjoy the hotel's restaurant. There are six different preparations of herring to get you going, followed by a "Dragør Plate" of mixed meats and pâtés, tender schnitzels, homemade soups, and a selection of *smørrebrød* (open-faced sandwiches) at lunch.

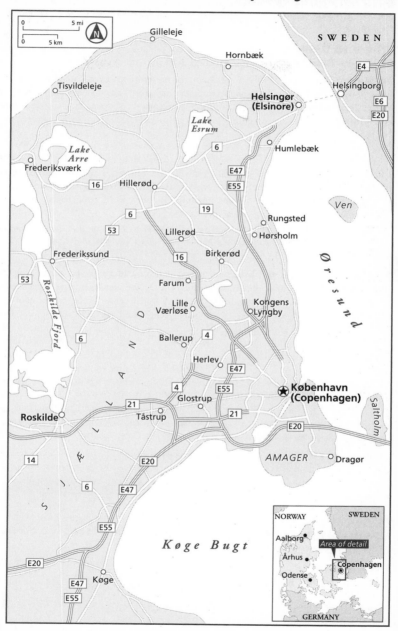

Drogdensvej 43, DK-2791 Dragør. © **32-53-05-00.** Fax 32-53-04-99. www.badehotellet.dk. 34 units. DKK838–DKK1,044 ($142–$178/£84–£104) double. AE, DC, MC, V. Bus: 30, 33, or 73E. **Amenities:** Restaurant; lounge; laundry service; nonsmoking rooms; rooms for those w/limited mobility. *In room:* TV, minibar.

Where to Dine

The Dragør Badehotel (see above) also offers excellent cuisine.

Restaurant Beghuset DANISH   Even on the most rushed of visits, we like to schedule at least one meal at this old-fashioned dining room, which not only serves good, home-cooked food but also is a nostalgic reminder of Denmark of yesterday. This cafe and restaurant on a cobblestone street in the center of town looks like an idyllic cottage. To reach the restaurant section, you walk through the cafe. Although the menu changes every 2 to 3 months to accommodate seasonal items, a weary traveler in search of sustenance will be tempted by such selections as fish soup, Swedish caviar, thinly sliced smoked lamb with a balsamic dressing on a bed of seasonal greens, and fresh oysters. Main courses include a divinely cooked guinea fowl braised in red wine served with bacon of veal (their own invention) and herbs, and Dragør plaice roasted in butter and served with either parsley sauce or a bacon-thyme sauce, just like grandmother used to bake.

Strandgade 14. © **32-53-01-36.** www.beghuset.dk. Reservations recommended. 1-course lunch DKK79–DKK228 ($13–$39/£7.90–£23); 3-course lunch DKK298 ($51/£30); dinner main courses DKK198–DKK238 ($34–$40/£20–£24). AE, DC, MC, V. Tues–Sun noon–3pm and 6–9pm. Bus: 30, 33, or 73E.

Strandhotel DANISH ★   In spite of its name, this establishment no longer accepts overnight guests but is one of the finest restaurants in Dragør, offering a more imaginative cuisine than the standard (yet good) Danish fare featured at the Beghuset (see above). Strandhotel is still going strong, but it's been a long time since Frederik III used to drop by for a bowl of the chef's eel soup. Even Søren Kierkegaard used to come here to brood.

At lunchtime, an ample spread of *smørrebrød* is served, although other offerings include filet of pork in paprika sauce, a savory smoked filet of eel, fried or poached plaice, and a delectable trout with almonds. At dinner the chefs tempt you with such dishes as grilled tuna with raspberries or oven-baked whitefish served in a banana leaf, the flavor enhanced by a saffron cream sauce.

Strandlinbyn 9, Havnen. © **32-53-00-75.** www.dragorstrandhotel.dk. Reservations recommended. Main courses DKK118–DKK218 ($20–$37/£12–£22); lunch *smørrebrød* DKK46–DKK99 ($7.80–$17/£4.60–£9.90); "quick lunch" DKK198 ($34/£20). AE, DC, MC, V. Daily 9am–9:30pm. Closed Nov–Mar. Bus: 350S.

HUMLEBÆK (LOUISIANA MUSEUM)
30km (19 miles) N of Copenhagen

The area running along the coast north of Copenhagen is called both the Danish Riviera and Millionaire's Row. Some of the wealthiest people in Denmark live in palatial homes between Copenhagen and the town of Humlebæk. But the only reason most visitors come to this former fishing village, unless they have a private invitation, is to visit the world-famous Louisiana Museum, our favorite art center in all of Denmark.

Essentials

GETTING THERE   By Train   Humlebæk is on the Copenhagen–Helsingør train line; there are two trains per hour that leave Copenhagen's main railway station heading toward Humlebæk (trip time: 40 min.). Once you reach Humlebæk, the Louisiana Museum is a 10-minute walk.

By Bus Take the S-tog train, line A or B, to Lyngby station. From there, take bus no. 388 along the coast road. There's a bus stop at the museum.

By Car Follow the Strandvej (coastal road no. 152) from Copenhagen. The scenic drive takes about 45 minutes.

Seeing the Sights

Louisiana Museum of Modern Art ★★★ (Kids) A lot of Americans think this
museum for some odd reason was named for the state of Louisiana. Actually the museum's name came from the fact that the first owner of the estate here, Alexander Brun, had three wives. Bizarrely, each of his spouses was named Louise. In a spacious old park with a panoramic view across Øresund to Sweden, this is one of the greatest museums of modern art in the Nordic world. The modest collection of Scandinavian art that opened here in 1954 has grown and grown with bequests and donations, and future architects have added more galleries onto the existing 19th-century villa.

The museum opened with works by the COBRA group, the name of artists from the cities of *CO*penhagen, *BR*ussels, and *A*msterdam. These original works are displayed along with some of the finest paintings and sculpture by international artists such as Calder, Dubuffet, Max Ernst, Giacometti, Picasso, and Warhol.

The museum has one of the largest exhibition spaces in Europe, and major exhibitions of contemporary art are staged here. There is also an extensive program of concerts, lectures, films, discussions with authors, and public debates. Children find their own haven here, especially at the **Børnehuset,** or children's house, and the **Søhaven,** or Sea Garden. The museum's cafe is on a terrace with Alexander Calder's sculptures.

Gl. Strandvej 13. ✆ **49-19-07-19.** www.louisiana.dk. Admission DKK90 ($15/£9) adults, DKK80 ($14/£8) students, free for children 18 and under. Tues–Fri 11am–10pm; Sat–Sun 11am–6pm. Closed Dec 24–25 and Dec 31.

Where to Dine

Louisiana Café DANISH Since 1772 there has been an inn on this spot, feeding
wayfarers of yore who took horse and carriage along the coast heading for Helsingør. Today much of yesterday has been swept away and what remains is this cafe-restaurant, which is the best and also the most convenient place for lunch, lying only a short walk from the museum. If you're so enthralled with the museum that you're still around at dinnertime, you can also dine here before heading back to the heart of Copenhagen.

We've always found the food satisfying in an old-fashioned sort of way, although we never feel we have to call the editors of *Gourmet* magazine on our cellphones. At lunch, most diners dig into a range of open-faced sandwiches—usually three will satisfy. At night you can partake of recipes based on tried-and-true dishes such as a platter-size wiener schnitzel. Veal also comes in medallions with a rich morel sauce. Herring is dressed up with a sherry sauce, and deep-fried filet of plaice comes with shrimp just recently caught off the coast.

Gl. Strandvej 13. ✆ **49-19-07-19.** Reservations recommended. Main courses DKK88–DKK138 ($15–$23/£8.80–£14). AE, DC, MC, V. Tues–Fri 11am–9:30pm; Sat–Sun 11am–5:30pm.

RUNGSTEDLUND: HOME OF KAREN BLIXEN
21km (13 miles) N of Copenhagen

Between Copenhagen in the south and Helsingør in the north, the second-most-important stopover is this elegant town where many Danes come in the summer to rent cottages, which they often surround with flower gardens. By all means, make the museum of Louisiana your first major stopover, but if time remains, you can pay your respects to one of the greatest of all Scandinavian writers (see below).

GETTING THERE **By Train** From Copenhagen's Central Railroad Station, trains run to Rungsted Kyst every 30 minutes. However, since this rail stop is still 1km (about 1/2 mile) from the museum, it is better to take the train to Klampenborg, where you can board **bus** no. 388, which offers frequent service to a bus stop about a block from the entrance to the museum.

By Car Head north from Copenhagen along the E4 to Helsingør until you reach the turnoff east marked RUNGSTED.

The Museum

Ever since we discovered the writings of Isak Dinesen in high school, we've been devoted fans. She remains our favorite Danish writer (forgive us, Hans). Since the 1985 release of *Out of Africa,* starring Robert Redford and Meryl Streep, thousands of fans have visited the former home of Baroness Karen Blixen, who wrote under her maiden name, Isak Dinesen. Her home, Rungstedlund, at Rungsted Strandvej III (℃ **45-57-10-57**), is midway between Copenhagen and Helsingør on the coastal road.

Karen's father, Wilhelm Dinesen, purchased the estate in 1879. She left in 1914 for Kenya when she married Sweden-born Bror van Blixen Finecke, but returned in 1931 and stayed until her death in 1962. It was at Rungstedlund that Blixen wrote her first major success, *Seven Gothic Tales,* which we consider more memorable than *Out of Africa.* She also wrote collections of stories, *Winter's Tales* and *Last Tales,* here. Before Blixen's father acquired the property, it was called Rungsted Kro, attracting travelers going north from Copenhagen to Helsingør.

Blixen wrote in Ewald's Room, named in honor of poet Johannes Ewald, who stayed at the place when it was an inn. Before her death, Blixen established the Rungstedlund Foundation, which owns the property and its 16-hectare (40-acre) garden and bird sanctuary. The gardens have long been open to the public, but in 1991 the foundation invited Queen Margrethe to open the museum.

In one part of the museum is a small gallery with exhibits in oil, pastel, and charcoal—all by Blixen. The museum is filled with photographs, manuscripts, and memorabilia that document Blixen's life in both Africa and Denmark.

Visitors pay DKK40 ($6.80/£4) to enter, although children 11 and under go free. It's open May to September, Tuesday to Sunday 10am to 5pm; October to April, Wednesday to Friday 1 to 4pm and Saturday and Sunday 11am to 4pm.

Blixen is buried in the grave at the foot of Edwaldshøj, a hill on the estate.

Where to Dine

Restaurant Nokken ★★ DANISH/SEAFOOD On a summer night, we always like to sit out here enjoying a drink on the terrace overlooking the harbor of Øresund, taking in a picture-postcard vista of yachts and sailboats returning to the shoreline under an amber-and-pink nighttime sky. Another reason for coming here is that the elegant restaurant serves some of the best food along the Danish Riviera. The setting is amid light-grained paneling and nautical accessories, a short walk downhill from Karen Blixen's house. You'll find it near the sea-battered piers next to the harbors, a fact that gives it a raffish feeling despite its reputation for well-prepared, savory fish and seafood. There's a bar near the entrance that's a hangout for boat owners and local millionaires, and when you eventually get hungry, head for the dining room. The specialty is a seafood platter piled high with mussels, shrimp, oysters, and lobster. There are also fresh fish dishes, including filets of lemon sole with hollandaise sauce, or you can try the roasted, herb-scented Danish lamb, or the scampi with sweet-and-sour sauce. The cuisine is generous, uncomplicated, and always market fresh.

Rungsted Havn 44. ✆ **45-57-13-14.** www.nokken.dk. Reservations recommended. Lunch platters DKK85–DKK195 ($14–$33/£8.50–£20); dinner main courses DKK115–DKK235 ($20–$40/£12–£24); fixed-price menu DKK385–DKK510 ($65–$87/£39–£51). AE, DC, MC, V. Daily noon–4:30pm and 5:30–10:30pm.

North Zealand

Most visitors, with their clock ticking, dash north of Copenhagen to chase after "Hamlet's ghost" at Helsingør—and that's it for North Zealand. But as the famous author Isak Dinesen (aka Karen Blixen) might have said, "That would be a shame—stick around a bit and discover some wonder."

We don't want to oversell North Zealand, because its charms are subtle and it might be a little too slow paced and idyllic for those who want more excitement in their vacation. But the queen of Denmark, who's rich enough to go anywhere, often comes here for a royal vacation. In fact, in July, like another queen in London, she opens her summer palace at Fredensborg, inviting the public in to see how the other half lives. That's why the province is called "Royal North Zealand." And its overall allure is more posh, more stylish, and a lot more interesting (at least in terms of who comes here, and who owns the local real estate) than are the landscapes of the less densely populated, more agrarian, and less wealthy South Zealand.

Hamlet and the queen aren't the only fun things. Just across the sound from Sweden, North Zealand is riddled with sandy seashores, studded with lakes, peppered with fishing villages, and layered with unspoiled woodlands. With Mercury-like feet, you can see most of the goodies in only 2 days. Of course, you'll want to pay your respects to Isak Dinesen (or Karen) at Rungstedlund, even if you aren't so sure of who she was. The Louisiana Museum of Modern Art at Humlebæk is one of the most renowned modern-art museums in Denmark and one of our favorite bastions of contemporary art in all of Europe (trust us, we've seen them all).

For information on the Dinesen abode and Louisiana, see "Side Trips from Copenhagen," in chapter 6.

We've read books on the famous arctic explorer Knud Rasmussen, and a visit to his home near Hundested will give you a vicarious thrill if you're the adventurous type. Devotees of architecture head for the cathedral at Roskilde, the old capital of Denmark. And, once here, you can also take a look at the Viking Ship Museum, reliving the saga of those raping, pillaging men who used to descend on England for some loot, some virgins, and an all-around good time, swilling down tankard after tankard of English brew before continuing with their dirty deeds.

Don't overlook the possibility of a beach outing, although you may at first think the water is better suited for polar bears. Wherever you stay in North Zealand, you are not far from a beach. A blue flag flying over the beach indicates that its waters are clean. Danes can be seen frolicking in the nude—they're a shameless bunch—on the beach during their too-short summer days. But they're not just fair-weather friends. Even on a blustery autumn afternoon, or when the Nordic winds of spring are still cold, you'll find them walking along the strands, smelling the fresh air, and listening to the crashing of waves. They even visit their beaches on crisp, fresh winter days for long walks. In fact, it was our Danish friends who taught us the glory of a beach stroll in winter, a custom we've been addicted to ever since.

If you can't make it to Norway, you can sample "Fjord Country" in Denmark. Around the fjords of Roskilde and Isefjord are charming towns such as Hundested, with its beautiful light (praised by artists)

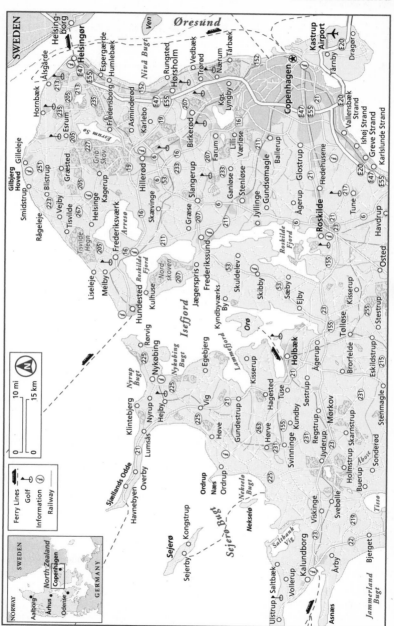

and its bustling harbor, and Frederiksværk, with its canal system. On the gentle banks of Isefjord, you'll find such lively centers as Holbæk and the already-mentioned Roskilde itself ("the town of kings").

For North Zealand rail information, you can call the main station in Copenhagen (p. 70). For train and bus information within Denmark, call © **70-13-14-15.**

---

1 HILLERØD

35km (22 miles) NW of Copenhagen

We don't expect you to fall in love with Hillerød. Unless you've consumed a lot of Danish beer, it can be a bit dull. We come here not only because it's a transport hub for North Zealand, especially for those connecting to trains heading for the north shore beaches, but to see its sprawling castle of Frederiksborg.

After a fire swept over it in 1859, even the royal family found the repairs too costly. They gave it up to the Carlsberg beer baron, J. C. Jacobsen, and he spearheaded the move to create the extravagant palace you see today.

You can spend at least an 1½ hours here wandering through its chambers before falling in love with the baroque gardens out back and wishing, with a greedy eye, they were yours to romp in.

Even if you don't like palaces and gardens, the ideal time to arrive here is in summer for the Viking Festival (see below).

If you, like us, are into long walks, you've come to the right place. Hillerød, in the heart of North Zealand, is surrounded by some of the most beautiful and extensive woodlands in the country. Christian IV used to ride through here back in 1602, and you can follow his trails. Space is too cramped here for us to go into all the best walks and trails to follow, but the tourist office will give you a leaflet outlining "the best of the best." Even the dour philosopher Søren Kierkegaard reveled in the tranquillity of these forests.

To the south sprawl the woodlands of **Store Dyrehave,** but we prefer the northern stretch of **Gribskov,** the second-largest forest in Denmark. The woodlands are still rich in game, and we take delight in spotting the pale, tailless roe deer. It's estimated there are some 800 fallow deer here, each distinguished by its white-speckled hide.

If you don't like to walk, you can also ask the tourist office for another leaflet, *Bicycle Routes in North Zealand.* Routes drawn on the map follow the most scenic paths, roads, and forest trails.

The forests of Gribskov front our favorite North Zealand lake, **Esrum Sø.** If you like bathing in admittedly chilly waters, sailing a boat, or fishing, you've come to the right place. The parklands of Fredensborg Slot (see later in this chapter) lie on the eastern shore of the lake, where chances are good in summer that you can hook up with one of the concessions featuring sailing trips on this gorgeous lake.

ESSENTIALS

GETTING THERE   The S-tog from Copenhagen arrives every 10 minutes throughout the day (trip time: 40 min.).

By Train   Trains link Hillerød with Helsingør in the east, and there are also rail links with Gilleleje and Tisvildeleje.

By Bus   Hillerød has good bus connections with the major towns of North Zealand: bus no. 305 from Gilleleje; bus nos. 306, 336, and 339 from Hornbæk; and bus nos. 336 and 339 from Fredensborg.

By Car   From Copenhagen, take Route 16 north.

VISITOR INFORMATION   The **tourist office,** Cristiansgade 1 (ℂ **48-24-26-26**), is open Monday to Wednesday 10:30am to 5:30pm, Thursday to Friday 10:30am to 4:30pm, and Saturday 10:30am to 2pm.

SPECIAL EVENTS   Every summer some 250 men, women, and children revert to their wild past. They don their Viking costumes and go on a rampage, re-creating the drama of the Viking age when the mere expression "the Vikings are coming" sent terror throughout a land about to be conquered. **Frederikssund Vikingespil (Viking Festival)** ★★★ is the big event of the Danish summer. If possible, try to adjust your schedule to take in the fun. Visit **www.vikingespil.dk** for more information or call ℂ **47-31-06-85.**

Frederikssund, a town 13km (8 miles) southwest of Hillerød and 48km (30 miles) northwest of Copenhagen, stages the 2-week Vikingespil in late June and early July. Nordic sagas are revived—and the record is set straight about who "discovered" America 5 centuries before Christopher Columbus. The festival features a series of plays, medieval and modern, about the Vikings.

The traditional play is performed nightly at 8pm, and a Viking banquet follows. Tickets for the festival are DKK140 ($24/£14) adults, DKK45 ($7.70/£4.50) children 5 to 12 (it's not suitable for children 4 and under). The dinner costs DKK175 ($30/£18) adults, DKK110 ($19/£11) children 5 to 12. Trains depart for Frederikssund at 20-minute intervals from Copenhagen's Central Railroad Station (trip time: 50 min.), and there are enough trains back to Copenhagen after the spectacle ends to allow commutes from the capital. From the station at Frederikssund, it's a 20-minute walk to the site of the pageant. For details, contact the tourist information office in Copenhagen or phone the Frederikssund Tourist Office (ℂ **47-31-06-85**).

SEEING THE SIGHTS

Frederiksborg Slot (Frederiksborg Castle) ★★★

We don't like giving labels to places that are designed to mislead. Don't fall for that hype about Frederiksborg Castle being "the Danish Versailles." Versailles, it isn't. It *is* the most beautiful royal residence in Denmark. Surrounded by a moat, the *slot* (castle) was constructed on three islands in a lake. Like Kronborg, it was built in Dutch Renaissance style (red brick, copper roof, sandstone facade). The oldest parts date from 1560 and the reign of Frederik II. His more extravagant son, Christian IV, erected the main part of the castle from 1600 to 1620. Danish monarchs used it for some 2 centuries. From 1671 to 1840, Danish kings were crowned in Christian IV's chapel, which is still used as a parish church. Since 1693, it has been a chapel for the knights of the Order of the Elephant and of the Grand Cross of Danneborg. Standing in the gallery is an old organ built by Esaias Compenius in 1610. Every Thursday from 1:30 to 2pm, the chapel organist plays for museum visitors.

Since 1878, the castle has housed **Det Nationalhistoriske Museum (the Museum of National History).** Founded by the brewer J. C. Jacobsen as part of the Carlsberg Foundation, it encompasses the Great Hall and the former Audience Chamber of Danish monarchs. The museum contains the best collection of portraits and historical paintings in the country, all the stiff-necked greats and the wannabes. You can explore 70 of its rooms, each with paintings, gilded ceilings, and tapestries covering entire walls. The

Visiting a Medieval Monastery's Remains

The ruins of an Augustinian monastery, **Abelholt Klostermuseum**, Abelholt 4
(☎ **48-24-34-48**), aren't everyone's cuppa, but if you're a doctor or a devotee of
eerie medieval ruins, consider a visit. You reach the site of this monastery,
founded in 1175, by driving west of Hillerød for 6km (3³/₄ miles)—it's signposted.
If you got sick in North Zealand centuries ago, you tried to make your way here,
as the local monks had various methods used in healing.

An on-site museum explains the primitive living conditions of the time, and
archaeologists have dug up skeletons of the former monks that are now on display and could be rented out for a horror flick. Healing methods used by these
early monks are also exhibited. You can wander through a garden adjoining the
museum to see the types of medicinal herbs grown. Admission is DKK20
($3.40/£2), free for those 12 and under. Hours are from March to October Tuesday
to Sunday 11am to 4pm.

20th-century collection on the third floor is a bit livelier, with its chronologically
arranged exhibits. There are portraits and paintings here, but somehow the photographs
are even more intriguing.

The castle is a 15-minute walk or a short taxi ride from the train station.

In Frederiksborg Slot. ☎ **48-26-04-39**. www.frederiksborgmuseet.dk. Admission DKK60 ($10/£6) adults,
DKK15 ($2.60/£1.50) children 6–15, free for children 5 and under. Nov–Mar daily 11am–3pm; Apr–Oct
daily 10am–5pm. Bus: 701 from Hillerød Station.

Frederiksborg Castle Garden ★★ For decades these gardens were used by three
kings of Denmark, including Frederik IV, Christian VI, and Frederik V. They were
designed by Johan Cornelius Krieger in just 5 years, from 1720 to 1725. In a flight of
fancy, he got carried away, creating a cascade with water canals and fountains, along with
promenades, groves of trees, and even a parterre sporting royal monograms to flatter the
egos of his patrons.

After many years in decay, however, the gardens have been recreated as they were in
their baroque heyday. As many as 65,000 box plants and 166 pyramid-shaped yews have
been planted in the parterre, while 375 limes and 7,000 hornbeam plants create the
avenues and groves. The cascade floor consists of nearly half a kilometer (¹/₄ mile) of
dressed granite stones. During the summer, the Frederiksborg Castle Garden forms the
venue for several recurring concerts, maypole celebrations, and other cultural events.

Rendelæggerbakken 3. ☎ **48-26-04-39**. Free admission. May–Aug daily 10am–9pm; Sept and Apr daily
10am–7pm; Oct and Mar daily 10am–5pm; Nov–Feb daily 10am–4pm. Bus: 701 from Hillerød Station.

SHOPPING

This is not a compelling reason to come to Hillerød, but you might be surprised at how
many goods there are to buy. In the town center is the sprawling **SlotsArkaderne ★**
shopping center, close to Frederiksborg Castle, with an entrance on Nordstensvej. Its distinctive interior design has been hailed throughout Denmark. It is definitely shopper-friendly.
Within the center are some 50 specialty shops, in one of the most beautiful shopping malls
in Europe. Open Monday to Friday 10am to 7pm and Saturday 10am to 4pm.

There are a number of specialty stores throughout the town. Right in front of the castle, **Sweater House,** Slangerupgade 1 (② **48-25-51-25**), offers the town's best selection of Scandinavian sweaters, often in blue-and-white patterns. Because Danish toys enjoy world renown, you might want to check out the selection at **Fætter BR,** SlotsArkaderne 27 (② **48-26-07-55**).

WHERE TO STAY

The **Hillerød Tourist office** (see above) offers a wide range of excellent, yet inexpensive, B&Bs in and around town. These are mostly seasonal openings, and some owners open one year and not the other; but the list in the tourist office is always current.

Although the hotel recommended below is fine, many guests prefer the more glamorous Fredensborg Store Kro (see below).

Hotel Hillerød With its smart, sleek Danish design, this is the town's best choice for overnighting. Okay, so its low-slung design and features might remind you of a motel on the outskirts of a large American city. Even so, the hotel is furnished both sensibly and comfortably, and all the bedrooms are well maintained, with Danish modern pieces and neatly kept bathrooms with shower units. Most of the accommodations come with a small kitchenette, as well as a private terrace. Breakfast is the only meal served; and, even if there are any shortcomings here, the attentive staff makes up for it. The location is a 3-minute walk from the town's commercial center.

Milnersvej 41, DK-3400 Hillerød. ② **48-24-08-00.** Fax 48-24-08-74. www.hotelhillerod.dk. 113 units, 62 w/kitchenette. DKK1,160–DKK1,260 ($197–$214/£116–£126) double, DKK3,495 ($594/£350) suite. Rates include breakfast. AE, DC, MC, V. **Amenities:** Restaurant; lounge; laundry service; dry cleaning; nonsmoking rooms; rooms for those w/limited mobility. *In room:* TV, minibar, coffeemaker, hair dryer, trouser press, safe.

WHERE TO DINE

Café Copenhagen DANISH/INTERNATIONAL Set on the main square of Hillerød, this joint makes one of the best stopovers for lunch if you're racing through the area during the day, returning to Copenhagen that evening. At midday, expect the usual array of freshly made salads, burgers, and sandwiches. During the day this place mainly functions as a cafe and restaurant, where good-tasting menu items include New Orleans–style barbecue, grilled shrimp, well-stuffed club sandwiches, and succulent pastas. However, when the food service winds down, beginning around 7pm, it transforms itself into a bar designed for drinking, talking, and flirting. We like it best then. Action spills over onto an outdoor terrace, and every Friday and Saturday an annex room is transformed into a dance club, **Club Annabell,** which can get quite rowdy. Entry is DKK50 ($8.50/£5); a bottle of Carlsberg goes for DKK40 ($6.80/£4). No one under age 21 is allowed inside.

Torvet 4. ② **48-26-04-05.** Fixed-price meals DKK90–DKK225 ($15–$38/£9–£23). AE, DC, MC, V. May–Sept Mon–Sat 2–11pm; Oct–Apr Tues–Sat noon–7pm. Bar until 2am year-round.

Slotskroen ★ DANISH After calling on the Queen, we always like to pop in here for lunch. It's been going strong since it opened its doors in 1795 and is the oldest tavern in town. But it's also kept abreast of the times in both its menu selections and its decor. Nowadays, food is served only at lunchtime (although on rare occasions, dinner is offered). Within a trio of cozy and historic-looking dining rooms, some of whose windows open onto direct views of the nearby castle, you can enjoy access to typical Danish dishes including several kinds of open-faced Danish sandwiches, *frikadeller* (Danish rissoles or meatballs), and freshly made salads. There's also an outdoor terrace for use during warm weather.

Slotsgade 67. © **48-20-18-00.** Main courses DKK65–DKK175 ($11–$30/£6.50–£18). AE, DC, MC, V. Daily noon–5pm.

Spisestedet Leonora ★ DANISH   Since the 1970s, this well-managed tavern has flourished in the former Frederiksborg Castle stables. Don't panic—the original smell is long gone. It's the most sought-after dining spot in town for anyone visiting the castle, partly because of its array of carefully crafted open-faced sandwiches. The place also serves succulent grilled meats, especially Danish lamb; homemade crisp, fresh salads; and platters of homemade, warm dishes, the kind your Danish grandmother used to make. These platters are big enough to make a meal unto themselves.

Frederiksborg Slot. © **48-26-75-16.** www.leonora.dk. Main courses DKK150–DKK170 ($26–$29/£15–£17); lunch plate DKK59–DKK115 ($10–$20/£5.90–£12); *smørrebrød* DKK59–DKK108 ($10–$18/£5.90–£11). DC, MC, V. Daily 10am–5pm. Closed 1 week at Christmas. Bus: 701 or 702.

HILLERØD AFTER DARK

The best place to go is the **Café Copenhagen** (see "Where to Dine," above), which transforms itself into **Club Annabell** on Friday and Saturday nights.

ON THE FRINGE: A RENAISSANCE CASTLE & MODERN ART

You're in for a treat if you've budgeted an hour or two to drive over to **Selsø Slot** ★, Selsøvej 30 at Hornsherred (© **47-52-01-71**), the first Renaissance-style castle built in 1575. Of course, all that baroque styling you see today is from 1733. The owners couldn't leave a good thing alone. Selsø is one of the few private manor houses in Zealand that can be thoroughly explored, yet it seems little publicized and most visitors pass it by without knowing it's there.

The Great Hall is still as it was in 1733 when those new decorators came through, adding touches such as ornate plaster ceilings, fine paintings, and 4-meter (13-ft.) marble panels. You can also wander down to the vaults from 1560, and even see the old manor kitchen and its open fireplace and scullery. A dungeon below the gatehouse is a bit spooky. Kids delight in a room devoted to them with its hundreds of tin soldiers. Before heading here, ask at the tourist office about orchestral concerts staged here. Hopefully, you'll get to see one for yourself. The setting's perfect. Hillerød makes a good center for exploring neighboring attractions.

From the center of Hillerød, take Route 6 south, following the signs to Copenhagen. At Route 53, turn west. Fifty-five kilometers (34 miles) from Hillerød you'll come to Selsø Slot. The location at Hornsherred is east of Skibby, south of Skuldelev, and 56km (35 miles) west of Copenhagen.

Admission is DKK50 ($8.50/£5) adults, DKK10 ($1.70/£1) children. The castle is open mid-June to mid-August, daily 11am to 4pm; and mid-August to late October, Saturday and Sunday 1 to 4pm (closed otherwise).

Frederikssund (see above) is usually visited at the time of its Viking pageant. But the opening of an art museum here in 1957 made the hamlet a year-round attraction. The **J. F. Willumsen's Museum,** Jenriksvej 4 (© **47-31-07-73;** www.jfwillumsensmuseum.dk), is devoted to the paintings, drawings, engravings, sculpture, ceramics, and photographs of the well-known Danish artist J. F. Willumsen (1863–1958), one of Denmark's leading symbolists, who spent most of his creative years in France. The museum also displays the works of other artists which were once part of Willumsen's private collection. Hours are year-round Tuesday to Sunday 10am to 5pm. Admission is DKK40 ($6.80/£4) adults, DKK20 ($3.40/£2) students, free for children 14 and under. From Hillerød, take Route 6 south, following the signs to Copenhagen. At Route 53 head west. The total distance from Hillerød is 40km (25 miles).

2 FREDENSBORG ★

9.5km (6 miles) W of Helsingør; 40km (25 miles) N of Copenhagen

The great time to visit is in July, when the queen graciously opens the doors of Fredensborg Slot (palace) to visitors from around the world. Elizabeth II of England has a lot more money, a lot more paintings, and much more precious furnishings, but the Danish queen's summer abode is impressive as well, though not as grand as Frederiksborg Slot (see above), with which it is often confused.

On the southeast shore of Esrum Sø, the country's second-largest lake, Fredensborg is more than a royal palace. Many visitors rush through, visiting the palace and then departing immediately. However, you can stay and dine in the area and enjoy a number of other attractions as well (see below).

The first inhabitants of the town were people who helped serve the royal court. But over the years others moved in, and today the town is a lively little place even when the Queen isn't in residence. To Denmark, it occupies a position somewhat similar to Windsor in England. The town is home to some 40 specialty shops.

The palace is a major backdrop for events in the life of the royal family—weddings, birthday parties, and the like. Heads of states from many of the countries of the world are received here when they pay state visits. And foreign ambassadors present their credentials to the monarch here as well.

ESSENTIALS

GETTING THERE   **By Train**   From Copenhagen's Central Railroad Station, frequent trains run to Fredensborg, but there are no buses.

By Car   From Copenhagen, head north on the E55 toward Helsingør, turning west on Route 6.

VISITOR INFORMATION   **Fredensborg Turistinformation,** Slotsgade 2 (© 47-31-06-85), is open Monday to Friday 10am to 5pm, Saturday 10am to 1pm.

EXPLORING THE AREA

Esrum Sø ★ not only is the second-largest lake in Denmark, but also is exceptionally deep: 22m (72 ft.) in some places. Since 1949, the land around the lake has been protected by the government. It is a winter feeding ground for large numbers of waterfowl. You can enjoy a trip on the lake if for no other reason than to admire the flocks of noble swans—there's not an "Ugly Duckling" among them.

If the weather is good enough and there's enough business to warrant its departure, a local outfitter, **Færgefart Bådudlejning på Esrum Sø,** Skipperhuset, in the village of Sørup (© 48-48-01-07), leads tours in an open boat through the lake's shallow waters. The emphasis is on ecology, and the tour is conducted in Danish with halting English and German explanations added afterward. The duration of the tour is around 45 minutes, and the cost is DKK60 ($10/£6).

Esrum Kloster, Klostergade 11, Esrum (© 48-36-04-00), was founded in 1151 and has a long and ancient history, especially when it was the most powerful Cistercian monastery in Scandinavia. Eleven monks arrived to lay the foundation stone of what later became the abbey, surrounded by forest, meadows, lake, and fields. The Middle Ages come alive here as you view the second-floor exhibit of the monastic period.

The mounted exhibition gives you an idea of the layout of the monastery and the everyday life of the monks. The exhibition on the main floor deals with Esrum Abbey after the Reformation. The cloisters underwent many changes, becoming a royal hunting lodge, a base for a regiment of dragoons, a stud farm for horses, and even a post office and district tax office. As a result of King Frederik II's horse-breeding interests, the fabled Frederiksborg horse was produced, highly prized for its skill and stamina.

In addition to the exhibitions, regular concerts and theatrical performances are staged here, both inside and outside the monastery.

The abbey is open January 5 to May 8 Thursday to Sunday 10am to 4pm; May 9 to June 30 and August 1 to October 23 Tuesday to Sunday 10am to 4pm; July Tuesday to Sunday 10am to 5pm (Thurs until 9pm); October 24 to December 18 Thursday to Sunday 10am to 4pm. It's closed December 19 to January 4. Admission is DKK45 ($7.70/£4.50), DKK20 ($3.40/£2) for children 5 to 15, free for children 4 and under.

From Fredensborg, you can get to Esrum by bus (marked ESRUM), getting off at Hovedgaden. From here, walk for less than half a kilometer (¼ mile) along the Klostergade, which leads you to the entrance of the abbey. Motorists can take Route 205 north from Fredensborg.

From Hillerød to Esrum, you can catch bus nos. 305, 306, or 331, a 25-minute ride, for around DKK35 ($6/£3.50).

Fredensborg Slot ★

This is the summer residence of the Danish royal family. Once it was called the palace of "the parents-in-law" of Europe. King Christian IX and Queen Louise had sons and daughters sitting on thrones in many of the royal houses of Europe, and they would gather in the summer months to catch up on royal gossip and scandals.

Although the palace has been added onto many times, it still retains its baroque, rococo, and classic features.

When the queen is in residence today, visitors assemble at noon to watch the changing of the guard—but don't expect this ceremony to match that of Buckingham Palace in London. On Thursdays, except in July, the queen often appears to acknowledge a regimental band concert in her honor.

The Danish architect J. C. Krieger built the palace for King Frederik IV. Originally there was only the main building with a Cupola Hall. Over the years, the palace was extended with such additions as the Chancellery House and the Cavaliers Wing. Though hardly one of the impressive royal palaces of Europe, it has its own charm, especially in the Domed Hall and the Garden Room.

The palace opens onto a 275-year-old **baroque garden ★★**. A public part of the palace garden is open year-round daily 1 to 5pm, but the private, reserved royal garden and Orangery are open only limited hours in July. These are some of the largest and best-preserved gardens in Denmark. Note how strictly symmetrical and geometrical the shapes are. Drawing on Italian designs for their inspiration, Frederik IV and J. C. Krieger laid out the palace gardens in the 1720s. In the 1760s, Frederik V redesigned the garden, adding elements from French baroque horticulture.

Slottet. © **48-48-18-35.** Admission DKK50 ($8.50/£5) adults, DKK25 ($4.30/£2.50) children 5–14, free for children 4 and under. Joint ticket for the Palace and the Orangery and Herb Garden DKK60 ($10/£6)

WHERE TO STAY

Endruplund Country House ★ (Finds)   This little hidden-away charmer was created
from a farmhouse that stood here in the early part of the 20th century. It's been run by
the same family since 1926, and is a comfortable little oasis for those seeking old-fashioned Danish ambience. It is set less than a kilometer (¹/₂ mile) northeast of Fredensborg's
center. Today, you'll find comfortable, somewhat eccentric rooms, each personalized by
the hardworking efforts of the inn's owner, Karen Windinge, whose critically acclaimed
dried-flower arrangements are artfully scattered throughout her comfortable and eclecti-
cally decorated guesthouse. No meals are served other than breakfast.

Holmeskovvej 5, DK-3480 Fredensborg. ℭ **48-48-02-38.** Fax 48-48-35-17. www.countryhouse.dk. 17
units, 11 w/private bathroom. DKK380 ($65/£38) double w/shared bathroom; DKK440 ($75/£44) double
w/private bathroom. MC, V. From Fredensborg's center, follow the signs to Helsingør. **Amenities:** Breakfast room; lounge. *In room:* No phone.

Fredensborg Store Kro ★★   A 10-minute walk from the train station and 5 minutes from Esrum Lake, this is one of the most venerable old inns in Zealand, and a
personal favorite of ours, lying a 10-minute walk from the train station or a 5-minute
leisurely stroll from Esrum Lake. It was commissioned in 1723 by Frederik IV. Because
it is right next door to Fredensborg Castle, many guests of the royal family once stayed
here. No two rooms are alike, but all are equally charming, as taste and elegance rule
throughout. Ask for a room with a view of the palace—although only five are available,
and they are of course the most requested. In 1997, President Clinton dropped in to the
inn for a look when he was visiting the queen at Fredensborg. The hotel restaurant, **Anna
Sophie,** is the finest in the area (see "Where to Dine," below).

Slotsgade 6, DK-3480 Fredensborg. ℭ **48-40-01-11.** Fax 48-48-45-61. www.storekro.dk. 49 units.
DKK1,500–DKK1,700 ($255–$289/£150–£170) double; DKK2,300 ($391/£230) suite. Rates include break-
fast. AE, DC, MC, V. Bus: 336 or 733E. **Amenities:** Restaurant; bar; room service; laundry service; dry cleaning; rooms for those w/limited mobility. *In room:* TV, Wi-Fi, hair dryer.

WHERE TO DINE

Anna Sophie ★★ DANISH/FRENCH   Should the queen accept your invitation for
a meal, take her here. Hopefully, the weather will be cooperative. That way, you can dine
outside in the garden, idyllic on a summer night. Otherwise, you can retreat into the
elegant dining room, which is also fit for a queen. The cooking is not only delectable—
it's often inspired. The chef assumes that when it comes to lunch appetizers, everybody
likes herring. We certainly do, especially the herring plate with three variations on this
fish. At night the starters grow more elaborate, including a lightly smoked foie gras with
dried goose breast and a rhubarb compote. The sautéed lamb is always perfectly prepared
with baked plum tomatoes and a savory sauce. The chef always bakes a special cake of
the day for dessert.

Slotsgade 6. ℭ **48-40-01-50.** Reservations recommended. Main courses DKK225–DKK230 ($38–
$39/£23). AE, DC, MC, V. Daily noon–3pm and 6–10pm.

Da Oscar ITALIAN   This small family-run restaurant a short walk from Fredensborg
Castle has a lot of panache, verve, and sensitivity. Originally built in the 1930s, the
premises might remind you of a small-scale villa. Inside you'll find a trio of cozy dining
rooms, a cuisine that focuses on Italian dishes, and food items that include succulent

pastas and freshly caught fish. The pastry chef makes a tempting array of goodies every day, big on calories and taste, horrible on your Kate Moss waistline. Grilled Danish lamb and savory pizzas are also offered. At any time, if the more substantial offerings don't appeal to you, you can order any of at least a dozen artfully contrived *smørrebrød* (open-faced sandwiches).

Slotsgade 3A. (48-48-01-25. www.daoscar.dk. Reservations recommended. Main courses DKK182–DKK220 ($31–$37/£18–£22); fixed-price menu DKK319–DKK360 ($54–$61/£32–£36). MC, V. Daily 5–11pm.

Restaurant Skipperhuset ★★ (Finds DANISH/FRENCH Picture this: alfresco dining on Lake Estrum. Not only that, but you're actually on the grounds of the royal summer residence of the queen. In the 18th century, this site was the royal boathouse. Part of the experience of dining at this restaurant is the path you'll use to reach it—a long promenade lined with trees originally laid out as one of the decorative avenues associated with Fredensborg Slot. Today this much-altered boathouse is a well-respected restaurant where cuisine manages to combine elements of the best of Danish and French traditions. The cooks here have experience and an expert sense of precise, clear flavors. Menu items we continue to enjoy include breast of chicken stewed with young vegetables and summer cabbage; fried mackerel with spinach, apples, olives, and lemon-thyme sauce; and a dessert specialty of stewed rhubarb with sugared biscuits.

Skipperallee 6. (48-48-17-17. www.skipperhuset.dk. Reservations recommended. Main courses DKK68–DKK348 ($12–$59/£6.80–£35); fixed-price menus DKK348 ($59/£35). DC, MC, V. Tues–Sun noon–6pm.

3 HELSINGØR: IN SEARCH OF HAMLET ★

40km (25 miles) N of Copenhagen; 24km (15 miles) NE of Hillerød; 72km (45 miles) NE of Roskilde

Does it really matter to the pilgrims flocking to this town that Hamlet never existed? Or that William Shakespeare never visited Helsingør? To the pilgrims wanting to see "Hamlet's Castle," the power of legend is what really matters.

Don't be disappointed if you arrive by train or bus. Make your way through the noisy, congested crowds and the fast-food stalls and move deeper into Helsingør. Once you do that, you'll find that it has a certain charm, with a market square, medieval lanes, and old half-timbered and brick buildings, many constructed by ships' captains in the heyday of the 19th-century shipping industry.

In 1429, King Erik of Pomerania ruled that ships passing Helsingør had to pay a toll for sailing within local waters. The town quickly developed into the focal point for international shipping, bringing in a lot of revenue. King Erik also constructed the Castle of Krogen, later rebuilt by Christian IV as the Castle of Kronborg. For a while, Helsingør prospered and grew so much that it was the second-largest town in the country.

Today much of the town's prosperity depends on those free-spending Hamlet devotees and that sliver of water between Denmark and Sweden, with ferries leaving frequently for Helsingborg.

ESSENTIALS

GETTING THERE **By Train** There are frequent trains from Copenhagen (trip time: 50 min.).

By Car Take E-4 north from Copenhagen.

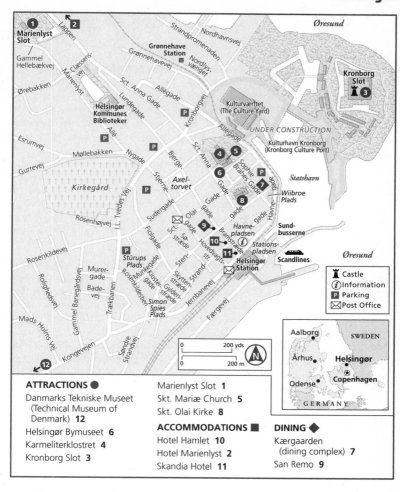

ATTRACTIONS ●

Danmarks Tekniske Museet
(Technical Museum of
Denmark) **12**
Helsingør Bymuseet **6**
Karmeliterklostret **4**
Kronborg Slot **3**

Marienlyst Slot **1**
Skt. Mariæ Church **5**
Skt. Olai Kirke **8**

ACCOMMODATIONS ■

Hotel Hamlet **10**
Hotel Marienlyst **2**
Skandia Hotel **11**

DINING ◆

Kærgaarden
(dining complex) **7**
San Remo **9**

By Ferry Ferries ply the waters of the narrow channel separating Helsingør (Denmark) from Helsingborg (Sweden) in less than 25 minutes. They're operated around the clock by **Scandlines** (© **33-15-15-15;** www.scandlines.dk), which charges DKK42 ($7.20/£4.20) each way for a pedestrian without a car, and DKK275 ($47/£28) each way for a car with up to nine persons inside. Between 6am and 11pm, departures are every 20 minutes; 11pm to 6am, departures are timed at intervals of 40 to 80 minutes. The process is simple and straightforward: You simply drive your car onboard and wait in your car. Border formalities during the crossing between Denmark and Sweden are perfunctory, and although you should carry a passport, you might not even be asked for it.

VISITOR INFORMATION   The **tourist office,** at Havnepladsen 3 (© **49-21-13-33;** www.visithelsingor.dk), is open Monday to Friday 10am to 5pm, and Saturday 10am to 2pm; June 20 to August 31 Monday to Friday 10am to 5pm, and Saturday 10am to 3pm.

SEEING THE SIGHTS

Danmarks Tekniske Museet (Technical Museum of Denmark) ★ (Finds)   Did

you know that rich Danes were driving an automobile, the Hammelvognen, back in 1888? They were and it's on display here. Would you like to see what the world's first typewriter looked like? You can do so here. There's even the world's first electromagnetic sound recorder (tape recorder) on display. Steam engines, antique electric appliances, bicycles, vintage cars, and the oldest Danish airplanes are on display here. The location is in the southern part of town in a former iron foundry.

Although there are many exhibits, including a pewter workshop, we are most intrigued by the 30 or so airplanes, ranging from gyrocopters to helicopters. Our favorite is called the "Danish Edison," an invention of J. C. Ellhammer. Danes will tell you he made the first flight in Europe in 1906. Regrettably, if this is true, his feat was never recorded.

Fabriksvej 25. © **49-22-26-11.** www.tekniskmuseum.dk. Admission Jan 2–Apr and Oct 1–Dec 30 DKK50 ($8.50/£5) adults, DKK25 ($4.30/£2.50) children 10–15, free for children 4–13; May–Sept DKK65 ($11/£6.50) adults, DKK35 ($6/£3.50) children 4–13. Tues–Sun 10am–5pm.

Helsingør Bymuseet   This Renaissance townhouse was built in 1520 by Carmelite

friars as a hospital for foreign sailors suffering from diseases; time has erased that sad history. Today it's the "attic" of Helsingør, a magnificent Renaissance townhouse filled with the city's relics. Children, or at least little girls, gravitate to the collection of 200 antique dolls. There is also a fine-scale model of Helsingør in 1801. The banquet hall on the main floor is filled with the chief goodies, artifacts left over from the golden age of Helsingør when it was a major shipping center. As for some of those portraits, they evoke the type you hide in your own family attic. In the basement are relics of the Middle Ages, best left undisturbed in our view.

Helsingørsgade 65. © **49-28-18-00.** Admission DKK20 ($3.40/£2) adults, free for children 17 and under. May–Oct Tues–Fri and Sun noon–4pm, Sat 10am–4pm.

Kronborg Slot ★★★   There is no evidence that Shakespeare ever saw this sandstone-

and-copper Dutch Renaissance–style castle, full of intriguing secret passages, but he made it famous in *Hamlet.* If Hamlet had really lived, it would have been centuries before Kronborg was built (1574–85). You're to be forgiven if you suddenly burst into Richard Burton's famous soliloquy of "to be or not to be." After all, *Hamlet* is the most frequently performed drama in the world, a historical challenge to all great actors such as Sir John Gielgud and Lord Laurence Olivier. Count yourself lucky if you missed Mel Gibson's pathetic attempt to play the Mad Dane in the 1990 movie directed by Franco Zeffirelli, who should have known better. Except for "Mad Mel," the film had a great cast, with Glen Close as Gertrude, Alan Bates as Claudius, and Paul Scofield as "the Ghost."

The castle, on a peninsula jutting out into Øresund, was restored in 1629 by Christian IV after it had been gutted by fire. Other events in its history include looting, bombardment, occupation by Swedes, and use as a barracks (1785–1922). The facade is covered with sandstone, and the entire castle is surrounded by a deep moat—but no dragon. You approach the castle via a wooden bridge and by going through Mørkeport, a gate from

A Hamlet "Sommer" in the Courtyard of Kronborg

Some 4 centuries have gone by since the Bard wrote *Hamlet,* but the age-old drama is still performed here in August in the courtyard of the so-called Hamlet's Castle, Kronborg. That great theatrical couple Laurence Olivier and his wife Vivien Leigh performed *Hamlet* here, as have many other theatrical greats since 1816. Tickets for this event cost DKK250 ($43/£25). For ticket information, contact **Helsingør Teaterkontor,** Havnepladsen 3 (℗ **49-20-08-11.** The box office is open Monday to Friday noon to 4pm.

the 16th century. Here you'll see an octagonal tower, the Trumpeters Tower, one of the landmarks of town. This will lead you to the main courtyard of Kronborg.

Note: Instead of entering the castle at once, you can walk around the moat to the waterfront, where you can view a spectacular vista of the Swedish coast. At the platform—backed by massive bronze guns—Hamlet is said to have seen the ghost of his father, shrouded in pea-soup fog.

The starkly furnished Great Hall is the largest in northern Europe. Originally, 40 tapestries portraying 111 Danish kings were hung around this room on special occasions. They were commissioned by Frederik II and produced around 1585. Only seven remain at Kronborg; the rest have disappeared except for seven in the Nationalmuseet in Copenhagen. The church, with its original oak furnishings and the royal chambers, is worth exploring. The bleak and austere atmosphere adds to the drama. Holger Danske, a mythological hero who is believed to assist Denmark whenever the country is threatened, is said to live in the basement. That "hero" didn't emerge when Nazi storm troopers invaded Denmark on Hitler's orders, but the legend, like the legend of Hamlet, still persists. Also on the premises is the **Danish Maritime Museum** (℗ **49-21-06-85**), which explores the history of Danish shipping. Unless you're really nautical, you might skip this if you're rushed for time. However, that would mean you'd miss seeing the world's oldest surviving ship's biscuit, dating from 1852. There is also an impressive collection of model ships and other sailors' memorabilia. More intriguing are relics of Denmark's colonial past in the West Indies (Caribbean), West Africa, Greenland, and even India.

Guided tours are given every half-hour October to April. In summer you can walk around on your own. The castle is less than a kilometer (½ mile) from the rail station. On November 30, 2000, Kronborg was added to UNESCO's World Heritage List.

Kronborg. ℗ **49-21-30-78.** www.kronborgcastle.com. Admission DKK65–DKK85 ($11–$14/£6.50–£8.50) adults, DKK25–DKK65 ($4.30–$11/£2.50–£6.50) children 6–14, free for children 5 and under. Joint ticket for the tower and the Danish Maritime Museum DKK50 ($8.50/£5) adults, free for children 17 and under. May–Sept daily 10:30am–5pm; Apr and Oct Tues–Sun 11am–4pm; Nov–Mar Tues–Sun 11am–3pm. Closed Dec 25.

Marienlyst Slot ★   Kronborg is all militant in its architecture and ghostly in its literary associations. But Marienlyst Slot, built by French architect N. H. Jardin from 1759 to 1763, is a place where you might actually live. In fact, up until 1953, it was a private residence before being turned into a museum. The location is 1km (⅔ mile) north of Helsingør. Allow 30 minutes or so to wander in the well-landscaped park surrounding the Slot. There's a panoramic view of the Sound from the top of a steep slope behind the palace.

In the 16th century, King Frederik II used this site for his summer gardens before the present palace was constructed. The interior is in the Louis XVI style, with a collection of lackluster paintings. One intrigued us as an oddity: The painting is half Venice, half Copenhagen. To lure English romantics in the 19th century, locals claimed that "Hamlet's grave" could be found in the garden out back. Thinking Hamlet was an actual prince, these visitors were instructed "to think melancholy thoughts."

Marienlyst Allé 32. ℂ **49-28-18-30.** www.museerne.helsingor.dk. Admission DKK30 ($5.10/£3) adults, free for children 17 and under. Tues–Sun noon–4pm.

Skt. Mariæ Kirke ★   Too often neglected by those Hamlet-crazed visitors, this former Carmelite monastery is one of the best preserved in the North of Europe. Rumor has it, the monks here used to flagellate themselves inside its walls like that albino monk did in the controversial film *The Da Vinci Code.*

The church was built between 1430 and 1500, and much of its original architecture remains. You can see the newly renovated organ that was used by the famous baroque composer Dietrich Buxtehude from 1660 to 1668. Murals dating from the 1480s have also been restored, and there is an impressive altarpiece from 1637. The interior contains two galleries, a royal gallery and a rococo gallery, dating from the 17th and 18th centuries. After the Reformation, the monastery was dissolved and converted into a retirement home.

Inside the walls of the ecclesiastical compound is the **Karmeliterklostret Monastery ★**, which can be visited on a guided tour. After the monks were booted out, this building was turned into a hospital specializing in brain surgery. With so little known about brain surgery in those days, you can imagine how botched the operations were.

In case you get asked on some trivia TV quiz, the body of the notorious Dyveke, mistress of Christian II, was buried here upon her death in 1517. Local gossips claimed that the king "wore her out."

The monastery lies near the intersection of Havnegade and Kronborgvej.

Skt. Annagade 38. ℂ **49-21-17-74.** Free admission. Mon–Sat 9am–noon; Thurs 4–6pm. Guided tours May 16–Sept 15 Mon–Fri at 2pm. DKK25 ($4.30/£2.50) adults, DKK10 ($1.70/£1) children 10–15, free for children 9 and under.

Skt. Olai Kirke   After a visit to the monastery above, and only if time remains, you can walk nearby to see this church, which is actually the cathedral of Helsingør. It was named after the patron saint Olai, a Norwegian king (spelled "Olav" in Norwegian) who died in 1030. Throughout the church are illustrations of this saintly king slaying the dragon of paganism.

The present building dates from 1559, constructed on the site of a small Romanesque church from the 1200s.

At the dawn of the 21st century, restorers opened many of the burial chambers here, discovering very well-preserved mummies. Had Danish monks learned the secrets of the Egyptians? After these long-dead corpses were studied, they were sealed away once more and buried beneath a floor of concrete and tile to "safeguard the peace of the dead now and forever."

Architecturally, the christening chapel and the baptistery of this spired church are worth a brief inspection. Also take in the ornately decorated altar. Sankt Olai takes up a city block between Stengade and Sankt Olai Gade.

Skt. Annagade 12. ℂ **49-21-04-43.** Free admission. May–Aug Mon–Sat 10am–4pm; Sept–Apr daily 10am–2pm.

WHERE TO STAY

Hotel Hamlet   Renovations have taken away from some of the old-fashioned character of this long-enduring favorite, but have made it more comfortable than ever. The location near the harbor makes it a convenient address for ferryboats arriving from Sweden. Overhead beams were left intact, and the dark wood furnishings and forest-green walls add a bit to the ambience. The bedrooms are standard and comfortable, but not especially alluring.

Bramstrasse 5, DK-3000. ℂ **49-21-05-91.** Fax 49-26-01-30. www.hotelhamlet.dk. 36 units. DKK1,095 ($186/£110) double, DKK1,645 ($280/£165) family unit. AE, DC, MC, V. **Amenities:** Restaurant; bar; nonsmoking rooms. *In room:* TV.

Hotel Marienlyst ★   On the western outskirts of town beyond the castle, this hotel is about as close to Las Vegas as you'll get in Denmark. Even if you don't like its flashy neon aggressiveness, it's the best and most comfortable place to stay in town. Composed of three buildings, its headquarters and oldest core were built around 1850, while the largest of its annexes went up in the mid-1970s. With a panoramic view over the gray sea toward Sweden, this hotel contains a glossy outbuilding with one of only six gambling casinos in Denmark. Rooms are a study in sleek Nordic styling—comfortable and beautifully maintained. The bathrooms are neatly kept, with tub/shower combinations. Many rooms have balconies or terraces, and 86 have a view of the sound. The suites and apartments have a kitchen and dishwasher.

Nordre Strandvej 2, DK-3000 Helsingør. ℂ **49-21-40-00.** Fax 49-21-49-00. www.marienlyst.dk. 222 units. DKK1,335–DKK1,900 ($227–$323/£134–£190) double; DKK2,135 ($363/£214) suite. Rates include breakfast. AE, DC, MC, V. Bus: 340. **Amenities:** 2 restaurants; bar; casino; indoor heated pool; children's pool and water slide; fitness center; spa; room service; massage; babysitting; laundry service; dry cleaning; nonsmoking rooms; rooms for those w/limited mobility. *In room:* TV, Wi-Fi, hair dryer.

Skandia Hotel (Value)   Attracting the economy-minded, this hotel provides simple but clean and cost-conscious accommodations in an amply proportioned building erected in 1922. Only half of its rooms have been renovated, so your opinion of this hotel may depend on your room assignment. Naturally, the renovated ones go first. Rooms are neat and functionally furnished. Ask for one on the fifth floor if you'd like a good view of the sound. If you need to make a phone call, you can do so at the reception desk. The hotel lies behind a redbrick facade along a street running parallel to the port near the bus and train station and the departure point for the ferryboat to Sweden.

Bramstræde 1, DK-3000 Helsingør. ℂ **49-21-09-02.** Fax 49-21-09-54. www.hotelskandia.dk. 44 units, 9 w/private bathroom. DKK750 ($128/£75) double w/shared bathroom; DKK850 ($145/£85) double w/private bathroom; DKK1,050 ($179/£105) 3-bed family rooms w/shower. DC, MC, V. **Amenities:** Lounge; nonsmoking rooms. *In room:* TV, Wi-Fi, no phone.

WHERE TO DINE

Typical Danish hot meals, such as *hakkebof* (hamburger steak), *frikadeller*, rib roast with red cabbage, cooked or fried flounder or herring, and *æggekage* (egg cake) with bacon, are served in the local restaurants. In Helsingør you'll also find many fast-food places, and you won't want to miss the celebrated ice-cream wafers.

San Remo DANISH   A down-to-earth self-service establishment that nevertheless sports crystal chandeliers, the San Remo offers 35 different meals, including *frikadeller* and potatoes. The fare is robust, filling, and cheap—nothing more. The cafeteria is set in a traffic-free shopping mall half a block from the harbor, in a Dutch-inspired building dating from 1904.

Stengade 53 (at Bjergegade). ① **49-21-00-55.** Main courses DKK69–DKK88 ($12–$15/£6.90–£8.80). MC, V. June–July daily 9am–9pm; Aug–May daily 10am–8pm. Bus: 801 or 802.

A Dining Complex

Kærgaarden is the setting for a trio of international restaurants in what was Helsingør's Customs House back in 1770. This complex enjoys the dining monopoly in Helsingør and is frequented by passengers going to and from Sweden. Kærgaarden offers **Gringo's Cantina** (① **49-26-14-47;** www.gringos.dk), a Mexican restaurant where main courses cost DKK118 to DKK189 ($20–$32/£12–£19), with a fixed-price menu going for DKK159 to DKK169 ($27–$29/£16–£17). There is also the very competent **Bamboo** (① **49-21-22-82**), a Chinese restaurant offering main courses for DKK115 to DKK179 ($20–$30/£12–£18). Both are open daily from noon to 10pm. All accept American Express, Diners Club, MasterCard, and Visa.

4 HORNBÆK

50km (31 miles) N of Copenhagen; 12km (7¹/₂ miles) west of Helsingør

New Englanders may sing of Cape Cod, but when the summer winds blow, islanders like to head for Hornbæk for "sea, suds, and sex," as one habitué told us. A 500-year-old fishing hamlet turned modern holiday resort, Hornbæk is one of the best places for a vacation on the north coast of Zealand—sometimes called the Kattegat coast. Coastal woodlands, heath, and sand dunes make for a uniquely Danish holiday.

Hornbæk has the best beach along the north coast, a wide expanse of soft white sands that runs the full length of the resort, set against a backdrop of beach grass and sand dunes. *Rosa rugosa,* a wild pink rose that flourishes in this salty air, blooms here all summer. The beach is pristine and is beautifully maintained; all the kiosks and facilities lie inland from the dunes.

The light found in Hornbæk attracted and continues to attract artists to this fishing hamlet. In 1870, the town was discovered by such artists as Kristian Zartmann, P. S. Krøyer, Viggo Johansen, and Carl Locher—all names you've never heard of unless you were born in Denmark. Krøyer often depicted the work of fishermen at sea and down the shore. Locher was so fascinated with his marine subjects that he lived at Hornbæk from 1881 to 1889; his home still stands at Østre Stejlebakke but is not open to the public.

ESSENTIALS

GETTING THERE   By Train   From Helsingør (see earlier in this chapter), which has frequent connections to Copenhagen, trains arrive about twice an hour during the day, pulling into the station at Hornbæk (trip time: 22 min.).

By Bus   Bus no. 340 journeys here about once an hour, taking 30 minutes.

By Car   Drive northeast along the coastal road (Rte. 237) from Helsingør, following the signs to Hornbæk and/or Gilleleje.

VISITOR INFORMATION   Providing information for the area, **Hornbæk Turistbureau,** Vester Stejlebakke 2A (① **49-70-47-47;** www.hornbaek.dk), is found inside the local library. Hours are Monday 10am to 7pm, Tuesday to Friday 10am to 5pm, Saturday 10am to 2pm.

Tips Insider's Tip

After you've explored the town of Hornbæk and hit the beach, consider taking a trail through a vast tract of public forest, **Hornbæk Plantage** ★, 3km (1¾ miles) east of the center of Hornbæk. The tourist office will give you a free map outlining the best hiking trails. You'll come across Scotch broom, wild roses, and hundreds of pine trees as you follow one of the trails along the coast. We recommend the coastal trail because of its more dramatic scenery, although some of the hiking routes cut inland.

FUN ON THE BEACH & ELSEWHERE

Hornbæk Beach is the big attraction, and swimming conditions are good. The dunes protect the beach from heavy winds. Danes, often from Copenhagen, flock here in summer, but there's always space for sunbathing. The beach offers views over the sea toward Kullen, the rocky promontory jutting out from the Swedish coast.

The municipality cleans the beach daily, and for several years it has been voted one of the cleanest beaches in Scandinavia. A host of activities are available, including water biking or even nude romping. Windsurfing can be arranged at **Surfudlejning** (© 49-70-33-75), at Drejervej 19. Kiosks sell food and drinks; there are toilets, and, for persons with disabilities, boardwalks that are wheelchair-friendly lead to the sea.

The **Havnen** or **Hornbæk Harbor** is a modern, well-equipped harbor with mooring for 200 boats. It lies next to "shanty town," a collection of huts where fishermen check their tackle or hang flatfish out to dry. Facilities with showers are beside the harbor master's office. Charters for fishing trips can be arranged here, and the harbor here is the starting point of an annual Zealand regatta in June.

If you've arrived by train from Helsingør, the harbor is only a 5-minute walk from the depot. Head down Havnevej. After crossing the dunes, you're on the beach, and we hope the day is a sunny one.

At the harbor, you'll see a monument honoring the poet Holger Drachmann, who died here in 1908.

If you'd like to walk through the village, you'll come upon some old fishermen's cottages still standing, and a church from the 17th century with many votive ships hanging from the ceiling. Votive ships are scaled-down replicas that have been blessed by a priest or minister and are designed to honor the sacrifices of men who labor at sea. The church was built in 1737 to take the place of two buildings that were blown down in fierce winds. A bit inland, many Danes have erected summer villas. City officials have planted tree plantations to give shelter from the frequent gales.

SHOPPING

The best outlet for handicrafts is found at **Sylvest Stentøj,** Klosterrisvej 2, Havreholm (© 49-70-11-20), which specializes in beautiful handcrafted stoneware.

WHERE TO STAY

Ewaldsgaardeny Value   Small-scale and deliberately rustic, this hotel prides itself on its role as a simple boardinghouse with few if any of the extras of a full-fledged hotel. It was originally built in 1814 as a post office, with enough stables to house the horses needed for keeping mail deliveries timely. You'll be thrown into a closer series of contacts with the other guests here than in a more anonymous setting, thanks to the small dimensions and rather cramped rooms. Each of these is outfitted with a combination of wallpaper and painted surfaces, sometimes in bright colors, and contains many of the trappings of a thoughtfully decorated private home. Overall, thanks to genuine cheerfulness and thoughtful management, you can have a happy and successful overnight stay here.

Johs. Ewaldswej 5, DK-3100 Hornbæk. ©/fax **49-70-00-82.** 12 units, all w/shared bathroom. DKK765 ($130/£77) double. Rates include breakfast. V. *In room:* No phone.

Havreholm Slot ★ (Finds) The most elaborate and best-accessorized hotel in Hornbæk—and our personal favorite—occupies what was originally built in the 1870s as the private home of a lumber baron and paper manufacturer, Valdemar Culmsee. Designed with a mock-fortified tower and vaguely ecclesiastical Victorian-style ornaments, it sits 4km (2¹/₂ miles) south of Hornbæk, within a large expanse of privately owned field and forest. Overnight accommodations are in a series of independent bungalows set on the hillsides sloping down to a widening of the river on which the property sits. Each is cozy and attractively decorated in a way befitting an upscale private home.

Klosterrisvej 4, Havreholm, DK-3100 Hornbæk. © 49-75-86-00. Fax 49-75-80-23. www.havreholm.dk. 30 units. DKK1,300 ($221/£130) double; DKK2,254 (383/£225) suite. AE, DC, MC, V. Take bus from central Hornbæk marked HAVREHOLM. **Amenities:** Restaurant; bar; 2 pools (1 indoor heated); 9-hole golf course; squash court; fitness room; Jacuzzi; sauna; laundry service; dry cleaning; nonsmoking rooms; solarium; rooms for those w/limited mobility. *In room:* TV, Wi-Fi, minibar, hair dryer, trouser press, safe.

WHERE TO DINE

Havreholm Slot ★ FRENCH/INTERNATIONAL Food-savvy yacht owners and their cronies head for the most appealing restaurant in the region, lying in the previously recommended Havreholm Slot hotel, in a grand 19th-century dining room whose original accessories remain for the most part intact. Part of its allure for art historians and Danish nationalists derives from the wall murals commissioned in 1872 by the owner of the house and painted by Danish artist Joakim Skovgaard. The result was an interpretation of the Creation and the Garden of Eden in 12 panels. In addition to the mural-decked dining room, there are three other dining areas, each with a fireplace. A well-trained chef produces the best food in town, with menu items that change with the seasons. The finest examples include a salad of fresh mussels, fresh salmon served with a vegetable terrine, breast of chicken delectably cooked with mushrooms and red-wine sauce, and an especially fine choice, roasted oxtail in red-wine sauce.

Klosterrisvej 4, Havreholm. © **49-75-86-00.** Reservations recommended. Fixed-price menus DKK200 ($34/£20) for 1 course, DKK325 ($55/£33) for 2 courses, and DKK480 ($82/£48) for 3 courses. AE, DC, MC, V. Daily noon–2pm and 6–9pm.

Hornbæk Bodega DANISH/INTERNATIONAL Set near the water, in a century-old building in the center of town, this deservedly popular place resembles an English pub more closely than anything else in Hornbæk. Surrounded by forest green walls, you'll be seated on the black leather upholstery of what used to serve as seats for an old-fashioned English train. No one will mind if you drop in for a drink. But if you're hungry, menu items include lots of American-derived items such as well-stuffed club sandwiches and juicy burgers, and such Danish standards as *frikadeller,* fish filets with shrimp and asparagus, liver pâté with bacon and mushrooms, and fried plaice. Fried plaice is to the Dane what Dover sole is to the English.

A.R. Friisvej 10. ✆ **49-20-00-12.** Reservations not accepted. Main courses DKK199–DKK249 ($34–$42/£20–£25). DC, MC, V. June–Aug Sun–Thurs 11am–midnight, Fri–Sat 11am–4am; Sept–May Mon–Fri 5–11pm, Sat–Sun 5pm–2am.

Søstrene Olsen ★ DANISH/CONTINENTAL   Imagination is not this restaurant's strong point, but if you want time-tested dishes, prepared to lip-smacking delight, this is the place to dine. Set near the sea, close to the center of town, the building that houses this restaurant was originally constructed in the 1880s as the summer home of a wealthy woman who spent most of her winters in Copenhagen. Today, it's a winner, partly because of the flavorful cuisine that emerges on steaming platters from the hardworking kitchen staff. The well-chosen menu is changed every 2 weeks and is seasonally adjusted. We like the gratin of lobster with an herby green sauce so much it's hard to sample any other dish. But Danish friends recommend the filets of monkfish served with fresh shrimp and "liquefied" spinach, or the mussels marinara, a heaping bowl seasoned just right. Danes delight in the fried eel with mashed potatoes like grandma made, but you may happily settle instead for the tender filet of Danish beef with a savory tomato cream sauce.

Øresundsvej 10. ✆ **49-70-05-50.** Reservations recommended. Main courses DKK240–DKK289 ($41–$49/£24–£29); fixed-price dinner DKK448 ($76/£45). AE, DC, MC, V. Daily noon–4pm and 5:30–9pm. Closed Dec–Mar.

HORNBÆK AFTER DARK

Two of the busiest and most oft-mentioned watering holes in Hornbæk are particularly active during the summer months. Our preferred choice, and the more historic of the two, is **Hornbæk Bodega,** A.R. Friisvej 10 (✆ **49-70-28-88**), a previously recommended restaurant (see above). Set within what was originally conceived as the town's movie theater, it attracts socializing young Danes like a magnet every evening as the dinner service begins to wind down. Come here for a drink of beer or schnapps, or for some dance music if your visit happens to fall on a Friday or Saturday night (10pm to around 5am year-round). When there is dance music, a cover charge of DKK50 ($8.50/£5) pays for the first drink. The Bodega's most visible competitor is **Café Paradiso,** Havnevej 3 (✆ **49-70-04-25**). This is a lively and hell-raising English-inspired pub that offers live music every Friday and Saturday night 9pm to 5am, with no cover.

---

5 GILLELEJE

59km (37 miles) N of Copenhagen; 30km (19 miles) NW of Helsingør

The great philosopher Søren Kierkegaard used Gilleleje as an escape from his world—and so can you. In World War II, it became the port for yet another escape, as Danish Jews fled here from the Nazis. The daring local fishermen in their colorful wooden-hulled fishing boats—sometimes under heavy gunfire—transported the refugees into neutral Sweden.

The northernmost town in Zealand, Gilleleje offers Blue Flag beaches (meaning their waters are not polluted), the leafy glades of the nearby Gribskov forest in the south, and a typical Danish landscape with straw-roofed houses and a large fishing harbor. In all, there are 14km (8²/₃ miles) of coastline with plenty of sandy beaches for water lovers of all ages.

Gilleleje Harbor is the center of local life. As soon as dawn breaks, fishing boats of all sizes make their way into North Zealand's largest industrial port, and they can be seen unloading their catch. Look for the fish auction hall to see the night's catch being sold in a unique language understood only by the initiated. There are many smokehouses along the harbor used for smoking the fish.

Later you can go for a walk in the town itself, with its many small and large shops. On Thursdays and Saturdays, you can experience a Zealand *mylder* (market), when the town square becomes a marketplace with stalls and booths vying to take your kroner. Horse-drawn carriage rides and street music provide an added bonus.

ESSENTIALS

GETTING THERE   **By Train**   During the day, two trains an hour arrive from Hillerød (trip time: 30 min.), and there is also frequent service from Helsingør (40 min.).

By Bus   Buses link all the towns of North Zealand. For example, bus no. 340 links Gilleleje with Hornbæk (20 min.), and with Helsingør (50 min.). Bus no. 363 links Gilleleje with Tisvildeleje, but the awkward route takes about an hour. The bus and train depot in Gilleleje adjoin each other. It's only a 5-minute walk from the bus and train stations down to the harbor.

By Car   Follow Route 237 west from Helsingør (see earlier in this chapter).

VISITOR INFORMATION   The **Gilleleje Turistbureau** is at Gilleleje Hovedgade 6F (© **48-30-01-74;** www.visitgribskov.dk). June to August, it's open Monday to Saturday 10am to 6pm; September to May, it's open Monday to Friday 10am to 4pm and Saturday 10am to noon.

EXPLORING THE AREA

When you tire of the beaches, take a stroll through the old town, with its narrow streets and well-preserved old houses, no two alike. In the center of town stands the Sladrebænken, or "gossip bench," where you can rest and spread some rumors.

From the harbor, you can take the signposted Gilbjergstien path, offering panoramic views over the sea. This will take you to the **Søren Kierkegaard Stone,** a monument to Denmark's most renowned philosopher. As long ago as 1835, he was one of the first visitors to appreciate the beauty and tranquillity of this place. If you want to get existential while standing here, you can repeat his words: "I often stood here and reflected over my past life. The force of the sea and the struggle of the elements made me realize how unimportant I was."

But most summer visitors come here for the beaches. Gilleleje has an unbroken coastline on either side, stretching from Gilbjerg to Kullen, running from Kattegat in the north to Øresund in the southeast. The city has lifeguards posted in several places along the coast. Many of the bathing beaches have modern toilets, little kiosks, and, often, good restaurants. Several beaches also have ramps leading down to the water for the benefit of wheelchair users.

Within a green space adjacent to the sea, an area that forms part of the landscaping around the recommended Gilleleje Museum and the town's public library, stands a bronze statue called *Teka Bashofar Gadol,* a Hebrew phrase meaning "Let the mighty shofar proclaim." The statue was donated by a wealthy Israeli patron of the arts, Yul Ofer, and was unveiled in the spring of 1997 to commemorate the flight of Danish Jews from the Nazis in 1943. Gilleleje was the point of departure for some 2,000 Jews who fled to Sweden from the town and other places along the North Coast. Risking their own lives, people in the town and country harbored Jews until they could secure passage on a ship to Sweden.

From a 19th-century fishermen's house to artifacts of the Middle Ages, curators have thrown relics of their past into a somewhat disorganized cultural stew at the **Gilleleje Museum,** Vesterbrogade 56 (℗ **48-30-16-31**). The museum traces the development of the area from the early Middle Ages, although some exhibits go back before recorded history. Panoramas present both shorebirds and migratory birds. The museum, along with Gilleleje's library, is housed in the **Pyramiden,** the Pyramid cultural center where traditional and modern buildings have been integrated into a harmonious whole. There is a fascinating exhibit related to the rescue of the Danish Jews in 1943. The museum is open year-round, Tuesday to Sunday, 1 to 4pm. Admission costs DKK30 ($5.10/£3) for adults; children ages 18 and under are free.

Less than a kilometer (½ mile) east of town stands the world's first coal-fired lighthouse, **Nakkehoved Østre Fyr,** Fyrvej 20 (℗ **48-30-16-31**). Dating from 1772, it has been restored and turned into a nautical museum. You can drive there—its location 2.5km (1½ miles) east of town is marked from the town center (follow the signs marked NAKKEHOVED ØSTRE FYR). But the more invigorating method of reaching the lighthouse involves walking along a coastal footpath beginning in Gilleleje at Hovedgade on the east side of the fishing museum. It's open only June to September, Wednesday to Monday 1 to 4pm, charging an admission of DKK15 ($2.60/£1.50) for adults; children ages 11 and under are free.

Fiskerhuset (Old Fisherman's House) and **Skibshallen** (Ship Hall) are at Hovedgade 49 (℗ **48-30-16-31**). "We've always looked to the sea," a local fisherman told us. "It's sustained our lives. Sometimes it took the lives of our brave men, but, even so, the sea and the food it gave us has always made it our faithful friend, although it gets turbulent at times." This is a restored fisherman's dwelling from the 1820s. The Hall presents the history of fishermen in the area from the Middle Ages to the present day, using the fishing hamlets between Hundested and Helsingør as the points of departure. The museum—on the main street—uses a variety of panoramic scenes, models of the boats, and exhibits on trades associated with fishing, to reveal how the industry has dominated local life. The hours and prices are the same as those previously mentioned for the lighthouse.

At Dronningmølle, the **Rudolph Tegnersmuseum** ★, Museumsvej 19, in Villingerød (℗ **49-71-91-77;** bus: 340), is set 7km (4⅓ miles) southwest of Gilleleje. You can reach it by driving southwest along the coastal route (no. 237) and then following the signs pointing south to the museum from Dronningmølle. Surrounded by heather-covered hills that might remind you of Scotland (although this region of Zealand is often referred to as "Russia"), this museum is devoted to the artist Rudolph Tegner (1873–1950). "So why should I come here to see the works of what's-his-name?" you might ask. Tegner is worth discovering, as his art is provocative with disturbing elements. "He makes you think," the curator told us. "Isn't that reason enough to come here?" At the end of your visit, you'll have to answer the big question for yourself: Was Tegner, born in 1873, the great artist he considered himself to be, an art megalomaniac, a crazy genius, or the world's worst sculptor? Fourteen of his bronzes are displayed in an adjacent sculpture park, 17,000 hectares (42,000 acres) of protected countryside. The museum houses Tegner's collection of 250 sculptures in plaster, clay, bronze, and marble, some of monumental proportions. Selected pieces of furniture from the artist's home and a sarcophagus containing his body make the museum a monument to this individual and controversial avant-garde artist. It's open April 15 to May, Tuesday to Sunday noon to 5pm; June to August, Tuesday to Sunday 9:30am to 5pm; September to the third Sunday in October,

Tuesday to Sunday noon to 5pm. It's closed the rest of the year. Admission costs DKK45 ($7.70/£4.50) for adults and is free for children under age 12.

SHOPPING

There are more shops in Gilleleje, per capita, than virtually any other small town in Zealand. At least part of that is attributable to the discretionary income of many of the well-heeled vacationers who flock here, or perhaps it's the tradition of buying and selling antiques that has been a part of the civic consciousness here since the 1960s. In any event, a walk up and down the length of the **Vesterbrogade** will reveal lots of small boutiques whose collective inventories might enrich the aesthetics of your home or office.

J.S. Antiques, Ferlevej 55–57, Ferle (✆ **49-71-79-79**), is one of the biggest and most visible antiques stores in town. Another store that has garnered a devoted clientele from all around the world because of its knowledge of antique Danish porcelain, especially Royal Copenhagen, is **Antik Ulla,** Vesterbrogade 46 (✆ **48-30-07-58**).

Know before you begin your barnstorming of Gilleleje's antiques stores that opening hours are relaxed to the point of being almost chaotic. In *most* cases, shops open daily except Monday and Tuesday, roughly 11am to 4 or 5pm, depending on business and the mood of the shopkeeper. Most, however, maintain extensions of the phone numbers listed that ring in their homes, so a call in advance will sometimes do the trick in getting a shop to open.

WHERE TO STAY

Hotel Strand If you were a bathing beauty who arrived in your bulky swimming costume for a dip in 1896, you wouldn't recognize this long-established hotel today. It's kept abreast of the times, but in doing so has lost a lot of its original architectural adornment. Nonetheless, if you're not a romantic, you'll find a well-managed hotel with functionally furnished, yet comfortable, rooms. Most of the fairly spacious bedrooms contain private bathrooms with showers; only a handful of occupants have to use the corridor bathrooms. Bookings are heavy in summer, so reserve well in advance. The Strand is aptly named, as it lies only a 2-minute walk from the sands and the old fishing harbor.

Vesterbrogade 4D, DK-3250 Gilleleje. ✆ **48-30-05-12.** Fax 48-30-18-59. 25 units, 22 with bathroom. DKK990 ($168/£99) double w/private bathroom; DKK820 ($139/£82) double w/shared bathroom; DKK1,100 ($187/£110) suite. Rates include breakfast. AE, DC, MC, V. **Amenities:** Breakfast room; bar; lounge; laundry service; dry cleaning; nonsmoking rooms. *In room:* TV, Wi-Fi, minibar (in some), fridge (in some), hair dryer.

WHERE TO DINE

Brasseriet ★ DANISH The setting is evocative: a yellow-brick building moving into its second century. Once it was a general store serving the fishing industry at the harbor. Today its hardworking staff attracts an array of visitors who come for the good-tasting food but like to avoid more formal dining choices. As so many Danish restaurants "go French," the owners here claim there's nothing wrong with serving their own version of regional food. Therefore, you get such classics as plaice sautéed in butter and served with new potatoes, chopped parsley, and browned butter. This is perhaps the most frequently served fish dish in the country. For something more exotic, order the steaming mussels flavored with saffron and fresh herbs. Each night a seafood kebab offers the market-fresh catch of the day studded with shrimp and scallops. The meat eater can take delight in the beautifully marbled and tender rib-eye steak. If you'd like to dine light at lunch, you can order *smørrebrød* along with freshly made salads.

Nordre Havnevej 3. ℂ **48-30-21-30.** Reservations recommended. Lunch *smørrebrød* DKK50–DKK135 ($8.50–$23/£5–£14); main courses DKK165–DKK210 ($28–$36/£17–£21). AE, DC, MC, V. Daily noon–4pm and 6–9:30pm.

Fyrkroen ★ DANISH When the lights go on in the harbor and the cool (often chilly) breezes blow in from Sweden, there is no more romantic place to be than sitting at a table at this first-class restaurant. You not only get panoramic views of the sea but also can enjoy the restaurant's historic charm. Back in 1772, the setting was a lighthouse. A low-slung, white-painted stone building was erected adjacent to the lighthouse for the restaurant itself. If the weather is right, try for a table on the alfresco terrace or else retreat indoors to enjoy the nautical decor of ships and the sailors who manned them.

Using market-fresh ingredients, the chef gives each dish a personal stamp. The kitchen still prepares homemade soups every day, none better than the shrimp. You might also start with some delectable smoked salmon or a freshly made salad with crisp lettuce. The steaks are tender to the fork and the palate, but most diners opt instead for such freshly caught fish as halibut, salmon, and perch, which, more or less, can be cooked to your specifications.

Fyrvejen 29. ℂ **48-30-02-25.** www.fyrkroen.dk. Reservations recommended, especially when weather is clear. Main courses DKK65–DKK149 ($11–$25/£6.50–£15); fixed-price menus DKK288–DKK388 ($49–$66/£29–£39). DC, MC, V. May–Oct daily noon–9pm; Nov–Dec and Mar–Apr Thurs–Sun noon–9pm. Closed Jan–Feb. From Gilleleje drive 4km (2½ miles) west, following signs to Hornbæk.

---

6 TISVILDELEJE

59km (37 miles) NW of Copenhagen; 25km (16 miles) W of Helsingør; 18km (11 miles) NW of Hillerød; 71km (44 miles) N of Roskilde

If heather-covered hills, gloriously wide sandy beaches backed by low dunes, and a forest of dramatic wind-tormented trees is your idea of a good time, make it to the seaside village of Tisvildeleje. We find it the most idyllic along the coast, the perfect place for a writer to complete that novel (more likely a screenplay these days). Tisvildeleje—the largest settlement in the region known as Tisvilde—opens onto the broadest stretch of white sandy beaches in Zealand, although the waters, even in July, will be too cold for you if you're accustomed to Florida-like temperatures. The best beach is less than 1.5km (1 mile) west of the center of the resort. It has a changing room and toilets and also a spacious parking lot.

People also come here for walks through **Tisvilde Hegn,** a wind-swept forest of heather-covered hills and trees twisted by the cold Nordic winds.

ESSENTIALS
GETTING THERE By Train From Hillerød, trains run to Tisvildeleje once an hour during the day (trip time: 30 min.).

VISITOR INFORMATION Tisvilde Turistinformation, Banevej 8 (ℂ **48-70-74-51**), is open Monday to Saturday 9am to 4:30pm and Sunday 10am to 3pm, but only from June to August.

GETTING AROUND Bike rentals are available at **Servicehjørnet,** Hovedgade 54 (ℂ **48-70-71-06;** www.visitgribskov.dk). You can rent one for DKK90 ($15/£9) per day.

To the west of the center, running alongside Tisvilde Hegn, one of Denmark's largest forests, is a 1.2km (³/₄-mile) stretch of white sandy beaches lapped by clean salty waters and fringed by dunes and woodland. The surroundings here are exceptionally clean and unspoiled. Volunteers work to see that this whole area of coastline is the most thoroughly inspected and litter-free in Denmark. A blue flag flies over the beach, meaning that the waters are not polluted.

In town you can visit **Tibirke Kirke,** Tibirke Kirkevej (© **48-70-77-85**), which is open Monday to Saturday 8am to 4pm, with Sunday devoted to a church service. Admission is free. This church was probably built around 1120 on a pagan site. In the latter part of the 14th century, it was enlarged and the nave provided with arches. At that time, the small Roman windows were replaced with larger Gothic ones. In the middle of the 15th century, a larger choir also replaced the original one. The tower was built during the first half of the 16th century, but has been reconstructed many times since. During a period of terrible sand drifts, the church was laid waste. But it was eventually restored, and in 1740 a baroque altarpiece was added, with a picture by J. F. Krügell depicting the Last Supper.

At the foot of the church is a spring that may have been the place where pilgrims came in olden days.

Tisvilde Hegn is enchanting and usually windblown. The forest is crossed with many trails, our favorite being a dirt path south to Troldeskoven, a distance of about 2.5km (1.5 miles). Nordic winds have turned the trees into "sculptures" of rather haunting shapes—one is called "Witch Wood." The tourist office (see "Visitor Information," above) will provide trail maps.

SHOPPING

Every Saturday between June and September, 10am to 2pm, a large, lively flea market, **Tisvilde Loppemarked** (Tisvilde Flea Market), is held at Birkepladsen, in front of Tisvildeleje's railway station. This is the time locals empty their attics, divesting themselves of things they might have inherited or acquired and don't really want. There's also a collection of crafts and, in some cases, used clothing.

WHERE TO STAY

Kildegaard ★ Finds   It's down-home and friendly, a most comfortable place to stay at a reasonable price. This is an engaging and likable small hotel whose owners, the Tetzschner family, work hard to create an intimate, cozy environment for guests who tend to return year after year. The centerpiece of the complex is a century-old farmhouse whose space is supplemented with outbuildings. Guests spend their days swimming at the nearby beach, playing volleyball or sleeping in hammocks strung across the garden, and enjoying a menagerie of family pets. Rooms are unpretentious and summery, and each is outfitted with a mishmash of simple contemporary furniture. Dinner platters are served only to residents who request them in advance. The establishment is located in the heart of town, a short walk from the tourist information office.

Hovedgaden 52, DK-3220 Tisvildeleje. © **48-70-71-53.** www.kildegaard-tisvildeleje.dk. 27 units, all w/ shared bathroom. DKK720 ($122/£72) double. Rates include breakfast. No credit cards. **Amenities:** Dining room; lounge. *In room:* No phone.

Tisvildeleje Strand Hotel   If your needs are a little grander than Kildegaard can provide, then check into what locals call "the Strand." This is one of the few structures in Tisvildeleje that preceded the building boom of the 1920s, when wealthy Copenhagen families bought up much of the seafront and constructed summerhouses. Conceived in 1897 as a grocery store and livery stable, it has been rebuilt and expanded many times until it reached its present form: four interconnected buildings encircling a verdant courtyard and a massive chestnut tree. Don't expect a lot of amenities to amuse and entertain you, as the focus is on beach life (the sea is only 90m/295 ft. away) and walks in the nearby forest. Rooms are functionally comfortable, summery, and unpretentious.

Hovedgaden 75, DK-3220 Tisvildeleje. © **48-70-71-19.** Fax 48-70-71-77. www.strand-hotel.dk. 29 units, 8 w/private bathroom. DKK695 ($118/£70) double w/shared bathroom; DKK895–DKK1,295 ($152–$220/£90–£130) double w/private bathroom. Rates include breakfast. MC, V. **Amenities:** Restaurant; bar; lounge. *In room:* No phone.

WHERE TO DINE

Bio-Bistro ⓥⒶⓛⓤⓔ DANISH/INTERNATIONAL   "We will feed you well, and at a good price, but we don't expect you to call the gourmet magazines if you eat with us." That was a waiter's candid appraisal of this well-respected dinner-only bistro next to a movie theater. It offers food that is praised by the owners of various B&Bs in town without restaurants of their own. In a setting that's vaguely reminiscent of the kind of brasserie you might expect in Paris or Lyons, you can order good-tasting lunches (sandwiches, burgers, croque-monsieur), but only during the peak of midsummer. Like many regional restaurants, the bistro serves mainly French and Danish dishes—and does so rather well, in our view. The chicken with wine sauce is always a dependable choice, but we find the salmon with a mousseline sauce even more alluring. The tender, well-cooked steaks served here are a good advertisement for Danish beef.

Hovegården 38. © **48-70-41-91.** Main courses DKK100–DKK235 ($17–$40/£10–£24). MC, V. June–Aug daily 6–10pm; Sept–May Fri–Sat 6–10pm.

7 ROSKILDE ★★

32km (20 miles) W of Copenhagen

If you have only 1 day for North Zealand, we'd skip the highly touted and touristy "Hamlet's Castle" and make the trek to Roskilde instead. It's that special.

Next to Copenhagen, this is Zealand's second-largest town, with one of its longest histories, dating back to 998. It's true that much of this thriving town is devoted to industry, but there are many remnants of its illustrious past as a royal residence in the 10th century and the spiritual capital not only of Denmark but of Northern Europe in the 12th century. The Vikings used Roskilde Fjord to sail in from the open sea after their conquests.

Royal tombs, Viking boats, and one of northern Europe's biggest open-air rock festivals keep the visitors coming.

Roskilde, once a great ecclesiastical seat, was Denmark's leading city until the mid–15th century. Today the twin spires of **Roskilde Cathedral** stand out from the Danish landscape like elegantly tapered beacons. These towers are the first landmark you see when approaching the city that celebrated its 1,000th anniversary in 1998.

Roskilde may be centuries past its peak, but it is no sleepy museum town. It's filled with a dynamic student community, boutique-filled walking streets, several landmarks and major sights, and a population of more than 52,000 people who call themselves Roskildenser.

Toward the end of the first millennium (A.D.), the Vikings settled the area, drawn, no doubt, by its sinuous coastline, where they could launch their ships. In 1957, divers in the Roskilde Fjord came upon shards of wood and reported their findings. Their discovery turned out to be bigger than anyone imagined. Here, sunken and mud-preserved, were five Viking ships that presumably had been put there to block the passage of enemy ships.

Archaeologists began the painstaking job of building a water-tight dam and draining that section of the fjord, while keeping the chunks of splinters of wood wet enough so as not to cause them to disintegrate. Splinter by splinter they began the reconstruction and reassembly of the boats—a process that continues today. You can see their efforts on display at the **Viking Ship Museum** (see below), a modern museum that contains the five ancient ships.

Between A.D. 990 and A.D. 1000, Roskilde's prominence grew, becoming the home of the royal residence. By the 11th century, a Catholic church and a Bishop's Seat resided at Roskilde, which was to remain Denmark's capital until the Reformation in 1536.

At that time all the parish churches were abolished and the Catholic hierarchy disappeared. The government and the monarchy moved to Copenhagen. Nonetheless, at its peak, Roskilde's importance was expressed in its architecture. By 1150, it was surrounded by an embankment and a moat, inside of which stood 12 churches and a cathedral. In 1170, Bishop Absalon built a new church on the site where Harald Bluetooth had erected his church 2 centuries before. Though it took 300 years to construct, and was subsequently burned, destroyed, ravaged, and rebuilt, Absalon's cathedral laid the foundation for the existing Roskilde Cathedral or Domkirche, which today is a UNESCO World Heritage Site.

ESSENTIALS

GETTING THERE **By Train** Trains leave three times an hour from Copenhagen's Central Railroad Station on the 35-minute trip to Roskilde.

By Bus Buses depart from Roskilde several times daily from Copenhagen's Central Railroad Station.

By Car Take the E-21 express highway west from Copenhagen.

VISITOR INFORMATION The **Roskilde-Egnens Turistbureau,** Gullandsstræde 15 (© 46-31-65-65; www.visitroskilde.com), provides pamphlets about the town and the surrounding area. The office is open August 23 to March 31 Monday to Thursday 10am to 5pm, Friday 9am to 4pm, and Saturday 10am to 1pm; April 1 to June 27 Monday to Friday 9am to 5pm and Saturday 10am to 1pm; June 28 to August 22 Monday to Friday 9am to 6pm and Saturday 10am to 2pm.

SPECIAL EVENTS The **Roskilde Festival** ★★ (© 46-36-66-13; www.roskilde-festival.dk) is one of Northern Europe's best outdoor concerts. We first discovered it when we journeyed here to see David Bowie. It is held June 29 to July 2 on a large grassy field, attracting fans of rock and techno music. To get information on the festival—dates and performances—call the above number or contact the Roskilde-Egnens Turistbureau (see above).

SEEING THE SIGHTS

Roskilde Domkirke ★★★ There's no church in Copenhagen, or anywhere else in Denmark for that matter, to rival this towering edifice. This cathedral made Roskilde the spiritual capital of Denmark and northern Europe. Today it rises out of a modest townscapelike a mirage—a cathedral several times too big for the town surrounding it.

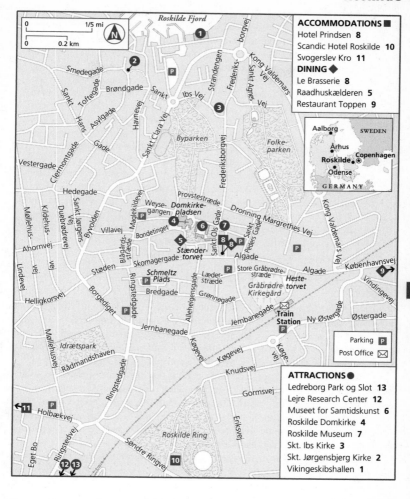

Construction started in 1170, when Absalon was bishop of Roskilde. Work continued into the 13th century, and the building's original Romanesque features gave way to an early Gothic facade. The twin towers weren't built until the 14th century.

Today the cathedral's beauty goes beyond a single architectural style, providing almost a crash course in Danish architecture. Although damaged by a fire in 1968, the cathedral has been restored, including its magnificent altarpiece.

The Domkirke is the final abode of 38 Danish monarchs whose tombs are here, ranging from the modest to the eccentric. Not surprisingly, Christian IV, the builder king who was instrumental in the construction of nearly all of Copenhagen's famous towers and castles, is interred in a grandiose chapel here with a massive sculpture of himself in

Czarina's Remains Returned to Russia

A historical footnote occurred in Denmark at the Roskilde Cathedral in 2006. In a bizarre episode, the remains of Czarina Maria Feodorovna, the mother of Russia's last emperor, made her final journey from Roskilde to St. Petersburg. Her saga began at birth, in 1847, when she was born Princess Dagmar, the daughter of Denmark's King Christian IX and Queen Louise. She was later to marry Alexander and convert to the Russian Orthodox faith. She had six children, one of whom was Nicholas II, who became czar in 1894 and was executed a year after the Bolshevik Revolution. Fleeing from the Imperial capital, Maria Feodorovna made it to the Crimean Peninsula, where a British navy ship took her to London. She continued to Copenhagen, where she lived until her death in 1928. Buried at Roskilde, she rested along with other Danish royalty. In September of 2006 she was transferred to St. Petersburg, where she was reburied with relatives in the Peter and Paul Cathedral. Until the day she died, she refused to believe that her husband and children had been executed in 1918, 16 months after Czar Nicholas had abdicated the throne. "She is reunited with her beloved family once again," said Dimitry Romanoc, an 80-year-old retired bank clerk and distant relative.

combat, a bronze likeness by the Danish sculptor Bertel Thorvaldsen. In humble contrast is a newer addition, from 1972, of the simple brick chapel of King Frederik IX, which stands outside the church. This chapel is octagonal in shape and decorated with hand-painted tiles designed by the architects Johannes and Inger Exner and Vilhelm Wohlert. Other notable tombs include the white marble sarcophagus of Queen Margrethe I.

In King Christian I's Chapel, which dates from the 15th century, there is a column marked with the heights of several kings. The tallest monarch was Christian I, at 2.1m (6 ft. 9 in.). This, no doubt, was an exaggeration, as his skeleton measures only 1.9m (6 ft. 2 in.). A large, bright cupola graces the late-18th- and early-19th-century chapel of King Frederik V. Note also the Gothic choir stalls, each richly and intricately carved with details from both the Old and New Testaments.

The gilded winged altar in the choir was made in Antwerp in the 1500s and was originally intended for Frederiksborg Castle. Pictures on the wings of the altar depict scenes from the life of Jesus, ranging from the Nativity to the Crucifixion. Following the fire, the renowned artist Anna Thommesen created a new altar cloth.

For us, the most charming aspect of the cathedral is its early-16th-century clock poised on the interior south wall above the entrance. A tiny St. George on horseback marks the hour by charging a dragon. The beast howls, echoing through the cavernous church, causing Peter Doever, "the Deafener," to sound the hour. A terrified Kirsten Kiemer, "the Chimer," shakes in fright but pulls herself together to strike the quarters.

Insider's tip: Free concerts on the cathedral's pipe organ, which dates from the 1500s, are often presented at 8pm on Thursdays in summer. They are featured less frequently throughout the rest of the year. Check with the tourist office.

Domkirkestræde 10. © **46-35-16-24.** www.roskildedomkirke.dk. Admission DKK25 ($4.30/£2.50) adults, DKK15 ($2.60/£1.50) children 10–15, free for children 9 and under. Apr–Sept Mon–Sat 9am–5pm, Sun 12:30–5pm; Oct–Mar Tues–Sat 10am–4pm, Sun 12:30–4pm. Bus: 602, 603, or 604.

Vikingeskibshallen (Viking Ship Museum) ★★

If the cathedral weren't reason enough to visit Roskilde, the Viking ships displayed here certainly are. These types of ships sailed to England, to Hamburg on the German coast, and—dare we speculate?—even to the east coast of North America. Displayed here are five vessels found in Roskilde Fjord and painstakingly pieced together from countless fragments of wreckage. It's presumed that the craft were deliberately sunk about 20km (12 miles) north of Roskilde at the narrowest section of the fjord to protect the settlement from a sea attack. The discovery was relatively unpublicized until 1957, when the Danish National Museum carried out a series of underwater excavations.

A merchant cargo ship used by the Vikings, a small ferry or fishing boat, and a Danish Viking warship similar to the ones portrayed in the Bayeux Tapestry are also displayed, and a longship—a Viking man-of-war that terrorized European coasts—was also discovered. Copies of Viking jewelry may be purchased in the museum gift shop, and there's also a cafeteria.

To understand the attraction better, you can see a short film, *The Ships of the Vikings,* about the excavation and preservation of the ships and the building and navigation of *Roar Ege,* a Viking ship replica.

In 1997, the Viking Ship Museum opened a museum harbor for its collection of Nordic vessels, including *Roar Ege,* plus another Viking ship replica, *Helge Ask.* The museum's restored sloop, *Ruth,* is also moored here. And workshops where you can try your hand at old maritime crafts, such as rope- and sail-making, woodworking, and other activities, are located opposite the Boat Yard.

Vindebader 12. © **46-30-02-00.** www.vikingeskibsmuseet.dk. Admission May–Sept DKK95 ($16/£9.50) adults; Oct–Apr DKK55 ($9.40/£5.50) adults; free for children 16 and under. Daily 10am–5pm. Bus: 216 or 607.

Roskilde Museum

We didn't give this place any stars, and no one will beat you if you skip it; but we always find something intriguing here. Take the strange-looking pictures that satirist Gustav Wied took of his family, for example, or what passed for children's toys in the Middle Ages. Located 90m (295 ft.) from the Town Square, this museum, in a former merchant's house, features exhibits of the celebrated Hedebo embroidery, and regional costumes. Displays also include an *aurochs* (an ancient European ox) skeleton, a unique Viking tomb, and a large number of medieval finds from the town. The museum also has a grocer's courtyard, with the shop in operation.

Skt. Ols Gade 15–18. © **46-31-65-00.** www.roskildemuseum.dk. Admission DKK25 ($4.30/£2.50) adults, free for children 17 and under. Daily 11am–4pm. Closed Dec 24–25 and Dec 31–Jan 1. Bus: 601, 602, 603, or 605.

Museet for Samtidskunst (Museum of Contemporary Art)

This is the artistic center of Roskilde. Invariably, there's always a presentation of interest to "culture vultures." In a beautiful palace from the 18th century, this museum of modern art has frequently changing exhibitions, together with performances, films, and dance and classical-music concerts. It also houses a screening room, presenting programs with Danish and foreign artists. "The Palace Collections" are also housed here, displaying objets d'art and paintings that rich Roskilde merchants and their families collected in the 18th and 19th centuries. Such local fat cats as the Brunns and the Borchs amassed an astonishing array of art and antiques on display today.

Stændertorvet 3D. ℂ **46-31-65-70.** www.mfsk.dk. Admission DKK30 ($5.10/£3) adults, DKK15 ($2.60/£1.50) seniors, free for children 9 and under. Tues–Fri 11am–5pm; Sat–Sun noon–4pm. Bus: 601, 602, 603, or 605.

More Attractions

The **St. Jørgensbjerg quarter** was originally a small fishing village, and a number of old, half-timbered houses, some with thatched roofs, remain. These houses cluster around **Skt. Jørgensbjerg Kirke,** Kirkegade, which stands on the top of a hill with a panoramic view of Roskilde Fjord. This is one of the oldest and best-preserved stone buildings in Denmark. The nave and choir of the church date from the beginning of the 12th century, but the walled-up north door is even older, possibly dating from 1040. Slender billets, found only in wooden churches, are in the corners of the church and in the center of the nave. A model of a *kogge,* a medieval merchant vessel, has been engraved in a wall. The church is open only June 22 to August 31, Monday to Friday 10am to noon. To get here from Roskilde, take bus no. 607 toward Boserup.

The same bus will deliver you to **Skt. Ibs Kirke** ("The Church of St. James"), Skt. Ibs Vej (ℂ **46-35-29-66**), also in the north of Roskilde. Although no longer in use as a church, this ruin dates from around 1100. Abolished as a church in 1808, it was later a field hospital and a merchant's warehouse. Regrettably, the merchant destroyed the tower, the chancel, the porch, and the church vaults of this medieval relic, though he spared the nave. It is open for visits only April 4 to October 17, from sunup to sundown.

Nearby Attractions

Ledreborg Park Og Slot ★   One of the last remaining aristocratic families of Denmark, the Holstein-Ledreborgs, still live in this castle and are willing to share their treasures with you in fair weather. A baroque manor house and French/English-style park 7km (4¹⁄₃ miles) southwest of Roskilde and 43km (27 miles) west of Copenhagen, Ledreborg is one of the best-preserved monuments in Denmark. Built by Johan Ludwig Holstein, a minister to Christian IV, the Holstein-Ledreborg family has owned this 33-room house with a landscaped garden and 88-hectare (217-acre) park for eight generations. Between 1741 and 1757 it was turned from a farmhouse into a baroque manor. Inside are a collection of 17th- and 18th-century antiques and a gallery of Danish paintings. It's approached by a 6km (3³⁄₄-mile) alley of lime trees, some 2 centuries old. Near the manor is a grave dating from the late Stone Age, approximately 3000 B.C.

Allé 2, Lejre. ℂ **46-48-00-38.** www.ledreborgslot.dk. Admission DKK75 ($13/£7.50) adults, DKK45 ($7.70/£4.50) children 3–14. Mid-June to Aug daily 11am–5pm; May to mid-June and Sept Sun 11am–5pm. Closed Oct–Apr. From Copenhagen's Central Railroad Station, take the direct train to Lejre, which leaves hourly and takes 35 min.; from Lejre station, take the 3-min. bus no. 233 to the castle and park. From Roskilde, frequent buses go to Lejre, followed by the short bus ride to the castle and park. Combined ticket for Ledreborg Park Og Slot and Lejre Research Center (see below) DKK130 ($22/£13) adults, DKK70 ($12/£7) children.

Lejre Research Center ★ (Kids)   Imagine being able to wander back into a village reconstructed from the Iron Age. Not only that, but getting to see workers, wearing the costumes of the era, going about their daily chores. You're even invited to take part in these activities. Such a thing is possible if you head here and have some 2 hours to spare. Eight kilometers (5 miles) west of Roskilde, this archaeological research center, Lejre Research Center, is the site of a reconstructed Iron Age community on 10 hectares (25 acres) of woodland. The main feature is clay-walled and thatch houses built with tools just as they were some 2,000 years ago. Staffers re-create the physical working conditions as they thatch Iron Age huts, work fields with *ards* (oxen-pulled plows), weave, and make pottery by an open fire. They also sail in dugout canoes, grind corn with a stone, and bake in direct fire. Visitors can take part in these activities. Jutland black pottery is produced here, and handicrafts and books are for sale at the gift shop. There are tables where you can enjoy a picnic lunch.

Slagealléen 2, Lejre. (*©* **46-48-08-78.** www.lejre-center.dk. Admission DKK100 ($17/£10) adults, DKK60 ($10/£6) children 3–11. Tues–Fri 10am–4pm; Sat–Sun 11am–5pm. Closed mid-Sept to Apr. Take the train from Copenhagen to Lejre, then bus no. 233 to the center. From Roskilde, there are frequent buses to Lejre; then take bus no. 233.

A Boat Tour of the Roskilde Fjord

Roskilde Fjord ★★ is one of the longest and largest in Denmark. A sail will take you along the same watery road that Viking ships used to traverse. The shores of this narrow fjord are peppered with tranquil landscapes set against a backdrop of rolling hills. Forests, windswept reeds, low-lying meadows filled with Danish cows, and little villages along the way greet you as you sail along.

You'll get a leisurely waterside view of the southern parts of Roskilde Fjord by participating in one of the frequent warm-weather tours offered aboard the *Sagafjord,* a steamer from the 1950s whose profile evokes a paddle-wheel steamer on the Mississippi. You can opt for either a lunch or a dinner cruise (2–2¹/₂ hr., and 3¹/₂ hr., respectively), or a shorter midafternoon cruise (90 min.), depending on your schedule. Regardless of what you select, you'll pay a base rate of DKK95 ($16/£9.50), after which your (optional) food costs are extra. A fixed-price lunch aboard the vessel costs DKK255 ($43/£26), with evening meals ranging from DKK295 to DKK475 ($50–$81/£30–£48). Tours are conducted April to October only. They operate daily in June, July, August, and September, and, depending on the schedule, 3 to 5 days a week in April, May, and October. Cruises depart from a prominently signposted (SAGAFJORD TOURS) pier in Roskilde Harbor. For schedules, information, and reservations, contact **Rederiet Sagafjord,** St. Valbyvej 154 (*©* **46-75-64-60**; www.sagafjord.dk).

SHOPPING

The best streets for shopping are the pedestrian thoroughfares **Algade** and **Skomagergade.** Of these, we find that Skomagergade has the best shops. From the 12th century, its name, which literally means "shoemaker street," was where the cobblers of Roskilde plied their trade in the Middle Ages.

At either end of the street, a **triskelion** within a circle has been placed in the pavement. The symbol is three curved lines radiating from the center. It comes from the coins struck in Roskilde from 1018 to 1047. Today this silver coin has been re-created by one of the goldsmiths of Roskilde and is sold as a piece of jewelry at the tourist office (see "Visitor Information," above).

The best time for shoppers to be in Roskilde is for the **market days** every Wednesday and Saturday morning (go after 8am). Fresh fruit and vegetables of the season are sold from stalls on Stændertorvet, the main square by the cathedral, along with many stalls hawking fresh fish and Danish cheese. You can purchase the makings of a picnic, along with beautiful pieces of jewelry, and even mugs and pottery. Vendors also peddle a number of well-made children's clothes.

Roskilde also abounds in specialty shops, notably **Bydr. Lützhøfts,** Købmandsgård, Ringstedgade 6–8 (© **46-35-00-61**), a cozy old grocer's shop selling herring and other delicacies across the counter. The interior of the shop looks as it did during the 1920s, and goods for sale are typical of that era. The building at Ringstedgade 8 is a butcher's shop, **Slagterbutikken O. Lunds,** selling goods made according to recipes from about 1920. You can also explore the merchant's yard with 18th- and 19th-century buildings. Sometimes exhibitions are staged here—for example, depictions of merchants and trade in Roskilde over the past 1,000 years. This shop is open Monday to Friday 11am to 5pm and Saturday 10am to 2pm. Even if you don't purchase anything, this is one of the town's tourist attractions.

The town also has very excellent buys in handicrafts. Head first for **Glasgallerjet** ★, Skt. Ibs Vej 12 (© **46-35-65-36**), a former gasworks near the harbor that now houses the open workshop of a glass blower. Here, the glass blower, who displays marvelous skill, shapes the most beautiful glasses, dishes, vases, and other items. Spectators are able to watch the transformation of a lump of melted glass into a beautiful Danish handicraft on sale at the gallery.

An unusual selection of crafts is found at **Jeppe,** Skomagergade 33 (© **46-36-94-35**), which is run collectively by 20 craftspeople from Roskilde and its environs. They make and sell their own crafts. These are definitely nonfactory goods, and exhibitions are always changing.

SWIMMING

You can swim both in- and outdoors in the Roskilde area, although outdoors might be a bit cool if you're not a Dane. There are several small bathing beaches along Roskilde Fjord, notably **Vigen Strandpark,** directly north of the town. Here you'll find a sandy beach with a jetty, set against the backdrop of green salt meadows. The blue flag flying at this beach means the waters are not polluted.

If you'd like to swim indoors, head for the **Roskilde Badet,** Bymarken 37 (© **46-31-63-63;** bus: 601 toward Vindinge from the center). Admission is DKK30 ($5.10/£3) adults, DKK15 ($2.60/£1.50) children 5 to 15, free for children 4 and under. Hours are Monday and Wednesday 1 to 6pm, Tuesday and Thursday 1 to 8:30pm, Friday 1 to 6:30pm, Saturday 7am to 4pm, and Sunday 8am to 1:30pm. Closed July 1 to 25.

WHERE TO STAY

Hotel Prindsen ★   Although surpassed by the Scandic (see below), the Prindsen has been an enduring favorite for 100 years. We still stay here on occasion and find that it has kept up with the times, even though its foundations date from 1695. Today it offers medium-size, smartly furnished rooms with bathrooms containing tub/shower combinations. Though a bit small, all in all the rooms are cozy nests. We prefer the five rooms on the top floor that have a view of the fjord. All the guest rooms in the newer wing are decorated in a Nordic style with wooden floors. Those in the older section are furnished in a more classic style. Take your choice, as rooms in both sections are equally comfortable. Our favorite pocket of posh here is the extremely spacious and elegant Hans Christian Andersen suite.

Algade 13, DK-4000, Roskilde. © **46-30-91-00.** Fax 46-30-91-50. www.hotelprindsen.dk. 76 units. DKK1,390–DKK1,595 ($236–$271/£139–£160) double; from DKK1,850 ($315/£185) suite. Rates include breakfast. AE, DC, MC, V. Bus: 602 or 603. **Amenities:** Restaurant; bar; sauna; room service; laundry service; dry cleaning; nonsmoking rooms. *In room:* TV, Wi-Fi, minibar, hair dryer, trouser press.

Scandic Hotel Roskilde ★   If you don't mind being housed outside the historic core, this chain-run hotel from 1989 is the best in town if you like modern decor and good facilities. If you're seeking a more romantic atmosphere, head for Svogerslev Kro (see below). Rooms are average size, typically furnished, and very comfortable, with medium-size bathrooms. The hotel also has a good restaurant serving Danish and international dishes, plus a bar. It's on the ring road less than a kilometer (½ mile) south of the green belt, Roskilde Ring, on the southern outskirts of the city.

Søndre Ringvej 33, DK-4000 Roskilde. ✆ **46-32-46-32.** Fax 46-32-02-32. www.scandichotels.com. 98 units. DKK800–DKK1,450 ($136–$247/£80–£145) double; DKK1,490–DKK1,650 ($253–$281/£149–£165) suite. Rates include breakfast. AE, DC, MC, V. Free parking. **Amenities:** Restaurant; bar; fitness center; sauna; children's playroom; babysitting; laundry service; dry cleaning; nonsmoking rooms; solarium; rooms for those w/limited mobility. In room: TV, Wi-Fi, minibar, hair dryer, iron, trouser press.

Svogerslev Kro ★ (Finds)   If you've seen those touristy pictures of a thatched-roof Danish inn, with timeworn and exposed wooden beams, and want to stay in such a place yourself, head here as we so often do. We like to wander around the little village of Svogerslev at night, far removed from the bustle of Copenhagen. Since 1727, this old-time inn has been welcoming visitors who make the 4km (2½-mile) journey west of Roskilde's center. Rooms are medium size (some are a bit small), decorated in modern Danish styling, and well maintained. Many open onto the inn's garden and come equipped with tub/shower combinations. The well-respected kitchen serves open-faced sandwiches at lunch and an array of international dishes at night, including regional specialties. If you're adventurous, request the fried eel; if not, you might happily settle for the breast of guinea fowl with fresh herbs and a red-pepper cream sauce. The chef's stew is made with bacon, onions, and mushrooms, in a paprika sauce. You can always count on baked salmon and some good steak dishes. After a good night's rest under the eaves, you'll be fortified to continue with us on our journey through Denmark.

Hovedgaden 45, Svogerslev, DK-4000 Roskilde. ✆ **46-38-30-05.** Fax 46-38-30-14. www.svogerslevkro. dk. 18 units. DKK900 ($153/£90) double. Rates include breakfast. AE, DC, MC, V. Bus: 602 with hourly connections to the town center. **Amenities:** Restaurant; bar; laundry service; dry cleaning. In room: TV, hair dryer.

Nearby Accommodations

Gershøj Kro ★ (Finds)   A visit here is like wandering back in time to experience Denmark as it used to be. The only problem with this atmospheric hotel is that it's open to individual travelers only 3 months a year, farming out its simple and old-fashioned rooms to members of corporate conventions the rest of the time. If you're lucky enough to arrive during midsummer, you'll be welcomed at an inn (dating from 1830) that's only a few paces from the docks of the fishing hamlet of Gershøj. Expect old-fashioned charm and a restaurant that's known for the variety of ways in which it prepares a time-tested local favorite, eels hauled in from the harbor. June to August, the restaurant is open daily for lunch and dinner.

Havnevej 14, Gershøj, DK-4050 Skibby. ✆/fax **47-52-80-41.** 11 units, all w/shared bathroom. DKK700–DKK1,100 ($119–$187/£70–£110) double. Rates include breakfast. MC, V. Free parking. Closed Sept–May. From Roskilde, drive 14km (8⅔ miles) NW, following the signs to Frederikssund. **Amenities:** Restaurant; bar. In room: No phone.

Osted Kro & Hotel   Frankly, we prefer Gershøj or Svogerslev Kro (see above), but you might not always get into those establishments. View Osted Kro as a lovely consolation prize. There has been a hotel on this site since 1521, functioning as a refreshment stopover for travelers migrating between Roskilde and Ringsted. The roadside inn you'll see today is much newer than that, with a rebuilt original core and a modern annex (constructed in 1985) that holds the establishment's 16 deliberately old-fashioned rooms. Don't expect too many distractions here; other than a restaurant and bar, there isn't a lot to do. Nonetheless, meals are savory and prepared according to old-time Danish recipes.

Hovedvejen 151B, Osted, DK-4000 Roskilde. ℭ **46-49-70-41.** Fax 46-49-70-46. www.ostedkro.dk. 16 units. DKK875 ($149/£88) double. Rates include breakfast. AE, DC, MC, V. From Roskilde, drive 12km (7½ miles) south along Rte. 151, following the signs to Ringsted. **Amenities:** Restaurant; lounge. *In room:* TV.

Skuldelev Kro   A final choice for aficionados of old Danish inns is this solid and reliable choice. In all the years we've been publicizing it, we've yet to get a complaint about it. It is set behind a pale yellow facade in the hamlet of Skuldelev, less than 1.5km (1 mile) from the sea. This Danish inn was built in 1778 and was reconfigured and upgraded from a virtual ruin in the early 1990s. Since its reopening, several branches of Denmark's governmental bureaucracy have designated it as the site for some of their conferences. When one of these isn't going on, you can rent any of the simple but comfortable rooms, with well-kept bathrooms.

Østergade 2A, Skuldelev, DK-4050 Skibby. ℭ **47-52-03-08.** Fax 47-52-08-93. www.hotel-skuldelevkro. dk. 31 units. DKK750 ($128/£75) double. Rates include breakfast. AE, MC, V. From Roskilde, take Rte. 53 north for 26km (16 miles), following the signposts to Skibby. **Amenities:** Restaurant; bar; outdoor pool; sauna; nonsmoking rooms. *In room:* TV, hair dryer.

WHERE TO DINE

La Brasserie ★ STEAK/DANISH/INTERNATIONAL   We've always found this first-rate restaurant, in the previously recommended Prindsen, to be one of the best places in town for dining. The food is well-prepared with market-fresh ingredients. The staff is perhaps the friendliest and most helpful in town, and the decor is in a stylish bistro style, like something in modern Paris. Everything is prepared from scratch, and handpicked Danish raw materials are used whenever possible. The chefs even get their butter from a special dairy; their herring is cured for 8 months in Iceland, and their virgin olive oil comes from a small privately owned farm near Madrid.

It's simple and standard but ever so good, as evidenced by the grilled entrecote with baked herb butter, baked potato, and grilled tomatoes. For a hefty, succulent meal, opt for the sirloin steak cut from Angus beef. Tiger prawns are a delightful concoction served with a raw tomato salsa with lime and cilantro flavorings. Chicken breast with homemade pesto is another reliable dish, as is a lamb kebab marinated in garlic and rosemary. In fair weather, you can dine outside.

Algade 13. ℭ **46-30-91-00.** Reservations recommended. Main courses DKK140–DKK298 ($24–$51/£14–£30). AE, DC, MC, V. Daily noon–10pm.

Raadhuskælderen ★ DANISH   Savvy foodies will often direct you to one of the oldest restaurants in Roskilde, a dining room at the street level of a building erected in 1430 across the street from the town's cathedral. Although it's tempting to remain within the vaulted interior, there's also an outdoor terrace that is pleasant during midsummer, especially because of its view of the cathedral. Menu items are carefully prepared using very fresh ingredients. Some of the chef's best dishes include salmon steak with tartar sauce and grilled and marinated filet of young chicken with sautéed vegetables and a cream sauce flavored with ginger and citrus. Rack of lamb is delectably roasted and served with a sauce made from fresh summer berries.

Stændertorvet, Fondens Bro 1. ✆ **46-36-01-00.** http://raadhuskaelderen.dk. Reservations recommended. Main courses DKK164–DKK258 ($28–$44/£16–£26); lunch main courses DKK128–DKK198 ($22–$34/£13–£20). DC, MC, V. Mon–Sat 11am–11pm.

Restaurant Toppen DANISH   We knew a travel writer who once wrote a book about where to dine with a view. We like views too, but we like the food to be good as well. Both the view and good food are possible at Toppen. At the top of a 1961 water tower, 84m (276 ft.) above sea level, Restaurant Toppen offers a panoramic view of the whole town, the surrounding country, and Roskilde Fjord—all from the dining room. Begin with a shrimp cocktail served with dill and lemon. Main dishes include sirloin of pork a la Toppen with mushrooms and a béarnaise sauce. For dessert, try the chef's nut cake with fruit sauce and sour cream. The restaurant is less than 1.5km (1 mile) east of the town center between Vindingevej and Københavnsvej. The water tower doesn't revolve electronically, but some clients, in the words of the management, "get the feeling that it's turning if they drink enough." There's a free elevator to the top.

Bymarken 37. ✆ **46-36-04-12.** www.restauranttoppen.dk. Reservations recommended. Main courses DKK78–DKK169 ($13–$29/£7.80–£17). DC, MC, V. Mon–Fri 3:30–11pm; Sat–Sun noon–10pm. Bus: 601.

A Nearby Place to Dine

Langtved Færgekro ★ (Finds) DANISH   Frankly, with its romantic setting, this inn could probably get away with serving hot dogs. Fortunately for us, it offers so much more. This isolated Danish inn, a short walk from the hamlet of Munkholm Bro, 5km (3 miles) southwest of the town of Kirke Såby, was inaugurated 250 years ago when a need arose to feed passengers on a nearby ferryboat route. Clients who appreciate a walk in the surrounding forest or along the nearby shoreline before or after enjoying a meal in this historic dining room favor this black-and-white half-timbered restaurant. The seasonal menu items have received several awards for their flavors. The best examples include crepes stuffed with baby shrimp, feta cheese, and herbs; marinated salmon with homemade bread; tender steak with fried onions; and either freshly caught halibut or plaice with hollandaise sauce.

Munkholmvej 138. ✆ **46-40-50-53.** Reservations recommended. Main courses DKK210–DKK240 ($36–$41/£21–£24). No credit cards. Fri–Sun noon–8pm. 5km (3 miles) SW of Kirke Såby; from Roskilde, drive 26km (16 miles) NW, following the signs to Holbæk and then to Munkholm Bro.

ROSKILDE AFTER DARK

One of the most consistently fun and popular nightlife venues in Roskilde is the **Gimle Musikcafe,** Ringstedgade 30 (✆ **46-35-12-13**), where the trappings and ambience of a battered English pub combine with recorded—and in rare instances live—music. A 5-minute walk west from the center of town, it serves simple lunches and dinners, endless steins of Danish and international beer, and a dose of good cheer that's often welcomed by the many regulars—often young—who define this place as their "local."

8

South Zealand & Møn

North Zealand and South Zealand

are a study in contrasts. The great drama and all the three-star man-made attractions, such as "Hamlet's Castle" or the cathedral at Roskilde, lie in the north, and naturally that's where hordes of visitors go. We don't dispute this obvious choice. If you have only 2 or even 3 days for Zealand, the north is a more rewarding target.

But if you have at least 2 days extra to spare, you can take in all the highlights of South Zealand, as travel times are short between sightseeing targets. Zealand may be the largest of all Danish islands, but it is only about the size of the state of Delaware. Even if you have only a day for South Zealand, you can visit it using Copenhagen as your base. If that's the case, we recommend that you confine your trip to the ancient "witch-burning," medieval city of Køge and the offshore island of Møn, both of which can be seen in just 1 day.

Sjælland Syd (its Danish name) is today called a "land of mist and moods," with its prehistoric monuments and ancient towns. Its "cities" are really overgrown towns, and it is blanketed with rolling farmlands, blighted in places by necessary industry. It is also filled with white sandy beaches opening onto rather cold waters.

The land is also filled with medieval churches (we've selected the best of them) and a 1,000-year-old ring fortress at Trelleborg (p. 221). There are often festivals of fine food and music throughout the summer, and there are seemingly endless sailing clubs, which give the ports a real maritime atmosphere, filled with the heady scents of seaweed and tar.

Before Copenhagen or Roskilde emerged, South Zealand loomed large in history as the seat of the Valdemar dynasty of Danish kings. It was also a power player in the Middle Ages and Denmark's ecclesiastical center. In the 1600s, some of the most epic battles between Sweden and Denmark took place here, especially in the seas off Køge. One of Denmark's greatest moments of shame came in 1658, when King Gustav of Sweden marched across the fields of South Zealand heading for Copenhagen. Once here, he forced a treaty that nearly cost Denmark its sovereignty.

Motorists from Køge in the east, heading to Korsør in the west (perhaps to cross the bridge over the Great Belt into Funen), would be wise to steer clear of the dull E20 motorway and follow the scenic and greener Route 150, which will take you through South Zealand's best villages and farmlands.

For Zealand rail or bus information, you can call © **70-13-14-15.**

---

1 KØGE ★

40km (25 miles) S of Copenhagen; 24km (15 miles) SE of Roskilde

The best-preserved medieval town on the island of Zealand lives in infamy as the town that "barbecued" old ladies suspected of witchcraft. "You had your Salem, Massachusetts, and we Danes, regrettably, had our Køge," a Danish historian once told us. The witch burning took place during the 17th century at the Torvet, the market square.

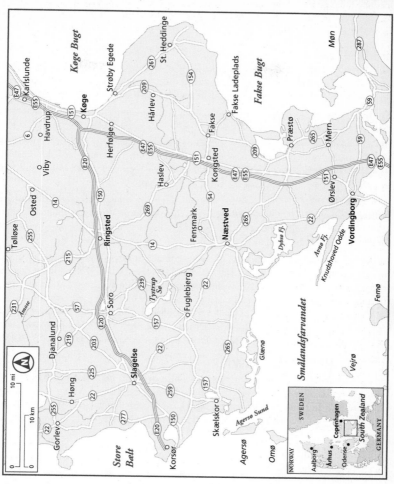

    In about 3 hours, you can explore this old port city on Køge Bay, lying on the east coast of South Zealand. The city was granted a charter by King Erik VI in 1288, but its fame is of another day. The area grew up and prospered because of its natural harbor, becoming a bustling hub of seafaring trade with Germany and a thriving fishing center, exporting its fresh catches to feed the hungry masses of Copenhagen.

    Every Danish schoolboy (or -girl) knows the story of the Battle of Køge Bay, fought here in 1677, one of the major conflicts in the eternal wars with Sweden. The Danish admiral Niels Juel defeated the attacking Swedish navy, thwarting their attempt to conquer Denmark. This made him a national hero, like Admiral Nelson to the British.

Køge, a bustling city of 40,000 with a modern commercial harbor, is visited mainly because it has preserved the narrow, historic streets of its inner core. A fire in 1633 leveled many of the buildings, but others were spared to greet visitors today—and still others were restored to their original appearance.

ESSENTIALS

GETTING THERE **By Train** Take the S-tog extension from Copenhagen, with service every 20 minutes throughout the day (trip time: 35 min.). You can also reach Køge by train from Roskilde (25 min.), and there are also rail links with Næstved (35 min.).

By Bus Bus no. 21 departs for Køge frequently from Copenhagen's Central Railroad Station.

By Car From Copenhagen, head south along the express highway E47/E55. Motorists from Roskilde can take Route 6, connecting with Route 151 south into the heart of Køge. Parking is available at Torvet (but only for an hour at a time); you'll find less restrictive parking at Havnen, north of the yacht harbor.

VISITOR INFORMATION Guided tours of Køge are arranged through the **Tourist Office,** Vestergade 1 (© **56-67-60-01;** www.visitkoge.com), open year-round Monday to Friday 9am to 5pm; June to August Saturday hours are 9am to 2pm; off-season, Saturday hours are 10am to 1pm.

GETTING AROUND **By Bicycle** While at the tourist bureau, you can ask for a free brochure published by the Dansk Cyklist Forbund (Danish Cyclists' Union). It's in English and outlines five biking tours of the nearby area, ranging from a 40km (25-mile) tour that features Vallø Slot (see "Easy Excursions from Køge," later in this chapter), to a 6km (3.75-mile) route that visits the grave of Danish philosopher Nikolai Frederik Grundtvig.

For bike rentals in Køge, contact **HH-Cykler,** Nørre Blvd. 59 (© **56-65-06-10;** www.hhcykler.dk), costing DKK75 ($13/£7.50) per day, plus a deposit of DKK450 ($77/£45).

EXPLORING THE TOWN

Many Copenhageners, especially those with a boat or yacht, flock to **Køge Bay ★★★** in the summer, the way New Yorkers go to the Hamptons. We find the town very sleepy in winter; but in summer, it bursts into bloom and its population swells. The bay is one vast pleasure-boat harbor set against a backdrop of beaches that we find bone-chilling even in July.

The harbor is only a short walk from the medieval center, and it has the same appeal for the people of Køge as Nyhavn does for Copenhageners. We enjoy the atmosphere here and like watching the action in the busy harbor, which is filled with Baltic freighters, fishing boats, and pleasure craft of all types. If you walk to the North Pier, you'll find a number of eating places and cafes in old-fashioned houses, where you can relax over a meal or order a cold Danish beer.

Opening onto the bay is a monument commemorating the battle in Køge Bay. You'll see it standing some 9m (30 ft.) high near the harbor. This granite obelisk bears the names of maritime heroes Niels Juel and Ivar Huitfeldt. Huitfeldt commanded the *Danebrog,* which burst into flames when bombarded by Swedish forces in 1710.

Before taking a look at the bay, wander the medieval streets of Køge's **Gamle Stan ★★★**, or Old Town. You'll pass fish markets selling freshly caught flatfish, herring, and eel. Stroll through the town parks and surrounding woodland and peek into the courtyards of the old buildings left from the Middle Ages. In summer, live street entertainment will amuse you (giving a few kroner to the young musicians is always appreciated, of course).

The best street for wandering is **Kirkestræde,** lined with graceful old houses. A small building on the street, no. 20, is reputed to be the oldest half-timbered house in Denmark, dating back to 1527. A couple of porch stones from the Middle Ages, said to be the only pair in Denmark in their original position, are in front of a house at Smedegarden 13, near an ancient tree.

Of the town's churches, **Sankt Nicolai Church,** Kirkestræde 29 (© **56-65-13-59**), 2 blocks north of Torvet, is a Gothic structure dating from 1450, named after St. Nicholas, patron saint of mariners. History records that King Christian IV watched the Battle of Køge, in which Niels Juel sank many Swedish vessels, from the church tower. The church has a number of art treasures, including an altarpiece by Lorents Jørgensen and 100 tombs of Køge merchants. Note the carved angels on the pews—they are without noses, thanks to drunken Swedish troops who in the 1600s came this way, cutting off the noses with their swords. What sorry fun that must have been for them. Look for a little brick projection at the east end of the church tower. Called *Lygten,* it was for centuries a place where a burning lantern was hung to guide sailors safely back into the harbor. From mid-June to late August, hours are Monday to Friday 10am to 4pm, Sunday noon to 4pm; off-season, Monday to Friday 10am to noon. Admission is DKK10 ($1.70/£1).

On the north side of the Torvet (market square) is the **Køge Rådhus ★★**, believed to be the oldest town hall in Denmark still in use. The building in the rear was erected very early in the 17th century to serve as accommodations for King Christian IV on his trips between the royal palaces in Copenhagen and Nykøbing F (the "F" refers to the island of Falster). You can wander into the courtyard at the town hall to see a modern sculpture created by Jens Flemming Sørensen.

A path for walkers and cyclists leads along the Køge River with access from the center in several places. Go here to enjoy some peace and quiet—and take along a picnic lunch if the weather's fair. There are several delis in town where you can pick up some open-faced sandwiches and drinks to take along. At a park, **Lovparken,** only a 5-minute walk from the Torvet, a wooden bridge takes you across the river, where you have a panoramic view of the riverside and its gardens.

The coastline near Køge offers several fine spots for bathing. Directly north of Køge you'll come upon a land of dunes and lyme grass, with a sandy beach on **Ølsemagle Revle.** Near the city center, **Køge Sydstrand,** or south beach, offers camping sites, and a bit farther south, the beach at **Strøby Ladeplads** is ideal for windsurfers.

Among specific attractions, consider a visit to the following:

Køge Museum ★ As provincial museums go, this is the best in South Zealand, and it can be visited in less than an hour, an especially amusing thing to do on one of the many rainy afternoons in Køge. The museum lies in an old merchant's home from 1610; it is surrounded by a beautiful garden near the town square and is devoted to the cultural history of South Zealand. It consists of six well-furnished rooms and a kitchen with implements used between 1640 and 1899. Displays of costumes, textiles, carriages, farm equipment, crafts from artisan's guilds, and other historical artifacts of the area are featured. Curiously, there's a windowpane where H. C. Andersen scratched the words OH, GOD, OH, GOD IN KØGE. The museum also displays many mementos and personal items belonging to this spinner of fairy tales. The museum also has a desk once owned by

Nikolai Frederik Grundtvig, the Danish philosopher and theologian who used to live on the outskirts of Køge. Also on display are hundreds of silver coins, forming a treasure-trove that may have been hidden for safekeeping during the wars with Sweden in the 1600s. There's also a collection of 322 coins from all over Scandinavia and Europe—the oldest coin is a Palatinate taler from 1548. Your museum ticket, incidentally, is valid—if you use it on the same day—for admission to Vallø Slot, a charming castle that's recommended separately at the end of this section, under "Easy Excursions from Køge."

Nørregade 4. ⓒ **56-63-42-42.** Admission DKK30 ($5.10/£3) adults, free for children 15 and under. June–Aug daily 11am–5pm; Sept–May Tues–Sun 1–5pm.

Kunstmuseet Køge Skitsesambling ★ ⟨Finds⟩   Changing exhibitions and a rather large permanent collection of sketches, sculpture, and contemporary Scandinavian art draw visitors to this art museum devoted mainly to sketches. Its most viewed work is a series of studies that sculptor Edvard Eriksen did for *The Little Mermaid* statue in Copenhagen that's always being decapitated by someone. But there's so much more—some 7,500 models and studies of both paintings and sculptures, the latter conceived mainly for public parks in the country. In English the museum's name translates as "art and sketch collection." What makes this museum unique is that it traces the artist's creative process from conception to execution, from the advent of the idea to the unfolding of the "vision." Original drawings, clay models, and even mock-ups of a particular work are included so that the public can see how a piece of art looks while it's still in the conceptual stage. This approach is particularly fascinating for us to see when a piece of art undergoes a tremendous conceptual change along the way.

Nørregade 29. ⓒ **56-67-60-20.** www.skitsesamlingen.dk. Admission DKK30 ($5.10/£3) adults, DKK15 ($2.60/£1.50) children 5–15, free for children 4 and under. Thurs–Tues 10am–5pm; Wed 10am–8pm.

SHOPPING

We try to time visits to Køge on market days, which take place on Wednesday and Saturday (it's best to go in the morning) at the main market square, **Torvet** ★★, the best-preserved market square from the Middle Ages in Denmark. The town is crowded with people from the countryside, many of whom have products to sell, including fruits, vegetables, Danish cheese, and smoked fish, as well as handicrafts and even secondhand goods. If you have a choice of days, we have found that the Saturday market is livelier. You can wander from stall to stall as street musicians—most often jazz artists—entertain you from courtyards nearby.

The best and largest selection of Danish gifts is found at **Jørgen Müller,** Torvet 3–5 (ⓒ **56-65-25-80**), on the market square. Here you can pick up Georg Jensen silver, exquisite Royal Copenhagen porcelain, Holmegaard glass—you name it. The best selection for women's fashion is **Rokkjoer,** Torvet 2 (ⓒ **56-65-02-58**), which has an impressive array of continental coats, blouses, and dresses—many in what they call "oversize."

For South Zealand antiques, the best outlet is **Antik Bahuset,** Brogade 16E (ⓒ **56-66-17-19**), selling old furnishings, pewter, brass, and a lot of pre-1900 items. It's open only Saturday 10am to 1pm, unless you call for an appointment. Another good antiques store is **Tamalat Antik,** Brogade 22 (ⓒ **56-65-63-10**), with a wide selection of furniture, and good buys in paintings, jewelry, glass, and porcelain. Finally, **Krybben,** Torvet 19 (ⓒ **56-63-02-01**), offers a wide selection of clothing, crafts, shoes, and antiques—an odd mixture, but intriguing nonetheless. A special feature of Krybben is an upstairs gallery exhibiting the works of a talented local painter, Anne Kureer.

For the novelty alone, you might want to visit **Købmandshandel,** Vestergade 6 (© **56-66-30-67**), a grocer's shop of yesterday. Two hundred different sorts of tea, spices from around the world, and everything from olive oils to licorice root to rock candy are on sale—you'll even find syrups, fruity jams, and handmade candles in rainbow colors.

Køge used to be known for its goldsmiths. Thriving since 1979, **Guldsmedien Ejvind Sørensen,** Nørregade 31 (© **56-66-19-91**), is in a charming old building dating from 1612. A selection of gold and silver jewelry is sold here.

For the very best of Scandinavian, especially Danish, design, not only furnishings but also home accessories, head for **Hjelm's Bolighus,** Nørregade 32 (© **56-65-06-30**), the leading design outlet in Køge for more than 4 decades.

WHERE TO STAY

Because of the demand from business travelers, some of these hotels charge higher rates in winter, granting discounts for tourists in summer.

Centralhotellet Køge (Value)   It calls itself a hotel, but it's really a glorified B&B hiding behind a pale blue facade in the heart of town, only a few feet from the tarmac of the street. There's the feeling of a cozy but restored 19th-century house here. Even though it's less well equipped than any other hotel in town, it's reasonably comfortable and most affordable—in fact, the best deal we find in town. The bedrooms are small and rather basic—and you can forget electronic extras such as TVs—but it's a good choice if you want only a bed for the night. Three of the bedrooms come with a tiny bathroom with shower; otherwise, you can use the facilities in the corridor.

Vestergade 3, DK-4600 Køge. © **56-65-06-96.** Fax 56-66-02-07. www.centralhotellet.dk. 12 units, 3 w/ private bathroom. DKK380–DKK650 ($65–$111/£38–£65) double w/shared bathroom; DKK750 ($128/£75) double w/private bathroom. Rates include breakfast. MC, V. **Amenities:** Breakfast room; bar; lounge. *In room:* No phone.

Hotel Hvide Hus   Washington isn't the only place with a White House. The White House (its English name) in Køge lies less than a kilometer (^{1}/2 mile) east of the center, and is a good choice for motorists. Built in 1963 at the height of the Cold War, it reflects the dull architecture of that era, rising two floors in white brick with an angular, glass-and-chrome style. Its most winning features are the panoramic views from its windows of the Bay of Køge, and a beach which lies about 180m (600 ft.) away. The midsize bedrooms are brightly decorated and furnished in Danish modern style, with well-kept tiled bathrooms. The Helnan International Hotel chain recently took over the hotel, and since has improved the service and ambience.

Strandvejen 111, DK-4600 Køge. © **56-65-36-90.** Fax 56-66-33-14. www.hotelhvidehus.dk. 126 units. DKK1,475–DKK1,875 ($251–$319/£148–£188) double; DKK2,900 ($493/£290) suite. Rates include buffet breakfast. AE, DC, MC, V. **Amenities:** Restaurant; bar; sauna; room service; laundry service; dry cleaning; nonsmoking rooms; rooms for those w/limited mobility. *In room:* TV, Wi-Fi, minibar, hair dryer.

Hotel Niels Juel ★   The town's best address since 1989 opens onto the harborfront, and is the place where we always lay our heads in modern comfort. Both the midsize bedrooms and the public lounges are designed with Feng Shui—the famous Chinese interior concept—in mind. Each of the rooms is well maintained and comfortably furnished, with tiled bathrooms. On-site are a cozy bar and a first-class restaurant, Quintus, offering Danish and French food, including fresh salmon, oysters, and mussels, which we find the most tantalizing items on the menu. On the ground floor, hotel guests are often invited for wine tastings from a well-stocked cellar, and there is also a library where guests relax while reading periodicals. The hotel is a safe, reliable, and substantial choice, and the staff is particularly helpful.

Toldbodvej 20, DK-4600 Køge. ✆ **56-63-18-00.** Fax 56-63-04-92. www.hotelnielsjuel.dk. 50 units. Sept–June DKK1,295 ($220/£130) double; July–Aug DKK925 ($157/£93) double; year-round DKK1,695 ($288/£170) suite. Rates include breakfast. AE, DC, MC, V. **Amenities:** Restaurant; bar; wine cellar; sauna; laundry service; dry cleaning; nonsmoking rooms; rooms for those w/limited mobility; solarium. *In room:* TV, Wi-Fi, minibar, hair dryer.

Vallø Slotskro ★ (Finds) This is one of the more enchanting little B&Bs on the southeast coast of Zealand, and it's surrounded by some of the most evocative landscapes on the island at a point 8km (5 miles) south of Køge near Vallø Slot (p. 214), a Renaissance castle from the 16th century. That's not all. The building was ordered built by a king, Christian VII, in 1781, for overflow guests he didn't want running underfoot at his own castle abode. The years have brought changes architecturally—not all successful—and what awaits you today is a well-run guesthouse where each of the small-to-midsize bedrooms is decorated and furnished individually, all comfortably appointed. Only seven come with private bathrooms, each with a tub/shower combination, the occupants of the other rooms sharing the adequate corridor facilities. The best rooms here—and these are assigned first—are those with more space and such extras as minibars, Jacuzzis, and four-poster antique beds.

Slotsgade 1, DK-4600 Køge. ✆ **56-26-70-20.** Fax 56-26-70-71. www.valloeslotskro.dk. 13 units, 7 w/private bathroom. DKK750 ($128/£75) double w/shared bathroom; DKK975 ($166/£98) double w/private bathroom. Rates include breakfast. AE, DC, MC, V. Free parking. **Amenities:** Restaurant; bar. *In room:* TV, minibar.

WHERE TO DINE

Horizonten Café & Restaurant ★★ DANISH/FRENCH On a summer day when the sun's shining, we always request a table on the terrace overlooking the harbor that has played such a major role in Denmark's naval history. This is Køge's premier dining room; the chef and his kitchen brigade are devoted to the memorable dishes they turn out. They are especially skilled with Danish seafood, and whenever possible they use fresh Danish ingredients, although they freely "plagiarize" recipes from the continent, mostly from France. We have found that their fixed-price menu is the best offered by any major restaurant in South Zealand. Most clients wisely request that their fish be grilled, and it's done almost to perfection here and to your specifications. "Americans generally like their fish too dry," the chef told us. "Danes prefer it more juicy." After we devoured the halibut meunière and all the goodies served—yummy desserts, freshly made crisp salads, and vegetables cooked "to the point," never mushy—the summer day was ours.

Havnen 29A. ✆ **56-63-86-28.** Reservations required. Main courses DKK205–DKK220 ($35–$37/£21–£22); fixed-price menus DKK450 ($77/£45). AE, DC, MC, V. Tues–Sun 6pm–midnight.

Restaurant Arken DANISH/FRENCH The chefs here may not be quite as dazzling as those manning the stoves at Horizonten, but they will also feed you well. They, too, have a terrace overlooking the smaller of Køge's two harbors. This 1979 big-windowed restaurant is called "the Ark," because its architecture is like a large wooden boat that would have made Noah green with jealousy. The interior is flooded with sunlight and decorated with varnished wood that evokes the paneling you might find aboard a yacht. During warm weather, we've often seen visitors from Germany devouring the fried eel with stewed potatoes. The cooks aren't interested in show-stopping dishes but prefer to stick to old Danish favorites such as *frikadeller* (meatballs), fresh grilled salmon in a butter sauce, and sautéed beefsteak with mashed potatoes and golden fried onions.

Køge Lystbådehavn 21. © **56-66-05-05.** www.restaurant-arken.dk. Reservations recommended. Main courses DKK168–DKK238 ($29–$40/£17–£24); fixed-price menu DKK228 ($39/£23). DC, MC, V. Daily 11:30am–10pm.

Skipperkroen ★ DANISH/INTERNATIONAL Sailors, yachters, and summer campers flock here for platters of hearty, good-tasting food within a restored 1600s building set across the road from Køge's harbor. Summer laughter and noise resound through the restaurant, where diners enjoy beer, wine, and Danish food. The drinking and dining overflow onto an outdoor garden with tables in summer, but for most of the year clients dine inside in one of two areas. The cooks are loyal to Danish products whenever they are available, both freshly caught fish and vegetables from the countryside. Plaice regularly appears on the menu, and, when the chefs get fancy, they dress it up with fresh shrimp and asparagus, even chunks of lobster meat. The cooks elevate the Danish staple of *biksemad* (beef hash with potatoes and onions, traditionally made with whatever happened to be lurking in a family's larder) to a high art form. Here, a platter of *biksemad*, with the promise of as many refills as you want, makes this one of the best dining deals in town.

Havnen 25. © **56-65-02-64.** Main courses DKK175–DKK215 ($30–$37/£18–£22). AE, DC, MC, V. Daily 10am–11pm.

KØGE AFTER DARK

Begin your nightly pub-crawl, as the locals do, at **Toldboden,** Havnen 27 (© **56-65-50-75**), built between 1833 and 1847. Carlsberg is served on draft, and you can also order Guinness, downing your suds in a summer courtyard. Live music is presented every Friday evening and on Saturday afternoons, but mostly it's a place to gather and meet the locals.

Our favorite spot to meet friends for a friendly chat at night is **La Fontaine,** Torvet 28 (© **56-65-51-00**), which somehow always manages to have the coldest beer in town. It's right on the market square by the old fountain and stays open Sunday to Thursday 10am to midnight, and Friday and Saturday 10am to 2am—late hours for sleepy Køge.

For young people, the hottest place to be at night is the **Ritz Rock Café,** Torvet 22 (© **56-65-33-77**), which is Køge's version of the fabled Hard Rock cafes. People come here for the dance music and to eat and drink, partaking of the American and Tex-Mex cuisine. On a busy night, it holds up to 1,000 patrons. On the ground floor, you'll find the most impressive sound and light equipment, whereas the second floor is smaller and more formal, attracting a more mature clientele.

One of the most charming places for a quiet drink at night is **Hugos Vinkælder,** Brogade 19 (© **56-65-58-50**), which opens its courtyard in fair weather. This cozy little wine bar retreat is found in the cellar of an antique building dating from 1392. Filled with atmosphere, it always has a well-chosen selection of wine, which it will sell by the half-bottle if desired. Open Monday to Thursday 10am to 11pm, Friday and Saturday 10am to 1am.

Ask at the tourist office what's on the bill at **Køge Bugt Kulturhus,** Portalen 1 (© **43-97-83-00**); the Køge Bay Cultural Center is the venue for a wide range of concerts and theatrical performances. An exhibit of Danish and international art is displayed in its exhibition hall. Tickets for all types of cultural events are sold at the tourist office. Of course, you might want to skip the theatrical performances if you don't speak Danish, but concerts and other entertainment might interest English speakers.

EASY EXCURSIONS FROM KØGE

Vallø & Its Castle ★

This hamlet of mustard-yellow houses and cobblestone streets from the Middle Ages gets our vote as the most charming in South Zealand, lying only 7km (4¹/₃ miles) south of Køge. Off the beaten path, it's visited by those wanting to wander through the gardens of the redbrick **Vallø Slot,** dating from 1586 but rebuilt after a fire in 1893. Originally the palace housed "spinsters of noble birth," but today it is used for housing pensioners. You can't go inside but you can wander through the well-landscaped gardens, with their little lakes, moats, rare trees, and rose and dahlia flower beds. The castle is surrounded by 2,800 hectares (6,920 acres) of woods and ponds and also enveloped by 1,300 hectares (3,210 acres) of cultivated fields that flow gradually to the coast. Charging no admission, the gardens are open April to October 10am to dusk.

GETTING THERE   By Train   Vallø station is two stops from Køge.

By Car   Head south on Route 209, turning right onto Billesborgvej and left onto Valløvej.

By Bicycle   Bicycling is the ideal way to reach Valløvej, as there's a cycle route signposted from Køge.

The Chalk Cliffs of Stevns Klint ★

If you, like us, sometimes prefer to wander off the beaten track, we suggest an afternoon exploring **Stevns Peninsula,** lying only 24km (15 miles) south of Køge, near Rødvig. The attraction here is the chalk cliffs of **Stevns Klint** (admittedly, they don't compare to the White Cliffs of Dover).

This chalk escarpment extends along the coastline, opening onto a panoramic vista of the sea, and it's one of our favorite places to wander and explore during an afternoon in southeast Zealand. The most stunning white chalk crag rises 43m (141 ft.) in the vicinity of Højerup. In the hamlet of Store Heddinge, you'll come across a little church, **Højerup Kirke,** built here in 1357. Legend claims this church was erected by fishermen in gratitude for having been rescued at sea. There's another legend about this church as well. The sea continues to erode the chalk cliffs, and locals claim that each New Year's Eve, the church moves a fraction inland to keep from falling into the sea. In 1928, it didn't move far enough and the choir collapsed, but the church has since been reinforced and made relatively safe. Hours are daily 10am to 5pm, but only May to September.

For more information about the area, consult the **Turistbureau** in Stevns at Havnevej 21 (✆ **56-50-64-64;** www.stevnsinfo.dk). It is generally open in summer Monday to Friday 9am to 5pm, Saturday 9am to 4pm.

GETTING THERE   By Train and Bicycle   To get to Stevns Klint from Køge, take the train to Rødvig, where you'll rent a bicycle from the tourist office. From here, it's only about 5km (3 miles), heading east, following the signs to Højerup, to the cliffs. This is an easy bike ride and offers the best way to experience the bracing sea air and wind-swept panoramas.

By Car   From Køge to Stevns Klint, take Highway 261 to the village of Store Heddinge, then detour to the cliffs, following the signs to Højerup.

(Fun Facts) Zealand's Link to the Continent

On June 14, 1998, one of the world's largest bridge links opened on the west coast of Zealand near the town of Korsør. Queen Margrethe II was here to cut the ribbon shortly before driving across the 18km-long (11-mile) **Great Belt Bridge.** After 10 years of construction, Zealand is linked to the mainland of Europe via Funen, which already has a bridge link to Jutland on the mainland. From Jutland, you can drive south into Germany.

The bridge has cut traveling time across the Belt by more than 1 hour compared to the ferries, which ceased operations with the opening of the bridge. At a speed of 105kmph (65 mph), crossing the Great Belt into Funen now takes only 10 minutes. By contrast, crossing by ferry took 1 hour, not including the waiting time at the port and embarkation and disembarkation from the ferries. For crossing the bridge, a one-way fare for a private car costs DKK205 ($35/£21). About 23,000 cars now cross the bridge each day.

The rail link across the Great Belt was opened in 1997, and since then Danish State Railways has seen a 60% rise in passenger volume on trains across the Great Belt.

Besides joining east and west Denmark, the bridge link across the Great Belt represented the first stage of an improved infrastructure between Scandinavia and the rest of Europe. The **Øresund Fixed Link** between Denmark and Sweden opened in 2000, establishing even more vital links between Copenhagen and Malmö, southern Sweden's largest city. With three million people living within a 50km (31-mile) radius of the link, the region has the largest population concentration in Scandinavia.

For more information about the bridge, call ✆ **33-93-52-00.**

2 RINGSTED

69km (43 miles) SW of Copenhagen; 24km (15 miles) W of Køge; 16km (10 miles) E of Sorø; 28km (17 miles) N of Næstved

"Our glory was of another day," the curator of a local museum told us. "But life must go on." He was referring to both the days of those "raping, pillaging Vikings" who made Ringsted a major settlement and also an era during the Middle Ages when Ringsted was a powerful ecclesiastical center.

A sleepy provincial town today, this modern center of 30,000 people makes an ideal base for touring South Zealand, offering excellent rail and road conditions. Route 14 from Næstved (see below) to Roskilde intersects the east-west highway (E20) from Køge to Korsør, where you can take the bridge over the Great Belt into Funen.

As late as the 4th century, Ringsted was the site of "the thing," or *Landsting*, as the regional governing body was called, where justice was dispensed. In Torvet, the market square, you can still see a trio of three stones, the *Tingstener*, or "thing stones," recalling the days when Ringsted was a center of power in Denmark. Also on the square is a 1930s statue of Valdemar I, sculpted by Johannes Bjerg.

In times gone by, Ringsted was where Valdemar kings and many of their successors were laid to rest, in Skt. Bendts Kirke (St. Benedict's Church), dating from the 12th century.

After a long period of slumber following the loss of its royal patronage, Ringsted revived again in the 19th century with the coming of the railway.

You could base in Ringsted for 2 nights if you want to use it as a center for exploring **Næstved** and **Slagelse** (see below), two neighboring towns within easy reach, both of which are of historic interest.

ESSENTIALS

GETTING THERE   **By Train**   Trains run frequently from Roskilde (trip time: 18 min.). Dozens of daily trains from Copenhagen pass through to Roskilde (see chapter 7, "North Zealand"). There are also rail connections from Næstved (20 min.). The center of Ringsted can be reached in a 10-minute walk north from the train depot.

By Car   Ringsted lies on Route 150 just off of the E20 motorway coming in from Copenhagen in the east or Funen in the west. From Roskilde, follow Route 14 to Ringsted.

VISITOR INFORMATION   The **Ringsted Turistbureau,** Nørregade 100 (© 57-62-66-00), stands opposite Skt. Bendts Kirke. May to August, its hours are Monday to Friday 10am to 5pm and Saturday 10am to 2pm. Off-season hours are Monday to Friday 10am to 5pm, and Saturday 10am to 1pm. The tourist office will advise you of the best cycling routes in the Ringsted area.

EXPLORING THE TOWN

Skt. Bendts Kirke ★★   The Domkirke at Roskilde (see chapter 7) is the major ecclesiastical site of Zealand, but this church has been the site of royal burials for 150 years. It was constructed by King Valdemar I (1157–82) on the site of a previous abbey. His original intent was that the church serve as a burial site for his father, Duke Knud Lavard, who was slain by Magnus the Strong, son of King Niets (1104–34). The beloved Knud Lavard was entombed here, beginning a tradition of using the church as a burial site for the Valdemar dynasty. In 1169, Knud Lavard was canonized by the pope. The tradition of burying kings and queens of Denmark here continued until 1341. Valdemar I's larger motive in building the church was to use it to bring together the influences of the Catholic hierarchy and the Valdemar dynasty.

In the early 20th century, ill-advised restorers altered the style of the original church, but much remains from the Middle Ages, even the 11th-century travertine blocks from the older abbey church built on this site.

In 1885, King Frederik VII ordered that the royal tombs be unsealed. In a church chapel, you can see the treasures found in these tombs, including a lead tablet from the tomb of Valdemar the Great, plus silks from the grave of Valdemar the Victorious. The tombs themselves—marked by a series of flat stones—were buried beneath the nave on the aisle floor. Such notables as Valdemar III and his queen, Eleonora; the twice-married Valdemar II with his queens, Dagmar and Benegærd; Knud VI; Valdemar I and his queen, Sofia; and the already-mentioned Duke Knud Lavard are all entombed here. Many long-forgotten royals suffered the indignity of having their tombs removed to make way for later royal personages. Chief among these was the beloved Queen Dagmar, born a princess in Bohemia and still revered in Danish folk ballads. Much loved by the people of Denmark, she died prematurely in 1212. When her grave was removed to make way for the tomb of Erik VI (Menved) and his Queen Ingeborg, a gold cross with

detailed enamel work was found. The **Dagmar Cross** is believed to date from around
1000. Today it is displayed in the National Museum in Copenhagen, but local jewelry
shops sell replicas of this pendant. Today, brides marrying in Skt. Bendts often wear
replicas of the Dagmar Cross.

In the choir and on the cross vaulting, you can see some notable chalk paintings. Some
of Zealand's best church frescoes are in the nave, especially a series depicting events in the
life of King Erik IV. He was called "King Ploughpenny," because of a tax he imposed on
ploughs throughout his kingdom. These frescoes were painted at the beginning of the
14th century in a failed attempt to have the king canonized (the pope declined). One
fresco shows Queen Agnes, wife of Erik IV, seated on a throne; another immediately to
her left depicts the murder of Erik IV, his attackers stabbing him with a spear. In another
fresco, the king's corpse is being rescued at sea by fishermen.

Other notable features in the church include pews from 1591 with dragon motifs. The
richly adorned altarpiece is from 1699, and the even older pulpit dates from 1609. The
baptismal font ★ is the oldest relic of all, believed to date from some time in the 1100s.

Sankt Bendtsgade. 𝄉 **57-61-40-19.** Free admission. May to mid-Sept daily 10am–noon and 1–5pm;
mid-Sept to Apr daily 1–3pm.

Ringsted Museum   This is another one of Denmark's provincial museums and is of
such minor interest it could easily be skipped. Instead of the museum, we gravitate to the
restored 1814 Dutch windmill next door, which is still in working order, grinding
organic flour sold at a kiosk on-site. You can also stop for a coffee at the cafe before ducking inside the museum of local culture and history, presenting artifacts to illustrate the
life of the locals long since departed. We learned more about the history of local farming
than we wanted to know.

Køgevej 41. 𝄉 57-61-69-00. http://historienshus.ringsted.dk. Admission DKK25 ($4.30/£2.50) adults, free
for ages 18 and under. Tues–Sun 11am–4pm. Closed Jan.

SHOPPING

Ringsted has a number of specialty shops. A covered shopping center, **Ringsted Centret,**
Nørregade 15 (𝄉 **57-67-38-05**), stands right in the middle of town, enabling you to
shop and browse without having to worry about the weather. This is where you'll find
the widest array of Danish products in various stores. The best place to go for copies of
the Dagmar Cross (see Skt. Bendts Kirke, above) is **Klints Guld & Sølv,** Torvet 2 (𝄉 **57-
61-01-83**). The cross comes in gold, silver, and gold with enamel. In 1683 the cross—
believed to date from 1000—was discovered when Queen Dagmar's tomb site was
moved. Today nearly all brides married in Ringsted wear a reproduction of this cross,
which makes an intriguing piece of jewelry even if you aren't a bride.

WHERE TO STAY

Scandic Hotel Ringsted ★ (Kids)   Short on character, but big on comfort, this four-
story redbrick hotel, lying a 5-minute walk south of the town center, opened in 1986,
and no challenger has risen since to unseat it as the king hostelry of town. Despite the
fact that it's newer and a lot less historic than the also-recommended **Sørup Herregård**
(see below), we prefer it for its location near the town center and because the staff is a lot
better organized. Its public areas host many of the region's conventions and business
meetings, which is hardly a recommendation for the average visitor—in fact, we don't
like to stay here at those busy times. The midsize bedrooms are streamlined in a Danish
modern sort of way, with writing tables, functional furniture, and tile bathrooms with

shower units. There's a respectable, rather standard restaurant on-site, which serves Danish dishes for lunch and dinner. This is one of the best hotels for families in the area, and kids are given a "surprise" when checking in and later can enjoy organized activities planned just for them.

Nørretorv 57, DK-4100 Ringsted. ℂ **57-61-93-00.** Fax 57-67-02-07. www.scandichotels.com. 75 units. DKK1,350–DKK1,450 ($230–$247/£135–£145) double. Rates include breakfast. AE, DC, MC, V. **Amenities:** Restaurant; bar; fitness center; sauna; children's playroom; laundry service; dry cleaning; nonsmoking rooms; solarium. *In room:* TV, Wi-Fi, minibar, coffeemaker (in some), hair dryer, trouser press (in some).

Sørup Herregård ★ (Finds)   If you're a motorist, and you like your hotels with a lot more character and atmosphere than Scandic (see above), drive 6km (3³/₄ miles) east of town to a restored old manor house surrounded by 385 hectares (951 acres) of rolling fields and forests. Of course, the redbrick manor didn't have 102 units, as does today's hotel, but modern wings were added in the 1980s with lots of glass allowing light to stream into the interior during those rare sunny days. The midsize-to-spacious bedrooms are conservatively but comfortably decorated in Danish modern, with small but well-appointed bathrooms. Public rooms evoke an upscale private home of the lord of the manor.

Sørupvej, DK-4100 Ringsted. ℂ **57-64-30-02.** Fax 57-64-31-73. www.sorup.dk. 102 units. DKK1,198 ($204/£120) double; DKK2,050 ($349/£205) suite. Rates include breakfast. AE, DC, MC, V. **Amenities:** Restaurant; bar; indoor heated pool; tennis court; sauna; room service; laundry service; dry cleaning; nonsmoking rooms; solarium; rooms for those w/limited mobility. *In room:* TV, Wi-Fi, minibar, hair dryer.

WHERE TO DINE

Italy & Italy ★ ITALIAN   Thanks to good, market-fresh food and an emphasis on the olive oil–based cuisine of Italy, this is the most consistently popular restaurant in Ringsted, and well deserving of its celebrity. It sits very close to Ringsted's most famous church, in a dining room that's flooded with sunlight from big windows and lined with paintings that commemorate the architectural grandeur of Italy. Menu items cover all aspects of a well-orchestrated Italian meal, and include marinated seafood and vegetarian antipasti, and such succulent pastas as lasagna and fettuccine with Bolognese sauce. Two specialties that we've noted that the cooks do very well are medallions of veal Skt. Elisabeth, flamed in cognac, and a strong, powerful-tasting but nonetheless appealing plate of tender veal with a Gorgonzola sauce.

Torvet 1C. ℂ **57-61-53-53.** www.italy-italy.dk. Reservations recommended. Pizza DKK69–DKK89 ($12–$15/£6.90–£8.90). AE, MC, V. Mon–Wed noon–10pm; Thurs–Sat noon–11pm; Sun 5–10pm.

Rådhus Kro DANISH   The cooks at this restaurant don't set out to win awards, their main intent being to give you a satisfying meal made with fresh ingredients—everything offered at an affordable price. The inn is set across the street from the Rådhus (City Hall), but isn't really the *kro* (inn) of the Rådhus, as its name suggests. Erected in the mid-1980s, it occupies a modern-looking building short on style and character. Diners include many of the town's locals who have one or two meals here a week, especially members of the business and government communities.

There is a certain attention to detail and a proud professionalism, but what you get are such familiar dishes as filet of pork with white sauce and those boiled potatoes Danes are so fond of, or else a "competent" veal steak in a mushroom sauce. Norwegian haddock occasionally appears on the menu, and it's jazzed up with a red-wine sauce.

Skt. Bendtsgade 8. ℂ **57-61-68-97.** Reservations recommended. Main courses DKK149–DKK220 ($25–$37/£15–£22). AE, DC, MC, V. Mon–Sat 11am–8:45pm; Sun 3–8:45pm.

You'll find pubs in virtually every neighborhood. Our favorite is the **Kong Valdemar Pub,** Nørregade 5 (© **57-61-81-32**), an antique-looking watering hole that has welcomed generations of drinkers to its paneled interior. Established in 1999, **Crazy Daisy,** Skt. Hansgade 31 (© **57-61-25-47;** www.ringsted.crazydaisy.dk), is a two-floor drink and dance emporium that contains an active bar area, sometimes with live music, on its street level, and a busy dance club upstairs. Every night owl in town between the ages of 20 and 40 is likely to show up here to enjoy relaxed conversation and hot music. It's open only Friday to Sunday, 11pm to around 5am, charging a cover of DKK60 ($10/£6) per person.

---

3 SLAGELSE

99km (62 miles) SW of Copenhagen; 37km (23 miles) SE of Kalundborg; 19km (12 miles) NE of Korsør; 32km (20 miles) W of Ringsted

In the Middle Ages, this was a major trading center, with trade routes to Næstved in the south, Copenhagen in the east, and Kalundborg in the north. In the 11th century, the town had its own mint, and its municipal charters were granted in 1288. Slagelse lies in the heart of Viking country and is the best center for visiting the nearby fortress at Trelleborg (see below).

Today the town of some 36,000 people is prospering, thanks largely to a lively economy. The area around here might be called Hans Christian Andersen Country, like Odense in Funen: The writer attended the local grammar school for several years but found the town a "nuisance." The school was founded after the Reformation and remained important until it closed in 1852.

After its heyday in the Middle Ages, Slagelse declined considerably, the victim of various wars and some raging fires that burned its major buildings. But with the coming of the rail lines, the economy recovered. Canning factories, distilleries, and breweries beefed up its economy.

Today it's a major city of West Zealand, a route along the important traffic artery, the E20, linking Copenhagen with the bridge across the Great Belt into Funen and the continent. Though often bypassed by rushed motorists, Slagelse has a number of treasures for those interested in the Viking period.

ESSENTIALS

GETTING THERE   By Train   Slagelse lies on the main east-west rail line between Copenhagen and the neighboring island of Funen (its subsequent link to the continent), and trains run here frequently (trip time: 1 hr.). There are also easy connections from Roskilde (35 min.) and from Korsør, near the bridge over the Great Belt (12 min.).

VISITOR INFORMATION   A 10-minute walk south of the train depot, the **Slagelse Turistbureau,** Løvegade 7 (© **58-52-22-06;** www.vikingelandet.dk), provides information about its own attractions and Trelleborg (see below) to the west. It's also helpful in hooking you up with any activities you may want to pursue and in providing directions for hiking and walking. Hours are Monday to Friday 10am to 5pm and Saturday 10am to 3pm, mid-June to August. Off-season, it's open Monday to Friday 10am to 5pm and Saturday 10am to 1pm. The tourist office can arrange rooms in private homes with prices DKK200 to DKK400 ($34–$68/£20–£40) per person for a B&B, plus a DKK10

($1.70/£1) booking charge. You can rent bikes here or at **HJ Cykler,** Løvegade 46 (C **58-52-28-57**), costing DKK25 to DKK60 ($4.30–$10/£2.50–£6) per day.

EXPLORING THE TOWN

If you follow the street, **Fisketorv,** it will lead to **Gammel Torv,** which, for many decades, was the thriving main square of town and a meeting place of locals. It's said that Queen Margrethe I crowned her 6-year-old son, Oluf, on this spot.

Slagelse possesses two historic churches and a minor museum, but, frankly, most sightseers use the town merely as a base for exploring the Viking reconstruction at **Trelleborg** (see below). If you're covering both Slagelse and Næstved in 1 day, you might skip the attractions in the center of Slagelse if you're pressed for time.

Skt. Mikkels Kirke St. Michael's Church dominates the town center. On the tallest hill in Slagelse, construction on this medieval church began in 1333, the architects preferring the Gothic style, using red brick made locally, in the construction. It was once the most important place for worship in town, but by the 1870s the townspeople seemed to have deserted it. Over the decades it had fallen into serious despair before a group of loyal church members raised the money for its restoration. If it was ever filled with art, it isn't anymore, but it does have a historic memorial, honoring the brave members of the Danish Resistance movement in World War II. A noted Danish sculptor, Gunnar Slot, designed this memorial in 1959, and next to it is the church's other most noteworthy sculpture. Simply entitled *Woman* (and so it is), it is the work of Keld Moseholm Jørgensen.

Rosengade 4. C **58-52-05-11.** Free admission. Daily 8:30am–5pm.

Skt. Peders Kirke If you like your churches dripping with more antiquity than Skt. Mikkels, then check out St. Peter's Church. Originally built in the Romanesque style around 1150, it was later—and regrettably—given a Gothic overlay. The vestry and porch came later, around 1500, and the present tower is from 1664, when it was reconstructed after the original collapsed. Of chief interest is a series of graves from the Middle Ages, which can be seen in a section that was once used for armament storage. The "big name" tomb here is that of St. Anders, who died in 1206, the first in a long line of vicars and one of the town's founding fathers. His tomb is in the northern tier of the church.

Bredegade 7A. C **58-52-08-81.** Free admission. Daily 9am–5pm.

Slagelse Museum The town museum is relatively dull, not unusual for the provincial market towns of Denmark. Lying south of Nytorv, the main commercial square of town, this 1984 museum brings together exhibits devoted to both arts and crafts, as well as industry. Everybody gets in on the act here—the grocer, the carpenter, the joiner, the blacksmith, and even the barber. It's sort of a mishmash of everything valuable the town owned, including an exquisitely set dining table from the 19th century.

Bredegade 11. C **58-52-83-27.** Admission DKK30 ($5.10/£3) adults, DKK10 ($1.70/£1) children 15 and under. June 15–Aug daily noon–4pm; Sept–June 14 Sat–Sun noon–4pm.

SHOPPING

Slagelse is home of the **Vestsjællands Center,** Jernbanegade 10 (C **58-50-63-90**), a shopping mall with about 40 stores strong on Danish design and clothing, among other utilitarian shops.

If you're in the market for gold and silver jewelry, as well as the elegant products of Georg Jensen and Royal Copenhagen, the best outlet is **Guildsmed Carl Jensens,** Rosengade 17 (C **58-52-02-97**). But don't expect any discounts, as we found the prices charged here about the same as those of Copenhagen.

Finally, **Bahne** (℃ 58-52-00-75) is located in the shopping complex in the heart of Slagelse and the Royal Danish Porcelain Factory. Again, prices are similar to what you'd pay in Copenhagen.

WHERE TO STAY

Hotel Frederik den II   In spite of its regal name, this sprawling, redbrick motel-style establishment is far better than the Bates Motel, but really no more than a refueling stop. Motorists stop here for the night, as the hotel lies a 10-minute drive south of the center at the junction of Route 22 and the E20 highway leading to Korsør and the neighboring island of Funen. Rooms are relatively small, but comfortably furnished in a standardized Danish modern way with tiny tiled bathrooms. The accommodations on the ground floor open onto private patios, and those upstairs open onto their own balconies. The on-site restaurant and bar is nothing special but will feed you well with Danish regional dishes.

Idagårdsvej 3, DK-4200 Slagelse. ℃ **58-53-03-22.** Fax 58-53-46-22. www.fr2.dk. 72 units. Mon–Fri DKK1,300 ($221/£130) double; Sat–Sun DKK963 ($164/£96) double; DKK1,500–DKK1,700 ($255–$289/£150–£170) suite for 2. AE, DC, MC, V. **Amenities:** Restaurant; bar; sauna; laundry service; dry cleaning; nonsmoking rooms; rooms for those w/limited mobility. *In room:* TV, hair dryer.

WHERE TO DINE

Pulcinilla ITALIAN   We won't pretend that this will be the finest Italian meal you've ever been served, but the food is well prepared with fresh ingredients, and it's good as a change of pace if you've tired of too much Danish fare. This likable dinner-only trattoria stands in the heart of Slagelse, with a white-walled interior whose roster of Italian art includes a blown-up version of the *Mona Lisa*. Menu items are flavorful and fun, and include a number of pizzas and pastas such as lasagna and fettuccine Bolognese, freshly made soups and crisp salads, with such standard main courses as veal parmigiana and entrecote with pepper sauce.

Rosengade 7C. ℃ **58-53-08-07.** Reservations recommended. Main courses DKK159–DKK229 ($27–$39/£16–£23). DC, MC, V. Daily 5–11pm.

SIDE TRIPS: MEDIEVAL RUINS & VIKING RECONSTRUCTION

Slagelse makes a good base for exploring one of Scandinavia's major Viking reconstructions, Trelleborg, as well as a center for exploring Antvorskov, the ruins of a former royal palace and monastery. While still based at Slagelse, you can view both of these attractions in 1 busy day.

Trelleborg ★★

Although it's merely a mock representation, you can experience Viking life as lived 1,000 years ago at **Trelleborg Allé** (℃ 58-54-95-06), the reconstructed fortress of **Trelleborg.** Trelleborg is the best preserved of the quartet of Viking ring fortresses in Denmark. Expect an agenda-loaded schedule once you arrive: You can feel replicas of Viking tools, see household items used by Mrs. Viking, view the inevitable weapons of the day, soak up the atmosphere in a re-created Viking house, and, best of all, enjoy the beautiful Danish countryside surrounding Trelleborg. You can also take part in various events staged throughout the summer, including longbow archery, Viking cooking, sailing, martial arts, games, a Viking pageant, and a Viking market.

A reconstructed Viking house at the entrance was built in the Viking stave style, with rough oak timbers rising above mud floors. Warriors and their families used the earthen benches inside for both sitting and sleeping. The central hearth, as in this house, usually had an opening in the roof for venting smoke. This house and other reconstructions were based on finds excavated from an actual settlement on this site, dating from 1000 to 1050.

The ring fortress consisted of a circular rampart with wooden stakes inserted in the earth, and it could be entered through four different gates. From these entrances, four lanes led to the heart of the fortress. This divided the ring into four quadrants, with about 16 houses laid out in each quadrant. A moat protected the eastern side of the fortress, whereas two small rivers and a marshland secured the other three sides.

The Trelleborg Museum contains a shop selling reproduction Viking jewelry, books on the era, a film room, Viking exhibitions, ship models, ancient artifacts, and a cafe. The 20-minute video shown here will help you understand Trelleborg better before you actually explore it.

It is open Saturday to Thursday 10am to 5pm, and you can allow at least an hour for a visit, perhaps more if you find the site intriguing. Admission is DKK55 ($9.40/£5.50) adults or free for ages 18 and under.

GETTING THERE   By Car   Trelleborg is 6km (3³/₄ miles) west of Slagelse. Follow Strandvejen until its end at the village of Hejininge, where you'll see signs for Trelleborg, which is less than a kilometer (¹/₂ mile) away.

By Bus   You can take bus no. 312 from Slagelse right to the gate. There are several buses daily.

By Bicycle   You can cycle your way to Trelleborg on a rented bike from Slagelse. The tourist office will give you a brochure outlining points of interest along the cycle trail.

Antvorskov

Today only the ruins of this former monastery and royal palace can be viewed, but much of Danish history happened on this spot, 2km (1¹/₄ miles) south of the center of Slagelse near the road to Næstved. In 1164, King Valdemar I founded a monastery here, dedicated to the Order of St. John of Jerusalem. In time it became the major seat of the Order of St. John throughout the Nordic countries.

The monastery's chief legend centers on Hans Tausen (1494–1561), who preached a sermon in Antvorskov that paved the way for the Reformation in Denmark. This renegade monk, who trained at Antvorskov, then one of the richest monasteries in the country, became a disciple of Martin Luther, whom he had heard preach in Wittenberg. Tausen became so inflamed at the abuses of the Catholic Church that he delivered a fiery speech upon his return to Antvorskov.

When the Reformation did come, the king confiscated Antvorskov, and it eventually was turned into a hunting manor. In time, it fell into disrepair, its buildings sold or carted off. When it was deemed unsafe, the monastery church was torn down. The E20 motorway from Copenhagen buried about half of the former grounds of the monastery, but you can still see some of the brick foundations.

Don't expect a formalized museum if you opt to visit this site, as it's little more than a ruin, with no guardian, no fence or barricades, no telephone contact point, no formal hours, and no admission fee.

GETTING THERE   By Bicycle   To reach the site from Slagelse, follow Slotsalleén from the heart of town, turning right when you reach the end of this road, and then follow the signposts into Antvorskov.

Birkegårdens Haver ★

This is a large, privately owned park set in one of the most beautiful parts of Southwest Zealand, 23km (14 miles) north of Slagelse. The grounds contain a stunning **Japanese garden** ★ designed by the Danish landscape architect H. C. Skovgård, and also a young oak forest with a woodland lake. There are plenty of benches throughout the park, and packed lunches may be eaten in the courtyard garden. Here you can also see cows being milked, horses grazing, and goats, rabbits, and calves that come right up to you. There are also a playground for children, a cafe offering refreshments, and a kiosk selling ceramics, porcelain, and jewelry. Birkegårdens Haver lies at Tågerupvej 4, at Tågerup, near Kongsted (© **58-26-00-42**). It's open from April 10 to September 12 daily 10am to 6pm (July–Aug to 9pm). Admission is DKK80 ($14/£8) for adults, DKK70 ($12/£7) for seniors, DKK20 ($3.40/£2) for children 2 to 14, free for children 1 and under.

GETTING THERE By Car To reach the gardens from Slagelse, drive north for 27km (17 miles) from the town center, following the signs that point to Kalundborg.

---

4 NÆSTVED

80km (50 miles) SW of Copenhagen; 25km (16 miles) S of Ringsted; 35km (22 miles) SE of Slagelse

As your car roars on through rolling farmland and undiscovered villages, you come to the largest town in South Zealand, at the mouth of the Suså River, which made it a major Hanseatic port back in medieval times. The Danes themselves come here to enjoy the series of lakes and woodland that lie to the west and south of the town. Some visitors also like to go boating on the **Karrebæk Fjord,** forming a waterway linking Næstved with the scenic Karrebæksminde Bay.

Although there is industry here that sprouted up when the railway line came through in the 19th century, there is much of historic charm as well. The average foreign visitor can spend 2 to 3 hours exploring the historic core, with its Gothic churches, before setting out to take in the treasures of the environs.

Næstved sprouted up around a Benedictine monastery, whose buildings today house Herlufen, Denmark's most famous boarding school, similar in prestige to Eton in Britain. Today it's a garrison town and home to the **Gardehussar Regiment** or Hussars of the Household Calvary. The best time to catch these guards is on Wednesday morning when they ride through the center of town amid much fanfare.

Today much of the outlying area of the town is industrial, devoted to such businesses as timber, paper, engineering, and even ceramics. But in the immediate surroundings, beyond the fringe of town, lie a number of charming places to visit, ranging from manors to mansions, and from abbeys to beautiful parks (see "Easy Excursions," below).

ESSENTIALS

GETTING THERE By Train Næstved lies on two major train routes, one going via Ringsted (trip time: 20 min.), the other going via Køge (38 min.). Of course, Køge (see section 1) and Ringsted (see section 2) enjoy frequent rail connections from Copenhagen.

By Car From Copenhagen, head south along E55 (also known as E47), cutting west along Route 54 into Næstved.

VISITOR INFORMATION South of Axeltorv, **Næstved Turistbureau,** Havnen 1 (© **55-72-11-22;** www.visitnaestved.com), is open January to June 14 and September to

December, Monday to Friday 9am to 4pm, Saturday 9am to noon; June 15 to 30 and August, it's open Monday to Friday 9am to 5pm, Saturday 9am to 2pm; July it's open Monday to Friday 9am to 6pm, Saturday 9am to 2pm.

GETTING AROUND   By Bicycle   Bicycling is especially popular in Næstved, thanks to a relatively flat landscape and the fact that everyone in town seems to view it as a part of everyday life. You can pick up a bike from **Brotorvets Bicycles,** Brotorvet 3 (© **55-77-24-80**), costing DKK40 to DKK100 ($6.80–$17/£4–£10) a day, plus a DKK100 ($17/£10) deposit.

EXPLORING THE TOWN

Our favorite pastime here is a canoe ride on the River Susä, with its calm waters, running through the west side of Næstved. It doesn't have rapids and its current is negligible, so maneuvering by canoe is fairly easy. On summer weekends, the river is crowded with others who like to go canoeing too. Boats can be rented at **Susä Kanoudlejning,** Næsbyholm Allé 6, near Glumsø (© **57-64-61-44**), costing DKK100 ($17/£10) per hour or DKK370 ($63/£37) per day. The outlet for rentals lies at Slusehuset, at the southern end of Rådmanshavn.

As you stroll through the town, you'll come upon antique buildings, the most notable of which is **Apostelhuset,** a half-timbered house on Riddergade (just south of Skt. Mortens Kirke) that dates from the Middle Ages. "Apostle House" has carved figures of the apostles on the beams of its 16th-century facade; each carries an object that symbolizes his martyrdom. These are some of the oldest, and certainly the best-preserved, timber-frame carvings in the country. Nearby you'll see **Løveapoteket,** an old pharmacy in a restored half-timbered structure from 1853. The building is in the Dutch Renaissance style, and medicinal herbs and spices are still grown in a garden out back.

The central square of town is **Axeltorv,** and all of the major sights of town are within a short walk of this historic area. These include the following:

Næstved Museum   Just when you thought you couldn't face another Danish provincial museum, along comes this one, which is better than most. Allow about an hour to visit its location north of Axeltorv, where it is divided into two sections. The best exhibits are in the town's oldest building, formerly the 14th-century **Helligåndshuset** or "House of the Holy Ghost," which used to be the town hospital. Its collection is known for its medieval woodcarvings, although some contemporary works are also featured, and other artifacts illustrate the agricultural history of the region and the tools the peasants used. The second section, **Boderne,** at Skt. Peders Kirkeplads, displays local silver and crafts, including Holmegaard glass made locally. The buildings housing this section of the museum are period pieces, made of medieval brick with arched windows imbedded in mortar. Called *Stenboderne,* these 15th-century "stone booths" are the only remaining medieval terrace houses in Denmark. Craftspeople used to occupy them before they were turned into a museum.
Ringstedgade 4. © **55-77-08-11.** Admission DKK30 ($5.10/£3) adults, free for children 17 and under. Tues–Sun 10am–4pm.

Skt. Mortens Kirke   With a facade of red brick similar to that of St. Peter's, this church is of minor interest but worth 20 minutes or so of your time. It's found halfway between the rail terminal and that landmark square Axeltorv. Inside, the artistic highlight is a towering altar that was carved in 1667 by Abel Schrøder the Younger. The pulpit of the church is even older, dating from sometime in the early 1600s, and is the work of the artist's father, Abel Schrøder the Elder.
Kattibjerg 2. © **55-73-57-39.** Free admission. July–Aug Mon–Fri 2–5pm; Sept–June Tues–Fri 9–11am.

Skt. Peder Kirke   Dating from the early 1200s, St. Peter's Church is the largest Gothic church in Denmark, lying just to the south of Axeltorv. When it was restored in the 1880s, wall paintings from 1375 were uncovered in the choir area, one depicting Valdemar IV and his consort, Hedwig, kneeling at a penitent's stool. A Latin inscription reads, "In 1375, the day before the feast of St. Crispin, King Valdemar died—do not forget that!" You can also see a choir screen by Abel Schrøder the Elder (ca. 1600), plus an impressive crucifix by an unknown artisan dating from the 1200s and a pulpit dated 1671.

Skt. Peders Kirkeplads. (C) **55-72-31-90.** Free admission. May–Sept Tues–Fri 10am–noon and 2–4pm; Oct–Apr Tues–Fri 10am–noon.

SHOPPING

There's plenty of shopping in Næstved itself, with no fewer than three major shopping centers. Every day in summer, the streets in the heart of town echo with the sounds of a jazz band, and there's a market at **Axeltorv** Wednesday and Saturday mornings. All the shopping malls in Næstved stage free exhibitions and shows.

The best mall is the **Næstved Stor-Center,** Holsted Allée ((C) **55-77-15-00;** bus: 2), the major shopping center for all of South Zealand, attracting shoppers from Møn, Falster, and various hamlets for many kilometers around. Located less than a kilometer (¹/₂ mile) north of the center, it's dominated by the giant Bilka supermarket (it's so large that they refer to it as a "hypermarket"). The mall's more than 50 specialist shops sell handicrafts, glass, jewelry, clothing, gifts, and dozens of other items.

WHERE TO STAY

Hotel Kirstine ★ (Finds)   The second-most-appealing hotel in Næstved originated in 1745, when a local alderman created it as a venue for town meetings in a carpenter-derived design that's part neo-Classical, part country baroque. Throughout most of the 1800s, it functioned as the home of the town's mayors, until around 1909, when it was transformed into a hotel that strictly prohibited any kind of alcohol on its premises, a policy long since abandoned. Today, the site is a half-timbered and romantic-looking monument to the elegant country life, thanks to a meticulous allegiance in all the public areas to a kind of well-scrubbed, prosperous-looking integrity that many visitors associate with rural Denmark. The midsize bedrooms are conservatively furnished and decorated, each with a private tiled bathroom. There's glamour in some of the richly accessorized public areas, but only comfort in the bedrooms.

Købmagergade 20, DK-4700 Næstved. (C) **55-77-47-00.** Fax 55-72-11-53. www.hotelkirstine.dk. 31 units. DKK975 ($166/£98) double; DKK1,300 ($221/£130) suite. Rates include buffet breakfast. AE, MC, V. **Amenities:** Restaurant; bar; laundry service; dry cleaning. *In room:* TV, Wi-Fi, minibar, hair dryer, safe.

Hotel Vinhuset ★★ (Finds)   The most distinctive and best hotel in the region was built in 1768 atop vaulted cellars that monks used to store wine as long ago as the 1400s. And although the site has always had a tradition of housing overnight guests and the worldly goods of an order of monks, it entered the world of modern tourism in earnest sometime after World War II, when it was transformed into a first-class hotel across the square from Sankt Peders Kirke. Inside, Persian carpets, antique furniture, and a romantic atmosphere add to the allure. The midsize-to-spacious rooms are comfortable, high-ceilinged, and outfitted with a combination of modern furniture—especially good beds—and reproductions of antiques. Even if you're not a guest, consider dining at this old hostelry (see below).

Skt. Peders Kirkeplads 4, DK-4700 Næstved. (C) **55-72-08-07.** Fax 55-72-03-35. www.hotelvinhuset.dk. 57 units. DKK1,025 ($174/£103) double; DKK1,495 ($254/£150) suite. Rates include breakfast. AE, DC, MC, V.

Amenities: Restaurant; bar; room service; babysitting; laundry service; dry cleaning; nonsmoking rooms. *In room:* TV, hair dryer.

Mogenstrup Kro   This is an old Danish *kro* that has been putting up wayfarers for more than 2 centuries. It has a steady stream of customers, often weekenders escaping the congestion of Copenhagen. In 2008, it was completely renovated, with an opening scheduled for some time in 2009. Even though it underwent extensive refurbishment, it remains a traditional country inn, but with a library lounge and an open-hearth fire, plus a small spa. Bedrooms are exceedingly comfortable and well furnished, but prices listed below are subject to change. Good Danish country cooking is still a feature in its on-site restaurant.

Præstø Landevej 25, DK-4700 Næstved. ✆ **55-76-11-30.** Fax 55-76-11-29. www.firsthotels.com. 99 units. DKK1,350 ($230/£135) double. Rates include breakfast. AE, DC, MC, V. **Amenities:** Restaurant; bar; spa; sauna; room service; laundry service; dry cleaning; nonsmoking rooms; rooms for those w/limited mobility. *In room:* TV, Wi-Fi, minibar (in some), hair dryer.

WHERE TO DINE

Restaurant Le Boeuf ★   DANISH/FRENCH   In the previously recommended Hotel Vinhuset, the town's best restaurant lies within an 18th-century setting that originally was a warehouse for wine. Both the roast Danish beef and the duckling are superb here, as the chefs are known for selecting the finest ingredients at the market that day. They can get fancy with their sauces but also turn out down-home fare, such filet of plaice in a parsley butter sauce. Desserts are made fresh daily and are scrumptious.

In the Hotel Vinhuset, Skt. Peders Kirkeplads 4. ✆ **55-72-08-07.** Main courses DKK128–DKK198 ($22–$34/£13–£20); fixed-price menus DKK254 (43/£25) for 2 courses, DKK294 (50/£29) for 3 courses, DKK324 (55/£32) for 4 courses. AE, DC, MC, V. Mon–Sat noon–3pm and 7–9:30pm.

NÆSTVED AFTER DARK

Each of the hotels recommended above maintains a bar, but in addition to those, you'll find easy access to at least three pubs, any of which might act as a backdrop for some drinks, dialogue, and people-watching. The watering holes follow an unpredictable, frequently changing schedule that incorporates an hour or two of live music, usually on Friday and/or Saturday nights, beginning around 9pm. However, everything in town is very spontaneous, so be alert to whatever musical venue your hotel staff says is happening during the time of your arrival. A worthwhile bet for nautical atmosphere and camaraderie is **Rådhus Kroenm,** Skomagerrækken 8 (✆ 55-72-01-56), rivaled only by **Underhuset Bar,** Axeltorv 9 (✆ 55-72-79-19). Equally appealing is another pub, **Step Inn,** Ramsherred 14 (✆ 55-77-01-08).

EASY EXCURSIONS

Herlufsholm is known to educators throughout Europe as the site of a famous prep school, less than a kilometer (¹/₂ mile) northwest of the center of Næstved. It was founded at the dawn of the 13th century as a Benedictine monastery known as Skovkloster. The monastery, abandoned at the time of the Reformation, was transformed into the **Herlufsholm Academy,** Herlufsholm Allée (✆ **55-75-35-00;** www.herlufsholm.dk; bus: 6A). To reach it from Næstved, follow the Slagelsevej from the town center. You can wander around the grounds, assuming you don't interrupt the flow of the academics; but if your time is limited, the crown jewel of the academy grounds is the monastery church, **Stiftskirke Herlufsholm.** Constructed in the late Middle Ages, it is one of the oldest brick churches in Denmark. It's noteworthy for its tombs, especially those of Admiral

Herluf Trolle, who left an endowment to the monastery, and his wife, Birgitte Goye. The ivory Gothic crucifix inside dates from around 1230; the baroque pulpit was the creation of Ejler Abelsen in 1620. The church, which has an unusually wide nave, can be visited daily—except during religious services—during daylight hours. Admission is free.

One of the many stately homes surrounding Næstved is **Gavnø Slot & Park** ★, Gavnørej (© **55-70-02-00;** bus: 1A). Located 4km (2¹/₂ miles) south of town, it lies on a peninsula, on the opposite bank of the Karrebækfjord. The old rococo castle is surrounded by a delightful botanical garden and is also the site of **Butterfly World,** where exotic tropical butterflies are allowed to fly free. A former nunnery, Gavnø reverted to private ownership in 1584. When Otto Thott (1703–85) took over the property, he had it converted into the rococo-style mansion you see today. Thott also accumulated one of the largest picture collections and private libraries (about 140,000 volumes) in Denmark. The premises also contain a valuable altar and pulpit carved by Abel Schrøder the Elder. Although part of the interior remains a private residence, some sections of the castle can be visited. The best time to visit is when the tulips bloom in spring, these flowers later giving way to ornamental shrubs and roses. A ticket that combines admission to the castle, the castle gardens with its butterfly collection, and a nearby church (Gavnø Kirke) that has been associated with the castle for many generations costs DKK80 ($14/£8) adults, DKK50 ($8.50/£5) for children 11 and under. All three places are open only May to August, daily 10am to 4pm.

The manor house that we'd like to own is **Gisselfeld Slot** ★, Gisselfeldvej 3, Haslev (© **56-32-60-32**), a beautiful, step-gabled, brick Renaissance home dating from 1557. If you visit, you'll be wandering in the footsteps of Hans Christian Andersen, who found inspiration here for his fairy tale *The Ugly Duckling.* Although it has been much altered and changed over the centuries, it forms an impressive sight today, set in a well-laid-out park that evokes the countryside of England, with a fountain, a small lake, a grotto, and even a waterfall. You will have to be content to view the house from the outside, but you can wander through one of Denmark's finest private gardens, with some 400 different species of trees and bushes, including a rose island and a bamboo grove. The gardens are at their best in the late spring. The gardens can be visited daily 10am to 5pm (mid-June to mid-Aug to 6pm). It costs DKK30 ($5.10/£3) for adults, free for children 11 and under. The only time the interior can be visited is during July, when guided tours can be arranged, on a rotating and oft-changing schedule that must be reconfirmed prior to your arrival.

The little town of Vordingborg, 27km (17 miles) south of Næstved, was a powerhouse back in the Middle Ages, and the place where Denmark's first constitution was written. "It's our Philadelphia," the tourist manager told us.

Most visitors arrive to see the fabled "Goose Tower," once part of the sprawling royal castle and fortress that stood here during the Middle Ages. The 14th-century **Gåsetårnet** ★★, Slotsruinen 1 (© **55-37-25-54**), is the best-preserved medieval tower in Scandinavia, the only structure remaining intact from the Valdemar era. The tower gets its name from 1368, when the king, Valdemar IV, ordered that a golden goose be placed on top of the tower to show his disdain for a declaration of war against Denmark by the Hanseatic League of Germany. He was hoping to suggest that the threats coming from the Hanseatic League were no more ominous to him than a flock of cackling geese. The pointed copper roof of the 37m (121-ft.) tower is still crowned by a golden goose, and the tower, of course, remains the town's landmark and source of historic pride. From the top of the tower, a panoramic view of the countryside unfolds. In its heyday, the fortress had seven more towers, but they were demolished over the centuries. In recent years excavations have uncovered the ruins of the castle. Queen

Margrethe visited in 1997 to view the excavation of a Viking quay. Visiting hours are June to August daily 10am to 5pm; off-season, Tuesday to Sunday 10am to 4pm.

VORDINGBORG AFTER DARK

A good place to begin your evening is **Amigo Bar,** Algade 35 (*©* **55-37-60-65**), right in the center of town. It seems to attract the most simpatico crowd. The best alehouse is nearby: **Slots Kroen,** Algade 119 (*©* **55-37-02-61**). A lot of the locals will also direct you to **Willy Nilly,** Algade 1 (*©* **55-34-20-40**), a friendly English pub that seems to have the coldest beer in town, attracting a 20-to-40 age group. It's also the site of **Prinsen Diskotek,** Algade 1 (*©* **55-34-20-40**), which opens at 10 or 11pm, often staying open until 3 or 4am. It rarely charges a cover.

---

5 MØN

128km (80 miles) S of Copenhagen

In World War II almost every music hall in England had singers promising that bluebirds would return to the White Cliffs of Dover when the world was free. On the island of Møn, which also has spectacular white cliffs, it was the peregrine falcon that returned after a mysterious disappearance that lasted for the remaining 25 years of the 20th century. Off the coast of Southeast Zealand in a "corner" of Denmark, the island of Møn lures visitors with its white chalky cliffs, the 120m (394-ft.) **Møns Klint** that stretches for some 6km (3³⁄₄ miles), rising dramatically from the Baltic Sea. Møns Klint was formed by the Baltic, and made up of ice-transported chalk masses and glacial deposits formed from calcareous ooze 75 million years ago. The ooze enclosed shells of marine animals that are now fossils. The glacial deposit originated partly as boulder clay deposited by inland ice and partly as bedded clay and sand containing mussels. The boulders on the beach long ago dropped from the cliff and have been rounded by wave erosion.

Although Møn's white chalk cliffs are its main appeal, once you get here you'll find an island of rustic charm and grace well worth exploring. Fewer than 12,000 people live here, and the residents of Møn zealously guard their natural environment where the beauty of their landscapes remains largely unspoiled. Sheltered by dunes, the white sandy beaches are a summer attraction, so it's not just the wild cliffs that draw visitors here. The island also boasts beautiful forests with a wide variety of wildlife and a trio of churches with the best frescoes in the country (more about that later), plus a lively market town in Stege.

Møn is also known for the prehistoric remains that are scattered about the island. For detailed information, the tourist office (see "Visitor Information," below) publishes a booklet called *Prehistoric Monuments of Møn.* Several Neolithic chambered tombs known

---

(Finds) Pottery Sales

As you drive about Møn, note the many signs advertising *keramik.* On this slow-paced island, people everywhere seem to have taken up ceramics and pottery and are only too willing to sell their products to you. This interest in ceramics originated because of the rich clay deposits found here.

as "giants' graves" were discovered. As the legend goes, the western part of the island was ruled by a "jolly green giant" called the Green Huntsman, and the eastern part of the island was the domain of another giant, Upsal.

Møn lies at the eastern edge of the Størstrommen, a channel dividing the island of Zealand and the island of Falster.

ESSENTIALS

GETTING THERE   By Car   Cross over from the island of Zealand on the Dronning Alexandrines Bridge, then proceed through the old country town of Stege.

VISITOR INFORMATION   The local tourist office, **Møns Turistbureau,** Storegade (© 55-86-04-00), is open Monday to Friday 10am to 5pm and Saturday 9am to noon.

GETTING AROUND   Because bus service on the island is meager, you'll need a car or bike to explore.

By Bicycle   Many Danes prefer to explore Møn by bike. The best trail to follow is the signposted bike route going from the capital, Stege, to Møns Klint. Ask at the tourist office for a pamphlet outlining the best cycling tours of the island, which take in all of

Møn's principal attractions. In Stege, bikes can be rented at **Dækaingen Cykler,** Storegade 91 (© **55-81-42-49**). Rates average DKK60 ($10/£6) a day.

STEGE ★: THE ISLAND'S CAPITAL

Time seems to have forgotten this sleepy little capital, and that is part of its charm. To the surprise of first-time visitors, Stege has preserved its moat and ramparts from the Middle Ages, whereas other Danish towns have torn them down. One of its original trio of town gates, **Mølleporten,** is still here to greet guests as in olden days. Mølleporten, which once allowed (or prohibited) entry to the town, stands on Storegade. Meaning "mill gate" in English, the gate bears a resemblance to the Stege church tower, and is made of red brick and lined with horizontal strips of white chalk from (where else?) Møns Klint.

After crossing the bridge from "mainland" Zealand on Route 59, take an immediate left and follow the road to the ancient market town of Stege, which is the ideal gateway to the island and the source of the best information about Møn (see "Visitor Information," above).

Exploring the Town

Known for its primitive frescoes, **Stege Kirke ★**, Kirkepladsen (© **55-81-40-65**), is one of the largest churches in the country, with a massive tower striped in brick and chalk. Its oldest section, built in the Romanesque style, dates from the early 1200s and was constructed by the ruler of the island, Jakob Sunesen, who was a member of the powerful Hvide family. In the latter 1400s, the church was expanded to its present size.

The principal nave is flanked by two smaller naves on each side and is filled with pointed arched windows and high vaulted ceilings. Rich frescoes by the Master of Elmelunde are found in the choir and main nave. Long covered with whitewash, they were discovered and restored in 1892. Many are quite whimsical in nature; and in the post-Reformation era, Lutheran ministers found the frescoes too evocative of Catholic themes, and ordered that they be whitewashed. Although this sounds bad, it was the whitewashing that actually preserved the frescoes so that they can still be enjoyed today. They were restored under the supervision of Denmark's national museum. Charging no admission, the church is open April to September Tuesday to Sunday 9am to 5pm; October to March Tuesday to Sunday 9am to 1pm.

Next to the old Mølleporten, or town gate, stands **Empiregården,** Storegade 75 (© **55-81-40-67**), housing the rather elegant **Møn Museum,** a repository of local cultural history. The collection is rich in artifacts from the Middle Ages, including coins and old pottery, but it also goes back to the Stone Age, displaying such items as ancient fossilized sea urchins. The museum also exhibits Møn house interiors from the 1800s. It's open Tuesday to Sunday 10am to 4pm, charging DKK40 ($6.80/£4), free for children 10 and under.

Shopping

The island is known for its ceramics and pottery, whose production keeps dozens of artisans working long hours. One of the best places to see and buy some of the goods produced here include a warehouse-size emporium 4km (2¹/₂ miles) east of Stege, on the road leading to Møns Klint. **Ympelese,** Klintevej 110 (© **55-81-30-05**), stocks some of the most appealing handmade candles in Zealand, as well as a variety of ceramic pots, plates, and vessels. There's even men's, women's, and children's clothing for sale, some of it fabricated by local seamstresses, and some of it designed to protect its wearer from the midwinter gales that sweep in from the Baltic and North Seas.

Where to Stay & Dine

Hotel Ellens Cabaret   This oddly named hotel is the site of a weekend cabaret that is pure country, certainly not of the "come to the cabaret" sophistication that would attract a Danish Liza Minnelli. One local told us that the humor is strictly for the islanders and even Copenhageners wouldn't understand it. But if you can get past this beer-and-booze attraction, you'll find a three-story motel-style building, standing at the edge of town near the sea. Bedrooms are fairly streamlined and small to midsize, the most desirable with large windows opening onto balconies. The bar, with its large-screen TV, attracts a lot of sports fans and traveling salespeople.

Langelinie 48, DK-4780 Stege. (✆ **55-81-54-54.** Fax 55-81-58-90. 27 units. DKK900 ($153/£90) double. Rates include breakfast. MC, V. **Amenities:** Bar; nightclub; lounge; laundry service; dry cleaning. *In room:* No phone.

Præstekilde Kro & Hotel ★★   This is the most opulent and glamorous hotel on Møns—partly because of its upscale comforts and partly because of its association with the island's nearby golf course, opening onto a view of the Bay of Stege. Built in the early 1970s in a rambling compound of big-windowed, low-slung buildings, it lies 5km (3 miles) east of Stege, about 2.5km (1¹/₂ miles) from the nearest beach, Strand Wengensgaardsvej. Bedrooms are not as plush as we would prefer, considering the public lounges, but, though small, they are tastefully and comfortably furnished.

The restaurant has big-windowed views over the surrounding scenery, offering conservative Danish cuisine in the form of fresh fish and such specialties as meatballs and hash. It's one of the few fully functioning restaurants that remains open throughout the year in this remote part of Denmark. Food is served daily 12:30 to 4pm and 6 to 9pm, with lunch going for DKK60 to DKK135 ($10–$23/£6–£14). Fixed-price menus are offered at dinner: DKK225 ($38/£23) for 2 courses, DKK265 ($45/£27) for 3 courses, DKK310 ($53/£31) for 4 courses, and DKK365 ($62/£37) for 5 courses.

Klintevej 116, DK-4780 Stege. (✆ **55-86-87-88.** Fax 55-81-36-34. www.praestekilde.dk. 46 units. DKK1,145–DKK1,245 ($195–$212/£115–£125) double; DKK1,400–DKK1,500 ($238–$255/£140–£150) junior suite. Rates include breakfast. AE, DC, MC, V. **Amenities:** Restaurant; bar; indoor heated pool; sauna; room service; laundry service; dry cleaning; nonsmoking rooms; solarium. *In room:* TV, Wi-Fi, minibar, hair dryer.

Stege After Dark

Persons under age 25 on the island are quick to point out that there are no full-time dance clubs on Møn, unless a local church or civic group opts to hold a youth-group gathering in a communal basement somewhere. In lieu of that, the most convivial gathering place is the bar at the previously recommended **Præstekilde Kro & Hotel,** Klintevej (✆ **55-86-87-88**). Here you'll find an inkling of big-city style a la Copenhagen, but not so much that you won't realize that you're far from urban life. Still, the drinks taste good, and you're likely to meet a handful of other urbanites to swap stories with.

ULVSHALE ★★ & NYORD

After leaving Stege, you can follow a minor little road directly north 6km (3³/₄ miles) with signposts that will lead you to Ulvshale, or "Wolf's Trail" in English, a peninsula jutting west toward Zealand. It's one of the most beautiful spots on Møn, now preserved as a nature reserve, with gnarled old trees and rare birds, such as snipe, razorbills, water rails, and others, which prefer to live on the mud flats. Ulvshale boasts one of the best beaches on the island and it also is home to one of the few virgin forests left in the country. The chilly beach is Ulvshale Strand, and the main road, Ulvshalevej, runs right along it. The forest is crisscrossed with a network of hiking routes.

Once at Ulvshale you'll see a bridge connecting Møn with the little offshore island of **Nyord.** You can walk across the bridge to get to this tiny speck of an island, which means "New Word" in English. It's been set aside as a sanctuary for rare birds, including rough-legged buzzards, snow buntings, hen harriers, and others. The birds are seen mainly in the east marshes. On the north side of the road, about a kilometer (²/₃ mile) after crossing the bridge, you'll come to a tower that is the best vantage point for watching the birds, and the bridge itself is also a good bird-watching site.

The little village on the island is called **Nyord,** too, and it's a time capsule from the 1800s, with old thatched houses. Other than a tiny yacht harbor and a little church from 1846, there aren't a lot of attractions, but it's such an idyllic place it's worth the effort to get here.

After a look at the birds, head back in the direction of Stege, but when you see a turnoff to Keldby, follow the signs into this hamlet, 5km (3 miles) east of Stege.

KELDBY

This agrarian community is mainly visited by those who want a look at **Keldby Kirke ★**, Præstegårdstræde 1, Keldby (© **55-81-33-05**). Built of brick between 1200 and 1250, this is one of the island's special churches, celebrated for its frescoes that span 200 years, the oldest dating from 1275, with both Old and New Testament scenes included. No church in Denmark quite equals Keldby in medieval frescoes—note especially the dramatic representation of Cain and Abel and the horror show depicting Armageddon. Shepherds pictured with their flocks create a more bucolic scene. In addition to the frescoes, the church contains a number of other treasures, notably a carved pulpit dated 1586, and, in the vaulting, paintings by the Master of Elmelunde, including a tender depiction of Joseph preparing gruel for his newly born infant son. A tombstone at the north side of the church dates from the mid-14th century. Admission is free, and the church can be visited April to September daily from 7am to 4:45pm, off-season daily 8am to 3:45pm.

If you have time after viewing the church, visit the manor **Hans Hansens Gård,** Skullebjergvej 15 (© **55-81-40-67**), which lies about 1.5km (about a mile) south of Keldby Church. (Follow the signs to Keldbylille to reach it.) Dating from 1800, this is a thatch-covered building whose wings enclose an inner courtyard. Originally conceived as a farmhouse, it's the home of Møns Museumsgården, a monument that depicts what family life was like for homesteaders during the 1800s. The farm was kept in the same family for generations. When its last owner, a bachelor, Hans Hansens (for whom the property is named), died, he willed it to the people of Møns, who converted it into a museum. Furniture and utensils used by the Hansens family are on display. Open April to September, Tuesday to Sunday 10am to 4pm, charging DKK35 ($6/£3.50) for admission.

The highway (Rte. 287) continues directly east to Elmelunde.

ELMELUNDE

This tiny rural hamlet, roughly equivalent to Keldby in size and layout, is 7km (4¹/₃ miles) east of Stege and is the site of the island's second-most-visited church, **Elmelunde Kirke ★**, Klintevej, Elmelunde (© **55-81-33-05**). Dating from around 1080, it's one of the oldest stone churches in Denmark. During the Romanesque era, the nave was expanded. In the early 1300s, the distinctive tower was added, transforming it into a prominent landmark for sailors coming in from the turbulent sea. The interior of the church is known for its frescoes painted by the Master of Elmelunde. Here this rather mysterious artist left some of his masterpieces, including *Last Judgment, St. Peter with the Key to Heaven, Christ in Majesty, St. Paul with a Sword,* and his charming *Entry into Jerusalem,* along with the more sobering *Flagellation of Christ.*

He also painted lighter subjects, including autumn harvest and some plowing-the-fields scenes. Other frescoes depict Adam and Eve being thrown out of the Garden of Eden. The feudal lord Corfitz Ulfeldt and his consort, Queen Leonora Christina, donated the altar and pulpit. The intricately carved and painted altar dates from 1646; the pulpit was created about 3 years later. The carved pulpit is supported entirely on a figure of St. Peter. In 1460, the three-pointed vaults (seen over the altar) were added, and the Master of Elmelunde painted them as well. Admission free, the church is open daily 8am to 4pm.

Where to Stay

Hotel Elmehøj This place, one of the most stately-looking guesthouses in Møn, has a real down-home feel, lying 4km (2¹/₂ miles) inland between Stege and Møns Klint, adjacent to the stop for buses that interconnect the two. The hotel actually started life in 1928 as a retirement home but was later successfully converted into a hotel. In 1991, it was acquired by Brit Olifent, a woman born and reared on Møn, who runs it today with her husband, Jonathan, who was born in Perth, Australia. Rooms are simple and very well maintained, with few frills and a sense of regimented orderliness. There's little to do on the property, other than taking promenades in the well-tended garden, exploring the nearby beach and forest, and visiting the 12th-century interior of the Elmelunde church, a short walk away. A communal TV room and a public kitchen that some guests use to prepare light lunches and snacks are on the premises.

Kirkebakken 39, Elmelunde, DK-4780 Stege, Møn. ⓒ 55-81-35-35. Fax 55-81-32-67. www.elmehoj.dk. 23 units, all w/shared bathroom. DKK490 ($83/£49) double. Rates include breakfast. MC, V. Closed Jan. **Amenities:** Breakfast room; lounge; laundry service; dry cleaning. *In room:* No phone.

Where to Dine

Kaj Kok ★ (Finds) DANISH Good country cooking consistently lures us to this big-windowed restaurant from the 1970s, lying a kilometer (²/₃ mile) from the hamlet of Elmelunde. Many locals praise it for its well-prepared versions of time-honored Danish specialties, and we agree with their enthusiasm. You'll recognize it by its red facade and a large garden in which tame goats munch on vegetables. The interior's modernity is disguised by a roster of old-fashioned decorative accessories. Launch yourself with the likes of a well-flavored garlic-laced crab bisque or else the smoked salmon. You won't shed tears of joy but might still delight in the filet of halibut in a white-wine and parsley sauce or a particularly flavorful version of pepper steak, with just the right "bite." Lighter appetites appreciate the *smørrebrød* (open-faced sandwiches), which usually sell for DKK40 ($6.80/£4) each.

Klintevej 151, Elmelunde. ⓒ **55-81-35-85.** Reservations recommended. Main courses DKK50–DKK200 ($8.50–$34/£5–£20). No credit cards. Daily 2–8pm. Closed Sept–Apr Mon–Wed.

LISELUND

After a meal at Kaj Kok, head east along Route 287 through the hamlet of Borre, where you'll pass a brick church built in the early 1200s. Continue through the village but turn left at the signpost to Sømarke. The next road to the right leads to Sømarkedyssen. At this point you'll come upon a round dolmen crowned by a huge capstone over an open chamber. From here there's a panoramic view over the entire island. After a look at the dolmen, continue on the same road, going left up a very narrow lane. At the peak, turn right along the road for about 90m (300 ft.), which will lead to the entrance of Liselund.

This thatched palatial summer home from 1795 is surrounded by lovely park grounds with artificial lakes and canals in the northeastern part of the island. H. C. Andersen wrote *The Tinder Box* while staying at the Swiss Cottage here. The park is called a "folly" of the 18th century, when it was constructed by Bosc de la Calmette, a royal chamberlain who was inspired by Marie Antoinette's Hamlet at Versailles. You can buy refreshments at a small chalet filled with antlers and antiques. The admission-free park is open daily until sunset year-round.

Other structures in the park were destroyed by a rockfall in 1905, but guided tours of the **Gamle Slot** (Old Castle) are available. Call ℂ **55-81-21-78** for more details. Inside you'll find an architectural mélange of styles, with tiny canopied beds, a *trompe l'oeil* painting, and a Monkey Room painted with a jungle scene. Visits are possible Tuesday to Friday and Sunday, at 10:30 and 11am, 1:30 and 2 pm. Admission is DKK30 ($5.10/£3) adults, DKK10 ($1.70/£1) for children 10 to 15, free for children 9 and under.

Where to Stay & Dine

Liselund Ny Slot   Don't let the *slot* (castle) reference in the name of this place mislead you—Buckingham Palace it isn't. Set amid the trees and rolling hills of a national park, this manor house was built in 1887 as an annex to a much older castle. Since the transformation of the original castle into a museum, most of the region's overnight guests seek accommodations in the yellow-colored stucco walls and soaring tower of the Ny Slot (New Castle). Rooms are simple but bright, outfitted with minimalist furniture and neatly kept bathrooms with shower units, offering views over fields, forests, a pond with swans, and the sea. Many of the public areas have high, frescoed ceilings that evoke a sense of the place's original grandeur.

You don't have to stay at the hotel to eat lunch in the establishment's basement-level cafe (served noon–6pm), or for dinner in the more formal dining room (6:30–8pm). Menu items include standard preparations of Danish lamb in rosemary sauce, Baltic or North Sea fish, and steaks. There's also an occasional Chinese or Asian dish to break the monotony. The restaurant is open daily in summer, with an occasional (unscheduled) closing 1 or 2 days a week in winter.

Langebjergvej 6, DK-4791 Borre. ℂ **55-81-20-81.** Fax 55-81-21-91. www.liselundslot.dk. 17 units. DKK1,640 ($279/£164) standard double; DKK2,150 ($366/£215) in the tower. Rates include breakfast. MC, V. **Amenities:** Dining room; cafe; lounge. *In room:* No phone.

MØNS KLINT ★★

After a visit or even an overnight stay at Ny Slot, drive back to Route 287 and follow the road east to the highlight of the tour, **Møns Klint.** These impressive white chalk cliffs (see section 5, "Møn") stretch for several kilometers, with a sheer drop of 120m (394 ft.) at their highest point. Formed by glacial deposits combined with the action of a turbulent sea, they are one of the most dramatic natural sights in Denmark. Møns Klint was pocked throughout with nearly 100 Neolithic burial mounds. Paths lead through woodland to the towering edge of the cliffs, where one of the most panoramic views ★★★ in all of Denmark awaits you. For decades photographers have delighted in capturing the image of these brilliantly white cliffs against the azure blue of the sea. When the sun is out, the scene is especially breathtaking.

Footpaths are cut into the cliffs, and visitors are fond of hiking these towering trails. It takes about an hour's walk to appreciate the magnificence of the site. There's a wide expanse of beech trees along the top of the cliffs, providing shelter for rare plants, including 20 species of orchids hidden in the undergrowth. For the best view, follow the signs to the peak called Sommerspiret, and hope that the sky is clear at the time of your visit. Fossils of marine animals—some long extinct—have also been discovered on the beach below these cliffs. Two steep flights of steps lead from both Storeklint and Jydeleje down to the sea, but be prepared for an exhausting climb back to the top. Once you're at the bottom, you can join Danish families who hunt for blanched fossils on the beach, usually sea urchins. Captains at sea use the cliffs as a navigational point because they stand out from Zealand's relatively flat topography.

The most dramatic hike, of course, is along the towering cliffs. But if time remains, you can also hike through **Klinteskoven** (Klinte Forest), a woodland area that grows right up to the edge of the cliffs. Horse trails and a network of paths have been cut through this forest. Trails start from the edge of the cliffs, and the best track to follow is about a kilometer (^{2}/$_3$ mile) west of Storeklint, which will take you to Timmesø Bjerg. Here you'll see the ruins of a castle built around 1100. If you visit, facilities for tourists are found at Storeklint, including a cafeteria and a parking lot, along with some routine souvenir kiosks.

At **Rent-A-Horse,** Langebjergvej 1 (© **55-81-25-25**), an outfitter near a local youth hostel at Møns Klint, you can book 1^1/$_2$-hour guided horseback tours of Møns Klint or the bay at its base, the Klinteskoven. Equestrian treks are priced at DKK350 ($60/£35) per person per 1^1/$_2$ hours (including a guide).

KLINTHOLM HAVN

Returning to the parking lot at Møns Klint, you can continue south along a minor little road to the hamlet of Sandvej. Once here, turn right at the T-junction in the direction of Mandemarke. Before reaching this village, take a left turn down a lane marked KLINTHOLM HAVN. This will take you to an old village on the coast with a bustling fishing harbor and a modern marina. The seaside village, a bit of a holiday center, opens onto Hjelm Bay. It's best to visit here on a sunny day, as Klintholm Havn is mainly known for its beach.

Many wealthy Germans use the marina here to station their yachts. One harbor is filled with fishing boats, the other with these yachts, and the beach runs in both directions from these two harbors. We prefer the beach extending to the east, as it's well maintained and set against a backdrop of low-lying dunes; the sands aren't pure white, however, but more of an oyster gray. But if you want to venture into these usually cold waters, the safest swimming is on the beach extending to the west of the harbors. At the marina are public toilets and showers.

Where to Dine

Chances are you'll be in the area for lunch. There are a few slightly formal places to eat, but our suggestion for a meal is to walk east along the coastal road from the fishing harbor until you come to a little outlet called **Klintholm Røgeri.** Here you can purchase fried or smoked fish and wash it down with a cold Carlsberg. This is an ideal place to enjoy a picnic, and there are picnic tables on-site.

SIGHTS IN WEST MØN

After a visit to Møns Klint, you'll have to take the same route back into Stege. But there are other attractions in Møn if time remains. From Stege, head south along Route 287 to **Grønjægers Høj,** an impressive long barrow surrounded by a stone circle, 6km (3^3/$_4$

miles) south of Stege near the hamlet of Æbelnæs. Called "The Hill of the Green Hunts-man," it's a Stone Age "passage grave." Nearly 150 large stones surround the megalithic tomb with three chambers, one of the largest such gravesites in all of Scandinavia.

The third church of Møn to have been decorated by the Master of Elmelunde lies in the area. To reach it, continue on Route 287 to Damsholte, then go left on a minor road following the sign to **Fanefjord Kirke** ★, Fanefjordkirkevej, Fanefjord (✆ **55-81-70-05**). The frescoes in the chancel date from the mid-14th century, but the rest are by the master himself. The cycle of paintings was called *Biblia Pauperum,* or "Bible of the poor," since many of the peasants who formed the congregation did not read. Most of the themes were taken from the Old and New Testaments, and others are loosely based on Christian legends.

Depicted are the *Adoration of the Magi,* the *Baptism of Jesus,* the *Birth of Jesus,* and the *Annunciation,* among other subjects. *The Slaughter of the Innocents* is particularly moving. The most fun and amusing fresco is *St. George and the Dragon.* In the choir arch are some frescoes from the High Gothic period, around the mid-14th century, depicting St. Mar-tin and St. Christopher, among other subjects, with St. Christopher seen carrying Christ across a fjord. The imagination that went into these frescoes shows amazing creativity and massive talent, and the refinement of color is also a remarkable achievement. They are well worth the detour here to reach them. The Gothic-styled church is open Monday to Saturday 7am to 4pm; admission is free.

One final attraction remains for Møn, and it's actually an island unto itself. The island of **Bogø** at the southwestern edge of Møn is reached by continuing along Route 287. A causeway leads to what is called "The Island of Mills." Once many mills peppered the little island, but now there's only one remaining, **Bogø Molle,** which was constructed in 1852 and looks like a windmill from Holland.

Other than its bucolic charm, there isn't a lot to see and do on Bogø, but it has some of the most unspoiled scenery around and makes for a satisfying drive.

In the little hamlet, you can pass by a medieval village church with some late-15th-century murals, but you will have seen better and more intriguing churches if you've already toured Møn. It isn't necessary to return to Møn to get back to Zealand. You can drive straight through Bogø until you come to the Farø bridges, which will connect you with Copenhagen in the north or to Falster in the south.

As you approach the ramp to the bridges, you'll see the **Farobroen Welcome Center,** with a cafeteria, money-exchange office, and toilets, and at the tourist kiosk here you can pick up brochures about Denmark if you wish to continue your journey into other parts of the country.

9

Bornholm

Bornholm is for connoisseurs and an acquired taste. We had discovered all of Denmark before getting around to Bornholm, writing it off as a Baltic island where Danish families who can't afford a Mediterranean holiday go to romp on the sandy beaches in summer. But after coming to know Bornholm in greater depth, we eventually succumbed to its peculiar charm.

The most hurried visitor to Denmark will still pass it by, and it's damn hard to get an accommodation in July and August unless you make reservations well in advance. Most of the holiday flats want a full week's booking, and very few foreign visitors, except perhaps Germans, have so much time to devote to Bornholm.

We like to skip the overcrowded summers altogether and visit in either the late spring or early fall, when Bornholm appears at its most dramatic seasonal change. Of course, that means you'll have to forego beach life, but the waters, even in July or August, are just too cold for us. Perhaps we grew spoiled after living for so many years in the Florida Keys.

Surrounded by the Baltic Sea, astride the important shipping lanes that connect St. Petersburg with Copenhagen and the Atlantic, Bornholm sits only 37km (23 miles) off the coast of Sweden, but about 153km (95 miles) east of Copenhagen and the rest of Denmark. Prized as a strategic Baltic military and trading outpost since the early Middle Ages, and sadly the site of many bloody territorial disputes among the Danes, Germans, and Swedes, it's home to 45,000 year-round residents. An additional 450,000 visitors arrive during the balmy months of summer. Besides tourism, which is growing rapidly, the economy relies on trade, fishing, herring processing, agriculture, and the manufacture of ceramics.

Thanks to the island's deep veins of clay, ceramics has been a major industry since the 1700s.

Covering a terrain of granite and sandstone is a thin but rich layer of topsoil; the island's rock-studded surface is made up of forests and moors. The unusual topography and surprisingly temperate autumn climate—a function of the waters of the Baltic—promote the verdant growth of plants: figs, mulberries, and enough lavish conifers to create the third-largest forest in Denmark (right in the center of the island). This forest, Almindingen, has the only rocking stone which still rocks. Rocking stones are giant erratic boulders weighing up to 40 tons that were brought to Bornholm by the advancing glaciers during the last Ice Age. In addition, one of Denmark's largest waterfalls, Døndalen, lies in the north of Bornholm in a rift valley and is best viewed from spring to fall.

The island covers 945 sq. km (365 sq. miles), and most of the inhabitants live along 140km (87 miles) of coastline. Not only do the flora and fauna differ in many respects from the rest of Denmark, but its geology is unique as well. The island is divided into two geologic zones: 1,500-million-year-old bedrock to the north and a 550-million-year-old layer of sandstone to the south. The best beaches of Bornholm lie in the southwestern section of the island, between the towns of Balka and the main beach town of Dueodde.

Bornholmers traditionally have been fishermen and farmers. Today their villages are still idyllic, evocative of the old way of life in their well-kept homesteads, as are fishing hamlets with their characteristic smokehouse chimneys, often used for smoking herring.

The island is still sparsely populated. Grand Canary, a Spanish island off the coast of Africa, for example, is the same size as Bornholm, but while that resort hosts some two million residents in high season, the greatest number of people ever seen on Bornholm at one time is 100,000.

Because of its location at the crossroads of warring nations, Bornholm has had a turbulent history, even as recently as 1945. Strongholds and fortified churches protected local inhabitants when the island was a virtual plaything in the power struggle between royal and religious forces. It was plundered by pirate fleets, noblemen, and the Hanseatic towns of Pomerania. It didn't experience peace until after it revolted against Swedish conquerors at the end of Denmark's war with Sweden in 1658. A group of liberators shot the island's Swedish Lord, and the Bornholmers handed their land over to the king of Denmark.

On a more modern and rather fanatical note, the liberation of Bornholm—unlike the rest of Denmark—was slow to come in 1945. Even when the Nazis had surrendered, the local German commandant on Bornholm refused to give up the island to the Allies. In response, the Soviets rained bombs down on Rønne and Nexø (the two main towns) and then invaded the island and occupied it for several months before returning it to the crown of Denmark. During the long Cold War, the Danes indulged in a little payback time with the Russians. Bornholm became one of NATO's key surveillance bases, spying on what Ronald Reagan called "The Evil Empire."

The island's cuisine is obviously influenced by the surrounding sea. Baltic herring, cod, and salmon are the traditional dishes. One of the most popular local dishes is called Sun over Gudhjem, a specialty of smoked herring topped with a raw egg yolk in an onion ring. It's served with coarse salt and chives, or, most often, radishes. In autumn, the small Bornholm herring are caught and used for a variety of spiced and pickled herring dishes. Another local dish is salt-fried herring served on dark rye bread with beetroot and hot mustard. When it comes to food, those Bornholmers are a hearty bunch.

ESSENTIALS
Getting There

By Ferry The most popular means of reaching the island from Copenhagen is the 7-hour ferryboat ride. Maintained by the **Bornholmstraffiken** (© **56-95-18-66;** www.bornholmstrafikken.dk), these ferries depart year-round from the pier at Kvæsthusbroen, once per evening, at 11:30pm, with scheduled arrival the following morning at 6:30am. Late-June to mid-August there's an additional departure at 8:30am every day except Wednesday. Passage costs DKK23 ($3.90/£2.30) per person each way. These ferries are most often used to transport a car from Copenhagen, which costs DKK168 ($29/£17) each way.

Tips   **Hassle on Bornholm**

Don't expect to enjoy a holiday on Bornholm without some inconvenience: Boats from Copenhagen take either 5¹/₂ or 7 hours each way. And if you plan to visit in midsummer, firm reservations are essential because of the large numbers of Danes who come for the sandy beaches and the Baltic sunshine.

Bornholm Ferries, Havnen, at Rønne (© **56-95-18-66**), operates 2¹/₂-hour ferries from Ystad on the southern coast of Sweden, with up to four departures daily. These ferries have tax-free shops onboard. A car with a maximum of five passengers costs DKK180 ($31/£18) each way. You can also travel from Sassnitz-Mukran (Rügen) in north Germany for a 3¹/₂-hour crossing to Bornholm, arriving at Rønne. Tax-free shopping is also found onboard during this crossing. From Germany, one-way passage for a car with a maximum of five passengers is DKK905 to DKK1,375 ($154–$234/£91–£138). Each of these ferries has a restaurant or bistro featuring a buffet with Danish and Bornholm specialties.

By Plane   Cimber Air (© **70-10-12-18;** www.cimber.dk) has about nine flights a day from Copenhagen to Bornholm's airport, 5.5km (3¹/₂ miles) south of Rønne. Depending on restrictions, round-trip fares range from DKK687 to DKK1,880 ($117–$320/£69–£188).

Visitor Information

The tourist office, **The Bornholm Welcome Center,** Kystvej 3, Rønne (© **56-95-95-00;** www.bornholm.info), is open June to August daily 9am to 7:30pm; April, May, September, and October Monday to Friday 9am to 4pm, Saturday 9am to noon; November to March Monday to Friday 9am to 4pm.

Getting Around

By Car   The best place on the island for car rentals is **Europcar,** Nodre Kystvej 1, in Rønne (© **877/940-6900** in the U.S., or 56-95-43-00; www.europcar.com). Its least expensive rentals begin at DKK2,640 ($449/£264) per week, including unlimited mileage and insurance coverage, as well as the government tax. In addition, **Avis** is located at Snellemark 19, in Rønne (© **800/230-4898** in the U.S., or 48-71-29-65).

By Bicycle   During sunny weather, biking around the island is almost as popular as driving. If you want to do as the Danes do, rent a bike; the prices are pretty much the same throughout the island—about DKK60 ($10/£6) a day. A suggested bike-rental company in Rønne is **Bornholms Cykleudleijning,** Nordre Kystvej 5 (© **56-95-13-59;** www.bornholms-cykeludlejning.dk). It's open daily 8am to 4pm and 8:30 to 9pm.

EXPLORING THE ISLAND

Even if you have a car available, you might want to take a bike tour (see "Seeing the Sights," below). Ask at any tourist office for a map of the island's more than 190km (120 miles) of bicycle trails, and divide this tour into several days, hitting the highlights mentioned below at your own pace.

The tour begins at Rønne, but you could join in at almost any point; basically, the route goes counterclockwise around the island's periphery. Be aware that Bornholm's highways do not have route numbers; even though some maps show the main east-west artery as Route 38, local residents call it "the road to Nexø."

1 RØNNE

Your arrival point is Rønne, the capital of the island, but not the most compelling reason to visit Bornholm. There are far more rewarding targets away from the main town, which lies on the western coast facing the island of Zealand and is the site of the major harbor and airport.

But, once here, you'll find Rønne has a certain charm as you walk its historic Gamle Stan (Old Town), with its cobblestoned streets flanked by cross-timbered houses, many of them brightly painted in such "sunshine colors" as yellow and orange.

The best streets for seeing Bornholm as it used to be are **Laksegade** and **Storegade,** plus the triangular sector lying between **Store Torv** and **Lille Torv.** You'll find even more charm in many of the island's smaller towns or hamlets.

Because of Soviet aerial attacks in 1945, most of Rønne was left in shambles, so what you see today is essentially a modern town with a population of some 15,000 people. The parents of today's inhabitants rebuilt Rønne wisely in the postwar years, opting for an old-fashioned architectural look, which makes most of the houses look older than they actually are.

If you arrive by ferry, you'll notice **St. Nicolai Church,** dedicated to the patron saint of seafarers, on Harbor Hill, towering over the small South Boat Harbor just below. It wasn't until the 18th century that locals moved ahead with plans for a large trading harbor here. Even today the harbor is still expanding to service ferries and the many cruise ships that call at Rønne in increasing numbers.

Should you experience that rare hot day in Denmark, you'll find that vast stretches of sand lie both south and north of Rønne. These beaches are popular with Danish families, many from Copenhagen, in summer.

SEEING THE SIGHTS

If you have a car or are a great biker, you can also view some attractions in the environs. **Borgårdsten** lies 9km (5²/₃ miles) north of Rønne along the road to the hamlet of Hasle. This is the most significant runic stone on the island. First found in 1868, it dates from the beginning of the 12th century. Some long-ago Viking inscribed SVENGER HAD THIS STONE PLACED HERE FOR HIS FATHER TOSTE AND FOR HIS BROTHER ALVLAK AND FOR HIS MOTHER AND SISTERS. Apparently, women weren't considered important enough to list their names.

If you visit Borgårdsten, you can continue for 2.5km (1¹/₂ miles) up the coast to the little port of **Hasle,** with its stone church from the 1300s and a half-timbered tower. Inside the church is an intricately carved and painted altar, the work of an unknown Lübeck artist, dating from the mid-15th century. In July a "herring festival" is celebrated here.

If you'd like to check out a west-coast Bornholm beach, you'll find the best one south of Hasle. It's quite sandy and set against a backdrop of pine trees.

While at Hasle, you can see five smokehouses in a row, lying on the coastline. One of the smokehouses (which can be visited free) is preserved as it was originally built in 1897, the **Silderøgerierne I Hasle,** Sdr. Bæk 16–20 (© **56-96-44-11**). In one of the other smokehouses, you can watch herring and other kinds of fish being smoked the traditional way, in open chimneys. Afterward you can purchase smoked fish, pick up a beer, and find a nearby spot for an idyllic and quintessential Bornholm experience.

The major and more clearly defined attractions of Bornholm include the following:

Bornholms Museum ★ To open this museum, islanders raided their attics for any curiosities that might be of interest to the general public, and they came up with a number of objects of intrigue, ranging from antique toys of the 19th century to gold objects discovered while farmers were plowing their fields. Even Roman coins are on display. The nautical exhibits are decked out like a ship's interior. Installed in what used to be the major hospital on the island, the museum traces the history of Bornholm's unique position in the

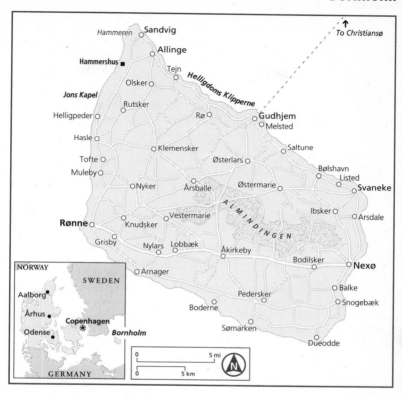

Baltic through displays on archaeology, folkloric costumes, ethnology, and seafaring and agrarian traditions. Several rooms are outfitted with 19th-century antique furniture, island-made silverware, and accessories. Of special interest is the collection of Bornholm-made clocks, copied from a shipment of English clocks that was salvaged from a Dutch shipwreck in the late 1700s. Because Bornholm is known for its ceramics and glassware, it is entirely predictable that there are nearly 5,000 pieces of glassware and handcrafted ceramics.

Skt. Mortensgade 29. (✆ **56-95-07-35.** www.bornholmsmuseum.dk. Admission DKK50 ($8.50/£5) adults, free for children 17 and under. Mid-May to mid-Oct Mon–Sat 10am–5pm; mid-Oct to mid-May Mon–Sat 1–4pm.

Ericksson's Gård (Farm) ★ (Finds) This is the most enchanting private home we've found on Bornholm, and the public can visit it and wander through its beautiful garden. Set on the outskirts of Rønne, just a short walk from the town center, this is the island's best-preserved example of an old-fashioned farm—the kind that once flourished on Bornholm. Originally constructed in 1806, it's a half-timbered, tile-covered building filled with antique furniture and oil paintings, many of them by the well-known Danish artist Kristian Zahrtmann. Some of the objects inside the house commemorate the marriage of a descendant of the farm's original owners—the Ericksson family. An Ericksson daughter married the Danish poet Holger Drachmann (1846–1908), whose works are studied by virtually every schoolchild in Denmark. Finally you can explore the remarkable **garden** ★★★, which horticulturists admire for its 160 species of nonhybrid roses and flowers. It's best seen in July.

Laksegade 7. ✆ **56-95-87-35.** Admission DKK50 ($8.50/£5) adults, free for children 16 and under. July to mid-Aug daily 10am–5pm; mid-Aug to mid-Oct Mon–Sat 10am–5pm. Closed mid-Oct to June.

Forsvarsmuseet   Today this museum attracts World War II buffs like us. But originally, the citadel was built in 1650 for defensive purposes, in the southern part of town. With its massive round tower, this old castle is like an armed fortress, with all its guns, blades, weapons, war maps, and models of fortification. There are even military uniforms of the men who fought each other, plus a rare collection of antique armaments. By far the most intriguing exhibitions depict the Nazi occupation of the island from 1940 to 1945, followed by the aerial bombardment of Rønne and Nexø by the Soviet air force. The Soviets occupied the island when the Nazis either were killed or fled for their lives. Although the Soviets left in the spring of 1946, it was done with reluctance. Stalin felt that Bornholm would have made a great center for spying on the west.

Kastellet Galløkken. ✆ **56-95-65-83.** Admission DKK30 ($5.10/£3) adults, DKK20 ($3.40/£2) children 4–16, free for children 5 and under. June–Oct Tues–Sun 11am–5pm.

Hjorth's Fabrik (Bornholm Ceramic Museum) ★   Bornholm has long been famed for its beautiful ceramics, and this "working ceramics museum" showcases the craft better than any other place on the island. The unusual geology of Bornholm includes deep veins of clay that potters have appreciated for many generations. Since the 1700s, hundreds of island residents have produced large numbers of unusual pots, plates, and cups—many of which are whimsical and highly idiosyncratic reminders of another way of life. In 1858, a small-scale factory, Hjorth's Ceramics, was established to make pottery from the island's rich deposits of clay, surviving until 1993. In 1995, this museum was established in the company's original factory, a solid building dating back to 1860. Inside, you'll find an intriguing hybrid between an art gallery and an industrial museum. You'll see the island's best examples of the dark-brown, yellow, and gray pottery that was produced in abundance beginning in the 1700s; samples of the dishes and bowls made by the Hjorth company over the years; and some of the work of Bornholm's modern-day potters. Throughout the year, several ceramic artists maintain studios inside, casting, spinning, or glazing pots in full view of visitors. Just follow the path of clay. Women descendants of the fourth generation of the Hjorth family run the museum. The museum shop sells modern-day replicas of Hjorth ceramics, and many exhibits trace the production process from start to finish. We once purchased a cherished "heirloom" set of old-fashioned pharmacy jars here.

Krystalgade 5. ✆ **56-95-01-60.** Admission mid-Apr to mid-Oct DKK50 ($8.50/£5) adults, free for children 17 and under; mid-Oct to mid-Apr DKK13 ($2.20/£1.30) adults, free for children. May–Oct Mon–Fri 10am–5pm, Sat 10am–2pm; Nov–Apr Mon–Fri 10am–5pm, Sat 10am–1pm.

SHOPPING

Despite its isolation in the middle of the Baltic, Bornholm offers many opportunities for acquiring some serious merchandise. Most of the island's shops line the streets funneling into the Lille Torv and the Store Torv. Part of the fun for us involves wandering aimlessly from shop to shop, but if you want specific addresses and ideas, consider any of the following.

Want to offer some flowers to the object of your most recent affections? Head for **Lil-liendal Plantecenter,** Sagavej 1 (© **56-95-47-24**). Some of the most unusual and eccentric kitchen- and housewares in Bornholm are available at **Inspiration,** Lille Torv 1 (© **56-95-01-11**). Expect Danish functionalism combined with wrought iron, glass, ceramics, textiles, and wood; much of it is made within Scandinavia.

If you're looking for a garment of any degree of formality for the child or kids you left behind, the best clothing store on the island is **Kids' Shop,** Skt. Mortensgade 4 (© **56-91-00-17**). Is your camera running out of film? Film supply or development is available at **Ilsted Bech,** Snellmark 25 (© **56-95-00-23**).

A major outlet for some of the art glass produced in abundance on Bornholm is **Per-nille Bülow Glas,** Lille Torv (© **56-95-43-05**).

The island is known for its unique Bornholmer grandfather clocks. The tradition began in 1744, when a Dutch ship was stranded on the way from Helsingør in Denmark to Tallinn in Estonia. In its hold were five clocks and a cask with weights for them. Dexterous young men made models of the clocks and, in so doing, founded a Bornholm clockmaking tradition, a craft that virtually disappeared at the end of World War II. The craft has now been revived, and the island's largest clockmaker workshop is located in Rønne. **Nye Bornholmerure** ★★, Torneværksvej 26 (© **56-95-31-08**), sells the finest handmade grandfather clocks in Denmark, although they can be very expensive depending on the model. These clocks sound the hour with music—everything from Mozart to Andrew Lloyd Weber.

Many Swedes come over to Bornholm just to shop for the island's famous ceramics. **Michael Andersen** ★★, Lille Torv 7 (© **56-95-00-01**), still preserves the old ceramics-making traditions but manufactures many modern products as well.

The island's best goldsmith—and he's a stunning talent—is Jørn-Ole Thomsen, who works at **Guldhuset** ★★★, Bornholmercentret (© **56-95-02-70**), on Store Torv. Thomsen makes fine jewelry not only for the local shop but also for Georg Jensen, the world-famous silver and goldsmith company.

WHERE TO STAY

The island is essentially a fair-weather destination, and most hotels are likely to be closed in winter except for a few die-hards.

Hotel Griffen ★ (Kids) Even though it was constructed in the dull architectural era of the '70s, its buildings have a certain style, designed to evoke 18th-century hip-roofed manor houses. Two of the four buildings contain the bedrooms, which are separated from the dining, drinking, and convention facilities in the other structures. Lying in the heart of Rønne, a 5-minute walk to the beach and the town center, the hotel is also close to a busy summer marina. We especially like the way the architects added plenty of windows so guests can take in views of the Baltic in many directions. Some rooms have floor-to-ceiling windows and glass doors. The small-to-midsize bedrooms are furnished in a modern but minimalist style, each comfortable and tasteful. We are especially fond of their "Sunset Menu," serv ed every evening between 5 and 9pm, and based on the "freshest and best" found at the market that day, most often seafood from Baltic waters.

Ndr. Kystvej 34, DK-3700 Rønne. © **56-95-51-11**. Fax 56-95-52-97. www.krohotel.dk. 140 units. DKK1,045–DKK1,195 ($178–$203/£105–£120) double; DKK1,800 ($306/£180) suite. AE, DC, MC, V. **Amenities:** Restaurant; bar; indoor heated pool; kids' pool; use of tennis courts at Radisson; sauna; room service; Wi-Fi (in lobby). *In room:* TV, hair dryer.

Hotel Ryttergården ★ (Kids) This is one of the best hotels—it's more of a holiday resort, really—on Bornholm, lying 2km (1¼ miles) south of Rønne. It is the most scenically located hotel in the area, enjoying its closeness to a sandy beach, a golf course, and woodland offering dozens of walks and hikes along the coast. Built in stages between 1986 and 1998, the compound of angular, big-windowed modern structures evokes a boxy, modern airport terminal with an ample use of glass.

The interior warms considerably, and you have a choice of standard doubles or else one-level holiday apartments, often booked by six persons, which makes them ideal for families. The midsize-to-spacious units have sleek, modern styling, with comfortable and tasteful Danish furnishings in blond wood, with sliding glass doors opening onto balconies fronting the sea. Guests enjoy drinks in an international bar with a starlit ceiling, later patronizing the 150-seat restaurant serving first-rate Danish and international cuisine with a focus on fresh seafood.

Strandvejen 79, DK-3700 Rønne. ℂ **56-95-19-13.** Fax 56-95-19-22. www.hotel-ryttergaarden.dk. 103 units, 28 apts w/kitchenette. DKK825–DKK995 ($140–$169/£83–£100) double; rates include breakfast. Apts for up to 6 occupants DKK3,295–DKK5,595 ($560–$951/£330–£560) per week, without breakfast, plus an obligatory one-time fee of DKK375 ($64/£38) for cleaning. AE, DC, MC, V. Closed Oct–Apr. Bus from Rønne: 23 or 24. **Amenities:** Restaurant; bar; indoor heated pool; tennis court; fitness center; sauna; laundry service; dry cleaning; nonsmoking rooms; solarium; rooms for those w/limited mobility. *In room:* A/C, TV, minibar, hair dryer, trouser press.

Radisson Hotel Fredensborg ★★ (Kids) There are hotels on Bornholm with more atmosphere and charm, but this chain hotel is clearly the market leader for international luxury. Of course, luxury is a relative term. What passes for luxe living on Bornholm wouldn't make the grade in Copenhagen. One of the few hotels on the island to remain open all year, Fredensborg lies in a wooded, tranquil location adjacent to a beach and less than a kilometer (½-mile) south of Rønne harbor. Its Danish modern style from the 1960s wouldn't win architectural awards, but its midsize-to-spacious bedrooms are the island's best appointed, each comfortable and tasteful with a private balcony or terrace overlooking the Baltic. The suites are really apartments with full kitchens, most often rented to families with small children. Some of the best food in Rønne is served at the well-respected **De 5 Ståuerna** restaurant here, specializing in Danish/French cuisine (see below). Guests are allowed to use the pool at the previously recommended Griffen.

Strandvejen 116, DK-3700 Rønne. ℂ **800/333-3333** in the U.S., or 56-96-44-44. Fax 56-90-44-43-14. www. bornholm.radissonsas.com. 72 units. DKK1,225–DKK1,525 ($208–$259/£123–£153) double; DKK1,475–DKK1,675 ($251–$285/£148–£168) suite. Rates include buffet breakfast. AE, DC, MC, V. **Amenities:** Restaurant; bar; tennis court; sauna; room service; babysitting; laundry service; dry cleaning; nonsmoking rooms. *In room:* TV, Wi-Fi, minibar, hair dryer.

Sverres Small Hotel (Value) "Small Hotel" is an apt description for this ocher-colored antique building, which had its origins as a coaching inn, putting up wayfarers since 1850. It's tried to keep up with the times with some modern improvements. It lies in the center of Rønne only 200m (656 ft.) from the yacht-clogged harbor. The place is well maintained and an unpretentious choice if you don't mind the 1km (⅔-mile) trek to the best nearby beach. In keeping with the hotel's name, the bedrooms are small, but comfortably and tastefully furnished. Breakfast is the only meal served, although the neighborhood around the hotel offers a few dining choices.

Snellmark 2, DK-3700 Rønne. ℂ **56-95-03-03.** Fax 56-95-03-92. www.sverres-hotel.dk. 22 units, 12 w/ private bathroom. DKK460 ($78/£46) double w/shared bathroom; DKK550–DKK630 ($94–$107/£55–£63) double w/private bathroom. MC, V. Rates include breakfast. **Amenities:** Breakfast room; lounge; room service. *In room:* TV, no phone.

De 5 Stâuerna ★★ DANISH/FRENCH/INTERNATIONAL   When we once told our Bornholm dining companion we were giving this restaurant two Frommer stars, he protested, "Give it three—be more generous!" But we're stubbornly sticking by our original position. It is, however, the best and the most upscale restaurant on the island, with a clientele that tends to select it for celebratory meals and family gatherings. Its name translates as "the five rooms," each of which is outfitted in a rustic country-Danish style. There's always a platter of the proposed fish of the day, which is usually fried in butter and served with new potatoes—a style that Bornholmers have witnessed since their childhood. Other more elaborate options include Hereford beefsteak prepared *cordon bleu* style, with salted cured ham and Emmenthaler cheese; tournedos of beef flambéed in Calvados and served with apples and onions; an exotic sautéed filet of ostrich with Mexican pimentos and peppers; marinated and minced beefsteak with chilies; and a dish that we personally prefer more than almost anything else on the menu: Bornholm lamb served with a sauce concocted from rosemary, olive oil, and tarragon.

In the Radisson Hotel Fredensborg, Strandvejen 116. ℂ **56-90-44-44.** Reservations recommended. Main courses DKK250–DKK375 ($43–$64/£25–£38); 4-course fixed-price menu DKK275–DKK365 ($47–$62/£28–£37); fish buffet DKK365 ($62/£37) Thurs–Fri 6–8:30pm. AE, DC, MC, V. Daily 11:30am–9:30pm.

Rådhuskroen ★ (Finds) DANISH   This is the most visible and, in its own way, most charming restaurant in Rønne, although it doesn't use the pricey ingredients or employ the expensive chefs hired by the previously recommended De 5 Stâuerna. It's situated in the darkened and intimately illuminated cellar of the Town Hall, a 140-year-old building with a long history of feeding island residents—and feeding them well—in a cozy setting protected from blustering midwinter winds. Wall sconces cast romantic shadows over a collection of antique furniture and accessories, as a well-trained staff serves fresh and creative dishes, such as filet of salmon in a "summer sauce" of fresh tomatoes, chives, and herbs, and two different sizes of tender and beefsteak ("Mr. Beef" and "Mrs. Beef").

Nørregade 2. ℂ **56-95-00-69.** Reservations recommended on weekends. Main courses DKK125–DKK200 ($21–$34/£13–£20). AE, DC, MC, V. Mon–Sat noon–3pm and 5–9pm.

RØNNE AFTER DARK

Its role as Bornholm's largest settlement forces Rønne into the sometimes unwanted role as nightlife capital of the island. But don't expect too much glitter, as things on Bornholm tend to stay quiet.

For high-energy members of the under-30 generation, the most visible and popular dance club on the island is **Red Barone,** Skt. Mortensgade 48, in Rønne (ℂ **56-95-06-88**). Victim to oft-changing ownership within the past decade, it offers high-volume mania that's associated with nightlife in bigger cities. The venue is a dark-painted, much-used environment with prominent bars, battered sofas and chairs, and a dance floor lit by colored lights that just might tempt you to get up and dance. A DKK40 ($6.80/£4) cover charge is imposed on Friday and Saturday; other times, entrance is free. If you're less interested in hanging out with the young crowd, consider a pint of Guinness at **O'Malley's Irish Pub,** Store Torvegade, in Rønne (ℂ **56-95-00-16**), where clients older than 30 appreciate the Celtic conviviality and the recorded music.

Calm, cool, and mellow, **Dr. Jazz** ★, Snelle Mark 26 (ℂ **56-95-50-26**), is Bornholm's leading emporium of jazz, which is produced by local combos as well as groups imported from other parts of Europe. Expect a crowd of drinkers and smokers over 25, and a spontaneity that can be rather charming. It's open daily 11pm to 5am. There's usually no cover charge.

FROM RØNNE TO NEXØ

From Rønne, drive east along the island's modern highway, A38, following the signs toward Nexø. Stop in **Nylars** (about 5km/3 miles from Rønne), a town that's known as the site of the best-preserved of Bornholm's four round churches. The **Nylarskirke** (© 56-97-20-13), built around 1250 and rising prominently from the center of a community with no more than about 50 buildings, contains frescoes that depict the Creation and the expulsion of Adam and Eve from the Garden of Eden. The cylindrical nave has three floors, the uppermost of which was a watchman's tower in the Middle Ages. You can also view two fragments of a runic stone. From Rønne, you can take bus no. 6 if you don't have a car; the bike path from Rønne to Åkirkeby also passes by the church. Admission is free May to October 20, Monday to Friday 9am to 5pm.

Continue driving another 5km (3 miles) east until you reach **Åkirkeby,** the only inland settlement of any size. With an economy based on farming, the hamlet is small-scale and sleepy, and is Bornholm's oldest settlement (its town charter dates from 1346). The little town was important in medieval times when islanders had to move inland to avoid attacks from enemies at sea. Bornholm's regional council met here until 1776, and Åkirkeby was also the ecclesiastical center of Bornholm.

It's also home to the island's oldest and largest church, **Åkirke,** Torvet (© 56-97-41-03), originally built around 1250. This church isn't as eccentric as some of the others. It's a sandstone-fronted monument built with defense in mind, as you'll note from the small windows. Inside, a Romanesque baptismal font is incised with runic inscriptions believed to be carved by the master craftsman Sigraf on the island of Gotland. Other runic inscriptions appear on the cloverleaf-shaped arches. The church is open daily 10am to 4pm, charging DKK10 ($1.70/£1) for visitors.

Åkirkeby is a good point to cut inland if you wish to see some of Bornholm's woodlands, among the densest in Denmark, with forests filled with oak, hemlock, fir, spruce, and beech trees. The tourist office in Rønne (see "Visitor Information," earlier in this chapter) will give you a map outlining the best of the trails that cut through Bornholm's largest forest, **Almindingen,** in the center of the island. It can be reached by following a signposted road north from Åkirkeby. The forest is also the location of the island's highest point, **Rytterknægten,** a 160m (525-ft.) hill with a lookout tower, Kongemindet, with a staircase you can climb for a panoramic view of the dense woodlands.

You can also pick up information at a minor, rarely used tourist office that's much less visible than the island's main office in Rønne. It's the **Sydbornholms Turistbureau,** Torvet 2 (© 56-97-45-20; www.visitdenmark.com), at Åkirkeby. Mid-May to mid-September, it's open Monday through Friday 9am to 6pm and Saturday 8am to 1pm. The rest of the year, hours are Monday to Friday 10am to 6:30pm, closed Saturday and Sunday.

A minor museum for devoted automobile fans is the **Bornholms Automobilmuseum,** Grammegardsvej 1 (© 56-97-45-95; www.bornholmsautomobilmuseum.dk), displaying vintage cars and motorcycles, plus some farm equipment and tractors that highlight the 20th century's advances in agrarian science. Antique cars and tractors derive from such manufacturers as Delahaye, Opel, Ford, Adler, Singer, Jaguar, and Fiat. It's open May to October, Monday to Saturday 10am to 5pm. The rest of the year it's closed, and admission costs DKK40 ($6.80/£4) adults, DKK20 ($3.40/£2) ages 5 to 15.

From Åkirkeby, cut southeast for 4.5km (2³/₄ miles), following the signs to **Pedersker**, a hamlet with only three shops (which close down during the cold-weather months). Six kilometers (3³/₄ miles) later you'll reach **Dueodde,** the name of both a raffish beachfront community and the entire region around the southernmost tip of the island. The village of Dueodde marks the southern edge of a stretch of coastline that is the finest beach on the island. The oceanfront bounty—and the best beaches on the island—stretch north-ward and eastward to the town of **Balka,** 5km (3 miles) beyond, encompassing stretches of white sand with grains so fine that they were used for generations to fill hourglasses. The towns themselves are little more than backdrops for seasonal kiosks and a scattering of holiday homes for mainland Danes and Swedes. Most of the landscape is a virtual wilderness of pine and spruce trees, salt-tolerant shrubs, and sand dunes, some of which rise more than 12m (40 ft.) above the nearby sea.

The focal point of this southeastern coastline is the **Dueodde Fyr** (Dueodde Light-house), the tallest lighthouse on the island, built in 1962 to warn ships away from the extreme southern tip of the island. Weather permitting, you can climb to its top during daylight hours May to October for a fee of DKK5 (85¢/50p), which you pay directly to the lighthouse keeper. For information, call the tourist office in Dueodde (℃ **56-49-70-79**).

From Dueodde, continue along the coast in a northeasterly direction, passing through the unpretentious fishing hamlets of **Snogebæk** and **Balka.** Immediately north of Balka, the road will deliver you north to Nexø, the second major town of the island after Rønne, opening onto the eastern coast facing Sweden.

---

2 NEXØ ★

Nexø, 48km (30 miles) northeast of Rønne, has a year-round population of 3,900, which makes it the largest fishing port on the island. As is the case with Rønne, we like to wander around only for 2 hours or so before pressing on to the countryside. It's not an unattractive town, because, after Soviet bombings in 1945, its demolished buildings were reconstructed more or less in the style of the 17th and 18th centuries. The 11th-hour World War II bombings of the town's once-fabled 900 antique buildings is the stuff of local legend—just ask any old-timer.

In May 1945, Nexø was heavily bombed by the Russians during 2 days of horror; this happened several days after the rest of Denmark had been liberated from the Nazis. Nexø was a final holdout of Nazi soldiers in the closing days of the war. Ironically, Bornholm was the last area of Denmark to get rid of its Russian "liberators," who didn't completely evacuate the island until 1946.

Before exploring the area, you can pick up good information at the **Nexø-Dueodde Turistbureau,** Sdr. Hammer 2A (℃ **56-49-70-79**). May to August, it's open Monday to Friday 10am to 5pm and Saturday 9am to 2pm. The rest of the year, it's open Monday to Friday 10am to 5pm and closed Saturday and Sunday.

One of the town's more eccentric and idiosyncratic monuments is the **Nexø Museum,** Havnen (℃ **56-49-25-56**), open only May to October, daily 10am to 4pm. For an entrance fee of DKK35 ($6/£3.50), you'll see displays of fishing-related equipment that has sustained the local economy, and memorabilia of the Danish author Martin Ander-sen (1869–1954)—better known as Martin Andersen Nexø, a pen name he adopted in honor of his native village. His novel *Pelle the Conqueror,* set in Bornholm and later made into an Oscar-winning film, revealed how Danish landowners in the early 20th century exploited Swedish newcomers to the island. Admittedly, this is hardly a subject that will interest most people, and you may want to pass it by in favor of outdoor fun, which is what Bornholm is all about.

WHERE TO STAY

In this southeastern corridor of Bornholm, you aren't limited just to Nexø. In summer, you can also stay at the seaside hamlets of **Dueodde** or **Snogebæk,** immediately south of Nexø. These are more scenic places to stay, and they also open onto the island's best beaches. Dueodde is Bornholm's number one beach area, and the entire stretch of coast is filled with rolling dunes and endless strips of white sand. Snogebæk is a little seaside settlement with holiday homes, but there's no village attached to Dueodde. For the most part, residents who live in Dueodde or Snogebæk use Nexø for their services and supplies. All these destinations are essentially summer ones, and most of the places to stay close for the winter.

At Nexø

Hotel Balka Strand   This is the only hotel along Bornholm's beach-fringed eastern coast that remains open year-round, so it stays busy even in midwinter, usually with conferences. Originally built in the 1970s and doubled in size in 1992, the hotel on its exterior could easily fit into any number of towns in America's heartland. There's nothing particularly Bornholmian about it; rather it's imbued with a more international aura. The government gives it four stars, based more on comfort and facilities than any particular winning atmosphere. Nonetheless, the hotel staff is helpful and personal in their welcome, and the building is laid out in a one-story format about 150m (490 ft.) from one of the island's best bathing beaches, adjoining a protected nature preserve ideal for walks or hikes. The neatly kept midsize bedrooms are comfortably and tastefully furnished in Danish modern (if you travel in Denmark, you invariably get Danish modern in the bedrooms). A standard but good cuisine is served in a big-windowed dining room, where most Danish-style dinners conclude with live music, dancing, or some form of entertainment.

Boulevarden 9, DK-3730 Nexø. ✆ **56-49-49-49.** Fax 56-49-49-48. www.hotelbalkastrand.dk. 95 units, half w/kitchenettes. DKK995 ($169/£100) double; DKK1,150 ($196/£115) double w/kitchenette. Rates include breakfast and dinner. MC, V. From Nexø, drive 2.5km (1½ miles) south along the coastal road, following the signs to Balka and Dueodde. **Amenities:** Restaurant; bar; outdoor heated pool; tennis court; sauna; room service; laundry service; dry cleaning; nonsmoking rooms; rooms for those w/limited mobility. *In room:* TV, Wi-Fi, hair dryer, safe.

Strandhotel Balka Søbad (Kids)   This hotel is designed for those seeking summer fun at one of Bornholm's prettiest sandy beaches, the waters of which lie no more than 90m (295 ft.) from the hotel's door. A compound of five white-painted buildings were modern in 1972 and 1976 when they were first constructed and aren't as fresh as they were, but the hotel's maintenance is still good. The clientele consists mostly of families with children, many of which can be seen renting a bike to go on self-generated tours of the island. The midsize-to-spacious bedrooms are furnished in plain but comfortable Danish modern with a balcony or private terrace in most cases. For the higher price, you often get a second bedroom, ideal for the family trade.

Vestre Strandvej 25, DK-3730 Nexø. ✆ **56-49-22-25.** Fax 56-49-22-33. www.hotel-balkasoebad.dk. 106 units. DKK895–DKK1,640 ($152–$279/£90–£164) double. Rates include breakfast. MC, V. Closed Nov–Apr. From Nexø, drive 3km (1¾ miles) south, following the signs to Snogebæk. **Amenities:** Restaurant; bar; outdoor heated pool; tennis court; sauna; laundry service; dry cleaning. *In room:* TV, kitchenette (in some).

At Snogebæk

Snogebæk Hotelpension (Value) This little boardinghouse began life as a rustic farmhouse at the turn of the 20th century, but in an expansion in the 1980s, it turned itself successfully into a small hotel with motel-style wings that extend into a garden. Set about a kilometer (²/₃ mile) west of the center of Snogebæk, we find it a refreshing place to stay. It lies inland about a kilometer (²/₃ mile) from the nearest good beach, and it is near many good walking and hiking trails. The farmhouse's old, beamed interior was converted into a restaurant and social center for guests. The rooms are comfortable enough though hardly plush—in fact, about as basic as we'd want to recommend with small shower-only bathroom units. The rooms would be more claustrophobic if they didn't open onto well-maintained greenery that surrounds the hotel. The on-site restaurant serves Danish fare, with a lot of fish based on the catch of the day. Surprisingly, such a simple place has one of the best hotel pools sheltered under an enclosed greenhouse-style canopy.

Ellegade 9, DK-3730 Snogebæk. (𝒞 **56-48-80-80.** Fax 56-48-81-31. www.zzz-zzz.dk. 25 units. DKK640–DKK1,300 ($109–$221/£64–£130) double. Rates include breakfast. MC, V. Closed Oct–Apr. **Amenities:** Restaurant; bar; indoor heated pool. *In room:* TV.

At Dueodde

Dueodde Badehotel ★ (Kids) This hotel is very much a family affair, which could be a turnoff for romantic duos seeking a more secluded Bornholm hideaway. Well-designed and tasteful, this two-story motel-like structure was built in 1978 and remains the most southerly hotel in Bornholm, set in a private pine-wood forest. It's surrounded by scrub-covered sand dunes and is a short walk from the beach, one of the finest in Europe and riddled with sand dunes and a wide stretch of fine, white sand. If only the water were warmer, it would be perfect. When the weather is bad, guests have access to a public indoor swimming pool just 400m (1,312 ft.) from the hotel. Each accommodation is laid out something like an efficiently designed suite aboard a cruise ship, with compact dimensions, a color scheme of blue and white, modern furniture, and, in every case, a separate seating area and a balcony or terrace. Each has a neatly kept bathroom equipped with a shower unit. Families often book the apartments, which come in various sizes, although all of them have an up-to-date kitchen. There's a comfortable restaurant serving Danish meals and open to the general public.

Poulsker, DK-3730 Nexø. (𝒞 **56-48-86-49.** Fax 56-48-89-59. www.dueodde-badehotel.dk. 48 apts w/ kitchenette. DKK950–DKK1,370 ($162–$233/£95–£137) double. AE, DC, MC, V. Closed Nov–Apr. From Nexø, drive 9km (5²/₃ miles) south along the coastal road, following the signs for Dueodde. **Amenities:** Restaurant; bar; cafe; tennis court; sauna; kids' playground; coin-operated laundry; nonsmoking rooms; rooms for those w/limited mobility. *In room:* TV, kitchenette, safe.

Hotel Bornholm (Kids) This hotel is one of the most idyllic for families who don't require a lot of luxury. The beach here is good for kids because the waters are usually calm and shallow for some 100m (328 ft.) out. Built between 1972 and 1982 in a dull architectural style, the hotel evokes a roadside motel in the States. Its saving grace is a verdant garden, and each unit opens directly on this greenery replete with roses, flowering shrubs, and small patches of lawn, giving the impression of camping out in a natural setting.

The rooms, ranging from midsize to spacious, are durable, efficient, and practical—designed for hard use by occupants who spend most of their holiday on the beach. Each unit comes with a small but well-kept bathroom with a tub/shower combination. Families and even "friendly friends" (those who don't mind living as a family unit) have a choice of 44 apartments or 7 cottages, and, naturally, we go for those cottages, which offer more privacy and living space.

Pilegårdsvej 1, Dueodde, DK-3730 Nexø. ☎ **56-48-83-83.** Fax 56-48-85-37. 44 apts, 7 cottages. DKK1,125–DKK2,200 ($191–$374/£113–£220) double; DKK2,975–DKK6,275 ($506–$1,067/£298–£628) cottage for 4 people. Rates include breakfast; half-board DKK200 ($34/£20) extra per person per day. MC, V. Closed Oct–Apr. From Nexø, drive 5.5km (3¹/₂ miles) south along the coastal road, following the signs to Dueodde. **Amenities:** Breakfast room; bar; 2 heated pools (1 indoor); tennis court; exercise room; sauna; coin-operated laundry. *In room:* TV, safe.

WHERE TO DINE
At Nexø
Hotel Balka Strand DANISH   The cuisine, although not richly varied, is always reliable, especially in its selection of fish and seafood from the Baltic. We've found the portions quite large, filling, and most satisfying, and you can often dance at least part of the night away to live music. Although residents of the (previously recommended) hotel occupy much of its dining room, this restaurant opens its doors to nonguests who phone ahead for reservations. Within an airy, sparsely decorated dining room, you can enjoy such traditional menu items as marinated or fried herring; various kinds of omelets; soups, such as a creamy borscht; a standard fried steak with onions; and, best of all, a roster of fresh fish that includes our favorite—halibut with herbed wine sauce. Dessert might be a slice of chocolate layer cake, or perhaps a flan inspired by the chef's vacation visit to Spain.

Boulevarden 9. ☎ **56-49-49-49.** Reservations required for nonguests. Main courses DKK120–DKK180 ($20–$31/£12–£18); 3-course set dinner DKK140 ($24/£14); Wed buffet DKK188 ($32/£19). AE, DC, MC, V. Daily noon–3pm and 6:30–9:30pm.

Tre Søstre ★★ DANISH/SEAFOOD   Outside Rønne, there is no restaurant on the island that serves finer food than "The Three Sisters," standing right at the bustling little harbor of Nexø. The large dining room was created from a former storage warehouse, and it's named for the model of an old Danish ship on display. The decor honors artists of Bornholm, and even the ceramic plates and candlesticks are locally made by craftspeople on the island working through long, dark winters. Island artist Kirsten Clemann, quite well known locally, created the ceramic fish suspended from the ceiling.

The rustic, somewhat nautical decor sets the stage for the tasty seafood you are likely to be served here. We take delight in the fresh turbot, which is roasted and served with "fruits of the sea"—in this case shellfish. The grilled salmon is equally delectable and is served with a homemade hollandaise (this chef knows how to make hollandaise!). Nothing is finer, however, than the sautéed scampi splashed with cognac and flavored with curry powder and fresh garlic. The meat eater can always order a standard grilled sirloin of beef with mushroom sauce.

Havnen 5. ☎ **56-49-33-93.** Reservations recommended. Main courses DKK125–DKK197 ($21–$34/£13–£20). AE, DC, MC, V. Daily 11:30am–10pm.

At Snogebæk
Den Lille Havfrue ⟨Value⟩ DANISH   The cookery here is always reliably good tasting, and never makes any pretense of being anything more than it is. In other words, the cooks have no "shame" in serving plain old codfish with boiled potatoes and onions. "Most Danes grew up on that dish," one of the cooks told us. "Why not serve it?" Housed in a cozy, modern building erected in the 1980s, this is one of the least-pretentious but solidly good restaurants on the island. Local artist Kirsten Kleman accents its

woodsy setting with dozens of pottery pieces. The hardworking staff will suggest any of various fish and meat dishes, including salmon with lobster sauce (a perennial favorite), beefsteak and calf's liver, and broiled plaice with lemon and parsley-butter sauce. The menu includes an ample selection of homemade soups, fresh salads, and desserts based on recipes that some cook's grandmother must have taught him.

Hovedgaden 5, Snogebæk. © **56-48-80-55.** Reservations recommended. Main courses DKK170–DKK229 ($29–$39/£17–£23). AE, DC, MC, V. Daily 5–10pm. Closed Oct–Apr.

3 SVANEKE ★

After Nexø, the topography of the island gradually changes from tawny sandstone to a more heavily forested area with thin topsoil, deep veins of clay, and outcroppings of gray granite. From Nexø, drive 5.5km (3½ miles) north along the coastal road, following the signs to Svaneke, Denmark's easternmost settlement, with fewer than 1,200 year-round residents, lying 20km (12 miles) east of Rønne.

An idyllic retreat from the urban life of Copenhagen, this is the one settlement where we'd like to anchor if we lived on Bornholm. Many writers, sculptors, and painters have acquired homes in Svaneke, a former fishing village and the most photogenic town on Bornholm. In 1975, it won the European Gold Medal for town preservation. Its most famous citizen was J. N. Madvig, Denmark's influential philologist, who was born here in 1804.

The little town bears some resemblance to certain eastern regions of the Baltic with which it has traded, and it still has many 17th- and 18th-century cottages along cobblestone streets leading to the harbor, where fishing boats bob idyllically at anchor. Sights are few here and easily covered on foot. It's the appealing town itself, filled with red-tile buildings, that's the attraction. The town's main square is the **Torv.** Directly south of here is **Svaneke Kirke,** which has a runic stone dating from the mid-14th century. The church itself was largely reconstructed in the 1800s and is only of minor interest.

In and around the area are a number of windmills, including an old post mill on the north side of town. At a point 3km (1¾ miles) south of Svaneke, in the hamlet of **Årsdale,** there is an old working windmill where corn is still ground and sold to locals.

For information about the area, contact **Svaneke Turistbureau,** Storegade 24 (© **56-49-70-79;** www.svaneke.net), open Monday to Friday 10am to 4pm.

SHOPPING

Bornholm's east coast, particularly around Svaneke, contains the highest percentage of artists, many of whom display their creations within such art galleries as **Gallerie Hvide Hus** ★, Rand Kløvej 15, Saltuna (© **56-47-03-33**). Set midway between Svaneke and Gudhjem, it specializes in crafts, ceramics, and paintings, usually by Danish or Swedish artists, many of whom reside on the island. On the antiques front, **Svaneke Antikvitet-shandel,** Kirkebakken 4 (© **56-49-60-91**), is one of the most appealing stores on Bornholm, with an inventory of nautical memorabilia, plus some of the curios and furnishings that long-ago merchant ships hauled here from all parts of the world.

WHERE TO STAY

Hotel Østersøen ★ (Finds) This is one of the oldest hotels on the island, having opened in 1873, when a former merchant's house was rebuilt as a hotel. In 1990, major construction took place again when the compound was converted to holiday apartments, each furnished with an individual character and containing a separate entrance opening onto a beautiful courtyard garden. Families settle in for a week, using the place as a base for exploring Bornholm. Rich with many of the architectural quirks of its original construction 400 years ago as a farmstead, this complex of apartments with kitchenettes is more charming and more authentically old-fashioned than its nearby competitors. It sprawls along a goodly portion of Svaneke's harbor, wrapping itself around three sides of an open-air courtyard. Apartments contain an appealing blend of old-fashioned buttresses, modern kitchenettes, and summery, airy furnishings. Overall, the venue is comfortable, cozy, and attractively positioned.

Havnebryggen 5, DK-3740 Svaneke. ✆ **56-49-60-20.** Fax 56-49-72-79. www.ostersoen.dk. 22 apts. DKK2,595–DKK5,500 ($441–$935/£260–£550) double per week; DKK3,195–DKK6,500 ($543–$1,105/£320–£650) quad per week. Obligatory end-of-rental cleaning fee of DKK400 ($68/£40) for 2 persons, DKK500 ($85/£50) for 4. AE, DC, MC, V. **Amenities:** Lounge; outdoor heated pool; laundry service; dry cleaning. *In room:* TV, kitchenette.

Pension Solgården   The only problem with this solidly built, family-style guest-house is that it's open only 3 months a year, during the peak of midsummer. It was originally conceived in the 1930s as the quintessential redbrick schoolhouse, with a panoramic position adjacent to the sea, 3km (1³/₄ miles) south of Svaneke, beside the road leading south to Nexø. The small but cozy rooms are outfitted with the kind of furnishings you might see in a college dormitory of long ago. This place is one of the bargains of the area, especially if you're willing to forego a private bathroom and settle for the quite adequate hallway facilities. There's a dining room serving good, wholesome Danish meals, but it's open only to residents of the hotel. Outside you'll find lawns strewn with tables for sea gazing and sun worshiping.

Skolebakken 5, DK-3740 Svaneke. ✆ **56-49-64-37.** Fax 56-49-65-37. 18 units, 9 w/private bathroom. DKK590–DKK650 ($100–$111/£59–£65) double w/shared bathroom; DKK690–DKK750 ($117–$128/£69–£75) double w/private bathroom. Rates include breakfast. No credit cards. Closed Sept–May. **Amenities:** Dining room; lounge. *In room:* No phone.

Siemsens Gaard ★   This is a hotel with a history, its origins going back to the great day of the sailing ships in the Baltic, beginning around 1650, when it opened as a merchant's store that supplied sailors. It's named for Johan P. Siemsens, who, in 1827, married the widow of a rich merchant. As an inn, it dates from 1687, welcoming a visit by the Danish king, Christian V, and naval hero Admiral Niels Juel. In the 1930s, it was rebuilt as a hotel. In the early 1990s, however, lightning struck one of the two buildings, burning it to the ground, and necessitating a rebuilding of about half of the hotel rooms. Today, you'll face a hotel with old and new rooms; both types are cozy and rustically appealing as weather-tight getaways. Its location a few steps from the Svaneke harbor adds a lot of charm to this property, as does the publike cocktail lounge and restaurant (see "Where to Dine," below). The hotel is entirely nonsmoking.

Havnebryggen 9, DK-3740 Svaneke. ✆ **56-49-61-49.** Fax 56-49-61-03. www.siemsens.dk. 50 units. DKK975–DKK1,500 ($166–$255/£98–£150) double. Rates include breakfast. AE, DC, MC, V. **Amenities:** Restaurant; bar; sauna; room service; coin-operated laundry. *In room:* TV, hair dryer, iron, trouser press, safe.

WHERE TO DINE

Siemsens Gaard ★ (Value) DANISH   Set directly on the Svaneke harbor, the building that contains this restaurant is one of the oldest in town. Half-timbered, and with a pale yellow facade, it serves the best food in the area. The artfully rustic dining rooms have thick walls and harbor views that evoke early-20th-century Denmark. If you're not sure what to order at lunch, consider a medley of *smørrebrød* (open-faced sandwiches) that some culinary experts think are almost too attractive to eat. An average lunch might consist of two or three of these. More substantial fare might include a selection of herring arranged onto a platter, steaming bowls of cream-of-shellfish soup, smoked and marinated salmon with crème fraîche, voluptuous grilled monkfish or haddock with herbs and red-wine sauce, and a dessert specialty of crepes with almond cream and fresh berries.

Havnebryggen 9. (C) **56-49-61-49.** Reservations recommended. Lunch main courses DKK94–DKK148 ($16–$25/£9.40–£15); dinner main courses DKK198–DKK258 ($34–$44/£20–£26); lunch *smørrebrød* DKK198 ($34/£20). AE, DC, MC, V. Daily 7am–10:30pm.

FROM SVANEKE TO GUDHJEM

From Svaneke, you can leave the Baltic coastline and head inland through the northern outskirts of the third-largest forest in Denmark, **Almindingen.** (The western part of this forest is best explored by heading north from Åkirkeby; see "From Rønne to Nexø," earlier in this chapter.) Dotted with creeks and ponds, and covered mostly with hardy conifers, it's known for the profusion of its wildflowers—especially lily of the valley—and well-designated hiking trails. Head first for **Østerlars,** home to the largest of the island's distinctive round churches, the **Østerlarskirke,** at Gudhjemsveg 28 ((C) **56-49-82-64;** bus: 9 from Gudhjem). It's open early April to mid-October, Monday to Saturday 9am to 5pm, charging DKK10 ($1.70/£1) adults; children 15 and under enter free. The Vikings originally built it around 1150, using rocks, boulders, and stone slabs. The church was dedicated to St. Laurence and later enlarged with chunky-looking buttresses; it was intended to serve in part as a fortress against raids by Baltic pirates. Inside are several wall paintings that date from around 1350, depicting scenes from the life of Jesus.

After exploring the area and dipping south along forest roads, you can follow the signposts to **Østerlars,** southwest of Gudhjem, or else drive back along the coast to Svaneke and take the coastal road northwest into Gudhjem.

4 GUDHJEM ★

If you're in this little town on a summer's day, you'll know why it's called "God's Home." Tiny cross-timbered houses in bright colors flank the cobblestone streets. The fig and mulberry trees, plus the steep slopes, give it a vaguely Mediterranean feeling. Boats clog the harbor, and for lunch you go for the alder-smoked golden herring from one of the local smokehouses—and the day is yours.

From Østerlars, drive 3km (1³/₄ miles) north, following the signs to Gudhjem, a steeply inclined town that traded with the Hanseatic League during the Middle Ages. Most of its population died as a result of plagues in 1653 and 1654, but Danish guerrilla fighters and sympathizers, following territorial wars with Sweden, repopulated the town some years later.

Before setting out to explore the area, you might want to call first at the **Gudhjem Turistbureau,** Åbogade 9 ((C) **56-48-52-10;** www.gudhjem.nu), a block inland from the harbor. It's open only in summertime, May to September. May to mid-June, and mid-August to September, hours are Monday to Saturday 9am to 3pm. During the peak of midsummer, from mid-June to mid-August, hours are Friday to Wednesday 10am to 3pm.

Especially charming are Gudhjem's 18th-century half-timbered houses and the 19th-century smokehouses, known for their distinctive techniques of preserving herring with alder-wood smoke. Its harbor, blasted out of the rocky shoreline in the 1850s, is the focal point for the town's 1,200 permanent residents.

Gudhjem Museum   Frankly, we find the temporary art exhibits and the outdoor sculptures more intriguing than the permanent collection of locomotives and other rail-related memorabilia housed here in an old station that existed from the early 20th century until 1952. Its exhibits depict the now-defunct rail line that once crisscrossed the island. But if you're a railroad buff, you'll really get off on this museum's nostalgic "remembrance of things past," to borrow from Marcel Proust.

Stationsvej 1. ℂ **56-48-54-62.** Admission DKK25 ($4.30/£2.50) adults, DKK10 ($1.70/£1) children 6–19, free for children 5 and under. Mid-May to mid-Sept Mon–Sat 10am–5pm, Sun 2–5pm. Closed mid-Sept to mid-May.

Landsbrugs Museum (Bornholm Agricultural Museum)   This is a timbered, thatched-roof farmhouse that originally was built in 1796, and it's been preserved much as it was back then. The farmhouse and its surrounding garden is a journey back in time. You can go inside the brightly colored interior of the house, which has been preserved with artifacts that were used by its occupants in the 1800s. Outside it's like Ma and Pa Kettle on the farm, the barnyard complete with pigs, goats, cows, and chickens. On-site is a little shop selling woolen sweaters and wooden spoons, as well as some of the tastiest jars of homemade mustard we've found in Denmark.

Melstedvej 25. ℂ **56-48-55-98.** Admission DKK50 ($8.50/£5) adults, free for children 16 and under. Mid-May to mid-Oct Tues–Sun 10am–5pm. Closed mid-Oct to mid-May. 1km/²/₃ mile south of Gudhjem.

SHOPPING

For some of the best glass objects in the area, head for **Gallerie Baltic See Glass** ★, Melstedvej 47 (℃ **56-48-56-41**), lying 3km (1³/₄ miles) south of Gudhjem along the coastal road. Although much of this glass has practical value, some works are so stunningly beautiful that they should be treated like objects of art. One of the best art galleries in the area is **Gallerie Kaffslottet,** Duebakken 2 (℃ **56-48-56-18**), which displays the finest works from local artists, some of whom are expats from Copenhagen who have escaped from the urban jungle.

WHERE TO STAY

Gudhjem Hotel & Feriepark   To stay in this holiday apartment complex, you have to agree to a booking of 3 or 4 days, which is enough time to explore Bornholm in depth. The location is south of Gudhjem, about midway between that town and its satellite hamlet of Melsted; the hotel is a 5-minute walk from either center. Most guests can be found during the day enjoying the wide, sandy expanse of beach lying a few steps from the hotel, or else taking in the view from the summer terrace. The complex consists of tastefully designed, masonry-sided cottages, each with a sky-lit terra-cotta roof and a cement-paved patio extending the living area out onto the carefully clipped lawns. The living isn't fancy—strictly utilitarian though comfortable. Apartments come with two bedrooms, each equipped with two single beds, plus a living room with a sofa converting at night into a bed for a cozy twosome. The bathrooms are small but well kept, with a shower unit, not a tub. There are small markets nearby where you can purchase food to

cook in your fully equipped kitchen. If you want more style and glamour, book into the
Jantzens (see below).

Jernkåsvej 1, DK-3760 Gudhjem. © **56-48-54-44.** Fax 56-48-54-55. www.hotelgudhjem.dk. 102 apts.
DKK700–DKK750 ($119–$128/£70–£75) double. Supplemental charges include DKK175 ($30/£18) for
electricity, a nominal fee for the rental of linens and towels, and a 1-time cleaning charge of DKK325
($55/£33). Discounts available for stays of more than 3 days. MC, V. Closed Nov–Apr. **Amenities:** Lounge;
outdoor heated pool; 2 tennis courts; sauna; coin-operated laundry. *In room:* TV, kitchen.

Jantzens Hotel ★★ (Value)   This is where we like to hang our hat, and it's one of the
best deals on the island—not only affordable but filled with an old-fashioned charm and
many grace notes, including an idyllic terrace and rose garden in the rear, which fronts a
trio of small cottages with private terraces. Opened in 1872, the buttercup-yellow structure with wrought-iron balconies opens onto the Baltic Sea. The owners have recaptured
the ambience of the early 1900s, with hardwood floors and rattan furnishings. Bathrooms were added as an afterthought and are a bit cramped, but adequate for your needs.
All the bedrooms come with a small refrigerator. You don't have to journey outside at
night but can dine at the on-site Andi's Kokken, serving a Danish and French menu.
What do we like most about the cook here? As we were hiking one summer day, we came
across him picking fresh berries in a nearby meadow, so we knew in advance what dessert
to order that night.

Brøddeg 33, DK-3760 Gudhjem. © **56-48-50-17.** www.jantzenshotel.dk. 16 units. DKK975–DKK1,150
($166–$196/£98–£115) double. Rates include breakfast. MC, V. Closed Nov–Apr. **Amenities:** Restaurant.
In room: TV (in some).

Melsted Badehotel   This is a classic Bornholm beach hotel that satisfies the needs of
all but the most demanding clients. Originally built in 1942, during the darkest days of
World War II, in a boxy format with white-painted bricks and soft blue trim, this is the
most prominent and visible building in the seaside hamlet of Melsted, a kilometer (²/₃
mile) south of Gudhjem. Part of its allure derives from its location just 12m (39 ft.) from
the edge of the sea—occupants of its well-maintained and cozy rooms can hear the
sounds of the surf throughout the night. Most of the rather small rooms have private
terraces or balconies. If you'd like more space and grander comfort, opt for one of the
apartments in a half-timbered house next to the hotel. These apartments are attractively
and comfortably furnished and one of the best deals on the island, the largest unit sleeping four adults and two to three kids. There's a coffee shop/bistro that serves simple
lunches every day when the hotel is open, but never dinner. Much of this establishment's
conviviality is exhibited on the wooden terrace that extends out over the sands, where
outdoor tables, sun parasols, and chairs provide a space for sunbathing, people-watching,
and dining on meals from the hotel's bistro. The hotel is entirely nonsmoking.

Melstedvej 27, DK-3760 Gudhjem. © **56-48-51-00.** Fax 56-48-55-84. www.melsted-badehotel.dk. 18
units. DKK1,135–DKK1,440 ($193–$245/£114–£144) double; DKK1,650–DKK1,750 ($281–$298/£165–
£175) apt. Rates include breakfast. DC, MC, V. Closed Nov–Apr. Bus: 7. **Amenities:** Restaurant; cafe;
lounge. *In room:* TV.

WHERE TO DINE
Bokulhus ★ DANISH   For the best food locally, head to this converted 1932 private
home, lying only a 5-minute walk from the harbor. Its name derives from the Bokul,
which in Gudhjem refers to the highest elevation in town—an undulating, gentle knoll.
It was built in 1932 as a private home. Menu items are authentically Danish and, in
many cases, designed so that a platter of food is all most warm-weather diners really want.

The best example is a *Dansk-platte,* which is loaded with herring, salmon, an assortment of cheeses, chickpeas, and hand-peeled shrimp. Other well-prepared choices include beef tournedos with baked sweet peppers, yellowfin tuna with saffron sauce, and veal cutlets with potatoes and a shallot and parsley sauce. There's nothing imaginative about this fare, but it's good tasting, wholesome, and market fresh.

Bokulvej 4. ℭ **56-48-52-97.** www.bokulhus.dk. Reservations recommended. Lunch DKK55–DKK128 ($9.40–$22/£5.50–£13). Dinner main courses DKK105–DKK285 ($18–$48/£11–£29). AE, DC, MC, V. Wed–Mon 11:30am–10pm. Closed mid-Oct to mid-Apr.

GUDHJEM AFTER DARK

Consider a drink at the **Café Klint,** Egn Mikkelsensvej (ℭ **56-48-56-26**), where a cozy ambience that might remind you of a Danish version of an English pub welcomes you with pints of ale in an old-fashioned setting. And for something a bit more electronic, with more emphasis on rock-'n'-roll music, have a drink or two at the **Café Gustav,** St. Torv 8 (ℭ **56-91-00-47**), where at least one or two of the many artists living on the island's east coast are likely to congregate.

FROM GUDHJEM TO ALLINGE

For our next journey, head west along the coastal road. Between Gudhjem and Allinge, a distance of 14km (8²/₃ miles), you'll enjoy dramatic vistas over granite cliffs and sometimes savage seascapes. The entire coastline here is known as **Helligdoms Klipperne** (Cliffs of Sanctuary), for the survivors of the many ships that floundered along this granite coastline over the centuries.

Midway along the route, the **Bornholms Kunstmuseet** (Art Museum of Bornholm), Helligdommen (ℭ **56-48-43-86;** www.bornholms-kunstmuseum.dk), which opened in 1993, contains the largest collection of works by Bornholm artists, including Olaf Rude and Oluf Høst. It's open June to August, daily 10am to 5pm; April, May, September, and October, Tuesday to Sunday 10am to 5pm; November to March, Tuesday and Thursday 1 to 5pm, Sunday 10am to 5pm. Admission is DKK70 ($12/£7) adults, DKK50 ($8.50/£5) for students and seniors, free for children ages 18 and under. From the rocky bluff where the museum sits, you can see the isolated and rocky island of **Christiansø** (see below), about 11km (6³/₄ miles) offshore, the wind-tossed home to about 120 year-round residents, most of whom make their living from the sea.

---

5 CHRISTIANSØ ★

This is where TomKat should have gone for their honeymoon. Even Brooke Shields, trying to present her wedding gift of a blender, wouldn't have found them here in this remote outpost of 100 islanders, much less the paparazzi.

The island is only 500m (1,640 ft.) long and can be explored in about an hour. Should there be too much "excitement" on Christiansø, you can walk over a footbridge to the smaller island of **Frederiksø,** which is so tranquil that it seems asleep. Christiansø and Frederiksø are the only inhabited islands in the Ertholmene archipelago, the others being set aside as bird sanctuaries.

Both Christiansø and Frederiksø are spring breeding grounds for eider ducks. Not only are cars forbidden on the island, but so are cats and dogs, each viewed as a predator to the rich bird life here, which includes puffins.

This remote place used to be a vital link in Denmark's defense when Christian V established a naval fortress here in the wake of a Swedish invasion in 1658. By the 1850s, when Sweden was no longer viewed as an enemy, the naval forces withdrew and the island went into a long decline, which continues to this day. The naval cottages housing the sailors were taken over by fishermen who still eke out a living here. A few artists, seeking a retreat from the world, have also established little studios here.

Other than the island's beauty, the only major—and clearly visible—sight is the **Store Tårn** (Great Tower) on Christiansø. Constructed in 1684, it measures 25m (82 ft.) in diameter and has a century-old **lighthouse** that offers the most panoramic view of the island. If you pay DKK4 (70¢/40p), you can scale the stairs to the top—that is, if anybody is around to let you in; things are very laid back here. An even grander thrill is a walk along the once-fortified stone walls with their cannon-studded batteries.

Lille Tårn (Little Tower) lies on Frederiksø and dates from 1685. It's been turned into a small museum of local artifacts that holds almost no interest at all—some old cannons, fishing equipment, ironworks, and fishing gear. We suggest you skip it.

Ferryboats depart from the "mainland" of Bornholm one to seven times a day, depending on the season. For ferry schedules from Allinge and Gudhjem, call ✆ **56-48-51-76;** from Svaneke, ✆ **56-49-64-32.** Round-trip transit of 60 to 90 minutes costs DKK168 ($29/£17).

If you become enchanted with Christiansø and want to move in, at least for the night, there is one charming accommodation.

WHERE TO STAY & DINE

Christiansø Gæstgiveriet ★ Finds Of all the places we recommend in this guide, this is the ultimate retreat for the escapist. There is no better place for an off-the-record weekend. Once the home of a naval commander, the 18th-century, solidly built house is the only place to stay on the island. The small bedrooms are decorated in a style that evokes a private home as it might have looked in 1910. Bedrooms are comfortably furnished, but you must share the corridor bathrooms with the other guests—no great hardship. Residents and day-trippers meet in the nautically decorated bar on-site, and there is also a good restaurant serving typically Danish meals, most often seafood. Even if you aren't staying here, you might visit for lunch—platters cost from DKK80 to DKK100 ($14–$17/£8–£10). At dinner the fare is more elaborate, with main courses going from DKK78 to DKK178 ($13–$30/£7.80–£18). The only entertainment you'll find here is what you'll create for yourself, talking with fellow guests, or exploring the local bird and wildlife habitats. Don't even consider, especially during July and August, heading out here from Bornholm without an advance reservation, as it's very popular in midsummer. These accommodations are entirely nonsmoking.

DK-3740 Christiansø. ✆ **56-46-20-15.** Fax 56-46-20-86. 6 units. DKK950 ($162/£95) double. Rates include breakfast. V. Closed mid-Dec to mid-Feb. **Amenities:** Restaurant; bar; coin-operated laundry. *In room:* No phone.

6 ALLINGE & SANDVIG

Continue driving northwest until you reach the twin communities of **Allinge** and **Sandvig.** Allinge, whose architecture is noticeably older than that of Sandvig, contains 200- and 300-year-old half-timbered houses built for the purveyors of the long-ago herring trade, and antique smokehouses for preserving herring for later consumption or for export abroad.

The newer town of Sandvig, a short drive to the northwest, flourished around 1900, when many ferryboats arrived from Sweden. Sandvig became a stylish beach resort, accommodating guests at the Strandhotellet.

The forest that surrounds these twin communities is known as the **Trolleskoe** (Forest of Trolls), home to wart-covered and phenomenally ugly magical creatures that delight in brewing trouble, mischief, and the endless fog that sweeps over this end of the island.

From Allinge, detour inland (southward) for about 4km ($2^{1}/_{2}$ miles) to reach **Olsker**, site of the **Olskirke** (Round Church of Ols), Lindesgordsvej (© **56-48-05-29**). Built in the 1100s with a conical roof and thick walls, it's the smallest of the island's round churches. It was painstakingly restored in the early 1950s. Dedicated to Skt. Olav (Olav the Holy, king of Norway, who died in 1031), it looks something like a fortress, an image that the original architects wanted very much to convey. June to September, and October 17 to 18, it's open Monday to Saturday 2 to 5pm; April and May, and October 1 to 16, it's open Monday to Friday 10am to 1pm. It's closed the rest of the year. Entrance costs DKK10 ($1.70/£1).

Now retrace your route back to Allinge and head northward toward Sandvig, a distance of less than a kilometer ($^{1}/_{2}$ mile). You'll soon see **Madsebakke,** a well-signposted open-air site containing the largest collection of Bronze Age rock carvings in Denmark. Don't expect a building, any type of enclosed area, or even a curator. Simply follow the signs posted beside the main highway. The carvings include 11 depictions of high-prowed sailing ships of unknown origin, and were made in a smooth, glacier-scoured piece of bedrock close to the side of the road.

From here, proceed just less than a kilometer ($^{1}/_{2}$ mile) to the island's northernmost tip, **Hammeren,** for views that—depending on the weather—could extend all the way to Sweden. Here you'll see the island's oldest lighthouse, **Hammerfyr,** built in 1871.

WHERE TO STAY IN SANDVIG

Strandhotellet ★★ Finds   There is a romantic nostalgia about this place. In 1896, it was built as stables but a decade later was converted to the largest and most stylish hotel in Bornholm. Those days are gone forever. Today the venerable old hotel is a remote outpost and a reminder of days gone by, when Sandvig was a viable port and commercial center, before losing out to Rønne. The hotel offers three floors of spartan accommodations with lots of exposed birch wood and (in most cases) sea views.

Strandpromenaden 7, DK-3770 Sandvig. © **56-48-03-14.** Fax 56-48-02-09. 49 units. DKK650–DKK1,400 ($111–$238/£65–£140) double; DKK580–DKK1,700 ($99–$289/£58–£170) suite. AE, DC, MC, V. **Amenities:** Restaurant; bar; sauna. *In room:* TV.

WHERE TO DINE IN SANDVIG

Strandhotellet Restaurant   DANISH/SEAFOOD   Today's hotel dining room, attracting both residents and visitors to the island, grew out of a 1930s dance hall and supper club that once flourished here. The chefs have to import a lot of their produce but use whatever is fresh at the local markets. Start, perhaps, with the smoked filet of wild salmon with a savory tomato tapenade, and then follow with a platter of various fish, the actual dish varying depending on the catch of the day. The meat devotee will also find a few good choices, such as beef medallions with a ragout of fresh vegetables.

Strandpromenaden 7, Sandvig. © **56-48-03-14.** Lunch main courses DKK59–DKK79 ($10–$13/£5.90–£7.90); dinner main courses DKK169–DKK189 ($29–$32/£17–£19). AE, DC, MC, V. Daily noon–10pm.

For our final adventure, turn south, following the signs pointing to Rønne. After less than a kilometer (¹/₂ mile), you'll see the rocky crags of a semiruined fortress that Bornholmers believe is the most historically significant building on the island—the **Hammershus Fortress** ★, begun in 1255 by the archbishop of Lund (Sweden). He planned this massive fortress to reinforce his control of the island. Since then, however, the island has passed from Swedish to German to Danish hands several times; it was a strategic powerhouse controlling what was then a vitally important sea lane. The decisive moment came in 1658, when the Danish national hero Jens Kofoed murdered the Swedish governor and sailed to Denmark to present the castle (and the rest of the island) to the Danish king.

Regrettably, the fortress's dilapidated condition was caused by later architects, who used it as a rock quarry to supply the stone used to construct some of the buildings and streets (including Hovedvagten) of Rønne, as well as several of the structures on Christiansø, the tiny island 11km (6³/₄ miles) northeast of Bornholm. The systematic destruction of the fortress ended in 1822, when it was "redefined" as a Danish national treasure. Much of the work that restored the fortress to the eerily jagged condition you'll see today was completed in 1967. Hammershus escaped the fate of the second-most-powerful fortress on the island, Lilleborg. Set deep in Bornholm's forests, Lilleborg was gradually stripped of its stones for other buildings, after its medieval defenses became obsolete.

Some 4km (2¹/₂ miles) south of Hammershus—still on the coastal road heading back to Rønne—is a geological oddity called **Jons Kapel** (Jon's Chapel); it can be seen by anyone who'd like to take a short hike (less than 1km/¹/₂ mile) from the highway. Basically it's a rocky bluff with a panoramic view over the island's western coast, where, according to ancient legend, an agile but reclusive hermit, Brother Jon, preached to the seagulls and crashing surf below. For those who would like to enjoy a panoramic view, signs point the way from the highway.

From here, continue driving southward another 13km (8 miles) to Rønne, passing through the hamlet of **Hasle** en route. And so ends our discovery of the island. If you followed us all the way, you've seen the best of Bornholm.

Funen

After Copenhagen and after a visit to "Hamlet's Castle" in North Zealand, nearly all foreign visitors head for **Odense,** the capital of the island of Funen (*Fyn* in Danish), lying to the west of Zealand. And rightly so. Hans Christian Andersen was born in Odense, and houses and memorabilia associated with him are the big attractions.

But there is so much more here, including the most fantastic island in Scandinavia, little old "time warp" Ærø of the southern coast. Hop gardens, Viking runic stones, orchards of fruit trees, busy harbors, market towns, swan ponds, thatch-roof houses, once-fortified castles, and stately manor homes invite exploration by car.

Funen has some 1,125km (700 miles) of coastline, with wide sandy beaches in some parts, and woods and grass that grow all the way to the water's edge in others. Steep cliffs provide sweeping views of the Baltic or the Kattegat.

Although ferryboats have plied the waters between the islands and peninsulas of Denmark since ancient times, recent decades have seen the development of a network of bridges. In 1934, the first plans were developed for a bridge over the span of water known as the **Storebælt** (Great Belt), the 19km (12-mile) silt-bottomed channel that separates Zealand (and Copenhagen) from Funen and the rest of continental Europe. After many delays caused by war, technical difficulties, and lack of funding, and after the submission of 144 designs by engineers from around the world, construction began in 1988 on an intricately calibrated network of bridges and tunnels.

On June 14, 1998, her majesty, Queen Margrethe II, cut the ribbon shortly before driving across the Great Belt Bridge. The project incorporated both railway and road traffic divided between a long underwater tunnel and both low and high bridges. (The rail link has operated since 1997.) Only some aspects of the Chunnel between England and France are on par with the staggering scale of this project.

Visitors can view exhibitions about the bridge at the **Great Belt Exhibition Center (℃ 58-35-01-00),** located at the entrance to the bridge and hard to miss. It's open July to August, Wednesday to Monday 11am to 4pm, and the admission is free.

1 NYBORG: GATEWAY TO FUNEN

130km (81 miles) W of Copenhagen; 34km (21 miles) E of Odense

One of the oldest towns in Denmark, founded 7 centuries ago, Nyborg lies at the western terminus of the Storebælt bridge and is the easternmost town on the island of Funen. Local residents thought the opening of the bridge would boost tourism, but that has happened only marginally. Most motorists, especially foreigners, rush through town en route to Odense to pay their respects to the memory of Hans Christian Andersen.

That's a shame, really, because Nyborg is deserving of at least 2 hours of your time, which will allow you to visit its old **Torvet** (the market square in the center), the ruins

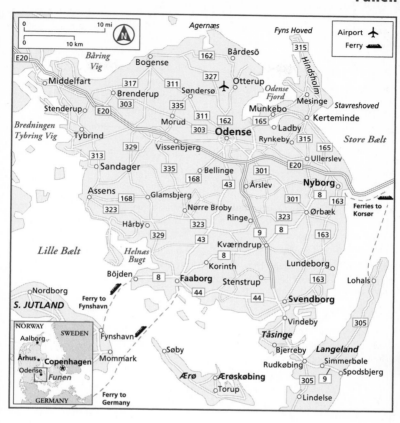

of a medieval castle, and some cross-timbered old houses. Like so many other cities or towns of Denmark, Nyborg was more strategic in the Middle Ages than it is today.

Its location in the middle of the trade route between Zealand in the east and Jutland in the west helped boost its importance. In medieval times, about 1200 to 1413, Nyborg was the capital of Denmark. Medieval buildings and well-preserved ramparts are testaments to that era. Nyborg's town square, the Torvet, was created in 1540, when a block of houses was demolished to make room for the royal tournaments of Christian III.

In summer, Denmark's oldest open-air theater, **Nyborg Voldspil,** is the setting for musicals or operettas under the leafy beeches on the old castle ramparts. Throughout the summer, classical music concerts (featuring international soloists) are performed in the castle's Great Hall. Inquire at the tourist office (see "Essentials," below) for further details.

Dating from the mid-1600s, the "Tattoo" is an ancient military ceremony with musical accompaniment. This old custom has been revived to honor the corps who played an important role in the Schleswig wars in 1848 and again in 1864. In tribute to the old corps, the present-day Tattoo participants wear a green uniform with its characteristic

> **(Tips) Around the Island by Rail & Bus**
>
> Funen has a good system of buses and trains that fan out from the central depot in Odense in all directions. Although public transport obviously takes longer than driving a car, it's possible to see the highlights of Funen without your own vehicle. It's also possible to base yourself in Odense, and visit the island's intriguing towns, such as Svendborg, as day trips. See the individual town listings for more details. For rail information or schedules throughout Funen, call ℂ **70-13-14-15,** and for bus routes on the island, call the tourist office (ℂ **65-31-02-80**).

cap, or *chakot*. The corps marches through the center of town at 9pm each year on June 30, thereafter every Tuesday in July and August.

ESSENTIALS

GETTING THERE   By Train or Bus   You can reach Nyborg by train or bus (via ferry). Trains leave Copenhagen every hour, and there's frequent bus service from Copenhagen as well. From Odense, east-bound trains arrive two times an hour.

VISITOR INFORMATION   The **Nyborg Turistbureau,** Torvet 9 (ℂ **65-31-02-80;** http://nyborgturist.dk), is open June 15 to August, Monday to Friday 9am to 5pm and Saturday 9am to 2pm; September to June 14, Monday to Friday 9am to 4pm and Saturday 9:30am to 12:30pm.

GETTING AROUND   Bus nos. 1, 3, and 4 serve all in-town destinations listed below.

SEEING THE SIGHTS

Mads Lerches Gård (Mads Lerches House) ★   Of all the places in Funen, this 1601 house, the former home of Mads Lerche, the town mayor, provides the best insight into what life was like in the 17th century—that is, if you had some money in the bank. The house, painted a reddish pink, is filled with exhibitions on local history, but far more intriguing than that are the antiques-filled period chambers spread over 30 rooms on two floors. There's even a small brewery on-site, which every home in the 1600s should have had but didn't.

Slotsgade 11. ℂ **65-31-02-07.** www.museer-nyborg.dk. Admission DKK30 ($5.10/£3) adults, DKK25 ($4.30/£2.50) students, free for children up to 17. Apr–May and Sept–Oct 21 Tues–Sun 10am–3pm; June and Aug Tues–Sun 10am–4pm; July Tues–Sun 10am–5pm. Closed Oct 22–Mar. Bus: 1, 3, or 4.

Nyborg Slot (Nyborg Castle) ★   This hardly compares to Windsor Castle in England but to the Danes it's just as important; yet it comes as a disappointment that there's so little left to evoke all the momentous historical events that occurred here in the Middle Ages. Dating from 1170, this is one of the oldest of Denmark's royal castles. Originally it was built to defend the country from the Wends of North Germany. King Erik Glipping signed Denmark's first constitution in this moated castle in 1282, and Nyborg became the seat of the Danish Parliament, the Danehof, until 1413, when Copenhagen took over.

In a regrettable decision, much of the Slot was demolished in 1722 to provide building materials for Odense Castle. Nonetheless, part of the original ramparts remain. From these bastions, Danes rained down hot tar on their invaders. If you walk these ramparts today, you'll have a **panoramic** view ★ of Nyborg and the sea. The terrace in front is still

lined with bronze guns facing the town center. The town gate, **Landporten** ★, can still
be seen just north of the castle.

Most intriguing is the still-remaining **Danehof** ★, the hall where Parliament met. The
walls are painted with geometric murals, and there is an extensive collection of armaments such as guns and swords, suits of armor (rather impressive), and old royal paintings
(not too impressive). Other rooms open to view include the King's Room, the Knights'
Hall, and even the apartment once occupied by the royal kids, heirs apparent to the
throne.

Slotspladen. ℭ **65-31-02-07.** www.museer-nyborg.dk. Admission DKK30 ($5.10/£3) adults, DKK25
($4.30/£2.50) students, free for children 16 and under. Apr–May and Sept–Oct 21 Tues–Sun 10am–3pm;
June and Aug Tues–Sun 10am–4pm; July Tues–Sun 10am–5pm. Closed Oct 22–Mar. Bus: 1, 2, or 3.

Vor Frue Kirke   The Church of Our Lady, as it's called in English, is still a place of
worship even though it dates from the Middle Ages. Unfortunately, restorers and decorators descended on the church in 1870 and completely changed it, so we're not able to see
the purity of its original simple architectural details. Even so, it's still a worthy place to
wander about for 30 to 45 minutes. We found that the greatest treasure here is a **baroque
pulpit** ★ in stunning detail, the work of Odense-born Anders Mortensen in 1653. He
depicted some of the epic moments in the Bible, including the Baptism of Christ, the
Birth of John the Baptist, the Transfiguration, and both the resurrection and the Ascension, the subject of countless medieval paintings.

The Gothic spire of the church is a landmark for miles around, and the interior is split
into a trio of aisles and endowed with woodcarvings, carved old epitaphs, candelabra, and
model ships. The elegant wrought-iron gate you see was forged in 1649 by Casper
Fincke, the court-appointed craftsman to King Christian IV. The most evocative aspect
of the church, which we discovered while strolling about Nyborg one night, is that at
9:45pm the Watchman's Bell from 1523 is still rung, a tradition that dates back for
centuries. Lying at the end of Kongegade in the town center, Vor Frue Kirke can be
entered through its south door. Nearby at Adelgade and Korsbrodregade stands a large
stone-built house, **Korsbrodregården,** dating from 1396. This was the Chapter House
of the Order of St. John, its vaulted cellar converted today into a gift shop.

Adelgade. ℭ **65-31-16-08.** Free admission. Daily 9am–6pm.

SHOPPING
The open workshop of the town's most talented potter and ceramicist can be visited at
Ida Rostgård, Holken Havn 1 (ℭ **65-30-23-02**).

WHERE TO STAY
Hotel Hesselet ★★★   Such an elegant hotel of a high international standard comes
as a surprise in this sleepy, provincial town. One of the most stylish hotels in Funen,
outclassing most of those in Odense itself, is idyllically set among beech trees, opening
onto a view of the Great Belt with its Storebælt suspension bridge. Opt for a room with
a view of this sea spectacle, or else you'll be assigned an accommodation opening onto a
forest.

Inside, the hotel creates a glamorous aura in its public lounges with its use of Asian
artifacts and plush Oriental carpets, its large fireplace, its sunken living rooms, and a cozy
library lined with leather-bound volumes. Bedrooms are sumptuously furnished and spacious, each with tasteful appointments and the best bathrooms of any hotel along the east

coast of Funen, coming with granite floors, double wash basins, bathtubs, and separate shower cabins, plus plenty of toiletries.

Even if you're not a guest, consider a meal here preceded by an aperitif on the patio or by the open fireplace in cold weather. A first-rate chef, Tina Møhring Madsen composes her dishes incorporating fresh seasonal produce.

Christianslundsvej 119, DK-5800 Nyborg. © **65-31-30-29.** Fax 65-31-29-58. www.hesselet.dk. 47 units. DKK1,680–DKK1,880 ($286–$320/£168–£188) double; DKK2,400–DKK3,000 ($408–$510/£240–£300) suite. Rates include breakfast. AE, DC, MC, V. Free parking. **Amenities:** Restaurant; bar; indoor heated pool; 2 tennis courts; sauna; room service; babysitting; laundry service; dry cleaning; nonsmoking rooms; solarium; rooms for those w/limited mobility. *In room:* TV, Wi-Fi, minibar, hair dryer, safe.

Hotel Nyborg Strand ★ (Kids The only thing that turns us off about this hotel, managed by Best Western, is its tendency to book noisy conference groups. That's the bad news. The good news is that it's a most recommendable choice in summer when there are no conventions. For years, it was the flag bearer in Nyborg, since 1899 in fact, until that "upstart," the Hesselet (see above) came along to absorb all the glory. The location near a forest-blanketed beach lies less than a kilometer (¹/₂ mile) from the train station. At the water's edge, the hotel, like its rival, opens onto a fine view of the bay and the Great Belt Bridge.

They cost more; but the junior suites in the hotel tower not only command the most panoramic views through their round windows but also have private balconies, and one comes with a private sauna. The midsize-to-spacious standard rooms also have great views and are tastefully and comfortably furnished. A brigade of skilled cooks offer a choice of two restaurants, the accurately named **Panorama,** with a formal French/Danish cuisine, and the more informal and family-friendly **Bistro,** specializing in grills. It also has the largest and best salad buffet in town. All menus are adjusted to take advantage of the best produce of any season.

Østersvej 2, DK-5800 Nyborg. © **800/528-1234** in the U.S., or 65-31-31-31. Fax 65-31-37-01. www. nyborgstrand.dk. 300 units. Mon–Thurs DKK1,130–DKK1,522 ($192–$259/£113–£152) double; Fri–Sun DKK724–DKK1,036 ($123–$176/£72–£104) double; DKK2,052–DKK2,444 ($349–$416/£205–£244) junior suite. Rates include breakfast. AE, MC, V. Closed Dec 16–Jan 3. **Amenities:** 2 restaurants; bar; indoor heated pool; fitness center; sauna; room service; babysitting; laundry service; dry cleaning; nonsmoking rooms; rooms for those w/limited mobility. *In room:* TV, Wi-Fi, hair dryer, iron.

WHERE TO DINE

Central Cafeen ★ DANISH/FRENCH When we first discovered this restaurant many years ago, we were put off by its name of "Central Café." Only after dining here did we discover that this is one of the finest restaurants along the east coast of Funen, set directly across the street from City Hall, in a house from 1787 that has contained some kind of restaurant since 1854. With a sense of local history and a deep-seated pride, it offers four separate, cozy dining rooms, each outfitted with sepia-toned photographs of four generations of Danish monarchs, plus a quirky collection of ladies' hats tucked museum-style in glass cases.

The composition of the fixed-price menus changes every month to take advantage of seasonal produce. First-rate ingredients are used, often fresh shrimp and lobster. Begin, perhaps, with a bowl of the creamy lobster bisque, going on to the fried plaice with a lobster-and-shrimp sauce. Roasted salmon appears with fresh spinach, and meat eaters gravitate to the fried pork cutlets in a parsley sauce. The sumptuous desserts are made daily, and there is an impressive but pricey wine list to back up the cuisine.

NYBORG AFTER DARK

The town's most consistently popular bar and pub is **Café Anthon,** Mellemgade 25
(© **65-31-16-64**), where sports enthusiasts, students, and anyone who happens to want
to be convivial gather in a publike ambience that's cozy and warm. It's open daily
10:30am to 8pm. For the release of spontaneous energy on a dance floor, head for **Crazy
Daisy,** Strandvejen 10 (© **63-31-08-28**), open Friday and Saturday 11pm to dawn.

---

2 ODENSE: BIRTHPLACE OF
HANS CHRISTIAN ANDERSEN ★★

96km (60 miles) W of Copenhagen; 34km (21 miles) W of Nyborg; 43km (27 miles) NW of Svendborg

Many people make their living off Hans Christian Andersen and all the visitors his
memory brings to Odense. But the town never seemed to appreciate the boy until the
world discovered his writing. In some respects, he was treated like Salzburg treated
Mozart. Actually, the storyteller had a very unhappy childhood in Odense and left as
soon as he was old enough to make his way to Copenhagen.

His cobbler father was always out of money, and had been forced to marry Hans's
ill-tempered, peasant mother when she was 7 months pregnant. The Andersen grandmother was insane and, as noted by Andersen himself, was a pathological liar. No wonder
the boy wanted to get out of Odense.

But those unpleasant memories are long gone today, and Odense is proud of its world-
famous son, hawking souvenirs of him and dusting off the writer's memorabilia for each
new generation. This ancient town, the third largest in Denmark, has changed greatly
since Andersen walked its streets. But its historic core still evokes the fairy-tale town that
Andersen knew so well.

In the heart of Funen and home to more than 185,000 inhabitants, Odense is one of
the oldest cities in the country, with a history stretching back some 1,000 years. The city's
name stems from two words—*Odins Vi* (Odin's shrine), suggesting that the god Odin
must have been worshiped here in pre-Christian times. Long before Odense became a
pilgrimage center for fans of Andersen, it was an ecclesiastical center and site of religious
pilgrimage in the Middle Ages.

Odense today is not just a fairy-tale town, but an industrial might in Denmark, its
harbor linked by a canal to the Odense Fjord and thus the Great Belt. It's a center of
electro-technical, textile, steel, iron, and timber production.

In summer, Odense takes on a festive air, with lots of outdoor activities, including all
types of music, drama, and street theater taking place on its squares and in its piazzas.
Cafes and pubs are lively day and night.

ESSENTIALS

GETTING THERE   By Train or Bus   You can easily reach Odense by train or bus from
Copenhagen, as about 12 trains or buses a day leave Copenhagen's Central Railway Station for Odense (trip time: 3 hr.).

FUNEN

10

ODENSE

By Car   From Nyborg, head west on E20 to Allerup and then follow Route 9 north to Odense.

VISITOR INFORMATION   **Odense Tourist Bureau** is at Rådhuset, Vestergade 2A (✆ **66-12-75-20**; www.visitodense.com). It's open mid-June to August, Monday to Friday 9am to 6pm, Saturday and Sunday 10am to 3pm; September to mid-June, Monday to Friday 9:30am to 4:30pm and Saturday 10am to 1pm.

GETTING AROUND   **By Bus**   Bus no. 2 serves all in-town destinations listed below. A typical fare is DKK16 ($2.70/£1.60).

SEEING THE SIGHTS

Less than a kilometer (¹/₂ mile) west of the city center is **Superbowl,** Grøneløkkenvej (✆ **70-11-11-55**; bus: 91 or 92), a complex of amusements and diversions that are entirely devoted to popular American culture. It incorporates facilities for indoor go-cart racing, an indoor version of American-style miniature golf, several bowling alleys, and a small-scale collection of rides and games inspired by the theme parks of Florida. Each individual attraction within the park maintains its own hours and entrance policies, but the best way to appreciate this site's activities is to head here anytime daily between 10am and 6pm, when, for an all-inclusive fee of DKK80 ($14/£8), you'll have unlimited access to all of them.

Brandts Klædefabrik (Brandt's Textile Mill) ★   An antique textile factory has been successfully converted into an artifact- and art-filled compound with four museums spread across its precincts. You can spend 3 or more hours here and only scratch the surface of its exhibits. At the very least you should ascend to the roof terrace for a panoramic view of Odense. The **Danish Museum of Printing** and the **Danish Press Museum** (✆ **66-12-10-20**) show the development of the printing press in the country for at least 3 centuries. The museum also houses papermaking, bookbinding, and lithography workshops. Also on-site is the **Kunsthallen Brandts** (✆ **66-13-78-97**), the art gallery filling four spacious rooms that once housed weaving machines. The exhibitions vary here depending on the season. Some of these have been of world-class interest, with stunning displays of paintings and sculpture, even avant-garde Danish design. Of special interest is a library of art films open to the viewing public. The **Museum of Photographic Art** (✆ **66-13-78-97**), the only one of its kind in the country, offers not only a permanent collection but at least 10 special exhibits a year. Exhibits go all the way back to August 19, 1839, the official "birthday" of photography in Denmark. Christian Tuxen Falbe, a former marine officer, was the first Dane to make daguerreotypes in Paris, sending them back to his patron in Copenhagen, Prince Christian Frederik (later King Christian VIII). Finally, **The Time Collection** (✆ **65-91-19-42**; www.tidenssamling.dk) allows you to travel through time by following its exhibitions of housing interiors and changing fashions. The exhibits focus on six interior designs, typical living rooms from the beginning of the 20th century until the '70s. You're allowed to actually enter the room and sit on the furniture. You can even play the old gramophones. Nostalgic fashion shows are presented on certain occasions.

Brandts Passage 37–43. ✆ **65-20-70-70.** www.brandts.dk. Combined ticket DKK70 ($12/£7); DKK35–DKK40 ($6–$6.80/£3.50–£4) for each attraction. Free for children 17 and under. July–Aug daily 10am–5pm; Sept–June Tues–Sun 10am–5pm.

Bymuseet Møntegården (Odense City Museum) ★   Not the typical dull city museum with dusty artifacts, of which we've seen too many, this museum traces Odense's

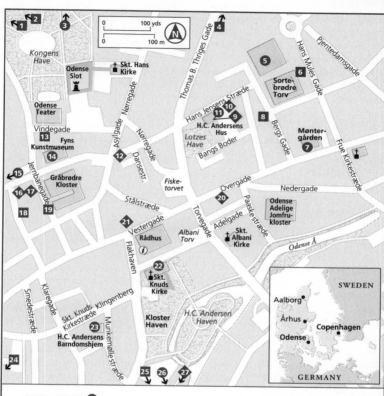

ATTRACTIONS ●
Brandts Klædefabrik **17**
Bymuyseet Møntegården **7**
Carl Nielsen Museet **5**
Danmarks Jernbanemuseum **3**
Den Fynske Landsby **26**
Fyns Kunstmuseum **14**
H.C. Andersen's Barndomshjem **23**
H.C. Andersens Hus **11**
Skt. Knuds Domkirke **22**
Superbowl **15**

ACCOMMODATIONS ■
Best Western Hotel Knudsens Gaard **25**
City Hotel Odense **6**
Clarion Hotel Plaza **1**
Comfort Windsor Hotel **13**

First Hotel Grand **19**
Hotel Ansgar **2**
Hotel Domir / Hotel Ydes **18**
Næsbylund Kro **4**
Radisson SAS H.C. Andersen Hotel **8**
Scandic Hotel Odense **24**

DINING ◆
Carlslund **2**
Den Gamle Kro **20**
Den Grimme Æling **10**
La Brasserie **16**
Målet **17**
Marie Louise **21**
Restaurant Klitgaard **12**
Sortebro Kro **27**
Under Lindetræt **9**

FUNEN

10

ODENSE

history back to the Viking era and has a number of half-timbered houses from the 1500s and 1600s you can actually walk through. In a snug little alleyway off the main courtyard stands a row of workmen's cottages from the same period. The museum is particularly rich in artifacts from the Middle Ages, and there are interiors from the 17th and 18th centuries, as well as exhibits that go right up to the 1950s. In the Nyborgladen—the open storehouse of the museum—there are thousands of items exemplifying everyday life from the Middle Ages to the present day. These artifacts cover a vast range, with exhibits from the Middle Ages, including church carvings, rare archaeological digs unearthed on Funen, and rooms filled with period furnishings, mostly from the 19th century, and even church carvings. The exceptional **coin collection** ★ spans the millennium, showcasing such rare numismatic items as coins minted during the Danish rule over Estonia.

Overgade 48–50. ⓒ **65-51-46-01.** http://museum.odense.dk. Free admission. Tues–Sun 10am–6pm.

Carl Nielsen Museet   Judge Carl Nielsen by his great music, not his purple prose, as evoked by such rhapsodic lines about the Funen landscape as "Even trees dream and talk in their sleep with a Funen lilt." At the Odense Concert Hall, you can learn about the life and music of Denmark's greatest composer, Carl August Nielsen (1865–1931), the second-most-famous son to come out of Odense.

This towering musician developed a unique polytonal and contrapuntal musical form; his operas include *Saul and David* in 1903 and *Maskerade* in 1906. He also composed symphonies, concertos, and choral and chamber music. Nielsen single-handedly "woke up" Danish music after its sleepy decline of decades. In the museum, you can listen to some of his greatest works, even a polka he penned as a child before joining the Odense Military Band as a trumpet player at the tender age of 14.

A biographical slideshow brings to life once again this cultural icon, whose six symphonies and several operas, as well as his hymns and popular songs (many of which are patriotic) are still played around the world today.

Nielsen married a famous sculptor of her day. She changed her name to Anne Marie Carl-Nielsen, strangely keeping her husband's first name in her full name. Although hardly as well known as her husband, she created works still on view in Denmark, including her equestrian statue of Christian IX that stands outside the Royal Stables in Copenhagen.

Although "Anne and Carl," as they were known to their intimates, remained married until he died, they had long periods of marital strife, including a lengthy separation and mutual accusations of infidelity.

Claus Bergsgade 11. ⓒ **65-51-46-01.** http://museum.odense.dk. Free admission. Tues and Fri 4–8pm; Sun noon–4pm.

Danmarks Jernbanemuseum (Railway Museum) ★ (Kids)   This is one of the best transportation museums in Scandinavia, appropriately located adjacent to the Odense train station. It's a very active museum and not some dull depot of long-abandoned locomotives, although there are those here too, the best of which is a **royal carriage** ★ that once carried his majesty King Christian IX.

From the first train in Denmark, dating from 1847, until more modern times, the history of locomotives and carriages is on display, even a "B-Machine," a moving vehicle from 1869. A replica of a 19th-century train depot is on view along with two dozen engines and various saloon cars. Model ferries, buses, model railway tracks, and even Wagons-Lits restaurant cars and ferries are on view. The entire family can go on the minitrains and take a simulated ride in a large diesel locomotive.

Dannebrogsgade 24. ⓒ **66-13-66-30.** www.jernbanemuseum.dk. Admission DKK60 ($10/£6) adults, DKK24 (4.10/£2.40) children 10–15, free for children 4 and under. Daily 10am–4pm.

Den Fynske Landsby (Funen Village) ★★ (Kids) If Hans Christian Andersen

himself were to come back to life and land in this village, he'd feel that the world had never changed. This is the Danish version of Scotland's mystical "Brigadoon," where some 30 buildings, dating from the 17th to the 19th century, keep alive the village milieu of yesterday, with half-timbered houses, flower gardens, a communal pond, and a grazing cow (or goat) that characterized village life of long ago.

In a scenic setting in the Hunderup Woods, these old buildings include a tollhouse, weaver's shop, windmill, farming homestead, vicarage, village school, brickworks, and the inevitable jail. Each was reassembled on this site and authentically furnished. You can visit workshops to see craftspeople, including a basket maker, a spoon cutter, a weaver, and the village blacksmith.

As an added treat, plays and folk dances are staged at a Greek-style theater. The best way to get here is to ignore the bus suggestion below and take a boat from Munke Mose in Odense down the river to Erik Boghs Sti. After you disembark, it's a 15-minute scenic walk to the museum. A one-way fare is DKK40 ($6.80/£4) for adults or DKK30 ($5.10/£3) for children 10 to 15, free for children 9 and under.

Sejerskovvej 20. ℰ 65-51-46-01. Admission DKK60 ($10/£6) adults, free for children 16 and under. Mid-June to mid-Aug daily 9:30am–7pm; Apr to mid-June and mid-Aug to mid-Oct Tues–Sun 10am–5pm; mid-Oct to Mar Sun 11am–3pm. Bus: 21 or 22 from Flakhaven.

Fyns Kunstmuseum (Funen Art Museum) ★ The founding fathers of one of the oldest, largest, and best art museums outside of Copenhagen wanted it to be a miniature version of the Statens Museum for Kunst in the Danish capital. Opening the Odense museum in the early 1880s, they long ago succeeded in their ambition. Their once-stated goal of "a little bit of everything" is clearly on display today, with a collection dating from 1750 to the present, going from the classics to abstract modern. The permanent exhibitions are beefed up with special shows presented several times a year, some of them world-class in interest, depth, and perspective (often devoted to themes featuring one artist or a collective group such as the French Impressionists). There are some fine sculptures but it is Danish painting that is clearly the star attraction here. Predictably the largest array of paintings is devoted to the artists of Funen, particularly Peter Hansen and Johannes Larsen. Our favorite painting here is the evocative, powerful *Udslidt*, meaning "worn out," the work of the enormously talented H. A. Brendekilde.

Jernbanegade 13. ℰ 65-51-46-01. www.museum.odense.dk. Admission DKK40 ($6.80/£4) adults, free for children 16 and under. Tues–Sun 10am–4pm.

H. C. Andersens Barndomshjem (H. C. Andersen's Childhood Home) (Kids) Visit Andersen's humble childhood abode, where the fairy-tale writer lived from 1807 to 1819. From what is known of Andersen's childhood, his mother was a drunken, superstitious washerwoman, and Andersen was a gawky boy, lumbering and graceless, the victim of his fellow urchins' cruel jabs. However, all is serene at the cottage today; in fact, the little house with its tiny rooms has a certain unpretentious charm, and the "garden still blooms," as in *The Snow Queen*. The museum is only mildly diverting, worth no more than 15 or 20 minutes of your time.

Munkemøllestræde 3. ℰ 65-51-46-01. http://museum.odense.dk. Admission DKK25 ($4.30/£2.50) adults, free for children 16 and under. June–Aug daily 10am–4pm; Sept–May daily 11am–3pm.

H. C. Andersens Hus (H. C. Andersens Museum) ★★ (Kids) Though not the rival of the Shakespeare properties in Stratford-upon-Avon, the object of most Funen pilgrimages is to the house of the greater spinner of fairy tales himself, Hans Christian

FUNEN

10

ODENSE

Andersen. When it opened in 1908, it became one of the first museums in the world focusing on the life and work of a single author. In various memorabilia, such as hundreds of documents, manuscripts, and reprints of his books in 100 languages (including Zulu), you learn of the writer's life from his birth as the son of a poor cobbler in Odense, to his hard times in Copenhagen, until his eventual debut upon the world stage.

We even learn about some aspects of his love life, as when he fell for Jenny Lind, "the Swedish Nightingale," who did not return his affection. Letters to such fellow famous writers as Charles Dickens are also on exhibit. The storyteller lives again as you get to see some of his "props," such as his famous walking stick, Fred Astaire–like top hat, and battered portmanteau.

On one visit, we encountered an Arab journalist who claimed "Andersen stole his fairy tales from *The Arabian Nights*." That provocative statement simply isn't true. It'd be better to say that he was "influenced" by the Arabian classic.

Bangs Boder 29. ✆ **65-51-46-01.** http://museum.odense.dk. Admission DKK60 ($10/£6) adults, free for children 16 and under. June 16–Aug daily 9am–6pm; Sept–June 15 Tues–Sun 10am–4pm.

Skt. Knuds Domkirke ★ Dating from the 13th century, this is the only purely Gothic cathedral in Denmark. It was named after King Knud (Canute), who reigned from 1080 to 1086. Of a certain ghoulish interest in the crypt is the skeleton of Knud II, who was slain in 1086 by farmers angered at the taxes he'd imposed on them. Amazingly, he was canonized 15 years later when the furor had died down. The crypt lay buried for centuries until it was rediscovered and opened in the 1870s, at which time tombstones of several royal personages were discovered. The *kirke*'s chief treasure—indeed the finest piece of art on Funen—is the intricate wooden **altar** ★★★ in gold leaf, carved by Claus Berg, the German sculptor, in 1526. The 5m (16-ft.) triptych is practically luminous—no doubt because of its whitewashed walls—and it contains some 300 intricately carved figures, the central panel of which depicts the Crucifixion. All this work was done at the bequest of Queen Christina. Other notable treasures include some wrought-iron pieces by Caspar Fincke, who was the official craftsman to King Christian IV.

Klosterbakken 2. ✆ **66-12-03-92.** www.odense-domkirke.dk. Free admission. Apr–Oct Mon–Sat 10am–5pm, Sun and holidays noon–2pm; Nov–Mar Mon–Sat 10am–4pm.

Nearby Attractions

Carl Nielsens Barndomshjem (Carl Nielsen's Childhood Home) Thirteen kilometers (8 miles) from Odense, the childhood house of the famous composer is now a museum and archive of his life. Nielsen lived here until his confirmation in 1879. He was born as one of a dozen children to a poor peasant family, his father a house painter and amateur musician. For more about Nielsen's early days, you can read a delightful memoir called *My Childhood on Funen*. Two studies have been made into commemorative rooms, where the collections illustrate the composer's life.

Odensevej 2A, near Lyndelse. ✆ **65-51-46-01.** http://museum.odense.dk. Admission DKK25 ($4.30/£2.50) adults, free for children 17 and under. Tues–Sun 11am–3pm. Closed Oct–Apr. Bus: 960 or 962.

Egeskov Castle ★★★ This moated Renaissance island castle is the best preserved of its type in Europe. Plan to spend at least a morning or an afternoon viewing the castle and its historical gardens. Constructed in 1554, it is still privately owned and still inhabited by the descendants of Henrik Bille, who purchased the castle in 1784. The location of Denmark's most splendid fortified manor is outside of the town of Kværndrup, lying 29km (18 miles) south of Odense.

The castle was built on oak pillars in the middle of a small lake, for which thousands of oak trees in the neighboring forests were cut down.

The most dramatic story in the castle's history is about an unfortunate maiden, Rigborg, who was seduced by a young nobleman and bore him a child out of wedlock. Banished to the castle, she was imprisoned by her father in a tower from 1599 to 1604.

Because of private living quarters, only some of the castle is open to view, including the restored **Great Hall** ★★, which is now a venue for chamber music concerts on 10 summer Sundays beginning in late June and starting at 5pm. The inhabitants of this castle were great hunters, and you can visit a hunting room with some of their most prized trophies, including elephant tusks and the heads of tigers. You can also view precious antiques and classical paintings.

For us the spectacular **gardens** ★★★ in the 12-hectare (30-acre) park are even more beautiful than the interior. Laid out in the 1730s, the gardens are among the most dramatic in Denmark. The **Fuchsia Garden** ★★★ contains the largest collection of fuchsias in Europe, about 75 different species. The English Garden with its tree-studded green lawns sweeps down to the streams and the castle lake. In summer, the rose beds are a delight to behold, the prize flower being the pink "Egeskov Rose." At a kiosk on-site you can purchase rose jelly. There is also a maze made of cut beech hedges several centuries old, and it's the world's largest maze.

Also on the grounds is a museum of antique cars, old airplanes, and even horse-drawn carriages.

Egeskovgade 18, Kværndrup. ℂ **62-27-10-16**. www.egeskov.dk. Admission including castle, park, and maze DKK175 ($30/£18) adults, DKK92 ($16/£9.20) children 4–12; park, maze, and museum DKK120 ($20/£12) adults, DKK67 ($11/£6.70) children 4–12; free for children 3 and under. July park daily 10am–8pm, castle daily 10am–7pm; June and Aug park daily 10am–6pm, castle daily 10am–5pm; May and Sept park and castle daily 10am–5pm. Closed Oct–Apr. Train: From Odense or Svendborg every hour. Bus: 920 from Nyborg.

Frydenlund (Kids) Sometimes when we've had enough of H. C. Andersen and his fairy tales, we like to secure the makings of a picnic lunch and escape to this bird sanctuary and park 20km (12 miles) southwest of Odense near the village of Tommerup. Some 200 different species of pheasants, ducks, geese, storks, ostriches, parrots, owls, and other birds from all parts of the world live here. There are more than 120 aviaries and some 20 parkland areas in an old farm setting, with many flowers, bushes, and trees. You can enjoy coffee and homemade pastries in the cafe on-site.

Skovvej 50, Naarup, near Tommerup. ℂ **64-76-13-22**. www.frydenlund.net. Admission DKK60 ($10/£6) adults, DKK30 ($5.10/£3) children 10–15, free for children 9 and under. Daily 10am–6pm.

Ladbyskibet Admittedly, the ruins of a 10th-century Viking ship, discovered in 1935, don't equal those vessels discovered in the Oslofjord and displayed on Oslo's Bygdøy peninsula. But if you're not going on to Oslo, this is your best shot at seeing what one of those ships that terrified the coastal settlers of Britain looked like. "The Vikings are coming!" was a scream heard throughout the land.

This is one of the few Viking ships discovered to date in Denmark. Archaeologists are puzzled as to why more Viking ships haven't been unearthed because they were used as coffins for burying chieftains. In this one, the corpse of the pagan chieftain buried was never found, just the bones of nearly a dozen horses and dogs. Other utensils, believed to be of use in Valhalla, were also interred with the corpse. Remains of the ship are displayed in a burial mound along with replicas from the excavation (the originals are in the National Museum of Copenhagen).

Vikingevej 123, Ladby. ⓒ **65-32-16-67.** www.kertemindemuseer.dk. Admission DKK40 ($6.80/£4) adults, free for children 17 and under. May 15–Sept 14 daily 10am–5pm; Mar–May 14 and Sept 15–Oct daily 10am–4pm; Nov–Feb Wed–Sun 11am–3pm. Bus: 482 from Kerteminde. 19km (12 miles) northeast of Odense.

SHOPPING

Inspiration Zinch ★, Vestergade 82–84 (ⓒ **66-12-96-93**), offers the widest selection of Danish design and handicrafts on the island of Funen. All the big names are here, everything from Royal Copenhagen to Georg Jensen, but you will also come across younger and more modern designers, with whose names you might be unfamiliar. In the heart of the old town, opposite Hans Christian Andersen's house, you'll find a display of Danish crafts and Christmas decorations in a typical atmosphere of Old Funen, at **Klods Hans,** Hans Jensens Stæde 34 (ⓒ **66-11-09-40**). Another outlet is **Smykker,** 3 Klaregade (ⓒ **66-12-06-96**), which offers museum copies of Bronze Age, Iron Age, and Viking jewelry—all made in gold, sterling silver, and bronze in the outlet's own workshop. **College Art,** Grandts Passage 38 (ⓒ **66-11-35-45**), has assembled a unique collection of posters, lithographs, silk-screens, original art, and cards. The best gallery for contemporary art is **Galleri Torso,** Hasselvej 25 (ⓒ **66-13-44-66**). Finally, if none of the above shops has what you want, head for **Rosengårdcentret** at Munkerisvej and Ørbækvej (ⓒ **66-15-91-18;** www.rosengaardcentret.dk). It's Denmark's biggest shopping center, with nearly 110 stores all under one roof.

WHERE TO STAY

Some hotels in Odense charge higher rates in winter because of the demand from business travelers at that time.

Expensive

Clarion Hotel Plaza ★★★   This is Odense's classiest address with far more personality, atmosphere, and glamour than its closest rival, the also-recommended Radisson SAS (see below). One of Funen's most alluring hostelries, the Plaza lies less than .5km (¼ mile) outside of the town center, yet only a 5-minute walk from the train station. A stately place to stay, it fronts the city's finest and leafiest park, Kongens Have.

After checking in and inspecting the formal lounges, an old-fashioned early-20th-century elevator takes you to the midsize-to-spacious bedrooms, many of which evoke life in an English country home, opening onto scenic views. The rooms are handsomely decorated, often with antique reproductions, and they escape the curse of too much Danish modern, each coming with a tiled bathroom with a tub/shower combination. The hotel's terrace overlooks the park and a garden. A first-class cuisine of both Danish and international specialties is served in the Plaza's formal restaurant, known for its attentive service and impressive wine list.

Østre Stationsvej 24, DK-5000 Odense. ⓒ **877/424-6423** in the U.S., or 66-11-77-45. Fax 66-14-41-45. www.hotel-plaza.dk. 68 units. July–Aug DKK871 ($148/£87) double, DKK1,940 ($330/£194) suite; Sept–June DKK1,143–DKK1,345 ($194–$229/£114–£135) double, DKK1,945 ($331/£195) suite. Rates include breakfast. AE, DC, MC, V. Free parking. Bus: 31, 33, 35, or 36. **Amenities:** Restaurant; bar; room service; laundry service; dry cleaning; nonsmoking rooms. In room: TV, Wi-Fi, minibar, hair dryer, safe.

Radisson SAS H.C. Andersen Hotel ★★   It may lack the nostalgic charm of the Plaza, but commercial travelers find this first-class hotel more convenient with a livelier roster of facilities, including a casino. In summer, fans of Andersen from abroad fill its 1960s Nordic-style bedrooms near a former Hans Christian Andersen residence in the

heart of the city. This redbrick hotel, one of the finest on the island of Funen, welcomes you into a plant-filled lobby and a glass-roofed reception area, where you encounter the most efficient staff in Odense.

The tasteful, conservatively decorated, and comfortably appointed bedrooms come in a variety of sizes—some large, others, especially the singles, a bit cramped—with the most tranquil rooms opening onto the interior. Each of the bathrooms, though small, is well equipped with thoughtful extras such as makeup mirrors.

Overlooking the market square, the hotel's formal restaurant is known for catering to special requests, such as vegetarian or other diets. It serves a refined international and Danish cuisine and does so exceedingly well, using market-fresh ingredients.

Claus Bergs Gade 7, DK-5000 Odense. ✆ **800/333-3333** in the U.S., or 66-14-78-00. Fax 66-14-78-90. www.radissonsas.com. 145 units. DKK1,595–DKK1,895 ($271–$322/£160–£190) double. Rates include breakfast. AE, DC, MC, V. Bus: 4 or 5. **Amenities:** Restaurant; bar; fitness center; sauna; room service; laundry service; dry cleaning; nonsmoking rooms; casino; solarium; rooms for those w/limited mobility. *In room:* TV, Wi-Fi, minibar, hair dryer, safe.

Scandic Hotel Odense ★ (Kids) This chain-run hotel is sort of a glorified roadside motel, dating from 1986, when it was built 5km (3 miles) southwest of the city center in an industrial neighborhood that's convenient to the E20 express highway. Motorists, especially families, are attracted to it because of its comfortable midsize bedrooms, many of which sleep up to two adults and two children. The rooms are in a three-story, low-slung building, with contemporary Danish modern decor, plus a good-size bathroom with shower unit. You don't have to go back into town for dinner, as the hotel operates a good restaurant on-site serving both Danish and international dishes. There is a big playroom with a large selection of books and toys.

Hvidkærvej 25, DK-5250 Odense SV. ✆ **66-17-66-66.** Fax 66-17-25-53. www.scandichotels.com. 100 units. DKK850–DKK1,590 ($145–$270/£85–£159) double; DKK1,550–DKK2,190 ($264–$372/£155–£219) suite. Rates include breakfast. AE, DC, MC, V. Bus: 835 or 840. **Amenities:** Restaurant; bar; fitness center; sauna; children's playroom; room service; babysitting; laundry service; dry cleaning; nonsmoking rooms; solarium; rooms for those w/limited mobility. *In room:* TV, Wi-Fi, minibar, hair dryer, trouser press.

Moderate

Best Western Hotel Knudsens Gaard This is a serviceable chain-operated hotel—and not a lot more—and still imbued with a slight aura of 1955, when it first opened less than a kilometer (1/2 mile) south of the town center. Once it was a half-timbered old Danish farmhouse, but those days are long gone. Today it attracts many families in town to check out the H. C. Andersen sights. Even so, it is not especially geared to families. The previously recommended Scandic (see above) caters better to kids. Nevertheless, the compact bedrooms are comfortably furnished, each containing a neatly kept bathroom. The on-site restaurant serves a standard and affordable cuisine.

Hunderupgade 2, DK-5230 Odense. ✆ **800/780-7234** in the U.S., or 63-11-43-11. Fax 63-11-43-01. www. bestwestern.com. 77 units. DKK995–DKK1,395 ($169–$237/£100–£140) double. Rates include breakfast. AE, DC, MC, V. **Amenities:** Restaurant; bar; room service; laundry service; dry cleaning; nonsmoking rooms; rooms for those w/limited mobility. *In room:* TV, Wi-Fi, minibar, hair dryer.

City Hotel Odense This hotel is down the pecking order from those previously recommended, but you forget all that as you sit out on summer furniture enjoying one of the best panoramic views of the city. Built in 1988, the hotel offers standard comforts and an affordable price without generating any raves. Lying only 2 blocks from the train station, this hotel often caters to conventions. Its midsize bedrooms are comfortably but rather blandly furnished, in an uninspired style. There is a certain coziness here even in winter, when you can sit in the lounge enjoying a cup of coffee in front of an open fire. Other than breakfast, no meals are offered, although a 300-year-old Danish inn, Den Gamle Kro, run by the same owner, serves flavorful meals a 5-minute walk away.

Hans Mules Gade 5, DK-5000 Odense. ✆ **66-12-12-58.** Fax 66-12-93-64. www.city-hotel-odense.dk. 43 units. DKK995–DKK1,095 ($169–$186/£100–£110) double; DKK1,195 ($203/£120) apt. Rates include breakfast. AE, DC, MC, V. Bus: 41 or 42. Free parking. **Amenities:** Breakfast room; bar; game room; laundry service; dry cleaning; nonsmoking rooms. *In room:* TV, Wi-Fi, hair dryer.

First Hotel Grand ★ ⒱ⓐⓛⓤⓔ   In those halcyon Belle Epoque days of 1897, this grand hotel opened near the rail depot to greet arriving passengers from Copenhagen. At that time it was the grandest hotel in town, losing that position in 1915 to the Clarion Hotel Plaza (see above), which is still the market leader today. But the Grand holds its own and is our second choice for Odense, rising four floors in a brick-built structure shaped like a triangle and studded with old-fashioned dormers. The ground-floor reception will provide you with an ornately shaped brass key for your bedroom door. Bedrooms, in the 19th-century tradition, are large, and each is comfortably furnished, with an adjoining good-size bathroom. On-site are a relatively good restaurant serving Danish regional food and a cozy bar that makes an ideal place for a rendezvous.

Jernbanegade 18, DK-5000 Odense. ✆ **66-11-71-71.** Fax 66-14-11-71. www.firsthotels.com. 138 units. DKK925–DKK1,425 ($157–$242/£93–£143) double; DKK1,125–DKK1,988 ($191–$338/£113–£199) suite. Rates include breakfast. AE, DC, MC, V. Parking DKK60 ($10/£6). **Amenities:** Restaurant; bar; sauna; room service; laundry service; nonsmoking rooms. *In room:* TV, Wi-Fi, minibar, hair dryer.

Hotel Ansgar ⓀⒾⒹⓈ   In 1902, when this hotel opened a 5-minute walk from the train depot, it attracted clean-living, nondrinking Christian clients. But those religious associations are long gone, and even some hard-drinking Danes check in here today. The original founders would shout hell and damnation, because there's even a bar on-site. Behind a brick-and-stone facade, the hotel has been considerably renovated, with the installation of modern furniture and double-glaze windows to cut down on the traffic noise. As befits the style of the hotel's era, the rooms range from small to spacious, each comfortably furnished with Italian pieces, and each with adequate and well-kept bathrooms with tub/shower combinations. The staff does much in summer to attract the family trade, even giving kids a coupon for free ice cream. A wide range of dishes from both the Danish and international kitchens is served, and one of the best food values in town is the restaurant's two-course fixed-price dinner at DKK150 ($26/£15).

Østre Stationsvej 32, DK-5000 Odense. ✆ **66-11-96-93.** Fax 66-11-96-75. www.hotel-ansgar.dk. 64 units. June–Aug DKK675–DKK825 ($115–$140/£68–£83) double; Sept–May DKK1,145 ($195/£115) double. Rates include breakfast. Extra bed DKK150 ($26/£15). AE, DC, MC, V. Free parking. Bus: 31, 33, 35, or 36. **Amenities:** Restaurant; bar; children's playroom; laundry service; dry cleaning; nonsmoking rooms. *In room:* TV, Wi-Fi, minibar, hair dryer.

Inexpensive

Comfort Windsor Hotel   Even though its prices have risen in recent years, this is still viewed as an affordable choice, since most of its bedrooms are at the lower end of the price scale. Since 1898, this cozy, well-furnished, redbrick hotel building has come as a welcome relief to travelers who arrive at the rail station. The Windsor, in spite of its royal name, was never regal in any sense, but is a decent, well-run, and inviting hotel. Comfortably furnished and tasteful, it offers high-ceilinged bedrooms that are well maintained and tasteful, although small for our tastes. Furnishings are in sleek, not very exciting, Danish modern, with double-glazing on the windows to cut down on the street noise.

DKK888–DKK1,145 ($151–$195/£89–£115) double. Rates include breakfast. AE, DC, MC, V. **Amenities:**
Restaurant; bar; laundry service; dry cleaning; nonsmoking rooms. *In room:* TV, Wi-Fi, minibar.

Hotel Domir/Hotel Ydes (Value)   When antiquities dealer Eigil Johns opened what
is now the Domir, he romantically called it "The Gaslight," evocative of the street lighting of the time. A few years later, the Ydes was opened nearby. Today, these are still among
the finest affordable lodgings in Odense and are under the same ownership. If there is no
room at one, chances are you'll be housed in the other. Each hotel has comfortable but
small rooms, with the Ydes (28 rooms) focusing a bit more on old-fashioned decor, and
the Domir (35 rooms) going for brighter colors and a more indulgent approach to pop
culture. Every room has a well-kept bathroom with a shower unit. You'll have a greater
sense of camaraderie at the Domir, where a live receptionist will check you in; at the Ydes,
a TV monitor will beam you the instructions from the manager (who works in the
Domir).

Hans Tausensgade 11 and 19, DK-5000 Odense. © **66-12-14-27** and 66-12-11-31. Fax 66-12-14-13.
www.domir.dk; www.ydes.dk. 60 units. Domir DKK645–DKK745 ($110–$127/£65–£75) double; Ydes
DKK595 ($101/£60) double. Rates include breakfast. AE, DC, MC, V. **Amenities:** Breakfast room; bar. *In
room:* TV, Wi-Fi, trouser press.

Næsbylund Kro   For greater tranquillity, many motorists like to stay out of town. If
so, our choice for such lodgings is this *kro* (inn), lying 4km (2¹/₂ miles) north of Odense.
The Danish word *kro* often suggests an antique inn, but in this case the compound is
modern, dating from 1983. It's basically a roadside motel, with midsize bedrooms, many
with balconies, and each furnished in a conservatively modern style, although the look is
somewhat impersonal. For an overnight stopover, it's just fine, but there are far more
attractive places to go for the rest of your stay in Funen. In a separate building, the
Carolinenkilde restaurant serves dinner nightly 5 to 9:30pm.

Bogensevej 105–117, DK-5270 Odense. © **66-18-00-39.** Fax 66-18-29-29. www.naesbylundkro.dk. 53
units. DKK795 ($135/£80) double; DKK1,200 ($204/£120) suite. Rates include breakfast. AE, DC, MC, V. Bus:
91 or 92. **Amenities:** Restaurant; lounge; indoor pool. *In room:* TV, Wi-Fi.

WHERE TO DINE
Expensive
Den Gamle Kro ★ DANISH/FRENCH   For all we know, Hans Christian Andersen
used to drop into this place—after all, it's been serving food and drink to the locals since
1683, and at one time or another nearly every resident of Odense has eaten or drunk
here. Set a 5-minute walk from the center, it is unusual architecturally in that it was
constructed within the courtyard of several antique buildings, but has been modernized
with its timeworn stone capped by a sliding glass roof.

A cellar-level bar is lined with antique masonry and the street-level restaurant rests
under centuries-old beams. The food has remained consistently good over the years, and
we've often dropped in for lunch for some of the best *smørrebrød* (open-faced sandwich)
selections in town, especially when shrimp and dill is stacked on top of a freshly baked
bread.

If you return for dinner, you'll find some of the best fixed-price meals in town. There's
nothing you're served here that you haven't tasted before, including beef tenderloin flavored with herbs or herb-sprinkled trout sautéed in butter, but the ingredients are market
fresh and skillfully prepared by the kitchen staff, who also serve yummy, freshly made
desserts.

Overgade 23. ℂ **66-12-14-33.** Reservations recommended. Main courses DKK79–DKK258 ($13–$44/£7.90–£26); fixed-price meals DKK298–DKK418 ($51–$71/£30–£42). AE, DC, MC, V. Mon–Sat 11am–10:30pm; Sun 11am–9:30pm. Bus: 2.

Le Brasserie ★ FRENCH/ASIAN   For years this restaurant was fondly known as LPC, or "La Petite Cuisine," and it's still here, only with a name change. It offers the same bistro fare that you might find in a provincial town somewhere in the heart of France. Set on a narrow, partially covered passageway in the heart of town, it features contemporary-looking decor and a soothing color scheme. The only change is that some of the dishes are inspired by an Asian fusion cuisine such as the marinated duck breast, which is delectable. The basically French menu is composed only after the shopping at the market is completed so that everything will be fresh. We can't predict what you will be served, but expect such delights as marinated wild Scottish salmon with pickled watercress and a mild mustard sauce with passion fruit oil. Thinly sliced scallops are "escorted" with foie gras, wild watercress, and slices of pickled pumpkin. For a main course, the chef proposes a delicious duet of Danish veal and French duck aromatically served with anise-poached fennel, or else the crisp fried filet of redfish with roasted artichoke hearts.

Brandts Passage 13. ℂ **66-14-11-28.** Reservations recommended. Main courses DKK169–DKK180 ($29–$31/£17–£18). DC, MC, V. Tues–Sat 5:30–10pm. Bus: 2.

Marie Louise ★★★ FRENCH/INTERNATIONAL   You'd have to return to Copenhagen to order French food as fine as that served here in an antique house sheltering one of the smallest and most exclusive—also the best—restaurants in Odense.

Its dining room is a white-walled re-creation of an old-fashioned country tavern, although closer inspection reveals a decidedly upscale slant to the furnishings, accessories, silver, and crystal. A polished staff serves well-planned dishes based mainly on French recipes, with more and more international recipes appearing on recent menus.

The chef prepares dishes with a certain precision and sensitivity, as evoked by such delectable specialties as a salmon-and-dill mousse with shrimp sauce. Most savvy diners order the fresh fish dishes of the day, perhaps turbot in Riesling or a champagne sauce. The chef gets an extra point for that divine lobster he served us in Danish country butter. An array of enticing desserts is laid out like works of art for your selection.

Lottrups Gård, Vestergade 70–72. ℂ **66-17-92-95.** Reservations recommended. Main courses DKK340–DKK410 ($58–$70/£34–£41). V. Mon–Sat noon–midnight. Closed July. Bus: 2.

Restaurant Klitgaard ★★★ Ⓕⁱⁿᵈˢ CONTINENTAL/DANISH   Although Marie Louise is still number one in Odense, this 1998 restaurant is the most innovative in town, serving a cuisine that is cutting edge—and not traditional like the time-honored favorite. The setting is woodsy and appealing in monochromatic tones of brown and beige, with room for only 30 guests at a time. The feeling you might get, except for its view over the other buildings of Odense's historic core, is that of a Tuscan farmhouse. Jacob Klitgaard, born about 30km (19 miles) from the town of Svendborg, is the chef and very hip namesake of this place, personally selecting impeccably fresh ingredients, many of them produced or cultivated in and around Odense. Menu items make ample use of both foie gras and shellfish. Ingredients such as herbs come from the restaurant's own kitchen garden, and produce is sourced from local growers, breeders, and local game hunters. Inspired by the bounty of Funen, you are likely to be served roast trout with a rosemary-scented olive oil, or else a saltwater catfish with a ragout of basil-flavored minestrone. The chef also keeps his customers happy with such marvelous dishes as braised pheasant with wild mushrooms in a beer sauce or else fricassee of guinea fowl with savory herb sauce.

Sortebro Kro (Value) DANISH/FRENCH   Even though it serves good food, this is a very touristy inn because it lies just outside the entrance to Funen Village (p. 269). The open-air culture museum is about 2.5km (1¹/₂ miles) south of the center. Sortebro was a coaching inn from 1807, but later in its life was moved to this location. The interior is an attraction in its own right: long refectory tables, sagging ceilings with overhead beams, three-legged chairs, florid handmade chests, and crockery cupboards. Expect a vast array of meat, poultry, and seafood dishes, plus a groaning table filled with freshly made desserts. The chef creates classic, time-tested dishes based on the freshest and finest produce from the Funen countryside.

Sejerskovvej 20. © **66-13-28-26**. www.sortebro.dk. Reservations required. Main courses DKK315–DKK385 ($54–$65/£32–£39). AE, DC, MC, V. Mon–Sat noon–10pm; Sun noon–5pm. Closed Dec 23–26. Bus: 21 or 22 from Flakhaven.

Under Lindetræet ★ DANISH/INTERNATIONAL   In summer, make your way past the artists who invariably sit out sketching the home of Hans Christian Andersen to this inn from 1704 located across the street from the storyteller's museum. Since the 1960s, it's been a landmark and local favorite. Since everyone visits *The Ugly Duckling*'s home, it's the most popular restaurant in town. That could mean it is no more than a tourist trap. It isn't—rather, it's one of the finest restaurants in town with a menu based on fresh, first-class ingredients. Skillfully prepared dishes include tender Danish lamb, filet of plaice with butter sauce, escallop of veal in sherry sauce, fried herring with new potatoes, and an upscale version of *skipperlabskovs*, the famed sailors' hash. The atmosphere is Old World, and in summer, meals and light refreshments are served outside under linden trees.

Ramsherred 2. © **66-12-92-86**. www.underlindetraet.dk. Reservations required. Main courses DKK95–DKK225 ($16–$38/£9.50–£23); fixed-price menus DKK330–DKK675 ($56–$115/£33–£68). AE, DC, MC, V. Mon–Sat noon–2:30pm and 6–9:30pm. Closed July 4–24. Bus: 2.

Moderate

Carlslund ★ DANISH   This restaurant's reputation rests on its famous country omelet, *aeggekage*, which is topped with crispy bacon curls and chives. Of course, you must not be a cholesterol watcher to devour this fluffy concoction. It's consumed with rye bread, and Danes often eat it between shots of aquavit. The restaurant, housed in an 1860 building with low ceilings, stands in a wooded area on the border of town. It's one of the most atmospheric places to dine in the Odense area. If you don't opt for the egg cake, you can sample many other dishes such as marinated herring with curry salad, fresh smoked salmon with asparagus, and even "the green platter," consisting of vegetables in season. Steaks and calf's liver appeal to the meat eater, and you can also order a whole pan-fried plaice with a prawn and asparagus sauce.

Fruens Bøge Skov 7. © **66-91-11-25**. www.restaurant-carlslund.dk. Reservations required. Main courses DKK115–DKK195 ($20–$33/£12–£20). DC, MC, V. Daily noon–10pm.

Inexpensive

Den Grimme Æling ★ (Kids) DANISH   Part of its charm derives from its name (which translates as "The Ugly Duckling"), and its location is very close to the former home of Hans Christian Andersen. It's set on a cobblestone street in Odense's historic core, in an ocher-colored building from around 1850 that emulates an old-fashioned

Danish *kro*. Attracting a large family trade, it specializes in well-stocked buffets manned by uniformed staff members who will cook your steak, fish, omelet, or whatever into virtually any Danish-inspired configuration you want. There are no *smørrebrød,* but because the buffet contains a roster of sliced cheeses, breads, meats, and condiments, you can always make your own. The staff speaks excellent English, and if buffet dining appeals to you, you might have a wonderful time here, as we always do.

Hans Jensens Stræde 1. (C) **65-91-70-30.** www.grimme-aelling.dk. DKK126 ($21/£13) buffet. MC, V. Daily noon–2:30pm and 5:30–10:30pm.

Målet DANISH   This is the leading sports pub in town and also a restaurant serving an acceptable (predictably not gourmet) cuisine. Don't expect the high-tech, big-screen bombast of sports bars you might visit in the U.S. Instead, you'll see a cramped bar for around 15 drinkers in one corner, two small-screen TVs projecting sports events from around the world, and years of collected memorabilia pertaining to soccer. No one will mind if you simply drink your way through the evening with the locals. But if you want a meal, try the house specialty, a large portion of pork schnitzel, served with potatoes, and prepared in any of 10 different ways. Otherwise, you can order fish or beefsteak, and even an occasional vegetarian dish, but the schnitzels are simply the most appealing dish in the house. *Målet,* incidentally, translates as "soccer goal post," and management has erected one as an admittedly ugly decorative centerpiece in a prominent position against one wall.

Jernbanegade 17. (C) **66-17-82-41.** Reservations recommended. Main courses DKK55–DKK135 ($9.40–$23/£5.50–£14); 2-course set menu DKK125 ($21/£13), 3-course set menu DKK160 ($27/£16). No credit cards. Tues–Sat 11am–11pm.

ODENSE AFTER DARK

There are lots of cultural events in Odense, foremost among which are performances by the **Odense Symphony Orchestra.** Throughout much of the year, concerts are presented in the **Carl Nielsen Hall,** Claus Bergs Gade 9 ((C) **66-12-00-57** for ticket information). Tickets cost DKK70 to DKK220 ($12–$37/£7–£22), depending on the event. During the warm-weather months, the orchestra's role is less formal. In August, for example, the group is more likely to play outdoors at the marketplace in front of the vegetable stands. Because of their location, these performances have been referred to as "the Vegetable Concerts." In August, on Saturdays at 11am, the orchestra presents free live music at Skovsoen park.

Boogies, Nørregade 21–23 ((C) **66-14-00-39**), attracts the most mixed crowd in town, including some of Odense's gay and lesbian population, who blend in with an otherwise straight clientele

At Odense's railway station, **Frank A.'s Café,** Jernbanegade 4 ((C) **66-12-27-57**), operates as a cafe throughout the day, and as such, draws a respectable crowd of drinkers and diners who appreciate the tasty Danish platters, which cost from DKK79 to DKK225 ($13–$38/£7.90–£23). But the real heart and soul of the place doesn't become visible until after 10pm, when all pretenses of culinary skill are abandoned, and the cafe becomes one of the loudest, wildest, and most raucous nightlife venues in town. Then, live music— Brazilian, Latin, or simple rock 'n' roll—transforms the room into everybody's favorite rendezvous. Come here to be convivial, amid a setting that's loaded with kitschy bric-a-brac and dozens of single or wannabe-single local residents. Food service is daily 10am to 10pm; nightlife action runs 10pm to at least 3am, and sometimes later.

43km (27 miles) S of Odense; 146km (91 miles) W of Copenhagen; 25km (16 miles) E of Faaborg

Svendborg, with 42,000 residents, is the second-biggest town in Funen and a major commercial and touristic hub for South Funen, but it has none of all that fairy-tale overlay that Odense hypes. It's a sailors' town—beloved of Danish yachties—and has had a long history as a maritime center. Until 1915, it was the home port for a big fleet of sailing ships because of its position on the beautiful Svendborg Sound, which provides convenient access to Baltic ports.

Although shipbuilding is a ghost of itself, there are still a couple of shipyards left that construct wooden-hulled ships and are around to repair visiting yachts plying the waters off the coast of South Funen.

Frankly, we'd spend only a night here as the islands of Ærø and Tåsinge (see later in this chapter) are more alluring. But if you give Svendborg a day, you'll find much to do.

You'll see yachts, ketches, and kayaks in the harbor. The town still retains some of its medieval heritage, but much of it has been torn down in the name of progress and industry.

Today Svendborg is a lively modern town, with museums, constantly changing art exhibitions, and sports. It has swimming pools, beaches, and a yachting school. Its best beach, **Christiansminde,** is one of several in Funen flying the blue flag that indicates nonpolluted waters.

Svendborg is also a market town, and on Sunday morning, you visit the cobblestone central plaza where flowers and fish are sold. Wander through the many winding streets where brick and half-timbered buildings still stand. On **Ragergade,** you'll see the old homes of early seafarers. **Møllergade,** a pedestrian street, is one of the oldest streets in town, with about 100 different shops.

Literary buffs know that the German writer Bertolt Brecht lived at Skovsbo Strand west of Svendborg from 1933 to 1939, but he left at the outbreak of World War II. During this period, he wrote *Mother Courage and Her Children,* which is still performed all over the world.

ESSENTIALS

GETTING THERE   By Train   You can take a train from Copenhagen to Odense, where you can get a connecting train to Svendborg, with frequent service throughout the day.

By Car   From our last stopover in Odense, head south on Route 9, following the signs into Svendborg.

VISITOR INFORMATION   Contact the **Svendborg Tourist Office,** Centrumpladsen (© **62-21-09-80;** www.visitsydfyn.dk), open June 20 to August 21, Monday to Friday 9:30am to 6pm and Saturday 9:30am to 2pm; January 2 to June 19 and August 22 to December 22, Monday to Friday 9:30am to 5pm and Saturday 9:30am to 12:30pm; closed December 23 to January 1.

GETTING AROUND   By Bus   Bus no. 200 serves all in-town destinations listed below, except for Vester Skerninge Kro, for which you need a car.

By Bike   Bike rentals for hotel guests, at DKK60 ($10/£6) per day, can be obtained at the Hotel Svendborg, Centrumpladsen 1 (© **62-21-17-00;** bus: 200 or 204). Biking routes and maps are available at the tourist office.

Anne Hvides Gård This cross-timbered house looks a little tipsy, like it's had too much to drink, lying as it does in the center of the Torvet, the old market square. Actually it's the oldest secular house in Svendborg, dating from 1558 and operated today as a branch of the County Museum. This is another one of those "let's raid the attic to see what we can find" types of museums. Its most dramatic features are the re-creations of interiors from the 18th and 19th centuries, and there are plenty of silver objects, glassware, copper and brass utensils, and the inevitable faience. Temporary cultural exhibitions are also presented here.

Fruestræde 3. ℂ **62-21-34-57.** www.svendborgmuseum.dk. Free admission. Apr–Sept Tues–Sun 11am–3pm; off-season by arrangement with the main office.

Naturama Formed from a zoological collection started in 1935, Naturama was greatly expanded, changing its name from the zoo to a new moniker based on "nature" and "drama." In both skeletons and mounted animals, the exhibition raids the land, sea, and air, including the great whales of the North Atlantic—in fact, Naturama is Denmark's largest display of not only whales but also other sea mammals. The center also displays the largest forest mammals in Scandinavia, including everything from bears to bison. Advanced lighting techniques, sound, and even films supplement the exhibitions. On top of the building, you'll be introduced to 500 woodland birds, everything from eagles to owls, from Woody Woodpecker to the most beautiful of songbirds.

Dronningemæn 30. ℂ **62-21-06-50.** www.naturama.dk. Admission DKK100 ($17/£10) adults, DKK70 ($12/£7) seniors, free for children 17 and under. Mid-June to mid-Aug daily 10am–5pm; mid-Aug to mid-June Tues–Sun 10am–5pm. Bus: 205, 206, or 208.

Skt. Jørgens Kirke Only the Church of Skt. Nicolai (see below) exceeds the beauty of St. George's church, whose origins go back to the 12th century when it was originally a chapel for lepers who were forced to live outside the town in an attempt to control spread of the disease. The church itself was named for that fearless knight St. George, patron of lepers. The core of the church is a Gothic longhouse with a three-sided chancel from the late 13th century. During restoration of the church in 1961, an archaeological dig of the floor disclosed traces of a wooden building believed to be a predecessor of the present house of worship.

Strandvej 97. ℂ **62-21-14-73.** www.sctjoergens.dk. Free admission. Mon–Fri 8am–4pm.

Skt. Nicolai Kirke Svendborg's oldest church is situated among a cluster of antique houses off Kyseborgstræde, in the vicinity of Gerrits Plads just south of the market square. Built of bricks before 1200 in the Romanesque style and last restored in 1892, its redbrick walls and white vaulting complement the fine altarpiece by Joachim Skovgaard in 1894. The magnificent **stained-glass windows** ★ were designed by Kræsten Iversen during Denmark's darkest days in recent history, the Nazi occupation that lasted from 1940 to 1945. Nearby, you can admire a statue by Kai Nielsen (1820–1924), a native son who went on to greater glory and became a famous sculptor.

Skt. Nicolajgade 2B. ℂ **62-21-28-54.** Free admission. May–Aug daily 10am–3pm; Sept–Apr daily 10am–noon.

Viebæltegård Time for a confession. We view this museum as being of such minor interest that we rarely give it more than 30 or 40 minutes. If the day is sunny, we prefer to come here to enjoy a picnic lunch in the museum garden. The headquarters for the county museum is housed in a former poorhouse/workhouse from 1872, the only one of

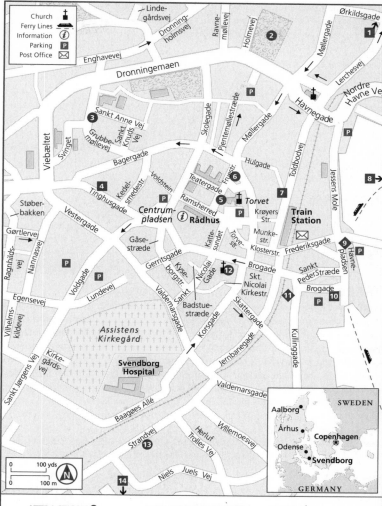

Church ✝
Ferry Lines 🚢
Information ⓘ
Parking P
Post Office ✉

Lindegårdsvej
Dronningholmsvej
Enghavevej
Ravnemøllevej
Holmevej
Ørkildsgade
Møllergade
Lerchesvej
Dronningemaen
Havnegade
Nordre Havne Vej
Skolegade
Pjentemøllestræde
Møllergade
Sankt Anne Vej
Sankt Knuds Vej
Grubbemøllevej
Viebæltet
Svinget
Bagergade
Hulgade
Toldbodvej
Jessens Mole
Kedelsmedestr.
Voldstein
Teatergade
Frue Str.
Tinghusgade
Ramsherred
Torvet
Train Station
Støberbakken
Centrumpladsen
Rådhus
Krøyers Str.
Munkestr.
Havnepladsen
Gørtlervej
Vestergade
Gåsestræde
Kattesundet
Torvestr.
Klosterstr.
Frederiksgade
Ragnhildsvej
Nannasvej
Gerritsgade
Kysseborgstr.
Sankt
Nicolai Gade
Skt. Nicolai Kirkestr.
Brogade
Sankt Peder Stræde
Havnepladsen
Brogade
Egensevej
Voldgade
Lundevej
Valdemarsgade
Badstuestræde
Korsogade
Skattergade
Kullinggade
Vilhelmskildevej
Assistens Kirkegård
Jernbanegade
Svendborg Hospital
Valdemarsgade
Kirkegårdsvej
Sankt Jørgens Vej
Baagøes Allé
Willemoesvej
Herluf Trolles Vej
Strandvej
Niels Juels Vej

Aalborg
Århus
Odense
Copenhagen
Svendborg
SWEDEN
GERMANY

0   100 yds
0   100 m

FUNEN
10
SVENDBORG

ATTRACTIONS ●
Anne Hvides Gård **6**
Naturama **2**
Skt. Jørgens Kirke **13**
Skt. Nicolai Kirke **12**
Viebæltegård **3**
Vor Frue Kirke **5**

ACCOMMODATIONS ■
Hotel Æro **10**
Hotel Christiansminde **8**
Hotel Garni **7**
Hotel Svendborg **4**
Majorgården **1**
Missionshotellet Stella Maris **14**

DINING ◆
Restaurant Marco Polo **11**
Svendborgsund **9**

its kind still existing in Denmark. The complex of "social welfare" buildings has been converted into museums of history, displaying artifacts from ancient times to the Middle Ages, including finds from fields around Svendborg and South Funen in general. More intriguing is to visit the crafts workshops on-site, watching goldsmiths, potters, and printers at work, and there's also an on-site museum shop that has some wonderful crafts for sale.

Grubbemøllevej 13 (near Dronningemæn). (C) **62-21-02-61.** www.svendborgmuseum.dk. Admission DKK40 ($6.80/£4) adults, free for children 17 and under when accompanied by an adult. Open year-round Tues–Sun 10am–4pm.

Vor Frue Kirke   On the hill where the old Castle Swineburg stood, this Romanesque-Gothic church, dating from 1253, has a carillon of 27 bells, which ring four times a day. From the tourist office at Torvet, walk up the steps leading to the rise on which the church stands, overlooking the Old Town and the harbor, for a grand view. The church has a late-16th-century pulpit and altar, but nothing else to hold your attention for very long.

Frue Kirkestræde 4. (C) **62-21-01-35.** Free admission. Daily 8am–4pm.

SHOPPING

The widest selection of Danish design, from household utensils to prestigious china from Royal Copenhagen, and even silver from Georg Jensen, is found at **Inspiration Zinck,** in the Svendborg Bycenter, Tinghusgade ((C) **62-22-35-93**). The best source of glass is **Glasblæseriet,** Brogade 37 ((C) **62-22-83-73**), where glass can be blown to your own design specifications. Of course, regular glass products, created by others, are also for sale.

WHERE TO STAY

Hotel Ærø (Value   Extensive renovations have turned Svendborg's oldest hotel into an acceptable choice once again for overnighting. Even if you don't stay here, consider it for a dinner, as it serves what is arguably the most authentic Danish cuisine in town, including those ping-pong-size meatballs, known as *frikadeller,* a large platter containing plaice with hollandaise, and many meat dishes, as well as several *smørrebrød* selections. All the bedrooms are decorated in the romantic English style, evocative of the 19th century. In addition to the cozy restaurant and hotel, there is a pub, **Hvalfisken,** where you can order beer from many countries, especially Ireland, Britain, and Belgium, while listening to live music. Sailors and guests mingle freely. The location is at the harbor where the ferry pulls in.

Brogade 1 Ærøfaergen. (C) **62-21-07-60.** Fax 63-20-30-51. www.hotel-aeroe.dk. 33 units. DKK975 ($166/£98) double, DKK1,250 ($213/£125) suite. Extra bed DKK250 ($43/£25). Rates include breakfast. DC, MC, V. **Amenities:** Restaurant; pub; room service; laundry service; bike rentals. *In room:* TV.

Hotel Christiansminde   According to photographs we saw, the history of this hotel dates from 1830, although in its present reincarnation the building was constructed in the 1970s, lying 3km (1³/₄ miles) east of Svendborg's center on a grassy knoll close to the sea. Many visitors come here for a summer holiday beside the beach; others arrive as part of corporate conventions whose sponsors rent virtually every room for inspiration-building discussions over long weekends. Midsize rooms have balconies or private terraces, and functional, unpretentious, yet comfortable furniture. Some contain small kitchens, although there's no additional cost for such added luxuries. There are a restaurant and a series of convention rooms with up-to-date electronic and broadcast facilities. Walks into Svendborg are made easier thanks to a network of hiking trails, most of which avoid active roadways. Other than that, there aren't a lot of sport facilities and diversions at this property—only easy access to the great Danish outdoors and the nearby sea.

Christiansmindvej 16, DK-5700 Svendborg. © **62-21-90-00.** Fax 62-21-60-82. www.christiansminde.dk.
98 units. DKK1,070–DKK1,270 ($182–$216/£107–£127) double. Rates include breakfast. AE, DC, MC, V.
Closed Jan–Mar. Bus: 201 from Svendborg. **Amenities:** Restaurant; lounge; laundry service; dry cleaning;
solarium. *In room:* TV, Wi-Fi.

Hotel Garni   If you're not supposed to judge a book by its cover, perhaps you'll extend
the same courtesy to this hotel, one of the most affordable in town, long attracting the
frugal traveler to its location opposite both the rail and bus stations. Behind a plain
facade, it is a bastion of comfort and convenience, its front rooms opening onto the
harbor. The small-to-midsize bedrooms are more inviting than stylish, and though the
furnishings are in plain Nordic design, they are nonetheless suitable for an overnight stay.
Only breakfast is served, but it's a generous one; and there are many taverns and restaurants nearby for lunch or dinner.

Toldbodvej 5, DK-5700 Svendborg. © **62-21-17-00.** Fax 62-21-90-12. www.hotel-garni.dk. 18 units.
DKK750 ($128/£75) double. Rates include breakfast. MC, V. Bus: 200, 208, or 980. **Amenities:** Breakfast
room; lounge; Wi-Fi (in lobby). *In room:* TV, hair dryer.

Hotel Svendborg ★   Built in the 1950s, this hotel nonetheless is stylish inside and
offers the best accommodations in Svendborg, the rooms spread across four floors above
the commercial core of town. It's never been our favorite, as we prefer more evocative or
romantic addresses, but, during the 2 nights we spent here, we were exceedingly comfortable and found the English staff helpful and informative about the area. The bedrooms
range from small to spacious, and each is furnished in a tasteful Scandinavian modern
design with excellent bathrooms. The eight apartments, each with kitchen, can be rented
to one to four guests. On-site is the first-class restaurant, **Krinsten,** serving menus based
on the seasons.

Centrumpladsen 1, DK-5700 Svendborg. © **62-21-17-00.** Fax 62-21-90-12. www.hotel-svendborg.dk.
133 units (8 apts). DKK1,145–DKK1,345 ($195–$229/£115–£135) double; DKK1,870–DKK2,420 ($318–
$411/£187–£242) suite; DKK1,520 ($258/£152) apt for 2; DKK1,820 ($309/£182) apt for 4. Rates include
breakfast. AE, DC, MC, V. Free parking. Bus: 200 or 204. **Amenities:** Restaurant; bar; room service; laundry
service; dry cleaning; nonsmoking rooms; rooms for those w/limited mobility. *In room:* TV, Wi-Fi, minibar,
hair dryer, safe.

Majorgården ★ (Finds)   It had to happen. We just had to find a cozy nest on Funen
that we liked above all others—and this is it. On the coast road, 11km (7 miles) from
Svendborg and 30km (19 miles) from Nyborg, such illustrious Danes as tenor Lauritz
Melchior have cherished this 1761 white-brick inn. Outside, a bower of roses grows
against the walls, low white tables on the lawn are great for sipping coffee, and a little
pond at the rear is filled with ducks. An old horse stable has been turned into a congenial
bar. The rooms sit above the restaurant under the roofline. If you're just driving by, stop
in for a "plate of the inn"—two kinds of herring, plaice, meatballs, meat sausages, liver
paste, and cheese. A large selection of fish and meat dishes is also available. Fixed-price
menus cost DKK145 to DKK195 ($25–$33/£15–£20), and meals are served every day
noon to 9:30pm.

Landevejen 155, DK-5883 Oure. © **62-28-18-19.** Fax 62-28-18-13. 4 units, all w/shared bathroom.
DKK475 ($81/£48) double. Rates include breakfast. MC, V. Bus: 910 from Svendborg and Nyborg. **Ameni-
ties:** Restaurant; bar; lounge. *In room:* No phone.

Missionshotellet Stella Maris ★ (Value)   A Danish countess with a staff of 18
servants once occupied this 1904 estate, naming it Stella Maris, meaning "Star of the
Sea," because of its location southwest of the city in a lovely old-fashioned seaside villa.

This old-fashioned world of charm and nostalgia is today one of the undiscovered allures of Svendborg, with its English-style drawing room (with piano), overstuffed chairs, and antiques. Surrounded by well-landscaped gardens, it offers midsize-to-spacious bedrooms, each with an individual color scheme, or else rose wallpaper and white-lace curtains. The rooms in front opening onto Svendborg Sound are the more expensive options, and you can follow a private path leading directly to the water.

Kogtvedvænget 3, DK-5700 Svendborg. ℂ **62-21-38-91.** Fax 62-22-41-74. www.stellamaris.dk. 26 units, 19 w/private bathroom. DKK535–DKK765 ($91–$130/£54–£77) double w/shared bathroom; DKK810–DKK1,050 ($138–$179/£81–£105) double w/private bathroom. Rates include breakfast. DC, MC, V. Bus: 202. From Svendborg head west along Kogtvedvej. **Amenities:** Breakfast room. *In room:* No phone.

WHERE TO DINE

Restaurant Marco Polo ★ ITALIAN   Housed in a former ironmonger's smithy, this appealing and congenial restaurant serves the best food in town. It just happens to be Italian, not Danish. Chef and owner Mr. Nikolaj is the host with the most, attracting foodies to his dining room at the edge of Svendborg's harbor. Perhaps the steady stream of locals want to remember some sunny holiday in Italy by dining here. To get you going, the chef might tempt with his ravioli and a freshly made pesto and tomato sauce. A well-crafted mating of products comes together in the golden brown roasted chicken with a Gorgonzola sauce. Our favorite of his pastas is a delectable fettuccine with strips of salmon, and we are forever tempted by the grilled lamb entrecote when it comes in a whisky sauce.

Kullinggade 1B. ℂ **62-22-92-11.** Reservations recommended. Main courses DKK149–DKK189 ($25–$32/£15–£19). MC, V. Mon–Sat 5–10pm.

Svendborgsund DANISH/FRENCH   Many Danes, often sailors and visiting yachters, come here just to drink in the separate bar area, but the food in the restaurant is good and wholesome, the cooks following recipes familiar to their grandmothers. In summer, the terrace is a magnet, and you can sit out taking in a picture-postcard view of all the ferryboats, trawlers, and pleasure yachts in the harbor. The waterfront restaurant is the oldest in town, built of white-painted stone in the 1830s and lying about a 5-minute walk south of the center of town. The food is for the meat-potatoes-and-onion crowd—in fact, that is the most popular dish to order here. It's called *biksemad* in Danish. The chef specializes in fresh fish, and does so exceedingly well, but he also provides a few dishes for the carnivore, notably some tasty pork chops or tender Danish lamb.

Havnepladsen 5A. ℂ **62-21-07-19.** www.restaurantsvendborgsund.dk. Reservations recommended. Main courses DKK128–DKK228 ($22–$39/£13–£23); lunch *smørrebrød* DKK48–DKK115 ($8.20–$20/£4.80–£12). MC, V. Daily 11am–10pm.

SVENDBORG AFTER DARK

The most popular dance club in town, with the most appealing clients, is **Crazy Daisy,** Frederiksgade 6 (ℂ **62-21-67-60**). Outfitted with bright lights and loud music deriving from Los Angeles, New York, and London, it spreads its clients—mostly people ages 20 to 35—over two floors that have easy access to three separate bars. Upstairs is disco music from the 1980s; downstairs, the dance music is newer, more cutting edge, and more experimental. It's open only on Wednesdays, Fridays, and Saturdays 10pm till dawn. Cover is DKK50 ($8.50/£5). Attracting a diverse age group, the town's best pub, Børsen, Gerritsgata 31 (ℂ 62-22-41-41), is also the largest. The tavern itself dates from 1620. We like its old-style atmosphere, but as the night ages, the patrons grow younger and rowdier. And during the warm-weather months, the outdoor decks of the ship **Orangi,** Jessens Mole (© **62-22-82-92**), is a late-night venue for drinks and live jazz, but only May to September, daily from 9pm to around 1am.

NEARBY ATTRACTIONS
On Thurø ★

Too often overlooked by the hurried visitor, this horseshoe-shaped island is one of the most beautiful off the coast of Funen. Its beautiful gardens and fruity orchards have earned it the justified title of the "Garden of Denmark." In 1 scenic hour, you can explore about all there is to see here. The island used to belong to the manor house, Bjornemose; but the Thurineans wanted liberty, so they joined together to buy back Thurø in 1810, an event commemorated by a stone proclaiming freedom from manorial domination.

It's the island itself that's the attraction, because of its scenic beauty. However, if you want a specific target to visit, make it the little **Thurø Kirke** (© **62-20-50-92;** open daily 7:30am to 4pm, charging no admission. The best beaches can be found at Smør-mosen, Thurø Rev, and Grasten. When you take the causeway over from Funen, you'll be entering another world.

On Tåsinge ★★

Ærø (see section 5, later in this chapter) is the major tourist attraction of Funen, outside Odense, but the lesser known island of Tåsinge is for lovers, the most romantic hideaway in all of Denmark. Although sleepy, it is still the largest island in the South Funen archipelago, and it's been connected to Funen by the Svendborg Sound Bridge since 1966. The location is only 3km (1³/₄ miles) south of Svendborg via the bridge, but a distance of 43km (27 miles) south of Odense.

Route 90, which is the main road, crisscrosses the island, but we'll let you in on a secret: When you see a signpost marked TÅSINGE, take it to the northeastern sector of the island. Once here, you'll find the "skipper town" of **Troense ★★**, one of the best-preserved and most idyllic villages in all of Denmark. Many half-timbered houses in gay colors still stand on **Badstuen** and **Grønnegade ★**, the latter declared by many makers of landscape calendars "the prettiest street in Denmark." While exploring Troense, you can also dart in for a quick look at the town's maritime museum, **Søfartssamlingerne I Troense** (p. 286). You can also visit **Valdemars Slot** nearby (see below).

The island was the setting for a famous tragic love story depicted in the 1967 film *Elvira Madigan*. After checking out of a hotel in Svendborg, Danish artist Elvira Madigan and her lover, Sixten Sparre, a Swedish lieutenant, crossed by ferry to Tåsinge, where together they committed suicide. The Romeo and Juliet of Denmark were buried in the Landet Kirkegård, Elvira Madigansvej, at Landet, in the middle of Tåsinge, where many brides, even today, throw their wedding bouquets on the couple's graves. The 100th anniversary of the death of these two lovers was widely observed in 1989 throughout Scandinavia; many ballads were written to commemorate the date.

The island is best explored by car—follow Route 9 and drive over the causeway—or you could take local bus no. 980. You can also take the vintage steamer MS *Helge* (© **62-21-09-80** for information), which departs several times daily from the harbor at Svendborg. The steamer operates from May 7 to September 5. A one-way ticket costs DKK50 ($8.50/£5); a round-trip, DKK100 ($17/£10). Tickets are sold onboard or at the Svendborg Tourist Office (see earlier in this section).

Bregninge Kirkebakke (Bregninge Church Tower)   Lying on Route 9, the small village of Bregninge doesn't have the charm of Troense, but it's a rewarding target for those who want to stop over here and climb its church tower for one of the greatest **panoramic views** ★★★ in all of Denmark, a clear sweep (that is, on a fair day) of Funen and its southern archipelago. To the south are the Bregninge Hills, whose wooded slopes are popular for outings. Originally Romanesque, the church has a porch that dates from the 16th century, and its north wing was built in the 18th century. Inside you'll see a Romanesque granite font, a head of Christ on the north wall dating from about 1250, and a 1621 pulpit with rich ornamentation. In the porch is a tombstone with arcade decoration, the image of a vicar, and runic letters. Except for that view from the tower, it's not much of an attraction, but you may want to give it 20 minutes or so. After seeing the church, you can also visit Tåsinge Skipperhjem og Folkemindesamling (see below).

Kirkebakken 1, Bregninge. © **62-22-50-37.** Admission to tower DKK5 (85¢/50p) adults, DKK2 (35¢/20p) children 10–15, free for children 9 and under; free admission to church. Tower daily 6am–10pm. Church Apr–Sept Mon–Sat 8am–6pm, Sun 8am–noon; Oct–Mar Mon–Sat 8am–4pm, Sun 8am–noon. Bus: 980 from Svendborg.

Sofartssamlingerne I Troense (Maritime Museum of Troense)   Funen sailors once traversed the trade routes from Scandinavia to China and East India. Along the way, they picked up rare curiosities of all shapes and sizes (some of which are too erotic to put on display), and many of those long-ago artifacts, often from the early 19th century, have been put on display here. It's a museum that has such mismatched exhibits as Sunderland china, rope-work art, and Staffordshire figures, along with model ships and figureheads. Surely you'll find something to amuse you here, as we always do. This museum, a branch of the County Museum, is housed in a 1790s school, with a rooftop belfry.

Strandgade 1, Troense. © **62-22-52-32.** Admission DKK25 ($4.30/£2.50) adults, free for children 15 and under. May–Oct daily 10am–5pm. Cross the causeway to Tåsinge, turn left and then left again, heading down Bregingevej toward the water; turn right at Troensevej and follow the signs to the old port of Troense and to the village school (now the museum) on Strandgade.

Tåsinge Skipperhjem og Folkemindesamling (Tåsinge Museum)   The young Romeos and Juliets of Denmark today go to this 1826 former school building to bathe in the aura of memorabilia linked to the tragic love affair of Lt. Sixten Sparre and the artist Elvira Madigan depicted in film and literature. How romantic can you get? "The death of these tragic lovers in 1889, who chose suicide to separation, is a story that will live forever in Denmark," the curator assured us. In addition to memorabilia of these lovers, you can see another one of those flotsam-and-jetsam type exhibits that Danes like to collect before opening museums. The inevitable ship models or ships in a bottle are here, along with ancient coins and other not-very-intriguing artifacts from the attics of Tåsinge. In another building, you can see what a typical sea captain's house looked like some 100 years ago.

Kirkebakken 1, Bregninge. © **62-22-71-44.** www.taasinge-museum.dk. Admission DKK40 ($6.80/£4) adults, free for children 15 and under. June–Aug daily 10am–5pm. Bus: 980 from Svendborg. From Valdemars Slot (see below), turn right by 2 thatched cottages and left again at the next junction; follow the signs to Bregninge.

Valdemars Slot (Valdemar's Palace) ★★ ⓚⒾⒹⓈ   Although not quite as stellar an attraction as Egeskov (p. 270), this palace is our second favorite on Funen, and it looms large in history, having been given to naval hero Niels Juel for his third victory over the

Swedes in 1678. The castle itself was built between 1639 and 1644 by Christian IV for his son, Valdemar, in a romantic style, and is still occupied today by a charming, handsome couple, Caroline and Rory Fleming, who welcome guests (some groups) to stay overnight.

You can eat here after enjoying one of four museums, including a big-game trophy room, a toy museum, and a yachting museum. Children take special delight in the toy museum, whose collection covers the past 125 years. Along with several thousand toys, there are books, comics, and other delights for kids, such as model cars. By far the most intriguing are the room interiors themselves, filled with artifacts and antiques. Guests today treat the property better than the Swedish soldiers who once occupied it, sending the copper roof back home to Sweden to make bullets and stabling their horses in the church.

Valdemars Slotskirke (Valdemar's Castle Church), in the south wing, cleaned up by Admiral Juel, was consecrated in 1687, and has been used for worship ever since. Two stories high, it's overarched by three star vaults and illuminated by Gothic windows.

Slotsalléen 100, Troense. ☎ **62-22-61-06.** www.valdemarsslot.dk. Admission DKK90 ($15/£9) adults, DKK45 ($7.70/£4.50) children 4–12, free for children 3 and under. Apr–June and Aug daily 10am–5pm; July daily 10am–6pm; Sept Tues–Sun 10am–5pm; Oct 1–19 Sat–Sun 10am–5pm. Take the MS *Helge* from Svendborg Harbor. By car, from Troense, follow Slotsalléen to the castle.

Where to Dine

Restaurant Slotskælderen DANISH/FRENCH   In a wing of the main attraction of Tåsinge, Valdemars Slot, you can dine like royalty or else more democratically at a bistro. Inside the thick stone walls of one of the region's most foreboding castles, this restaurant is divided into an unpretentious Danish bistro and an upscale French restaurant. The bistro serves such down-home dishes as schnitzels, *lobscouse* (hash), and roulades of beef with Danish beer and akvavit. The views over the tidal flats and sea are better from the restaurant, but most visitors prefer the informality and lower prices of the bistro. For more elegant dining, with formal place settings, you can enjoy haute cuisine like that served in the best of Paris's luxe restaurants, feasting on venison in the autumn, a delicate foie gras, a velvety lobster bisque, and only the choicest cuts of tender beef.

In Valdemars Slot, Slotsalléen 100, Troense. ☎ **62-22-59-00.** Restaurant 3-course menu DKK358 ($61/£36), 6-course menu DKK498 ($85/£50); bistro main courses DKK80–DKK128 ($14–$22/£8–£13). MC, V. June to mid-Sept daily 11:30am–5pm; Apr–May and mid-Sept to mid-Dec Tues–Sat 11am–9pm. Closed mid-Dec to Mar.

---

4 FAABORG ★

25km (16 miles) W of Svendborg; 179km (111 miles) W of Copenhagen; 37km (23 miles) S of Odense

Far removed from the commerce and industry of Svendborg, Faaborg is more a sleepy dream of long ago. It's a "Gone with the Wind" situation, as its heyday was in the 1600s when it was a thriving harbor town containing one of the country's biggest commercial fleets.

Today you can wander those same streets where wealthy merchants and shipbuilders lived. The best collection of these crisscrossed, half-timbered houses in pastel colors is along **Adelgade, Tarngade,** and **Holkegade.** For some reason, many homeowners like to plant hollyhock around their doorways.

Funen has more attractive villages, but Faaborg is its most beautiful small town, lying on the sunny south coast and a magnet for Danish and German sunbathers in summer.

In the Middle Ages, Faaborg was a fortified town, with a castle and defensive walls, which were torn down, although you can still see some of the fortifications in the western gate on Vestergade. The West Gate, dating from the 1400s, lies 500m (1,640 ft.) north of Torvet.

Gamle Stan (Old Town) is centered around the Torvet (market square), where you can enjoy a coffee in a cafe while taking in Funen's most controversial sculpture, the bronze fountain, *Ymerbrønd,* by Kai Nielsen. For more information about the original, refer to the Faaborg Museum, below.

ESSENTIALS

GETTING THERE   By Bus   From Odense, bus nos. 960, 961, and 962 run hourly from sunrise to about 11pm (trip time: 1¼ hr.). Bus no. 930 from Svendborg also arrives frequently throughout the day (40 min.). The bus station lies on Banegårdspladsen, site of the old rail train depot at the southern rim of town. *Note:* There is no longer **train service** to Faaborg.

By Car   From Svendborg, head west on Route 44; from Odense, go south on Route 43.

VISITOR INFORMATION   The **Faaborg and District Tourist Association,** Banegård-spladsen 2A (**©** **62-61-07-07**), is open May to mid-September Monday to Saturday 9am to 5pm, Sunday 10am to 3pm.

GETTING AROUND   You can cover the sites below **on foot** from the Faaborg bus station with the exception of Korinth Kro, which can be reached by **bus** no. 930.

SEEING THE SIGHTS

Den Gamle Gaard (The Old Merchant's House)   Hans Christian Andersen came this way, falling in love with Riborg Voigt, the daughter of a rich merchant. The relationship was brief, but he maintained a longing and infatuation for her that lasted most of his life. In one room of this museum are personal mementos of his stay here, even a lock of his hair.

There's much more here than that, however, including 22 rooms that are decorated mostly with antiques from the 19th century, along with displays related to life even as far back as the 1700s. The house itself dates from 1725 and was established as a museum back in 1932, complete with glassware, china, and faience, much of it left over from the days when Faaborg was an important trading and shipping center.

In the town center, near the marketplace and harbor, the museum also displays some beautiful textiles and embroidery, but these are of such minor interest they rarely hold one's attention. There is one ghoulish-looking exhibit of a hearse carriage that carried the dead for burial back in the 1800s.

Holkegade 1. **©** **63-61-20-00.** www.fkm.nu. Admission DKK30 ($5.10/£3) adults, free for children 13 and under. May 15–Sept 15 daily 10:30am–4:30pm; Sept 16–Oct 31 Sat–Sun 11am–3pm. Closed Nov 1– May 14.

Faaborg Museum ★   This collection of the works of Funen artists, known for depicting the "dusky light of the overcast Danish sky," was founded in 1910 by a wealthy art patron with what to us at least is the most amusing nickname in Denmark—"Mads Tomato." Actually, he was named Mads Rasmussen. All the major Funenite artists are represented here with their best works, including painters Jens Birkholm, Karl Schou, Harald Giersing, Anna Syberg, Alhed Larsen, and Christine Swane. But the real show-stopper of the group is the sculptor Kai Nielsen (1882–1924), whose bronze fountain

Ymerbrønd ★★★ is found here. We know of no other piece of sculpture in Denmark that is as controversial as this one, and it caused a rage among local citizens when first shown. The sculptor depicts a naked giant suckling at the udder of a bony cow which licks a baby. Denounced as obscene by some critics, Ymer Wall (its English name) was praised by others for its originality. A copy stands on the Torvet, the main market square of town. The museum is installed in an impressive neoclassical building with a rotunda, which was once a former winery.

Grønnegade 75. ℂ **62-61-06-45.** www.faaborgmuseum.dk. Admission DKK50 ($8.50/£5) adults, free for children 17 and under. Apr–Oct daily 10am–4pm; Nov–Mar Tues–Sun 11am–3pm.

Klokketårnet   In the center of town near the marketplace stands Faaborg's major landmark, an old belfry which is all that remains from the Church of St. Nicolai, the town's first church, which was built in the 16th century but demolished by 1600 because of structural flaws. For reasons known only to themselves, the town fathers did not rebuild the church but kept the belfry, whose carillon bells play hymns four times a day. Visitors are allowed to climb the tower in summer for a view of the town.

Tarnstræde. ℂ **63-61-20-00.** Admission DKK10 ($1.70/£1) adults, free for children 15 and under. Mon–Fri 11am–4pm; Sat 10am–1pm. Closed mid-Sept to mid-June.

WHERE TO STAY

Faaborg Fjord ★   This is a modern year-round resort that is one of the largest and best in the area, opening onto one of Funen's most famous fjords at a location in its own parklike setting at the eastern edge of Faaborg. Because of its size, it has more facilities than most in the area, including an indoor heated pool and a fitness center. The bedrooms are midsize to spacious, each with comfortable furniture in Danish modern. Opening onto a panoramic view of the water, the first-class restaurant hires chefs skilled in a French-inspired Danish cuisine, and they purchase locally caught fish and produce at the market and seasonally adjust their menus.

Svendborgvej 175, DK-5600 Faaborg. ℂ **62-61-10-10.** Fax 63-60-61-60. www.hotelfaaborgfjord.dk. 126 units. DKK875–DKK1,295 ($149–$220/£88–£130) double. Rates include breakfast. AE, DC, MC, V. **Amenities:** Restaurant; bar; indoor heated pool; fitness center; sauna; laundry service; dry cleaning; nonsmoking rooms; rooms for those w/limited mobility. *In room:* TV.

Falsled Kro ★★★   The epitome of a Danish roadside inn, this former 15th-century smuggler's inn has been converted into a premier Relais & Châteaux property, the finest hotel in Funen. When Hans Christian Andersen passed through here, he wrote, "It was glorious out in the country." And so it is today. In fact, much of the landscape around here is as the 19th-century Funen artists depicted it. Perhaps our most delightful memory of a stay here is when the owner allowed mushroom gatherers with their baskets to come onto the property and pick wild mushrooms, including cèpes, horn of plenty, chanterelles—some with an apricot aroma—and field mushrooms tasting of aniseed. The most delectable of all, morels, are available as early as the month of April.

The *kro* offers tradition and quality in its colony of beautifully furnished thatched buildings clustered around a cobblestone courtyard with a fountain. The spacious rooms are often furnished with antiques, and some of the units are in converted outbuildings, others in cottages across the road. Regardless of your room assignment, expect the comfort to be equal. The inn is filled with grace notes, such as stone fireplaces, and, as a piece of enchantment, a lovely garden leads to the water and the yacht harbor. The *kro* not only is the finest address on the island, better than anything in Odense, but also offers the island's premier restaurant (see below).

FUNEN

10

FAABORG

Assensvej 513, Falsled, DK-5642 Millinge. © **62-68-11-11.** Fax 62-68-11-62. www.falsledkro.dk. 20 units. DKK1,650–DKK2,800 ($281–$476/£165–£280) double; DKK3,000–DKK3,250 ($510–$553/£300–£325) suite. AE, DC, MC, V. Bus: 930. **Amenities:** Restaurant; bar; 24-hr. room service; babysitting; laundry service; dry cleaning; Wi-Fi (in lobby). *In room:* TV, minibar, hair dryer.

Hotel Mosegaard ★ Finds

Here is a rare chance to live on a genuine Funen farm in a compound built around a quadrangle and converted into a modern hotel with an inviting atmosphere and complete comfort. The hotel lies in a tranquil, isolated spot in a setting of field and woodland opening onto the sea at a point 5km (3 miles) east of Faaborg. Most of the clients are the Danes themselves, some of whom book in here with their families for a week or more.

The small-to-midsize bedrooms are well maintained, tastefully and comfortably furnished—all rather snug and cozy. The most desirable accommodations open onto a sea view and contain private balconies. The cuisine is Danish regional fare, with such familiar dishes as roast veal with boiled potatoes or breaded plaice meunière with fresh lime. Fixed-price meals in the hotel's informal, family-style dining room go for DKK235 ($40/£24) for two courses or DKK295 ($50/£30) for three courses.

Nabgyden 31, DK-5600 Faaborg. © **62-61-56-91.** Fax 62-61-56-96. www.hotelmosegaard.dk. 22 units. DKK745–DKK1,095 ($127–$186/£75–£110) double. Rates include breakfast. AE, DC, MC, V. **Amenities:** Restaurant; breakfast room; lounge. *In room:* TV, hair dryer (in some).

Hvedholm Slot ★★

Would you like to stay in a romantic castle mentioned in the writings of Hans Christian Andersen? The choice is yours. One of the region's most evocative castles enjoys a recorded history going back to 1231, and a sweeping view over the fjord and the Faaborg harbor. The grand and ornate brick-and-sandstone facade you'll see today was rebuilt during the late 19th century, when it gained the soaring tower and elaborate gables and ornamentation that make it so charming. When its owners ran out of money after World War I, the contents were sold at auction by the Danish government, and the site functioned as a mental hospital beginning in 1928. In 1996, it was bought by a team of bold and imaginative entrepreneurs, Gorm Lokdam and Ann Vibeke, who added it to their already-functioning chain of three other stately hotels in Denmark. Today, you'll find a tasteful medley of conservative reproductions vaguely inspired by the stately homes of England. Bedrooms are spacious and comfortably and tastefully furnished, containing well-kept bathrooms.

Breakfast and dinner are the only scheduled meals, although someone on the staff might prepare you a platter of food around noontime if you ask.

Hvedholm Slot 1, DK-5600 Faaborg. © **63-60-10-20.** Fax 63-60-10-29. www.royalclassic.dk. 42 units. DKK1,100–DKK1,300 ($187–$221/£110–£130) double. Rates include breakfast. AE, DC, MC, V. Bus: 920 from Faaborg center stops .5km (1/3 mile) from hotel. 7km (4 1/3 miles) west of Faaborg; follow Rte. 8 and signs for Bøjden. **Amenities:** Restaurant; room service; laundry service; dry cleaning; rooms for those w/ limited mobility. *In room:* TV, hair dryer, minibar.

Korinth Kro Value

This is one of the oldest inns in Funen, dating back to 1801 when it first opened its doors as a *kro*. Before that, this 1758 building had been a school teaching weaving to local farm girls. Today it still exudes an old-fashioned aura, although it's been brought up-to-date with modern amenities. Bedrooms are midsize to spacious, each with comfortable, tasteful furnishings; most of them come with a small private bathroom with shower. Occupants of the bathroomless rooms share adequate corridor facilities. The good country cooking attracts locals and nonresidents alike to a location 8km (5 miles) northeast of Faaborg along Route 8.

Reventlowsvej 10, DK-5600 Faaborg. ℂ **62-65-10-23.** Fax 62-65-24-00. 26 units, 17 w/private bathroom. DKK595 ($101/£60) double w/shared bathroom; DKK775 ($132/£78) double w/private bathroom; DKK925 ($157/£93) suite. Rates include breakfast. DC, MC, V. Bus: 930. **Amenities:** Restaurant; bar. *In room:* TV.

Steensgaard Herregårdspension ★ (Finds)   It doesn't pretend to have the glamour of Falsled Kro or Hvedholm Slot, but Steensgaard is the best place in Funen that is evocative of a bygone manorial life. This brick-and-timber house is set in an area of scenic beauty with a private lake and nearly 10 hectares (25 acres) of lovely parkland with old trees and a game reserve, lying at the foot of the so-called "Funen Alps." About 6.5km (4 miles) northwest of Faaborg, the oldest section dates from 1310, possibly earlier. The midsize-to-spacious rooms are comfortably and tastefully furnished, often with antiques, and all units contain well-kept bathrooms. Even if you're just passing through for the day, consider a stopover here for either lunch or dinner, as you get atmosphere and good food at an affordable price. Dinner is served nightly 6:30 to 9:30pm. If you aren't a guest, you should reserve a table. You can also visit for lunch daily 12:30 to 2pm. Some of the best dishes include champagne soup, roe deer with juniper berries, and salmon *en papillote* with local herbs. Fresh from the sea, Danish lobster or baby shrimp are also featured.

Steensgaard, DK-5642 Millinge. ℂ **62-61-94-90.** Fax 63-61-78-61. www.herregaardspension.dk. 20 units. DKK1,275–DKK1,775 ($217–$302/£128–£178) double. Rates include breakfast. AE, DC, MC, V. Bus: 920 or 930. **Amenities:** Restaurant; bar; tennis court; room service; laundry service; dry cleaning; non-smoking rooms. *In room:* Minibar, hair dryer.

WHERE TO DINE

Falsled Kro ★★★ DANISH/FRENCH   Not only is this previously recommended inn the finest on the island of Funen, but it is one of the premier choices for cuisine outside Copenhagen. Moneyed, cosmopolitan Danes, along with savvy foodies from abroad, book in here for a gourmet weekend. The chefs know how to work wonders with fresh ingredients, and they grow many of their own vegetables, and secure the best game from hunters in the autumn. As a sign of their extreme dedication to cuisine, the owners also breed quail locally, cooking the birds to perfection in a port-wine sauce.

The chefs even bake their own delectable breads and rich, yummy cakes, and back up all their food with the most impressive—but also pricey—wine *carte* on the island.

Some of the restaurant's most noted dishes are among the simplest, as evoked by a succulent salmon smoked on the premises in one of the outbuildings. Flavor and harmony combine in the fish-and-shellfish soup with sorrel, and the spicy lobster "Tiger Lee" borrows "the best secrets" from Asian cuisine. Also deserving of your attention is a warm salad of smoked haddock with roast eggplant. The chef's seafood platter is a gift to put before Neptune, and French duck liver with wild rice and the saddle of rabbit are hard to resist.

Assensvej 513, Falsled, Millinge. ℂ **62-68-11-11.** Reservations required. Main courses DKK290–DKK650 ($49–$111/£29–£65); 3-course fixed-price menu DKK370 ($63/£37); 6-course fixed-price menu DKK950 ($162/£95). AE, DC, MC, V. Mon noon–2:30pm; Tues–Sun 6:30–9pm. Closed Mon Oct–Mar.

Restaurant Klinten ★ DANISH   Come here as we do for dining with a view, either on the terrace or through big windows opening onto a panoramic view of a verdant offshore island. The forest setting for this restaurant is near the sea, about half a kilometer (1/3-mile) east of the center of Faaborg. Fortunately, the cooks here don't depend just on that view, but imbue dishes with a lot of flavor and show respect for fresh ingredients. On the terrace is a barbecue grill with a bar of freshly made salads, and, on occasion, the cooks stage an all-you-can-eat barbecue.

In a relaxed and friendly setting, you can try the fresh salmon in puff pastry with spinach and lobster as a divine appetizer. You can later, as a main course, sample such well-loved dishes as spicy steak in a tomato sauce, served with a medley of fresh vegetables, or else fresh salmon cutlet in a well-made white-wine sauce. Desserts are country fresh and rich in calories, but a delight to the palate.

Klintallée 1. © **62-61-32-00.** www.klinten-faaborg.dk. Reservations recommended. Main courses DKK169–DKK225 ($29–$38/£17–£23); fixed-price dinner DKK249–DKK298 ($42–$51/£25–£30). DC, MC, V. Daily 9am–10pm. Bar open until 11pm.

Tre Kroner DANISH This is the oldest pub and restaurant in Faaborg, with a pedigree going back to 1821, when it was established as an inn, and a stone-sided architectural layout that dates back to sometime in the 1600s. The venerable, informal, and somewhat cramped setting is the first to be cited by townsfolk as a cozy site for drinks. Meals focus on traditional Danish recipes, and include a lunchtime roster of *smørrebrød,* platters of herring, homemade soups, and freshly tossed salads. All this is predictable fare, which some Danes never tire of day after day. Dinners are more elaborate, but the cooks still stick to time-tested recipes, including some longtime favorites such as grilled steaks, calf's liver with onions, and roasted pork with braised red cabbage. Occasionally they get fancy and pour a brandy sauce over the chicken breasts and fresh mushrooms.

Strandgade 1. © **62-61-01-50.** Reservations recommended. Lunch main courses DKK45–DKK95 ($7.70–$16/£4.50–£9.50); dinner main courses DKK129–DKK145 ($22–$25/£13–£15). MC, V. Mon–Fri noon–10pm; Sat 11am–10pm; Sun noon–9pm. Bar daily 10am–11pm or midnight, depending on business.

FAABORG AFTER DARK

Our leading choice for a drink in comfy and historic surroundings is the previously recommended restaurant **Tre Kroner.** Even during peak dinner hours, someone is likely to be here just for drinks, and after the rush of the evening meal service ends (around 9:15pm), the entire place is reinvented as a hard-drinking pub until closing at around midnight.

A viable competitor for the after-dark favors of Faaborgians is **The Train,** Banegårdspladsen 21 (no phone), occupying a former movie theater. Its pub section opens daily at noon and continues until at least midnight. Live music is heard on Fridays and Saturdays 9pm till closing. A weekend nightclub transforms the place into a rock-'n'-roll emporium every Friday and Saturday 10pm to around 6am, and admission to the club ranges from DKK30 to DKK70 ($5.10–$12/£3–£7).

5 ÆRØ ★★★

29km (18 miles) across the water S of Svendborg; 176km (109 miles) W of Copenhagen; 74km (46 miles) S of Odense

If this small Danish island, off the southern coast of Funen, didn't exist, Hans Christian Andersen would have invented it. It's that special. Its capital of Ærøskøbing is a Lilliputian souvenir of the past. Walt Disney must have gone through this town with a paintbrush and a bucket of rainbow colors.

Many of Denmark's offshore islands are dull and flat with redbrick market towns best passed through hurriedly. But Ærø is a place in which you'll want to linger, wandering its sleepy one-lane roads, walking the cobblestone streets of its hamlets—or merely spending a day at the beach. The best sands are along the northern and eastern coastlines. Take your pick. Chances are, even in July, you'll end up with a strip of sand all to yourself.

The place is small so it's easy to get around—30km (19 miles) long and 8km (5 miles) at its widest point. The number of windswept "souls" is also small, no more than 7,000 hearty islanders, with fewer than a thousand centered in the capital of Ærøskøbing itself.

There are only three towns that could even be called that. If time is fleeting, explore only **Ærøskøbing,** the best preserved town of 18th-century Denmark. The largest town is the ancient seaport of **Marstal,** where mariners once set out to conquer the Seven Seas. Its maritime glory a distant memory today, it has a bustling marina and a shipyard that still makes some wooden vessels as in Viking days. Yachters sail into **Søby,** the third town with a still-active shipyard and a sizable fishing fleet. Everyone's lifeblood here seems drawn from the sea.

Small fishing harbors, wheat fields swept by the winds, storybook hamlets of half-timbered houses, a dilapidated church or two from the Middle Ages, beer gardens filled with raucous laughter during the too-short weeks of summer, old windmills, and yacht-filled marinas make Ærø the kind of island you search for—but rarely find—in all of Scandinavia. Sure, Ærø is all clichéd charm, but a cliché wouldn't be that unless it existed once in time. A local resident put it this way: "We didn't change after our seagoing hey-day in the 17th century. We were too poor to modernize. When we finally started earning money centuries later, we were a valuable antique, and we learned there was money to be made from visitors who wanted to see Denmark the way it used to be."

ESSENTIALS

GETTING THERE **By Ferry** The only way to reach Ærø is by ferry; car ferries depart Svendborg six times daily (trip time: 1 hr.). For a schedule, contact the tourist office or the ferry office at the harbor in Svendborg. Bookings are made through **Det Æroske Færgegraf-Ikselskab** in Ærøskøbing (© **62-21-09-80**). An average car can be transported for DKK392 ($67/£39) round-trip; a passenger, DKK178 ($30/£18) round-trip.

GETTING AROUND **By Bus** It's best to take a car on the ferry as there's limited bus service on Ærø (© **62-53-10-10** in Ærøskøbing for bus information). Bus no. 990 runs every hour on the hour in the afternoon between Ærøskøbing, Marstal, and Søby, but there's only limited morning service. Tourist offices (see below) provide bus schedules, which change seasonally. Tickets are DKK70 ($12/£7) for the day and can be bought on the bus.

If you'd like to take a bus tour of the island, call **Jesper "Bus" Jensen** (© **62-58-13-13**). His bus holds 12 to 14 passengers, costing DKK450 ($77/£45) for a 3-hour mini-mum.

EXPLORING THE ISLAND

Most visitors go to Ærøskøbing, or perhaps Marstal, then return to the pleasures of south Funen. But if you like to cycle or have rented a car in Funen, you can explore the southern tier of the island, going from Marstal, the port in the east, all the way to Søby at the northern and far western tip of Ærø. There are several attractions along the way, although you can just enjoy the landscape for its own idyllic beauty.

Take the coastal road going west from Marstal (signposted VEJSNÆS). From here continue west, following the signs to Store Rise, where you can stop and visit **Rise Kirke,** originally a Romanesque church dating from the latter part of the 12th century. Later, vaults were added and the church was enlarged twice, the last time in 1697. The altarpiece inside dates from 1300 and depicts the suffering and resurrection of Christ. Its carved work is from the town of Schleswig, now in northwestern Germany. The tower is similar to that of the church at Bregninge. It was originally roofed in oak tiles but these were replaced in 1957. In the churchyard wall, facing the vicarage garden, an old porch known as "the Monks Door" (ca. 1450) can be seen.

In a field in the rear of the church, you can view **Tingstedet,** a 54m (177-ft.) Neolithic passage grave believed to be at least 5,000 years old. Archaeologists have claimed that the cuplike markings in the biggest stone (close to the church) indicate the site may have been used by a "fertility cult." A footpath leading from the church to the Neolithic site only a short walk away is clearly marked.

If you'd like to break up the driving tour, you can drive less than a kilometer (¹/₂ mile) south of the village to **Risemark Strand,** one of the island's few sandy beaches. Many of the other beaches on Ærø consist of shingles.

Cycling around the Island

Ærø is one of the best islands in Denmark for cycling because of its low-lying terrain and scenic paths. Local tourist offices provide maps outlining routes for DKK20 ($3.40/£2), and you can use these maps for bike rides but also for walks. Numbers 90, 91, and 92 mark cycle trails around the coast. Bike rentals cost DKK50 ($8.50/£5) a day, and rentals in Ærøskøbing are available at the **Ærøskøbing Vandrerhjem,** Smedevejen 15 (☎ **62-52-10-44**); at Marstal at **Nørremark Cykelforretning,** Møllevejen 77 (☎ **62-53-14-77**); and at **Søby Cykelforretning,** Langebro 4A (☎ **62-58-18-42**).

The road continues west to Tranderup, where you can visit **Tranderup Kirke,** a Romanesque building with Gothic vaulting. Inside, the large carved figure depicting Mary and the infant Jesus dates from around the 14th century and is one of the oldest ecclesiastical pieces on the island. The triptych is from around 1510, and the large mural over the chancel arch reveals the date of its execution in 1518. Originally, the spires of Tranderup resembled those of Bregninge (see below). But they were rebuilt in a neoclassical style in 1832; the largest bell was cast in 1566 and is still in use.

After a visit follow the signs west to the village of **Vodrup,** which originally was founded in the 13th century and is mentioned for the first time in 1537 as "Wuderup." The village disappeared in the 17th century, when the land became part of Vodrup Estate. When the estate was dissolved, the village came back.

The cliffs at Vodrup, **Vodrup Klint ★★,** have an unusual geology: Large blocks of land have slipped down and resemble huge steps. The soil lies on top of a layer of gray clay, which can be seen at the base of the cliffs by the beach. The layer of clay is full of snail and cockleshells, left here by the sea. Water seeping down through the earth is stopped by the clay. When the clay absorbs enough water, it becomes so "movable" that it acts as a sliding plane for the layers above. The last great landslide here occurred in 1834.

Vodrup Klint is one of the most southerly points in Denmark, attracting creatures such as lizards and many species of plants that thrive here—the carline thistle grows on these cliffs, blooming from July to September. An unusual characteristic of the cliffs is a proliferation of springs, where water bubbles out by the foot of the slopes. When the cattle need water, farmers need only push a pipe into the cliff face and let the water collect in a pool.

Fyn County has bought the cliffs, roughly 35 hectares (86 acres), and set them aside for the use of the public, which has access to the area. Animals are allowed to graze the fields in the summer months, and you can walk on all areas of the land. Cycle trail 91 runs right past Vodrup Klint, so it's often a stopover for bikers.

The route continues west to Bregninge and **Bregninge Kirke,** a 13th-century building with grandiose vaults that were added during the late 15th century. Its impressive spire shows the influence of east Schleswig (Germany) building traditions, and is roofed with oak tiles. The murals inside date from around 1510—one, for example, depicts the Passion of Christ, another the life of John the Baptist. The magnificent **triptych** ★ dates from shortly before the Reformation, and was made by the German sculptor Claus Berg. The crucifix in the nave is from the latter Middle Ages, and the 1612 pulpit was executed in the Renaissance style.

After your visit along the southern part of Ærø, you can continue northwest into Søby.

ÆRØSKØBING ★★★

The neat little village of **Ærøskøbing** is a 13th-century market town, which came to be known as a skippers' town in the 17th century, with its small gingerbread houses, intricately carved wooden doors, and cast-iron lamps. Few Scandinavian towns have retained their heritage as well as Ærøskøbing. In the heyday of the windjammer, nearly 100 commercial sailing ships made Ærøskøbing their home port.

Lying in the middle of the island, the town looks as if it were laid out by Walt Disney—in fact, it's often known as "the fairy-tale town" because it looks more like a movie set than a real town. Filled with cobblestone streets, hollyhocks, and beautifully painted doors and windows, the town invites wandering and exploring at random.

During the summer, its shops, cafes, and restaurants are bustling with life. At the old market square you can still see the pumps that supplied the town with its water until 1952; they are still in working order. The marina and nearby beach are ideal spots for enjoying outdoor activities. At the end of a busy day, we suggest you stroll over to the **Vesterstrand,** where the sunset (in our view) is the most romantic and evocative in all of Denmark.

The town of Ærøskøbing was founded in the 12th century, and it was granted town privileges in 1522 on orders of King Christian II. As visitors wander through the town, many wonder why the houses are still original and weren't torn down to make way for modern structures. The main reasons were the hard times and poverty that prevented many citizens from tearing down their old structures and rebuilding. However, when prosperity did come, the locals realized their old buildings were a treasure, so instead of tearing them down they restored them—and they're waiting for you to see them today. Preservation societies are particularly strong on the island.

Essentials

VISITOR INFORMATION The **Ærøskøbing Turistbureau,** Vestergade 1 (© **62-52-13-00;** www.visitaeroe.dk), is open June 15 to August, Monday to Friday 9am to 4pm, Saturday 11am to 3pm; September to June 14, Monday to Friday 10am to 3pm, Saturday 10am to 1pm.

Seeing the Sights

Ærøskøbing Kirke, Søndergade 43 (© **62-52-11-72**), was built between 1756 and 1758 to replace a rather dilapidated church from the Middle Ages. In the present reconstructed church, the 13th-century font and the pulpit stem from the original structure, and were donated by Duke Philip of Lyksborg in 1634, the year he bought Gråsten County on the island of Ærø. The year before, he had inherited the market town of Ærøskøbing and an estate in Vodrup. The altarpiece is a copy of Eckersberg's picture hanging in Vor Frue Kirke in Svendborg. The colors selected for the interior of the church, along with the floral motifs, were the creation of Elinar V. Jensen in connection with an extensive restoration project carried out in 1950. The church can be visited every day 8am to 5pm; admission is free.

Flaskeskibssamlingen, Smedegade 22 (© **62-52-29-51**), is a nautical museum dedicated to the seafaring life documented by Peter Jacobsen's ships in bottles, which represent his life's work. Upon his death in 1960, at the age of 84, this former cook, nicknamed "Bottle Peter," had crafted more than 1,600 bottled ships and some 150 model sailing vessels built to scale, earning him the reputation in Ærøskøbing of "the ancient mariner." The museum also has Ærø clocks, furniture, china, and carved works by sculptor H. C. Petersen. Admission is DKK25 ($4.30/£2.50) adults, DKK10 ($1.70/£1) children 3 to 15, free for children 2 and under; open daily 10am to 5pm.

Ærø Museum, Brogade 35 (© **62-52-29-50**), is the best local museum, found at the corner of Nørregade and Brogade. In the old days it was inhabited by the bailiff, but today you'll find a rich exhibit of the island's past. The collection includes antiques and paintings from the mid-1800s. It's open Monday to Friday March 19 to October 22, 10am to 4pm; off-season hours are Monday to Friday 10am to 1pm. Admission is DKK20 ($3.40/£2).

Of minor interest, **Hammerichs Hus,** Gyden 22 (© **62-52-29-50;** www.arremus.dk), at the corner of Brogade and Gyden, is the home of sculptor Genner Hammerich and now a museum with a collection of his art and tiles. The half-timbered house also has period furnishings, antiques, and china, all gathered by the artist in Funen and Jutland. In one of the rooms you'll find a pair of porcelain dogs, which were brought home from England by sailors. Prostitutes placed these dogs on their windowsills; if the dogs faced each other, callers were welcome. Because prostitutes were not allowed to charge for their "favors," they sold the dogs to their customers instead. It's said that the North Sea is paved with porcelain dogs that the sailors did not dare bring home. It's open June to August, daily noon to 4pm; admission is DKK25 ($4.30/£2.50).

Shopping

Shopping options in Ærøskøbing blossom like flowers in summer, but are greatly reduced after the crush of seasonal tourists retreats. Two particularly worthwhile options remain open most of the year: **Ærøskøbing Antiks,** Vestergade 60 (© **62-52-10-32**), sells a remarkable collection of antiques, many of them nautical in their inspiration, and some of them imported from faraway St. Petersburg, Estonia, or northeastern Germany during Ærø's maritime heyday. Gift items, souvenirs of Ærø, newspapers, and books in Danish, German, and English are available from **Creutz Boghanel,** Vestergade 47 (© **62-52-10-22**). And in addition to those year-round staples, some of the best shopping is available simply by wandering among the seasonal kiosks and boutiques that line either side of the Søndergade and the Vestergade, the town's main shopping emporiums.

Where to Stay

Hotel Ærøhus ★   Cozy intimacy and nostalgia are combined at this classic Danish inn, with many traditional features from its past, such as copper kettles hanging from the ceiling and warm lamps glowing, but it has modern amenities as well. We like to hang out here on a summer evening at the barbecue grill that keeps glowing long after everyone has been fed. An old-fashioned lounge, a typical Danish courtyard, and a luxuriant garden are part of the allures of this place.

The midsize-to-spacious bedrooms are traditionally furnished in a vaguely French boudoir style for the most part; most of them come with private bathrooms with shower, although some units lack facilities and guests share the adequate corridor bathrooms. The good island cooking, based on fresh produce, is a reason to stay here, and tables are placed on the terrace in summer. Offering live music on most summer weekends, the inn lies a 3-minute walk from the harbor.

Vestergade 38, DK-5970 Ærøskøbing. ⒸⒻ **62-52-10-03.** Fax 63-52-31-60. www.aeroehus.dk. 30 units, 18 w/private bathroom. DKK800 ($136/£80) double w/shared bathroom; DKK1,250 ($213/£125) double w/ private bathroom. Rates include breakfast. MC, V. Free parking. **Amenities:** Restaurant; bar. *In room:* TV, hair dryer, safe.

Pension Vestergade 44 ★ (Value

One of the most historically appealing buildings of Ærøskøbing is in the center of the village, 180m (591 ft.) from the ferryboat piers, within an antique (ca. 1784) half-timbered structure that the Danish historical authority considers almost sacrosanct. This allegiance to maintaining the building in its pristine original condition has restricted its owner, English-born Susanna Greve, from adding private bathrooms to its venerable interior. This enormous apricot-colored building was built by a local sea captain for his two daughters, and it's divided into two almost exactly equal halves. Only half of the house is occupied by this B&B. (The other half is the home of a local doctor, and is not open for view.) Within Susanna's half, you'll find scads of Danish and English antiques, substantial and bracing breakfasts, and midday coffee that's served every day. The inn maintains five bathrooms, each opening onto corridors and public areas, for six accommodations, more than most other B&Bs in Denmark, so most visitors find the bathroom situation acceptable.

Vestergade 44. DK-5970, Ærøskøbing. ⒸⒻ **62-52-22-98.** www.pension-vestergade44.dk. 6 rooms, none w/private bathroom. DKK780–DKK930 ($133–$158/£78–£93) double. No credit cards. *In room:* Dataport, Wi-Fi, no phone.

Where to Dine

Ærøskøbing Røgeri (Value SMOKED FISH

The setting is anything but glamorous, and your meal will be served on paper plates with plastic knives and forks. And if you're looking for wine to accompany your meal, forget it, as the beverage of choice is beer. Nevertheless, this is one of the most popular places in town, a culinary landmark that patrons describe with nostalgia and affection. Set beside the harbor in a raffish-looking house built in the old Ærø style, it serves only fresh fish that has been smoked (usually that morning) in electric and wood-fired ovens on the premises. You specify what kind of fish you want (salmon, herring, filet or whole mackerel, trout, or shrimp) and which of a half-dozen seasonings you want (dill, parsley, pepper, paprika, garlic, or "Provençal"); then you carry your plate to outdoor seating overlooking the harbor, or haul it back to wherever you're staying. The most expensive thing on the menu is a slab of fresh-smoked salmon accompanied by bread, butter, and a portion of potato salad; the least expensive is a make-it-yourself *smørrebrød* that includes a smoked herring, a slice of rough-textured bread, and Danish butter.

Havnen 15. ⒸⒻ **62-52-40-07.** Platters DKK24–DKK65 ($4.10–$11/£2.40–£6.50). No credit cards. May–Aug daily 10am–6pm (until 8pm mid-June to mid-Aug). Closed Sept–Apr.

Restaurant Mumm ★ AMERICAN/INTERNATIONAL

In a simple house, with its foundation dating from 1780, this restaurant enjoys a reputation for well-prepared dishes that sometimes carry a North American (or at least an international) flavor. Inside, you'll find a pair of dining rooms; the less formal one offers a view into a very busy kitchen. There's also a terrace set up in the garden in back, where parasols and candles usually adorn the outdoor tables. The restaurant offers an unusual combination of

American- and Danish-style dishes (a former owner was a chef at a Florida resort). There's a copious salad buffet, well-flavored steaks, and an abundance of seafood (most of which comes from local waters), including filet of plaice, grilled salmon with hollandaise sauce, sole in parsley-butter sauce, and various preparations of shrimp and snails.

Søndergade 12. ✆ **62-52-12-12.** Main courses DKK188–DKK198 ($32–$34£19–£20). AE, DC, MC, V. June–Aug daily 11:30am–2:30pm and 6–9:30pm; May and Sept Tues–Sun 11:30am–2:30pm and 6–9:30pm. Closed Oct–Apr.

Ærøskøbing After Dark

In summertime, you'll find sidewalk cafes and bars that come and go with the seasons (and that sometimes don't return the following year) along either side of the Vestergade and the Søndergade. One of the most reliable and enduring of these seasonal joints is the **Café Andelen,** Søndergade 28A (✆ **62-52-17-11**), which presents live jazz that begins around 9pm most nights June to August. Two year-round pubs that are favored by local residents and fishermen are **Aarebo Pub,** Vestergade 4 (✆ **62-52-28-50**), which offers some kind of live music every Friday and Saturday throughout the year, and its nearby competitor, **Landborgården Pub,** Vestergade 54 (✆ **62-52-10-41**), which is a site just for drinking and socializing for all ages.

MARSTAL ★

Marstal is the second city—really, an overgrown town of 2,500 people—standing at the eastern end of the island. Its marina is busy in summer with yachts, and there's even a shipyard, but its glory days are long gone. Back in the 1800s, as many as 300 merchant ships called Marstal their home port.

The harbor is protected by a granite jetty, forming one of Denmark's largest yacht basins. It's idyllic for all with nautical interests, but if you have time for only one town on Ærø, make it Ærøskøbing (see above). Otherwise, wander the streets of Marstal for an hour or two, the names of which still evoke the town's seafaring past—**Skonnertvej, Barkvej,** and **Galeasevej** (Schooner, Bark, and Ketch roads).

Seeing the Sights

In summer, consider an offbeat side trip to **Birkholm Island,** which is ideal for exploring, relaxing, and swimming. Twice a day a mail boat takes a limited number of passengers on this 45-minute trip from Marstal. Except for service and utility vehicles, there are no cars allowed on the island. For information and reservations, call **Birkholm Færgen** at ✆ **40-58-03-59.** The price of round-trip passage from Marstal to Birkholm Island is DKK70 ($12/£7) for adults, DKK35 ($6/£3.50) for ages 12 and under.

Maren Minors Minde   This is the once-prosperous, once-private home of a successful sea captain, Rasmus Minor, whose other bequests to Ærø included an orphanage and a retirement home. In the 1950s, his widow, Maren Minor, willed the house and its collection of nautical artifacts to the municipality as a museum. It's not much of a sight, but in its own way is some kind of immortality for the captain. If he hadn't given his home, his name would certainly be forgotten today. Give it 20 minutes or so. Although Minor always declared his love for his native Ærø, he eventually left the island and sailed for a new life in the United States.

Teglgade 9. ✆ **62-53-23-31.** Admission DKK40 ($6.80/£4) adults, DKK10 ($1.70/£1) children 5–15, free for children 4 and under. Daily 10am–3pm. Closed Sept–May.

Marstal Kirke   Built in 1738, the church was enlarged twice—once in 1772, by adding an extension, and later in 1920, with a tower to commemorate the reunification of southern Jutland with Denmark. Seven votive ships inside indicate the growth of shipping in the town from the 18th to the 20th century, and Marstal's close links to the sea. The font dates from the Middle Ages, and the blue color of the benches symbolizes the sea and eternity, whereas the red colors of the altar and pulpit evoke the blood shed by Christ. Red is also the color of love. Carl Rasmussen, a maritime artist who usually specialized in the motifs of Greenland, painted the 1881 altarpiece, depicting Christ stilling a storm. In the old churchyard are memorials and tombstones honoring the sailors of Marstal who died at sea during two world wars.

Kirkestrade 14. ⓒ **62-53-10-80.** Free admission. Daily 9am–5pm.

Marstal Søfartsmuseum ★ This museum is an evocative reminder of Marstal's heyday as a center of shipping. It's larger than you expect, spread across a trio of old buildings with three dozen different showrooms illustrating a maritime past. It has Funen's best collection of ship models, more than 200 in all, plus 100 "bottle ships," even full-size boats and a lot of junk Danish sailors of yore picked up in foreign ports, often while cavorting with prostitutes. At least the museum reveals what some of these sailors thought were objects valuable enough to bring home with them.

We are drawn to the works of an island-born artist, Carl Rasmussen, who sailed to Greenland and was captivated by its landscapes and its turbulent sea. He painted a large collection of works, some of which are on view today. Of course, some of the rooms are more worthwhile than others, especially when you get to see the 19th-century parlors of skippers of yore. There are many antiques and a lot of nautical memorabilia to check out. Some of these types of museums are boring, but this one has much to intrigue you, including an on-site shop selling unusual gifts and souvenirs.

Prinsensgade 1. ⓒ **62-53-23-31.** www.marmus.dk. Admission DKK45 ($7.70/£4.50) adults, free for children 17 and under. Oct–Apr Tues–Fri 10am–4pm, Sat 11am–3pm; May and Sept daily 10am–4pm; June and Aug daily 9am–5pm; July daily 9am–8pm.

Shopping

Marstal's most densely packed shopping streets are the **Kirkestræde** (which is transformed into a pedestrians-only walkway July–Aug) and **Kongensgade.** Many of the boutiques and kiosks that flourish there during midsummer disappear altogether the rest of the year, so the best way to appreciate the shopping scene involves spontaneously dropping in and out of boutiques as they catch your fancy. The best, and most enduring, venue for souvenirs from Ærø and the rest of Denmark is **Emerto,** Kirkestræde 10 (ⓒ **62-53-13-91**). Its owner, Bille Knusen, accumulates porcelain, crystal, woodcarvings, nautical memorabilia, and pots and pans into an all-inclusive emporium. Nearby is **Fruhøst,** Kongensgade 22 (ⓒ **62-53-24-09**), a store specializing in odd bits of handmade paraphernalia that for the most part are made on Ærø. Owner Elizabeth Jørgensen sells weavings, homemade wine, homemade chocolates, candles, and bric-a-brac.

Where to Stay

Hotel Ærø Strand ★ Surrounded by sea grass and sweeping vistas of the water, this first-class hotel is the largest and most up-to-date on the island, even though it opened back in 1989. It is a 5-minute walk from the center and less than half a kilometer (¼ mile) from the beach. The hotel is about the only place on Ærø that could be called a holiday resort, offering midsize-to-spacious bedrooms, each decorated in Danish modern set against pastel-colored walls, and each containing a sleek tiled bathroom. The suites are twice the size of the regular rooms and worth the extra money if you can afford it.

The restaurant is right by the harbor, and during the day fishermen can be seen bringing in the catch. In winter you can retreat to one of the cozy nooks inside, or else dine in summer close to the giant heart-shaped swimming pool.

Egehovedvej 4, DK-5960 Marstal. © **62-53-33-20.** Fax 62-53-31-50. www.hotel-aeroestrand.dk. 100 units. DKK1,890 ($321/£189) double; DKK2,390 ($406/£239) suite. Rates include breakfast. DC, MC, V. Free parking. Closed Dec 20–Jan 2. Bus: 990 to Marstal. **Amenities:** Restaurant; bar; dance club; indoor heated pool; tennis court; Jacuzzi; sauna; Wi-Fi (in lobby); solarium. *In room:* TV.

Hotel Marstal   This is a classic Danish waterfront inn, drawing more locals and visitors to its drinking and dining facilities than it does to the rather Spartan bedrooms upstairs. The location is in the town center, and the look is a bit nautical, with a ship's wheel on the wall along with old-fashioned wood-beamed ceilings and subdued lighting. You may want to dine here even if you're not an overnight guest (see below). The small-to-midsize bedrooms are well maintained and functionally furnished in Danish modern, two with windows that open onto a view of the sea—naturally, these are the most frequently requested. Bathrooms are a bit small but tidily kept and equipped with tub/shower combinations; otherwise, you can use one of the corridor bathrooms.

Droningstræde 1A, DK-5960 Marstal. © **62-53-13-52.** www.hotelmarstal.dk. 18 units, 12 w/private bathrooms. DKK600–DKK1,175 ($102–$200/£60–£118) double. Rates include breakfast. MC, V. **Amenities:** Restaurant; bar. *In room:* TV, no phone.

Where to Dine

Den Gamle Vingård ★ DANISH   On the Torvet (main square) of Marstal, this restaurant is set in a relatively new building, despite the fact that its name means "the old vineyard." It is, nonetheless, one of the best restaurants in Marstal, with engravings and oil paintings of antique ships and lots of woodsy-looking memorabilia of old Ærø. Your meal might consist of something as simple as pasta or pizza, or more substantial fare, which includes tender steaks, veal, chicken, fried filet of pork, or any of a half-dozen kinds of fresh fish. Each is prepared with the sauce suited to its individual flavors: Salmon, for example, is grilled and accompanied by an herb-and-butter sauce; herring is best either marinated, or fried and served with a lime-vinegar sauce. Plaice, depending on the mood of the chef, might be stuffed with shrimp and asparagus.

Skolegade 15. © **62-53-13-25.** Reservations recommended. Pizzas and pastas DKK75–DKK95 ($13–$16/£7.50–£9.50); main courses DKK108–DKK198 ($18–$34/£11–£20). No credit cards. May and Sept daily 5–10pm; June–Aug daily noon–10pm. Closed Oct–Apr.

Hotel Marstal Restaurant ★ STEAKS/SEAFOOD   The other leading restaurant in town is this dark-toned replica of an English pub, where lots of varnished paneling, flickering candles, and nautical accessories contribute to a general coziness at all times of the year. There's lots of beer on tap, as well as a menu that focuses on grilled steaks, some of them with pepper sauce; veal *cordon bleu;* and fresh seafood that might have arrived that morning from local fishermen. Especially flavorful are any of the beef dishes, or the grilled salmon steak with potatoes, asparagus, and either a lemon-butter or hollandaise sauce.

Dronningestræde 1A. © **62-53-13-52.** www.hotelmarstal.dk. Reservations recommended. Main courses DKK104–DKK178 ($18–$30/£10–£18); fixed-price menus DKK110–DKK175 ($19–$30/£11–£18). AE, DC, MC, V. Daily noon–2pm and 4–9pm.

Marstal After Dark

Our favorite pub in Marstal is **Toldbohus,** Prinsensgade 7 (© **62-53-15-41**), which opens every day at 8am and transforms from a cafe into a bar and pub as the day progresses. People of all ages converge here in a convivial atmosphere.

South Jutland

This is a tough call for us to make, but if you have time to visit only one part of the peninsula of Jutland, we'd opt for the south as opposed to central and northern Jutland. Each has its peculiar charm, but South Jutland can be a joyful celebration in summer, with its old seafaring towns, miles of sandy beaches, North Sea islands, and Jutland's oldest and most beautiful town, Ribe.

South Jutland (*Syd Jylland* in Danish) is the part of Denmark that's on Continental Europe, with Germany its immediate neighbor to the south. As the southernmost part of the Jutland peninsula, it is dotted with heather-covered moors, fjords, farmlands, lakes, and sand dunes. It's 400km (250 miles) from the northern tip of Jutland to the German frontier, and the North Sea washes up on kilometers of sandy beaches, making this a favorite holiday place.

The meadows of Jutland are filled with rich bird life and winding rivers, and nature walks are possible in almost all directions. Gabled houses in the marshlands of South Jutland add to the peninsula's charm. The two most popular vacation islands are **Rømø** and **Fanø,** off of the southwestern coast. Here many traditional homes of fishermen and sea captains have been preserved. Of all the towns of South Jutland, none has more particular appeal and charm for the visitor than **Ribe,** fabled for its storks' nests.

You can do as the Danes do and cycle through the countryside of South Jutland, which is crisscrossed by a fine network of bicycle paths. Stop in at one of the tourist offices and pick up a detailed map of the region, which often outlines the best bike paths.

A dike evocative of the Netherlands stretches along the coast of southwest Jutland, built to protect the land here from the tempestuous North Sea. Nature lovers flock here to enjoy walks along the Wadden Sea, and at low tide they can even explore the seabed itself. You can also bicycle along the dike, but the westerly winds make this a difficult run.

Some of the finest beaches in northern Europe are found in South Jutland, especially on the island of Rømø. When the winds blow, these long beaches are ideal for kite flying. In the little villages and towns, the past meets the present as you walk along narrow, cobbled streets, admiring the half-timbered houses that look as if they've emerged from a Hans Christian Andersen fairy tale. To experience an authentically Danish meal, order the traditional lunch of pickled herring, rye bread, and schnapps.

There are many museums of local history, showing you how life was lived long before you arrived. Many include workshops where artisans still practice the old crafts—for example, the lacemaking that made Tønder famous in the 18th century.

Mainly, South Jutland is a place to go to recharge your batteries.

1 KOLDING

208km (129 miles) SW of Copenhagen; 71km (44 miles) NW of Odense; 82km (51 miles) N of the German border; 70km (43 miles) SW of Århus

Our South Jutland adventure begins in the gateway city of Kolding, nestled on the scenic **Kolding Fjord.** The sixth-largest city in Denmark can become an overnight stopover or else the object of a short visit of 2 to 3 hours, depending on your schedule.

There are more young designers running around the streets of Kolding than even in Copenhagen itself, as it is home base for the **Danish School of Art & Design,** attracting students from throughout Scandinavia who dream of becoming the Arne Jacobsen of tomorrow. The center is comparable to the Parsons School of Design in New York. Many devotees of art and design visit Kolding just to see the **Trapholt Museum for Moderne Kunst** (p. 303), devoted to 20th-century and modern art.

Kolding is hardly one of the "must-see" sites for Jutland, but tourism is on the rise, mainly because of its hilltop castle, that modern art museum, and its historic Gamle Stan (Old Town) in the center. If you'll ignore the industrial suburbs, the cobblestoned streets and gaily painted half-timbered houses make a visit worthwhile. The center is surrounded by thriving industries such as iron, engineering, and textiles.

Dating from 1321, Kolding was a battleground in the Middle Ages, which led to the erection of Koldinghus Slot (castle) in 1248. The town stood as disputed territory of Schleswig-Holstein, which is now part of Germany. Prussian troops wanted to make it part of the German empire but by 1864 at the signing of the Treaty of Vienna, it was returned to Danish hands, except for its Nazi occupation from 1940 to 1945.

ESSENTIALS

GETTING THERE   By Train   Trains run frequently between Kolding and Padborg on the northern German border (trip time: 70 min.). Frequent trains also arrive from Frederikshavn in the north of Jutland (4 hr.). Trains also cut across Jutland, reaching Esbjerg in the west in just under an hour.

By Car   After taking the bridge from Funen in the east, follow Route 161 into Kolding. If you're already in West Jutland, perhaps in Esbjerg, you can cut across Jutland along motorway E20 until you reach Kolding as you near the east coast.

VISITOR INFORMATION   Kolding Tourist Information, Akseltorv 8 (© 76-33-21-00; www.visitkolding.dk), is open Monday through Friday 9:30am to 5:30pm and Saturday 9:30am to 2pm.

SEEING THE SIGHTS

Kolding Fjord ★ attracts anglers, swimmers, and boaters, and **Kolding Marina** is one of the largest in Denmark. The fjord is also lined with beaches with plenty of recreational areas.

The town's main attractions include the following:

Geografsisk Have og Rosehave (Geographical Garden) ★ Finds   An idyllic spot, but most often overlooked by visitors, is this "Garden of Eden" on the southern border of the town, housing some 2,000 species of trees and shrubs from all over the globe, including North and South America, and what used to be Burma. It's the perfect place for a picnic lunch either on the grounds or at one of the on-site garden pavilions. This vast nursery, the creation of green thumb Axel Olsen, also is home to the largest **bamboo grove** ★★ in Northern Europe.

Chr. d. 4 Vej. © **75-50-38-80.** Admission DKK50 ($8.50/£5) adults, DKK25 ($4.30/£2.50) children 10–16, free for children 9 and under. Daily 10am–6pm.

Koldinghus Slot ★★   This castle from the Middle Ages is the most happening spot in town. We'd visit it for no other reason than to see the **panoramic view** ★★ of the

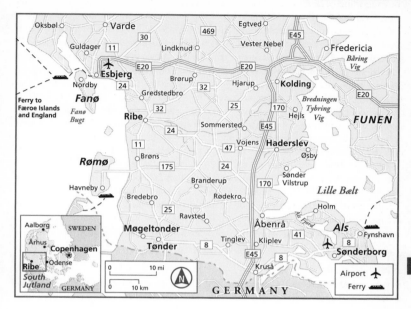

fjord and the town from its observation deck. But there is so much more here, even cultural events such as classical music concerts presented every Thursday evening (inquire at the tourist office for details). These take place in the Great Hall.

The last royal castle built in Jutland, the domain of King Erik Glipping, the castle became a royal residence, although its original purpose was as a defense against the Duchy of Schleswig to the south. Christian IV spent much of his boyhood here, adding a landmark tower in 1600. Fire and bombardment has destroyed the castle over the years, but it always bounced back, its oldest sections dating from around the mid-1400s. In 1808, Denmark was allied with France under Napoleon Bonaparte. Napoleon commanded Spanish troops because his brother occupied the Spanish throne, and at the time Spanish soldiers were billeted in Koldinghus Slot. The Spanish soldiers, not used to Danish winters, built a roaring fire that not only kept them warm, but set the castle on fire.

Until 1890, the castle was left in ruins. A north wing was restored to house a museum. Reconstruction continued slowly over much of the 20th century, with the Christian IV tower restored by 1935. The exterior has a baroque facade evocative of the 18th century. Today the castle shelters a **Historical and Cultural Museum,** with exhibitions tracing the town's history. The castle is rich in Romanesque and Gothic sculptures, plus such handcrafted articles as silver, stoneware, and porcelain. A special exhibit documents the wars against Prussia from 1848 to 1850 and in 1864.

Rådhustrasse. 🕐 **76-33-81-00.** www.koldinghus.dk. Admission DKK65 ($11/£6.50) adults, DKK35 ($6/£3.50) students, free for children 12 and under.

Trapholt Museum for Moderne Kunst (Museum of Modern Art) ★★★ This

is one of Denmark's greatest museums outside of Copenhagen. After you've viewed too many badly lit and dusty country museums throughout Denmark, it's refreshing to visit this sprawling complex that's been incorporated into its landscape opening onto scenic views over Kolding Fjord. Housing one of the country's most sophisticated collections of visual arts, sculpture, furniture design, applied art, and design produced after 1900, the museum is a stunner with state-of-the-art lighting and floor-to-ceiling windows. The **ceramic art collection ★★** is one of the finest in the country, the works often called "studio pieces." All the pioneers in Danish ceramic art are represented here, including Jais Nielsen and Gutte Eriksen.

Begun in 1988, the **furniture collection ★** charts Danish design from the 1900s to the present day, with a broad selection from the kingpin of them all, Arne Jacobsen. The museum also stages special exhibits where the best in new Danish furniture design is on parade. A full array of Danish painters can be viewed, from the COBRA movement to abstract artists of today. The works of one of our favorite Skagen artists, Ann Ancher, are particularly impressive. Pieces of sculpture by leading Danish artists are viewed in the museum garden. Near the main entrance is the Museum Shop, where many items on sale have been produced exclusively for Trapholt by leading Danish designers.

Overlooking the fjord, a cafe with a summer terrace features a selection of hot main dishes, salads, and homemade cakes.

Æblehaven 23. © **76-30-05-30.** www.trapholt.dk. Admission DKK65 ($11/£6.50) adults, free for children 17 and under. Daily 10am–5pm. Closed Dec 21, 24, and 25.

SHOPPING

A network of pedestrian streets flanked with shops lies in the town center. On Tuesday and Friday, 7am to 1pm, there's an open-air market at Akseltorv, where traders sell flowers, fruit, vegetables, cheese, fish, and much more.

One of the largest shopping malls in Denmark, **Kolding Storcenter,** Skovvangen 42 (© **75-50-96-06;** www.koldingstorcenter.dk), lies 4km (2¹/₂ miles) north of Kolding's center (follow the signs to Vejle from the town center). Home to some 60 shops, it attracts an astonishing 80,000 visitors a week. In a style that evokes a megamall in California, it's especially crowded whenever it's raining, when hundreds of local residents come here just to hang out.

Another intriguing shopping possibility is the **Kolding Antiques & Stall Market,** held at Haderslevvej and Sdr. Ringvej on Saturday and Sunday 10am to 5pm.

The best art galleries in town are **Galleri Elise Toft,** Låsbygade 58 (© **20-96-54-14**), and **Galleri Pagter,** Adelgade 3 (© **75-54-09-30**).

WHERE TO STAY

Comwell Kolding ★ Finds This hotel is not exactly a spa, but it's the best in the area for R & R as well as the active life. Opening onto a small lake northwest of the town center, it does have a small spa as well as a pool. The staff will hook you up to play at two nearby 18-hole golf courses or else will rent you a bike for trailblazing through the beautiful forest, Marielundskoven.

The hotel is a showcase for Danish modern design, with exposed and varnished pinewood trim with touches of brass, big windows opening onto views, and cozy public areas, including a wood-burning fireplace in one lounge. The bedrooms are tastefully and comfortably furnished, also in a contemporary Danish design, and they are decorated in bright, cheerful colors and well maintained. First-class international and Danish cuisine are served in the on-site restaurant, Repos, and you can also enjoy lighter fare and drink in the bar with an unusual name: Jes or No.

Skovbrynet 1, DK-6000 Kolding. © **76-34-11-00.** Fax 76-34-12-00. www.comwell.com. 180 units. DKK1,530–DKK1,730 ($260–$294/£153–£173) double; DKK2,030 ($345/£203) suite. Rates include breakfast. AE, DC, MC, V. Bus: 1, 5, or 6. **Amenities:** Restaurant; bar; indoor heated pool; exercise room; spa; sauna; room service; laundry service; dry cleaning; nonsmoking rooms; solarium. *In room:* TV, dataport, Wi-Fi, minibar, hair dryer.

Hotel Byparken (Kids)

The owners of this hotel built it in 1972 as a motel right next to the city park, Legeparken, which offers many free activities for children of all ages, such as rides, video games, and biking. It's a good base for touring South Jutland as it lies just 3km (1³/₄ miles) from the express highway. Outside it's not distinguished architecturally, although the owners have done much in recent years to make the interior more relaxing and cozy in the public rooms. Each of the midsize bedrooms is furnished in standard Danish modern with comfortable, tasteful furnishings. The best deal here is one of the renovated junior suites with more living space and a more upmarket decor. The staff can make arrangements for you to use the spa and Slotssøbadet (which includes a water slide and pools) lying just a few minutes' walk from the hotel.

Byparken, DK-6000 Kolding. © **75-53-21-22.** Fax 75-50-40-64. www.hotelbyparken.dk. 76 units. DKK1,094–DKK1,245 (186–$212/£109–£125) double; DKK1,145–DKK1,595 ($195–$271/£115–£160) junior suite. Rates include breakfast. AE, DC, MC, V. **Amenities:** Restaurant; bar; fitness center; access to nearby spa; sauna; room service; laundry service; dry cleaning; nonsmoking rooms; rooms for those w/ limited mobility. *In room:* TV, Wi-Fi, safe.

Kolding Byferie ★★ (Kids)

Although right in the heart of Kolding's Gamle Stan (Old Town), this is a series of modern cement-and-glass buildings erected in 1994 and shaped into different architectural forms, including squares, rectangles, octagons, circles, and stars—we kid you not. Many of the "flats" open onto a scenic view of Lake Slotssøen and the castle, Koldinghus. The apartments, each tastefully and comfortably furnished, come in various sizes, housing from two to eight visitors, which makes them ideal for families traveling together. Children not only will find a playground on-site, but also will enjoy the location near the watersports center and baths at Slotssøbadet. The staff is one of the most helpful in the area, and will give touring guidance, or even rent you a bike for the day. A 3-night booking is preferred, which means you can use the hotel as a base for day tours of South Jutland, visiting some of the towns we'll discuss later.

Kedelsmedgangen 2, DK-6000 Kolding. © **75-54-18-00.** Fax 75-54-18-02. www.kolding-byferie.dk. 85 units. DKK795–DKK895 ($135–$152/£80–£90) double. AE, DC, MC, V. **Amenities:** Restaurant; indoor heated pool; bike rentals; playground; nonsmoking rooms. *In room:* TV, Wi-Fi, full kitchen, safe.

Koldingfjord Hotel ★★

You're close to town but can still feel you're in the country if you check into this vast compound at the edge of the fjord and surrounded by beautiful beech forests. Formerly a Radisson SAS hotel, this is the most appealing hotel in the region, lying on the opposite bank of Kolding Fjord, a 5km (3-mile) drive from the center. The ostentatious and somewhat grandiose complex began life in 1911 as a neo-Classical palace erected on 20 hectares (49 acres) of forested land. After a stint as a hospital and later a school, the site was transformed into a first-class hotel in 1988. Each of the midsize-to-spacious bedrooms is individually designed in a combination of classic decor and modern Danish design. Rooms open onto views, of either the forest or the fjord, and are spread across the main building and three of the original outbuildings, each offering "separate but equal" facilities. Also on the premises are a brand-new, very large convention center and a recommended restaurant (see "Where to Dine," below).

Fjordvej 154, Strandhuse, DK-6000 Kolding. © **75-51-00-00.** Fax 75-51-00-51. www.koldingfjord.dk. 134 units. DKK1,365–DKK1,865 ($232–$317/£137–£187) double; DKK1,965–DKK2,265 ($334–$385/£197–£227) junior suite. AE, DC, MC, V. From Kolding, follow the signs to the E45; before you reach it, detour northward along the Lushojalle and drive 3km (1³/₄ miles). **Amenities:** Restaurant; bar; indoor heated pool; tennis court; sauna; room service; laundry service; dry cleaning; nonsmoking rooms; solarium; rooms for those w/ limited mobility. *In room:* TV, Wi-Fi, minibar, hair dryer, trouser press.

Saxildhus Hotel ★★   Although the competition is keen today, since 1915 this architecturally graceful hotel was the traditional choice, lying right at the train station. With its dormer-studded rooftop, valuable antiques, and painted beams, it's been our preferred stopover for years. We applaud the postmillennium renovations that have returned some of the bedrooms to those glory days before World War II. Not all the bedrooms are the same—some have nostalgic decor with antique mahogany four-poster beds, and others are furnished in Danish modern. As befits a hotel of its day, bedrooms come in various sizes, but each is equipped with a good-size private bathroom with a tub/shower combination. Even if you're not a guest, consider stopping off at the hotel restaurant, as it features superb Danish regional specialties, most of which come from the sea.

Banegårdsplatz, DK-6000 Kolding. ℂ **75-52-12-00.** Fax 75-53-53-10. www.saxildhus.dk. 87 units. DKK1,180–DKK1,510 ($201–$257/£118–£151) double; DKK1,760 ($299/£176) suite. Rates include buffet breakfast. AE, DC, MC, V. **Amenities:** 2 restaurants; bar; 24-hr. room service; laundry service; dry cleaning; nonsmoking rooms. *In room:* TV, Wi-Fi, minibar.

WHERE TO DINE

Hotel Koldingfjord ★   DANISH/CONTINENTAL   The menu is adjusted seasonally because the cooks like freshness, such as lobster with asparagus, which the chef called his "*terroir* specialty." If a dish from the sea could be labeled "earthy," we'd give the honor to the gratin of fresh tuna with a ragout of fish roe. The chef also makes the most of local produce in such dishes as a warm salmon pudding with fresh spinach or a crabmeat bouillon with fresh tomatoes. The filet of monkfish—a delectable offering—comes with either a citrus sauce or else beurre blanc. The dessert specialty consists of a medley of summer berries with freshly made vanilla cream.

Fjordvej 154, Strandhuse. ℂ **76-20-86-66.** Reservations recommended. Main courses DKK198–DKK248 ($34–$42/£20–£25). Fixed-price menus DKK298 ($51/£30) for 2 courses, DKK368 ($63/£37) for 3 courses, DKK428 ($73/£43) for 4 courses, and DKK498 ($85/£50) for 5 courses. AE, DC, MC, V. Daily noon–2pm and 6–10:30pm. From Kolding, follow the signs to the E45; before you reach it, detour northward along the Lushojalle and drive 3km (1³/₄ miles).

Repos DANISH/FRENCH   The only drawback to this well-orchestrated restaurant is its lack of a view over the nearby lake. Other than that, the place is cozy, inviting, and appealing, thanks to well-prepared food. The copious lunchtime buffet (the best in town) includes an all-Danish medley of hot and cold dishes that feature *frikadeller* (meatballs), many different preparations of herring, freshly made salads, casseroles, an impressive collection of fresh-baked breads, and an artful medley of Danish and European cheeses. Our favorite dish here is North Sea turbot with white asparagus stalks, baby cabbage, and a reduction of fresh tomatoes. You might also find other delectable dishes offered, especially a ragout of anglerfish with scallops and fresh vegetables. A classic Dover sole meunière is on the menu, as is a tender, flavorful tournedos of beef "perfumed" with onions and confit of sweet red peppers.

In the Hotel Comwell, Skovbrynet 1. ℂ **76-34-11-00.** Reservations recommended. Lunch DKK100–DKK180 ($17–$31/£10–£18); dinner main courses DKK225–DKK275 ($38–$47/£23–£28); fixed-price dinners DKK300–DKK525 ($51–$89/£30–£53). AE, DC, MC, V. Mon–Sat noon–2pm and 6–10pm. Bus: 1, 5, or 6.

Three sites compete with one another for the title of most popular nightlife option in Kolding. They include the **English Pub,** A. L. Passagen (© **75-50-80-44**), open Monday to Friday 2pm to 2am, Saturday 2pm to 4am, and Sunday 2 to 8pm, serving hundreds of pints of English and Danish beer every night until closing. Equally popular, but with shorter hours, is the **Crazy Daisy,** Jernbanegade 13 (© **75-54-16-88**), a pub and nightclub that's open for drinking every night 9pm to midnight, and which becomes a dance club every Tuesday, Friday, and Saturday night 9pm to around 4am. A fashionable venue that combines hi-tech decor with food service and occasional bouts of live jazz is the **Blue Café,** Lilletorv (© **75-50-65-12**). Light platters of passable food are served daily 10am to around 9:30pm; cappuccino, wine, beer, and schnapps are available every day till at least midnight, and sometimes later, depending on the size of the crowd.

AN EASY EXCURSION FROM KOLDING

Directly to the south of Kolding, a distance of 9km (5²/₃ miles)—follow the signs pointing to Christiansfeldt—is one of the most powerful but understated monuments of Denmark, **Skamilingsbanken.** A rolling hill that rises to a height of 113m (370 ft.), it commemorates the survival of the Danish language and the Danish nation against German incursions throughout the centuries. Its location marks the frontier between Denmark and North Schleswig, a hotly contested territory that was bounced around between Germany and Denmark repeatedly throughout modern times. In 1920, as part of the settlement at the end of World War I, the Danish-German border was moved 82km (51 miles) to the south, where it has remained ever since. Today, few Danes can articulate the reason for the emotion associated with this site. For reasons of tact, since the 1960s, the site has been downplayed within the Danish national psyche. Beginning in 1998, it has been the site of a concert presented the first Sunday in August, for which the Royal Danish Opera travels down from Copenhagen to present operatic works by archetypal German and Danish composers Richard Wagner and Karl Nielsen. The event is free, with further details available at the tourist office in Kolding (see earlier in this section).

---

2 HADERSLEV ★

248km (154 miles) SW of Copenhagen; 31km (19 miles) S of Kolding; 51km (32 miles) E of Ribe

This is not an imperative stopover on one's itinerary for South Jutland, but if you have 2 hours or so, it's a rewarding visit. If it's a choice between Kolding and Haderslev, make it Kolding. Some visitors see Kolding in the morning, reserving Haderslev for an afternoon checkout.

At the head of the **Haderslev Fjord,** this appealing town of 32,000 inhabitants is known for having one of the oldest and best-preserved historic cores in Denmark. In 1995, it was awarded the Europa Nostra Prize for its old, beautifully restored buildings, which center around Torvet, the historic market square in the center. In spite of some minor attractions, there's nothing better here than walking through its narrow cobblestone streets with buildings dating back all the way to 1570. In 1971, the people of Haderslev launched this massive preservation effort to save their Gamle Stan (Old Town), and they succeeded beautifully.

Although built on the banks of a fjord, Haderslev actually lies 15km (9¹/₃ miles) inland. It has always depended on trade for its livelihood, and by 1292 it already had a city charter. Christian I came here in 1448, signing a charter that allowed him to become king of Denmark. Another Christian (this time King Christian IV) came here in 1597 to celebrate his wedding to Anne-Catherine of Brandenburg. From 1864 to as late as 1920 Haderslev was part of the duchy of Schleswig-Holstein and controlled by Prussia (and later Germany). When the Duchy of Schleswig was divided in 1920, Haderslev became part of Denmark, and remains so to this day.

ESSENTIALS

GETTING THERE   By Train   The nearest train depot is at the town of Vojens. It is possible to arrive by train at Vojens, then take a 30-minute bus ride over to Haderslev.

By Bus   Bus no. 34 runs hourly between Kolding and Haderslev (trip time: 45 min.).

By Car   From Kolding, head south on Route 170 or go east from Ribe along Routes 24 and 47.

VISITOR INFORMATION   The **Haderslev Turistbureau,** Norregade 52 (© **73-54-56-30;** www.haderslev-turist.dk), is open January 2 to March, Monday to Friday 9:30am to 4:30pm; April to mid-June and September to December 22, Monday to Friday 9:30am to 4:30pm, Saturday 9:30am to 12:30pm; mid-June to August, Monday to Friday 9:30am to 6pm and Saturday 9:30am to 2pm.

EXPLORING THE AREA

Haderslev is situated in a **subglacial stream trench** ★ that is 24km (15 miles) long and stretches from the Little Belt to the neighboring town of Vojens. A beautiful landscape has been created by nature. In 1994, Denmark's second-largest nature reserve opened south of Haderslev Dam, stocked with fallow deer. Near the reserve, the large marsh area of Hindemade was flooded, and today the whole area has a rich bird and animal life. Hindemade has been designated a bird sanctuary by the European Union, and you can walk about in the area along the Tunneldal paths, which run through most of the subglacial trench between Haderslev and Vojens.

   Back in the center of Haderslev, you can wander through the town's historic core, an area so well preserved it was voted "European Town of the Year" in 1984. The old town grew up around its Domkirke (see below), which stands on high ground.

Ehlers-samlingen (Ehlers Collections) ★   The Ehlers family set out to collect pottery from the Middle Ages to the present and ended up with one of the biggest collections in Europe. All of this vast array can be seen in this historic timber-framed building from 1577, which has preserved many of its original decorative wall panels. You can also see many antique domestic utensils and some 16th-century wall paintings.

Slotsgade 20. © **74-53-08-58.** Admission DKK25 ($4.30/£2.50) adults, free for children 15 and under. Tues–Fri 10am–5pm; Sat–Sun 1–5pm. Closed Mon in winter.

Haderslev Domkirke ★★   The origins of this redbrick cathedral go back to the 13th century; but over the years it's been torn down, rebuilt, destroyed, rebuilt, and so on, so what you see today is a mishmash of styles. The transept and nave are the most ancient parts of the cathedral, dating from the mid-13th century. Many additions, however, were made over the years, including the bronze font from the late 1400s and a baroque pulpit added in 1636. A restored Sieseby organ has a beautifully clear sound, and is played regularly. At the altar you'll see a Romanesque crucifix, probably from the beginning of the 14th century, and statues of Mary and John along with alabaster figures of the Apostles. The church played an important part in the Reformation, becoming the first Lutheran church in the country. A disastrous fire swept over the Domkirke in 1627, destroying much of the building, but a restoration was completed by 1650. When Haderslev reunited with Denmark in 1920, a new diocese was established, making the Domkirke a true cathedral. In August, concerts are given on the previously mentioned organ at 8pm on Tuesday and at 4:30pm Friday. These days might vary, depending on the availability of performers, so a call in advance to the tourist office might clear up any confusion. The Friday concert is usually free, while admission to the Tuesday concert is DKK80 ($14/£8).

Torvet. (C) **74-52-36-33.** Free admission. May–Sept Mon–Sat 10am–5pm, Sun 11:30am–5pm; off-season daily 10am–3pm.

Haderslev Museum This two-part museum is only of passing interest and need occupy less than an hour of your time. Lying a kilometer (²/₃ mile) northwest of the market square, Torvet, it contains one of South Jutland's most extensive collections of archaeological artifacts, most of which were dug up from nearby bogs. The best parts are the reconstructed street scenes of the 19th century and the entire re-created and antiques-filled rooms. Adjacent to the museum is a small open-air museum with an old farmstead, several period structures, and even a windmill.

Dalgade 7. (C) **74-52-75-66.** Admission DKK30 ($5.10/£3) adults, free for children 17 and under. June–Aug Tues–Sun 10am–4pm; off-season Tues–Sun 1–4pm.

SHOPPING

One of the most appealing shops in Haderslev is **Stentebjerg,** Storegade 8 ((C) **74-52-02-09**), which specializes in pottery from the region and from throughout Denmark. For more options on how to make your home or apartment look a little more Danish, head for **Stolen,** Møllepladsen 2 ((C) **20-16-02-16**).

WHERE TO STAY

Hotel Harmonien ★★ Established in 1793, this is one of the oldest and most historic hotels of South Jutland, receiving its share of royal visitors over the years, ranging from King Christian VII in the 1800s to today's Queen Margrethe II. Much of the historic atmosphere has been maintained, although the hotel has been completely modernized over the years. The staff is one of the most hospitable we've encountered in Jutland, advising about touring in the area and attending to your personal needs. Even so, much of the allure of this place still derives from its cozy restaurant (see "Where to Dine," below). The midsize-to-spacious bedrooms are attractively and tastefully decorated with a combination of Danish modern and antiques. There is no array of spas or gyms here, but plenty of charm and lots of comfort—and that's why we love it so.

Gåskærgade 19, DK-6100 Haderslev. (C) **74-52-37-20.** Fax 74-52-44-51. www.harmonien.dk. 33 units. DKK1,300–DKK1,990 ($221–$338/£130–£199) double. Rates include breakfast. AE, DC, MC, V. **Amenities:** Restaurant; bar; room service; laundry service; dry cleaning; nonsmoking rooms. *In room:* TV, hair dryer.

Hotel Norden ★★ Harmonien may have the history, but Norden offers the most facilities in the area and is also the best and most scenically positioned, placed directly by the sea on a beautiful lake with a view to the cathedral. To make the place more charming and personal, the owners of the hotel have placed original oil paintings and sculptures by the internationally known Robert Jacobsen throughout. As a curiosity, Jacobsen coated with pure gold the motorcycle from the world champion Ole Olsen, which can be seen in the reception. The midsize-to-spacious bedrooms are done in a stylish Danish modern,

SOUTH JUTLAND

11

HADERSLEV

with the best units, called VIP rooms, costing more, but worth it if you want the ultimate in local comfort.

Storegade 55, DK-6100 Haderslev. © **74-52-40-30.** Fax 74-52-40-25. www.hotel-norden.dk. 68 units. DKK1,145–DKK1,445 ($195–$246/£115–£145) double. Rates include breakfast. AE, DC, MC, V. **Amenities:** Restaurant; bar; indoor heated pool; exercise room; sauna; room service; laundry service; dry cleaning; nonsmoking rooms; solarium; 1 room for those w/limited mobility. *In room:* TV, minibar, hair dryer, trouser press.

WHERE TO DINE

Restaurant Harmonien ★ DANISH/INTERNATIONAL There isn't culinary greatness here, but you get the sense that the kitchen staff really cares about the meals it serves guests. The 19th-century setting in the town center is both charming and historic, and the dining room is frequented by royalty. This is the coziest place in the area for a fine Danish meal without too much emphasis on big-city glamour. The long and narrow dining room has only 10 tables and an oversized fireplace that's ablaze in the evening. The kitchen staff prepares dishes that are well crafted and expertly seasoned, including venison with red-wine sauce or a tournedos of beef with several kinds of peppercorns. The repertoire is familiar—no inventiveness or experimentation here—but the "classics" are done with great competence, including Dover sole meunière or roasted breast of duck with a piquant sauce.

In the Hotel Harmonien, Gåskærgade 19. © **74-52-37-20.** Reservations recommended. Main courses DKK168–DKK192 ($29–$33/£17–£19). Daily 11:30am–10pm. AE, DC, MC, V. Closed Dec 20–Jan 4.

Restaurant Svanen ★ DANISH/FRENCH This hotel restaurant is in a neck-and-neck race for culinary supremacy with the previously recommended Harmonien. Unlike the antique dining room of the Harmonien, the Norden offers a modern, airy, high-ceilinged, and spacious setting, which is decorated with art. The food is flawlessly prepared and beautifully presented by a helpful staff, which is both unobtrusive and prompt. Some of the most successful dishes emerging from the kitchen include North Sea turbot roasted with lemon juice and wine and served with white asparagus and braised cabbage. We also recommend that you try the Danish veal cutlet with ham, shallots, parsley, and a morel sauce, or the delectable noisettes of lamb sautéed in virgin olive oil and served with a Dijon mustard sauce and Swiss-style *spätzle* (egg noodles).

Storegade 55. © **74-52-40-30.** Reservations recommended. Main courses DKK100–DKK300 ($17–$51/£10–£30). AE, DC, MC, V. Daily 6–10pm.

HADERSLEV AFTER DARK

Most of the after-dark activities in town take place at one of only two hangouts. One of them, **Buch's Vinstue,** Nørregade 9 (© **74-53-09-53**), is an old-fashioned Danish beer and wine house that gets very crowded with friends and acquaintances from throughout the district. They select it as a rendezvous point for ongoing discussions about politics, art, business, or just casual conversation. It opens daily at 2pm, closing at 1am. A competitor that's a bit more modern in its approach to entertainment is **Huset,** Nørregade 10 (© **74-53-43-73**). Opening around 6pm, it functions as a well-used bar most nights, except on Thursdays and Fridays, when live music is presented beginning around 10pm; it closes at 2am. There's never any cover charge, and the under-40 residents of Haderslev tend to flock to the changing musical fare at this local landmark.

3 TØNDER ★

277km (172 miles) SW of Copenhagen; 77km (48 miles) S of Esbjerg; 85km (53 miles) SW of Kolding; 195km (121 miles) SW of Århus

Tønder, on the banks of the River Vidå, is called the capital of the marshland, the oldest town in Denmark holding official town rights, with a municipal charter granted in 1243. In medieval times, it was an important port and a place of disembarkation for horses and cattle. Its surrounding marshland, even Tønder itself, was often flooded by the North Sea. By the middle of the 15th century, townspeople started to erect dikes. But the end result was that Tønder lost its position as a port. The sea eventually receded, leaving Tønder landlocked.

In the 17th century, the townsfolk turned to lacemaking, and eventually 12,000 lace-makers were employed in and around the town. The many rich lace dealers built the beautiful patrician houses adorning the streets today.

From 1864, Tønder and the region of North Schleswig were part of Germany. But a plebiscite in 1920 led to the reunion of North Slesvig with Denmark. Even so, Tønder is still influenced by German traditions, as it is only 4km (2¹/₂ miles) north of the German frontier. The town still has a German school, kindergarten, and library, and a German vicar is attached to Tønder Christ Church.

ESSENTIALS

GETTING THERE By Train The train depot lies on the west side of Tønder, less than a kilometer (¹/₂ mile) from Torvet (the market square) and reached by going along Vester-gade. Monday to Friday, trains arrive every hour during the day from Ribe (trip time: 50 min.) and Esbjerg (trip time: 1¹/₂ hr.). There's less frequent service on Saturday and Sunday.

By Car From Kolding (see earlier in the chapter), take Route 25 southwest to the junction with Route 11, which will carry you for the final lap to the turnoff for Tønder, reached along Route 419 heading west.

VISITOR INFORMATION The **Tønder Turistbureau,** Torvet 1 (© 74-75-51-30; www.visittonder.dk), is open June 15 to August Monday to Friday 9am to 5pm and Saturday 9am to noon. Otherwise, hours are Monday to Friday 9am to 4pm and Saturday 9am to noon.

GETTING AROUND By Bicycle Tønder Campingplads, Holmevej 2A (© 74-72-18-49), rents bikes and, mid-May to mid-August, water bikes from DKK70 ($12/£7) a day. Bicycling maps are available at the tourist office.

SPECIAL EVENTS Beginning rather modestly in 1975, the **Tønder Festivalen,** Vestergade 80 (© 74-72-46-10), held every year August 25 to 29, has turned into an international musical event. The Tønder Festival, covering a wide range of music styles, presents musicians from all over the world playing blues, bluegrass, Cajun, zydeco, jazz, gospel, and traditional Irish, Scottish, English, and American folk music. Names as well as unknowns play their instruments in the streets, squares, pubs, and on seven official stages. More than 25,000 visitors flock to Tønder annually for this event. Tickets cost DKK90 to DKK350 ($15–$60/£9–£35).

To see the antique homes built by the lacemakers during the heyday of Tønder's prosperity, wander up and down the main street, which changes its name several times: **Østergade** becomes **Storegade,** and finally **Vestergade.** Most of these stately mansions, which are characterized by richly carved portals, were built in the 17th and 18th centuries. The actual lacemakers lived on the smaller side streets, Uldgade and Spikergade, and their houses were more modest, but still worthy to explore. Most of these houses on the latter two streets were built in the 1600s with bay windows. Actually, in our view, **Uldgade ★** is the most colorful street in Tønder. A narrow cobblestone lane, it is in many ways the street in Tønder most evocative of old Denmark.

All that remains of the ancient **Tønder Castle,** victim of border wars with the Germans, is this gatehouse housing the local history of the area, including its lacemaking heyday, with lacy baptismal gowns and fragile doilies of another era. The collection of tiles is exceptional, as they were hand-painted in the Netherlands and brought back home by sailors from the 1600s and 1700s, when they were used as ballast. Once they were in Tønder, locals used them to decorate their homes. Other artifacts and exhibits include regional costumes and even elegant table silver owned by prosperous merchants in the area. The wooden figure with cane, *Kagmand,* once stood at the Torvet, the marketplace. At one time any citizen who had committed a crime was tied to this figure and publicly whipped—real S&M stuff.

In the same building as the Tønder Museum is the **Sønderjyllands Kunstmuseum,** which holds a fine collection of Danish surrealistic art and a collection of contemporary works. Besides the permanent exhibitions, changing art shows are staged here as well.

Follow a glass corridor to the old water tower, which has been converted into a museum:

Museumstårnet & H. J. Wegner udstilling (Tower Museum and H. J. Wegner Exhibit)

In 1995, the town's old water tower was converted into an exhibition center for the works of the celebrated furniture designer, native son H. J. Wegner, whose designs during the 1950s and 1960s were precursors of the style that became known as Danish modern. His best-known design is called—rather simply—"The Chair." If you're of a certain generation, you may have seen this chair during the famous Nixon/Kennedy debates. Both presidential aspirants sat in Wegner's chair, a debate that some historians claim cost Nixon, with his five o'clock shadow, the election. The top floor of the tower offers panoramic views over the surrounding marshlands.

Kongevej 55. (𝄯 **74-72-89-89.** Admission DKK45 ($7.70/£4.50), free for children 12 and under. May–Oct daily 10am–5pm; off-season Tues–Sun 1–5pm.

Kristkirken (Christ's Church) ★

Religious lace merchants and cattle barons in the surrounding area were devout followers of this church and used part of their personal treasures to richly decorate the interior, which is one of the finest in Denmark in terms of furnishings and art from the Renaissance and baroque eras. The present church dates from the end of the 16th century, although the 50m (164-ft.) tower is actually from the earlier Skt. Nicolai Kirke that stood on this spot before it became too small. Inside the church are a mid-14th-century font, a pulpit from 1586, and a series of memorial tablets, some dating from the 1400s.

Kirkepladsen. (𝄯 **74-72-20-80.** Free admission. Mon–Sat 10am–5pm.

Dröhse's Hus (Dröhse's House)

In this little museum—strictly for aficionados in our opinion—Tønder pays homage to its lacemaking past. Other exhibits focus on artifacts of the area, including antique furniture and glass. The museum is only of passing interest, and you may not want to give it more than 20 minutes unless you plan to take up lacemaking.

Storgade 14. (*C* **74-72-49-90**. Admission DKK20 ($3.40/£2) adults, free for children 15 and under. Apr–Dec Mon–Fri 10am–5pm, Sat 10am–1pm.

SHOPPING

According to long tradition, the shopkeepers of Tønder—dressed in old-fashioned costumes—arrange a pedestrian-zone market in the center of town July 17 and 18. On Saturday, the final market day, there are live music and drinks in the main square, Torvet. Another shopping adventure occurs on August 1, when there's a feast in the pedestrian zone. Shops remain open until 10pm, offering amusements to visitors, with plenty of food and drink, climaxed by a concert in the main square.

On Tuesday and Friday, local vendors sell fish, fruit, cheese, and fresh vegetables in the main square. We always like to gather the makings for a picnic here, to be enjoyed later in the marshland surrounding Tønder.

For such a small town, Tønder has a large number of specialty shops. Many Germans drive across the border to shop here. Various gifts and souvenirs can be purchased at **Andersen & Nissen,** Storegade 26 ((*C* **74-72-13-42**).

Back in 1671, **Det Gamle Apotek** (The Old Pharmacy), Østerg 1 ((*C* **74-72-51-11**; www.det-gamle-apotek.dk), opened as a pharmacy. But today it's been converted into one of the best Danish handicrafts shops in the area, although the landmark antique structure was left as it used to be, just restored. Even the medicine jars and pharmaceutical equipment are intact, except instead of headache remedies and cures for the gout, you get Danish glassware, handmade ceramics, and various other quality crafts. **Din Grønne Skobutik,** Østergade 3 ((*C* **74-72-48-93**), features one of the best collections of women's shoes in town, everything from high heels to the kinds of boots a woman might want for treks through the marshes and forests of Denmark.

Gaveboden, Østergade 10–12 ((*C* **74-72-58-29**), sells sweaters—the kind of garments that ward off the fog and damp of a Danish winter yet still manage to make a wearer look appealing. Specialties of the store include alpaca, Angora, and woolen tops with unusual patterns, including plaids. There's even a scattering of garments by Finnish designer Marimekko.

WHERE TO STAY

Bowler Inn (**Kids**)   If you're a bowler, this is your number one place to stay in all of Denmark. Adjoining the hotel is a series of 10 state-of-the-art bowling alleys, even two other lanes set aside for young children, as they are equipped with "ball walls" to prevent the ball from going off the lane. Rental of a bowling alley for up to six players costs DKK100 to DKK145 ($17–$25/£10–£15), depending on the time of day. Even if you're not a bowler, consider staying here as the midsize bedrooms are tastefully furnished in Danish modern, each with a private bathroom with shower unit. Just north of the city center, the Bowler Inn also contains an English-inspired pub attracting bowlers (but of course) and a good family-style restaurant serving mostly Danish regional specialties.

Ribe Landevej 56, DK-6270 Tønder. (*C* **74-72-00-11**. Fax 74-72-65-11. www.hotelbowlerinn.dk. 10 units. DKK795 ($135/£80) double. Rates include breakfast. AE, DC, MC, V. **Amenities:** Restaurant; bar. *In room:* TV, Wi-Fi, minibar.

Hostrups Hotel ★   On the banks of the Vidæn River, this classically designed hotel dates from 1904, when it was erected on the southern tier of town. Today it projects an aura of calm, manicured charm, alluring to those who seek a bastion of tranquillity in the "capital of the marshlands." As befits a hotel of its era, bedrooms come in widely different sizes, shapes, and decor, but all of them are comfortable, and tastefully furnished. We've found the staff most helpful in guiding you for outings and excursions. An informal on-site restaurant and bar specializes in good-tasting Danish specialties with a scattering of continental dishes.

Søndergade 30, DK-6270 Tønder. © **74-72-21-29.** Fax 74-72-07-26. www.hostrupshotel.dk. 18 units. DKK490–DKK725 ($83–$123/£49–£73) double. Rates include breakfast. AE, DC, MC, V. **Amenities:** Restaurant; bar; Wi-Fi (in lobby). *In room:* TV, hair dryer.

Hotel Tønderhus ★★   This is Danish country living at its best, even superior to the also highly recommended Hostrups. A government-rated, four-star hotel, it is a family-run operation that we've always found most welcoming and inviting. The hotel was built in 1943, which is unusual in itself in that this was the time of the Nazi occupation—not a good time to be opening hotels in Denmark. In 1986, the owners extended the hotel with 21 rooms, and again in 1993 they added a dozen more units. In 2004 the hotel was so successful that they added another two dozen rooms. We still prefer the older and more spacious rooms in the main house, enjoying the bathrooms with the large tubs. However, the modern rooms are comfortable and tasteful as well, many with balconies. Tradition or Danish modern—the choice is yours.

A basement-level party room with a glass ceiling was originally a cistern. A glass-sided cafe serves tasty snacks and coffee, and the cozy restaurant is so good that we're recommending it separately even if you aren't staying here.

Jomfrustien 1, DK-6270 Tønder. © **74-72-22-22.** Fax 74-72-05-92. www.hoteltoenderhus.dk. 65 units. DKK995–DKK1,395 ($169–$237/£100–£140) double. AE, DC, MC, V. **Amenities:** Restaurant; lounge; room service; laundry service; dry cleaning. *In room:* TV, Wi-Fi, minibar, hair dryer, trouser press.

WHERE TO DINE

Hotel Tønderhus ★ DANISH   This is a model of successful innkeeping, in not only the previously recommended hotel, but also the restaurant, which uses the finest ingredients handled with a razor-sharp technique by the kitchen chefs. In an artfully old-fashioned setting, accessorized with rustic farm implements, you can order copious portions of such tried-and-true Danish specialties as cold potato soup with bacon and chives, fried fish cakes, a platter of assorted marinades of tangy herring, tender brisket of beef with horseradish, and a savory afterthought that might include fried Camembert with black currant jam. Between the lunch and dinner hour, the place remains open for coffee, tea, drinks, and a selection of such cold platters as marinated herring with various types of Danish cheeses.

Jomfrustien 1. © **74-72-22-22.** Main courses DKK199–DKK289 ($34–$49/£20–£29); fixed-price menus DKK279–DKK329 ($47–$56/£28–£33). AE, DC, MC, V. Daily noon–2pm and 6–9:30pm.

Torvets Restaurant ★ (Finds DANISH   The stately main floor of this former 1930s bank is divided into a formal, antiques-laden restaurant and a less elegant bistro where food is cheaper and culinary pretensions are a lot lower. In the bistro, you can order platters of *smørrebrød* (open-faced sandwich), pastas, pizzas, and cold assortments of Danish cheese, herring, and fresh vegetables. In the restaurant, expect more elaborate concoctions that change with the season. As a former dining companion told us, "I grew up on mother's fried plaice with hollandaise sauce and boiled potatoes, and I'm still ordering it today. Why not?" Why not indeed. If you want something more exciting, try the grilled trout with roasted fresh tomatoes, Danish shrimp, asparagus recently picked from the

fields, and button mushrooms. The chef "stuffs" a steak with roast onions, bacon, and
mushrooms—and it's quite a savory concoction. The staff also serves a roasted salmon
"spiced up" for more flavor.

Storegade 1. © **74-72-43-73.** www.tonder-net.dk/torvet. Reservations recommended in restaurant
only. Restaurant main courses DKK96–DKK268 ($16–$46/£9.60–£27); bistro platters DKK36–DKK114
($6.10–$19/£3.60–£11). AE, DC, MC, V. Daily noon–11pm.

TØNDER AFTER DARK

There isn't much activity here at night. Your best bet is **Hagge's Musik Pub,** Vestergade
80 (© **74-72-44-49;** www.hagges.dk), which lies opposite the post office. You can order
pub grub and both Irish and Danish beer on draft here. Although it's not a nightly event,
it's a frequent venue for live music, including blues, jazz, and Danish or Scottish folk.
Open Tuesday to Thursday 4 to 11pm; Friday 3 to 11pm; Saturday noon to 11pm.

A VISIT TO OLD-WORLD MØGELTØNDER

Even if you have to skip Tønder itself, head for the little village of **Møgeltønder** ★★,
only 4km (2¹⁄₂ miles) west of Tønder via Route 419. Bus no. 66 from Tønder runs here
about every hour during the day (trip time: 10 min.).

Once at Møgeltønder, you'll find a charming old-world village, which filmmakers have
called "a fairy-tale setting." Its long and narrow street, **Slotsgade** ★★, is lined with low
gabled houses, some with thatched roofs and most dating from the 1700s. The street is also
planted with a double row of lime trees, making it even more colorful and photogenic.

At the end of the street stands a small castle, **Schackenborg Slot,** which can be viewed
only from the outside, as it's owned by the Queen of Denmark and currently functions as
the principal residence of her younger son, Prince Joachim. After his marriage to Hong
Kong–born Alexandra, in 1995, the couple lived here until their divorce. Today, Prince
Joachim wanders the lonely castle alone, although many attractive young women write him
daily, volunteering to become his "new princess." The king presented Field Marshall Hans
Schack with the castle in 1661, in the wake of his victory over the Swedes during the battle
of Nyborg. Although security is tight and you can't visit the interior of the castle, you can
tour the moat-enclosed grounds that begin on the opposite side of the street. June, July, and
August, two 30-minute tours are conducted daily at 2 and 2:30pm. The price is DKK30
($5.10/£3) for adults, DKK25 ($4.30/£2.50) for children 5 to 15, for the carefully supervised trek. The rest of the year, visits to the gardens are not possible.

At the other end of the Slotsgade stands the 12th-century **Møgeltønder Kirke,** Slotsgade (© **74-73-89-40**), which contains frescoes—the oldest from 1275—under the chancel's arch. In the chancel itself are some mid-16th-century frescoes. The altarpiece is
probably early 16th century, and you can also see such treasures as a Romanesque font, a
late-17th-century baroque pulpit, and a church organ made in Hamburg in 1679. The
admission-free church is open daily from 8am to 4pm, closing at 3pm October to March.

Where to Stay

Schackenborg Slotskro ★★★ **(Finds)**   After checking in here, you can always tell the
folks back home that you were the guests of the Danish royal family. This venerable, thick-
walled 17th-century structure is set on the historic, picture-perfect main street of the
hamlet Møgeltønder. Owned, but not operated, by the queen's son, Prince Joachim, the
Royal-licensed coaching inn takes great pains to project an aura of aristocratic well-being
and glamour, despite occasional streamlined, modern touches in an otherwise old-world
setting. Princess Alexandra, now divorced from the prince, personally decorated each of the

bedrooms. Each room is named after one of the palaces or fortresses of Denmark and contains a condensed history of its namesake. Both the furnishings and the bathrooms are tidily kept. Expect a relatively luxurious Danish manor house at its most intimate. Even if you opt not to spend the night, consider a meal in the formal **dining room,** which, frankly, is a lot more appealing than the hotel (see "Where to Dine," below).

Slotsgaden 42, Møgeltønder, DK-6270 Tønder. © **74-73-83-83.** Fax 74-73-83-11. www.slotskro.com. 25 units. DKK1,225–DKK1,525 ($208–$259/£123–£153) double. Rates include buffet breakfast. AE, DC, MC, V. **Amenities:** Restaurant; bar; car rental; room service; laundry service; dry cleaning; nonsmoking rooms. In room: TV, hair dryer, safe.

Where to Dine

Schackenborg Slotskro ★★★ DANISH/INTERNATIONAL   The most stylish and prestigious restaurant in South Jutland lies on the street level of the inn owned by Prince Joachim. In an ocher-colored dining room that reeks of 18th-century elegance, you'll be seated at formally accessorized tables. The restaurant is famous for a distinctive specialty—salmon soufflé encased in a fish mousse. Yours will come with a number indicating where it falls on the historical tally (at this writing, the restaurant had served more than 72,000). Another specialty that we like equally is quail in Madeira sauce, along with various versions of market-fresh seafood and fish. The chefs cook with a flawless technique, using local ingredients and seasonal produce. For us, dining here is about not just the cuisine, but the "regal experience." Expect a leisurely, rather elegant reflection of the image that's preferred by Denmark's royal family, and a bit of social posturing on the part of the other guests.

Slotsgaden 42, Møgeltønder. © **74-73-83-83.** Reservations recommended. Main courses DKK168–DKK248 ($29–$42/£17–£25); fixed-price menus DKK328–DKK798 ($56–$136/£33–£80). AE, DC, MC, V. Daily noon–2pm and 6–8:30pm. Closed Dec 1–28.

A TRIP TO LØGUM KLOSTER & MEMORIES OF A MONASTERY

In sad decline today, our final excursion is through a marshy plain to an abbey that knew its greatest days in the Middle Ages. Journey to the hamlet of Løgum, 18km (11 miles) north of Tønder. (From Tønder, follow the road signs to Ribe, then to Kolding and, a bit later, to Løgum Kloster.) **Løgum Kloster (Løgum Abbey),** Klostervej (© **74-74-41-65**), once competed with Tønder as a lacemaking center. Built in what was then an uninhabited area, the abbey—today an ecclesiastical administrative center—was founded in 1173. Once impressive in size, the abbey today has been reduced to its east wing, with the sacristy, library, chapter house, and church remaining. Constructed from red brick, the abbey church grew and changed over a period of years from 1230 to 1330. It was built when Europe was changing from the Romanesque to the Gothic style, so the abbey reflects both periods of architecture. In the nave are traces of frescoes, and other treasures include a winged altar and elegantly carved choir stalls from the early 16th century, and a reliquary with wings and a Gothic triumphal cross (ca. 1300). Opposite the main building stands a 24m (79-ft.) tower with a carillon named in honor of King Frederik IX. It strikes a concert every Wednesday at 8pm (only June–Aug).

Between May and October, the admission-free abbey church can be visited Monday to Saturday 10am to 6:30pm; Sunday noon to 5pm. The rest of the year it's open Monday to Saturday from 10am to 4pm and Sunday noon to 4pm.

288km (179 miles) SW of Copenhagen; 15km (10 miles) W of Skærbæk; 5km (3 miles) N of Sylt

We've never recovered from our first visit here, when we saw three Anita Ekberg–style blondes chasing a Danish man into the sand dunes. Germans, some sans clothing, flock to this North Frisian island for nude sunbathing like that practiced on their own island of Sylt to the immediate south.

In summer, it's a wild romp, straight, gay, or whatever, but it settles down for a long winter nap when the cold winds blow in from North Sea. Rømø is the largest Danish island in the North Sea, which borders its western shore. The east coast faces the Danish mainland and is bounded by tidal shallows, and the northwest corner of the island is a restricted military zone. In all, Rømø is 9km (5²/₃ miles) long and 6.5km (4 miles) wide.

Wild and almost constantly windswept, Rømø is separated from Germany by the Lister Dyb (Lister Deep) body of water. Midway between Ribe and Tønder, Rømø is connected to the mainland by a 10km (6¹/₄-mile) causeway that passes over a panoramic marshland filled with wading seabirds and grazing sheep in summer. Exposed to the North Sea, the western edge of the island is the site of the best sandy beaches and is a magnet for windsurfers. The most popular beach area is at Lakolk on the central western coastal strip. Here the beach is under a kilometer (¹/₂ mile) wide. The main hamlets are on the eastern coast along a 6km (3³/₄-mile) stretch from the causeway south to the little port of Havneby.

ESSENTIALS

GETTING THERE   **By Train**   Skærbæk is linked by rail to the towns of Tønder, Ribe, and Esbjerg.

By Bus   You can take a bus south from Ribe to Skærbæk and then bus no. 29 across the tidal flats to Rømø.

By Car   Take the 10km (6¹/₄-mile) stone causeway from mainland Jutland, a half-hour's drive on Route 175 from either Tønder or Ribe (there are no tolls en route).

By Ferry   If you'd like to continue your trip to Sylt from Rømø, a car ferry departs six times daily from the Danish fishing village of Havneby to the far northern German town of List (trip time: 1 hr.). For schedules and more information, call **Rømø/Sylt Linie** (© **74-75-53-03**). The price for a car (up to five passengers) is DKK320 to DKK400 ($54–$68/£32–£40), depending on the size of the car.

VISITOR INFORMATION   **Rømø Turistbureau,** Havnebyvej 30 (© **74-75-51-30;** www.romo.dk), is open June to August daily 9am to 6pm. It's closed every Sunday off season November to April.

ⓜ**Moments**   **Wildlife on Rømø**

Many visitors come to Rømø to seek out its plentiful bird life on the west coast, which is also home to some 1,500 seals. You can see them sunbathing during the day.

GETTING AROUND **By Bicycle** The best way to get around Rømø is by bike. Rentals, costing from DKK50 ($8.50/£5) a day, are available at **Garni,** Nørre Frankel at Havneby (© **74-75-54-80**).

SEEING THE SIGHTS

The island of Rømø has one of the widest **beaches** in Denmark flying the blue flag (indicating nonpolluted waters). The nude beach, frequented by Germans, is at Sønderstrand on the southwestern tip of the island. Windsurfing is popular here, mainly on the west coast, the best area being at the southern side of Lakolf. *Note:* Windsurfers must bring their own equipment to Rømø, as there is no outlet locally to rent equipment.

Other than the beaches and windsurfing, the most popular outdoor pursuit is horseback riding, available at **Rømø Ranch,** Lakolk Strand (© **74-75-54-11**), a stable right on Lakolk Beach. It offers rides to experienced as well as novice riders, and most jaunts take place right on the beach, for DKK105 ($18/£11) per hour.

At the rear of the tourist office (see "Visitor Information," above), you'll find the **Naturcentret Tønnisgård,** Havnebyvej 30 (© **74-75-52-57**; www.tonnisgaard.dk), in an old thatched farmhouse from the island of Rømø. It contains modest displays of the island flora and fauna, and there is also a cafeteria serving drinks and Danish pastries. Tønnisgård is open Monday to Friday 10am to 4pm except November to January. Admission is DKK15 ($2.60/£1.50) adults and DKK5 (85¢/50p) children 14 and under. The center also conducts 90-minute nature tours of the local wetlands June to September. Four or five of these depart every day during that period, depending on demand, for DKK50 ($8.50/£5) adults, DKK25 ($4.30/£2.50) children 13 and under. Phone ahead for schedules and departure times.

Other attractions include **Kommandørgården** (The National Museum's Commander House), Guvrevej 60, in the hamlet of Toftum (© **74-75-52-76**). The house dates from 1748 and is evocative of the great prosperity enjoyed by ship commanders in the sailing heyday of Rømø in the 18th century. The house is fully restored, including its panels, ceilings, and doors. The walls are covered with Dutch tiles and the furnishings are lavish. About 50 sailors from Rømø served simultaneously as captains on Dutch and German ships that sailed on whaling expeditions to Greenland. May to September the house is open Tuesday to Sunday 10am to 5pm. In October it's open Tuesday to Sunday 10am to 3pm and closed off-season. Admission costs DKK15 ($2.60/£1.50) adults, DKK10 ($1.70/£1) seniors and students, free for children 15 and under.

In the village of **Jurve,** there is a fence of whale jawbone made in 1772, which has been preserved and is now under the protection of the National Museum in Copenhagen. As no wood or stone was available on the island at the time, the locals made use of this unusual building material, a remnant of the whaling ships' catches in Greenland.

Rømø Kirke at Kirkeby also merits a visit. The church was originally built in the late Gothic style, but was greatly extended in the 17th and 18th centuries. It is consecrated to St. Clemens, the patron saint of seafarers, and contains a number of ship models, as well as three large chandeliers, all donated by sailors. Admission is free, and it is open year-round Tuesday to Friday 8am to 4pm.

SHOPPING

At the center of the island in Kongsmark, Rømø's major gallery is known by its English name **Art House,** Gamle Skolevej, 8A (© **74-75-61-36**). Here you can experience and purchase Danish and European handicraft products. April to October, a new exhibition of glass and pottery by leading Danish and international artisans is presented every month. If

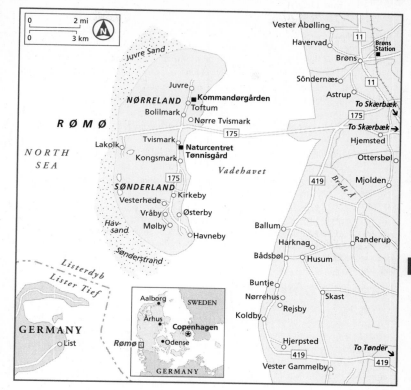

weather allows, you can enjoy freshly brewed coffee and other refreshments in a beautiful garden surrounding the Art House. The only way to stop in is by appointment.

WHERE TO STAY

Danland RIM & Feriecenter   If you want to spend a few days devoted to a beach holiday on Rømø, this is the best choice without breaking the bank. Germans fleeing here from the North Sea's highest-priced island of Sylt claim that the tariffs charged here were prevalent in Germany 20 years ago. This is the largest and most visible hotel on Rømø, with a northern European clientele (Danish, Dutch, and German) that tends to stay for several days or more. The setting is a compound of gabled brown-brick houses. Inside, you'll find angular modern furnishings, lots of exposed wood, neatly kept bathrooms, and an overall unfrilly, anonymous setting. Don't expect verdant gardens or forests, as the venue is based on the fragile ecology of tenacious sea grasses that grow under streaming sunlight and almost constant ocean winds. There's easy access to the largest beach in northern Europe, a windswept stretch of sand almost 3km (1³/₄ miles) wide by 7km (4¹/₃ miles) long. Unlike many other apartment-style beachfront hotels in Denmark, this one remains open year-round.

Vestergade 159, DK-6792 Rømø. © **74-75-57-75.** Fax 74-75-57-36. www.feriecenter-rim.dk. 207 units. DKK350–DKK1,300 ($60–$221/£35–£130) house for 1–6 occupants. AE, DC, MC, V. **Amenities:** Nonsmoking rooms; solarium. *In room:* TV, kitchenette.

Kommandørgården ★ (Kids) Far superior to Feriecenter, this is the island's best holiday resort, offering you a choice of living styles—hotel rooms, a fully equipped apartment, or an Abe Lincoln log cabin. The hotel rooms are rather standard—nothing special here, but the apartments are generous in size, with beds for two to four guests, including bunk beds for families traveling with kids. Added features include a private terrace or balcony with garden furniture and a large shared barbecue by the pool. Log cabins house two adults and two children, with a terrace filled with garden furniture and a barbecue, each coming with a kitchenette. In some cases, a bathroom is shared by other guests at the campsite. Other better-equipped cabins contain their own bathroom. Of all the hotels of Rømø, this one offers the most activities, including beach sailing, trips by horse carriage, and rides on Icelandic horses. A special feature is a small Tepidarium, which is said to "rid your body of toxins." On-site dining is possible, though many families prefer to cook their own meals in their apartment rentals.

Havnebyvej 201, Mølby DK-6792. © **74-75-51-22.** Fax 74-75-59-22. www.kommandoergaarden.dk. 83 units. DKK825–DKK1,095 ($140–$186/£83–£110) double; DKK850–DKK1,200 ($145–$204/£85–£120) apt; log cabins DKK845–DKK1,195 ($144–$203/£85–£120). MC, V. Free parking. **Amenities:** 3 restaurants; bar; cafe; 2 pools (indoor and outdoor); 2 volleyball courts; 2 playgrounds; laundry service; nonsmoking rooms; rooms for those w/limited mobility. *In room:* TV, Wi-Fi, kitchenette (in apts and cabins), beverage maker, hair dryer.

WHERE TO DINE

Otto & Ani's Fisk SEAFOOD You'll find this place either authentic and appealingly raffish, or hopelessly informal, depending on your temperament. Expect a self-service format in a brown-brick building that's among the least stately looking in Rømø. English-speaking proprietor Susan Jensen will help you select from a Danish-language menu that lists various platters of fish, most of which compose a filling meal in their own right. Some taste treats include everything from a fresh filet of cod served sandwich-style, with fresh home-baked bread, butter, and a handful of freshly peeled shrimp, to a dinner-sized filet of sole with baked potato, mixed salad, and—again—a handful of shrimp. Beer or wine might accompany your meal, which you'll consume either at picnic tables set up outside or in a severe all-white room. Despite its shortcomings, the place has thrived for more than a dozen years because of its low prices and fresh fish.

Havnepladsen, Havneby. © **74-75-53-06.** Main courses DKK65–DKK155 ($11–$26/£6.50–£16). No credit cards. Apr–Oct daily 11am–9pm.

RØMØ AFTER DARK

There are very few options for nightlife on this island that is notoriously sleepy, even by the Danish island standards. Our best suggestion is to have a drink and do some dancing at **Make Up Diskotek,** Lakolk Butikstorv (© **74-75-59-23**), open summer only Thursday to Saturday 10pm to 4am and Sunday to Wednesday 10:30pm to 2am. Cover is DKK65 ($11/£6.50).

150km (93 miles) SW of Århus; 298km (185 miles) W of Copenhagen; 47km (29 miles) N of Tønder

This is one of Denmark's oldest towns, and if you have to miss all the other cities of Jutland, spend a night here, where local residents ponder the question, "Will the storks return on April 1?" Every year some storks—now an endangered species—fly to Ribe to build their huge nests on top of the red-roofed, medieval, half-timbered, and crooked houses of Ribe which flank the narrow cobblestone lanes.

One of New York's most legendary citizens, Jacob A. Riis, was born in Ribe. When "the town's prettiest girl" broke his heart, he headed for New York in 1870. Once here, he was shocked by the city's inhumane slums, which he wrote about in his first book in 1890, *How the Other Half Lives*. A friend of Theodore Roosevelt, Riis was offered the job of mayor of the city but turned it down to pursue his efforts to get a million people off the streets and into decent housing. For such work, he became known as "the most beneficial citizen of New York." In time, he returned to Ribe, where "the prettiest girl" said yes this time. His former residence lies at the corner of Skolegade and Grydergade, a plaque marking his former abode.

As a former port, Ribe was an important trading center during the Viking era (around A.D. 900) and became an Episcopal see in 948, when one of the first Christian churches in Denmark was established here. It was also the royal residence of the ruling Valdemars around 1200.

In medieval days, sea trade routes to England, Germany, Friesland, the Mediterranean, and other ports linked Ribe, but then its waters receded. Today it's surrounded by marshes, much like a landlocked Moby Dick. On a charming note, the town watchman still makes his rounds—armed with his lantern and trusty staff—since the ancient custom was revived in 1936.

ESSENTIALS

GETTING THERE   By Train   There's hourly train service from Copenhagen (via Bramming). The schedule is available at the tourist office.

By Car   From Kolding (see earlier in this chapter), head west across Jutland on the E20 motorway, but cut southwest when you reach Route 32, which will carry you into Ribe.

VISITOR INFORMATION   The **Ribe Turistbureau**, Torvet 3 (🕐 **75-42-15-00;** www. ribetourist.dk), is open June 15 to August, Monday to Friday 9am to 5:30pm, and Saturday 10am to 2pm; April to June 14 and September to October, Monday to Friday 9am to 5pm and Saturday 10am to 1pm; and November to March, Monday to Friday 10am to 4:30pm and Saturday 10am to 1pm.

GETTING AROUND   By Bicycle   If you'd like to bike your way around the area, you can rent bikes for DKK65 ($11/£6.50) at **Ribe Vandrerhjem** (Youth Hostel), Skt. Pedersgade 16 (🕐 **75-42-06-20**).

SEEING THE SIGHTS

Gamle Stan ★★★   The historic core of Ribe is the gem of all Old Towns on the peninsula of Jutland. Beginning at the **Torvet ★★★** or old market square, you can fan out in all directions, covering most of the major streets or lanes of interest within 2 hours, maybe more if you have the time. The well-preserved Ribe of the Middle Ages surrounds the cathedral, the Ribe Domkirke (see below).

Instead of wandering at random, you can visit the tourist office, which sells a copy of a guided walking tour of Ribe for DKK10 ($1.70/£1). Our favorite hotel (Dagmar) and our favorite Ribe restaurant (Weis Stue) open onto the main square.

From Torvet many streets radiate out—take **Skolegade,** for example, opening onto the west side of the Domkirke. Riis spent his final decade on the street at **Hans Tausen's House,** which dates from the early 17th century. A plaque marks the spot.

To the east of Torvet lies **Skt. Catharine Kirke** (p. 324), the only remaining church built before the Reformation.

Arm yourself with a tourist-office map and discover other streets that evoke the Middle Ages, of which **Fiskergade** is one of the most evocative, with its offshoot alleys that lead to the riverfront. Talk about narrow alleys.

Det Gamle Rådhus (Town Hall Museum)   Perhaps the most exciting thing to look at in Denmark's oldest existing town hall are storks building a nest on top. You'll be lucky if you chance upon this. Originally built in 1496, the Town Hall Museum today houses some rather unimpressive artifacts and archives from Ribe's illustrious past. These include a gruesome 16th-century executioner's axe, ceremonial swords, the town's money chest, antique tradesmen's signs, and a depiction of the "iron hand," still a symbol of police authority.

Von Støckends Plads. (℃) **76-88-11-12.** Admission DKK60 ($10/£6) adults, free for children 17 and under. June–Aug daily 1–3pm; May and Sept Mon–Fri 1–3pm. Closed Oct–Apr.

Ribe Domkirke ★★   Denmark's earliest wooden church, built around A.D. 860, once stood on this spot. In 1150 it was rebuilt in the Romanesque style, opening onto the main square of town, but over the years has been remodeled and altered considerably. The **south portal** ★ remains a rare example of Danish Romanesque sculpture, and is known for its carved tympanum depicting the *Descent of Christ from the Cross.* Most of the *kirke* was built of a soft porous rock (tufa) found near the German city of Cologne and shipped north along the Rhine River. Before the Dom was completed, 100 years would go by. Several Gothic features such as arches were later added, but the overall look is still a Rhineland Romanesque. The wide nave is flanked by aisles on both sides, and the church is surmounted by a dome. The interior holds treasures from many eras, including mosaics, stained glass, and frescoes in the eastern apse by the artist Carl-Henning Pedersen, who created them in the 1980s. Older treasures include an organ designed by Jens Olufsen in the 1600s, plus an elaborate altar from 1597 by the renowned sculptor Kens Jens Asmussen.

The Devil, or so it is said, used to enter the Domkirke through the **"Cat's Head Door"** ★★, once the principal entryway into the church. The location is found at the south portal of the transept. The triangular pediment depicts Valdemar II and his queen, Dagmar, positioned at the feet of Mary and her infant son. Talk about tradition: Daily at noon and 3pm the cathedral bell still tolls in mourning of Dagmar's death during childbirth.

For the most **panoramic view** ★★ of Ribe and the surrounding marshes, climb the 248 steps to the cathedral tower left over from 1333. A watchman once stood here on the lookout for floods, which frequently inundated Ribe.

Torvet (town center) off Sønderportsgade. (℃) **75-42-06-19.** www.ribe-domkirke.dk. Admission DKK10 ($1.70/£1) adults, DKK5 (85¢/50p) children 3–14. June–Aug daily 10am–5pm; May and Sept daily 10am–5pm; Oct–Apr Mon–Sat 11am–3pm, Sun 1–3pm.

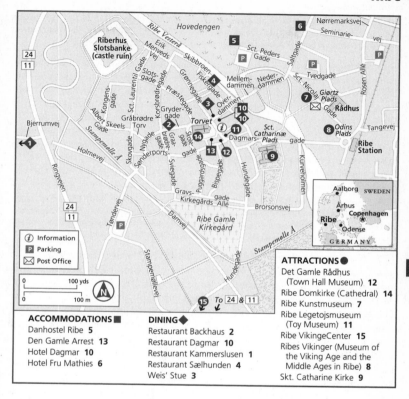

ATTRACTIONS ●
Det Gamle Rådhus
(Town Hall Museum) **12**
Ribe Domkirke (Cathedral) **14**
Ribe Kunstmuseum **7**
Ribe Legetøjsmuseum
(Toy Museum) **11**
Ribe VikingeCenter **15**
Ribes Vikinger (Museum of
the Viking Age and the
Middle Ages in Ribe) **8**
Skt. Catharine Kirke **9**

ACCOMMODATIONS ■
Danhostel Ribe **5**
Den Gamle Arrest **13**
Hotel Dagmar **10**
Hotel Fru Mathies **6**

DINING ◆
Restaurant Backhaus **2**
Restaurant Dagmar **10**
Restaurant Kammerslusen **1**
Restaurant Sælhunden **4**
Weis' Stue **3**

Ribe Kunstmuseet (Ribe Art Museum)   Of minor interest, this museum with its more than 600 paintings and sculpture is dedicated to art from various epochs in Danish history, from around 1750 to 1940, which marked the beginning of the Nazi occupation. There are masterpieces from artists from all the major eras in Danish painting—the Golden Age, the Realistic Period, the Skagen and Funen artists, Modernism, and the period "between the wars." The Golden Age is best evoked by P. C. Skovgaard's *Møns Cliff* (1852), the Skagen painters by Michael Archer's *Baptism of the Painter's Daughter* (1888). The museum is housed in a stately villa in a garden on the Ribe River, the former residence of a factory owner built from 1860 to 1864 based on drawings made by the royal surveyor L. A. Winstrup.

Skt. Nicolai Gade 10. (✆ **75-42-03-62.** Admission DKK40 ($6.80/£4) adults, free for children 17 and under. July–Aug daily 11am–5pm; Sept–Dec and Feb 12–June Tues–Sun 11am–4pm. Closed Jan–Feb 11.

Ribe Legetøjsmuseum (Toy Museum) ★   The only problem with taking your children to this museum is in convincing them that none of the several thousands of toys made from 1850 to 1980 is for sale. Spread across two floors—there are more than 500 dolls alone—the collection ranges from toy cars to the first horseless carriages to today's model cars. There are also wooden toys, old games, robots, antique teddy bears, and much more.

Von Støckens Plads 2. ✆ **75-41-14-40.** Admission DKK35 ($6/£3.50) adults, DKK15 ($2.60/£1.50) children 3–12, free for children 2 and under; family ticket DKK100 ($17/£10). Jan–Mar and Nov–Dec Mon–Sat 1–4pm; Apr–May and Sept–Oct daily 1–5pm; June–Aug daily 10am–noon and 1–5pm.

Ribe VikingeCenter ★   You don't see too many Vikings running around Ribe anymore except at this center, 2km (1³/₄ miles) south of the center. Just follow your nose: The smell of baking bread will lure you here. The bread is baked over open fires by women dressed in early medieval costumes. Such crafts as pottery making and leather work are demonstrated, but it's the falconry demonstrations that lure the visitors. The aim of the center is to reenact Ribe's Viking age, and locals do so by reconstructing buildings, costumes, utensils, tools, and equipment—even the food. Horses, cows, sheep, hens, and geese run about as in olden days. The centerpiece of the re-created town is a "great house" revealing an early Danish manor reserved for the town's most powerful baron. Other buildings from around 1050 can also be entered.

Lustrupvej 4. ✆ **75-41-16-11.** www.ribevikingecenter.dk. Admission DKK75 ($13/£7.50) adults, DKK35 ($6/£3.50) children 3–14, free for children 2 and under. May–June and Sept Mon–Fri 10am–3:30pm; July–Aug daily 11am–5pm. Guided tours in English are offered May–June and Sept daily at 10:10am; July–Aug daily at 11:10am. Tours cost DKK200 ($34/£20) for 30 min. or DKK375 ($64/£38) for 1 hr.

Ribe Vikinger (Museum of the Viking Age and the Middle Ages in Ribe)   This museum showcases Ribe in both its Viking era and its medieval epoch. Beginning in the year 700, when a marketplace was established on the banks of the Ribe River, thousands of archaeological finds have been dug up to reveal how the Vikings lived and traded with Europe to the south. Pottery and even skeletons are exhibited from the Middle Ages when Ribe was one of Denmark's major commercial towns. Justice was harsh in those times, as you can see from the re-created Debtors' Prison, with its spiked maces, thumbscrews, and executioner's swords. Most bizarre of all is a multimedia room, Wodan's Eye, where you can explore the Viking age via computer, lights, and sound. A Viking marketplace from around 800 is re-created, as well as a church from around 1500.

Odins Plads. ✆ **76-88-11-22.** www.ribesvikinger.dk. Admission DKK60 ($10/£6) adults, free for children 17 and under. Apr–June and Sept–Oct daily 10am–4pm; July–Aug Thurs–Tues 10am–6pm, Wed 10am–9pm; Nov–Mar Tues–Sun 10am–4pm.

Skt. Catharine Kirke ★   The Spanish Black Friars (Dominicans) came to Ribe in 1228 and began constructing a church and chapter house (the east wing of a monastery). Parts of the original edifice can still be seen, especially the southern wall. The present church, near Dagmarsgade, with nave and aisles, dates from 1400 to 1450, the tower from 1617. Only the monks' stalls and the Romanesque font remain from the Middle Ages, with the delicately carved pulpit dating from 1591, the ornate altarpiece from 1650. The brothers were kicked out in 1536, at the time of the Reformation, and in time the complex became both an asylum for the mentally ill and, later, a wartime field hospital. You can walk through the cloisters and see ship models and religious paintings hanging in the southern aisle. Tombstones of Ribe citizens from the Reformation and later can be seen along the outer walls of the church.

Skt. Catharine's Plads. ✆ **75-42-05-34.** Free admission to church; cloisters DKK5 (85¢/50p) adults, DKK1 (15¢/10p) children 13 and under. May–Sept daily 10am–noon and 2–5pm; Oct–Apr daily 10am–noon and 2–4pm. Closed during church services.

You can evoke yesteryear by riding a horse-drawn **carriage** through the cobblestone streets of Ribe. In summer, you can hire a carriage in Torvet, the central market square. The cost is DKK65 ($11/£6.50) per person for a ride of about 15 minutes, with carriages holding up to five passengers each. For more information, call ℂ **75-42-19-94.**

Anglers and fishermen head for **Storkesøen,** an interconnected trio of artificial lakes that are kept well-stocked with fish, especially trout. Known for their appeal to escapists and for their verdant beauty, they lie less than 1.5km (³/₄ mile) south of Ribe. A permit allowing 4 consecutive hours of fishing costs DKK105 ($18/£11); 6 hours cost DKK145 ($25/£15); 9 hours go for DKK205 ($35/£21); and a permit good for 20 hours of fishing is priced at DKK470 ($80/£47). For more information, contact Storkesøen, Haulundvej 164 (ℂ **75-41-04-11**).

SHOPPING

Ribe has some of the best shopping in Jutland. The best selection of antiques is at **Antik Gaarden,** Overdammen 5 (ℂ **75-44-19-47**). The best clothing store is **Mr. Lundgaard,** Saltgade 3 (ℂ **75-42-42-40**), which has the town's largest selection, everything from high-quality clothes to Marlboro classics, catering to both women and men. A wide range of footwear for adults and children is available at **Sara Sko,** Skoringen Ribe, Tømmergangen 3 (ℂ **75-42-11-24**). At **Ribe's Broderi & Garn,** Dagmarsgade 4 (ℂ **75-42-16-75**), you'll find the finest selection of needlework—some of the pieces are exquisite—and woolen items. **Bentzons Boghandel,** Mellemdammen 16 (ℂ **75-43-57-51**), is the best bookstore, with many English-language titles. **Alisson-Dansk Naturkosmetik,** Nederdammen 32 (ℂ **75-41-09-01**), is an intriguing store with a varied selection of products from a well-known Danish company, Alisson of Denmark, which makes skin-care and cosmetic products.

If your tastes run to handicrafts, gifts, and souvenirs, you'll find that Ribe is loaded with boutiques. The most amusing outlet is **Ryk Ind,** Sønderportsgade 7 (ℂ **75-42-29-69**), which is stuffed with gifts—everything from classic model cars to china dolls. A large assortment of artwork, porcelain, glass, paper collages, and mobiles, plus other decorative items for the home, is sold at **Overdammens Idebutik,** Overdammen 5 (ℂ **75-42-14-14**). For generations, Ribe citizens have patronized **Børge Bottelet Guldsmedie,** Mellemdammen 14 (ℂ **75-42-02-26**), for exquisite jewelry.

WHERE TO STAY

Weis Stue and Restaurant Backhaus (see "Where to Dine," below) also rent rooms. Parking at the following hotels is available on the street.

Danhostel Ribe ⓥⁿ𝐥ᵘᵉ   In the heart of Ribe, this brick-built hostel is one of the finest in Jutland, attracting families, backpackers, and groups. A total of 40 rooms are spread out over three floors, each with a private bathroom with shower. Most of these open onto views of the medieval town and the distant marshland. The standard bedrooms can be rented as family rooms for up to five guests. Otherwise, single guests can rent a bed in a room shared by others. All the bedrooms have allergy-free pillows and comforters, and there is bed linen for rent.

Ribehallen, Skt. Peders Gade 16, DK-6760 Ribe. ℂ **75-42-06-20.** www.danhostel-ribe.dk. 40 rooms w/ private bathroom, 152 beds. DKK300–DKK600 ($51–$102/£30–£60) per person. No credit cards. **Amenities:** Cafeteria; nonsmoking rooms; guest kitchen. *In room:* No phone.

Den Gamle Arrest ★★ (Finds)   Among hotels, this is the most amazing job of recycling on the peninsula of Jutland. The town jail from 1546 to 1989 has been turned into a hotel of charm albeit with some cramped "jail cells." Right on the main square of town, it was constructed from the same russet-colored bricks as the town's more prestigious addresses. On the top floor the rooms are . . . well, "cozy," with sloping attic walls. There are also various prison cells on the second floor, but how did a bridal suite with a four-poster manage to appear on the ground floor? The prison garden courtyard has been transformed into a sensuous garden with fragrant roses, trickling fountains, and stone sculptures. The brick walls bear the prisoners' inscriptions, including their names, addresses, the date and year, even the length of their sentences, and, of course, their longing for wine, women, and song.

Torvet 11, DK-6760 Ribe. ℂ 75-42-37-00. Fax 75-42-37-22. www.dengamlearrest.dk. 12 units, 2 w/private bathroom. DKK590–DKK640 ($100–$109/£59–£64) double w/shared bathroom; DKK790–DKK990 ($134–$168/£79–£99) double w/private bathroom. Rates include breakfast. No credit cards. **Amenities:** Restaurant; bar. *In room:* TV (in some), no phone.

Hotel Dagmar ★★★   The most famous hotel in Denmark outside Copenhagen is also the oldest in the country, dating from 1581. Converted from a private home in 1850, it's also the most glamorous hotel in South Jutland, taking its name from the medieval Danish queen. The bedrooms have been carefully restored, respecting the hotel's age while adding modern conveniences. Most of the units, as befits a building of this vintage, have low ceilings, sloping floors, and windows with deep sills. Textiles are in autumnal colors, and the walls are decorated with original paintings. Each bedroom is also individually decorated and comes in various shapes and sizes. Dagmar also offers the best food in Ribe; see "Where to Dine," below.

Torvet 1, DK-6760 Ribe. ℂ 75-42-00-33. Fax 75-42-36-52. www.hoteldagmar.dk. 50 units. DKK1,195–DKK1,595 ($203–$271/£120–£160) double. Rates include breakfast. AE, DC, MC, V. **Amenities:** 3 restaurants; bar; room service; laundry service; dry cleaning; nonsmoking rooms. *In room:* TV, Wi-Fi, minibar, hair dryer, safe.

Hotel Fru Mathies (Value)   For those who like to travel the B&B route, this is one of the best choices in town—and extremely affordable. Set behind a bright yellow stucco facade, a very short walk from the city's pedestrian zone, this hotel was named after its present guardian and supervisor, *Fru* Inga Mathies. There's a shared TV/living room on the premises, and the small bedrooms are simple but cozy affairs with a modest number of old-fashioned accessories. Breakfast is the only meal served, and it's generous and satisfying, fit fortification for a morning of wandering the streets of Ribe.

Saltgade 15, DK-67660 Ribe. ℂ 75-42-34-20. Fax 75-41-02-44. 6 units, 4 w/private bathroom. DKK650 ($111/£65) double w/shared bathroom; DKK700 ($119/£70) double w/private bathroom. Rates include breakfast. AE, DC, MC, V. **Amenities:** Breakfast room; bar; lounge. *In room:* TV, minibar, no phone.

WHERE TO DINE

Restaurant Backhaus DANISH   This place has served as a restaurant or an inn for as long as anyone in Ribe can remember. Today, steaming platters of all-Danish food arrive in generous portions at reasonable prices. Menu specialties include a Danish platter containing artfully arranged presentations of herring, cheeses, and vegetables that taste wonderful with the establishment's earthy, rough-textured bread. Tomato soup with sour cream comes with a surprising but refreshing dab of horseradish. The chef tells us that the most frequently ordered dish is tender pork schnitzels with boiled potatoes and braised red cabbage, a favorite of German visitors. However, we found that the sautéed

strips of beef tenderloin with fried onions hit the spot better on one cold, windy, rainy
day. Dessert might be a hazelnut pie with vanilla ice cream.

On the premises are seven simple rooms, stripped-down but comfortable hideaways that
are well maintained. With breakfast included, doubles cost DKK550 ($94/£55). With the
exception of about a week every year at Christmas, the hotel is open year-round.

Grydergade 12. © **75-42-11-01.** Reservations recommended. Main courses DKK102–DKK182 ($17–
$31/£10–£18). MC, V. Daily 11am–9:30pm. Closed 1 week around Christmas.

Restaurant Dagmar ★★ DANISH/INTERNATIONAL Honoring a beloved
medieval queen, this restaurant opposite the cathedral is a major stopover for those making the gastronomic tour of Denmark. Its four dining rooms are a 19th-century dream
of ornate furnishings and objets d'art, a tribute to the heyday of the Belle Epoque. In
such fancy surroundings, they could get away with ordinary food, but the chefs showcase
a varied cuisine that is refreshingly authentic in that it's based on the best of market-fresh
ingredients in any season. Care, craftsmanship, and a concern for your palate go into
every dish served by the best staff in town.

We opt for one of the two fresh North Sea fish dishes of the day as they are just caught
and prepared with flavor without spoiling their natural taste. The scallops are topped
with a sweet-potato crisp, and in autumn we go for the sautéed stuffed quail with mushrooms accompanied by beurre blanc sauce. We feel the chefs shine brighter with their
regional cuisine, but they also borrow freely from international larders, serving a tender
veal tenderloin with one of the tastiest shallow mousses we've ever sampled—plus a
delectable port-wine sauce as well.

In the Hotel Dagmar. © **75-42-00-33.** Reservations required. Main courses DKK165–DKK265 ($28–
$45/£17–£27); fixed-price lunch DKK165–DKK245 ($28–$42/£17–£25); fixed-price dinners DKK425
($72/£43) for 3 courses, DKK585 ($99/£59) for 6 courses. AE, DC, MC, V. Daily noon–10pm.

Restaurant Kammerslusen ★ (Finds) DANISH Quite by accident we discovered
this place while driving through the marshlands, and we've been loyal customers ever
since. This restaurant lies between the seacoast and the canal that connects Ribe to the
sea; to reach it, drive 15km (9¹⁄₃ miles) east of Ribe, across flat and sandy terrain, until
you reach this redbrick, old-fashioned-looking hideaway. There's no public transport to
this place. The cooking is always reliable and tasty, and it's easy to understand why this
place has blossomed into a local favorite. Menu items derive from long-standing regional
traditions, and include fried filets of eel with white sauce and new potatoes, poached red
salmon with au gratin potatoes, and a popular house specialty of grilled steak with barbecue sauce and fried onions. There's nothing too fancy here, nothing you've not had
before, but we like the congenial premises, the old-fashioned flavors, and the sense of a
nostalgic charm that hangs over the place.

Bjerrumvej 30. © **75-42-07-96.** Fax 75-42-29-32. www.kammerslusen.dk. Reservations recommended.
Main courses DKK145–DKK290 ($25–$49/£15–£29); fixed-price menu DKK235 ($40/£24). DC, MC, V. Daily
11am–9pm.

Restaurant Sælhunden ★ DANISH/INTERNATIONAL One of the most
evocative and cheerful restaurants in Ribe occupies a venerable but cozy brick building
whose history goes back to 1634. Set beside the river that flows through Ribe, within full
view of the craft that kept its commerce alive during its mercantile heyday, it has flourished as a restaurant since 1969. Today, you're likely to find an engaging staff hailing from
every corner of Europe, and an old-fashioned format whose size is doubled during mild
weather thanks to an outdoor terrace. The cuisine is based on fresh ingredients and, for

the most part, sticks to tried-and-true favorites so beloved by the Danish palate, including smoked salmon or platters of ping-pong-size meatballs. The dish that most locals seem to order is the fried filets of plaice with boiled potatoes, a dish that—no doubt—their mamas made for them. Other items include at least three kinds of steaks that feature T-bone, French-style entrecôte, and something known as "English steak." A local delicacy is smoked and fried dab, a flat fish not unlike flounder that flourishes in the local estuaries. No one will mind if you come here just for a beer or a simple snack. In summertime, it's one of the closest approximations in town to the kind of beer garden you might expect to find in Hamburg.

Skibbroen 13. © **75-42-09-46.** Reservations recommended. Main courses DKK135–DKK229 ($23–$39/ £14–£23). MC, V. Daily 11am–10pm. Beer served till 11pm.

Weis Stue ★ DANISH   For old-fashioned dining in a mellow atmosphere of long ago, there is no better place in Ribe than this small, charming, brick-and-timber inn sitting on the market square near the cathedral and the Hotel Dagmar which owns it. Originally built in the 1500s, the half-timbered inn you see today dates mainly from 1704. The food here is plentiful and well prepared, based on the best from field, air, and stream.

When in Denmark, we always do as our fellow Danish diners do and launch a repast with marinated herring with raw onions and the always-divine little shrimp they serve with mayonnaise. For something more substantial, we join our fellow guests in feasting on smoked Greenland halibut with scrambled eggs, a local favorite, as is the liver paste with mushrooms. For more standard dishes, you can order a very good filet of beef flavored with onions. We ended our meal, as did our dining companions, with a selection of Danish cheese and almost found ourselves agreeing with our hosts—"It's the best in the world."

The inn also has four upstairs guest rooms that are cozy but don't have private bathrooms. A double costs DKK695 ($118/£70), including breakfast.

Torvet 2. © **75-42-07-00.** www.weis-stue.dk. Reservations recommended. Main courses DKK155–DKK235 ($26–$40/£16–£24); 2-course fixed-price menu DKK178 ($30/£18). AE, DC, MC, V. Daily 11am–10pm.

RIBE AFTER DARK

The Hotel Dagmar, on the market square, is the most happening place in Ribe. If it's winter, visit their cellar-level restaurant, **Vægterkælderen** (© 75-42-14-00), the place to enjoy a good meal in informal and traditional surroundings, or else to savor a glass of frothy, newly drawn ale in the company of locals. The kitchen serves homemade pickled herring, fresh fish dishes, and juicy steaks, but many locals just come in for a drink. In the summer months, you might want to sit outside in the Dagmar's courtyard, enjoying the **Pavillionen** (© 75-42-00-33). Hot drinks are served on cooler days, but if it's hot you can order draft beer or lemonade. Light summer meals, including fresh fish, are served. You can listen to the bells in the cathedral tower, admire the storks in their nests, and, if you're still around at 10 o'clock at night, see the night watchman as he prepares for his rounds.

The market square is also the home of the **Stenbohus Pub & Bar,** entered at Stenbogade 1 (© 75-42-01-22), where live music can be heard at least once a week—folk, rock, soul, or blues. Otherwise, it's one of the most congenial taverns in town to meet locals over a glass of beer with a good head on it. Vægterkælderen (see above) is a classier joint for a drink; this one is more informal, attracting a more youthful crowd.

328

SOUTH JUTLAND

11

RIBE

A SIDE TRIP TO MANDØ ★

The island of Mandø, 10km (6¼ miles) off the coast of Jutland southwest of Ribe, is one of the most tranquil island hideaways in Denmark. Surrounded by the Wadden Sea, it has remained almost untouched by tourism, partly because of the awkwardness involved in getting here. Other than privately owned watercraft, the only way to reach the island is via a bumpy stone-and-gravel drive (the Låningsvejen) that's completely submerged during high tide, usually twice a day.

Under normal conditions, and whenever seas aren't particularly rough, access is possible some 15 to 18 hours during every 24-hour period in summertime. The island itself is a low-lying marshland that's protected from erosion by a man-made dike that surrounds it. Massive sandbanks and dunes that are infertile, uninhabited, and completely surrounded by water during high tides, and that change their size and locations after storms, also protect the island.

To reach Mandø from Ribe, drive 10km (6¼ miles) southwest of town to the coastal hamlet of Vester Vedsted, which marks the beginning of the Låningsvejen. The distance from Vester Vedsted to Mandø is 11km (6¾ miles), of which 5.5km (3½ miles) are submerged by the high tides of the Wadden Sea. If you respect the clearly posted safety notices and the schedule of tides, a conventional car can make the trip out to Mandø without incident. You can also get there as a passenger in the **Mandø Bussen (Mandø Bus),** a heavy-duty tractor-bus that's equipped with large-tread tires. It departs from the parking lot just to the west of Vester Vedsted at least twice a day May to September, charging DKK60 ($10/£6) per passenger. Except under optimum circumstances, it doesn't run at all from October to April. For information about departure times, call either the tourist office in Ribe (p. 321) or the Mandø Bussen at ⓒ **75-44-51-07.**

The first recorded mention of Mandø appeared in 1231, when it was claimed in its entirety by the Danish monarch. In 1741, the inhabitants purchased the island from the king at auction. Then, and throughout the rest of the 18th and 19th centuries, the island's men were involved with shipping while the women took care of the farms. In 1890, the island's population was 262; today, the island has a year-round population of only 70.

A few meters from where the bus stops in Mandø village stands **Mandøhuset** (ⓒ **75-42-60-52**), an old skipper's home, now a lackluster museum of local artifacts. Entrance is DKK15 ($2.60/£1.50) adults and DKK5 (85¢/50p) children, and visits are possible Monday to Friday 10am to 4pm.

To the south stands **Mandø Kirke** (ⓒ **75-44-51-80**), dating from 1639. The entrance costs DKK30 ($5.10/£3), but you have to call ahead to have the church opened. An old mill, built in 1860, can be seen in the northern part of the village.

Birders flock here to see thousands of breeding pairs, including eider ducks, sandpipers, and oystercatchers.

The tidal flats on the island are neither land nor sea. One moment they are dry, but for 6 hours a day they are covered by vast quantities of water. These flats are spawning grounds for several species of edible fish, including plaice and cod. It is estimated that every year 10 to 12 million birds fly over these tidal flats. These flats are Denmark's largest nature reserve. For those who like bird-watching, the spring and autumn migration periods are the best times to visit.

If you look anywhere to the southwest of Mandø, you'll get a view of what's sometimes referred to as Denmark's largest desert, an uninhabited expanse of sand dunes surrounded like an island by tidal flats that are submerged during high tides and storms. With borders and *prieler* (channels) whose positions are constantly changing because of storm and wave actions, the dunes and sand deposits are known as **Koresand.** Although a visit in winter is not advisable, during calm seas in summer, the site attracts ecologists and bird-watchers as part of twice-per-week half-day tours that are arranged by the same entrepreneurs who manage the above-mentioned **Mandø Bussen** (*(C)* **75-44-51-07** for reservations and departure times).

Tours depart from and return to Mandø in open trailers drawn by tractors that resemble the Mandø Bussen. En route, you'll pass some of the largest seal colonies in the Baltic. (These are most active during Aug.) You'll also be able to see the island of Rømø to the south and the island of Fanø to the northwest. There's usually a chance to search for amber on the beaches of Koresand, depending on the waves and the weather. The whole experience covers about 25km (16 miles) and takes about 2 hours, and the cost of the excursion is DKK80 ($14/£8) adults and DKK60 ($10/£6) children 11 and under.

6 FANØ ★★

47km (29 miles) NW of Ribe; 282km (175 miles) W of Copenhagen

Off the coast of South Jutland, Fanø, at least in our view, is the most beautiful of all North Sea islands—and we've sailed to all of them. It is the one place in Denmark which we most prefer for some R & R. Perhaps you will join us in the fun, which is what Fanø is all about. Go here to enjoy the outdoors and nature, ducking into the man-made attractions only if it's a rainy day.

Consisting of a landmass of some 54 sq. km (21 sq. miles), with a population of 3,500, it is known for its white sandy beaches, which have made it a popular holiday resort in summer. Set against a backdrop of heath-covered dunes, the best beaches are in the northwest, mostly in and around the hamlets of Rindby Strand and Fanø Bad.

Nordby, where the ferry arrives, is a logical starting point for exploring the island of Fanø. Here you'll find heather-covered moors, windswept sand dunes, fir trees, wild deer, and bird sanctuaries. From Ribe, Fanø makes for a great day's excursion (or longer if there's time).

Sønderho, on the southern tip, and only 14km (8²/₃ miles) from Nordby, with its memorial to sailors drowned at sea, is our favorite spot—somewhat desolate, but that's its charm.

It was a Dutchman who launched Denmark's first bathing resort at Nordby in 1851. It consisted of a raft on which some bathing huts had been set up. The bathers entered the huts, undressed, put on different clothes, pulled down an awning to the water's surface, and bathed under the awning. How modest of them.

Until 1741, Fanø belonged to the king, who, when he ran short of money, sold the island at auction. The islanders themselves purchased it, and the king then granted permission for residents to build ships, which led to its prosperity. From 1741 to 1900, some 1,000 sailing vessels were constructed here, with the islanders often manning them as well. Inhabitants built many beautiful houses on Fanø with monies earned, and some of these thatched Fanø homes stand today to greet visitors. There are some charmers in the northern settlement of Nordby, but more gems in the south at Sønderho.

Although Nordby and Sønderho are the principal settlements, beach lovers head for the seaside resort of **Fanø Bad,** which is also a popular camping area. From Fanø Bad, the beach stretches almost 4km (2¹/₂ miles) to the north. Swimming here is absolutely safe, as a sandy bottom slopes gently into the North Sea, and there are no ocean holes and no dangerous currents.

Fanø adheres to old island traditions almost more than any other island in Denmark, with the exception of Ærø. As late as the 1960s, some of the elderly women on Fanø still wore the "Fanø costume," the traditional dress, although today you'll see it only at special events and festivals. This dress originally consisted of five skirts, but today's costumes are likely to have only three. When the skirt was to be pleated, it was wet, laced up, and sent to the baker, who steamed it in a warm oven.

ESSENTIALS

GETTING THERE   By Car and Ferry   From Ribe, head north on Route 11 to Route 24. Follow Route 24 northwest to the city of Esbjerg, where you can board a ferry operated by **Scandlines** (© 70-10-17-44; www.scandlines.dk for information and schedules). May to October, ferries depart Esbjerg every 20 minutes during the day (trip time: 12 min.). In winter, service is curtailed, with departures during the day every 45 minutes. A round-trip ticket costs DKK40 ($6.80/£4) adults or DKK20 ($3.40/£2) children 5 to 15, and one average-size car, along with five passengers, is carried for DKK385 to DKK425 ($65–$72/£39–£43) round-trip.

VISITOR INFORMATION   The **Fanø Turistbureau,** Færgevej 1, Nordby (© 70-26-42-00; www.visitfanoe.dk), is open Monday to Friday 9am to 4pm, Saturday 9am to 1pm, and Sunday 11am to 1pm, except from June 6 to August 23, when hours are Monday to Friday 9am to 6pm, Saturday 9am to 7pm, and Sunday 9am to 5pm.

GETTING AROUND   By Bus   Local buses meet passengers at the ferry dock, criss-crossing the island about every 40 minutes, with vastly curtailed service in winter. The bus will take you to the communities of Nordby in the north and Sønderho in the south, with stops at Rindby Strand and Fanø Bad. For information, call **Fanø Rutebiler** at Sønderho (© 75-16-40-10), or pick up a bus timetable at the tourist office.

By Bicycle   Many visitors like to explore Fanø by bike, and rentals cost from DKK70 ($12/£7) per day, at **Unika Cykler,** Mellemgaden 12 (© 75-16-24-60).

SPECIAL EVENTS   A summer highlight on Fanø is **Fannikerdagene,** the second weekend in July, which offers traditional dancing, costumes, and events connected with the days when sailing ships played a major part in community life. If you miss the festival, try to be on Fanø the third Sunday in July for **Sønderho Day.** The high point of the festival day is a wedding procession that passes through the town to the square by the old mill. Traditional costumes and bridal dances are some of the attractions.

SEEING THE SIGHTS

Most explorations of the island begin where the ferry docks at the settlement of Nordby. While here, and before setting out to explore the rest of Fanø, you can stop in at the **Fanø Skibsfarts-og Dragtsamling** (Fanø Shipping & Costume Collection), Hovedgaden 28 (© 75-16-22-72). The museum traces the maritime heyday of the island in the 19th century, its boom period, when Fanø had the largest fleet outside of Copenhagen. Exhibits reveal that husbands often left their families for years at a time for a life at sea. The maritime collection incorporates many ship models, details of Fanø's fleet, and displays depicting a sailor's life aboard ship and in port. The costume collection shows both the working dress of the island women and those special costumes they wore for festivals. May to September, the museum is open daily 11am to 4pm. Off-season, it's open Monday to Saturday 11am to 1pm. Admission is DKK20 ($3.40/£2) adults and DKK10 ($1.70/£1) children under age 12.

Housed in a 300-year-old building, the **Fanø Museum,** Skolevej 2 (no phone), houses a comprehensive collection of period furniture, utensils, tools, and other island artifacts. There's also an exotic collection of mementos sailors have gathered on their voyages. The museum is open in June, Monday to Saturday 10am to 1pm, and July and August, Monday to Friday 11am to 4pm and Saturday 10am to 1pm. In September, it's open Monday to Friday 10am to 1pm. Admission is DKK20 ($3.40/£2) adults, DKK10 ($1.70/£1) children under age 12.

Near the most southerly tip of the island, in the settlement of Sønderho, you can visit the island's most beautiful building, **Sønderho Kirke,** Strandvejen (✆ 75-16-40-32), open daily during daylight hours, with free admission. The church has a strong maritime influence—in fact, it displays 14 votive ships, more than any other church in Denmark. The baroque altarpiece dates from 1717, the pulpit from 1661, and the organ loft with a painting from 1782. This is an assembly-hall church, seating some 800 members of a congregation.

While at Sønderho you can also visit **Fanø Kunstmuseum** (Fanø Art Museum), Norland 5 (✆ 75-16-40-44; www.fanoekunstmuseum.dk), which in 1992 opened in Kromanns Hus, a former store and factory. The old shop dating from 1868 has been restored and now serves as the entrance to the museum. Fanø attracted a number of artists who moved here, and this museum showcases their most outstanding paintings, the collection based on pictures first assembled by Ruth Heinemann, who founded an art association on Fanø. The museum shows art inspired by the Frisian coast, past and present, with both permanent and temporary exhibitions. April 3 to October, it is open Tuesday to Sunday 2 to 5pm, charging DKK30 ($5.10/£3) or DKK15 ($2.60/£1.50) children under age 12.

Less than half a kilometer (¹/₄ mile) north of Sønderho, on the road to Nordby, stands the **Sønderho Mølle,** Vester Land 44 (✆ 75-16-44-29), a restored windmill. Once islanders were obliged to use the crown's mill at Ribe, but in 1701 they received permission to construct one here. Several mills have stood on this site since then, and one burned down in 1894 but was replaced by another the following year, which was in use until 1923. A preservation-minded group purchased the mill in 1928 and restored it. It's open to the public June 26 to August 29 and during October, daily 3 to 5pm; and from August 30 to September 30, Wednesday, Saturday, and Sunday 3 to 5pm. Admission is DKK20 ($3.40/£2) adults or DKK10 ($1.70/£1) for children 11 and under.

Hannes Hus, Østerland 7 (✆ 75-16-44-29), is one of the most typical of old Fanø structures, and it's in Sønderho, which contains Denmark's highest proportion of protected buildings. Hannes Hus faithfully maintains the atmosphere of a 17th-century captain's home. Hanne, a captain's widow, and her daughter, Karen, lived here until 1965, when it was acquired by the Village Trust. Inside are original furnishings, a stove, pictures, a sheep stable, and souvenirs from the captain's travels. Here's your chance to see what a Fanø sailor's private home looked like. It's open July and August, daily 3 to 5pm, and September, Saturday and Sunday 3 to 5pm. Admission is DKK20 ($3.40/£2) adults, DKK10 ($1.70/£1) children under age 12.

SHOPPING

For an antiques store, combined with a flea market, head for **Vestergårdens Antik,** Vestervejen 47 (✆ 75-16-68-00), also at Nordby. For the best collection of the tiles for which the island is known, shop at **Den lille butik,** Landevejen 3 (✆ 75-16-43-58), at

Sønderho. You'll also find an array of exquisite silk items, many of them handmade, at **Jane Heinemann,** Landevejen 15 (© **75-16-42-90**), also at Sønderho. The best art gallery is at Sønderho: **Galleri Anne,** Østerland 15 (© **75-16-43-05**), is open in July and August, Monday to Friday noon to 3pm. Island artists are showcased here.

WHERE TO STAY

Hotel Fanø Badeland (Kids)   This hotel takes no chances with the quite likely possibility that fog or rain might ruin the swimming. Although it sits on Fanø's western edge, close to one of the best beaches on the island, it has the added benefit of a glass-enclosed complex of indoor pools creating an impressive array of year-round swimming options. Located 3km (1³/₄ miles) south of the hamlet of Nordby, it was built amid windswept scrubland. The midsize rooms are urban-looking, minimalist, and angular, with well-kept shower-only bathrooms and small kitchenettes nestled into the corners of the living rooms. Each has either one or two bedrooms outfitted with simple, durable furniture and no-nonsense accessories. The atmosphere is rather impersonal, not snug and cozy, but it's perfectly suited for families who want to spend most of their time outdoors, enjoying comfortable living and plenty of facilities when they nestle in for the night. You'll pay an additional DKK65 ($11/£6.50) per person for a package containing sheets and towels, unless you opt to bring your own.

Strandvejen 52–56, DK-6720 Fanø. © **75-16-60-00.** Fax 75-16-60-11. www.fanoebadeland.dk. 126 units. DKK825–DKK965 ($140–$164/£83–£97) 1-bedroom unit for up to 4 occupants; DKK985–DKK1,425 ($167–$242/£99–£143) 2-bedroom unit for up to 6 occupants. Discounts offered for stays of 5 nights or more. MC, V. Bus: 631. **Amenities:** Restaurant; bar; swimming complex; tennis court; fitness center; sauna; room service; laundry service; dry cleaning. In room: TV, kichenette.

Sønderho Kro ★★★   This is an unbeatable choice. Dating from 1722, it is one of Denmark's oldest inns—not only that, but one of its most charming and atmospheric. A Relais & Châteaux property, the thatch-roof inn in the heart of the village of Sønderho is the best we've ever encountered in South Jutland. There's also a beautiful garden where guests drink and dine on a summer night in the shade of towering trees.

Niels and Birgit Steen Sørensen are the "hosts with the mostest" on Fanø, pampering guests and feeding and housing them in elegant style. The building is under the protection of the National Museum, which closely supervised its expansion in 1977. Each of the bedrooms comes in a different shape and size, and each is individually decorated in a tasteful way. The windows open onto views over a nearby dike, the marshlands, and the North Sea. Lace curtains, lovely tapestries, and four-poster beds add to the old-fashioned allure.

Guests meet in the first-floor lounge, opening onto views of tidal flats. The *kro* (inn) lies 13km (8 miles) south of the Nordby ferry dock, where a bus carries nonmotorists the final distance into Sønderho.

Kropladsen 11, Sønderho, DK-6720 Fanø. © **75-16-40-09.** Fax 75-16-43-85. www.sonderhokro.dk. 13 units. DKK1,250–DKK2,050 ($213–$349/£125–£205) double. Rates include full breakfast. AE, DC, MC, V. Free parking. **Amenities:** Restaurant; lounge; room service (7am–10pm); laundry service; dry cleaning. In room: TV, hair dryer.

WHERE TO DINE

Café Nanas Stue ★ (Finds) DANISH   If it's a summer night and you're on Fanø, head to this 1855 half-timbered farmhouse for a rollicking good time. It's likely that a group of local musicians will be playing typical island music using such instruments as the harmonica and the bagpipe. You get not only entertainment, but a display of tiles as well: The cafe is also the site of the **Fanø Tile Museum,** and its walls and handmade wood cupboards are filled with Dutch blue-and-white tiles brought by Fanø sailors from the 1600s to the 1800s. Each tile depicts a representational scene, often taken from the Bible.

Wooden tables fill up with both islanders and visitors who come here to enjoy a typical Fanø kitchen that offers regional specialties. At lunch you can partake of those Danish open-faced sandwiches—count on three making a really satisfying meal. At night you can enjoy more elaborate fare such as a tender and perfectly cooked pepper steak topped with a cognac sauce. Other tasty dishes include shrimp and salmon with asparagus or else a "Paris steak" with such accompaniments as horseradish and capers. Most habitués finish off their repast by asking the bartender to make his specialty, which is a powerful *akvavit* ("water of life") flavored with coffee beans, vanilla, and orange zest.

Sønderland 1. ℂ **75-16-40-25.** www.nanas-stue.com/cms. Reservations recommended. Main courses DKK148–DKK238 ($25–$40/£15–£24). MC, V. July–Sept Tues–Sat 11am–midnight, Sun 11am–5pm; off-season Fri–Sun 5pm–midnight.

Kromann's Fisherestaurant DANISH/GERMAN

Far from the fancy *kros* of Fanø, this is a local hangout where the cookery is solid, filling, reliable, and affordable—nothing more, nothing less. But isn't that enough? In the heart of the village, near its famous church, this restaurant occupies a redbrick building originally constructed as a private house during the early years of World War I. Menu items include a wide roster of meats and fish, especially plaice and salmon, which the chef prepares in any of at least three different ways. There are also shrimp, crayfish, and fried eel served in the traditional way—with potatoes and parsley. Obviously there's nothing served that taxes the imagination of the chef, but the food is fresh and well flavored.

Kropladsen, Sønderho. ℂ **75-16-44-45.** Reservations recommended. Main courses DKK128–DKK180 ($22–$31/£13–£18). No credit cards. Easter–Oct daily noon–3pm and 6–9pm. Closed Nov–Easter.

Sønderho Kro ★★★ INTERNATIONAL

Over the years, we have found no finer cuisine in South Jutland than that served here. It's as bracing and fresh as the North Sea breezes that blow this way. A Relais & Châteaux property, this is the most prestigious and elegant restaurant on the island. The setting is adjacent to the harbor within what was established as an inn in 1722; it has gained steadily in influence and glamour ever since. Your meal is likely to include some form of smoked fish, prepared in-house with smoke from juniper wood, in a custom-built oven whose construction was inspired by designs perfected by the Inuit of Greenland.

Only the best local produce is used by the hotel chefs, who make their own jams and preserves. You can purchase some of the hotel's products to take home—like strawberry jam with almonds and French black-currant liqueur. All of their dishes are superb, especially some of the best beef sausage you are likely to taste—it's also smoked with juniper wood. A juniper-schnapps sausage and a superb smoked leg of lamb are also likely to be offered. These meats are without artificial coloring and have a low-fat content. Move on to an array of perfectly prepared dishes, a splendid gourmet feast that comes as a surprise in a country inn. Save room also for one of the harmoniously composed desserts. The international wine list is no less delightful than the friendly, efficient service.

Kropladsen 11, Sønderho. ℂ **75-16-40-09.** Reservations required. Main courses DKK108–DKK348 ($18–$59/£11–£35); fixed-price menus DKK380–DKK820 ($65–$139/£38–£82). AE, DC, MC, V. Apr–Sept daily noon–2:30pm and 6–9pm; Oct–Mar Thurs–Tues noon–2:30pm and 6–9pm.

FANØ AFTER DARK

Your best bet is any event sponsored by the **Fanø Jazzklub,** Bavnebjergtoft 7 (© **75-16-28-52**), at Fanø. The club has various events in summer, and the tourist office keeps a schedule. Tickets cost DKK70 to DKK110 ($12–$19/£7–£11) and can be purchased at the door.

Don't expect glitter or glamour on Fanø, as virtually everyone who lives here seems to believe in honest industry and an early-to-bed kind of entertainment agenda. In Sønderho, a fun bar is **Nanas Stue** (© **75-16-40-25**), which is lively and comfy with live music and good food.

12

Central Jutland

The central part of Jutland cuts across a broad swath of the country, extending from the gateway city of Fredericia in the south to Viborg and Limfjord (a large inland fjord) in the north. The east side of Central Jutland is more populous than the west, which is a wide plain of windswept moors bordered by a rugged coastline of beach flats and sand dunes.

Small farms and rich fertile land characterize the rolling hills of the central belt's eastern shores. But since the 19th century, much of the land in the west has also been reclaimed; great parts of it have been transformed into pastureland and fields against the competition of North Sea winds.

Central Jutland contains some of the most sparsely populated regions of Denmark, although it has cities too—notably Århus (the largest city in the region), as well as Silkeborg, Randers, and others.

It is also one of the most hospitable regions of Denmark. Locals are proud of a landscape that ranges from wide expanses of heath to lovely fields of heather to charming towns. Central Jutland also has some of the best beaches in Denmark, with vast stretches of white sand. Art museums, galleries, concerts, and beautiful old churches add to the allure.

The best towns in east Central Jutland are Jelling, Vejle, and Århus. If you'd like to base your travels in the Lake District, favorite spots include Ebeltoft, Silkeborg, and Ry. In the interior, Randers makes the best stopover, and if you want a base on the central west coast, make it Ringkøbing.

Jelling is one of the most historic spots in Denmark, and **Legoland** is Jutland's most visited attraction. The liveliest and most diverse cultural scene is found in Århus, Denmark's second-largest city with some quarter of a million residents.

For rail and bus information to any town, call © **70-13-14-15.**

---

1 VEJLE ★

199km (124 miles) W of Copenhagen; 72km (45 miles) SW of Århus; 30km (19 miles) N of Kolding; 25km (16 miles) NW of Fredericia; 27km (17 miles) E of Billund

Admittedly, there are more enticing destinations in Central Jutland than the ancient old city of Vejle. But there is a certain charm here which you'll soon discover if you stop over for 2 or 3 hours.

The setting of the city is spectacular, against a backdrop of tree-clad hills facing the Kattegat, that body of water that separates the island of Funen from mainland Jutland. Lying near the top of the blue waters of the Vejle Fjord, the thriving town invites hikes into its tall wooded slopes, fertile dales, and deep gorges. This area of Central Jutland has long been known for its scenic beauty and hilly countryside, and Vejle is smack in the middle of it.

One evocative moment we experienced in Vejle was the chiming of an old Dominican monastery clock. The clock still chimes even though its monastery is gone with the wind, having given way in the 1800s to the construction of the town's imposing City Hall.

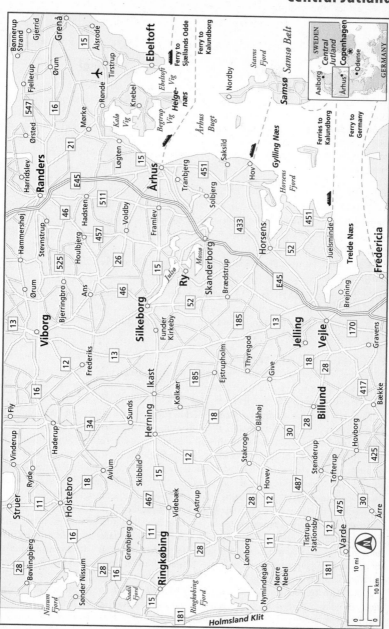

Lying in a sheltered hollow, the city has a thriving economy based on exports of sausage, textiles, and chewing gum, among other products, as well as an ever-increasing tourist industry. Highway 3 goes through the town, and the railway also brings passengers and goods here.

Vejle is close to the coast of East Jutland, and lies north of Kolding and northwest of Fredericia. The entire Vejle region stretches from the Vejle Fjord through Grejsdalen to Jelling, going through the river valley of Vejle Adal to Egtved.

The town was granted its charter in 1327. But wars with Prussia hurt its economy, and Vejle suffered great hardship in the 1600s due to the Black Plague and economic deprivation brought on by wars. In the 1820s, the construction of a new harbor brought it increased prosperity. By that time, the making of *akvavit* (schnapps) played an important role in its economy. In the wars of the 19th century with Schleswig-Holstein in the south, Vejle was occupied several times by German troops, and until 1956, it was a garrison town.

ESSENTIALS

GETTING THERE By Train Trains arrive frequently throughout the day from Copenhagen, as Vejle is on the main Jutland line. The town also has good rail links to the other major towns in Jutland—it's only 45 minutes by rail to Århus or 35 minutes to Kolding.

By Car If you've used Fredericia as your gateway to Central Jutland, follow Route 28 northwest into Vejle.

VISITOR INFORMATION The **Vejle-Egnens Turistbureau,** Banegårdspladsen 6 (© 76-81-19-25; www.visitvejle.dk), is open June to August, Monday to Friday 9am to 5pm, Saturday 10am to 1pm; off-season, Monday to Friday 10am to 4pm, Saturday 10am to noon.

SEEING THE SIGHTS

Charming small squares, old houses, courtyards, and pedestrian streets provide the town center with a distinctive atmosphere. Even from the center of town, there are views of the blue waters of Vejle Fjord and its forest-clad hills.

The chief attraction is **Sankt Nicolai Kirke** ★, Kirketorvet (© 74-62-53-80; www.aabenraasogn.dk), a 10-minute walk from the tourist office. The Gothic church is one of the town's oldest buildings, its north wall dating back to the mid–13th century. The church contains one of Denmark's finest bog findings, an **Iron Age woman** ★★ from 450 B.C., discovered in the Haraldskaier bog in 1835. She can be seen through a glass-topped case. Many guidebooks report that this is the preserved body of the Viking queen Gunhilde. However, recent scientific studies have shown that the corpse is much older, dating from the early Iron Age. The skulls of 23 beheaded robbers caught in the Nørreskoven woods some 3 centuries ago have been gruesomely bricked into the outer north wall of the church. Special features of the church include a classical reredos (the screen behind the altar), the work of sculptor Jens Hiernoe in 1791, plus a 16th-century Renaissance pulpit and a processional crucifix. Admission free, it's open Monday to Friday 9am to 5pm, Saturday and Sunday 9am to noon.

Vejle Kunstmuseum ★, Flegborg 16 (© 75-72-31-99; www.vejlekunstmuseum.dk), comes as a surprise for such a provincial town. Many large Danish towns have provincial art museums, but it's rare to find works by such famous Old Masters. Of course, Danish art from the beginning of the 20th century to the millennium is what's primarily showcased. The museum's prize is a remarkable **self-portrait of Rembrandt** ★★ dating from 1563. Founded back in 1899, the museum houses some 12,000 prints and drawings, including foreign prints from 1450 to 1800. The treasure-trove here is 2,000 prints and drawings, forming the **Eckardts Sambling Collection** ★★, donated at the turn of the 20th century, providing the reason for the museum to come into existence. The collection comprises Old Master prints by Albrecht Dürer, among others, and there are some 50 prints from Rembrandt alone. Just to see this collection is reason enough to visit the museum in the first place. Landscape painting is a strong feature here, including some rare art from the Danish-affiliated and faraway Faroe Islands. Admission is DKK40 ($6.80/£4) adults, DKK30 ($5.10/£3) seniors, and free for ages 18 and under; hours are Tuesday to Friday 11am to 4pm, Saturday and Sunday 10am to 5pm.

A far less intriguing museum, **Vejle Museum,** Flegborg 18 (© **75-72-31-99;** www.vejlekunstmuseum.dk), adjacent to the art museum, could be skipped if time is running short. It also was founded in 1899, offering an exhibit called "Man and Nature—Archaeology in the Vejle Area." Exhibits trace the history of Vejle over the past 8 centuries, including life in the Middle Ages, Vejle as a 17th-century theater of war, and, finally, Vejle's rise as an industrial town. We were not overly enchanted, but you might find it of passing interest, charging DKK40 ($6.80/£4) adults, DKK30 ($5.10/£3) seniors, and free for those 18 and under. The museum is open Tuesday to Sunday 10am to 4pm.

For your farewell to Vejle, you can take a moving stairway in town up to the "mountain" known as **Munkebjerg,** to the southeast of Vejle. At an elevation of 90m (300 ft.), you'll enjoy a panoramic view of Vejle and the fjord. The yew—that most Scandinavian of trees—and other rare trees and plants can be seen here.

If you have a car, arm yourself with a good map (available at the tourist office) and explore **Grejsdalen,** 7km (4¹⁄₃ miles) from Vejle. This valley is one of Denmark's most beautiful areas, with densely wooded hillsides and many lookout points. The preserved part of the valley is also the home of a richly varied bird life. Near Grejs itself are some limestone deposits resembling cliff caverns.

SHOPPING

The main pedestrian zone in the heart of town features more than 220 specialty shops, restaurants, and department stores, so there's a wealth of shopping opportunities here, more so than nearly any other place in Jutland.

The best and most innovative ceramics are sold at **Ulla Møller,** Havnegade 21 (© **75-83-71-21**). For a gift shop featuring local crafts, head to **Allehånde,** Søndergade 14 (© **75-83-83-66**).

WHERE TO STAY

Best Western Torvehallerne ★   Its construction in 1993 was viewed as a vital part of the success of the Torvehallerne—Vejle's largest conglomeration of cultural, dining, drinking, and nightlife facilities. Consequently, in any season or weather, you'll be able to migrate from your room at this three-story hotel through the big-windowed, green-house-inspired spaces of the market hall for diversions of the kind you might expect in a mall in California. Rooms are well maintained and comfortable, and contain angular, modern furnishings that are both comfortable and tasteful, along with small private bathrooms with neatly tiled shower units. In spite of its charms, we still gravitate to the Munkebjerg.

In the Torvehallerne, Kirketorvet 12, DK-7100 Vejle. 🕾 **800/780-7234** in the U.S., or 79-42-79-10. Fax 79-42-79-01. www.torvehallerne.dk. 43 units. DKK895–DKK1,195 ($152–$203/£90–£120) double. Rates include breakfast. AE, MC, V. **Amenities:** 2 restaurants; bar; room service; laundry service; dry cleaning; nonsmoking rooms; rooms for those w/limited mobility. *In room:* TV, Wi-Fi, minibar, hair dryer.

Golden Tulip Vejle ★★★ This is one of the most modern and state-of-the-art hotels in Central Jutland, and is even better than the superb Munkebjerg. It rises 11 stories and is in a central location in the heart of town. Inside, you'll find all the amenities that several corporations would need to host simultaneous conventions. The public lounges are spacious and decorated in Danish modern, as are the midsize-to-large bedrooms, which are both comfortably and tastefully furnished, with small bathrooms coated with tiles. Because of its first-class restaurant on-site, many visitors eat in at night.

Dæmningen 6, DK-7100 Vejle. 🕾 76-40-60-00. Fax 76-40-60-01. www.goldentulip.com. 102 units. DKK1,099–DKK1,450 ($187–$247/£110–£145) double; extra bed DKK200 ($34/£20). Rates include breakfast. AE, DC, MC, V. **Amenities:** Restaurant; bar; exercise room; sauna; room service; babysitting; laundry service; dry cleaning; nonsmoking rooms; 1 room for those w/limited mobility. *In room:* TV, Wi-Fi, minibar, hair dryer, iron, trouser press.

Munkebjerg Hotel ★★ One of the most stylish and prestigious hotels in the region, with the most panoramic setting, and a professional and sensitive staff that's capable of dealing with delicate temperaments. South of the center, it sits in isolated but contemporary grandeur on a panoramic hilltop within the Munkebjerg Forest. Expect dramatic, impeccably maintained public areas in a big-windowed and angular modern style, and very comfortable, soothing accommodations that range from midsize to spacious. Rooms are flooded with sunlight thanks to sliding glass windows, and offer private balconies overlooking the forest. The furniture is soft and comfortable, with deep cushions, and each is midsize. From the three large suites with Jacuzzi and a separate living room, there is a panoramic view of the fjord.

Munkebjergvej 125, DK-7100 Vejle. 🕾 76-42-85-00. Fax 75-72-08-86. www.munkebjerg.dk. 158 units. DKK1,575–DKK2,075 ($268–$353/£158–£208) double; DKK2,575–DKK3,875 ($438–$659/£258–£388) suite. Rates include buffet breakfast. AE, DC, MC, V. From Vejle's center, drive 7km (4¹⁄₃ miles) south, following the signs to Vejle Sid. **Amenities:** 3 restaurants; 2 bars; casino; indoor heated pool; gym; sauna; room service; babysitting; laundry service; dry cleaning; nonsmoking rooms. *In room:* TV, Wi-Fi, minibar, hair dryer.

WHERE TO DINE

Treetops Restaurant ★★ DANISH/INTERNATIONAL This restaurant in the previously recommended Munkebjerg Hotel is celebrated throughout the region for its contemporary glamour and its devotion to fine cuisine. A meal is always prefaced with a guided tour of the establishment's wine cellar, where a glass of something tasty is part of the experience. After that, a table is prepared within a high-ceilinged room that's spanned with artfully arranged tree limbs that provide a cozy, forestlike tone. Menu items change frequently, but count on the ingredients being first-rate and market fresh. Finely balanced sauces are one of the culinary highlights here. Our appetizer contained two of our favorite foods—smoked salmon and foie gras. For a hearty regional dish guaranteed to put hair on your chest, try the breast of goose with pork jaw. More tempting to most diners are a succulent version of filet of lamb roasted with garlic and served with a lemongrass sauce or tournedos of veal with ratatouille and a flavoring of balsamic vinegar. The pastry chef always manages to delight, with such concoctions as white chocolate mousse with mango and pistachio.

In the Munkebjerg Hotel, Munkebjergvej 125. 🕾 **76-42-85-00.** Reservations required. All main courses DKK295 ($50/£30); 4-course fixed-price menu DKK595 ($101/£60); 8-course fixed-price menu DKK790

VEJLE AFTER DARK

At the **Casino Munkebjerg Vejle,** Munkebjergvej 125 (© 76-43-50-00), you can play roulette, blackjack, the slot machines, and—if you're willing to learn—"Viking poker." A photo ID is required to gain entrance, and there is an admission fee of DKK50 ($8.50/£5). The major cultural venue for the city is the **Musik Theatret Vejle,** Vedels-gade 25–31 (© 79-43-20-20), the setting for operas, musicals, shows, and theater. You can check with the tourist office (see "Visitor Information," above) to see if any events at the time of your visit appeal to you.

Also consider a visit to the complex **Torvehallerne,** Kirketorvet 10–16 (© 79-42-79-00). A large, spacious palm garden, Væksthuset, forms the center of a complex that includes restaurants, a hotel, a cafe, a stage, and a pub. There is always something going on here—jazz, dancing under the palm trees, concerts, or theatrical performances. We can't predict what will be going on at the time of your visit, but it's always a lively place to drop in on at night.

Vejle is also a town rich in pub life, our favorite being **Seven Oaks,** an old English-style pub at Dæmningen 42G (© 75-72-07-77). Another good choice is the dance club **Crazy Daisy,** Nørregade 65–67 (© 75-83-61-33).

---

2 JELLING ★

11km (6³/₄ miles) NW of Vejle; 144km (89 miles) W of Copenhagen

It seems almost impossible to wander this sleepy little village today and realize that it was the site of riotous pagan festivals and celebrations. At the peak of the Viking era, a thousand years ago, Jelling was the Danish Royal Seat, the birthplace of the Danish monarchy. Although the site of Gorm the Old's castle has never been discovered, he was the first in a millennium-long string of Danish kings that continues today in an unbroken line to Queen Margrethe herself.

Gorm the Old and his son, the amusingly named "Harald Bluetooth," left behind two large burial mounds and two runic stones from their reigns. In 1994, these Viking monuments were declared a World Heritage Site. Bluetooth is a towering figure in Danish history, having driven the Swedes from his lands and having begun the conversion of his people from pagan rituals to Christianity. See the box "Discovering a Viking Past" for more details.

Most visitors come for the meager glimpse into the secrets of the Viking era, but some remain to wander around the village of Jelling itself, which enjoys idyllic surroundings set against a backdrop of forests and lakes.

ESSENTIALS

GETTING THERE   By Train and Bus   Jelling is a 20-minute train ride from Vejle on the run to Struer and Herning. Trains depart about once an hour Monday to Friday, less frequently on weekends. Connections are possible by bus no. 211 from Vejle's bus station.

By Car   From Vejle, take Route A18 north. If you're using Fredericia as your gateway to Central Jutland, go to Vejle first, then continue into Jelling.

Discovering a Viking Past

In the center of town, **Jelling Kirke** ★ (© 75-87-16-28) was erected at the beginning of the 12th century, and is one of the oldest churches in Denmark. The church is visited mainly because of its two well-preserved runic stones, which sit outside the door. You should look inside the church as well to see its restored 12th-century frescoes. Admission is free, and the church is open Monday to Friday 10am to 5pm, and Saturday 10am to 2pm. It's closed for visits on Sunday because of Mass. You can attend Mass then, but casual sightseeing in the church is discouraged when it's being used as a place of worship.

Both **Gorm the Old** (883–940) and his son, **Harald Bluetooth** (935–85), lived in Jelling, and they left behind two large burial mounds and two runic stones—one small, one large. The small stone bears the inscription KING GORM MADE THESE SEPULCHRAL MONUMENTS TO THYRA, HIS WIFE, THE GRACE OF DENMARK. The large stone is inscribed KING HARALD HAD THESE SEPULCHRAL MONUMENTS MADE TO GORM, HIS FATHER, AND THYRA, HIS MOTHER, THE HARALD WHO CONQUERED ALL DENMARK AND NORWAY AND MADE THE DANES CHRISTIANS.

The latter part of the inscription has often been called Denmark's baptismal certificate, though this is something of an exaggeration. But King Harald and his people were undoubtedly converted to Christianity, even if it was a century before the country as a whole can be said to have become Christian.

The north's oldest depiction of Christ is seen over this part of Harald's runic lettering. The Christ-like figure appears with his arms spread out but without a cross. This may have been because the artist at the time wanted to depict Christ as a victorious Viking king—hence no cross. The significance of the other depiction on the stone isn't known. It shows a snake locked in deadly combat with a mythical animal. The stones, decorated in the typical Viking style, with interlacing leaf and creeper-work, were originally painted in bright colors.

Excavations of the two barrows began in 1820, when the north barrow was dug up. It revealed a burial chamber but no human remains, only a few objects and fragments, including a silver goblet, later dubbed the Jelling goblet. It's thought that grave robbers may have plundered the site over the years. In 1861 King Frederik VII, who had a keen interest in archaeology, excavated the south barrow, but it didn't even have a burial chamber. It is now believed that both Gorm and Thyra had been buried in the north mound and that the empty south barrow was merely a memorial mound.

In modern times, the area beneath the church was excavated, and archaeologists discovered the remains of three wooden churches. The oldest was King Harald's and was even bigger than the present Jelling Kirke, earning the nickname "the Cathedral of the Viking Age."

The discovery of a burial chamber beneath the choral arch revealed human bones, but they were in complete disorder, indicating that they had been moved. The skeletal remains are believed to be those of Gorm, which were probably moved over from the north mound when Harald became Christian. It has never been determined where Queen Thyra was reburied.

www.visitvejle.com), is open daily June to August, 10am to 5pm. it is also open Tuesday to Sunday in September 10am to 4pm, and Tuesday to Sunday in October 10am to 1pm.

WHERE TO STAY

Jelling Kro ★ (Value   The most evocative and appealing hotel in town occupies the dignified yellow-fronted premises of what has functioned since 1780 as a *kro* (old-fashioned inn). Capped with a terra-cotta roof and positioned in the center of town, across from the country's most famous burial site, the hotel offers a well-recommended restaurant (see "Where to Dine," below). Each of the comfortable, well-maintained rooms is slightly different from its neighbor, and all have a shared bathroom. If you opt to stay in this hotel, know in advance that you'll share it with good company. In 1842, just before an overnight visit from the Danish king, it was reclassified as one of only about 30 hotels in Denmark suitable then and thereafter for overnight visits from a Danish monarch.

Gormsgade 16, DK-7300 Jelling. © **75-87-10-06.** Fax 75-87-10-08. www.jellingkro.dk. 6 units, all w/ shared bathroom. DKK695 ($118/£70) double. Rates include breakfast. AE, MC, V. Bus: 214. **Amenities:** Restaurant. *In room:* TV, no phone.

WHERE TO DINE

Jelling Kro ★ (Value DANISH   Good, wholesome cookery greets visitors in Jelling to pay homage to a Viking past. The most appealing restaurant in Jelling is in the previously recommended hotel. The dining room is much more modern than the historic setting would imply. Menu items usually stress fish that's parceled out into several kinds of platters, served either as a starter or in a more elaborate form as a main course configured into a "symphony of fish." Although the composition of each platter changes according to availability, you can almost always expect an emphasis on marinated salmon and fresh shrimp. Other excellent dishes include cream of leek soup with bacon, tournedos of beef garnished with mushroom stew and potato dish of the day, or breast of chicken with white-wine sauce.

Gormsgade 16. © **75-87-10-06.** Reservations recommended. Lunch main courses DKK42–DKK99 ($7.20–$17/£4.20–£9.90); dinner main courses DKK88–DKK182 ($15–$31/£8.80–£18). AE, MC, V. June–Aug daily noon–4pm and 5–9pm; Sept–May Wed–Sun noon–4pm and 5–9pm.

---

3 BILLUND ★ & LEGOLAND ★★

228km (142 miles) W of Copenhagen; 59km (37 miles) NE of Esbjerg; 27km (17 miles) W of Vejle

The "Disneyland of Denmark," Legoland, an amusement park less than a kilometer ($^{1}/_{2}$ mile) north of the small Central Jutland town of Billund, is the second-most-visited tourist attraction in the country, after Tivoli in Copenhagen. Since it opened in 1968, some 28 million visitors from around the world have arrived. It can be a lot of fun if you're traveling as a family. Adults exploring Denmark without children in tow might want to seek other diversions (unless, of course, they are hard-core Lego aficionados).

ESSENTIALS

GETTING THERE   **By Plane**   Planes fly into **Billund Airport,** just across the road from Legoland—a 5-minute walk from the arrival lounge to the park. **SAS** (© **800/221-2350** in North America, or 32-32-22-33 in Billund; www.flysas.com) has frequent daily flights from Copenhagen (26 flights a week from Copenhagen). **Sterling Airlines** (© **70-10-84-84;** www.sterling.dk) has direct flights from London and Stockholm, to Billund.

By Bus   There is no train service. Rail passengers get off at Vejle (see earlier), then take a bus marked LEGOLAND for the final lap of the journey. In summer, more buses run from Vejle, and there is also bus service from Esbjerg (© **75-16-26-00**).

By Car   After crossing the bridge linking Funen and Jutland, continue northwest toward Vejle on the E20, linking up with Route 18, which connects with Route 28 going west into Billund.

LEGOLAND ★

Legoland theme park (**www.legoland.dk**) is constructed from—what else?—plastic Lego blocks, and boasts 50 "fun activities." The greatest attraction is Castleland, which opened in 1997. Home to the King's Castle, a faux-medieval fairy-tale castle, it offers an action-adventure ride on one of two 212-seat "dragons" that fly around this re-created world. On the upper floor is the Knight's Barbecue, a restaurant decorated with suits of armor and shields.

Miniland is the second major attraction, with miniature models of famous buildings and monuments from around the world. The entire medieval town of Ribe is re-created, for example, as is Amalienborg Castle in Copenhagen. Other thematic attractions in the park include Legoredo Town, a re-creation of a western town with an Indian camp and a sheriff's office, plus Pirateland, where you can take a boat trip through caves. There's even a Lego Safari, where children steer small zebra-striped jeeps on a ride through a faux savanna. There are dozens of amusement rides, mostly for children, including merry-go-rounds and Ferris wheels. All the rides, including the miniature train and boat trips, are included in one admission price.

Hours are subject to change based on seasonal and weather conditions. Always call for the latest information before heading here. In general, the park is open Monday to Friday in April, May, September, and October from 10am to 8pm. In June and the last days of August, it is usually open daily 10am to 8pm. At the time of peak visitation, July to late August, hours are daily 10am to 9pm. Admission is DKK259 ($44/£26) for those 13 to 59, or DKK229 ($39/£23) for ages 3 to 12; free for children 2 and under. For more information, call © **75-33-13-33**.

WHERE TO STAY

Hotel Legoland ★ Kids   This is the only hotel associated with Jutland's most famous theme park, and as such, it does a thriving summer business renting overnight accommodations to families with children. In fact, we find it the most kid-friendly hotel in Denmark. During the winter, the clientele shifts to more of a business-oriented crowd that checks in as part of an ongoing schedule of corporate conventions. It was originally built in 1968, and it's predictably permeated with a Legoland theme. There are lots of Disney-style Legoland sculptures in the lobby, and a chipper and perky multilingual staff that's often preoccupied with the care, feeding, and amusement of children. Like everything else in Legoland, a bit of this goes a long way, especially if you happen to be traveling without children. Rooms have less of an emphasis on the Legoland theme than you'll find in the public areas. Suites are larger, and contain minibars. In 2000, the hotel opened up an additional wing with 22 "Kids' House Rooms," ideal for families. Some of the rooms, suitable for boys, are called "Knights' Rooms," whereas those for little girls are

known as "Princess Rooms." Both of these types of rooms feature a mock wooden castle
door in the middle of a wall that converts to a bunk bed.

Aastvej 10, DK-7190 Billund. © **75-33-12-44.** Fax 75-35-38-10. www.hotellegoland.dk. 176 units. DKK2,225–DKK3,000 ($378–$510/£223–£300) double; DKK3,925 ($667/£393) junior suite. Rates include breakfast and 2 days' admission to Legoland. AE, DC, MC, V. Free shuttle bus to the hotel from the airport at Billund. **Amenities:** Restaurant; bar; gym; room service; laundry service; dry cleaning; nonsmoking rooms. *In room:* TV, Wi-Fi, minibar (in suites), hair dryer, iron, trouser press.

WHERE TO DINE

Le Petit ★★ DANISH/INTERNATIONAL   By creating this luxe restaurant in 1998, the owners more or less admitted that you can carry the kiddie theme too far. So instead of another pirate's restaurant or one with a Viking dragon decor, they went upmarket and created a first-rate international restaurant. Le Petit especially appeals to the corporate convention crowd, whose clients dominate when the kiddies go back to school. Consequently, you might be relieved to discover a mostly adult crowd in this attractively formal venue within the resort's only hotel. The decor is urbane and postmodern, and cuisine draws its inspiration from big-city venues. Don't expect a wide variety of menu items, as there might be only three or four starters, main courses, and desserts. Examples include roe of salmon garnished with red onions and sour cream, *Bündnerfleisch* (air-dried beef) with Parma ham served with exotic lettuces and marinated artichokes, a savory ragout of halibut and shellfish in a saffron sauce with wild rice, tuna steak with fresh spinach in a pasta basket on a bed of tomato sauce, and a succulent version of tenderloin of lamb with *Rösti* potatoes with rosemary-flavored gravy and glazed onions.

In the Hotel Legoland, Aastvej 10. © **75-33-12-44.** Reservations recommended. Lunch DKK89–DKK128 ($15–$22/£8.90–£13); main courses DKK88–DKK254 ($15–$43/£8.80–£25). AE, DC, MC, V. Daily 11am–10pm.

4 RINGKØBING ★

320km (199 miles) W of Copenhagen; 9km (5²/₃ miles) E of the North Sea; 85km (53 miles) W of Silkeborg; 100km (62 miles) W of Århus

Århus and Silkeborg (see later in this chapter) justifiably attract more visitors, but count yourself lucky if you can spare a day for one of Denmark's most attractive towns left over from the Middle Ages.

We used to exclude Ringkøbing from our Danish itinerary until a broken vehicle forced us to overnight here one rain-lashed night. In the morning, the sun broke through, and we set out to discover the charms, both obvious and hidden, of Ringkøbing, and have been including it on our stopovers ever since. The physical setting alone is dramatic, lying to the east of the gigantic **Ringkøbing Fjord,** which is separated by a narrow strip of land, Holmsland, from the turbulent North Sea to the west.

This old market town, lying on the north side of the lagoonlike Ringkøbing Fjord, is the seat—albeit tiny, with only 9,000 inhabitants—of the regional government. Its oldest known municipal charter dates from 1443, but the earliest archaeological finds establish its origins some time around the mid–13th century. At that time there was no outlet from the western end of Liim Fjord to the North Sea, so Ringkøbing Fjord was the only natural harbor in the area. It became one of the most important harbor cities on the west coast of Denmark, with trading links extending to Norway, Germany, and Holland.

In time, though, especially during the 17th century, the approach at Nymindegab began to fill with sand and move south. With the opening of the West Jutland trunk line in 1875, shipping for Ringkøbing stopped almost immediately, leaving the town to reinvent itself. It wasn't until a lock at Hvide Sande was constructed in 1931 that Ringkøbing was once again assured of a passage to the North Sea. However, its role as a port for ships was never to return to its former glory. It did, however, become the first small town in Denmark to provide free universal education.

That falloff in commerce is what has kept Ringkøbing looking as old-fashioned and splendid as it does today. The townspeople also have a lively, cooperative spirit. For example, they have a beachcombing event to clean the town's 11km (6¾ miles) of coastline to ensure that the blue flags (symbol of unpolluted waters) fly over their beaches in summer.

ESSENTIALS

GETTING THERE **By Train** Ringkøbing lies on the main rail lines between Esbjerg (trip time: 1¼ hr.) and Struer (1 hr.).

By Car From Silkeborg (see later in this chapter), continue west along Route 15 into Ringkøbing.

VISITOR INFORMATION **Ringkøbing Turistbureau,** Torvet (© 70-22-70-01; www.ringkobingfjord.dk), is open mid-June to August, Monday to Friday 9:30am to 5pm, Saturday 10am to 2pm; September to mid-June, it's open Monday to Friday 9:30am to 5pm and Saturday 10am to 1pm.

GETTING AROUND **By Bicycle** The surrounding scenic flatlands are ideal for cyclists. Bikes can be rented at **Børgensen Cykler,** Nørredige 10 (© 97-32-36-01) for DKK50 to DKK60 ($8.50–$10/£5–£6) per day.

SEEING THE SIGHTS

Ringkøbing's townscape takes its characteristic look from houses mostly built from 1700 to 1800. The dominant building style—dark red houses with white cornices and semi-hipped rooftops—developed in the late 18th century. Ringkøbing's leading citizens were its merchants, whose large houses lined the narrow streets, particularly **Algade** and **Østergade.** Some have remained in a well-preserved condition, especially the addresses of Nørregade 2 and Algade 4–6. Much effort still goes into preserving Ringkøbing's mellow old-town atmosphere, and a walk through the town's narrow cobblestone streets brings its own reward.

If you're standing at the Torvet (marketplace) seeking a way to the harbor, the obvious choice is **Vester Strandgade** ★. This is an old street whose earliest homes date from the early 1800s. The street was always known for its merchants, including a plumber, butcher, baker, grocer, and shoemaker, as well as a bike shop and an inn. We always like to smell fresh bread from the local bakery and to stop for a delicious Danish pastry at a coffee shop, chatting with the locals.

For us, no visit is complete without time spent wandering **Ringkøbing Harbor** ★, dating from 1904, when it was a bustling fishing port until the town lost out to Hvide Sande to the south. Today, it's much sleepier and filled with yachts, smaller pleasure craft, and fjord fishing boats. You can see fishermen from Ringkøbing Fjord pulling in here with their catch of the day, earmarked for private homes or restaurants. We like to attend the daily auction at 9:30am in a red-painted wooden structure at the harbor's edge. Here salmon, trout, flounder, perch, eel, and sea trout are hawked to the highest bidder and might be resting on your plate if you stick around Ringkøbing for dinner.

At the edge of the town center, **Alkjær Lukke** is a lovely park, idyllic for a picnic lunch. Ducks quacking in the pond tell you they want to be fed. In the airy beech woods, the forest floor is covered with wood anemones, buttercups, and lilies of the valley. It's a good place to stop and enjoy "the sound of silence."

The town's main attraction—other than the town itself—is **Ringkøbing Museum Østerport,** Herningvej 4 (© **97-32-16-15;** www.ringkobing.dk). A few blocks east of the Torvet, this museum is a virtual attic of local history, including coins and ecclesiastical artifacts, ships' figureheads, and even pictures of stranded ships in the North Sea. Someone at the museum is likely to show you what a chastity belt from 1600 looked like. We find the most intriguing exhibits to be those devoted to Ludwig Mylius-Erichsen (1872–1907), who led an expedition to Greenland in 1906. Regrettably, he died on the return journey. July and August, the museum is open daily 11am to 5pm; September to June, Monday to Sunday 11am to 5pm. It's closed Friday during off-season. Admission costs DKK40 ($6.80/£4) adults, free for ages 18 and under.

SHOPPING

Some of the town's most sophisticated ceramics are sold at **Keramikkens Hus,** Ndr. Ringvej 14 (© **97-32-05-88**).

One of the most intriguing shopping prospects is not in Ringkøbing itself, but directly south of the town at the hamlet of Stauning. Follow the secondary road along the east side of Ringkøbing Fjord until you come to the village, where you'll see a sign indicating **Bousøgaard ★,** Bousøvej 6, Stauning (© **97-36-91-72**). This is an old thatched West Jutland farm with four wings. The attractive barn is an art gallery, the biggest in West Jutland, with oils, graphics, and sculptures by well-known Danish artists. There's also an on-site potter's workshop, where the old potter's craft is still practiced. Next to the workshop is a museum of Danish decorated pottery from the 1800s to about 1950. Hours are Monday to Saturday 11am to 5pm.

WHERE TO STAY

Hotel Fjordgården ★ (Kids) Head for the Hotel Ringkøbing for an older pedigree but check in here for greater comfort and superior facilities. The best hotel in Ringkøbing lies less than half a kilometer (^{1}/$_4$ mile) north of the town center, on sandy flatlands 8km (5 miles) from the coast. Built in 1967 in a sprawling, generously proportioned format with between one and two stories, white walls, and a prominent brown roof, it has more comfortable accommodations—and better dining—than any competitor. Rooms are good size with firm beds, small but spanking-clean bathrooms, and big windows that grant views over the surrounding land and seascape. Many of the units are large enough to use as family rooms. The hotel boasts an indoor subtropical water land, with spa, sauna, children's pool, and water slide.

Vesterkær 28, DK-6950 Ringkøbing. © **97-32-14-00.** Fax 97-32-47-60. www.hotelfjordgaarden.dk. 98 units. DKK1,325 ($225/£133) double; DKK1,625 ($276/£163) suite. AE, DC, MC, V. **Amenities:** Restaurant; bar; indoor heated pool; gym; spa; sauna; room service; laundry service; dry cleaning; nonsmoking rooms; solarium. *In room:* TV, Wi-Fi, minibar, coffeemaker, hair dryer.

Hotel Ringkøbing Set on a cobble-covered square in the heart of town, near a quartet of linden trees, this is the second-oldest hotel in Jutland, established in its present format in 1833. The hotel is cozy but somewhat kitschy. Rooms are banal, even a bit dowdy, thanks to overly frilly bedcovers and clumsy attempts at gussying up relatively plain spaces. Two are in a nearby annex, and all units contain a private bathroom with shower. On the premises are an English-style pub serving lots of suds and occasional live rock-'n'-roll sessions and a restaurant.

Torvet 18, DK-6950 Ringkøbing. ℭ 97-32-00-11. Fax 97-32-18-72. www.hotelringkobing.dk. 53 units. DKK895–DKK1,195 ($152–$203/£90–£120) double; DKK1,795–DKK2,195 ($305–$373/£180–£220) suite. Rates include breakfast. DC, MC, V. **Amenities:** 2 restaurants; bar; gym; laundry service; dry cleaning. *In room:* TV, Wi-Fi, hair dryer, iron.

WHERE TO DINE

Restaurant Helten ★ DANISH/INTERNATIONAL   This is the showplace dining room of the only government-rated four-star hotel in Ringkøbing, and as such, you receive more internationally conscious culinary finesse, and more diligent service, than elsewhere in town. Within a very modern dining room with a view of the dunes and the sea, you'll find a lunch venue centered around the most appealing buffet in town. Look for a savory collection of homemade soups, salads, open-faced sandwiches, Danish cheeses, smoked meats and fish, seasonal berries, and pastries. Dinners are more elaborate. We highly recommend, when it's available, a platter of smoked *helten* (a small herring-shaped fish that's the restaurant's namesake). Found only in the nearby fjord, and traditionally served salted or smoked, it's prized as one of the unusual delicacies of Denmark. Among the menu items we've enjoyed here is fried North Sea plaice with brown butter, or else the fresh salmon cutlet with vegetables, pasta, and herb butter. Also delectable is the guinea fowl with mushroom fricassee.

In the Hotel Fjordgården, Vesterkær 28. ℭ 97-32-14-00. Reservations recommended. Dinner main courses DKK172–DKK210 ($29–$36/£17–£21); fixed-price dinner menus DKK260–DKK325 ($44–$55/£26–£33). AE, DC, MC, V. Mon–Fri 7am–10pm; Sat 7am–1:30pm; Sun 7am–9pm.

EXPLORING RINGKØBING FJORD ★

Long, straight, sandy beaches, nature reserves, drifting North Sea sands, and heather-covered dunes create a dramatic West Jutland landscape on the narrow isthmus running south from Ringkøbing along Route 181. To reach the road that takes you along the western side of the fjord, head directly east of Ringkøbing along Route 15, turning south when you see the junction with Route 181, going to the small town of Hvide Sande.

Hvide Sande

Midway along the isthmus, Hvide Sande (whose name translates as "white sands") is a typical West Jutland fishing town, founded in 1931, when it grew up around the large lock and sluice between the North Sea and Ringkøbing Fjord. Today, with its splendid beach on the seaside, it's the fifth-largest fishing port in Denmark. A path follows along the windswept dunes between the sea and Ringkøbing Fjord, with panoramic views in all directions.

The most intriguing attraction here is the picturesque fishing harbor, the heartbeat of the town. Catches of fish are unloaded at the auction building here. The auction is held every Monday to Friday at 7am, and again at 10am if the catch is heavy. A small nod or a lifted eyebrow is caught immediately by the auctioneer, and the purchase is registered. When the fish is sold, the catch is taken by truck for processing at local plants or exported directly in large refrigerated vans.

While in the area, you can visit the **Vestkyst Akvariet** (also known as Fiskeriets Hus), Nørregade 2B (ℭ 97-31-26-10; www.fiskerietshus.dk), a museum devoted to anything and everything to do with fishing. The museum has a saltwater aquarium with fish from both the North Sea and Ringkøbing Fjord. It also includes tanks for large fish such as piked dogfish, rays, and big gadoids. April to October, the fish are fed every Tuesday and

Windsurfing on Ringkøbing Fjord

Ringkøbing Fjord is one of the most popular places for windsurfing in the north of Europe. The area has Denmark's excellent breezes, and the shallow fjord waters are ideal for beginners. When the wind blows from the west, it comes in directly from the North Sea. Having passed the dunes, it accelerates across the fjord, creating a strong and constant wind. A wind from the east brings heat and sun, which in turn ensures increasing winds in the afternoon, so that surfing is generally possible every day. The wind is strongest in March, April, September, and October.

The best conditions are found at Hvide Sande, the venue for international and national speed weeks. This is the largest center around the fjord, with Denmark's best shallow water area for speed and slalom surfing. The center has a well-stocked shop with a school providing windsurfing instruction, equipment for hire, and a cafeteria with wind gauge. You'll be kept up-to-date on weather forecasts. You can stop in at **Westwind Nord** (*©* **97-31-25-99;** www.westwind. dk), where you can get an introductory 3-hour course for DKK360 to DKK895 ($61–$152/£36–£90). They also rent gear in summer months.

Friday at 3:30pm. Displays also include fishing tackle, and children can go on a voyage in the wheelhouse of a real cutter. While below deck, visitors experience the cramped conditions under which fishermen live at sea. April to October, it's open daily 10am to 5pm; November to March, daily 10am to 4pm. Admission is DKK50 ($8.50/£5) adults, DKK25 ($4.30/£2.50) children 4 to 12.

At Hvide Sande you'll find information available at **Holmsland Klit Turistforening,** on the premises of the **Vestkyst Aquarium,** Nørregade 2B (*©* 97-31-18-66). The office is open year-round, Monday to Friday from 9am to 4pm. From June to August, it's also open Saturday noon to 5pm and Sunday 11am to 4pm.

Where to Dine in Hvide Sande

Restaurant Slusen SEAFOOD/DANISH   In a building from the 1940s, directly astride the harbor, this is the most appealing restaurant in Hvide Sande, thanks to well-conceived cuisine and a helpful staff. Menu items include fried filets of plaice or turbot, different preparations of herring and salmon, a succulent seafood platter, and filets of catfish with mustard sauce. Lobster is available, kept fresh in an on-site aquarium. The dessert specialty is a Grand Marnier soufflé served on a purée of fresh peaches. The helpings are generous, the food is flavorful, the fish is fresh and well prepared, and the price is right. Not only that, but the staff assured us that readers will have "great fun" here. What more could you ask?

Bredgade 3. *©* **97-31-27-27.** Reservations recommended. Main courses DKK189–DKK400 ($32–$68/£19–£40); fixed-price menu DKK320 ($54/£32). AE, DC, MC, V. Daily 1–4pm and 5–10pm. Closed Oct–Mar Sun 5–10pm and Mon.

Tipperne Nature Reserve ★

You can continue south to Nymindegab, the gateway to the isthmus, if you're coming from Esbjerg. In times gone by, Nymindegab was the home of a small fishing harbor.

From here you can explore **Tipperne Nature Reserve.** A small road, signposted from Nymindegab, leads into this tiny peninsula jutting into Ringkøbing Fjord. The flats and water surrounding the peninsula are one of the best bird sanctuaries in West Jutland. The area's bird life is protected to establish undisturbed breeding. Today it is a favorite stop-over for migratory birds. During both spring and autumn, thousands of ducks, geese, and waders stop here to rest. In July and August, when migration is at its peak, the sandpiper, curlew, snipe, and golden plover are some of the many species to be seen here. In the winter season, the swan, Denmark's national bird, is one of the species finding shelter at Tipperne. April to August, the bird reserve is open to visitors Sunday 5 to 10am only. September to March, the reserve can be visited every Sunday 10am to noon. You should continue by car until you reach a building marked TIPPERHUSET. You're not allowed to stop until you come to the parking lot, but once here you can climb a viewing tower to observe the birds. A 1.5km (1-mile) nature path departs from the bird tower, and all walking in the area is restricted to this one path to protect bird life.

5 RY ★

256km (159 miles) W of Copenhagen; 24km (15 miles) SE of Silkeborg; 35km (22 miles) SW of Århus

In the heart of Jutland, the little old town of Ry makes a less commercialized center than Silkeborg (see below) for visiting the mid-Jutland Lake District, one of the most beautiful areas of Denmark. Ry lies in a rural setting of extensive forests and rolling hills, valleys, gorges, and lakes, all linked by the Gudenå (also spelled Gudenåen), the longest river in Denmark. The region is filled with numerous sites of historical interest, including old churches, abbey ruins, villages with thatched roofs, and a number of small museums. Other than a walk through the town of Ry itself, there aren't many notable sights in the historic center. We use Ry as a base, branching out to see attractions in its environs.

ESSENTIALS

GETTING THERE By Train   Ry lies on the main rail route linking Silkeborg (trip time: 20 min.) and Århus (trip time: 30 min.). There's also a bus from Århus, but it takes twice as long.

By Car   From Silkeborg (see below), take Route 15, heading east, and following the signs to Århus. Veer right (south) when you reach the town of Låsby, following the signs to Ry.

VISITOR INFORMATION   The **Ry Turistbureau,** Klostervej 3 (© **86-69-66-60;** www.visitry.dk), is open June 15 to August 31, Monday to Saturday 9am to 4:30pm. Off-season hours are Monday to Friday 9am to 4pm and Saturday 9am to noon.

GETTING AROUND By Bicycle   For many Danes, the only way to see the lake district and its little hamlets is by bike. **Ry Cykel,** Skanderborgvej 19 (© **86-89-14-91**), will rent you a bike for the day for DKK75 ($13/£7.50).

By Canoe   Instead of a bike, you might prefer to explore the river and the beautiful lakes in the area by canoe. Brochures about canoeing are available from the Ry Turistbureau or from **Ry Kanofart,** Kyhnsvej 20 (© **86-89-11-67**), which will rent you a canoe for DKK300 ($51/£30) per day.

A 10-minute drive west of Ry via Route 445, **Himmelbjerget (Sky Mountain)** ★ is the most visited spot in the Lake District. You can also get here by taking bus no. 104 from the train station at Ry. Himmelbjerget rises 147m (482 ft.) above sea level, the highest point in Denmark. In 1871, the Danish crown obtained the property and turned it over to the people of Denmark as a sightseeing attraction.

Himmelbjerget towers majestically over the surrounding countryside, when viewed not only from the lake, but from the many footpaths in the woods as well. Two modern tourist boats, the *Viking* and the *Turisten,* run summer cruises between Ry and Himmelbjerget. For information and schedules, call ℂ **86-82-88-21** in Ry. The one-way cost is DKK55 ($9.40/£5.50) adults and DKK35 ($6/£3.50) children 3 to 12.

Himmelbjerget Tower, rising 25m (82 ft.), was designed by the architect L. P. Fenger and erected in commemoration of King Frederik VII, who, on June 5, 1849, gave the Danish people a new constitution. From the tower you'll have the most panoramic view of the area. It's open daily May and June, 10am to 5pm; July, 10am to 9pm; August to September 15, 10am to 6pm. From September 16 to October, it's open only on Saturday and Sunday from 10am to 5pm. Admission is DKK10 ($1.70/£1).

Even more than Ry, we are attracted to the hamlet of **Gamle Ry (Old Ry)** ★, directly west of Ry along Route 461. This is called the "village of kings and springs." The name "Ry" comes from *rydning,* Danish for "clearing." In the Middle Ages this was a spiritual center of Denmark because of its "holy springs." The village gets its royal associations through Frederik II, who built a mansion here in 1582.

From the center you can follow a sign directing you to Skt. Sørens spring in Rye Sønderskov (Rye Southwood). This is a wonderful walk through a subglacial stream trench, called Jammerdalen, or "The Vale of Tears." The water of this spring, thought to have curative powers, attracted many pilgrims, launching Gamle Ry on its heyday of medieval glory. In gratitude, pilgrims contributed to the funding of a granite church on the nearby hill where the present Skt. Sørens Kirke is situated. After the Reformation, when the pilgrimages stopped, the church fell into disrepair. In 1912, a rich farmer had the old tower reconstructed. The original church was the scene of the election of Christian III as king of Denmark on July 4, 1534, leading to the collapse of the Catholic Church in Denmark.

From the church, you go east past a mill to **Galgebakken** (The Gallows Hill), a protected nature reserve set in lovely heather-clad hills.

East of Gamle Ry, if you cross the Gudenå at Emborg Bridge, you will come to the ruins of the largest Cistercian abbey in Denmark, the **Øm Kloster** (monastery). In the 12th century, a group of Cistercian monks left the Vitskøl Kloster monastery in Himmerland and arrived at Øm, where they founded the Øm Kloster monastery in 1175. The Cistercians were skilled farmers who preferred sites in forests and remote areas, where their hard work turned barren land into exemplary farms. During the Reformation, the monastery ceased to exist and the lands were taken over by the king. The monastery itself was pulled down. However, excavations in modern times have revealed one of the best-preserved ground plans of a medieval monastery to date. There is a little museum here open April, May, September, and October, Tuesday to Sunday 10am to 4pm; June to August, Tuesday to Sunday 10am to 5pm. The cloister is always closed on Monday. Admission is DKK40 ($6.80/£4) adults, free for ages 18 and under. This minor museum has a historical medical exhibition, an herb garden, and a collection of skeletons discovered in the area. The plants in the herb garden date back to the days when the monastery flourished here. We find it an evocative, nostalgic place worthy of your discovery. For information, call ℂ **86-89-81-94** or visit www.klostermuseet.dk.

You can take Route 461 south from Gamle Ry until you see the turnoff east to the hamlet of Emborg. This takes you to **Mossø,** the largest lake in Jutland. To the west of the lake are the Højlund Forest and the Sukkertoppen Hill, rising 108m (354 ft.).

The longest watercourse in Denmark, the **Gudenå,** also passes through Mossø en route from Tinnet Krat to Randers Fjord. Closer to the river are valley terraces created by water that melted after the Ice Age. The sandy surfaces are covered with heather and coniferous plants, but make for poor farmland.

Mossø is the habitat of many types of birds. The sanctuary at Emborg Odde is a breeding site for a colony of black-headed gulls, which are extremely aggressive, thus providing protection from predators. The black-necked grebe takes advantage of this and breeds among the gulls. In the late summer, grebes can be seen along the edges of the reed banks, feeding on small animals.

WHERE TO STAY

Gamle Rye Kro ★ Finds   Our favorite nest and the most historic hotel in Ry lies in the satellite town of Gamle Ry. The place looks like a large white farmhouse, set 180m (590 ft.) north of the village church and the town market square. It has a history stretching back 400 years, to the time when pilgrims heading for the nearby (now ruined) monastery extolled the healing powers of local springs. Don't expect your accommodations—or even the public rooms—to drip with a sense of antique nostalgia, as much of the inn's historic charm was erased during its renovations in the early 1990s. Overall, however, there's a sense of hospitality from the youthful and entrepreneurial staff, and a restaurant with good regional Danish cooking (see "Where to Dine," below).

Ryesgade 8, DK-8680 Ry. ℂ **86-89-80-42.** Fax 86-89-85-46. www.krohotel.dk. 20 rooms. DKK750 ($128/£75) double. AE, DC, MC, V. From Ry, drive 5km (3 miles) southwest, following the signs to Gamle Ry. **Amenities:** Restaurant; indoor heated pool; fitness room; laundry service; dry cleaning; nonsmoking rooms; solarium. *In room:* TV, no phone (in some).

Hotel Himmelbjerget ★ Kids   Set at a higher altitude than any other hotel in Denmark, this charming, rustic, old-fashioned venue has changed little, despite subtle modernizations, since it was built in 1922. It lies 7km (4¹/₃ miles) northwest of the center of Ry, on a rocky plateau of its own, within a 10-minute walk of the Himmelbjerget Tower. Rooms retain some of their old-time paneling and accessories, and in many cases have terraces or balconies overlooking the nearby tower or the fields, lakes, and forests. Each has a writing table and twin beds that can be separated or moved together. On the premises are a bar and an appealing restaurant that serves generous portions of conservative, time-tested Danish recipes (see "Where to Dine," below). On-site is a children's cafeteria with direct access to a playground. The hotel's name, incidentally, translates from the Danish as "Heaven Mountain." It's not quite that, but is a worthy contender nonetheless.

Ny Himmelbjergvej 20, DK-8680 Ry. ℂ **86-89-80-45.** Fax 86-82-00-68. www.hotel-himmelbjerget.dk. 18 units, all w/shared bathroom. DKK675 ($115/£68) double. Rates include breakfast. AE, DC, MC, V. Bus: 411. **Amenities:** Restaurant; cafeteria; bar; kids' playground; laundry service; dry cleaning.

Nørre Vissing Kro ★   Set 11km (6³/₄ miles) northwest of Ry, amid rolling farmlands dotted with stately trees, this century-old inn has received many awards for the excellence of its cuisine. (See "Where to Dine," below.) It also maintains artfully decorated and stylish rooms, each with a small tiled bathroom. Each has a scattering of rustic antiques that were in most cases acquired within Jutland. There are few amenities per se; but the staff is very hip, and we find the owners charming.

Låsbyvej 122, Nørre Vissing, DK-8660 Skanderborg. ⓒ **86-94-37-16.** Fax 86-94-37-57. www.nr-vissing-kro. dk. 16 units. DKK845–DKK995 ($144–$169/£85–£100) double. Rates include breakfast. DC, MC, V. Drive north from Ry, following the signs from Låsby; at Låsby, turn southwest, following the signs to Nørre Vissing. **Amenities:** Restaurant; bar; room service; public Internet; nonsmoking rooms. *In room:* TV.

Ry Park Hotel Set in the center of Ry, this is one of the oldest *and* newest hotels in town. Originally built in 1888, it was radically reconfigured into a more streamlined and comfortable venue a century later. About 20 rooms are in a comfortable annex across the road. We find the accommodations in the annex more sterile and prefer to stay in the main building. Regardless of your room assignment, all units come with a small private bathroom with tub or shower. Regrettably for the casual visitor, the inn is frequently reserved for conventions. If one is not taking place, the more relaxed and less harassed staff can arrange many sports for you, including fishing, canoeing, kayaking, cycling, and yachting.

Kyhnsvej 2, DK-8680 Ry. ⓒ **86-89-19-11.** Fax 86-89-12-57. www.ryparkhotel.dk. 76 units. DKK890– DKK1,250 ($151–$213/£89–£125) double. Rates include breakfast. AE, DC, MC, V. **Amenities:** Restaurant; bar; indoor heated pool; sauna; room service; laundry service; dry cleaning; nonsmoking rooms. *In room:* TV, hair dryer, iron, safe.

WHERE TO DINE

Gamle Rye Kro ★ (Finds) DANISH It's the always-reliable grandmotherly Danish cookery—and not the hotel rooms (see above)—that attracts a steady stream of visitors and locals to one of the oldest inns in the region. Although the place has been renovated and modernized a little too much for our tastes, the generous portions of food are still traditional. Menu items include all the Danish staples, such as *frikadeller* (meatballs), platters with several different preparations of herring, smoked salmon with chive-flavored cream sauce, roasted pork with red cabbage and onions, Dover sole meunière, and filet of plaice stuffed with asparagus and baby shrimp. Fried eel is even available on occasion.

Ryesgade 8. ⓒ **86-89-80-42.** Reservations recommended. Main courses DKK100–DKK200 ($17–$34/ £10–£20). AE, DC, MC, V. Daily noon–10pm. From Ry drive 5km (3 miles) southwest, following the signs to Gamle Ry.

Nørre Vissing Kro ★★★ FRENCH/ITALIAN/DANISH This is one of the most sophisticated and urbane restaurants in Jutland, with a string of awards for its culinary excellence and flair. Most of the dinner guests combine their meal with an overnight stay (see above). Luncheons, however, tend to include greater numbers of guests en route to somewhere else, and are lighter and less elaborate. The dining room is a spacious, all-blue affair dotted with country antiques and artfully chosen accessories. Menu items change with the seasons. A well-conceived meal, however, might include foie gras with cherry sauce served on a bed of sautéed summer cabbage, poached lobster with a spinach flan and orange sauce, a medley of French and Italian cheeses, and a layer cake stuffed with summer berries marinated in rum, served with strawberry sorbet. There is a robust quality to the cuisine, yet each dish is imbued with a subtle texture that only a master chef— one who knows how to turn simple, natural produce into a gastronomic experience of unmistakable quality—can achieve.

Låsbyvej 122, Nørre Vissing, Skanderborg. ⓒ **86-94-37-16.** Reservations recommended. Main courses DKK125–DKK225 ($21–$38/£13–£23); fixed-price menus DKK295–DKK610 ($50–$104/£30–£61). AE, DC, MC, V. Daily noon–3pm and 6–9pm. Drive north from Ry, following the signs to Låsby; at Låsby, turn southwest, following the signs to Nørre Vissing.

Restaurant Himmelbjerget DANISH   At a higher altitude than any other in Denmark, this is an appealingly old-fashioned restaurant where white napery, high ceilings, and old-world service are still offered. The recipes haven't changed in a century—and that's exactly what the locals depend upon when they book a table here. Menu items include most traditional Danish specialties, including marinated salmon with mustard and dill sauce and fresh-baked bread, filet of beef with onions and red-wine sauce, filet of veal with fresh vegetables and mushroom sauce, cold potato soup with bacon and chives, brisket of beef with horseradish sauce, or tenderloin of beef with fried onions. Any of these might be followed by selections from a carefully arranged platter of Danish cheeses.

Ny Himmelbjergvej 20. (©) **86-89-80-45.** Reservations recommended. Main courses DKK165–DKK270 ($28–$46/£17–£27). AE, DC, MC, V. Daily 10am–10pm. Bus: 411 from Ry.

6 SILKEBORG

43km (27 miles) W of Århus; 279km (173 miles) W of Copenhagen; 37km (23 miles) S of Viborg

If you go on a TV trivia quiz show and are asked the question "How old is the oldest man in the world and where does he reside?" remember that the answer, hopefully for $100,000, is the "Tollund Man," who is in pretty good shape, having been born 2,400 years ago. He resides in Central Jutland in the little town of Silkeborg. To make his acquaintance, read on.

In the heart of the Danish lake district, this town of 35,000 opens onto the waters of Lake Longsø, where we like to go for a stroll at night to see the largest color fountain in Scandinavia. If you don't like the lake (highly unlikely), there is always the Gudenå River, the longest in Denmark. The Danes themselves come here to go canoeing, hiking through the surrounding hills, or boating on the lake. Silkeborg has some notable attractions, as we will soon see, but many locals prefer it for the joy of its setting "in the great outdoors," as a local proudly informed us.

In 1845, Michael Drewsen, whose statue is seen in the heart of town on the Torvet (main square), built a paper mill here on the east side of the river, and in time other industries sprouted up, leading to great prosperity for the town. Unlike some little towns of Denmark, with their narrow cobblestone streets, Silkeborg is spaciously laid out. A progressive town, it is scenic, historic, but also modern, with a vast shopping district of 200 specialty stores, the largest marketplace in Central Jutland, a multiplex cinema, dozens of restaurants, and a convention center.

ESSENTIALS

GETTING THERE   From Århus, follow Route 15 west to Silkeborg. If you aren't driving, there's frequent train service from Copenhagen via Fredericia.

VISITOR INFORMATION   The **Silkeborg Turistbureau** is at Godthåbsvej 4 (© **86-82-19-11;** www.silkeborg.com). It's open June 15 to August, Monday to Friday 9am to 5pm, Saturday and Sunday 10am to 2pm; September, October, and April to June 14, Monday to Friday 9am to 4pm, Saturday 10am to 1pm; November to March, Monday to Friday 10am to 3pm. In December, the office is also open Saturday 10am to 1pm.

GETTING AROUND   Numerous **bus routes** service the city; all local buses depart from the stop on Fredensgade. There's no number to call for information. Tickets cost DKK18 ($3.10/£1.80) per individual ride.

Although we can never resist the charms of the **Tollund Man** (see "Silkeborg Museum," below), the greatest adventure for us is to sail aboard the world's last coal-fired paddle steamer, the *Hjejlen* ★★★, which has been sailing since 1861. It follows the route of the Gudenå River, going along a waterway of about 150km (100 miles) through Jutland's lake district. Himmelbjerget, or "Sky Mountain" (p. 351), is the major attraction along the route. Departures are daily from Silkeborg harbor at 10am and again at 2pm from mid-June to mid-August, with a round-trip costing DKK110 ($19/£11) for adults or DKK80 ($14/£8) for children 3 to 12. For schedules and more information, call **Hjejlen Co., Ltd.,** Havnen (✆ **86-82-07-66**).

AQUA Ferskvands Akvarium og Museum ★ (Kids) North Europe's largest freshwater aquarium is called "the inside-out aquarium." Now just what does that mean? The circular building is placed in the waters of the lake, which makes it a reverse aquarium, with you inside it. Through the large seascape windows, you can look into the lake and watch both fish and water plants. In a beautiful park at AQUA, you can observe bird life with plenty of beavers around to amuse you. We forego the ferocious pikes to find fun with the diving ducks.

The spookiest part is called "The Bog," a dark, mysterious place where the big carp dwells, as does the tench and the elusive eel. Rare European otters can be seen hunting live fish in "The Otter Lake." One section, "The Darkness of the Night," is devoted to nocturnal animals that come out in moonlight, especially the Danish owl. This section also boasts AQUA's largest indoor aquarium with its "dancing eels," along with zander, sturgeon, crayfish, and the freshwater turbot. Another section of the park is set aside for children where they can actually feel the big sturgeon, carp, flounder, or other fish. You can have lunch or picnic in the park or pay a visit to the AQUA Café.

Vejsøvej 55. ✆ **89-21-21-89**. www.ferskvandscentret.dk. Admission DKK95 ($16/£9.50) adults, DKK55 ($9.40/£5.50) children 3–12. July and Aug daily 10am–6pm; off-season Mon–Fri 10am–4pm, Sat–Sun 10am–5pm.

Silkeborg Kunstmuseum (Silkeborg Museum of Art) ★★ This is one of the great provincial art museums of Scandinavia. The moment you arrive you know you're in for something special when you are greeted by two large ceramic walls by Jean Dubuffet and others. In one of the most beautiful areas of Silkeborg, in old parkland bordering the banks of the Gudenå River, Asger Jorn, a leading figure in 20th-century European art, donated his impressive collection of 5,000 paintings by 150 artists he collected up until his death in 1973. Many of the works were by his friends, artists he met in Paris "between the wars."

Jorn is famous today for having founded the fabled COBRA group, based on the first letters of Copenhagen, Brussels, and Amsterdam, where most of the artists originated. The Jorn collection includes impressive works by Le Corbusier, Léger, Max Ernst, Dubuffet, Miró, and Picasso.

Jorn himself was a virtual Renaissance man when it came to art, excelling in painting, sculpture, ceramics, tapestries, drawings, and graphics. His *Moon Dog* from 1953 is amusing, but he is at his most frightening in his masterpiece, *Stalingrad* ★★.

The museum is also richly imbued with an important collection of Danish art ★ from the 20th century. Of the COBRA group and their paintings, Jorn once said, "We are in violent reaction against the social disorder brought about by war. We also renounce all other artistic trends of our day." The privately owned gallery supplements its permanent collection with changing exhibitions of paintings and sculpture.

Gudenåvej 9. ✆ 86-82-53-88. www.silkeborgkunstmuseum.dk. Admission DKK60 ($10/£6) adults, free for children 17 and under. Apr–Oct Tues–Sun 10am–5pm; Nov–Mar Tues–Fri noon–4pm, Sat–Sun 10am–5pm. Bus: 10.

Silkeborg Museum　One of the world's greatest human treasures from antiquity is the world-famous and much-photographed **Tollund Man ★★★**. Discovered in a peat bog in 1950, he is the most perfectly preserved human being to have survived the ages. When he lived during the Iron Age (roughly 500 B.C. to A.D. 500), the great city of Athens was in decline, the second Punic War was being fought, the finishing touches were being put on the Great Wall of China, and Hannibal was trying to get those damn elephants to cross the Alps.

Just how well preserved is the Tollund Man? When his body was discovered, locals called the police, thinking it was a recent murder. You can even see the wrinkles in his forehead. He had good cause for wrinkles. His head capped by fur, the Tollund Man was strangled by a plaited leather string, probably as part of a ritual sacrifice for a successful peat harvest. He was also a vegetarian, as scientists have determined, his last meal consisting of flax and barley.

Sleeping near the Tollund Man for centuries is the **Elling Woman ★★**, whose body was discovered in 1938 about 60m (200 ft.) from where the Tollund Man was later discovered. Wrapped in a sheepskin cape, she had been hanged with a leather thong, the V-shaped furrow still to be seen around her neck today. Scientists estimate that she was about 25 years old when she died in 210 B.C., probably the result of another ritual sacrifice.

After seeing these rather gruesome sights, you can admire the setting of the museum in a manor house by the Gudenå River, directly east of the Torvet. The building itself dates back to 1767 and is the oldest structure in Silkeborg.

In addition to its gruesome corpses, the museum displays exhibits devoted to regional history and local handicrafts, especially an antique glass collection, the renowned **Sorring ceramics ★**. Interiors have been arranged to illustrate antiques from the mid-19th century.

The museum also has a special exhibition of a clog maker's workshop, a collection of stone implements, antique jewelry, and artifacts from the ruins of Silkeborg Castle. In the handicraft and Iron Age markets, artisans use ancient techniques to create iron, jewelry, and various crafts.

Hovedgaardsvej 7. ✆ 86-82-14-99. www.silkeborgmuseum.dk. Admission DKK45 ($7.70/£4.50) adults, free for children 18 and under. May to mid-Oct daily 10am–5pm; mid-Oct to Apr Sat–Sun noon–4pm. Bus: 10.

Nearby Attractions
Jysk Automobilmuseum (Jutland Car Museum) ★　Ever since a long-ago friend let us drive custom-made 1920s cars, originally created for silent-screen vamps around Hollywood, we've been addicted to vintage cars. Outside Silkeborg at the village of Gjern, our fantasies live again with a collection of 150 vintage vehicles made as far back as 1900 and as recently as 1950. Many rare European and American vehicles and motorcycles can be viewed, not only the Rolls Royce and Maserati, but also the famous Renault Taxis de la Marne or a V12 Cadillac or the 1947 Crosley. A local mechanic, Aagi Louring, not only collected these vehicles but restored them to working order, opening the museum in 1967.

Skovvejen, Gjern. ✆ 86-87-50-50. www.jyskautomobilmuseum.dk. Admission DKK70 ($12/£7) adults, DKK30 ($5.10/£3) children 6–14, free for children 5 and under. May 16–Sept 15 daily 10am–5pm; Apr 1–May 15 and Sept 16–Oct 31 Sat–Sun and holidays 10am–5pm. Closed Nov 1–Mar. Bus: Take the bus marked RANDERS from Silkeborg. 15km (9¹⁄₃ miles) northeast of Silkeborg, it's accessible by following the

SHOPPING

The main market is held at **Torvet** (town square) on Saturday mornings, starting around 7am. It's always best to go before noon. A smaller market begins about the same time every Wednesday at **Nørretorv.** Among specialty stores, **Bon Sac,** Søndergade 2C (© **86-82-60-55**), has an intriguing collection of fashionable leather goods. **Inspiration,** Østergade 5 (© **86-82-50-11**), offers a large array of gift items for the home.

WHERE TO STAY

The Silkeborg Turistbureau (© **86-82-19-11;** www.silkeborg.com) can book you into nearby **private homes.**

Moderate

Gl. Skovridergaard ★   This historic and luxurious complex would be a complete delight if it weren't conference-crazed. Rooms during the peak of winter might not always be available if a convention is booked. But when midsummer arrives, and most Frommer's readers are in the Silkeborg area, a stay here can be one of the most rewarding in Central Jutland. The location itself is idyllic—close to the Gudenå River. Set within a well-maintained park, the hotel originated in the 1700s, when the manager of the surrounding game reserve and forest built a well-appointed home for himself. In the mid-1980s, under the ownership of Silkeborg's largest bank (which books at least 30% of all convention space for its own managers and staff members), it was expanded into the convention center and hotel you'll see today.

Rooms are larger than you might expect, and filled with comfortable furnishings. Cafe tables are set up on the hotel's verdant lawns during mild weather, and the hotel's restaurant offers well-prepared, carefully choreographed meals.

Marienlundsvej 36, DK-8600 Silkeborg. © 87-22-55-00. Fax 87-22-55-11. www.glskov.dk. 68 units. DKK1,375 ($234/£138) double; DKK1,670 ($284/£167) junior suite. Rates include buffet breakfast. AE, DC, MC, V. From Silkeborg, drive less than a kilometer (¹/₂ mile) south of town, following the signs to Horsens. **Amenities:** Restaurant; bar; sauna; room service; babysitting; laundry service; dry cleaning; nonsmoking rooms. *In room:* TV, Wi-Fi, minibar (some units), coffeemaker, hair dryer, iron (in some).

Hotel Dania ★   If you want modernity, plus facilities, check into the Radisson SAS (see below). But if you desire tradition, you could find no better choice than the town's oldest hotel, dating from 1848. Much improved over the years, it's been modernized without losing its charm. The bedrooms overlook either the lake or the Torvet, the main square of town. Antiques fill the corridors and reception lounge, but the midsize-to-spacious guest rooms have been decorated in Danish modern, each unit containing a neatly kept bathroom. Outdoor dining on the square is popular in the summer, and the **Underhuset** restaurant serves typical Danish food along with Scandinavian and French dishes. The hotel's dining room is physically one of the longest restaurants in Denmark.

Torvet 5, DK-8600 Silkeborg. © 86-82-01-11. Fax 86-80-20-04. www.hoteldania.dk. 49 units. DKK1,512 ($257/£151) double; DKK1,725–DKK2,480 ($293–$422/£173–£248) suite. Rates include breakfast. AE, DC, MC, V. Free parking. Bus: 3. **Amenities:** Restaurant; bar; room service; babysitting; laundry service; dry cleaning; nonsmoking rooms. *In room:* TV, minibar, hair dryer, trouser press, safe.

Radisson SAS Hotel ★★★   In hotels, this is the best case of recycling in all of Central Jutland. It was converted from a historic, 150-year-old paper factory into the most modern and up-to-date hotel in the area. The location is not quite as central as the

Dania, but the Radisson rises right by the harbor, a short walk from attractions, shops, and restaurants. The chain hotel is also a favorite venue in Silkeborg for conferences, as the town's concert and theater facility, Jysk Musik & Teaterhus, lies nearby. The hotel offers the finest and most modern doubles and suites in Greater Silkeborg, successfully combining Danish modern with traditional styling, including state-of-the-art bathrooms with tub/shower combinations. When it's snowing outside, the lobby bar with its fireplace is the best place to be in Silkeborg. During fair weather, the restaurant, with its spacious terrace offering panoramic views of the Remstrup River, is a favorite spot.

Papirfabrikken 12, DK-8600 Silkeborg. © **88-82-22-22.** Fax 88-82-22-23. www.radissonsas.com. 100 units. DKK1,365–DKK1,450 ($232–$247/£137–£145) double; DKK1,995–DKK2,400 ($339–$408/£200–£240) suite. Rates include continental breakfast. AE, DC, MC, V. **Amenities:** Restaurant; bar; sauna; room service; laundry service; dry cleaning; nonsmoking rooms; rooms for those w/limited mobility. *In room:* A/C, TV, Wi-Fi, minibar, fridge, hair dryer, iron, Jacuzzi (in suites).

Scandic Hotel Silkeborg ★ (Kids) This chain-run hotel hardly has the glamour of the Radisson, but it is one of the better choices in the area for overnighting, especially for motorists, as it lies 2.5km (1¹⁄₂ miles) west of the town center in a residential neighborhood surrounded by fields and forests. The hotel has a certain charm and family appeal, with its playroom for kids and indoor heated pool. Bedrooms are small to midsize, each furnished in a chain format of Danish modern, with well-equipped tiled bathrooms. In winter, commercial travelers dominate the clientele, giving way by midsummer to vacationers from abroad. The hotel dining room, **Guldanden** (Golden Duck), is a glamorous spot serving Danish and international cuisine.

Udgårdsvej 2, DK-8600 Silkeborg. © **86-80-35-33.** Fax 86-80-35-06. www.scandic-hotels.dk/silkeborg. 117 units. DKK1,090–DKK1,390 ($185–$236/£109–£139) double; DKK1,390–DKK1,690 ($236–$287/£139–£169) suite. AE, DC, MC, V. Bus: 3 from rail station. **Amenities:** Restaurant; bar; indoor heated pool; gym; sauna; children's playroom; laundry service; dry cleaning; nonsmoking rooms; solarium; rooms for those w/limited mobility. *In room:* TV, Wi-Fi, minibar, coffeemaker (in some), iron, trouser press.

Inexpensive
Kongensbro Kro ★★ Although a tavern stood on this site from 1663, it was little more than a ruin when members of the Andersen family bought and rebuilt it in 1949. The family's matriarch, Else, authored five Danish-language cookbooks during her active years here, and became something of a legend throughout Denmark. Today the charming and well-kept inn is directed by her son, Øle, and his hardworking staff. Accommodations are pleasant and cozy, and all contain private bathrooms.

Meals are served daily noon to 3pm and 6 to 9pm. A two-course fixed-price menu is available at lunch and dinner for DKK245 to DKK295 ($42–$50/£25–£30), although most serious gastronomes opt for a la carte meals. The inn lies between Ans and Århus, about a 10-minute drive north of Silkeborg.

Gamle Kongevej 70, DK-8643 Ans By. © **86-87-01-77.** Fax 86-87-92-17. www.kongensbro-kro.dk. 15 units. DKK995–DKK1,500 ($169–$255/£100–£150) double. Rates include breakfast. AE, DC, MC, V. Closed Dec 23–24 and Dec 31–Jan 15. **Amenities:** Restaurant; room service; laundry service; dry cleaning; nonsmoking room. *In room:* TV.

Svostrup Kro ★ (Finds) The hotel advertises itself as "sweet as the good ole times"—and so it is. This is one of the least-modernized inns around Silkeborg, with more of its original architectural features than many of its competitors. On farmland between the Gudenå River and the Gjern hills, it was built in the 1600s as a bargeman's inn and designated by the Danish monarchy in 1834 as one of the inns suitable for a visit from the Danish king. Because of its authenticity and its hardworking, tactful staff, it's sought out by aficionados of old Danish inns, who appreciate its antique paneling and an interior that evokes the Denmark of long ago. Rooms contain appealing antique (or at least old) furnishings, with charmingly dowdy touches. The restaurant is open 7am to 11pm every day. Many of the food items include old-fashioned Danish cuisine such as herring platters with new potatoes, or fried steak with onions. Others are more modern, such as venison steak braised with red wine, and served with caramelized apples, nuts, celery, mushrooms, and a confit of baby onions.

Svostrupvej 58, Svostrup, DK-8600 Silkeborg. © **86-87-70-04.** Fax 87-57-23-26. www.svostrup-kro.dk. 15 units. DKK995 ($169/£100) double; DKK1,195 ($203/£120) suite. Rates include breakfast. AE, DC, MC, V. Bus: 313 from Silkeborg. From Silkeborg, drive 10km (6¼ miles) north, following the signs to Randers and then the signs to Svostrup. *In room:* No phone.

WHERE TO DINE

Piaf ★ (Finds) MEDITERRANEAN The most exotic and deliberately counterculture restaurant in town occupies a solid, 80-year-old brick building in the historic core. It was named after the uncanny resemblance of its owner, Anni Danielsen (who's known for her fondness for black dresses), to the late French chanteuse Edith Piaf. Artwork within the restaurant is offset with brick walls, potted plants, poster-image testimonials to the late Gallic sparrow, and deliberately mismatched tables, plates, ashtrays, and accessories. Lunch platters tend to be light, airy, and flavorful; dinners, more substantial with excellently chosen ingredients—always fresh—deftly handled by a skilled kitchen staff. Both are inspired by the tenets of Spanish, Greek, Provençal, and Italian cuisine. Look for heaping platters of paella, roasted lamb with rosemary, carpaccio, and sliced veal, with bowls of bouillabaisse. What's the only item you're likely not to find on the menu? Pork, since it reminds most of the clients of the cuisine served in Denmark during their childhood, and which is consequently something avoided within this consciously exotic setting.

Nygade 31. © **86-81-12-55.** www.restaurant-piaf.dk. Reservations recommended. Fixed-price menus DKK298–DKK990 ($51–$168/£30–£99). DC, MC, V. Tues–Sat 6–10pm.

Spiesehuset Christian VIII ★★ DANISH/FRENCH The best restaurant in Silkeborg, this establishment was founded in 1992 in what was originally a private house built in the late 1700s. It seats only 30 people in a dining room painted in what the owners describe as the color of heaven (cerulean blue), accented with modern paintings. "Give the chef a toque!" our dining companion once urged, before we explained the Frommer's star system. "You'll shed tears of joy over the lobster ravioli." The dish doesn't make us cry, but we have praise for the chef. We also think his carpaccio of marinated sole and salmon with a saffron sauce has a touch of brilliance, as does the filet of beef with truffle

The Riverboat Jazz Festival

In late June of every year, you'd think you were in pre–Hurricane Katrina New Orleans. For 4 days, the sounds of jazz music—Dixieland, swing, gospel, big band, street parades, and jam sessions—fill the air. The festival takes place on the town squares, in the streets, and on the lakes, but most of all in four great tents erected for the occasion, two at the harbor, one on Bindslevs Plads, and another on Torvet (the main square). Concerts at these tents are always free. Jazz lovers from all over Europe flock here. For more information, contact the Turistbureau (see earlier in this chapter) or log on to **www.riverboat.dk.**

sauce. The multifariously flavored medallions of veal come stuffed with a purée of wild duck and herbs. Of course, you can go for the classics, none better than the tender rack of Danish lamb with garlic sauce.

Christian VIII Vej 54. ℭ **86-82-25-62.** Reservations required. Main courses DKK185–DKK305 ($31–$52/£19–£31). AE, DC, MC, V. Mon–Sat 4–10pm.

SILKEBORG AFTER DARK

Available at any bar in town is *Neptun,* the local brew. According to a panel of expert tasters in Paris in 1986, it was then the world's best beer. Since that time, it's been challenged by other suds, but as any loyal native of Silkeborg will tell you, all other beers "taste like p—." We don't dare complete the word, but it rhymes with *hiss.*

Rather historic is the **Underhuset Pub,** part of the dining and drinking facilities within the also-recommended Hotel Dania, Torvet 5 (ℭ **86-82-01-11**), which is charmingly old-fashioned. The town's swankiest bar is in the previously recommended Radisson SAS (see above). It was designed by Botikken, a well-known retail design store, and is the trendiest place for a drink in town.

7 ÅRHUS ★★★

159km (99 miles) NE of Fanø; 175km (109 miles) W of Copenhagen; 43km (27 miles) E of Silkeborg

Some locals call it "the world's smallest city." Actually, it is the second-largest city in Denmark and the capital of Jutland. Because Copenhagen is so far to the east, Århus has also been called "the capital of the West." A large student population makes for a vast cultural life, which reaches its peak in late summer when visitors flock here for an arts festival.

There is much to see and do. More than any man-made attractions in Århus, we like its bustling life, which takes place in the best bars in Jutland and in its sidewalk cafes. There are sandy beaches nearby and a number of museums. Even more than the actual museums to explore, you can experience Århus life with a close encounter by walking its cobblestone streets and taking a picnic lunch to one of the city parks on a sunny day.

The city's economic growth today is based on communications, the food industry, electronics, textiles, iron and steel, and Danish design, as well as the harbor, which is now the second most important in Denmark, rivaled only by Copenhagen.

Originally Århus was a Viking settlement, founded as early as the 10th century; its original name, Aros, meaning estuary, comes from its position at the mouth of a river, Århus Å. The town experienced rapid growth and by 948 it had its own bishop. An Episcopal church was built here in 1060, and a cathedral was started at the dawn of the 13th century. This prosperity came to a temporary end in the late Middle Ages when the town was devastated by the bubonic plague. The Reformation of 1536 also slowed the growth of Århus. But the coming of the railway in the 19th century renewed prosperity, which continues to this day.

Try to plan at least a full day and night here—or two if you can spare the time.

ESSENTIALS

GETTING THERE   By Plane   Århus Airport is in Tirstrup, 43km (27 miles) northeast of the city. **SAS** (ℭ **800/221-2350** in North America, or 70-10-20-00 in Århus; www.aar.dk) operates some 12 flights a day from Copenhagen, Monday to Friday, and

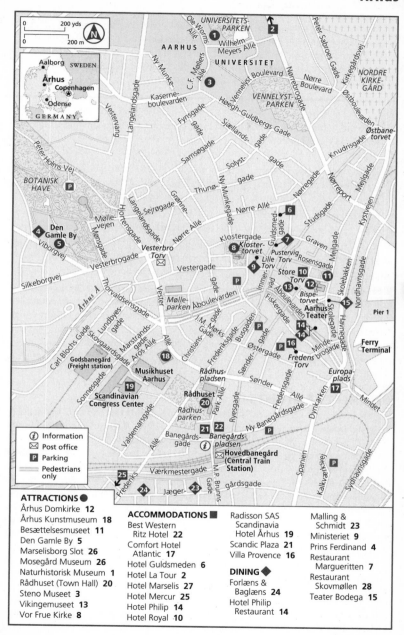

0 200 yds
0 200 m

AARHUS
UNIVERSITETS-PARKEN
Ole Worms Allé
Wilhelm Meyers Allé
UNIVERSITET
Peter Sabroes Gade
NORDRE KIRKE-GÅRD

Aalborg SWEDEN
Århus
Copenhagen
Odense
GERMANY

Ny Munke-
C.F. Møllers Allé
Vennelyst Boulevard
Nørre Boulevard
Nørrebrogade
Østboulevarden
Kirkegårdsvej

Kaserne-boulevarden
Høegh-Guldbergs Gade
VENNELYST PARKEN

Vestervang
Langelandsgade
Fynsgade
Sjællands-gade
Samsøgade
Solyst-gade
Østbane-torvet
Knudrisgade

Peter Holms Vej

BOTANISK HAVE
Thunø-gade
Ny Munkegade
Nørregade
Nørreport
Kystvejen
Meilgade

Langelandsgade
Møllevangs-gade
Grønne-gade
Sejrøgade
Nørre Allé
Nørre Allé
Guldsmed-gade
Studsgade
6

Den Gamle By
4
5
Viborgvej
Mølle-vejen
Vesterbro Torv
Klostergade
Kloster-torvet
8
Graven
Pustervig
Lille Torv
7

Silkeborgvej
Vesterbrogade
Vestergade
Vestergade
gade
9
Store Torv
10
Rosensgade
Meilgade
Nordhavnsgade
11

Århus Å
Thorvaldsensgade
Vester
Mølle-parken
Åboulevarden
Immervad
13
Torv
12
Bispe-torvet
Aarhus Teater
15
Pier 1

Carl Blochs Gade
Lundbyes-gade
Skovgaardsgade
Marstrands-gade
Aros Allé
J.M. Mørks Gade
Christians-gade
Fredensgade
Busgaden
Fiskergade
14
14
Havnegade
Skolebakken
Skolegade

Godsbanegård
(Freight station)
18
Musikhuset Aarhus
Rådhus-pladsen
Østergade
16
Fredens Torv
Minde-brogade
Ferry Terminal

Sønnesgade
19
Scandinavian Congress Center
Rådhuset
20
Rådhus-parken
Sønder Allé
Ryesgade
Ny Banegårdsgade
Fredensgade Allé
Dynkarken
Europa-plads
17
Mindet

Valdemarsgade
Sønder Allé
21
22
Banegårds-gade
Banegårds-pladsen
Hovedbanegård (Central Train Station)
Spanien
Kalkværksvej
Sydhavnsgade

25
Frederiks gade
Værkmestergade
M.P. Bruuns
gade
gårdsgade
24
Jæger-
23

Information
Post office
Parking
Pedestrians only

ATTRACTIONS ●
Århus Domkirke **12**
Århus Kunstmuseum **18**
Besættelsesmuseet **11**
Den Gamle By **5**
Marselisborg Slot **26**
Mosegård Museum **26**
Naturhistorisk Museum **1**
Rådhuset (Town Hall) **20**
Steno Museet **3**
Vikingemuseet **13**
Vor Frue Kirke **8**

ACCOMMODATIONS ■
Best Western
  Ritz Hotel **22**
Comfort Hotel
  Atlantic **17**
Hotel Guldsmeden **6**
Hotel La Tour **2**
Hotel Marselis **27**
Hotel Mercur **25**
Hotel Philip **14**
Hotel Royal **10**

Radisson SAS
  Scandinavia
  Hotel Århus **19**
Scandic Plaza **21**
Villa Provence **16**

DINING ◆
Forlæns &
  Baglæns **24**
Hotel Philip
  Restaurant **14**

Malling &
  Schmidt **23**
Ministeriet **9**
Prins Ferdinand **4**
Restaurant
  Margueritten **7**
Restaurant
  Skovmøllen **28**
Teater Bodega **15**

Value **The Århus Card**

The **Århus Card** allows unlimited travel by public transportation and free admission to many museums and attractions. It also includes a 2¹/₂-hour guided tour. A 2-day pass costs DKK169 ($29/£17) for adults and DKK69 ($12/£6.90) for children 3–12. The Århus Card is sold at the tourist office, many hotels, camping grounds, and kiosks throughout the city.

about 6 on Saturday and Sunday. SAS also operates an afternoon flight most days between Århus and London. An airport bus runs between the train depot at Århus and the airport, meeting all major flights. The cost of a one-way ticket is DKK90 ($15/£9).

By Train About five or six trains a day travel between Århus and Copenhagen (trip time: 4¹/₂ hr.). Some 20 trains a day connect Aalborg with Århus (1 hr., 40 min.). From Frederikshavn, the North Jutland port and ferry-arrival point from Norway, some 20 trains a day run to Århus (3 hr.).

By Bus Two buses daily make the run to Århus from Copenhagen (4 hr.).

By Car From the east, cross Funen on the E20 express highway, heading north at the junction with the E45. From the north German border, drive all the way along the E45. From Frederikshavn and Aalborg in the north, head south along the E45.

VISITOR INFORMATION The tourist office, **Tourist Århus,** Banegårdspladsen 20 (© **87-31-50-10**; www.visitaarhus.com), is open June 26 to September 10 Monday to Friday 9:30am to 6pm, Saturday 9:30am to 5pm, and Sunday 9:30am to 1pm; September 11 to April 30 Monday to Friday 9am to 4pm, Saturday 10am to 1pm; May 1 to June 25 Monday to Friday 9:30am to 5pm and Saturday 10am to 1pm.

GETTING AROUND A regular bus ticket, valid for one ride, can be purchased on the rear platform of all city buses for DKK18 ($3.10/£1.80).

SEEING THE SIGHTS

For the best introduction to Århus, head for the town hall's tourist office, where a 2¹/₂-hour **sightseeing tour** leaves daily at 10am June 24 to August 31, costing DKK80 ($14/£8) per person (free with the Århus Card; see above).

In addition to the more major museums listed below, you can visit two museums on the grounds of Århus University, Nordre Ringgade. One is **Steno Museet,** C. F. Møllers Allé (© **89-42-39-75**; www.stenomuseet.dk; bus: 2, 3, or 4), which displays exhibits documenting natural science and medicine. You'll see beautiful 19th-century astronomical telescopes, a 1920s surgical room, and some of the first computers made in Denmark in the 1950s. Posters, models, and do-it-yourself experiments, including tests of Galileo's demonstrations of gravity and of electromagnetism, are also on display. In addition, you can walk through an herbal garden with some 250 historical medicinal herbs. There is also a Planetarium, with daily shows Tuesday to Sunday at 11am, 1pm, and 2pm, or Saturday and Sunday at noon and 2pm. Hours for the museum are Tuesday to Sunday 10am to 4pm (until 7pm Oct–Mar), costing an admission of DKK45 ($7.70/£4.50), with children 17 and under admitted free.

Also at the university is a **Naturhistorisk Museum,** Block 210, Universitetsparken (© **86-12-97-77**; www.naturhistoriskmuseum.dk; bus: 2 or 3), filled with mounted animals from all over the world, some of which are displayed in engaging dioramas. The collection of Danish animals, especially birds, is unique within Denmark. Skeletons, minerals, and a display devoted to the evolution of life are some of the other exhibits. It's open daily 10am to 4pm (to 5pm July–Aug). It's closed on Mondays November to March. Admission is DKK50 ($8.50/£5) adults, and free for children 17 and under.

Århus Domkirke (Cathedral of St. Clemens) ★   As European city cathedrals go, the Domkirke at Århus is low on the totem pole. When it was built in 1201 in the Romanesque style, it probably had greater style. But in the 1400s, after a fire, it was rebuilt in the Gothic style, with a soaring whitewashed nave that makes it the longest in Denmark, practically as deep as its spire is tall (96m/315 ft.). Today's Gothic interior is relatively plain except for one of the few pre-Reformation survivors, a grand **tripartite altarpiece** ★★, by the noted Bernt Notke. The pipe organ is from the 1700s. Behind the altar is a painted glass window, the creation of Emmanuel Vigeland, brother of the more celebrated Gustav Vigeland of Norway. In shades of lavender and black, among other colors, chalk frescoes date from medieval times, depicting scenes from the Bible. Our favorite is a depiction of St. George slaying that dragon to save a princess in distress. Also depicted is the namesake of the church, St. Clement, who drowned with an anchor around his neck, making him the patron saint of sailors. The best for last: Climb the tower for a **panoramic view** ★★ over Århus and its surrounding area. (After the cathedral, we suggest a visit to the nearby medievalesque compound at Vestergade 3, with half-timbered buildings, rock garden, aviary, and antique interiors.)

Bispetorvet. ℂ **86-20-54-00.** Free admission. May–Sept Mon–Sat 9:30am–4pm; Oct–Apr Mon–Sat 10am–3pm. Bus: 3, 11, 54, or 56.

Århus Kunstmuseum (Århus Museum of Art) ★   Crouching down and looking at you from 5m (16 ft.) above is Ron Mueck's controversial sculpture of a boy, called simply *Boy* ★★★, which is eerily lifelike. This avant-garde sculpture sets the tone for one of the best provincial art museums in all of Denmark. The collection is strong on Modernism from the turn of the 20th century to the 1960s.

The museum is also strong on paintings from the so-called Golden Age of art in Denmark in the 1800s. The Romantics, the Realists, the Impressionists—they are all here, along with contemporary works not only from Denmark but from such countries as the United States and Germany as well. The museum is spread over several floors, which are linked by a footbridge. On the top floor is a first-class restaurant and rooftop patio, from which panoramic views of Århus can be seen. Often a venue for temporary exhibitions, the museum owns about 10,000 pieces of art, the oldest of which date from 1770.

Aros Allé 2, Århus C. ℂ **87-30-66-00.** www.aros.dk. Admission DKK90 ($15/£9) adults, free for children 17 and under. Tues–Sun 10am–5pm (Wed to 10pm). Bus: 2 or 3.

Besættelsesmuseet (Occupation Museum)   Dating from 1857 in what was the old town hall and police station, this building had a grim role to play in World War II. It was here that the Nazis interrogated prisoners and subjected them to torture in the cellars now housing this museum that illustrates the dramatic events of the German takeover of the city in 1940 until liberation in 1945. This was the Gestapo headquarters during the war. In the basement of the building, this Occupation Museum details a most troubled time, depicting Allied air raids on Århus, weapons, documents, World War II photo displays, guns, and even instruments of torture. The museum also describes sabotage carried out by the local resistance movement. One display documents Allied, Nazi, and Danish propaganda.

Mathilde Fibigers Have 2. ℭ **86-18-42-77.** www.besaettelsesmuseet.dk. Admission DKK30 ($5.10/£3) adults, free for children 11 and under. June–Aug Tues–Sun 11am–4pm; off-season Sat–Sun 11am–4pm. Bus: 3 or 7.

Den Gamle By (The Old Town) ★★★ (Kids) Outside of Copenhagen, this is Denmark's only government-rated three-star museum, a journey back to yesterday as you wander through a Danish market town as it appeared in olden days. More than three million visitors descend on this museum where history comes alive. More than 75 historic buildings, many of them half-timbered, were uprooted from various locations throughout the country and placed down here to illustrate Danish life from the 16th to the 19th century in a re-created botanical garden. The open-air museum differs from similar attractions near Copenhagen and Odense in that this one focuses more on rural life. Visitors walk through the authentic-looking workshops of bookbinders, carpenters, hatters, and other craftspeople. There is also a pharmacy, a school, and an old-fashioned post office. A popular attraction is the Burgomaster's House, a wealthy merchant's antiques-stuffed, half-timbered home, built at the end of the 16th century. Be sure to see the textile collection and the Old Elsinore Theater, erected in the early 19th century. The museum also houses a collection of china, clocks, delftware, and silverware. Summer music programs are staged, and there are a restaurant, tea garden, bakery, and beer cellar. Many activities and programs are designed especially for kids.

Viborgvej 2. ℭ **86-12-31-88.** www.dengamleby.dk. Admission DKK50–DKK100 ($8.50–$17/£5–£10) adults, free for children 17 and under. Sept–Oct and Apr–May daily 10am–5pm; June–Aug daily 9am–6pm; Nov–Dec and Feb–Mar daily 10am–4pm; Jan daily 11am–3pm. Bus: 3, 14, or 25.

Moesgård Museum ★ It's not quite the rival of the Tollund Man in Silkeborg (see earlier in this chapter), but this manor house museum shelters the 2,000-year-old **Grauballe Man** ★★★, whose well-preserved body was found in a bog. Apparently, the poor wretch had been sacrificed to some pagan gods. Discovered in 1952, Mr. Grauballe was so well preserved that you can still see the wrinkles on his face. Centuries of "life" in the bog tanned his skin, making it very brown and leatherlike. The museum lies in a 100-hectare (247-acre) forest about 8km (5 miles) south of Århus. It's really a Prehistoric Museum with exhibits on archaeology, featuring digs from the area, and ethnography.

If you take the Prehistoric Trail through the forest, you will come to reconstructed houses from the Viking area, even prehistoric houses and grave monuments. A still-active water mill stands on the grounds.

The Viking Market in July and the Willow Festival in August attracts visitors from all over Denmark (ask at the tourist office above for exact dates). As part of the landscape, a path leads to **Moesgård Strand,** the best sandy beach outside Århus.

Moesgård Manor, Moesgård Allé 20, Højbjerg. ℭ **89-42-11-00.** www.moesmus.dk. Admission DKK60 ($10/£6) adults, free for children 17 and under. Apr–Sept daily 10am–5pm; Oct–Mar Tues–Sun 10am–4pm. Bus: 6 from railway station. Positioned 9km (5²/₃ miles) south of Århus's center.

Rådhuset (Town Hall) Just before the outbreak of World War II, Arne Jacobsen, one of Denmark's greatest designers, drew up the plans for this Town Hall. Built between 1936 and 1941 to commemorate the 500th anniversary of the Århus charter, it's been the subject of controversy ever since. For us, it's too raw and functional to earn our press. The outer skeleton of the building evokes scaffolding that was abandoned, although the interior has light, open spaces and plenty of glass. It can be seen only on a guided tour. An elevator (and 346 steps) runs to the top of the 60m (197-ft.) tower, where a carillon occasionally rings. *Note:* The guided tour at 11am includes the tower. The elevator and stairs are open three times a day: 11am, noon, and 2pm.

Vikingemuseet   In the Viking era, a rampart protected Århus, and in 1963 some archaeologists went digging to find whatever they could to learn of life in centuries past. The finds were impressive, including many artifacts, even a human skeleton. Remains of the town's Viking walls can still be seen. The most precious artifacts of the Viking era are displayed in the basement of Unibank, close to the cathedral. You'll find reconstructions of Viking houses—that is, a stave church and one of the small pit houses found during the excavation at the site. Objects illustrate how life went on in this bustling merchant city from its foundation in about A.D. 900 until around 1400.

Skt. Clemens Torv 6. ⓒ **89-42-11-00.** www.vikingemuseet.dk. Free admission. Mon–Wed and Fri 10am–4pm; Thurs 10am–5:30pm. Bus: 3, 11, 54, or 56.

Von Frue Kirke ★   "The Church of Our Lady," lying to the northwest of Århus Domkirke, was built between the 13th and 15th centuries but was originally part of a Dominican priory. The original Århus Cathedral was erected on this site in 1060. Today's church, built of red brick, has a largely whitewashed interior. It's mainly a Gothic building with frescoes and a significant altarpiece from the workshop of Claus Berg, painted in 1520. The altarpiece depicts a scene from the Passion, in a stunningly expressive style that is often compared to the work of Pieter Bruegel the Elder. Restoration work was begun here in the 1950s, and the crypt of the original Romanesque church from 1060 was uncovered under the chancel. Its early date makes it the oldest vaulted building in all Scandinavia. This vaulted crypt is now virtually "a church within a church." In addition, a chapter house, which once was a hospital for the elderly in the Reformation era, has been dedicated as a church and incorporated into the general structure. So "Our Lady" is actually three churches in one. Wall paintings from the Middle Ages adorn the walls of the chapter house. Because of all these multiple layers beneath the surface, Von Frue Kirke is often likened to a Russian matryoshka doll.

Frue Kirkeplads. ⓒ **86-12-12-43.** www.aarhusvorfrue.dk. Free admission. Sept–Apr Mon–Fri 10am–2pm, Sat 10am–noon; May–Aug Mon–Fri 10am–4pm, Sat 10am–noon. Bus: 7, 10, or 17.

Nearby Attractions

The summer residence of Denmark's royal family, **Marselisborg Slot** ★, at Kongevejen 100, less than 2.5km (1½ miles) south of Århus's center (bus: 1, 18, or 19), is one of the most famous and symbolic buildings in Denmark. If you visit at noon on days Her Majesty and family are in residence, you can see the changing of the guard. It's announced on the local news and in the newspapers when Her Majesty is here. The royal family has used this white manor house since 1902.

It is not possible to visit the interior of the palace, but the castle grounds, even the Queen's rose garden, are open to the public admission-free 9am to 5pm when the castle is not occupied.

The setting is a large forest belt stretching for some 10km (6¼ miles) along the coast. The entire area is ideal for hikes, as nature trails have been cut through the forests. Bikers also like the terrain. Less than 1.5km (1 mile) from the royal palace on the main road south lies **Dyrehaven** (deer park), a protected forest area where you can see fallow deer, and even sika. The more elusive wild roe deer also live here, as well as wild boar, although you're unlikely to spot the latter. For more information visit www.kongehuset.dk.

CENTRAL JUTLAND

12

ÅRHUS

Clausholm ★★   Seventeenth-century Clausholm is a splendid baroque palace, one of the earliest in Denmark. It was commissioned by Frederik IV's chancellor, whose adolescent daughter, Anna Sophie, eloped with the king. When Frederik died, his son by his first marriage banished the queen to Clausholm, where she lived with her court until her death in 1743.

The rooms are basically unaltered, but few of the original furnishings remain. The salons and ballroom feature elaborate stucco ceilings and decorated panels, and an excellent collection of Danish rococo and Empire furnishings has replaced the original pieces. The Queen's Chapel, where Anna Sophie and her court worshiped, is unchanged and contains the oldest organ in Denmark. In 1976, the Italian baroque gardens were reopened, complete with a symmetrically designed fountain system.

Clausholm is about 13km (8 miles) southeast of Randers and 31km (19 miles) north of Århus.

Voldum, Hadsten. ✆ **86-49-16-55.** www.clausholm.dk. Admission (including guided tour) DKK70 ($12/£7) adults, free for children 13 and under. Castle July only daily 11am–4pm; park May–Sept only daily 11am–4pm. Bus: 221 from Randers.

The Museums at Gammel Estrup ★   One of the most elegant Renaissance manors in Central Jutland lies 39km (24 miles) northeast of Århus. Today this compound of buildings is the site of the **Jutland Manor House Museum,** complete with a great Hall, a chapel, and richly decorated stucco ceilings; and the **Danish Agricultural Museum,** which celebrates the role of Danish farming over the past thousand years. The entire compound dates from the 14th century, but the structures you see were extensively rebuilt and remodeled in the early 1600s. Expect a glimpse into medieval fortifications, baronial furnishings, the changing nature of tools and machines used during Danish plantings and harvests, and an enormous sense of pride in Denmark and its traditions.

Jyllands Herregårdsmuseum, Randersvej 2, Auning. ✆ **86-48-34-44.** www.gl-estrup.dk. Admission DKK75 ($13/£7.50) adults, free for children 17 and under. Agricultural Museum Jan–Mar and Nov–Dec Tues–Sun 10am–3pm; Apr–June and Sept–Oct daily 10am–5pm; July–Aug daily 10am–6pm. Manor House Museum Apr––Oct daily noon–4:30pm. Bus: 119. From Randers, take Rte. 16 east to Auning.

Rosenholm Slot (Rosenholm Castle) ★   One of Jutland's stateliest Renaissance manors was built in 1559 on a small island in the middle of a lake. Stone lions guard the bridge that leads to the castle where the Rosenkrantz family has lived for more than 4 centuries. The four-winged castle is encircled by 14 hectares (35 acres) of landscaped parkland. We find Rosenholm far more impressive than the queen's more modest digs at Marselisborg (see above). The Great Hall is graced with a portrait of King Frederik V, and most of the other salons and galleries are furnished and decorated in a Moorish-inspired Spanish style—or else with rococo adornments (a bit much at times). The Winter Room is walled with leather, and French and Flemish tapestries, some 3 centuries old, adorn the Tower Room and the Corner Room. The castle is 21km (13 miles) north of Århus and a kilometer (²/₃ mile) north of the village of Hornslet.

Hornslet. ✆ **86-99-40-10.** www.rosenholmslot.dk. Admission DKK60 ($10/£6), free for children 5 and under. June 1–19 Sat–Sun 11am–4pm; June 20–Aug 31 daily 11am–4pm. Closed Sept–May. Bus: 119 or 121 from Århus.

SHOPPING

Århus is the biggest shopping venue in Jutland, with some 400 specialty stores, each of them tightly clustered within an area of about 1.3 sq. km (¹/₂ sq. mile). The centerpiece of this district is the Strøget, whose terminus is the Store Torv, dominated by the Århus Domkirke. You might try a large-scale department store first. One of the best is **Salling,** Søndergade 27 (℃ **86-12-18-00**), with some 30 specialty boutiques, all under one roof. A wide range of articles for the whole family is sold here, including body-care items, clothing, gifts, toys, music, and sports equipment. **Magasin du Nord,** Immervad 2–8 (℃ **86-12-33-00**), is the largest department store in Scandinavia, in business for more than 125 years. The staff will assist foreign visitors with tax-free purchases.

"The greatest silversmith the world has ever seen," is the praise often used to describe **Georg Jensen,** Søndergade 1 (℃ **86-12-01-00**). A tradition since 1866, Georg Jensen is known for style and quality, producing unique silver and gold jewelry, elegant clocks and watches, and stainless steel cutlery, among other items. A leading goldsmith, **Hingelberg,** Store Torv 3 (℃ **86-13-13-00**), is the licensed Cartier outlet, and offers a wide selection of top-quality designer jewelry.

Galleri Bo Bendixen, Store Torv 14 (℃ **86-12-67-50**), offers the brilliantly colored designs of Bo Bendixen, the famous Danish graphic artist. The shop also sells a wide range of gifts and garments for children and adults. **Volden 4 Kunsthåndværk,** Volden 4 (℃ **86-13-21-76**), specializes in top-quality applied art, and glass made by some of the leading artisans of the country. Silver, copper, and brass ornaments are for sale, as are exclusive bronze candlesticks.

Bülow Duus Glassblowers, Studsgade 14 (℃ **86-12-72-86**), is a working glass-blowing shop open to the public. At an attractive old house in the heart of the city, you can watch the fascinating work of glass blowing. Drinking glasses, candlesticks, bowls, and other items are for sale. For traditional Danish pottery, head for **Favlhuset,** Mølles-tien 53 (℃ **86-13-06-32**).

If you haven't found what you're looking for after all that, head for **Inspiration Buus,** Ryesgade 2 (℃ **86-12-67-00**), which sells top-quality gifts, kitchenware, tableware, and toiletry articles, much of it of Danish design.

WHERE TO STAY

Low-cost accommodations in this lively university city are limited. Those on a modest budget should check with the tourist office in the Rådhuset (℃ **87-31-50-10**) for book-ings in **private homes.**

Depending on the day of the week or the time of the year you check in, rooms in many of the hotels labeled inexpensive aren't inexpensive at all, but more moderate in price.

Expensive

Hotel Marselis ★   This is the most scenically located, isolated, and nature-conscious of the grand modern hotels of Århus, thanks to a long, narrow layout that rambles along a grass-covered bluff, a few steps from the sea, about 5km (3 miles) south of the city center. Built of earth-colored bricks in 1967, it plays up its views over the water and an interior decor that's the most nautical of all the hotels in the area. Rooms are smaller and less imaginatively decorated than those in, for example, the SAS Radisson, but overall, the setting is better with the windows opening onto views of the water. Corporate con-ventions sometimes come here, but less often than the hotel would really like.

The **Restaurant Marselis** and its bar, the **Café Nautilus,** provide food, piano music, drink, and a log-burning fireplace. A less formal dining and drinking venue, open only during mild weather, is the **Beach Café,** whose tables are arranged on a sunny terrace. This is one of the few modern hotels in Århus with its own swimming pool, an indoor affair with big windows overlooking the sea.

Strandvejen 25, DK-8000 Århus C. © **86-14-44-11.** Fax 86-14-44-20. www.marselis.dk. 101 units. DKK950–DKK1,600 ($162–$272/£95–£160) double; DKK2,150 ($366/£215) suite. Rates include buffet breakfast. AE, DC, MC, V. Bus: 6. **Amenities:** Restaurant; bar; indoor heated pool; gym; sauna; room service; laundry service; dry cleaning; solarium. *In room:* TV, Wi-Fi, minibar, hair dryer.

Hotel Philip ★★★ (Finds)

This hotel represents a dream come true for its famous owner. This discovery offers the finest accommodations in Århus and some of the best lodgings in Central Jutland, a 5-minute walk from the bus station. The hotel is owned by Marc Rieper, a former player on the Danish soccer team, who headed the ball at the crossbar—narrowly missing a goal—in the final moments against Brazil during the semi-finals of the 1998 World Cup. Opening onto a canal, the building housing this boutique hotel has been vastly renovated, each accommodation turned into a luxury suite. The six regular suites have been lavishly decorated in a French and Italian style, and the two remaining suites on the top floor are even more luxuriously equipped in a romantic style. Jutlanders on their honeymoon often book this pair of suites. All the suites are spacious, containing Oriental carpets and works of art. The service is the best in Århus—for example, you're greeted with fresh flowers. Even if not a guest, consider a meal at the Hotel Philip's on-site **restaurant.** See "Where to Dine," below.

Åboulevarden 28, DK-8000 Århus. © **87-32-14-44.** Fax 86-12-69-55. 8 units. DKK1,495 ($254/£150) suite. Rates include breakfast. DC, MC, V. **Amenities:** Restaurant; cafe; bar; room service; laundry service; dry cleaning; nonsmoking rooms. *In room:* TV, Wi-Fi, minibar, hair dryer, iron, safe.

Hotel Royal ★★★

For the best in modern facilities, check into the Radisson SAS (see below). But for traditional extravagance and royal luxury, make this aptly named hotel your choice. This is the most glamorous accommodation in town, attracting such cultural greats of yesterday as Marian Anderson and Arthur Rubenstein or such current celebs as Madonna and Sting (but not in the same suite). The gilt date on its neo-baroque facade commemorates the hotel's establishment in 1838. There have been numerous additions and upgrades since. The Royal stands close to the city's symbol, its cathedral. A vintage elevator takes you to the guest rooms, many of them quite spacious. Beds are refurbished and accommodations are fitted with high-quality furniture, carpeting, and fabrics. The ground floor houses the Royal Scandinavian Casino and night club, offering such games of chance as international roulette, blackjack, and seven-card stud poker.

Stove Torv 4, DK-8000 Århus. © **86-12-00-11.** Fax 86-76-04-04. www.hotelroyal.dk. 102 units. DKK1,745 ($297/£175) double; DKK1,995–DKK2,195 ($339–$373/£200–£220) suite. Rates include breakfast. AE, DC, MC, V. Parking DKK200 ($34/£20). Bus: 56 or 58. **Amenities:** Restaurant; bar; casino; sauna; room service (7am–10pm); babysitting; laundry service; dry cleaning; nonsmoking rooms. *In room:* TV, Wi-Fi, minibar, beverage maker, hair dryer.

Radisson SAS Scandinavia Hotel Århus ★★★

This is one of the most modern and dynamic hotels in Denmark, and a city showplace that municipal authorities show off to visiting dignitaries. It was built in 1995 above the largest convention facilities in Jutland, and is the most popular convention hotel in the region. Of course, for that reason we like it less. However, should you arrive when a convention isn't taking place, the hotel can be a honey. Bedrooms occupy floors 4 to 11 of a glass-and-stone–sheathed tower that's visible throughout the city. Lower floors contain check-in, dining, drinking, and convention facilities. The standard bedrooms are outfitted in plush upholstery with bright colors. Each has a tasteful decor that's different from its immediate neighbor, incorporating Scandinavian, English, Japanese, or Chinese themes. Costing more are the upgraded business-class rooms, with newspaper delivery, turndown service, and free entrance to the fitness suite.

Margrethepladsen 1, DK-8000 Århus C. © **800/333-3333** in the U.S., or 86-12-86-65. Fax 86-12-86-75. http://aarhus.radissonsas.com. 234 units. DKK950–DKK1,695 ($162–$288/£95–£170) double; from DKK2,500 ($425/£250) suite. Rates include breakfast. AE, DC, MC, V. Bus: 1, 2, 6, or 16. **Amenities:** Restaurant; bar; fitness center; sauna; room service; massage; babysitting; laundry service; dry cleaning; nonsmoking rooms; rooms for those w/limited mobility. *In room:* TV, Wi-Fi, minibar, hair dryer, trouser press, safe.

Scandic Plaza ★ (Kids)   The massive bulk of this chain-run hotel rises imposingly in the heart of the city, and we think it's a most reliable and comfortable choice for overnighting, without reaching the pinnacle scaled by the Radisson SAS. Actually, it opened in 1930 but has been vastly improved and enlarged since that time. The hotel never escapes the "chain format" of its bedroom decor, but the furnishings are first-class and the decoration is tasteful, with well-maintained private bathrooms. The on-site Restaurant Brazil comes as a surprise with its Latin cuisine. Before dinner, head for the cozy bar, where six exotic cocktails await your selection every evening along with the standard beer and liquors. This is one of the best hotels for families traveling with children, as it offers a playroom with all those games, toys, books, and crayons that kids demand. There's even a wooden train to amuse.

Banegårdspladsen 14, DK-8500 Århus C. © **87-32-01-00.** Fax 87-32-01-99. www.scandic-hotels.com/aarhus. 162 units. DKK950–DKK1,150 ($162–$196/£95–£115) double; from DKK1,450 ($247/£145) suite. Rates include breakfast. DC, MC, V. Bus: 3, 17, 56, or 58. **Amenities:** Restaurant; bar; fitness center; Jacuzzi; sauna; kids' playroom; room service; laundry service; dry cleaning; nonsmoking rooms. *In room:* TV, Wi-Fi, minibar, hair dryer, iron, safe.

Villa Provence ★ (Finds)   Living up to its name, this small hotel brings a touch of sunny Provence to a tranquil square in Århus. A designer hotel built in the style of Southern France, Villa Provence offers well-designed bedrooms and suites, each individually furnished in the Provençal style. The taste level is set in the stylish lounge, where you can order an aperitif. Another oasis is the courtyard in the rear, with its tall lime trees and cobblestones. Decorated with 1940s French movie posters, the bedrooms have traditional quilts resting on wrought-iron beds which sit on wide-planked oak floors. In the periwinkle-colored cafe, guests order a breakfast which ranges from Italian cold cuts to French cheese to Greek yogurt with honey.

Fredens Torv 12, DK-8000 Århus. © **86-18-24-00.** Fax 86-18-24-03. www.villaprovence.dk. 36 units. DKK1,195–DKK2,200 ($203–$374/£120–£220) double; DKK2,200–DKK2,800 ($374–$476/£220–£280) suite. Rates include breakfast. AE, DC, MC, V. **Amenities:** Breakfast room; room service; laundry service. *In room:* TV, Wi-Fi, hair dryer.

Moderate

Best Western Ritz Hotel ★★ (Value)   Since 1932, when this hotel first opened its doors, it's been known for its fair-value rooms, its comfort, and its helpful staff. The good news is that it has been carefully restored and redecorated, with the original architecture still intact. Tradition is respected here. Don't be misled by the "Ritz" in its title. The Århus version is far less grand. The hotel takes its name from a large painting in its Art Deco restaurant that depicts the superswanky Ritz in Paris. The hotel offers midsize-to-spacious bedrooms, which are rated "standard" and "standard plus." The main difference between the two is that the standard plus units are larger, with bathtubs as well as a shower and a big comfortable queen-size bed (or twins), and some of these superior units also have a private balcony.

Banegårdspladsen 12, DK-8000 Århus. © **800/528-1234** in the U.S., or 86-13-44-44. Fax 86-13-45-87. www.hotelritz.dk. 67 units. DKK1,350–DKK1,595 ($230–$271/£135–£160) double. Rates include breakfast. AE,

DISC, MC, V. Free parking. Bus: 3, 17, 56, or 58. **Amenities:** Restaurant; cafeteria; laundry service; dry cleaning; nonsmoking rooms. *In room:* TV, Wi-Fi, hair dryer.

Comfort Hotel Atlantic   This is a standard, durable choice for overnighting, though it lacks the style and glamour of some of our previous selections. Since its opening in 1964, it's provided good comfort and a fair price in one of the city's tallest buildings, rising 11 floors, with good views from the top-floor bedrooms, some of which open onto a balcony with a view of the water. Bedrooms range from small to midsize, but each is tastefully and agreeably furnished. Breakfast is the only meal served, although there are many eateries nearby—the helpful staff will advise. They will also arrange for you to have access to a nearby health club and tennis courts.

Europlads 10–14, DK-8000 Århus. ℂ **86-13-11-11.** Fax 86-13-23-43. www.choicehotels.dk. 102 units. DKK1,101–DKK1,295 ($187–$220/£110–£130) double; DKK1,425–DKK1,595 ($242–$271/£143–£160) suite. Rates include breakfast. AE, DC, MC, V. Bus: 3. **Amenities:** Breakfast lounge; bar; access to nearby tennis court; access to nearby healh club; laundry service; dry cleaning; nonsmoking rooms. *In room:* TV, Wi-Fi, minibar, hair dryer, safe.

Inexpensive
Hotel Guldsmeden ★ ⟨Value⟩   In its price range, this small, intimate hotel is our favorite hideaway in Århus. This affordable choice lies in a former town house from the 1800s that was completely renovated and turned into a cozy little place. We like to stop off here in the summer, when the garden is at its peak, and enjoy breakfast on the terrace outdoors. It's the best and healthiest breakfast in town—all organic, with fresh fruit, muesli, and the like. The bedrooms are small to midsize, and each is furnished tastefully, most often cheerfully, in soothing shades. Some of the rooms contain a small bathroom with shower; in units without bathrooms, corridor facilities suffice.

Guldsmedgade 40, DK-8000 Århus. ℂ **86-13-45-50.** Fax 86-13-76-76. www.hotelguldsmeden.dk. 27 units, 20 w/private bathroom. DKK895 ($152/£90) double w/shared bathroom; DKK1,250 ($213/£125) double w/private bathroom; DKK1,595 ($271/£160) suite. Rates include buffet breakfast. AE, DC, MC, V. **Amenities:** Breakfast room; lounge. *In room:* TV, Wi-Fi.

Hotel La Tour ⟨Kids⟩   If you're not too demanding, this is quite a good choice, especially for families on a holiday. Since its construction in 1956, and its rebuilding in 1986, this hotel has followed a conscious policy of downgrading (yes, downgrading) its accommodations and facilities from a once-lofty status to a middle-brow formula. The result is a hotel that's far from being the best in town—viewed, we imagine, as a great success by the management—that attracts hundreds of foreign visitors. The hotel, housed in an unimaginative two-story building, is 3.5km (2¼ miles) north of Århus center. It offers well-maintained, simple bedrooms with small bathrooms. There is a patio-style restaurant serving competently prepared Danish and international food, as well as a bar, and a children's playroom (open May–Sept only).

Randersvej 139, DK-8200 Århus. ℂ **86-16-78-88.** Fax 86-16-79-95. www.latour.dk. 101 units. DKK785–DKK875 ($133–$149/£79–£88) double; DKK1,175 ($200/£118) suite. Rates include breakfast. AE, DC, MC, V. Bus: 2, 3, or 11. **Amenities:** Restaurant; bar; room service; laundry service; dry cleaning. *In room:* TV, Wi-Fi, minibar, hair dryer, safe.

Hotel Mercur   For motorists, this is one of the most ultramodern hotels in town, 4km (2½ miles) south of the center and less than a kilometer (½ mile) from the park that surrounds Queen Margrethe's summer house (Marselisborg Slot). Overall, it's warmer and cozier than some of its most visible competitors. Rooms are masculine looking and conservatively contemporary with views that encompass panoramas over the town and the seacoast. Some have narrow, rarely used balconies. There are a restaurant, the **Mercur,** and a bar on the premises, both of which are appealing and warmly decorated. There are also two bowling alleys in the hotel's cellar, and a larger bowling alley complex a few blocks away. A shopping mall, Viby Centret, with about 50 shops, is found on Skander-borgvej, a short walk from the hotel. In spite of its name, this hotel is not associated with the French-based chain.

Viby Torv, DK-8260 Århus, Viby J. ℂ **86-14-14-11.** Fax 86-14-46-41. www.hotel-mercur.dk. 107 units. DKK895–DKK1,050 ($152–$179/£90–£105) double, from DKK1,050 ($179/£105) suite. Rates include buffet breakfast. AE, DC, MC, V. Bus: 5, 15, or 25. **Amenities:** Restaurant; bar; laundry service; dry cleaning; nonsmoking rooms. *In room:* TV, Wi-Fi.

WHERE TO DINE
Very Expensive
Malling & Schmidt ★★★ SCANDINAVIAN   Thorsten Schmidt is the most imaginative chef cooking in Jutland. Who else combines goat cheese and smoked herring ice cream—and makes it taste delectable? In the kitchen, he has an almost scientific approach to ingredients, putting them under a microscope to create new taste sensations. All the raw ingredients are found only in the Nordic countries. He uses such elements as grape-seed oil, dehydrated pumpkin, kippers emulsion, pickled cloudberries, seaweed, Swedish caviar, organic linseed oil, and, in one dish at least, unbaked bread to combine with his main ingredients. These include Danish sausage, raw vegetables, shellfish, and various other ingredients. The description of some of his products sound off-putting, but the taste sensation is there in almost every dish.

81 Jægergårdsgade. ℂ **86-17-70-88.** Reservations required. Fixed-price menus DKK565 ($96/£57) for 5 courses, DKK695 ($118/£70) for 7 courses, DKK995 ($169/£100) for special "Aroma Menu." AE, DC, MC, V. Wed–Sat 6pm–midnight.

Expensive
Forlaens & Baglaens ★ TAPAS   For a change of taste adventure, head for this authentic Spanish restaurant where you can consume delectable delicacy after delicacy under vintage enameled lamps dangling overhead like bonbons. Only a 5-minute walk from the main rail station, the restaurant is in the center of town. You can order the best tapas in Central Jutland here, most of them fish-based. Tapas—meat, vegetable, and seafood—can be ordered separately, or you might prefer the set dinner which begins with a before-dinner cocktail and concludes with an after-dinner cocktail. The dinner includes three tapas and two glasses of wine. The chefs make a divine aioli and a savory couscous, along with curry soup with chutney, a fennel salad, pork filets, chorizo, and calamari, among many other offerings.

23 Jægergårdsgade. ℂ **45-86-76-00.** Reservations recommended. Fixed-price menu DKK425 ($72/£43); individual tapas DKK89–DKK120 ($15–$20/£8.90–£12). V. Tues–Sat 5–9:30pm; Sun 4–9pm.

Hotel Philip Restaurant ★★★ DANISH/FRENCH   In the most exclusive hotel in Århus, a delightful restaurant is imbued with a romantic atmosphere and serves quality food prepared with the best and freshest of ingredients—an unbeatable combination. Tables are placed on beautiful hardwood floors, and elegantly set and lit by brass candle-holders. The ceiling is adorned with a metal tapestry in the Art Nouveau style, and the walls are painted dark but brightened with summery yellow ornaments.

The front part of the restaurant, as can be viewed from the street, is decorated as an elegant cafe, with the luxurious dining found in the rear. Inventiveness goes hand in hand with solid technique. The kitchen also takes full advantage of the region's riches, with seafood predominating.

We like the way the chefs seasonally adjust the menu to take advantage of the best produce in any month—fresh asparagus in late spring, the finest of game dishes in the autumn, and always—but always—the freshest catch of the day. We can't recommend specific dishes because they are forever changing. But take that old standby cannelloni. As an example of the chef's technique, he stuffs it with Serrano ham, seafood, and Danish cheese—and that's not all. He serves it with truffles. Cannelloni will never taste the same again. Appetizers and desserts, as well as the meat and poultry dishes, have always tasted sublime to our palates.

Åboulevarden 28. © **87-32-14-44.** Reservations required. Main courses DKK175–DKK295 ($30–$50/£18–£30). DC, MC, V. Mon–Sat noon–10:30pm.

Prins Ferdinand ★★★ DANISH/INTERNATIONAL   This is the only restaurant in town to give Philip a run for its kroner. Its name is actually a reference to the notoriously carousing Prince Frederik (1792–1863), who spent most of his nights in Århus gambling or pursuing wine and women. On the edge of Århus's historic center in a former tea salon, this is one of the city's finest restaurants. It was established in 1988 by different owners, but is run today by the hospitable Tonny Hansen and Martin Lemvig, who welcome the local business community and also the most discerning of visiting foodies into their lovely luxe restaurant. In two pink-toned dining rooms laden with flickering candles and flowers, you can order a platter of fresh smoked salmon served with tartare of salmon and pepper-cream sauce, turbot with Russian caviar and a drizzle of olive oil, sea devil with lobster prepared Thai-style with lemongrass, or boneless pigeon stuffed with fresh gooseliver served with a raspberry sauce. A dessert specialty is pears cooked with elderberries and served with vanilla ice cream, nougat, and almonds. The restaurant's array of dessert cheeses, the most unusual array in Jutland, includes artisan creations produced by small farmers.

Viborgvej 2. © **86-12-52-05.** www.prinsferdinand.dk. Reservations recommended. Fixed-price lunch menus DKK225–DKK295 ($38–$50/£23–£30); fixed-price dinner menus DKK475–DKK775 ($81–$132/£48–£78). AE, DC, MC, V. Tues–Sat noon–3pm and 6–9pm. Bus: 3.

Moderate

Restaurant Margueritten ★ (Finds DANISH/FRENCH/ITALIAN   One of the town's better restaurants was carved out of what used to be stables for horses that pulled the carriages through Århus. It's a cozy place for lunch, and an ideal venue for a romantic dinner under old beamed ceilings. Old Danish furniture enhances the ambience, and in summer a beautiful little garden in the rear is open. This isn't grandmother-type cooking, as the fare is as modern as tomorrow, but it always uses the freshest regional produce. Chefs offer such dishes as guinea fowl with a stuffing of tiger shrimp; the distinctive flavor comes from the marinade of yogurt and tandoori spices. Some of the best dishes we found on the menu included filet of wild pork with a balsamic chocolate sauce (yes, you read that right), medallion of beef in a cognac sauce with mixed vegetables, and a tangy breast of duck with a raspberry sauce and fresh plums which have been marinated in port. The English-speaking waitstaff is polite and helpful.

Guldsmedgade 20. © **86-19-60-33.** Reservations required. Lunch main courses DKK65–DKK139 ($11–$24/£6.50–£14); 1-course fixed-price menu DKK179–DKK195 ($30–$33/£18–£20); 2-course menu DKK239 ($41/£24); 3-course menu DKK269 ($46/£27). Mon–Sat 11:30am–11pm.

Inexpensive

Ministeriet (Value) DANISH/MEDITERRANEAN   This small and cozy inn with a courtyard is in the old Klostertorv across from Frue Kloster Abbey. You'll invariably stumble upon the charming old place if you're out sightseeing. It's a cafe-style place serving very good food, with lots of fish such as plaice, offered at reasonable prices. The chefs offer various menus depending on the season, using fresh Danish produce whenever available. There's a strong Mediterranean influence here.

Klostertorvet 5. (C) **86-17-11-88.** www.ministeriet.org. Reservations required. Main courses lunch DKK60–DKK100 ($10–$17/£6–£10); fixed-price dinner menus DKK250 ($43/£25). AE, DC, MC, V. Mon–Sat 9:30am–1pm; Sun 10am–6pm. Bus: 1, 2, 6, or 9.

Restaurant Skovmøllen ★ (Finds) DANISH/INTERNATIONAL   Since it was constructed of straw, wood, and stone more than 300 years ago, this building has functioned as a farmhouse, a gristmill, and a simple cafe. It's set beside the Giber River, 10km (6¼ miles) south of Århus, close to the Moesgård Museum. Beneath a beamed ceiling and frequent reminders of old-time Denmark, you can order typically Danish platters at lunchtime, and straightforward, not particularly esoteric dishes that are just a bit more cosmopolitan at night. Lunches might include meatballs, *smørrebrød* (open-faced sandwiches), herring platters, or roasted pork with onions and braised cabbage. Dinners are more elaborate, featuring shrimp cocktails, steak with french fries, stuffed filets of plaice with new potatoes, and salmon chops with garlic-flavored butter sauce. The place is always dependable, the cookery always reliable, but its main allure is that it's a charming, country-flavored getaway from the city center.

Skovmøllenvej 51. (C) **86-27-12-14.** www.skovmollen.dk. Reservations recommended. Main courses DKK85–DKK110 ($14–$19/£8.50–£11); fixed-price menus DKK245 ($42/£25). MC, V. June–Aug Tues–Sun noon–6pm; Sept–May Fri–Sun noon–5pm. From downtown Århus take bus no. 6.

Teater Bodega DANISH   Originally established at a different address in 1907, Teater Bodega in 1951 moved across the street from both the Århus Dramatic Theater and the Århus Cathedral. Here in its new setting it offers an amusing dining ambience for local actors and theatergoers, its walls covered with illustrations of theatrical costumes and other thespian memorabilia. The food is solid and flavorful in the Danish country style. Various kinds of Danish hash, including *biksemad,* are served along with regular or large portions of Danish roast beef. Although the beef dishes are good, a waiter once assured us that most locals go for a platter of the freshly caught plaice or flounder. "Fish is the faithful friend to the Danish palate," he so accurately claimed.

Skolegade 7. (C) **86-12-19-17.** www.teaterbodega.dk. Reservations recommended. Main courses DKK78–DKK226 ($13–$38/£7.80–£23); lunch *smørrebrød* DKK52–DKK138 ($8.90–$23/£5.20–£14); 3-course fixed-price lunch or dinner DKK265 ($45/£27). DC, MC, V. Mon–Sat 11am–11:30pm. Bus: 6.

ÅRHUS AFTER DARK

The city of Århus has the richest and most varied cultural life in Jutland. Its chief attraction, and a major venue for cultural events, is the Musikhuset Århus (see below). The Århus Symphony Orchestra and the Danish National Opera perform here frequently, among other attractions. For a look at what's happening here and in other venues, pick up a copy of the monthly booklet *What's On in Århus* at the tourist office (see "Visitor Information," earlier in this chapter).

Cultural Århus

You'll have to speak Danish to enjoy most productions at the **Århus Theater,** Bispetorv ((C) **89-33-23-00**), which has five stages with a total of 1,200 seats. It was designed by

Hack Kampmann and opened in 1900. Local actors and visiting stars entertain in a wide repertoire early September to mid-June.

Svalegangen, Rosenkrantzgade 21 (© **86-13-88-66**), presents an up-to-date repertoire, the latest in Danish drama, music, cabaret, modern dance, and guest artists. The company stages about 40 productions annually. **Entré Scenen,** Grønnegade 93B (© **86-20-15-36**), is an experimental feature of Århus's dramatic life. A varied range of performances, often by foreign artists, appeals to a wide spectrum of ages here. Guest opera and dance theater productions are also staged at **Gellerupscenen,** Gudrunsvej 78 (© **86-25-03-66**).

Opened in 1982, **Musikhuset Århus,** Thomas Jensens Allé (© **89-40-90-00**), is the home of the Århus Symphony Orchestra and the Danish National Opera. Tickets for most events range from DKK50 to DKK1,000 ($8.50–$170/£5–£100). Programs are presented on the great stage, the small stage, and the cabaret stage, as well as in the amphitheater and on the foyer stages, where free performances are presented year-round. The foyer, open daily 11am to 9pm, is the site of the box office, an information desk, a cafe/restaurant, and souvenir shops.

Dance Clubs

The most popular, charming, and fun dance club in town is **Train ★**, Toldbodgade 6 (© **26-12-58-00**), where a crowd that's under 35 or 40-ish dances on any of three floors of what used to be a warehouse down beside the waterfront. The top floors feature disco music from the '70s and '80s; the middle and lower levels are devoted to an English-style pub and louder, more jarring techno. The site is also a venue, at irregular intervals, for live concerts. There's sometimes, but not always, a cover charge that can range from DKK45 to DKK80 ($7.70–$14/£4.50–£8), depending on what's on that night.

Barhopping

Århus abounds in bars and taverns, most of which charge no cover unless there's live music on special nights. The oldest hostelry in town, **Thorups Kælder,** Store Torv 3 (© **86-12-04-14**), was founded by Cistercian monks in the 13th century. Here you can quench your thirst in historic surroundings. You'll find us at our favorite bar and cafe, **Café Under Masken,** Bispegade 3 (© **86-18-22-66**), next door to the Royal Hotel. This is the creation of a well-known local artist, Hans Krull, who designed the iron sculptures adorning the gateway to the hotel. If Salvador Dali were alive and could see the decor, he would call it surreal. Krull and some of his patrons apparently picked up the flotsam and jetsam of the world for decor. The only Aussie bar in Århus, **The Billabong Bar,** Skolegade 26 (© **86-13-27-15**), is a typical Outback-style bar, its raw edge adding to its charm. There's live music every weekend, and sports fans gather here to watch major events on TV, all the time sipping Australian beverages. **Gyngen,** Mejlgade 53 (© **86-19-22-55**), is the venue for rock, techno, and the like.

Bryggeriet Skt. Clemens ★, Kannikegade 10–12 (© **86-13-80-00**), is a combined brewery and public house which offers freshly tapped, frothy draft beer brewed in coppers in the cellar, matured, and served in glasses. The bartender's special is a 1-liter *kwak glas* (a round-bottomed glass held upright on a wooden stand). Regardless of which beer you select, this glass is designed for massive consumption. In addition to the pub, you can also order various Danish dishes here if you decide to stick around and dine.

Gays and lesbians gather to dance and enjoy the cafe at **Pan Club,** Jægergårdsgade 42 (© **86-13-43-80**). The cafe is open Friday and Saturday 10pm to 6am; the dance club is open Friday and Saturday 11pm to 5am. Cover is DKK60 ($10/£6) after midnight.

An Amusement Park

Tivoli-Friheden, Skobrynet (© **86-14-73-00;** www.friheden.dk; bus: 4), is a pale imitation of the Tivoli in Copenhagen; the scale is much smaller here, but there is some of the same sense of fantasy. Set in a forest about 3.5km (2¹/₄ miles) south of Århus, it's bright and modern, appealing to families and couples from the city and the surrounding communities. Entertainment includes an open-air theater, art shows, concerts, clowns, rides, and a scattering of restaurants. The park is open only mid-April to mid-August. Although the park opens every day at noon, the rides and attractions don't open until 2pm. Everything closes down at 11pm. Admission is DKK65 ($11/£6.50) adults, DKK45 ($7.70/£4.50) children 4 to 11.

8 EBELTOFT ★

96km (60 miles) E of Silkeborg; 53km (33 miles) NE of Århus; 335km (208 miles) W of Copenhagen

Wandering the cobblestone streets of Ebeltoft is like going back to a town 200 years ago. Why has so little changed in its historic core? That's because this town of half-timbered houses had a long slumber of about 2 centuries, when it economically stagnated. When it woke up in the 1960s, it found its old buildings and streets had become a tourist attraction. So instead of tearing down buildings, locals restored them with their increased prosperity.

Meaning "apple orchard" in Danish, Ebeltoft is the capital of the Mols hill country, an area of great scenic beauty in Central Jutland. Allow at least 3 hours to wander its streets—in some cases, hidden-away lanes—and to explore its old inns. Sometimes a ruddy-faced fisherman will consent to have his picture taken, assuring you that he is still following the same profession as his grandfather.

Ebeltoft's Viking-age wooden "dragon boats" have given way to expensive yachts in the harbor today. Life at Ebeltoft developed around this beautiful harbor and its scenic bay, Ebeltoft Vig.

In the Middle Ages, Ebeltoft was a thriving port, enjoying trade with Germany, Sweden, and, of course, Copenhagen. However, in 1659, after a dispute, the Swedish army invaded, sacking the port and setting fire to the merchant fleet. Ebeltoft never really recovered from this almost-fatal blow until it became a tourist destination in the 1960s. Ironically, it was Swedish tourists who first discovered the antique charms of Ebeltoft, with its timber-framed buildings topped with red tile roofs.

ESSENTIALS

GETTING THERE By Train and Bus   There's no direct train service to Ebeltoft. From Copenhagen, take the train (via Fredericia) to Århus; at Århus Central Station, board bus no. 123 for Ebeltoft.

By Car   From Silkeborg head east on Route 15 through Århus and continue around the coast, then follow Route 21 south to Ebeltoft.

VISITOR INFORMATION   Contact the **Ebeltoft Turistbureau,** Strandvejen 2 (© **87-52-18-00;** www.visitdjursland.com), open June 15 to August Monday to Saturday 10am to 6pm and Sunday 11am to 4pm; and September to June 14 Monday to Friday 9am to 4pm and Saturday 10am to 1pm.

GETTING AROUND By Bicycle   Bikes can be rented at **L&P Cykler,** Nørre Allé 5 (© **86-34-47-77**), open Monday to Friday 8am to 5:30pm, Saturday 8am to noon. Rental fees cost around DKK60 to DKK80 ($10–$14/£6–£8) per day.

Det Gamle Rådhus (The Old Town Hall)   This is the smallest town hall in Denmark. It looks like something erected just for kindergarten children to play in—a 1789 building, blackened half-timbering, a redbrick with timbered facade, and a bell tower. Its museum houses an ethnographic collection from Thailand and artifacts from the town's history. It's in the town center north of Strandvejen.

Torvet. (© 86-34-55-99. Admission DKK25 ($4.30/£2.50) adults, free for children 17 and under. Apr–Aug daily 10am–5pm; Sept–Oct Tues–Sun 11am–3pm; Nov–Mar Sat–Sun 11am–3pm.

Fregatten Jylland ★   Moored at the harbor, the *Jylland* is the oldest man-of-war in Denmark (1860) and the world's longest wooden ship at 71m (233 ft.). The vessel is an impressive monument to Ebeltoft's maritime heyday, and the restoration of the three-masted ship was financed by Mærsk McKinney Møller, a local shipping tycoon. Stand on the bridge and gun deck, imagining the harbor 2 centuries ago, and, down below, check out the captain's room and the galley with several miniature sea-battle scenarios on display.

Strandvejen 4. (© 86-34-10-99. www.fregatten-jylland.dk. Admission DKK95 ($16/£9.50) adults, DKK45 ($7.70/£4.50) children 4–12, free for children 3 and under. Jan 2–Mar 21 and Oct 25–Dec 30 daily 10am–4pm; Mar 22–June 13 and Aug 23–Oct 24 daily 10am–5pm; June 14–Aug 22 daily 10am–7pm.

Glasmuseet Ebeltoft (Ebeltoft Glass Museum)   Unless you have a fascination with glass, you might want to pass by this attraction. At Ebeltoft harbor stands one of Denmark's most important glass museums, housed in a building that was once a customs and excise house. It displays both decorative and functional glass, ranging from the symbol-laden works of Swedish glass guru Bertil Vallien to the luminous gold pavilions of Japanese artist Kyohei Fujita. The artists exhibited decide which of their pieces they want to represent their work; this has resulted in a large permanent exhibition. May to September young glass students work with blowing irons and modern "syrupy" blobs of glass in the museum garden.

Strandvejen 8. (© 86-34-17-99. Fax 86-34-60-60. www.glasmuseet.dk. Admission DKK60 ($10/£6) adults, DKK10 ($1.70/£1) children 6–12, free for children 5 and under. Jan–June and Aug–Dec daily 10am–5pm; July daily 10am–7pm. Closed Dec 24–25, Dec 31, and Jan 1.

Vindmølleparken (Windmill Park)   Don Quixote chased windmills across the plains of La Mancha, and you can follow in his tracks by heading to this offbeat attraction. Five kilometers (3 miles) south of Ebeltoft, adjacent to the ferryboat terminal, 16 windmills sit on a curved spit of land open to gusts of wind from the Baltic to generate electricity for some 600 families. To see it, drive south of town, following the signs toward the hamlet of Øer, or the signs pointing to the ferryboat to Zealand. If you phone in advance, in some rare instances, a free 30-minute guided tour during open hours can be arranged by the city council.

Færgehavnen. (© 89-52-11-11. Free admission. Mon–Fri 10am–4pm.

SHOPPING

Since the mid-1980s, Ebeltoft has become Denmark's "glass kingdom." There are no fewer than six local glassworks producing and selling blown-glass items. At several of the studios, it's possible to see the workshops where glass bowls, vases, wine glasses, and beautiful dishes are created in the glowing furnace. You can visit various workshops and purchase glass at such outlets as **Glasværkstedet,** Skindergade 5 (© 86-34-08-89); **Glaspusteriet,** Kystvejen 169 (© 86-34-49-58); and **Ebeltoft Glas,** Nedergade 19 (© 86-34-35-66).

WHERE TO STAY

Hotel Ebeltoft Strand ★ (Kids) This hotel is the best choice in the town center, although summer visitors will find the swanky Molskroen (see below) along the coast more inviting. Constructed in 1978, the comfortable, well-furnished guest rooms often have a private balcony or terrace, overlooking Ebeltoft Bay or the Mol hills. Each of the units, painted in pastel-like Nordic colors, comes with a well-kept bathroom. Family rooms can be composed by joining another room, with an extra bed for kids (provided they are under the age of 18). Kids have their own room but with a connecting door leading to where their parents sleep. In winter, guests retreat to a cozy lounge with a fireplace; in summer, the terrace with a view of the water is preferred. The restaurant serves the best lunch buffet in town, and the chef relies on the fresh produce of the season to create an enticing menu. The location is a 5-minute drive from the ferry dock and a 15-minute jaunt from Tirstrup Airport.

Nordre Strandvej 3, DK-8400 Ebeltoft. © **86-34-33-00.** Fax 86-34-46-36. www.ebeltoftstrand.dk. 72 units. DKK1,245 ($212/£125) double. Rates include buffet breakfast. AE, DC, MC, V. Free parking. Bus: 123 from Århus. **Amenities:** Restaurant; bar; indoor heated pool; kids' playroom; room service; laundry service; dry cleaning; nonsmoking rooms; rooms for those w/limited mobility. *In room:* TV, Wi-Fi, minibar, hair dryer, safe.

Molskroen ★ (Finds) Perched northwest of Ebeltoft on the coast, this half-timbered structure began life in 1923 as a private manor, but has been expanded and altered over the years. It's the best place to stay in the area. Many rooms have terraces overlooking Mols Hills, and a fine white sandy beach is only 100m (328 ft.) away. The *kro* is in the center of an area of summer houses mostly built in the 1920s and 1930s. The midsize guest rooms are now sleek, functional, and most comfortable, with freshly tiled bathrooms. Ten of the bedrooms are found in the annex, a redbrick building with a tiled roof. Accommodations here are every bit as good in the main building. Nine of these annex accommodations are individually furnished junior suites set on two floors, with four beds in each room, making them suitable for families. Even if you're not a guest, consider a stopover at the on-site French restaurant.

Hovegaden 16, Femmøller Strand, DK-8400 Ebeltoft. © **86-36-22-00.** Fax 86-36-23-00. www.molskroen. dk. 18 units. DKK1,580–DKK1,880 ($269–$320/£158–£188) double; DKK2,400–DKK3,500 ($408–$595/£240–£350) suite. Rates include breakfast. AE, DC, V. Free parking. Closed Dec 24–Jan 8. Bus: 123 from Århus. **Amenities:** Restaurant; bar; room service; babysitting; laundry service; dry cleaning; rooms for those w/limited mobility. *In room:* TV, fax, Wi-Fi, minibar, hair dryer, safe.

WHERE TO DINE

Harriet ★ DANISH/FRENCH/ITALIAN Our favorite restaurant in Ebeltoft, occupying a former general store built in 1775 in the heart of town, presents a sophisticated, carefully choreographed cuisine. Lunches include stable and relatively conservative platters, the most popular of which are salmon fish cakes with salad and fresh bread, or plates piled high with an assortment of various preparations of herring. Dinners are more elaborate, with menus that change frequently, according to the season, but which might include veal roasted with a ragout of locally picked forest mushrooms, veal cutlets in wine sauce, or filets of plaice with lemon-butter sauce. Any of these can be preceded by such exotica as Mediterranean-inspired carpaccio Piemontese with truffle oil, or hot pecorino cheese drizzled with hot maple syrup.

Adelgade 62. © **86-34-44-66.** Reservations recommended. Main courses DKK185–DKK295 ($31–$50/£19–£30); 2-course fixed-price menu DKK245 ($42/£25). AE, DC, MC, V. Daily 11:30am–10pm.

Restaurant "Mellem Jyder" ★ DANISH   The oldest and most historically evocative restaurant in Ebeltoft occupies a half-timbered building (ca. 1610), a few steps from the old Town Hall. Inside, you can order a roster of ultratraditional Danish dishes whose authenticity seems to go well with the antique setting. The chefs don't have any great surprises up their sleeves but turn out the tried-and-true, dishes such as filet of sole meunière or marinated salmon with dill sauce. They still make that old-fashioned sailors' favorite, Danish hash—*biksemal.* Desserts are nothing special. On afternoons, a beer garden in back—like you might expect in neighboring Germany—is popular during mild weather.

Juulsbakke 3. ⓒ **86-34-11-23.** Reservations recommended. Main courses DKK105–DKK195 ($18–$33/£11–£20); 3-course fixed-price menu DKK225 ($38/£23). MC, V. Daily noon–8pm.

EBELTOFT AFTER DARK

The best place to gather in the evening is **Den Skæve Bar,** Overgade 23 (ⓒ **86-34-37-97**), an English-style pub in a building dating from 1683. This is often the venue for live music, including folk, rock, blues, and jazz.

North Jutland

13

"Why do we live here in such a rugged environment?" asked a painter in Skagen, who answered his own question: "The real Denmark is a winter day at the North Sea with the wind blowing back your hair and making your skin salty, a trip in the autumn forest to gather mushrooms, or a romantic stroll in the newly leafed beech forest."

The first visitors arrived in North Jutland some 4,000 years ago in a land created by the Ice Age some 10,000 years earlier. Many places in Vendsyssel (the name of the province) still bear traces from the Stone Age, the Iron Age, and certainly the Viking Age. You can see history at many ancient monuments and relics of antiquity on display in the area.

In 1859, Hans Christian Andersen said it best: "If you are a Painter then follow us here, here are Subjects for you to paint, here is Scenery for Writing." In the 19th century, the Skagen painters—the Danish equivalent of the French Impressionists—were attracted to North Jutland for its intense light, the region's natural surroundings, the sea, and the people. Many of their paintings can be seen at the Skagens Museum. Some of their homes have been turned into museums.

After a long slumber, the towns of North Jutland are more alive than ever. Young people, who used to head for the bright lights of Copenhagen, often remain in the area of their birth, bringing new energy to its once-dull towns and hamlets.

Separated from the rest of Jutland (and also the mainland of Europe) by the Limfjord, North Jutland is a land unto itself. It's a landscape of North Sea beaches, coastal hamlets, fishing harbors, and wild heaths. It has only one large city, Aalborg, which lies at the narrow point of Limfjord, plus a number of midsize towns, notably Frederikshavn. Any of these would be a suitable base for exploration, but for scenic beauty we'd choose Skagen, at the northernmost boundary of Denmark, which has long attracted some of Denmark's leading artists and artisans.

Because of bridges linking Funen with Zealand and Jutland, you can drive to North Jutland from Copenhagen in 4¹/₂ hours.

1 MARIAGER ★

58km (36 miles) N of Århus; 341km (212 miles) NW of Copenhagen

There's a little nugget of a town that thrives in North Jutland that is most often overlooked by visitors on their trek to the more famous Aalborg. For a preview of Denmark

---

 Getting to North Jutland

For rail information to any town in North Jutland, call © **70-13-14-15;** for bus schedules, © **98-11-11-11.**

of long ago, nothing evokes a time gone by in all of North Jutland more than the charming little town of Mariager overlooking the Mariager Fjord, an idyllic setting.

The locals certainly adore summer roses—planting them everywhere along their cobblestone streets and in front of their half-timbered, red-roofed antique structures. If your time is short and you want to see the most picturesque streets, stroll down **Kirkegade** and **Postgården.** But the best collection of buildings with crisscross timbers envelops the **Torvet ★★**, the market square in the exact center of town. Some of our rival guidebooks (we won't name them) ignore Mariager completely—and that is a shame as it deserves at least a morning or an afternoon of your time.

Mariager was only a small fishing hamlet at the ferry crossing on the way between Randers and Aalborg before the foundation of Bridgettine Abbey in 1410. The abbey led to a flourishing trade and commerce in the area, and the town became a popular resort for the worshiping nobles. However, with the coming of the Reformation in 1536, the tide turned. When Mariager was granted its city charter in 1592, only 500 inhabitants remained. Many of the old buildings constructed in Mariager's heyday remain for us to appreciate today. Industrialization did not come until 1960, and by that time the town had become preservation-minded, as a walk through its cobbled streets will reveal.

ESSENTIALS

GETTING THERE   By Train and Bus   There are no direct trains to Mariager. Trains run from Aalborg to Hobro, east of Mariager, every 30 minutes, and from Århus to Hobro hourly. Take the bus from Hobro. Buses to Mariager run hourly from Hadsun, Hobro, or Randers. The ride on all three takes about a half-hour.

By Car   From Randers, take the E45 north, then head east at the junction of Route 555.

VISITOR INFORMATION   The **Mariager Tourist Association,** Torvet 1B (✆ **98-54-13-77;** www.visitmariagerfjord.dk), is open June 15 to August Monday to Friday 9am to 5pm, Saturday 9am to 2pm; off-season hours generally are Monday to Friday 9:30am to 4pm, Saturday 9am to noon. It is closed on Saturday from November to January.

SEEING THE SIGHTS

Mariager is connected to the Baltic via the **Mariager Fjord ★★★**, a deep but narrow saltwater inlet favored by sailors and yachters because of its smooth surface. You can sail aboard a small-scale cruise ship, the *Svanen,* as it circumnavigates the western recesses of the fjord. About four times a day, the ship touches down at such towns as Mariager, Hadsun, and Hobro, taking 2¹/₂ hours for a complete circuit that's priced at DKK100 ($17/£10) per person. You can get off at any of five villages en route, and wait for the next boat to pick you up 2 hours later and carry you on to the next town. There's a cafeteria onboard, and a sun deck where guests can improve their suntans during the short Nordic summer. Call ✆ **98-54-14-70** for more information.

Another ride you may not want to miss is aboard the smoke-belching **Mariager-Handest Veteranjernbane,** Ny Havnevej 3 (✆ **98-54-18-64**), which takes riders on an hour-long joy ride from Mariager to the village of Handest. After a stopover of half an hour, the little steam train makes the return journey to Mariager. The summer-only train departs daily at 11am, noon, 2pm, and 3pm, charging DKK80 ($14/£8) for a round-trip ticket. For more information visit **www.jernbaner.dk/mhvj**.

Although it's the old town itself that is the most alluring attraction, you may want to call on the abbey church, Mariager Kirke, Klostervej (✆ **98-54-15-95**), which was

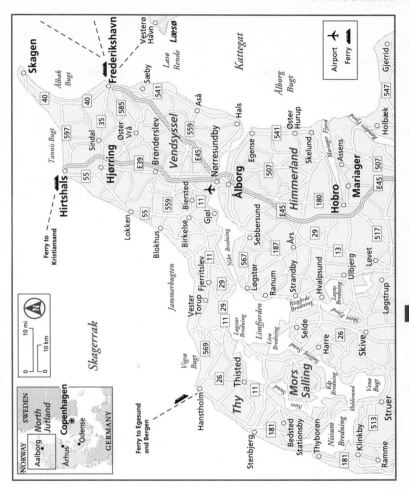

constructed in the 15th century as part of a nunnery. It was given to the town as its parish church following the Reformation. Although it has been largely reconstructed over the years, it's still a fine and lofty building with a magnificent carved altarpiece depicting the Last Supper and the Crucifixion, surrounded by 11 of the apostles. A memorial tablet to the last abbess can be seen in the south transept. Hours are Monday to Saturday 8am to 3:30pm; admission is free.

One of the most beautiful buildings in Mariager is an 18th-century merchant's house, now the **Mariager Museum,** Kirkegade 4B (*©* **98-54-12-87**). In the museum, you can see an attractive collection of domestic utensils and tools. The museum also contains relics from the ancient history of both Mariager and the surrounding district. Of special interest is a minireconstruction of the abbey and its church, an exhibit established in 1981 in connection with the 500th anniversary of the church. Frankly, the antique building itself is more intriguing to us than the rather lackluster exhibits inside. If you're pressed for time, you can hop, skip, and jump by its doorstep, just enjoying its 1700s facade. It's open May 15 to September 15, daily 1 to 5pm. Admission is DKK25 ($4.30/£2.50) adults; free for children 14 and under.

Even if you like to take a shaker and sprinkle extra salt on your food before tasting it, a visit to a salt museum may not be your idea of a good time. It's not at all surprising to learn that when the **Danmarks Saltcenter★** (Kids) (Havnevej; ℂ **98-54-18-16**) opened in 1998 it became the only science center in Denmark devoted to salt. But the museum is far more of an adventure than you might think. Salt, formed some 250 million years ago, was once considered such an invaluable ingredient for food it was called "white gold." Of course, it's so commonly available today, and in such wide use, that doctors and new cookbooks try to get us to cut down on its usage. Lying on the harbor at Mariager, close to the water, the museum traces the methods for extracting salt since the Middle Ages. You can explore in the tunnels of the salt mine and experience what it was like to work in a mountain salt mine a century ago. You can watch a foreman at the salt works boil the salts in a boiling hut as they did in the Middle Ages. That's not all. You can actually float in the **Dead Sea Pool★**, the liquid of which is 30% salt. The curiosity of the museum is a collection of salt cellars that have been entered into the *Guinness Book of World Records*. The salt garden is planted with plants that obviously can tolerate salt, and this is the setting for the museum's Salt Café, where, naturally, dishes connected with salt are served. There are also many activities for children, including, among others, shallow pools in the outdoor water playground. Tickets are DKK90 ($15/£9) adults, DKK70 ($12/£7) children 3 to 11, and free for children 2 and under. Hours are June 19 to August 8 daily 10am to 6pm; January 3 to June 18 and August 9 to December 23 Monday to Friday 10am to 4pm, Saturday and Sunday 10am to 5pm. Closed December 24 to January 2.

WHERE TO STAY

If you can't find a hotel room, the **Mariager Tourist Association** (ℂ **98-54-13-77**; www.visitmariagefjord.dk) will help book you into a private home or boardinghouse.

Hotel Postgården ★ There is just no contest about where to stay here. This old charmer—known for its warm hospitality, comfort, tradition, and elegance—is clearly the leader of a very limited pack. The most authentically historic hotel in Mariager has extended hospitality to travelers since it was established in 1710, in the heart of town, near the main square and Town Hall. It was restored in 1982 and has been upgraded many times since. The building's facade and public areas, especially its pub and restaurant, are the most popular places in town. About two-thirds of the rooms have been stripped of their historic charm and upgraded to a modern international style that nonetheless is still comfortable and cozy. If you insist on antique decor, request room no. 305 (one that the hotel usually assigns to anyone claiming to be a honeymooner); or, to a lesser extent, room nos. 201, 203, or 307. Even if you don't stay here, stop in for the best food and drink in town (see below).

Torvet 6A, DK-9550 Mariager. ℂ **98-54-10-12.** Fax 98-54-24-64. www.hotelpostgaardenmariager.dk. 14 units. DKK797 ($136/£80) double. Rates include breakfast. AE, DC, MC, V. **Amenities:** Restaurant; bar; sauna. *In room:* TV, Wi-Fi.

Motel Landgangen (Value) We've obviously made our preference known for the Postgården, but if for some reason that hotel is fully booked (a likely possibility in

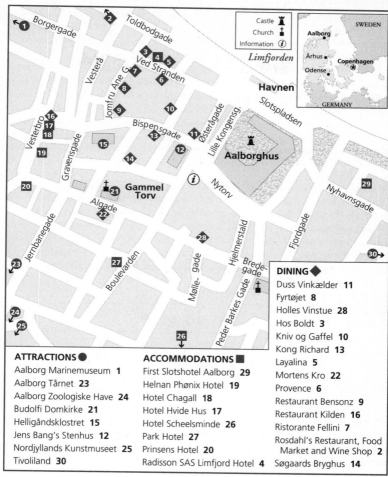

Castle ♟
Church ✝
Information ⓘ

Limfjorden

Havnen

Slotspladsen

SWEDEN
Aalborg
Århus • Copenhagen ✪
Odense •
GERMANY

Aalborghus

Gammel Torv

NORTH JUTLAND

13

MARIAGER

DINING ◆
Duss Vinkælder **11**
Fyrtøjet **8**
Holles Vinstue **28**
Hos Boldt **3**
Kniv og Gaffel **10**
Kong Richard **13**
Layalina **5**
Mortens Kro **22**
Provence **6**
Restaurant Bensonz **9**
Restaurant Kilden **16**
Ristorante Fellini **7**
Rosdahl's Restaurant, Food Market and Wine Shop **2**
Søgaards Bryghus **14**

ATTRACTIONS ●
Aalborg Marinemuseum **1**
Aalborg Tårnet **23**
Aalborg Zoologiske Have **24**
Budolfi Domkirke **21**
Helligåndsklostret **15**
Jens Bang's Stenhus **12**
Nordjyllands Kunstmuseet **25**
Tivoliland **30**

ACCOMMODATIONS ■
First Slotshotel Aalborg **29**
Helnan Phønix Hotel **19**
Hotel Chagall **18**
Hotel Hvide Hus **17**
Hotel Scheelsminde **26**
Park Hotel **27**
Prinsens Hotel **20**
Radisson SAS Limfjord Hotel **4**

midsummer), this motel provides alternative accommodations—and good ones at that. Set beside the river, a 5-minute walk north of the abbey, this is not a dreary motel, even though its white exterior and simple architecture date from the late 1960s. Rooms are cozy and inviting, well kept and neat, including the bathrooms. The place is even better known for its restaurant, which features Danish specialties and comfy furniture with a view of the water. It's open in summer daily noon to 8pm, and off-season Friday to Sunday noon to 8pm.

Oxendalen 1, DK-9550 Mariager. ⓒ **98-54-11-22.** 6 units. DKK650 ($111/£65) double. Rates include breakfast. AE, DC, MC, V. **Amenities:** Restaurant; bar. *In room:* TV.

Restaurant Postgården DANISH/FRENCH Many diners appreciate this restaurant for its old-time decor and the sense of intimacy created by its small but bustling dining rooms. During mild weather, tables are set up outside. There's nothing particularly avant-garde about the food served here. Luncheon favorites include such tried-and-true favorites as *smørrebrød* (open-faced sandwiches) piled high with baby shrimp or Danish ham, and platters of herring or roasted pork with red cabbage and new potatoes. Dinners are more elaborate and might feature such good-tasting dishes as bacon-wrapped salmon with fettuccine in a saffron sauce or else lemon sole with crab in a lime-laced white-wine sauce with dill potatoes. A special treat is the marinated leg of duck with sautéed cabbage and mushrooms served in a sweet pepper sauce with a potato soufflé.

In the Hotel Postgården, Torvet 6A. (C) **98-54-10-12.** Reservations recommended. Lunch main courses DKK92–DKK145 ($16–$25/£9.20–£15); dinner main courses DKK116–DKK235 ($20–$40/£12–£24); fixed-price menus DKK155–DKK320 ($26–$54/£16–£32). AE, DC, MC, V. Daily 11am–9pm.

MARIAGER AFTER DARK

The town's most consistently popular pub is in the **Hotel Postgården,** Torvet 6A ((C) **98-54-10-12**). Within a room sheathed with old-fashioned paneling, near a bar with antique-looking beer pulls, you'll find an animated crowd of office workers and the after-dinner set taking refuge from the confines of their homes, with lots of options for meeting and making new friends. Open daily 11am to 11pm, it serves platters of food, including herring, that taste good with the Carlsberg, and which cost DKK30 to DKK65 ($5.10–$11/£3–£6.50).

NORTH JUTLAND

13

AALBORG

2 AALBORG ★

132km (82 miles) NW of Ebeltoft; 383km (238 miles) W of Copenhagen

We won't pretend that Aalborg is our favorite city in Jutland—Århus is. But once in this city opening onto the Limfjord, we always manage to have a good time, and so will you if you avail yourself of all its attractions, especially some of those in the environs. We like to stand at Aalborg harbor, watching ships head out for sea, sailing to faraway Iceland and even the Faroe islands, and most definitely to Britain and Ireland.

The largest city in North Jutland, Aalborg is known worldwide for its akvavit. Although essentially a shipping town and commercial center, Aalborg makes a good base for sightseers, with its many hotels and attractions, more than 300 restaurants, and diverse nightlife.

History is a living reality in Aalborg. The city was founded 1,000 years ago when the Viking fleets assembled in these parts before setting off on their predatory expeditions. The city's historic atmosphere has been preserved in its old streets and alleys. Near the Church of Our Lady are many beautifully restored and reconstructed houses, some of which date from the 16th century.

Not far from Aalborg, on the west coast of North Jutland, some of the finest beaches in northern Europe stretch from Slettestrand to Skagen. The resort towns of **Blokhus** and **Løkken** are especially popular with Danes, Germans, and Swedes.

ESSENTIALS

GETTING THERE   By Plane You can fly from Copenhagen to Aalborg; the **airport** ((C) **98-17-11-44;** www.aal.dk) is 6.5km (4 miles) from the city center.

By Train There is frequent train service from Copenhagen by way of Fredericia to
Århus; there you can connect with a train to Aalborg, a 90-minute ride.

By Bus Aalborg's bus station is the transportation center for North Jutland and is served from all directions. For all bus information in North Jutland, call **Nordjyllands Trafikselskab** (✆ **98-11-11-11**).

By Car From Ebeltoft, follow Route 21 north until you reach the junction with Route 16. Drive west on Route 16 until you come to E45, which runs north to Aalborg.

VISITOR INFORMATION The **Aalborg Tourist Bureau** is at Østerågade 8 (✆ **99-31-675-00;** www.visitaalborg.com). It's open June and August, Monday to Friday 9am to 5:30pm, Saturday 10am to 1pm; September to May, Monday to Friday 9am to 4:30pm, Saturday 10am to 1pm. In July it is open Monday to Friday 9am to 5:30pm, Saturday 10am to 4pm.

GETTING AROUND For bus information, call ✆ **98-11-11-11.** Most buses depart from Østerågade and Nytorv in the city center. A typical fare costs DKK16 ($2.70/£1.60), although you can buy a 10-trip tourist pass for DKK110 ($19/£11) to ride on all the city buses for a day. Information about bus routes is available from the *Aalborg Guide,* which is distributed free by the tourist office.

SPECIAL EVENTS The **Aalborg Carnival ★★** , scheduled each year on May 25 and 26, is one of the major events of spring in Jutland. Streets are filled with festive figures in colorful costumes strutting in a parade. Up to 100,000 people participate in this annual event, marking the victory of spring over winter's darkness. The whole city seems to explode in joy. There's also the **Aalborg Jazz and Blues Festival** August 13 to 19. Jazz fills the whole city at dozens of clubs, although most activity centers on C. W. Obels Plads. Every year on the Fourth of July, Danes and Danish Americans meet to celebrate America's **Independence Day** in the lovely hills of Rebild.

SEEING THE SIGHTS

Aalborg Marinemuseum ⟨**Kids**⟩ If you've ever fantasized about having a close encounter with the dinghy that Queen Margrethe sailed in while still a princess, here is your chance. Seriously, this museum is more enthralling than that, as it gives you a hands-on experience with the interior of a submarine, *Springeren,* which is primed and ready for action. The 23m (75-ft.) sub was one of the last to be designed and built in Denmark. Also on-site is the torpedo boat *Søbjørnen,* the world's fastest such boat. You can see the inspection ship, *Ingolf,* that was on active duty in the bone-chilling waters around Greenland until 1990. Other exhibits depict life at sea, the port of Aalborg, and activities at the Aalborg shipyard. At the Café Ubåden (submarine), you can order food and drink. There's also a playground on-site.

Vester Fjordvej 81. ✆ **98-11-78-03.** www.aalborgmarinemuseum.dk. Admission DKK75 ($13/£7.50) adults, DKK35 ($6/£3.50) children 6–14, free for children 5 and under. May–Aug daily 10am–6pm; off-season daily 10am–4pm. Bus: 12 or 13.

Aalborg Tårnet (Aalborg Tower) Whenever we visit a city or town, and if there is a lookout point, we always head there first for a panoramic overview. In Aalborg, that perfect view (that is, if it's a clear day) is seen from this tower, rising 105m (344 ft.) into the air. Reached by stairs or elevator, its view takes in everything from the smokestacks to the beautiful Limfjord. Weather permitting, you can see the North Sea and even Rold Forest in the south. The tower itself is no beauty—rather ugly in fact—but it does have its rewards, including its location on a hill in back of the Nordjyllands Kunstmuseum and at the border of Mølleparken, the best woodland for walking or hiking in the area.

Søndre Skovvej, at Skovbakken. ℂ **98-77-05-11**. www.aalborgtaarnet.com. Admission DKK25 ($4.30/£2.50) adults, DKK15 ($2.60/£1.50) children 3–14, free for children 2 and under. Apr–June daily 11am–5pm; July–Aug 8 daily 10am–7pm; Aug 9–Sept 26 and Oct 14–Oct 22 daily 11am–7pm. Closed Oct–Mar, except for 1 week in Oct. Bus: 11, 14, or 16.

Aalborg Zoologiske Have (Aalborg Zoo) ★★ (Kids)

We've seen bigger and better zoos in our lives, but this remains one of our favorites because of its success in the breeding of near-extinct animals such as the Siberian tiger. More than 1,300 animals are on parade here, including crocs, zebras, tigers, giraffes, polar bears, and orangutans. Apes and beasts of prey are kept under minimal supervision. They live in such simulated conditions as an African savanna or a rainforest from South America. With the opening of a large playground, Oasen, for children, kids can romp around like the resident monkeys. Other adventures include a riverbank for crocs, a pampa for anteaters, or a forest full of bears.

Mølleparkvej 63. ℂ **96-31-29-29**. www.aalborg-zoo.dk. Admission DKK115 ($20/£12) adults, DKK60 ($10/£6) children 3–11, free for children 2 and under. Jan–Feb and Nov–Dec daily 10am–2pm; Mar daily 10am–3pm; Apr and Sept–Oct daily 10am–4pm; May–Aug daily 9am–6pm. Last ticket is sold 1 hr. before closing. Bus: 11. 4km (2½ miles) south of Aalborg.

Budolfi Domkirke (Cathedral of St. Budolf)

Even if you don't visit this church, you'll be made aware of its presence. A carillon makes beautiful music daily every hour from 9am to 10pm, when it mercifully shuts down to allow the early-to-bed crowd to get some sleep. This elaborately decorated and whitewashed cathedral is dedicated to the patron saint of sailors. The baroque spire of the church is Aalborg's major landmark. The church you see today is the result of 800 years of rebuilding and expansion. On the south wall is a fresco depicting St. Catherine of Alexandria and some grotesque little centaurs. Look for the altarpiece from 1689 and the pulpit from 1692—both carved by Lauritz Jensen. The marble font from 1727 was a gift to the church. Note too the gallery in the north aisle with its illustrations of the Ten Commandments. A similar gallery in the south aisle illustrates the suffering of Christ and also bears the names of a number of prominent Aalborg citizens from around the mid–17th century, which seems to be of no interest to anyone anymore. A series of cocks crow the hour from four matching clock faces on the church's tower.

Algade. ℂ **98-12-46-70**. Free admission. Bus: 3, 5, 10, or 11. June–Aug Mon–Fri 9am–4pm, Sat 9am–2pm; Sept–May Mon–Fri 9am–3pm, Sat 9am–noon.

Helligåndsklostret (Monastery of the Holy Ghost)

Once when we were doing a magazine article on the Danish resistance movement during the Nazi occupation from 1940 to 1945, our trail led us to this site, often called the "Aalborg Kloster." Here we learned that it was the secret headquarters of the "Churchill Club," which was the first Resistance group established in Denmark to fight the Nazi menace. This vine-covered monastery is the oldest social-welfare institution in Denmark, as well as the oldest building in Aalborg. Built near the heart of town in 1431 and designed with step-shaped gables, it contains a well-preserved rectory, a series of vaulted storage cellars—some of which occasionally functioned as prisons—a whitewashed collection of cloisters, and a chapter house whose walls in some areas are decorated with 16th-century frescoes. The complex can be visited only as part of a guided tour.

C. W. Obels Plads. ℂ **99-30-60-90**. Guided tour DKK40 ($6.80/£4) adults, DKK10 ($1.70/£1) children 3–12. Guided tour late June to mid-Aug Mon–Fri 1:30pm. Bus: 1.

Jens Bangs Stenhus (Jens Bang's Stone House) ★   This is the finest example
of Renaissance domestic architecture in the north of Europe. This glittering six-floor
mansion, built in 1624, once belonged to a wealthy merchant, Jens Bang. Bang was
gifted but also argumentative and obstinate. He deliberately made his house rich with
ornamentation and ostentation as a challenge to the other good citizens of the town. It
was rumored that he avenged himself on his many enemies by caricaturing them in the
grotesque carvings on the facade of the house. In spite of his wealth, he was never made
a member of the town council, and to this day his image is depicted on the south facade
sticking his tongue out at the Town Hall. The historic wine cellar, Duus Vinkjælder, is
the meeting place of the Guild of Christian IV. On the ground floor is an old apothecary
shop. The mansion itself is still privately owned and is not open to the public.

Østerågade 9. Bus: 3, 5, 10, or 11.

**Nordjyllands Kunstmuseet (Museum of Modern and Contemporary
Art)** ★ (Kids)   This building is a prime example of modern Scandinavian architecture.
Built from 1968 to 1972, it was designed by Elissa and Alvar Aalto and Jean-Jacques
Baruël as a showplace for 20th-century Danish and international art. The nucleus of the
collection dates from 1850 but it's been added to over the years with many purchases and
bequests. The Carlsberg Foundation, those beer barons, have donated some of the most
notable works, including William Scharff's *Nocturne Series* and J. F. Willumsen's *War
Invalids.* We find that the museum's most romantic picture is Harald Slott-Møller's
Spring (1901). The greatest treasure-trove of art came from two dental technologists,
Anna and Kresten Krestensen, who amassed a notable collection of Danish and international art from 1920 to 1950. In later years, as funds became available, the museum
purchased works by great international artists including Fernand Léger, Max Ernst, and
Wassily Kandinsky. Many events are staged for children, including picture hunts, family
tours, and children's museum exhibits. On the ground floor is a good cafe overlooking
the sculpture park. In 1994, artist Paul Gernes decorated the walls of the cafe, which
serves a light lunch menu and open-faced sandwiches. Ask about musical concerts frequently staged here all year.

Kong Christians Allé 50. (© **98-13-80-88.** www.nordjyllandskunstmuseum.dk. Admission DKK40
($6.80/£4) adults, free for children 17 and under; free admission in Dec. Tues–Sun 10am–5pm (Feb–Apr
and Sept–Nov Tues to 9pm).

Nearby Attractions

Less than 4km (2¹/₂ miles) north of Aalborg, you'll find some of the oldest grave sites in
all of Scandinavia, not just those of the Viking era but even Iron Age burial grounds. The
Viking settlement of Nørresundby is the location of more than 700 cremation graves,
and contains the charred remains of more than 150 Viking boats and ships that were
ceremonially burned as part of the cremations. Set within a park, the excavations are
open to the public year-round 24 hours a day. Most of the graves are marked with stones
placed in the form of a triangle, an oval, or a ship. The deceased person was usually
cremated. North of the burial ground lay the associated village, where the finds include
the remains of houses, fences, wells, and fire pits. The area was subject to drifting sand.
About A.D. 1000, the whole burial ground became covered with sand, which meant that
the stone markings and even a newly plowed field were preserved until this day.

   Further details about the excavations are on view in the **Lindholm Høje Museet,**
Lindholmsvej 65 (© **96-31-04-10;** www.nordjyllandshistoriskemuseum.dk; bus: 2).
The museum contains archaeological finds from the excavations and illustrates how the

inhabitants of Lindholm Høje lived at home and traded abroad. It is open Easter to mid-October daily 10am to 5pm; mid-October to Easter Tuesday through Sunday 10am to 4pm. Admission costs DKK30 ($5.10/£3) adults, DKK15 ($2.60/£1.50) children 5 to 11, free for children 4 and under.

Voergård Slot ★★, Voergård 6, Dronninglund (*©* **98-86-71-08**; www.voergaard slot.dk), is enveloped by Denmark's widest moat, and is one of the best preserved Renaissance castles in the land. Its oldest section was constructed in 1481, its most "recent" in 1590. What makes this a special place is that it is furnished with an exceptional **collection of European art and furniture ★★★**, including paintings by Goya, Rubens, El Greco, and Raphael. The antique treasures come from the eras of Napoleon, Louis XIV, and Louis XVI. A special section displays some of the **personal furniture ★★** of Marie Antoinette. Two magnificent sideboards with gilted bronze plates and ornaments by Gouttiers were made by cabinetmaker Riesener for Louis XVI's court. Many of these rare treasures came from Count Ejnar Oberbech-Clausen, who took over Voergård in 1955 and filled it with art, antiquities, and furniture, making it one of the most spectacular private homes in Denmark.

Denmark's most famous ghost, Ingeborg Skeel, still resides at the castle, or so locals believe. As the owner of the castle, she is said to have drowned the architect, Philip Brandin, in the moat to prevent him from building a castle as splendid as Voergård ever again. Admission costs DKK70 ($12/£7) adults, DKK25 ($4.30/£2.50) children. Take the E45 from Aalborg, cutting east on Route 559 to Droningland, and then follow the signs to Voergård Slot. May 1 to June 13 and August 21 to October 17, it's open Saturday 2 to 5pm, Sunday 10am to 5pm; July 10 to 18, daily 10am to 5pm.

Americans who are in Jutland for the Fourth of July should make a beeline to the **Rebild National Park,** 29km (18 miles) south of Aalborg. On these heather dunes, Danes, Danish Americans, and Americans celebrate America's Independence Day. The program often features opera singers, folk dancers, choirs, and glee clubs, together with well-known speakers.

A 1-hour drive from Aalborg takes you to the resort town of **Blokhus** and the broad white beaches of the North Sea coast. Not far from here is a 50-hectare (124-acre) amusement park, **Fårup Sommerland & Waterpark** (*©* **98-88-16-00**; www.faarupsommer land.dk; bus: 200). Expect lots of noise, lots of families, and lots of emphasis on good, clean fun in a style that might remind you of a small-scale version of Disneyland. It's open mid-May to early September, daily 10am to 7pm. Admission: May 12 to June 23 DKK165 ($28/£17), seniors 65 and over DKK90 ($15/£9); June 24 to early September DKK195 ($33/£20), seniors 65 and over DKK120 ($20/£12); free for children 2 and under. Admission is reduced in late afternoon; see website for further details.

For Family Fun

Tivoliland ★★, Karolinelundsvej (*©* **98-12-33-15**; www.tivoliland.dk), is an amusement park for the entire family, with lots of snap and sparkle, although a pale imitation of the more famous one in Copenhagen. A tradition since 1946 in the center of Aalborg, it's one of the most attended attractions in North Jutland. In addition to rides, there are beautiful gardens with thousands of flowers and fantastic fountains. You've seen it all before, but it's still an amusing and delightful way to spend an evening, as you can take everything from a flying carpet ride to a spin on Scandinavia's only boomerang roller coaster (which screws and loops both forward and backward). China Town is one of the most visited attractions, containing such features as the China dragon, the fun house, and a cycle fun rail. Other attractions include a Gravity Tower, with a 55m (180-ft.) free fall, and a Hall of Mirrors, a labyrinth showing you amazing dimensions of yourself. An open-air stage, restaurants, a pizzeria, dancing areas, and sing-alongs—it all makes for one big day. The attraction is open May to June daily noon to 9pm; July to September 6 daily 10am to 10pm. Admission is DKK195 ($33/£20) adults, free for children 2 and under. However, you'll pay separately for the various attractions, with tickets ranging from DKK10 to DKK50 ($1.70–$8.50/£1–£5). An unlimited ticket for all rides, good for 1 day only, costs DKK195 ($33/£20).

SHOPPING

This North Jutland city abounds in specialty stores. For the best collection of gold and silver jewelry, patronize **Aalborg Guld & Solvhus,** Gravensgade 8 (© **98-16-57-11**). The most sophisticated handicrafts—many quite amusing—are sold at **Lange Handicrafts,** Hjelmerstald 15 (© **98-13-82-68**). To watch a glass blower in action, and perhaps make some purchases, go to **Glaspusteriet,** Nørregade 6 (© **98-13-01-20**).

The largest shopping center in North Jutland lies about 6.5km (4 miles) south of Aalborg's center. The **Aalborg Storcenter,** Hobrovej 452 (© **98-18-23-10;** bus: 11, 14, or 16), contains at least 50 specialty shops and kiosks, as well as the all-inclusive **Bilka Department Store** (© **98-79-70-00**).

Aalborg also has some other department stores that bring a vast array of Danish merchandise together under one roof, including **Salling,** Nytorv 8 (© **98-16-00-00;** bus: 1, 11, or 14), with 30 specialty shops. It has the city's largest selection of fashion, plus lots of other good stuff, including books and toys. A major competitor is **Magasin,** Nytorv 24 (© **98-13-30-00;** bus: 1, 11, or 14). **Gavlhuset,** Algade 9 (© **98-12-18-22;** bus: 16 or 18), has a little bit of everything—Indian silver, "dancing beans," old Kilim carpets, masks from around the globe, knitted goods, "gods" in bronze, exotic spices, wooden toys in bright colors, and even African woodcarvings. To look at and perhaps purchase some of the city's best contemporary art, head for **Galerie Wolfsen,** Tiendeladen 6 (© **98-13-75-66**).

WHERE TO STAY

The **Aalborg Tourist Bureau** (© **99-31-675-00;** www.visitaalborg.com) can book a room for you in a private Danish home—double or single, with access to a shower. Bed linens are included in the price, and all rooms are situated within the city limits and reached by bus. In July and August, the peak tourist months, Helnan Phønix slashes its rates and becomes a moderately priced choice, because it's primarily a business hotel, and for them, high tourist season is their low season. Although many rooms at the Limsford Hotel are labeled expensive, the hotel rents dozens of more affordable accommodations as well.

Expensive

First Slotshotel Aalborg ★   You can have a drink while taking in views of the beautiful Limfjord. Although down several notches from other recommended choices in this category, this is still a comfortable, tasteful, and well-designed hotel. Since its opening in 1986, it's been a preferred choice to stay for those seeking a central location near the harbor. Tired of their yachts, the boating crowd often stops over here for a real bath and a real meal. The location is also close to the major attractions of town. Bedrooms are larger than those of the average Danish hotel, and they have extrawide beds and plenty of space to store your possessions. Some of the accommodations can easily be converted into family units.

Rendsburggade 5, DK-9100 Aalborg. © **98-10-14-00.** Fax 98-11-65-70. www.firsthotels.com. 154 units. DKK748–DKK1,548 ($127–$263/£75–£155) double; DKK1,548–DKK1,800 ($263–$306/£155–£180) suite.

Rates include buffet breakfast. AE, DC, MC, V. Free parking. Bus: 1, 3, 5, or 7. **Amenities:** Breakfast lounge; bar; gym; sauna; breakfast-only room service; laundry service; dry cleaning; nonsmoking rooms; solarium; rooms for those w/limited mobility. *In room:* TV, Wi-Fi (in most), minibar.

Helnan Phønix Hotel ★★★   In the town's most sumptuous mansion, you'll find the oldest, largest, most historic, and most prestigious hotel in Aalborg, lying close to the bus station. It originated in 1783 on the main street of town as the private home of the Danish brigadier general assigned to protect Aalborg from assault by foreign powers. In 1853, it was converted into a hotel. Today, it appears deceptively small from Aalborg's main street, and very imposing if you see its modern wings from the back. Bedrooms are tastefully and elegantly appointed with dark wood furnishings. Some of the rooms have exposed ceiling beams, and all of them are equipped with neatly tiled bathrooms. The hotel's restaurant, **Brigadieren,** serves a sophisticated Danish and international cuisine.

Vesterbro 77, DK-9000 Aalborg. ⓒ 98-12-00-11. Fax 98-10-10-20. www.helnan.dk. 210 units. Summer DKK955 ($162/£96) double, DKK2,500 ($425/£250) suite; winter DKK1,075–DKK1,495 ($183–$254/£108–£150) double, DKK2,500 ($425/£250) suite. AE, DC, MC, V. Parking DKK50 ($8.50/£5). **Amenities:** Restaurant; bar; gym; Jacuzzi; sauna; room service; massage; laundry service; dry cleaning; nonsmoking rooms; solarium. *In room:* TV, Wi-Fi, minibar, hair dryer, safe.

Hotel Hvide Hus ★   If you're willing to forego the antique charms of the Phønix, or prefer a more modern high-rise address, then the Hvide Hus is one of the most viable candidates for overnighting. The first-rate "White House Hotel" is in Kilde Park, about a 12-minute walk from the heart of Aalborg and close to the bus station. Many international businesspeople now stay here instead of at the traditional Phønix. In cooperation with well-known galleries, the hotel is decorated with works by some of Denmark's leading painters. The guest rooms are well furnished in fresh Scandinavian modern style; all have private balconies with a view of Aalborg. The restaurant **Kilden** and the bar **Pejsebar** are both on the 15th floor and offer city views.

Vesterbro 2, DK-9000 Aalborg. ⓒ 98-13-84-00. Fax 98-13-51-22. www.hotelhvidehus.dk. 198 units. Mon–Fri DKK1,495–DKK1,595 ($254–$271/£150–£160) double, DKK2,445 ($416/£245) suite; Sat–Sun DKK995 ($169/£100) double, DKK2,445 ($416/£245) suite. Rates include buffet breakfast. AE, DC, MC, V. Free parking. **Amenities:** Restaurant; bar; room service; massage; babysitting; laundry service; dry cleaning; nonsmoking rooms. *In room:* TV, Wi-Fi, minibar, hair dryer, trouser press.

Radisson SAS Limfjord Hotel ★★   Check into the Phønix for traditional comfort and into the Radisson SAS for the modern comfort of its up-to-date facilities. This is the most avant-garde hotel in town—a five-story yellow-brick structure with huge expanses of glass in a streamlined Danish modern layout. In the center of town, a 3-minute walk east of the cathedral, the hotel opens onto the famous Limfjorden Canal. It's near Jomfru Anegade, a street packed with bars and restaurants. The public rooms are sparsely furnished with modern, streamlined furniture. Many of the midsize-to-spacious bedrooms overlook the harbor, and each is well maintained with tasteful, comfortable furnishings. The suites are blessed with a Jacuzzi. The hotel offers some of the best drinking and dining facilities in town, and its casino is a lively hub of nighttime action.

Ved Stranden 14–16, DK-9000 Aalborg. ⓒ 800-333-3333 in the U.S., or 98-16-43-33. Fax 98-16-17-47. www.radissonsas.com. 188 units. DKK1,445–DKK1,655 ($246–$281/£145–£166) double; DKK2,275 ($387/£228) suite. Rates include breakfast. AE, DC, MC, V. Parking DKK85 ($14/£8.50). Bus: 1, 4, 40, or 46. **Amenities:** Restaurant; pizzeria; bar; casino; fitness center; sauna; 24-hr. room service; laundry service; dry cleaning; nonsmoking rooms; rooms for those w/limited mobility. *In room:* TV, Wi-Fi, minibar, hair dryer, trouser press; Jacuzzi (in suites).

Moderate

Hotel Scheelsminde ★ Finds We'll let you in on a secret: For a stopover in Aalborg, we often like to drive out of town for 4km ($2^1/_2$ miles) south to an old but beautifully restored manor house from 1808. If you've been doing the whirlwind tour of Jutland, this is one of the best places we've found to wind down, enjoying total comfort, fresh air, and a market-fresh regional cuisine. A modern extension was built to accommodate tasteful, comfortably furnished, and completely up-to-date bedrooms, with the restaurant remaining inside the original manor. During the day you can go for walks through the hotel's large private grounds.

Scheelsmindevej 35, DK-9100 Aalborg. ℂ **98-18-32-33.** Fax 98-18-33-34. www.scheelsminde.dk. 96 units. DKK1,095–DKK1,695 ($186–$288/£110–£170) double. Rates include breakfast. AE, DC, MC, V. Bus: 5 or 8. **Amenities:** Restaurant; bar; indoor heated pool; gym; sauna; room service; laundry service; dry cleaning; nonsmoking rooms; room for those w/limited mobility. *In room:* TV, Wi-Fi, minibar, hair dryer.

Park Hotel ★ This hotel has been putting up wayfarers who arrive at the rail terminus opposite the building since 1917. One of the oldest hotels in the city, the Park (not to be confused with Park Inn Chagall) became so popular that a modern block of tasteful, comfortable rooms was added when an extension was tacked on in 1990. The original architectural details of the main building remain relatively intact in spite of modernization. Today the hotel enjoys a well-deserved reputation for its coziness and comfort, with personal service a hallmark. On-site is a first-class restaurant and bar, and in summer guests spill out onto chairs in front of the hotel.

J. F. Kennedys Plads 41, DK-9100 Aalborg. ℂ **98-12-31-33.** Fax 98-13-31-66. www.park-hotel-aalborg.dk. 81 units. DKK1,015–DKK1,130 ($173–$192/£102–£113) double; DKK1,450 ($247/£145) suite. Rates include buffet breakfast. AE, DC, MC, V. **Amenities:** Restaurant; bar; room service; laundry service; dry cleaning; nonsmoking rooms; rooms for those w/limited mobility. *In room:* TV, Wi-Fi, hair dryer.

Inexpensive

Chagall Ever since the 1950s, this hotel has been an affordable choice in pricey Aalborg. In honor of its namesake, most of the bedrooms have reproductions of Marc Chagall's paintings. As a grace note, the hotel offers an inner courtyard where you can sit out in summer, enjoying the far-too-few nights of warm weather. The midsize bedrooms are designed in sophisticated Danish modern, with such features as individual climate control. On-site is a cafe-style area in the lobby where breakfast is served.

Vesterbro 36–38, Postboks 1856, DK-9000 Aalborg. ℂ **98-12-69-33.** Fax 98-13-13-44. www.hotel-chagall.dk. 89 units. DKK780–DKK880 ($133–$150/£78–£88) double. Rates include breakfast. AE, DC, MC, V. **Amenities:** Breakfast lounge; fitness center; Jacuzzi; sauna; laundry service; dry cleaning; nonsmoking rooms; solarium. *In room:* TV, Wi-Fi (in some), minibar, coffeemaker, hair dryer.

Prinsen Hotel Value Local residents often cite the Prinsen to us as "the place we store our relatives when we don't have room at home." They seem to know they'll get a square deal here. Opposite the railroad station, this 1906 landmark doesn't have the glamour of our previous choices, but it's still a good deal in our opinion. The small-to-midsize bedrooms, in spite of their age, are decorated in a light, modern Danish style, with comfortable, tasteful furnishings. The hotel may be aging, but it's kept up-to-date with the times with frequent renovations and modernizations. There is a family-style welcome here, and we like the touch of providing free coffee, tea, or hot chocolate (especially welcoming when you come in on one of the frequent snowy nights).

Prinsensgade 14–16, DK-9000 Aalborg. ℂ **98-13-37-33.** Fax 98-16-52-82. www.prinsen-hotel.dk. 40 units. DKK675–DKK995 ($115–$169/£68–£100) double. Rates include buffet breakfast. AE, DC, MC, V. Free parking. Closed Dec 23–Jan 1. Bus: 1, 3, or 5. **Amenities:** Breakfast lounge; bar; Jacuzzi; sauna; laundry service; dry cleaning; nonsmoking rooms; solarium. *In room:* TV, Wi-Fi, hair dryer.

WHERE TO DINE

Jomfru Anegade is the most famous restaurant-filled street in Jutland. If you can't find good food here, you didn't try. It's got something for most palates and most pocketbooks.

Expensive

Hos Boldt ★ DANISH/FRENCH We once knew this place as a good tavern filled with suds-loving drinkers. The setting, in a building from the 1800s, was always antique, and the family owners have kept the rooms deliberately old-fashioned. In 1992, they decided to transform the place into an upmarket restaurant while keeping the quaint atmosphere of antique furniture and candles. One of our closest friends in Aalborg claimed that "this is my favorite, a pet spot I keep coming back to." His reason is obvious, as the food is consistently good. Menu items change with the season and the availability of ingredients. If featured, the lobster bisque seems the peak among all other appetizers. One intriguing main course is salmon presented with various preparations. The sea bass is cooked in a salt crust to preserve its aroma and its juices, and the tender rack of Danish lamb is made even more savory with the rosemary-laced wine sauce that comes with it. You just might smack your lips at the steamed freshly caught turbot with a julienne of leeks, or the consommé of veal with herbs and quail eggs—a real gourmet dish.

Ved Stranden 7. ℂ 98-16-17-77. Reservations recommended. Main courses DKK248–DKK298 ($42–$51/£25–£30); fixed-price menus DKK358 ($61/£36). AE, DC, MC, V. Mon–Sat 5pm–midnight. Bus: 1, 4, 40, or 46.

Kong Richard ★ DANISH/FRENCH Although under separate management, this restaurant occupies the street-level floor of the previously recommended Radisson SAS Hotel. We first discovered this place when it occupied a 1737 warehouse in another location. We were impressed then, and we're even more impressed with the restaurant after its move into sleeker, more sophisticated surroundings. The skilled chefs produce five- and six-course menus that change nightly and feature the best of Danish reginal produce. A typical set menu might begin with smoked salmon flavored with ginger, followed by a soup, perhaps a medley of celery, parsnips, carrots, and lobster tail. You're given a choice of a main dish—perhaps sautéed duck breast or beef tenderloin. The pastry chef makes a different confection every night, such as chocolate tort.

Ved Stranden 14–16. ℂ 98-12-39-99. Reservations recommended. 5-course menu DKK375 ($64/£38); 6-course menu DKK490 ($83/£49). AE, DC, MC, V. Tues–Fri 11:30am–3:30pm and 5:30pm–midnight; Sat 5:30pm–midnight. Bus: 1.

Mortens Kro ★★★ (Finds) FRENCH/DANISH This artful restaurant is the domain of Morten Nealsen, the most gifted chef in Aalborg. It is the best place to dine in the city, offering classic dining chairs and luxurious sofas. The chef wanted a "New York look but with Parisian ambience," the latter evoked by the champagne bar. The rustic brickwork and glass and steel form a backdrop for fine dining. DJs entertain during the weekends. This is really a top-rate restaurant with a lot of flair. The results are achieved with well-rehearsed rules of cooking technique, and the classic schooling of French cuisine has been beautifully blended with Danish flavors. Passionately fond of his trade, the chef is the supreme professional. To get you launched, he takes great care with his appetizers, as evoked by such choices as a seafood plate with a sauté of mint- and lemon-flavored rice noodles. For a main course, the chef has several surprising delicacies up his sleeve. Try his filet of seawolf marinated with chili and lemon and served with a golden saffron risotto. The fresh lobster is divine—boiled to perfection and served with a lemon-flavored homemade mayonnaise that is so good we wanted to bottle it. Our favorite dessert is the passion fruit sorbet with pieces of rose hip served in a meringue "nest" with rose-hip syrup.

Mølleå 4–6, Mølleå Arkaden. (C) **98-12-48-60.** www.mortenskro.dk. Reservations recommended. Main courses DKK189–DKK198 ($32–$34/£19–£20); fixed-price menus DKK548–DKK848 ($93–$144/£55–£85). DC, MC, V. Mon–Sat 5:30–10pm. Bus: 3, 5, 10, or 11.

Restaurant Kilden ★ DANISH/INTERNATIONAL   Set on the second-highest (15th) floor of the Hotel Hvide Hus, in the center of town near the bus station, this is a contemporary, stylish, and highly recommended restaurant that draws crowds of office workers to its attractively priced luncheon buffet, and both local residents and hotel guests to its smoothly choreographed evening meals. Some of its allure derives from the views that sweep over the nearby municipal park (the Kilden Park, after which the restaurant is named) and the seacoast. Menu items are all elegant dishes, beautifully prepared, using the freshest ingredients possible. Each year the chefs make their reputations anew with such classics as lobster soup or a tender, well-flavored pepper steak. The medallions of veal become a delicacy when "married" to a truffle sauce, and the roasted rack of lamb with garlic sauce almost bursts with flavor.

In the Hotel Hvide Hus, Vesterbro 2. (C) **98-13-84-00.** Reservations recommended. Main courses DKK200–DKK225 ($34–$38/£20–£23); fixed-price menus DKK328–DKK385 ($56–$65/£33–£39). AE, DC, MC, V. Daily noon–10pm.

Rosdahls ★★ MEDITERRANEAN/DANISH   One of the most exclusive seafood restaurants in town, Rosdahls is housed in an old converted sugar warehouse right down on the Limfjord River, close to the heart of the city. The fish arrive each day from auction in Hanstholm, and other raw goods are delivered from the Danish countryside as well as France and Italy. In spite of its rustic setting, this is one of the most elegant restaurants in town, with Philippe Starck chairs. There is also a wine and tapas bar adjoining. The best of seasonal ingredients go into the fusion cuisine that blends Danish flavors with the Mediterranean kitchen. Specialties include the chef's home-smoked bacon, tureen of smoked eel, pasta with pumpkin and sage, and halibut with chanterelles. A fresh food market takes place here every Saturday between 9am and 2:30pm.

Strandvejen 6. (C) **98-12-05-80.** Reservations required. Main courses DKK185–DKK265 ($31–$45/£19–£27); 4- to 7-course fixed-price menus DKK380–DKK725 ($65–$123/£38–£73). DC, MC, V. Tues–Sat noon–3pm and 6–10pm.

Moderate

Kniv og Gaffel ★★ FRENCH/DANISH   This is a romantic choice for dining, housed in the oldest preserved citizen's house, dating from 1552, in Aalborg. The street takes its name from Maren Turis, a woman who lived here in the 16th century and was accused of witchcraft, tried, but found not guilty. Those terrifying memories are long erased today—you'll experience only lots of atmosphere, and wonderful food served by candlelight. Its old oak tables fill up every night, and the wooden floors are buckled and slanted with age. The house specialty is thick steaks, the best in Aalborg, although you can order an array of other dishes as well, each prepared with first-rate ingredients plucked from the markets that very morning. On our most recent rounds, we enjoyed fresh Norwegian salmon baked with mushrooms and served with a béarnaise sauce. The chicken breast platter is delectably cooked here with homemade basil and tomato sauce and served with a garden salad and baked potato.

Maren Turis Gade 10. 🕐 **98-16-69-72.** Reservations recommended. Main courses DKK65–DKK192 ($11–$33/£6.50–£19). DC, MC, V. Mon–Sat noon–midnight. Bus: 1, 3, or 5.

Provence ★ DANISH/FRENCH This is Aalborg's foremost purveyor of Danish cuisine that's influenced in almost every case by the culinary traditions of France. Across from the Radisson SAS in the center of town, it offers a cozy, small-scale brown-and-white interior that's illuminated by a stained-glass skylight. The only complaint ever expressed is that its younger staff is not as well trained as those at some of its competitors. Even though the service isn't always faultless, the cuisine itself usually is, as the food is classical and always reliable. A wonderful menu begins with a tasting of the sea, with fresh Danish lobster appearing in a cocktail or in a velvety soup laced with cognac. The cuisine lately seems touched with a special grace, including a Dutch sole with a salmon soufflé and fresh spinach or a "fired" sea bass with a leek sauce. As on most elegant French menus, tournedos appear in their own juices or layered with foie gras. We are not that enthralled with the dessert list, our dining companion complaining that the chocolate mousse brought back "memories of the nursery."

Ved Stranden 11. 🕐 **98-13-51-33.** Reservations recommended. Main courses DKK200–DKK278 ($34–$47/£20–£28); fixed-price menus DKK219–DKK348 ($37–$59/£22–£35). AE, DC, MC, V. Sun 5–10pm; Mon–Sat 11am–10pm. Bus: 2, 12, or 13.

Restaurant Benzons ★ DANISH/FRENCH The inviting decor, summer terrace, attentive service, and finely honed cuisine make this pair of restaurants the very best on a street crammed with places to eat. The same kitchen prepares the tempting specialties served in the downstairs bistro and in the more formal upstairs restaurant. The menu, prices, and hours are the same in both. Appetizers include the best chunky lobster soup in the region, served with sour cream; sautéed Skagen shrimp; and delectable fish pâté. The main courses are prepared with equal flair, as you'll realize by savoring the roast breast of duck with Madeira sauce. The chefs also captivated our taste buds with the tender Dijon-style beef.

Jomfru Anegade 8. 🕐 **98-16-34-44.** Reservations required. Main courses DKK65–DKK145 ($11–$25/£6.50–£15); fixed-price menus DKK125–DKK140 ($21–$24/£13–£14). AE, DC, MC, V. Daily 11:30am–11:30pm.

Ristorante Fellini SOUTHERN ITALIAN Although not quite as superb as the previously recommended Il Mulino, this is another chance to break from too constant a diet of Danish food. As good as the local food is, change is always nice, or so we think as we head for this trattoria run by a hardworking staff in the center of Aalborg. The staff comes from Campania, the region around Naples, so they are skilled in preparing succulent Mediterranean cuisine. Their display of fish and marinated vegetable antipasti is Aalborg's finest. No pasta tastes better to us than their spaghetti *con vongole* (with clams). Nightly you face a choice of fresh shellfish mingled with the catch of the day. Though the fish may come from the North or Baltic Seas, it's prepared with Italian verve, especially the risotto *alla pescator* (with both shellfish and fish) and the grilled shrimp resting on a bed of fresh radicchio. There's also a succulent version of lamb roasted with herbs and potatoes in a style perfected over the centuries by cooks in the highlands of Italy's south-central regions.

Vestergade 13. 🕐 **98-11-34-55.** Main courses DKK145–DKK200 ($25–$34/£15–£20); 3-course fixed-price menu DKK289 ($49/£29). AE, DC, MC, V. Mon–Sat 11:30am–11pm; Sun 5–10pm. Bus: 1 or 2.

Duus Vinkjælder DANISH   The atmospheric setting alone would justify a visit here, but fortunately the snacks are also good and most affordable. This old-world 1624 cellar lies beneath one of the most famous private Renaissance mansions (Jens Bangs Stenhus), a 2-minute walk east of the cathedral. It features a selection of beer and wine (ever had Rainwater Madeira?), but it's a bit skimpy on the food. It's more of a snack restaurant and a wine bar than a full-fledged restaurant. However, you can order a plate of Danish *biksemad* (hash), a burger, or perhaps some pâté.

Østerågade 9. ℂ **98-12-50-56.** Snacks DKK100–DKK120 ($17–$20/£10–£12); wine by the glass DKK42 ($7.20/£4.20). MC, V. Mon–Fri 11am–midnight; Sat 10am–2am.

Fyrtøjet DANISH/INTERNATIONAL   This cozy, small restaurant in the center of town never pretends to be more than what it is—an affordable food joint with competently prepared, filling dishes made with fresh ingredients. The cooks never scale any culinary heights, but we've always left here satisfied, especially after sampling the house specialty, an *almueplatte* (peasant's plate) with marinated herring, curry salad, two warm rissoles, cold potato salad flecked with fresh chives, and a deep-fried Camembert cheese with black currant jam. Sitting one night under a glass-covered courtyard, as the rains came down, our party sampled what was on each other's plates and dug into some tasty main courses that included a tender, cognac-flavored pepper steak, a savory roast breast of duck, and a freshly caught plaice stuffed with tiny Danish shrimp.

Jomfru Anegade 17. ℂ **98-13-73-77.** www.fyrtorget.dk. Reservations recommended. Main courses DKK120–DKK225 ($20–$38/£12–£23). AE, DC, MC, V. Daily 11:30am–10pm. Bus: 1, 3, 5, or 15.

Holles Vinstue DANISH   Much of the cookery here is designed to appeal to old Norsemen of the North Sea instead of foodies. We come here mainly to sample wine by the glass. In most Danish restaurants, the tax on a bottle of wine is so high that if you purchase one you'll be putting someone's kid through college. With an inviting atmosphere, welcoming a convivial crowd (often young), this combined wine bar/restaurant combo serves the best *smørrebrød* in town until 3pm. We found that many dishes are designed to help you brace for the cold winds blowing in from the north—a platter-size Wiener schnitzel, for example, or some "granny" stews and hashes. Lighter fare is available if you order one of the various omelets or the filets based on the catch of the day. The location is one of the most convenient in town, lying just a 4-minute walk west of Nytorv.

Algade 57. ℂ **98-13-84-88.** Main courses DKK55–DKK120 ($9.40–$20/£5.50–£12); smørrebrød from DKK32 ($5.50/£3.20). Mon–Fri 11am–8pm; Sat 11am–4pm. Bus: 1, 3, or 5.

Layalina LEBANESE   *Layalina* means "our pleasant nights" in Arabic. Its owners are Lebanese, and they have decorated the restaurant warmly with handmade Middle Eastern artifacts. Exotic dishes (at least by Danish standards) such as shish kebab and hummus are served in an atmosphere of genuine Middle Eastern hospitality. The house special is three brochettes with lamb, meatballs, and spicy sausage. Two other house specials include a vegetarian dish of hummus, eggplant, falafel, and sautéed cauliflower, or chicken on a brochette flavored with a sauce with Asian spices. Although a true Lebanese might find fault with the cookery here, it comes as a wonderful change of pace for most of us after too many nights of unvarying Danish cuisine.

Ved Stranden 7–9. ℂ **98-11-60-56.** www.layalina-aalborg.dk. Main courses DKK169–DKK239 ($29–$41/£17–£24); 2-course fixed-price menu DKK129–DKK139 ($22–$24/£13–£14); 3-course menu DKK139 ($24/£14). MC, V. Mon–Thurs and Sun 5–10pm; Fri–Sat 5–11pm. Bus: 1, 4, 40, or 46.

NORTH JUTLAND

13

AALBORG

Søgaards Brewery DANISH This microbrewery is on two levels—on the ground level are found two large copper boilers, where the air is permeated with a hops scent. In the cellar is the brewery itself, where one can watch the brewing process through a glass wall. After a tour of the brewery, you can eat lunch or a supper, feasting on barbecue ribs, Danish beef, freshly caught fish, game in autumn, and Danish dairy products. The meats are especially good, as the brewery even has its own on-site butcher shop.

CW Obels Plads 1A. © **98-16-11-14.** www.soegaardsbryghus.dk. Reservations recommended. Light meal w/tour DKK175 ($30/£18) per person. MC, V. Daily 11am–9:30pm.

AALBORG AFTER DARK

Hot summer days and long, mild evenings are ideal for open-air concerts of various kinds. Each year Aalborg hosts several major rock concerts in **Mølle Park,** with up to 16,000 attending. There are also rock concerts in **Skovdalen,** behind Nordjyllands Kunstmuseum, all through the summer. **Kilden Park** is also a setting for summer concerts. Information about these summer concerts becomes available at the tourist office (see "Visitor Information," earlier in this chapter) beginning in April.

The home of the Aalborg Symphony Orchestra is **Aalborg Kongres og Kultur Center,** Europa Plads 4 (© **99-35-55-55;** bus: 15), north of Kilden Park. Opera and ballet performances are also presented here. The tourist office keeps complete data on all cultural events staged here.

Dance Clubs

Young people gravitate to **Musik Keller,** in the basement of the previously recommended restaurant Provence, Ved Stranden 11 (© **98-13-51-33**). Neither the wildest nor the most conservative club in town, it's a bit staid by New York standards, although its DJ plays the most recent music arriving from London, Los Angeles, and elsewhere. There's never any live music, however. Admission is free, and the Keller is open Friday and Saturday 9:30pm to 6am.

Rendez-Vous, Jomfru Anegade 5 (© **98-16-88-80**), offers drinking facilities on its street level, and a dance floor upstairs, attracting university students and folks under 40. Or head for **Cube,** Jomfru Anegade 10 (© **98-10-33-10**), a bar and dance club that's open every Friday and Saturday 11pm to 6am.

3 FREDERIKSHAVN

64km (40 miles) NE of Aalborg; 381km (237 miles) NW of Copenhagen; 40km (25 miles) S of Skagen

Most visitors use Frederikshavn as a ferryboat terminus for trips to and from Norway. Playing host to some three million passengers annually, the port is the busiest international ferry terminal in all of Jutland. Unless you're passing to and from Norway, there are far more glamorous destinations in Jutland, which have already been documented.

There is a good chance you'll be passing through this town—briefly, at least. Because it's such a vital link for so many passengers, we're including information about this port of some 26,000 people, the largest town in North Jutland north of Aalborg.

A relatively young town, it has a number of attractions but few historic sites. At first glance, however, you'll think the whole town is one vast supermarket, filled with Swedes or Norwegians on shopping expeditions. Danish food products are cheaper here than they are back in Sweden or Norway.

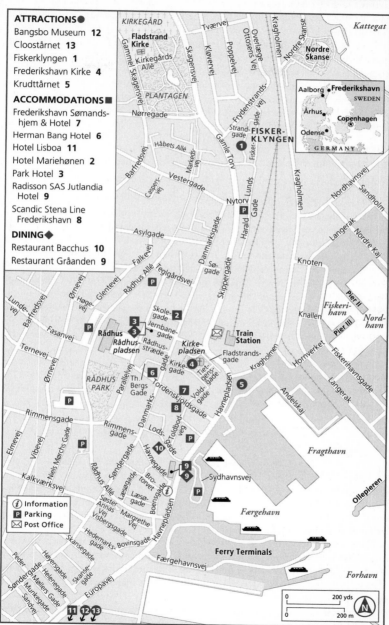

ATTRACTIONS●
Bangsbo Museum **12**
Cloostårnet **13**
Fiskerklyngen **1**
Frederikshavn Kirke **4**
Krudttårnet **5**

ACCOMMODATIONS■
Frederikshavn Sømands-
   hjem & Hotel **7**
Herman Bang Hotel **6**
Hotel Lisboa **11**
Hotel Mariehønen **2**
Park Hotel **3**
Radisson SAS Jutlandia
   Hotel **9**
Scandic Stena Line
   Frederikshavn **8**

DINING◆
Restaurant Bacchus **10**
Restaurant Gråanden **9**

ⓘ **Information**
🅿 **Parking**
✉ **Post Office**

NORTH JUTLAND

13

FREDERIKSHAVN

A strong maritime aura permeates the town, and there are seven municipal harbors alone where the ferries leave or arrive from Norway and Sweden. Just north of Frederikshavn lies the fishing hamlet of Standby, where most of the famous "Frederikshavner plaice" are landed.

In the Middle Ages, the fishing settlement here was called Fladstrand. During the Thirty Years' War, the site became a defense entrenchment, and in time a powder tower surrounded by a wall was erected. But it wasn't until as late as 1818 that Fladstrand was granted its municipal charter and the new name of Frederikshavn. In addition to tourists, ferry passengers, and shoppers from other Scandinavian countries, Frederikshavn also depends on fishing to spark its economy, and is the site of such industries as iron foundries, shipbuilding, and engineering.

ESSENTIALS

GETTING THERE   **By Train**   Trains leave from Aalborg hourly during the day.

By Bus   Frequent buses run between Aalborg and Frederikshavn.

By Car   Head north from Aalborg along the E45 to Frederikshavn.

By Ferry   Stena Line (© 96-20-02-00; www.stenaline.co.uk), one of Europe's largest and most reliable ferryboat operators, runs the two most popular routes in and out of town. Passengers to and from Norway have the option, with or without their cars, of a daily, 8-hour ferryboat transit between Frederikshavn and Oslo. Depending on the season, pedestrians pay from DKK175 to DKK360 ($30–$61/£18–£36) each; transport of a car with its driver costs from DKK700 to DKK2,300 ($119–$391/£70–£230) round-trip, depending on the season and the size of the car. Be warned in advance that southbound boats originating in Oslo depart after dark, and consequently, all passengers are required to rent an overnight cabin for the 9-hour transit. Cabins, each suitable for two passengers, rent for DKK810 to DKK1,880 ($138–$320/£81–£188) each. Stena also maintains five ferryboats a day between the Swedish port of Gothenburg and Frederikshavn. Transit time is between 2 and 3 hours, depending on the boat, all of which are capable of transporting cars. Pedestrians pay DKK150 to DKK225 ($26–$38/£15–£23) each way. Transport of a car with its driver, depending on the speed of the boat and the season, costs DKK850 to DKK1,580 ($145–$269/£85–£158). If you're traveling with a car during the midsummer crush, between mid-June and August, advance reservations are advised. Stena also operates three catamaran crossings every day that are much faster than the ferries.

VISITOR INFORMATION   The **Frederikshavn Turistbureau**, Skandiatorv 1 (© 98-42-32-66; www.toppenafdanmark.dk), near the ferry dock, is open January 2 to June 23 and August 21 to December 30 Monday to Friday 9am to 4pm, Saturday 11am to 2pm; June 24 to August 20 Monday to Saturday 9am to 6pm, Sunday 9am to 2pm.

SEEING THE SIGHTS

Although most of Frederikshavn is modern, the oldest part of town, **Fiskerklyngen,** lies to the north of the fishing harbor. Here you'll encounter a number of 17th-century houses, each well preserved. You can also see a former military fortification, **Norde Skanse** (North Entrenchment), which was constructed by the troops of Wallenstein during the Thirty Years' War.

Opposite the railway station rises Frederikshavn's most famous symbol, **Frederikshavn Kirke,** Kirkepladsen (© 98-42-05-99; www.frederikshavnkirke.dk). Most of this church dates from 1690, although it was significantly rebuilt in 1892. Inside you can see its major attraction, an altarpiece painted by Michael Ancher, the Skagen artist. The cemetery at the church contains graves of both Allied and German soldiers killed in World War II. Admission is free, and the church is open Tuesday to Saturday 9am to noon.

You can climb the whitewashed gun tower, **Krudttårnet,** at Havnepladsen (© **98-43-19-19**), a remnant of the famed citadel that stood here in the 1600s. The tower actually stood at another place in Frederikshavn, but when the shipyards had to be expanded it was moved here instead of being torn down. The former gunpowder magazine, built of stone in 1688, has been turned into a Museum of Military History, displaying weapons from the 17th to the 19th century. Admission is DKK25 ($4.30/£2.50), free for children 17 and under. Hours are June to mid-September Tuesday to Sunday 10am to 5pm.

Another tower worth a visit is **Cloostårnet** (© **98-48-60-69**), lying 4km (2¹/₂ miles) southwest of town at an altitude of 165m (541 ft.) above sea level. This observation tower rises 60m (197 ft.) above that, offering panoramic views over the sea and the countryside of Vendsyssel. An elevator will take you to the top, and in fair weather you can see most of the surrounding district. Admission is DKK20 ($3.40/£2) adults or DKK10 ($1.70/£1) children. Hours are May to mid-June Wednesday to Monday 1 to 5pm, Saturday and Sunday 10am to 5pm; mid-June to mid-August daily 10am to 5pm; mid-August to August 31 Wednesday to Monday 1 to 5pm. Closed the rest of the year.

Bangsbro Museum ★ Kids One of the premier open-air museums of Jutland, this place is in a wooded area beside the Deer Park, 3km (1³/₄ miles) south of the town center, and contains a cluster of 18th-century buildings near the remnants of a moated 14th-century manor house. Of special interest is an old barn built in 1580, one of the oldest in Denmark, which houses antique farm equipment and implements. The main house has such curiosities as a collection of handicrafts made from human hair, a display of relics from World War II, and a nautical section including ship models, figureheads, and other mementos. An early ship, *Ellingå,* similar to the vessels used by the Vikings, is in one of the buildings. It's the reconstructed remains of a Viking-style merchant ship excavated 5km (3 miles) north of Frederikshavn. Linked to the museum is the Bangsbo Botanical Gardens, with an herb garden and a deer park, plus a playground for the kids.

Dronning Margrethesvej 6. © **98-42-31-11.** www.bangsbo-museum.dk. Admission DKK40 ($6.80/£4) adults, free for children 17 and under. June–Oct daily 10:30am–5pm; Nov–May Tues–Sun 10:30am–5pm.

SHOPPING

Frederikshavn is an active shopping town, with boutiques and emporiums that line both sides of the **Gågade,** one of the longest all-pedestrian streets in Denmark.

One of the most intriguing shopping possibilities, **Dot Keramik** is at Skagensvej 270, Nielstrup, Standby (© **98-48-14-10**), 7km (4¹/₃ miles) north of Frederikshavn. Here you'll find a wide display of hand-thrown ceramics, plus an array of applied art, gift articles, and intriguing decorations. At **Birgitte Munch ★**, Daanmarksgade 42C (© **98-43-80-66**), you can see the town's most talented goldsmith producing jewelry according to the best traditions of workmanship. A wide range of high-quality, locally designed jewelry is on sale.

WHERE TO STAY

In case you miss the boat and need a room, the Frederikshavn Turistbureau (see above) will book you into a private home, if you'd prefer that to a hotel.

Radisson SAS Jutlandia Hotel ★★ This is the largest and the best-rated hotel in town, and as such, it's the site where members of the Danish royal family have stayed during several of their visits. It's also the closest hotel to the dock where the ferryboats pull in. The lobby, a study in high-ceilinged, 1960s-style architecture, is one of the best examples of Scandinavian design of any hotel in town. Ranging from midsize to spacious, the bedrooms are the best furnished and most comfortable in town, beginning with the cheapest—the standard doubles—and ranging upward to deluxe suites. The decor is harmonious, with a perfect match in colors and natural materials. One exceptional accommodation is the Thai Suite, the largest in the building, outfitted in carved teakwood furniture.

Postboks 89, Havnepladsen, DK-9900 Frederikshavn. © **800-333-3333** in the U.S. or Canada, or 98-42-42-00. Fax 98-42-38-72. www.radissonsas.com. 95 units. DKK1,130–DKK1,530 ($192–$260/£113–£153) double; DKK1,480–DKK2,480 ($252–$422/£148–£248) suite. Rates include breakfast. AE, DC, MC, V. **Amenities:** Restaurant; bar; health club; sauna; room service; babysitting; laundry service; dry cleaning; nonsmoking rooms; rooms for those w/limited mobility. *In room:* TV, Wi-Fi, minibar, hair dryer.

Scandic Stena Hotel Frederikshavn ★ (Kids) Different from all other hotels in North Jutland, this longtime favorite has a special feature, Aqualand, where you can splash your way down water slides and enjoy foaming waterfalls, summery wavelets (even in the dead of winter), and even a "water flame." Talk about family fun—no wonder kids like it so. The hotel is made even more attractive to families with its playroom with the usual—balls, building bricks, crayons, a slide—but, get this, even a cinema for kids. In the center of town, near the pedestrian shopping area and not far from the harbor, this 1987 hotel, one of the largest hotels in Denmark outside of Copenhagen, is not as fancy or as highly rated as the Jutlandia. Rooms are well furnished and well maintained; and some can be converted into three- or four-bed accommodations, so the Stena has long been a favorite with families. Good food is served in the hotel's premier dining room, **Det Gulge Pakhus,** or you can dine more informally in the **Brasserie Søhesten.**

Tordenskjoldsgade 14, DK-9900 Frederikshavn. © **98-43-32-33.** Fax 98-43-33-11. www.scandic-hotels.com. 213 units. DKK1,090–DKK1,890 ($185–$321/£109–£189) double; DKK2,415–DKK2,715 ($411–$462/£242–£272) suite. AE, DC, MC, V. **Amenities:** 2 restaurants; bar; nightclub; indoor heated pool; gym; sauna; children's playroom; room service; massage; laundry service; dry cleaning; nonsmoking rooms; rooms for those w/limited mobility. *In room:* A/C, TV, Wi-Fi, minibar (some units), hair dryer, iron, trouser press.

Moderate

Frederikshavn Sømandshjem & Hotel (Kids) (Value) Everyone from families on vacation to sailors check into this hotel offering one of the best deals in town. In the center of town, near the shopping area and close to the harbor, this old-fashioned hotel was founded in 1880 as the Seamen's Mission. However, restored in 2003, it offers some of the best lodgings for your kroner in town. Many of its functionally furnished bedrooms can be converted into three- or four-bed rooms suitable for families, although this hotel is hardly the family favorite that the Scandic Stena (see above) is. The restaurant serves good Danish food of the meat-and-potatoes-with-gravy variety.

Tordenskjoldsgade 15B, DK-9900 Frederikshavn. © **98-42-09-77.** Fax 98-43-18-99. www.fshotel.dk. 53 units. DKK695–DKK995 ($118–$169/£70–£100). Rates include breakfast. AE, DC, MC, V. **Amenities:** Restaurant; laundry service; dry cleaning; nonsmoking rooms. *In room:* TV, Wi-Fi, hair dryer.

Hotel Lisboa Outfitted in a blue-and-white color scheme, and with polished stone floors of the type you might expect in a hotel in Portugal, this hotel was named in honor of a holiday that its founders had taken in Lisbon just before the hotel's construction in 1958. In 1978, it was enlarged with an annex. In many hotels, the annex contains less desirable rooms, but in the case of the Lisboa they are larger, more modernized, and better furnished. With good views of the sand dunes and the beach, it appeals to a nature-loving, escapist crowd year-round. Rooms are spartan and uncomplicated, with comfortable but strictly functional furniture. Public areas and the restaurant are outfitted with the blue-and-white abstract paintings of Danish artist Peder Meinert.

Søndergade 248, DK-9900 Frederikshavn. ✆ 98-42-21-33. Fax 98-43-80-11. www.lisboa.dk. 32 units. DKK799–DKK899 ($136–$153/£80–£90) double. Rates include breakfast. MC, V. From Frederikshavn, take bus no. 1, 2, 3, or 4. **Amenities:** Restaurant; bar. In room: TV, Wi-Fi, hair dryer.

Park Hotel ★   An atmospheric choice with a certain charm, this hotel was built in 1880 in a combination Old French and Old English style. Many of the handsomely furnished midsize rooms have marble bathrooms. Only the suites have tubs in the bathrooms; the doubles contain showers. The Park is known for its gourmet restaurant, **Gastronomen,** which serves an international cuisine. The hotel doesn't just wait until dinner to feed you well; we found its breakfast buffet the most bountiful in town. In fair weather (not guaranteed in Denmark), breakfast—or even dinner on a warm summer night—can be served in a courtyard. On our last visit, we could imagine we were in the south of France.

Jernbanegade 7, DK-9900 Frederikshavn. ✆ 98-42-22-55. Fax 96-20-17-98. www.parkhotelfrederikshavn. dk. 30 units, 20 w/private bathroom. DKK500–DKK700 ($85–$119/£50–£70) double w/shared bathroom; DKK600–DKK1,100 ($102–$187/£60–£110) double w/private bathroom; DKK1,300–DKK1,700 ($221–$289/£130–£170) suite. Rates include breakfast. AE, DC, MC, V. **Amenities:** Restaurant; bar; room service; laundry service; dry cleaning; nonsmoking rooms. In room: TV, Wi-Fi, minibar, hair dryer, iron, safe.

Inexpensive

Herman Bang Hotel ★ (Value   As the Hoffmann Hotel, it was founded in 1882 and is today the oldest hotel in town. The hotel is now named for the well-known author Herman Bang, who used to be a frequent visitor back in the days when the hotel was a bohemian hangout, attracting writers and painters. Under new management, the hotel experienced not only a name change but a wholesale renovation, making it better than it ever was in its past. The midsize bedrooms are attractively furnished and maintained, each with a tiled bathroom. As a grace note, the private bathrooms are candlelit and you can recline in luxurious comfort, using the aromatic oils and stimulating mineral salts. That's not all—the hotel has the best spa facilities in town, both indoor and outdoor. The spa is aptly named "Seventh Heaven." On-site is a good family-style restaurant that offers not only breakfast, but lunch and dinner also, inspired by both American and Italian cuisine.

Tordenskjoldsgade 1, DK-9900 Frederikshavn. ✆ 98-42-21-66. Fax 98-42-21-07. www.hermanbang.dk. 54 units. DKK795–DKK1,295 ($135–$220/£80–£130) double; DKK1,595–DKK1,795 ($271–$305/£160–£180) suite. Rates include breakfast. AE, DC, MC, V. **Amenities:** Restaurant; spa. In room: TV, Wi-Fi, hair dryer, iron.

Hotel Mariehønen   More people come here to dance at the bar, **Sussi & Leo,** to recorded music than they do to stay in the rooms. But if you've danced yourself out, you can sleep in comfort at an affordable price here. This hotel is among the most convenient in town, only 5 minutes from the ferry terminal and 3 minutes from the train depot. Most of its guests are passengers waiting overnight to catch ferries to Oslo or Gothenburg. A family-run hotel, Mariehønen offers rooms that are basic, functionally although comfortably furnished, and well maintained, some coming with a small bathroom with shower. There's no restaurant, but there are several places to eat nearby.

Scoolagade 2, DK-9900 Frederikshavn. ℂ **98-42-01-22.** Fax 98-43-40-99. www.hotelmariehoenen.dk. 32 units, 18 w/private bathroom. DKK490–DKK525 ($83–$89/£49–£53) double w/shared bathroom; DKK690–DKK890 ($117–$151/£69–£89) double w/private bathroom. Rates include buffet breakfast. AE, DC, MC, V. **Amenities:** Restaurant; bar (w/dancing). *In room:* TV.

WHERE TO DINE
Expensive
Restaurant Grå-Ander ★★ (Finds) FRENCH   Only fixed-price menus are offered, and they're the best and most finely honed in the area. This is the best-recommended dining room in Frederikshavn, with a reputation that the managers of the Hotel Jutlandia work hard to maintain. There's room inside for only 34 diners, who enjoy their meal in a dining room with windows overlooking the blue-gray expanse of the sea. Menu items are based on inspirations from France, and might include such starters as a seafood cocktail, a spinach crepe, or smoked duck breast. Two dishes to rave about include lemon sole in a ragout of mussels and curried cream, and quail with foie gras and a red-wine flambé. Dessert might be a raspberry Napoleon with a honey parfait and chocolate sauce. The staff are justifiably proud of their food and the service they provide, which are both excellent. There are many luxury ingredients on the menu but prices are not as daunting as you might fear.

In the Hotel Jutlandia, Havnepladsen. ℂ **98-42-42-00.** Reservations recommended. Fixed-price 2-course menu DKK188 ($32/£19); 3-course menu DKK280 ($48/£28); 4-course menu DKK325 ($55/£33). AE, DC, MC, V. Mon–Sat 6–10pm.

Inexpensive
Restaurant Bacchus MEXICAN/ITALIAN   View this more as a place for food on the run between ferryboat stopovers than as a venue for serious dining. Set near the harbor within a simple building dating from the 1850s, this is an unassuming, unpretentious bistro. Although there's a well-chosen wine list, it's a lot less comprehensive than you might assume from the restaurant's name. Within an old-fashioned dining room with only 40 seats, you can order such standard fare as pizza, succulent pastas, burritos, and a spicy chili con carne.

Lodsgade 8A. ℂ **98-43-29-00.** Reservations recommended. Main courses DKK100–DKK115 ($17–$20/£10–£12); fixed-price dinner DKK80–DKK180 ($14–$31/£8–£18). AE, DC, MC, V. Mon–Sat 5–10pm.

FREDERIKSHAVN AFTER DARK
In Frederikshavn, nightlife simmers away in quiet, not particularly demonstrative ways, most visibly at the **John Bull Pub,** Havnepladsen (ℂ **98-42-42-00**), a clone of an English pub adjacent to the Jutlandia Hotel.

---

4 SKAGEN ★★

104km (65 miles) NE of Aalborg; 485km (301 miles) W of Copenhagen

Since the 19th century, Skagen—pronounced *skane*—has been the leading artists' colony of Denmark. As is inevitable in such cases, hordes of tourists followed in the footsteps of the artists to discover the northernmost tip of Jutland on its east coast. A sort of "bony finger" of land points into the North Sea at the second-biggest fishing port in Denmark.

We find the combination today of Nordic sailors—Skagen has been a fishing port for centuries—and a colony of artists an intriguing mix. At least the two disparate elements make for lively conversation in the bars. The early artists were more isolated here, but the coming of the railway in 1890 opened up Skagen to the world with its link to the terminus of Frederikshavn.

By the end of July, the visitors are in retreat, and Skagen happily reverts to the locals again. We've spent hours here in both September and October wandering the heather-covered moors, the undulating stretches of dunes, and some of the best, but not the warmest, beaches in Europe. We particularly like to stand at the point where the North Sea meets the Baltic, the subject of countless landscape paintings. It's not unknown to have visitors applaud the spectacular sunsets here.

One of the founders of the Skagen School of Paintings, the poet and artist Holger Drachmann (1846–1908), once said, "Unlike so much of the rest of Europe, Skagen still retains its soul."

ESSENTIALS

GETTING THERE   **By Car**   Take the E45 northeast to Frederikshavn. From there, head north on Route 40 to Skagen.

By Train   Several trains a day run from Copenhagen to Århus, where you connect with another train to Frederikshavn. From Frederikshavn there are 12 daily trains to Skagen.

VISITOR INFORMATION   The **Skagen Turistbureau** is at Vestre Strandvej 10 (© 98-44-13-77; www.skagen-tourist.dk). Open January 3 to March 31 and November 1 to December 23 Monday to Friday 10am to 4pm, Saturday 10am to 1pm; April, May, and August 29 to October 30 Monday to Friday 9am to 4pm, Saturday 10am to 2pm; June 1 to 26 and August 1 to 28 Monday to Saturday 9am to 5pm, Sunday 10am to 2pm; and June 27 to July 31 Monday to Saturday 9am to 6pm, Sunday 10am to 4pm.

SEEING THE SIGHTS

Since it opened in 1907, **Skagen Havn** (Skagen Harbor) ★ has been one of the major attractions of the town. It's seen at its best when the boats come back to land their catches (times vary). For early risers, the fish auction at the crack of dawn is a popular attraction. Mid-May to mid-October, the oldest part of the harbor is a haven for the boating crowds centered around one of the marinas. Many yachting people in Jutland use Skagen as their favorite harbor haven.

Gammel Skagen (Old Town) ★ lies 2.5km (1½ miles) from Skagen Havn. Signs point the way. Originally, Gammel Skagen was the fishing hamlet—that is, until Skagen Havn opened in 1907. Today, Gammel Skagen is a little resort town with large beach hotels that are mainly timeshares.

An attraction worth exploring is **Rådjerg Mile,** a migrating dune moving at the rate of about 11m (36 ft.) annually. Located 16km (10 miles) south of town, it can be reached via Kandestederne. This dune was formed on the west coast in the 16th century during the great sand drift that characterized the landscape until the 20th century. The dune continues to move yearly, eastward toward the forest.

Den Tilsandede Kirke (Sand-Buried Church)   This church buried in sand dunes 1.5km (1 mile) south of town is an amusing curiosity. The only part that's visible is the upper two-thirds of the tower. When Hans Christian Andersen visited in 1859, he called the church "The Pompeii of Skagen." The only things hidden under the dunes are the remnants of a wall and the old floor and perhaps the baptismal font. By 1775, the church had fallen into disrepair and was used by fewer and fewer members. By 1795, it was closed down; in 1810, it was partly demolished, the stones sold to people in the area as building materials for their private houses. Today, red stakes in the ground indicate the placing and extent of the nave and vestry.

(✆ **98-44-43-71.** Admission DKK10 ($1.70/£1) adults, DKK5 (85¢/50p) children 5–12. June–Aug daily 11am–5pm; Sept–May Sat–Sun 11am–5pm.

Drachmanns Hus   Built in 1828, the house was home to poet and artist Holger Drachmann until his death in 1908. Now a museum, it's filled with mementos of the artist. On his first visit to Skagen in 1872, he fell in love with the village and its surroundings—"Here there is sand, more sand, nothing but sand. And then, here there is the sky with large floating clouds, and finally the sea, Kattegut's shining surf on one side and the distant roar of the North Sea on the other." Following many illnesses and professional disappointments, Drachmann died and was buried in the sand dunes around Skagen.

Han Baghsvej 21. (✆ **98-44-51-88.** www.drachmannshus.dk. Admission DKK30 ($5.10/£3) adults, free for children 14 and under. June 1–14 and Sept 16–Oct 16 Sat–Sun 11am–3pm; June 15–Aug 15 daily 10am–5pm; Aug 16–Sept 15 daily 11am–3pm. Closed Oct 17–May.

Michael og Anna Ancher Hus ★   If you visit the Skagens Museum (see below), you will see work by talented artists Michael and Anna Ancher, who originally purchased this house back in 1884. After their daughter, Helga, died in the 1960s, it was converted into a museum of their work. It's preserved rather like it was in the lifetime of these artists. Michael painted the doors throughout the house, and some 240 paintings by all three family members adorn the walls. In the parlor, the antique oil lamps and the lace curtains speak of a time long ago. Bathed in the fabled light of Skagen, Anna's studio still contains the easel she abandoned upon her death.

Markvej 2–4. (✆ **98-44-30-09.** Admission DKK60 ($10/£6) adults, free for children 14 and under. May–Sept daily 10am–5pm; Apr and Oct daily 11am–3pm; Feb–Mar and Nov Sat 11am–3pm. Closed Dec–Jan.

Nordsømuseet ★★★   The denizens of the deep who live in the North Sea come alive for you here in the town of Hirtshals. The main attraction of this two-story Oceanarium is the giant aquarium itself, containing some 4.5 million liters of seawater. Visitors can gaze upon an 8m-high (26-ft.) column of water or view the "ocean" through an aquarium window, the thickest in the world.

The large aquarium has been designed to house fish of the North Sea. Through the huge windows viewers can watch fascinating schools of herring, mackerel, gar, and horse mackerel, and see them react as predatory fish approach. Among other large creatures, several species of North Sea sharks can be viewed. Each day divers feed the shoal fish and the sharks and describe life in the aquarium to visitors.

The museum is devoted to modern Danish sea fishing, detailing man's exploitation of the North Sea—for better or worse. Displays of the daily lives of fishermen, equipment, and vessels are placed alongside exhibits depicting the resources of the North Sea. Seals are common along the coast of Denmark, but you seldom spot them. However, in the on-site seal pool, you can observe the animals at close range—above as well as underwater. Feeding times for the seals are daily at 11am and 3pm.

Willemoesvej, Hirtshals. (✆ **98-94-44-44.** www.nordsoemuseet.dk. Admission DKK120 ($20/£12) adults, DKK50 ($8.50/£5) children 3–11, free for children 2 and under. July–Aug daily 10am–6pm; Sept–June daily 10am–5pm. From Skagen take Rte. 40 south to the junction with Rte. 597 heading west into Hirtshals, a distance of 50km (31 miles).

Skagen By- & Egnsmuseum (Skagen Open-Air Museum) This museum, a 15-minute stroll from the train depot, is evocative of a time long gone. The lifesaving station here reminds us of how the seas sometimes violently clash in the depths of winter, as demonstrated by the dramatic photographs of ships and men in distress. In this open-air museum, the homes of both well-to-do fishermen and their poorer cousins were moved here to demonstrate how life was lived in Skagen from 1830 to 1880. A maritime museum is filled with nautical memorabilia, and an original Dutch windmill is all that's left of the many that used to dot the landscape.

P. K. Nielsensvej 8–10, Fortidsminderne. © **98-44-47-60.** www.skagen-bymus.dk. Admission DKK35 ($6/£3.50) adults, free for children 17 and under. May–June and Aug–Sept Mon–Fri 10am–4pm, Sat–Sun 11am–4pm; July Mon–Fri 10am–5pm, Sat–Sun 11am–4pm; Mar–Apr and Oct Mon–Fri 10am–4pm; Nov–Feb Mon–Fri 11am–3pm.

Skagens Museum ★★★ (Finds) The glory days of the artists of the Skagen School of painting live again at this impressive museum. The apogee of their art was created from the beginning of the 1870s until the turn of the 20th century. The Skagen artists were inspired by naturalism and open-air painting, their favorite motif being the fishermen working on local beaches or their quaint cottages. The artists came to celebrate the North Sea landscape, everything bathed in that special light that seems to exist in Skagen.

The major artists of this period included Michael Ancher (1849–1909) and his wife, Anna Ancher (1859–1935). You'll also see works by another of the school's leading painters, P. S. Krøyer (1851–1909), plus many more—the entire collection consists of 1,800 paintings, sculptures, drawings, and graphic works. The museum opened its doors in 1928 but with only 325 works of art.

Brøndumsvej 4. © **98-44-64-44.** www.skagensmuseum.dk. Admission DKK80 ($14/£8) adults, free for children 17 and under. May–Sept daily 10am–5pm; Apr and Oct Tues–Sun 11am–4pm; Nov–Mar Wed–Fri 1–4pm, Sat 11am–4pm, Sun 11am–3pm.

SHOPPING

Since so many artists live in Skagen, many visitors purchase art here. The best gallery is **Galerie Skagen,** Trondsvej 16 (© **98-44-44-25**), which also has a tasteful collection of handicrafts. The most sophisticated collection of pottery is found at **Skagen Potteri,** Skt. Laurentivej 27 (© **98-44-69-29**). Stunningly designed modern jewelry is sold at **Smykkekunstner,** Skt. Laurentivej 48 (© **98-44-11-08**), in Gammel Skagen. Some of Jutland's finest glass pieces—often works of art—are on display and for sale at **Skagen Glasværksted,** Skt. Laurentivej 95 (© **98-44-60-50**).

WHERE TO STAY

Color Hotel Skagen ★ (Finds)
This is more of a place to settle in for 2 or 3 days for a beach holiday, exploring the North Sea coast, than for an in-and-out overnight stopover. Southwest of Skagen, beside the only road leading into town from the rest of Jutland, this sprawling, one-story hotel lies 2km (1¼ miles) from the sea. Alone on sandy flatlands, it possesses an almost otherworldly sense of isolation. Unlike many of its competitors, which cater to families with children, this place appeals mostly to couples. Built in 1969, the hotel has a formal restaurant. The spacious, attractively furnished guest rooms contain hardwood floors, padded armchairs, and big windows. Of the accommodations, 45 are listed as apartments, which are rented only for 3 days at a time except during midsummer, when they are rented per week.

Gammel Landevej 39, DK-9990 Skagen. © **98-44-22-33.** Fax 98-44-21-34. www.skagenhotel.dk. 153 units. DKK975–DKK1,976 ($166–$336/£98–£198) double; DKK2,800 ($476/£280) suite; DKK6,500–DKK22,500

($1,105–$3,825/£650–£2,250) apt per week. AE, DC, MC, V. From Skagen, drive 2km (1¼ miles) southwest along Rte. 40. **Amenities:** Restaurant; bar; outdoor heated pool; fitness center; sauna; room service; non-smoking rooms; rooms for those w/limited mobility. *In room:* TV, Wi-Fi, hair dryer, safe.

Finns Hotel Pension   Originally built in 1909 in a style that the owner refers to as "a Norwegian wood house," this old-fashioned Danish homestead is designed like houses that Scandinavian immigrants made popular during the 19th century in American states such as Minnesota. In a residential neighborhood of Skagen, a 10- to 15-minute walk northeast of center and a 3-minute walk from the beach, it's furnished with old furniture and antiques. Many rooms have beamed ceilings and a charming but vaguely claustro-phobic allure. Our only warning involves a rigidity on the part of the hardworking managers and staff, who establish very clear-cut rules for new arrivals; they aren't noted for their flexibility, and maintain an aggressive "take it or leave it" approach to their unique hotel. If you give advance notice, they'll prepare a three-course evening meal, which is served only to residents, for a price of DKK325 ($55/£33) per person. If you agree to this, on pain of severe reproach, don't be late for dinner. Children 14 and under are not accepted.

Østre Strandvej 63, DK-9990 Skagen. © **98-45-01-55.** Fax 98-45-05-55. www.finnshotelpension.dk. 6 units, 3 w/private bathroom. DKK700 ($119/£70) double w/shared bathroom; DKK850–DKK975 ($145–$166/£85–£98) double w/private bathroom. Rates include breakfast. MC, V. Closed Oct–Mar. **Amenities:** Dining room. *In room:* No phone.

Ruth's Hotel ★★★   This is a bastion of both comfort and gastronomy—its restau-rant, in fact, is one of the greatest outside Copenhagen. Located in the sand dunes of Old Skagen, it stands by the beach just 4km (2½ miles) from the center of modern Skagen. It takes its name from its founders, Emma and Hans Christian Ruth. The bedrooms are superior to anything at Skagen, beautifully furnished and designed, exuding spaciousness and light. Some units have a Jacuzzi. A private balcony or terrace opens onto a view of the sea.

The spa is one of the best in Jutland, complete with solarium, sauna, Turkish baths, therapy pool, and gym. The hotel restaurant, **Ruth's Gourmet,** is one of the top five in the country outside of Copenhagen, yet we hesitate to recommend it because it requires reservations a month in advance. If you're lucky enough to get a table, you'll be rewarded with Chef Michel Michaud's repertoire of sublime dishes, which embrace the best of fine French cuisine and tradition, with a carefully chosen wine carte. You stand a better chance of dining on the airy, sunlit terrace of the on-site Brasserie; the food here is watched over by Chef Michaud himself.

Hans Ruths Vej 1, Gammel Skagen, DK-9990 Skagen. © **98-44-11-24.** Fax 98-45-08-75. www.ruths-hotel. dk. 26 units. DKK1,700–DKK2,150 ($289–$366/£170–£215) double; DKK1,950–DKK3,350 ($332–$570/£195–£335) suite. AE, DC, MC, V. **Amenities:** Restaurant; brasserie; bar; heated indoor pool; gym; spa; sauna; limited room service; laundry service; solarium. *In room:* TV, Wi-Fi, hair dryer.

Strandhotellet/Strandhuset ★   This hotel at Gamle Skagen is for wild romantics who like the wind from the North Sea blowing through their hair. Built in 1912 as a holiday home, it lies only a stone's throw from the sea and incorporates the dunes and buildings of a historic farm into the main building. The compound also contains four other outbuildings, each with an individual atmosphere. The newest addition is Strand-huset, which was built in the 1990s with a prominent hip roof. The suites with kitchens within Strandhuset are evocative of a tasteful private summer home. Everything has a warm, cozy atmosphere, helped along by the original works of art on the walls, the wicker furnishings, and the painted wood furnishings. Breakfast is served within a semicircular greenhouse-style extension jutting out from one end of the house.

Jeckelsvej, Gammel Skagen, DK-9990 Skagen. © **98-44-34-99.** Fax 98-44-59-19. www.strandhotellet. glskagen.dk. 14 units, 6 suites w/kitchenette. DKK1,575–DKK1,950 ($268–$332/£158–£195) double; DKK1,950–DKK2,275 ($332–$387/£195–£228) junior suite; DKK2,650–DKK3,200 ($451–$544/£265–£320) senior suite. AE, DC, MC, V. 4km (2¹⁄₂ miles) south of Skagen. **Amenities:** Restaurant (summer only); bar; room service. *In room:* TV, Wi-Fi, hair dryer, iron.

WHERE TO DINE

Skagen Fiske Restaurant ★★ SEAFOOD   One of the best-known fish restaurants in Jutland occupies the red-sided, gable-roofed building that was erected directly beside the harbor in 1907. You'll enter a bar on the establishment's street level, where the floor is composed of the actual beachfront—nothing more than sand. Climb to the nautically decorated dining room one floor above street level for meals. Lunches usually include flavorful platters that might contain fish cakes, Norwegian lobster, peel-your-own-shrimp, three different preparations of herring, or grilled filets of sole with lemon sauce. Dinners are more elaborate, consisting of whatever fish has been hauled in that day by local fishermen, prepared any way you specify, with virtually any sauce that's reasonably available.

Fiskehuskai 13. © **98-44-35-44.** www.skagen-fiskerestaurant.dk. Reservations recommended. Lunch platters DKK30–DKK55 ($5.10–$9.40/£3–£5.50); dinner main courses DKK270–DKK298 ($46–$51/£27–£30); fixed-price menus DKK325–DKK495 ($55–$84/£33–£50). AE, DC, MC, V. Daily 6–10:30pm. Closed Jan–Feb.

Appendix: Fast Facts, Toll-Free Numbers & Websites

1 FAST FACTS: DENMARK

AMERICAN EXPRESS Amex is represented throughout Denmark by **Nyman & Schultz,** Nørregade 7A (© **33-13-11-81;** bus: 34 or 35), with a branch in Terminal 3 of the Copenhagen Airport. Fulfilling all the functions of American Express, except for foreign exchange services, the main office is open Monday to Thursday 8:30am to 4:30pm, and Friday 8:30am to 4pm. The airport office remains open until 8:30pm Monday to Friday. On weekends and overnight on weekdays, a recorded message, in English, will deliver the phone number of a 24-hour Amex service in Stockholm. This is useful for anyone who has lost a card or travelers checks.

AREA CODE The international country code for Denmark is **45.** For international calls, dial **00,** then the country code (**44** for Britain, **1** for the United States or Canada).

ATM NETWORKS See "Money & Costs," p. 38.

BUSINESS HOURS Most **banks** are open Monday to Friday from 9:30am to 4pm (Thurs to 6pm), but outside Copenhagen, banking hours vary. **Stores** are generally open Monday through Thursday from 9am to 5:30pm, Friday 9am to 7 or 8pm, and Saturday noon to 2pm; most are closed Sunday.

CAR RENTALS See "Toll-Free Numbers & Websites," p. 412.

CURRENCY See "Money & Costs" on p. 38.

DRINKING LAWS To consume alcohol in Danish bars, restaurants, or cafes, customers must be 18 or older. There are no restrictions on children 17 and under who drink at home or, for example, from a bottle in a public park. Danish police tend to be lenient unless drinkers become raucous or uncontrollable. There is no leniency, however, in the matter of driving while intoxicated. It's illegal to drive with a blood-alcohol level of 0.8 or more, which could be produced by two drinks. If the level is 1.5, motorists pay a serious fine. If it's more than 1.5, drivers can lose their license. If the level is 2.0 or more (usually produced by six or seven drinks), a prison term of at least 14 days might follow. Liquor stores in Denmark are closed on Sunday.

DRIVING RULES See "Getting There & Getting Around," p. 32.

DRUG LAWS Penalties for the possession, use, purchase, sale, or manufacturing of drugs are severe. The quantity of the controlled substance is more important than the type of substance. Danish police are particularly strict with cases involving the sale of drugs to children.

DRUGSTORES They're known as *apoteker* in Danish and are open Monday to

Thursday 9am to 5:30pm, Friday 9am to 7pm, and Saturday 9am to 1pm.

ELECTRICITY Voltage is generally 220 volts AC, 50 to 60 cycles. In many camping sites, 110-volt power plugs are also available. Adapters and transformers may be purchased in Denmark. It's always best to check at your hotel desk before using an electrical outlet.

EMBASSIES All embassies are in Copenhagen. The embassy of the **United States** is at Dag Hammärskjölds Allé 24, DK-2100 Copenhagen (✆ 33-41-71-00). Other embassies are the **United Kingdom,** Kastelsvej 40, DK-2100 Copenhagen (✆ 35-44-52-00); **Canada,** Kristen Berniskows Gade 1, DK-1105 Copenhagen K (✆ 33-48-32-00); **Australia,** Dampfærgevej 26, DK-2100 Copenhagen (✆ 70-26-36-76); and **Ireland,** Østbanegade 21, DK-2100 Copenhagen (✆ 35-42-32-33).

EMERGENCIES Dial ✆ **112** for the fire department, the police, or an ambulance, or to report a sea or air accident. Emergency calls from public telephone kiosks are free (no coins needed).

HOLIDAYS Danish public holidays are New Year's Day, Maundy Thursday, Good Friday, Easter Sunday, Easter Monday, Labor Day (May 1), Common Prayers Day (fourth Fri after Easter), Ascension Day (mid-May), Whitsunday (late May), Whitmonday, Constitution Day (June 5), Christmas Day, and Boxing Day (Dec 26).

INSURANCE **Medical Insurance** For travel overseas, most U.S. health plans (including Medicare and Medicaid) do not provide coverage, and the ones that do often require you to pay for services up front and reimburse you only after you return home.

As a safety net, you may want to buy travel medical insurance, particularly if you're traveling to a remote or high-risk area where emergency evacuation might be necessary. If you require additional medical insurance, try **MEDEX Assistance** (✆ 410/453-6300; www.medexassist. com) or **Travel Assistance International** (✆ 800/821-2828; www.travelassistance. com; for general information on services, call the company's **Worldwide Assistance Services, Inc.** at ✆ 800/777-8710).

Canadians should check with their provincial health plan offices or call **Health Canada** (✆ 866/225-0709; www.hc-sc. gc.ca) to find out the extent of their coverage and what documentation and receipts they must take home in case they are treated overseas.

Travelers from the U.K. should carry their European Health Insurance Card (EHIC), which replaced the E111 form as proof of entitlement to free/reduced-cost medical treatment abroad (✆ **0845/606-2030;** www.ehic.org.uk). Note, however, that the EHIC covers only "necessary medical treatment." For repatriation costs, lost money, baggage, or cancellation, travel insurance from a reputable company should always be sought (www.travelinsuranceweb. com).

Travel Insurance The cost of travel insurance varies widely, depending on the destination, the cost and length of your trip, your age and health, and the type of trip you're taking, but expect to pay between 5% and 8% of the vacation itself. You can get estimates from various providers through **InsureMyTrip.com** (✆ **800/ 487-4722**). Enter your trip cost and dates, your age, and other information, for prices from more than a dozen companies.

U.K. citizens and their families who make more than one trip abroad per year may find that an annual travel insurance policy works out cheaper. Check **www. moneysupermarket.com**, which compares prices across a wide range of providers for single- and multitrip policies.

Most big travel agencies offer their own insurance and will probably try to sell you their package when you book a holiday.

Think before you sign. **Britain's Consumers' Association** recommends that you insist on seeing the policy and reading the fine print before buying travel insurance. **The Association of British Insurers** (✆ **020/7600-3333;** www.abi.org.uk) gives advice by phone and publishes Holiday Insurance, a free guide to policy provisions and prices. You might also shop around for better deals: Try **Columbus Direct** (✆ **0870/033-9988;** www.columbusdirect. net).

Trip Cancellation Insurance Trip-cancellation insurance will help retrieve your money if you have to back out of a trip or depart early, or if your travel supplier goes bankrupt. Trip cancellation traditionally covers such events as sickness, natural disasters, and Department of State advisories. The latest news in trip-cancellation insurance is the availability of expanded hurricane coverage and the "any-reason" cancellation coverage—which costs more but covers cancellations made for any reason. You won't get back 100% of your prepaid trip cost, but you'll be refunded a substantial portion. **TravelSafe** (✆ 888/885-7233; www.travelsafe.com) offers both types of coverage. **Expedia** (www.expedia. com) also offers any-reason cancellation coverage for its air-hotel packages. For details, contact one of the following recommended insurers: **Access America** (✆ 866/807-3982; www.accessamerica.com); **Travel Guard International** (✆ 800/826-4919; www.travelguard.com); **Travel Insured International** (✆ 800/243-3174; www. travelinsured.com); and **Travelex Insurance Services** (✆ 888/457-4602; www. travelex-insurance.com).

LANGUAGE Danish is the national tongue. English is commonly spoken, especially among young people. You should have few, if any, language barriers. The best phrase book is *Danish for Travellers* (Berlitz).

LOST & FOUND Be sure to tell all of your credit card companies the minute you discover your wallet has been lost or stolen and file a report at the nearest police precinct. Your credit card company or insurer may require a police report number or record of the loss. Most credit card companies have an emergency toll-free number to call if your card is lost or stolen; they may be able to wire you a cash advance immediately or deliver an emergency credit card in a day or two. Visa's emergency number outside the U.S. is ✆ 410/581-3836; call collect. American Express cardholders should call collect ✆ 336/393-1111. MasterCard holders should call collect ✆ 314/542-7111. If you need emergency cash over the weekend when all banks and American Express offices are closed, you can have money wired to you via **Western Union** (✆ 800/325-6000;** www.westernunion.com).

MAIL Most post offices are open Monday through Friday from 9 or 10am to 5 or 6pm and Saturday from 9am to noon; they're closed Sunday. All mail to North America is sent airmail without extra charge. Mailboxes are painted red and display the embossed crown and trumpet of the Danish Postal Society.

NEWSPAPERS & MAGAZINES English-language newspapers are sold at all major news kiosks in Copenhagen but are much harder to find in the provinces. London papers are flown in for early-morning delivery, but you may find the *International Herald Tribune* or *USA Today* more interesting. Pick up a copy of *Copenhagen This Week,* printed in English, which contains useful information.

PASSPORTS The websites listed provide downloadable passport applications as well as the current fees for processing applications. For an up-to-date, country-by-country listing of passport requirements around the world, go to the "International Travel" tab of the U.S. Department of State at **http://travel.state. gov**. International visitors to the U.S. can obtain a visa application at the same website. *Note:* Children are required to present a passport when entering the United States at airports. More information on obtaining a passport for a minor can be found at **http://travel.state.gov**. Allow plenty of time before your trip to apply for a passport; processing normally takes 4 to 6 weeks (3 weeks for expedited service) but can take longer during busy periods (especially spring). And keep in mind that if you need a passport in a hurry, you'll pay a higher processing fee.

For Residents of Australia You can pick up an application from your local post office or any branch of Passports Australia, but you must schedule an interview at the passport office to present your application materials. Call the **Australian Passport Information Service** at ℂ **131-232,** or visit the government website at www.passports.gov.au.

For Residents of Canada Passport applications are available at travel agencies throughout Canada or from the central **Passport Office,** Department of Foreign Affairs and International Trade, Ottawa, ON K1A 0G3 (ℂ **800/567-6868;** www.ppt.gc.ca). *Note:* Canadian children who travel must have their own passport. However, if you hold a valid Canadian passport issued before December 11, 2001, that bears the name of your child, the passport remains valid for you and your child until it expires.

For Residents of Ireland You can apply for a 10-year passport at the **Passport Office,** Setanta Centre, Molesworth Street, Dublin 2 (ℂ **01/671-1633;** www.irlgov.ie/iveagh). Those under age 18 and over 65 must apply for a 3-year passport. You can also apply at 1A South Mall, Cork (ℂ **21/494-4700**), or at most main post offices.

For Residents of New Zealand You can pick up a passport application at any New Zealand Passports Office or download it from their website. Contact the

Passports Office at ℂ **0800/225-050** in New Zealand or 04/474-8100, or log on to www.passports.govt.nz.

For Residents of the United Kingdom To pick up an application for a standard 10-year passport (5-yr. passport for children 15 and under), visit your nearest passport office, major post office, or travel agency, or contact the **United Kingdom Passport Service** at ℂ **0870/521-0410** or search its website at www.ukpa.gov.uk.

POLICE Dial ℂ **112** nationwide.

SAFETY Denmark is one of the safest European countries for travelers. Copenhagen, the major population center, naturally experiences the most crime. Muggings have been reported in the vicinity of the railway station, especially late at night, but crimes of extreme violence are exceedingly rare. Exercise the usual precautions you would when traveling anywhere.

SMOKING August 15, 2007, was D-day for Danish smokers. A smoking ban took effect, against cigarettes, cigars, and pipes, which can no longer be enjoyed in any public buildings or private businesses. The ordinance covers restaurants, shops, schools, bars, public transport, entertainment establishments, and places of employment. The World Health Organization estimates that 30% of all Danes smoke.

TAXES The 25% VAT (value-added tax) on goods and services is known in Denmark as *moms* (pronounced "mumps"). Special tax-free exports are possible, and many stores will mail goods home to you, circumventing *moms*. If you want to take your purchases with you, look for shops displaying Danish tax-free shopping notices. Such shops offer tourists tax refunds for personal export. This refund applies to purchases of at least DKK300 ($51/£30) for U.S. visitors. Danish Customs must stamp your tax-free invoice when you leave the country. You can receive your refund at Copenhagen's Kastrup International Airport when you depart. If you go by land or sea, you can receive your refund by mail. Mail requests for refunds to Danish Tax-Free Shopping A/S, H. J. Holstvej 5A, DK-2605 Brøndby, Denmark. You'll be reimbursed by check, cash, or credit- or charge-card credit in the currency you want.

For the refund to apply, the DKK 300 ($51/£30) must be spent in one store, but not necessarily at the same time. Some major department stores allow purchases to be made over several days or even weeks, at the end of which receipts will be tallied. Service and handling fees are deducted from the total, so actual refunds come up to about 19%. Information on this program is available from the Danish Tourist Board (see "Visitor Information," in chapter 3).

A 25% *moms* is included in hotel and restaurant bills, service charges, entrance fees, and repair bills for foreign-registered cars. No refunds are possible on these items.

TIME   Denmark operates on Central European Time—1 hour ahead of Greenwich Mean Time and 6 hours ahead of Eastern Standard Time. Daylight saving time is from the end of March to the end of September.

TIPPING   Tips are seldom expected. Porters charge fixed prices, and tipping is not customary for hairdressers or barbers. Service is built into the system, and hotels, restaurants, and even taxis include a 15% service charge in their rates. Because of the service charge, plus the 25% *moms*, you'll probably have to pay an additional 40% for some services!

Consider tipping only for special services; some Danes would feel insulted if you offered them a tip.

TOILETS   All big plazas, such as Town Hall Square in Copenhagen, have public lavatories. In small towns and villages, head for the marketplace. Hygienic standards are usually adequate. Sometimes men and women patronize the same toilets (signs read TOILETTER or WC). Otherwise, men's rooms are marked HERRER or H, and women's rooms are marked DAMER or D.

USEFUL PHONE NUMBERS U.S. Department of State Travel Advisory ✆ 202/647-5225 (manned 24 hrs.)

U.S. Passport Agency ✆ 202/647-0518, and **U.S. Centers for Disease Control International Traveler's Hotline** ✆ 404/332-4559.

WATER   Tap water is safe to drink throughout Denmark.

---

2 TOLL-FREE NUMBERS & WEBSITES

MAJOR U.S. AIRLINES
(*flies internationally as well)

American Airlines*
✆ 800/433-7300 (in U.S. and Canada)
✆ 020/7365-0777 (in U.K.)
www.aa.com

Continental Airlines*
✆ 800/523-3273 (in U.S. and Canada)
✆ 084/5607-6760 (in U.K.)
www.continental.com

Delta Air Lines*
✆ 800/221-1212 (in U.S. and Canada)
✆ 084/5600-0950 (in U.K.)
www.delta.com

Northwest Airlines
✆ 800/225-2525 (in U.S.)
✆ 870/0507-4074 (in U.K.)
www.flynaa.com

United Airlines*
✆ 800/864-8331 (in U.S. and Canada)
✆ 084/5844-4777 (in U.K.)
www.united.com

US Airways*
✆ 800/428-4322 (in U.S. and Canada)
✆ 084/5600-3300 (in U.K.)
www.usairways.com

Virgin America*
✆ 877/359-8474
www.virginamerica.com

MAJOR INTERNATIONAL AIRLINES

Air France
✆ 800/237-2747 (in U.S.)
✆ 800/375-8723 (U.S. and Canada)
✆ 087/0142-4343 (in U.K.)
www.airfrance.com

Air India
✆ 212/407-1371 (in U.S.)
✆ 020/8745-1000 (in U.K.)
✆ 91 22 2279 6666 (in India)
www.airindia.com

Alitalia
✆ 800/223-5730 (in U.S.)
✆ 800/361-8336 (in Canada)
✆ 087/0608-6003 (in U.K.)
www.alitalia.com

American Airlines
✆ 800/433-7300 (in U.S. and Canada)
✆ 020/7365-0777 (in U.K.)
www.aa.com

British Airways
✆ 800/247-9297 (in U.S. and Canada)
✆ 087/0850-9850 (in U.K.)
www.british-airways.com

China Airlines
✆ 800/227-5118 (in U.S.)
✆ 022/715-1212 (in Taiwan)
www.china-airlines.com

Continental Airlines
✆ 800/523-3273 (in U.S. and Canada)
✆ 084/5607-6760 (in U.K.)
www.continental.com

Finnair
✆ 800/950-5000 (in U.S. and Canada)
✆ 087/0241-4411 (in U.K.)
www.finnair.com

Iberia Airlines
✆ 800/722-4642 (in U.S. and Canada)
✆ 087/0609-0500 (in U.K.)
www.iberia.com

Icelandair
✆ 800/223-5500 (in U.S. and Canada)
✆ 084/5758-1111 (in U.K.)
www.icelandair.com
www.icelandair.co.uk (in U.K.)

Japan Airlines
✆ 012/025-5931
www.jal.co.jp

Lan Airlines
✆ 866/435-9526 (in U.S.)
✆ 305/670-9999 (in other countries)
http://plane.lan.com

Lufthansa
✆ 800/399-5838 (in U.S.)
✆ 800/563-5954 (in Canada)
✆ 087/0837-7747 (in U.K.)
www.lufthansa.com

Olympic Airlines
✆ 800/223-1226 (in U.S.)
✆ 514/878-9691 (in Canada)
✆ 087/0606-0460 (in U.K.)
www.olympicairlines.com

Swiss Air
✆ 877/359-7947 (in U.S. and Canada)
✆ 084/5601-0956 (in U.K.)
www.swiss.com

Turkish Airlines
✆ 90 212 444 0 849
www.thy.com

United Airlines
☎ 800/864-8331 (in U.S. and Canada)
☎ 084/5844-4777 (in U.K.)
www.united.com

US Airways
☎ 800/428-4322 (in U.S. and Canada)
☎ 084/5600-3300 (in U.K.)
www.usairways.com

Virgin Atlantic Airways
☎ 800/821-5438 (in U.S. and Canada)
☎ 087/0574-7747 (in U.K.)
www.virgin-atlantic.com

CAR-RENTAL AGENCIES

Auto Europe
☎ 888/223-5555 (in U.S. and Canada)
☎ 0800/2235-5555 (in U.K.)
www.autoeurope.com

Avis
☎ 800/331-1212 (in U.S. and Canada)
☎ 084/4581-8181 (in U.K.)
www.avis.com

Budget
☎ 800/527-0700 (in U.S.)
☎ 800/268-8900 (in Canada)
☎ 087/0156-5656 (in U.K.)
www.budget.com

Enterprise
☎ 800/261-7331 (in U.S.)
☎ 514/355-4028 (in Canada)
☎ 012/9360-9090 (in U.K.)
www.enterprise.com

Hertz
☎ 800/645-3131
☎ 800/654-3001 (international)
www.hertz.com

Kemwel (KHA)
☎ 877/820-0668
www.kemwel.com

Thrifty
☎ 800/367-2277
☎ 918/669-2168 (international)
www.thrifty.com

MAJOR HOTEL & MOTEL CHAINS

Best Western International
☎ 800/780-7234 (in U.S. and Canada)
☎ 0800/393-130 (in U.K.)
www.bestwestern.com

Clarion Hotels
☎ 800/CLARION [252-7466] or
  877/424-6423 (in U.S. and Canada)
☎ 0800/444-444 (in U.K.)
www.clarionhotel.com

Comfort Inns
☎ 800/228-5150 (in U.S. and Canada)
☎ 0800/444-444 (in U.K.)
www.comfortinn.com

Crowne Plaza Hotels
☎ 888/303-1746
www.ichotelsgroup.com/crowneplaza

Hilton Hotels
☎ 800/HILTONS [445-8667]
  (in U.S. and Canada)
☎ 087/0590-9090 (in U.K.)
www.hilton.com

Holiday Inn
☎ 800/315-2621 (in U.S. and Canada)
☎ 0800/405-060 (in U.K.)
www.holidayinn.com

InterContinental Hotels & Resorts
☎ 800/424-6835 (in U.S. and Canada)
☎ 0800/1800-1800 (in U.K.)
www.ichotelsgroup.com/intercontinental

Marriott
☎ 877/236-2427 (in U.S. and Canada)
☎ 0800/221-222 (in U.K.)
www.marriott.com

Quality Inn
🕾 877/424-6423 (in U.S. and Canada)
🕾 0800/444-444 (in U.K.)
www.qualityinn.com

Radisson Hotels & Resorts
🕾 888/201-1718 (in U.S. and Canada)
🕾 0800/374-411 (in U.K.)
www.radisson.com

Ramada Worldwide
🕾 888/2-RAMADA [272-6232]
   (in U.S. and Canada)
🕾 080/8100-0783 (in U.K.)
www.ramada.com

Sheraton Hotels & Resorts
🕾 800/325-3535 (in U.S.)
🕾 800/543-4300 (in Canada)
🕾 0800/3253-5353 (in U.K.)
www.starwoodhotels.com/sheraton

INDEX

See also Accommodations and Restaurant indexes, below.

GENERAL INDEX

Aalborg, 384–396
  accommodations, 389–392
  getting around, 385
  nightlife, 396
  restaurants, 2, 392–396
  shopping, 389
  sights and attractions,
    385–389
  traveling to, 384–385
Aalborg Carnival, 31, 385
**Aalborg Guld & Solvhus
  (Aalborg), 389**
**Aalborg Jazz and Blues
  Festival, 385**
**Aalborg Kongres og Kultur
  Center, 396**
Aalborg Marinemuseum, 385
Aalborg Storcenter, 389
**Aalborg Tårnet (Aalborg
  Tower), 385–386**
**Aalborg Zoologiske Have
  (Aalborg Zoo), 386**
**Aarebo Pub (Æroskobing),
  298**
AARP, 44
**Abelholt Klostermuseum,
  174**
Above and Beyond Tours, 44
Access-Able Travel Source, 43
Accessible Journeys, 43
Accommodations, 53–55
  best, 5–6
  green-friendly, 46
Active vacations, 50–51
  best, 8
**Adventure travel
  operators, 48**
Æro, 292–300
**Æro Museum (Æroskobing),
  296**
Æroskobing, 7, 293, 295–298
Æroskobing Antiks, 296
Æroskobing Kirke, 295–296
**Æroskobing Vandrerhjem
  (Æro), 294**

Air travel
  to Denmark, 32–33
  green-friendly, 46
Åkirke (Åkirkeby), 246
Åkirkeby, 246
**Alisson-Dansk Naturkosme-
  tik (Ribe), 325**
**Alkjær Lukke (Ringkobing),
  347**
Allehånde (Vejle), 339
Allinge, 257
**Almindingen (Bornholm),
  246, 253**
Amager Beach Park, 163
**Amager Museum (Dragor),
  164**
**Amaliehavn (Copenhagen),
  146**
**Amalienborg Palace (Copen-
  hagen), 124–128, 146**
**The Amber Specialist
  (Copenhagen), 151**
American Express, 39, 408
  Copenhagen, 75
**Amigo Bar (Vordingborg),
  228**
**Andersen, Hans Christian, 5,
  135, 137, 227, 234, 379**
  Copenhagen
    grave, 139–140
    residences, 139, 146
    statue, 143
  Faaborg, 288
  Odense, 265
    H. C. Andersens Barn-
      domshjem (Child-
      hood Home), 269
    H. C. Andersens Hus
      (H. C. Andersens
      Museum), 269–270
**Andersen & Nissen (Tonder),
  313**
**Anne Hvides Gård (Svend-
  borg), 280**
Antik Bahuset (Koge), 210
Antik Gaarden (Ribe), 325
Antik Ulla (Gilleleje), 192

Antvorskov, 222
Apostelhuset (Næstved), 224
**AQUA Ferskvands Akvarium
  og Museum (Silkeborg), 355**
Aquariums
  AQUA Ferskvands Akvar-
    ium og Museum
    (Silkeborg), 355
  Danmarks Akvarium (Den-
    mark's Aquarium; Copen-
    hagen), 141
Architecture, 24, 25
Area code, 408
Århus, 360–375
  accommodations, 2–3,
    367–371
  getting around, 362
  nightlife, 373–375
  restaurants, 3, 371–373
  shopping, 366–367
  sights and attractions,
    362–366
  traveling to, 360, 362
  visitor information, 362
Århus Card, 362
**Århus Domkirke (Cathedral
  of St. Clemens), 363**
Århus Festival Week, 31
**Århus Kunstmuseum (Århus
  Museum of Art), 363**
Århus Theater, 373–374
**Arken Museum for Moderne
  Kunst (Arken Museum of
  Modern Art; Copenhagen),
  135**
Årsdale, 251
Art, 24–25
Art galleries
  Aalborg, 389
  Århus, 367
  Bornholm, 251
  Copenhagen, 151
  Fano, 333
  Kolding, 304
  Romo, 318–319
  Skagen, 405
Art House (Romo), 318–319

Assistens Kirkegård (Assistens Cemetery; Copenhagen), 139–140
ATMs (automated-teller machines), 38–39
Australia
  customs regulations, 30
  embassy, 409
  passports, 411
Axel Musik (Copenhagen), 155
Axeltorv (Næstved), 224, 225

B ackroads, 45
Bahne (Slagelse), 221
Bakken Amusement Park (Copenhagen), 140, 141
Bakkens Hvile (Copenhagen), 140
Bald & Bang (Copenhagen), 151–152
Balka, 247
Ballet and Opera Festival (Copenhagen), 30
Bangsbro Museum (Frederikshavn), 399
Beaches, 50
  Hornbæk, 186, 187
  Koge, 209
  near Copenhagen, 163
  Romo, 317, 318
Bed & breakfasts (B&Bs), 53
Bellevue, 163
Bentzons Boghandel (Ribe), 325
Besættelsesmuseet (Occupation Museum; Århus), 363
Best Western hotel chain, 55
Biking, Ribe, 321
Biking and bike rentals, 8, 50
  Æro, 294–295
  Copenhagen, 74–75, 149–150
  Mon, 229
  Tisvildeleje, 193
  Tonder, 311
  tours, 48
Bilka Department Store (Aalborg), 389
Billabong Bar (Århus), 374
Billetnet (Copenhagen), 156
Billund, 343–345
Bird-watching, 177, 271, 350
Birger Christensen (Copenhagen), 153, 154
Birgitte Munch (Frederikshavn), 399
Birkegårdens Haver, 223

Birkholm Færgen, 298
Birkholm Island, 298
Blixen, Baroness Karen (Isak Dinesen), Rungstedlund, 168
Blokhus, 388
Blue Café (Kolding), 307
Blue Marble Travel, 48
Boderne (Næstved), 224
Boghallen (Copenhagen), 151
Bogo, 236
Bogo Molle, 236
Boingo, 52
Boiz Bar (Copenhagen), 161
Bon Sac (Silkeborg), 357
Boogies (Odense), 278
Books, recommended, 26
Bookstores, Copenhagen, 75, 151
Borgårdsten (near Ronne), 240
Borge Bottelet Guldsmedie (Ribe), 325
Bornholm, 237–259
  brief description of, 58
  exploring, 239
  getting around, 239
  traveling to, 238–239
  visitor information, 239
Bornholm Agricultural Museum (Landsbrugs Museum; Gudhjem), 254
Bornholm Ferries, 239
Bornholms Automobilmuseum, 246
Bornholms Kunstmuseet (Art Museum of Bornholm) (Helligdommen), 256
Bornholms Museum (Ronne), 240–241
Bornholmstraffiken, 238
The Bornholm Welcome Center (Ronne), 239
Botanisk Have (Botanical Gardens; Copenhagen), 131
Bousogaard (Ringkobing), 347
Brandts Klædefabrik (Brandt's Textile Mill; Odense), 266
Brecht, Bertolt, 279
Brede House (Copenhagen), 139
Brede Værk (Copenhagen), 139
Bredgade (Copenhagen), 150
Bregninge Kirke, 295

Bregninge Kirkebakke (Bregninge Church Tower; Tåsinge), 286
British Airways, 32
Bruun Rasmussen (Copenhagen), 151
Bruuns Bazaar (Copenhagen), 153
Bryggeriet Skt. Clemens (Århus), 374
Buch's Vinstue (Haderslev), 310
Budolfi Domkirke (Cathedral of St. Budolf; Aalborg), 386
Bülow Duus Glassblowers (Århus), 367
Business hours, 408
Bus tours, 48
Bus travel, within Denmark, 36–37
Butterfly World (near Næstved), 227
Bydr. Lützhofts (Roskilde), 202
Bymuseet Montegården (Odense City Museum), 266, 268

C afé Andelen (Æroskobing), 298
Café Anthon (Nyborg), 265
Café Gustav (Gudhjem), 256
Café Klint (Gudhjem), 256
Café Paradiso (Hornbæk), 189
Café Under Masken (Århus), 374
Café Zirup (Copenhagen), 160
Calendar of events, 30–31
Camping, 8
Canada
  customs regulations, 30
  embassy, 409
  health insurance, 409
  passports, 411
Canoeing, Næstved, 224
Carbon offsetting, 46
Carl Nielsen Hall (Odense), 278
Carl Nielsen Museet (Odense), 268
Carl Nielsens Barndomshjem (Carl Nielsen's Childhood Home; near Odense), 270
Carlsberg Brewery (Copenhagen), 149
Carnival in Copenhagen, 30
Car rentals, 37
  green-friendly, 46

Car travel
to Denmark, 33
within Denmark, 37
self-drive tours, 48
Casino Munkebjerg Vejle, 341
Castles and manor houses, accommodations in, 53–54
Castles and palaces, best, 9
Cathedral of St. Budolf (Budolfi Domkirke; Aalborg), 386
Cathedral of St. Clemens (Århus Domkirke), 363
Cellphones, 51
Centers for Disease Control and Prevention, 41
Centralhjornet (Copenhagen), 161–162
Central Jutland, 336–378
Ceramics and pottery. *See* Pottery and ceramics
Chalk cliffs
Mons Klint, 228, 234–235
Stevns Peninsula, 214
Charlottenborg Palace (Copenhagen), 146
Charlottenlund Slot (Hellerup), 141
Children's Museum (Copenhagen), 131
Christiania (Copenhagen), 9, 72, 159
Christiansborg (Copenhagen), restaurants near, 114–115
Christiansborg Slot (Christiansborg Palace; Copenhagen), 132–133, 158
Christianshavn (Copenhagen), 72, 158
Christiansminde (Svendborg), 279
Christianso, 256–257
Church of the Holy Ghost (Helligåndskirken; Copenhagen), 143
Cirkusbygningen Wallmans (Copenhagen), 159–160
City Bike (Copenhagen), 150
Claustholm (near Randers), 366
Climate, 30
Cloostårnet (Frederikshavn), 399
Collection of Antiquities (Copenhagen), 133
College Art (Odense), 272

Copenhagen, 69–169
accommodations, 1, 77–95
active sports, 149–150
American Express, 75
business hours, 75
currency exchange, 75
dentists, 75
doctors, 75
emergencies, 75
finding an address in, 71
gay and lesbian clubs, 161–162
getting around, 73–75
hospitals, 76
Internet access, 76
layout of, 70–71
lost property, 76
luggage storage and lockers, 76
neighborhoods in brief, 71
newspapers, 76
nightlife, 2, 155–163
organized tours, 148–149
parking, 74
pharmacies, 76
police, 76
pornography and sex industry, 162–163
post office, 76
restaurants, 1–2, 95–119
safety, 76
shopping, 2, 150–155
side trips from, 163–169
sights and attractions, 120–149
taxes, 76
taxis, 74
toilets, 76
transit information, 76
traveling to, 70
visitor information, 70
walking tours
guided, 149
self-guided, 143–148
what's new in, 1–2
Copenhagen Card, 73
Copenhagen Cathedral (Vor Frue Kirke), 135
Copenhagen Excursions, 148
Copenhagen Jazz Festival, 31, 141
Copenhagen JazzHouse (Copenhagen), 160
Copenhagen Opera House, 156–157
Copenhagen This Week, 155
Copenhagen Tourist Information Center, 70
Copenhagen Zoo (Zoologisk Have), 142

Cosy Bar (Copenhagen), 162
Cox & Kings, 48
Crazy Daisy (Kolding), 307
Crazy Daisy (Nyborg), 265
Crazy Daisy (Ringsted), 219
Crazy Daisy (Svendborg), 284
Credit cards, 39–40
Creutz Boghanel (Æroskobing), 296
Crossing Latitudes, 48
Crystal and glass. *See* Glass objects and crystal
Cube (Aalborg), 396
Currency and currency exchange, 38, 40
Customs regulations, 29–30
Cyclists' Touring Club, 49

Dagmar Cross (Ringsted), 217
Danehof (Nyborg), 263
Danish Agricultural Museum (near Århus), 366
Danish Cultural Institute, 49
Danish Cycling Federation (Dansk Cyklist Forbund), 48, 50
Danish design, 6–7, 126–127
Copenhagen, 125
Danish Design Centre, 135–136
Kunstindustrimuseet (Museum of Decorative and Applied Art), 129–130
shopping, 151–153
Danish School of Art & Design (Kolding), 302
Koge, 211
Odense, 272
Svendborg, 282
Danish Design Centre (Copenhagen), 135–136
Danish Disability Council, 42–43
Danish Immigrant Museum (Iowa), 49
Danish Maritime Museum (Helsingor), 183
Danish Museum of Printing (Odense), 266
Danish National Association for Gays and Lesbians, 43
Danish Opera House (Copenhagen), 148
Danish Press Museum (Odense), 266
Danish School of Art & Design (Kolding), 302

Danish Tourist Board, 29
Danish Union of Wind-
gliders, 51
Danmarks Akvarium (Den-
mark's Aquarium; Copen-
hagen), 141
Danmarks Jernbanemuseum
(Railway Museum;
Odense), 268
Danmarks Saltcenter
(Mariager), 382
Danmarks Tekniske Museet
(Technical Museum of Den-
mark; Helsingor), 182
Danska Kroer og Hoteller, 54
Dansk Bed & Breakfast, 53
Dansk Cyklist Forbund (Dan-
ish Cycling Federation),
48, 50
Dansk Drageflyver Union, 51
Dansk Jodisk Museum
(Copenhagen), 136
Dansommer, 54
Dan Wheel (Copenhagen),
149–150
Davids Samling (Copenha-
gen), 130
DDC Shop (Copenhagen), 152
Deep vein thrombosis, 41
Den Fynske Landsby (Funen
Village; Odense), 269
Den Gamle By (Old Town;
Århus), 364
Den Gamle Gaard (The Old
Merchant's House;
Faaborg), 288
Den Hirschsprungske Sam-
ling (Hirschsprung Collec-
tion; Copenhagen), 132
Den Kongelige Afstobn-
ingssamling (Royal Cast
Collection; Copenhagen),
136
Den lille butik (Fano),
332–333
Den Lille Havfrue (The Little
Mermaid; Copenhagen),
128–129, 148, 149, 210
Den Rode Pimpernel
(Copenhagen), 157
Den Skæve Bar (Ebeltoft),
378
Den Tilsandede Kirke
(Skagen), 403–404
Design. See Danish design
Det Danske Udvandrer-
arkiv, 49
Det Gamle Apotek (Tonder),
313

Det Gamle Rådhus (Old Town
Hall; Ebeltoft), 376
Det Gamle Rådhus (Town
Hall Museum; Ribe), 322
Det Kongelige Teater (Royal
Theater), 146, 157
Det Nationalhistoriske
Museum (Museum of
National History; Freder-
iksborg), 173
DFDS Seaways, 35
Dinesen, Isak (Baroness
Karen Blixen), Rungsted-
lund, 168
Din Gronne Skobutik
(Tonder), 313
Disabilities, travelers with,
42–43
Dot Keramik (Frederikshavn),
399
Dr. Jazz (Ronne), 245–246
Drachmanns Hus (Skagen),
404
Dragor, 7, 73, 163–166
Dragor Museum, 164
Drinking laws, 408
Driving rules, 37
Dröhse's Hus (Dröhse's
House; Tonder), 312–313
Drug laws, 408
Drugstores, 408–409
Dueodde, 247, 249–250
Dueodde Fyr, 247
Dyrehaven (near Århus), 365

Eating and drinking, 27–28
Ebeltoft, 7, 375–378
Ebeltoft Glass Museum (Glas-
museet Ebeltoft), 376
Economy-class syndrome, 41
Ecotourism, 45
Egeskov Castle (Kværndrup),
270–271
Ehlers-samlingen (Ehlers Col-
lections; Haderslev), 308
Elderhostel, 44
Electricity, 409
Elling Woman, 356
Elmelunde, 232–233
Elmelunde Kirke, 232–233
Elvira Madigan (film), 285
Embassies, 409
Emergencies, 409
Emerto (Marstal), 299
Empiregården (Stege), 230
English Pub (Kolding), 307
Entré Scenen (Århus), 374
Entry requirements, 29

Ericksson's Gård (Farm;
Ronne), 241–242
Esrum Kloster, 178
Esrum So, 172, 177
Ethical tourism, 45
Eurailpass, 33–35
European Health Insurance
Card (EHIC), 41, 409
Experimentarium (Hands-On
Science Center; Copenha-
gen), 141–142

Faaborg, 287–292
Faaborg Museum, 288–289
Færgefart Bådudlejning på
Esrum So (Fredensborg),
177
Fætter BR (Hillerod), 175
Fall Ballet Festival (Copenha-
gen), 31
Families with children
Copenhagen
attractions, 140–142
hotels, 90
restaurants, 104
information and resources,
44–45
suggested itinerary, 66–68
Family History Library, 49
Fanefjord Kirke, 236
Fannikerdagene (Fano), 331
Fano, 330–335
Fano Bad, 330–331
Fano Jazzklub, 335
Fano Kunstmuseum (Fano
Art Museum), 332
Fano Museum, 332
Fano Skibsfarts-og Dragt-
samling (Fano), 331–332
Fano Tile Museum, 334
Farm holidays, 54
Farobroen Welcome
Center, 236
Fårup Sommerland & Water-
park (near Blokhus), 388
Favlhuset (Århus), 367
Films, 26–27
Fire Festival Regatta
(Silkeborg), 31
Fishing, 8, 50
Storkesoen, 325
Fiskerhuset (Gilleleje), 191
Fiskerkylyngen (Frederik-
shavn), 398
Flaskeskibssamlingen
(Æroskobing), 296
Flying Wheels Travel, 43

Food and cuisine, Bornholm, 238
Forsvarsmuseet (Ronne), 242
Frank A.'s Café (Odense), 278
Fredensborg, 177–180
Fredensborg Slot, 178–179
Frederiksberg (Copenhagen), 73
    accommodations, 95
    restaurant, 117
Frederiksborg Castle Garden, 174
Frederiksborg Slot (Frederiksborg Castle), 173–174
Frederiksborg Svommehal (Copenhagen), 150
Frederikshavn, 396–402
Frederikshavn Kirke, 398–399
Frederikskirke (Marmorkirken or Marble Church; Copenhagen), 138, 148
Frederikso, 256
Frederikssund, 173
Frederikssund Vikingespil (Viking Festival; Hillerod), 173
Fregatten *Jylland* (Ebeltoft), 376
Friendship Force, 54
Frihedsmuseet (Museum of Danish Resistance, 1940-45; Copenhagen), 129, 148
Frilandsmuseet (Open-Air Museum; Copenhagen), 139
Frommers.com, 47
Fruhost (Marstal), 299
Frydenlund (near Tommerup), 271
Fuchsia Garden (Kværndrup), 271
Funen, 260–300
    brief description of, 58
Funen Art Museum (Fyns Kunstmuseum; Odense), 269
Funen Festival, 31
Funen Village (Den Fynske Landsby; Odense), 269
Fyns Kunstmuseum (Funen Art Museum; Odense), 269

Galerie Asbæk (Copenhagen), 151
Galerie Skagen, 405
Galerie Wolfsen (Aalborg), 389
Galgebakken (Ry), 351

Galleri Anne (Fano), 333
Galleri Bo Bendixen (Århus), 367
Gallerie Baltic See Glass (Gudhjem), 254
Gallerie Hvide Hus (Saltuna), 251
Gallerie Kaffslottet (Gudhjem), 254
Galleri Elise Toft (Kolding), 304
Galleri Pagter (Kolding), 304
Galleri Torso (Odense), 272
Gamle By (Old Town; Århus), 364
Gamle Rådhus (Old Town Hall; Ebeltoft), 376
Gamle Rådhus (Town Hall Museum; Ribe), 322
Gamle Ry (Old Ry), 351
Gamle Slot (Liselund), 234
Gamle Stan (Old Town)
    Koge, 208–209
    Ribe, 321
    Tåsinge, 288
Gammel Skagen, 403
Gammel Strand (Copenhagen), 144
Gammel Torv (Ringsted), 220
Gardehussar Regiment, 223
Gåsetårnet (Vordingborg), 227–228
Gasoline, 37
Gaveboden (Tonder), 313
Gavlhuset (Aalborg), 389
Gavno Slot & Park (near Næstved), 227
Gays and lesbians
    Århus, 374
    Copenhagen, 161–162
    information and resources, 43–44
Gefion Springvandet (Gefion Fountain; Copenhagen), 128
Gellerupscenen (Århus), 374
Geografsisk Have og Rosehave (Geographical Garden; Kolding), 302
Georg Jensen
    Århus, 367
    Copenhagen, 155
    Ronne, 243
Georg Jensen Damask (Copenhagen), 152
Gilleleje, 189–193
Gilleleje Harbor, 189–190
Gilleleje Museum, 190, 191
Gimle Musikcafe (Roskilde), 205

Gisselfeld Slot (Haslev), 227
Glasblæseriet (Svendborg), 282
Glasgallerjet (Roskilde), 202
Glasmuseet Ebeltoft (Ebeltoft Glass Museum), 376
Glaspusteriet (Aalborg), 389
Glass objects and crystal, 7
    Århus, 367
    Copenhagen, 154
    Ebeltoft, 376
    Glasmuseet Ebeltoft (Ebeltoft Glass Museum), 376
    Gudhjem, 254
    Roskilde, 202
    Skagen, 405
    Svendborg, 282
Global Refund, 150
Gold. See also Jewelry
Golf, 8, 50
Gråbrodretorv (Copenhagen)
    restaurants, 113–114
    shopping, 150
Grauballe Man, 364
Great Belt Bridge, 215
Great Belt Exhibition Center, 260
Grejsdalen, 339
Gribskov, 172
Gronjægers Hoj (near Æbelnæs), 235–236
Gudenå, 352
Gudhjem, 253–256
Gudhjem Museum, 254
Gudhjem Turistbureau, 253
Guildsmed Carl, Slagelse, 220
Guildsmed Carl Jensens (Slagelse), 220
Guldhuset (Ronne), 243
Guldsmeden Ejvind Sorensen (Koge), 211
Gyngen (Århus), 374

H aderslev, 307–310
Haderslev Domkirke, 308–309
Haderslev Fjord, 307
Haderslev Museum, 309
Hagge's Musik Pub (Tonder), 315
Hamlet (Shakespeare), 182–183
Hammeren, 258
Hammerfyr (Hammeren), 258
Hammerichs Hus (Æroskobing), 296
Hammershus Fortress, 259

Hang gliding, 51
Hannes Hus (Fano), 332
Hans Hansens Gård (Keldby), 232
Hans Tausen's House (Ribe), 322
Hartmann's Selected Estate Silver & Jewelry (Copenhagen), 155
Hasle, 240, 259
Havnen (Hornbæk Harbor), 187
H. C. Andersens Barndomshjem (H. C. Andersen's Childhood Home; Odense), 269
H. C. Andersens Hus (H. C. Andersens Museum; Odense), 269–270
Health concerns, 40–42
Health insurance, 41, 409
Helligåndshuset (Næstved), 224
Helligåndskirken (Church of the Holy Ghost; Copenhagen), 143
Helligåndsklostret (Monastery of the Holy Ghost; Aalborg), 386
Helligdoms Klipperne, 256
Helsingor, 3, 180–186
Helsingor Bymuseet, 182
Herlufsholm, 226
Herlufsholm Academy, 226
Hillerod, 172–177
Himmelbjerget, 351
Himmelbjerget Tower, 351
Hingelberg (Århus), 367
Hirschsprung Collection (Den Hirschsprungske Samling; Copenhagen), 132
Historical and Cultural Museum (Kolding), 303
History of Denmark, 11–24
  books about, 26
  postwar, 23–24
  prehistory and the Romans, 13–14
  Scandinavian union, 17–18
  16th century, 18–19
  19th century and the Napoleonic Wars, 20–21
  12th-14th centuries, 15–17
  Vikings, 14–15
  wars with Sweden, 19–20
  World War I and economic chaos, 21–22
  World War II and Nazi occupation, 22–23

Hitler, Adolf, 129
Hjelm's Bolighus (Koge), 211
Hjortespring Boat (Copenhagen), 133
Hjorth's Fabrik (Bornholm Ceramic Museum; Ronne), 242
Hojbro Plads (Copenhagen), 144
Hojerup Kirke (Store Heddinge), 214
Holiday Care Service, 43
Holiday homes, 54
Holidays, 409
Holmens Kirke (Copenhagen), 138
Holy Ghost, Church of the, 143
Home exchanges, 55
Home furnishings, Copenhagen, 154–155
Home Link, 55
Home stays, 54
Hornbæk, 186–189
Hornbæk Beach, 187
Hornbæk Bodega, 189
Hornbæk Plantage, 187
Horseback riding
  Mon, 235
  Romo, 318
Horse-drawn carriage rides, Ribe, 325
Hotel Booking Service (Copenhagen), 77
Hotel Postgården (Mariager), 384
Hotels. See Accommodations
The House (Copenhagen), 152
HovedBanegården (Central Railway Station; Copenhagen), 70
Hugos Vinkælder (Koge), 213
Humlebæk, 166–167
Huset (Haderslev), 310
Hvide Sande, 348
Hvids Vinstue (Copenhagen), 161

IAMAT (International Association for Medical Assistance to Travelers), 41
Icelandair, 32
Ida Rostgård (Nyborg), 263
Illum (Copenhagen), 153
Illums Bolighus (Copenhagen), 154
Ilsted Bech (Ronne), 243

Indre By (Old Town; Copenhagen), 72
  sights and attractions, 134–135
  walking tour, 143–144
Industriens Hus (Copenhagen), 74
Inns, 54
Inspiration (Ronne), 243
Inspiration (Silkeborg), 357
Inspiration Buus (Århus), 367
Inspiration Zinch (Odense), 272
Inspiration Zinck (Svendborg), 282
Institute of International Education (IIE), 49–50
Insurance, 409–410
Interhostel, 49
International Association for Medical Assistance to Travelers (IAMAT), 41
The International Ecotourism Society (TIES), 45
International Gay and Lesbian Travel Association (IGLTA), 44
Internet access, 52
Intervac USA, 55
InTouch USA, 51
INTRAV, 44
The Invented City, 55
IPass network, 52
Ireland
  embassy, 409
  passports, 411
Iron Age woman (Vejle), 338
Itineraries, suggested, 58–68

Jailhouse Copenhagen, 162
Jane Heinemann (Fano), 333
Japanese garden, Birkegårdens Haver, 223
Jelling, 341–343
Jelling Kirke, 342
Jens Bangs Stenhus (Jens Bang's Stone House; Aalborg), 387
Jeppe (Roskilde), 202
Jewelry
  Aalborg, 389
  Copenhagen, 155
  Koge, 211
  Ronne, 243
  Skagen, 405
Jews, Danish, 129
  Teka Bashofar Gadol (Gilleleje), 190

J.F. Willumsen's Museum (Hillerod), 176–177
Jogging, Copenhagen, 150
John Bull Pub (Frederikshavn), 402
Jons Kapel (near Hammershus), 259
Jorgen L. Dalgaard (Copenhagen), 152
Jorgen Müller (Koge), 210
J.S. Antiques (Gilleleje), 192
July 4th (Rebild), 31
Jurve, 318
Jutland, brief description of, 56
Jutland Car Museum (Jysk Automobilmuseum; Gjern), 356
Jutland Manor House Museum (near Århus), 366
Jylland, Fregatten (Ebeltoft), 376
Jysk Automobilmuseum (Jutland Car Museum; Gjern), 356

K ære Ven (Copenhagen), 155
Kærgaarden (Helsingor), 186
Karmeliterklostret Monastery (Helsingor), 184
Karrebæk Fjord, 223
Kastellet (Copenhagen), 128–129
Kastrup Airport (Copenhagen), 70
Keldby, 232
Keldby Kirke, 232
Keramikkens Hus (Ringkobing), 347
Kids' Shop (Ronne), 243
Kierkegaard, Soren, 135
  grave of (Copenhagen), 139–140
  Soren Kierkegaard Samlingen (Copenhagen), 140
  Stone (Gilleleje), 190
Kilden Park (Aalborg), 396
Kildeskovshallen (Copenhagen), 150
Kirkestræde (Koge), 209
Klassik Moderne Mobelkunst (Copenhagen), 152
Klinteskoven (Mon), 235
Klintholm Havn, 235
Klints Guld & Solv (Ringsted), 217
KLM, 32

Klods Hans (Odense), 272
Klokketårnet (Faaborg), 289
Knights Hall (Copenhagen), 130
Kobenhavns Bymuseet (Copenhagen), 140
Kobenhavns Cyker (Copenhagen), 149
Kobenhavns Cyklebors (Copenhagen), 75
Kobmandshandel (Koge), 211
Koge, 206–215
Koge Bay, 208
Koge Bugt Kulturhus (Koge), 213–214
Koge Museum, 209–210
Koge Rådhus (Koge), 209
Koge Sydstrand, 209
Kolding, 301–307
Kolding Antiques & Stall Market, 304
Kolding Fjord, 302
Koldinghus Slot (Kolding), 302–303
Kolding Marina, 302
Kolding Storcenter, 304
Kommandorgården (Romo), 318
Kongelige Bibliotek (Royal Library; Copenhagen), 136–137
Kongelige Stalde & Kareter (Copenhagen), 132
Kongens Have (Copenhagen), 130
Kongens Nytorv (Copenhagen), 143
  accommodations near, 77–83
  restaurants near, 95, 98–106
  walking tour, 144, 146–148
Kong Valdemar Pub (Ringsted), 219
Koresand, 330
Korsbrodregården (Nyborg), 263
Kristkirken (Tonder), 312
Kronborg Slot ("Hamlet's Castle;" Helsingor), 182–183
Krudttårnet (Frederikshavn), 399
Krybben (Koge), 210
Kunsthallen Brandts (Odense), 266

Kunstindustrimuseet (Museum of Decorative and Applied Art; Copenhagen), 129–130
Kunstmuseet Koge Skitsesambling, 210

L adbyskibet (Ladby), 271–272
Læderstræde (Copenhagen), 150
La Fontaine (Copenhagen), 160
La Fontaine (Koge), 213
Landborgården Pub (Æroskobing), 298
Landporten (Nyborg), 263
Landsbrugs Museum (Bornholm Agricultural Museum; Gudhjem), 254
Landsforeningen for Bosser og Lesbiske (LBL), 43
Landsforeningen for Landboturisme, 54
Langebro (Copenhagen), restaurant, 117
Lange Handicrafts (Aalborg), 389
Language, 410
Lavendelstræde (Copenhagen), 143
Learning vacations, 49–50
Ledreborg Park Og Slot (Lejre), 200
Legoland (Billund), 344
Lejre Research Center, 200–201
Library Bar (Copenhagen), 160–161
Lille Tårn (Frederikso), 257
Lilliendal Plantecenter (Ronne), 243
Lindholm Hoje Museet, 387–388
Liselund, 233–234
The Little Mermaid (Den Lille Havfrue; Copenhagen), 128, 148, 149, 210
Logum Kloster (Logum Abbey), 316
Longso, Lake, 354
Loppen (Copenhagen), 159
Lost and found, 410
Louisiana Museum of Modern Art (Humlebæk), 166–167
Loveapoteket (Næstved), 224
Lovparken (Koge), 209

Lufthansa, 32
Lurblæserne (Copenhagen), 124
Lysberg, Hansen & Therp (Copenhagen), 154

Madsebakke, 258
Mads Lerches Gård (Mads Lerches House; Nyborg), 262
Mads Norgaard (Copenhagen), 153
Magasin
    Aalborg, 389
    Copenhagen, 153
Magasin du Nord (Århus), 367
Magstræde (Copenhagen), 144
Mail, 410
Make Up Diskotek (Romo), 320
Mando, 329–330
Mandohuset (Mando), 329
Mando Kirke, 329
Maps, 29
Maren Minors Minde (Marstal), 298
Margrethe, Queen, birthday of (Copenhagen), 141
Maria Feodorovna, Czarina, 198
Mariager, 379–384
Mariager Fjord, 380
Mariager-Handest Veteranjernbane, 380
Mariager Museum, 381–382
Marienlyst Slot, 183–184
Maritime Museum of Troense (Sofartssamlingerne I Troense; Tåsinge), 286
Marselisborg Slot (near Århus), 365
Marstal, 293, 298–300
Marstal Kirke, 298–299
Medical insurance, 41, 409
Medicinsk-Historisk Museet (Medical History Museum; Copenhagen), 148
MedjetAssist, 41
The Men's Bar (Copenhagen), 162
Michael Andersen (Ronne), 243
Michael og Anna Ancher Hus (Skagen), 404
Midsummer's Night, 31
Moesgård Museum (Århus), 364

Mogeltonder, 315
Mogeltonder Kirke, 315
Mojo Blues Bar (Copenhagen), 160
Molle Park (Aalborg), 396
Molleporten (Stege), 230
MOMS (VAT), recovering, 150, 411–412
Mon, 228–236
Monastery of the Holy Ghost (Helligåndsklostret; Aalborg), 386
Money and costs, 38–40
Mon Museum (Stege), 230
Mons Klint, 228, 234–235
Mosso, 352
MossRehab, 43
Mr. Lundgaard (Ribe), 325
Munkebjerg, 339
Munthe plus Simonsen (Copenhagen), 153
Museet for Samtidskunst (Museum of Contemporary Art; Roskilde), 199–200
Museum of Contemporary Art (Museet for Samtidskunst; Roskilde), 199–200
Museum of Danish Resistance, 1940-45 (Frihedsmuseet; Copenhagen), 129
Museum of Decorative and Applied Art (Kunstindustrimuseet; Copenhagen), 129–130
Museum of Modern and Contemporary Art (Nordjyllands Kunstmuseet; Aalborg), 387
Museum of Modern Art (Trapholt Museum for Moderne Kunst; Kolding), 303–304
Museum of National History (Det Nationalhistoriske Museum; Frederiksborg), 173
Museum of Photographic Art (Odense), 266
Museum of the Viking Age and the Middle Ages in Ribe (Ribe Vikinger), 324
The Museums at Gammel Estrup (near Århus), 366
Museumstårnet & H. J. Wegner udstilling (Tower Museum and H. J. Wegner Exhibit; Tonder), 312
Music, 27
Musikhuset Århus, 374
Musik Keller (Aalborg), 396
Musik Theatret Vejle, 341

Naestved, 3
Næstved, 223–228
Næstved Museum, 224
Næstved Stor-Center, 225
Nakkehoved Ostre Fyr (Gilleleje), 191
Nanas Stue (Fano), 335
NASA (Copenhagen), 157
Nationalmuseet (National Museum; Copenhagen), 133
National Registration Center for Study Abroad (NRCSA), 50
Naturama (Svendborg), 280
Naturcentret Tonnisgård (Romo), 318
Naturhistorisk Museum (Århus), 362–363
Newspapers and magazines, 410
New Zealand
    customs regulations, 30
    passports, 411
Nexo, 246–251
Nexo, Martin Andersen, 247–248
Nexo-Dueodde Turistbureau, 247
Nexo Museum, 247–248
Nielsen, Carl
    Carl Nielsens Barndomshjem (Carl Nielsen's Childhood Home; near Odense), 270
    Museet (Odense), 268
Nikolaj Kirke (Copenhagen), 143
Nordby, 330
Norde Skanse (Frederikshavn), 398
Nordjyllands Kunstmuseet (Museum of Modern and Contemporary Art; Aalborg), 387
Nordsomuseet (Skagen), 404
Normann Copenhagen (Copenhagen), 152
Norrebro (Copenhagen), 72–73
    restaurants, 115–116
Norremark Cykelforretning (Æro), 294
North Jutland, 379–407
North Zealand, 170–205
Norwegian Coastal Voyage Inc., 35
Novasol AS, 54
Now, Voyager, 44

Nyborg, 260–265
Nyborg Slot (Nyborg Castle), 262–263
Nyborg Voldspil, 261
Ny Carlsberg Glyptotek (Copenhagen), 121, 124
Nye Bornholmerure (Ronne), 243
Nyhavn 17 (Copenhagen), 161
Nyhavn (Copenhagen), 146, 158
  accommodations near, 77–83
  restaurants near, 95, 98–106
Nyhavn/Kongens Nytorv (Copenhagen), brief description of, 71–72
Nylars, 246
Nylarskirke (Nylars), 246
Nyman & Schultz (Copenhagen), 75
Nyord, 232
Nytorv (Copenhagen), 143

O ccupation Museum (Besættelsesmuseet; Århus), 363–364
Odense, 7, 265–278
  accommodations, 272–275
  getting around, 266
  restaurants, 275–278
  shopping, 272
  sights and attractions, 266–272
  traveling to, 265–266
  visitor information, 266
Odense Symphony Orchestra, 278
The Old Merchant's House (Den Gamle Gaard; Faaborg), 288
Old Ry (Gamle Ry), 351
Old Town (Indre By; Copenhagen), 72
  sights and attractions, 134–135
  walking tour, 143–144
Old Town Hall (Det Gamle Rådhus; Ebeltoft), 376
Olsemagle Revle (Koge), 209
Olsker, 258
Olskirke, 258
O'Malley's Irish Pub (Ronne), 245
Om Kloster (Ry), 351–352
Orangi (Svendborg), 285
Oresund Fixed Link, 215

Orlogsmuseet (Royal Naval Museum; Copenhagen), 137
Osterlars, 253
Osterlarskirke, 253
Overdammens Idebutik (Ribe), 325

P alm House (Copenhagen), 131
Pan Club (Århus), 374
Pan Club (Copenhagen), 162
Pantomime Theater (Copenhagen), 156
Paragliding, 51
Park City (Copenhagen), 74
Passports, 410–411
Paustian (Copenhagen), 155
Pedersker, 247
Pernille Bülow Glas (Ronne), 243
Petrol, 37
Police, 411
Politikens Boghallen (Copenhagen), 75
Porcelain, Copenhagen, 154
Pornography, Copenhagen, 162–163
Pottery and ceramics
  Ehlers-samlingen (Ehlers Collections; Haderslev), 308
  Frederikshavn, 399
  Hjorth's Fabrik (Bornholm Ceramic Museum; Ronne), 242
  Mon, 228
  Ringkobing, 347
  Ronne, 243
  Silkeborg Museum, 356
  Skagen, 405
  Trapholt Museum for Moderne Kunst (Museum of Modern Art; Kolding), 304
Præstekilde Kro & Hotel (Stege), 231
Prinsen Diskotek (Vordingborg), 228
Pyramiden (Gilleleje), 191

R ADAR (Royal Association for Disability and Rehabilitation), 43
Rådhus (Town Hall), Copenhagen, 124
Rådhuset (Town Hall), Århus, 364–365

Rådhus Kroenm (Næstved), 226
Rådhuspladsen (Copenhagen), accommodations near, 83–89
Rådhuspladsen (Town Hall Square; Copenhagen), 143
Rådjerg Mile (Skagen), 403
Railway Museum (Danmarks Jernbanemuseum; Odense), 268
Rebild National Park, 388
Red Barone (Ronne), 245
Rendez-Vous (Aalborg), 396
Rent-A-Horse (Mons Klint), 235
Restaurants, 6, 46. See also Restaurants Index
Ribe, 3, 7, 321–330
Ribe Domkirke, 322
Ribe Kunstmuseet (Ribe Art Museum), 323
Ribe Legetojsmuseum (Toy Museum; Ribe), 323–324
Ribe's Broderi & Garn, 325
Ribe VikingeCenter, 324
Ribe Vikinger (Museum of the Viking Age and the Middle Ages in Ribe), 324
Riis, Jacob A., 321, 322
Ringkobing, 345–350
Ringkobing Fjord, 345–346, 348–350
Ringkobing Harbor, 346
Ringkobing Museum Osterport, 347
Ringsted, 215–219
Ringsted Centret, 217
Ringsted Museum, 217
Rise Kirke (Store Rise), 293–294
Risemark Strand, 294
Ritz Rock Café (Koge), 213
Riverboat Jazz Festival (Silkeborg), 359
RoadPost, 51
The Rock (Copenhagen), 157
Rokkjoer (Koge), 210
Romo, 317–320
Romo Kirke, 318
Romo Ranch, 318
Ronne, 239–247
Rosenborg Slot (Rosenborg Castle; Copenhagen), 130–131
Rosendahl (Copenhagen), 152–153
Rosengårdcentret (Odense), 272

Rosenholm Slot (Rosenholm Castle; near Århus), 366
Rosenthal Studio-Haus (Copenhagen), 154
Roskilde, 195–205
Roskilde Badet, 202
Roskilde Cathedral, 195
Roskilde Domkirke, 196–199
Roskilde Festival, 31, 196
Roskilde Fjord, 201
Roskilde Museum, 199
Round Tower (Rundetårn; Copenhagen), 134–135
Royal Association for Disability and Rehabilitation (RADAR), 43
Royal Cast Collection (Den Kongelige Afstobningssamling; Copenhagen), 136
Royal Collection of Coins and Medals (Copenhagen), 133
Royal Copenhagen Porcelain
    Copenhagen, 154
    Slagelse, 220
Royal Danish Ballet (Copenhagen), 157
Royal Danish Opera (Copenhagen), 157
Royal Library (Kongelige Bibliotek; Copenhagen), 136–137
Royal Museum of Fine Arts (Statens Museum for Kunst; Copenhagen), 131
Royal Naval Museum (Orlogsmuseet; Copenhagen), 137
Royal Theater (Det Kongelige Teater; Copenhagen), 146, 157
Ruby (Copenhagen), 161
Rudolph Tegnersmuseum (Gilleleje), 191–192
Ruesch International, 40
Rundetårn (Round Tower; Copenhagen), 134–135
Rungstedlund, 167–169
Rust (Copenhagen), 158
Ry, 350–354
Ryk Ind (Ribe), 325
Rytterknægten, 246

S afety, 42, 411
Sailing, 51
Salling (Århus), 367
Salling (Aalborg), 389
Sandvig, 257–258
Skt. Annæ Plads (Copenhagen), 146

Skt. Bendts Kirke (Ringsted), 216–217
Skt. Catharine Kirke (Ribe), 322, 324
Skt. Ibs Kirke (Roskilde), 200
Skt. Jorgensbjerg Kirke (Roskilde), 200
Skt. Jorgens Kirke (Svendborg), 280
Skt. Knuds Domkirke (Odense), 270
Skt. Mariæ Kirke (Helsingor), 184
Skt. Mikkels Kirke (Slagelse), 220
Skt. Mortens Kirke (Næstved), 224
Sankt Nicolai Kirke
    Koge, 209
    Vejle, 338
Skt. Nicolai Kirke (Svendborg), 280
Skt. Olai Kirke (Helsingor), 184
Skt. Peder Kirke (Næstved), 225
Skt. Peders Kirke (Slagelse), 220
Skt. Sorens Kirke (Ry), 351
Sara Sko (Ribe), 325
SAS (Scandinavian Airlines Systems), 32, 36
SATH (Society for Accessible Travel and Hospitality), 43
ScanAm World Tours, 48
Scandinavian Tourist Board, 29
Scanrail Pass, 34
Scantours Inc., 48
Schackenborg Slot (Mogeltonder), 315
Seasons, 30
Self-drive tours, 48
Selso Slot, 176
Senior travel, 44
Servas, 54–55
Seven Oaks (Vejle), 341
Ships and ferries to Denmark, 35
Shopping
    best buys, 6–7
    shipping and recovering VAT (MOMS), 150
Silderogerierne I Hasle, 240
Silkeborg, 354–360
Silkeborg Kunstmuseum (Silkeborg Museum of Art), 355–356
Silkeborg Museum, 356

Silver objects, 7, 389. *See also* Jewelry
    Copenhagen, 155
Singles Travel International, 45
Single travelers, 45
Skagen, 402–407
Skagen By- & Egnsmuseum (Skagen Open-Air Museum), 405
Skagen Glasværksted, 405
Skagen Havn, 403
Skagen Potteri, 405
Skagens Museum, 405
Skamilingsbanken, 307
Skibshallen (Gilleleje), 191
Skovdalen (Aalborg), 396
Slagelse, 219–223
Slagelse Museum, 220
Slagterbutikken O. Lunds (Roskilde), 202
SlotsArkaderne (Hillerod), 174
Slotsgade (Mogelteonder), 315
Slots Kroen (Vordingborg), 228
Slutterigade (Copenhagen), 143
Smoking, 411
Smykkekunstner (Skagen), 405
Smykker (Odense), 272
Snaregade (Copenhagen), 144
Sneaky Fox (Copenhagen), 153
Snogebæk, 247, 249, 250–251
Soby, 293
Soby Cykelforretning (Æro), 294
Sofartssamlingerne I Troense (Maritime Museum of Troense; Tåsinge), 286
Sol og Strand, 54
Sonderho, 330
Sonderho Day (Fano), 331
Sonderho Kirke (Fano), 332
Sonderho Molle (Fano), 332
Sonderjyllands Kunstmuseum (Tonder), 312
Soren Kierkegaard Samlingen (Copenhagen), 140
Soren Kierkegaard Stone (Gilleleje), 190
South Jutland, 301–335
South Zealand, 206–228
Specialkobmanden (Copenhagen), 151

426 Statens Museum for Kunst (Royal Museum of Fine Arts; Copenhagen), 131
Stege (Mon), 230
Stege Kirke (Mon), 230
Stena Line, 35
Stenbohus Pub & Bar (Ribe), 328
Steno Museet (Århus), 362
Stentebjerg (Haderslev), 309
Step Inn (Næstved), 226
Stevns Klint, 214
Stiftskirke Herlufsholm (Herlufsholm), 226–227
St. Jorgensbjerg quarter (Roskilde), 200
St. Nicolai Church (Ronne), 240
Stolen (Haderslev), 309
Storebælt (Great Belt), 260
Store Dyrehave, 172
Store Heddinge, 214
Store Tårn (Christianso), 257
Storkesoen, 325
Stroby Ladeplads (Koge), 209
Stroget (Copenhagen), 71, 125, 143, 150
Sundby Swimming Pool (Copenhagen), 150
Superbowl (Odense), 266
Surfudlejning (Hornbæk), 187
Suså Kanoudlejning (Næstved), 224
Sustainable tourism, 45–48
Svalegangen (Århus), 374
Svaneke, 251–253
Svaneke Antikvitetshandel (Bornholm), 251
Svaneke Kirke, 251
Svendborg, 3, 279–287
Sweater House (Hillerod), 175
Swimming
Copenhagen, 150
Roskilde, 202
Sydbornholms Turistbureau, 246
Sylvest Stentoj (Hornbæk), 187

Tamalat Antik (Koge), 210
Tåsinge, 285
Tåsinge Skipperhjem og Folkemindesamling (Tåsinge Museum), 286
Taxes, 411
Teatermuseet (Copenhagen), 137–138

Teka Bashofar Gadol (Gilleleje), 190
Telephones, 51
Thorups Kælder (Århus), 374
Thorvaldsens Museum (Copenhagen), 134
Thuro, 285
Thuro Kirke, 285
Tibirke Kirke (Tisvildeleje), 194
TIES (The International Ecotourism Society), 45
Tilsandede Kirke (Skagen), 403–404
The Time Collection (Odense), 266
Time zone, 412
Tingstedet, 294
Tipperne Nature Reserve, 349–350
Tipping, 412
Tisvilde Hegn, 193
Tisvilde Hegn (Tisvildeleje), 194
Tisvildeleje, 193–195
Tisvilde Loppemarked (Tisvildeleje), 194
Tivoli-Friheden (near Århus), 375
Tivoli Gardens (Copenhagen), 144
accommodations near, 83–89
nightlife, 156
restaurants, 118–119
sights and attractions in and around, 121, 124
special and free events, 141
Tivoli Glassalen (Copenhagen), 156
Tivoliland (Aalborg), 388–389
Tivolis Koncertsal (Copenhagen), 156
T-Mobile Hotspot, 52
Toilets, 412
Tojhusmuseet (Royal Arsenal Museum), 134
Toldboden (Koge), 213
Toldbohus (Marstal), 300
Tollund Man, 356
Tonder, 311–316
Tonder Castle, 312
Tonder Festivalen, 311
Torvehallerne (Vejle), 341
Torvet (Koge), 210
Tourist offices, 29
Tours, special-interest, 48–50

Tower Museum and H. J. Wegner Exhibit (Museumstårnet & H. J. Wegner udstilling; Tonder), 312
Town Hall Museum (Det Gamle Rådhus; Ribe), 322
Toy Museum (Ribe Legetojsmuseum; Ribe), 323–324
Train (Århus), 374
The Train (Faaborg), 292
Train travel
to Denmark, 33–35
within Denmark, 36
Tranderup Kirke (Æro), 294
Transportation, green-friendly, 46
Transportation around Denmark, 36–37
Trapholt Museum for Moderne Kunst (Museum of Modern Art; Kolding), 303–304
Travel Buddies Singles Travel Club, 45
TravelChums, 45
Traveler's checks, 39
Travel Health Online, 41
Traveling to Denmark, 32–35
Travel insurance, 409–410
Tre Kroner (Faaborg), 292
Trelleborg, 221–222
Trelleborg Allé, 221–222
Trip cancellation insurance, 410
Troense, 285
Trolleskoe, 258
Tycho Brahe Planetarium (Copenhagen), 142

Ulla Moller (Vejle), 339
Ulvshale, 231–232
Underhuset Bar (Næstved), 226
Underhuset Pub (Silkeborg), 360
United Kingdom
adventure travel operators, 48
customs regulations, 30
for disabled travelers, 43
embassy, 409
health insurance, 409
passports, 411
rail passes for British travelers, 35
sustainable tourism, 47
traveling to Denmark from, 32, 35
travel insurance, 410
visitor information in, 29

United States
    adventure travel
      operators, 48
    customs regulations, 30
    embassy, 409
    passports, 410–411
    traveling to Denmark
      from, 32–33
    visitor information in, 29

Værelsænvisningen
    (Copenhagen), 77
**Valdemars Slot (Valdemar's
    Palace; Tåsinge), 286–287**
**Valdemars Slotskirke (Valde-
    mar's Castle Church;
    Tåsinge), 287**
Vallo, 214
Vallo Slot, 214
**VAT (value-added tax), 150,
    411–412**
Vega (Copenhagen), 158–159
Vejle, 336–341
Vejle Kunstmuseum, 338–339
Vejle Museum, 339
Vesterbro (Copenhagen), 72
    restaurants, 116–117
**Vestergårdens Antik
    (Fano), 332**
**Vesterstrand (Æroskobing),
    295**
Vestkyst Akvariet, 348–349
**Vestsjællands Center
    (Slagelse), 220**
**Viebæltegård (Svendborg),
    280, 282**
**Vigen Strandpark (Roskilde),
    202**
**Vikingbus (Copenhagen),
    148**
Vikingemuseet (Århus), 365
**Vikingeskibshallen (Viking
    Ship Museum; Roskilde),
    196, 199**
**Vikingespil (Frederikssund),
    173**
**Viking Festival (Freder-
    ikssund), 31**
**Viking Festival (Freder-
    ikssund Vikingespil; Hille-
    rod), 173**
Vikings, 4–5
    art, 24
    history of, 14–15
    Jelling, 341, 342
    Ladbyskibet (Ladby),
      271–272
    Norresundby, 387
    Ribe, 324

Roskilde, 196
Trelleborg, 221–222
Vikingemuseet (Århus),
    365
**Vindmolleparken (Windmill
    Park; Ebeltoft), 376**
Visitor information, 29
Visit Scandinavia Pass, 36
Vodrup, 294
Vodrup Klint, 294
**Voergård Slot (Dronnin-
    glund), 388**
**Volden 4 Kunsthåndværk
    (Århus), 367**
Volunteer travel, 47–48
Von Frue Kirke (Århus), 365
Vordingborg, 227
**Vor Frelsers Kirken (Copen-
    hagen), 138–139**
Vor Frue Kirke
    Copenhagen (Copenhagen
      Cathedral), 135
    Nyborg, 263
    Svendborg, 282

Walking, 51
Water, drinking, 412
Wayport, 52
Websites, 29
    traveler's toolbox, 52
Western Union, 410
**White chalk cliffs. See Chalk
    cliffs**
Wi-Fi access, 52
**Willumsen, J. F., Museum
    (Hillerod), 176–177**
**Willy Nilly (Vordingborg),
    228**
**Windmill Park (Vind-
    molleparken; Ebeltoft), 376**
Windsurfing, 209
    Ringkobing Fjord, 349
    Romo, 318
**Wonderful Copenhagen
    Tourist Information &
    Booking Center, 53**
**World Clock (Copenhagen),
    124**
**World War II and Nazi occu-
    pation, 22–23**
    Besættelsesmuseet (Occu-
      pation Museum;
      Århus), 363
    Forsvarsmuseet (Ronne),
      242
    Frihedsmuseet (Museum of
      Danish Resistance, 1940-
      45; Copenhagen), 129

Ympelese (Mon), 230

Zealand, brief description
    of, 56
**Zoologisk Have (Copenhagen
    Zoo), 142**

ACCOMMODATIONS

**Absalon Hotel og Absalon
    Annex (Copenhagen), 91**
Alexandra (Copenhagen), 83
Ascot Hotel (Copenhagen), 87
**Avenue Hotel (Copenha-
    gen), 95**
**AXEL Hotel Guldsmeden
    (Copenhagen), 90**
**Bertram Hotel Guldsmeden
    (Copenhagen), 83–84**
**Best Western Hotel Knudsens
    Gaard (Odense), 273**
**Best Western Ritz Hotel
    (Århus), 369–370**
**Best Western Torvehallerne
    (Vejle), 339–340**
Bowler Inn (Tonder), 313
**Carlton Hotel Guldsmeden
    (Copenhagen), 87–88**
**Centralhotellet Koge
    (Koge), 211**
Chagall (Aalborg), 391
**Christianso Gæstgiveriet,
    257**
**City Hotel Nebo (Copenha-
    gen), 89**
City Hotel Odense, 273–274
**Clarion Collection Hotel Nep-
    tun (Copenhagen), 80**
**Clarion Collection Mayfair
    (Copenhagen), 90–91**
**Clarion Hotel Plaza (Odense),
    272**
Color Hotel Skagen, 405–406
**Comfort Hotel Atlantic
    (Århus), 370**
**Comfort Hotel Esplanaden
    (Copenhagen), 81–82**
**Comfort Windsor Hotel
    (Odense), 274–275**
Comwell Kolding, 304–305
**Copenhagen Admiral
    Hotel, 82**
Copenhagen Crown, 89
**Copenhagen Island Hotel,
    93–94**
Copenhagen Plaza, 84
Copenhagen Strand, 82

428

CPH Living (Copenhagen), 94
Danhostel Copenhagen City, 94–95
Danhostel Ribe, 325
Danland RIM & Feriecenter (Romo), 319–320
Den Gamle Arrest (Ribe), 326
DGI-byen's Hotel (Copenhagen), 88, 90
Dragor Badehotel, 164, 166
Dueodde Badehotel, 249
Endruplund Country House (Fredensborg), 179
Ewaldsgaardeny (Hornbæk), 187–188
Faaborg Fjord, 289
Falsled Kro (Faaborg), 289–290
Finns Hotel Pension (Skagen), 406
First Hotel Grand (Odense), 274
First Hotel Vesterbro (Copenhagen), 84
First Slotshotel Aalborg, 389–390
Fredensborg Store Kro, 179
Frederikshavn Somandshjem & Hotel, 400
Front Hotel Copenhagen, 80
Gamle Rye Kro (Ry), 352
Gershoj Kro, 203
Gl. Skovridergaard (Silkeborg), 357
Golden Tulip Vejle, 340
Grand Hotel (Copenhagen), 84–85
Gudhjem Hotel & Feriepark, 254–255
Havreholm Slot (Hornbæk), 188
Helnan Phonix Hotel (Aalborg), 390
Herman Bang Hotel (Frederikshavn), 401
Hostrups Hotel (Tonder), 313–314
Hotel Æro (Svendborg), 282
Hotel Ærohus (Æroskobing), 296–297
Hotel Ærø Strand (Marstal), 299–300
Hotel Ansgar (Copenhagen), 91
Hotel Ansgar (Odense), 274
Hotel Balka Strand (Nexo), 248
Hotel Bornholm (Dueodde), 249–250

Hotel Byparken (Kolding), 305
Hotel Christiansminde (Svendborg), 282–283
Hotel Dagmar (Ribe), 326
Hotel d'Angleterre (Copenhagen), 77, 80, 90
Hotel Dania (Silkeborg), 357
Hotel Domir/Hotel Ydes (Odense), 275
Hotel Ebeltoft Strand (Ebeltoft), 377
Hotel Ellens Cabaret (Stege), 231
Hotel Elmehoj (Elmelunde), 233
Hotel Fano Badeland, 333
Hotel Fjordgården (Ringkobing), 347
Hotel Fox (Copenhagen), 88, 90
Hotel Frederik den II (Slagelse), 221
Hotel Fru Mathies (Ribe), 326
Hotel Garni (Svendborg), 283
Hotel Griffen, 243
Hotel Guldsmeden (Århus), 370
Hotel Hamlet (Helsingor), 185
Hotel Harmonien (Haderslev), 309
Hotel Hesselet (Nyborg), 263–264
Hotel Hillerod, 175
Hotel Himmelbjerget (Ry), 352
Hotel Hvide Hus (Aalborg), 390
Hotel Hvide Hus (Koge), 211
Hotel Jorgensen (Copenhagen), 93
Hotel Kirstine (Næstved), 225
Hotel La Tour (Århus), 370
Hotel Legoland (Billund), 344–345
Hotel Lisboa (Frederikshavn), 400–401
Hotel Mariehonen (Frederikshavn), 401–402
Hotel Marienlyst (Helsingor), 185
Hotel Marselis (Århus), 367–368
Hotel Marstal, 300
Hotel Mercur (Århus), 370–371
Hotel Mosegaard (Faaborg), 290

Hotel Niels Juel (Koge), 211–212
Hotel Norden (Haderslev), 309–310
Hotel Nyborg Strand, 264
Hotel Opera (Copenhagen), 82–83
Hotel Ostersoen (Svaneke), 251–252
Hotel Philip (Århus), 368
Hotel Postgården (Mariager), 382
Hotel Prindsen (Roskilde), 202
Hotel Ringkobing, 347–348
Hotel Royal (Århus), 368
Hotel Ryttergården (Ronne), 244
Hotel Skt. Petri (Copenhagen), 80–81
Hotel Scheelsminde (Aalborg), 391
Hotel Selandia (Copenhagen), 92
Hotel Strand (Gilleleje), 192
Hotel Svendborg, 283
Hotel Tonderhus (Tonder), 314
Hotel 27 (Copenhagen), 88
Hotel Vinhuset (Næstved), 225–226
Hvedholm Slot (Faaborg), 290
Ibsens Hotel (Copenhagen), 90, 92–93
Jantzens Hotel (Gudhjem), 255
Jelling Kro, 343
Kildegaard (Tisvildeleje), 194
Kolding Byferie, 305–306
Kommandorgården (Romo), 320
Kong Arthur (Copenhagen), 89, 90
Kongensbro Kro (Silkeborg), 358
Kong Frederik (Copenhagen), 85
Korinth Kro (Faaborg), 290–291
Liselund Ny Slot, 234
Majorgården (Svendborg), 283
Maritime (Copenhagen), 83
Marriott Copenhagen, 94
Melsted Badehotel (Gudhjem), 255
Missionshotellet Stella Maris (Svendborg), 283–284

Mogenstrup Kro (Næstved), 226

Molskroen (Ebeltoft), 377

Motel Landgangen (Mariager), 382–383

Munkebjerg Hotel (Vejle), 340

Næsbylund Kro (Odense), 275

Norre Vissing Kro (Ry), 352–353

Osted Kro & Hotel, 203–204

Park Hotel (Aalborg), 391

Park Hotel (Frederikshavn), 401

Pension Solgården (Svaneke), 252

Pension Vestergade 44 (Æroskobing), 297

Phoenix Copenhagen (Copenhagen), 81

Præstekilde Kro & Hotel (Stege), 231

Prinsen Hotel (Aalborg), 391–392

Radisson Hotel Fredensborg (Ronne), 244

Radisson SAS H.C. Andersen Hotel (Odense), 272–273

Radisson SAS Hotel (Silkeborg), 357–358

Radisson SAS Jutlandia Hotel (Frederikshavn), 400

Radisson SAS Limfjord Hotel (Aalborg), 390

Radisson SAS Royal (Copenhagen), 85

Radisson SAS Scandinavia Hotel (Copenhagen), 86

Radisson SAS Scandinavia Hotel Århus, 368–369

Ruth's Hotel (Skagen), 406

Ry Park Hotel, 353

Saga Hotel (Copenhagen), 92

Saxildhus Hotel (Kolding), 306

Scandic Copenhagen, 86–87

Scandic Hotel Odense, 273

Scandic Hotel Ringsted, 217–218

Scandic Hotel Roskilde, 203

Scandic Hotel Silkeborg, 358

Scandic Palace Hotel (Copenhagen), 86

Scandic Plaza (Århus), 369

Scandic Stena Hotel Frederikshavn, 400

Schackenborg Slotskro (Tonder), 315–316

71 Nyhavn (Copenhagen), 81

Siemsens Gaard (Svaneke), 252

Skandia Hotel (Helsingor), 185

Skuldelev Kro, 204

Snogebæk Hotelpension, 249

Sonderho Kro (Fano), 333

Sorup Herregård (Ringsted), 218

The Square (Copenhagen), 87

Steensgaard Herregårdspension (Faaborg), 291

Strandhotel Balka Sobad (Nexo), 248

Strandhotellet (Sandvig), 258

Strandhotellet/Strandhuset (Skagen), 406–407

Sverres Small Hotel (Ronne), 244

Svogerslev Kro (Roskilde), 203

Svostrup Kro (Silkeborg), 358–359

Tisvildeleje Strand Hotel, 194–195

Vallo Slotskro (Koge), 212

Villa Provence (Århus), 369

RESTAURANTS

Æroskobing Rogeri, 297

Alberto K. (Copenhagen), 107

Anna Sophie (Fredensborg), 179

Atlas Bar/Restaurant Flyvefisken (Copenhagen), 108

Axelborg Bodega (Copenhagen), 110

Bamboo (Helsingor), 186

Bio-Bistro (Tisvildeleje), 195

Bof & Ost (Copenhagen), 113

Bokulhus, 255–256

Brasserie Le Coq Rouge (Copenhagen), 102

Brasseriet (Gilleleje), 192–193

Café à Porta (Copenhagen), 102

Café Copenhagen (Hillerod), 175

Cafeen Nikolaj (Copenhagen), 144

Café Ketchup (Copenhagen), 119

Café Lumskebugten (Copenhagen), 100, 148

Café Nanas Stue (Fano), 333–334

Café Sorgenfri (Copenhagen), 110

Café Victor (Copenhagen), 102–103

Café Zeze (Copenhagen), 104–105

Cap Horn (Copenhagen), 103

Carlslund (Odense), 277

Central Cafeen (Nyborg), 264–265

Chili (Copenhagen), 110

Copenhagen Corner, 104, 109

Da Oscar (Fredensborg), 179–180

Den Gamle Kro (Odense), 275–276

Den Gamle Vingård (Marstal), 300

Den Grimme Æling (Odense), 277–278

Den Lille Havfrue (Snogebæk), 250–251

De 5 Ståuerna (Ronne), 245

Divan II (Copenhagen), 118–119

Domhus Kælderen (Copenhagen), 111

Duus Vinkjælder (Aalborg), 395

Era Ora (Copenhagen), 95, 98

Færgekroen (Copenhagen), 119

Falsled Kro (Faaborg), 291

Forlaens & Baglaens (Århus), 371

Formel B. (Copenhagen), 117

Fox Kitchen and Bar (Copenhagen), 107

Fyrkroen (Gilleleje), 193

Fyrtojet (Aalborg), 395

Gamle Rye Kro (Ry), 353

Geranium (Copenhagen), 103–104

Godt (Copenhagen), 98

Gringo's Cantina (Helsingor), 186

Harriet (Ebeltoft), 377

Havreholm Slot, 188

Holles Vinstue (Aalborg), 395

Horizonten Café & Restaurant (Koge), 212

Hornbæk Bodega (Hornbæk), 188–189

Hos Boldt (Aalborg), 392

430 Hotel Balka Strand (Nexo),
250
Hotel Koldingfjord (Kolding),
306
Hotel Marstal Restaurant,
300
Hotel Philip Restaurant
(Århus), 371–372
Hotel Tonderhus (Tonder),
314
Husmann Vinstue (Copenha-
gen), 111
Italy & Italy (Ringsted), 218
Jelling Kro, 343
Kaj Kok (Elmelunde), 233
Karriere (Copenhagen),
116–117
Kiin Kiin (Copenhagen), 116
Klintholm Rogeri (Klintholm
Havn), 235
Kniv og Gaffel (Aalborg),
393–394
Kobenhavner Cafeen (Copen-
hagen), 104, 111
Kong Hans Kælder (Copenha-
gen), 98
Kong Richard (Aalborg), 392
Krogs Fiskerestaurant
(Copenhagen), 114–115
Kromann's Fisherestaurant
(Sonderho), 334
La Brasserie (Roskilde), 204
L'Alsace (Copenhagen), 104
Langtved Færgekro (near
Munkholm Bro), 205
Layalina (Aalborg), 395
Le Brasserie (Odense), 276
Le Petit (Billund), 345
Le Saint-Jacques (Copenha-
gen), 106
Le Sommelier (Copenhagen),
100
Under Lindetræet (Odense),
277
Louisiana Café (Humlebæk),
167
Målet (Odense), 278
Malling & Schmidt (Århus),
371
Marie Louise (Odense), 276
Ministeriet (Århus), 373
Mortens Kro (Aalborg),
392–393
MR (Mads Reflund; Copenha-
gen), 99
Murdoch's Books & Ale
(Copenhagen), 114
NOMA (Copenhagen), 99

Norrebro Bryghus (Copenha-
gen), 115–116
Norre Vissing Kro (Ry), 353
Nyhavns Færgekro (Copen-
hagen), 105
Otto & Ani's Fisk (Romo), 320
Parnas (Copenhagen), 105
Pasta Basta (Copenhagen),
114
The Paul (Copenhagen), 118
Pavillionen (Ribe), 328
Peder Oxe's Restaurant/
Vinkælder Wine Bar
(Copenhagen), 113–114
Piaf (Silkeborg), 359
Pierre André (Copenha-
gen), 99
Prins Ferdinand (Århus), 372
Provence (Aalborg), 394
Puk's Restaurant (Copenha-
gen), 112
Pulcinilla (Slagelse), 221
Pussy Galore's Flying Circus
(Copenhagen), 116
Raadhuskælderen (Roskilde),
204–205
Rådhus Kro (Ringsted), 218
Rådhuskroen (Ronne), 245
Repos (Kolding), 306
Restaurant Arken (Koge),
212–213
Restaurant Bacchus (Freder-
ikshavn), 402
Restaurant Backhaus
(Ribe), 326–327
Restaurant Beghuset
(Dragor), 166
Restaurant Benzons
(Aalborg), 394
Restaurant/Café Nytorv
(Copenhagen), 104,
105–106
Restaurant Dagmar (Ribe),
327
Restaurant Els (Copenhagen),
100–101
Restaurant Grå-Ander (Fred-
erikshavn), 402
Restaurant Harmonien (Had-
erslev), 310
Restaurant Helten (Ringkob-
ing), 348
Restaurant Himmelbjerget
(Ry), 354
Restaurant Kammerslusen
(Ribe), 327
Restaurant Kilden (Aalborg),
393

Restaurant Klinten (Faaborg),
291–292
Restaurant Klitgaard
(Odense), 276–277
Restaurant Le Boeuf, 226
Restaurant Marco Polo
(Svendborg), 284
Restaurant Margueritten
(Århus), 372
Restaurant "Mellem Jyder"
(Ebeltoft), 378
Restaurant Mumm (Æroskob-
ing), 297–298
Restaurant Nokken (Ore-
sund), 168–169
Restaurant Postgården
(Mariager), 384
Restaurant Sælhunden
(Ribe), 327–328
Restaurant Skipperhuset
(Fredensborg), 180
Restaurant Skovmollen
(Århus), 373
Restaurant Slotskælderen
(Tåsinge), 287
Restaurant Slusen (Ringkob-
ing), 349
Restaurant Svanen (Hader-
slev), 310
Restaurant Toppen (Rosk-
ilde), 205
Ristorante Fellini (Aalborg),
394
Riz Raz (Copenhagen), 112
Rosdahls (Aalborg), 393
Salt (Copenhagen), 101
San Remo (Helsingor),
185–186
Schackenborg Slotskro
(Tonder), 316
Siemsens Gaard (Svaneke),
252–253
Skagen Fiske Restaurant, 407
Skindbuksen (Copenhagen),
106
Skipperkroen (Koge), 213
Slotskælderen (Copenha-
gen), 112
Slotskroen (Hillerod),
175–176
Sogaards Brewery (Aalborg),
396
Sonderho Kro, 334
Soren K (Copenhagen), 109
Sortebro Kro (Odense), 277
Sostrene Olsen (Hornbæk),
189
Spiesehuset Christian VIII
(Silkeborg), 359–360

Spisestedet Leonora (Frederiksborg Slot), 176
St. Gertruds Kloster (Copenhagen), 112–113
Strandhotel (Dragor), 166
Strandhotellet Restaurant, 258
Sult (Copenhagen), 109–110

Svendborgsund (Svendborg), 284
Teater Bodega (Århus), 373
Thorvaldsen (Copenhagen), 115
Torvets Restaurant (Tonder), 314–315
Treetops Restaurant (Vejle), 340–341

Tre Kroner (Faaborg), 292
Tre Sostre (Nexo), 250
Umami (Copenhagen), 101–102
Vægterkælderen (Ribe), 328
VIVA (Copenhagen), 117
Weis Stue (Ribe), 328

FROMMER'S® COMPLETE TRAVEL GUIDES

Alaska
Amalfi Coast
American Southwest
Amsterdam
Argentina
Arizona
Atlanta
Australia
Austria
Bahamas
Barcelona
Beijing
Belgium, Holland & Luxembourg
Belize
Bermuda
Boston
Brazil
British Columbia & the Canadian
  Rockies
Brussels & Bruges
Budapest & the Best of Hungary
Buenos Aires
Calgary
California
Canada
Cancún, Cozumel & the Yucatán
Cape Cod, Nantucket & Martha's
  Vineyard
Caribbean
Caribbean Ports of Call
Carolinas & Georgia
Chicago
Chile & Easter Island
China
Colorado
Costa Rica
Croatia
Cuba
Denmark
Denver, Boulder & Colorado Springs
Eastern Europe
Ecuador & the Galapagos Islands
Edinburgh & Glasgow
England
Europe
Europe by Rail

Florence, Tuscany & Umbria
Florida
France
Germany
Greece
Greek Islands
Guatemala
Hawaii
Hong Kong
Honolulu, Waikiki & Oahu
India
Ireland
Israel
Italy
Jamaica
Japan
Kauai
Las Vegas
London
Los Angeles
Los Cabos & Baja
Madrid
Maine Coast
Maryland & Delaware
Maui
Mexico
Montana & Wyoming
Montréal & Québec City
Morocco
Moscow & St. Petersburg
Munich & the Bavarian Alps
Nashville & Memphis
New England
Newfoundland & Labrador
New Mexico
New Orleans
New York City
New York State
New Zealand
Northern Italy
Norway
Nova Scotia, New Brunswick &
  Prince Edward Island
Oregon
Paris
Peru

Philadelphia & the Amish Country
Portugal
Prague & the Best of the Czech
  Republic
Provence & the Riviera
Puerto Rico
Rome
San Antonio & Austin
San Diego
San Francisco
Santa Fe, Taos & Albuquerque
Scandinavia
Scotland
Seattle
Seville, Granada & the Best of
  Andalusia
Shanghai
Sicily
Singapore & Malaysia
South Africa
South America
South Florida
South Korea
South Pacific
Southeast Asia
Spain
Sweden
Switzerland
Tahiti & French Polynesia
Texas
Thailand
Tokyo
Toronto
Turkey
USA
Utah
Vancouver & Victoria
Vermont, New Hampshire & Maine
Vienna & the Danube Valley
Vietnam
Virgin Islands
Virginia
Walt Disney World® & Orlando
Washington, D.C.
Washington State

FROMMER'S® DAY BY DAY GUIDES

Amsterdam
Barcelona
Beijing
Boston
Cancun & the Yucatan
Chicago
Florence & Tuscany

Hong Kong
Honolulu & Oahu
London
Maui
Montréal
Napa & Sonoma
New York City

Paris
Provence & the Riviera
Rome
San Francisco
Venice
Washington D.C.

PAULINE FROMMER'S GUIDES: SEE MORE. SPEND LESS.

Alaska
Hawaii
Italy

Las Vegas
London
New York City

Paris
Walt Disney World®
Washington D.C.

FROMMER'S® PORTABLE GUIDES

Acapulco, Ixtapa & Zihuatanejo
Amsterdam
Aruba, Bonaire & Curacao
Australia's Great Barrier Reef
Bahamas
Big Island of Hawaii
Boston
California Wine Country
Cancún
Cayman Islands
Charleston
Chicago
Dominican Republic

Florence
Las Vegas
Las Vegas for Non-Gamblers
London
Maui
Nantucket & Martha's Vineyard
New Orleans
New York City
Paris
Portland
Puerto Rico
Puerto Vallarta, Manzanillo & Guadalajara

Rio de Janeiro
San Diego
San Francisco
Savannah
St. Martin, Sint Maarten, Anguila & St. Bart's
Turks & Caicos
Vancouver
Venice
Virgin Islands
Washington, D.C.
Whistler

FROMMER'S® CRUISE GUIDES

Alaska Cruises & Ports of Call

Cruises & Ports of Call

European Cruises & Ports of Call

FROMMER'S® NATIONAL PARK GUIDES

Algonquin Provincial Park
Banff & Jasper
Grand Canyon

National Parks of the American West
Rocky Mountain
Yellowstone & Grand Teton

Yosemite and Sequoia & Kings Canyon
Zion & Bryce Canyon

FROMMER'S® WITH KIDS GUIDES

Chicago
Hawaii
Las Vegas
London

National Parks
New York City
San Francisco

Toronto
Walt Disney World® & Orlando
Washington, D.C.

FROMMER'S® PHRASEFINDER DICTIONARY GUIDES

Chinese
French

German
Italian

Japanese
Spanish

SUZY GERSHMAN'S BORN TO SHOP GUIDES

France
Hong Kong, Shanghai & Beijing
Italy

London
New York
Paris

San Francisco
Where to Buy the Best of Everything

FROMMER'S® BEST-LOVED DRIVING TOURS

Britain
California
France
Germany

Ireland
Italy
New England
Northern Italy

Scotland
Spain
Tuscany & Umbria

THE UNOFFICIAL GUIDES®

Adventure Travel in Alaska
Beyond Disney
California with Kids
Central Italy
Chicago
Cruises
Disneyland®
England
Hawaii

Ireland
Las Vegas
London
Maui
Mexico's Best Beach Resorts
Mini Mickey
New Orleans
New York City
Paris

San Francisco
South Florida including Miami & the Keys
Walt Disney World®
Walt Disney World® for Grown-ups
Walt Disney World® with Kids
Washington, D.C.

SPECIAL-INTEREST TITLES

Athens Past & Present
Best Places to Raise Your Family
Cities Ranked & Rated
500 Places to Take Your Kids Before They Grow Up
Frommer's Best Day Trips from London
Frommer's Best RV & Tent Campgrounds in the U.S.A.

Frommer's Exploring America by RV
Frommer's NYC Free & Dirt Cheap
Frommer's Road Atlas Europe
Frommer's Road Atlas Ireland
Retirement Places Rated

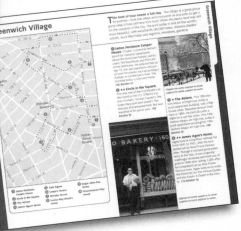

A Guide for Every Type of Traveler

Frommer's Complete Guides

For those who value complete coverage, candid advice, and lots of choices in all price ranges.

Pauline Frommer's Guides

For those who want to experience a culture, meet locals, and save money along the way.

MTV Guides

For hip, youthful travelers who want a fresh perspective on today's hottest cities and destinations.

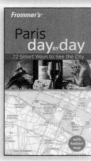

Day by Day Guides

For leisure or business travelers who want to organize their time to get the most out of a trip.

Frommer's With Kids Guides

For families traveling with children ages 2 to 14 seeking kid-friendly hotels, restaurants, and activities.

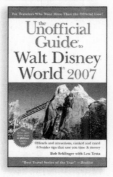

Unofficial Guides

For honeymooners, families, business travelers, and others who value no-nonsense, *Consumer Reports*-style advice.

For Dummies Travel Guides

For curious, independent travelers looking for a fun and easy way to plan a trip.

Visit Frommers.com

WILEY
Now you know.

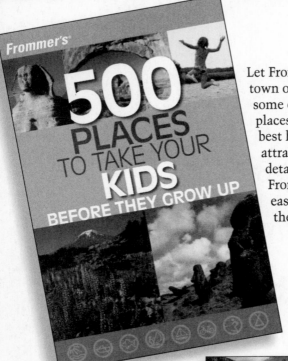

Authority Is Relational

Rethinking Educational Empowerment

CHARLES BINGHAM

STATE UNIVERSITY OF NEW YORK PRESS

Published by
STATE UNIVERSITY OF NEW YORK PRESS, ALBANY

© 2008 State University of New York

For information, contact State University of New York Press, Albany, NY
www.sunypress.edu

Production by Kelli W. LeRoux
Marketing by Anne M. Valentine

Library of Congress Cataloging-in-Publication Data

Bingham, Charles, 1961–
    Authority is relational : rethinking educational empowerment / Charles
Bingham.
        p. cm.
    Includes bibliographical references and index.
    ISBN 978-0-7914-7403-7 (hardcover : alk. paper)
    1. Education—Philosophy.   2. Authority.   I. Title.

LA134.B56 2008
370.11'5—dc22   2007033900

10 9 8 7 6 5 4 3 2 1

Contents

Acknowledgments   vii

Introduction: Authority Is Relational   1

1. Texts and the Authority Relation   17

2. The Literary Relation of Authority   41

3. Relating to Authority Figures Who Are Not There   65

4. When Faced with Authority   87

5. Questioning Authority   111

6. Paulo Freire and Relational Authority   129

Notes   153

References   165

Index   169

Acknowledgments

My thanks go to Sasha Sidorkin, Donna Kerr, Cathryn Sedun, Stephen Haymes, and Claudia Ruitenberg, whose thoughtful conversation and insightful thinking have made this book possible.

The introductory chapter includes material reworked from "Authority Is Relational" in *No Authority Without Relations* (New York: Peter Lang, 2004). Chapter 1 includes a version of "I Am the Pages of the Text I Teach: Gadamer and Derrida on Teacher Authority," *Philosophy of Education*, 2001. Chapter 2 includes material reworked from "The Literary Life of Educational Authority," *Journal of Philosophy of Education*, Vol. 40, no. 3 (2006). Parts of chapter 3 appeared in a different version in "Language and Intersubjectivity: Recognizing the Other without Taking Over or Giving In," *Philosophy in the Contemporary World*, Vol. 6, nos. 3–4 (Fall–Winter 1999). Chapter 4 includes revised versions of the following essays: "Pragmatic Intersubjectivity, or, Just Using Teachers," *Philosophy of Education*, 2004; and, "Who Are the Philosophers of Education?" *Studies in Philosophy & Education*, Vol. 25, no. 1 (2005). Chapter 5 contains material first published in "The Hermeneutics of Educational Questioning," *Educational Philosophy and Theory*, Vol. 37, no. 4 (2005). Chapter 6 includes a version of "Paulo Freire's Debt to Psychoanalysis: Authority on the Side of Freedom," *Studies in Philosophy and Education*, Vol. 21, no. 6 (2002).

Introduction

Authority Is Relational

I have been a university professor for quite a few years now. I still can't let my students out of class early. I continue to keep them in class until the last scheduled minute, but that is not necessarily what I *want* to be doing. Why do I say that I "still" cannot let them out early? Because I hope to let them out early some day. I would truly like to let them out early, but I have an aversion to doing so.

It is not hard to pinpoint my aversion. It comes from the years prior to my role as a university professor, years during which I taught in high school and junior high school classrooms. My experience as a teacher during these early years was marked, as I assume many school-teachers' experience has been, by an insistence on watching the clock, and by making every minute count. Authority figures at schools where I worked would insist on timeliness. Principals and assistant principals would remind us teachers to use every minute of class time. Messages such as, "Teachers, do not let your students into the halls until the bell has rung," could be heard daily over school loudspeakers.

In addition to being told to keep our students busy for every minute of each class, we were also told to keep ourselves busy until the last minute of the school day. We were warned, during faculty meetings, not to leave the school premises until the last school bell sounded. At one school where I worked, the windows of the principal's office looked out, strategically, onto the faculty parking lot. The principal could easily tell whose car was gone before three o'clock and whose was not. This principal would give the whole faculty stern warnings when the parking lot was beginning to look "too empty" at the end of the school day.

I once asked a colleague at my university if he has the same hesitance to letting students out of class early. To my surprise, he told me that he lets his students out of class early if the class discussion gets to a low

1

point. He said he considered the end of the class period not to be a set time; rather, class closure should reflect the pedagogical aims of the instructor. If learning has ceased, class time should be over. I on the other hand seem to have issues with time. It is clear to me that the authority structure in which I was apprenticed has gotten under my skin.

So I do still worry about classroom time "on task." But what interests me about these worries goes further. There is more to say than "this thing called authority has gotten under my skin." Indeed, the usual way of talking about authority is to say that authority is some "thing" to which we *succumb*. Yet, while my retentive tendencies are indeed a way of succumbing to intercom announcements and to the watchful eyes of principals, I find this simplistic understanding of my ingrained habits to be impoverished in many ways. While it might be true that one succumbs to authority, it is also true that authority operates in ways that need *not* be explained along the lines of domination and acquiescence to one who "has" this "thing" called authority. While it may be true that my current classroom practices *can* be seen as a matter of acquiescing to the authority of former administrators, it is also true that my current habits can be described in another way that is more fruitful. What interests me about my worries with time is the fact that these worries can also be understood as a matter of *relation*.

As a teacher, I seem to have gotten used to a certain *relation* to authority. I tend to relate to my students in the same way that I am used to relating to the authority figures I have answered to before. Authority, I would say, is not as much a matter of control (how my own authority figures have controlled me, how I control my students as an authority figure myself) as it is a matter of the relation that has been established between authority figures and myself, between me and my students. To break with past authority figures in this case would entail a certain defiance on my part, yes. But that defiance would not be simply "saying no to power." That defiance is more profoundly a willingness to change the sorts of *relations* that I am used to. To continue to be influenced by authority would be to continue with a relation that I have gotten used to. To act differently would be to change a relation to which I have become accustomed.

The aim of this book is to think about authority in terms of relation. It is my aim to look at scenarios of authority in ways that problematize, augment, and redefine prevalent notions of how authority works. For, current educational conceptions of authority assume that authority is primarily a thing that people have, a thing that is wielded by individuals who are in positions of power. Scholarly renditions and folk notions of authority alike thing-ify authority and describe it as a substance that is possessed by people in power who, in turn, use that thing, that authority, over others who are not in power.[1] Thus, it is common to hear statements such as, "That person has a lot of authority because she is a teacher," or, "Unfortunately I do not have much authority since I am only a student." Authority is usually construed as a possession to which one who lacks power either succumbs or does not succumb. In contrast, if we understand authority as a relation (as opposed to a thing), then an entirely new set of questions emerges. An entirely new sort of analysis is called for. Tired analyses of authority as a "thing" have outlived their usefulness.

CURRENT CONCEPTIONS OF AUTHORITY AS SUBSTANCE: THE PROGRESSIVE, THE TRADITIONAL, THE CRITICAL

Take, for example, recent scholarly debate about educational authority. Such debate over authority usually ends up in an impasse precisely because it treats authority as such a "thing." On one hand, progressivists hold that authority is best dealt with by giving it up.[2] In progressive camps of educational thought, it is assumed that authority is harmful to the student. It is thought that the more authority a teacher has, the less chance the student will have to gain autonomy or agency. In the context of progressive education, one hears such things as, "How can we share authority with our students?" "How can we try not to be authority figures in classrooms?" and "She is a very personable teacher; she really doesn't flaunt her authority."

The traditional argument, on the other hand, holds that authority must be embraced. Traditionalists contend that authority is a moral good that comes when one acquires knowledge and institutional responsibility. Following this line of thought, a teacher is a beneficent authority figure because of what she knows, because of her classroom role in loco parentis. The traditional argument asks us to recognize that some folks are in a position to help others.[3] Can authority be wrong if it is employed in a thoughtful manner? Authority, following this traditionalist logic, is completely acceptable as long as one uses one's authority to help those who are not in authority. By using one's authority, one can cultivate the capacities of those who are themselves not yet authority figures.

Against the backdrop of a progressive rejection of authority and the traditional acceptance, the critical argument maintains that authority *must* be used, but only for the purposes of teaching for social justice.[4] The critical argument suggests a qualified use of authority. It is qualified in that it does not embrace authority per se, but embraces only the authority of those who speak for social justice. So unlike the traditional perspective that advocates the practical necessity of the various versions of educational authority (personal, institutional, scientific, cultural, etc.), the critical perspective encourages only those versions of authority that promote freedom and social change. And unlike progressive perspectives, the critical perspective does not assume that the use of authority is somehow *naturally* at odds with social justice. The critical argument advocates the use of authority when teaching for human freedom is at stake.

Progressives argue against authority. Traditionalists embrace it. Criticalists embrace it at certain times. Granted, these are stereotyped positions that I have laid out, it is certainly true that these positions tend to treat authority as a "thing." These three positions consider authority to be a sort of zero-sum commodity. It is said that the more authority one person has, the less another person has, that authority is a substance to be rejected or embraced, a thing that is either bad or good. I am not saying that these three positions do not offer important insights into the use and abuse of authority. Certainly, each of these positions makes some sense in their respective rejection, embrace, and qualified embrace of authority *as substance*. Yet, when these positions are taken, I am struck by the extent to which each is hamstrung by the assumptions they make about the thing-ified nature of authority. Certainly, if authority were a thing, then I would have to agree with the critical perspective. Yet, it is my contention that authority is in fact not a thing. It is a relation.

Let me say it again: These three positions, as well as most prevalent explanations of authority, make a fairly primitive ontological presumption regarding authority. They presume that authority is a thing. According to these sorts of explanations, the same mistake is made that a folk-meteorologist might make if he or she were to assume that wind is itself a substance. To be sure, one can take the position that wind is a substance in and of itself. And to the extent that one takes that position, it might even make sense to wonder if more wind is a good or bad thing. It might make sense to wonder if we should try to stop the wind on certain occasions, or if we should try to increase the wind on other occasions. Yet, from a more sophisticated, more accurate position, one should understand that wind is in fact a movement of air. It is a movement of air that exists in relation to the differing temperatures of various land masses and bodies of water. It exists in relation to differences in atmospheric pressures. The wind exists only in relation to other circumstances. With a more sophisticated understanding of the wind, there is no meteorological sense in the endeavor to create more wind, or to create less wind. There is only sense in asking how the wind acts in relation to different events.

It is the same with authority. The common sorts of arguments either embracing or decrying authority fail to deal with the most important of all questions concerning authority, namely: How does authority work *in relation*? So I propose that we think about educational authority in a way that is uncommon at present. I propose that we consider how educational authority operates. For while progressivists argue against it, while traditionalists embrace it, and while criticalists warn about using it judiciously—while these various perspectives on the 'substance' are being articulated, none of them look deeply into the question of *How?* To ask the question *How?* is a different matter altogether than arguing for or against. To ask *How?* is to look for models that illustrate the workings of authority as relation. In the chapters that follow, I examine a few such models.

Let me offer another example. This one was told to me by one of my university students. A university sophomore, let's call her Julie, told the following story in class. Julie is at school to become a teacher. And, as a student who will soon be a teacher, she pays close attention to her own relationships vis-à-vis teachers so that she might learn from them habits that would benefit her own teaching. She told this story to illustrate the ways in which some university professors are sympathetic to the genuine experiences of students while some are not.

Julie had just encountered a traumatic experience. Her grand-mother had passed away. She had been very close to her grandmother when she was a child, though she was separated now from her by quite a distance, having moved out of state to attend university. Julie spent a week away from school to attend the funeral and to be with her family in this time of mourning. And, as it so happened, she did not inform her professors about her absence until after she returned to school, until she was once again in attendance at the courses where she had been absent.

Julie was quite apprehensive before returning to her classes. She did not want to be seen as making excuses for the coursework she had missed, and she felt a bit guilty for not contacting her instructors earlier. But at the same time she wanted to let her professors know that she had been absent for a very legitimate reason, for an event that was much more significant than any week's worth of lectures.

On the first day of her return, she approached her English profes-sor after class. She told the professor the reason she did not attend the previous week's classes. The professor acted in a very sympathetic manner. She did not say a word to Julie about the absence itself, not a word about Julie's classwork. Rather, she asked if Julie had been close to her grandmother, to which Julie said yes. Julie told her of how they used to play card games together in her childhood. The professor also asked if Julie needed anything in order to get through this rough time. Julie and her English professor stood at the front of an empty classroom: "If there is anything I can do for you," the professor said, "please let me know." Julie thanked her for her kind words.

Julie contrasts this first reception to a different sort that she faced upon explaining her absence to her history professor. As in the previous class, Julie told her history professor about her absence.

The history professor said this: "Well, you know that you missed last week's quiz don't you?"

"Yes," Julie responded.

"Well, you're going to have to make that up within two days."

"Alright," Julie said.

"And," her professor said, "I'll need to have a written verification of your absence. I'll need that note before you can actually take the make-up quiz. That's my policy for every student no matter how extenuating the circumstances."

Julie responded that she would do so. But as she recounted this story to me, she added a couple of details about what went through her mind as this incident unfolded. Julie explained: "As my history teacher was talking, I became so angry with her for ignoring my feelings, for being so unsympathetic. She lost all credibility in my view. After that, I refused to work hard in that class. She lost her authority as a teacher over me."

What intrigues me about this story is a bit different than what intrigued Julie. While Julie was intrigued by the different affective relationships that were established by these two professors, I am more interested in the small detail that Julie included about the way she treated the professor who was so unsympathetic to the tragic experience she had gone through. For, as Julie explained, her instructor's callousness caused her to discount her authority from that time forward. I am interested in this discounting because it points to an aspect of educational authority that is so often overlooked, the aspect of relation. Educational authority is generally treated as a monologic rather than a dialogic experience. It is rarely investigated with an eye to its enactment as a circuit.

Julie's small detail is significant because it goes against so much educational thought. The bulk of educational thought assumes that authority is located solely in the hands of instructors. That is to say, it assumes that Julie is not a key player in the workings of authority, and that her sort of small detail is just that, small and insignificant. I contend, though, that Julie *is* a key player in the relation of authority. Because authority is a relation, there is not just one person who "has" authority and one who does not. Rather, each person is involved. Both Julie *and* her professor are involved in the relation of authority. It is my contention in this book that Julie's experience must be listened to. Her experience shows us that there is a certain circuitry to authority. Authority gets enacted in circuits where each participant has a role to play, where authority is not simply a monological enactment, where it takes the participation of at least two people for authority to gain purchase. It works as a circuit instead of working unidirectionally or monologically.

CONCEPTIONS OF AUTHORITY AS NONRELATIONAL: MONOLOGICAL AUTHORITY

I have mentioned current conceptions that treat authority as a substance rather than as a relation—the progressive, the traditional, and the critical conceptions. Indeed, one way to construe authority as something other than relation is to treat authority as a substance that is possessed by people. However, this understanding of authority as substance is closely related to another assumption that is made about authority: that authority is monological. To assume that authority is a thing is first to assume that it stands alone in spite of human relations. But oftentimes, there is an accompanying assumption that authority is held and applied by one person only, that it is monological. In spite of the fact that experiences such as Julie's happen all the time, an unquestioningly monological understanding of authority has dominated, and continues to dominate, many educational and noneducational accounts.

Such a monological view of authority can be traced back at least as far as its Kantian inheritance. Indeed, as evidenced in his pivotal article of 1784, entitled "What Is Enlightenment?" Immanuel Kant shows that the entire project of Western Enlightenment is grounded in a monological understanding of authority. In this article, Kant encourages his readers to have the courage *not* to rely on the authority of others. As he notes,

> Enlightenment is man's emergence from his self-imposed immaturity. Immaturity is the inability to use one's understanding without guidance from another. This immaturity is self-imposed when its cause lies not in lack of understanding, but in lack of resolve and courage to use it without guidance from another. *Sapere Aude!* [dare to know] "Have courage to use your own understanding!"—that is the motto of enlightenment.[5]

According to Kant, then, authority comes at individuals from above, from the unilateral direction of one who has authority *toward* one who has none. In Kant's analysis of authority, it is up to the individual to either submit to such authority, or, to have the courage to be "mature" by using one's own reason. One must fight the authority of others by using the authority of one's own reason. In this Kantian formulation of Enlightenment, there is no mention that authority is in any way affected by the individual's reaction to that authority. Authority may be directed at one person from another, it may be directed from an institution or tradition toward a person. But, authority remains monological in the Kantian tradition. For Kant, the best (the most "mature") way to deal with authority is to ignore it and to use one's own authority instead. Kant thus sets up a zero-sum game of authority the likes of which I have described in the context of progressive, traditional, and critical approaches to educational authority. Kant's conception of authority depends on a thing-ification of authority. And in addition, it assumes that authority works through an atomistic, monological relation between those "in" authority and those who are "faced with" authority.

In more recent educational thought, too, authority continues to be treated as a monologic entity. Interestingly, the monologic account of authority continues in full force even for thinkers who are otherwise thoroughly dialogic in their orientation to education! For example, monologic authority makes a particularly interesting appearance Paulo Freire's seminal work, *Pedagogy of the Oppressed.*[6] This appearance is interesting given the fact that Freire is otherwise so successful at advocating a relational form of pedagogy. For Freire, authority is virulently monologic even at a time when there is to be reciprocity in the teacher/student relation. In Freire's dialogic education,

> The teacher is no longer merely the-one-who-teachers, but one who is himself taught in dialogue with the students, who in turn while being taught also teach. They become jointly responsible for a process in which all grow. In this process, arguments based on "authority" are no longer valid; in order to function, authority must be on the side of freedom, not against it.[7]

Even as Freire advocates an education that scissors back and forth between teacher and student, authority itself remains a one-sided possession of individuals who are free.

It is actually the work of Freire that has made me the most attuned to the deeply entrenched, indeed the seemingly irrational, insistence that authority needs to be understood as monologic. His work has made me realize how important it is to rediscribe authority in a relational way. Why the work of Freire? Because he protests too much. His proclamation that arguments over authority will disappear in dialogic education is just a little bit too neat. His proclamation that authority simply jumps over to the side of freedom is in fact a very obvious crack in his own well-formulated methodology, and it performs the following unfortunate maneuver: (1) Monologic education is full of authority.

(2) Authority in such a monologic education is wrong. (3) Dialogic education must replace monologic education. (4) Since dialogic education promotes freedom, authority will switch to the side of education that promotes freedom. It is as if authority is just one of those monological things that will change for the better when educational actors engage with each other in a dialogic way.

Interestingly, Freire supposes that authority remains monological, remains on one side, even when educational interactions become dialogic. He supposes that authority works monologically *against* freedom when it is oppressive, and monologically *for* freedom when it is liberatory. For Freire, the object of dialogic education is to change the nature of authority from freedom-crushing to freedom-enhancing, even while authority remains essentially monologic. In contrast to Freire, I contend that authority is always already dialogical in nature. Freire's understanding of authority is steeped in the Enlightenment tradition inaugurated by Kant even while his vision of the human person is intersubjective in ways that Kant could not have endorsed. Freire does not entertain the possibility that there could be dialogic authority. Indeed, dialogic experiences with authority such as Julie's are pushed aside even by such a dialogic educator as Freire.

SPEAKERS AND LISTENERS

At a very basic level, even during a simple exchange of words between two people, authority gets enacted in relational ways. When a person speaks, I listen. What happens when I listen? The relation of authority begins. When I listen to another, I partake in authority. I partake as I halt my own speech long enough for the other to speak. When I listen, the other does not listen but speaks instead. I listen, the other speaks. Through my listening, I enact a relation of authority. Through the other's speaking, she enacts authority as well. Authority is not a "thing" lying in wait. It is not first "possessed" by the speaker, then "used." Authority does not happen until we, the listener and speaker, enter a relation.

When I listen, I partake in the relation of authority. When another speaks, she partakes also. Neither of us "has" authority. Neither of us "succumbs" to authority. Rather, we create the relation of authority within the speaking and within the listening. The relation of authority would be incomplete without listener. It would be incomplete without the speaker. To speak to no one is to be outside of authority. To listen to no one is to be outside of authority. Authority is not present until the speaker is listened to. It is not present until the listener is spoken to. Authority comes to exist when the relation is made. Until the relation is made, authority is not yet present.

An important example of the authority relation between speaker and listener can be found in Louis Althusser's *Ideological State Apparatuses*.[8] Althusser describes the experience of a person who is hailed by a policeman on the street, a person who is *talked to* by another who is in authority. When such a hailing takes place, it is not simply the policeman who enacts authority. Indeed, the role of the person being hailed is just as central to the enactment of authority as the role of the policeman. For what is interesting about this sort of hailing is that the policeman might be calling to *anyone* on the street when he calls out, "Hey, you there." Yet, in spite of the fact that he might be calling on just anyone, the hailing takes effect when the one who is being hailed responds by acknowledging that the anyone is *he* rather than someone else. Althusser narrates this event as follows:

> There are individuals walking along. Somewhere (usually behind them) the hail rings out: "Hey, you there!" One individual (nine times out of ten it is the right one) turns round, believing/suspecting/knowing that it is for him, i.e. recognizing that "it really is he" who is meant by the hailing. But in reality these things happen without any succession. The existence of ideology and the hailing or interpellation of individuals as subjects are one and the same thing.[9]

While Althusser focuses on the ideology at work, I want to focus on the authority at work. In this example, the police man is a figure of authority. The person on the street has his back to the policeman. He does not even know for sure that the policeman is a policeman. He does not even know for sure that it is *he* who is being hailed by the policeman. Yet in spite of all of this ambiguity, the man turns around because he assumes that it is he who is being hailed. When he does turn around, he becomes "interpellated" into (quite literally, "called into") the position of being named as "you" by the policeman. Importantly, the authority of the policeman is not a preexisting authority. It is clearly not preexisting since the policeman's authority qua policeman is not known until after the man has turned around, until after the man has himself participated in the relation of authority.

Any authority that the policeman might have over the man who believes he is being called cannot have been in existence before the turn of the man. For, before that turn, it is not at all clear that it is *this* man over whom the policeman has authority. It is the turn itself that establishes the policeman's authority per se, and it is the turn itself that establishes that the policeman "has" authority over this particular man. It is in fact the man's participation in the relation of authority that establishes both the existence of the policeman's authority and its direction (being ultimately directed at the man by virtue of the man's turn toward it). As I have stated above, it is the listening and the acceptance of the relation itself that establishes authority. The authority was not actually present until a relation has been established between speaker and listener.

Franz Fanon provides another excellent example of the authority relation between a listener and a speaker, this time in the context of a racist colonial regime. In *Black Skins/White Masks*, Fanon describes a black man's reaction to the call of a white boy on the streets of Paris. Fanon recalls being hailed as a black man by a white boy:

> [A boy calls out] "Dirty Nigger!" Or simply, "Look, a Negro!"
> I came into the world imbued with the will to find a meaning in things, my spirit filled with the desire to attain to the source of the world, and then I found that I was an object in the midst of other objects.
> Sealed into that crushing objecthood, I turned beseechingly to others. . . . I was indignant; I demanded an explanation. Nothing happened. I burst apart. Now the fragments have been put together again by *another self.*[10]

The boy may have hailed him by saying, "Dirty nigger," or he may have hailed him by saying simply, "Look, a Negro." Whatever the case, being hailed as a black man on the streets of a racist white regime causes the black man to listen, to be entered into a racist relation with white authority. As Fanon recounts this incident, he reminds us how devastating such an encounter can be for a black man. In a racist world, being called out as a black man, either viciously or as a simple matter of fact, is a threat and a derogation.

Fanon reminds us that in a racist world it really doesn't matter whether the words used to hail are "dirty nigger" or simply "hey you." Whatever the case, the black man's hearing of the white boy's hail creates a relation of authority between the white boy and the black man that is devastating in its psychological import. Certainly the white boy "has" little authority before he does the hailing. Perhaps just as certainly, the white boy "has" little or no authority even after the hailing. It is not that one (white) person has authority and the other (black) person has none. It is rather that a relation of racist authority is established as soon as one (white) person speaks and another (black) person listens.

In a racist world, racist authority is not enacted until a relation is established. That is not to say that racist authority is somehow less odious or less oppressive because it exists in relation rather than as

some sort of preexisting "thing" or "substance." Emphatically and viciously, racist authority diminishes the agency and freedom of those
who are marked as people of color in a racist world. It does so through
relation. Indeed racist authority obtains its particular viciousness *because* it is relational. Racist authority is not something abstract: It establishes real hierarchies and concrete instances of domination between
real people who have flesh-and-blood relationships.

If these two examples described by Althusser and Fanon seem
extreme, then let me go back to a simpler example of listening and
speaking. This example comes from an exchange that can be heard
every day in thousands of classrooms across the world. It happens when
roll is taken on the first day of class. On the first day of class, a teacher
looks at her roll sheet and calls out, "Deborah Williams?" At the sounding of her name, Deborah answers, "Here." Before the calling, Deborah
is a name on a piece of paper. She is a faceless place-marker, a student-
to-be, a name whose person might well be a mistake on the classroom
roster. The name might well stand for an absence that might never be
present in class. Before the answering, the authority of the teacher over
this Deborah Williams is hypothetical at best. Before the answering,
Deborah has every opportunity to opt out of her role as student vis-à-
vis this teacher. Before the answering, Deborah may decide that she
does not like the teacher's manner. She may decide to absent herself
from this particular class by standing up and telling the teacher that she
is in the wrong class. She may not reveal that she is indeed assigned to
be a student in this class. It is only through the answering of Deborah
that authority becomes enacted between the teacher and herself.

AGENCY AND RELATIONAL ANALYSIS

Once again, I want to emphasize that authority gets enacted whenever
one person speaks and another person listens. But what's more, I would
even say that authority gets enacted *whenever there is a relation* between two or more people. Just as there is no way to avoid the enactment of authority once one has gained the ear of another, so, too, is
there no way to avoid the enactment of authority once two or more
people have entered into a relation with each other. As soon as there is
a relation between human beings, there is authority. That is to say,
relation is a *sufficient* condition for the existence of authority. As well,
the enactment of authority does not happen until there is a relation
between two or more people. That is to say, relation is also a *necessary*
condition for the existence of authority. While it may seem surprising
that the commonplace, even benign, experiences of listening and speaking are sufficient events for the enactment of authority to happen, I

want to go much farther: authority is enacted whenever there is relation among people, no matter how benign or commonplace the relation is.

To realize that authority is enacted even during those seemingly benign moments when one person speaks and another person listens, to realize moreover that authority is enacted whenever there is a relation between people—to realize these matters puts us on a very different course of analysis with regard to authority. First of all, an analysis that looks at authority as relational must stop asking the same tired questions about authority that have been asked for so many centuries under so many guises. Those tired questions are, Is authority a good thing or a bad thing? Must we embrace authority or dismiss authority? Should authority figures give over their authority or cling to it? Certainly, these tired questions have been asked with good intent. From Immanuel Kant, to Paulo Freire, to progressive, traditional, and critical theorists, these sorts of questions have been asked in order to figure out how to deal with authority. They have been asked in order to figure out how to increase freedom and agency when human beings are faced with authority.

Yet, when authority is understood as relation, then a different sort of analysis is required. Authority, like the wind that we encounter when we walk outside, is not something that will go away. It is not something that can be avoided. Authority as relation is not to be eschewed or embraced per se. Rather, it must be analyzed on its own terms of reference. Does this mean that we must abandon the Enlightenment search for freedom and agency when it comes to authority? Absolutely not. It simply means looking elsewhere than to the tired questions that have been asked for so long to so little avail. Indeed, in the chapters that follow, I will be concerned precisely with questions of human freedom and human agency. Yet, these questions will be pursued on the assumption that authority takes place in relation rather than on the side of one person who clearly "has" authority in his possession.

To begin looking at the theoretical work that helps to unpack the relational life of authority, let me borrow from Michel Foucault's analysis of power. Foucault reminds us that power is *productive* in nature. For Foucault, power is not only a restraining force that works against people. It is not only a force that people need to break down in order to gain more freedom. Power is also constitutive. It constitutes people's freedom at the same time that it constrains their freedom. Power may sometimes be oppressive, but it also makes a double gesture: it often insinuates itself into the very pleasures that it serves to repress. In this way, power cannot said to be primarily repressive. It is both repressive and active in the lives of individuals who are enabled by power at the same time that they are constrained by it. Power "doesn't only weigh on us as a force that says no," but it also "traverses and produces things, it induces pleasure, forms knowledge, produces discourse."[11] For Foucault, then, it can never be a question of "saying no" or "saying yes" to power. Even in the "saying no" or "saying yes" power is already at work.

Foucault also points out that, when it comes to power, the most important thing we can do is to separate power from capacity.[12] That is to say, we must analyze power in a way that does not assume that agency and freedom are always at odds with power. In fact, because power both constitutes and constrains, human capacity cannot be the same as power. Sometimes, human capacity will be decreased by power but sometimes it will be increased by power. There is not a simple either/or binary when it comes to taking a stand vis-à-vis power. Power does not *either* constrain *or* enhance human capacity. Thus, Foucault encourages us to separate power from capacity in order that we might analyze power in a thorough manner without prejudicing our analysis by assuming that power is only that which diminishes human capacity. If we presume, beforehand, that power is that-which-diminishes-human-capacity, then our analysis of power will be hamstrung by such a presumption.

Foucault's insights into power ring true for authority. Authority, because it is a relation, works on all sides of human interaction. Authority produces as well as constrains. Let me go back to my own example of being reticent to let students out early. A relational understanding of authority will entertain the possibility that authority was working with me as well as working against me. Authority affects classroom practices in two senses. It affects them in the sense that it changes them, yes; but it also affects them in the sense that it puts them into use. For example, using the entire class period has become a working part of how I understand pedagogy in my own classroom. Using the entire class period changes the ways I plan lessons. It gives rise to affective investments about the quality of education I provide. (I am actually *proud* that I use the entire class period.) The *entire* block of classroom time is a platform upon which my pedagogical sensibilities find a certain orientation. The authority that constrains my options also gives meaning of my options.

So, it is important for any relational analysis of authority to follow Foucault in his advice to separate capacity from power. In my own analysis, I too want to separate capacity from authority. When people engage in a relation of authority (and as I have been arguing, all relations are relations of authority), we must be able to distinguish between the types of authority relations that enhance capacity from those that diminish capacity. It is not true, as most Enlightenment conceptions of authority would have it, that human agency is automatically diminished when there is a relation of authority. Sometimes relations of authority will be dominating, but sometimes such relations will be agentive. What we should stay away from is the assumption that capacity is linked in fixed, non-agentive ways to the exercise of authority. It is most important to determine those instances when human capacity can be enhanced even as the relation of authority is being enacted. Authority relations can lead to domination and submission, *or* they can lead to reciprocity and agency. Indeed, as the following chapters will show, I am concerned with detailing the ways that authority relations can lead to human agency even when authority itself is as unavoidable as the wind that blows.

I have said that all relation entails authority and that all authority entails relation. Of course, such a claim sounds immense. Such a claim is indeed immense. It is too immense for the educational analysis that I want to carry out in this book. In the chapters that follow, I will be concerned with some very specific instances of the authority relation that one encounters in educational circumstances. I will be concerned, in chapter 1, with the textual relation of authority. Chapter 2 will consider how authority relations must be understood as literary and linguistic. Then in chapter 3, I will look into the educational authority that gets enacted when teachers (as authority figures) are not present, are not in the same room, with the students they have been teaching. In chapter 4, I will look into the ways that students can use the authority relation to their own advantage, the ways that students can "use" teachers. In that chapter, I will return to the work of Michel Foucault (among others) as part of an elaboration on the ways that students can use authority to enhance capacity and agency. Chapter 5 will be concerned with the ways that authority gets enacted through the process of questioning and answering in education. And finally, chapter 6 will explore the matter of relational authority in the context of the critical pedagogy of Paulo Freire. In the end, this book does not attempt to make a grand statement that solves all questions about educational authority. It is an attempt to look at a few, and only a few, of the salient practices in education where relational authority is at stake. It is an attempt to isolate a few instances of educational authority and to show ways in which such instances can lead to human agency especially on the part of students.

CHAPTER 1

Texts and the Authority Relation

Recently, I began one of my university courses in a way that was for me unusual. I told the students that one of the books we were going to read was new to me, that I had never read it before. I justified my choice of the book, and the fact that I had not read it yet, by mentioning that it had come highly recommended by two colleagues whom I respected very much and who had read it in manuscript form. And it was a brand new book, I told my students, hot off the press. Thus, I thought it reasonable that we read the book together. We would learn from each other.

Actually, what was unusual for me was that I *told* my students this. I had, when teaching a course, read texts with my students, for the first time, quite a few times. But I had never prefaced a course by admitting that we would do so.

The students seemed to take the admission in stride, until the day we discussed the book. One student, let's call him Darrel, was visibly upset with the book. His classroom comments were highly critical of the text. And while he spent some time in class offering judicious and well-argued critiques of the book, it seemed as if he was biding his time, holding back. Darrel finally burst out, "You know, I promised myself I wasn't going to say this, but I don't think this book has anything to offer to teachers, to schools, or to anyone concerned with education. This book has nothing to offer educators, Dr. B!"

This sort of critique is not what was remarkable, though. Many other students critique texts that I have chosen. They are encouraged to do so and should do so. What surprised me happened about a week

17

later when I was talking with Darrel in the hallway. Going out of his way to explain his outburst in the previous week's class, Darrel said that he still did not think the book was useful for educators. "But what bothered me even more," he said, "was that you had not even read the book before you assigned it. That's what got to me."

What struck me about Darrel's comment was mainly that I had never had my own authority as a professor positioned in quite this way, between flattery and condemnation, between all-knowing and unknowing, between progressive and traditional, between one who learns along with his students and one who lets them learn something wrong, between the 782 books on the shelves of my office that I had read and this one that I *hadn't* read. Given these encounters with Darrel, both in class and out, I am sure that my own teaching authority was in play, but I was not quite sure how.

In this chapter, I want to examine the authority relation and the place of texts therein. Why look first to texts? Because it is important to start examining the relation of educational authority not in general, but with an eye toward the context in which such authority gets enacted. In education, this context is, quite literally, a *con*-text, a "with text." The text is an integral part of the educational relation of authority. For, authority comes in many forms: familial authority, legal authority, religious authority, institutional authority, state authority... Yet, not all of these noneducational forms of authority include a use of the written word. I examine here the place of texts in the authority relation because texts are an inevitable component of *educational* authority. When authority gets enacted in education, it is most often through the use of texts.

Indeed, as I will put forth in this chapter, the text enters the relation of education authority in some complicated ways. For, texts are not only *used* as part of this relation. In addition, texts become an integral part of the relation itself. Students and teachers engage with texts and these texts become, to a greater or lesser extent, a part of them. In this regard, it is worthwhile to note another etymological link: The very word, *authority*, has its history in matters of *author*-ship. Who writes what, and who reads what, are central to authority, and especially central to educational authority. It is thus very important to look at the place of the book deep within relations of educational authority. The place of the book in the relation of educational authority is not a distant one. Students and teachers are intertwined with the book when authority gets enacted. The relation of authority in education makes us readers and authors. It ties us in organic ways to the text. Authority in education is thus not only a relation between people who use texts; it is also a relation between people who are in the process of becoming, themselves, textual. To partake in educational authority is to partake in authorship.

To think about the place of the book, this chapter will outline two theoretical frameworks for interpreting the textual nature of authority: one based on the hermeneutics of Hans-Georg Gadamer and one based Jacques Derrida's logic of the "supplement."[1] By outlining these two frameworks, I try to shed some light on the complicated link between teaching authority and the text. I find that the works of both Gadamer and Derrida are vital in teasing out the messy relationship between the learner, the teacher, and the book. It is this messy relationship that I believe my student Darrel was pointing out. For Gadamer, the authority of the text is separate from, and preferable to, the authority of the teacher. Gadamer sees a difference between textual authority and human authority. He sees the former as more beneficial and the latter as less beneficial. However, Derrida sees more of an organic link between the two. I therefore use Derrida's logic of the supplement to extend the Gadamerian analysis. Derrida reminds us that we are an actual part of the texts we teach.

As well, this chapter will examine a work of literature that helps to further elucidate the place of texts within the authority relation. I will examine the play, *My Country! My Africa!*, written by Athol Fugard and set in South Africa during the Apartheid regime.[2] Fugard's play offers a powerful lens for further analysis of the central, yet complicated, role that texts play within relations of educational authority. His play reminds us that texts bear not only on the relation between a student and his or her teacher, but also on larger social movements where authority is at stake, social movements such as the anti-Apartheid struggle in South Africa.

GADAMER ON AUTHORITATIVENESS VERSUS AUTHORITARIANISM

Gadamer's analysis of teaching authority is based on his more general understanding of hermeneutic authority. So I begin with synopsis of hermeneutic authority as described by Gadamer. Hermeneutic authority, as a part of the to-and-fro interchange between text and interpreter, derives from the cultural "horizon" upon which a text rests in order to make sense to the reader, in order to lay claim on the reader. According to Gadamer, the authority of a given text rests in its ability to be understood within a set of cultural and historical cues that are available for understanding not only because they wait to be discovered within the closed pages of the text, but also because they draw upon a tradition of understanding that is to some extent already shared with the reader or interpreter of the text. (Such a tradition may be shared either consciously or unconsciously.) For Gadamer, authority is thus not merely a way of describing the quality of the knowledge or theory or narrative that a text imparts. Authority is also a description of the extent to which a book participates in a conversation whose language the reader is familiar with. Following Gadamer, a book is authoritative to the extent that it is informative and to the extent to which it lends itself to a cultural and historical understanding that takes place between the reader and the book.

That is not to say that authority works only in positive ways, however. As Gadamer points out, there are certainly times when authority contributes to rigid thinking, when it promulgates prejudices. He notes,

> If the prestige of authority displaces one's own judgment, then authority is in fact a source of prejudices. But this does not preclude its [authority's] being a source of truth, and that is what the Enlightenment failed to see when it denigrated authority.[3]

Authority is certainly in a position to restrict freedom, but it is also in a position to let freedom run its course by allowing a conversation to take place. In his later work, Gadamer gives names to two different kinds of authority, the sort that is restrictive and the sort that is productive. He points out that if a person is "authoritarian," then he or she draws upon institutional power and hierarchical position in order to demonstrate authority. For Gadamer, this sort is restrictive. But he also points out that if one is "authoritative," then one draws upon superior knowledge and insight, upon cultural traditions that allow conversations to take place instead of shutting them down.

"The word 'authoritative,'" writes Gadamer,

> precisely does not refer to a power which is based on authority. It refers, rather, to a form of validity which is genuinely recognized, and not one which is merely asserted. . . . Anyone who has to invoke authority in the first place, whether it be the father within the family or the teacher in the classroom, possesses none.[4]

Authoritativeness is a quality that depends upon learning and knowledge, upon texts and shared cultural understandings. Authoritativeness, unlike authoritarianism, is a productive version of authority. And, following this distinction, a teacher should be authoritative, but should not be authoritarian. An authoritative teacher, like a text that "speaks" with authority, can lay claim to a wide array of knowledge, draws upon a wide cultural horizon that serves as backdrop for a conversation in which curriculum becomes intelligible to students.

What is significant here is precisely the link that Gadamer makes between teaching and authoritativeness. He points out that teaching authority can be construed from a hermeneutic viewpoint, from an appeal to the cultural and historical horizons that make understanding available in the first place. Critiquing the Enlightenment's "subjection of authority to reason," Gadamer asks us to reconsider the possibility that teaching authority is not necessarily a bad thing, and that a student's being made subject to teaching authority is not necessarily a loss of freedom.[5] Yes, it is oppressive if one exercises authority over another by virtue of institutional position. Yes, the Enlightenment tendency to es-chew authority is valid when the authority of church or state or school impinges on one in a way that is a threat to personal autonomy or the use of reason. However, Gadamer points out that there are elements of authority that are useful and empowering as well. Just as the authority of a text derives in part from a larger cultural horizon that actually makes the text intelligible to begin with, so too, for Gadamer, teaching authority derives in part from a shared set of understandings. He argues that the cultural and historical background that supports teaching au-thority is empowering rather than hindering as it contributes to the growth of others rather than curtailing their freedom.

What I find interesting about Gadamer's hermeneutic understand-ing of authority is that it points to the territory that is at stake in my student's comments. Gadamer's analysis suggests that teaching author-ity, if it is to be empowering instead of hindering, should be based upon the knowledge of the teacher, that teaching authority is shored up by the books the teacher has read. Following Gadamer, one can envision the authoritativeness so vividly depicted in many professors' offices today: all of the books behind the professor's desk, those books that she has read with such care, serve to shore up authority in a legitimate way. Looked at in this way, the book that I did not read before the course started is missing from the shelf. My authoritativeness is weakened and illegitimate to the extent that I had not read the text long before.

Gadamer's analysis of authority distinguishes "genuine" authority from nongenuine authority by separating the knowledge-based-ness of authoritativeness from the power-based-ness of authoritarianism. If we were to follow Gadamer here, we would conclude that knowing the text backward and forward and keeping one's aims "genuine" vis-à-vis stu-dents (aiming to impart knowledge rather than aiming to manipulate) is the basis of valid teacher authority. Along these lines it is perfectly rea-sonable to suggest that the professor acts authoritatively by assuming full responsibility for the book, for *reading* the book before it appears on the syllabus, for taking authoritative (as opposed to authoritarian) responsibility for the book. Being authoritative by knowing the book well is a primary responsibility the professor has for his or her students. *Not* reading the book beforehand, but assigning it nevertheless, Gadamer's analysis implies, the professor practices authoritarianism; the professor relies on her institutional position, not on her firsthand knowledge of the work, to convince the student to read that text. This is the sort of authoritarianism that Darrel had every right to question.

As I see it, though, Gadamer's analysis of teaching authority stops short of being able to provide a more nuanced understanding of Darrel's complaint. While Darrel's complaint makes a lot of sense when set against Gadamer's distinction between authoritativeness and authoritarianism, his complaint also points to the limitations of the way in which Gadamer applies his own hermeneutic project to the matter of teaching authority. For when Gadamer speaks of the two types of teaching authority, he creates an either/or scenario that forces an instructor into a corner: either he has genuine knowledge, or he employs institutional power. In this way, Gadamer's thinking on teacher authority contradicts the much more nuanced thinking of his overall hermeneutic project. While Gadamer's overall project is concerned with the incredibly complex interpretive relationship between people and texts, his thinking on teacher authority ghettoizes the teacher/text relationship into a matter of good and bad authority.

Teacher authority should not be split into the two categories of authoritativeness and authoritarianism and then left at that. Such dichotomizing forces an explanation of Darrel's complaint that is too simplistic. What is needed is a way to push farther into the teacher's relation to the text in order to see if Darrel's complaint might be something other than a complaint about authoritarianism. In other words, there is a need to push Gadamer's educational thinking along.

I AM THE MISSING PAGES OF THE TEXT I TEACH

Jacques Derrida, with his notion of the "supplement," opens an important brief on this question of how teaching authority relates to the text. In a very straightforward sense, the teacher can be construed as a supplement to the text, as a welcome addition that makes the text itself more intelligible to the student. This understanding of the instructor-as-supplement follows a long tradition of educational thought that calls upon the teacher to clarify curriculum for students, to make texts more available to their understanding. It's important to think more thoroughly about this role of the instructor as supplement, and that can be done with the more complex notion of supplementarity that Derrida introduces, especially in *Of Grammatology*.[6]

As Derrida points out, the straightforward understanding of supplementarity is limited. The supplement must not be construed solely as something that is *in addition* to a given text. The process of supplementarity entails a double gesture that must be thought in its doubleness. The supplement to a text must be construed both as something that adds to that text *and* as something that makes that text whole, that both augments and completes.

For Derrida, remembering this doubleness of supplementary is absolutely essential. To forget the supplement's doubleness is to practice a forgetfulness of textual complexity. To begin with, a textual supplement enriches a text by bringing it more fully into the light of day, into the realm of human understanding, into presence. Noting this first role of the supplement, Derrida writes,

> The supplement adds itself, it is a surplus, a plenitude enriching another plenitude, the *fullest measure* of presence. It cumulates and accumulates presence. It is thus that art, *techne*, image, convention, etc., come as supplements to nature and are rich with this entire cumulating function.[7]

But also, the supplement instills itself as a *natural* part of that which it supplements. We might think here of a person who takes a vitamin supplement. The vitamin supplement is an addition, yes, but it stands in for a *natural* lack. It becomes a *natural* part of the body. So for Derrida,

> the supplement supplements. It adds only to replace. It intervenes or insinuates itself *in-the-place-of*; if it fills, it is as if one fills a void. If it represents and makes an image, it is by the anterior default of a presence.[8]

More than a merely an add-on by which a presence such as a text is made more present, the supplement also instills itself as a necessary part of the text. The supplement represents the text, yes, but in doing so it also becomes part of the text's economy, part of its very health.

One way to begin considering the link between supplementarity and pedagogy is to remember that teachers are in a relation to their texts that to some extent parallels the complicated relationship between the spoken and the written word. Teachers are often called upon to relate or facilitate the written word by spoken means. This oral/written distinction has connections with Derrida's project. For Derrida, the logic

of supplementarity follows from his critique of philosophers who prioritize either the spoken or the written word. Long-standing paradigms of
linguistics such as Rousseau's or Hegel's or Saussure's have tended to
prioritize either the spoken or the written pole of the speaking/writing
binary. Speaking is taken to be either the ideal form of writing or its
messy human counterpart. The written word is often considered to be
merely a conduit for the spoken or, conversely, what is spoken is often
considered to be merely a conduit for the written word.

But, as Derrida points out, language theory has been unwilling to
think about the ways that writing actually infects the spoken work and,
vice versa, the ways in which spoken word continues to infect language.
There is no way to cleanly separate the spoken from the written because
neither of them works *simply* as a conduit for the other. The spoken
word has a written-ness that can no longer be left out of consideration;
the written word has a spoken-ness that will not go away. To put it very
simply, the word *period* now has an ordinary meaning based on its
grammatical function ("I am done with this book, period!") and the
word "ain't" *is* now in the dictionary. Both the period (".") and "ain't"
have become supplementary. This cross-infection of the spoken/written
has ramifications for the teacher/text relationship.

While the above is a general (and admittedly cursory) description
of supplementarity, it is interesting, and germane to this discussion of
my student's concern, that Derrida links his notion of supplementarity
more explicitly to pedagogy in his analysis of Rousseau's *Emile*. For
Derrida, pedagogy is fundamentally grounded in a tradition of
supplementarity, in a tradition of putting the instructor in place of a
parent, of supplementing parental teachings. Reading *Emile*, Derrida
notes that pedagogy functions within an economy where "it is indeed
culture or cultivation [supplied by the instructor] that must supplement
a deficient nature, a deficiency" that cannot be adequately supplied by
the parent.[9] Quoting Rousseau, Derrida goes on to say that "[a]ll organization of, and all the time spent in, education will be regulated by this
necessary evil: 'supply [suppleer] . . . [what] . . . is lacking' and to replace Nature."[10] Pedagogy is an endeavor caught up in the logic of
supplementarity: children need to be given their supplements not only
because they lack a certain amount of knowledge, but also because such
knowledge completes them and becomes inseparable from them. Education is both *an addition to* and *a natural part of* childhood; the
instructor's role is an addition to the parent's and is itself parental; the
classroom both contributes to certain habits of nature and creates a
naturalness out of certain habits.

This Derridian discussion of supplementarity is not as far from
Darrel's concern as it might seem. What is striking and provocative in

Darrel's comment is that there is a logic of supplementarity that works alongside of or, to stay with Derrida's theme, seems to supplement, such a straightforward discussion of authority as Gadamer's. For while there is a sense in which pedagogical authority must depend upon the instructor's grounding in textual knowledge, in what Gadamer names the "genuine knowledge" of the "traditionary text," there is also a sense in which the instructor and the text stand within an economy of supplementarity that makes the instructor both *an addition to* the text and *an integral part of* the text. Following Derrida's logic of supplementarity, Darrel's experience of lack when he discovered that the book had not been read by me is not only a matter of disgust with the teacher's lack of authoritativeness. It is also a reminder that the book is somehow incomplete without the instructor's presence. The book experiences the teacher not only as an extension of itself, but as a supplement that it cannot do without. Like the teacher whose introduction of culture into the "natural" family life of the child becomes part and parcel of that "natural" family life, the instructor whose job it is to supplement the text also becomes part and parcel of the very text whose message she attempts to convey. When I complain that my teacher has not read the book, I am not only complaining that she is not authoritative enough; I am complaining also that the book is missing some pages.

Comparing Gadamer's description of "authoritativeness" to Derrida's understanding of "supplementarity" is instructive. While both versions link up with Darrel's concern about the relation of the book to teacher authority, this comparison points out how Gadamer relies on a one-way understanding of authoritativeness that is limiting. For Gadamer, the movement of text and textual tradition runs from historical tradition, through texts, then out to the mouth and fingers of the instructor. The instructor is a conduit for the message of tradition and for the message of the text. That is not to say the text of the tradition must be conservative or regressive; only that the movement is from what has been previously known to what the student is to learn. The pedagogical problem, as I see it, with Gadamer's understanding of authority is not that it depends upon tradition in any regressive sense. Indeed, the textual authority upon which I build my syllabus, and upon which I speak, may be based on progressive or even radical education. The problem with this understanding of authority is that it depends upon a pedagogical movement that is one-way.

In contrast, Derrida's logic of the supplement highlights the two-way movement that complicates the teacher's position with respect to the text. The teacher participates in more than a one-way trajectory from tradition to text to teacher to student. She is also a complicatedly *real* part of the text that he teaches. Teachers and students are in a relation with their texts. When I teach subject matter, I am not only a representative of, nor only an addition to, the tradition from which I have constructed my syllabus; I am also an active part of that tradition. I act as a spokesperson of the book that I may or may not have read, but I also push the book this way or that way as if I am one of its chapters. This supplementary understanding of the teacher's role vis-à-vis the text suggests that Darrel's critique was more than a claim that I wasn't properly prepared to teach the text, more than a claim that I was not authoritative enough; it was also a claim that the text itself was somehow lacking a part of itself without which it would fail to be whole. Because the supplement is both an addition to, and a part of; because of this, my disconnection from that text threatened the authority of the book itself. My *not*-reading was a weakening of the book.

BEING CONTENT

So I consider it important to follow Derrida's logic of supplementarity when it comes to the complicated connection between teacher and texts. I have been inspired by Darrel's challenge. It was a challenge that I assumed initially to be a questioning of my authority, but that I now see as a questioning of the authority relation between me and the book that I hadn't read. I think it is too easy for educators to think along one-way lines when it comes to curriculum, authority, and pedagogy. It is too easy for educators to assume, like Gadamer, that pedagogical authority is primarily a matter of deploying one's knowledge of curriculum in a judicious manner. Following Derrida's lead, we must also think about the relation of pedagogical authority vis-à-vis the text. Because, as the instructor, I am part of the educational text, it follows that, in spite of the way I teach, I nevertheless have an active role in constructing the way educational texts are read by my students. Assuming that Derrida has a (supplementary) point, it is impossible for a student to read a classroom text without, in some way, reading me. Thus, the habits that students form around reading curriculum are going to reflect, at least in part, the habits they form around reading *me*.

To make this notion of "reading the instructor" more specific, imagine that I am a white man and that I have chosen to read Toni Morrison's *Playing in the Dark* with my class.[11] (To summarize inadequately, Morrison's text is an analysis of how the white racist imagination that has come to structure canonical literary works in the United States.) Having assigned this text, the problem of teacher authority rests not only on whether I have understood the text deeply enough, on whether I can refrain from *forcing* the text on my students. It refers also to how I, as a white man, become part of the text's own analysis.

Morrison's text, as complicated as this may seem, becomes in my class a text that is co-authored in black and white, by Morrison and me. To become educated about Morrison's argument means, at least in my class, also to become educated about how a white man can be in relation to that argument.

When I teach Morrison's text, and when I do so with the logic of the supplement in mind, I must be cognizant of the perlocutionary (to borrow John Austin's term) effects that I put into play as a white man who teaches that text.[12] Being part of that text, I will also be part of the ways in which my students read that text now and in the future. As part of that text, my whiteness will be a barrier for some students and an invitation for others. Importantly, I cannot shirk that barrier status, or that invitational status. That status will not go away by laying the onus of learning on my students nor will it go away by presenting the text as if I am merely a conduit through which my students reach text directly. The white perspective that I bring to this text on white racism will be part of the lesson that this text teaches. And conversely, if my teaching strategy is to act as if I do not have a perspective on this text, then the message this text sends may very well be that a white person has no pages to add to Morrison's text. Whatever I say—even if I say nothing—speaks pages about a white understanding of the racist imagination.

To return to the objections raised by Darrel, I now have a deeper respect for the validity of his reaction. It now seems to me that there are at least two distinct reasons for his response. On one hand, it may have been that Darrel was reacting to what he thought of as a particularly authoritarian act on my part. Here I am following Gadamer: because authority becomes authoritarian when not based on genuine knowledge, it is entirely justified to accuse an instructor of resorting to authoritarianism when he chooses texts based not on knowledge, but upon his institutional position. Following a Gadamerian logic, my choosing of that text can justifiably be criticized because it depended more on my institutional power to set curriculum than it did upon my genuine knowledge of the text. On the other hand, Darrel may have been reacting to the textual incompleteness that my admission revealed. Here I am following Derrida: because the instructor resides in a position of supplementarity vis-à-vis her text, curriculum is simply not complete unless it is supplemented by the instructor's own authoritative voice. Pedagogical authority can be described as the authority that books borrow from teachers. Because I had not read the book before I assigned it, the *text's* authority became permanently marred in this student's eyes. Along with Derrida, a case can be made that Darrel knew the text he had purchased was missing some pages.

SUPPLEMENTARITY AGAINST THE BACKDROP
OF PREDOMINANT PEDAGOGIES

One way or another, both of these versions of textual authority (the authoritative and the supplemental) show how the book supplements the teacher. On the one hand, we have a picture of a teacher who enacts authority because he or she has the ability to draw upon the authority of the book. Drawing upon the authority of the book rather than drawing upon the authority of one's position as teacher, is, at least according to this first version, a helpful way to enact authority. In this first picture, we find that the teacher has a choice to make between the extrinsic and the intrinsic. Either she can put in play the external authority of the institution to which she belongs, or, she can enact the internal authority that comes with the book's knowledge. In this first picture, there is a difference in distance between the illegitimate, institutional authority that one might enact and the legitimate, textual authority that one might enact. One is far away, while the other is close. It is in this way that the authoritarian person draws on an authority that is distant while the authoritative person enacts authority that is close. The judicious enactment of authority deals with knowledge that is close at hand, with a text that is sutured in tight.

On the other hand, we have a picture of a teacher who stands in a certain relation with the text that she teaches. In this picture, there is also something that is far away and something that is close. This something is the *same* thing. It is the book. When one thinks of the teacher as a spokesperson for the book, as a voice for the written text, then the book seems far away from the teacher. The spokesperson can stand at a great distance because she is merely an echo of what the book says. She is like the stereo speaker that can stand at a great distance from wherever the recording itself is being played. When, however, one thinks of the teacher as a spokesperson who is part and parcel of the book's presentation, then the teacher and the book turn out to be located at the same place. When the spoken word is taken to be central to the written word, then the teacher is closely bound to the text that is being taught.

Indeed, a lot of educational theory about authority hinges on the sort of relation that exists between teachers and texts. In the introductory chapter, I gave a brief overview of three different orientations toward educational authority: the progressive, the traditional, and the critical. I described the progressive orientation as a complete dismissal of authority, the traditional orientation as an embracing of authority, and the critical orientation as a pragmatic embracing of authority, an embracing that endorses authority as long as that authority serves liberatory purposes. Actually, each of these three orientations also includes an orientation toward the relation that exists between teachers and texts. Let me explain.

The progressive orientation toward educational authority assumes that texts need little support from teachers. Progressives assume for the most part that texts can stand on their own, can speak for themselves. Thus, in classrooms inspired by progressive pedagogy one often finds a rather hands-off approach to the content matter of the texts being learned. In such classrooms it is most often assumed that the text is better learned if it is kept separate from the instructor, if it is dealt with by the student, for the student, rather than by the teacher, for the student. To give one small example, I need only recall the responses that I have received from progressive educators when they have listened to me tell my story about Darrel. I am not exaggerating when I say that most of my *progressive* colleagues who have listened to my story have doubted whether Darrel's complaint was legitimate. Those colleagues who call themselves progressive have, for the most part, few qualms about teaching a book that one has not already read. After all, from the progressive perspective, it is not the teacher's role to offer direct instruction on a text's content. To put this in terms of the teacher's relation to the text: the progressive teacher keeps his or her distance from the texts that are being learned. The progressive orientation sees the relation between teacher and text as a distant one.

If the progressive orientation construes the relation between teacher and text as a distant one, the traditional orientation is just the opposite. For traditionalists, it is just fine for teachers to teach the content matter of a book. After all, the use of authority for such a benign purpose— that of teaching texts—is perfectly acceptable. Indeed, because students seem to benefit from the direct use of pedagogical authority by the teacher, the use of such authority is more than acceptable; it is pedagogically necessary. It is necessary in that it aids in the learning of texts. And because of this pedagogical necessity, traditionalist theory carries with it a perspective on the proximity of teacher to text. Because of the necessity of pedagogical intervention on the part of the teacher, the traditional teacher is a *confrere* of the text. The teacher keeps the text close at hand.

As one might expect, the critical perspective blends the progressive and the traditional. From the viewpoint of the criticalist, the ultimate aim of education is to foster a healthy distance between text and teacher. The steady-state at which a critically educated student eventually arrives is one where the student no longer depends upon the authority of the teacher to shore up her own knowledge of the text. However, from the critical perspective, the student may not be able to arrive at such a steady-state on her own. Why? Because hegemonic ideology prevents the student from reading texts properly. While the criticalist might want to keep her distance from the text, while she might hold such a distance as an ideal, she knows that, in fact, hegemonic ideology requires her to intervene in the student's reading of the text. If students are to read texts on their own, as in the progressive tradition, they might not be able to see past the implicit ideology of those texts. Hence the necessity of an enlightened, critical educator who can help students to see past ideology and into the "true" message of the text. As one might expect, the criticalist is a mixture of progressive distance from the text and traditionalist proximity. She tries to be distant from the text, but is willing to be close to the text when such proximity is required in order to debunk hegemonic ideology.

Once again, I have stereotyped these three positions—the progressive, the traditional, and the critical—unreasonably. I have done so for heuristic purposes. Indeed, these stereotypes are not far off the sorts of general orientations that guide many a thoughtful teacher. By explicating these three ways that educational authority gets positioned vis-à-vis the text, I have wanted to show the various ways that texts enter into the relation of educational authority. Texts are part and parcel of the authority relation. Depending upon how one theorizes the authority relation, depending upon the orientation that one takes toward pedagogy, texts can be construed as either more central or less central to that relation.

TEXTUAL AUTHORITY AND RELATION

Actually, I would say that each of these positions gets it all wrong. A text is not to be distanced from the teacher because one is progressive, held tight because one is conservative, nor held tight strategically because one is a criticalist. In contrast, I would take up Derrida's position, namely, that texts *always* supplement the one who teaches. In contrast to the orientation of these three popular positions, the teacher is always part and parcel of the text that is being taught—even if he or she has not read the text! A mistake is made by the progressive, traditional, and critical orientations alike. Their mistake is twofold. First, these orientations assume that one's relation to a text is somehow voluntary, that it is based upon the will of the teacher, upon either the unwillingness of the teacher to teach the text through direct instruction, or upon his willingness to do so. On the contrary, the will of the teacher has very little to do with the teacher's textual authority. Teachers supplement texts whether or not they *want* to do so, as the story of Darrel so clearly illustrates. Teachers are always already close to their texts, but this has nothing to do with some traditionalist orientation that advocates direct instruction based on the teacher's knowledge of the text. Teachers are always already close to their texts because the pedagogical relation of authority is thoroughly textual.

Second, these orientations are off the mark because they see the text as a matter of monological authority (coming from the teacher) rather than as part of a *relation* of authority. As is the case when progressive, traditional, and critical educators treat authority as a substance, when these folks theorize the place of the book, they do so solely from a teacher-sided perspective. That is to say, these perspectives assume that it is the distance or proximity of the teacher to the text that is paramount. They assume that the decision of the teacher to stay close (in the case of traditional and critical orientations) to the book, or the decision of the teacher to stay far (in the case of progressive orientations) from the book, is primarily the teacher's. Following these three conceptions of the textual life of authority, it is the teacher's stance vis-à-vis the text that is paramount. The student is hardly involved.

Yet in contrast to this picture of a teacher who has monological authority over the educational life of the text, let's remember Darrel (and for that matter Julie, too). Darrel is intimately involved in the way his instructor gets positioned in relation to the text. Far from being the passive recipient of the teacher's textual orientation, students (and not only Darrel, but all students) are integral to the ways in which teachers get configured as supplements. As I have argued above, teachers are supplemental to texts whether or not they choose to be, whether or not they disavow their role as textual authorities. It is precisely because of the fact that students construe their teachers as textual authorities that teachers become supplemental to their texts. In this way, the textual authority of teachers is relational: students impute textual authority to teachers whether teachers "want" that authority or not.

DISCOUNTED SUPPLEMENTARITY

In this section I would like to further illustrate the textual relation by looking more closely at instances when students discount the teacher and the text. One of the problems with discussions of educational authority, a problem that I tried to articulate in rehearsing the "common" assumptions held about authority, is that they tend to focus too narrowly on the teacher side of the educational relation. Such discussions tend to be monological. Indeed, when I examined my own interaction with Darrel and the supplemental position it put me in vis-à-vis an educational text, I still focused too narrowly on the ties between teacher and book. Surely, this teacher/book tie means something to the student as well. If the teacher is tied to the book, how does this bear on the one who is receiving the education? What circumstances lead a student to

break with supplemental authority? When is supplementarity an intrusive aspect of the authority relation rather than a benign one? What are
the political dimensions of the tying-together of the teacher and the
book? How can student resistance be understood in light of such tying?

To further explore this matter, I turn to Athol Fugard's play *My
Children! My Africa!*[13] Fugard's play is set in the fascist South African
regime during the Apartheid era. It explores the relationship between
two high school students and one of their teachers. Thami, a black
South African student and Isabel, a white South African student of
Afrikaaner descent, attend different high schools. They come into contact, though, because each has been chosen to take part in a literary
competition, a competition that tests their respective knowledges of
English literature.

Mr. M is their coach. He is a black South African and is a teacher
of English at Thami's school. Although he is a black South African
teaching in an all-black school, he helps to coach an extracurricular
literary competition in which the teams are comprised of both blacks
and whites. Thus, although Thami is Mr. M's student in an all-black
school while Isabel attends an all-white school, Mr. M coaches both
Thami and Isabel after school hours as they prepare together for the
competition. Isabel ventures into a black neighborhood where she has
never been before in order to take advantage of Mr. M's coaching.

The play is set in the late 1980s when there is considerable student
resistance, in schools and on the streets, against the Apartheid government. It is this militant anti-Apartheid unrest that serves as a political
backdrop for the play. Although the play starts out during a time when
students are attending school regularly, as the play progresses, students
have begun to show their resistance by boycotting the black high school
where Thami attends and where Mr. M teaches. They are refusing to
attend school in order to force reform in the Apartheid system. By the
end of the play, Mr. M, being himself opposed to the boycott, gives
names of some of the boycotting students to the police. Mr. M, the
teacher, becomes Mr. M the informer. He is denounced as such by the
boycotting students. Toward the end of the play, he is killed by an angry
mob because of his status as an informer. This happens in spite of
Thami's efforts to make a public apology in his name. Let this suffice
as an introduction to the play. In what follows, I want to use some of
the words of the characters in this play to investigate the relation between students and textual authority.

To get at this relation, let us first examine the textual authority of
the teacher in Fugard's play, Mr. M. In particular we can look at the
way he stands as a supplement in relation to the English literature that
he teaches and that forms the basis for his coaching of Thami and

Isabel. As the play unfolds, we learn about Mr. M's unwavering love of the texts he teaches. In the terms I have presented in this book, we learn that he has become part and parcel of the texts he teaches. He and they have entered a supplemental relation. For example, as play proceeds Mr. M reveals to us that his entry into the teaching profession is marked not only by a desire to teach young people, but more importantly by a desire to supplement the experiences of his own life with the experiences that he reads about in books. He has decided to enter the teaching profession because he believes that a lifelong apprenticeship to books will serve him better than any other sort of career might do. He decides to follow a career of teaching because he believes that a career of reading will, in fact, change him for good.

Mr. M's decision to take up a career of books is described as follows. I quote at length Fugard's beautiful rendering of this decision:

> This was my home, my life, my one and only ambition . . . to be a good teacher!. . . . That ambition goes back to when [I] was just a skinny little ten-year-old pissing on a small gray bush at the top of the Wapasberg Pass. . . .
>
> I went to the teacher who was with us and asked him: "Teacher, where will I come to if I start walking that way?" . . . and I pointed. He laughed. "Little man," he said, "that way is north. If you start walking that way and just keep walking, and your legs don't give in, you will see all of Africa! Yes, Africa little man! You will see the great rivers of the continent: the Vaal, the Zambesi, the Limpopo, the Congo and then the mighty Nile. You will see the mountains: the Drakensberg, Kilimanjaro, Kenya and the Ruwenzori. And you will meet all our brothers: the little Pygmies of the forests, the proud Masai, the Watusi . . . tallest of the tall and the Kikuyu standing on one leg like herons in a point waiting for a frog." "Has teacher seen all that?" I asked. "No," he said. "Then how does teacher know it's there?" "Because it is all in the books and I have read the books and if you work hard in school little man, you can do the same without worrying about your legs giving in."
>
> He was right Thami. *I* have seen it. It is all there in the books just as he said it was and I have made it mine.[14]

In this moving passage, Mr. M tells of the ways that books have become part of his very life. By choosing teaching as a career, he has had the chance to go on the very same journeys of the mind that his former teacher had been able to go on. Importantly, his choice to become a teacher was made precisely because being a teacher would require a rigorous assimilation of books. He knew early on that becoming engrossed in books would change his life, that such a textual profession would take him places both literally and metaphorically. Mr. M is indeed a dedicated teacher. He follows through with this teacherly ambition to let books change his life. Having been a teacher for decades, he is now able to say, in a very supplementary way, "It is all there in the books just as he said it was and I have made it mine."[15] Mr. M has let the teacherly reading of books supplement his life experience. He and the books he has read are now intertwined.

The books that Mr. M has read also supplement his life experience in a particularly political way. During this time of political upheaval and student resistance in the South African townships, he has clung to the notion that learning itself will set the stage for political change in a way that no other political activities will be able to do. He maintains that the words used by those in the South African freedom movement are very weak compared to the articulate political phrases that a well-educated person can construct. Says Mr. M:

> Slogans don't need much in the way of grammar do they. . . .
> [*Picks up his dictionary. The stone in one hand, the book in the other*] You know something interesting, Thami . . . if you put these two on a scale I think you would find that they weighed just about the same. But in this hand I am holding the whole English language. This . . . [*the stone*] is just *one* word in that language. It's true! All that wonderful poetry that you and Isabel tried to cram into your beautiful heads . . . in here![16]

Weighing the stone and the dictionary together, Mr. M demonstrates that even his political strategies are supplemented by, are shaped by, the books that he values so much. His strategy for changing the South African political system is tied to the books that he has taught, and learned from, over the course of his teaching. For Mr. M, these books, and the articulate language they represent, are linked not only to his authority as a teacher but to the authority that he claims to have about how politics should be conducted. The educational authority of Mr. M's texts has gotten under his skin even when it comes to politics.

Mr. M's relation to his texts is quintessentially "traditional" if the traditional orientation toward texts can be said to entail a fairly blind faith that canonical texts carry the moral weight to change things for the better in this world. It is also a traditional orientation in the sense that this teacher assumes it to be his role to pass down the wisdom of these canonical texts, to "stay close" to his texts as I have described earlier. Indeed, Mr. M has good reason to stay close to his texts. He has been a successful teacher who has "seen" the great rivers and mountains of Africa, who has made them his own as a result of the texts to which he has been devoted. This experience alone is proof enough, at least for Mr. M, that texts carry a moral weight to change people's lives for the better. And, when it comes to political change, Mr. M's belief in the power of texts seems to have borne fruit as well. For, by coaching Thami and Isabel, a black student and a white student, together, Mr. M has successfully caused the color line of Apartheid to be crossed. His coaching of Thami and Isabel, and their surprising friendship in spite of Apartheid laws, proves Mr. M's position: that social change can be effected when people of different races use literary texts as a common ground for gathering.

At least at the personal level, and in one small instance of the political arena, it must be admitted that Mr. M and his texts have, together, created the circumstances for moral change in the world. They have enriched Mr. M's life and they have enabled a subversive engagement between a black and a white student to occur in spite of a fascist Apartheid regime. With the aid of Mr. M and his favorites—Coleridge, Wordsworth, Byron, Keats, Arnold, Shelley—Thami and Isabel forge a close friendship during a time when their paths might otherwise not cross at all. It might be said, from the two versions of textual authority that we looked at earlier, that Mr. M has been admirably authoritative (rather than authoritarian) and that the educational texts he has been involved with have been a true supplement to his life. Mr. M holds a traditional reverence for his texts, one that keeps texts close at hand. And, his supplementary relation to his texts has benefited both himself and his students.

LESSONS FROM ATHOL FUGARD

However, from the perspective of Thami, Mr. M's prize student, the supplementary relationship between teacher and text looks quite different. Indeed, Fugard's entire play hinges upon Thami's *relation* to Mr. M's text-driven authority. For, Thami's relation to Mr. M's text-driven authority cannot be extricated from the authority of the great number young black students (and young black *former* students who have already quit school), people who, like Thami, want a different version of authority than Mr. M has in mind. Thami does not have a straightforward respect for the textual authority of his teacher. Thami knows that Mr. M's textual authority does not have power to change society. He knows that Mr. M's moral stance is in conflict with the political action needed to change a country steeped in racist laws. Mr. M himself describes this conflict:

> Respect for authority, right authority, is deeply ingrained in the African soul. It's all I've got when I stand there in Number One [his classroom]. Respect for my authority is my only teaching aid. If I ever lost it those young people will abandon their desks and take to the streets.[17]

Thami is one of those young people who will take to the streets.

From Thami's perspective, the authority of Mr. M does not stand alone; it stands in competition with the authority of those students who decide to take to the streets. From Thami's perspective, there is a choice to make about *which* authority he will enter into a relation with. As the play progresses, Thami's political place in the anti-Apartheid struggle becomes more firmly affixed "to the streets." Mr. M's literary knowledge, his supplementary relation to the texts he teaches, is discarded by Thami in favor of more pressing political commitments. Speaking of Mr. M, Thami says that "[h]is ideas about change are the old-fashioned ones. And what have they achieved? Nothing. We are worse off now than we ever were. The people don't want to listen to his kind of talk anymore."[18] In Thami's eyes, the "old fashioned" quality of his teacher's authority undermines its more positive potential. Thami is faced with the textual authority of his teacher and the political authority of his comrades. He chooses to authorize the latter rather than the former. This, in spite of the benevolent, textual authority of Mr. M, authority which, as we have seen, does change lives for the better, at least on some small scale.

Let us draw a few insights from Fugard's play. First, the relation of the student to the authority of the teacher/text does not only depend upon the sincerity of a teacher's engagement with the text. Indeed, Mr. M is sincere to the core about his teaching, about his love for literature, about the potential for literature to actually *create* experience and opportunity. Mr. M has concrete experience from his own life that literature can make one's life more worth living. Because of his own life experience, he assumes that he can change his student's life for the better in the same way. He is sure of this fact:

> He is my favorite. Thami Mbikwana! Yes, I have waited a long time for him. To tell you the truth I had given up all hope of him ever coming along. Any teacher who takes his calling seriously dreams about that one special pupil, that one eager and gifted young head into which he can pour all

that he knows and loves and who will justify all the years of frustration in the classroom.[19]

Mr. M hopes to "point to Thami and say: And now ladies and gentlemen, a full university scholarship if you please."[20]

Truly, Mr. M's "textual sincerity" fills this drama with pathos. Mr. M is a tragic figure whose tragic flaw is his devotion to the written word. His devotion is especially tragic because he assumes that his "best" student will necessarily follow him in his textual footsteps. Mr. M makes the same assumption that so many good-intentioned, well-read teachers make. He assumes that if his authority is enacted in a sincere way, with the right texts, then his "best" students are sure to benefit. He believes this so much that he is willing to become an informer against his students' political activities with the hope that his students will go back to the classroom and learn what he has to teach them. He loses his life by clinging to these good intentions. His good intentions with respect to his texts have little bearing on the efficacy of the authority relation that is enacted between him and his students.

A second insight to draw from Fugard's play is one that I have briefly touched upon in the introductory chapter. It is that educational authority works in circuits. And, the student has an active (rather than a passive) role in this *circuit* of authority. Yes, Thami is the prize student of Mr. M, the student Mr. M hopes to influence the most through his great love for the written word. Yet at the same time, Thami is also the student who has the most ability to either authorize of de-authorize Mr. M's teaching. Thami's status as Mr. M's "best" student not only signifies that Mr. M's hopes are pinned on Thami. It also signifies that the very authority Mr. M so cherishes, the authority of the canon, or the written word—this very authority depends upon Thami's own authorization for it to be enacted. When Thami decides that Mr. M's ways are too old-fashioned, when he decides to authorize the actions of his comrades rather than the books of his teacher, then the textual authority that Mr. M would like to enact falls flat. In spite of Mr. M's sincere engagement with his texts, and in spite of his belief that book learning is the only way to prevent students from taking to the streets, Thami takes to the streets anyway.

Fugard's play teaches this general lesson about the authority relation between students and teachers and texts: Authority works in a circuit from teacher to student and from student to teacher. It works through a circuit of *authorization*. It is not the case that the teacher is the only one to enact authority. Authority does not start from the teacher and then go toward the student. Rather, authority is borne out of an authorizing circuit that gets established between the teacher, and the student, and the text. For authority to be enacted, it is not enough for there to be a show of textual authority on the side of the teacher. It is not enough for the teacher to know her books through and through. It is not enough for the teacher to act in authoritarian ways. It is not enough for her to have good authoritative intentions. The teacher always needs to be authorized by the student just as much as she needs to enact authority. Indeed, we might even say that authority has not been initiated by the teacher until it has been authorized by students. This concept of circuitry is central for understanding how textual authority gets configured from a student's perspective, and it is central for a more general analysis of authority's relationality. To say it again: authority works in a circuit. The authority of one person comes into being because it is authorized by another person. This notion of circuitry will be especially important later on when we look into the authority of questioning and when I offer an extension of Paulo Freire's conception of authority.

A final insight to draw from Fugard's play takes us back to Derrida's notion of the supplement. The insight is this: from the perspective of a student, sometimes texts can become *too* supplemental to the teacher. I have mentioned that Mr. M's tragic flaw stems from his extreme devotion to the canon and in his extreme belief that book-learning will change both his own life and the lives of his students for the better. That is from Mr. M's perspective. From Thami's perspective, Mr. M's supplemental relationship to his texts looks a bit different. As we saw above, Thami thinks that his teacher's "ideas about change are the old-fashioned ones. And what have they achieved? Nothing. We are worse off now than we ever were. The people don't want to listen to his kind of talk anymore."[21] Interestingly, Mr. M is being understood by Thami differently than he might want to have himself understood. Somehow, the "old-fashioned" books that Mr. M reads get linked in Thami's mind (and in the minds of those who have Thami's ear) to "old-fashioned" ways of acquiescing to Apartheid laws, which in turn get linked to "old-fashioned" ways of teaching and learning. I do not think that Mr. M means to be "old-fashioned" in the derogatory sense that the students have in mind. Mr. M surely wants to change the Apartheid regime. After all, he facilitates the color-line crossing friendship of Thami and Isabel.

Yet notwithstanding Mr. M's intentions, he has become indelibly marked as old-fashioned by Thami and his comrades. From the perspective of Thami, he has become "hyper-supplemented." Mr. M stands as a dramatic metaphor for the many teachers who become so inexorably branded by students with such labels as "the old-fashioned English teacher," or "the Darwinian science teacher," or "the jock physical education teacher," or "the laissez faire education professor." While Mr.

M's status as symbol of an old order is surely more rich and complicated than the simplistic labeling of a teacher who teaches a certain subject matter, what I want to stress here is the way in which such labeling must be taken seriously as it effects the ways students authorize and de-authorize teachers. Mr. M is de-authorized because he is perceived as "hyper-supplemented" and inflexible. Thinking back to the example of Julie that I offered in the previous chapter, we could say that she de-authorized her history professor in much the same way. That is, once she found out that his only concern was for his own curriculum, once she found out that he was so hyper-supplemented as not to see that her grief was a significant pedagogical concern, then she de-authorized both him and the history he wanted to teach her. From the perspective of a student, one's authority is not always shored up by proximity to one's subject matter.

This chapter has tried to pay attention to the place of curriculum in the educational relation of authority. If the introductory chapter was a general outline of how we might think of educational authority in terms of relation, this chapter examined an inevitable component of that relation—the written word. To restate the point that I have been building to: the relation of authority can be understood at a textual level. Teachers are supplementary to texts in a Derridean sense. Because we are supplementary to texts, we cannot disavow our role as textual authorities. When students read texts, their teachers are inevitably involved. Whether teachers take an active role in interpreting texts for students, or whether teachers take a passive role by trying to let students interpret texts for themselves, students nevertheless authorize teachers to be part and parcel of the curriculum. Educators cannot escape this fact no matter how progressive we might aim to be. Because authority in education is primarily a textual relation, teachers and students are in relation to texts just as much as they are relation to each other. In the next chapter, I will go one step farther by asking, "What sort of relation is this, this relation of authority?" As I will show in the chapter that follows, the relation of authority is a literary relation.

CHAPTER 2

The Literary Relation of Authority

If authority is a relation, what is this relation like? In this chapter, I will make the case that the authority relation is like a literary relation. To consider how one relates to authority in education, it is best to consider how one interprets literature. With this in mind, I will retell a short story by Franz Kafka. I will use Kafka's story, and Jacques Derrida's interpretation of that story, to show the authority/literature connection. Also in this chapter, I will examine how we must change the ways we currently conceive of communication. By doing so, I will extend the brief remarks made in the introductory chapter about the authority that gets enacted when people speak and listen to each other. As I will show, current, "thingified" conceptions of authority are hamstrung by the "sender-receiver" model of communication. I suggest that we reconceptualize communication itself as a matter of interpretation. Doing so, we can once again foreground the fact that authority is a relation. It is a relation through and through, even in its speaking and listening.

EDUCATIONAL AUTHORITY IN KAFKA: FORCE WITHOUT SIGNIFICANCE

In Franz Kafka's tale, *Before the Law*, a man from the country approaches a building where a doorkeeper is standing watch.[1] In front of the building, the man asks if he might be allowed inside in order to meet "the Law" that resides therein. The doorkeeper tells the man that he cannot admit the man at the moment, but it is possible that the man

41

will be allowed to enter later. The door to the law is open during this inquiry, but when the countryman tries to peer through, he is met with laughs by the doorkeeper. The man is dismayed: "The Law, he thinks, should be accessible to every man and at all times."[2] The man is told that there are more doors inside and more doorkeepers even more powerful than this one. The man from the country is relentless, though. He waits for days and years. He gives gifts to the doorkeeper on occasion but to no avail. Finally, the man grows old and approaches death, still waiting to be let in to the law. At the end of his life he asks why there has been no one else who has joined him, during all those years, to seek admittance to the law. To this, the doorkeeper answers that "this door was intended only for you. I am now going to shut it."[3]

The short stories and novels of Franz Kafka, having introduced into the English language the term *Kafkaesque*, are famous for the enervating, paralytic mood they evoke. Kafka's narratives generally present the struggles of a protagonist who is faced with a pressing condition, but the protagonist generally does not know the *content* of that condition. The man in search of the law in the short story under consideration; the man who is being punished but does not know why he is being punished in *"In the Penal Colony"*; the man who is trying to get into *The Castle* but does not know how; the man in *The Trial* who is served with papers to appear at a trial without being told of the accusation against him—in most cases, Kafka's fiction tells of a protagonist who is highly compelled but unaware exactly what his compulsion *is*.[4] Giorgio Agamben has accurately called this Kafkaesque predicament "being in force without significance."[5] There is a lot of force in Kafka's fiction. His protagonists are highly motivated. What the significance of their motivation is, though, is always difficult to discern.

It is striking to me how easy it is to discern this Kafkaesque quality in so many cases where authority is being enacted. Especially when *educational* authority is being enacted, such authority often borders on the Kafkaesque. I do not consider it a stretch to think about the many instances when educational authority impinges on students and teachers as instances that have "force without significance." From the student perspective, one need only think of the processes by which one obtains degrees, diplomas, and grades. As many a student can tell you, one works for a degree, perhaps for years and years. When the degree is finally obtained, there often lingers a certain dissatisfaction that the precise thing that one coveted for so long is really not much more than a shiny piece of paper with fancy print. One tends to wonder, in the end, if there was really any content to the very goal of all that travail. To be sure, on the way toward that goal, a student often projects into the degree, the diploma, or the certificate a magical sort of content. But in the end, haven't most students felt a sort of Kafkaesque realization that there was plenty of force to the degree, but not so much significance? This parallel between Kafkaesqueness and student experience seems to break down only insofar as Kafka's protagonists feel this lack of significance *even on the way toward* their goals. While in education, students usually sense that authority is hollow only once they have experienced the full dose of what authority has to offer, Kafka's characters are persecuted with such hollowness from the very beginning.

From the teacher's perspective, one might think of the authority enacted when grades are given. Haven't many teachers felt the intense irony of the grading procedure? To be sure, grading is one of the central processes by which teaching authority is enacted. But is there not a distinct lack of *content* to grading? While grades are, at least as far as institutional rhetoric is concerned, supposed to reflect the achievement of students, it is really very difficult to say that grades actually do such a thing. As most teachers would, I think, acknowledge, one never actually knows how much a student has, or has not, learned. A teacher can hardly hope to know some of the more intangible aspects of student learning, such as whether the student puts her learning to use some time in the future, or whether the student uses that learning to shape her future life in empowering ways.

Grades are also said to have significance insofar as they motivate students. But the final grade at the end of an academic semester, however full of force it is, is particularly lacking in such motivational significance. At such an endpoint, the grade can no longer serve its ostensible purpose as motivator because there is nothing to be motivated *for* when the course is already completed! And even when interim grades are given out, say, as the academic semester progresses, isn't there often a certain Kafkaesque sense in which the grades have a lot of force but very little content? Grades really do not *mean* much of anything. Many experienced teachers will say, if not in these precise terms, that they have felt a sort of Kafkaesque pang when they allot grades. As one long-time primary school teacher recently told me, "When it comes giving grades, I often feel like a charlatan."

Or, one can think about the forceful, yet content-less, quality that typifies the teaching of the famous educator Socrates. When, in the *Meno*, Socrates acts as a "torpedo fish," when he refuses to give content to his interlocutors but instead answers their questions with more questions of his own, he enacts the sort of educational authority that leaves them, much like the man in Kafka's story, without anywhere to go.[6] Or when Socrates says that he is the wisest of the Athenians because he knows not how *much* he knows, but rather how *little* he knows, he certainly enacts a very powerful—yet content-less—show of authority.[7]

And again, when in the *Meno* he uses his skill at questioning to evoke from the slave boy geometrical knowledge without teaching him anything *new*, there is a sense in which the authority of Socrates comes not from any meaning, but from some sort of pure force.

It *might* even be said that the Greek doctrine of *anamnesis*, far from being an obtuse and unbelievable myth of the existence of some collective memory, is more properly conceived as that enigmatic quality of educational authority that Kafka illustrates so well.[8] What I mean by this is that perhaps the Greeks noticed exactly what Kafka noticed about authority. Perhaps they noticed the many instances when authority seems to function even in the absence of propositional meaning. Upon noticing such a magical occurrence, it is not at all unreasonable, at least in a society where myths are common, to explain away such a thing with recourse to mythology. If meaning seems to come from nowhere, then the myth of collective memory is a fine way to explain just where "nowhere" is located. And another point is to be made about Socratic themes. Take the elenchus, or, "Socratic Method." The force of the enlenchus, with its refusal to give answers, with its refusal to give meaning—this force can well be described in the same way that Agamben describes Kafka's world. The enlenchus is full of "force without significance."

AUTHORITY AND THE LITERARY RELATION

So in Kafka's fiction, we can see the beginnings of an analysis of *how* the authority relation works. Following the examples of authority that fill the works of Kafka, I would say that educational authority most often works on the basis of a certain "force without significance." In order to further illustrate the force without significance of educational authority, it is helpful to look at Jacques Derrida's analysis of Kafka. Following Derrida, we can understand the force without significance of educational authority as the same sort of authority enacted through the reader's encounter with literature. The workings of authority are indebted to the sort of *relation* that occurs when one encounters literature. So in the case of "Before the Law," the man from the country is not only unsuccessful at understanding and gaining access to "the Law," where the law is an example of authority. In addition, the man from the country also typifies the reader of literature who does not understand, and thus cannot gain access to, a piece of literature. "The man from the country," writes Derrida, "had difficulty in grasping that an entrance was singular or unique when it should have been universal, as in truth it was. He had difficulty with literature."[9]

Derrida thus draws the helpful analogy between authority in general, and the authority of literature. He draws an analogy that helps to elucidate the precise distinction that I am, in this work, trying to make between authority that gets enacted relationally and other, more static, substance-oriented understandings of authority. Why did the man from the country have difficulty with the authority of literature? He had difficulty with it because he understood authority as a substance rather than as a relation. He thought it was some *thing* that lay in wait behind a closed door. Relating to authority, like relating to literature, can never be a matter of getting at some thing that a piece of literature "possesses."

WRONG APPROACHES TO LITERATURE

To repeat, I am trying to describe the authority relation as a literary one. There are, of course, good ways and bad ways to approach literature. Let me describe the bad ways because they will, later, help to shed some light on educational authority. There are three common, but mistaken, ways that people approach literature. First of all, there is the tendency to judge the authority of a literary work by its content. Oftentimes it is said that a great literary work is great because of the story it tells, because it is said to embody some universal human theme, because it has content that is authoritative. Yet, as any good reader of literature will tell us, such a content-bound judgment is bound to fail. Take, for example, two stories that are about the exact same thing, one that is judged "literary" and another that is not. It may very well be the case that the same "facts" that are included in a great piece of literature are also included in another, derivative piece of writing that is not considered literary. Content alone is never a guarantee that a piece of writing will be admitted into a literary canon.

Secondly, consider the attempt to judge the literary worth of a work by making an assessment based on the *form* of a piece. While it is often said that a literary work is distinguished by the *way* it is written, such a basis for judgment is also bound to fail. It may very well be the case that two works are written with the same flair, with the same voice. Still, their status as "literature" may be quite different. The authority of a piece of literature does not reside in its style alone. Style and form are easy to duplicate. As many a copycat author is aware, two works may be written in the same style, but even so, one of those two works, the one written by the copycat, may never end up being deemed literary. When it comes to discerning literary authority, the very thing that seems so central to a great piece of fiction—its style and its form—is not enough to provide an "entrance" for the work. Form, like content, is not a sufficient condition for the enactment of literary authority.

Remarking on the content and form of literary authority, Derrida reminds us that, in reality, the authority of literature lies elsewhere:

"What differs from one work to the other," notes Derrida, "is not its *content*, nor is it the *form* (the signifying expression, the phenomenon of language or rhetoric). It is the movements of framing and referentiality."[10] While content and form are both important, these elements alone, or even together, do not constitute the literary authority of a work. Why? Because "the movements of framing and referentiality" that indeed convince us that a work is authoritative cannot be so easily pinned down to one element or the other. Authority is not a "thing" to be found behind this "door" of content or that "door" of form. Rather, it is in the relation of "framing and referentiality" that the authority of literature resides. The authority of literature is always established in relation, in the relation that is established between readers and the literary works they read. It may be the case that content and form come into play as one deems a work to be great, but authority gets enacted more through the deeming than through the content or the form per se.

Third, there are often attempts made to assess literary authority by looking to authorship. As is the case with great content and great form, it is often assumed that a great author makes a work great. Hence, it might be said that William Faulkner's novels are among the great works of literature primarily because of Faulkner's status as a formidable novelist. This sort of assessment falls flat too, though. It may be the source of great consolation to the copycat author to sigh and say, "Well, I can write just as well as William Faulkner but I just lack the notoriety. I lack his great name." But while this sort of writerly resentment might massage the ego of a copycat, the truth of the matter is that Faulkner himself has written lesser works that have never been authorized with the status of "masterpiece." Many an author has written that "one great novel" only to fall into obscurity because his or her other works were never granted such "great" status. Who an author is is no guarantee of authority. Once again, authority does not reside "behind some door," at least not in the form of the author's identity.

So literary authority has "framing and referentiality" at its core, rather than the authoritative "things" of content, form, or authorship. When a person encounters literary authority, it is *unlikely* that one can discern the nature of that authority by scrutinizing *what it is* (its content) or *how it is presented* (its form) or *who is behind it*. As Derrida notes, "Thus one never acceded directly to the law or to persons, one is never *immediately* before any of these authorities; as for the detour, it may be infinite."[11] One never has *direct* access to literary authority. Faced with literary authority, one is primarily faced with the ways that such authority is instantiated in the people who enact, interpret, embody, and employ that authority. "One cannot reach the law, and in order to have a *rapport* of respect with it, *one must not* have a rapport with the law, *one must interrupt the relation*. One must *enter into relation* only with the law's representatives, its examples, its guardians."[12] In literature, as in education, authority is a relation of force without significance.

WRONG APPROACHES TO EDUCATION

But how does this Derridean understanding of literary authority inform, in a practical way, the matter of educational authority? Educational authority, I propose, is at present wrongly construed. At present, we tend to assess educational authority in the same mistaken ways that *bad* readers construe literary authority. We, too, try to look behind the "doors" of content, form, and authorship.

First, there is a common tendency to focus on content when it comes to questions of authority. As I have outlined earlier in this study, many serious analyses of educational authority focus mainly on the role of content, on the role of the texts that are taught by teachers. Many such analyses deem educational authority to be "great" when the texts that are taught are "great." Such an orientation toward "great" curriculum guides the progressive, traditional, and critical perspectives alike. Following the progressive program of education, authority is doing the right thing when teachers get out of the way and let great texts speak for themselves. Following the traditional program, authority is valid when it is used to shore up the knowledge embodied in great texts. Following the critical program, authority is valid when great texts are understood in ways that debunk hegemonic ideology. Yet, what these perspectives on authoritative content overlook is that content per se cannot possibly be the source of educational authority. If content were a sufficient source of educational authority, then education as we know it would not even be necessary. What I mean by this is that one can find "great" texts almost anywhere: in libraries, in bookstores, online, on the shelves of studies, living rooms, and bedrooms. Anyone can read a great text anywhere. The mere fact that one has read a great text hardly signifies that educational authority has been enacted.

There is also a common tendency to judge educational authority by virtue of its form. That is to say, there is a tendency to judge authority by looking to the quality of instruction. This sort of judgment has its pitfalls as well. It is by no means true that a teacher who has carried out his or her lesson in the best manner has necessarily contributed at all to the education of even one student! As many a teacher will testify, all of the best techniques are bound to fall on deaf ears at one point or another. Quite simply, there is no one teaching style, and there is not even any specific combination of teaching styles, which will guarantee that one's students become well educated. In spite of all the technicist, rationalist, optimistic educational research into the ways that education can be delivered more effectively by teachers, there is simply no guarantee that "good" instruction will suffice. Authority can never be judged by quality of instruction because quality of instruction is itself a dubious notion. As in the case of the copycat author who tries to copy the work of a master writer, there is no certainty that copying the "best practices" of other teachers will lead to an educative experience on the part of the student.

Too, there is a mistaken tendency to judge educational authority by its author, by who does the teaching. Let me bring in my own observations here, as a teacher of nineteen years. Over the years as I have listened to many students talk about their teachers, the one thing that always rings true is that the authority of any particular teacher always differs according that teacher's particular relation to particular students. It is not uncommon for a teacher with certain highly idiosyncratic pedagogical techniques to win a highly prestigious award for university teaching. Often, this very teacher is detested by as many students as she is loved. Her idiosyncrasies are harmful as well as helpful. Educational authority cannot be attributed to authorship, to the teacher, in any consistent way at all. Quite simply, one student's super-teacher is often another's worst teacher. This is just as sure as the fact that the author of one great novel is likely to write a flop now and again.

Like the authority of literature, education authority tends to be judged by content, form, and authorship—by curriculum, technique, and teacher identity. Yet when we so judge educational authority, we make the same mistake that an ill-informed reader of literature makes. We make the mistake of looking for authority "behind some door" as if it is a substance or a thing just waiting to be revealed. When we so judge educational authority, we ignore the fact that authority must be construed as a relation. It must, as Derrida says, be construed as a matter of "framing and referentiality." If we treat educational authority as a relation akin to the literary relation, then we must look past the individual qualities that texts, pedagogies, and teachers are said to "possess." We must look at the "force" of such a relation rather than its "significance." We must look at its movements rather than at its steadfast qualities. We must examine *how it reads* rather than *what it is*.

THEN WE ARE ALL FROM THE COUNTRY

So let us return to Kafka's story. It seems that we can now describe the countryman as a sort of student. The man stands before the law in much the same way a student stands before educational authority. In this new version of Kafka's tale, we might say that there is a student who is barred entrance to authority. Why is he barred entrance? It is because he mistakenly thinks that the primary attribute of educational authority is that it is generally available. He thinks that authority is somewhere within, that it is written inside on a tablet, like some moral code.[13] He believes that if only he is patient enough, then he will be let in and will be able to discern authority's true content. But, this student of Kafka's can never gain entry into the house of educational authority. He remains frustrated. He never learns that in reality authority has no specific content. In truth, it has no identifiable form. This student's misunderstanding of the nature of authority leads to his continued desire to get through an open door. This student has a problem with educational authority in the same way that many people "have a problem with literature." He believes that it is his role to figure out exactly "what" authority is.

It is a mistake on the part of the student to think that facing authority entails facing a canon of knowledge that is already there. It is a mistake to think that a particular body of knowledge is waiting to be understood in a particular way. When faced with authority, one should not ask to gain such straightforward entrance. One will never gain such an entrance. Instead, one should understand that authority has no steadfast life. It has no "truth" that is set in stone behind a door. Authority is always a movement that can never be pinned down. It is a movement between content, form, and teacher. Because authority is a movement, the student must understand that he will never be able to gain *direct* entrance. But if our student can never gain direct entrance, then what *can* he do? Or to put this question in more broad terms: How might students and teachers negotiate the relation of authority given that it has such a literary life?

Rather than trying to gain direct entrance, a student might do much better to engage in the very staging of authority, to engage in its referentiality, to engage in the effects it has on him or herself. A student might understand that confronting education is much like gaining access to a great novel. To access the authority of a novel, one does not dwell strictly on its content, nor does one dwell strictly on its form, nor does one dwell strictly on what so-and-so (say, a teacher) says about the novel. Let us say, for example, that this student is a reader of James Joyce. To read and interpret Joyce's *Ulysses*, it is absolutely insufficient to understand its content. Its content is, after all, only one life in the day of a fairly unremarkable man, Leopold Bloom. To read and interpret *Ulysses*, it is also completely insufficient to know that, in its form, *Ulysses* is a metaphor for Homer's epic poem. To read and interpret *Ulysses*, it is furthermore insufficient to learn precisely who James Joyce, the writer, was. Likewise, it is insufficient to learn precisely what Dr. X, the professor, has to say about the novel. To read and interpret *Ulysses*, one must engage in a relation with all of the factors that allow one to be moved by the reading. One must enjoy the story. One must make one's own judgments about its worth. One must arrive at an interpretion of the novel in a way that is ultimately unlikely to be the same interpretation that one finds somewhere in some certain place, behind some door.

This student would do well to proceed without the illusion that *Ulysses*, just because it has been assigned for a course, has some authority that is thing-ified or concrete. This student would do well to take an example from many a devoted novel reader. It is not a coincidence that many readers of novels do so late at night in the comfort of their bedrooms, and indeed that they do not discuss the contents of the novel with anyone else. The successful interpreter of a novel ultimately meets the authority of the novel through his or her own personal acts of "staging and referentiality." Reading a novel successfully, one will enter a personal relation with the mechanisms of literary authority. One will enter into a relation with the authority that canonizes novels and satisfies readers. One will enter a personal relation with the "doorkeepers" of literary insight rather than coming to know precisely "what" or "who" they are.

Any student who encounters classroom curriculum should proceed in this same literary light. Faced with a way to "enter" curriculum, the student might best be aware that it will not be solely a matter of knowing the content of what is being taught. Nor will it be strictly a matter of knowing the *form* of curriculum, of being taught correctly. Nor will it be strictly a matter of having direct access to the author, of having direct access to the teacher. In fact one does not "enter" curriculum in such a straightforward way. Rather, one must enter an interpretive relation wherein the person who learns acts as her own guide, as her own literary interpreter, doing her own "staging" and her own establishing of "referentiality."

This is not to say that the learner should not look to outside sources in order to interpret curriculum. Indeed, it may be precisely by means of outside sources that a student finds insight that will bear on her own interpretations. One may go to a teacher. One may go to a text of reference. One may go to a dictionary. One may go to a friend, to an instructional text, to a text of criticism, etc. But while it may be in one of these sources where one finds the means to stage an interpretation, it will never be in these sources where one reaches some authoritative source. Authority in education is a relation that gets enacted in the interpretive act itself, in the act of learning. It is not a thing that lies hidden waiting to be found. A student will never "reach" educational authority, but he or she does have the chance, like the reader of a novel, to stage an event of curriculum that becomes meaningful and enriching. Like the novel reader who is transformed because of her own personal interpretation of a work, the student's own interpretation of curriculum is the only way that she can partake in the relation of authority. This is not to say she will "enter the house" of authority. She will, though, achieve a *relation* with one or more of its doorkeepers.

THE TEACHER AND THE LITERARY RELATION

But if the student never has direct access to authority, does that mean that the teacher *does* have direct access? Not at all. A literary understanding throws into question many current assumptions about the educational authority of the teacher. For example, educational accounts of authority often assume that a teacher who has more authority is one who does a lot more direct instruction of content. It is often said that dialogic pedagogies or progressive pedagogies are able to eschew authority because they do not force-feed students with content. Informed by our literary understanding of authority, this is simply wrongheaded. Authority can never reside in the content itself, nor in that content's delivery. This very popular, scholarly-accepted perspective makes the same mistake as Kafka's countryman made. It assumes that authority lies behind the door. It assumes that authority is sequestered knowledge. Scholarly arguments about whether or not to use such "authority" will never get anywhere because they misconstrue the way that authority is necessarily an interpretive relation. Such descriptions of teacher authority are as ill-conceived as are the notions of the student who assumes she can access that venerable, carved-in-stone version of authority.

The authority of the teacher does not depend upon the extent of the teacher's knowledge, nor does it depend upon the approach the teacher takes to his or her subject, nor does it depend upon who the teacher is. Haven't many teachers had the same experience that the countryman has had? Is it not a common feeling to be barred entrance to teaching authority? Are there not many times when one just can't get through to one's students? I, for one, have felt like the countryman. With regard to content: How often do we wrongly assume that if the content is clear, then the rest of teaching and learning will take care of itself? After a feeling of being barred entrance, many teachers make the following content-based mistake: they just try all the harder to make the content clear to their students. With regard to teaching methods: How often do we wrongly assume that some innovative approach to teaching will make learning possible where none was possible before? With regard to teacher identity: How often do we wrongly assume that a teacher lacks authority because he is too young, because he is has not established a good enough reputation, because he is not as likeable as another teacher of the same course? Yet how many teachers never become successful when in fact their reputation and experience should have gained them "entrance" long ago? When teaching the novels of Toni Morrison, for example, one can know all there is to know about Morrison. One can polish up one's teaching style to be as shiny as can be. One can have years and years of experience. These matters of content, form, and identity do not guarantee that a student's interpretation of Morrison will be profound. Matters of content, form, and identity will not guarantee a teacher access to authority because authority is not a particular thing waiting to be accessed.

Authority only gets enacted through a meaningful interpretation on the student's part. It is the student who must actually practice the "staging and referentiality" of this interpretation. The best that the teacher can do is to act as an aid to the reader. Of course, it may happen that it is precisely the content knowledge or the teaching style of the teacher that the student uses to make her interpretation meaningful. Or it may not happen that way. If, at least, a teacher knows that content, style, and identity are not sufficient, then he or she will not make the same mistake as Kafka's countryman. He or she will not continue to expect that the aim of the teacher is to "let in" the student. As teachers, we should not aim to "give over" authority, nor should we aim to "keep" our authority. Authority is not a substance that one "has." The best we can do is to avoid making the same mistake as the man from the country. We can avoid trying to "get through" to our students. And, we can help students to avoid making the same mistake by pointing out that they will never "get through" to us. They will never "get through" to some illusory authority that the teacher is supposed to "have."

Does all this mean that we can no longer talk about the content of teaching? Can we no longer talk about pedagogy? Can we no longer talk about the charisma of the teacher? This is not my point at all. Indeed, texts are central (as I have argued in the previous chapter), pedagogy is absolutely necessary, and teacher charisma a boon. Of the three, I would say that texts are the most important. But . . . this choice has nothing to do with the authority that might wrongly considered to be inherent in any one of the three. Rather, the text is preferable to the other two because it is more likely to lend itself to *interpretation*. The texts that teachers teach are preferable because they are already situated within a set of discursive practices that encourage reading and interpretation, *not* because of some mistaken stereotype of a pure, nonauthoritative experience of knowledge acquisition on the part of the student. Given the deferred, interpretive life of a student's interaction with texts, the act of reading is more likely to enable one to participate in the literary life of educational authority. Teachers should favor texts, but this is not because texts are some "source" of authority. Texts are not behind the door. They remain in front of it. Teachers, like students, should settle for the foyer. To be let in need not be the aim.

To recap, I have so far offered a description of authority that asks us to stop thinking of authority as a matter of substance, style, and identity, and asks us to start thinking of it as a matter of interpretation and reading. There is no stable, authoritative meaning behind the door over which the doorkeeper stands guard. There is actually no way to enter the room guarded by the doorkeeper. The entranceway itself is the venue where one learns, where one becomes educated. The entranceway is also where one teaches. One can't "get in." One can at best, one can only, enter a relation with the doorkeeper. When the doorkeeper (or the teacher) says to the man (or to the student), "This door was intended only for you," it makes sense to settle for the door.

BUT WHY DO WE ASSUME THAT SOME THING IS BEHIND THE DOOR?

All of this said, why is it such a common presumption that authority is located somewhere in particular? Why are there so many countrymen among us who assume that authority is a "thing" that is waiting somewhere behind a door? Why do people ignore the interpretive life of the authority relation? To get at an answer to this question, I want to look to language itself. For it seems to me that common presumptions about authority are actually based on even more fundamental presumptions about what it means to speak and to listen. That is to say, because authority is most often *communicated*, there are some very deep presumptions about communication itself that tend to derail how we understand authority. Communication itself is much more of an interpretive event than is commonly realized. Therefore, when authority is construed as a substance rather than an interpretive relation, this misunderstanding is itself guided by a misunderstanding of language where language is said to be the transfer of a *substance* between autonomous human actors, that substance being *meaning*.

To this end, I take a bit of a detour through language theory in the pages that follow. Once we understand that communication is *not* solely about the transfer of meaning, but is rather a matter of authoritative staging and interpretation, then we can see that the relation of authority is indeed literary from the ground up, from the very basic acts of listening and speaking all the way up to the more refined enactments of educational authority that take place between student and teacher.

THE SENDER-RECEIVER MODEL

One of the most common ways to understand human communication is according to the "sender-receiver" model. Following such a model, it is assumed that language is a tool, a "thing," that is used by human actors to communicate with one another. As such, when human beings have ideas, they use the tool of language to send their ideas to one another. John Stewart has argued that this tool-like understanding of language has been one of the primary philosophical commitments to which philosophers of language have adhered. He describes this "tool commitment" as follows:

> Historically, of course, the primary use of the language tool has been viewed as the communication of thoughts or ideas. Among others, Locke underscored the importance of the communicative function of language, and the eighteenth-century theorist John Horne Tooke would not even grant "language" status to the solitary mental naming that some of his predecessors had analyzed. Horne Tooke argued that the fact that the purpose of language is "to communicate our thoughts" should "be kept singly in contemplation . . ."[14]

George Lakoff and Mark Taylor, commenting on how many people talk of language, describe the use of the "conduit metaphor."[15] According to this metaphorical description of language, "The speaker puts ideas (objects) into words (containers) and sends them (along a conduit) to a hearer who takes the idea/object out of the word/containers." It is the sending and the receiving part of this metaphor that I would like to highlight. It is not only in high philosophy, but it is in our everyday speech, too, where the sender-receiver model is assumed. As Taylor notes, the following sorts of conduit metaphors are used all the time: "It's hard to *get* that idea *across to* him"; "Your reasons *came through* to us"; and, "I *gave* you that idea."[16] These are just a few examples of many other common ways of talking that echo the sender-receiver conception of language.

So according to the sender-receiver model, human beings first have something in mind to communicate. They put their thoughts into language, into words, and then those words are sent to other human beings. The process of communication, then, is often construed as if we communicate via something like a pneumatic tube. First a person thinks a thought. Then that person puts that thought into words. The persons then sends those words to another person via pneumatic tube. The person at the other end of the communication receives those words. He or she deciphers those words, and thus understands what was on the sender's mind. According to this sender-receiver model, it is assumed that language communicates a world of ideas that can easily be transmitted from one person to another.

The sender-receiver model of communication is well ensconced in a modernist, Enlightenment conception of human beings as autonomous actors. Following this conception, a person is an atomistic entity who has ideas, thoughts, intentions, and ambitions. A person can exist just fine on his or her own. In fact, the Enlightenment conception of the self insists that people *should* exist on their own. As Stewart notes of the tool orientation toward language, "[T]he contemporary emphasis on language as an instrumental tool reflects the Cartesian cogito and the irreducible distinction between the subject and the objects that subjects allegedly encounter, construct, and manipulate."[17] And as I have pointed out with respect to Kant, the enlightened person is encouraged to think, act, and live autonomously. It is through the use of one's own reason, as opposed to living through a reliance on the guidance of others, that one rises from a state of immaturity to a state of maturity.

Of course, the Enlightenment conception of self does not object to people communicating with one another. People must communicate in order to live happy lives. Not even a stereotyped version of Kant's autonomous, "mature" person could be said to live without communicating with others. This is where the sender-receiver model of communication fits so well with Enlightenment notions of autonomy. According to the sender-receiver model, people need not be in reciprocal or mutually enhancing relations in order to communicate. Rather, people can stand at a fair distance from one another. The pneumatic tube acts as a buffer between people. One person has her thoughts and another person has her thoughts. They learn about each other's thoughts by means of the tool of language. Language enables one to learn what another person is thinking. After learning what the other is thinking, one can use one's own reason, one's enlightened "mature" reason, to decide which path to take.

The sender-receiver model is a modernist, Enlightenment model. Alphonso Lingis has underscored this fact by describing the sender-receiver model of communication as the sort that takes place in modern, "rational communities."[18] For Lingis, there are two main types of communities: rational communities and communities of difference. It is in the former type of community that communication is thought of according to the sender-receiver model. In what Lingis calls rational communities, people gather together on the assumption that they have something in common to say to each other. People gather together because they believe that they all share a common enough language to understand the various ideas, the various viewpoints, that various members of the rational community have. Lingis notes the following about the rational community of communication:

> Each one speaks as a representative of the common discourse. His own insights and utterances become part of the anonymous discourse of universal reason.
>   This discursive practice then invokes a human community in principle unlimited. A community in which each one, in facing the other, faces an imperative that he formulate all his encounters and insights in universal terms, in forms that could be the information belonging to everyone.[19]

In the rational community, which is the sort of community that the modern, liberal state is based on, people use the public sphere to "send messages" to one another in a common language. Thus, the very idea of the modern, rational community is based on the assumption that language is the public tool that will be used to send ideas that can be understood by all as long as those ideas are communicated well enough. When I send a message about an idea that I have in mind, that message will, in a rational community, be understandable to many, many people. Many people will be able to share in the common language that conveys my meaning.

Three important observations are to be made about the authority relation and the sender-receiver model of communication. The first is this: common understandings of authority are based on this same simplistic sender-receiver model of communication. That is to say, authority is usually treated as if it is the bearer of a message. When people talk about authority, and when they theorize about it, they refer to a person who "has" authority. It is assumed that such a person communicates her ideas to someone who does not "have" such authority. It is further assumed that if the person communicates her ideas well enough to the other, then that other can "get" authority if she has understood clearly. My point here is that the sender-receiver metaphor about how language communicates ideas is the same metaphor that guides common presumptions about how authority gets "passed" from one person to another. Just as people assume that some specific idea gets transferred through each utterance, so, too, people assume that some specific type of authority can be transferred through an utterance.

The second observation follows from the concept of the rational community to which Lingis introduces us. It is this: when a person is said to "have" authority, then it is assumed that his or her authority can be understood by many people. It is assumed that such authority is able to be understood by the members of a rational community who share a common language. Just as in the case of person's ideas that are "sent" by language to all who share that common language, so too is it assumed that authority exists within a "rational community" whose interlocutors are able to understand one another. Authority, like an idea that one sends to another in a rational community of one common language, is assumed to make sense to a lot of people.

I want to illustrate this by way of an example from my own teaching. Yet, I am sure that my own experience is hardly unique. As a university professor, I sometimes expound in class upon some of my own ideas. Oftentimes students ask me questions about those ideas. Tellingly, even when I state that those are *my own* ideas, students go on to ask where they can do further reading about those ideas. I will say it again: in spite of my claim that these are my own unique ideas, students very often insist that they want other sources to go to in order to learn more about those ideas! Now, by giving this example, I am not trying to belittle my students in any way. Indeed, a student who wants to do further study about some educational concept that I raise is the very sort of student I, for one, want to be teaching. However, this student who insists that my own ideas must have origins elsewhere does so because she assumes that there must be some rational community from which my ideas emanate. She assumes that there must be some common language that she has not been exposed to yet. Indeed, many students assume that there must be some common rational community of scholars who authorize the speaking teacher.

As will have been guessed by now, I am no fan of the sender-receiver model of rational communication. Here is a third observation: this model contradicts itself. The contradiction is this: even when authority is ostensibly denounced, the specter of authority always returns in the form of an assumed rational community. Even when the Enlightenment model of communication eschews authority, it advocates a common language that is, itself, a forceful form of authority. So the Kantian imperative to "have the courage to think on your own" depends upon a rational community that does not let one think on one's own! Let me say this a different way. Think about the students of mine who want to find out where I "really" get my ideas. Because they assume that there is a rational community behind my speaking, my speaking can never become "mature." Like good Kantians, they know that one can never speak on one's own. Yet also like good Kantians, they want me to be an authority in my own right. The Enlightenment sender-receiver model assumes that we all rely on the authority of the rational community at the same time that it eschews reliance on authority.

So back to the question, "But why do we think some *thing* is behind the door?" In order to explain this resilient belief, I have tried to explicate some of the erroneous communicative assumptions surrounding authority. People tend to think that there is some *thing* behind the door in the same way that people tend to think that there is some *person's idea* behind each word that is spoken. People tend to think that authority is a substance because they cling to the modernist belief that if authority is being communicated then there must be some specific "thing" that is being sent to someone else.

People tend to think that there is some thing behind the door because they tend to think that communication arises from an established rational community. Going back to the example of my own students who, when I am talking about my own ideas, make the assumption that there must be some rational community somewhere from which I am speaking, it seems that people both want to get away from authority and at the same time want to insist that there is, after all, some "rational" authority that one cannot get away from. No matter how much one wishes to be mature, one still assumes that the key to maturity is just behind somebody else's door. This happens because people assume that communication is rational and that communication is mainly about ideas that lie in wait to be understood.

Two questions follow from this discussion, and I will address these questions by way of concluding this chapter on the literary life of authority. The first is: Is there an alternative model of communication? Is there one that is different from the sender-receiver model, one that better describes how relational authority works? The second is: If there is such an alternative model, how, exactly, does it help us to understanding the educational relation of authority?

AUTHORITY AND PERFORMATIVE COMMUNICATION

In contrast to the sender-receiver model of communication, we should rather think of authority according to a model of performative communication. Such a model can be distinguished from a sender-receiver model in a number of ways, some of which I will outline here. To begin with, a performative model construes that *the saying itself* is just as important as *what is said*. Take for example the utterance of a teacher. When a teacher speaks, there is certainly something in particular that is being said by her. Yet at the same time, it is the speaking itself that establishes a relation between herself and her class of students. Following the sender-receiver model, we might have assumed that *what is said* by the teacher is the most important thing, that the most important thing is the thought that is communicated to the class. In contrast, a performative account of communication helps us to understand that the speaking itself is important. The performative model helps us to remember that when a teacher addresses her class, she establishes a role by her very speaking. She may be taking roll. She may be giving a lesson no one understands. She may have taught some mathematics skill without knowing exactly how she got her point across. Whatever the case, the relation between her and her students will most often be established by *the fact that she has said something* rather than *what she has said.*

The performative model of communication differs in another major way from the sender-receiver model. In the sender-receiver model, it is assumed that a clear and consistent understanding of the speaker's intent is the most important aspect of communication. On the performative model, though, it is assumed that differences in understanding are just as important as consistencies in understanding. So when someone says something to me, one way of looking at what has been said is that it is my job to understand (and to understand correctly) what has been said to me. But another way of looking at communication is to realize that my interpretation of what has been said may very well *never* be quite the same as what the speaker intended to mean.

Following a performative model of communication, it is not a *problem* that I have not understood exactly what the speaker had in mind. Such a misunderstanding is part and parcel of what it means to communicate. Indeed, as Hans-Georg Gadamer has intimated, every understanding is also, in part, a misunderstanding.[20] According to the performative model, it cannot be the role of language to transport via pneumatic tube, safely and securely, the intended meaning of one speaker to the attentive ears of her listener. Why? Because language operates as much on misunderstanding as it does on understanding. It may be that a listener *mis*understands a speaker as much as she understands him. A sender-receiver conception of communication might hold at this point that the two have not communicated. From the performative perspective, this sort of phenomenon *is still communication.* It is perhaps the most common version of communication.

Furthermore, the performative perspective acknowledges that there are many circumstances when communication takes place not because of the knowledge that someone has in mind but because of the unique, perlocutionary circumstances that surround that communication.[21] In other words, sometimes communication happens because of the circumstances of the speaker and listener rather than because of any specific knowledge that is conveyed from one to the other. The quintessential example of this, offered by J. L. Austin, is when a minister pronounces a couple "husband and wife." When a minister does so, the *effect* of the pronouncement does not depend upon the knowledge or understanding of the speaker and his or her listeners. Rather, the *effect* depends upon staging and referentiality. It depends upon the circumstances surrounding what the minister has to say. It depends upon how the minister's words get interpreted.

It is not difficult to see how much the performative conception of communication bears on educational authority. If authority is relational, it is precisely because authority gets enacted in a performative, rather than a sender-receiver, way. Let me go back to the example of the teacher who takes roll, who teaches a lesson that is not clear to her students, or who has taught a math skill while not knowing exactly how she got her point across. When a teacher takes roll, it is truly not *what is said* that is important, at least not as far as authority is concerned. What is important when roll is taken is *that something is said*. As far as authority is concerned, there is little import whether the student whose name is called out is present or absent on that particular day. Of little import is whether or not the name called out is the name of a student who never planned to attend class. Of little import is whether or not the name that is called is a mistaken name, one generated by a computer glitch. Of little import is whether or not the teacher makes up a fictitious name to call and then calls that name in order to dupe the students in the class. As far as authority goes, the specific content of the roll call does not bear on the fact that the roll was called by a teacher and that students were listeners to that roll call. Authority gets enacted—with all its absences, presences, and potential mistakes—because roll was called, because a relation was established. It hardly matters that some name in particular, or even some "correct" name, was said during the roll call.

A performative understanding of authority thus helps us to understand the many instances when a teacher teaches a lesson that is not clear. If we were to cling to the sender-receiver model of authority, it might follow that authority has not succeeded, that it is somehow lessened, when a teacher is not able to communicate what she wants to communicate. This is simply not so: authority does not increase or decrease in direct proportion to what is learned "correctly" in the classroom. There are very often cases where much is learned that was not intended. In an English class, there might be an insightful reading of a piece of literature that is based on what the student *thought* the teacher said rather than what the teacher actually said. In a science class, there might be a mistaken, but nevertheless sensible, interpretation of the reasons behind an eclipse of the moon. In a math class, there might be an algorithm learned "incorrectly," an algorithm that solves the given math problem just as well. In any of these cases, as in many others where misunderstanding causes an understanding of its own, it can in no way be said that the enactment of authority has been lessened by such a misunderstanding. The relation of authority functions as much on misunderstanding as on understanding. As in instances of performative communication, it is the learning from another person, no matter what has been learned, for right or for wrong, that constitutes the relation of authority.

Take the example of a math teacher who, after trying to no avail to teach a certain mathematical technique to a particular student, decides to use other, affective means to inspire this student: "You are great at mathematics. Don't give up just because I'm not having one of my best teaching days!" In instances such as this, at least when they do turn out to be successful, it seems as though education happens through osmosis, or maybe by magic. However it happens, one is often hard-pressed to come up with a logical solution. In instances such as this, there is a striking similarity, if not an equivalence, between the educational relation of authority and the performative moment of authorization described by Austin. When the minister says, "I pronounce you married," and the teacher says, "You are great at mathematics," the same performative event results, or at least it can result if the circumstances are "felicitous."[22] Just as two partners "become" married by virtue of this pronouncement, it is altogether possible that a student will "become" great by virtue of what the teacher has said to him or her. Or at least (in a less momentous sense), it may be the case that the student will become "great" enough to learn the mathematics in spite of the teacher's inadequate methods. In such cases, it is the performative relation that typifies the workings of authority, even when there may be no sender-receiver explanation for the learning that took place.

Eric Santner, for example, has noted the following about performativity, especially in a literary context:

> [A] work is endowed with a life beyond the order of knowledge, beyond a merely additive history of tastes and style. Such "redemptive" reading can, to borrow the language of speech-act theory, never be reduced to a purely constative act of noting the positive features of the work but depends instead on a dimension of performativity.[23]

In this passage, Santner is describing the way that works of literature can bring human beings to new levels of awareness. As Santner notes, literature brings such new levels of awareness in a performative way. Literary works are "endowed with a life beyond the order of knowledge," beyond what one can say about content and style. I would add to Santner's comments that education works in the same performative way. Educational authority calls to us in ways that bring new levels of awareness. Teachers and students are also "endowed with a life beyond the order of knowledge."

Santner goes on to describe how each performative reading of a work is different from its previous reading:

> What makes a work of art inexhaustible, subject to multiple interpretations, is not simply an excess of content or information that, because of the limits of every human consciousness, requires multiple readings to "bring it out"; rather, this much noted inexhaustibility depends on the fact that every reading is, on a certain level, a kind of *creation ex nihilo*. The details supporting a strong reading of a work only become visible retroactively, in light of the performative gesture that intervenes into its history of reception. In a certain sense, these details were not there before . . . [24]

Let me put Santner's thoughts in terms of educational authority. In education, what makes the experience of learning inexhaustible is not the vast content that the teacher might bring into the classroom day after day. It is not the ability of the teacher to encourage students to think in many different ways about that vast content. The inexhaustibility of authority rests rather in the way in which something can be created from scratch when teacher and student meet. When teacher and student meet in order to study something, a performative gesture "intervenes." In a sense, certain details of the curriculum may not have been there before this intervention. Or, to go back to a phrase that I have used earlier, through the performative intervention of authority, teacher and student "become the missing pages" of the text that is taught.

Indeed, it is necessary to look beyond the sender-receiver model of communication. Authority is a relation that acts performatively. Therefore, authority gets enacted through interpretation rather than through clear communication. It is not that someone "has" authority and then communicates her ideas clearly by virtue of that authority. Instead, authority gets enacted through communication itself. It gets enacted through the communicative relation. Authority depends more on *the being said* than it depends on *what is said*. This becomes obvious when we notice that authority gets enacted through misunderstanding as often as it gets enacted through understanding.

Looking beyond the sender-receiver model of communication brings us full circle, back to the countryman in front of Kafka's door. The countryman assumes that there is some authority figure behind the door. He assumes that there is a person who "has" authority. The man assumes that this person will communicate something to him. The countryman wants to be the receiver of a message that will be sent by this authority figure. The countryman does not understand that authority is a relation that acts performatively rather than through some sender-receiver model.

When a person takes part in the relation of educational authority, it is the relation itself that educates. It is the relation, rather than some predetermined content. One becomes educated through the interplay of content, style, and identity. One becomes educated through interpretation rather than through clarity. And the interpretation to which I am referring is particularly literary. Of course, to say that "the relation itself educates" is to force another matter into play. Namely, we must ask whether people must be *present* during this relation. Is it possible to have an authority relation when an authority figure is absent? This question will guide the chapter that follows.

CHAPTER 3

Relating to Authority Figures Who Are Not There

So far in this book I have dealt with relation in terms of authority figures who are *present*. However, when we think about the authority figures to whom we relate, don't we have relations with many who have left the picture? Are we not constantly relating to authority figures whom we remember? Whom we anticipate meeting in the future? Whom we know about but only rarely come into contact with? Indeed, might it be the case that we do *more* relating to those authority figures who are absent than to those who are present? In this chapter, I will investigate this particularly *lingering* aspect of the educational authority. I will argue that what lingers is actually central to educational authority. Absence has bearing on presence. And contrariwise, I maintain that presence has bearing on absence. Non-presence and presence are two symbiotic components of authority.

Let me draw on one example of absence from my own education: I was first introduced to the novelist Toni Morrison during my undergraduate education, in a course taught by Professor Denise Depuis. Under the thoughtful guidance of Professor Depuis, I came to cherish Morrison's writing, and especially her famous novel *Beloved*. Indeed, from the time of that course up until now, even when I am not in the presence of Professor Depuis, the warm image of her comes flooding back to mind each time I pick up a book written by Toni Morrison.

There are certainly variations on this sort of experience. Perhaps one learns to run, with grace and style, under the watchful eyes of a certain coach Hoffman. And then from time to time, when venturing to the park for just a short jog, the memory of coach Hoffman and his running tips hovers in the mind's eye, reminding one that a swifter run is always in store by letting the shoulders hang low, by keeping the fingers relaxed. Or maybe it's the memory of the person from whom one learned to play chess, or perhaps it is one's mathematics teacher, or one's philosophy of education instructor. If one has indeed gone through a truly educative experience in the presence of a teacher, isn't there often a parallel experience that is once removed from that teacher, a lingering memory of that teacher even though we are no longer in his or her presence?

THE PRESENTIST FALLACY

Unfortunately, current educational accounts of authority are hamstrung by a markedly *presentist* orientation.[1] A presentist orientation tends to address authority as if authority is always in the ideal state of being around. The presentist orientation focuses on instances when students are *face-to-face* with the authority of the teacher. Lost in this face-to-face focus is an account of the ways that authority reverberates *after* the classroom experience. There are a number of drawbacks to the presentist orientation, some of which I want to mention here. First, it ignores the fact that I have been trying to explain above, the fact that people are often affected by the authority relation when authority figures go away then come back, or when they go away permanently. Second, because the presentist orientation focuses on authority as if it is present, the nuances of difference between absent and present authority are lost.

Most damagingly, the presentist orientation runs into the following dilemma: On the one hand, it is naïve to say that the authority relation stays around, *in the exact same form as if it were still present*, when the student and teacher are no longer in each other's company. On the other hand, it is equally naïve to say that authority needs little attention since the harm it causes, or the good it does, are only temporary. In the first case, we would be saying that every student is affected for a lifetime by each authority with whom he or she comes into contact. The first conclusion is certainly wrong: many students go through an entire course of twelve, sixteen, or more years of education being little, if at all, affected by those who are in positions of educational authority. The second conclusion is equally wrong: many people are affected in permanent ways by an authority figure who has gone away. A presentist orientation gets stuck between the Scylla of permanent presence and the Charybdis of permanent absence.

But what happens when the two polar opposite presentist assumptions about authority (that face-to-face authority remains, as if present, indefinitely, or, conversely, that authority has force only when students

are face-to-face with teachers) are inadequate? Between these two extreme presentist assumptions, how might we consider the effects of authority that is present at some times and absent at others? How might we
describe authority that sometimes lingers and sometimes does not? How
might we describe a more complex interaction between the presence and
absence of authority? What happens when we leave the presentist orientation behind, and look at the life of the authority relation that comes
and goes, that has *various* effects in its comings and goings?

ABSENT AUTHORITY, PYCHIC PRESENCE

For anyone who knows a bit about psychoanalysis, it will be clear that
we are delving into matters of the psyche. Key concepts in psychoanalysis help to explain the force of authority figures who are not around.
Psychoanalytic concepts given to us by Freud, concepts such as transference, countertransference, the Oedipal struggle, melancholia—these
and many more psychoanalytic notions deal with the relations we have
with authority figures who have left the picture. Transference: when one
relates to a new authority figure in the same way one used to relate to
a similar figure in the past. Countertransference: when an authority
figure relates to a person not in authority the same way he or she has
done with another such person in the past. The Oedipal struggle: the
struggle that a child has with a parental authority figure, a struggle that
has repercussions throughout one's life even when the parent is not
around. Melancholia: when a deceased authority figure casts a bleak
shadow over the life of one who mourns.[2]

Indeed, I find that the best lens one can use to look into authority
figures who are no longer around is a psychoanalytic one. And so this
chapter will be indebted to a particular psychoanalytic viewpoint, the
viewpoint of Jessica Benjamin.[3] Benjamin's work offers an understanding of how educational authority might actually straddle the spaces of
presence *and* non-presence. As Benjamin reminds us, the experience of
an other may at first be a matter of being with that other. But ultimately, it is also a matter of *not* being with the other. Benjamin's work
helps to flesh out the relation between people who experience authority
in various ways, in absence as well as in presence.

Let us begin with presence and work our way toward absence.
According to Benjamin, the circuit of recognition is inaugurated when
the newborn looks up at the face of the caregiver in search of a warm,
confirming presence. In these first instances of life, the young person
learns the significance of the caretaker's presence. The caretaker's presence becomes a comforting one, one that will encourage both agency
and autonomy on the part of the child. When the child goes to play

with a toy, for example, she often looks for recognition from an author-ity figure. Notes Benjamin, "Now, when the infant reaches excitedly for a toy, he looks up to see if mother is sharing his excitement; he gets the meaning when she says, 'Wow!' "[4] In the caretaker's presence, the child derives encouragement and agency as the caretaker offers proof that the child's playing is important. The caretaker authorizes the child. He or she demonstrates with a "Wow!" that the child has done something important in the world.

While this account is focused on the life of a child, it isn't unrea-sonable to claim that this process of *presentist* recognition, this process of affirmation in the presence of an other, continues throughout adult life. Such a process is certainly at work when one is faced with the authority of a teacher. When we look to a teacher for affirmation of our learning, we are not unlike that child who excitedly reaches for a toy in anticipation that his caretaker will say, "Wow!" When a runner runs her hardest under the watchful eye of coach Hoffman, will she not look to that coach for a sign of affirmation? Will she not want to know that the coach shares her feeling of accomplishment? In the presence of a teacher, a student experiences the other's authority, the other's recogni-tion for the learning she has done. In the presence of a teacher, the student gains a shared sense of experience. And, "The sense of shared feeling about the undertaking [or, the learning] is not only a reassur-ance, but is, itself, a source of pleasurable connection."[5] That is to say, the presence of an other is more full than the presence of oneself alone. In the presence of an other, one gains recognition from an authority figure that one cannot attain on one's own.

But this experience of presence with an other can also be described as the beginning of non-presence. Yes, recognition by an authority fig-ure is initially dependent upon an authority who is actually *there*. But, this initial act of being affirmed in the flesh for a swift run or a subtle interpretation of a literary passage, such an initial act will certainly be followed by further efforts at running, further efforts at reading, further efforts when the teacher is no longer present. And, during such times of non-presence, is it not the case that the other is still with us to some extent? Is it not the case that the authority figure lingers as a powerful agent of affirmation, even at a time far removed from the actual expe-rience under her watchful eye? The student is still bound with the teacher who has offered affirmation in the past, just as the child con-tinues to be bound with his caregiver even into adulthood. The expe-rience of presence with an other is already the beginning of non-presence with the other. For, when we are no longer in the physical presence of an authority figure, that authority figure still lingers in what Benjamin calls "inner space." Outward contact with the other always entails the beginning of an *inward contract* with the Other.

At this point it might seem easy to say that the case is closed, that the problem of the authoritative remnant is not such a problem after all. One might say at this point that the remnant is always at work because the unconscious is always at work. One might say that educational thought has been hamstrung by a metaphysics of presence because it has refused to sufficiently admit the pedagogical role the unconscious. But this is not my point at all.

My point here is not simply to restate a common psychological insight, the insight that one's relation to an authority figure becomes internalized in the form of unconscious bonds with him or her. My aim here is rather to unpack how the workings of such inner bonds might be more involved with educational interactions than is commonly acknowledged. For, it is not just that there is an educationally important remnant that lingers in the inner world of the student once the teacher is no longer present. In addition, the remnant plays a significant role within the *ongoing* process of education. The remnant, while indeed facilitating the presence of a non-presence when the student is out of reach of the teacher, is also an anchor point by which further interaction with the teacher will become meaningful. In other words, the remnant has a second role. The remnant actually affects the real experience of the student once he or she comes face to face with that teacher from whom she has been absent for some time.

I turn once again to the circuit of recognition to limn this second role. Following Benjamin, we should note that there are two main components to interhuman relations: the "intrapsychic," and the "intersubjective."[6] *Intrapsychic* life is the life of mental holdings, the life of the remnant. But intersubjective life is the real-life counterpart to the remnant. It is that part of experience that puts the remnant to the test. When one comes face to face with an authority figure, such face-to-face-ness serves as a foil to the isolated experience of the remnant, where one could formerly manipulate the authority figure, where the other used to be my own private other. Thus, a remnant is always the remnant of a specific other, an other who is likely to take one aback when intersubjective contact is reestablished. As such, there is always a give-and-take between the remnant, on the one hand, and fleshly contact with the other, on the other. Human experience is not primarily intrapsychic, as much psychoanalytic thought would have it. Nor is human experience based primarily on the interaction with the "real" authority figure, as so much presentist thought would have it. Human experience is a give and take between the remnant and the real.

Let us follow this present/absent theory of authority once again from the beginning, starting from a presentist conception, then moving to a version of the remnant, and then back again from the remnant to the real. When I come into contact with a teacher, I do so with a certain neediness. The teacher is important for my own growth as a person. I look to the teacher for recognition, for sustenance, for encouragement. I need the teacher to act as a mirror, reflecting who I am and who I am becoming. It is such an other, the teacher, who lets me know that my own actions are valuable, and that I am a person who has an affect on other people in this world. Yet at the same time, experiencing the authority figure's presence is bound to be unsettling. Indeed, the other is a separate "center of self," to borrow Benjamin's phrase.[7] The teacher as other is someone whom I do not control. Thus, while the teacher may offer me confidence and agency, she will doubtless shock me at some time. She will sometimes react in ways that I don't expect, sometimes in ways that do not offer me the recognition that I want. I will, after all, fail the authority figure's test from time to time. Thus, it is dangerous to depend wholly on the teacher. Such dependence will, at the end of the day, leave me tethered to an other whom I don't control. The teacher is a danger as well as a source of agency.

Vis-à-vis such a situation of danger and agency, the inner life of the remnant offers a buffer. When I leave the presence of the teacher, I am left with an inner conception of what the teacher has to offer me. This inner conception will be more under my control, more malleable to my needs, my wants, my autonomous actions. As Benjamin notes, "This 'inside' is the internal version of the safe transitional space (open space) that allows us to feel that our impulses come from within and so are authentically our own."[8] The remnant is under our control. The remnant is a version of authority that lets us replay the sort of recognition that we need from the other, even in the absence of that other. The inner life affords us an arena for play, for creativity, for experimentation, and for learning that is sheltered from the vicissitudes of the fleshly teacher. Under the watchful eyes of a teacher remnant, a teacher *whom I control*, I can practice my own ways of being, my own autonomous actions, without the threat of a teacher who might disappoint. In this way, the very nonpresence of the teacher is as central to the development of agency as the presence of that teacher. The remnant, cut from the same cloth as the real, functions as a prosthetic authority figure.

But as recognitive theory reminds us, the inner life contributes to agency only if it is ultimately tested in the real world. While the remnant is a safe space, one where I am in control, the remnant remains a space *of fantasy* unless it is tested against the real. Real agency cannot be fostered solely by remnants because agency is ultimately enacted in real life. In order for the teacher's recognition of me to count, she must have the real-life, presentist opportunity *not* to offer me recognition. In order for my agency to count, that agency must be tested in circumstances that could in fact end in disappointment. Thus, the remnant and the real exist in a symbiotic relationship. The inner life of the remnant cannot exist successfully on its own. An exclusively inner life leads to pathology, where playful imaginings of the remnant are never given a reality check, where the other is always a smiling face. Similarly, the intersubjective life cannot exist successfully on its own. A life experienced solely on the outside affords no zone of safety, no place where agency can be fostered without being constantly under threat, no place where the authority figure is not bound to surprise me *too much*. An exclusively outer life also leads to pathology, where submission to the whims of authority is the order of the day.

Think again of the thoughtful literary instruction of Professor Depuis, or the skilled coaching of Mr. Hoffman. While we described these teachers, at first, as a source of looming, beneficent presence, it is important now to amend that picture. On the one hand, yes, these teachers represent sources of inspiration, sources of educational agency, a warm cup of tea on a cold winter's day, if you will. The teacher, as a non-present, unconscious figure, continues to act as an active agent of motivation for his or her former student, *but not only because the teacher may have been an excellent teacher*. For, the teacher-as-remnant was once a teacher-in-the-flesh, a teacher who certainly had ups and downs of his or her own, who may not, in reality, have been the same inspiring figure that we now remember. Thus, the remnant serves a very important role in mitigating between, on the one hand, the active influence that a teacher has over his or her pupil, and, on the other, the safe space that is necessary to assimilate, to experiment with, and to make one's own the knowledge and abilities that the "real" teacher has to offer. The real teacher, by virtue of her role as an authority, always has the potential to influence his or her pupil *too much*, to nip agency in the bud, perhaps even by willful domination of her student. The remnant of authority acts as a buffer in times of non-presence. It enables students to effect a modicum of control over the teacher's authority. In the space of non-presence, the teacher is freeze-framed; the recognition that she offers can be invoked or disinvoked in order to decrease the threat of domination.

But let us think further about the remnant of authority and its real counterpart, about Professor Depuis and Mr. Hoffman as they were, but also about how they might be when they return. What is most educative may indeed *not* be the safe inner space afforded by the remnant. While the remnant may provide a mechanism for the agency of a student vis-à-vis an authority figure who is not present, isn't there also a sense in which education has already ended if the one-who-educates is once and for all relegated to a freeze-framed role? While it may be true that a student feels good about the remnant, that a student is eager to engage with the subject matter (Toni Morrison, running) associated with the smiling remnant, isn't it also true that the freeze-framed remnant has also lost the educative ability to challenge, to provoke, *to lead out* in the etymological sense of *educare*? It is at this point that I would say Professor Depuis and Mr. Hoffman should no longer be described as good teachers. Rather than still being effective teachers, they are, rather, set-in-stone objects in our memories, more monu/mental, if I can partake in this bit of punning, than they are educative.

In fact, what may be of more educational significance than the experience of the remnant is the symbiotic relation between the remnant and the real. Following the logic of recognition theory we should note that, while the remnant is a buffer to the real, being a buffer does not guarantee that the remnant contributes, on its own, to student agency. While the relation of non-presence with Professor Depuis is certainly a safer relation to have than the more unanticipatable relation that one has with her in the flesh; while the remnant of her "thoughtful guidance" may be a happy illusion of classroom experiences that were much more filled with tension, misrecognition, and domination than our unconscious chooses to recall; even so, a happy illusion is not necessarily a safe illusion in the long run. When the remnant of authority becomes the sole vehicle by which to gauge the extent to which one has become educated, the result is a solipsistic, inner-oriented educational experience that is dominated by private imaginings.

Consider cases where the remnant of authority tends to run rampant: Don't many of us know someone who always presents his or her educational reminiscences in glorious terms, but who, in a sort of performative contradiction, seems to be distinctly uneducated, decidedly unwise? For a student to *truly* learn from the lessons offered in the presence of Professor Depuis, the remnant of that teacher must be given a reality check. After one spends some time away from the presence of Professor Depuis, the real Professor Depuis must be encountered again in person in order for the student to gauge whether he can benefit from the real teacher in ways that are anything like the ways he benefited from her remnant. Without such a further encounter, the student's experience of the remnant may become tarnished by the nagging doubt that he or she might not be able to handle the fleshly experience that, ultimately, cannot be avoided since we are social beings. If a student stays solely in the realm of the authoritative remnant, then education stops.

EDUCATIONAL STOPOVERS:
BETWEEN THE REMNANT AND THE REAL

So I would ultimately like to argue for the interdependence of presence and non-presence when it comes to educational authority. It seems that education is necessarily influenced by instances of authoritative presence *as well as* by instances of authoritative non-presence. Why? Because the remnant is central to the real just as the real is central to the remnant. By this I don't mean that we should mysteriously know what our students are up to even when they are not in our presence. Nor do I mean that we should discount the significance of the time students spend *with* teachers.

What I mean, rather, is that we should pay more heed to the importance of educational stopovers, to those times when teachers and students leave each others' presence, and those times when they return to each other once again. Too often, these liminal moments are seen as unimportantly transitional, secondary to the times when students and teachers are actually in each other's presence, or, in more progressivist moments, secondary to the times that students are on their own, encountering what John Dewey calls "experience."[9] To put this another way, let's say that any consideration of the ends of education should also take into account the fact that education needs to have ends, many ends. It also needs to have many new beginnings. Authority should leave and then come back, leave and then come back. Education must have numerous ends and numerous beginnings if students and teachers are to take advantage of the give-and-take that is necessary between the remnant and the real.

In fact, it is important to note that this give-and-take between the remnant and the real is actually a very accurate description of day-to-day relations as they are practiced in our educational institutions. What I mean by this is that educational institutions have, for the most part, a certain rhythm. Students engage with teachers sometimes daily, sometimes weekly, and then there is time built in for them to be away from their teachers. As the logic of the remnant shows us, the time spent away from the teacher is more than a time for one to complete one's exercises. It is more than a time to complete one's reading. It is more than a cooling-off period away from the pressures of school. Time spent away from the teacher can also be an unconscious reenactment of the ways that one experiences authority in the flesh. And while the unconscious reenactment of the teacher's presence will be part of the student's inner world, a part of that over which the student has complete control, it is important for the growth of the educational relation that there be time together to augment inner experience with outer reality. The student must come once again into contact with the "real" authority figure in order that inner images do not come to dominate.

This particular way of construing the comings and goings (the "ends") of education casts a different light on the day-to-day rhythm of educational interactions with authority. The actions of the teacher are important, yes. But, it is in the oscillation between presence and non-presence, and back again, where such actions gain their significance. Is it not interesting that so much educational research treats the school as a petri dish of presence, while the actual rhythm of education so clearly enacts a back-and-forth between the remnant and the real? Especially when it comes to the matter of authority, the school should not be treated as a petri dish of presence.

Of course, there is a paradox that is certainly present (and certainly also non-present) when we delve into the role of the remnant and the real of educational authority. *The paradox, clearly stated, is this*: successful educational authority always depends upon presence *and* absence. Thus, one finds real difficulties when one tries to describe "successful" authority. For, to describe successful educational authority, one can only describe that which is describable, that which is *present*. So, just when one is in a position to describe an instance of "successful" authority, just then, it may be that authority is no longer successful precisely because it has become solely a matter of presence. At the moment when authority is present, freeze-framed, and describable, the educative role of authority may have already passed.

One might thus wonder if my fond reminiscence of Professor Depuis is not actually more of a testament to the fact that she no longer has a role in educating me than it is a testament to what she once had to offer me as an educator. Such a reminiscence leaves me with a profound remnant, but with little in the way of a reality check. After a consideration of the give-and-take between authority's absence and its presence, I must wonder if a *truly great teacher* isn't rather one who has refused to make a lasting impression on us. Or at the very least, isn't she one who is remembered as a bit enigmatic? Isn't she one who continues to be troublesome because unexpected? Isn't she one who continues to force an engagement with the real rather than a fond recalling of the ideal?

PRESENCE AND ABSENCE, THE SPOKEN AND THE WRITTEN

A few years ago, I was speaking to a colleague about a philosophy conference that we were both going to attend. She mentioned how happy she was that there were to be no simultaneous presentation sessions. She was happy that everyone would be present to listen to everyone else's papers. She was pleased that papers were not to be given in different rooms at the same time because, she said, "this way, everyone will be able to listen, and perhaps respond, to every paper." I think her observation goes right to the heart of an important relational notion that many people hold dear. For many, it is very important to have face-to-face dialogue instead of simply reading the hard copy. Colleagues come together in order to learn. We come together to see each other. We come together to hug or shake hands. All of this is facilitated by the shared experience of living dialogue.

My colleague's comment is about presence and absence. It is also about dialogue versus reading. In many people's eyes, dialogue is how people become most *present* to one another. The question I pursue in the pages that follow in this chapter is this: What is the role of speaking, as opposed to the role of reading, in the authority relation? I pursue this question to add nuance to a few themes that I have already been looking into in the previous pages of this study. First, I have already started an investigation into the place of texts within the relation of authority. That investigation was based mainly on curricular texts that have been written by people *other* than the teacher. This account of written texts will expand that initial investigation and open it up to texts and other communiqués that are written by the teacher herself. Second, I have already made the claim that a relational understanding of language is central to a relational understanding of authority. Thus, what follows will augment the performative account of communication that I have already offered, showing how language works, within the performance of an authority relation, to negotiate the presence and absence of speakers and listeners. What follows is based on an account of authority in the realm of academia. However, I am confident that what is examined here should be clearly applicable to the authority relation as it occurs in many educational settings.

To address the question of speaking and writing in the authority relation, I will look into two more versions of the role that language plays in human relations. These two understandings of language augment the performative account described earlier without falling back into the sender-receiver model that we should rightly reject. The first version derives from the phenomenological work of Maurice Merleau-Ponty. I will detail Merleau-Ponty's account of language and relationality, but show that it has several limitations. Then, I will pick up on some of the work done in the previous pages by examining the psychoanalytic perspective on speech provided by Jessica Benjamin's intersubjective psychoanalysis. Intersubjective psychoanalysis highlights the importance of present/absent interaction. By looking into Benjamin's theory of language, I will show that her viewpoint fills in some important gaps in what I call Merleau-Ponty's "traditional" view of speech. Ultimately, I will come back to my colleague's observation on listening to one another, as opposed to simply reading each other's papers, at conferences. Her observation was quite correct: we *are* well met at conferences such as the one we both attended. Sometimes hard copies simply will not do. The living relation of authority is most appropriately brought alive through the performative enactment that occurs via the living word.

THE PROBLEM OF INTERSUBJECTIVITY

Before jumping right into language, though, let us start with the more general philosophical "problem of intersubjectivity." Intersubjectivity has been the concern of a wide range of philosophers who have wanted to know how one subject recognizes another subject. In phenomenological terms, the question is posed like this: If the other is constituted within one's own ego, then how can we account for the specificity of the other? How can I constitute an other who is self-constituting? Won't the other's self-constituting just be a version of my own self-constituting? Is there a way to understand the experience of relationality other than merely saying, "I really don't know the other; all I know is my own version of the other"?

Edmund Husserl, for example, addresses the problem of intersubjectivity in his *Cartesian Mediations*.[10] There, he employs the notion of "pairing" to show how the ego attains intersubjectivity. Pairing is a developmental answer to the predicament of intersubjectivity. As Husserl explains, pairing happens early in the ego's development, and it sets the stage for intersubjectivity later in life. The mother (or whoever the nurturer is) makes available the child's first "apperceptive" experience of otherness.[11] In words that are not as phenomenologically technical, we might say that the mother, or caretaker, is vaguely experienced both as other and as part of the ego. According to Husserl, the two members of this pair "found phenomenologically a unity of similarity and thus are always constituted precisely as a pair."[12] This is before the ego constitutes itself as a separate ego. Then, even after self-constitution, the ego continues to constitute others by analogy to the self-mother pair. The other is like the mother, who was, and still is, like me. The more mature, self-consituting ego understands others to be self-constituting also. A mature other can be self-constituting because others can be like me—just as the mother was once like me.

Some followers of Husserl are not sure that the origin of intersubjectivity can be situated at the primordial stage, just before self-constitution of the ego. Even if the self-other analogy begins early on, the problem of solipsism ensues later. Later on, when the self-constituting other is recognized to be just like me, then hasn't her self-constituting turned out to be a version of my own self-constituting? Pairing may have started *before* self-constituting, but it still ends up there. A developed ego loses the *vague* perception of pairing. However, its pairing now happens within the realm of self-constitution—which leads us back to the original predicament of intersubjectivity. As Maurice Merleau-Ponty reminds us, "To be conscious is to constitute, so that I cannot be conscious of another person, since that would involve constituting him as constituting."[13] Husserl does not get past the problem of solipsism.

MERLEAU-PONTY'S TRADITIONAL VIEW OF RELATIONAL LANGUAGE

Following up on his objection to Husserl's developmental, "pairing" explanation of intersubjectivity, Merleau-Ponty looks to language. He argues that language provides the bedrock of intersubjectivity. In his essay entitled "The Phenomenology of Language," Merleau-Ponty shows how language provides a medium for intersubjectivity.[14] I will call his conception the "traditional" view of intersubjective language. The traditional view points out two dimensions of language.[15] The first dimension is *not* intersubjective: language forms a set of cultural signifiers that are commonly understood among people who share that language. In this dimension, a word is understood to be an object, just like a stone or a table. Just as we share some understanding of what an object such as a stone is, we also share some understanding of what a word is, what it means. This first dimension of language is not properly intersubjective because, according to the phenomenological view, intersubjectivity means recognizing another subject, another self. Just because two subjects recognize a common object in language, that does not necessarily mean that they recognize *each other*. Intersubjectivity is not guaranteed just because two people recognize common objects or share common meanings.

The second dimension of language brings us into the realm of intersubjectivity. It does so as follows: When I speak, I give to language the unique quality of my intended meaning. And when an other speaks, she also gives to language the unique quality of her intended meaning. In this second dimension, language is no longer an object in the sense that a stone is an object. Instead, language is a uniquely *linguistic* object insofar as it lets an other demonstrate her subjectivity. A Merleau-Ponty explains, spoken language serves to "reverse my ordinary relationship to objects and give certain ones of them the value of subjects."[16] If an other picks up a stone, the stone remains the same stone just as it would remain the same stone if I (as opposed to the other) were to pick it up. When the other picks up a stone, that picking-up does not convince me that an other's consciousness is different from my own. When an other speaks, though, she invests language with a unique meaning that I could not replicate. It is as if she has changed the stone's stoneness in a way that I could never have done. Through using language, the other convinces me of her specific subjectivity. Language, in its second dimension, is thus a vehicle for intersubjectivity, for relation.

While this traditional view of language and intersubjectivity is appealing, I would like to point out several of its limitations. First of all, this view of language is not longitudinal, to borrow a term from the social sciences. The traditional view does not explain why we keep speaking with others over a long period of time. What I mean is, If the ego recognized the specificity of an other once, why would one keep speaking with the other? In terms of the comment made by my colleague with regard to our conference, if I have already been to one of someone's presentations, why not just read the hard copy of that person's thoughts from then on? Or in terms of a love relationship, should I quit speaking with my partner in person just because we have come to an intersubjective realization of each other's consciousnesses? Speaking seems to be an ongoing project, but why? The traditional view of intersubjective language does not answer this question.

Second, the traditional view of language does not account for the speaker behind the speech. If speech is a *vehicle* for intersubjectivity, then there is still a unique subject *behind* the speech that needs to be dealt with. Speech may help us to recognize the specificity of another subject, but what if I have problems with that other subject? What if that other subject is threatening to me? In the traditional view of intersubjective speech, it seems that speech is a means for establishing a *positive* relation with the other; speech leads to empathy. Does speech have any function when the other is someone I do *not* want to recognize? To return again to the experience of attending a conference and to listening to papers, is there some reason to speak with a presenter whose views I loathe?

A third limitation follows directly from the second. What if the subject behind the speech is *too* appealing? What if an other's unique subjectivity threatens to engulf my own uniqueness? Following the traditional view, it seems that speech serves to clarify the specificity of the other, and thus to intensify the other's charm. In the case of one who attends a conference, why would I speak with an other who threatens to overshadow me with the appeal of her views, with the logic of her arguments?

And because I want ultimately to relate an intersubjective theory of language to the problem of relational authority, let me translate these three objections into terms that speak to the communication that takes place with an authority figure. If language acts according to this traditional intersubjective model, why, once I have ascertained the authoritative status of the person with whom I speak, would I ever need to listen to such an authority figure again? Couldn't I just accept, after that initial ascertainment, that every other thing I hear from, or about, that person is equally authoritative? Would authority ever need to be enacted more than once between two people? Or, if language does serve to establish a relational understanding of an authority figure, mightn't my potential fear of an other be an inordinate deterrent to communication in cases where I guess, beforehand, that the other has the potential to dominate me? Or conversely, following my third objection to the traditional view, mightn't language be the royal road to domination? Mightn't communication with an authority figure turn out to be too convincing, too enticing, to the point where one abandons one's own stance through engaging in the relation of authority?

I sense that Merleau-Ponty is quite justified in claiming that language is a key element for attaining intersubjectivity, for recognizing an other as a subject in her own right. And, I am quite sure that the traditional view goes much farther toward establishing language's intersubjective role than the more common sender-receiver understanding of communication. However, recent work in intersubjective psychoanalysis offers a more helpful view of language's intersubjective role. Specifically, intersubjective psychoanalysis sheds light on the three limitations of the traditional view that I have described. It also highlights the importance of everyday dialogue at a conference such as the one I have been referring to.

LANGUAGE AND THE REMNANT

Intersubjectivity in psychoanalytic discourse, it will be recalled, relies upon a distinction between *intrapsychic* space and *intersubjective* space. Defining the term *intersubjectivity*, Benjamin says that it "refers to that zone of experience in which the other is not merely the object of the ego's need/drive or cognition/perception but has a separate and equivalent center of self."[17] This distinction—between the other recognized as object and the other recognized as subject—is the distinction between the intrapsychic and the intersubjective. Whereas intrapsychic space involves internal, psychic manipulation of the other, intersubjective space involves recognition of the other as a subject with agency. According to Benjamin, the other always remains an object if she remains only in the psychic realm. Intersubjectivity ensues when we confront the other "out there in the real world," on his or her own terms.

It is easy to see the essential similarity between the phenomenological version of intersubjectivity, *à la* Husserl, and the psychoanalytic version. For each version, intersubjectivity consists in recognizing the other *as autonomous subject*. There is, however, a difference in how objects are construed by these two versions. In the psychoanalytic view, the other-as-object is manipulated in intrapsychic space, while the other-as-subject resides "out there in the real world." In the phenomenological view, though, the other-as-object does not reside in a *different* space than the other-as-subject. In this latter view, they both reside in the same world of "intended" others. Another difference that characterizes the psychoanalytic view is that it does not consider intersubjectivity to be an automatic state of human consciousness. Instead, intersubjectivity is an achievement. We sometimes refuse intersubjectivity, or intersubjectivity is avoided because it is unbearable. Since confronting the other as a subject with agency can be threatening, often it is more comfortable to experience the other as an object under our control. In such cases, we disregard the other-as-subject and represent him as an object in the psyche.

Because of this last difference, a psychoanalytic understanding of intersubjectivity suggests that, often, the self becomes swollen with objectifying representations of the other. Unfortunately, if our relation to the other resides mainly in intrapsychic space, then the self will experience a sudden crisis when faced with an other who proves to be a subject with agency. In this case, if the other acts in an unanticipated way, I will feel *doubly* threatened because I do not anticipate its agency. In the face of this double threat, I will feel *my own* subjectivity diminished. In order to avoid this sudden threat, in order to be an autonomous subject in my own right, I must accept that intrapsychic representations of the other are *not* equivalent to the autonomous other "out there in the real world." I can only be an autonomous subject if I can negotiate between the intrapsychic realm and the intersubjective realm.

This is where language comes to play a different role than the one suggested by Merleau-Ponty. Language facilitates the move between intrapsychic space and intersubjective space.[18] Language makes use of symbols.[19] As such, it enables us to practice going from reality to symbol, and from symbol to reality, over and over. This oscillation between symbol and reality happens because language itself is a way to negotiate between the intrapsychic and the intersubjective realms. That is to say, just as the other can be either intrapsychically constructed, or, can be recognized as an actual, living subject; so, too, can language freeze-frame thoughts and actions and thus offer a dual status for people with whom we come into contact. Language works within a system that can offer steadfast words to substitute for less steadfast living beings. Take for example the word, *Grandma*. This word offers a steadfast, freeze-framed sign of the living woman who is one's grandmother. Language negotiates between objects in the outside world and our inside representations of those objects. Language "constitutes a space of fluctuating convergence and divergence between inner and outer," to borrow the words of Benjamin.[20]

Let me offer an example, from my own life, of this outside/inside use of language. My daughter, Olivia, when she was two years old, was just at the point of entering the realm of language. At that point, her use of language was limited, although it was already very helpful to her. For example, sometimes she and I would visit her grandparents even though we did not spend a lot of time around them on a daily basis. Nevertheless, even when Olivia was away from her grandparents, she was able to use language to conjure up images of them that would bring a smile to her face. For instance, when I would speak to Olivia of a nearby zoo that we had visited together with her grandparents, a smile would come to her face as she would say, "Grandma Grandpa zoo." "Yes," I would tell her, "Grandma and Grandpa were at the zoo with us." Even before Olivia had stepped completely into language, she could use language as a system to negotiate between what was present and what was absent. She could use language to negotiate between inner representations of her grandparents and outer experiences with them in real life.

According to Benjamin's view—the view that language provides a symbolic space for play, for practicing the transition from intersubjective to the intrapsychic, and back again—Olivia's evocation of her grandparents enables her to do two things: First, it enables her to let go of her grandparents, allowing them to be independent subjects who come and go as they please. In other words, Olivia can accept the departure of her grandparents because she has words that evoke their presence even in their absence. Conjuring up the image of her grandparents by saying their names, Olivia can smile even though they are not under her direct control. This first use of language allows her to practice moving from the intersubjective realm to the intrapsychic realm as she changes Grandma and Grandpa into intrapsychic representations. Second, language enables her to negotiate the return of Grandma and Grandpa when she finally sees them again. When they return, Olivia will be reminded that her intrapsychic image of Grandpa and Grandma—the picture in her mind that their names evoke—is, perhaps, not the same as their physical presence. Whereas their images can be evoked almost at will, Grandpa and Grandma really only come back when they want to. Upon their return, she will once again be reminded that they are autonomous subjects. This second use of language helps her to move from intrapsychic space to intersubjectivity.

Another important role of language between subjects is the role of mediation.[21] This is not the simple role of "softening reality" as some would have it who unthinkingly say, "Sticks and stones can break my bones but words can never hurt me." Rather, it is the complex role of negotiating the tension between inner and outer life. For example, if I am in face-to-face contact with an other, I may feel threatened by his or her aggression. I may feel overwhelmed by the force of his or her physical presence, or I may feel overwhelmed by the force of his or her argument. Language's symbolization enables me to create a safe haven even during such an onslaught of the other. Let us say that I have stage fright just before speaking with a person whose ideas and writings I have long revered. I can use strategies of linguistic symbolization to keep myself fortified, to temper the anxiety that threatens to overcome my very being. I may say to myself, "She is just like any other person. She is made of flesh and blood like my daughter, and I am never afraid to interact with my daughter." In this way, the symbolic quality of language enables one to mediate the incursion of an other onto the agency of self. It is not that language *never* allows the other to affect the self. If the other could not affect the self, then the other would not be an agentive subject, and intersubjectivity would cease. It is, rather, that language enables the self to be affected without being lost.

As the above examples show, language does work in the realm of the subject/object pair, in the ongoing relational problem of how subjects come to recognize others as more than mere objects. Intersubjectivity, as it gets elaborated in the psychoanalytic tradition, always happens in juxtaposition to intrapsychic activity. That is to say, there is never pure intersubjectivity nor is there pure intrapsychic life. There is only oscillation between the two. Similarly, human language exists in oscillation between the symbolic and the real. Language is neither pure symbol nor is it pure object. Rather, language acts in ways that parallel the inner/outer split. And as long as language has referents, language will be integral to intersubjectivity.

BETWEEN THE PAPER AND THE WORD

What has all this to do with education? With authority? In education, there is often a choice to be made between absence and presence. It takes the form of a choice between the paper and the word. In education, one must constantly negotiate between written pronouncements and living dialogue. When a student reads what a teacher has written, there is absence. When a student talks with a teacher, there is presence.

Students submit essays, term papers, written tests, written exams, as well as other forms of written texts that are read by teachers. Teachers give out notes. They deliver prepared lectures. They offer students written evaluations. They hand out opinion papers and essays that they themselves have written. They give out grades. All of these are set-in-stone forms of communication. These documents and pronouncements are severely limiting if they are not accompanied by dialogue. Dialogue is central to the educational relation. The relation will certainly entail hard copies, but it should utilize more fluid aspects of communication, too. In this way, the teachers with whom students interact have a chance to return with unexpectedness, with surprise.

In classrooms, we have missed something very important if we overfocus on the written documents that are exchanged between student and teacher. Yes, it may be the case that texts are thoughtfully submitted, thoughtfully critiqued, thoughtfully graded and assessed. Yes, it may be the case that student and teacher are "happy" that an even-handed relation of authority has been enacted through such exchanges of text. However, it must be remembered that fully functioning authority depends upon the dynamic interchange between the written and the spoken. This happens just as every relation depends upon the dynamic interchange between the remnant and the real. Dialogue about what has been written is as important as the physical return of a teacher who has been absent. The speaking teacher is always a "supplement" to what has been written.

But what is the use of dialogue if a teacher threatens to overwhelm me with his or her allure? As I have tried to show earlier, the psychic life of language actually helps to *mediate* between self and other. Speaking with an other provides a symbolic space for interaction that can temper the aggression of an other toward the self. If I speak with someone whose otherness threatens to engulf me, then the words we exchange can become objects for my manipulation. Using the symbolic, intrapsychic qualities of language, I can achieve a certain distance from the other, a distance that helps to attenuate the onslaught of that other. In cases where the other is threatening, the linguistic distance of dialogue can help me to keep my own subjectivity intact. So while it might seem at first glance that I should *not* speak with an other who might be threatening to me, in fact, language serves to help us through those times when we are about to be engulfed by another person's ideas, by another person's presence. Dialogue can serve to de-ossify the seemingly overwhelming quality of an other's ideas.

When student and teacher come together, the relational nature of language makes space for agency. Dialogue between student and teacher can offer something much different than what the student had suspected was "behind the door." To be engaged in dialogue is not simply to be exposed in an unadulterated manner to the perspectives, ideas, and opinions of another person. Quite the contrary, dialogue may serve to mitigate some elements of the authority relation that might be quite rigid without such dialogue. As counterintuitive as this may seem, please consider the following: when the other threatens to engulf me with his rigid opinions; when the other seems to have me in an authoritative relation where I feel squelched—just then it may be that I can use dialogue with the other to my benefit, to the enhancement of my own capacity.

And what about instances when the other seems repulsive? It might seem as if there is little reason to speak with a person whose written viewpoints I simply cannot stand. Such a rejection of dialogue with a loathsome other is based on the premise that dialogue will only serve to accentuate an other's loathsomeness. Actually, it is not necessarily the case that the "real" other is as anticipatable as the carved-in-stone written other. Yes, I may dislike the substance of a person's writings. However, there is always a difference between the fleshly author and that which he or she writes. There will always be a *dis*continuity between authorship and the spoken word. The spoken word is a supplement to the written word in both senses of "supplementarity." The spoken will not only have natural connections to the written word, but it will have post-natural additions to the written word too. There is little reason to think that the author's fleshly interaction with me will be synonymous with her text's influence on me. For, the intersubjective nature of language is such that dialogue opens up new symbolic qualities that depend upon the relation between speakers as much as they depend upon what the author has written in the past.

So it is not necessarily the case that the authority that gets enacted between teacher and student in dialogue will be the same as the authority that has been enacted by means of teacherly pronouncements. If a student decides, beforehand, that a teacher's objectionable lecture, or the objectionable comments that a teacher makes on a student's work, will be synonymous with the authority that gets enacted through conversation with that same teacher, this is a mistake. Dialogue between student and teacher itself opens up new vistas that may not be as loathsome as one might anticipate.

Once again, what I am trying to say is this: there is a dynamic interaction between teacher pronouncements, on the one hand, and student-teacher dialogue, on the other, that closely parallels the dynamic between absence and presence. It may be that the very antidote to the loathsomeness of the other comes from an experience that might at first glance be foreshadowed as an experience even more loathsome. It may be that talking with the other is less objectionable, and more agentive, than could ever have been imagined from a distance where distilled pronouncements seem to rule the day.

THE SIGNIFICANCE OF BOTH ABSENCE AND PRESENCE

For some, this chapter may seem inconclusive. It may seem at this point that I am advocating the benefits of *both* presence *and* absence. It may seem that there is no way to decide whether the authority relation gets enacted most prominently when there is presence, or most prominently when there is absence. In fact, *there is no way* to decide. I began this chapter by noting that current understandings of authority focus too much on presence. They certainly do. So, if it has accomplished anything, this chapter has served to make the reader aware of the place of absence within the authority relation. Please note, though, that I do not claim that there is any clear-cut way to decide *which* is more significant to the authority relation, presence or absence. What I have attempted to show is, first, that absence is significant, and second, that the real and the remnant are symbiotically related, each living off of the other.

Another way of stating this is to say that there is no "behind the door" to presence and absence. There is no preordained essence to either one. Rather, presence and absence (or, alternatively, authority in dialogue and authority that has been distilled into written pronouncements) are significant to the extent that they are related to each other. Each gains its educational import in its performance, rather than behind the door. Hence the ongoing nature of both presence and absence. The nature of presence and absence in the authority relation is always *to be* worked out.

Acknowledging presence and absence yields new insight into the workings of student agency vis-à-vis their teachers. Once we know that the impact of the authority relation depends upon the dynamic interaction between presence and absence, we also know that there is plenty of wiggle room for students to configure their relationships to authority *even when teachers are not around.* Thus, students should not only be encouraged to gain voice and confidence when they speak with teachers face to face. They should also be encouraged to gain the agency when they experience the remnants of teachers. This can happen as student rethink the freeze-framed effects of teachers who have made their impact through marks, through written communications, and through teacherly lectures. Cognizance of the remnant, and of its interaction with the real, reminds us that what one does with educational authority on one's own is just as important as how one experiences that authority in the flesh. Such cognizance reminds us that students have much control over the effects of educational authority.

Educators should make it clear to students that students have power to treat authority as they see fit. There is a particular opportunity to do so when authority figures are not around. The relation between presence and absence is one that should depend, to a large extent, upon the actions of students. As a student, how I relate to a Professor Depuis, to a coach Hoffman, or to a history teacher such as Julie's, is to a large extent under my own control, at least when such figures of authority are not around. And even when such authority figures do come back into the picture, I have a chance, myself, to alter the effect that their return has on me. For, the return of an authority figure can depend greatly on my stance toward him or her while he or she was away. The wiggle room between presence and absence affords great space for student agency.

It is the more general matter of student agency vis-à-vis authority that will be the subject of the next chapter. There, I will outline some of the ways that we might encourage students to be active participants in the authority relation. I will look into how students can "use" the relation of authority to their benefit. I will look into how students might "use" their teachers in ways that are agentive. In addition, I will examine how students can use *larger* forces of authority to their benefit, these forces being: the force of natural inclination, the force of acculturation, and the force of tradition.

CHAPTER 4

When Faced With Authority

Let us now look into the ways that we might orient ourselves toward authority. For, if authority is a relation, then it is not enough to say how authority operates. Nor is it enough to say which kinds of authority (non-present as well as present, textual as well as spoken) are involved in the authority relation. We must also ask what role we have to play when we are faced with authority. In the face of authority, what do we *do*? What might students do?

There are at least two ways to approach how we orient ourselves toward authority. First, we can think about how we face an other who is in authority. We can think about how we treat that other. Second, we can think about how we face authority when authority is bigger than an other, when authority is a societal force or a cultural tradition. We can consider when authority is a larger entity, rather than being a *specific* other. Of course how one orients oneself toward an other in authority, and how one orients oneself toward larger societal forces—these are immense topics, each one of them. In this chapter, I want to bite off just a small nibble from each of these immense topics. With regard to the other who is in authority, I will describe the benefits of "using" authority figures to our educational advantage. This "using" I will call "pragmatic intersubjectivity." With regard to how one treats oneself when facing larger forces of authority, I will explain some of the educational benefits of tending to one's own agency in such circumstances. To do this, I will be drawing upon the philosophical tradition of "self-fashioning."[1]

PRAGMATIC INTERSUBJECTIVITY,
OR, JUST USING TEACHERS

Pragmatism has long held sway in educational thought, especially in North America. While the "consequences of pragmatism" in education are many, one central tenet seems to emerge as influential again and again.[2] Here I am referring to the pragmatist notion of making all educational ends into means for further educational ends.[3] Such pragmatism gains purchase in educational thought because education is, after all, an ever-growing, never-ending project where curricular achievements lead to further curricular achievements. To make ends into means into further ends just keeps the ball rolling in a very educational sort of way. As John Dewey put it, "[T]he central problem of an education based upon experience is to select the kind of present experiences that live fruitfully and creatively in subsequent experiences."[4]

Of course, this tenet of pragmatism does not really apply to *people*. To my knowledge, Dewey never went so far as to say that people should use other people. He never said that it would be all right to turn a person into a means to a further end. In this way, John Dewey follows Immanuel Kant's moral dictum that every rational creature must be treated as an end in himself. Kant condemns the use of others. His condemnation is enmeshed with his understanding of autonomous selfhood, and with the dignity of such selfhood. As Kant puts it, "Man and, in general, every rational being exists as an end in himself and not merely as a means to be arbitrarily used by this or that will. . . . This principle . . . of every rational creature as an end in itself is the supreme limiting condition on freedom.[5] And Dewey toes a good, Kantian, moral line. He leaves *people* out of his pragmatism.

But let us be immoral for a bit. Let us bring people into the pragmatist picture. Let us bring students and teachers into this picture just for the sake of argument. I want to make the case that Dewey *should have* embraced pragmatism all the way down to the personal level. I want to suggest that, at least in the case of students and teachers, there should be some using going on. In particular, students should be using their teachers as means to further ends. Such a move of making human beings into means to further ends, of making teachers into means for the further ends of students, of going against Kant's categorical imperative, we might call "pragmatic intersubjectivity." Or, we might call it *just using people* in education.

Let us be immoral by arguing against the morality of Kant. Why might it be okay for one person to use another? Why might it be all right for one *not* in authority to use one who *is* in authority? Why should we *not* follow Kant's moral imperative? Well, from the standpoint of relational authority, Kant's order not to use another is, quite simply, impossible to follow! When it comes to the authority relation, Kant makes a faulty assumption to begin with. He assumes that the self is autonomous in its most "mature" state. In his response to the question, "What is Enlightenment?" Kant encourages each person to use his or her own authority in his or her own way. "Have the courage to use the authority of your own reason," Kant exhorts.[6] He assumes that human beings are fundamentally autonomous, and thus he imagines that how we relate to authority must honor the autonomy within each of us. Well, when it comes to the relation of authority, Kant picks the pan up by the wrong handle. I say this because once one realizes (contra Kant) that human beings are relational vis-à-vis authority, then relation, whether it be a dependency on others, or whether it be an instrumental use of others, is *not* something that we can simply choose to avoid. The moral pan should rather be picked up by its intersubjective handle.

Unlike Kant, we should take as a given that human beings exist in relation, and that the only optional matter is *how* we engage with another person. While Kant envisions an authority that one can engage with alone, we should envision the relation of authority as one wherein we *inevitably* use one another, at least to some extent. As I have been trying to argue throughout this work, human beings are always *already* relational, especially when authority is at play.

USING THE OTHER: NIETZSCHE, FOUCAULT, WINNICOTT

When we go against Kant, it may, at first blush, seem a bit immoral. But we are in good company. There is good philosophical grounding for the concept of pragmatic intersubjectivity. For example, Friedrich Nietzsche has responded to Kant's use-aversion with the bold statement that " 'autonomous' and 'moral' are mutually exlusive."[7] Nietzsche turns the Kantian moral imperative on its head. He does so by showing how moral decisions are always imbedded in a moral calculus that is already intersubjective. For Nietzsche, a person's moral decision is not something that is decided upon by the autonomous individual and then carried out in the fashion that the autonomous individual sees fit. A moral act is not carried out solely by the intention of the autonomous actor. On one's own, it is not actually possible to choose what is right or what is wrong. Rather, what is "right" or "good" is always already involved in a moral calculus that has been begun before the human actor has even considered making a moral choice. For Nietzsche, moral goods are always saturated with significance because of human obligations and human power struggles that have taken place in the past.

So in his famous example of early Christian morality, Nietzsche argues that some "moral" habits such as abstinence and moderation were deemed "moral" not out of autonomous free choice.[8] They were deemed "moral" only because they were forced on the early Christians by the ruling class. Under pressure from the other, Nietzsche maintains, one makes a virtue out of necessity. Moral decisions derive from intersubjective experience rather than from the free intentions of autonomous selves. Or to repeat his bold claim, " 'autonomous' and 'moral' are mutually exlusive."[9]

To put Nietzsche's observations in terms of means and ends, we can say that other people are *already* being used as means when we consider how to live well. Why? Because moral acts take place in the intersubjective realm. In stark contrast to Kant's aversion to using people, Nietzsche reminds us that somebody is going to be used in a certain way when we decide how best to act. Moral decisions are made possible precisely because somebody has been, or somebody will be, used. Systems of moral thought, even such large systems as Christianity, are always already predicated upon people being used.

We are also in the company of Michel Foucault. Foucault pushes Nietzsche's thought along. He demonstrates that it is not only the moral realm that is based on using others. More than that, all human subjectivity is born out of such relations. Human flourishing itself is a matter of subjection. For Foucault too, the Kantian ideal of human autonomy is a mistaken one. The telos of human selfhood is not that of becoming autonomous and staying autonomous. Instead, human selfhood always owes its existence to various cultural practices of dependency upon others. The self is situated by bio-power, by the power of surveillance, by confessional techniques, by epistemic regimes, by governmental hierarchies, etc.[10] For Foucault, human selfhood lives and breathes through processes of subjection. It is not that the self arrives on the scene first, and is then fettered by the power of others. Nor is it that the self is first indebted to the power of others and then proceeds to free itself from power little by little. Instead, the power of others constitutes the self to begin with, and it continues to form who the self is as time progresses. Power creates the self *and* fetters the self, doing both at the same time. For Foucault, the self is "the product of the relation of power."[11] As such, the only way for the human being to flourish is for him or her to work *within* the various relations of power.

To look ahead for a moment, we might say that the student's experience at school is one of those subjectifying processes that Foucault claims are central to human subjectivity. For Foucault, being a subject means being subjectified, and being a subject at school means being subjectified at school. Now, what this means for the student is that the only way to obtain agency in a place such as school is to engage with the subjectifying processes already at work. It is only possible to flourish by means of using the power-laden tools at hand. What I want to suggest in this chapter is that one of the subjectifying processes at school is the teacher-student relationship. Interaction with the teacher is one of those educational sites where student subjectivity is constituted. As such, one way for student flourishing to occur is through the strategic use of that site. Using teachers is one way to attain agency within the subjectifying processes of schooling.

D. W. Winnicott is keeping us company as well. Winnicott assails Kant from a psychoanalytic standpoint.[12] His insights not only bolster the "immoral" stance that I am putting forth here, but they provide a very practical way to think about how students might use authority in educational settings. For Winnicott, human agency is formed against the backdrop of using other people. As the child develops a sense of self, he or she does so by experimenting with the absence and presence of a primary caregiver. The child needs the presence of a caregiver in order to have a space that is safe for experimentation, creativity, and acquisition of new skills. She needs someone to fall back on when things fail. Yet the child also needs the absence of a caregiver insofar as she must be able to experiment, to create, and to acquire new skills *on her own*. The child needs spaces where the caregiver is there, but the child also needs spaces where the caregiver is not there. In order to establish these sorts of spaces, the child must sometimes call her caregiver to her side. At other times, she must banish the caregiver from her sight so that she can test what she can do alone. In both of these circumstances, the child must "use" the other in order to set the stage for growth. The child must manipulate the presence of an other so that the other is around sometimes and not around at others. The child must call on the other sometimes. At other times she must either implicitly or explicitly ask the other to leave. So even though the young child is in the process of establishing her own autonomy, this process includes an other. It includes the use of an other.

And as Winnicott points out, this practice of using others is not just a childhood matter. Throughout life, and in many different arenas, agency is *not* gained in a passive, nor in an isolated, way. It is through the active "use" of others that one flourishes. When we "use" other people, we call them to our sides or we banish them from our midst. And we must do so in an active way. If the other seeps in and out of our presence on her own volition, then *she* has control over how I can gain agency. It is only through *my own* use of others that I can create the circumstances where I am both dependent on, yet independent of, another person who serves as my guide.

So we need to use others in order to gain agency. Of course, this is not the end of the story. After all, not all people will let themselves be used. Not every person I meet will agree to both be at my beck and call and to be absent when I see fit. There must be a *relation* at work between the person who sometimes needs an other, and an other who accepts the challenge of being around at those particular times. For this other who is willing to be around, Winnicott introduces a concept that is very important for us, educationally speaking. It is the concept of the "good enough" mother. The good enough mother is the object of use. She is the person who avails herself to be used by another. She is the person who understands that another person needs her to be present at times and absent at others. If I am a good enough mother, I understand that my presence and absence are central to the autonomy, creativity, and thoughtfulness of the other. I understand that being around may not always be easy. For example, sometimes the other will try to "destroy" me.[13] Sometimes the other will try to banish me from his or her presence. And at such times, I may have a desire to leave the other for good. But, as a good enough mother, I must have the fortitude to stay the course. I may need to go away at times, even at times when I do not want to go away. And yet, I must be willing to bring myself back into the picture later in order that the other might use me again. In Winnicott's terms, the other may try to "destroy" and banish me, but I must be able to "survive" the other's destruction of me. The idea of being "good enough" is related to the fact that I must be able to be around when need be, but I must also be able to be absent when need be.[14]

EDUCATIONAL IMPLICATIONS:
THAT TEACHERS MIGHT BE GOOD ENOUGH

Let us now think "immorally" with regard to education. Unfortunately, the use of teachers by students is very much ignored as an educational theme. I suspect this is because modern educational thought is still steeped in a Kantian understanding of moral life. As if to underscore this point, I have had the following experience while I have been writing about this anti-Kantian way of approaching authority: as I have shared this idea of students using teachers with fellow teachers, a response I often get is, "I hope you are not suggesting that students use teachers in an instrumental way." To respond, I prefer to make the following point: "Actually, human beings always operate in ways that are *already* instrumental. There is no way for human beings to become autonomous enough that they might *not* use each other in instrumental ways." That is not to say that students should *harm* teachers by using them. Pragmatic intersubjectivity need not be a slippery slope to harming others. Using others is, simply, how human beings gain agency.

Indeed, ignoring the use of others has been detrimental to educational thought. A dire result of such ignoring has been the advent of Pollyanna-esque narratives of educational progress. Take theories of teaching, for example. They tend to cling to the assumption that there is still a lot of progress to be made so that teachers might better facilitate student learning and student agency. While we try to squeeze the last drops out of our teaching, there is little attention paid to the interhuman mechanisms that allow teaching to be successful in the first place. Student learning and student agency do not happen in schools unless students use other people in ways that facilitate such learning and agency. Pedagogical practices, no matter how much they improve, are of little use if students do not set the stage for their own flourishing through the use of others. Teaching may get better and better, but students will not put teaching to good use unless they are able to use the presence/absence of teachers in ways that enrich students' educational experience.

Educators cling to such silly progress narratives precisely because they do not consider the *use* of teachers by students. When there is no conception of students using teachers, then it follows that educators must carry out whatever progress is to be made. But such user-phobic narratives of progress ignore the fact that teachers are not actually perfectible. Let's face it: there are many teachers who won't ever be *super*. From a Kantian perspective, this seems like a dreadful fact. ("Our children will not all be able to have *the* best teacher, how awful.") In contrast, a *using* perspective suggests that many students will be able to flourish even if their teacher is not *the* best. Indeed, many students *do* flourish even when they do not have the best teachers. Don't we all know of students who have flourished in spite of mediocre teachers? Haven't many students had educational experiences that, while not being at all exemplary, were used by them in agentive ways? Students flourish in many unexpected circumstances. They often flourish precisely because they know how to *use* a given teacher in ways that address their own needs. It may often be the case that teachers need only be good enough, rather than super.

In fact, Winnicott has outlined the intersubjective dynamics that are at stake when a teacher is just "good enough." Drawing on Winnicott's concept of the "good enough mother," we might say that the good enough teacher is one who provides the circumstances for the student to use the teacher's presence (and absence) for her own flourishing. If the student is able to situate herself toward the teacher so that she learns, experiences, and attains agency in ways that would not have been possible without the teacher, then the teacher has acted in a way that is good enough. The "good enough mother" is one who meets, but does not exceed, the needs and demands of her child. Likewise, the good enough teacher is one who meets, but does not exceed, the needs and demands of his or her student.

Importantly, being good enough may have little to do with whether a teacher is perfect, super, or even just good. Being good enough *may* mean being perfect or super, but it may not. Because being a good enough teacher has more to do with the *student's* actions than with the teacher's abilities, it is wrong to say that the progress of pedagogy lies mainly in the hands of teachers. The good enough teacher is one who proves to be enough of a presence so that the student can be sure that she has a person to fall back on if needed, but also enough of an absence so that the student can gain educational agency that is all her own. What is clear about the role of the good enough teacher is that it cannot come to pass without the activity of the student. The good enough teacher, once she has taken on the present/absent role that is required by the student, cannot actually get any better.

In response to this anti-Kantian conception of student agency, one major objection might be raised right away. It might be said that this is nothing but a reformulated argument for educational merit. It might be suggested that pragmatic intersubjectivity is just another way of saying that education is really up to the individual aspirations of students. Is the notion of the "good enough" teacher simply a way of abdicating institutional responsibility for educating students? Does pragmatic intersubjectivity suggest that it is completely up to students to find ways to use teachers in an agentive way? Is this akin to the conservative argument that folks should pull themselves up by their bootstraps?

Not at all. By arguing that current narratives of educational progress are lopsided, I am not arguing that we should give up on making education better, and that it is up to students to flourish for themselves. I am not arguing that there is no more work to be done, but rather that the work that needs to be done should start focusing on the heretofore neglected issue of how students might be encouraged to use teachers. Far from offering a conservative solution, I want to suggest that the only way for progressive education to succeed is for us to take seriously Dewey's pragmatism. Let us take his pragmatism to the intersubjective realm. Educational theory should, at least for a while, stop thinking about what it means for teachers to be great, and start thinking more thoroughly about what teachers can do to set up a "good enough" platform so that students might become empowered to use teachers.

And another objection might be raised. It might be argued that students are already doing too much using, that many students slide through educational experiences, using schools and teachers as a means to get other things in life. Indeed, many students use other people in order to get a grade, get a diploma, and move on with life. This is not the sort of "use" that I am advocating. When students use teachers and schools in this way, there is a denigration of educational experience. In such cases, education is treated as if it is not a part of life, as if it can be *used* to enhance some "real life" that ultimately lies outside of the school. On the contrary, the use of others that I am advocating is one that makes educational experience itself part and parcel of "real life" self-flourishing. And please note, the "get a diploma and move on with life" type of use is already rife in our present Kantian environment. This type of use will hardly be increased simply by introducing the notion of "using teachers" into educational practice. If anything, the type of use that I am advocating may entice students to use education for purposes that are much more immediate than "getting ahead in life," for purposes that are more agentive.

STRATEGIES FOR "USING" AUTHORITY IN EDUCATION

Here, then, are a few strategies to facilitate the use of teachers. First, it is important for educational institutions to stress the notion of student flourishing through the use of others. It is striking that most schools do not advocate such a basic concept. While education has long treated student flourishing as a central aim, there has been remarkably little advocacy for schools as places where students tend to their own empowerment. When student empowerment is advocated, such advocacy is usually focused on the ways that educators might empower students. It is not only educators who need to empower students; empowerment cannot be done all on the teacher's side. Students need to think of teachers and schools as centers of authority, authority they can use to increase their own agency.

Secondly, students must be encouraged to find the right teacher, the one whom they can benefit from greatly. Such a situation is rare in educational institutions as they now exist. Students are not currently encouraged to befriend teachers based on the extent to which those teachers might help them flourish. Such befriending means more than getting the teacher that you really want for a particular class. It means more than listening to other students' opinions of a particular teacher or professor, and then choosing the instructor accordingly. It means that a student might find a teacher who is truly important to him or her, and then continue to go back to that teacher time and time again, whether in a classroom setting or for more informal conversation. In fact, it strikes me that educators really *do* know about this process of "using." However, we do not currently think about it deeply enough, nor do we theorize it in any sustained way. Educators know that those students who flourish as a result of their education are usually the ones who go out of their way to make extra contact with one or more of their instructors. Students should be encouraged to seek out instructors who are "good enough" for their own particular needs wherever they might find them. This may mean that students seek out teachers who are not their "official" teachers, and it may mean that they do so at times that are not "official" class times. The encouragement of students to use instructors should come both at the institutional level and at the classroom level. Students should be introduced early and often to the notion that they can use teachers in schools in order to gain agency, in order to flourish.

Third, there should be venues and times for students to link up with teachers whom they want to use. It is certainly not the case that all students, once introduced to the notion of using teachers, will avail themselves of this practice on their own. The asymmetry in the teacher-student relation is a great barrier to what I am suggesting. Students may avoid such a relation of use out of the hesitancy that comes when one is faced with authority. Therefore, institutional changes must be made that encourage students to use teachers. Certainly, the practice of keeping office hours, and the practice of connecting with students between classes and after school, these practices are already conducive to the use of teachers. Yet, it is presently the case that very few students avail themselves of using teachers during these times. These times are often taken up by more practical concerns such as making up assignments that have been missed, or obtaining clarification about a concept that was not understood during class. The problem with office hours and in-between times is not that they are inappropriate times for students to use teachers, but that these times too easily float from the work of flourishing to the work of classroom catch-up. In order to encourage the use of teachers, it must be well articulated by the educational institution that educational downtimes are times when student flourishing takes precedent over makeup coursework. Students should be encouraged to use these times, and these teachers, for their own purposes rather than for the purposes that have been laid out by the course syllabus.

Fourth, teachers might be oriented toward this perspective of "being used" early on in their training. At least two aspects of "being used" need to be considered, both of which go against the grain of much teacher preparation. To begin with, being willing to be used also means being willing not to be used, paradoxical as this might sound. Teachers must understand that they will never be used by all of their students. Some students will choose to use someone else instead. In these cases, it is imperative that the teacher be willing to let go. From the Kantian perspective of teacherly perfectibility and educational progress, it may be very difficult to accept that I, as a teacher, may not be in a position to empower the very person I would most like to empower. However, from the anti-Kantian perspective of using others, it is quite possible that I, as a teacher, may have a favorite student who simply chooses to flourish with the help of another rather than with my help. As Winnicott notes, human beings cannot use many people at once.[15] Self-flourishing usually depends upon just a few significant others.

Finally, teachers will, themselves, need to be introduced to the concept of being "good enough." A teacher who knows how to help students flourish will know that student flourishing is ultimately something that must be enacted by the student. Once again, this is a paradoxical concept: in order to help a student flourish, the teacher must know that the student *must help herself to the help of the teacher*, and that this is better perfected by the student than by the teacher. Ultimately, this means that a teacher may never need to be "really good." To be "really good" can interfere with whatever the student might do on her own. Instead, the teacher needs to know how to be just "good enough." It may be necessary to warn teachers that being just good enough may not be as fun as being super. As a good enough teacher, one may or may not get recognition for what one does. This is not an easy notion to accept in a profession that prides itself on the meager consolation that student gratitude offers to employees whose wages are embarrassingly low. To be sure, educators and students are most often caught up in a Kantian calculus of autonomous perfectibility. Authority figures need to be used. They need not be perfect.

SELF-FASHIONING IN THE FACE OF AUTHORITY

In my analysis of relational authority, I have so far focused mainly on interpersonal relations, on intersubjectivity. The only nonhuman element of authority that I have so far entered into our discussion has been the educational text. Now I would like to broaden this enquiry by examining one's relation to larger forces of authority, to forces that have influenced students over the course of centuries. If it is true that authority functions as a relation; and if it is true, as I have tried to show so far in this study, that it is possible for students to gain agency within authority relations, doing so through engagement with other people (both present and absent), and with texts—if these things are true, then one would suspect too that it is possible for students to gain agency through relations with other, larger forms of authority. That agency can be attained in these latter cases I take to be true. To this end, I will now attempt to outline in broad strokes what it takes to attain agency in relation to some potent educational forces. Such agency I call "self-fashioning."[16]

Kieran Egan has argued that education has been overwhelmingly susceptible to three major forces, that educators cling steadfastly to three aims: to follow the natural inclinations of the student, to acculturate the student, and to equip the student with a certain foundation of knowledge.[17] Following Egan, we might say that there are three overarching sources of authority in education, sources that are not human, sources that do not dwell in the body of the teacher. Rather, these are sources of authority that are in the educational air, and have been for many centuries. These sources of authority are, to state them concisely: nature, culture, and knowledge. Egan comes up with these three sources of authority by looking at Rousseau's idea that one should be educated according to one's natural inclinations, at the traditionalist idea that education should pass on tried and true cultural goods, and at Plato's academic idea that there are certain pure forms of knowledge to be learned.

In fact, there is a clear-cut philosophical tradition that speaks to our relation to nature, culture, and knowledge. There is a philosophical tradition that aims to deal directly with the various forces of authority at work in this educational triumvirate. It is the tradition of self-fashioning as manifest in the works of two thinkers to whom we have already been introduced: Friedrich Nietzsche, and Michel Foucault. As I will show here, these philosophers of self-fashioning show quite clearly what it means to gain agency in the face of the educational influences of nature, culture, and knowledge. Philosophers of self-fashioning, on whom the remainder of this chapter will focus, deserve our attention because, both in the writing that they dedicate specifically to education and in their other more general philosophical texts, they offer ways that one might negotiate nature, culture, and knowledge in order to enhance the living of one's life. For the philosophical tradition of self-fashioning, life itself is a matter of negotiating these three forces. And, as such a trajectory of thought shows, living one's life fully, to fashion a self, entails negotiating the authority of these life forces. It entails embracing the contradictory forces of culture, nature, and knowledge in order to become who one is. It entails negotiating the paradoxical forces of authority one faces through the becoming of a person, which, in other terms, might be called becoming well-fashioned.

What is interesting to me about these philosophers of self-fashioning, and what I think is important for educational thought, is that they treat these themes at the personal level of the one educated. They ask us to negotiate these contradictory impulses as such impulses arise throughout the course of our lives. By asking us to undergo such negotiations, by showing us how such negotiations are to proceed, these self-fashioners are looking at the primary predicaments of education from the inside out rather from the outside in. For, if it is true, as Egan argues, that educational activity has been hamstrung by clinging to this authoritative triad, it is also true that such educational activity has been clinging to this triad from the outside in. Gazing in at the fishbowl, one can see the whirl of a contradiction. Gazing in at the fishbowl, the conflicting authorities of nature, culture, and knowledge may seem too much to deal with. Yet, there are also times when one must take the perspective of the fish who looks out. Self-fashioners are aquatic philosophers. They are educational thinkers par excellence because they offer advice for the most significant person in education, the one who is to be educated. These aquatic philosophers show us that it is always possible for a student to engage in a relation with authority, no matter how daunting that source of authority might seem.

In the pages that follow, it is my aim to look closely at how Nietzsche and Foucault deal with the contradictory authorities of nature, culture, and knowledge. I will give an in-depth account of the specific ways that Nietzsche and Foucault use these three forces to shape their own lives, and to offer, by extension, a form of self-management that is germane to our own lives. Further, I will point to some concrete ways that self-fashioning might be brought into the practices of those who are being educated.

SELF-FASHIONING: A NIETZSCHEAN PERSPECTIVE

Nietzsche and the Natural

Addressing the theme of self-fashioning, Alexander Nehamas has noted that "Expressions like 'creating' or 'fashioning' a self sound paradoxical. How can one not already have, or be, a self if one is to engage in any activity whatever? How can one not already have, or be, a self if one is even to be conscious of the experiences and views one is supposed to integrate?"[18] Central to any project of self-fashioning is certainly this paradox that Nehamas has noted, namely, that a person who wants to partake in self-fashioning is already in an untenable position. In such a position, one desires to fashion something, a self, yet it is that very self that is already setting the terms for such a fashioning. In such a case, if there is a self to be fashioned, then that self will not be the same self once it has been fashioned. Thus, the self that one becomes will be a different self than the self that one was before. Under such conditions, one is no longer the same self as the one that set the conditions for self-fashioning, and so it is difficult to say whether one can claim that the self is, in fact, what did the fashioning. Under such circumstances, we are left wondering what, if anything, in human life is natural.

Indeed, the project of self-fashioning starts with very different premises about human nature than those premises that are assumed to cause the above paradox. There is a different orientation toward what is natural about the self and what is not. In the work of Friedrich Nietzsche, for example, we find a form of selfhood that actually inverts the above paradox. For Nietzsche, human conceptions of self are based on an overvaluing of selfhood that is particular to the human animal. It is the hubris of the human animal to assume that there is such a thing as a self that one can identify as an unchanging, natural element. The self, Nietzsche reminds us, is "that little changeling."[19] Selves are no more steadfast than any other natural element, no more steadfast than, say, a tree, or a cloud, or a river. The self is not necessarily selfsame from one period of time to the next, no more selfsame than a tree that grows into a different form or a cloud that depletes itself as it rains. What is natural about a self, is, in fact, precisely that it changes, that it is a "little changeling." Selfhood, from a Nietzschean perspective, makes the above paradox uncomplicated rather than paradoxical. Whereas self-fashioning seems paradoxical from the perspective of the natural, steadfast self; from the perspective of the changeling self, such a practice is altogether reasonable.

The problem of the natural in Nietzsche is not solved so easily, though. It is a shallow reading of Nietzsche that posits him as the champion of pure overcoming, as the unfettered self-fashioner. For in Nietzsche, there is also an insistence that there be something steadfast in people. Nietzsche says of "a well-turned out person" that such a person, "has a taste only for what is good for him, his pleasure, his delight cease where the measure of what is good for him is transgressed. . . . He exploits bad accidents to his advantage; what does not kill him makes him stronger. . . . He is always in his own company, whether he associates with books, human beings, or landscapes . . ."[20] In these famous lines, Nietzsche reminds us that the self, even if protean in nature, needs to remain steadfast enough so that one can choose what one values in oneself. If one is to lead a healthy life, then one must be able to discern and cultivate those facets of life that are most healthy. So while it may seem that Nietzsche is at times advocating a view of the self that is completely malleable, it is also the case that he identifies the importance of seeing enough order in one's self to enhance its positive elements while rejecting its negative ones. For Nietzsche, the natural is ever-changing; but, for the purposes of a life well lived, one must interpret out of that change just enough order so that one can "be many things and in many places in order to be able to become one thing—to be able to attain one thing."[21]

Nietzsche on Culture

When Nietzsche refers to being "in his own company," we can also discern his unique stance toward culture. It is in this stance that Nietzsche shows us a brilliant alternative to the two views of culture that are prevalent in today's educational discourses. In current educational thought, culture is usually treated either as a flimsy adjunct to the more serious natural determinants of genetics and psychological hardwiring, or, in the case of social constructivist approaches, it is treated as that which principally influences natural development. Nietzsche's stance, as exemplified in his statement, "He is always in his own company, whether he associates with books, human beings, or landscapes . . ." is quite different from both the essentialist and the constructivist perspectives. How might one, engaged in the project of self-fashioning, think of culture? One might think of it as a self-projection. When one is faced with culture, one is faced not with an impediment to self-formation, nor with the only mode of self-formation available. Rather, one is faced with the various ways that one's self becomes manifest outside the boundaries of the limits of one's body. When one reads, one is to be looking for aspects of self that resonate with the reading. When one is with others, one is to look for the shades of one's fashioning self that inhere in other human beings. Even when one looks at the wonders of nature, one is to look not for what is exterior to the self but for what one can see of oneself in such wonders. Culture is to be used as a mirror held before the self.

Nietzsche's stance toward culture is also addressed in his educational writings. In *Schopenhauer as Educator*, for example, he argues that the benefit of education will never be realized until such a time when education can contribute to the greatness of great individuals.[22] This is precisely to say that the acculturation carried out by educators should be a reverse-mirror acculturation. Education should expose students to the cultural accoutrements that bring out the best of the best in students, that promote the flourishing of the great individual. His model of the great individual was, of course, himself, under the influence of Schopenhauer. It is true that Nietzsche was at this time against the sort of acculturation he saw in democratically oriented education. Education of the masses, he thought, would be an awful leveling-out process for humanity. What is interesting from the point of view of relational authority, though, is *not* Nietzsche's critique of democratic acculturation per se, but rather what such a critique shows us about how Nietzsche conceived of culture in an educational context. For Nietzsche, the acculturation offered by educators need not be construed

as an imposition on the "natural." Rather, the culture that education
brings to the student should be approached as "a higher concept of
culture," a conception wherein culture is that which helps the self become healthy and strong.[23] Such an acculturation will build "the hardest
self-love, self-discipline," and self accomplishment.[24]

And what of navigating the natural together with the cultural?
Under Nietzsche's description, this navigation takes an interesting turn.
For, what turns out to be "natural" about one's self, what turns out to
be a deep description of human selfhood, is the fact that the human self
is a protean commodity whose steadfastness is merely a psychological
necessity to be tolerated as a sort of orienting force. What turns out to
be cultural are those elements in the world at large that might be used
to benefit the greatness of individuals. As such, there is still a profound
difference between the natural and the cultural, but there is not a contradiction per se. Nature is that which must take enough respite from
the vicissitudes of the truly random acts of nature so as to have a
potential that is identifiable. Culture, in its turn, instead of being at
odds with nature, and also instead of *defining* the natural as some
versions of constructivist thought might have it, is that which increases
the potential of the natural. To navigate the natural and the cultural is
to stick with a version of self just long enough to take advantage of the
outward circumstances that increase one's human capacity.

The most striking elements of this Nietzschean approach are found
in such statements as this: "My formula for greatness in a human being
is *amor fati*: that one wants nothing to be other than it is, not in the
future, not in the past, not in all eternity."[25] Nature and culture are to
be construed not as monolithic entities to which human selves are yoked,
but as two possible objects toward which the human being might turn
with psychological intensity. *Amor fati*, love of fate, has a characteris-
tically Nietzschean ambivalence toward the natural and the cultural
worlds. One is left wondering whether what is advocated is a love of
one's natural lot, or whether it is a love of one's cultural allotment. And
then as if to make the distinction between the natural and the cultural
even less important, there is the added psychological nuance that human beings should hone in themselves the capacity to *embrace* these
objects as one embraces any other object of affection. Nature and culture, whichever of them is actually being referred to, are light matters,
matters that we might embrace or cast off at our choosing. To navigate
well, we should embrace both. The same ambivalent lightness is evident
in the inside-out teleology of Nietzsche's injunction, "Become who you
are," and in the introjected causality of his claim, "Thus I willed it."[26]
In such statements Nietzsche urges us to navigate the natural and the
cultural, and he suggests how: we must embrace such injunctions and
such claims whenever possible.

Nietzsche on Knowledge

As for knowledge, Nietzsche's position is most easily summarized by the following health warning: knowledge can be dangerous to one's health. Just look at Nietzsche's critique of knowledge acquisition and his championing of forgetfulness. With regard to acquisition, Nietzsche reminds us that it can often happen, in fact does often happen, that the more one pursues knowledge, the less one has a chance to cultivate the self in healthy ways. Commenting on scholars, and by extension all those who spend much of their lives in the pursuit of knowledge, Nietzsche notes the following: "We are unknown to ourselves, we men of knowledge—and with reason. We have never sought ourselves."[27] Here we are reminded, in a somewhat lighthearted way, of the absent-minded professor, or of Socrates who was known to lose himself in thought for hours at a stretch. But Nietzsche is quite serious about this matter. He has studied the *psychology* of epistemology and notices that human beings tend to lose touch with themselves when they dedicate themselves to learning.

> "The objective man," writes Nietzsche, "is indeed a mirror: he is accustomed to submit before whatever wants to be known, without any other pleasure than that found in knowing and 'mirroring'; he waits until something comes, and then spreads himself out tenderly lest light footsteps and the quick passage of spiritlike beings should be lost on his plane skin."[28]

When one becomes focused on knowledge, one can become a human mirror, unable to look selfward. At least that is the health risk of knowledge acquisition. We people of knowledge "are necessarily strangers to ourselves, we do not comprehend ourselves . . . we are not 'men of knowledge' with respect to ourselves."[29] Nietzsche's words here are self-explanatory.

To complement this critique of knowledge acquisition, Nietzsche offers a self-fashioning strategy—the strategy of forgetting. On the flip side of learning, there is forgetting, forgetting that has been historically denigrated as a sort of epistemological lack, forgetting which Nietzsche instead champions as a necessary antidote to the experience of being turned into a human mirror. One can recuperate one's self-focusing strength, and one can get rid of unhealthy, knowledge-focusing habits. This has been done in the past by people who are willing to practice forgetfulness. Nietzsche remarks that it "is the sign of strong, full natures in whom there is an excess of the power to form, to mold, to recuperate and to forget."[30] He reminds us of the French author "Mirabeau, who had no memory for insults and vile actions done him and was unable to forgive simply because he—forgot."[31] To forget, rather than being a sign of weakness, is, for self-fashioners, a positive way to deal with the agglomeration of knowledge that tends to turn us away from our selves.

AN EDUCATIONAL STRATEGY OF SELF-FASHIONING

Faced With the Authority of Nature

At this point, I should make it more clear how such a philosophy of self-fashioning, concerned as it is with authorities natural, cultural, and epistemological, is important for educational practices. It seems to me that education *writ large* has a certain reticence to think about these themes even though these themes are so inescapably involved in teaching and learning. For example, with regard to human "nature," I would submit that, as we go through educational experiences, we, as learners, need ways to think about what we might do with our "natural" capacities. I would submit, along with Nietzsche, that one cannot get away from making judgments about what one is good at learning, what one does well, what one likes to learn, as well as what one is not good at, what one does not do well, what one does not like to learn. We are, to go back to Nehamas's point, beginning in all educational instances with a self, and it would be very difficult *not* to make certain judgments about that self. When learning to speak a foreign language, for example, does one not right away make judgments about whether one is good at speaking that foreign language? And even once that initial judgment is made, do we not make further judgments about what particular aspects of learning that foreign language we are good at? Are we not constantly making judgments such as, "I am very good at conjugating verbs, but not so good at memorizing vocabulary?" To make a judgment such as "I am good at conjugating verbs," or "I am not good at conjugating verbs" is precisely to make a statement about what one's *natural* capacities are.

My point here is not to show the various ways that one identifies something natural in one's capacities as a learner, but rather to say how important it is to take such an act of identification as a specific theme in education. When it comes to what seems natural and what does not so seem, one should have an educational strategy. Such a strategy should entail at least two steps. The first is the simple identification of what one does well and what one does not. This first step is already too common.[32] But the second step is one that is so well illustrated by philosophies of self-fashioning: one should have a stance and a mode of conduct vis-a-vis the natural. Yes, judgments about what comes naturally are all but unavoidable in education. However, it is possible that such judgments can themselves be used as an educational tool to increase one's human capacity. When I discover that I *naturally* enjoy reading poetry more than I enjoy reading novels, that is only a preliminary judgment on the natural. Questions that follow are the more important questions such as, "What do I make of this enjoyment?" "Is this an enjoyment that I want to cultivate?" "Is this an enjoyment that I want to inhibit?" "Is this enjoyment one that is tied to other enjoyments that I might bundle together in order to enrich how I live my life?" Secondary questions such as these do not just assess the natural. They make the natural an integral part of how one fashions one's self.

By taking the "natural" self as something to be fashioned, one willingly ignores, or one chooses to forget, to borrow Nietzsche's idea, disciplinary practices that hinder one's flourishing. Instead, one makes of one's life an artwork. One treats matters of self as if they are matters of shaping, fashioning, embellishing, and elaborating. This treatment is in direct opposition to procedures that would identify, quantify, and "treat" the human being. In fact, the difference between the two senses of the English word *treat*, serves to underscore the difference between self-fashioning and just plain living one's life. When one lives a modern life, one tends to become enmeshed in disciplinary systems. One is diagnosed and often "treated" by juridico-medico discourses. Yet self-fashioning offers another way to "treat" oneself. One stands back from oneself and treats oneself as a painter would treat her painting. One chooses what formulas to apply to the self, and what formulas to shed. In the disciplinary treatment, one is subjected to steadfast remedy. In the self-fashioning treatment, one partakes in self-molding.[33]

Faced With the Authority of Culture

A strategy with respect to culture is similarly important for educational flourishing. Just as one might identify a natural inclination, one will certainly be able to identify educational agendas that stem from cultural imperatives. And these cultural imperatives may not be in sync with what one enjoys to do, or with what one can easily do. A strategy of self-fashioning, however, will serve to highlight, and build upon, the cultural-ness of these cultural imperatives. In other words, a person with a self-fashioning orientation will recognize that the cultural has a form that must be juxtaposed with the natural. In the case of acculturation, too, there should also be a two-part strategy.

The first part would consist of the student identifying those aspects of education that are thoroughly cultural, those aspects that clearly go against the grain of one's natural inclinations, those aspects that seem to be public interventions rather than private blossomings. However, this first step in self-fashioning would be initiated by the student rather than the educator. The first step in self-fashioning would entail identifying aspects of acculturation that truly rub one the wrong way. Are there not always requirements in education that one simply does not agree with, that are said to be necessary because one will not "fit" in society without so conforming? Perhaps the matter at hand is as simple as the quality of one's handwriting. Perhaps it is a more central aspect of one's identity such as forced gender conformity. Perhaps one has a reaction against being a responsible citizen. A first step would be to make such identifying part and parcel of the student's educational experience.

Once again, this first step is not enough. It is not enough for one to identify such cultural norms. Educational rhetoric aimed at "producing thoughtful consumers," "developing responsible citizens," and "training students to succeed in the workplace"—such rhetoric has long identified acculturating ends. Educators have long taught students the requirements of culture. And certainly, students have long identified those aspects of acculturation against which they then choose to rebel. A second step to self-fashioning would entail moving beyond the Manichean binary of acceptance or rebellion. A second step would entail taking an active stance toward things cultural. While it may be that most of us have had a reaction to acculturating imperatives, and while it may be that some of us have resisted such imperatives over the course of our educational experience, how many of us have pushed forward with the myriad ways one might conduct oneself toward the cultural? Such questions as these might be asked about the cultural imperatives toward which one has an aversion: "Is this a cultural imperative that needs to be resisted? Would such resistance behoove me?" "If I do resist, do I want to resist in ways that avoid confrontation, or would it behoove me to *create* confrontation?" "Are there other cultural imperatives that are more important for me to resist than this one?" "Which resistances will be most healthy for me?"

At this point, the following objection might be made: Doesn't this sort of stance serve to depoliticize people? When we speak of what is most healthy "for me," does it not undercut the more admirable aim of educational acculturation? The aim of creating democratic citizens? To answer this objection, I turn to the work of Michel Foucault on self-fashioning.

Foucault points out that, actually, the goal of self-fashioning is as much about one's political orientation as it is about what might seem, at first blush, to be a matter of individualism. In educational interactions today, one is often hard-pressed to encourage serious political engagement on the part of students. Such failure may rest on a failure to understand the profound ways in which the political bears on practices of self. For the philosophers of self-fashioning, the self is the starting place for the ways one orients oneself toward freedom. Thus, practices of self are about the self per se, but they are also about the ways in which one orients oneself. One cannot orient oneself toward the political when the self is disregarded. Current thinking on the distance of the self from the political is the remnant of humanist, Cartesian thought that takes the self to be a thinking machine that thinks on other objects rather than on itself. This is what Foucault means by remarking that "there are more secrets, more possible freedoms, and more inventions in our future than we can imagine in humanism as it is dogmatically represented on every side of the political rainbow."[34] The political, as Foucault has shown in his genealogical works, serves to discipline and punish people at the level of self. Thus, for one to orient oneself toward freedom, one must work at the level of self at the same time that one works at the level of structural and cultural change.

Faced With the Authority of Knowledge

And toward knowledge, a self-fashioning education will also entail a strategy. The first step is to identify some of the ways that knowledge gets used in one's life. Let us take the example of a student who enjoys reading poetry. Questions such as these might be raised: What does my knowledge of poetry do for me as I live my life? How much of my life is spent reading poetry? Has poetry increased the quality of my life? Or, are there ways in which poetry has detracted from the quality of my life? Are there certain periods of my life when poetry has been more useful, certain periods where it has been less useful? These first-step questions are actually not at all common in modern thought, which tends to look at knowledge as benign. Philosophers of self-fashioning, and in particular Nietzsche, take a radical stance toward knowledge. Their stance is one that questions the very usefulness of knowledge if such knowledge does not increase the capacity of human beings. Following a self-fashioning strategy, one will not assume that learning poetry is necessarily beneficial. Knowledge of poetry, for example, is only beneficial to the extent to which it gets put to good use in one's life. Learning itself is not good use. Good use comes when learning enhances one's life.

A second self-fashioning relation toward knowledge might include the meta-understanding that knowledge can be as dangerous as it is beneficial. Certainly such an understanding flies in the face of modernist epistemologies. And, it flies in the face of current conceptions of education, especially ones that uphold knowledge accumulation as the litmus test of a successful education. Modern epistemologies, as inaugurated by Descartes' privileging of thinking over feeling, tend to have a the-more-knowledge-the-better orientation. This is all too evident in the push toward ever-increasing student achievement. If there is one atti-tude that philosophers of self-fashioning certainly have in common, it is the warning that knowledge is not innocuous.[35] Indeed, when it comes to knowledge, one who self-fashions may be willing to put reins on the mind. And this stance toward the mind will be different from the popu-lar mantra that we should enhance thinking skills rather than learn content. As a self-fashioner, even thinking skills may be dangerous if they are not in sync with what one needs to increase one's human capacity. To flourish as one who self-fashions, all things knowledge-based might be let go if need be.

Certainly, this sort of letting-go takes a great amount of courage. It takes courage to let go of one thought and pursue another. Michel Foucault has spoken about the courage to self-fashion one's thinking as follows:

> As to those for whom to work hard, to begin and begin again, to attempt and be mistaken, to go back and rework everything from top to bottom, and still find reason to hesi-tate from one step to the next—as to those in short, for whom to work in the midst of uncertainly and apprehension is tantamount to failure, all I can say is that clearly we are not from the same planet.[36]

These words were written at a time when Foucault was under attack for the change of course in his thinking. Some have claimed that he went back on his previous thinking when, in his later writings, he turned to self-fashioning. Yet, those who make such a claim have precisely failed to see the courage of thought that is entailed when one turns one's back on previous thought, when one takes one's self in a new direction.[37] Educational institutions are the sorts of places where the courage to think in new directions should be fostered. Self-fashioning will certainly entail courage of thought.

A third step is to self-fashion using the specific techniques with which education equips us. One such technique is fluency in writing. Philosophers of self-fashioning such as Nietzsche and Foucault, and as well others such as Socrates and Michel de Montaigne, have shown us that writing can well be used as a technique of self. With regard to writing, Foucault has noted the following:

> The main interest in life and work is to become someone else that you were not in the beginning. If you know when you

began a book what you would say at the end, do you think
that you would have the courage to write it?[38]

When he makes these sorts of statements, we are reminded that
the tool of literacy is a great aid to the project of self-fashioning. Such
a stance toward literacy is much different than a stance that advocates
"finding one's voice" through writing. Within a writerly pedagogy of
self-fashioning, one will become other than what one is in part through
the interchange that takes place between who one is to begin with and
who one's writing makes one become. This self-fashioning perspective
on writing is especially important given current educational strategies
vis-à-vis literacy. It is striking that while schools do tend to encourage
students to practice all the trappings of the writing profession—encouraging creativity, proper documentation, precise conceptual thought, etc.—
they tend not to encourage the very trait that makes literacy so very
important to those who are truly engaged with writing as a form of life.
Writing is a means to self-modulation. Writing can be, in the context of
an education oriented toward self-fashioning, a means to become who
one was not before.

DEEP IMPLICATIONS OF RELATIONAL AUTHORITY

Self-fashioning thus orients one toward the natural, the cultural, and
the epistemological.[39] Yet my point is not that one should first *identify*
the natural, the cultural, and the epistemological aspects of one's educational experience, and then make the best of one's education in light
of these findings. It is not that at all. For, the natural, the cultural, and
the epistemological can too easily be identified and taken as steadfast
attributes of one's educational experience. To identify such aspects only
is precisely to *stop* self-fashioning. My point is rather that one's stance
toward nature, culture, and knowledge needs to be *educated* all along
the way. In fact, I cannot imagine—at least not after having read such
self-fashioning thinkers as Nietzsche and Foucault—any reason to ever
assume that the matters of what should be one's stance toward nature,
culture, and knowledge could ever be ascertained once and for all. It is
precisely the brilliance of philosophers of self-fashioning that they show
how these fundamental educational concerns are actually lifelong problems. One's life cannot be identified first, and then practiced later. That
is the mistake made by one who lives one's life in a stilted way. Similarly,
one cannot be educated first, and then proceed to live one's life after
education has ended. Both self-fashioning and education proceed through
modulation. Self-fashioning and education proceed through an ongoing
engagement with the authority of nature, culture, and knowledge.

If this chapter has shown anything, it is that treating authority as a relation has deep consequences. To understand authority as a relation, we must rethink Kantian morality. We must rethink the popular educational focus on pragmatism. We must be willing to "use" other people. We must rethink how we orient ourselves toward larger bodies of authority. We must rethink how we choose to remember, and how we choose to forget. We must rethink how we understand the personal and the political. We must even rethink the self, itself. That is, we must rethink dearly held notions about self-integrity. We must wonder if self-constancy is so important after all. What I am trying to say here is that relational authority is not just about authority. It is also not just about relation. It is about a paradigm shift that requires serious changes in a Western belief system that has long used *non*relational authority as a fulcrum point for understanding human beings. To be sure, this chapter has only sent out feelers. It has only begun to intimate the myriad, deep, philosophical implications that follow once we embrace the relationality of authority. These sorts of deep implications deserve better treatment than I can give in this short book. For, the present study is not meant to be an extended treatise on modern philosophical trends, but is rather oriented toward authority in educational settings. With this aim in mind, the next chapter will address an educational matter whose boundaries are better defined. It will address the relation of authority when educators pose questions.

CHAPTER 5

Questioning Authority

I have always called myself a progressive educator. Thirteen years teaching in junior high and high schools. Eight years of university teaching. I have called myself a progressive educator in part because I have always liked the progressive orientation toward authority. As we have seen earlier in this book, the progressive position comes with definite assumptions about the nature of authority, about how authority is *not* a thing to be trusted. I have liked this progressive discomfort with authority. Along with embracing progressive pedagogy, I suppose I have embraced a few other progressive commonplaces. For example, over these twenty-one years, I have usually been sure, as I believe many progressive educators have been sure, that lecturing to my students is an unnecessary imposition of authority. I have been sure that asking students questions, and eliciting their answers, is less imposing than straightforward teacher-talk. I have understood questioning as a fair and just way for students to interact with authority, while I have understood lecturing as an un-needed showing-off of the teacher's knowledge. I have preferred the former. At least that *used to be* the case.

My confidence in questioning was shaken some time ago when I had a conversation with a friend of mine who was trained to be a lawyer at Harvard Law School many years ago. When I told her about the way I favored questioning over lecturing, her response was unqualified: "While there might be some merit to questioning, let me tell you . . . Socratic questioning, of the law school variety, is the most authoritarian form of education I have ever experienced. As law school students, we used to be cowered into submission. Law professors frightened us to death with their knowledge of the law, and with our own lack of knowledge. They did this all without *telling* us anything. It was all by questioning."

These remarks have certainly made me think. They have challenged one of the commonplace assumptions that I have been making for many years now. These remarks have reminded me that I, too, used to make some fairly *non*relational assumptions about authority. Let me explain. When I have, in the past, favored questioning over teacher-talk, I have been making the assumption that some forms of authority are more relational than others. I have been assuming that questioning is a more dynamic way for students to interact with the authority of the teacher, while lecturing is a static way for teachers to impose their authority. Yet now I notice something that I used to miss about the practice of questioning. It is this: if all authority is relational, then the distinction I used to make—the distinction between the authority of questioning being dynamic and the authority of a lecture being static—simply does not make sense. Authority is dynamic, period. Thus, if there is any benefit to educational questioning, it must come from the questioning interchange itself rather than from the fact that questioning is a "more relational" way of enacting authority. My friend's remarks, together with the relational conception of authority that I am offering in this book, suggest that the matter of educational questioning cannot be solved so easily. We must not be pre-satisfied, simply because it has become a progressive commonplace, that questioning is somehow impeccably beneficial in education.

In this chapter, I look into the authority that gets enacted through the question-answer exchange between teacher and student. Since this entire book is focused on the relation of educational authority, it is very important that we look at educational questioning. Why? Quite simply because if commonplace assumptions about authority map, in various ways, onto various teaching techniques, then such assumptions map onto the practice of educational questioning in the most direct way possible. Since the aim of this work is to challenge commonplace assumptions about authority, then there is no more practical way to go about it than investigating the relation of educational questioning. Today, various educational camps such as the three that I have mentioned before—the progressive, the traditionalist, and the critical—make commonplace assumptions about questioning. These assumptions derive from their respective stances toward authority. My aim is to break through the progressive commonplace that questioning students forms the basis of a kinder and gentler pedagogy. I also want to break through the traditional commonplace that lecturing is altogether unharmful. And I want to break through the critical commonplace that lecturing is unharmful as long as it aims toward social justice.

QUESTIONS AND THEIR HIDDEN STATEMENTS

This chapter's investigation of questioning will rely on the work of Hans-Georg Gadamer. Gadamer's work affirms, as I have mentioned above, that an investigation into the authority of questioning is highly instructive. Indeed, Gadamer goes so far as to say that "[t]o understand meaning, is to understand it as the answer to a question."[1] So he sees in questioning a wide range of ramifications including meaning itself. Gadamer's analysis helps us to understand that questions are more intimately connected to statements than we might think. In terms of education, it might seem easy to claim differences between a pedagogy of questions and other sorts of pedagogies, such as ones that mainly tell. It might indeed seem that a pedagogy that questions exercises less authority than a pedagogy that does not question. As a literature teacher, for example, one might tend to be confident that the use of a question, one that asks, "What do you think about such and such a passage?"— that such a question enacts less authority than the use of a statement that tells students, "This passage means such and such." However, as we shall see, Gadamer's analysis of the question shows that these sorts of assumptions need to be reconsidered.

Gadamer notes that the structure of the question puts finitude into play in the same way that the thought of one's own mortality puts the finitude of existence into play. Writes Gadamer,

> It is clear that the structure of the question is implicit in all experience. . . . From a logical point of view, the openness essential to experience is precisely the openness of being either this or that. It has the structure of a question. And just as the dialectical negativity of experience culminates in the idea of being perfectly experienced—i.e., being aware of our finitude and limitedness—so also the logical form of the question and the negativity that is part of it culminate in a radical negativity: the knowledge of not knowing.[2]

In the same way that notions of human finitude and death suggest the limits of what can be experienced, the use of a question intended toward an object presents us with the possibility that such an object may not exist as we originally thought. As Gadamer puts it, the question "breaks open the being of the object."[3] "The significance of questioning consists in revealing the questionability of what is questioned."[4] "The sense of every question is realized in passing through this state of indeterminacy, in which it becomes an open question."[5] In this way, the question presents us with mortality. It presents us with the possibility that existence, in the form of whatever object is subject to the question, is not as we heretofore thought. It presents us with the possibility of the death of the object as we know it. A question, in contrast to a statement, is posed in order to emphasize the possibility that an object may be otherwise. While a statement explains the living attributes of an object, a question presents us with the possibility that the object may not exist at all. While a statement confirms, a question disconfirms.

Another aspect of the question is that it actually contains a statement within. In a sense, it might be said that the statement is only a subset of the question. Let me explain this in Gadamerian terms. For Gadamer, the question is that which orients us toward a field of possible experiences. The question provides a framework for the sort of experience that a group of interlocutors will be in a position to think about. It provides us with what might be called a "spectrum of experience." In this way, a question is not simply a reminder that an object of questioning may cease to exist as we know it; it is not just a statement about the *limits* of experience. A question opens up possibility at the same time that it suggests the limits of possibility. As Gadamer puts it, "A question places what is questioned in a particular perspective."[6] A question situates, and it opens up an inroad with regard to the object.

Thus, the spectrum of experience begun by the question implies both a limit and a field of possibilities. The question suggests the limits of its answers at the same time that it asks for possible responses. A "Why?" question demands a "Because" response. A "Who" question demands that a person be named. "Posing a question," notes Gadamer, "implies openness but also limitation."[7] A question establishes the range of possible experiences that may come into play within the process of questioning and answering. When the question is answered, the spectrum of possible answers will be bound by the question. To put Gadamer's point succinctly, we might say that *every question contains the seed of its own answer*. A question implies its own statement.

THE "TRUE QUESTION"

And while it might seem that the question, described in the above way, overdetermines its own answer, Gadamer is quick to point out that it is possible to pose questions in such a way that the answer will not be overdetermined. He writes of the difficult, but possible, practice of asking what he calls a "true question." It is possible to question in such a way that the question itself, while sowing the seeds of its own answer, drives right for that spot where the answer is truly unknown to both the questioner and the respondent. In such a case, the questioner will ask about something she really does not understand:

To ask a [true] question means to bring into the open. The openness of what is in question consists in the fact that the answer is not settled. It must still be undetermined, awaiting a decisive answer. The significance of questioning consists in revealing the questionability of what is questioned.[8]

So for Gadamer, the hermeneutic, horizon-posing structure of the question does not preclude the questioner from creating space where she honestly searches for information from the other. While the questioner has a definite horizon from which she asks the question, there is still space within that horizon to query about that which is not yet known. As Gadamer says, "Discourse that is intended to reveal something requires that that thing be broken open by the question."[9] So, while my own understanding may limit the subject of my questioning to the objects that are within my cultural and historical purview, I will still be able to identify some objects within that purview as objects that I do not fully understand. I can cause an object, one that I only catch a glimpse of from my present horizon, to be "broken open." I can catch myself up short. I can identify objects that, while available to my understanding, are not fully understood without the help of an other. When I can cause an object to be "broken open," only then have I posed a "true question" about that object.

BUT CAN A TEACHER ASK A "TRUE QUESTION"?

What we must ask, though, is whether a *teacher* can ask such a true question. According to Gadamer, the act of posing a "true question" falls apart when it comes to teachers who actually have curricular aims. Teachers *do* have something in mind that they want their students to learn. We *do* want our students to know how to factor an algebraic equation. We *do* want our students to know that John Dewey was an American Pragmatist. We *do* want our students to be able to place Langston Hughes within the historical context of the Harlem Renaissance. While it may be possible for the ordinary person engaged in dialogue to ask "true" questions, questions that intend to *really* question, to break the object of question open, to truly put that object into question; while it may be possible for the ordinary person, from Gadamer's perspective it appears that the ordinary *teacher* is actually hamstrung by her commitment to conveying a certain body of knowledge. A teacher, as opposed to just any old someone, must choose questions with possible answers in mind. That is to say, it would be a very strange pedagogical situation if a teacher were to question her students without a preconceived notion of which answer she hopes to elicit from them. Teachers, after all, enact authority. A law school professor, as opposed to any old questioner, can be frightening because she knows exactly where her questions are to lead.

Another way to say this is that the pedagogical pressure to elicit *specific* answers from students, as opposed to any old answer, is the difference between general dialectic and pedagogy. It is certainly possible to imagine a teacher asking completely open-ended questions: "What did you think of the first chapter of Toni Morrison's *Sula*?" "What is your interpretation of John Dewey's notion of "experience" in his book *Experience and Education*?" "What do you think the answer to 2X + 8 = 0 is?" However, it ceases to be pedagogy and becomes general dialectic if the teacher does not intervene to steer answers in a direction that she favors.

With this sort of logic Gadamer surmises that it is not actually possible for a pedagogical question to be "true." Talking about the true question, Gadamer notes that there is a paradoxical difficulty with any true question that would be posed by a teacher. The paradox inheres in the fact that the teacher himself would have to disappear. As Gadamer puts it,

> Every true question requires an openness. Without it, it is basically no more than an apparent question. We are familiar with this from the example of the pedagogical question, whose paradoxical difficulty consists in the fact that it is a question without a questioner.[10]

That is to say, as soon as a teacher must ask a "true question," then she ceases to exist *as teacher*. So for Gadamer, the teacher can only pose false questions. If she poses true ones, then she ceases to exist. This is Gadamer's Cartesian motto of the questioning teacher: "I pose false questions; therefore, I exist."

TEACHERS CAN ASK TRUE QUESTIONS

But we should say more about "true questions" than Gadamer does. Gadamer intimates that teachers cannot pose true questions. Is he correct? I would say not. It is precisely at such a juncture that we should stop listening to Gadamer even while taking his notion of the "true question" to heart. In other words, we should heed his philosophical insight, but disregard his educational perspective. Gadamer moves in a very subject-centered direction with regard to the "true question." First, he describes the nature of a true question, its nature being that it cracks open the object. This description we should cling to. This description is very consistent with the "linguistic turn" of poststructuralist thought, the turn that gives ontological priority to the linguisticality of human experience. While language, in general, is constitutive of human experience, the question, in particular, is deconstitutive of the subject matter to which it refers.

However, when Gadamer claims that some folks can ask true questions while some cannot, he slips into the subject-centered assumption that language is ultimately a tool under the employ of human intentions. At this point he forgets the important lesson of his instructor, Heidegger, that language is the house of Being, rather than Being being the house of language.[11] When Gadamer claims that the pedagogical question presents us with a "paradoxical situation," we must note that Gadamer is making a subject-centered correlative to the linguistic structure of the question. At this point, he is indicating that some people will be less "true" in their questioning by virtue of what they *intend*. While it may be a fact that a teacher cannot have scot-free intentions, it is not a fact that these tainted intentions will automatically derail the deconstitutive nature of a question. A teacher can indeed "break open" an object. This is because a teacher's intentions do not completely determine the outcome of dialogue. In Gadamer's analysis, the notion of the "true question" becomes confused with the more subject-centered notion of *asking a question in a true way*. Can there be an educational scenario in which subject matter can be broken open? The answer is, "Yes." Teaching intentions will never be pure, it is true, but that does not mean that pedagogical questions will not break open the subject matter at hand. Teachers *can* pose true questions.

To make it clear how true questions can be posed, it is helpful to draw on Gadamer's own conception of language, and then to borrow a metaphor from Gilles Deleuze. As Gadamer's conception of language reminds us (perhaps as a reminder that his "paradox of the pedagogical question" is not such a paradox), language does not result from the intentions of individual speakers. Instead, language is enacted in the in-between space of dialogue with an other. Language is the practical consequence of intersubjective engagement, rather than the transition of messages from one interlocutor to another. As Gadamer himself writes, "[L]anguage is by nature the language of conversation; it fully realizes itself only in the process of coming to an understanding."[12] That is to say, language becomes what it truly is by way of its enactment within the to-and-fro of dialogue. Likewise, a question is only a question within the context of the interlocutors' engagement with that question. Thus, when a question is posed, it is on the field of human interaction where its "truth" is worked out. Whether a question is a "true question" will depend upon the subject matter that it "breaks open" during conversation. To say that a teacher's question is automatically "false" even before the dialogue has begun is to ignore the intersubjective life of language. It is to confuse the intention of speech with the communal enactment of conversation. A teacher *can* pose a true question because such a question is always poised to be enacted relationally, between teacher and student. Such a question is always poised to be worked out somewhere down the line, sometime after the question has been posed.

There is, of course, one more problem to be worked out with regard to the "true question" posed by a teacher. Given that a true question poses its own field of possibilities; given that a true question breaks open its subject matter; given that a teacher does have certain intentions; and, given that questioning gets worked out in the in-between of human dialogue—what, then, might "true" questioning look like in education? While the specificities of each interchange will vary, I want to offer the following Deleuzian metaphor.[13] A question, truly enacted, will be much like the rolling of dice. When a pair of dice is rolled, the field of possible outcomes is bounded, to be sure. Only combinations of one through six will result. At the same time, though, the object under consideration, the resulting combination, cannot be manipulated by the dice roller. Combinations will be "broken open" each time the dice are rolled. Of course, it cannot be said that the dice roller lacks intentionality. She wants the dice to roll, without doubt. My point here is that we can take the dice roller in this case to be the teacher who questions.

The main difference between questioning, on the one hand, and throwing dice, on the other, is the importance of keeping subject matter in play. Picture a pair of dice that is thrown into a wobbling box. These questioning dice, unlike others that might be thrown onto a stationary table, will be thrown by the teacher into a wobbling box that is held on one side by that teacher, and on the other side by the student. It is the interaction of teacher and student that must keep the question (the dice) in play for as long as the subject matter at hand requires a questioning attitude. Such a gaming process suspends the intentionality inherent in the philosophy of the subject, and it inaugurates an intentionality that does not want to know exactly what its own outcome will be. It signals a break from the sender/receiver model of language, and it requests an openness toward subject matter that searches for answers that are not necessarily known beforehand. Within the questioning process, the aim of communicants is not *erklären*, but rather *verstehen*. The aim of questioning is not to *explain*, but rather to *understand*.

A teacher *can* ask a true question in spite of Gadamer's claim that he or she can't do so. Gadamer's insight is that there is teacher authority being enacted in questioning scenarios. Unfortunately, he jumps to the conclusion that such authority keeps the teacher from being able to ask true questions. His insight is that the teacher's questions cannot have a pedagogical purpose without exercising the authority to steer answers in this direction or that. His mistake is to say that such authority spoils the essence of the question. With his insight we should agree; with the mistake we should not. The questioning process in education exercises authority as a sort of ontological prerequisite—this is the insight of Gadamer's that we should explore.

Let us approach this insight by first summarizing what we have learned about the difference between questioning and telling. While it is tempting, following progressivist sensibilities, to jump to the conclusion that questioning is a process that exercises less authority than telling, the situation now seems quite different. Telling relies on an exercise of authority—that is certainly true. Indeed, when a teacher tells his students, "This passage means such and such," or, "The answer to this problem is X = −4"—by such statements, a teacher is enacting authority to the extent that the student must accept these statements as true. However, as far as the exercise of authority goes, telling is not in fact different from questioning. While telling relies on an exercise of authority that guarantees the veracity of a teacher's statements, questioning also relies on an exercise of authority. Like telling, questioning would not have any grounds on which to proceed if it were not based on authoritative enactment. In this way, we cannot say that there is an appreciable difference between the authority of telling and the authority of questioning. Both pedagogical telling and pedagogical questioning enact authority as a prerequisite for *being pedagogical*. Without such an enactment of authority, educational telling would not effectively convince, and educational questioning would not properly steer.

But having said all this, I am not trying to say that we should settle into complacent equanimity. It is now tempting to claim that questioning is no more, and no less, overbearing than telling. It is tempting to say that it really does not matter whether we tell our students what they need to know, or whether we question them about curricular matters. After all, the question involves the same sort of authoritative steering that the statement does. Indeed, I would agree to this sort of equanimity to some extent. I think it is correct to say that when it comes to questioning and telling, neither one is inherently more imbalanced than the other. Questioning, per se, is not *more* innocuous than telling. But once we have said that questioning and telling in education are both enactments of authority, it is important to go farther. We must ask if questioning might be more dominating at some times than at others. When might questioning be, as my lawyer friend has said, "the most authoritarian form of education I have ever experienced"? When might it be less authoritarian? To address this matter, I turn, as I have a number of times in this book, to an analysis of language itself.

THE AUTHORITY OF QUESTIONING:
ITS SIGNIFIER AND SIGNIFIED

The linguistic distinction between the signifier and the signified sheds some light on instances when a question might be more authoritarian, and when it might be less so. A question is certainly different from other forms of speech. It is different from a statement. In a statement, there is a certain authoritative link between speaker and phrase. For example, if I, as a teacher, *state* "this passage from Ernst Gaines's novel means such and such," it is clear that the person who ensures such a statement to be true is I, the instructor. When I say that "this passage means such and such," I am the one who is obligated to stand behind what I say. In such a case, I am enacting authority. The statement is true to the extent that one trusts my authority as a teacher. It is true to the extent that a student enters into the authority relation that has been inaugurated by my statement. To put this in linguistic terms, the teacher, by virtue of being authorized, *signifies* some aspect of the world. When I am a teacher, my statement *signifies* the truth about Gaines's novel, and it does so by virtue of authority. In this sense, the instructor's statement takes the role of signifier while the truth about Gaines's novel is what is signified. What motivates the signifier/signified connection? By this I mean, why does my statement signify some truth, just as the word *chair* might signify some real chair? The instructor's statement signifies the signified because there is an enactment of authority. Authority is the glue that cements signifier and signified. It makes the pedagogical statement believable.

Compare this to *questioning*. When a teacher questions, it seems, at first blush, that the teacher gives over the signifier/signified pair to the student. When I, as teacher, ask a student, "What does this passage from Ernst Gaines's novel mean?" it seems that the question places the student in a position to signify the meaning of the passage. It seems as if the student's answer will now stand in relation to the truth of Gaines's text as the signifier does to the signified.

However, the difference between the signifier/signified pair of a teacher's statement, on the one hand, and the signifier/signified pair of a student's answer to a question, on the other, is that the latter pair does not exercise authority in the same way. When the student answers a question, there is no "glue" of authority. Instead, the teacher remains the one who applies the glue by means of steering the dialectic. As Gadamer has shown us, pedagogical questions are *pedagogical* precisely because they are enacted through authority. One does not "give over" authority by changing the way one talks, by changing from statement to question. One does not make glue available to the student, as it might seem at first glance. Instead of being a "giving over" of authority, questioning is a ventriloquizing of authority. The question makes authority seem to be on the side of the student, while in fact, the glue remains on the side of the teacher.

Questioning does not really give over the signifier/signified pair (together with its glue) to the student. The questioner retains a new, glued, signifier/signified pair even as he conceals that retention. When I ask about a certain passage, it is true that my words no longer signify the passage's meaning. It is true that my question no longer signifies some fact that I want my student to accept. However, questioning simply *personalizes* the signifier/signified pair. *Now my words signify the meaning of the question in my head. I am the text being interpreted by my question. My question signifies the meaning of me.* And in this new signifier/signified relation, it is still the teacher who is being authorized. As in the case of the statement, authority still shores up a certain signifier/signified relation. Because I enact authority in the process of asking the question, my question holds together. My question is now glued to *me*.

I find this signifier/signified relation between the teacher and her question to be very important. For, this relation goes a long way toward distinguishing between the forms of questioning that are more dominating and those that are less dominating. The question will be more dominating when the authority enacted during questioning is not readily visible to the student. When teachers act as if authority is being "given over" by posing a question, then they are hiding the authoritative workings of the question. This leads to domination. The authority of the question itself, the authority enacted as the teacher's words signify her own meaning—this authority should not be hidden from view. Questions dominate to the extent that one ventriloquizes without admitting that there is ventriloquism going on.

The problem with Socratic method that dominates does not rest solely in the fact that such a method uses forceful questions. It lies rather in the fact that the questioner stands in such a relation to the student that the authority of questioning is not open to critique. When the gluing of authority is elided from view, then questioning leads to domination. On the other hand, if the student is in a position to *question the question*, then such questioning is less dominating. Questioning will be less dominating when the student is able to recognize that there is no *natural* link between the signifier and signified, that there is no *natural* reason that the teacher should get to signify her own meaning. Questioning will be less dominating when the student is able to realize, instead, that there is "steering" lodged even in questions that seem innocuous, that there is authority being enacted even in questions. It will be less dominating when teacher and student wobble the box. The question itself must be on shaky ground.

NON-SUPERFICIALITY, HUMILITY, CIRCUITRY

So one way for a question to be less dominating is for the authority of the question to be exposed. How else can the question work in healthy ways? To answer this means proceeding with our hermeneutic inquiry. Three themes that such an inquiry offers I will call: non-superficiality, pedagogical humility, and circuitry.

By non-superficiality, I mean the hermeneutic insight that linguistic interaction, interaction such as questioning, is not simply a topical way to address the more serious matter of content. Questioning need not be conceived as just one way, among many, that a particular content can be broached. From the perspective of philosophical hermeneutics, the linguistic practice of questioning is instead intimately linked to the content at hand. That is to say, there is not a hierarchical relationship between language and being, between what we say and what our saying represents, between pedagogy and curriculum content. Instead, language and being are human states that are ontologically equal. Questioning and content are on the same ontological plane.

Gadamer explains this relation of language practices to human experience with this succinct statement in *Truth and Method*: "Being that can be understood is language."[14] That is to say, linguistic formations are not in a representational relation to human experience. A word does not signify a thing. Instead, a word, a phrase, and in the case that interests us here, a question, are all intrinsic to the being-understood of the thing. Linguistic forms are synonymous with the ways that human beings come to understand the things of this world. Following Gadamer, there would be no human understanding without the linguistic forms in which humans participate. And more specifically, there would be no questioning sorts of understandings if there were no questioning statements. "The coming into language of meaning," writes Gadamer, "points to a universal ontological structure, namely to the basic nature of everything toward which understanding can be directed."[15] In other words, linguistic forms are a necessary phase in the process of human understanding. Language is not a tool that is used to understand subject matter. Rather, language enacts subject matter. Language brings into being the understanding of subject matter. Or to let Gadamer state this point as he has put it in his interchange with Habermas around the scope of hermeneutics, "[T]here is no societal reality, with all its concrete forces, that does not bring itself to representation in a consciousness that is linguistically articulated. Reality does not happen 'behind the back' of language . . . reality happens precisely *within* language."[16]

Thus, the authority of the question is not superficial. A question is not a supplement to content in the sense that it is an annex, an addition enabling students to understand the more serious matter of content. Rather, questioning is a particular linguistic form that insinuates itself into the very content that is being understood. Questioning is a "supplement" to content in the more invasive sense that I have outlined in the fist chapter. A question becomes part and parcel of the content at the same time that it supplements. In this way, questioning cannot be said to be simply one mode, among others, by which curriculum is presented. It cannot be said that the question is a mere matter of presentation. For, questioning, as linguistic practice, is integral to that which is questioned. Questioning enacts the authority of content. It becomes part of the content, authorizing content into life.

In this sense, a question that empowers will be "non-superficial." When a question is posed, it should not be posed as a technique or as a method. It should rather be posed in the true spirit of exploration. Content can be authorized into life by the question, if the question is treated as it should be treated: as part of the emergence of content itself. A question that empowers will not be a test. It will not aim to expose what the student does not know. It will not even aim to show what the student *does* know. Its aim will be understanding itself. A question must not be treated as a mere adjunct to the more serious matter of learning content. To be empowering, a question will go to the depths of the subject matter under consideration. An empowering question will thus create new understandings. It will not serve as a teaching technique. It will not solidify understandings that the teacher already has in mind.

Another property of the question, one highlighted not only by hermeneutics but by Platonic dialogues as well, is the question's ability to encourage pedagogical humility on the part of the instructor. It is in the nature of the question to authorize such humility. Gadamer speaks to the humility that can be fostered by the question when he reminds us, in *Truth and Method*, of Socrates:

> Among the greatest insights that Plato's account of Socrates affords us is that, contrary to the general opinion, it is more difficult to ask questions than to answer them. . . . In order to be able to ask, one must want to know, and that means knowing that one does not know.[17]

Questioning, as we have seen, is different from stating to the extent that there must be some desire to break open the object in question. And in this desire to break open the object, there will necessarily be an admission that one does not know all about the object. To ask a question, one must *want* to know, and we should take this locution of wanting in both its senses. First, asking a question means that we *desire* to know. But also, asking a question means that we *lack* knowing something. To ask a question in this way is an admission of incompleteness. It is in this way that questioning enacts an authority that questions its own authority. A question throws its own authority into question.

Gadamer reminds us of the comic thematics of Platonic dialogues when Socrates' interlocutors mistakenly think that asking questions is easier than answering them: "When the partners in the Socratic dialogue are unable to answer Socrates' awkward questions and try to turn the table by assuming what they suppose is the preferable role of the questioner, they come to grief."[18] Questioning must not be considered a cavalier act, an act that can be carried out without thought or deference. While it may be easy to ask a question of another person when the aim of the question is to reaffirm self-knowledge, such a question, as we have seen, is no more a question than it is a statement. The matter of serious questioning, questioning that intends to break open the object, requires deference with regard to the object. Haven't we all had the experience, as teachers, where we find ourselves slipping into an *easy* mode of questioning, a mode where we ask a question whose answer we want parroted back according to what we already have in mind? In such a circumstance, isn't there a sense in which we feel that our question is not a question after all, but is actually a statement in disguise? As Gadamer notes, "To someone who engages in dialogue only to prove himself right and not to gain insight, asking questions will indeed seem easier than answering them."[19] Questioning that does not aim to subsume otherness in the name of the same is not easy. It entails the labor of identifying one's own ignorance.

The "true" question, then, gets enacted through a practice of deference. It is striking how such deference gets overlooked even in progressive pedagogies that claim to be student-centered. For instance, while there is much focus on the experience of the child in the work of Dewey, it is ironic that there is not mention of the existential humility that must accompany any serious inquiry that intends to put subject matter into question. One would think that being child-centered has the existential correlate of being teacher-decentered, but such is not necessarily the case in progressive pedagogy. For example, when Dewey stresses, in *The Child and the Curriculum*, how the teacher must "psychologize" the link between student and subject matter, there is no sense that humility is central to how educators approach their relation to student and subject matter. In fact, the opposite is more the case. Following Dewey, it is assumed that the teacher must know *more and more* in order to facilitate learning on the part of the child.[20] Indeed, the very group of educators whom we suppose we might look to for humility vis-à-vis the student lets us down. And the same is true in the more obvious cases of educators who hail from traditional and critical backgrounds. Rather than advocating humility, there is a tendency among progressives, traditionalists, and criticalists alike to stress the ways in which teachers need to know *even more*, that such a surplus of knowledge needs to be applied with great confidence by teachers if they are to educate students in today's rapidly changing world. But an analysis of the question reminds us that confidence and surplus are not altogether happy matters in the realm of education. And importantly, one can be authorized, by means of questioning, to affirm the significance of that which is *not* known.

Another aspect that questioning brings to the fore is the way authority *circuits* between self and other. By this I mean that a "true" question cannot actually be asked without beginning a circuit in which the original question is responded to by *another question* on the part of the student. As Gadamer reminds us, questioning puts the student and teacher into the mode of a circuit, a mode wherein each is the asker of questions. It is not simply that the teacher asks questions and the student responds. Rather, any response that is a genuine attempt on the part of the student to let the question speak to him or her, such a response will itself be a question. Thus, questions are not unidirectional. They run back and forth between teacher and student. A detailed hermeneutic explanation of this circuitry is in order since such back-and-forthness goes against commonsense understandings of questioning and responding.

Whereas a rough-and-ready sketch of questioning would, unproblematically, show the teacher questioning and the student answering, Gadamer maintains that such a question/answer exchange is not what actually happens when a teacher and a student are addressing questions in earnest. Actually, the question will be answered *by a question*. To see this, first recall how Gadamer understands the nature of questioning. Questioning is characterized primarily by the process of self-critique, or humility. It is enacted through the process of suspending one's own judgments in order to truly question some object, to admit the aspects of an object that one doesn't know. But as Gadamer reminds us, this process of suspending judgment is precisely what occurs also in the case *where one is the recipient of a question!* To be open to a question, one must also suspend one's particular point of view in order to make meaning out of the question that is posed. Thus, within the process of responding to a question, the structure of posing that same question also comes into play.

Gadamer explains this process as follows:

> Understanding begins . . . when something addresses us. This
> is the first condition of hermeneutics. We now know what this
> requires, namely the fundamental suspension of our own preju-
> dices. But all suspension of judgments and hence, a fortiori, of
> prejudices, has the logical structure of the question.[21]

In order for a question to be understood by the one to whom it is
posed, it is not enough for the question to be posed. In addition, the
person toward whom the question is intentioned must be open to the
question's meaning. That is to say, the one questioned must be just as
open to an exploration of the object in question as the questioner is
himself. To return to our metaphor of the wobbling dice box, the one
questioned must be involved in keeping the dice in play. Such openness
requires a "suspension of judgments and hence, a fortiori, of prejudices" that will allow space for the object to be scrutinized by the one
questioned. In order to entertain a question, one must put in check all
hasty judgments, all overdetermined understandings, about the object in
question. In short, one must undergo the same self-critique that the
questioner undergoes. "The essence of the question," notes Gadamer,
"is to open up possibilities and keep them open."[22] One must, in this
fundamental sense of acquiring a questioner's humility, *become* a questioner in order to understand a question.

To be more clear, let us work through this circuit from teacher to
student, and back again: To ask a question, the teacher must let her
guard down and admit that the object in question is not entirely understood. So when the teacher asks a question, she is approaching an
object in a particular way, in a way that emphasizes the extent to which
that object is unknown from her perspective. This is the only way a
teacher can approximate a "true" question, namely, from a stance of
humility that admits there are certain ways in which the object is unknown to her. But as Gadamer reminds us, the teacher's self-critique
applies not only to the teacher but to the student as well. Given that the
question is intended toward the student, the particular situatedness of
the teacher's self-critique has implications for the student's understanding of the question. The question gets its meaning from its particular
vantage point, its particular humility, the particular way in which it
"breaks open" the object. And, this particular self-critique cannot be
lost on the student without the question losing its meaning.

Gadamer explains the circuitry of the questioning process as follows: "To understand a question means to ask it. To understand meaning is to understand it as the answer to a question."[23] In other words,

the process of questioning, once begun by a person in a particular situation, requires that the recipient of the question must walk in the shoes of the questioner, must experience the questioner's particular situation. The one questioned must do more than simply acquire a questioner's humility. She must also acquire the particular humility that the questioner used to pose the question in the first place. The one questioned needs to be able to think through the question from the questioner's position, or, in other words, she must be in a position to pose the same question in the same way. This is to say nothing of answering the question. We need not know whether the one questioned is yet in a position to answer. The point here is that even to get to an understanding of the questioner's question, the one questioned must, herself, be in a position to pose a question (to roll the dice) that gets at the same questionableness that was proposed in the first place. The circuit of questioning, from the teacher to the student, creates a circuit in which questions always follow questions.

But let us once again take a step beyond Gadamer. Whereas Gadamer focuses on the circuitry of the question, it is possible to glean a significant insight about authority from this notion that the question reduplicates itself within the response of the one questioned. It is possible to consider the authority of pedagogical questions in a different light, namely, as an authority that authorizes further questions. The circuitry of questioning will prompt the teacher to listen closely to the student's response. In this way, after the initial question has been posed, the teacher is prompted to turn around and become the student of her own student. She is prompted to see the student response as an authoritative source. The teacher, by virtue of treating the student's response as a question (rather than treating it as an answer that is simply insightful or not, simply correct or incorrect), is prompted to search for the ways that the student's new question might lead to further learning. She is prompted to see her own question as the beginning of a circuit that begs for more questions. The authority of the question authorizes not only the meaning of content and the humility of the questioner. It also authorizes the questioning circuit to continue.

QUESTIONING AND THE AUTHORITY RELATION

In elementary school classrooms, in middle schools, in high schools, in universities, during music lessons and dance instruction, when parents teach their children, and at almost any time when education is taking place, questioning sooner or later comes into play. As I have tried to show in this chapter, questioning has ramifications for the authority relation, but not in the way that some people, including myself, have assumed. Questioning does not simply make the authority relation more gentle, nor does is simply intensify the authority relation. Instead, questioning has a circuitry of its own that may bear one way *or the other* on the authority relation. As I have shown, the circuitry of the question needs to be considered in light of hermeneutics, in light of language theory, and in light of the attitudes questioners and answerers adopt toward the object they are questioning. And as I have also shown, questioning in education cannot be distinguished so easily from other forms of interaction. Questioning is not so different from making statements as one might think.

Certainly, this last matter, the complicated relation between statements and questions, has implications for educators who claim that a pedagogy of questions is less authoritarian than a pedagogy of statements. One such educator is Paulo Freire, who will be the focus of the next chapter. In his work, *Pedagogy of the Oppressed*, Freire condemns the practice of narration in education, and praises instead his problem-posing method of pedagogy. As he says, much oppressive education is suffering from "narration sickness."[24] Oppressive educators narrate too much, and ask questions too little. After the work that has been done in this chapter examining the nuances of similarities and differences that exist between the authority of questions and statements, I do not think that Paulo Freire is remiss in coming to the initial conclusion that the authority of questioning is fundamentally different than the authority of narrating. I think his work simply needs to be augmented. Freire's work on problem-posing education goes part of the way toward explaining the relational life of authority. But, his work needs to be augmented with a theory of authority-in-relation, a theory of the sort that I have been proposing throughout this book. The final chapter will address this matter, in addition to offering some concluding remarks.

CHAPTER 6

Paulo Freire and Relational Authority

In his famous text on education, *Pedagogy of the Oppressed*, Paulo Freire makes a claim about authority that is very bold, yet seemingly uncomplicated. Freire claims that through *his* type of education there will no longer be any problems with authority. His type of education is a problem-posing form of pedagogy, one that aims to liberate students and teachers from the ideological and physical domination practiced by rulers and elites. In the problem-posing pedagogy of liberation that Freire describes, "arguments based on 'authority' are no longer valid." Instead, authority will "be *on the side of* freedom."[1] While this claim about authority is presented as uncomplicated, I would like to suggest that such a claim can only be made if we first delve into the *relations* involved in Freirean pedagogy. Further, I suggest that the relations involved in Freirean pedagogy are relations of the psyche. To understand authority in Paulo Freire, we must understand relation therein. To understand relation in Paulo Freire, we must understand relation as a psychic phenomenon.

In this chapter, I argue that Freirean education needs a psychoanalytic theory to deal with the relation of authority.[2] And by extension, I mean that any pedagogy which aims to enact authority in ways that enhance the capacity of students and teachers needs to take the psyche into account. Without recourse to psychoanalytic thought, Freire's work falls into a nonrelational, and more thoroughly liberal, understanding of authority. With a full-fledged use of psychoanalysis, though, Freire's thought establishes a way of understanding educational authority that

129

no longer falls into the either/or binary of authority on one side, and freedom on the other. Authority *can* advance the cause of freedom. It can do so if we understand authority as a psychic relation. It can do so if the authority relation does not succumb to the unwanted psychic extremes of domination and submission.

BANKING AUTHORITY WITHOUT THE PSYCHE

To begin with, though, I want to leave the psyche out of our conversation in order to highlight what Freire's treatment of authority is like *without* any reference to the unconscious. Such an approach I find useful in order to highlight certain gaps that exist when such an omission is made. This means describing "banking education," which is Freire's trope for educational authority, without referring to issues of psychic domination and submission. Without such referents, banking authority ends up being much like other liberal notions of authority. Theories of liberalism assume that authority is detrimental. Liberalism tends to refute *all* authority, with no room for compromise or nuance, because the elimination of authority is seen as the only avenue for attaining freedom. In such a schema, banking authority falls on the oppressive side of the dichotomous split between authority and freedom.

At the risk of repeating what is common knowledge, a restatement of Freire's banking model helps to show what kind of authority is at work therein. The banking model is remarkable for at least five oppressive operations. Each of these operations is enforced by the authority of the banking instructor. First, banking authority uses methods that force students into the passive position of an active/passive dichotomy. Some examples of this active/passive dichotomy are: "the teacher teaches and the students are taught," "the teacher knows everything and the students know nothing," "the teacher thinks and the students are thought about," and "the teacher disciplines and the students are disciplined."[3] In this binary of what-the-teacher-does and what-the-student-does, the teacher is always the initiator of pedagogical practice and the student is always the one for whom such practice is initiated. The banking instructor is an authority figure who takes the active position of oppressor. The student is in the passive position of the one who is oppressed.

Second, banking authority uses *epistemological* force to strip the learner of human agency. Describing the banking system, Freire shows the convergence of epistemological and existential agency. To know for oneself is also to *be* for oneself. And conversely, to have another person think in one's stead is to lack the ontological position of being completely human. When banking authority is used on a person, that "person is not a conscious being (*corpo consciente*); he or she is rather the possessor of *a* consciousness: an empty 'mind' passively open to the reception of deposits of reality from the world outside."[4] Fullness and emptiness are first of all descriptions of *knowledge* that has been acquired or not. At the same time, though, they are descriptions of the extent to which human *existence* is fully, or only partially, actualized. Banking authority forces epistemological passivity onto students, which is in fact no different from forcing them into existential passivity.

Third, banking authority is used to dominate the other by separating pedagogy into two parts. Splitting curriculum in an artificial manner, the preparation of content is done by the teacher only. The student does not witness that preparation, and thus the banker keeps the student out of the loop of human agency. Writes Freire,

> The banking concept (with its tendency to dichotomize everything) distinguishes two stages in the action of the educator. During the first, he cognizes a cognizable object while he prepares his lessons in his study or his laboratory; during the second, he expounds to his students about that object. The students are not called upon to know, but to memorize the contents narrated by the teacher.[5]

What the banking teacher does in his or her preparation of knowledge ensures that the student's relation to curriculum will not be an agentive one that *engages* with knowledge, but will rather be a passive one that *looks at* predigested knowledge. Students are force fed what Charles Schwab has called a "rhetoric of conclusions."

Banking authority also works as an ideological apparatus. Freire notes that "[b]anking education (for obvious reasons) attempts, by mythicizing reality, to conceal certain facts which explain the way human beings exist in the world."[6] Such education promotes commonsense understandings of the world that are not to be questioned. These are the "myths" to which Freire is referring. In a banking system, people do not "develop their power to perceive critically *the way they exist* in the world *with which* and *in which* they find themselves."[7] Instead, they see their world "as a static reality."[8] So banking authority creates static myths about the world. And, it also creates static myths about language. The very words that come to be used by teachers and students are shrouded in the common sense of dominant ideology. Within the banking system, students are not able to interrogate language. They cannot say "a true word."[9]

Moreover, banking authority sets up house inside of the student's consciousness, instilling its own slogans and its own policies *within* the student's worldview. Drawing on Hegel's Master/Slave dialectic, Freire describes this situation as the same as the consciousness of the slave who internalizes his or her master's values. Banking educators fill the oppressed "with slogans which create even more fear of freedom."[10] The oppressed, " 'housing' the oppressors within themselves . . . cannot be truly human."[11] This is because the oppressed are " 'beings for another.' "[12] "What characterizes the oppressed is their subordination to the consciousness of the master," and this subordination is augmented by the practice of banking authority, a practice that is quite happy to let students experience the world vicariously, as an inauthentic part of the student self.[13] After being banked, students can no longer think for themselves because their thinking is only borrowed from an other. Likewise, they can no longer *be* for themselves because their very being is borrowed from that other.

In short, banking authority uses various means to oppress the student. The banking system employs authority at the expense of the student's freedom. Such authority produces passive students, denies epistemological/existential agency, severs the student from knowledge production, fosters dominant ideologies, and introjects itself into student consciousness. As Freire points out, "The teacher confuses the authority of knowledge with his or her own professional authority, which she and he sets in opposition to the freedom of the students."[14] Authority, in the banking system, is antithetical to freedom.

HOW TO STOP BANKING?

A Familiar Refrain

Freire's analysis is convincing, and it forces a pressing question: How can educators combat this banking authority? I would like to begin answering this question by referring to a familiar refrain, one that I hear almost every time I expose my own students to this text by Freire. This refrain might seem familiar to those who remember reading Freire for the first time, or to those who have asked their students to read *Pedagogy of the Oppressed* in the classroom. The refrain is, "Stop banking." Indeed, this is one way to read Freire, namely, that his text is primarily a warning against the banking system. Along with this refrain, I usually get the message that what Freire wants teachers to do is give up authority in the classroom. To use the banking system, it is reasoned, means being authoritarian in the classroom. In order to give up the banking system, and to empower our students accordingly, authority must be yielded.

This refrain has a long history in the liberal tradition, echoed at least since Kant's *What is Enlightenment?* The refrain is that authority is always the enemy of freedom. As John Dewey points out in "Authority and Social Change," liberal notions that pit authority *against* freedom derive from the Enlightenment attempt to escape two very specific forms of authority: the Church and the State.[15] Yet, what started out as the rebellion of individuals against these specific censuring institutions became generalized into a "demarcation of two separate spheres, one of authority and one of freedom."[16] Dewey describes this process:

> The final result was a social and political philosophy which questioned the validity of authority in *any* form that was not the product of, and that was not sanctioned by, the conscious wants, efforts, and satisfactions of individuals in their private capacity—a philosophy which took the form of *laissez faire* in economics and all other social and political affairs. This philosophy claimed for itself the comprehensive title of liberalism.[17]

Authority and freedom are one of those binaries against which Dewey is always railing, and it is a binary that can, at first glance, seem to be what Paulo Freire is trying to underscore with his denunciation of the banking system.

But the results of such a liberal abdication of authority do not necessarily succeed, at least not in escaping the banking situations that Freire describes. Giving up authority, on the part of the instructor, does not necessarily lead to agency on the part of the student. It simply leads to less authority on the part of the instructor. When one stops exercising epistemological force, that does not *necessarily* lead to the other's existential agency. That the instructor is no longer the sole arbiter of ways of knowing does not guarantee that the student will become empowered as a knowledge seeker. Nor does showing students the preparation of content guarantee that the student will herself come any closer to the construction of knowledge. Giving up authority also does not guarantee that dominant ideology won't continue to trump progressive notions. And, abdicating authority may decrease the internalization of alienating positions; but, there is no guarantee that students will rid themselves of internalized otherness that has already taken place. In general, we can't know how an abdication of authority will empower students; we can only know that there has been a withdrawal. Liberalist assumptions about the withdrawal of authority are based on the false logic that if A works to the detriment of B, then not A will automatically foster the capacity of B.

Dialogics Against Banking

Freire's own answer to the problem of authority is, of course, the application of a dialogic, problem-posing pedagogy. For Freire, a dialogic approach helps dissolve the dehumanizing effects of banking authority, encouraging instead humanization. The dialogic approach is supposed to work against banking authority on all of the levels that I have outlined above. For the purposes of this analysis, though, I will focus on the most significant level, namely, the imbalance created by banking authority: the imbalance that pits teacher against student in a relation of one who is active (the teacher) versus one who is passive (the student). As Freire argues, this is the fundamental opposition that needs to be resolved: "[T]he practice of problem-posing education entails at the outset that the teacher-student contradiction to [sic] be resolved. Dialogic relations—indispensable to the capacity of cognitive actors to cooperate in perceiving the same cognizable object—are otherwise impossible."[18] Dialogic education is supposed to end the passive/active teacher-student dichotomy that characterizes banking pedagogy.[19] While the banking system activates teachers and pacifies students, the dialogic model will rectify this relationship. The teacher-student relationship will be subject to revision. Instead of teacher and student, there will be teacher/student and student/teacher.

Linking together the matters of dialogue, activity/passivity, and teacher authority, Freire writes:

> Through dialogue, the teacher-of-the-students and the students-of-the-teacher cease to exist and a new term emerges: teacher-student with students-teachers. The teacher is no longer merely the-one-who-teaches, but one who is himself taught in dialogue with the students, who in turn while being taught also teach. They become jointly responsible for a process in which all grow. In this process, arguments based on "authority" are no longer valid; in order to function, authority must be *on the side of* freedom, not *against* it.[20]

Notable in this passage, first of all, is that Freire is trying to get away from the liberal paradigm of authority, where authority is pitted against freedom. This is clearly implied in the claim that authority will be "*on the side of* freedom, not *against* it" in the dialogic approach. Yet also notable in this passage is Freire's own inability to actually get out of liberalism's authority versus freedom dilemma.

There are two ways that Freire fails to escape this dilemma. The first is that he fails to give up the very terms that are at stake. Freire's claim that "arguments based on authority are no longer valid" is still very much an argument based on authority. While Freire offers a different configuration of those terms, he does not get out of the general parameters that are already establish by the liberal conversation about authority.[21] While Freire troubles the authority/freedom binary by putting authority on the side of freedom, he does not give up the binary itself. He refutes the mutually exclusive nature of authority and freedom, but does not provide any nuance for understanding the difference between the two. It is at this point that Freire falls into what Michel Foucault has called "the trap of the Enlightenment."[22] By accepting the terms of the Enlightenment (in this case the authority-freedom dichotomy), one finds oneself in a position where it is not possible to escape the Enlightenment gambit without seeming to advocate an irrational position.

A second problem with Freire's solution to the freedom and authority dilemma is that he reconciles the pair simply by fiat—*let there be* authority on the side of freedom. But putting authority on the side of freedom does not ensure that authority will not continue to be oppressive. There have been many historical cases where a movement's authority, or the authority of an enlightened leader, continues to be oppressive in the very name of freedom. Freire knows this is a problem. He struggles with this concern in *Pedagogy of the Oppressed* when he wonders if someone could practice a banking education in the name of the oppressed. His conclusion is that it is *not* possible to liberate and to bank at the same time:

> In the revolutionary process, the leaders cannot utilize the banking method as an interim measure, justified on the grounds of expediency, with the intention of *later* behaving in a genuinely revolutionary fashion. They must be revolutionary—that is to say, dialogical—from the outset.[23]

But in response to this admonition against using the banking method even for expediency's sake, we must ask of Freire: What is the difference between "authority *on the side of freedom*" and "the banking method as an interim measure"? Within the discussion that has been established in *Pedagogy of the Oppressed* on the banking system as an authority-driven pedagogy, there is no substantive difference. Authority on the side of freedom is the same as the use of the banking method on the side of freedom. By putting authority on the side of freedom by fiat, the very notion of authority becomes hollowed out to the point where it is meaningless. Freire does not solve the authority/freedom dilemma because he does not offer a substantive account of what authority actually does once it is on the side of freedom.

Now, it is clear to me that Freire does not mean to say that the banking method should be on the side of freedom. What happens to Freire's account of authority is that it gets stuck in a nonrelational way of thinking. To say that authority will be on this side or that is to ignore the relational dynamics of authority. It is to remain under the spell of liberalism. It is to stop short of true dialogic thinking. Freire's pedagogy is relational. It is dialogical. Unfortunately, he does not push his relational thinking all the way through to the matter of authority. Authority will never be on the side of freedom because, as we have seen, authority is not some "thing" that takes sides. Let us rather say, *"The authority relation will foster freedom"*—such a statement is relational. Such a statement honors Freire's dialogic project. To give meaning to such a revised statement, we must take the psyche into account. In the above paragraphs, I have intentionally ignored Freire's allusions to psychoanalysis. The psychic life of problem-posing education is not fully developed in *Pedagogy of the Oppressed*. But it should be. Without it, Freire's account of authority stops short of being relational. To push Freire's relational thinking all the way through to the matter of authority, it is necessary to push farther with his psychoanalytic leanings.

PSYCHOANALYSIS IN PAULO FREIRE: FROM AUTHORITY TO BALANCE

When the metaphorics of *Pedagogy of the Oppressed* are scrutinized, it becomes apparent that there are too many allusions to psychoanalytic thought to ignore. Terms such as "domination," "submission," "unconsciously," "guilt," "alienation," " 'neurotically,' " "sadism," "masochism," "internalization," and "necrophilia" are used in ways that evoke psychoanalytic sensibilities. Moreover, Freire's text makes explicit use of the psychoanalytically inspired work of Eric Fromm, Herbert Marcuse, and Franz Fanon. Freire's seminal text is indeed indebted to psychoanalysis in many ways. Attention to Freire's psychoanalytic references yields a much more subtle understanding of the place of authority in dialogic education. Such attention yields a notion of authority that does not succumb to the "trap" of the Enlightenment. Attention to Freire's psychoanalytic stance points to a conception of *pedagogical authority as balance* that is Freire's unique contribution to the problem of authority vis-à-vis freedom in education.

Authority is explicitly considered from a psychoanalytic perspective in *Pedagogy of the Oppressed* as Freire relates Erich Fromm's psychoanalytic work on child rearing to the matter of domination in education. Paraphrasing Fromm, Freire comments on authoritarianism in the family:

If children reared in an atmosphere of lovelessness and op-
pression, children whose potency has been frustrated, do not
manage during their youth to take the path of authentic
rebellion, they will either drift into total indifference, alien-
ated from reality the authorities and the myths the latter
have used to "shape" them; or they may engage in forms of
destructive action.[24]

At stake here is the submission, of the child, a submission that is facilitated by the authority of a parent who dominates, using his or her
authority in a destructive way. Freire's point here is that banking authority reenacts the authoritarian ways of households.

Authoritarian instructors also force students into submission, into
a state of being dominated by the other. Freire goes on to describe the
teacher's role as one-who-dominates. Teachers, even if they mean well,
are too often caught in a psychic equation that is difficult to get out of
because the equation started long ago during their own submission as
children. Writes Freire,

Well-intentioned professionals (those who use "invasion" not
as deliberate ideology but as the expression of their own
upbringing) eventually discover that certain of their educational failures must be ascribed, not to the intrinsic inferior-
ity of the "simple men of the people," but to the violence of
their own act of invasion. Those who make this discovery
face a difficult alternative: they feel the need to renounce
invasion, but patterns of domination are so entrenched within
them that this renunciation would become a threat to their
own identities. To renounce invasion would mean ending
their dual status as dominated and dominators.[25]

The authority figure in the unhealthy banking system, like the parental
authority in an imbalanced family system, practices domination. Authoritarian instructors are caught replaying circuits of domination and
submission with their students.

FLESHING OUT THE CIRCUIT
OF DOMINATION AND SUBMISSION

To further unpack the relation between authority and domination/sub-
mission, it is helpful to look again at Jessica Benjamin's rendition of
psychoanalysis. Benjamin describes domination and submission in a
manner that glosses the intricacies of parental and teacher authority to

which Freire alludes. Her analysis, like Freire's, is based on an analysis of dialogic interaction between self and other. Also like Freire's, it is based on the sort of struggle for recognition that is described in Hegel's dialectic of recognition between master and slave.

As you will recall, Benjamin offers an account of the self as involved with the other in a struggle for recognition that may be balanced and healthy, or that may denigrate into a relationship of domination and submission. Self and other may find balance in their recognitive relations, or they may become stuck at the poles of oppressor and oppressed. What I will argue here, with the help of Benjamin, is that Paulo Freire's solution to the problem of authority finds its resolution in a psychoanalytic notion of *balance* between the poles of domination and submission.[26]

Recall that Benjamin describes an interaction between self and other that is grounded in the double life of self. For Benjamin, human encounter between self and other is best understood in terms of the intersection between the domain of fantasy and the domain of reality. Balance, domination, and submission all happen on the fault line between these two domains. One domain, it will be recalled, is that of fantasy. She terms this domain "intrapsychic" space. It is

> the inner world of fantasy, wish, anxiety, and defense; of bodily symbols and images whose connection defy the ordinary rules of logic and language. In the inner world, the subject incorporates and expels, identifies with and repudiates the other, not as a real being, but as a mental object.[27]

The bonds formed in intrapsychic space are based on my ego's needs and drives. They are based on my own way of understanding the world. These bonds are rigid. They congeal in the psyche if they are not tested by experiences that are not in my own psychic control.

This description of intrapsychic space resonates with Freire's own description of the objectification that happens in banking interaction. As Freire notes, "banking education begins with a false understanding of men and women as objects."[28] Such objectification happens, writes Freire borrowing the words of Eric Fromm, in the space of fantasy as the banking educator

> is driven by the desire to transform the organic into the inorganic, to approach life mechanically, as if all living persons were things. . . . Memory, rather than experience; having rather than being, is what counts. The necrophilous person [the banker] can relate to an object—a flower or person—

only if he possesses it; hence a threat to his possession is a
threat to himself; if he loses possession he loses contact with
the world. . . . He loves control, and in the act of controlling
kills life.[29]

The oppressor is one who objectifies the other. Such objectification
takes place as one controls the image of the other, holding the other in
the private space of fantasy, subjecting the other to one's own control,
killing the subjective life of the other.

Distinct from the objectifying bonds formed in intrapsychic space
are those formed in intersubjective space. These bonds are exterior to
the self. These bonds are experienced during fleshly encounters with the
other. As Benjamin explains, intersubjectivity "refers to that zone of
experience in which the other is not merely the object of the ego's need/
drive or cognition/perception but has a separate and equivalent center
of self."[30] An intersubjective bond is established when I interact with an
other who is *not* under my control, who is radically separate from me.
Whereas the intrapsychic bond involves internal, psychic manipulation
of the other, manipulation that turns the other into an *object* of fantasy,
the intersubjective bond involves recognition of the other as a subject
with agency.

This distinction—between the intrapsychic and the intersubjective—
is in fact akin to a similar distinction upon which Freire relies: Martin
Buber's distinction between the I-It and the I-Thou. Freire calls upon
Buber, noting that "the antidialogical, dominating *I* transforms the
dominated, the conquered *thou* into a mere *it*."[31] In such a relationship,
the self refuses to be with the other in an intersubjective way. In contrast to this *I* that treats the other as an *it*, Freire recommends "the
dialogical *I*." He points out that such an dialogical *I*

> knows precisely the *thou* ("not-*I*") which has called forth his
> or her own existence. He also knows that the *thou* which calls
> forth his own existence in turn constitutes an *I* which has in
> his *I* its *thou*. The *I* and the *thou* thus become, in the dialectic
> of these relationships, two *thous* which become two *I's*.[32]

A Thou, which Buber calls a "center of surprise," must be an other who
is unexpected and thus thoroughly out of the control of the I who
acknowledges this Thou.[33] It is this surprising, intersubjective Thou to
which Freire links his dialogic pedagogy.

Following this distinction that both Benjamin and Freire make
between the domain of fantasy and that of reality, we find that domination occurs when either of these two domains take over completely.

It is dangerous for self and other to live in a world that is primarily fantasy and objectifying, but it is likewise dangerous for self and other to live in a world that is full of too much unexpectedness, too much Thou-ness. Domination and submission follow from either extreme.

For example, when I interact with an other, domination can result if I continually cast the other in forms that are lodged in the psyche, in ways that are rigid. When I get used to such interaction, I will want to avoid the unpredictability of the other because I have become used to an other who fulfills my expectations. Confronting the other as a true subject with agency will become threatening because such an agentive subject will not be able to grant me the sort of recognition that I'm used to. It becomes more comfortable to interact with the other as an object that is under my own control. So I disregard the other-as-subject and represent her as an object in the psyche. In such a case, the self becomes swollen with objectifying representations of the other. And unfortunately, when my relation to the other resides mainly in intrapsychic space when faced with an other, then I will experience a sudden crisis whenever I am faced with the other in an intersubjective context. That is to say, when a relation is almost always as expected, it can be very startling for there to be unexpectedness all of the sudden. If the other acts in an unanticipated way, I may feel threatened because I do not anticipate her agency. In order not to feel threatened in this interchange, I will keep the other at bay, making sure that the recognition I receive is the sort that is comfortable for me, the sort that is static.

Conversely—and here is precisely where an extension of Freire's psychoanalytic work successfully departs from a liberal understanding of authority—it is also a mistake to be in an intersubjective circuit where the other is mainly unanticipatable. Such a relation also leads to domination. Let us say that the other resides mainly as *radically* other for me, that she is totally out of my control. Eventually, there will come a time when she seeks recognition from me. When I give recognition to an other who is unpredictable, to an other who does not represent for me some sort of stable image, then I will tend to give recognition that is random and subject to my own whims. That is to say, I must be able to see in the other some stable image, some specific other who needs recognition. If not, I will recognize randomly. In such a case of random recognition, the other will become subject to the vicissitudes of *my* unpredictability, to a randomness in recognizing that will be too unfamiliar to her. Even though I recognize the other, the recognition itself may be damaging in such an unpredictable case. Domination also results in such a case, when the other becomes dependent upon a recognitive encounter that cannot be anticipated because I can't be sure *whom* to recognize. Just opposite to the case where I cast the other in rigid terms and foist upon the other a recognition that is all my own, it is likewise dominating to be unpredictable in the granting of recognition. Such a situation also causes dependency on the one recognized.

DOMINATION AND SUBMISSION IN THE CLASSROOM

It is not hard to imagine such a relation of domination in the classroom. Let us say that I am a teacher and I know little about one of my students except what I can discern from his role *as my student*. This student certainly has a rich, unpredictable life that has little to do with what I know about him, but, nevertheless, I continue knowing this student only in the limited ways that he is permitted to interact with me within the particular parameters that I set up for the students in my class. Let us say that I keep the student in a banking relationship, and expect him to stay in such a role.

In such a relationship, it can be said that I have a relationship with that student that is based more on fantasy than on reality, more on the limited circumstances that I have predetermined while setting up my classroom than on the unpredictability and surprise that is part of human experience. In such a case, there will come a time that I give recognition to that student. In this case, the recognition that I give will tend to keep that student in his prescribed role. It will tend toward domination. I will give recognition from a perspective that is already dependent upon *me*. The other's recognition will be based on the "dependence that is the fruit of the concrete situation of domination," to borrow Freire's description. It will be based on the other's submission to my fantasy.

To put the issue of domination and submission in curricular terms, think of Freire's accusation that banking instructors separate instruction into two stages, the preparation and then the actual teaching. This sequential process is not itself the problem. To pretend that there will be absolutely no contemplation of curriculum "in the instructor's study or laboratory," is not, I believe, Freire's point.[34] His point is, rather, to note the long-term ill effects that such a process fosters. Such effects include domination on the part of the instructor, and submission on the part of the student. When instructors hide the preparation of content from students, the long-term effect of such hiding on the student is no different from the psychic process that leads to an imbalanced interchange between self and other. The instructor creates a rigid, preformulated curriculum. She creates a content that is solely under her control, one that is no different from an object of fantasy. In turn, the student must engage with this curriculum in the narrowly defined way that the instructor has prepared. The student, like the one dominated, must succumb to the objectifying grid of the preset curriculum. He must fall in line with the narrow workings of the other's preformulated fantasy.[35]

In such a curricular situation, the student, trapped in a circuit of succumbing to the fantasy-inspired curriculum of the instructor, has no chance to become an agent in the learning process. If agency does take place, if the student does engage with content *preparation*, then the instructor is not in a position to recognize the student as having partaken in worthwhile learning.[36] In that case, the instructor, having become used to recognizing only that which she has formulated in advance, will not recognize the validity of any learning that is not prepared under her control. Agentive learning will not "count," as the instructor is able to recognize only that learning which she has prearranged for the student. Curriculum will continue to be severed from its preparation because a cycle of domination and submission has set in.

Or, let us say that I am a teacher who "gives up authority." Let us say I assume from the start that my student should not be the subject of *my* understandings, that he should not be relegated to the student roles I have in mind for him. That does not undo the scenario of domination and submission; it only reverses its conditions. For, when I "grant" autonomy, agency, and unpredictability to my student, there will still come a time when the student seeks recognition from me. At such a time, the recognition I grant him will be arbitrary because it will be unpredictable. Ironically, my attempt to let the student free will make him just as submissive to my whims as he was previously to my fantasy.

AUTHORITY AND BALANCE

Examined in light of intersubjective psychoanalysis, authority can neither be insisted on nor given up. Both stances will lead to domination and submission. Rather, self and other must strike a balance where acknowledgment is practiced on two levels: the level of fantasy and the level of unpredictability. The challenge herein is to strike a balance that takes into account both the strong need for recognition built into the teacher/student relationship, *and* the omnipresent danger of becoming entangled in circuits of recognition that are either dominating or submissive. The teacher/student relation has a natural tendency to fall into stereotypical role playing that leads to domination and submission, *but* the liberal eschewing of authority also leads down a similar path.

The way out of domination and submission is built on balance. There must be a fluctuation in the self-other relation that at once encourages fantasy *and* reality. The teacher must be in a position to recognize the student as a separate center of self, one that is out of her own control. However, for such recognition to count, the student cannot be so far out of the teacher's control that she becomes a threat. There must be an oscillation, on the part of the teacher, between being in control and letting loose. And there must be such an oscillation on the side of the student, too. For recognition to count, the student must know that the teacher is predictable enough not to be threatening. Yet, the teacher must seem autonomous enough not to *have to* grant recognition. Recognition counts for the one recognized only when there is the option, on the part of the one recognizing, of not recognizing.

These psychoanalytic insights point precisely to what Freire is after when he argues that "authority must be *on the side of* freedom." To enhance freedom, authority must work against its own tendency to dominate the other. For authority to enhance freedom does not mean that it *is* freedom. It means rather that authority must be enacted more judiciously than has heretofore been considered. It must be deployed with an eye toward alleviating the bonds of domination and submission that characterize many educational interactions, and most oppressive situations.

For Freire, it is not authority that is the problem. The problem is rather the subservience that may result from authority that is exercised injudiciously. When Freire states that "arguments based on authority are no longer valid," this statement should *not* be read as a liberalist critique that assumes authority to be some problem in itself. Authority, without the concomitant subservience that sometimes results from its use, is no more of a problem in itself than the clanging piano is itself at fault for having been played awkwardly. Authority becomes a problem when it is used in ways that either rigidify the other or let the other loose completely. The judicious use of authority will strive to avoid the poles of dominance and submission. Its judicious use will subvert the banking tendency that employs authority to maintain the circuit of domination and submission. It is such a circuit, and not authority itself, that carries out the work of banking—producing passive students, precluding epistemological and existential agency, severing students from the production of knowledge, replicating dominant ideology, and installing the banking method in student consciousness.

Balance is as applicable to classroom authority as it is to psychic circuits of recognition. On the instructor's side, it is necessary to conscientiously allow for my own agency. There are certainly times when one must teach in the way one wants. But at the same time, it is necessary to realize that my position as educator must be tempered by the position of an other who is not under my control. For me to teach in a way that counts, I must stake out my own position, yet be willing to lose that position from time to time. Similarly, the student must be allowed by me to stake out her position, but must also be willing to lose that position from time to time. It is only by such a movement between the interior domain of one's own pedagogical agenda, and the exterior domain of the other's intellectual growth, that circuits of domination and submission will be kept at bay.

It will be argued at this point that I have started with the naïve reading of Freire, one that recommends giving up authority altogether, that I have made a detour through authority's relation to the psyche, and that I have merely come back to a more "balanced" approach to Freire, one that is ultimately not about the psychic dynamics of authority but more about some sort of "reasonable" conscious use of authority. I want to emphasize that this is not the case. When I advocate balance, I do not mean a happy medium where threat is avoided and the other remains within the realm of the anticipatable. I mean instead balance in the sense that a pendulum must be balanced, and not tilted to one side or the other, if it is to continue to oscillate. The circuit of recognition will entail oscillation. There will be times when authority seems uncontrollably lost, times when the other will seem to have taken over, times when the teacher, for instance, finds herself in a vulnerable position that threatens to engulf all reasonable progress within the classroom. Vulnerability will be inevitable. One cannot anticipate, with any accuracy, the times when the other will be unexpected and threatening. Authority without domination will oscillate toward vulnerability, and back again.

In short, authority must be seen as a dynamic and intersubjective process. When Freire describes an authority that enhances freedom, we must understand such authority in the same way that we understand the circuits of recognition that are fundamental to all self-other relations. Such authority does *not* enhance freedom when it gets stuck in an imbalance that leads to continued domination on the side of one person, and continued submission on the side of another. Such authority *does* enhance freedom when states of domination and submission are merely fleeting, fleeting to such an extent that they constitute momentary experiences of threat, vulnerability, omnipotence, and excess. During these moments, authority is at work in motion. It does not freeze into domination. Authority that enhances freedom is best judged by the extent to which vulnerability and excess are precisely *not* avoided. It can be judged by the extent to which vulnerability and excess are kept in motion, sometimes practiced by the self and sometimes by the other. This oscillation must never get stuck. Both teacher and students must practice excess. Both students and teachers must experience vulnerability.

Authority must be in flux, sometimes abdicated and sometimes claimed. It must be used, as Freire notes, so that "through dialogue, the teacher-of-the-students and the students-of-the-teacher cease to exist and a new term emerges: teacher-student with students-teachers."[37] It must be used on the fault line between fantasy and unexpectedness, between domination and submission, within the oscillation of excess and vulnerability, and thus "on the side of freedom."[38]

CONCLUSION

In this concluding chapter, I have ended up claiming something audacious. I have claimed that even the work of the great educator Paulo Freire stands to gain from a more thoroughly relational examination of authority. Indeed, this last chapter has been different from the rest. In this chapter I have tried to augment a long-standing educational program by using a relational approach to authority. In contrast, the preceding chapters have been more or less based on the *experience* of relational authority. I have examined the relation of authority between texts and people. I have examined the way that the relation of authority is like a literary relation. I have examined the relation of authority when the person in authority is no longer present. I have examined how one relates to larger, impersonal sources of authority. And I have examined how the authority relation bears on the use of questions. So instead of using relational authority to think through *experience*, this last chapter has used relational authority to think through a *theory*.

But to conclude this book, I would like to go back once again to lived experience. I would like to share just a few experiences from my own teaching and from my own life. I share these experiences in no particular order, yet they all have something in common. These reflections all invoke different insights to be gleaned from a relational perspective on authority. I trust that the reader of the pages that follow will be able to see how these reflections stem from the work that I have already done in the preceding chapters.

I leave these reflections for you to think about for this reason: if this book has done anything, it should have given the reader a way to understand authority differently. The ideas that have been put forth in this book should enable the reader to re-understand *any* instance when authority is in play. And so here I will offer just a few instances that come to mind. Here, I will be challenging myself to rethink a few instances of authority that I have come across. I do this because if one cannot rethink, in a relational way, *any and all* instances of authority, then the book fails. There should be no exception. After all, it is not just certain types of authority that are relational. *All* authority is so.

Recently I was teaching a graduate seminar on moral philosophy in education. We were discussing a passage in the book *I and Thou*, written by Martin Buber. Students were taking turns offering insights.

As one student offered comments, she used the pronoun "it" in a way that I did not understand. I asked her,

"What do you mean by 'it'? You used the word 'it' in your last sentence. I can't figure out what 'it' is referring to."

She replied, "I'm not sure what I mean."

Another student offered his comments. Once again, it happened. I interrupted him, asking, "Can you tell me what *you* mean by 'it'? As with Carol, I can't put my finger on the meaning of the word 'it' as you have used it."

He replied, "I think by the word 'it' I mean 'spirit' or 'language' or 'presence.' But I'm not positive."

I asked a third student for his insights because I could see in his eyes that he had something to say about the passage. He began to speak, but then stopped mid-sentence.

He said, "I don't know if I can go on with my idea because I was about to say 'it' and I know that you are going to ask me what 'it' means, and I don't know what the 'it' that I am going to say means.

At first I was frustrated that my previous questioning had caused a halt in the conversation. But then I smiled to myself because I realized that the questioning, and the halt, were very productive. This last interchange illustrates the way that authority can oscillate between teacher and student, especially when questions are asked by the teacher. Such oscillation is productive. It is important for questioning to exhibit reciprocity. In this instance, my student wobbled the box. He kept the dice rolling.

When the third student responded to me, he did not let himself be pigeon-holed by the question. Rather, he turned my question back onto me. He wondered what I intended by my question. He wondered if it was reasonable for me to come back at him with another question. He examined what the question might entail. He wondered, out loud, where I would be going with my question. He questioned my question. He turned my question into his own question. He caught *me* up short. He partook in the authority exchange rather than letting authority be a one-way relation.

Three years ago, my mother died. My mother was, quite simply, the most import figure of authority in my life. She was a moral authority for me. A social activist, she taught me to work against racism in all its forms. A white woman unafraid to go against the grain at a time when schools in many parts of the United States were segregated, she and a handful of other progessive, white parents had their children bussed into an all black elementary school. I was bussed to McCarver elementary school at the age of seven, and I will forever live by the anti-racist values that she embodies.

She was a pedagogical authority for me. My mother set a standard of teaching that I may never live up to, but will always strive to attain. She was not a teacher by profession. She did, though, have a teacherly way with people. One might call this way a matter of 'unconditional intellectual regard.' For my mother, the intellectual potential of her children was never to be challenged. Her children simply *could*. She let no one say differently. She let none of her children think otherwise.

Since she has passed away, I have come to know something I had never known before. My mother had all along been the authority figure to whom I had turned for guidance. It wasn't that I asked her in person for guidance, at least not after I became an adult. It was rather that she authorized me by being front-and-center in my memory, in my psyche. If I trained to run a marathon, I thought of my mother. If I attended a protest march, I thought of my mother. If I put on snow skis and skied gracefully down the hill, I thought of her smiling.

After she passed away, though, I must admit that her presence as an authority figure changed. I could no longer look to her without grief overshadowing. Try as I might, I could no longer look to her with the hope that she would authorize me in person. She was no longer the same sort of living authority. She is, and will always be, central to who I am. Yet, I have learned that I must look to others as well. My father is still alive and flourishing. He is slowly insinuating himself into that position of authority that my mother can now only hold in a certain way. He is becoming my living absence. Through this transition, it has helped me to know that authority is a relation. It has helped me to know that authority is a relation that depends upon presence as well as absence.

The reasons that I have written this book are many. One of them stems from interactions that I have had with university colleagues. If you learn anything as a university professor, it is that authority is always at stake when colleagues get together. This is in part because of the hierarchical nature of academic life. Academics are *always* being ranked in one way or another whether it is by one's scholarship, one's teaching ability, or, as in the case I want to recount, one's racial identity. Who gets authorized when professors have the occasion speak with each other is always a matter of tension. One specific occasion comes to mind.

At the university where I used to work, our college of education was replete with racial tension. African American and Latino faculty members were subject to personal and institutional racism. For example, one Latina faculty member, mistaken for a student worker because most of the student workers in our faculty were Latino, was asked by a white faculty member to make photocopies. Too, some white members of the faculty would complain when one African American faculty member, in particular, would speak out, when she would speak her mind. Some white members of the faculty accused her of bullying white women. Race was used as a wedge by some white faculty members to mark off those who had a right to speak out and those who didn't. Of course, the white accusers were the first to defend their own right to speak as forcefully as they wished.

Adding to the racial tension was a refusal by some white members of our faculty to acknowledge that significant racial tension *existed*. To them, racial tension among faculty members was a thing that should never be confused with the "real" racism that happens in less rarefied situations outside of academia. To them, "real" racism did not happen where people of color had already achieved an academic position of authority.

To make a long story short, the tension was so extreme that an outside consultant was called in by our dean. This consultant recommended that all faculty members participate in workshops to understand, and to talk about, the racism that was being experienced. I was asked by the dean to lead these workshops. The reason I was asked to do so was that I was seen as a white person who would not appear to represent one side or the other in any partisan way. Another way of saying this is that I was asked to lead these workshops because, if an African American person was leading them, then the authority of that person might have been undermined by a presumed bias. The dean told me that I had a certain authority enabling me to conduct this particular set of workshops. I "had" authority because of my whiteness.

Looking back on this experience, I now have a different understanding of the way that authority got enacted, through me, during these workshops. For, the reason that I was able to assume a place of authority is not *simply* because I was white. Indeed, some white folks on faculty would not have been able to assume such a place because they enacted a white identity that had already offended others. They would not have been able to assume such a place because they were the ones who had been accused of racism. Other white folks on faculty would not have been able to assume such a place because they had enacted a white identity that clearly sided with folks of color who had been the target of racism. In my case, it just happened that I was in a relational position, a position that happened to straddle, and, yes, have affinities with, both those who were offended and those who did the offending. It wasn't that I was white, nor was it that I had some "true" position, some "true" knowledge that enabled me to conduct these workshops. It was rather that I had a tenable *relation* with both factions. It was the relation itself that authorized me.

Throughout the writing of this book, I have had the unique opportunity to teach a large lecture class entitled "Education and Social

Issues." This opportunity has been unique in that it has challenged most of my prior assumptions about authority. In the past, I had always assumed that lecturing to ninety students entailed an unreasonable imposition of authority. After all, I have considered myself to be a progressive educator. Along with Paulo Freire, I have assumed that lecturing *to* students indicates a certain "narrative sickness."[39] I have assumed that dialogue *with* and *among* students is the preferable means of communication. Certainly, it is very difficult to have dialogue with as many as ninety interlocutors.

Yet, throughout these years of lecturing, I have also been struck by a certain paradox that puts into question the simple assumption that lecturing is a *wrong* imposition of authority. The paradox is this: On the one hand, I have felt uncomfortable lecturing to a large audience of students. I have felt uncomfortable because of the "banking method" that it entails. On the other hand, I have long enjoyed attending poetry readings. Often sitting in theatre audiences that have been even larger than the audience of my students in lecture class, I have enjoyed hearing the spoken word, the word of poetry, flowing from a poet on stage. It has long seemed paradoxical to me that I have not felt dominated or "banked" at poetry readings.[40] Yet at the same time, I have felt that my own lecturing to a large audience has been too much of an authoritarian imposition. I have wondered what the difference between a poetry reading and a lecture really is. Is there any difference at all?

During the first couple years of my lecture class, I figured that the only way for me to become more progressive in my pedagogy was to create dialogue in this large lecture setting. I created opportunities for my students to talk among themselves. I asked students to work in small groups to discuss the readings that had been assigned. I did everything I could to let students speak in class. Meanwhile, though, the authoritative paradox of the poetry reading continued to bother me. Why couldn't I be the poet? I often asked myself. Why is *my* authority so intrusive while the poet's is not?

More recently, I must admit that I have given up somewhat on my efforts to let student dialogue guide the flow of my lecture class. Quite simply, these efforts proved to be strained. Though I created the opportunity for students to talk among themselves in small groups, the students often remarked that such times were not very productive. While I took great pains to recreate the atmosphere of a more intimate dialogue, this large lecture setting hasn't allowed for true dialogue of the sort that is clearly attainable in smaller settings. I have found that one can't use a progressive template for pedagogy anywhere and everywhere.

In fact, I have now come to a different understanding of authority in this lecture class. I now lecture to this large group of students unabashedly. I have found that students are more profoundly moved by the spoken word of the lecture. I have found that students engage more deeply with the concepts presented. When students come to visit me in my office, or when we talk in the halls, they have more to say than before. Interestingly, the dialogue that we *do* have with each other is now less frequent, but is also more substantial. Students speak up in class in ways that didn't happen previously. They challenge my position right there in front of so many of their peers. They speak their minds. I listen. I do not need to be imposing about what I present in class. It is there for the taking, or for the walking away. At least this is my interpretation of what has happened as the years have progressed.

Now, I am not claiming to have become the poet. But the lesson of the literary relation is germane here. I am convinced that the relation of authority must be considered in a literary light. Even the authority relation establish by a professor in a large lecture class. I read my failure to successfully import progressive methodology as a comment on the literary life of authority. The quality of the authority relation, I would now say, never depends solely on some fixed method, just as the quality of a literary work never depends solely on some fixed style. A certain progressive methodology may facilitate a healthy authority relation, but it may not. In the same way, a certain free verse form of poetry may authorize the work of a poet, but it may not. The authority relation between teacher and student will benefit from different forms at different times. In this particular situation, I have found that the speaking voice of the teacher is the form of choice.

I would like to further explore the literary life of authority, the one outlined in chapter 2, with the following example.

One of the courses that PhD students are required to take in my department focuses on the history of educational thought. In this course, students are asked to read a series of texts considered to be canonical in Western education. They read Plato, John Locke, Jean-Jacques Rousseau, Mary Wollstonecraft, and John Dewey, among others. The aim of this course, as stated the course syllabus, is "to consider the major contributions to educational theory in their historical contexts."

Certainly, this list of authors raises profound questions about authority. And of course, such questions have already garnered lots of air time in academic discussions over the past decades. Questions such as the following arise: Who "has" the authority to say that these texts are "the major contributions"? Do these texts deserve the ("thingified") authority that is attributed to them? Which groups of people benefit from the ("thingified") authority that is attributed to these texts? Which types of education are authorized by such texts? Which types are not?

Though I have never taught this course, I have had the opportunity to talk with many students who have taken it. These students have had various reactions to the course and its content. Some, like Judith, have had a very positive reaction. She has related to me what a profoundly moving experience it has been to engage with these canonical authors. For Judith, her understanding of educational thought has been greatly enlarged because she can now pinpoint where competing conceptions of educational thought in the West originate. She is happy to know where the current debates over educational practices reside on a larger plain of various intellectual traditions.

For others such as Stephen, this course has been worthless. For him, this investigation of Western educational origins is just another exercise in the performance of hegemony. He would rather that we, as educators, move on. He has had enough of exploring a canon that has served to segregate and oppress.

I have also listened to professors and students who say they are tired of complaints such as Stephen's. Stephen is dismissed as being anti-intellectual, as being unwilling to engage in the intellectual work of learning from history. It is this dismissal of Stephen's perspective that I would like to look at more closely.

With the literary life of authority in mind, I find it difficult to jump to the conclusion that Stephen should be written off as anti-intellectual. For, such a writing-off entails a mistaken focus on content. Such a writing-off assumes that these canonical texts are somehow self-authorizing. It assumes that such works should be automatically authorized because of the rich content that they offer. Certainly, the content of Plato's *Republic* and the content of Emile's *Rousseau* are rich. About this there can be no question. The question is, rather, whether we can ever assume that content per se is sufficient for authority to gain purchase within the educational relation. The relation of authority depends not only upon content. It depends as well upon how things are taught, and who is doing the teaching.

Indeed, no work will ever authorize itself simply because it has a lot to say. This is true of classroom content just as it is true of great literary works. In education, content alone does not "have" authority. Instead, there will always be an interplay between three things: the way the text is presented, the content of the text, and the authority enacted by the instructor. All three of these variables will come into play when students read a classroom text. Students' involvement in the authority relation depends upon a combination of style, content, and personhood. Stephen may not be correct in dismissing these rich texts wholesale. However, the fact remains that the content of these texts may not suffice to bring him into an educative relation with authority. Sometimes, texts do not speak for themselves.

My daughter Olivia is now ten years old. She has started at a new school this year. At this new school, there has been an interesting shift in her confidence at mathematics. Whereas last year she didn't fair too well at mathematics, this year things are different. This year she will tell you that mathematics is her favorite subject. Last year, math was a distant last on her list of favorite subjects. At this new school, Olivia considers herself an authority at mathematics.

Having talked to Olivia about this newfound interest in math, I think I can pinpoint the time when things changed for her. It was on a day when the students in Olivia's class were doing what I call "long-multiplication"—multiplying multidigit numbers together. Olivia's teacher noticed that Olivia was using a different algorithm than the rest of the students in her class.

Olivia's teacher approached her and asked, "Olivia, will you show me the way you are doing your multiplication?"

"Yes," Olivia responded, "I do it like this. . . ." She showed the teacher her process.

"That's the old-fashioned algorithm, Olivia. That's exactly what I'm trying to teach to our class this year. Last year they used the new math algorithm, but the old-fashioned one is better. That's why I want all the kids learn your way.

Olivia, can you be our tutor this year? Can you help students who don't know your way of multiplying?"

"I can do that," Olivia responded.

Olivia tells this story with pride, and, yes, with authority. In my mind, this story points to one thing. It points to a new *relation* of authority, a relation that has authorized Olivia to be an expert at mathematics. It is not that a lightbulb suddenly went on this year in Olivia's mathematical mind. It is not that Olivia didn't "have" authority last year, but "has" it this year. After all, what Olivia "had" last year was exactly what she "has" this year, namely, a certain ability to do the long multiplication the old-fashioned way. It is the relation that has changed. Olivia's teacher was able to facilitate a relation between Olivia and her peers that put her in a place of authority.

I have offered here just a few examples from my own experience, and I have tried to think through them keeping in mind that authority is a relation. As it turns out, it is not difficult to think of authority in terms of relation. However, it still proves easy to fall back into the habit of thinking of authority as a thing, as a substance. It is a fact that each of the experiences above could be reframed in terms of who "had" authority, and what he or she did with that authority that he or she "had." Yet, I am hoping that this book has provided enough evidence to convince its readers not to fall back into the habit of treating author- ity as a substance. Authority is a relation. The evidence attests to this fact. If we continue to treat authority as a substance, it is a matter of habit rather than a matter of accuracy.

Notes

INTRODUCTION

1. Here I use the term *folk notion* to refer to a commonplace, widely accepted conception that gets used without questioning the presumptions of such a conception.

2. See Ira Shor, *Empowering Education : Critical Teaching for Social Change* (Chicago: University of Chicago Press, 1992); and *Critical Teaching and Everyday Life* (Chicago: University of Chicago Press, 1987).

3. See E. D. Hirsch, *The Schools We Need and Why We Don't Have Them* (New York: Anchor Books, 1999); Diane Ravitch, *The Schools We Deserve* (New York: Basic Books, 1985).

4. See Henry Giroux, "Authority, Intellectuals, and the Politics of Practical Learning," *Teachers College Record* 88, 1 (Fall 1986): 22–40; *Pedagogy and the Politics of Hope* (Boulder: Westview, 1997); *Schooling and the Struggle for Public Life* (Minneapolis: University of Minnesota Press, 1998).

5. Immanuel Kant, "What Is Enlightenment?" http://www.fordham.edu/halsall/mod/kant-whatis.html (Oct 2, 2005).

6. Paulo Freire, *Pedagogy of the Oppressed* (New York: Continuum, 1970).

7. Ibid., 61.

8. Louis Althusser, "Ideology and Ideological State Apparatuses (Notes toward an Investigation)," in Slavoj Zizek, *Mapping Ideology* (New York: Verso Press, 1994), 100–40.

9. Ibid., 31.

10. Franz Fanon, *Black Skins/White Masks*, trans. Charles Lam Markmann (New York: Grove Press, 1967), 109.

11. Michel Foucault, *The Foucault Reader*, ed. Paul Rabinow (New York: Pantheon Books, 1984), 61.

12. Ibid., 49.

CHAPTER 1. TEXTS AND THE AUTHORITY RELATION

1. The works I rely on here are Hans-Georg Gadamer, *Truth and Method* (New York: Continuum Books, 1995); *The Enigma of Health* (London: Polity

Press, 1996); and Jacques Derrida, *Of Grammatology*, trans. Gayatri Chakravorty Spivak (Baltimore: The Johns Hopkins University Press, 1974).

2. Athol Fugard, *My Children! My Africa!* (New York: Theatre Communications Group, 1989).

3. Ibid., 279.

4. Gadamer, *Enigma*, 119.

5. Gadamer, *Truth and Method*, 278.

6. See Jacques Derrida's discussion of supplementarity in *Of Grammatology*, 144–47. See also Charles Bingham, "I Am the Missing Pages of the Text I Teach: Gadamer and Derrida on Teacher Authority," *Philosophy of Education 2001* (Urbana-Champaign: Philosophy of Education Society, 2002), 265–72.

7. Derrida, *Of Grammatology*, 144–45.

8. Ibid., 145.

9. Ibid., 146.

10. Ibid., 146–47.

11. Toni Morrison, *Playing in the Dark: Whiteness and the Literary Imagination* (New York: Vintage, 1993).

12. See J. L. Austin, *How to Do Things with Words* (Cambridge: Harvard University Press, 1975).

13. Athol Fugard, *My Children! My Africa!* (Theater Communications Group, 1990).

14. Ibid., 67–68.

15. Ibid.

16. Ibid., 63–64.

17. Ibid., 24.

18. Ibid., 43.

19. Ibid., 23–24.

20. Ibid., 25.

21. Ibid., 43.

CHAPTER 2. THE LITERARY RELATION OF AUTHORITY

1. In Jacques Derrida, "Before the Law," in *Acts of Literature*, ed. Derek Attridge (New York: Routledge, 1992), 183, 184.

2. Ibid., 183.

3. Ibid., 184.

4. Franz Kafka, *The Metamorphosis, In the Penal Colony, and Other Stories*, trans. Willa and Edwin Muir (New York: Schocken, 1995); *The Castle*, trans. Mark Harman (New York: Schocken, 1998); *The Trial*, trans. Willa and Edwin Muir (New York: Schocken, 1984).

5. See Eric L. Santner, *On the Psychotheology of Everyday Life: Reflections on Freud and Rosenweig* (Chicago: University of Chicago Press, 2001), 40.

6. Plato, *Meno*, trans. G. M. A. Grube (Indianapolis: Hackett, 1976).

7. Plato, *The Last Days of Socrates: Euthyphro; The Apology; Creto; Phaedo* (New York: Penguin Classics, 1993).

8. Anamnesis refers to the Greek belief that human beings share a collective memory.

9. Derrida, "Before the Law," 213.

10. Ibid., 213.

11. Ibid., 196.

12. Ibid., 204.

13. I would like to thank reviewers at the *Journal of Philosophy of Education* for pointing this out.

14. John Stewart, ed., *Beyond the Symbol Model* (Albany: State University of New York Press, 1996), 20.

15. George Lakoff and Mark Taylor, *Metaphors We Live By* (Chicago: University of Chicago Press, 2003), 10.

16. Ibid., 11.

17. Stewart, *Beyond the Symbol Model*, 20.

18. Alphonso Lingis, *The Community of Those Who Have Nothing in Common* (Indianapolis: University of Indiana Press, 1994).

19. Ibid., 4.

20. Gadamer, *Truth and Method*, 268–69.

21. Austin, *How to Do Things With Words*. Austin does not even entertain the notion that same-sex couples can marry, too.

22. Ibid.

23. Santner, *Psychopathology*, 133. By "constative," Santner means the ordinary decoding of the literal meaning of a passage. By "redemptive," Santner means the religiously transformative reading of a passage.

24. Ibid., 133.

CHAPTER 3. RELATING TO AUTHORITY
FIGURES WHO ARE NOT THERE

1. Here I am again referring to mainstream educational accounts of authority, be they progressive, traditional, or critical, accounts that include: Kenneth Benne, "The Locus of Educational Authority in Today's World," *Teachers College Record* 88, 1 (Fall 1986): 15–21; Giroux, "Authority"; Patricia White, "Self-respect, Self-esteem, and the School: A Democratic Perspective on Authority," *Teachers College Record* 88, 1 (Fall 1986): 95–106; Emily Robertson, "Teacher Authority and Teaching for Liberation," *Philosophy of Education Society*, 1994, <http://www.ed.uiuc.edu/eps/ pes~yearbook/ 94_docs/roberso.htm> (June 10, 2000); Edward Sankowski, "Autonomy, Education, and Politics," *Philosophy of Education Society*, <http://www.ed.uiuc.edu/eps/pes~yearbook/ 1998/sankowski.html> (July 15, 2000).

2. See Jean Laplance and J. B. Pontalis, *The Language of Psycho-Analysis* (New York: W.W. Norton, 1974).

3. See Jessica Benjamin, *The Bonds of Love: Psychoanalysis, Feminism, and the Problem of Domination* (New York: Pantheon, 1988); *Like Subjects, Love Objects: Essays on Recognition and Social Difference* (New Haven: Yale

University Press, 1995); and *Shadow of the Other: Intersubjectivity and Gender in Psychoanalysis* (New York: Routledge, 1998).

4. Benjamin, *Bonds of Love*, 30.

5. Ibid., 31.

6. Ibid., 19ff.

7. Benjamin, *Like Subjects*, 30.

8. Benjamin, *Bonds of Love*, 43.

9. See John Dewey, *Experience and Education* (New York: Collier Books, 1963).

10. Edmund Husserl, *Cartesian Meditations*, trans. Dorian Cairns (The Hague: Martinus Nijhoff, 1970), 112–13.

11. For comments on this apperceptive process, see Kathleen M. Haney, *Intersubjectivity Revisited: Phenomenology and the Other* (Athens: Ohio University Press, 1994), 57–60.

12. Husserl, *Meditations*, 112.

13. Maurice Merleau-Ponty, *Phenomenology, Language, and Sociology: Selected Essays of Maurice Merleau-Ponty*, ed. John O'Neill (London: Heinemann, 1974), 81–94.

14. Ibid., 81–94.

15. Ibid.

16. Ibid., p. 91. Please notice that while this aspect of language sounds a bit similar to the sender-receiver model it is actually quite different insofar as language is not considered a neutral vehicle for the transfer of ideas but rather a uniquely linguistic medium that actually comes alive through the act of human communication.

17. Benjamin, *Like Subjects*, 30.

18. Ibid., 202–205; Benjamin, *Shadow of the Other*, 25–30.

19. Here, I am entering a contentious conversation about the more general question of whether or not language is a symbolic system. My position on this is as follows: language does make use of symbols, but it does so in a *functional, living* way. There are two points that I am trying trying to make here. First, I do not consider language to be a symbolic system, per se. That is to say, I do not consider language to be *only* a symbolic system. Language certainly acts in other nonsymbolic ways as well. Second, I do not consider language's use of symbols to be a use of "just" symbols in the sense that symbols are construed of as a lesser order of things, as an order of things that is somehow ontologically distinct and less important than things in the "real" world. Rather, language's symbols are part and parcel of the same real world where everything else resides. Language may use symbols, but these symbols are not lesser or greater, in fact have no ontological distinction, from the "real world" itself. For an introduction to this contentious debate, please see Stewart, ed., *Beyond the Symbol Model*; and John Stewart, *Language as Articulate Contact: Towards a Post-Semiotic Philosophy of Language* (Albany: State University of New York Press, 1995).

20. Benjamin, *Shadow of the Other*, 28.

21. Benjamin, *Like Subjects*, 202.

CHAPTER 4. WHEN FACED WITH AUTHORITY

1. See, for example, Alexander Nehemas, *The Art of Living* (Berkeley: University of California Press, 1998); Pierre Hadot, *Philosophy as a Way of Life*, ed. Arnold Davidson (Cambridge: Blackwell, 1995); and Michel Foucault, *Technologies of the Self: A Seminar with Michel Foucault*, ed. Luther H. Martin, Huck Gutman, and Patrick H. Hutton (Amherst: University of Massachusetts Press, 1988).

2. I take this phrase from Richard Rorty's *The Consequences of Pragmatism* (Minneapolis: University of Minnesota Press, 1982).

3. See Dewey, *Experience and Education*.

4. Ibid., 27–28.

5. Immanuel Kant, *Foundations of the Metaphysics of Morals* (New York: The Liberal Arts Press, 1959), 47–49.

6. Kant, "What is Enlightenment?"

7. Friedrich Nietzsche, *On the Genealogy of Morals* (New York: Vintage Books, 1967), 59.

8. Nietzsche, *Genealogy*.

9. Ibid., 59.

10. Here I am referring to the following texts by Foucault: "bio-power," in *History of Sexuality Vol. I: An Introduction* (New York: Pantheon, 1978); "surveillance" and "confessional techniques," in *Discipline and Punish: The Birth of the Prison* (New York: Pantheon, 1977); "epistemic regimes," in *The Order of Things: An Archaeology of the Human Sciences* (New York: Pantheon, 1971); and "governmental hierarchies," in *Technologies of the Self*.

11. Michel Foucault, *Power/Knowledge: Selected Interviews and Other Writings* 1972–1977 (New York: Pantheon, 1980), 74.

12. For a discussion on Winnicott's anti-Kantian stance, see Barbara Johnson, "Using People: Kant with Winnicott," in *The Turn to Ethics*, ed. Marjorie Garber, Beatrice Hanssen, Rebecca L. Walkowitz (New York: Routledge, 2000), 47–63.

13. See D. W. Winnicott, *Playing and Reality* (New York: Routledge, 1971).

14. Certainly, my account of Winnicottian "use" does not do justice to the overall psychoanalytic territory that Winnicott establishes through his analysis of using, destruction, survival, relating, play, potential space, transitional space, transitional objects, etc. That is to say, I have isolated the phenomenon of "use" without giving a proper account of the way that use is but a small part of a larger constellation of processes contributing to the psychic flourishing of individuals. This omission is carried out intentionally on the assumption that Winnicott's understanding of psychic flourishing is implied, even if not theoretically elaborated, in this chapter on using others. This chapter focuses not on the psychic life of using others, but on its conscious life. By omitting the unconscious thrust of Winnicott's work in this chapter, I am not trying to say that the psychic life of using others is not important, but that an analysis of the use of authority can cover important ground even before it gets to the more nuanced elements of psychic life.

15. *Playing*, 111 ff.

16. Once again, I am echoing the work of Alexander Nehemas, among others. See note 1 of this chapter.

17. See Kieran Egan, *The Educated Mind: How Cognitive Tools Shape Our Understanding* (Chicago: University of Chicago Press, 1997).

18. Nehemas, *The Art of Living*, 4.

19. Nietzsche, *Genealogy*, 45.

20. Friedrich Nietzsche, *Ecce Homo*, trans. Walter Kaufman (New York: Vintage Books, 1967), 224–25.

21. Ibid., 282.

22. Friedrich Nietzsche, "Schopenhauer as Educator," in *Unfashionable Observations*, ed. Ernst Behler (Stanford: Stanford University Press, 1995), 171–255.

23. Nietzsche, *Ecce Homo*, 277.

24. Ibid., 277.

25. Ibid., 258.

26. See Nietzsche, *Ecce Homo*, "Zarathustra," and *The Gay Science*, trans. Walter Kaufmann (New York: Vintage Books, 1974), 270.

27. Nietzsche, *Genealogy*, 15.

28. Friedrich Nietzsche, *Beyond Good and Evil*, trans. Walter Kaufman (New York: Vintage Books, 1966), 127.

29. Nietzsche, *Genealogy*, 15.

30. Ibid., 39.

31. Ibid.

32. Here I think of intelligence tests, career inventories, and all sorts of other tests that claim to make assessments of one's "natural" abilities and aptitudes. There is a loathesome, and fundamentally uneducative, result when one takes only this first step, when one assumes that such measures actually indicate what one has the capacity to do and what one does not.

33. Of course, it is important to recall that whatever seems "natural" in education may in fact be a human invention. Michel Foucault's work on prisons, asylums, military barracks, medical discourses, and schools has shown very clearly the powers that institutions such as schools have to shape the self, to make students into "docile bodies." As he reminds us, systems of power have their own ways of making us believe that this or that is "natural" to you or me. One such system is the discourse of psychology. Restrictive yet ubiquitous psychological discourses dominate human practices these days. They especially dominate educational practices.

Yet even if the natural is a human invention, such an invention can be a venue for self-fashioning and for human flourishing. For Foucault, the act of self-fashioning serves to mitigate against scientistic labeling, against statistical categorizing, against medicalizations of all kinds. He insists, especially in his later work, that self-fashioning can be a strategy toward whatever is deemed "natural" by power. He reminds us that self-fashioning is a way of refusing to be dominated, in this modern culture of ours, by systems of disciplinary power that tend to offer us limitations rather than freedoms. And, he reminds us that while power is indeed ubiquitous, it also produces its own resistances. Sites of power also produce sites that can effectively resist that power. Thus, for Foucault, we can use tactics of resistance precisely where power resides. With regard to the specific sorts of power mechanisms that one finds in institutions such as schools, mechanisms that produce docile, "natural" selves, it is not unreasonable to find in those same institutions sites for resisting the production of docile bodies. Self-fashioning is a strategy of resistance best practiced in the very places where "natural" selves are produced, in places such as schools.

34. Nietzsche, *Genealogy*, 15.

35. With Socrates' claim that he is the one who knows he does not know, with Montaigne's suggestion that the educated child should be "well-formed" instead of "well-filled," and with Foucault's practical return to the care of the self in his later work, we find a willingness to limit oneself when it comes to knowledge. See Michel de Montaigne's "On the Education of Children," in *Selected Essays*, ed. Blanchard Bates (New York: The Modern Library, 1949); David Hansen, "Well-Formed, Not Well-Filled: Montaigne and the Paths of Personhood," *Educational Theory* 52, 2 (Spring 2002); Michel Foucault, *The Use of Pleasure: The History of Sexuality, Volume 2*, trans. Robert Hurley (New York: Vintage Books, 1990); and *Technologies of the Self: A Seminar with Michel Foucault*.

36. Foucault, *History of Sexuality Vol. 2*, 7.

37. For a good essay on how Foucault changed his thinking, see John Rajchman, *Michel Foucault: The Freedom of Philosophy* (New York: Columbia University Press, 1986).

38. Foucault, *Technologies of the Self*, 9.

39. I have been advocating a philosophy of self-fashioning as a way to deal with the tensions that arise in education from the inevitable, and potentially contradictory, matters of nature, culture, and knowledge. To be sure, this investigation has not looked at enough of Nietzsche's thought with regard to these matters, nor has it investigated other self-fashioning philosophers such as Socrates and Montaigne who have much to teach us on these matters. But the aim here is not to exhaustively detail the natural, cultural, and epistemological insights that self-fashioning offers, but rather to identify a strand of thought that deserves to be explored further in the future. The aim of this investigation is to show that the trajectory of self-fashioning, a trajectory has been most thoroughly explored so far by Alexander Nehamas and Pierre Hadot, is perhaps the most important one that exists when it comes to the major problems that education poses. See especially Alexander Nehemas, *The Art of Living*; and, Pierre Hadot, *Philosophy as a Way of Life*.

Certainly, many have written on the educational insights to be gleaned from the various philosophers who happen to be philosophers of self-fashioning. But I am trying to foreground the educational significance of self-fashioning thought itself, rather than the specific thought of a Nietzsche or a Foucault per se. Clearly, this general approach to the theme of self-fashioning will not satisfy readers who want a detailed study of Nietzschean self-consitution, and Foucaultian agency, in education. For more detailed work on these educational matters I recommend my article "What Friedrich Nietzsche Cannot Stand About Education: Toward a Pedagogy of Self-Reformulation," *Educational Theory* 51,

3, as well as Chris Mayo's "The Uses of Foucault," *Educational Theory* 50, 1: 103–16.

CHAPTER 5. QUESTIONING AUTHORITY

1. Gadamer, *Truth and Method*, 375.
2. Ibid., 362.
3. Ibid., 262.
4. Ibid., 363.
5. Ibid.
6. Ibid., 362.
7. Ibid., 363.
8. Ibid.
9. Ibid.
10. Ibid.
11. See Heidegger's "Letter on Humanism," in *Martin Heidegger: Basic Writings, Second Edition* (San Francisco: Harper, 1993).
12. Gadamer, *Truth and Method*, 446.
13. See Gilles Deleuze, *Nietzsche and Philosophy*, trans. Hugh Tomlinson (New York: Columbia University Press, 1983).
14. Ibid., 474.
15. Ibid.
16. Hans-Georg Gadamer, *Philosophical Hermeneutics* (Berkeley: University of California Press, 1976), 35.
17. Gadamer, *Truth and Method*, 262–63.
18. Ibid., 263.
19. Ibid.
20. Here I am referring to Dewey's discussion in *The Child and Curriculum* (Chicago: University of Chicago Press, 1990), where he notes that the teacher must be concerned "with the subject matter as a related factor in a total and growing experience. Thus to see it is to psychologize it. It is the failure [of the teacher] to keep in mind the double aspect of subject matter which causes the curriculum and child to be set over against each other . . ." 201.
21. Gadamer, *Truth and Method*, 299.
22. Ibid.
23. Ibid., 375.
24. Freire, *Pedagogy of the Oppressed*, 72.

CHAPTER 6. PAULO FREIRE AND RELATIONAL AUTHORITY

1. Freire, *Pedagogy of the Oppressed*, 61.
2. Certainly, the problem of authority is of central concern to many versions of psychoanalysis. Such fundamental concepts of psychoanalysis as transference, the Oedipus complex, and shame are tied to issues of authority. And more specifically, the problem of authority within educational contexts has been written about in very interesting ways as of late. For examples of works

that address the interconnection of psychoanalysis, authority, and education, see especially Deborah Britzman's *Lost Subjects, Contested Objects: Toward a Psychoanalytic Inquiry of Learning* (Albany: State University of New York Press, 1999); Shoshona Felman's *Jacques Lacan and the Adventure of Insight: Psychoanalysis in Contemporary Culture* (Cambridge: Harvard University Press, 1987); and Appel's recent edited volume, *Psychoanalysis and Pedagogy* (New York: Bergin and Garvey, 1999). My concern in this essay is not, however, to explore the various understandings of authority, and more specifically educational authority, that have been analyzed in the literature of psychoanalysis. It is rather to take a particular version of psychoanalysis, one that is particularly suited to understanding Freire's work on authority, namely, Jessica Benjamin's intersubjective version, and to use it to understand his claims about how a liberatory authority might be configured.

I thus situate this chapter at the intersection of mainstream Freirean-inspired versions of critical pedagogy whose main proponent I consider to be Ira Shor (1987, 1992, 1996) on the one hand; and, on the other, those works cited above whose authors argue that psychoanalysis needs to inform the intersubjective dynamics of pedagogy. Ira Shor gives us very useful ways to employ Freirean pedagogy, but Jessica Benjamin's work lends further insight to the matter of critical authority.

3. Freire, *Pedagogy of the Oppressed*, 54.

4. Ibid., 56.

5. Ibid., 61.

6. Ibid., 64.

7. Ibid.

8. Ibid.

9. Ibid., 68.

10. Ibid., 176.

11. Ibid.

12. Ibid., 31.

13. Ibid.

14. Ibid., 54.

15. John Dewey, "Authority and Social Change," in *Authority and the Individual* (Cambridge: Harvard University Press, 1937).

16. Ibid., 171.

17. Ibid., 177–78.

18. Freire, *Pedagogy*, 60–61.

19. At this point, it is important for me to state my assumptions about epistemology vis-à-vis intersubjectivity in Freire. I take Freire to be very psychoanalytic in his understanding of epistemology. Thus, when Freire mentions that we are "cognitive actors" who share the same "cognizable object," I take him to mean that cognition is a means by which intersubjective relations get worked out. It is not clear to me that Freire works out the link between epistemology and intersubjectivity adequately. Hence, this essay. I thus locate Freire within the sorts of psychoanalytic thinking typified by D. W. Winnicott and Jessica Benjamin that points out the ways humans interact by means of

object relations, "cognizable object" relations. See, for example, Winnicott's *Playing and Reality*.

20. Freire, *Pedagogy*, 61.

21. Here I am referring to the Enlightenment version of authority that Kant introduces in his essay, "What Is Enlightenment." Therein, Kant argues that freedom and authority are at odds. He argues that one must have the audacity to use one's own reason in the face of authority. It is this understanding of freedom versus authority that I am also calling a "liberal" version, liberalism being broadly defined as the intersection of discourses that advocate individualism and the separation of private and public spheres, such advocacy being glued together by the assumption that authority is contrary to individual freedom.

22. Michel Foucault, "What is Enlightenment?" in *Michel Foucault: Ethics, Subjectivity, and Truth*, ed. Paul Rabinow (New York: The New Press, 1997), 312.

23. Freire, *Pedagogy*, 67.

24. Ibid., 136.

25. Ibid., 137.

26. While this essay addresses primarily the recognitive implications of Freire's work, I have elsewhere argued for the centrality of recognition in all of education. Please see Charles Bingham, *Schools of Recognition: Identity Practices and Classroom Practices* (Boulder: Rowman and Littlefield, 2001).

27. Jessica Benjamin, *The Bonds of Love* (New York: Pantheon, 1988), 20–21.

28. Freire, *Pedagogy*, 58.

29. Ibid.

30. Benjamin, *Like Subjects*, 30.

31. Freire, *Pedagogy*, 148.

32. Ibid.

33. Maurice Freedman, *The Confirmation of Otherness: In Family, Community, and Society* (New York: Pilgrim Press, 1973), 30.

34. Freire, *Pedagogy*, 61.

35. Since I am speaking here in terms of "fantasy" versus "reality," it is appropriate to point out now that this distinction is properly a psychoanalytic one. It might be argued, in a philosophical critique of this essay, that I have not made a proper distinction between the two. I would not respond to such a critique, though. This distinction is rather a matter of discursive suppositions. It is a primary supposition of psychoanalysis that there is such a distinction, and that is one of the suppositions upon which this psychoanalytic augmentation of Freire is based.

36. Certainly there are a wide variety of ways in which students might engage in content preparation, some being pedagogically successful and some not. I am not trying to say that all content preparation is fortuitous, but am rather taking the case where such preparation *is* successful in order to think through the psychic dynamics of authority.

37. Friere, *Pedagogy*, 61.

38. I am grateful to the thoughtful comments and stimulating conversation of Michael Dupuis, James Fusco, Felicia Michaels, and Stephen Haymes, who helped me during the preparation of this chapter.

39. Freire, *Pedagogy*, 51.

40. Here I am referring once again to the work of Paulo Freire. I am referring to the "banking system of education" that narrates whatever it wants to the student who is to be "filled" with knowledge of the teacher's choice.

References

Althusser, Louis. "Ideology and Ideological State Apparatuses (Notes toward an Investigation)." In *Mapping Ideology*, ed. Slavoj Zizek, 100–40. New York: Verso Press, 1994.

Appel, Stephen. *Psychoanalysis and Pedagogy.* New York: Bergin and Garvey, 1999.

Austin, J. L. *How to Do Things with Words.* Cambridge: Harvard University Press, 1975.

Benjamin, Jessica. *The Bonds of Love: Psychoanalysis, Feminism, and the Problem of Domination.* New York: Pantheon, 1988.

———. *Like Subjects, Love Objects: Essays on Recognition and Social Difference.* New Haven: Yale University Press, 1995.

———. *Shadow of the Other: Intersubjectivity and Gender in Psychoanalysis.* New York: Routledge, 1998.

Benne, Kenneth. 1986. "The Locus of Educational Authority in Today's World." *Teachers College Record* 88, 1 (Fall 1986): 15–21.

Bingham, Charles. "What Friedrich Nietzsche Cannot Stand About Education: Toward a Pedagogy of Self-Reformulation." *Educational Theory* 51, 3 (2001).

———. "I Am the Missing Pages of the Text I Teach: Gadamer and Derrida on Teacher Authority." *Philosophy of Education 2001*, 265–72.

———. *Schools of Recognition: Identity Practices and Classroom Practices.* Boulder: Rowman and Littlefield, 2001.

———. "Who are the Philosophers of Education?" *Studies in Philosophy and Education* 24, 1 (2005).

Britzman, Deborah. *Lost Subjects, Contested Objects: Toward a Psychoanalytic Inquiry of Learning.* Albany: State University of New York Press, 1999.

Deleuze, Gilles. *Nietzsche and Philosophy.* Trans. Hugh Tomlinson. New York: Columbia University Press, 1983.

Derrida, Jacques. "Before the Law." In *Acts of Literature*, ed. Derek Attridge. New York: Routledge, 1992.

———. *Of Grammatology.* Trans. Gayatri Chakravorty Spivak. Baltimore: The Johns Hopkins University Press, 1974.

Dewey, John. "Authority and Social Change." In *Authority and the Individual.* Cambridge: Harvard University Press, 1937.

————. *Experience and Education*. New York: Collier Books, 1963.

————. *The Child and Curriculum*. Chicago: University of Chicago Press, 1990.

Egan, Kieran. *The Educated Mind: How Cognitive Tools Shape Our Understanding*. Chicago: University of Chicago Press, 1997.

Fanon, Franz. *Black Skins/White Masks*. Trans. Charles Lam Markmann. New York: Grove Press, 1967.

Felman, Shoshana. *Jacques Lacan and the Adventure of Insight: Psychoanalysis in Contemporary Culture*. Cambridge: Harvard University Press, 1987.

Foucault, Michel. *The Order of Things: An Archaeology of the Human Sciences*. New York: Pantheon, 1971.

————. *Discipline and Punish: The Birth of the Prison*. New York: Pantheon, 1977.

————. *History of Sexuality I: An Introduction*. New York: Pantheon, 1978.

————. *Power/Knowledge: Selected Interviews and Other Writings 1972–1977*. New York: Pantheon, 1980.

————. *The Foucault Reader*. Ed. Paul Rabinow. New York: Pantheon Books, 1984.

————. *Technologies of the Self: A Seminar with Michel Foucault*. Ed. Luther H. Martin, Huck Gutman, and Patrick H. Hutton. Amherst: University of Massachusetts Press, 1988.

————. *The Use of Pleasure: The History of Sexuality, Volume 2*. Trans. Robert Hurley. New York: Vintage Books, 1990.

————. "What Is Enlightenment?" in *Michel Foucault: Ethics, Subjectivity and Truth*, ed. Paul Rabinow. New York: The New Press, 1997.

Freedman, Maurice. *The Confirmation of Otherness: In Family, Community, and Society*. New York: Pilgrim Press, 1973.

Freire, Paulo. *Pedagogy of the Oppressed*. New York: Continuum, 1970.

Fugard, Athol. *My Children! My Africa!* New York: Theatre Communications Group, 1989.

Gadamer, Hans-Georg. *Philosophical Hermeneutics*. Berkeley: University of California Press, 1976.

————. *Truth and Method*. New York: Continuum, 1994.

————. *The Enigma of Health*. London: Polity Press, 1996.

Giroux, Henry. "Authority, Intellectuals, and the Politics of Practical Learning." *Teachers College Record* 88, 1 (Fall 1986): 22–40.

————. *Pedagogy and the Politics of Hope*. Boulder: Westview, 1997.

————. *Schooling and the Struggle for Public Life*. Minneapolis: University of Minnesota Press, 1998.

Hadot, Pierre. *Philosophy as a Way of Life*. Ed. Arnold Davidson. Cambridge: Blackwell, 1995.

Haney, Kathleen M. *Intersubjectivity Revisited: Phenomenology and the Other*. Athens: Ohio University Press, 1994.

Hansen, David. "Well-Formed, Not Well-Filled: Montaigne and the Paths of Personhood." *Educational Theory* 52, 2 (Spring 2002).

Heidegger, Martin. "Letter on Humanism." In *Martin Heidegger: Basic Writings, Second Edition*. San Francisco: Harper, 1993.

Hirsch, E. D. *The Schools We Need and Why We Don't Have Them.* New York: Anchor Books, 1999.

Husserl, Edmund. *Cartesian Meditations.* Trans. Dorian Cairns. The Hague: Martinus Nijhoff, 1970.

Johnson, Barbara. "Using People: Kant with Winnicott." In *The Turn to Ethics*, ed. Marjorie Garber, Beatrice Hanssen, Rebecca L. Walkowitz, 47–63. New York: Routledge, 2000.

Kafka, Franz. *The Trial.* Trans. Willa and Edwin Muir. New York: Schocken, 1984.

———. *The Metamorphosis, In the Penal Colony, and Other Stories.* Trans. Willa and Edwin Muir. New York: Schocken, 1995.

———. *The Castle.* Trans. Mark Harman. New York: Schocken, 1998.

Kant, Immanuel. *Foundations of the Metaphysics of Morals.* New York: The Liberal Arts Press, 1959.

———. "What Is Enlightenment?" http://www.fordham.edu/halsall/mod/kant-whatis.html (Oct 2, 2005).

Lakoff, George, and Mark Taylor. *Metaphors We Live By.* Chicago: University of Chicago Press, 2003.

Laplance, Jean, and J. B. Pontalis. *The Language of Psycho-Analysis.* New York: W.W. Norton, 1974.

Lingis, Alphonso. *The Community of Those Who Have Nothing in Common.* Indianapolis: University of Indiana Press, 1994.

Mayo, Chris. "The Uses of Foucault" *Educational Theory* 50, 1 (2000): 103–16.

Merleau-Ponty, Maurice. *Phenomenology, Language and Sociology: Selected Essays of Maurice Merleau-Ponty.* Ed. John O'Neill. London: Heinemann, 1974.

de Montaigne, Michel. "On the Education of Children." In *Selected Essays*, ed. Blanchard Bates. New York: The Modern Library, 1949.

Morrison, Toni. *Playing in the Dark: Whiteness and the Literary Imagination.* New York: Vintage, 1993.

Nehemas, Alexander. *The Art of Living.* Berkeley: University of California Press, 1998.

Nietzsche, Friedrich. *Beyond Good and Evil.* Trans. Walter Kaufman. New York: Vintage Books, 1966.

———. *On the Genealogy of Morals.* Trans. Walter Kaufmann. New York: Vintage Books, 1967.

———. *The Gay Science.* Trans. Walter Kaufmann. New York: Vintage Books, 1974.

———. *Ecce Homo.* Trans. Walter Kaufman. New York: Vintage Books, 1989.

———. "Schopenhauer as Educator." In *Unfashionable Observations*, ed. Ernst Behler, 171–225. Stanford: Stanford University Press, 1995.

Plato. *Meno.* Trans. G. M. A. Grube. Indianapolis: Hackett, 1976.

———. *The Last Days of Socrates: Euthyphro; The Apology; Creto; Phaedo.* New York: Penguin Classics, 1993.

Rajchman, John. *Michel Foucault: The Freedom of Philosophy.* New York: Columbia University Press, 1986.

Ravitch, Diane. *The Schools We Deserve*. New York: Basic Books, 1985.

Robertson, Emily. "Teacher Authority and Teaching for Liberation." *Philosophy of Education Society 1994* <http://www.ed.uiuc.edu/eps/pes~yearbook/94_docs/roberso.htm> (June 10, 2000).

Rorty, Richard. *The Consequences of Pragmatism*. Minneapolis: University of Minnesota Press, 1982.

Sankowski, Edward. "Autonomy, Education and Politics." *Philosophy of Education Society* <http://www.ed.uiuc.edu/eps/pes~yearbook/1998/sankowski.html> (July 15, 2000).

Santner, Eric L. *On the Psychotheology of Everyday Life: Reflections on Freud and Rosenweig*. Chicago: University of Chicago Press, 2001.

Shor, Ira. *Empowering Education : Critical Teaching for Social Change*. Chicago: University of Chicago Press, 1992.

———. *Critical Teaching and Everyday Life*. Chicago: University of Chicago Press, 1987.

Stewart, John. *Language as Articulate Contact: Towards a Post-Semiotic Philosophy of Language*. Albany: State University of New York Press, 1995.

Stewart, John, ed., *Beyond the Symbol Model*. Albany: State University of New York Press, 1996.

White, Patricia. 1986. "Self-respect, Self-esteem, and the School: A Democratic Perspective on Authority." *Teachers College Record* 88, 1 (Fall 1986): 95–106.

Winnicott, D. W. *Playing and Reality*. New York: Routledge, 1971.

Index

absence, 65ff
agency, 3, 12ff, 67ff, 80, 82ff, 91ff, 130ff
Althusser, Louis, 10, 153n
amor fati, 102
anamnesis, 44
Appel, Stephen, 161n
Austin, J.L., 27, 59, 61, 154n, 155n
authority
  and absence, 65ff, 146–147
  arguments based on, 134
  and authoritarianism, 19ff, 35, 38, 111, 119, 128, 132, 136, 137, 149
  and authoritativeness, 19ff, 35, 38, 45ff, 50, 52, 53, 69, 72, 73, 78, 83
  authority-versus-freedom dilemma, 134–136
  and balance, 142–145
  the circuit of, 6, 7, 37, 38, 67, 69, 125–128, 137ff
  its content, form, and authorship 47–48
  of culture, 105–107
  and epistemology, 107–109
  as force without significance, 41–45
  and hermeneutics, 19–22, 113ff
  of knowledge, 107–109
  and language, 54–63
  and literature, 41–53, 61–63, 150–151
  and maturity, 7–8
  monological, 7–9
  of nature, 104–105
  and presence, 66ff
  and political action, 31–39
  and the psyche, 67ff, 136ff
  and questioning, 111ff
  and the spoken word, 9ff, 74ff, 149–150
  and supplementarity, 22–27
  and texts, 17ff
  as a thing or substance, 2ff, 31, 45, 52, 53, 58, 152
  types of: traditional, progressive, and critical: 3–4, 28ff
  use of, 87ff
autonomy, 3, 21, 55, 67, 89, 90, 91, 92, 142

banking education, 130ff
"Before the Law" (Kafka), 41ff
Benjamin, Jessica, 67ff, 79ff, 137–139, 155n, 156n, 161n, 162n
Benne, Kenneth, 155n
Bingham, Charles, 154n, 159n, 162n
Black Skins/White Masks (Fanon), 11
Britzman, Deborah, 161n
Buber, Martin
  I-It relationship and, 139
  I-Thou relationship and, 139

capacity, 14, 15, 83, 102, 105, 107, 108, 129, 133, 134
Cartesian Meditations (Husserl), 76

cogito, 55
communication
  and the sender-receiver model, 54ff
  and performativity, 58ff
communities of difference, 55
critical perspectives on authority,
  3–4, 24ff, 112, 125
culture, 105–107
curriculum, 21, 22, 26, 27, 39, 47ff,
  62, 123, 131, 141, 142

Deleuze, Gilles, 117, 160n
Derrida, Jacques, 19, 22ff, 38, 39,
  41ff, 154n, 155n
Dewey, John, 73, 88, 94, 124, 133,
  155n, 156n, 157n, 160n, 161n
dialogue, 8, 75, 79, 82ff, 115, 117,
  118, 123, 124, 134, 144, 150
domination and submission, 15,
  70–74, 78, 79, 130, 137ff

Egan, Kieran, 98, 158n
elenchus, 54
enlightenment, 7, 8, 9, 13, 14, 20,
  21, 55, 57, 89, 133, 135, 136
empowerment, 21, 43, 94ff, 123,
  132, 133
epistemology, 107–109

Fanon, Franz, 11, 12, 136, 153n
fantasy, 70, 138, 139, 140, 141,
  142, 145
Felman, Shoshana, 161n
forgetfulness, 103–104
Foucault, Michel, 13–15, 90–91, 98,
  99, 106–109, 153n, 157n, 162n
Freedman, Maurice, 162n
freedom, 4, 8, 9, 12, 13, 14, 20, 21,
  88, 107, 129ff
Freire, Paulo, 8, 9, 128ff, 153n,
  160n, 161n, 162n, 163n
Fugard, Athol, 32–38, 154n

Gadamer, Hans-Georg, 19–22, 25–
  27, 113ff, 153n, 154n, 155n,
  160n
Giroux, Henry, 153n, 155n
good enough mother, 93–97

good enough teacher, 93–97
grades, 43, 82

Hadot, Pierre, 159n
Haney, Kathleen M., 156n
Hansen, David, 159n
Heidegger, Martin, 117, 160n
hermeneutics, 19ff, 113ff
Hirsch, E.D, 153n
Husserl, Edmund, 76, 77, 79, 156n

Ideology and Ideological State
  Apparatuses (Althusser), 10
Ideology, 10, 29, 30, 47, 131, 133,
  137, 143
interpellation, 10
intersubjectivity, 76ff, 87ff, 97, 139
intrapsychic, 69, 79ff, 138ff

Johnson, Barbara, 157n

Kafka, Franz, 41ff, 154n
Kafkaesque, 42, 43
Kant, Immanuel, 7–9, 55ff, 88ff,
  133, 153n, 157n, 162n
knowledge, 107–109

Lakoff, George, 54, 155n
literature, 41–53, 61–63
  its content, form, and authorship,
  45–47
  its framing and referentiality, 46ff
language theory, 53ff, 113ff
Laplance, Jean, 155n
Liberalism, 56, 129, 130, 133ff,
  140, 142, 143
Lingis, Alphonso, 55, 56, 155n
linguistic turn, 116
literary relation, 41ff
  and the teacher, 51ff
  and the student, 48ff

maturity (and Enlightenment), 7, 55,
  58
Mayo, Chris, 160n
Meno (Plato), 43, 44
Merleau-Ponty, Maurice, 75, 77, 79,
  80, 156n

de Montaigne, Michel, 108, 159n
morality, 88ff
Morrison, Toni, 26, 27, 154n
My Children! My Africa! (Fugard), 32ff

nature, faced with the authority of,
    104–105
Nehemas, Alexander, 99, 104, 157n,
    158n, 159n
Nietzsche, Friedrich, 89, 90, 92, 98ff,
    108, 109, 157n, 158n, 159in

object relations theory, 67–70,
    80–82, 89, 91ff, 137–139
objectification, 80, 140, 141
oppressed, 130, 132, 135, 138
oppressor, 130, 134, 138, 139

pairing, 76, 77
Pedagogy of the Oppressed (Freire),
    128ff.
performativity, 58–63
Plato, 98, 123, 124, 150, 151, 154n
Playing in the Dark: Whiteness and
    the Literary Imagination
    (Morrison), 26
Pontalis, J. B., 155n
power, 2, 3, 13, 14, 19, 20, 21, 27,
    90, 91
pragmatism, 88
pragmatic intersubjectivity, 88ff
presence, 65ff
problem-posing education, 134–136
progressivism, 3–4, 7, 8, 13, 18, 25,
    28ff, 39, 47, 51, 94, 111, 112,
    124, 125, 133, 149, 150
psychoanalysis
    and absence, 67ff
    and Paulo Freire, 136ff
    and intersubjectivity, 69, 79ff,
        139–140
    and intrapsychic life, 69, 79ff,
        138ff
    and language, 79ff

questioning, 111ff
    and circuitry, 125–128, 145–146
    and throwing dice, 117–118, 126

false, 114–120
    and hidden statements, 113–114
    and steering, 116, 119, 120, 122
    and non-superficiality, 122–123
    true, 114–127
    and ventriloquism, 121
    and responding with a question,
        125–128

Rabinow, Paul, 153n
Rajchman, John, 159n
Ravitch, Diane, 153n
Robertson, Emily, 155n
Rorty, Richard, 157n
recognition, 67ff, 79ff, 137ff, 162n
rational communities, 55ff
reciprocity, 8, 15, 146
relation
    authority as, 2ff
    and balance, 142–145
    between self and culture, 105–107
    between self and nature, 104–105
    between self and knowledge,
        107–109
    with absent others, 65ff
    and questioning, 111ff
remnant, 69ff
Rorty, Richard, 157n

Sankowski, Edward, 155n
Santner, Eric L., 61, 62, 154n, 155n
self-fashioning, 97ff
sender-receiver model of language,
    54ff
Shor, Ira, 153n, 161n
signified and signifier, 120ff
Socratic Method, 43–44, 111–112,
    123–124, 159n
speech, 9ff, 74ff, 149–150
spoken and written word, 9ff, 74ff,
    149–150
Stewart, John, 54, 155n
submission (and domination), 15,
    70–74, 78, 79, 130, 137ff
supplementarity, 22ff
    and progressivism, 29
    and traditionalism, 29
    and criticalism, 29–30

Taylor, Mark, 54, 155*n*
traditionalism, 3–4, 28ff, 34, 98,
   112, 125
Truth and Method (Gadamer), 122, 123

using others, 87ff

"What is Enlightenment?" (Kant), 7,
   89, 133, 162*n*
"What is Enlightenment?" (Foucault),
   162*n*
White, Patricia, 155*n*
Winnicott, D.W., 89, 91ff, 157*n*